Continued

Featured Studies

Second Edition

SOCIAL PSYCHOLOGY

Stephen L. Franzoi

Marquette University

Boston   Burr Ridge, IL   Dubuque, IA   Madison, WI   New York   San Francisco   St. Louis
Bangkok   Bogotá   Caracas   Lisbon   London   Madrid
Mexico City   Milan   New Delhi   Seoul   Singapore   Sydney   Taipei   Toronto

DEDICATION

To the women in my life: Cheryl, Amelia, and Lillian,
To my parents, Lou and Joyce,
And to my brother and sister, Randy and Susie.
Together, and singly, they influence
the essential elements of my life.

McGraw-Hill Higher Education

A Division of The McGraw-Hill Companies

SOCIAL PSYCHOLOGY, SECOND EDITION

Copyright © 2000, 1996 by The McGraw-Hill Companies, Inc. All rights reserved. Printed in the United States of America. Except as permitted under the United States Copyright Act of 1976, no part of this publication may be reproduced or distributed in any form or by any means, or stored in a data base or retrieval system, without the prior written permission of the publisher.

This book is printed on acid-free paper.

1 2 3 4 5 6 7 8 9 0 QPH/QPH 0 9 8 7 6 5 4 3 2 1 0

ISBN 0–07–043494–8

Editorial director: *Jane E. Vaicunas*
Executive editor: *Mickey Cox*
Developmental editor: *Sharon Geary*
Senior marketing manager: *James Rozsa*
Project manager: *Joyce M. Berendes*
Senior production supervisor: *Mary E. Haas*
Design manager: *Stuart D. Paterson*
Photo research coordinator: *John C. Leland*
Senior supplement coordinator: *David A. Welsh*
Compositor: *Carlisle Communications, Ltd.*
Typeface: *10/12 Palatino*
Printer: *Quebecor Printing Book Group/Hawkins, TN*

Cover design: *Sean Sullivan*
Interior design: *Kristyn Kalnes*
Photo research: *Rose Deluhery*
Cover images: *Background image, Gray Buss/FPG International, first, second, and fourth image on right side of cover, Tony Stone Images, third image is from Corbis.*

The credits section for this book begins on page 597 and is considered an extension of the copyright page.

Library of Congress Cataloging-in-Publication Data

Franzoi, Stephen L.
    Social psychology / Stephen L. Franzoi. — 2nd ed.
      p. cm.
    Includes bibliographical references and index.
    ISBN 0–07–043494–8
    1. Social psychology.   I. Title.
  HM1033.F73   2000
  302—dc21   99–24520
                                   CIP

www.mhhe.com

Stephen L. Franzoi is an associate professor in the psychology department at Marquette University. Born and raised in Iron Mountain, Michigan, he received his B.S. in both psychology and sociology from Western Michigan University in 1975. After earning his Ph.D. in social psychology from the University of California at Davis in 1981, he spent three years at Indiana University in an NIMH-sponsored postdoctoral research program studying the self. During that time, he also served as the assistant editor of *Social Psychology Quarterly*. Since 1984 Dr. Franzoi has been a faculty member at Marquette University, where he teaches both undergraduate and graduate courses in social psychology and publishes primarily in the areas of body esteem, self-awareness, and personal relationships. Over the years, Dr. Franzoi has discussed his research in such media outlets as the *New York Times*, *USA Today*, National Public Radio, and the Oprah Winfrey Show. Because of his desire to apply social psychological knowledge to real-world problems, Dr. Franzoi regularly provides gender equity and multicultural workshops to schools and organizations, including NAACP-sponsored programs. With his students, he has also developed and presented social skills and achievement training workshops for the Milwaukee Boys and Girls Club and social service agencies promoting employment opportunities to the economically disadvantaged and recently incarcerated adults. Stephen and Cheryl Figg are parents of Amelia, age 12, and Lillian, age 9.

BRIEF CONTENTS

DETAILED CONTENTS

CHAPTER 1

SOCIAL PSYCHOLOGY AS A DISCIPLINE 3

PART ONE PERCEIVING PEOPLE AND EVENTS 35

CHAPTER **2**

THE SELF 37

CHAPTER **3**

SELF-PRESENTATION AND SOCIAL PERCEPTION 73

PART TWO   EVALUATING OUR SOCIAL WORLD   143

CHAPTER 4

SOCIAL COGNITION   111

CHAPTER 5

ATTITUDES   145

CHAPTER 6

PERSUASION   187

CHAPTER 7

**PREJUDICE AND
DISCRIMINATION   225**

PART THREE
UNDERSTANDING OUR PLACE WITHIN THE GROUP 267

CHAPTER 8

SOCIAL INFLUENCE 269

CHAPTER 9

GROUP BEHAVIOR   313

PART FOUR
INTERACTING WITH
OTHERS   349

CHAPTER 10

INTERPERSONAL ATTRACTION   351

CHAPTER **11**

INTIMATE RELATIONSHIPS **391**

CHAPTER **14**

THE PERSONAL RELEVANCE
OF SOCIAL PSYCHOLOGY **519**

evising a textbook is like renovating a building. The goal is to retain those designs and features that are essential in maintaining the integrity and attractiveness of the original product, while enhancing and updating the contents so that it will continue to serve a useful function. Just as successful architects base their renovations on the feedback of those who actually live in the buildings being restored, I have substantially based my "renovations" of this second edition on the opinions expressed by professors and students who used the first edition. For those of you who "inhabited" the first edition, I think you will find many familiar features among the various new additions. The primary goal of this updating process was to make the second edition of *Social Psychology* an even better structure where teaching and learning are fostered. I hope that you will find that I have succeeded in this endeavor.

RENOVATIONS IN THE SECOND EDITION

In writing the second edition, I evaluated every aspect of the book in terms of its contribution to effective teaching and learning. Described below are the primary pedagogical revisions.

INCREASED ATTENTION TO CRITICAL THINKING

One reason for initially undertaking this project was that I saw a need for an undergraduate text that would encourage students to critically examine their own social surroundings while they were simultaneously digesting social psychological theories and research. To accomplish this goal, in the first edition I regularly asked students questions in the text. These questions often invited students to guess a study's hypotheses, results, or alternative interpretation of findings. Further elaboration of text material was also encouraged by inserting questions into the captions of figures, tables, photos, and cartoons. For these text and caption questions, the answers usually could be found on the same text page. All of these attempts to foster student analysis are continued in the second edition. In addition, a new feature is that each chapter contains prominently displayed critical thinking sidebars in which the student reader is asked to critically analyze a particular topic under current discussion. Unlike the regular questioning, the answers to these sidebar questions are not contained in the chapter, but one possible answer to each question is contained in an end-of-book appendix.

EMPHASIZING CONNECTIONS WITH STUDENTS' LIVES AND CURRENT EVENTS

In teaching social psychology, professors are essentially trying to persuade their students that the information presented is a valuable way to understand social behavior and the process of living on this planet. There are compelling arguments in the message of social psychology, and most professors believe that if they can get students to critically analyze the message, they will become more competent in dealing with future life events. However, one thing that social cognition research tells us is something that good teachers have intuitively known for many years: Even students who enjoy intellectual stimulation will engage in lazy thinking when the material has little perceived relevance to their lives. In addition, this research further informs us that people who are typically lazy thinkers can become critical thinkers if they find the message content personally compelling and relevant. In writing the second edition, I endeavored to describe social psychological theory and research in such a way that students would be more likely to emotionally identify with the material. I encourage this identification by including more than twenty self-report questionnaires in the textbook and by directly asking the student readers to consider how the specific text material relates to their own lives. The self-report questionnaires are those currently used by researchers, and the results of studies employing them are part of the text material. Thus, as students learn about various social psychological theories and relevant research findings, they also learn something about themselves. Following are the questionnaires contained within each chapter.

SOCIAL PSYCHOLOGY IN APPLIED SETTINGS

Beyond self-report questionnaires, I also demonstrate to students how social psychology can be applied to their own lives by including an *Application Section* at the end of chapters 2 to 13. In these sections, which are generally two to three pages long, students learn how the theories and research in a particular area of social psychology can be applied to real-world settings. This end-of-chapter format allows many more applied topics to be discussed than in the typical social psychology textbook that has a very limited number of end-of-book application chapters. In addition, a new feature accompanying the application section is the *Featured Study* section. This Featured Study summarizes the purpose, method, and results of a recently published scientific article (within the past six years) that is relevant to the material covered in the applications section. These studies are described in the general format and style of a journal article, although they are much shorter and do not contain the statistical analyses. Following are the topics covered in the end-of-chapter application sections and their accompanying featured studies:

The Self
> Chapter 2: Do You Engage in Binge Drinking or Eating to Escape from Yourself?
> *Featured Study: Depletion of Self-Regulation Resources*

Self-Presentation and Social Perception
> Chapter 3: How Good Are You at Detecting Lies?
> *Featured Study: Telling Lies to Those Who Care*

Social Cognition
> Chapter 4: How Do You Explain Negative Events in Your Life?
> *Featured Study: Explanatory Style and Untimely Death*

Attitudes
> Chapter 5: How Do Reference Groups Shape Your Social and Political Attitudes?
> *Featured Study: The Persistence of Political Attitudes*

Persuasion
> Chapter 6: Can You Be Persuaded by Subliminal Messages?
> *Featured Study: Testing the Effectiveness of Subliminal Self-Help Tapes*

Prejudice and Discrimination
> Chapter 7: How Can Our Schools Both Reduce Intergroup Conflict and Promote Academic Achievement?
> *Featured Study: Student Cooperation and Prejudice Reduction*

Social Influence
> Chapter 8: Could You Be Pressured to Falsely Confess to a Crime?
> *Featured Study: Falsely Accepting Guilt*

Group Behavior
> Chapter 9: How Do Juries Make Decisions?
> *Featured Study: Defendant-Juror Similarity and Juror Judgments*

Interpersonal Attraction
> Chapter 10: How Can Social Skills Training Improve Your Life?
> *Featured Study: Mood Regulation Prior to Social Interaction*

Intimate Relationships
> Chapter 11: How Can You Cope with Jealousy?
> *Featured Study: Gender Differences in Jealous Responding*

CONTINUED COVERAGE OF DIVERSITY AND CULTURAL ANALYSIS

As in the previous edition, when discussing social psychological topics, I have taken great care to recognize the diverse nature of my readership. For example, in the self chapter, I analyze how ethnic minorities cope with racial intolerance by developing positive ethnic identities. In the chapter on prejudice and discrimination, different forms of racism are examined, as are strategies to promote racial tolerance in our schools. When examining intimate relationships, both heterosexual and homosexual friendships and romantic relationships are discussed, which helps the reader to better understand related issues, such as the avoidance of intimacy in heterosexual male friendships. In the examples used throughout the text, I use people from different countries around the globe and different ethnic groups within North American culture. Through these types of discussions and in the diverse examples given to illustrate the theories and principles of social psychology, I seek to foster in the writing a sense of inclusion for all readers.

When examining social behavior in a cross-cultural context, the particular aspect of culture highlighted is *individualism versus collectivism*. Why? Throughout the history of American social psychology, the concept of individualism has been an influential, yet unexamined, force directing our analysis of social life. All too often, American social psychologists have generalized their findings about social life in this country to all the inhabitants of the planet. Now, with the emerging influence of social psychology in Europe and in Third World countries, some of the basic assumptions of the relationship of the individual to the group have been questioned. This text includes discussions about how people from individualist and collectivist cultures respond to similar social situations, helping students to better understand the richness and flexibility of social life. This cross-cultural analysis is fully integrated into each chapter, rather than treated as a separate boxed insert or separate chapter.

ADDITION OF A SUMMARY CHAPTER

The last chapter in the second edition is titled "The Personal Relevance of Social Psychology." It is designed to help students better understand what they have learned about the psychology of social behavior in the hopes that this knowledge may prove useful beyond the classroom, specifically in their future careers and intimate relationships. This summary chapter is organized around the four sections of the text, and each book section "walk-through" includes one or two relevant, but not previously mentioned, research studies. This new information will further help students make connections between what they have learned and what they will soon be doing in their personal and professional lives. For students who are interested in learning more about how one becomes a social psychologist, this chapter ends with a brief overview of the profession as a career option, highlighting the process of graduate school education and career opportunities, and discussing the discipline's possible future interconnections with other disciplines.

SUPPLEMENTARY MATERIAL

The supplements listed here may accompany Franzoi, *Social Psychology,* second edition. Please contact your local McGraw-Hill representative for details concerning policies, prices, and availability as some restrictions may apply.

INSTRUCTOR'S MANUAL BY KRIS VASQUEZ, UNIVERSITY OF WISCONSIN-MADISON AND STEPHEN L. FRANZOI, MARQUETTE UNIVERSITY, COAUTHOR

The *Instructor's Manual* has been carefully revised and expanded in this edition to provide a variety of useful tools for both the novice and experienced professor of social psychology. Benefiting from the author's involvement in the revision, this edition includes for each chapter, a chapter overview, detailed chapter outline, and key terms and targeted learning objectives. These learning objectives are also used across the package in the test bank and study guide for better consistency in student learning. Complete lecture suggestions are provided for each major chapter concept. In addition, realistic classroom activities with handouts provide interesting suggestions for applying course material to students' lives. Further, the discussion questions are designed to promote critical thinking and target the concepts with which students may have the most difficulty. Finally, extensive media resources are included that can be utilized in a variety of ways to enliven the classroom. Included in the media resources are the McGraw-Hill Social Psychology Image Database, which is available in CD-ROM and online formats; an extensive list of web sites pertinent to the chapter material, which can be reached through hotlinks on the McGraw-Hill web site; and a variety of film and video selections for improved classroom planning. Additionally, there is an appendix on "Using Video in the Classroom" which provides detailed suggestions for applying some popular videos in a social psychology course.

TEST BANK BY KRIS VASQUEZ, UNIVERSITY OF WISCONSIN-MADISON

The *Test Bank* was expanded in this edition to include more than 2,100 questions written specifically for testing material in the main text. Questions include fill in the blank, matching, essay, and multiple-choice, which will give instructors a wide variety of choice in creating their testing and quizzing materials. In addition, all multiple-choice questions are identified by type (factual, conceptual, or applied) and level (easy, medium, difficult) for easier instructor editing.

COMPUTERIZED TEST BANK BY KRIS VASQUEZ, UNIVERSITY OF WISCONSIN-MADISON

This computerized test bank contains all of the questions in the print version and is available in both Macintosh and Windows platforms.

THE McGRAW-HILL SOCIAL PSYCHOLOGY IMAGE DATABASE CD-ROM

This set of 200 full-color images was developed using the best selection of our social development art and tables and is available in a CD-ROM format with a fully functioning editing feature, as well as on the text web site at http://www.mhhe.com/franzoi2. Instructors can add their own lecture notes to the CD-ROM as well as organize the images to correspond to their particular classroom needs.

POWERPOINT™ SLIDE PRESENTATION

This set of PowerPoint slides follows the chapter organization of *Social Psychology*, 2/e and includes images from the image database for a more effective lecture presentation.

WEB SITE

Please visit our social psychology web site for additional information on this title as well as text-specific resources and web links for both instructors and students. Our web site address is http://www.mhhe.com/franzoi2

ANNUAL EDITIONS—SOCIAL PSYCHOLOGY 1999/2000

Published by Dushkin/McGraw-Hill, these editions are a collection of forty-five articles on topics related to the latest research and thinking in social psychology. These editions are updated annually and contain helpful features including a topic guide, an annotated table of contents, unit overviews, and a topical index. An instructor's guide containing testing materials is available.

SOURCES: NOTABLE SELECTIONS IN SOCIAL PSYCHOLOGY

These selections are a collection of articles, book excerpts, and research studies that have shaped the study of social psychology and our contemporary understanding of it. The selections are organized topically around major areas of study within social psychology. Each selection is preceded by a head note that establishes the relevance of the article or study and provides biographical information on the author.

STUDENT STUDY GUIDE BY MICHELE ACKER, OTTERBEIN COLLEGE

The *Study Guide* has been revised substantially to reflect the changing needs of students as suggested in instructor/student reviews. Additionally, each chapter includes learning objectives, a chapter outline, flashcards, key terms, crossword puzzles, multiple-choice questions, essay questions, and a guide to Internet web sites relevant to that chapter, all aimed at helping students succeed in their social psychology course.

THE McGRAW-HILL SOCIAL PSYCHOLOGY SERIES

This popular series of paperback titles is written by authors about their particular field of expertise and are meant to complement any social psychology course. The series includes:

> Berkowitz, Leonard, *Aggression: Its Causes, Consequences, and Control*
> Brannigan, Gary G., and Matthew R. Merrens, *The Social Psychologists: Research Adventures*

Brehm, Sharon S., *Intimate Relationships,* second edition
Brown, Jonathon, *The Self*
Burn, Shawn M., *The Social Psychology of Gender*
Ellyson, Steve L., Amy G. Halberstadt, *Explorations in Social Psychology: Readings and Research*
Fiske, Susan T., and Shelley E. Taylor, *Social Cognition,* second edition
Milgram, Stanley, *The Individual in a Social World,* second edition
Myers, David G., *Exploring Social Psychology*
Pines, Ayala M., and Christina Maslach, *Experiencing Social Psychology: Readings and Projects,* third edition
Plous, Scott, *The Psychology of Judgement and Decision Making*
Ross, Lee, and Richard E. Nisbett, *The Person and the Situation: Perspective of Social Psychology*
Rubin, Jeffrey Z., Dean G. Pruitt, and Sung Hee Kim, *Social Conflict: Escalation, Stalemate, and Settlement,* second edition
Schroeder, David, Louis Penner, John Dovidio, Jane Piliavan, *The Psychology of Helping and Altruism: Problems and Puzzles*
Triandis, Harry C., *Culture and Social Behavior*
Zimbardo, Philip G., and Michael R. Leippe, *The Psychology of Attitude Change and Social Influence*

ACKNOWLEDGEMENTS

During the time I spent writing this text, many people have provided invaluable assistance and understanding. I first want to thank my family for not only supporting my writing efforts and forgiving my memory lapses during this time, but also for providing me with wonderful examples of social psychological principles that I used throughout the text. I also apologize to my daughters, Amelia and Lillian, for any future embarrassment I may cause them by retelling some of their life experiences in the book!

I also wish to thank the students in my social psychology courses at Marquette University who are the first to be exposed to my new stories of the social psychological enterprise. In addition, I would like to thank those students using my book at other colleges and universities who wrote me letters and e-mail concerning their reactions to what they read. The encouragement, enthusiasm, and criticism of all these students has made this revision much easier.

Appreciation is also extended to the many Internet-user members of the Society of Personality and Social Psychology who graciously responded to two important requests during the revision process: (1) sending me reprints and preprints of recent scientific articles describing recent advances in our understanding of social behavior, and (2) providing me with their opinions on where social psychology is headed as a discipline in the twenty-first century. Their response to the first request greatly aided me in offering a second edition of *Social Psychology* that incorporates exciting new research and theoretical developments. Their response to the second request about the future of social psychology closely corresponded to the opinions expressed by Steven Breckler, another SPSP member, who is also the social psychology program director at the National Science Foundation. These *Possible Future Connections* are summarized in chapter 14. The following are some of the SPSP members who responded to my requests:

Andrea Abele-Brehm
Universtat Erlangen, Germany
Christiane Alsop
Lesley College
Craig Anderson
University of Missouri-Columbia

Steven Breckler
National Science Foundation
Jerry Burger
Santa Clara University
Brad J. Bushman
Iowa State University

Jonathan Cheek
Wellesley College
Kristina DeNeve
Baylor University
Ed Diener
University of Illinois
Alice Eagly
Harvard University
Nicholas Epley
Cornell University
Stanley Feldstein
University of Maryland-Baltimore
Fred Fiedler
University of Washington
Joseph Forgas
University of New South Wales
Donelson Forsyth
Virginia Commonwealth University
James Friedrich
Willamette University
William Froming
*Pacific Graduate School of
Psychology*
Jack Glaser
Yale University
Donald Green
Yale University
Sharon Gross
University of Southern California
Mary Harris
University of New Mexico
Kwang-Kuo Hwang
National Taiwan University
William Ickes
University of Texas-Arlington
Kris Kelly
Western Illinois University
Herbert Kelman
Harvard University
Eric Klinger
University of Minnesota-Morris
Joachim Krueger
Brown University
Sonja Lyubomirsky
University of California-Riverside
Tara MacDonald
University of Wisconsin-Madison
James Maddux
George Mason University
Don McAdams
Northwestern University
Charles Miller
Northern Illinois University
Margo Montieth
University of Kentucky

Kris Moreno
Northwestern University
John-Paul Mulilis
*Penn State University-Beaver
Campus*
Darren Newtson
University of Virginia
Daphna Oyserman
University of Michigan
Paul Paulus
University of Texas-Arlington
Louis Penner
University of South Florida
Ashby Plant
University of Wisconsin-Madison
Thomas Postmes
*Amsterdam School of
Communications*
Jack Powell
University of Hartford
June Price-Tangney
George Mason University
Brian Quigley
Research Institute on Addictions
Bertram Raven
*University of California at
Los Angeles*
James Rest
*University of Minnesota-
Minneapolis*
Stan Sadava
Brock University
Mark Schaller
University of British Columbia
Todd Shackelford
Florida Atlantic University
Jeff Sherman
Northwestern University
Don Sharpsteen
University of Missouri
Dean Simonton
University of California-Davis
Sheldon Solomon
Skidmore College
Joseph Vandello
University of Illinois-Urbana
Paul Van Lange
Free University
Bas Verplanken
University of Nijmegen
Rex Wright
University of Alabama-Birmington
Ron Wright
University of Arizona
Vincent Yzerbyt
Catholic University of Louvin

Finally, I would like to thank my Acquisitions Editor, Mickey Cox and my Developmental Editor, Sharon Geary, for having sufficient confidence in this project to move it into production. I would also like to thank Editorial Assistant Sara Davis who coordinated the ancillary package for the text. Production Editor Joyce Berendes was a god send to me, always handling my anxieties and questions with a calming efficiency that not only strengthened the book but also enhanced my mental health. I had fun again working with Photo Research Editor Rose Deluhery who has a wonderful aesthetic sense when searching for just the right photographs to embellish text material. Stuart Patterson, Visuals/Design Specialist, made sure the book has the right "look" and that it would be pleasing to the reader's eye, while Sean Sullivan capped it off with a fine cover. Permissions Coordinator Sharon Geary adeptly secured the rights to a great deal of valuable material that is included in this text. Last but certainly not least, thanks to Jane Vaicunas, Executive Publisher, who had the wisdom and foresight to provide the necessary resources at all stages of development and production to make this a first-rate text.

The writing of this book was helped tremendously by the input of numerous reviewers who obviously care very much about the field of social psychology and about the art and craft of teaching. For their generous participation, I would like to thank:

REVIEWED MANUSCRIPT

Karin Ahlm
DePaul University

Matthew Berent
Idaho State University

Brad J. Bushman
Iowa State University

William Buskist
Auburn University

Diana Cordova
Yale University

Regina Conti
Colgate University

Eric Cooley
Western Oregon University

Keith E. Davis,
University of South Carolina at Columbia

Donna M. Desforges
University of Wisconsin-Stevens Point

Dorothee Dietrich
Hamline University

Roderick C. Gillis
University of Miami

Richard D. Harvey
St. Louis University

Michael Kernis
University of Georgia

Tracy L. Manning
Grossmont Community College

Joseph Marrone
Siena College

Karyn S. McKenzie
Georgetown College

Jeffery Scott Mio
California State Polytechnic University

John Phelan
Western Oklahoma State College

Lucy Robin
Indiana University

Daniel Sachau
Minnesota State University-Mankato

Connie Schick
Bloomsburg University

Charles G. Stangor
University of Maryland, College Park

JoNell Strough
West Virginia University

REVIEWED PROPOSAL

Brad J. Bushman
Iowa State University

Eric Cooley
Western Oregon University

Marti Hope Gonzales
University of Minnesota-St. Paul

Todd Heatherton
Dartmouth College

Melinda Jones
University of Pittsburgh at Bradford

Marianne LaFrance
Yale University

Rene Martin
University of Iowa

Robert Ridge
Brigham Young University

FOCUS GROUP

Karin Ahlm
  DePaul University
Monica Biernat
  University of Kansas
Keith E. Davis
  *University of South Carolina at
  Columbia*
William Gaeddert
  Plattsburgh State University

Rowland Miller
  Sam Houston State
Kathryn A. Morris
  Butler University
Robert Ridge
  Brigham Young University
Lee B. Ross
  Frostburg State

REVIEWED FIRST EDITION FOR SECOND EDITION

Mark Costanzo
  *Claremont McKenna College and
  Claremont Graduate University*
Harry Frank
  The University of Michigan-Flint
Russell Geen
  University of Missouri-Columbia
E. Keth Gerritz
  Wilmington College of Ohio
John H. Harvey
  University of Iowa
Elaine Hatfield
  University of Hawaii

Todd Heatherton
  Dartmouth College
Martin Kaplan
  Northern Illinois University
Marianne LaFrance
  Yale University
Louis Manza
  Lebanon Valley College
Mary Seay
  Allentown College
Rowena Tan
  University of Northern Iowa
Lawrence T. White
  Beloit College

TO THE STUDENT

I hope you enjoy reading this book. One of my main objectives in writing it was for you to experience how much fun it is to learn about the rich inner workings of our social world. The sole purpose of social psychology is to provide us with a better understanding of how the presence of other people influences our own thoughts, feelings, and behaviors. Social psychology can provide us with valuable insights about why people behave the way they do when in the social arena.

In my own social psychology classes, I tell my students many stories—stories about current events, stories about famous social psychological studies, and even stories about me and my family. By doing so, I hope to capture their imaginations in a way that will make learning enjoyable and relevant. For this textbook, I put some of these same stories on paper for you. When you read them, try to make personal connections between yourself and the material. I think this will help you develop a greater appreciation for the value of social psychology.

Whenever I teach, I learn a lot from my students about how to make the course better. I would like to have a similar opportunity to learn from you how I can improve this textbook. Your feedback about what you like or don't like about the book is important to me. To make it easy for you to provide this feedback, my school address, telephone number, and e-mail address are listed below. I will personally respond to all comments and questions.

Professor Stephen L. Franzoi
Department of Psychology
Marquette University
P.O. Box 1881
Milwaukee, WI 53201-1881
Telephone: (414)288-1650
E-mail: franzois@vms.csd.mu.edu

hapter outlines at the beginning of each chapter prepare you for the material to come.

Vivid, real-life stories introduce each major topic area. News events, historical incidents, or one of the author's personal experiences will help you, the reader, apply social psychological theories to the real world.

Key terms appear in bold type and are defined in context and in the page margin when they are first introduced. Key terms and their definitions can also be found in the end-of-book glossary.

Critical thinking exercises located within each chapter encourage you to carefully analyze a particular topic under current discussion. A possible answer to each question is contained in an end-of-book appendix.

Tables and figures throughout the text visualize information and clarify material.

Self-report questionnaires within each chapter promote a better understanding of the material at hand and help relate social psychological theories to situations we experience every day.

End-of-chapter *Application* sections show how the chapter's material can be used to solve real-life problems.

The *Featured Study* sections following each end-of-chapter application section describe recently published scientific articles that elaborate on the applications topic.

Section summaries at the end of each major chapter section review the major theories and terms covered in that section.

Suggested reading lists at the end of each chapter can help you find books about specific topics within social psychology and may be useful sources for research papers.

Web site resources are provided at the end of each chapter with descriptions of each site as it relates to the chapter content. The hot-linked web addresses can be found on the text web site at http://www.mhhe.com/franzoi2.

The closing chapter, "The Personal Relevance of Social Psychology," is designed to help you apply what you have learned about the psychology of social behavior beyond the classroom, specifically in your future careers and intimate relationships. This chapter ends with a discussion of social psychology as a career option, highlighting graduate school education and career opportunities, and discussing possible future interconnections with other disciplines.

SOCIAL PSYCHOLOGY

CHAPTER 1

SOCIAL PSYCHOLOGY AS A DISCIPLINE

t was a pleasantly mild Midwest day in 1974 in Kalamazoo, Michigan. I sat across from "Dave," a young and energetic man of 21, in a small, two-story house that was the residence or "ashram" of the local Divine Light Mission. Today was a red-letter day for me as an aspiring social scientist, and I wanted to be careful how I asked the question foremost in my mind. The Divine Light Mission was a neo-Hindu religious movement from India that had been receiving a lot of national attention since 1971. For the past two months I had been visiting the ashram on a regular basis, attempting to understand why so many people were attracted to this new Eastern religion. Dave had been a devoted member for more than two years, despite the protests of his family. I was a senior in college with a few social psychology courses under my belt and aspirations for graduate study in the discipline. Now I had the opportunity, with Dave's help, to observe some classic social psychological principles in operation.

In 1974, the Divine Light Mission claimed a worldwide membership of 6 million, with about 80,000 located in the United States. The leader of this new religious movement was a 16-year-old boy from India named Guru Maharaj Ji, who was hailed by his disciples (who were called "devotees") as being "Lord of the Universe" and "Divine Incarnation." Devotees believed that this young boy was about to usher in the New Age of Peace. Potential followers were promised salvation if they received the "Knowledge," which was described as being infinite and therefore unexplainable.

Although Guru Maharaj Ji touted himself as a divine entity, he was not immune to the allure of earthly pleasures. Rolls-Royces, Jaguars, airplanes, motorcycles, town houses and mansions staffed with servants, as well as an elaborate assortment of Batman comic books and squirt guns were but a few of the material indulgences of the Perfect Master. What allowed the young guru to live in such luxury were thousands of unsalaried devotees like Dave who coordinated a host of enterprises, including ten Divine Sales thrift stores, a "Cleanliness Is Next To Godliness" janitorial service, and a vegetarian restaurant in New York City. In addition to the income generated by these businesses, upon joining, all new members' financial assets were routinely funneled into the mission's accounts, as was any income earned from "worldly jobs."

Which brings me back to the question that I was considering as I sat across from Dave in the Kalamazoo ashram. The previous day, the national media had reported that Guru Maharaj Ji had skipped town and eloped with his secretary. Upon learning of this youthful, and decidedly ungodlike, flight of spontaneous passion, his mother had publicly pronounced that Guru Maharaj Ji was no longer the Perfect Master. Instead, she angrily proclaimed that his older brother was the new divine incarnation. Within one day's time, members of the religious movement were being told to believe that Guru Maharaj Ji had gone from being the Perfect Master of their 6-million-member mission to being spiritually "grounded" by his "Holy Mother." The question I was intent on asking Dave was how the members of the Kalamazoo ashram were going to reconcile this turn of events. After all, they had paid a high price to gain admission to this religious cult that promised them contact with divine salvation. Yet now the Mission that was their life's work and the seat of their spirituality was in danger of crumbling. Had Dave begun to question the spirituality of his guru and his own commitment to the Divine Light Mission?

Dave's reply was immediate and unwavering. He told me that these recent events were all part of the Perfect Master's plan of ushering in the New Age of

Imaginal figures can influence our thoughts, feelings, and actions. For example, seeing that the lead fictional character in Disney's Mulan overcomes immense obstacles to protect her family and country from an invading warlord and his army may inspire young viewers—especially girls—to persevere when they themselves face life challenges. What imaginal figures inspired you when you were a child? What imaginal figures—either real or fictional—influence you today?

Kurt Lev
refugee
instrum
psychol
scientifi

Why do
psychc
Hitler c
the
develop

Intera

An impc
psycholc
combine
and the
behavio

SOCIAL PSYCHOL
PSYCHOLOGY AN

You might be surprised to
known as social psycholo
Edward Jones (1998) point
the two is the psycholog
behavior, they do so from

The central focus of *p*
and how she or he respond
be due to people's interpro
ties and temperament. Eve
dynamics, they tend to ex
tion of social psychology i

In contrast, *sociologi*
vidual differences and the
the focus tends to be on la
conomic status, their socia
larger group variables p
interest to this discipline t
social psychologists are r
etal-based problems as p
branches of social psycho

Although there have
(Backman, 1983)—and e
offered at the University
tions make it doubtful th
an interdisciplinary socia
influence each other. The
impact of culture on soci
the sociological disciplin
attention to individual d
from the psychological
occurred over the years, t
differing, perspectives or

THE HISTORY O
REVEALS ITS A

As a scientific discipline,
of the growth occurring
By most standards, socia

Guru Maharaj Ji, 16-year-old leader of the Divine Light Mission, was supposed to be the spiritually perfect "Divine Incarnation." How do you think the followers of this "Perfect Master" would respond to his mother's pronouncement that he was no longer the divine incarnation?

Peace. If anything, Dave stated, Guru Maharaj Ji was now more in his thoughts than before, and he was even more certain that the New Age would be dawning soon.

Does Dave's strengthened conviction in the face of troubling counterevidence surprise you? Was his reaction different from what you might expect from a "normal" person? Was it irrational or perhaps even indicative of abnormality? Why was Dave ignoring or explaining away so much damning information about the Divine Light Mission and its leaders?

Had I not been exposed to the field of social psychology, I probably would have concluded that Dave's thinking might be best explained by an expert in abnormal psychology. Yet, at the time, I strongly suspected that his far-fetched rationalizations were more similar to the normal and all-too-ordinary thought processes of a person placed in a very untenable psychological position. Years ago, social psychologist Leon Festinger (1957) had outlined a theory to explain how our need to maintain consistency between our beliefs can often lead to irrational behavior. That is, if people simultaneously hold two thoughts that are inconsistent ("Guru Maharaj Ji is a god" and "Guru Maharaj Ji is a spiritual fraud"), this will create an uncomfortable psychological state that people will try to reduce or eliminate. The greater their investment in particular beliefs (for example, "Guru Maharaj Ji is a god"), the more difficult it is for people to divest themselves of these beliefs. Known as the theory of *cognitive dissonance* (see chapter 5), it captured the imagination of social scientists because it provided an explanation for how normally sane individuals can engage in some rather odd forms of thought and behavior due to being caught up in the circumstances at hand.

More recently, social psychologists have demonstrated how our self-concepts are very resistant to change, even when these self-beliefs are detrimental to our well-being (see chapter 2). In Dave's case, having so thoroughly committed himself to Guru Maharaj Ji and the Divine Light Mission, how could he be expected to do anything but rationalize and explain away evidence suggesting that his commitment was a mistake? It was not as though he had merely spent fifty cents on a candy bar and then had to admit that it wasn't very tasty. No, this admission would threaten the very core of his own self-definition and central values. The natural and self-protective thing to do would be to deny to others—and to himself—that he had made a mistake. From a social psychological perspective it made perfect sense.

WHAT IS SOC

As the preceding example
defies rational explanation
Most of the examples pro
Mission's, but they will cc
daily lives. You, the new
affinity to the subject ma
your daily experience in

SOCIAL PSYCHO
HOW WE ARE I

Gordon Allport, one of th
nition of the field that ca
discipline that uses scier
how the thought, feeling
imagined, or implied pr

To better understan
might the *actual presen*
behavior? Returning to
Divine Light Mission wa
renew their allegiance. F
strength in the presence
ence of others can influer
players have to the acti
Opposing fans often try
gesturing wildly in the h

Regarding how th
ings, and behavior, thir
something that ran cou
ally been present, did t
when Dave first learne
figured prominently i
young guru was thous
actions. Imaginal figu
events just as surely a
uals may even be pure
daughter, Lillian, tells
cartoon character who
tration of the power o

Finally, how can
you ever had the exp
speed limit, only to pa
"We're watching you
copter circling overhe
sure on the gas pedal

Based on this d
better understand the
(1989), a well-know
psychology as a "bri
means that social ps
political science, ecor
individual fits into th
of knowledge, in this
ogists, and anthropo

Social Psychology

The scientific discipline that attempts to understand and explain how the thoughts, feelings, and behavior of individuals are influenced by the actual, imagined, or implied presence of others.

In
Soc
der
con
val
of s

also use this inner experience to anticipate how rivals might behave in the future—perhaps in war or in social bargaining—thus giving them an advantage in these activities. Similarly, the development of language not only allowed our ancestors to better coordinate group activities, but they could also use this symbolic communication to discuss things not physically present, such as a herd of antelope or a band of hostile warriors (Dunbar, 1993). According to this *evolutionary* view, these two defining features of the self became the means by which our ancestors developed an adaptive advantage in their environment, thus increasing their chances of surviving and reproducing.

According to George Herbert Mead, the self develops as children learn to engage in symbolic interaction and role taking.

The "V" sign is the symbol of the unconquerable will of the occupied territories, and a portent of the fate awaiting the Nazi tyranny.

Winston Churchill, British prime minister during World War II, 1874–1965, message to the people of Europe on launching the "V" for Victory propaganda campaign, July 20, 1941

CONTEMPORARY SELF THEORIES ARE BASED ON THE INSIGHTS OF GEORGE HERBERT MEAD AND WILLIAM JAMES

Arguably, the most influential contributors to our understanding of the self were two early social theorists, psychologist William James and sociologist George Herbert Mead. In both James's and Mead's theories, the self is described as having two separate aspects, the self as knower (the *I*) and the self as known (the *me*). The "I" is the active perceiver, initiator, and regulator of action; the "me" is the knowledge one has about oneself. One way to think of these two discriminated self-aspects is that, no matter what you are conscious of, you—in the form of the "I"—are always the *subject* of awareness (the subjective self). Whenever consciousness becomes self-reflexive, you—in the form of the "me"—become the *object* of awareness (the objective self). To keep these two aspects of the self straight in your mind, repeat this phrase: Whenever I think about something, "I" am always the subject of consciousness, and one of the things I may be consciously attending to is "me."

MEAD AND THE DEVELOPMENT OF THE SELF

Mead asserted that a human infant is not born a self, but rather, a self *emerges* as a result of social interaction and role taking. Regarding social interaction, a critical ingredient in developing a self is learning to use symbols. *Symbols* are arbitrary signs of objects that stand in the place of those objects. Spoken or printed words are symbols—their symbolic nature is confirmed by the fact that the groupings of letters on this page are meaningful to you. A hand gesture can also be a symbol. We interpret others' gestures and act on the basis of this interpreted meaning. If we misinterpret, social interaction can become awkward.

The exact meaning assigned to each gesture will be substantially determined by the social context in which it takes place. A raised index finger in North American culture, for example, may mean that the gesturing person is asking for permission to speak to an assembled group, or that her sports team is "Number One," or that she would like others to look in the direction she is pointing. *Cultural context* can also significantly alter the meaning of a gesture, as is illustrated in figure 2.1.

In this symbolic interaction, participants must continually consider one another's ongoing acts and reorganize or adjust their own intentions in terms of the others' intentions. To be able to ascertain others' intentions, Mead argued that we must engage in *role taking*, which is imaginatively assuming the point of view of others and observing our own behavior (the "me") from this other perspective. Mead believed that it is through such symbolic interaction that humans cease to merely be passive responders to their social environment and, instead, become coactors in creating (and re-creating) their social reality.

According to Mead, the self develops as children acquire language ability and start taking the role of the other in their play activities. The roles they adopt in this *play stage* are those of specific others, such as parents and siblings, but Mead believed children at this stage could only adopt one role at a time. An example of role taking here would be a boy adopting the perspective of "Daddy" and reprimanding himself

FIGURE 2.1

Thumb extended up with closed fingers

In North America, Russia, and France, it normally means "Good job!" or "Excellent!"

In Nigeria it is a rude gesture, expressing strong disapproval.

In Japan, China, and Korea, it is used in counting and means "four."

Index finger at ear and rotated in a circle

In Argentina it means that someone is wanted on the telephone—probably a vestige of the old, hand-cranked phones.

In North America, Russia, Japan, France, and Germany, it means "Something is wrong with his (or her) head" or "They're crazy."

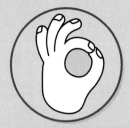

Thumb and index finger forming a circle

In Laos and France it means "Bad," "Zero," or "Worthless."

In Japan it means "money."

In North America and Russia it means "That's good!"

In Arab states (accompanied by a baring of the teeth) it expresses extreme hostility.

Gestures and Their Meaning Around the World

Source: Data from Morrison et al., 1994; and Schneller (1992).

for disobeying a family rule. It is in this role taking that children develop beliefs about themselves, which are largely a reflection of how they believe others evaluate them. This *reflected appraisal* is an important determinant of self-beliefs (Felson, 1989). As children mature, Mead stated that they learn to take the role of many others simultaneously and, as a result, the self becomes more cognitively complex. In this *game stage,* they can engage in complex activities (often in the form of games) involving the interaction of many roles. An example of role taking in the game stage would be someone playing baseball. To play effectively, one must understand how all the players on the field are related to one another, and one must be able to cognitively adopt these multiple roles simultaneously. Early in the game stage, Mead believed the multiple role taking involves mostly those who are physically present. However, as the self becomes increasingly complex, Mead stated that children begin to respond to themselves from the point of view of not just a number of discrete others, but from the perspective of society as a whole. By internalizing the attitudes and expectations commonly held by the larger society—what Mead called the *generalized other*—the person becomes a fully formed self.

JAMES AND THE SELF AS A PROCESS OF IDENTIFICATION

While Mead focused on cognitive factors and attempted to explain how the self develops, James focused on the mature self and its affective or emotional aspects. The way things become part of the "me," James argued, is through our *emotional identification* with them. Your body, your feelings, your beliefs and values are all part of your "me." But because what is part of the "me" is determined by emotional identification, your parents, siblings, friends, and lovers are also likely to be incorporated into your "me." Indeed, your clothes, your stereo system, and perhaps even your fuzzy little teddy bear could be elements in your "me." In this regard, the "me" includes not just that which is inside

An important aspect of William James's theory of the self was that things became a part of the "me" through our emotional identification with them.

your body, but anything that symbolizes and affirms who and what you are. This belief that the objective self can extend beyond the person is noteworthy, for it represents a break with the traditional assumption that people are separate, encapsulated egos.

James's notion of the identification process also illustrates his belief in the ever changing nature of the self. He contended that due to the evolving nature of life as reflected in our social relationships and material possessions, and the fallibility and reconstructive nature of our own memories, the objective self is not stable like a diamond, but rather, it is constantly changing—"we are dealing with a fluctuating material." The implication here is that our self of today is different, even if only subtly, from our self of yesterday.

Finally, James also believed that what we emotionally identify with will serve as the basis for judging our own self-worth. His formula for self-esteem was *success divided by pretensions,* meaning that self-esteem is a measure of one's successes relative to one's pretensions or concerns. Thus, if you emotionally identify yourself as a budding pianist, your self-esteem will be significantly determined by your success in piano activities, and not in how you perform in activities with which you do not identify (for example, soccer, sewing, carpentry).

SHADOWS OF OUR PAST IN CONTEMPORARY RESEARCH

Both James's and Mead's theories of the self have had a profound and continuing influence on social psychology, with James's writings reflecting the more affective or "hot" perspective on the nature of human behavior, and Mead's writings reflecting the more cognitive or "cold" approach (see chapter 1). Despite these different orientations, the contributions of both theorists revolve around a common theme: as social beings, we are aware of our self-aspirations and how our appearance and behavior are seen and judged by others. Through their work, James and Mead provided the path by which later theorists would explore, in more detail, central issues of social life, such as willpower and self-regulation (Mischel et al., 1996), self-awareness and self-discrepancy (Higgins, 1987), social identity (Tajfel, 1982), and self-presentation (Schlenker, 1980). Mead's idea that people creatively shape reality through social interaction forms the cornerstone for **symbolic interaction theory** in sociological social psychology (Gecas & Burke, 1995) and is echoed in the *social constructionist* perspective seen in the social sciences as a whole (Hermans et al., 1992). Contemporary social psychologists have also borrowed James's notion of self-expansion in their analysis of love (Aron et al., 1992) and people's identification with others' successes (Cialdini et al., 1976). Table 2.1 summarizes some of the similarities and differences between James's, Mead's, and contemporary self theories.

In the upcoming discussion of contemporary self theories and research, we will analyze the subjective self and the objective self, previously identified by James and Mead as the "I" and "me." Essentially the "I" is the self's *executive function:* it makes decisions, initiates behavior, and exerts control over the self and the environment. Our analysis of this executive function will focus on how we regulate our behavior through self-awareness, and how we process and evaluate self-relevant information.

Regarding James's and Mead's "me," this aspect of the self will be discussed using the term self-concept (Snodgrass & Thompson, 1997). **Self-concept** is the sum total of a person's thoughts and feelings that defines the self as an object. Put another way, self-concept is a "theory" of our personal behavior that we construct through social interaction (Epstein, 1973; Oyserman & Packer, 1996). Consistent with James's thinking, self-concept has no precise location or boundaries, but rather, is framed through identification. Thus, my two precious daughters Amelia and Lillian are very much a part of my self-concept. The ten-speed bike that carried me on a 3,000-mile, cross-country trek in the summer of 1977 was at the time also encompassed within my self-concept. Yet years later, this same bike, collecting dust

---

. . .We have the paradox of a man shamed to death because he is only the second pugilist or the second oarsman in the world. . . . Yonder puny fellow, however, whom everyone can beat, suffers no chagrin, for he has long ago abandoned the attempt to "carry that line."

William James, American psychologist and philosopher, 1842–1910

Symbolic Interaction Theory

A contemporary sociological theory, inspired by Mead's insights and based on the premise that people, as selves, creatively shape reality through social interaction.

Self-Concept

The sum total of a person's thoughts and feelings that defines the self as an object.

TABLE 2.1

Aspects of the Self

William James's Self Theory	George Herbert Mead's Self Theory	Contemporary Theories
Outlined the dimensions of the mature self, and contended that things become part of the self through *emotional identification*	Outlined how the self develops and contended that it was largely a *cognitive process*, brought about through symbolic interaction and role taking	Have expanded on the insights of these two past theorists
Term Used to Describe the Subjective Self	**Term Used to Describe the Subjective Self**	**Term Used to Describe the Subjective Self**
The "I": the self as active perceiver and initiator of action	The "I": the self as active perceiver and initiator of action	"Executive function": all cognitive and affective processes that initiate and regulate behavior
Term Used to Describe the Objective Self	**Term Used to Describe the Objective Self**	**Term Used to Describe the Objective Self**
The "me": the self as anything that symbolizes and affirms who and what one is	The "me": the self as seen from the imagined perspective of others	"Self-concept": the sum total of a person's thoughts and feelings that define the self as an object

in the garage, is not something with which I strongly identify. At best, the bike is now on the periphery of my self-concept.

In a very real sense, our self-concept is a grand self-portrait we paint and repaint throughout our lives—a little change here, a small alteration there, most of the time so insignificant that no one notices, least of all us. Sometimes as we paint, those who are important to us guide our hands, shaping the alterations. At other times, those who view the changed portrait express disapproval and we restore the old image. If we become sufficiently dissatisfied with the portrait and feel that we can no longer reliably paint, we may consult a master painter who will help us to create a more accurate and pleasing visage. In rare instances, as a result of dramatic changes in our lives, we may scrap the entire portrait and paint a new, very different self-concept.

In discussing self-concept, we must also keep in mind that it is not a dispassionate self theory. It consists of numerous evaluations of self as being good, bad, or mediocre. This evaluative aspect of the "me" is called **self-esteem.** Research indicates that people with low self-esteem have less clearly defined and stable self-concepts than people with high self-esteem (Setterlund & Niedenthal, 1993). The self-concepts of people with low self-esteem also appear to be less complex (Campbell et al., 1991) and less flexible (Paulhus & Martin, 1988). As you will soon learn, the favorability of people's self-evaluations play a significant role in shaping numerous life choices. Before reading further, spend a few minutes completing the self-esteem questionnaire in table 2.2.

Self-Esteem

A person's evaluation of his or her self-concept.

TABLE 2.2

Self-Esteem Scale

Instructions

Read each item below and then indicate how well each statement describes you using the following response scale:

0 = extremely uncharacteristic (not at all like me)
1 = uncharacteristic (somewhat unlike me)
2 = neither characteristic nor uncharacteristic
3 = characteristic (somewhat like me)
4 = extremely characteristic (very much like me)

_____ 1. On the whole, I am satisfied with myself.

_____ 2. At times I think I am no good at all.*

_____ 3. I feel that I have a number of good qualities.

_____ 4. I am able to do things as well as most other people.

_____ 5. I feel I do not have much to be proud of.*

_____ 6. I certainly feel useless at times.*

_____ 7. I feel that I'm a person of worth, at least on an equal plane with others.

_____ 8. I wish I could have more respect for myself.*

_____ 9. All in all, I am inclined to feel that I am a failure.*

_____ 10. I take a positive attitude toward myself.

Directions for Scoring

Half of the self-esteem items are reverse-scored; that is, for these items a lower rating actually indicates a higher level of self-esteem. Before summing all ten items to find out your total self-esteem score, recode those with an asterisk ("*") so that 0 = 4, 1 = 3, 3 = 1, and 4 = 0. Your total self-esteem score can range from 0 to 40, with a higher score indicating a higher level of self-esteem. Scores greater than 20 indicate generally positive attitudes toward the self; those below 20 indicate generally negative self-attitudes.

Source: From M. Rosenberg, *Conceiving the Self.* Copyright © 1979 Basic Books, New York, NY. Reprinted by permission.

SECTION SUMMARY

In both William James's and George Herbert Mead's theories, the *self* is described as having two separate aspects, the self as knower (the *I*) and the self as known (the *me*). Contemporary social psychologists have expanded on the insights of these two pioneers and made the study of the self an important aspect of their analysis of social behavior. *Self-concept* is our theory of our own personal behavior, while our evaluation of our self-concept is called *self-esteem*.

THE SELF AS BOTH TARGET OF ATTENTION AND ACTIVE AGENT

The self as the "I" is the initiator and regulator of behavior, yet, in the form of the "me," it is also the object of the "I"'s attention. Let's explore the interplay between the "I" and the "me" in the process of self-awareness and self-regulation.

SELF-AWARENESS IS A TEMPORARY PSYCHOLOGICAL STATE

Self-Awareness

A psychological state in which you take yourself as an object of attention.

Stop for a moment and think about your current mood. If you followed my suggestion, you just engaged in **self-awareness,** which is a psychological state in which you take yourself as an object of attention. To have a self-concept, you must be able to engage in self-awareness. Two different types of self-awareness have been identified. *Private self-awareness* is the temporary state of being aware of hidden, private self-aspects, whereas *public self-awareness* is the temporary state of being aware of public self-aspects. Being asked about your current mood, seeing your face in a small mirror, or feeling the hunger pangs of your stomach will likely cause you to become privately self-aware. Being watched by others, having your picture taken, or seeing your entire body in a full-length mirror can induce public self-awareness (Buss, 1980).

SELF-AWARENESS DEVELOPMENT

You might be surprised to know that we are not born with self-awareness ability, but rather, we develop it. Psychologists discovered this fact by placing a spot of rouge on babies' noses and then placing them in front of a mirror (Lewis & Brooks, 1978). Infants between the ages of 9 and 12 months treated their mirror image as if it was another child, showing no interest in the unusual rouge spot. Yet those around 18 months of age exhibited self-recognition—and thus, self-awareness ability—by staring in the mirror and touching the mysterious spot on their noses. Recognizing the image in the mirror as their own, they realized that they looked different. Based on such studies, it appears that self-awareness develops at about 18 months of age (Amsterdam, 1972).

SELF-AWARENESS IN OTHER PRIMATES

Research by Gordon Gallup and his coworkers suggests that we may not be evolution's only experiment in self-awareness. In one study, Gallup (1977) painted an odorless red dye on one eyebrow and one ear of anesthetized chimpanzees. When the chimps later looked into a mirror they immediately began to touch the red dye marks on their bodies, indicating that they recognized the image in the mirror as their own. These and other studies indicate that our primate cousins (chimpanzees, gorillas, and orangutans, but not monkeys)—and perhaps even dolphins—appear to possess self-awareness ability (Anderson, 1993; Gallup & Povinelli, 1993). Does this mean these animals also possess self-concepts? As yet, we don't know, but contrary to previous scientific beliefs, we humans may not have a monopoly on the self-concept.

PRIVATE AND PUBLIC SELF-AWARENESS EFFECTS

There are a number of consequences of inducing private and public self-awareness. One effect of private self-awareness is *intensification of affect,* meaning that any positive or negative feelings experienced when privately self-aware will be exaggerated (Scheier & Carver, 1977). Thus, if you are happy and become privately self-aware, your happiness will be intensified. Likewise, if angered, private self-awareness will result in more anger. A second consequence, *clarification of knowledge,* means that private events become clearer and more distinct, thus increasing your ability to accurately report on them (Gibbons et al., 1979). A third consequence of private self-awareness is *greater adherence to personal standards of behavior* (Froming et al., 1998). Thus, when privately self-aware, you are more likely to act in line with your personal beliefs than to conform to social pressures.

Regarding public self-awareness, one likely effect is *evaluation apprehension* when you realize you are the object of others' attention. This is because you have learned through experience that public scrutiny often results in either positive or negative outcomes. Evaluation apprehension is the reason you get butterflies in

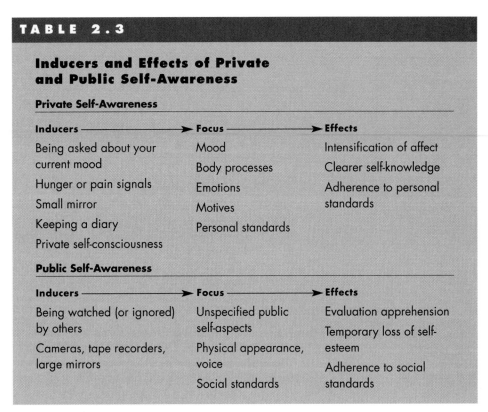

TABLE 2.3

Inducers and Effects of Private and Public Self-Awareness

Private Self-Awareness

Inducers ⟶	Focus ⟶	Effects
Being asked about your current mood	Mood	Intensification of affect
Hunger or pain signals	Body processes	Clearer self-knowledge
Small mirror	Emotions	Adherence to personal standards
Keeping a diary	Motives	
Private self-consciousness	Personal standards	

Public Self-Awareness

Inducers ⟶	Focus ⟶	Effects
Being watched (or ignored) by others	Unspecified public self-aspects	Evaluation apprehension
Cameras, tape recorders, large mirrors	Physical appearance, voice	Temporary loss of self-esteem
	Social standards	Adherence to social standards

Source: Based on Buss, 1980.

your stomach before making an important class presentation or calling that special person for a date. A second effect is a *temporary loss of self-esteem* due to realizing that there is a discrepancy between your ideal and actual public self. This explains why you feel badly after a failed presentation or date request. Finally, a third consequence of public self-awareness is *greater adherence to social standards of behavior*, meaning a heightened degree of conformity (Duval & Wicklund, 1972).

If you look at the consequences for both private and public self-awareness in table 2.3, do you notice something interesting? Whether behavior is more influenced by personal or social standards is at least partially determined by what aspect of the self is salient (private or public). This proposition is an important one to consider, for social scientists have long debated the importance of personal versus social standards. Some theorists have assumed that people are motivated primarily by a desire to meet personal goals and are responsive largely to their own attitudes and feelings (Maslow, 1970; Rogers, 1947). Others have argued that we are largely a reflected image of our social group and that prior to acting, we consider how we will be judged by others (Cooley, 1902; Goffman, 1959). As in most such debates, both perspectives are true in their own limited fashion. When privately self-aware, we tend to act in line with our personal standards, but social standards are more influential when we are publicly self-aware (Froming et al., 1982).

SELF-CONSCIOUSNESS IS A PERSONALITY TRAIT

As adults, we all have the ability to engage in either private or public self-awareness. However, when some stimulus induces self-awareness, that focus is only temporary. Besides becoming self-aware due to external stimuli, researchers have also determined that some people spend more time self-reflecting than others. This habitual tendency to engage in self-awareness is known as the personality trait of **self-consciousness.**

Self-Consciousness

The habitual tendency to engage in self-awareness.

Just as there are two types of self-awareness, there are also two types of self-consciousness. In 1975, Allan Fenigstein, Michael Scheier, and Arnold Buss developed the Self-Consciousness Scale to measure these two traits (see table 2.4). *Private self-consciousness* is the tendency to be aware of the private aspects of the self, while *public self-consciousness* is the tendency to be aware of publicly displayed self-aspects. These traits are two distinct tendencies; therefore, a person could either be very attentive to both sides of the self, attentive to one but inattentive to another, or relatively inattentive to both. Spend a few minutes completing the items in table 2.4 to learn more about your own levels of private and public self-consciousness.

PRIVATE SELF-CONSCIOUSNESS EFFECTS

Many of the effects of private self-attention are the same whether they result from the psychological state of private self-awareness or the personality trait of private self-consciousness (Scheier & Carver, 1980). Therefore, individuals high in private self-consciousness tend to experience greater intensification of affect, greater clarification of knowledge, and greater attention and adherence to personal standards of behavior than do their less self-conscious counterparts. A number of studies have also found that the self-concepts of those high in private self-consciousness are not only more accurate reflections of their actual behavior than those low in private self-consciousness, but they are also more complex and more in line with others' perceptions of them (Davies, 1994). Based on these findings, you might be wondering whether it's better to be high or low in private self-consciousness. Is it true that the more we learn about ourselves the better persons we become? Or are those people correct who sometimes warn us not to try to analyze our thoughts and feelings so much ("It will drive you crazy! You will make yourself unhappy and depressed!")?

On the plus side, Mark Davis and I have found evidence that those high in private self-consciousness are more likely to reveal private self-aspects to their friends and romantic partners, and this self-disclosure in turn reduces loneliness and increases relationship satisfaction (Davis & Franzoi, 1986). In addition, research by Jerry Suls and his colleagues indicates that the physical health of persons high in private self-consciousness is less likely to be adversely affected by stressful life events than is the health of low self-conscious persons (Mullen & Suls, 1982; Suls & Fletcher, 1985). One explanation for this finding is that people who regularly pay attention to their physiological states (an aspect of the private self) are more likely to become aware of early warning signs of illness-inducing stress, and thus are more likely to take precautionary steps to avoid the onset of illness.

On the negative side, other studies indicate that habitual attention to private self-aspects can be a contributing factor to depression (Hull et al., 1990; Ingram, 1990). Why might heightened private self-focus be associated with depression? One possible reason is that greater attention to private self-aspects intensifies a person's current emotional state, including depression. Thus, the *trait* of private self-consciousness or the *state* of private self-awareness might increase feelings of depression among those who are already depressed (Nix et al., 1995).

Taking these studies into account, it appears that there are both benefits and drawbacks to attending to our private self. Instead of high or low private self-conscious individuals being healthier than the other, they may simply represent different motivational orientations toward the self.

PUBLIC SELF-CONSCIOUSNESS EFFECTS

As with situationally induced public self-awareness, persons who are high in public self-consciousness tend to be more concerned about how others judge them (Fenigstein & Vanable, 1992), are more conforming to group norms (Yoshitake, 1990), and are more likely to withdraw from embarrassing situations (Froming et al., 1990) than those low in this trait. This tendency to comply with external standards encompasses physical appearance as well. A number of studies have found

TABLE 2.4

Measuring Private and Public Self-Consciousness

The personality traits of private and public self-consciousness are measured by items on the Self-Consciousness Scale (SCS: Fenigstein et al., 1975). To take the SCS, read each item below and then indicate how well each statement describes you using the following scale:

0 = extremely uncharacteristic (not at all like me)
1 = uncharacteristic (somewhat unlike me)
2 = neither characteristic nor uncharacteristic
3 = characteristic (somewhat like me)
4 = extremely characteristic (very much like me)

_____ 1. I'm always trying to figure myself out.

_____ 2. I'm concerned about my style of doing things.

_____ 3. Generally, I'm not very aware of myself.*

_____ 4. I reflect about myself a lot.

_____ 5. I'm concerned about the way I present myself.

_____ 6. I'm often the subject of my own fantasies.

_____ 7. I never scrutinize myself.*

_____ 8. I'm self-conscious about the way I look.

_____ 9. I'm generally attentive to my inner feelings.

_____ 10. I usually worry about making a good impression.

_____ 11. I'm constantly examining my motives.

_____ 12. One of the last things I do before I leave my house is look in the mirror.

_____ 13. I sometimes have the feeling that I'm off somewhere watching myself.

_____ 14. I'm concerned about what other people think of me.

_____ 15. I'm alert to changes in my mood.

_____ 16. I'm usually aware of my appearance.

_____ 17. I'm aware of the way my mind works when I work through a problem.

Directions for Scoring

Several of the SCS items are reverse-scored; that is, for these items a lower rating actually indicates a higher level of self-consciousness. Before summing the items, recode those with an asterisk ("") so that 0 = 4, 1 = 3, 3 = 1, and 4 = 0.*

Private self-consciousness. To calculate your private self-consciousness score, add up your responses to the following items: 1, 3*, 4, 6, 7*, 9, 11, 13, 15, and 17.

Public self-consciousness. To calculate your public self-consciousness score, add up your responses to the following items: 2, 5, 8, 10, 12, 14, and 16.

When Fenigstein, Scheier, and Buss developed the SCS in 1975, the mean college score for college students on private self-consciousness was about 26, whereas the average score of public self-consciousness was about 19. The higher your score is above one of these values, the more of this type of self-consciousness you probably possess. The lower your score is below one of these values, the less of this type of self-consciousness you probably possess.

that individuals high in public self-consciousness are more concerned about their physical appearance and believe appearance is important for smooth social interaction (Striegel-Moore et al., 1993). Although this concern reflects a global tendency to stereotype people based on their physical appearance (see chapter 10), those high in public self-consciousness are more likely to "judge the book by its cover" than the average person (Ryckman et al., 1991).

A good deal of the research investigating public self-consciousness has also explored private self-consciousness as well. How do these two traits interact in a public setting? As you might expect, people who are high on private self-consciousness and low on public self-consciousness are the ones most likely to act according to their true attitudes when among others. On the other hand, people who are high on public self-consciousness, regardless of their level of private self-consciousness, are much less likely to publicly act according to their true attitudes (Scheier, 1980). Therefore, it appears that even when people have an accurate understanding of their own attitudes as a result of their habitual private self-focus, being simultaneously high in public self-consciousness can lead to behavior that runs counter to those attitudes.

SELF-REGULATION IS THE SELF'S MOST IMPORTANT FUNCTION

Self-Regulation

The ways in which people control and direct their own actions.

Closely related to self-awareness is **self-regulation,** which refers to the ways in which we control and direct our own actions. How is self-regulation related to self-awareness? Simply put, you must be self-aware to engage in self-regulation. Research by Walter Mischel and his coworkers has analyzed how self-regulation provides people with the capacity to forgo the immediate gratification of small rewards to later attain larger rewards (Mischel, 1996). Anyone who has ever turned down a party invitation to study for an upcoming exam understands this particular self-regulatory process. People who learn how to delay gratification early in childhood are significantly better adjusted later in life—both academically and socially—than low self-regulators (Shoda et al., 1990).

Control Theory of Self-Regulation

A theory contending that, through self-awareness, people compare their behavior to a standard, and if there is a discrepancy, they work to reduce it.

In Charles Carver and Michael Scheier's (1981a) **control theory of self-regulation,** they contend that self-awareness allows us to assess how we are doing in meeting our goals and ideals. The core idea in control theory is a cognitive feedback loop (see figure 2.2), summarized by the acronym TOTE, which stands for the steps taken in self-regulation: Test-Operate-Test-Exit. In self-regulation, engaging in self-awareness allows us to compare how we are doing against some standard. This is the first test phase. When we are privately self-aware we will compare ourselves against a *private* standard (for example, our own values), but when we are publicly self-aware we will compare ourselves against a *public* standard (for example, our beliefs about what other people value). In the test phase, if we discover that we are falling short of the standard (for example, not studying enough), then we operate to change ourselves (we study harder). Soon, we self-reflect again—the second test phase—to see whether we are moving closer to reaching our standard. This test and operate cycle repeats itself until there is no longer a difference between our behavior and the standard. When we meet the standard, the control process is ended, we feel happy, and we exit the feedback loop. If repeated attempts to move closer to the standard fail, we will feel bad and eventually exit the loop (Carver & Scheier, 1990b).

Self-Discrepancies

Discrepancies between our self-concept and how we would ideally like to be (ideal self) or believe others think we should be (ought self).

What specifically happens to us emotionally when self-regulation doesn't lead to us meeting our standards? That is, how do we react when a discrepancy exists between our self-concept and how we would ideally like to be or believe others think we should be? Tory Higgins (1987) suggests that these **self-discrepancies** produce strong emotions. When we realize there is a discrepancy between our actual self and our *ideal self* (for example, "I wish I was more physically attractive"), we experience

FIGURE 2.2

Control Theory of Self-Regulation

According to the control theory of self-regulation, self-awareness provides the means by which we assess how successful we are in meeting our standards. When we become self-aware, we enter the first "test" phase. If we notice a difference between our actual behavior and our standards, we next enter the "operate" phase in which we try to change our behavior to match the standard. Soon, we again self-reflect—the second "test" phase—to discover whether we have reduced or eliminated the discrepancy. When there is no longer a difference between our behavior and the standard, we exit this control process.

It is not enough to understand what we ought to be, unless we know what we are; and we do not understand what we are, unless we know what we ought to be.

T. S. Eliot, American poet, 1888–1965

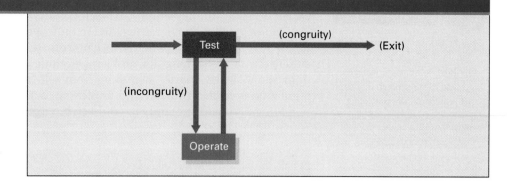

dejection-related emotions, such as disappointment, frustration, and depression. On the other hand, when we notice a discrepancy between our actual self and what we think we ought to possess (*ought self*) to meet our obligations and responsibilities (for example, "I should be helping my family out more financially"), we are vulnerable to *agitation-related emotions,* such as anxiety and guilt (Higgins et al., 1986). A number of studies have found that people with considerable self-discrepancies not only experience negative emotions but are often indecisive in their behavior, have unclear self-concepts, and experience a loss of self-esteem (Dana et al., 1997). The more important these self-discrepant attributes are to the self-concept, the greater are the negative emotions experienced (Higgins et al., 1994).

Based on our discussion thus far, it appears that attending to and meeting one's standards is an important function of the self. Although a high capacity for self-regulation appears to improve one's chances for success in life, there is evidence that self-regulating on one task makes it harder to immediately self-regulate on unrelated tasks (Baumeister et al., 1998). For example, Mark Muraven and his colleagues (1998) instructed some research participants to exercise self-control by suppressing their emotional reactions to an upsetting movie on environmental disasters. In contrast, other participants were either given no emotional control instructions or were told to increase their emotional responses by "really getting into the film." In this study, self-regulation was measured by determining how long participants would persist at a difficult physical task, namely squeezing a hand grip as long as possible. Such squeezing requires self-control to resist giving up and releasing the grip. Participants squeezed the grip both before (*pretest*) and after (*posttest*) watching the movie, and the difference between the pre- and posttest was the dependent measure of self-regulation depletion. Consistent with the hypothesis that self-regulation strength is weakened following the exercise of self-control, those who were told to control their emotions while watching the upsetting film exhibited self-regulation depletion as measured by the hand grip test. No such depletion was found in the other participants.

In explaining such findings, Roy Baumeister and his coworkers (1994) propose that controlling or regulating our own behavior is best conceptualized in terms of the following principles from a *strength model* of self-regulation:

1. At any give time, we only have a limited amount of energy available to self-regulate.
2. Each exercise of self-regulation depletes this limited resource for a period of time.
3. Right after exercising self-regulation in one activity, we will find it harder to regulate our behavior in an unrelated activity.

According to this self-regulation model, if Tameeka is on a diet and is also cramming for final exams, if she forces herself to study instead of going to a party, she should be more likely to give in to a "snack attack" later that evening. In a very

CRITICAL *thinking*

Spend a few minutes considering how self-regulation failure contributes to domestic violence. According to the strength model of self-regulation, when would a parent or a spouse be most likely to harm someone due to losing control of their emotions?

real sense, Tameeka's lack of willpower in dealing with food is a direct result of the earlier exertion and depletion of her self-control resources in the academic realm.

If self-regulation failure resulted in only people breaking their diets I would not be devoting page space to it here. Unfortunately, cultures throughout the world suffer from a broad range of problems—crime, drug addiction, teen pregnancy, domestic violence—partly stemming from self-regulation failure. Although self-regulation is often a difficult and unpleasant activity, learning how to exercise it will bring dividends not only to yourself, but to society as a whole.

SECTION SUMMARY

A prerequisite for self-concept development is *self-awareness. Private self-awareness* is the temporary state of being aware of our hidden, private self-aspects, while *public self-awareness* is the temporary state of being aware of our observable, public self-aspects. Engaging in private self-awareness leads to intensification of affect, clarification of knowledge, and greater attention and adherence to personal standards of behavior. Engaging in public self-awareness often leads to general uneasiness, a temporary loss of self-esteem, and a greater attention and adherence to social standards. We also differ in our tendencies to habitually engage in private and public self-awareness, and these personality traits are known as *private self-consciousness* and *public self-consciousness*. Closely related to self-awareness is *self-regulation*, which refers to the ways in which we control and direct our actions. The *control theory of self-regulation* states that, through self-awareness, we compare our behavior to a standard, and if there is a discrepancy, we try to reduce it. Although a high capacity for self-regulation is associated with success in life, exerting self-control on one task may make self-regulation immediately more difficult on other tasks.

THE SELF AS A KNOWLEDGE STRUCTURE

Self-awareness allows us to analyze our own thoughts and feelings, as well as anticipate how others might respond to us interpersonally. Through self-awareness, we develop a theory about ourselves, our self-concept. This self-knowledge summarizes information about us as objects in the world that help us better regulate our behavior and adapt to our surroundings (Higgins, 1996). Yet how is this self-information organized in memory?

SELF-SCHEMAS ARE THE INGREDIENTS OF SELF-CONCEPT

During the past twenty years, many social psychologists have expended considerable effort to better understand how information about the self is stored and categorized in memory. In describing this process, the computer has often been used as a metaphor: the subjective self (the "I") consists of program components, and the objective self (the self-concept or the "me") is the data aspect of the computer (Greenwald & Pratkanis, 1984).

To describe how self-knowledge is cognitively stored, investigators have borrowed the term *schemas* from cognitive psychology (Markus, Smith, & Moreland, 1985). **Schemas** are organized, repeatedly exercised patterns of thought about some stimulus, which are built up from experience and which selectively guide the processing of new information. They direct our attention to relevant

Schemas

Organized, repeatedly exercised patterns of thought about some stimulus, which are built up from experience and which selectively guide the processing of new information.

50   Part 1   Perceiving People and Events

FIGURE 2.3

Self-Schema Processing

In Markus's (1977) study of processing self-relevant information, those participants who had a self-schema for independence judged independent words much faster than they judged dependent words. The exact opposite was true of those who had a self-schema for dependence. How do you think these two groups of people might differ in other aspects of their lives relevant to this dependent/independent dichotomy?

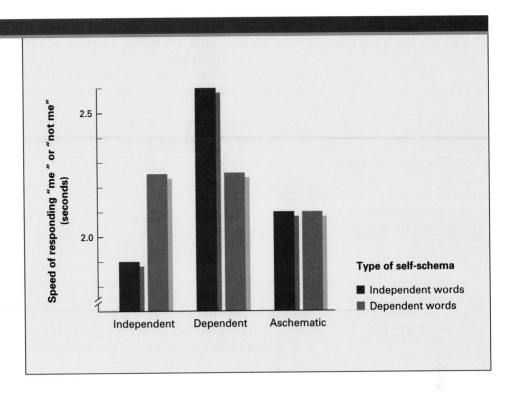

Self-Schemas

The many beliefs people have about themselves that constitute the "ingredients" of the self-concept.

information, giving us a framework for assessing it, and they provide categories for memory. You can have schemas about people, things, and events.

According to Hazel Markus (1977), the most important types of schemas are **self-schemas,** which are the many beliefs people have about themselves. Just as the self-concept has been previously described as a theory that people have about themselves, self-schemas can be thought of as the hypotheses of this self-theory. Any particular self-schema is a generalization about the self established through life experiences. For example, if a person possesses a self-schema of "sexiness," he or she considers this quality to be personally relevant and most likely has well-developed self-conceptions of this quality. How do you know if you possess such a self-schema? Markus states that people are self-schematic for qualities that are *important* to them, on which they think of themselves as *extreme* (high or low), and on which they are certain the *opposite* does not hold. In contrast, if people are not self-schematic for a particular quality, they are not invested in or concerned about it; it is not relevant to their self-concepts (they are *aschematic*). I would be willing to bet that actor Brad Pitt has a self-schema for sexiness, but Pope John Paul II is aschematic on this dimension.

Markus (1977) tested the effects of self-schemas on information processing by having college students rate themselves in terms of their independence/dependence. Those who rated themselves as decidedly independent (*independent schematics*) or decidedly dependent (*dependent schematics*), as well as those who didn't consider themselves possessing either quality (*aschematics*), were later recruited to participate in a seemingly unrelated study. Markus reasoned that possessing a schema would make it easier for people to process and recall from memory any information relevant to the schema. She therefore predicted that schematics would be able to decide faster whether adjectives relevant to their self-schema were descriptive of them than would aschematics, and that they would be able to recall more behavioral incidents from their past that were indicative of the self-schema.

In the study, trait adjectives associated with independence (for example, assertive) and dependence (for example, obliging) were projected on a screen one at a time, and participants were told to press a "me" button if the word was self-descriptive or a "not me" button if the word was not self-descriptive. Results are depicted in figure 2.3. As expected, independent schematics made faster judgments about words related to independence, and dependent schematics made faster judgments about words related to dependence. Aschematics' judgments about dependent- or independent-related adjectives did not differ at all. Schematics were also able to recall more incidents from their pasts in which they acted in line with their schema, while aschematics showed no such pattern of memory recall. This and other research supports the idea that self-schemas play a crucial role in explaining how potentially self-relevant information is processed, stored, and later recalled from memory.

If self-schemas influence information processing and memory recall, what determines which one of our self-schemas or which combination of them will be most influential at any given moment? For example, if you think of yourself as fun-loving, young, single, and intelligent, which, if any, of these self-schemas will affect how you process information at 8 P.M. on Saturday? Research by William McGuire and his colleagues indicates that *context* is a major determinant in activating certain self-schemas (McGuire et al., 1978). The aspect of the self-concept that becomes salient and activated in a particular setting is called the *spontaneous self-concept.* If at 8 o'clock on Saturday night you find yourself at a very dull college party, you are more likely to think of yourself as the fun-loving one rather than the intelligent, single, or young one. Likewise, if you are at a festive party celebrating the fiftieth wedding anniversary of two senior citizens, you may not think about the fact that you are fun-loving or intelligent, but you may be quite aware that you are young and single. The more often you are exposed to contexts that remind you that you possess a particular quality, the stronger that self-schema becomes.

This self-schema dependence on context has important implications for the nature of the self-concept. Whether or not a specific personal quality leads to a self-schema will largely depend on the degree to which it "stands out" in everyday interactions. If you are frequently reminded about a particular personal quality, a self-schema will likely develop. In this "context," I distinctly remember my first year in graduate school at the City College of New York. Having grown up in a small town in the ethnically homogenous region of the upper peninsula of Michigan, I was unprepared for the importance that many New Yorkers place on their own ethnicity. It seemed as if everywhere I went in the city, the first thing that people would ask me was, "Franzoi, what's that?" My initial reaction was to naively reply, "It's my last name." I had no self-schema for my ethnic background because it had little relevance in my hometown. Indeed, when my fourth-grade teacher asked us one day to identify our heritage, I mistakenly claimed to be Australian rather than Austrian. When corrected, my thought was that I was only a couple of letters off. In culturally diverse New York, however, one's ethnic background is more than a matter of the combination of letters; it is an important aspect of one's self-concept.

GENDER IDENTITY AND GENDER SCHEMAS ARE IMPORTANT ASPECTS OF SELF-CONCEPT

One evening as we sat eating our dinner, Amelia, who was 3 years old at the time, put her fork down, surveyed the table, then looked at me and announced, "Daddy? I'm a girl, and Mommy's a girl, and Lillian's a girl, but you're not a girl. You're a boy." Then, glancing over at our dog, Yocker, who was sleeping on the floor near my feet, she added, "And Yocker's a boy, too." Ignoring the possibility that my daughter had recognized some characteristics other than sex that helped her in categorizing me with the family dog (perhaps a tendency to stare off in space or to pant at the sight of food), I complimented Amelia on her ability to distinguish males from females.

Gender identity is fully developed by age 6 or 7, and then, many children use this identity when deciding which behaviors and activities are most appropriate for them. If my daughters are typical of girls their age, which of the two photographs do you think they most strongly identify with? Would it be that unusual if they identified more strongly with the shorts and caps than with the dresses? What if they were boys? Why would their identification with the "dresses" photo raise alarm bells among many adults? What do these different reactions suggest to you about gender socialization?

Gender Identity

The knowledge that one is a male or a female and the internalization of this fact into one's self-concept.

Gender Schema

A mental framework for processing information based on its perceived female or male qualities.

GENDER IDENTITY

This "Amelia story" describes an identification process that all children experience at approximately this age. This self-labeling, known as **gender identity,** is the identification of oneself as a male or a female and the internalization of this fact into one's self-concept. Knowing that "I am a girl" or "I am a boy" is one of the core building blocks in a child's developing self-theory (Intons-Peterson, 1988). Shortly after self-awareness develops—by the age of 2—children begin to acquire an understanding of gender (Katz, 1986). Two-year-olds can reliably sort photographs into female and male categories, but they cannot consistently name their own sex (Fagot, 1985). By age 3 or 4, they can correctly label themselves as male or female (gender identity), but they are still unaware that their biological sex is unchangeable (Coker, 1984). What Amelia demonstrated to us at the dinner table was that she could successfully categorize herself and others based on gender cues. Once gender identity has fully developed—around the age of 6 or 7—little if anything can change it (Money & Ehrhardt, 1972).

GENDER SCHEMA

When children develop gender identity they strive to act in ways consistent with this identity. According to Sandra Bem (1981, 1985), if a culture emphasizes distinctions between women and men, then children growing up in that culture learn to process information about themselves, other people, and even things and events according to their perceived gender associations. In other words, they develop a **gender schema,** which is a mental framework for processing information based on its perceived female or male qualities. Adults in the child's world help shape this developing gender schema by associating different objects and activities with one sex rather than the other. For example, in North American culture, personal characteristics such as physical attractiveness, cooperation and empathy, activities such as skipping rope and cooking, or even animals such as cats and birds come to be perceived as having a female connotation. On the other hand, physical strength, independence and aggressiveness, football, woodworking, dogs, and bears are perceived as having a male connotation.

Bem believes that the self-concepts of children become assimilated into this culturally derived gender schema as they learn which attributes are associated with their own sex and, hence, with themselves. At the same time children's self-concepts become linked to the gender schema, they also learn to evaluate their adequacy as a person in terms of how well their own personal attributes match the standards of the gender schema. Thus, boys are more likely to evaluate themselves in terms of their physical strength and competitiveness, while girls are more likely to evaluate themselves according to their physical attractiveness and ability to get along with others. As adults, many of us continue to define ourselves through these same gender-filtered lenses, regulating our behavior so it conforms to the culture's definition of maleness and femaleness.

Are you *gender schematic?* That is, do you habitually organize things in your mind according to gender categories? Do you try to keep your own behavior consistent with traditional gender standards? Actually, in most Western societies today, rigid gender attitudes and beliefs are increasingly being challenged, especially by college-educated adults and their children (Lottes & Kuriloff, 1994). One effect is that some people can be characterized as being relatively *gender aschematic:* they do not cognitively divide the world into female-male qualities, and gender is not of primary relevance to either their self-concepts or their perceptions of others (Bem, 1993). As you will discover in future chapters, unlike gender schematics who try to keep their own behavior consistent with stereotypical gender standards, gender aschematics exhibit a great deal more flexibility.

CULTURE SHAPES THE STRUCTURE OF SELF-CONCEPT

At the beginning of this chapter I asked you to contemplate who you are by describing yourself twenty times. Sociologists Manford Kuhn and Thomas McPartland devised this Twenty Statements Test (TST) in 1954 to measure self-concept. A common technique used to analyze TST responses (see Hartley, 1970) is to code each response into one of four categories: *physical self-descriptions* identify self in terms of physical qualities that do not imply social interaction ("I am a male"; "I am a brunette"; "I am overweight"); *social self-descriptions* identify self in terms of social roles, institutional memberships, or other socially defined statuses ("I am a student"; "I am a daughter"; "I am a Jew"); *attributive self-descriptions* identify self in terms of psychological or physiological states or traits ("I am intelligent"; "I am assertive"; "I am tired"); *global self-descriptions* identify self so comprehensively or vaguely that it doesn't distinguish one from any other person ("I am a human being"; "I am alive"; "I am me"). Return to your own TST responses and code each into one of these four categories. Which category occurs most frequently for you?

POSSIBLE HISTORICAL EFFECTS

Using this classification scheme, Louis Zurcher (1977) found that while American college students in the 1950s and early 1960s tended to describe themselves in terms of social roles, college students in the 1970s were more likely to identify themselves in terms of psychological attributes. This self-concept trend has continued (Trafimow et al., 1991) and coincides with a rise in individualistic attitudes among American young adults (Roberts & Helson, 1997). Do your own self-responses also fit this pattern?

Zurcher suggests that these self-concept and attitudinal changes are due to widespread cultural changes and upheavals beginning in the mid-1960s. For many Americans, the Vietnam War and the later Watergate scandals created a deep distrust of political institutions. Likewise, the recessions of the 1970s and early 1980s eroded people's faith that economic institutions could provide good-paying, secure jobs. The increasing divorce rate and weakening of the family unit, as well as growing problems in the educational system, created similar disaffection for these societal institutions. In reaction to this dissatisfaction, college students' tendencies to identify themselves more in terms of their own personal qualities, rather than in terms of institutional affiliations, may be an attempt to achieve a greater sense of control in a society where uncertainty often reigns.

TABLE 2.5

"I Am Special"	"A Letter To Children"
No one looks The way I do. I have noticed That it's true.	I wish you from your early age to be obedient to father and mother; respect teachers; to have good thoughts and good moral character.
No one walks The way I walk. No one talks The way I talk.	All in all, I wish you to be like uncle Lei Feng (a national hero), to grow up healthy. To grow up to be successors of revolution; well rounded in morality, intelligence, physically, and beauty.
No one plays The way I play. No one says The things I say. I am special, I am me. There's no one else I'd rather be.	Zhongyang, J. K. Y. (Ed.). (1984). *Song Qingling lun shaonian ertong jiaouyu (Song Qingling's essays on education for youth and children)*. Beijing: Jiaoyu chubanshe.
Author Unknown	

The poem on the left, posted at the hallway entrance to my daughters' elementary school, is a good illustration of how individualist cultures socialize children to think of themselves as being unique and "one of a kind." Next to the poem was a cutout of a snowflake and the accompanying words, "You're UNIQUE!" In marked contrast, the poem on the right, addressed to the children of China by the national leader of child and youth welfare, stresses obedience and respect as important values. As such, it reflects the time-honored Confucian ideal of the person as an insignificant self submitting to a significant larger (Chinese) collectivity. Which of these two poems best reflects the spirit of your own upbringing?

INDIVIDUALIST-COLLECTIVIST COMPARISONS

In addition to investigating changes in the structure of self-concept over time, researchers have also conducted cross-cultural comparisons (Markus & Kitayama, 1991). As stated in chapter 1, most of the world's population resides in collectivist cultures. It is not surprising, then, that numerous studies have found cross-cultural differences in TST responses: in general, American, Canadian, and European self-concepts are comprised of predominantly attributive self-descriptions, while people from collectivist countries such as China, Mexico, Japan, India, and Kenya have more social self-descriptions (Ip & Bond, 1995; Ma & Schoeneman, 1997). This research suggests that the differing cultural perspectives of individualism and collectivism affect the degree to which we identify with groups within society, and this identification process is reflected in basic differences in the nature of our self-concepts. Taken together, these studies indicate that the configuration of our self-concepts is shaped both by historical events and cultural context.

This differing view of the individual due to a culture's collectivist or individualist orientation not only shapes the configuration of self-conceptions, it also determines beliefs about how self-development should proceed (Greenfield, 1994). Within collectivist societies, childrearing practices tend to emphasize conformity, cooperation, dependence, and knowing one's proper place, whereas within more individualist societies, independence, self-reliance, and personal success are stressed. One consequence of these differing views is that in an individualist society, people develop a belief in their own uniqueness and diversity (Miller, 1988). This sense of individuality is nurtured and fostered within the educational system (see table 2.5), and its manifestation is considered to be a sign of maturity (Pratt, 1991). On the other hand, in a collectivist society, uniqueness and individual differences are often seen only as impediments to proper self-growth (Kim & Choi, 1994). Instead, the self becomes most meaningful and complete when it is closely identified with—not independent of—the group (DeVos, 1985). In collectivist China, for example, one consequence of this group focus is that educational theories and practices emphasize shaping children's personalities to best meet societal needs and goals (Pye, 1996). To employ the previous analogy of self-concept being the "grand portrait" we paint and repaint throughout life, in individualist cultures, people are given primary responsibility to paint their own grand portrait, while in collectivist cultures each person's self-portrait is expected to truly reflect a group effort.

CULTURAL VERSUS GENDER DISTINCTIONS

Gender socialization in North American culture has often been described as fostering the construction of an *independent* self-concept among males and a *relational* self-concept among females (Cross & Madson, 1997; Powlishta, 1995). To what degree are these gender differences in self-concept similar to the cultural differences we have just reviewed? That is, are American women's self-concepts similar to the self-concepts of people from collectivist cultures?

Actually, it appears that the similarities are more superficial than substantive. A five-culture study by Yoshihisa Kashima and his colleagues (1995) indicates that American and Australian women's self-concepts are not like Asians' self-concepts. Instead, what these researchers found was that while individualist-collectivist cultural differences are captured mostly by the extent to which people see themselves as acting as independent agents, gender differences are best summarized by the extent to which people regard themselves as *emotionally related* to others. What this suggests is that gender socialization has much more to do with encouraging girls to pay attention to the emotional "pulse" of their social relationships while discouraging boys from doing so, than it does in encouraging boys to act independent and girls to act interdependent. In other words, individualist-collectivist socialization has decidedly different effects on the nature of self-concept than does male-female socialization.

WHAT ABOUT BICULTURALISTS?

Although cultures can be characterized as being more oriented toward individualism or collectivism, not everyone living within a particular culture will have the same individualist-collectivist leanings. For example, even while living in a larger culture that promotes individualism, American Indians, African Americans, Mexican Americans, and Asian Americans are rooted in distinct cultural heritages that promote collectivist strivings (Gaines, 1995). The same is true of Jews and Arabs who live in Israel, where a Western individualist ideological system often conflicts with traditional Arab and Jewish collectivist cultures. Survey research by Daphna Oyserman (1993) indicates that individuals with such a *bicultural* background tend to view themselves and the world through both individualist and collectivist lenses. This dual view of oneself and the world can lead to internal conflict as the person attempts to reconcile individualist strivings with collectivist yearnings. As one Israeli Arab student explained these competing demands:

> When I am here in Jerusalem, I think of myself as a psychologist, I am trying to learn and to achieve professional goals, I have friends, and I live alone in a big house. I do not want to go home (to the village), get married, and have children. When I go home (to the village), I wonder what I ever saw in my life in the city; I experience a strong longing to return to my past, to be married and with children, living as a member of my nation. (Oyserman, 1993, p. 993)

How is this conflict best resolved? Based on recent studies of Pueblo, Navajo, and Korean-American/Canadian children and young adults, neither abandoning

FIGURE 2.4

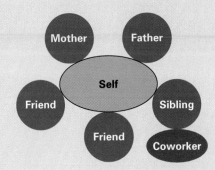

Individualist view

Collectivist view

The self should be independent of the group.

Self-concept is primarily defined by internal attributes.

People are socialized to be unique, to validate their internal attributes, to promote their own goals, and to "speak their minds."

Self-esteem is based on the ability to engage in self-expression and the ability to validate internal attributes.

The self should be dependent on the group.

Self-concept is primarily defined by social roles and relationships.

People are socialized to belong, to occupy their proper place, to engage in appropriate behavior, and to "read others' minds."

Self-esteem is based on one's ability to adjust to the group, restrain his or her own desires, and maintain social harmony.

How Is the Self Construed in Collectivist and Individualist Cultures?

The individualist view of the self so characteristic of Western cultures stresses independence, uniqueness, and the validation of internal attributes. In contrast, the collectivist view of the self typically found in non-Western cultures emphasizes dependence and adjustment of one's social roles to accommodate group goals. How might these two different views of the self lead to personal conflicts between individualists and collectivists when they interact with one another?

one's ancestral collectivist culture nor isolating oneself from the dominant individualist culture is good for mental health (Joe, 1994; Kim & Choi, 1994). Instead, successful biculturalism entails retaining ancestral values and practices while incorporating new values and practices from the dominant culture (see the section "Ethnic Identity of Minority Groups," pp. 63–64). This melding of the collectivist and individualist orientation not only benefits the health of biculturalists, it can also provide long-term benefits to society by infusing it with individuals who understand the value of both autonomy and social obligation (Oyserman et al., 1998).

Figure 2.4 outlines how cultural differences regarding individualism-collectivism may influence the structure of self-concept. Unfortunately, the degree to which individualists and collectivists differ in the way they conceive of themselves is just beginning to be understood. Furthermore, the self as a research topic has primarily been of interest to social scientists from individualist cultures, in which issues such as personal identity and self-boundaries are woven into the fabric of socialization. Because of this relative lack of understanding of cultural effects on the self, as you read the remaining sections in this chapter, please keep in mind that these findings are most confidently generalizable to cultures with an individualist orientation.

SECTION SUMMARY

Self-schemas are the many beliefs we have about ourselves, and they help us to process, store, and later recall self-relevant information. What determines which one of our self-schemas or which combination of self-schemas will be most influential at any given moment is largely determined by the social context. The self-schemas that are most likely to be salient in a given situation (our spontaneous self-concept) are those that make us unique or different from others. *Gender identity* is one of the core building blocks in self-concept, and children's self-concepts become assimilated into a culturally derived *gender schema*, which they use as a behavioral standard. The structure of self-concept is also shaped by historical events and cultural context, with collectivist self-concepts being identified more with societal institutions and individualist self-concepts being identified more with personal attributes.

SELF-ENHANCEMENT AND SELF-VERIFICATION

So far we have seen how self-concept is constituted and how attention to private and public self-aspects can affect thinking, feelings, and action. Yet what motivates the self? We have already discussed self-regulation and the desire to reduce self-discrepancies, so here we will analyze two widely studied self-motives, namely, the desire to enhance self-esteem and the desire to verify self-concept.

SELF-ENHANCEMENT AND SELF-VERIFICATION CAN BE CONFLICTING MOTIVES

Self-Enhancement

The process of seeking out and interpreting situations so as to attain a positive view of oneself.

Self-Verification

The process of seeking out and interpreting situations so as to confirm one's self-concept.

Self-esteem and self-contempt have specific odors; they can be smelled.

Eric Hoffer, U.S. social philosopher, 1902–1983

Over the years there has been an ongoing debate regarding self-evaluation and self-concept that is related to the hot and cold perspectives discussed in chapter 1. The **self-enhancement** perspective embodies the emotional, or hot, viewpoint of human nature and is based on the notion that people are primarily motivated to maintain high self-esteem (Dunning et al., 1995; Jones, 1973). According to this view, the need for self-enhancement will increase as one's negative self-evaluations increase. In contrast, the **self-verification** perspective (more generally known as the *self-consistency view*) reflects the cognitive, or cold, viewpoint. According to this view, people are motivated to maintain consistent beliefs about themselves, even when these self-beliefs are negative (Andrews, 1989; Swann, 1997). By verifying firmly held self-beliefs, people feel more secure that their social world is predictable and controllable.

For those with high self-esteem, there is no conflict between these two motives because receiving positive feedback verifies positive self-beliefs. However, for individuals with low self-esteem, these two motives often conflict: the need for self-enhancement causes those with low self-esteem to seek positive feedback, but that action conflicts with their desire to verify existing negative self-beliefs (Brown, 1993). Self-enhancement theorists contend that people with low self-esteem will seek out positive social feedback because it will bolster their self-esteem. In contrast, self-verification theorists argue that this positive feedback will create the fear in people with low self-esteem that they may not know themselves after all, and therefore, they will reject it. Which of these perspectives is correct?

J. Sidney Shrauger (1975) proposes that *both* the need for self-enhancement and the need for self-verification operate simultaneously, but the first operates in response to a person's feelings, while the second operates in response to a person's thoughts. That is, when judging social feedback about themselves, people's

FIGURE 2.5

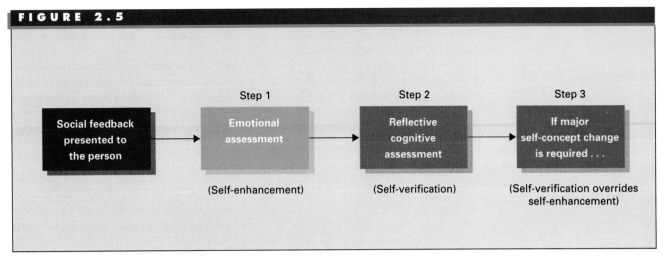

The Interplay Between Self-Enhancement and Self-Verification Motives

When confronted with positive feedback that contradicts a negative self-concept, how do people with low self-esteem resolve the conflict between self-enhancement and self-verification needs? Research (Swann, 1990; Swann et al., 1990) suggests that people follow a three-step process in resolving this conflict. In step 1, the initial reaction is to self-enhance. This is especially true when people are distracted or aroused. However, with more time to critically analyze the feedback (step 2), self-verification dominates thinking. In step 3, if internalizing this positive feedback will necessitate a major reassessment of their self-concept, the need for self-verification tends to override self-enhancement needs and people reject the feedback. Overall, recent studies suggest that low self-esteem people try to strike a balance in satisfying these two motives. They prefer to associate with people who make them feel better about themselves without seriously calling into question their current self-concepts. Why wouldn't people with high self-esteem have this same dilemma when given positive feedback from others?

emotional reactions ("Do I like it?") are based on whether the feedback bolsters their self-esteem (self-enhancement need), and their cognitive reactions ("Is it correct?") are based on whether it is consistent with their self-concepts (self-verification need). Thus, negative feedback that is expected will be considered more accurate, but self-enhancing feedback will be more satisfying. A number of studies support Shrauger's hypothesis that cognitive reactions to social feedback conform to self-verification needs and affective reactions conform to self-enhancement needs (Jussim et al., 1995; Swann et al., 1987). In these studies, people were presented with either favorable or unfavorable feedback about themselves. Although people felt better after receiving positive feedback than after receiving negative feedback (as predicted by the self-enhancement view), they accepted more responsibility for feedback consistent with their self-concepts than inconsistent feedback (as predicted by the self-verification view).

So which of these motives is the strongest, the need for self-enhancement or the need for self-verification? Based on a host of studies, some with contradictory findings (for example, Sedikides, 1993), the best current answer to this question is that it depends. As depicted in figure 2.5, self-enhancement appears to be the automatic and initially strongest response to favorable feedback (Sedikides & Strube, 1997), but self-verification is the slower, more deliberate, and perhaps more lasting response (Baumeister, 1998). When people first receive favorable evaluations, or when they are distracted or aroused, they tend to automatically self-enhance (Paulhus & Levitt, 1987), but when they have time to critically analyze the feedback, or are instructed to do so, they tend to self-verify (Krueger, 1998; Swann et al., 1990). To the casual observer who witnesses the person's initial delight in receiving praise from others, the need to self-enhance may seem the stronger of the two motives. However, later, once the warm emotional glow of the praise wears off, extra cognitive processing often results in self-verification overriding self-enhancement. For example, if you have low self-esteem and someone says you are absolutely wonderful, your initial reaction may be to accept this positive feedback and thereby increase your self-esteem. However, if you engage in more complex cognitive analysis, you may realize that internalizing this positive feedback will require a major reassessment of your self-concept, a task you may feel ill-equipped to accomplish. Faced with the possible upheaval caused by such a major self-reconstruction, you may well abandon self-enhancement and instead seek self-verification. Therefore, you reject the feedback and retain your original self-concept. If you hadn't analyzed the implications of the positive feedback, this incident probably would have ended with simple self-enhancement (step 1 in figure 2.5). Self-verification overrode self-enhancement only because of the later extra cognitive processing (step 2).

Finally, Seymour Epstein and Beth Morling suggest that the need for self-enhancement and the need for self-verification act as checks and balances on one another, and that it is only in cases of maladjustment that one need rampantly dominates the other (Epstein & Morling, 1995). For example, individuals with delusions of grandeur require self-enhancement to lord over self-verification to maintain their grand, yet faulty, self-beliefs. On the other hand, chronic depressives continually avoid self-enhancement so that they can verify their negative self-beliefs. Most regular folk, however, seek *compromises* between these two motives. Epstein and Morling's research suggests that when low self-esteem individuals receive positive or negative feedback from others, they automatically compare it with their own self-beliefs and prefer to associate with people who make them feel better about themselves without seriously disconfirming their current self-concepts (Morling & Epstein, 1997).

SELF-ESTEEM INFLUENCES WILLINGNESS TO TAKE RISKS

Based on our review thus far of self-esteem research, it appears that people with high self-esteem perceive their lot in life more optimistically than those with low self-esteem. That is, high self-esteem people expect others to verify their positive self-beliefs, while low self-esteem people expect the opposite. Does this different mind-set lead to differences in the willingness to take risks?

To answer this question, Robert Josephs and his colleagues (1992) had high and low self-esteem participants play a game in which they gambled real money for the opportunity to win more than $100. In the game, players chose among pairs of gambles that varied in risk and payoff. Each gamble pair was composed of a sure thing and a speculative gamble of equal or roughly equal expected value. Half of the pairs were framed positively as gains (for instance, $10 sure win versus 50 percent chance of winning $20), and half were framed negatively as losses (for instance, $10 sure loss versus 50 percent chance of losing $20). If players chose the sure thing, the person running the game noted their choice and moved on to the next pair. If players chose the risky prospect, the gamesperson rotated a bingo drum containing one hundred pieces (numbered 1–100) and removed one piece. If the number was less than or equal to the stated probability of the risky prospect, the outcome of the prospect occurred. So, for a 50 percent chance of winning $20, players had to draw a bingo piece numbered 50 or lower to win the $20. Players did not get to see these outcomes until they had made all their choices.

In the positively framed prospects, the sure gain would be the clear choice for those motivated to protect their self-esteem from threats. As you can see in figure 2.6, the gambling choices of the participants with low self-esteem reflected this choice pattern: they were 50 percent more likely to choose the sure gain than were those with high self-esteem. With the negatively framed prospects, however, the choice that minimizes threat is not clear, for both can be viewed as threatening. As a result,

FIGURE 2.6

Risky Decisions as Self-Esteem Threats

Josephs and his colleagues (1992) presented high and low self-esteem people with forced-choice gambling decisions of high and low risk to determine whether they would differ in the amount of risk they were willing to take. In the positively framed prospects, avoiding the risky option would be the clear choice for those who are motivated to protect their self-esteem from threats, which was the option generally taken by those low in self-esteem. For the negatively framed prospects, both choices are threatening, and high and low self-esteem participants chose each prospect 50 percent of the time. Thus, when prospects are framed positively, low self-esteem individuals appear to take fewer risks than high self-esteem individuals. Based on these findings, which of the two groups are more concerned with protecting self-esteem?

Source: Data from R. A. Josephs et al., "Protecting the Self from the Negative Consequences of Risky Decisions" in *Journal of Personality and Social Psychology*, 62:26–37, 1992.

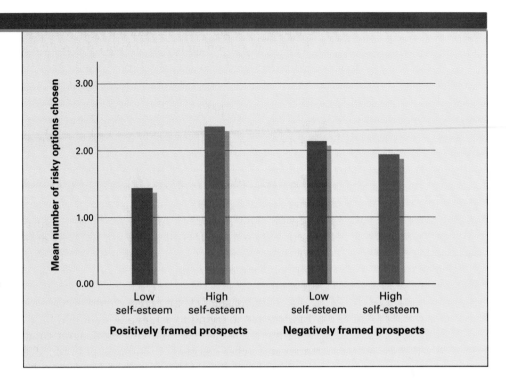

neither prospect should be preferred to the other by low self-esteem individuals. Results supported this expectation. Both high and low self-esteem participants chose each prospect 50 percent of the time. Therefore, when prospects are framed positively, individuals with low self-esteem appear to take fewer risks than individuals with high self-esteem.

Further studies in this series replicated these findings and suggest that people with low self-esteem lack the self-protective resources necessary to defend against self-esteem threats. Overall, they appear to be more concerned with self-esteem *protection* on an everyday basis than people with high self-esteem (Wood et al., 1994). But, you might be saying to yourself, what self-esteem do low self-esteem people have to protect? Is "low" self-esteem the same thing as "no" self-esteem? In a review of self-esteem studies, Roy Baumeister and his colleagues (1989) found that the vast majority of people who are identified as having low self-esteem generally do not see themselves as worthless, incompetent losers. Instead, they are people who evaluate themselves more *neutrally* than either very positively or very negatively. In most cases, it is only in comparison to the very positive evaluations of people with high self-esteem that these individuals can be described as having "low" self-esteem. Their low self-esteem is best understood as a weakly or inadequately satisfied desire for self-worth (Baumeister, 1993).

Viewed in this light, Diane Tice (1993) has argued that the best way to understand the motives of people with low self-esteem when they are faced with a self-enhancing opportunity is that they act like financial investors with limited resources who are presented with a moneymaking opportunity. In both instances, people of modest means tend to adopt a cautious, self-protective strategy. They don't try to attain terrific self-enhancement because they are too concerned about losing the modest assets they currently possess. In contrast, those with high self-esteem tend to act like wealthy, high-stakes speculators who can afford to risk some of their many assets. Thus, when presented with a self-enhancing opportunity, high self-esteem people are likely to take the risk and try to further enhance their self-regard. Every time they succeed, they reduce their self-discrepancies and move closer to realizing their ideal selves.

Unfortunately for those with low self-esteem, the need to protect their very modest self-regard sets in motion a cycle that in the long run reinforces their relatively low self-opinion and inhibits the realization of their possible selves. By consistently opting for less rewarding risks, in the short run they may guard against self-esteem threats due to failure, but over time they lose opportunities to experience self-enhancing grand success. Think about your own approach to risk taking. Do you hold on to a "sure thing," or do you instead make a grab for greater riches, be they material or psychological? How does your typical strategy of risk taking correspond to your level of self-esteem (refer back to table 2.2)?

THERE IS A DARK SIDE TO HIGH SELF-ESTEEM

Thus far we have discussed research that generally extols the virtues of high self-esteem. Indeed, in Western cultures there is a strong belief that high self-esteem is essential for mental health and good adjustment (Bednar et al., 1989). Perhaps due to this cultural belief, psychologists have been slow to study any possible negative effects of people wanting to feel good about themselves. Fortunately, that trend is reversing.

In the past few years, several studies have found evidence that there can be a hidden cost to trying to achieve or maintain high self-esteem: certain individuals with high self-esteem tend to react with aggression when someone challenges their favorable self-assessments (Baumeister et al., 1996; Blaine & Crocker, 1993). The source of this aggressive response appears to be a defensive reaction to avoid having to make any downward revision of self-esteem (Tangney et al., 1992).

What type of high self-esteem person is most likely to react in this aggressive manner? Research indicates that it is the *stability* of high self-esteem that determines whether threats to self-esteem lead to aggression (Kernis et al., 1993; Kernis & Waschull, 1995). People with *unstable* high self-esteem are the ones who become angry and hostile when others challenge their self-worth, while *stable* high self-esteem individuals are no more aggressive in such circumstances than low self-esteem people. The explanation for these findings is that, unlike stable high self-esteem people, those with unstable high self-esteem are not confident about that which they value so highly—namely, their own self-worth. As a result, they are much more dependent on having their self-worth regularly validated by others. When such validation is denied by social criticism, these unstable high self-esteem people react by attacking their critics (Bushman & Baumeister, 1998).

What this research suggests is that the emphasis in individualist cultures on feeling good about oneself has resulted in some people being so desirous of high self-esteem that they must constantly bolster and defend it in order for it to survive. When others don't comply with this need and, instead, threaten their self-esteem through social criticism, these unstable high self-esteem people are likely to respond by engaging in antisocial self-enhancement strategies. This is the dark side of high self-esteem.

SECTION SUMMARY

Two principal self-motivators are *self-enhancement* and *self-verification*. Self-enhancement appears to be the automatic and initially strongest response to favorable feedback, but self-verification is the slower, more deliberate, and perhaps more lasting response. Low self-esteem individuals take fewer risks than those high in self-esteem, but people with unstable high self-esteem tend to become angry and hostile when others challenge their self-worth.

THE SELF AS A SOCIAL BEING

Having examined the self as an object of attention and evaluation, and having explored some of the primary self-motives that impel us to action, it is now time to analyze how the self operates as a social being (Taylor, 1998). We will examine how our social identities constitute a very important aspect of our self-concepts, and how we protect our self-esteem in social relationships.

SOCIAL IDENTITIES ESTABLISH "WHAT" AND "WHERE" WE ARE AS SOCIAL BEINGS

Social Identities

Aspects of a person's self-concept based on his or her group memberships.

From our own personal experiences we all know that identification with a specific social group can have a great deal of importance for our self-concepts, especially when the group identified with is compared with other clearly defined social groups. In explaining this process of group identification, Henri Tajfel (1982) and John Turner (1985) have taken William James's notion of the social "me" and developed it into the concept of social identity. **Social identities** are those aspects of a person's self-concept based on his or her group memberships (Hogg & Abrams, 1988). They establish *what* and *where* the person is in social terms. For example, an Italian American living in the Bronx, a borough of New York City, would in all likelihood have social identities based on ethnicity and locale. Likewise, a woman who is a Canadian and an American Indian would probably feel a sense of identity with all three of these social groupings (gender, nationality, and race). By having a social identity, these individuals feel situated within a clearly defined group (Deaux et al., 1995).

ETHNIC IDENTITY OF MINORITY GROUPS

One of the consequences of group identification is an internalization of the group's view of social reality. Social identities provide members with a shared set of values, beliefs, and goals about themselves and their social world. As Mead might describe it, to have a social identity is to internalize the group within the individual, which in turn serves to regulate and coordinate the attitudes and behavior of the separate group members. However, if social identities are a representation of the group within the mind of the individual, what of those who live in a society in which their group is devalued by the larger culture? Don't they run the very serious risk of falling victim to a negative self-fulfilling prophecy?

Ethnic Identity

An individual's sense of personal identification with a particular ethnic group.

This is, in fact, the dilemma faced by members of social groups who have been subjected to prejudice, discrimination, and negative stereotypes (Crocker et al., 1994). One way minority groups have coped with this intolerance is by rediscovering their own ethnic heritage and actively rejecting the negative stereotypes in the larger culture (Kelman, 1998). **Ethnic identity**, which is a type of social identity, is an individual's sense of personal identification with a particular ethnic group (Hutnik, 1991). In a very real sense, ethnic identity is a state of mind, and acquiring it often requires considerable effort.

Jean Phinney (1991, 1993) has proposed a three-stage model of ethnic identity formation (see table 2.6). In stage 1, the *unexamined ethnic identity* stage, individuals often have not personally examined ethnic identity issues and may have incorporated negative stereotypes from the dominant culture into their own self-concepts. One negative consequence of internalizing these derogatory social beliefs into the self-concept is that people may experience low self-esteem and feelings of inadequacy (Clark & Clark, 1939; Phinney & Kohatsu, 1997). In contrast to those who are ignorant of ethnicity issues, some people in stage 1 may have been exposed to positive ethnic attitudes from others but have simply not incorporated them into their self-concepts.

In stage 2, *ethnic identity search,* people have an experience that temporarily dislodges their old-world view, making them receptive to exploring their own

A race of people is like an individual man; until it uses its own talent, takes pride in its own history, expresses its own culture, affirms its own selfhood, it can never fulfill itself.

Malcolm X, U.S. Muslim and Black nationalist, 1925–1965

One cannot be "an Indian." One is a Comanche, an Oneida, a Hopi. . . . We progress as communities, not as individuals. We want to maintain ourselves as communities, according to our group identity, not just as mere individuals or as amorphous "Indians."

La Donna Harris, Comanche writer, 1988

CRITICAL *thinking*

Does your ethnic heritage have relevance to who you are? If so, at what stage are you in Phinney's model? Is this an accurate portrayal of your own ethnic identity development? Are there aspects of the model that do not correspond to your own personal experiences?

Ingroup

A group to which a person belongs and that forms a part of his or her social identity.

Outgroup

Any group with which a person does not share membership.

TABLE 2.6

Stages in Ethnic Identity Formation

Stage 1: Unexamined ethnic identity. Lack of exploration of ethnicity, due to lack of interest or due to having merely adopted other people's opinions of ethnicity

Stage 2: Ethnic identity search. Involvement in exploring and seeking to understand the meaning of ethnicity for oneself, often sparked by some incident that focused attention on one's minority status in the dominant culture

Stage 3: Achieved ethnic identity. Clear and confident sense of one's own ethnicity; able to identify and internalize those aspects of the dominant culture that are acceptable and stand against those that are oppressive

Source: Based on Phinney, 1989.

ethnicity. In many cases, the catalyst for this exploration is a personal experience with prejudice (Sanders Thompson, 1991). In other instances, a person's more general search for personal identity in early adolescence kindles an interest in her or his ethnicity (Roberts et al., in press). Whatever the initial spark, this stage often entails an intense period of searching, in which people passionately consume ethnic literature and participate in cultural events. During stage 2, some individuals may also develop an *oppositional identity*, in which they actively reject the values of the dominant culture and denigrate members of the dominant group.

The third stage and culmination of this process is a deeper understanding and appreciation of one's ethnicity—what Phinney labels *achieved ethnic identity*. Confidence and security in a newfound ethnic identity allows people to feel a deep sense of ethnic pride along with a new understanding of their own place in the dominant culture. They are able to identify and internalize those aspects of the dominant culture that are acceptable (for example, financial security, independence, pursuit of academics) and stand against those that are oppressive (for example, racism, sexism). In this manner, the development of a positive ethnic identity functions not only to protect members of disparaged groups from continuing intolerance, but it also allows them to use this positive social identity to pursue mainstream goals and participate in mainstream life.

A number of studies support Phinney's view of the mental health benefits of ethnic identity development, among them being high self-esteem and a stable self-concept (Brookins et al., 1996; Phinney et al., 1997).[1] These findings indicate that it is individuals' own commitment and attitudes toward their ethnic group, rather than the evaluations of the group by the larger society, that influence self-esteem. Such positive social identities can short-circuit the negative effects that prejudice can inflict on self-esteem.

GROUP PERFORMANCE AND SOCIAL IDENTIFICATION

People not only categorize themselves as members of certain groups, they also categorize others as either members of these same groups or as members of other groups (Deaux, 1996). An **ingroup** is a group to which a person belongs and that forms a part of his or her social identity. An **outgroup** is any group with which the person does not share membership. In the course of daily activities, just as people compare their individual performance on a given task with the performance of others (see pp. 65–67 on self-evaluation maintenance), they also compare the performance of ingroup and outgroup members. When ingroup members succeed,

---

[1]This process of identity development in oppressed ethnic groups has parallels in other social groups that have historically been discriminated against, such as women, lesbians and gay men, and the disabled.

other ingroup members who played no role in this success respond with pride and satisfaction. Robert Cialdini has labeled this identification with and embracing of ingroup members' success as *basking in reflected glory (BIRGing)* and believes it is common in a variety of social arenas. Examples are fan reaction to their sports teams' victories, the pride ethnic group members have for other members' accomplishments, or the satisfaction that citizens express for their nation's military and political successes. When such successes occur, ingroup members often describe the success as "our victory." This process of reflected glory enhances individual self-esteem because people's social identity in this domain constitutes an integral part of their self-concept (Smith & Henry, 1996).

Although people tend to readily share in the successes of their ingroup members, what happens when failure is tasted by those with whom we identify? Do we embrace the defeat as readily as the victory? Hardly. In dealing with the failures of ingroup members, people typically react in two different ways. First, excuses are often made. For example, in sporting events, disheartened fans often blame poor officiating or injuries as the cause of their team's defeat (Hastorf & Cantril, 1954). In defending their team, fans are defending their own self-esteem (refer to chapter 7, pp. 239–240, for a more extensive discussion of ingroup bias).

A second reaction to ingroup member failure is psychological distancing, often referred to as *cutting off reflected failure (CORFing)*. In one study, Cialdini and his colleagues (1976) phoned students a few weeks after their college team had played a football game and asked them to describe the outcome. When the team had won, students were very likely to use the pronoun *we* in describing the team victory, but this pronoun was rarely used to describe a team defeat. Instead, following defeat, students tended to use the pronoun *they*, as in "They blew the game." This social identification with success and psychological distancing from failure—which is exactly the type of identification that William James contended was typical of the self—was clearly expressed by one particular student who exclaimed, "*They* threw away *our* chance for a national championship!"

Although fair-weather fans can CORF to their heart's content, what about those of us whose sports teams truly are an integral part of our self-concepts? Research by Edward Hirt and his coworkers (1992) suggests that a team's poor performance can significantly lower a fan's own self-evaluations. In one of their studies, college students who were avid fans of their school's men's basketball team watched live televised games in which their team either won or lost. Not only were the moods of these zealous fans lower following defeat, but their immediate self-esteem and feelings of competence were also depressed. What these findings suggest is that forming a strong allegiance to a team is a risky venture. Because true fans generally do not CORF, each season they subject themselves to an emotional roller coaster that must be ridden out, regardless of how exhilarating or nauseating the ride happens to be. CORFing would certainly provide psychological relief following a crushing defeat. Adopting a successful team would make life even easier for the long-suffering fan. But, the true fans could no sooner change teams than they could change their names—for better or worse, their team affiliation is an important social identity.

IN SOCIAL RELATIONSHIPS, SELF-ESTEEM IS MAINTAINED THROUGH SOCIAL REFLECTION AND SOCIAL COMPARISON

Thus far we have examined how our own moods and self-evaluations are influenced by the successes and failures of ingroup members. This link between the quest for self-esteem and social relationships has been further elaborated in Abraham Tesser's (1988) **self-evaluation maintenance model.** This theory primarily explains how we draw closer to or draw away from successful people we have a relationship with due to our desire to maintain self-esteem. According to Tesser,

---

Born into the
skin of yellow women
we are born
into the armor of warriors.

Kitty Tsui, Chinese American poet, 1989 from Chinatown Talking Story, in Making Waves: An Anthology of Writings By and About Asian American Women, ed. Asian Women United of California, Boston: Beacon Press, 1989, p. 132

All things being equal, you root for your own sex, your own culture, your own locality. . . . Whoever you root for represents you. And when he or she wins, you win.

Isaac Asimov, science fiction writer, 1920–1992

Self-Evaluation Maintenance Model

A theory predicting under what conditions people are likely to react to the success of others with either pride or jealousy.

We treat our favorite sporting teams' successes as if they are our own, and we suffer their defeats as well. What psychological term is used to describe what these hockey fans are experiencing while celebrating their team's victory?

© Lynn Johnston Productions Inc./Dist. by United Feature Syndicate, Inc.

in personal relationships, self-esteem is maintained by two social psychological processes: *social reflection* and *social comparison.* Social reflection, previously identified as BIRGing (see p. 65), is a process in which self-esteem is reinforced by identifying ourselves with the outstanding accomplishments of those close to us. In our daily conversations, we hear this reflection process when people tell us proudly about "My son, the banker" or "My best friend, who was on the 'David Letterman Show'." Social comparison, on the other hand, is a process in which our own accomplishments are evaluated by comparing them with those close to us, and our self-esteem suffers if we are outperformed (Kulik & Gump, 1997). As you can see, reflection and comparison produce opposite self-esteem results when others excel at some task: your self-esteem increases if you engage in reflection, but it decreases if you engage in comparison. The stronger the emotional bond between you and the successful person, the stronger the self-esteem effects for both reflection and comparison. Thus, you gain (or lose) more self-esteem if your best friend accomplishes some great task than if your former third-grade classmate does.

What determines whether you engage in reflection or comparison following someone else's success? One important factor is the *relevance* of the task to your self-concept (Morf & Rhodewalt, 1993). If your sister wins first prize in the state chess tournament, your self-esteem may increase due to reflection, but only if chess is not highly relevant to your own self-concept. If you also entered the contest and did poorly, it's likely that your sister's success will lower your self-esteem because it makes you look that much worse by comparison.

Another significant factor that influences whether you engage in reflection or comparison following someone else's success is your *certainty* about your abilities in the domain under question. A series of studies conducted by Brett Pelham and Jeff Wachsmuth (1995) found that when people hold uncertain beliefs about their abilities in an important domain, they are motivated to reduce this uncertainty by carefully comparing their abilities with those of close relationship partners. For example, if my wife wins great praise for her cooking and I am uncertain about how good of a cook I am, I may experience a loss of self-esteem in this area of my life due to social comparison. In contrast, once people develop very certain beliefs about their abilities in a given domain, Pelham and Wachsmuth found that they tend not to engage in social comparison. Instead, they tend to engage in the less effortful process of social reflection, in which the strengths and weaknesses of their close relationship partners reflect directly (rather than comparatively) on themselves. Returning to my previous example, if I am certain I am a good (or bad) cook, when my wife wins great praise for her cooking, I am more likely to bask in the reflected glory of this praise rather than use it as a basis for comparison. As a result, I experience a boost in my own self-esteem.

What about those instances when social comparison makes you look bad? How can you try to recover lost self-esteem? One way is to exaggerate the ability of those who outperform you (Alicke et al., 1997). By seeing your victor as truly outstanding, you can still perceive yourself as well above average. Another way to recover self-esteem is to compare yourself with those who are even less capable, a process known as *downward comparison* (Gibbons et al., 1994). Although high and low self-esteem people both engage in downward social comparison, they respond differently to it. When self-esteem is threatened by comparison with superior others, persons with low self-esteem benefit from downward comparison: they not only feel better, but they also perceive their less capable comparison targets as more similar to them and more likable than persons with high self-esteem. In contrast, downward comparison doesn't improve the mood of those with high self-esteem. Instead, they react negatively to the self-esteem threat by being more critical of the downward comparison targets (Exline & Lobel, 1997; Gibbons & McCoy, 1991). Thus, engaging in downward comparison only makes people with low self-esteem feel better. Perhaps simply realizing that there are others worse off than them may be sufficient to improve the mood of those who generally don't have a very favorable opinion of themselves.

Besides engaging in downward comparison, a second way to reduce self-esteem threat after comparing yourself with someone who has outperformed you is to reduce your closeness to this person (Pleban & Tesser, 1981). Salvaging self-esteem through such emotional distancing, however, usually exacts a high price on the relationship—it often ends. A third method of protecting self-esteem—and one that also preserves your relationship—is to change your beliefs so that the task is no longer important to your self-concept (Tesser & Campbell, 1982). Now, instead of comparing yourself with this superior person, you simply bask in his or her reflected glory. Let's return to your hypothetical sister, the budding chess master. Instead of her accomplishments making you feel bad and straining your relationship, by making chess a less defining aspect of your self-concept you can (through reflection) elevate your self-esteem. In this way, a decidedly different outcome is achieved: family ties and self-esteem prevail.

CRITICAL *thinking*

Our self-esteem will often be threatened when we compare ourselves with those superior to us on some task. However, a recent review of the literature indicates that upward comparison can sometimes lead to higher self-esteem (Collins, 1996). How do you think this particular self-enhancement effect might occur?

SECTION SUMMARY

A very important aspect of our self-concepts are the *social identities* we have with various groups. By having social identities, we feel situated within clearly defined groups, and we respond to their successes and failures much like we do to our own individual triumphs and defeats. The development of a specific type of social identity, namely, *ethnic identity*, can insulate us from the negative effects that prejudice would otherwise inflict on our self-esteem. According to the *self-evaluation maintenance model*, in personal relationships, self-esteem is maintained by two social psychological processes: *social reflection* and *social comparison*. Self-esteem is enhanced through social reflection when we associate ourselves with the outstanding accomplishments of others. Regarding comparison, self-esteem will be enhanced if we outperform our comparison partners, but it will be diminished if others outperform us. After reading the "Applications" section, review the self terms in table 2.7.

APPLICATIONS

DO YOU ENGAGE IN BINGE DRINKING OR EATING TO ESCAPE FROM YOURSELF?

s you have learned from reading this chapter, we all have the ability to engage in self-awareness. When we experience failure or a significant personal loss, we generally spend some time afterward in focused self-awareness as a means to better understand what happened. Although this self-focused answer seeking can be quite helpful, most of us soon disengage from intense introspection and return to our normal states of awareness. However, what happens when our failure or loss is very great, such that we can find no ready solution? In such instances, we may become depressed, which increases self-focus, which increases depression, and so forth (Pyszczynski & Greenberg, 1992). Thus, intense self-awareness can be thought of as both resulting from depression as well as contributing to it.

Unfortunately, one way depressed individuals sometimes try to break out of this negative self-aware state is by engaging in self-destructive behaviors that have the side-benefit of temporarily reducing self-awareness, and thereby, temporarily reducing depression. Binge eating and drinking are two activities that can be motivated by a desire to escape from self-awareness. They also are two of the most serious social problems faced by college students today (Reynolds et al., 1992; Vandereycken, 1994).

Regarding alcohol abuse, Jay Hull (1981) not only found evidence that alcohol reduces self-awareness, but that individuals high in private self-consciousness are more likely to use it to deal with negative information about themselves. In one study, undergraduate participants were given intelligence-related tests and were then randomly given either success or failure feedback (Hull & Young, 1983). Immediately following this feedback, they participated in a seemingly unrelated wine-tasting study. Although the amount of wine consumed by those low in private self-consciousness was not influenced by their previous success or failure, those high in private self-consciousness drank more wine after receiving failure feedback than after success feedback. In effect, consuming alcohol following failure temporarily caused the high private self-conscious individuals to act like low private self-conscious individuals—their degree of self-awareness was reduced and they were then not as attentive to their failure. Similar results have been found in adolescent alcohol abuse, where high private self-conscious students report drinking more if their academic performance is poor than less self-conscious students (Hull et al., 1986). What these studies suggest is that some people—especially high private self-conscious individuals—may use alcohol as a "psychological crutch" to avoid the chronic attention to their own private thoughts and feelings that causes emotional pain.

While alcohol seems to reduce self-awareness by physically interfering with complex cognitive functioning, other techniques can accomplish the same result by simply focusing attention narrowly on concrete, unemotional stimuli. By paying attention to simple, here-and-now movements and sensations, a person can divert attention away from troubling self-aspects (Steele & Josephs, 1990). This shift from self-awareness to "other-awareness" effectively allows the person to avoid the type of self-reflective activities that evoke unpleasant emotion (Baumeister, 1991). *Binge eating*, which involves episodes of huge amounts of food consumption, may serve this function for some people. That is, by redirecting attentional focus from the self to the simple acts of chewing, tasting, and swallowing, binge eaters may temporarily find relief from depression (Heatherton & Baumeister, 1991). Or, as one binger expressed it, "Eating can help me bury my emotions when I don't want to feel them" (Smith et al., 1989).

Ironically, although some people may engage in binge behavior to escape negative self-awareness, self-regulation theory contends that they must actually consciously engage in self-awareness if they desire to gain control over their self-destructive actions. The following three suggestions, derived from self-regulation theory, indicate how binge drinkers and eaters can work to change their behavior by employing self-reflective thought:

1. *Focus your awareness beyond the immediate situation.* An important mechanism in effective self-regulation of negative behavior is keeping attention focused beyond the immediate situation to more distant, long-range goals (Baumeister & Heatherton, 1996). This sort of situational *transcendence* is clearly an important factor in effective food or alcohol management, because it requires you to forgo the temporary relief of bingeing so that you will achieve your long-term goal of learning to eat and drink responsibly. By focusing on your long-range goal, the more-immediate goal of bingeing on cheesecake or beer becomes cognitively *reframed:* it becomes an

obstacle to your long-term goal rather than an appealing treat.

2. *Pay attention to cues that trigger undesirable behavior.* Certain stimuli in your social environment can serve as signals that you may be "sliding" down a path that leads to your undesirable behavior. The sooner you identify signals of impending undesirable behavior, the better chance you have of controlling your impulse to engage in that behavior (Wegner, 1994). Thus, if you know that arguments with family members have triggered binge behavior in the past, pay attention to your feelings when conversing with these people and try to defuse arguments before they get out of hand.

3. *Recognize when your resolve is weak.* As suggested by the *strength model of self-regulation* (p. 49), at any give time, you only have a limited amount of energy available to self-regulate. With this knowledge, be aware that you are going to find it hardest to keep yourself from bingeing with food or alcohol right after exercising a great deal of control in some other unrelated activity.

TABLE 2.7

Self Terms and Their Relation to One Another

The "I"

Self-Awareness

This is awareness directed toward oneself, and it can be focused on private self-aspects (e.g., emotions, motives, personal standards) or public self-aspects (e.g., physical appearance, self-presentations). The tendency to engage in this self-aware state is known as self-consciousness, and it too is described in private and public terms.

Self-Regulation

These are the ways in which we control and direct our own actions. You must be self-aware to engage in self-regulation.

The "Me"

Self-Concept

Due to self-awareness, we develop a theory about ourselves.

*   *Gender identity*: the knowledge that one is a male or a female.
*   *Self-schemas*: the "hypotheses" that make up self-concept.
*   *Spontaneous self-concept*: the aspect of the self-concept that is salient and activated in a particular setting.
*   *Social identities*: the aspects of the self-concept based on group membership.

Self-Esteem

We not only develop a theory of ourselves, but we also develop an evaluation of this theory. The need to enhance self-esteem is a primary motive but may not be as strong as the need to verify the self-concept. In social relationships, we can enhance self-esteem by basking in others' reflected glory or by comparing ourselves with those we outperform. High self-esteem people tend to know themselves better, are higher risk-takers, and can recover from failure better than those low in self-esteem.

FEATURED STUDY
DEPLETION OF SELF-REGULATION RESOURCES

Baumeister, R. F., Bratslavsky, E., Muraven, M., & Tice, D. M. (1998). Ego depletion: Is the active self a limited resource? *Journal of Personality and Social Psychology, 74*: 1252–1265.

Many crucial functions of the self involve making choices, inhibiting behavior, taking responsibility, and persevering in the face of adversity. This controlling or *self-regulating* aspect of the self was investigated in four separate experiments in this featured article, of which one (Experiment 1) will be described here. According to the strength model of self-regulation, each act of self-regulation depletes the limited energy available for this purpose. As a result, immediately after exercising self-regulation in one activity, people will find it harder to regulate their behavior in an unrelated activity. In Experiment 1, it was hypothesized that an act of self-control—in the form of resisting a delicious food treat—would make it harder for participants to later persist at a difficult and frustrating task.

METHOD

Participants were sixty-seven introductory psychology students (thirty-one male; thirty-six female) who received course credit for taking part in what was described as a taste perception study. The experimenter instructed participants to skip one meal before showing up for their individual session and to be sure they did not eat anything for at least three hours.

For each session, chocolate chip cookies were baked in the laboratory room, and thus, participants were greeted by a delicious aroma when they entered. Two foods were displayed on the table at which the participant was seated: a stack of the cookies combined with some chocolate candies, and a bowl of red and white radishes. The experimenter explained that chocolates and radishes had been selected for the taste perception study because they were both very distinctive foods. She further explained that the following day the participants' sensation memory for one of these foods would be tested (a deception).

Participants in the "radish" condition were asked to take about five minutes to eat at least two or three radishes while the experimenter was out of the room and not to eat any of the chocolate food. Participants in the "chocolate" condition were given similar instructions for the cookies and candies. It was assumed—and later confirmed by participants' own self-reports—that eating radishes in the presence of delicious chocolate treats required high self-regulation, while eating chocolates in the presence of radishes required low self-regulation. Participants' eating behavior was unobtrusively observed through a partially covered one-way mirror to verify that they only ate their assigned food.

After five minutes, the experimenter returned and asked the participants to provide her with some preliminary data that would help other researchers learn whether college students' problem-solving abilities differed from those of high school students. Unbeknownst to the participants, the problem-solving task—which consisted of geometric puzzles—was designed to be impossible to solve. This was done to evoke frustration in the participants. Although the problem-solving study was described as being unrelated to the taste perception study, in fact, how long the participants worked on the puzzles was the main dependent variable in the experiment. There also was a "no-food" control condition in which some participants skipped the food part of the experiment and were only asked to complete the problem-solving task.

RESULTS AND DISCUSSION

Consistent with the depletion hypothesis of the strength model of self-regulation, results indicated that the radish participants quit sooner on the frustrating problem-solving task and also tried to solve fewer puzzles than did the chocolate or control participants. The chocolate participants' task persistence did not differ from that of the control group. Self-reports following the problem-solving task also indicated that the radish participants felt more tired than the other two groups.

What do these results tell us? They do not tell us that eating chocolates instead of radishes (*low self-regulation*) improves persistence, because the chocolate-eating participants did not work any longer on the tasks than did the participants who ate no food at all. Rather, wanting to eat chocolates but forcing oneself to eat radishes (*high self-regulation*) seems to deplete some psychological resource that fuels self-regulation. These findings suggest that resisting temptation in one activity produces a subsequent drain on the ability to persist when faced with frustration on another activity. In general, this might mean that after successfully completing a difficult act of self-control, you would be well advised to rest before engaging in another activity requiring similar self-control.

 WEB SITES accessed through http://www.mhhe.com/franzoi2

Web sites for this chapter focus on the self, including cross-cultural research, an international society devoted to the study of the self, and information on the history of the self-concept in the social sciences.

Society for Cross-Cultural Psychology
This is the web site for an organization pursuing cross-cultural research from a multidisciplinary perspective.

International Society for Self and Identity
This is the web site for an interdisciplinary association of social and behavioral scientists dedicated to promoting the scientific study of the self. Users can find abstracts of unpublished articles and recent books.

Overview of Self-Concept Theories
This web page investigates the history of the self-concept in the social sciences. It also includes ideas for people who aspire to be counselors.

American Psychological Association
The web site for the American Psychological Association contains a web page which discusses the possibility that high self-esteem narcissists tend to be aggressive when criticized.

The President

C H A P T E R   3

SELF-PRESENTATION AND SOCIAL PERCEPTION

*I*n November of 1996 President Bill Clinton was reelected to a second term by a landslide vote. In early 1998, at the height of his popularity, he was accused of having had an extramarital affair with White House intern Monica Lewinsky. At first, Clinton vehemently denied the accusation. If you watched his televised denial, did you believe he was telling the truth? As the evidence mounted against him, Clinton reluctantly admitted to his family and to the public that there had been an "improper relationship" and that he had sinned. Following this acknowledgment, he asked a trio of ministers to counsel him about his spiritual and moral failures. Why do you think he sought such counsel? Was it a genuine attempt at repentance, or simply a calculated strategy to appease Congress and voters?

Of course, we all know that this matter did not end with spiritual healing. On December 19, 1998, the Republican-dominated Congress voted to impeach Clinton, despite the fact that the majority of Americans disagreed with this action. In defending their impeachment vote, Republicans presented themselves as protecting the country from a president whom they believed had broken numerous laws trying to conceal his sexual dalliances. To what degree did you believe that this was their primary motivation? Did you think that they may have been cynically using Clinton's indiscretion as an excuse to overturn the 1996 election? How did you perceive those Republican lawmakers who denounced the president as immoral, only to have their own extramaritial affairs exposed by the press?

Although this highly charged political event was unusual due to the threat of the removal from office of a sitting president, it is actually similar to events we face on a daily basis. That is, as *self-presenters,* we often consciously try to shape others' impressions. In turn, as observers, we often try to explain self-presenters' actions and gain insight into their motives and beliefs. The way we seek to know and understand other persons and events is known as **social perception.** This type of perception is not a single, instantaneous event, but rather comprises a number of ongoing processes, which can be roughly classified into two general areas: *impression formation* and *attribution.*

Impression formation is often based on rapid assessments of salient and observable qualities and behaviors in others. These judgments are obtained by attending to nonverbal cues, such as facial expressions and body posture, as well as incorporating more detailed and descriptive characteristics, such as traits, into an overall impression. What made Bill Clinton such an effective politician and campaigner was that, like Ronald Reagan, he was adept at changing his self-presentation style so that it "fit" the mood and expectations of the situation. He could present himself to people in such a way that they felt he understood their point of view.

Impression formation is usually just the first step of social perception. Often, we also want to understand what *causes* people to act in a particular manner. This *attribution process* goes beyond discerning people's current moods and feelings and attempts instead to use their past actions to predict future behavior. For example, when deciding whether to vote for Bill Clinton in the 1990s and Ronald Reagan in the 1980s, Americans examined these two men's past actions, both as private and public citizens. If they knew what these politicians were like as individuals, voters believed they could better predict how they would act as president. This chapter will introduce you to these two areas of social perception.

Yet, before we examine how we judge others, let us first step into the shoes of those we are judging. As so clearly demonstrated in the chapter 2 discussion of the

Social Perception

The way we seek to know and understand other persons and events.

self, whenever we interact with others our self-esteem may be enhanced or diminished, and our self-concepts may be confirmed or cast in doubt. How does this fact of social intercourse affect the way in which we present ourselves to others? And how do we—as social perceivers—use our knowledge as seasoned self-presenters to judge others' self-presentations?

SOCIAL INTERACTION AS "THEATER"

In social relationships, we often try to manage the impression we make on others by carefully constructing and monitoring our self-presentations (Leary, 1996). Indeed, sociologist Erving Goffman (1959) suggests that social interaction is like a theatrical performance, with the interactants being the actors on stage playing prescribed roles. While "on stage," people act out "lines" and attempt to maintain competent and appropriate self-presentations. In observing this performance, the audience generally accepts the presented selves at face value and treats them accordingly. The acceptance may not be genuine, but Goffman asserts that people have learned to keep their private opinions to themselves, unless self-presenters prove wholly incompetent. To do otherwise would disrupt the smooth flow of social interaction.

Because self-presenters sometimes worry about being judged incompetent, Goffman states that they often rehearse prior to the performance. They also rely upon "props" and take care to "set the stage" in order to present a more believable self. In preparing for a romantic dinner date, for instance, you might purchase your date's favorite wine, splash on some enticing cologne, and bring along a romantic CD as a gift (the props) that will later be played at the right moment to properly set the stage for your romantic self-presentation. You might even practice your romantic gazes and postures in front of a mirror or rehearse a romantic speech beforehand.

If this description of social life sounds a bit too contrived, reflect on your early teenage memories a moment, especially those when you were preparing for your first social dance or date. Today, as the mature and knowledgeable social actor that you are (or at least think yourself to be), you may have forgotten how contrived and stilted some self-presentations can be when not well learned. The more skilled we become in particular self-presentations, the less effort is necessary in executing them. Generally, in familiar situations our self-presentations are learned to the point that we don't have to think about impression management very much and can instead pay more attention to other matters (Baumeister et al., 1989).

T he world's a stage and most of us are desperately unrehearsed.

Sean O'Casey, Irish playwright, 1880–1964

Sociologist Erving Goffman contended that social interaction is similar to a theatrical performance, with people playing prescribed roles like actors on stage. In observing both theatrical and everyday "performances," the audience generally does not question the validity of others' presented selves because this would disrupt the "play." When President Bill Clinton's denial of a sexual affair with Monica Lewinsky was not accepted as truthful by many people, this particular "play" was indeed disrupted.

SELF-PRESENTATIONS ARE OFTEN CAREFULLY CONSTRUCTED AND MONITORED

Viewing social interaction as theater, how might you understand the actions of President Clinton and his Republican adversaries as the scandal and impeachment trial unfolded? Like actors on stage, their self-presentations were carefully planned and executed. At times Clinton sought to present a serene, business-as-usual image, while at other times he presented himself as a victim of partisan politics. In contrast, Republican lawmakers generally tried to present themselves as fair-minded judges and jurors. These are known as **strategic self-presentations**—conscious and deliberate efforts to shape others' impressions to achieve ulterior goals (Jones & Pittman, 1982).

There is nothing necessarily unsavory about strategic self-presentations—we all employ them. In general, we are most likely to use them when we are interacting with strangers or casual acquaintances and are concerned about making the right impression (Leary et al., 1994; Tice et al., 1995). When with our family and friends, our self-presentations are less likely to be strategic because impression management is probably no longer our goal. Instead, we are likely to engage in *expressive self-presentations,* where our principal desire is to express the important aspects of our self-concepts (Baumeister, 1982).

STRATEGIC SELF-PRESENTATIONS

When people try to shape the impressions of others to gain some ulterior goal, they often employ commonly recognized strategic self-presentations. One such strategy, *self-promotion,* attempts to convey positive information about the self either through one's behavior or by telling others about one's positive assets and accomplishments. People who use self-promotion want to be respected for their intelligence and competence, and thus, this strategy is commonly employed during job interviews (Stevens & Kristof, 1995). Although often effective in conveying a positive social image, self-promotion does not always result in desired consequences. This is because in addition to evaluating competence, perceivers also judge such interpersonal dimensions as likability and humility. Therefore, while self-promoters may be seen as competent, they also may be judged to be less likable because they are perceived to be bragging (Godfrey et al., 1986). To counter this social danger, astute self-promoters often acknowledge possessing certain minor flaws or shortcomings along with their many competencies (Baumeister & Jones, 1978). Boasting is considered to be a more masculine response following achievement, and thus, it isn't surprising that men are more likely than women to employ self-promotion (Miller et al., 1992).

A strategy that has much in common with self-promotion is *exemplification,* which is a self-presentation designed to elicit perceptions of integrity and moral worthiness, at the same time that it arouses guilt and emulation in others. Exemplifiers often come across as being absorbed by devotion to some cause and appear to be suffering for the welfare of others. Workers who encourage fellow employees to go home while they sacrifice personal time for the "good of the company," religious leaders who profess to "walk with the Lord," or politicians who tell their constituents that they will be a "moral beacon" in government are all displaying this form of strategic self-presentation. The danger of taking on the saintlike role is that one runs the risk of being perceived as hypocritical if actions deviate from this moral highground (Stone et al., 1997). Exemplifiers also run the risk of being socially shunned because some people experience guilt and shame while in their presence due to being reminded of their own shortcomings.

A strategy that overcomes some of the self-presentational problems of self-promotion and exemplification is *modesty.* To be modest is to underrepresent one's positive traits, contributions, or accomplishments. Modesty can be extremely effective in increasing one's likability, even while it preserves high levels of perceived competence and honesty (Baumeister & Ilko, 1995; Schlenker & Leary, 1982). In contrast to self-promotion, modesty is considered to be a more feminine response

---

Strategic Self-Presentation

Conscious and deliberate efforts to shape other people's impressions in order to achieve ulterior goals.

following achievement (Miller et al., 1992), and thus, it isn't surprising that women are not only more likely than men to employ it, but they also are more successful in using it (Wosinska et al., 1996). Despite the generally favorable response to modesty, you should only use it when others are aware of your successes and can recognize that an underrepresentation is taking place (Miller & Schlenker, 1985). For example, modesty will not be a particularly effective strategy for talented students to employ when trying to secure strong letters of recommendation from professors who are unaware of their many accomplishments. Instead, self-promotion should be used.

Humility is something I've always prided myself on.

Bernie Kosar, former NFL quarterback

When people want to coerce others into doing something, they might use *intimidation,* a self-presentation tactic of arousing fear and gaining power by convincing others that they are powerful and/or dangerous. This self-presentation strategy is the hallmark of strong-armed robberies and is also employed by athletes in such aggressive sports as football, hockey, and boxing. In its more subtle forms, intimidation is also used by parents. A frown combined with a lowered tone of voice and a pointed index finger is often sufficient in securing compliance from a child.

What if people lack the skills necessary for the preceding strategies? Under such circumstances, they may rely on *supplication.* In this technique, people advertise their weaknesses or their dependence on others, hoping to solicit help or sympathy out of a sense of social obligation. For example, an indigent alcoholic asking passersby for spare change relies on societal norms of empathy for those who are less fortunate. A less extreme example are students who repeatedly ask others for help in completing class assignments, stating that they don't understand the material. This technique, while effective in many circumstances, is fraught with psychological landmines. One danger is that people tend to "blame the victim" (Lerner, 1980), often believing their suffering is self-inflicted. Another danger is that even though supplicators often receive help and support, they will be privately judged as poorly functioning individuals (Powers & Zuroff, 1988). Not surprisingly, the final toll of advertising one's incompetence is often a loss of self-esteem.

Last, and most important, people can also manipulate our impressions of them by flattering us. This self-presentation strategy, known as *ingratiation,* is used to describe behaviors that are motivated by a desire to be liked (Jones & Wortman, 1973). Because flattery does indeed increase recipients' self-esteem, and hence, increases their liking for the flatterer, Jones (1990) calls ingratiation the most fundamental of all the strategies—"a pinch or two of ingratiation helps to leaven the other self-presentation strategies as well" (p. 185). Despite the potential rewards of ingratiation, like self-promotion, it is a double-edged sword. A meta-analysis of sixty-nine ingratiation studies found that while the recipient of ingratiation is positively affected by flattery, bystanders who observe the ingratiating self-presentation are more likely to question the motives of the flatterer (Gordon, 1996). These findings suggest that such disparaging terms as *brown-noser* and *apple polisher* are more likely to be used by observers of ingratiation than recipients. Table 3.1 describes some common self-presentation strategies.

CRITICAL *thinking*

Make a list of the different self-presentation strategies that you employed today. Under what circumstances and with whom were they used? Which ones achieved the desired effect? Was there one strategy that you frequently employed? If you didn't use any, why was this the case?

Embarrassment and Excuse Making Commonly Follow Failed Self-Presentations

Despite our tendency to rehearse prior to important social interactions, we sometimes prove to be incompetent in our self-presentations. For example, you could go into a job interview intending to convey intelligence and social skill, only to spill coffee all over yourself. In such instances when we are unable to project an appropriate public image, we often feel embarrassed. **Embarrassment** is an unpleasant emotion experienced when we believe that we cannot perform coherently in a social situation. When embarrassed, we typically blush, avert our gaze, lower our heads, touch our faces, and smile nervously (Keltner & Buswell, 1997).

Embarrassment

An unpleasant emotion experienced when we believe that we cannot perform coherently in a social situation.

How often does embarrassment occur? College students report being embarrassed at least once a week, while younger teenagers become embarrassed even

TABLE 3.1

Common Self-Presentation Strategies

	Attributions Sought	Negative Attributions Risked	Emotions to Be Aroused	Typical Actions
Self-promotion	Competent	Conceited	Respect	Performance claims
Exemplification	Worthy	Hypocrite	Guilt	Self-denial
Modesty	Likable and competent	Nonassertive	Affection and respect	Understatement of achievements
Intimidation	Dangerous	Blowhard	Fear	Threats
Supplication	Helpless	Stigmatized	Nurturance	Self-deprecation
Ingratiation	Likable	Brownnoser	Affection	Compliments and favors

Source: Partly based on Jones, 1990.

more often (R. Miller, 1995). Answer the items in table 3.2 to assess your own susceptibility to embarrassment. Mark Knapp and his colleagues (1986) asked people to recall embarrassing moments in their lives. Perhaps you can relate to the following account of a woman's ill-fated attempt to impress the parents of her fiancé:

> I was invited to my fiancé's home for a special dinner. It was the first time I had met everyone and I was trying to impress them. As we sat down to eat, his father turned to me and said, "I hope you'll say grace." I was so unsettled by this request that I immediately bowed my head and said, "Now I lay me down to sleep. . . . " (p. 40)

One common way to recover from these self-presentation lapses is to provide excuses. Offering excuses generally bolsters our mood, unless others don't buy the excuse (Mehlman & Snyder, 1985). In using excuses, we usually explain our self-presentation failures as being caused by external and uncontrollable events (Weiner et al., 1987). For example, if you show up an hour late for a date and blame your tardiness on a traffic jam, a flooded road, or a malfunctioning car, you have a better chance of maintaining a favorable self-presentation than if you say you were late because of watching a rerun of your favorite television program. In addition, an excuse must also be plausible to be effective. Claiming you arrived late because of a flooded road would not save a self-presentation if it was given on a clear sunny day. Thus, to reconstruct a desired self-presentation, the simple advice to excuse makers is to know your audience before offering up an excuse. The good news is that embarrassing situations are also unpleasant for onlookers, and thus, they often help us recover our self-presentations (Marcus et al., 1996).

Sometimes people do not wait for a self-presentation to fail before providing an excuse. Instead, they actually take steps beforehand to sabotage their performance, thereby setting themselves up for failure. For example, the night before an important exam, Barry may go to a party instead of studying. By choosing to socialize, he is greatly decreasing his likelihood of success. An observer of Barry's actions might conclude that his decision not to study was self-defeating. But someone versed in social psychological theory might suggest that his actions serve a second purpose: to protect his self-esteem. Putting barriers in the way of your success not only provides you with an excuse for failure, but it also will enhance your self-esteem if success is secured despite the handicap. Thus, creating obstacles

TABLE 3.2

Susceptibility to Embarrassment Scale

Instructions: Listed below are a variety of statements. Please read each statement carefully and indicate to the left of each item the extent to which you feel it applies to you using the following scale:

1	2	3	4	5	6	7
Not at all Like me						Very much Like me

_____ 1. I feel unsure of myself.

_____ 2. I don't feel comfortable in public unless my clothing, hair, etc. are just right.

_____ 3. I feel uncomfortable in a group of people.

_____ 4. I don't mind being the center of attention.*

_____ 5. I probably care too much about how I come across to others.

_____ 6. I feel inadequate when I am talking to someone I just met.

_____ 7. I feel clumsy in social situations.

_____ 8. I feel uncomfortable leaving the house when I don't look my best.

_____ 9. Sometimes I just feel exposed.

_____ 10. I feel humiliated if I make a mistake in front of a group.

_____ 11. I get flustered when speaking in front of a group.

_____ 12. I often feel emotionally exposed in public and with groups of people.

_____ 13. It is unsettling to be the center of attention.

_____ 14. I get tense just thinking about making a presentation by myself.

_____ 15. I have felt mortified or humiliated over minor embarrassment.

_____ 16. I am very much afraid of making mistakes in public.

_____ 17. I don't like being in crowds.

_____ 18. I do not blush easily.*

_____ 19. I often worry about looking stupid.

_____ 20. I feel so vulnerable.

_____ 21. I am concerned about what others think of me.

_____ 22. I'm afraid that things I say will sound stupid.

_____ 23. I worry about making a fool out of myself.

_____ 24. What other people think of me is very important.

_____ 25. I am not easily embarrassed.*

Scoring instructions. Before adding up your total score, ratings for the three "*" items should be reversed, so that 1=7, 2=6, 3=5, 4=4, 5=3, 6=2, and 7=1. The score range for the Susceptibility to Embarrassment Scale is 25 to 175. The mean score for college students is 92, with higher scores indicating higher degrees of embarrassability.

Source: From Kelly, K. M., & Jones, W. H. (1997). Assessment of dispositional embarrassability. *Anxiety, Stress, and Coping, 10:* 307–333.

the neighborhood™ Jerry Van Amerongen

Copyright 1982 The Register and Tribune Syndicate, Inc.

"Good Lord, Berlingham, any one of us could have mistaken this for a costume ball! . . ."

Self-Handicapping

A self-presentation strategy in which a person creates obstacles to his or her own performance either to provide an excuse for failure or to enhance success.

to success can not only *protect* self-esteem, it can also *enhance* it. These are the two primary motives underlying **self-handicapping,** a self-presentation strategy in which a person creates obstacles to his or her own performance (Berglas & Jones, 1978). Self-handicapping is more likely to occur when people are being evaluated on skills or attributes central to their self-concepts rather than on unimportant characteristics (Baumeister & Scher, 1988).

Of the two motives underlying self-handicapping, which is dominant? A series of studies by Diane Tice (1991) indicates that it depends on a person's level of self-esteem. She found evidence that individuals with high self-esteem handicap themselves to enhance their success, and they are largely unconcerned about protecting themselves against failure. In contrast, individuals with low self-esteem self-handicap to protect themselves from the negative implications of failure. Thus, the desire to further enhance self-esteem appears to motivate high self-esteem people to self-handicap, but it is the desire to protect self-esteem that appears to be the motivating force behind self-handicapping for those low in self-esteem.

Although it is unclear whether men are more likely than women to self-handicap, there is evidence that they use different *sorts* of handicaps. Men are more likely to handicap themselves either by not adequately preparing for a task or by using drugs or alcohol beforehand to inhibit their performance (Higgins & Harris, 1988). In contrast to this *behavioral self-handicapping,* women seem to prefer the less harmful *self-reporting handicapping:* before performing a task, they complain about stress-induced physical ailments (Hirt et al., 1991). These studies, then, suggest that male self-handicappers employ a more debilitating form of handicapping, while female self-handicappers generally use one that doesn't actually hamper their performance.

Research by Lawrence Sanna and Melvin Mark (1995) points to a possible hidden self-handicapping benefit. In their studies, participants actually performed better on intellectual tasks when they either were placed or placed themselves in situations where they (mistakenly) thought they were handicapped than when they thought they were not. This effect was strongest for those who were habitually high self-handicappers. These findings suggest that providing plausible excuses for inadequate performance *prior* to actual performance can sufficiently reduce anxiety so that people perform better than they would normally.

HIGH SELF-MONITORS ARE SOCIAL CHAMELEONS

We all use self-presentation strategies. However, some people are more likely to engage in strategic self-presentations than are others. According to Mark Snyder (1987), these differences are related to a personality trait called **self-monitoring,** which is the tendency to use cues from other people's self-presentations in controlling one's own self-presentations. Those who are high in self-monitoring spend considerable time learning about other people and tend to emphasize impression management in their social relationships (Fiske & Von Hendy, 1992; John et al., 1996). In 1974, Snyder published a Self-Monitoring Scale to measure this personality trait, and it has been studied extensively since that time.

Individuals who are high in self-monitoring are especially attuned to social cues concerning appropriate behavior in a given situation (Koestner et al., 1992). They are skilled impression managers who strive to perform whatever behavior projects a positive self-image, even if some degree of deception is required (see the end-of-chapter Applications section). In this regard, they tend to be extraverted, good actors, and willing to change their behavior to suit others (Briggs & Cheek, 1988; Chen et al., 1996). For example, when trying to initiate a dating relationship, high self-monitoring men and women behave in a chameleon-like fashion, strategically and often deceptively changing their self-presentations in an attempt to appear more desirable (Rowatt et al., 1998). On the Self-Monitoring Scale (Snyder, 1974), those high in self-monitoring would agree with such statements as:

> I'm not always the person I appear to be.
> I can look anyone in the eye and tell a lie with a straight face (if for the right end).
> I may deceive people by being friendly when I really dislike them.

On the other hand, individuals low in self-monitoring are less attentive to situational cues, and their behavior is guided more by inner attitudes and beliefs. As a result, their behavior is more consistent across situations. A likely reason for this consistency is that they more quickly access their attitudes from memory than do people high in self-monitoring (Snyder & Gangestad, 1982). They are also less interested than those high in self-monitoring in projecting a positive self-image that others will respect. People low in self-monitoring would agree with the following Self-Monitoring Scale statements:

> I can only argue for ideas that I already believe.
> I have trouble changing my behavior to suit different people and different
>   situations.
> At parties and social gatherings, I do not attempt to do or say things that
>   others will like.

Due to their greater attention to social cues, those high in self-monitoring are more socially skilled than those low in self-monitoring. They are better able to communicate and discern the meaning of emotions and other nonverbal behaviors. They also learn more quickly how to behave in new situations, and are more likely to initiate conversations (Snyder, 1979). On the negative side, people high in self-monitoring have less intimate and committed social relationships (Snyder & Simpson, 1984), and they tend to judge people more on superficial characteristics, such as physical appearance and social activities, rather than their attitudes and values (Jamieson et al., 1987).

Noting the differences between high and low self-monitoring, which orientation do you prefer? Perhaps you see high self-monitoring as being more socially adaptive because it allows one to better negotiate in an ever changing and complicated social world. Or maybe you view the chameleon-like nature of the high self-monitor as indicating a distasteful shallowness and instead prefer the principled

Self-Monitoring

The tendency to use cues from other people's self-presentations in controlling one's own self-presentations.

It is not whether you really cry. It's whether the audience thinks you are crying.

Ingrid Bergman, Swedish actress, 1915–1982

consistency of someone low in self-monitoring. Yet what you see as principled consistency, others may interpret as inflexibility. The safest and perhaps wisest conclusion to draw is that neither high nor low self-monitoring is necessarily undesirable unless it is carried to the extreme. Fortunately, pure high and low self-monitoring is rare—most of us fall somewhere on a continuum of these two extremes (Miller & Thayer, 1989).

At this point, you may be wondering how self-monitoring differs from the personality trait of public self-consciousness discussed in chapter 2 (pp. 46–48). Being high in self-monitoring is similar in some respects to being high in public self-consciousness—both have to do with a concern about and awareness of how others react to the self. The way they differ is that high self-monitoring, but not high public self-consciousness, describes individuals who are actively and effectively changing their behavior to adjust to the reactions and expectations of others. Individuals high in public self-consciousness may be aware of and concerned about themselves as social objects, but they are not necessarily sufficiently attentive to the subtle cues around them to structure their self-presentations in such a way as to manage the impressions others have of them. In addition, although people high in public self-consciousness are motivated more by a concern to avoid presenting themselves negatively, high self-monitors strive to achieve a favorable self-presentation in others' minds. Do these two different motives sound familiar? They should, for the social motives of high public self-conscious individuals are similar to the motives of people with low self-esteem, while the social motives of high self-monitors are similar to those of people with high self-esteem (see chapter 2, pp. 60–62).

SECTION SUMMARY

In social relationships, we often try to manage the impression we make on others by carefully constructing and monitoring our self-presentations. Common self-presentation strategies are *self-promotion, exemplification, modesty, intimidation, supplication,* and *ingratiation.* When these self-presentations fail, we experience *embarrassment* and often try to recover by offering excuses. *Self-handicapping* refers to actions that we take to sabotage our performance and enhance our opportunity to excuse anticipated failure. *Self-monitoring* is the tendency to use cues from other people's self-presentations in controlling our own self-presentations.

IMPRESSION FORMATION

Impression Formation

The process by which one integrates various sources of information about another into an overall judgment.

Now that we have walked in the shoes of the self-presenter, let us next view the social stage from the perspective of the audience. **Impression formation** is the process by which observers integrate various sources of information about others' self-presentations into a unified and consistent judgment (see Hamilton & Sherman, 1996). The process of forming impressions is viewed by social psychologists as a dynamic one, with judgments being continually updated in response to new information. It is analogous to building a "working model" of a person and then using this as a guideline in our actions toward him or her. The model works if our mental representation of the person accurately predicts his or her behavior.

Impression formation is not only a dynamic process; it is also integrative. By this I mean that each bit of information about a person is interpreted within the context of all the other information we have about her or him. Each information "bit" takes its character from the other "bits" as a whole. As you will soon discover, however, not all bits of information are created equal. Some bits will carry more weight and even orchestrate all the other bits into a coherent whole.

TABLE 3.3

Cross-Cultural Judgments of Six Primary Emotions: Percentage of Success Rate in Choosing the Correct Emotion

Nation	Happiness	Surprise	Sadness	Fear	Disgust	Anger
Estonia	90	94	86	91	71	67
Germany	93	87	83	86	61	71
Greece	93	91	80	74	77	77
Hong Kong	92	91	91	84	65	73
Italy	97	92	81	82	89	72
Japan	90	94	87	65	60	67
Scotland	98	88	86	86	79	84
Sumatra	69	78	91	70	70	70
Turkey	87	90	76	76	74	79
U.S.A.	95	92	92	84	86	81

Source: From P. Ekman et al., "Universals and Cultural Differences in the Judgments of Facial Expressions of Emotion" in *Journal of Personality and Social Psychology*, 53:712–717. Copyright © 1987 by the American Psychological Association. Reprinted by permission.

OUR IMPRESSIONS OF OTHERS ARE SHAPED BY THEIR NONVERBAL BEHAVIOR

Nonverbal Behavior

Communicating feelings and intentions without words.

First impressions are often based on self-presenters' **nonverbal behavior,** which involves communicating feelings and intentions without words. Whether a person smiles when greeted by another, whether a person's walk is "bouncy" or "purposeful," or whether one's gestures are expansive or constricted can provide important information in developing a working model of those we meet on a daily basis. Two of the more important nonverbal channels of communication are facial expressions and body movements.

FACIAL EXPRESSIONS

More than two thousand years ago, the Roman orator Marcus Cicero wrote that the "face is the image of the soul." Centuries later, Charles Darwin (1872) proposed that *facial expressions* not only play an important role in communication, but that certain emotional expressions are innate and thus are understood throughout the world. Studies conducted during the past thirty years provide support for Darwin's assertions (Ekman, 1994; Izard, 1994). For example, people from very different cultures have been found to manifest similar facial expressions when experiencing particular emotions (Keating et al., 1981). Regardless of whether they are from Western or non-Western societies, people can also reliably identify at least six primary emotions: happiness, surprise, anger, sadness, fear, and disgust (Buck, 1984; Matsumoto, 1992). In one of the most extensive studies of emotion recognition, Paul Ekman and his colleagues (1987) asked participants from ten different Western and non-Western cultures to identify the six primary emotions displayed by White men and women in a series of photographs. As you can see in table 3.3, across cultures there was a high percentage of agreement.

When Darwin proposed that certain emotional expressions are universally understood, it was within the context of introducing evolutionary theory to the sciences. He believed that this ability to recognize emotion from the observation of facial expressions was genetically programmed into our species and had survival value for us. How might this ability aid in species survival? One possibility is that being able to read the emotions of others by attending to facial expressions allows people to not only better predict their behavioral intentions ("Do they mean to harm me?"), but it also helps them to understand how others are interpreting the world ("Why are they afraid? Are we all in danger in this situation?"). This "survival value" hypothesis would predict that people do not attend equally to all facial expressions, but rather exhibit the most sensitivity to those that would give them the best chances of survival. In other words, people should be most attentive to facial expressions that signal potential danger.

Research by Christine Hansen and Ronald Hansen (1988) support the survival value hypothesis. In their study, they showed people pictures of crowds of faces to determine what facial expressions were most recognizable in such a clustered setting. In some pictures, all individuals had the same facial expression, and in other pictures there was one discrepant face. As Darwin would have predicted, participants spotted discrepant angry faces faster and more accurately than happy faces. The threatening faces appeared to "pop out of the crowd," while the nonthreatening faces were often overlooked. Besides anger, people are also extremely sensitive to facial expressions of fear (Lanzetta & Orr, 1986). Apparently, both of these facial expressions function as general danger cues, evoking anxiety and preparing people for self-protective action.

BODY MOVEMENTS

Besides facial cues, the body as a whole can convey a wealth of information. For example, research indicates that people who walk with a good deal of hip sway, knee bending, loose jointedness, and body bounce are perceived to be younger and more powerful than those who walk with less pronounced gaits (Montepare & Zebrowitz-McArthur, 1988). Besides providing information about one's age and strength, attention to body movements can also provide useful clues to a person's level of emotional arousal. Perhaps you have observed that when people become nervous they often spend a good deal of time touching, scratching, or rubbing various parts of their bodies. A number of studies have demonstrated that when people are emotionally aroused, they tend to engage in a greater number of such body movements than when they are calm (Harrigan, 1985; Harrigan et al., 1991).

A series of studies by Joel Aronoff, Barbara Woike, and Lester Hyman (1992) also suggest that people often infer underlying emotional states by reading the geometric patterns of bodies during social interaction. For example, in a creative analysis of dance characters in classical ballet, the researchers found that the body and arm displays of the threatening characters were more *diagonal* or *angular*, while those of the warm characters were more *rounded* (refer to figure 3.1). In subsequent studies, college students who were asked to evaluate various geometric shapes judged those with diagonal shapes to be more bad, powerful, and active than those that were rounded. What these findings suggest is that people may analyze the *shape* of large-scale body movements to better determine another person's behavioral intentions. It appears then that body movements, in addition to facial gestures, convey quite a wide variety of information to others that may well have a significant impact on the impression formation process. Yet although there are commonly shared meanings of many physical gestures, it is also true that people from different cultures often assign different meanings to the same physical movements. Table 3.4 provides a brief sketch of how certain nonverbal cues are interpreted differently around the world.

DO PEOPLE DIFFER IN USING NONVERBAL CUES?

Research indicates that people recognize the important role that nonverbal behavior plays in impression formation and often consciously employ nonverbal cues in their self-presentation strategies (DePaulo, 1992). For example, have you ever forced yourself to smile at someone you really didn't like? Or have you ever

You know about a person who deeply interests you more than you can be told. A look, a gesture, an act, which to everybody else is insignificant tells you more about that one than words can.

Henry David Thoreau, philosopher, author, naturalist, 1817–1862

FIGURE 3.1

Rounded, Diagonal, and Angular Body Displays

Based on an analysis of classical ballet dance movement and people's judgments of simple geometric shapes, Aronoff and his colleagues (1992) contend that rounded body postures convey warmth and friendliness to an observer, while diagonal and angled body postures imply threat and danger. Using this information, try a little experiment on your friends. Act out some diagonal and angled body displays for them, as well as some that are rounded. In this variation of "charades," what sort of emotions do they believe underlie each of these body displays?

Body display

Diagonal   Rounded

Arm display

Angled   Rounded

deliberately fixed someone with a cold, angry stare to convey your displeasure or your feeling of social dominance?

Whether you tend to use the forced smile over the cold stare may be associated with your gender socialization. During childhood, boys are generally discouraged from displaying vulnerable emotions (Blier & Blier-Wilson, 1989; Buck, 1977). A common warning given the weeping boy is that if such behavior persists, he runs the risk of being labeled a "sissy." Although expressing vulnerability is discouraged in boys, *anger expression* is not only more encouraged in boys than girls, but it is also the only emotion that is better communicated nonverbally by men than women. In contrast, *happiness expression* is the emotion most encouraged in girls (Brody, 1993). Consistent with this encouragement, women are not only better nonverbal communicators of happiness than men, but they are also better at masking disappointment with a positive expression (Davis, 1995). In thinking about your own upbringing, are your skills at constructing fixed stares and forced smiles consistent with these gender socialization patterns?

Besides these gender differences, one personality trait that identifies individuals who are more motivated to consciously use nonverbal cues in managing their social relationships is self-monitoring, which we discussed earlier in this chapter. In one study, Howard Friedman and Terry Miller-Herringer (1991) arranged for participants who were either high or low in self-monitoring to receive feedback indicating that they had done very well on a series of problem-solving tasks. In one condition, participants received this positive information in the presence of two other competitors who were told that they had not performed very well (these individuals were actually confederates). Because it is impolite to gloat about one's

TABLE 3.4

Cultural Differences in Certain Nonverbal Cues, or, A North American's Brief Guide to Avoiding International Misunderstandings

Although a number of facial gestures appear to convey universal meaning, here are some nonverbal cues that are more culture-specific. To avoid misunderstandings when traveling overseas, or when hosting an international visitor, North Americans should duly note that everyday gestures and accepted interaction patterns in this culture are not universally shared.

Shaking hands: North Americans are taught to shake hands as a friendly sign of greeting. A firm, solid grip is thought to convey confidence and good character. Japanese prefer greeting one another by bowing, Southeast Asians press their own palms together in a praying motion, and when Middle Easterners and many Asians shake hands, they prefer a gentle grip, because a firm grip suggests aggressiveness.

Touching: North Americans and Asians are generally not touch-oriented, and hugging is almost never done among casual acquaintances. In contrast, Latin Americans and those in the Middle East often embrace and hold hands as a sign of friendship.

Space relationships: North Americans generally maintain a distance of about thirty inches during normal social interaction. Asians tend to stand farther apart, and Latin Americans and Middle Easterners stand very close, often brushing up against one another. In those cultures where space relationships are small, moving away is interpreted as a sign of unfriendliness.

Eye contact: North Americans are taught to look others directly in the eye when conversing. Avoiding eye contact is considered to be a sign of shyness, disinterest, or weakness. In Japan and Korea, people are taught to avert the eyes and avoid direct eye contact. There, engaging in eye contact is considered intimidating, or perhaps a signal of sexual interest.

Source: Based on Axtell, 1991.

success in the company of those you have bettered, the researchers hypothesized that those high in self-monitoring would be more successful in hiding their expressions of joy when in the presence of their less fortunate competitors than would those low in self-monitoring.

Judges, watching videotape of the participants' faces as they received the good news in the presence of their competitors, rated that those high in self-monitoring did indeed exhibit fewer nonverbal signs of happiness than those low in self-monitoring. High self-monitors concealed their nonverbal expressions of joy by biting their lips or twisting their mouths to one side, presumably to prevent themselves from smiling. This study suggests that people high in self-monitoring are not only more attentive to their nonverbal behavior in social settings, but they are also better able to modify or suppress nonverbal gestures that might be considered socially inappropriate. In this respect, then, high self-monitors appear to be better at using their nonverbal behavior to convey a desired self-presentation to others.

CAN WOMEN "READ" NONVERBAL CUES BETTER THAN MEN?

Beyond the gender differences in using specific nonverbal cues, meta-analytic studies indicate that females are significantly more adept than males in *decoding* nonverbal communication. For example, in a review of seventy-five studies testing the ability of men and women to decode nonverbal behavior, Judith Hall (1978) found that 68 percent of the investigations reported superior female performance. Later meta-analyses found that this gender difference is greatest for decoding facial expressions, next largest for body cues, and smallest for correctly interpreting voice tone (Hall, 1984). The studies further suggest that this gender difference is not isolated in adult samples but can also be found in adolescents and children. Although these gender differences vary in size from study to study, females appear to be consistently better than males at decoding nonverbal cues (Brody & Hall, 1993).

As with emotional expression, social psychologists principally explain these gender differences in reading nonverbal cues by examining the different social roles played by females and males (Coats & Feldman, 1996). A **social role** is a cluster of socially defined expectations that individuals in a given situation are expected to fulfill. Social roles are (1) defined by society, (2) applied to all individuals in a particular social category, and (3) consist of well-learned responses by individuals. According to Alice Eagly's (1987, 1996) **social role theory,** the different social roles occupied by women and men lead to differences in the perception of women and men and in their behavior. In other words, because women and men typically operate in different domains within society—for example, women in the home and men in the world of paid employment—they engage in different patterns of behavior to properly play their roles. Female social roles require women to be more nurturing, friendly, and sensitive, while male social roles compel men to be more dominant, aggressive, and emotionally nonexpressive. In addition, because the social roles played by women tend to have lower status relative to male roles, Eagly contends that it is more important for women to learn to be accommodating and polite. Thus, by being more skilled at nonverbal communication, females are better able to understand people's feelings and thus increase their interpersonal comfort. This explanation is consistent with research indicating that regardless of gender, those who have less powerful social roles are more sensitive to the feelings of their superiors than vice versa (Snodgrass, 1992).

WE FORM PERSONALITY IMPRESSIONS WITH THE HELP OF CENTRAL TRAITS

In the early stages of impression formation, we make use of easily observable physical and nonverbal information (Park, 1986). However, as we learn more about others, our impressions become more abstract and less tied to their specific behavioral qualities (Sherman & Klein, 1994). Some of these more descriptive characteristics are *traits,* which are stable personal qualities such as "intelligent," "kind," and "unscrupulous." Because traits are so commonly used by us in forming impressions (Fiske & Cox, 1979), social psychologists have attempted to understand how they are combined to form a meaningful picture of a person. Do we simply add up the traits to a sum total, or do we average them together?

ADDITIVE OR AVERAGING MODEL?
To illustrate the differences between these two possible processes, imagine that you meet two people, Tanya and Kimberly. Based on conversations with both, you find them to be intelligent and humorous, two personality traits you evaluate very positively (let's say 9 points on a 10-point scale of evaluative positivity). You also think that Tanya is practical and modest, two traits you feel moderately positive about (6 points on a 10-point scale). Based on this information, would your overall impression of Tanya be more or less favorable than your impression of Kimberly? As illustrated in table 3.5, if you use an *additive model,* the extra, moderately positive information about Tanya's practicality and modesty would be summed with the very positive information about her intelligence and humor. As a result, you would judge her more favorably than Kimberly (+30 versus +18). However, with an *averaging model,* the moderately positive information about Tanya would be averaged with the extremely positive information and thus lower your overall impression of her. Using the averaging model, Kimberly would be evaluated more positively (+9 versus +7.5).

Social Role

A cluster of socially defined expectations that individuals in a given situation are expected to fulfill.

Social Role Theory

A theory that explains gender differences as being due to the different social roles occupied by women and men in society.

RITICAL *thinking*

As previously discussed, evolutionary theory contends that the ability to recognize emotion from the observation of facial expressions is part of our evolutionary heritage. How might an evolutionary theorist explain the gender differences in decoding nonverbal communication? That is, from an evolutionary perspective, why would it be more beneficial for females than males to have good nonverbal skills?

TABLE 3.5

Additive or Averaging Model of Traits?

Are traits added or averaged to form an overall evaluation of a person? The answer to this question determines whether Tanya will be viewed more or less favorably than Kimberly.

	Tanya	Kimberly
Trait	**Evaluation**	**Evaluation**
Intelligent	+9	+9
Humorous	+9	+9
Practical	+6	
Modest	+6	
	Overall Evaluation	**Overall Evaluation**
Additive Model	**+30**	+18
Averaging Model	+7.5	**+9.0**

Based on a number of studies, it appears as though the averaging model is a more accurate description of how traits are combined than the additive model. For example, Norman Anderson (1965) found that two strongly negative traits produced a more negative overall impression than two strongly negative traits combined with two moderately negative traits. Likewise, a moderately positive trait added to a very positive trait did not increase the overall impression and, in some circumstances, actually resulted in a less positive evaluation.

CENTRAL TRAITS

Although the averaging model predicts that traits are averaged into an overall impression, it is based on the assumption that all traits are equally important in the impression formation process. However, research by Solomon Asch in the 1940s indicates that not all traits are created equal, and therefore a simple averaging model will sometimes not account for the final overall impression. Asch believed that certain traits exerted a disproportionate influence on people's overall impressions, causing them to assume the presence of other traits. He called these dominant traits **central traits.**

In his classic study, Asch (1946) told participants they would hear a list of discrete traits that belonged to a particular person and that they should try to form an impression based on this information. For some participants, the following traits were then presented: intelligent-skillful-industrious-warm-determined-practical-cautious. For other participants, the trait *warm* was replaced with the trait *cold*, but otherwise everything else was identical. Those who had been told that the hypothetical person was warm rated him as significantly more *generous, humorous, sociable,* and *popular* than those who had been told that he was cold. In contrast to the effect of switching these two central traits, when Asch switched the traits *polite* and *blunt* from a similar list that people rated, the resulting impressions differed very little from one another.

Based on these results, Asch concluded that *warm* and *cold* are central traits that significantly influence overall impression formation. In a warm and caring individual, being industrious and determined would likely carry positive connotations, but in a cold and heartless individual these same traits carry very different, more negative, connotations. Thus, these central traits dramatically affect the *meaning* of the other characteristics of the person in question. In contrast to the influence of these central traits, whether people are considered polite or blunt is much less likely to alter social perceptions of their other traits.

Central Traits

Traits that exert a disproportionate influence on people's overall impressions, causing them to assume the presence of other traits.

In an elaboration of this research, Harold Kelley (1950) attempted to determine how these same traits might influence impression formation in a real-life situation. When students arrived at their college psychology class, they were greeted by a representative of the instructor who told them they were to have a guest lecturer that day. The representative led some students to believe that the soon-to-arrive lecturer was a rather warm person, and other students were led to expect a rather cold individual. The lecturer then appeared and led the class in a twenty-minute discussion. Results indicated that those given the "warm" preinformation not only consistently rated the lecturer more favorably than those given the "cold" preinformation, but they also interacted with him more in class discussion. Thus, the "warm" and "cold" descriptors not only shaped the students' impressions of the guest lecturer but also their behavior toward him.

In attempting to reconcile the averaging model to the central traits effect, Anderson (1968, 1981) proposed a *weighted averaging* model. According to this revised model, just as people assign certain scale values to traits, they also assign specific weights to traits, which determines their importance to the overall impression. For example, the traits *intelligent* and *humorous* may have equal scale values, but *intelligent* would carry more weight for a psychology department's graduate school admissions committee when evaluating applicants, while *humorous* would have more of an impact on the owner of a comedy nightclub when looking for a new act. Therefore, Anderson asserted that similar to the old averaging model, overall impressions are the average of all traits. Yet, consistent with the central traits effect, he added that some traits are given more weight than others in this averaging. Subsequent research has generally supported this weighted averaging view of impression formation (Kashima & Kereckes, 1994).

OUR PERSONALITY JUDGMENTS ARE OFTEN BASED ON BIASED THINKING

Health experts have grown increasingly alarmed about AIDS among young adults because most of this population are not practicing safe sex by using condoms (H. Miller et al., 1990). Why is this the case? A survey conducted by Diane Kimble and her colleagues (1992) found that young adults tend to have a well-developed and generally accepted set of ideas regarding which potential sexual partners are safe and which are not. Who are these sexually "safe" individuals? People whom one knows and likes are perceived not to be a risk. As one respondent summed up this view, "When you get to know the person . . . as soon as you begin trusting the person . . . you don't really have to use a condom" (p. 926). Risky people, on the other hand, are those one does not know well, who are older, and are overanxious for sex.

Kimble and her coworkers interpreted the young adults' tendencies not to practice safe sex with partners they knew and liked as being due to their reluctance to link the risk of disease with loving or caring relationships. Unfortunately, the criteria these people use to judge AIDS risk is totally unrelated to a person's HIV status. Individuals who operate from such a belief system run the very real risk of exposure to AIDS and possibly death.

IMPLICIT PERSONALITY THEORY

Where do such misguided judgments come from? As suggested by Asch's research on central traits, our knowledge about people is *structured* by our prior set of beliefs about which traits go together, and the resulting personality judgments we make often defy the rules of cold logic. These assumptions or naive belief systems that we have about the associations among personality traits are called an **implicit personality theory.** In these personality assumptions, we tend to assume that all good things occur together in persons and that all bad things do so as well, with little overlap between the two. Believing that an individual possesses one trait leads to the inference of other traits or behaviors assumed to be associated with the

Implicit Personality Theory

Assumptions or naive belief systems people make about which personality traits go together.

observed trait (Leyens, 1991). This is why many young adults perceive that someone whom they know and like could not be HIV-positive. This conclusion is arrived at because the alternative judgment is inconsistent with their assumptions about the relationships among traits and behaviors.

In an implicit personality theory, as in impression formation generally, there appears to be operating a principle of *evaluative consistency*—a tendency to view others in a way that is internally consistent. Even when contradictory information is made available, we still generally persist in viewing people as either consistently good or bad. In this effort toward consistency, we will often distort or explain away contradictory information.

Although implicit personality theories are commonly employed in making social judgments, some people rely on them more than others. Research by Chi-yue Chiu and his coworkers (1997) indicates that implicit theories are used more often by people who believe that personality consists of fixed, static traits than by those who believe that personality is dynamic and changing. This relation was found both in the individualist culture of the United States and in collectivist Hong Kong. These findings are important because they suggest that although implicit personality theories may be used by people around the world, there is a good deal of *individual* variation in the extent to which they are used. Additionally, findings by Chiu et al. point toward a possible *cultural* variation in the use of implicit personality theories. They found that more Americans than Chinese believe in fixed personality traits, which suggests that implicit personality theories are used more often by Americans.

POSITIVITY BIAS

Positivity Bias

The tendency for people to evaluate individual human beings more positively than groups or impersonal objects.

Another general evaluative bias operating in impression formation is to view people in a favorable light. Known as the **positivity bias,** it is the tendency for people to evaluate individual human beings more positively than groups or impersonal objects (Miller & Felicio, 1990). For example, in an analysis of more than 300,000 teacher evaluations, David Sears (1983) found that students rated 97 percent of their instructors as "above average," despite the negative experiences students often have in college classes. Why do we evaluate people so leniently? One possibility is that we feel better surrounded by good things, pleasant experiences, and nice people (Matlin & Stang, 1978) and therefore are motivated to see the world and others through "rose-colored glasses." A second possible explanation is that compared to groups or impersonal objects, people regard other human beings as relatively similar to themselves (Sears, 1983), and similarity heightens attraction (see chapter 10).

NEGATIVITY EFFECT

Negativity Effect

The tendency for negative traits to be weighted more heavily than positive traits in impression formation.

It may seem contradictory, but because people are biased toward perceiving others in a positive light, when they learn that someone has negative traits they place more weight on these unfavorable attributes in forming an impression of the person. Known as the **negativity effect,** it is the tendency of people to give more weight to negative traits than positive traits in impression formation (Vonk, 1993). This tendency to direct attention to negatively evaluated stimuli, like the tendency to notice fearful and angry faces in a crowd, is believed to have survival value for human beings (Pratto & John, 1991). Unfortunately, although this automatic vigilance may protect people from immediate harm, it may also contribute to harsher than warranted social judgments. The increasing use of "negative campaign ads" in politics is testimony to the power of the negativity effect. Even though such mudslinging is criticized by political commentators, research indicates that public opinion is shaped more by negative news about candidates than by positive news (Ansolabehere & Iyengar, 1995).

PRIMACY AND RECENCY EFFECTS

Primacy Effect

The tendency for the first information received to carry more weight than later information on one's overall impression.

There is one other simple and basic factor influencing impression formation, and it is related to the *order* in which we learn bits of information about someone. Known as the **primacy effect,** it is the tendency for the first information received to carry more

Research indicates that the first bits of information we learn about a person carry more weight in forming an overall impression than information learned later. Thus, if the woman in the photograph was described to you as intelligent, industrious, impulsive, critical, stubborn, and envious, your overall impression of her might be more favorable than if she was described an envious, stubborn, critical, impulsive, industrious, and intelligent. Although the information contained in these two descriptions is identical, Asch (1946) found that a hypothetical person described in the first manner was thought to be competent and ambitious, whereas a person described in the reverse order was considered overemotional and socially maladjusted.

Recency Effect

The tendency for the last information received to carry greater weight than earlier information.

weight in one's overall impression than later information. This effect was impressively demonstrated by Edward Jones and his colleagues (1968) when they had participants observe a confederate completing a thirty-item test of intellectual ability. As the confederate gave each answer, the experimenter publicly announced whether his response was correct. The confederate always answered fifteen questions correctly, but in one condition he would start off with many right answers and then end with many incorrect answers. In another condition, just the opposite would occur. At the end of the test, the participants predicted how well the confederate would do on the next thirty-item test, and to rate his intelligence. Even though the confederate always answered fifteen items correctly, he was rated as more intelligent and more likely to do well on the next test if he had started off with a number of correct responses rather than incorrect ones. See the accompanying photograph here for another example of how the primacy effect might operate in impression formation.

Why does early information figure more prominently than later information in our impression of others? One possible explanation is that the early bits of information we learn about another provide a cognitive *schema* or mental "outline," which we then use to process later information. If the later information contradicts this schema, we are likely to ignore it. Research suggests that the primacy effect is particularly strong when people are given little time to make judgments and are not under a great deal of pressure to be correct (Kruglanski & Freund, 1983).

Although the primacy effect regularly occurs in social perception, it can sometimes be reversed if people are warned against making hasty judgments or told that they will be asked to justify their impressions of a target person (Tetlock & Kim, 1987). In such circumstances, the last bits of information learned may be given greater weight than earlier information. This is known as the **recency effect.** Thus, if you have a shy friend whom you'd like to introduce to a potential romantic partner, you might guard against the primacy effect in the following manner. You could inform this person that your friend is somewhat shy and that her true personality doesn't always shine through in first meetings. If this person takes your advice, he will ignore some of the early awkwardness and social fumbling and pay more attention to what he learns about her after she feels more comfortable with him.

SECTION SUMMARY

First impressions are often based on self-presenters' nonverbal behavior, such as facial expressions, body movements, and posture. Throughout the world, people can also reliably identify at least six primary emotions: happiness, surprise, anger, sadness, fear, and disgust. We also often infer underlying emotional states by analyzing the shape of large-scale body movements during social interaction. Beyond attending to nonverbal behavior, in forming first impressions we also attend to personality *traits.* Instead of simply adding up or averaging these traits, we tend to employ a *weighted average.* In this mental computation, the traits are averaged together, but some of these traits are given more weight than others in this averaging. The traits that exert a disproportionate influence on the overall impression are called *central traits.* In judging others' personalities, we fall prey to a number of cognitive biases that involve viewing others in a way that is internally consistent. One bias, the *implicit personality theory,* is our assumption about which personality traits go together and which do not. Although we tend to assume that people possess positive personality characteristics (*positivity bias*), we also place more weight on negative traits when they are revealed (*negativity effect*), and we assign more importance to early information learned about others than later information (*primacy effect*).

MAKING ATTRIBUTIONS

In forming impressions of others, we attempt to determine what characteristics in each person explain their behavior and cause them to act the way they do. Yet in attempting to understand others, we do not solely focus on personality traits. In seeking explanations for their behavior we also consider the situational context, as well as the influence that others may have on them. Beyond trying to understand people as individuals, when we perceive events in general, we often are irresistibly drawn to understand *why* they unfold in the observed manner. This tendency is strongest when the events are the actions of other people and are unexpected, unusual, or distressing (Kanazawa, 1992). The process by which we use such information to make inferences about the causes of behavior or events is called **attribution.**

In the way of an example, let me describe an unexpected experience of my own. A few years ago after a snowstorm, I arrived home from work and noticed that our garbage had not been picked up. When I phoned the company, an exasperated woman replied to my query by sarcastically stating, "Well sir, with all the snow we had yesterday I would have thought people wouldn't have been stupid enough to put out their garbage today." Now, despite the public perception of psychologists as detached observers, constantly analyzing other people's behavior and motivation, this psychologist's response was not quite so analytical. Later, however, I wondered what caused her to act so rudely. Was she simply an insensitive person, or was it just a bad day for her?

About a year later, my garbage was not picked up again and I had to contact this woman a second time. Now there was no snowstorm. As I dialed, I wondered if I was about to be chastised again for yet another mental failing. To my relief, she was very cordial and apologetic. Based on this second conversation, I concluded that her previous behavior was most likely not due to some stable personality trait such as rudeness, but rather to an external, uncontrollable, and unstable event—the situational stress she experienced on that snowy winter day.

How did I arrive at this judgment, and how do people in general assign causal explanations for events? Studying the attribution process has been of primary concern to a number of social psychologists over the past forty years. Fritz Heider (1958) was the first social psychologist to formally analyze how people attempt to understand the causes behind behavior. He believed that everybody has a general theory of human behavior—what he called a *naive psychology*—and that they use it to search for explanations of social events.

In seeking attributions, Heider believed people are motivated by two primary needs: the need to form a coherent view of the world, and the need to gain control of the environment. Being able to predict how people are going to behave goes a long way in satisfying both of these needs. If we can adequately explain and predict the actions of others, we will be much more likely to view the world as coherent and controllable than if we have no clue to their intentions and dispositions. In satisfying these two needs, Heider asserted that we act much like *naive scientists*, rationally and logically testing our hypotheses about the behavior of others.

THE PRIMARY DIMENSION OF CAUSAL EXPERIENCE IS THE LOCUS OF CAUSALITY

In making causal attributions, by far the most important judgment concerns the *locus of causality*. According to Heider, people broadly attribute a given action either to internal states or external factors. An **internal attribution** (also called *person attribution*) consists of any explanation that locates the cause as being internal to the person, such as personality traits, moods, attitudes, abilities, or effort. An **external attribution** (also called *situation attribution*) consists of any explanation that locates the cause as being external to the person under scrutiny, such as the actions of others, the nature of the situation, or luck. In my "garbage" example, I ultimately made an external attribution about the woman's actions, explaining it due to the stress of the

Attribution

The process by which people use information to make inferences about the causes of behavior or events.

Internal Attribution

An attribution that locates the cause of an event to factors internal to the person, such as personality traits, moods, attitudes, abilities, or effort.

External Attribution

An attribution that locates the cause of an event to factors external to the person, such as luck, or other people, or the situation.

TABLE 3.6

Possible Causes of Academic Achievement due to Locus, Stability, and Controllability

| Controllability | Internal | | External | |
	Stable	Unstable	Stable	Unstable
Controllable	Typical effort	Temporary effort exerted for a particular exam	Some forms of teacher bias	Unusual help from others
Uncontrollable	Exerted ability	Mood	Exam difficulty	Luck

job brought on by adverse weather. For Heider and other attribution theorists, whether my explanation is correct or not is not the issue. Their task is not to determine the *true* cause of events, but rather to explain how people *perceive* the causes.

Besides making internal or external distinctions, people also attempt to answer other important attributional questions. Bernard Weiner and his colleagues expanded Heider's primary distinction between the internal and external locus of causality to include questions about stability and controllability (Weiner, 1986; Weiner et al., 1972). *Stable* causes are permanent and lasting, while *unstable* causes are temporary and fluctuating. This stable/unstable dimension is independent of the direction of causality. Some causes, called *dispositional,* are both internal and stable ("She insulted me because she is rude"). Other causes are considered to be internal but unstable ("She insulted me because she has a cold"). Likewise, some causes are seen as external and stable ("She insulted me because I, the external factor, rub people the wrong way"), while others are perceived as external and unstable ("She insulted me because the weather conditions that day made her job very difficult").

Although judgments of the locus and stability of causes are the most important in making attributions, a third dimension we often consider is the *controllability* of these causes. According to Weiner (1982), we think of some causes as being within people's control and others as being outside their control. The controllable/uncontrollable dimension is independent of either locus or stability. Weather is a good example of an uncontrollable factor.

Table 3.6 illustrates how these three dimensions might interact with one another in assigning causality to academic performance. For example, how much you generally study for exams would be considered an internal, stable, and controllable factor, while how much you *choose* to study for any particular exam would be an internal, unstable, and controllable factor. Sometimes a controllable factor like effort will only get you so far in academic achievement. Then we must consider internal factors that are seen as uncontrollable, such as innate intellectual ability (stable) and one's mood during exam time (unstable). External factors that are considered controllable might be rather stable, such as knowing that your teacher looks for specific definitions of terms and use of examples in test answers, or they might also be unstable, such as others deciding to help you prepare for an exam (this help is presumably under their control). Finally, the difficulty of tests given by the teacher would be perceived as being external, stable, and uncontrollable, while luck is an external, unstable factor typically perceived as uncontrollable.

The locus, stability, and controllability of causal attributions appear to be the primary dimensions employed when people explain events (Meyer & Koebl, 1982). For example, Weiner and his colleagues have demonstrated how these three dimensions are used by people to help them interpret requests for help, and how to view those who have stigmatizing diseases such as cancer and AIDS (Schmidt

& Weiner, 1988). Cross-cultural studies have also demonstrated that these dimensions are not only employed in individualist countries but in collectivist ones as well (Hau & Salili, 1991; Schuster et al., 1989).

Since Heider's initial formulations, other social psychologists have expanded upon his insights and developed formal attribution theories. The following pages focus on theories that have had the most influence on the field, and also discuss recent refinements in our understanding of the attribution process. These discussions will refer to *actors*, meaning the persons whose behavior we are attempting to understand.

CORRESPONDENT INFERENCE THEORY ASSUMES THAT PEOPLE PREFER MAKING DISPOSITIONAL ATTRIBUTIONS

Correspondent Inference

An inference that the action of an actor corresponds to, or is indicative of, a stable personal characteristic.

When we observe others, we not only attend to their behavior, but we are also aware of the *consequences* of the behavior. In developing correspondent inference theory, Edward Jones and Keith Davis (1965) were particularly interested in how people infer the cause of a *single* instance of behavior (for example, why did the garbage woman act rudely?). According to them, people try to *infer* from an overt action whether it *corresponds* to a stable personal characteristic of the actor. Thus, a **correspondent inference** is an inference that the action of an actor corresponds to, or is indicative of, a stable personal characteristic. For example, if Jane acts compassionately toward Bob, his correspondent inference would be that Jane is a compassionate person. But will Bob actually make a correspondent inference? Not always. If there are several plausible reasons why someone may have performed a certain act, correspondence is low, and therefore you cannot be confident about the cause of the act. However, if there is only one plausible reason to explain the act, correspondence is high and you will be confident in your attribution.

In explaining social events, Jones and Davis argued that people have a preference for making dispositional attributions (that is, those that are internal and stable), and that external attributions are merely default options, made only when internal causes cannot be found. The reason for this preference is the belief that knowing the dispositional attributes of others will enable one to better understand and predict their behavior. The problem in confidently making these attributions, however, is that social behavior is often ambiguous and the causes are not always readily apparent to the observer. Therefore, to guide them in their attempts to infer personal characteristics from behavior, Jones and Davis stated that people use several logical rules of thumb.

One such rule deals with the *social desirability* of the behavior. That is, people are much more likely to make dispositional attributions about behavior that is socially undesirable than about behavior that is desirable. This is the case because socially desirable behavior is thought to tell us more about the cultural norms of the group than about the personality of the individuals within that group. Yet when people are willing to break from these norms to act in a certain way, such unexpected behavior demands an explanation. When such action is taken, people realize that the social costs incurred by the actor may be great, and they are much more confident that the behavior reflects a stable and internal disposition (Jones et al., 1961).

Imagine that you are watching a number of candidates for political office addressing a meeting of Mothers Against Drunk Drivers (MADD). Every candidate voices support for tougher laws against those who drive while intoxicated. How confident would you be in concluding that the candidates' words truly reflect an underlying personal conviction? Now let's imagine that one of the speakers stands up and denounces the actions of MADD as an infringement on a citizen's pursuit of happiness. It's likely that you would be more confident that this candidate's words reflect his or her true convictions because they run so counter to prevailing societal norms.

Another rule considered by people is the actor's degree of *choice*. Actions freely chosen are considered to be more indicative of an actor's true personal characteristics

FIGURE 3.2   **95**

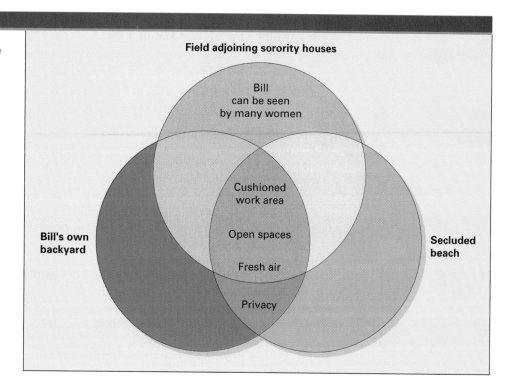

Why Did Bill Choose the Field as His Exercise Area? Looking for Noncommon Effects

Why Did Bill Choose the Field as His Exercise Area? Looking for Noncommon Effects

When there are a number of common effects for a given action, it is difficult to tell why people do what they do. However, when people engage in a behavior that has a noncommon effect—as is the case with Bill's decision to exercise next to the sorority houses—it is much easier to make a correspondent inference: Bill is an attention-seeker.

CRITICAL *thinking*

Why might someone argue that correspondent inference theory would not have been developed in a collectivist culture? Put another way, what indivdualist assumption is at the core of this theory?

than those that are coerced. Support for the freedom of choice factor comes from a study in which college students read a speech, supposedly written by a fellow student, that either supported or opposed Fidel Castro, the communist leader of Cuba (Jones & Harris, 1967). Some students were told that the student speechwriter had freely chosen her or his position, while others were told that the student was assigned the stated position by a professor. When asked to estimate what the student speechwriter's true attitudes were toward Castro, those who believed that the speechwriter had freely chosen her or his position were more likely to assume there was a correspondence between the student's essay (behavior) and her or his true attitudes.

According to Jones and Davis, we not only observe the social desirability of behaviors and the degree of choice of the actors, but we also analyze the actor's chosen behavior in the context of other potential behaviors. We then ask, "Is there some effect or outcome unique to the chosen behavior?" By comparing the consequences of the chosen behavior with the consequences of other actions not taken, people can often infer the strength of the underlying intention by looking for unique or "noncommon" consequences. This third rule of inference then, has to do with actions that produce *noncommon effects*—outcomes that could not be produced by any other action.

Research indicates that behaviors with unique noncommon effects result in stronger inferences about an actor's dispositions than behaviors with common effects (Ajzen & Holmes, 1976). For example, let's imagine Bill is looking for a place to lift weights and exercise. He is considering a spot in his backyard, a place on a secluded beach, and a field adjoining two sorority houses on campus. As illustrated in figure 3.2, some effects are common to any of these places (whichever he chooses, Bill will have a naturally cushioned work area and plenty of open space and fresh air). However, only one of these spots offers the opportunity for young women to watch him exercise. If Bill chooses the field as his exercise site, observers may likely conclude that he is an attention seeker. In drawing this conclusion, they are using the unique noncommon effect of Bill's behavioral decision to infer his personality traits.

Taking these rules into account, according to Jones and Davis's theory, people are most likely to conclude that other people's actions reflect underlying dispositional traits (that is, they are likely to make correspondent inferences) when the actions are perceived to (1) be low in social desirability, (2) be freely chosen, and (3) result in unique, noncommon effects.

THE COVARIATION MODEL EXPLAINS ATTRIBUTIONS DERIVED FROM MULTIPLE OBSERVATIONAL POINTS

The theory of correspondent inferences describes how we use certain rules of thumb in an attempt to infer dispositional (internal and stable) causes of behavior. However, the theory is generally applied only to single observations of behavior and only details the cognitive processes for making dispositional attributions. Yet it is quite clearly the case that many of our causal explanations are derived from an extended analysis of others and often result in attributions of causality *external* to the actor.

One theory that specifically attempts to explain attributions derived from multiple observational points and details the processes for making external, as well as internal, attributions is Harold Kelley's (1967) covariation model. Kelley agreed with Heider that human beings are rational and logical observers, acting much like naive scientists in the manner in which they tested their hypotheses about the behavior of others. Just as a scientist arrives at a judgment of causality by noticing that a particular variable is associated with a particular effect across a number of different conditions, Kelley believed that people make causal judgments about everyday events.

Covariation Principle

A principle of attribution theory stating that for something to be the cause of a particular behavior, it must be present when the behavior occurs and absent when it does not occur.

According to Kelley, people make attributions by using the **covariation principle.** This principle states that for something to be the cause of a particular behavior, it must be present when the behavior occurs and absent when it does not occur—the presumed cause and observed effect must "covary." If your boyfriend or girlfriend becomes cold and irritable only when you spend extended time with others, that is high covariation. If he or she is only occasionally cold and irritable when you spend extended time with others, that is low covariation. In attempting to assign a cause to the cold and irritable behavior, you would observe its covariation with as many potential causes as possible and attribute the effect to the cause with which it has the greatest covariance.

Our confidence in assigning a cause to some effect will be adversely affected if we cannot distinguish significant differences in the covariation between the effect we are interested in explaining and a number of possible causes. Kelley (1972) called this cognitive "fact" the **discounting principle.** Whenever there are several possible causal explanations for a particular event, we tend to be much less likely to attribute the effect to any particular cause (Morris & Larrick, 1995).

Discounting Principle

A principle of attribution theory stating that whenever there are several possible causal explanations for a particular event, people tend to be much less likely to attribute the effect to any particular cause.

In describing the locus of causality, Kelley elaborated on the internal/external dimension by further delineating external attributions into the *entity* and *circumstances*. The *entity* is the object toward which the actor's behavior is directed and can be another person or a thing. *Circumstances* are simply the conditions in which actions or events occur.

In assessing covariation, Kelley stated that people rely on three basic kinds of information. *Consensus* information deals with the extent to which others react in the same way to some stimulus or entity as the person whose actions we are attempting to explain. *Consistency* information concerns the extent to which the person reacts to this stimulus or entity in the same way on other occasions. Finally, *distinctiveness* information refers to the extent to which the person reacts in the same way to other, different stimuli or entities. Kelley's theory predicts that people are most likely to attribute another person's behavior to internal causes when consensus and distinctiveness are low but consistency is high. On the other hand, circumstance attributions are most likely when consensus and consistency are low and distinctiveness is high. When all three kinds of information are high, people are likely to make entity attributions.

Occasionally when I'm lecturing I notice a student has fallen asleep in class. Naturally, I wonder why. Did he have a bad night's sleep (circumstance attribution)? Is this a lazy and unmotivated student (internal attribution)? Am I that boring (entity attribution)? In table 3.7, I've outlined how Kelley's theory might predict specific

TABLE 3.7

Why Did the Student Fall Asleep in my Class?

| | Available Information | | | |
Condition	Consensus	Consistency	Distinctiveness	Most Common Attribution
1	Low—No other students fall asleep in my class	High—He has fallen asleep in previous classes of mine	Low—He falls asleep in other professors' classes	Internal: The student is lazy
2	High—Many students fall asleep in my class	High—He has fallen asleep in previous classes of mine	High—He doesn't fall asleep in other professors' classes	Entity: I'm a boring professor
3	Low—No other students fall asleep in my class	Low—He has not fallen asleep in previous classes of mine	High—He doesn't fall asleep in other professors' classes	Circumstance: The student didn't sleep well last night

attributions about this behavior. The covariation model predicts that I would seek an attribution by gathering consensus, consistency, and distinctiveness information. For consensus, I would look at the behavior of my other students: Is everybody on the verge of dozing off in my class? For consistency, I would consider this student's past classroom behavior: How attentive (or at least awake) has he appeared in previous class sessions? For distinctiveness, I would gather information about the student's behavior in other professors' classes: Does he fall asleep only in my class?

For an internal attribution to be made (Condition 1: The student is lazy), there must be evidence for low consensus and distinctiveness and high consistency. This attribution would be likely if none of my other students nod off, he falls asleep in other professors' classes, and he has fallen asleep in some of my previous classes as well. For an entity attribution to be made (Condition 2: I'm a boring professor), there must be evidence of high consensus, distinctiveness, and consistency. This attribution is likely if many students fall asleep in my class, and this particular student doesn't fall asleep in other professors' classes, even though he consistently dozes off in mine. A circumstance attribution would likely be made if consensus and consistency are low but distinctiveness is high (Condition 3). So if no one else is dozing off and he hasn't fallen asleep in previous classes of mine, or in other professors' classes, some unusual circumstance must have caused this behavior. Perhaps he didn't get enough sleep last night.

How accurate is the covariation model in explaining the attribution process? Empirical studies have generally supported the model, yet the three types of information do not appear to be equally influential (Chen et al., 1988). Of the three, consensus information has the weakest effect on attributions (Windschild & Wells, 1997; Wright et al., 1990). What this suggests is that, when trying to understand an actor's actions, we appear to primarily focus on information that can be obtained solely by attending to the actor (Was his or her behavior distinctive or consistent?), and pay less attention to information that requires us to also attend to other actors' actions (consensus information).

Both correspondent inference theory and the covariation model have significantly advanced the original insights of Heider by attempting to better understand how we make inferences about the causes of behavior. In its original form, correspondent inference theory dealt primarily with assigning meaning to *single instances* of behavior, whereas the covariation model was designed to explicitly explain how meaning is assigned to a *sequence* of behavior over time. Both theories assume that people are rational and logical observers, acting like naive scientists by testing hypotheses about the location of causality for social events. Yet how logical are we really in our daily attributions?

SECTION SUMMARY

In making causal attributions, the most important judgment concerns the locus of causality, which, broadly speaking, can be either *internal* or *external*. *Corresponding inference theory* describes how we use certain rules of thumb in trying to infer from some action whether it corresponds to a stable personal characteristic of the actor. These rules deal with the *social desirability* of the actions taken, the degree of *choice* of the actor in taking those actions, and the *noncommon effects* of the actions. Another theory that specifically attempts to explain attributions derived from multiple observations and details the processes for making external, as well as internal, attributions is the *covariation model*. From this perspective, for us to decide that some factor caused a particular action, this factor must be present when the action occurs and absent when it does not occur—the presumed cause and effect must covary. In assessing covariation, we rely on *consensus* information, *consistency* information, and *distinctiveness* information.

BIASES IN ATTRIBUTION

Based on the discussion thus far, the attribution process appears to be highly rational. However, although people seem to follow logical principles in assigning causality to events, this cognitive process—likened by some to a computer program—has some interesting and all-too-illogical human "bugs."

THE FUNDAMENTAL ATTRIBUTION ERROR DESCRIBES THE TENDENCY TO MAKE INTERNAL ATTRIBUTIONS OVER EXTERNAL ATTRIBUTIONS

As discussed in chapter 1, behavior is generally caused by an interaction of an individual's internal characteristics and external factors. However, in explaining other people's actions, we tend to locate the cause in terms of their dispositional characteristics rather than to what might be more appropriate situational factors. Lee Ross (1977) named this tendency to make internal attributions over external attributions for the behavior of others the **fundamental attribution error**.

Fundamental Attribution Error

The tendency to make internal attributions over external attributions in explaining the behavior of others.

Consider one example of this particular cognitive bias in operation. Ross and his colleagues (1977) devised a simulated TV quiz game in which students were randomly assigned to serve the role of "quizmaster" or "contestant." The quizmasters were told to think up ten challenging but fair questions, and the contestants were told to answer as many as possible. Under such conditions, the quizmasters were able to devise some rather tough questions and, on average, the contestants answered only four of the ten questions correctly. Despite the fact that the quizmaster role gave students playing that part a decided advantage, the contestants failed to discount or take this external factor into account in assigning a causal explanation for the quiz show's results. As you can see in figure 3.3, contestants saw the quizmasters as far more knowledgeable than themselves. Observers who watched the game, but were not directly involved in the outcome, also rated the quizmasters as more knowledgeable than the contestants.

FIGURE 3.3

Even though students playing the role of quizmaster held a decided advantage over contestants, the contestants failed to discount or take this external factor into account in assigning a causal explanation for the quiz show's results. Like the observers, the contestants judged the quizmasters as more knowledgeable than themselves. What might explain this fundamental attribution error?

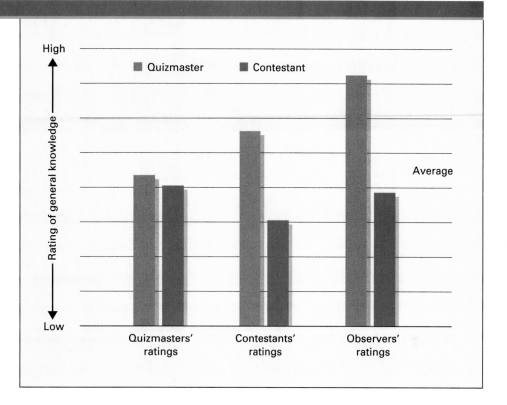

THE ROLE OF PERCEPTUAL SALIENCE

Why do we tend to engage in this sort of systematic bias? One possibility is that when another person is observed in a social setting, what is most *perceptually salient* is that particular person: their dynamic movements, their distinctive voice, and their overall physical presence. In comparison, the relatively static external forces that may actually cause those behaviors are less salient and therefore less likely to be factored into the attribution equation.

Shelly Taylor and Susan Fiske (1975) tested this hypothesis by varying the seating arrangements of six people who observed two actors engaging in a carefully staged, five-minute conversation. In each session, observers were seated so they faced either actor A, actor B, or both. This seating arrangement is illustrated in figure 3.4. Following the conversation, the observers were asked questions about the two actors to determine whom they thought had the most impact on the conversation. Results indicated that whichever actor they faced was the one the observers judged to be the more dominant member of the dyad. Further research has confirmed perceptual salience as a contributing factor to the fundamental attribution error (Krull & Dill, 1996).

IS THIS REALLY A "FUNDAMENTAL" ERROR?

Besides perceptual salience, another reason the fundamental attribution error exists is that our Western culture appears to provide us with a view of social reality that leads us to be more susceptible to committing such an error. As stated earlier in the text, our culture is based on the ideology of *individualism*, in which human beings are conceived as autonomous, internally driven creatures, not influenced by external forces. On the other hand, many non-Western cultures have a more collectivist perspective, stressing the relationship between the individual and her or his social roles and surroundings. These two different perspectives of social reality not only influence our self-concepts (see chapter 2), they shape our social perceptions as well.

FIGURE 3.4

**Perceptual Salience
and the
Fundamental
Attribution Error**

This is the seating arrangement for the two actors and six observers in the perceptual salience study. Taylor and Fiske found that observers rated the actor they could see most clearly as being the dominant contributor to the conversation. How do these findings help explain the fundamental attribution error?

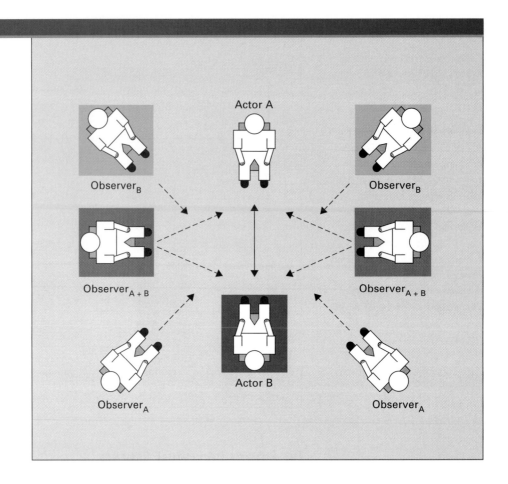

In a study that documented these cultural differences in attributional style, Joan Miller (1984) asked groups of American and Asian-Indian citizens of varying ages to explain the causes of positive and negative behaviors they had seen in their own lives. As figure 3.5 shows, in the youngest children of the two cultures (8- to 11-year-olds), there were no significant attribution differences. However, as the age of the participants increased, Americans made more dispositional attributions, and the Asian Indians made more external attributions. This study and others, strongly suggest that the fundamental attribution error is more common in individualist cultures than in those that are collectivist, and it is learned through socialization (Lee et al., 1996; Morris & Peng, 1994).

Whether perceptual salience, individualism, or a combination of these and other factors explain the fundamental attribution error, this particular bias can have significant social consequences. Attributing the behavior of others to internal factors allows social perceivers to block the actor's attempts to deny responsibility for negative events with which he or she is associated (Inman et al., 1993). For example, the tendency to disregard situational forces in explaining the plight of victims within our society (rape victims, street people, disadvantaged minorities, etc.) can result in a decidedly less-than-sympathetic response, because we hold these people responsible for their condition due to "bad" dispositions.

Even if our response is one of sympathetic caring for unfortunate others, the assignment of dispositional blame will influence the type of solutions we as a society implement for these people (Caplan & Nelson, 1973). That is, if we attribute the difficulties of unfortunate others to personal defects rather than to their circumstances, it is likely that the treatment programs will focus on changing individuals and not on improving the conditions of their social environment. Yet if the individuals in these treatment programs are members of particular social groups in which failure is often

FIGURE 3.5

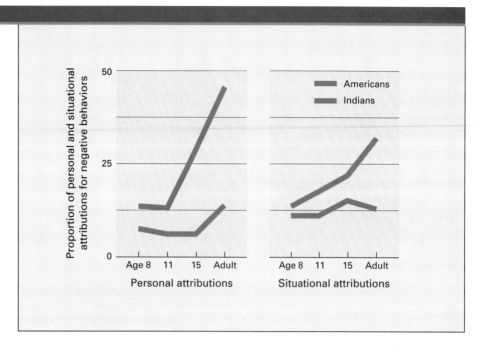

Asian-Indian and American participants of varying ages explained the causes of positive and negative behaviors they had seen in their own lives. Consistent with the fundamental attribution error, the individualist American adults made more dispositional than situational attributions for both positive and negative events. The exact opposite was true for the collectivist Asian-Indian adults. Among the younger children, no attribution differences were found. Why do you think there were differences between adults but not children in these two cultures?

due to discrimination rather than to personal defects (like ethnic minorities and women), our attempted interventions may prove to be psychologically damaging.

ACTORS GIVE MORE WEIGHT TO EXTERNAL FACTORS THAN DO OBSERVERS

When explaining the actions of others, we are especially likely to commit the fundamental attribution error. But when explaining our own behavior, we tend to give more weight to external (or situational) factors. This tendency to attribute our own behavior to external causes but that of others to internal factors is known as the **actor-observer effect** (Jones & Nisbett, 1972; Karasawa, 1995). For example, if Charisse is having a conversation with an attractive male stranger and her boyfriend, Singh, sees them from a distance, they may well arrive at different explanations for this social interaction. Although Charisse may attribute it to an external factor (the stranger was asking for directions), Singh may assign an internal cause (Charisse is infatuated with this guy!).

Actor-Observer Effect

The tendency for people to attribute their own behavior to external causes but that of others to internal factors.

Michael Storms (1973) created such conversational setups (minus the jealousy component) to test for the actor-observer effect. Employing a design similar to the previously discussed Taylor and Fiske (1975) study, Storms had four unacquainted research participants—two playing the role of observers and two playing the role of conversational actors—arranged in a seating pattern similar to the one shown in figure 3.6. The two actors were instructed to engage in a five-minute conversation, and the two observers were told to focus their attention on the actor they were facing. Two video cameras also separately recorded the facial expressions of the actors as they conversed. Immediately afterward, both the actors and the observers rated the actors' behavior along a number of dimensions, and then they were asked to indicate the degree to which the actors' behavior was determined by their personal characteristics and by the situation. Consistent with the actor-observer effect, the observers placed greater importance on *dispositional* factors when explaining the actions of the actor they were watching, whereas the actors emphasized *situational* factors when explaining their own behavior.

Why does the actor-observer effect occur? As with the fundamental attribution error, a likely possibility is perceptual salience. While engaged in a particular

FIGURE 3.6

Perceptual Salience and the Actor-Observer Effect

This is the seating arrangement for the two actors and two observers in Storms's (1973) perceptual salience study. Why would two actors who watched themselves on videotape following the conversation with the other actor make more dispositional attributions about their behavior?

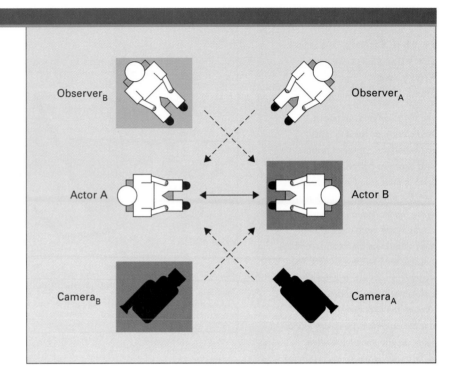

activity, the actor's attention is typically turned outward toward the situation, but the observer's attention is likely focused on the actor. Thus, what is salient for the actor (the situation) and what is salient for the observer (the actor) differs due to their perspectives in viewing the event.

If perceptual salience is important in the attribution process, what would happen if you manipulated this salience *after* the event had transpired but *prior* to observers and actors making any formal attributions? In another condition of Storms's study, he showed the videotapes to the participants before they made their attributions. Instead of seeing on tape what they had experienced live, however, some of them watched the *opposite* visual perspective. Thus, actors A and B saw their own faces, observer A saw actor B, and observer B saw actor A. What do you think resulted from this perceptual flip-flop?

In contrast to participants who saw on tape what they had experienced live, these *reversed-perspective* viewers no longer exhibited the typical actor-observer effect. Instead, the actors who had seen themselves made more dispositional attributions, and the observers made more situational attributions about the actor they had previously faced. These findings, along with others, not only demonstrate the power of perceptual salience in the attribution process, but they also demonstrate that if we manipulate the attention of the actors so that they become *self-aware*, they tend to place more importance on internal factors when explaining their own actions, and the actor-observer effect disappears (Arkin & Duval, 1975). In a very real psychological sense, when the actors engaged in self-awareness, they became observers of their own actions.

Keeping in mind how differing psychological perspectives—self-focused versus situation-focused—can influence perceptual salience, let us consider an extension of Storms's (1973) study by Mark Frank and Thomas Gilovich (1989). In their investigation, male and female college students engaged in a brief "get-acquainted" conversation with a stranger of their own sex. Immediately following this interaction, they rated their own behavior along similar dimensions used by Storms, and also assigned causality to these actions. Three weeks later, they returned and were asked to recall the previous conversation and to rate their behavior once again. This time they were also asked to indicate how they imagined the scene while recalling it—from their own perspective or from an "outside" viewpoint. The researchers predicted that if the actors remembered their actions from their own perspective, they would tend to make external attributions. However, if they remembered it from an "outside" perspective (that is, taking themselves as an object of attention), then it was hypothesized that they would make internal attributions. Results supported both hypotheses. The majority of actors remembered the scene from their own perspective. They also reported more external attributions on the second occasion than on the first. For those actors who remembered the scene from an outside observer's perspective, internal attributions were more likely.

In a second study, instead of allowing participants to spontaneously adopt an observer or actor perspective, Frank and Gilovich (1989) induced them to remember the get-acquainted conversation from either one perspective or the other. As in the previous study, those who were induced into the observer perspective made more internal attributions, while those induced into the actor perspective made external attributions. Taken together, these findings, along with Storms's manipulated self-awareness results, suggest that the differing perspectives typical of actors and observers is a significant cause of this particular attributional bias.

Although the actor-observer effect is a well-documented attributional phenomenon (Krueger et al., 1996), it is less likely to occur when the actors making the attributions have personalities or self-concept qualities that match the behavior being explained in a given situation (Robins et al., 1996). For example, if Shalini considers herself to be an extraverted person (a dispositional attribution), and acts very outgoing when introduced to a group of people, she is as likely to explain her behavior in dispositional terms ("I am talking a lot because I'm an extraverted person") as are those who are observing her behavior. Thus, despite the general tendency for the actor-observer effect to operate, personality and self-concept differences among individuals help explain why it does not occur in certain situations.

SELF-SERVING ATTRIBUTIONS ENHANCE AND PROTECT SELF-ESTEEM

Perhaps the best evidence that we are not coldly rational information processors is found in situations in which our own performance results in either success or failure. When such events transpire, where do you think we tend to assign the locus of causality? I probably do not need to cite numerous studies to convince you that the nature of the attribution process is decidedly self-protective in failure situations and self-enhancing in success situations. That is, we tend to take credit for positive behaviors or outcomes but to blame negative behaviors or outcomes on external causes (Olson & Ross, 1988). For example, when students receive a good grade on an exam, they are likely to attribute it either to their intelligence (an uncontrollable, yet stable, internal factor), their strong work ethic (a controllable, stable, internal factor), or a combination of the two (Bernstein et al., 1979). However, if they receive a poor grade on this exam, they tend to attribute it to an unreasonable professor (a stable, yet uncontrollable, external factor) or pure bad luck (an unstable, uncontrollable, external factor). This tendency to assign an internal locus of causality for our positive outcomes and an external locus for our negative outcomes is known as the **self-serving bias.** It is arguably the most robust of the attributional biases and has been documented cross-culturally, although it may be stronger in individualist societies than in those with a collectivist orientation (Kashima & Triandis, 1986).

Although the existence of this bias has been established, its origins have become the source of debate within the field (Knee & Zuckerman, 1996). The most agreed-upon explanation is that the self-serving bias allows us to protect self-esteem. If we feel personally responsible for successes or positive events in our lives but do not feel blameworthy for failures or other negative events, our self-worth is

Self-Serving Bias

The tendency to assign an internal locus of causality for our positive outcomes and an external locus for our negative outcomes.

likely to be bolstered. This self-enhancement explanation emphasizes the role of motivation in our self-serving biases. As was documented in chapter 2 on the self, most people have a strong desire to see themselves in a positive light, and sometimes this need can override the desire for accurate self-knowledge. If future studies find that people from collectivist cultures do indeed engage in the self-serving bias less than those from individualist cultures, this may mean that (1) collectivists have less of a need to protect self-esteem, and/or (2) the self-serving bias is more of an individualist coping strategy, less likely to be found in societies in which social support is widely available and collective coping is more likely.

Whatever future cross-cultural studies may find, the self-enhancement explanation is appealing in that it can also provide insight into how self-serving biases extend beyond ourselves to include our explanations of individuals or groups with which we identify (S. Miller, 1995; Mullen & Riordan, 1988). As discussed in chapter 2, self-esteem can be reinforced by associating ourselves with the success of others. In a psychological sense, those others with whom we strongly identify are part of our self-concept. When we observe their actions, we tend to ascribe their positive behaviors to internal factors and their negative behaviors to external factors. In so doing, we can "bask in the reflected glory" of their accomplishments and experience our own self-esteem benefits (Cialdini et al., 1976). This tendency to see the actions of ingroup members through the same "rose-colored glasses" as we view our own is a variation of the self-serving bias, known as the *ingroup bias*. As we will discuss more fully in chapter 7, ingroup biasing contributes to a host of social ills, such as sex and race discrimination.

In addition to the self-enhancement explanation, a second and more recent proposition claims that what is called the self-serving bias is actually a very rational information-processing outcome. These so-called self-serving attributions stem from our expectations for success in given situations (Taylor & Riess, 1989). The basic argument here is that people generally expect to succeed and therefore are more willing to accept responsibility when it occurs. Based on Kelley's covariation model, this explanation contends that when people do succeed, the success is low in distinctiveness and high in consistency; therefore, people will make an internal attribution. However, when people meet with failure, this event is considered unusual (high in distinctiveness and low in consistency), and they are therefore likely to make an external attribution. If others also fail on the same task, such high consensus will only strengthen an external attribution.

Whatever the ultimate cause, and despite the fact that self-serving attributional biases provide us with a less-than-accurate view of ourselves (and often other ingroup members), they may be quite adaptive cognitive strategies in many social settings. For example, attributing any current successes to enduring internal characteristics creates an expectation of future success in related tasks, increasing the likelihood that we will attempt new challenges (Taylor & Brown, 1988). Similarly, attributing repeated failures to external factors may well serve to maintain an optimistic belief in the possibility of future success, resulting in task persistence. Wilmar Schaufeli (1988), for instance, has found that unemployed workers seeking reemployment in the labor market have more success if they exhibit the self-serving bias in their job search (that is, not being hired for a particular job is attributed to external factors and not to internal ones such as incompetence).

In summary, then, people tend to assume more credit for success than responsibility for failure, and the most common explanation for this effect is motivational—a desire to enhance and protect self-esteem. It is also possible that this bias is not as illogical as previously perceived, and that it may be the result of rational information processing and our expectations for success. Although some of the more recent research supports the motivational view over the more cognitive perspective (Brown & Rogers, 1991), both may prove to be contributing factors.

APPLICATIONS

HOW GOOD ARE YOU AT DETECTING LIES?

 uring President Clinton's impeachment trial, Republican prosecutors wanted to directly question witnesses so they could look them in the eye and judge their credibility. Is this an effective strategy in truth-seeking? Do you believe that lying is common or uncommon for the average person? Would you be surprised to learn that research by Bella DePaulo and her colleagues indicate that, during an average week, people lie to about one-third of all of those with whom they interact? On average, people tell about ten lies per week, with the greatest lying committed by those who are more sociable, manipulative, and concerned about creating favorable self-presentations than others (DePaulo et al., 1996; Kashy & DePaulo, 1996). Most of the time, these untruths are told to benefit the liar (*self-centered lies*)

rather than benefiting someone or something else (*other-oriented lies*). Yet when people lie to spare others' feelings (other-oriented lying), these "kind lies" are usually reserved for those they like (Bell & DePaulo, 1996). Table 3.8 lists some of the characteristics of lying in everyday life.

Given that people sometimes try to conceal their true feelings and intentions from others, how do we—as social perceivers—respond to the possibility of such subterfuge? Erving Goffman (1959) contended that when we judge other people's self-presentations, we pay attention to two different types of social stimuli, which he called *expressions*. First, there are expressions that people freely "give" to others in what is typically thought of as their traditional communication patterns. These *expressions given* consist of the words and gestures that people are consciously trying to transmit to others.

Virtually everyone lies on an everyday basis. What sort of a lie is depicted here? Can you recall a recent incident when you told such a lie? What was your motivation for doing so? When do you last think you were the recipient of a "kind lie"?

Reprinted with special permission of King Features Syndicate.

TABLE 3.8

Lying by College Students and Community Members in Everyday Life

Number of lies told per week	10.4
Of all the people interacted with during the week, % lied to	34%
Percent who said they told no lies	5%
Reasons for lying	
Self-centered: Lie told to protect or enhance the liars psychologically, or to advance or protect the liars' interests	51%
Other-oriented: Lie told to protect or enhance other persons psychologically, or to advance or protect the interest of others	25%
Neither self-centered or other-oriented: To control an interaction, to entertain, to conform, or to simplify a response	24%
How was lie delivered?	
Face to face	79%
By telephone	20%
In writing	1%
Was lie discovered?	
No	59%
Yes	19%
Don't know	19%
Unclassified response	3%
Percent who said they would tell the lie again	77%

Source: Based on data in DePaulo et al., 1996

Besides these strategic gestures, there are also expressions that people "give off," which are mostly nonverbal in nature. *Expressions given off,* also known as *nonverbal leakage,* cover a wide range of behavior unintentionally transmitted and of which people are much less aware. The lack of gusto when chewing a host's poorly prepared meal and the tortured look behind your forced smile are examples of expressions given off.

The tendency to tune into this silent language of nonverbal behavior when we believe others are attempting to deceive us is a common strategy employed in judging social reality. Under such circumstances, we pay more attention to others' facial expressions, then body posture, and least of all words (Mehrabian, 1972). Apparently we assume that nonverbal information is more likely to reveal others' true feelings because it's less likely to be consciously controlled than is verbal information. This assumption appears to be true. In an analysis of accurate and inaccurate judges of deception, Ekman and Maureen O'Sullivan (1991) found that the inaccurate judges (30 percent accuracy or worse) focused on verbal cues, while the accurate judges (80 percent accuracy or better) attended more to nonverbal cues.

> The eyes have one language everywhere.
>
> George Herbert, English poet, 1593–1633

Although attending to nonverbal behavior can improve our ability to reveal the "lie" in others' self-presentations, not all nonverbal cues are equally instructive. One of the biggest mistakes we make is placing too much importance on the face to reveal deception. For example, we tend to believe that others do not smile when they lie, when in fact, smiling is a common device used by deceivers to hide their true feelings (Ekman et al., 1988). We also tend to be fooled by the *structure* of people's faces, falsely assuming that baby-faced individuals (large eyes and symmetrical facial features) and physically attractive persons are more honest than those with mature-looking and less attractive faces (Zebrowitz & Montepare, 1992; Zebrowitz et al., 1996).

Instead of focusing on the face, attending to other nonverbal cues appears to lead to more accurate social perception. For example, in one study, Ekman and Wallace Friesen (1974) showed a series of either pleasant or disgusting short films to a sample of female nurses and instructed them either to report their honest feelings about the film or to conceal their feelings. Hidden video cameras—some focused on the face and others focused on the body—recorded their behavioral expressions. These tapes were later viewed by participants acting as observers whose task it was to judge whether the nurses had been truthful or deceptive. Results indicated that observers who watched tapes focused on the face were not as accurate at detecting deception as were those who watched tapes focused on the body. Body movements that significantly predicted deception were "fidgeting" of the hands and feet, and restless shifts in body posture. This and other research suggests that when trying to deceive others, people's facial expressions are more likely to be self-monitored and controlled (expressions given) than are their other bodily movements (expressions given off).

Although nonverbal behavior generally provides more useful information about lying than verbal behavior, it is sometimes possible to detect deception by attending to certain changes in a person's speech patterns—what is known as *paralanguage*. Several studies indicate that when people lie, they tend to give shorter answers, the pitch in their voice often rises slightly, and their speech is slower and filled with many pauses ("ahs" and "uhms") and other sentence hesitations (Porter & Yuille, 1996; Stiff et al., 1989).

A meta-analysis of seventeen studies involving almost twenty-eight hundred participants found that our *confidence* in detecting deception does not predict our *accuracy* in distinguishing liars from nonliars (DePaulo et al., 1997). Even those who make these judgments for a living, such as judges, police officers, CIA polygraphers, and customs inspectors, generally do no better than chance (DePaulo & Pfeifer, 1986). Indeed, the best of the professional deception detectors, namely Secret Service agents, are successful only about 70 percent of the time (Ekman & O'Sullivan, 1991).

Taken as a whole, the research on deception tells us that despite the numerous deception signals available to us as social perceivers, we frequently make mistakes in judging whether others are being truthful. Deceivers succeed in duping us regardless of our sex, race, cultural background, socioeconomic status, or educational level. Perhaps the primary reason why we so often fail to detect deception is that, by and large, we tend to believe that others are basically honest (Zuckerman et al., 1981). In the final analysis, there is no one verbal or nonverbal channel that can be thought of as a lie detector. If a deceiver is well prepared and exercises great self-control, even attention to body fidgeting, posture shifts, and voice pitch will not necessarily separate truths from lies.

FEATURED STUDY
TELLING LIES TO THOSE WHO CARE

DePaulo, B. M., & Bell, K. L. (1996). Truth and investment: Lies are told to those who care. *Journal of Personality and Social Psychology, 71*: 703–716.

The feedback that people receive from others about their appearance, personality, behavior, or work often does not reflect the evaluators' true opinions. An important reason for such dishonesty may be that evaluators are more concerned about hurting others' feelings than in helping them correct their imperfections. In the present study, it was hypothesized that evaluators' concerns for hurting others' feelings, and their tendency to be dishonest in providing unfavorable feedback, would be most pronounced when the activity being evaluated was something with which the evaluatees strongly identified. It was further hypothesized that this social norm against hurting other people's feelings is so strong that explicitly telling evaluators to be polite and to try to avoid hurting another person's feelings would result in communications that were no different than if no instructions had been given.

METHOD

Participants were ninety-four introductory psychology students (forty-seven males and forty-seven females) who received course credit for volunteering to take part in a study described as being designed to help art students learn more about how art is perceived by ordinary people. First, participants were left alone in a room to choose their two most favorite and two least favorite paintings from a selection of nineteen paintings. They were then instructed to write a brief description about what they liked and disliked about each of the four paintings. The experimenter then informed participants that they would now discuss the four paintings with a female art student, and that this student may have actually painted some of the paintings herself. They were also told that the art student would not know that the participant had selected the four paintings, nor would she ever be shown the participant's written evaluations. During the subsequent conversation, the art student (a confederate of the experimenter) always claimed that one of the participant's two most favorite paintings and one of their two least favorite paintings were special to her in some way. In the *moderate investment* condition, the art student said that the painting was one of her favorites. In the *high investment* condition, the student claimed that the painting was one of her own. She volunteered this information just before asking what the participant thought of the painting.

Participants were randomly assigned to one of three instructional conditions. One third of them were instructed to be *honest* when discussing the paintings, another third were instructed to be *polite* and to try not to hurt the art student's feelings, and the final third were given *no instructions* about what to do. The participant and art student were left in the room alone while a hidden video camera recorded their interaction. Following this meeting, participants completed a questionnaire indicating how much liking they tried to convey to the art student, how honest they had been, and how comfortable they felt while discussing what they liked and disliked about the paintings. Participants were then debriefed about the true purpose of the study.

In the next phase of the study, undergraduate judges watched the videotapes of the painting discussions, and rated the participants' honesty, comfort, actual liking for the paintings, and degree of liking that the participants were trying to convey to the art student. Judges knew whether the paintings were special to the artists, but they did not know what the participants really thought of the paintings, nor did they know whether the participants were trying to be polite or honest. These ratings were then used, along with the participants' own evaluations and self-reports, in the subsequent statistical analyses.

RESULTS AND DISCUSSION

As predicted, when the paintings were thought to be very special to the art students (*high investment* condition), participants reported being more uncomfortable and more dishonest, but only for the disliked paintings. For these disliked paintings, they tried to convey more liking, and they exaggerated their liking more. The judges also thought that the participants were similarly more uncomfortable and dishonest when discussing the very special paintings. Although participants exaggerated their liking for disliked paintings dear to the heart of the art student, in most cases they did not rave about these paintings.

Support for the hypothesis that people conform to a politeness norm when providing feedback to others came from a number of sources. Based on the judges' perceptions, the uninstructed participants generally provided feedback to the art students that was just as distorted and dishonest as those conveyed by the participants who were told to be polite. Further, although participants seldom told outright lies (raving about a painting they strongly disliked), such lying was most likely when they were given no special instructions or were instructed to be polite.

Overall, these findings are directly relevant to decades of research indicating that our perceptions of others' views of us are not strongly related to their actual views. The present results suggest that what may account for these discrepancies are that people, out of concern for our feelings, are not very open and honest when communicating negative feedback about matters important to us.

WEB SITES accessed through http://www.mhhe.com/franzoi2

Web sites for this chapter focus on nonverbal communication and the history of attribution theory.

Dane Archer's Nonverbal Communication Web Page

Dane Archer's web page will introduce you to the topic of nonverbal communication and give you a chance to try to guess the meaning of some real nonverbal communication.

Facial Analysis Website

This web site highlights the work of many past and present researchers, including deBoulogne, Darwin, Ermiane, and Ekman.

Folk Explanations of Behavior

This web page reviews the history of attribution theory and discusses how people act like naive scientists when trying to understand others' actions.

C H A P T E R 4

SOCIAL COGNITION

CHAPTER OUTLINE

uppose you are visiting a city for the first time and have car trouble downtown in the dead of night. In desperation, you scan the faces of passing motorists, looking for someone who will get you out of this jam. How can you tell who will be your Good Samaritan? Can you seek help from the carload of teenagers who have passed by twice in the past five minutes? Or should you take a chance and try to flag down the neatly dressed and pleasant-looking young man driving the 1965 Chevy . . . who, on second glance, bears an uncanny resemblance to the character of Norman Bates in the movie *Psycho?* Just as you are bemoaning the fact that you don't know anything about the people whom you are about to ask for help, something in the distance catches your eye. It is a white car with lettering and an emblem on the door, and a panel of light flashers on the roof. Inside are two people wearing blue uniforms and badges. Despite the fact that you are certain they are carrying loaded guns and wooden clubs, you immediately step out in the street and signal them to stop. Are you crazy? You have never seen these two people before in your life, yet you believe they will help you. Why?

Later, upon returning to your hotel room, you turn on the television to unwind. On the city news, there is a report about a local train crash in which two women were killed. You learn that while one of the women was a regular passenger on the train, the other woman was a first-time rider who had been on board only because the busline she normally used was out on strike. While digesting this story, you realize that you feel sorrier for the first-time rider than for the regular commuter. Her death seems more tragic. Why?

Life is complicated. Nothing that you have learned thus far about the psychology of social interaction should argue against this statement. Faced with life's complications, and thrust into the world as both actors and observers, we try to make sense of it. In chapter 2 we examined how we develop a theory of ourselves, and in chapter 3 we examined how we form impressions of individuals and how we explain the causes of their behavior. In developing theories about ourselves and the world around us, we rely on **social cognition**, which involves how we actively interpret, analyze, remember, and use information about the social world (Berkowitz & Devine, 1995).

The social perception theories described in chapter 3 generally depict human beings as *naive scientists,* who are highly rational and logical information processors. Although these theories note that the social perception process has a number of "bugs" in it, none necessarily imply that people do not *try* to act logically and thoroughly in seeking social judgments. Yet it is true that people often do not systematically make careful observations to arrive at an explanation for events. Instead of sparing no "cognitive expense" in explaining social events, in this chapter we will examine how people often act like discount bargain shoppers who are always on the lookout for "blue-light specials." This alternative view of ourselves as social thinkers, known as the *cognitive miser perspective,* conceives of human beings as creatures more than willing to engage in timesaving mental shortcuts when trying to understand their social world (Fiske & Taylor, 1991).

How do we reconcile the naive scientist and the cognitive miser views of social cognition? The answer to this question is found by remembering the important role the self plays in human thought and action. Based on our discussions of the self in chapter 2, you realize that *self-awareness* and *self-regulation* allow us to

Social Cognition

The way in which we interpret, analyze, remember, and use information about the social world.

reflect on, plan, and control our thoughts and actions. In the realm of social thinking, social cognition theorists have recently contended that whether we act like naive scientists or cognitive misers is determined by what *motivates* us in a given situation (Kruglanski, 1996). While acknowledging that people sometimes take cognitive shortcuts, this **motivated-tactician model** proposes that we are flexible social thinkers who choose among multiple cognitive strategies based on our current goals, motives, and needs. For instance, if social judgment accuracy is the primary goal in a given situation, we will probably carefully assess information. However, if we need to make a quick decision and/or the issue in question is not that important to us, we may take cognitive shortcuts. Thus, what directs the nature and quality of our social thinking is the self and its motives. One of the primary strengths of the motivated-tactician model is that it attempts to integrate the "cold" information-processing approach with the "hot" motivational perspective of human nature (refer back to chapter 1, p. 17). As you will discover in your reading of this chapter, the hot-cold integration leads to a more complete explanation of our social thinking.

CATEGORIZATION AND STEREOTYPING

As much as you may desire to only respond to other people based on information you have personally learned about them as individuals, which was our topic of discussion in chapter 3, the complexity of our social environment often makes this an impractical—even undesirable—task. In situations where you must make quick judgments about others based on minimal information, you generally don't have the luxury of engaging in detailed impression formation. Luckily, we come equipped with alternative social judgment strategies.

WE ARE CATEGORIZING CREATURES

In our hypothetical nighttime dilemma, the reason you might respond in the manner described is because human beings spontaneously categorize things they experience. That is, to reduce and simplify the processing of information from our surroundings, we mentally group objects, ideas, or events that share common properties. For example, because certain objects such as roses, daffodils, and lilies share the same features and attributes (for example, petals, pistils, and anthers), we place them into the same cognitive concept or category, namely that of "flower." This natural tendency to categorize is also applied to people, a process called **social categorization** (Hampson, 1988). Like the heart that pumps life-giving blood throughout the body, or the lungs that replenish oxygen to this blood, the general scientific consensus is that humans could not survive without engaging in social categorization.

How do we mentally group things, including people, into their proper categories? The classical view was that category membership was determined by *defined features* (Bruner et al., 1956). For instance, if an animal has three body divisions, six legs, an external skeleton, and a rapid reproductive system, I would say it was an insect; if it lacks one or more of these features, I would not think of it as an insect. The problem with forming categories by definition is that many familiar categories have uncertain or *fuzzy* boundaries (Rosch, 1978). This fact makes categorizing some members of familiar concepts more difficult than others (Komatsu, 1992;). For example, most people consider a German shepherd more "doglike" than a chihuahua.

Research suggests that categorizing has less to do with the features that define all members of a concept and has more to do with the features that characterize the typical member (Labov, 1973). In the chapter-opening story, this is the reason I assumed you would quickly categorize the two uniformed and armed adults as police officers: they represent our culture's concept of people in this social

Motivated-Tactician Model

An approach to social cognition that conceives of people as being flexible social thinkers who choose among multiple cognitive strategies based on their current goals, motives, and needs.

Social Categorization

The classification of people into groups based on their common attributes.

We initially categorize people based on readily identifiable physical features. What features did you use to categorize the people in this photograph when you first looked at it? How many different social categories did you perceive?

Prototype

The most representative member of a category.

category. The *most* representative member of a category is known as a **prototype;** it is our mental model that "stands for" or symbolizes the category (Barsalou, 1991). Because a prototype is the category member that best represents the category for you, members of that category will vary in how closely they match the prototype. Thus, although patrol officers and undercover officers both fit into our social category *police officer,* for most of us, patrol officers are more "coplike." As you undoubtedly know from personal experience, failing to correctly categorize people because they don't resemble the prototype can lead to errors in decision making. This is why female doctors are more often mistaken for nurses than are male doctors, while male nurses are more likely than female nurses to be miscategorized as doctors. In both cases, the mistaken judgments are due to our culturally derived prototypes for these two professions.

As demonstrated in our examples, in social categorization, we tend to rely on readily apparent *physical features* when initially classifying people (Stangor et al., 1992). Some of the most universally salient physical features are those based on race, sex, age, and attractiveness. Because categorizing others by these physical features is done so frequently, it becomes habitual and automatic, often occurring without conscious thought or effort (Fiske & Neuberg, 1990).

SOCIAL CATEGORIZATION SETS THE STAGE FOR STEREOTYPED THINKING

Social categorization does not typically end with merely grouping people into different categories. Within these social categories, there often already are certain beliefs about the individuals' personalities, abilities, and motives. These social beliefs, which are often learned from others, are **stereotypes** (see Hilton & Hippel, 1996). Like other cognitive frameworks, stereotypes significantly influence how we process social information. That is, once a stereotype is activated from memory, we have a tendency to see people within that social category as possessing the traits or characteristics associated with the stereotyped group (Vonk & Knippenberg, 1995; Wyer, 1988). In this sense, stereotypes are fixed ways of thinking about people that put them into categories and don't allow for individual variation.

Stereotypes

Fixed ways of thinking about people that put them into categories and don't allow for individual variation.

STEREOTYPES AS PROBABILITY JUDGMENTS

If we believed that *every* member of a particular social group possessed *all* the attributes stereotypically associated with it, this sort of all-or-none thinking could easily be considered irrational. Going back to our hypothetical situation of seeking help from heavily armed police officers, very few of us believe that *all* police officers are helpful and fair-minded in their service to the community. Instead, most of us conceive of stereotypes as *probability judgments;* that is, they estimate the likelihood that individuals in specific social groups possess certain attributes (Karlins et al., 1969). Therefore, when you step out in the street to seek assistance from the individuals in the oncoming patrol car, it is because you believe that the probability is fairly high that they will fulfill your expectations for those in their occupational category. Although most research has focused on the inaccuracy of stereotypes, a number of studies also reveal that they often possess a "kernal of truth," and thus, can lead to accurate social judgments (Ashton & Esses, 1999; Lee et al., 1995). Yet what specific factors are most likely to activate stereotypes following social categorization?

FACTORS THAT ACTIVATE STEREOTYPES

After categorizing a person into a specific social grouping, physical appearance cues are especially important in either activating or defusing the stereotype process. Individuals whose physical characteristics closely match their culture's prototype for a particular social category are likely to be perceived as possessing the personal traits associated with that social category (McKelvie, 1993). Thus, for example, a man in North America with wide shoulders and a tapering V-shaped physique who also has a square jaw, small eyes, thin lips, and thick eyebrows is more likely to be thought of as being active, adventurous, forceful, independent, and coarse than a man with a pear-shaped body who has a round face, thick lips, high cheekbones, and long eyelashes. Similarly, when target persons who are known to be members of a particular social group do not come close to matching the *behavioral* prototype for that group, people are less likely to judge them based on that group's stereotype (Lord et al., 1991). Thus, if Antony is known to be gay, but is also known to be a "jock" who likes to hunt, fish, repair cars, and drink beer, he is less likely to be judged based on cultural gay stereotypes than someone who is simply known to be gay.

Besides qualities about the target person, certain situations are more likely to activate stereotypes. One situational factor that often activates stereotypes is the *target person's social category salience* (Deaux & Major, 1987). As you may remember from chapter 3, salience has to do with the degree to which a person stands out relative to others in a given situation. For instance, a woman's sex is more salient when she is in a numerical minority in a predominantly male work group. In groups in which one sex has numerical dominance, the minority sex not only receives a disproportionate amount of attention, they also are more likely to be evaluated in a gender-stereotypical fashion (Lord & Saenz, 1985). Another situational factor that can interact with the target person's social category salience is *self-esteem threat.* That is, when self-esteem is threatened, people will often negatively stereotype others who are present and who are members of a stigmatized group in order to restore their feelings of self-worth (Fein & Spencer, 1997; Spencer et al., 1998). Essentially, this is a special case of the downward comparison process described in self-evaluation maintenance theory (chapter 2, p. 67).

THE FUNCTIONS OF STEREOTYPED THINKING

In studying stereotyping, one question that social psychologists have pondered is what purpose it serves as a cognitive process. The quickness of stereotyped thinking is one of its most apparent qualities: being *fast*, it gives us a basis for immediate action in uncertain circumstances. In a very real sense, stereotypes are "shortcuts to thinking" that provide us with rich and distinctive information about individuals we do not personally know (Dijker & Koomen, 1996; Gilbert & Hixon, 1991). Not only

CRITICAL *thinking*

Imagine that you will soon be entering a social gathering exclusively populated by people of the other sex who are members of a group widely known to hold negative stereotypes toward your sex. Your goal is to create a favorable first impression. What could you actively do to reshape their social perceptions so that negative gender stereotypes are not activated? In crafting your answer, consider your physical appearance, social interaction style, and even who you might choose to accompany you to this gathering.

do stereotypes provide us with a fast basis for social judgments, but stereotyping also appears to "free up" cognition for other tasks (Macrae et al., 1994b). Thus, a second function of stereotyped thinking is that it is *efficient* and allows people to cognitively engage in other necessary activities. Daniel Gilbert (1989) suggests that this resource-preserving effect may have an evolutionary basis. That is, expending cognitive resources as cheaply as possible enables perceivers to redirect their energy to more pressing concerns. It is this speed and efficiency of stereotype-based information that apparently motivates people to rely on it over the more time-consuming method of getting to know a person as an individual (Pendry & Macrae, 1994).

Although stereotyping people can bring greater speed and efficiency to our social judgments, research indicates that these cognitive shortcuts also function to *inhibit* thought. For example, in one study, Galen Bodenhausen (1988) asked predominantly white college students to play the role of jurors in a mock court case. Some students were told the defendant was named Carlos Ramirez, and others were told that his name was Robert Johnson. Half of the students in each of these experimental conditions were given information about the case before learning the defendant's name, whereas the other half were given the case information afterward. Bodenhausen hypothesized that hearing the Hispanic-sounding name "Carlos Ramirez" *before* receiving the evidence would activate students' ethnic stereotypes, and this activation would bias their processing of the information. That is, he predicted that instead of "weighing the facts," these students would be more likely to pay attention to stereotype-consistent information than to stereotype-inconsistent information.

This is exactly what he found. The imaginary Carlos Ramirez was more likely to be found guilty than the imaginary Robert Johnson only when students learned the name *before* receiving the evidence. A later study in this series indicated that stereotypes appear to influence information processing by increasing the amount of attention and rehearsal to stereotype-consistent information. This study, along with others (Dijksterhuis & Knippenberg, 1996), suggests that one of the important reasons the activation of stereotypes often results in fast social judgments is that filtering social perceptions through a stereotype causes people to ignore information that is relevant but inconsistent with the stereotype. Thus, although stereotyping may be beneficial because it allows us to redirect our energies to other pressing cognitive activities, the cost appears to be that we may often make faulty social judgments about whomever we stereotype (Nelson et al., 1996).

GENDER KNOWLEDGE IS OFTEN BASED ON STEREOTYPES

Despite the many changes in the status of women that have occurred over the years, research provides little evidence of substantial changes in *gender stereotypes* (Deaux & Kite, 1993). For instance, a study by John Williams and Deborah Best (1982) indicates that people in twenty-five countries believe men are more dominant, independent, and adventurous than women, and women are believed to be more sentimental, submissive, and superstitious (refer to table 4.1).

The different personal attributes that males and females are assumed to possess are known as the general personality traits of *masculinity* and *femininity*, respectively. **Psychological masculinity** encompasses instrumental traits related to task completion and goal achievement in the public world of work, while **psychological femininity** deals with expressive personality traits related to caretaking and nurturance in the private world of the home. These gender stereotypes are found not only in many different cultures, but also among people of varying ages (including children as young as 5 years of age), marital statuses, and educational levels (Broverman et al., 1972; Ruble, 1983).

Alice Eagly and Mary Kite (1987) asked American college students to rate the probability that the people in twenty-eight countries possessed certain instrumental and expressive personality traits. It is interesting that the resulting stereo-

Labels are devices for saving talkative persons the trouble of thinking.

John Morley, English statesman and author, 1838–1923

Psychological Masculinity

Possession of instrumental personality traits.

Psychological Femininity

Possession of expressive personality traits.

Oh well, we say with a knowing lilt in our voice, that's a man for you. Or that's just the way women are. We accept, as a cosmic joke, the separate ways of men and women, their different levels of foolishness.

Carol Shields, U.S. author, 1994, The Stone Diaries, New York: Viking Press

TABLE 4.1

Cross-Cultural Gender Stereotypes

Listed below are the personality traits typically attributed to men and women in countries around the world, including nations in North and South America, Europe, Australia, and the Middle East. Which of these traits attributed to men and women would you consider to be positive? Negative? Which sex is associated with the more highly valued traits?

Men	Women
Courageous	Fearful
Severe	Softhearted
Dominant	Submissive
Strong	Weak
Independent	Dependent
Rude	Sensitive
Unemotional	Emotional
Stern	Sentimental
Daring	Superstitious
Adventurous	Affectionate
Progressive	Attractive
Robust	
Wise	
Enterprising	
Forceful	
Autocratic	
Active	
Aggressive	

Source: Data from J. E. Williams and D. L. Best, *Measuring Sex Stereotypes: A Thirty Nation Study,* Sage Publications, 1982.

types of different nationalities where sex was not specified tended to resemble the stereotypes of their men more than their women (refer to figure 4.1). In addition, the ratings of instrumental and expressive traits for the men of these countries exhibited quite a degree of variability, although the women in all these countries—except American women—were consistently rated low on instrumentality and high on expressiveness. These findings suggest that the women of different nationalities tend to be judged more by gender stereotypes than the stereotypes of their nationality, but the exact opposite appears to hold for the men.

Eagly and Kite explained these results as being due to the fact that the women in most of these countries have considerably less power and status than the men. As a result, their behavior is infrequently observed by foreigners, and that which is observed consists largely of domestic activities. When judging these nationalities, Americans' stereotypes reflect this different level of exposure to each nation's men and women. This also explains why American women were not rated gender-stereotypically. American college students interact with American women in varied roles and settings, and many of them belong to this sex category as well. Thus, when rating American women, they were rating either their own ingroup, or at least a group with which they had extended contact. These more positive perceptions of both female and male Americans is consistent with the type of ingroup evaluation biases discussed in chapters 2 and 7 (see p. 65 and p. 240).

FIGURE 4.1

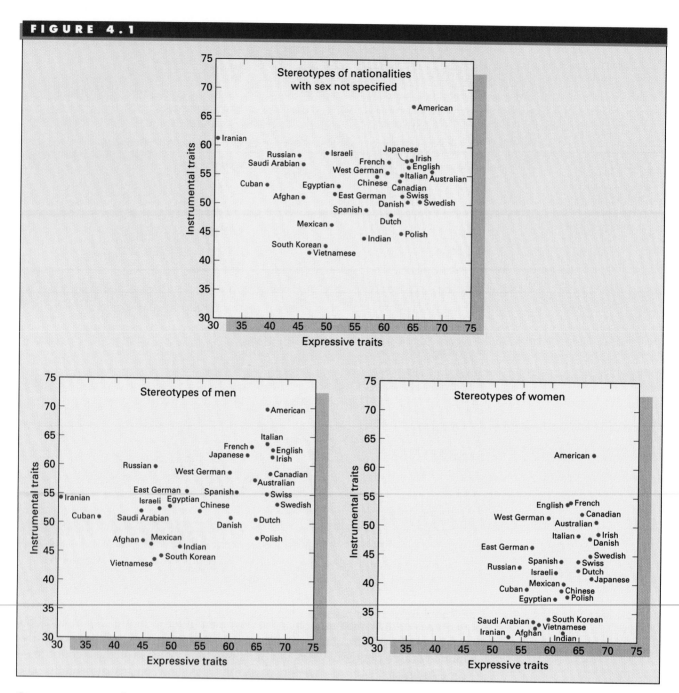

Stereotypes of Men and Women of Different Nationalities

When American college students rated the citizens in twenty-eight countries on personality dimensions related to instrumentality and expressiveness, the general stereotypes of the different nationalities tended to resemble the stereotypes of the men, not the women, in the countries. As you can also see, the ratings of instrumental and expressive traits for the men of these countries varied quite a bit, but the women were consistently rated low on instrumentality and high on expressiveness. What these findings suggest is that men are perceived in terms of nationality stereotypes, but women are perceived in terms of gender stereotypes. Based on your examination of these three figures, what nation's women were least likely to be perceived in terms of gender stereotypes?

TABLE 4.2

Illusory Correlation

If Harriet tends to selectively remember only those deceptive business relationships with Jews and the honest ones with non-Jews, she is likely to develop an illusory correlation that Jews are more dishonest in their business dealings than non-Jews. This is so, even though the percentages of actual instances of business deception in the two groups is equal (5%). Can you think of any illusory correlations that people may have about a group in which you are a member?

	Number of Business Relationships Person Has Been Exposed to in Their Lives	
	Deceptive Experiences	Honest Experiences
Jews	5	100
Non-Jews	25	500

STEREOTYPES ARE OFTEN BASED ON ILLUSORY CORRELATIONS

When we stereotype people, we associate certain characteristics with specific social groups. As an example, Harriet might believe that Jews are more deceptive in their business dealings than non-Jews. When asked why she holds this belief, Harriet might recall a set of pertinent cases of either business deception or honesty from her own personal experiences or from the experience of others. As you can see in table 4.2, in recalling these instances, Harriet remembers those few cases that conform to her stereotype of Jews, but she forgets or explains away all those that clash with it. Based on this selective recall of past cases, Harriet concludes that there indeed is an association between Jews and deception even though the correlation is no greater than it is for non-Jews. This example illustrates the power of an **illusory correlation,** which is the belief that two variables are associated with one another when in fact there is little or no actual association.

Sometimes we develop illusory correlations because we associate a group that usually doesn't receive much attention with something atypical or with an infrequent occurrence. In an experiment demonstrating this effect, David Hamilton and Robert Gifford (1976) asked participants to read information about people from two different groups, "Group A" and "Group B." Twice as much information was provided about Group A than about Group B, making Group B the smaller or "minority group" in the study. In addition, twice as much of the information given about both groups involved desirable behaviors rather than undesirable actions. Desirable information included statements such as, "John, a member of Group A, visited a sick friend in the hospital." An example of an undesirable statement was, "Bob, a member of Group B, dropped litter in the subway station."

Even though there was no correlation between group membership and the proportion of positive and negative information, participants perceived a correlation. As figure 4.2 shows, they overestimated the frequency with which Group B, the "minority group," behaved undesirably. Hamilton and Gifford explained these results by contending that people are more likely to associate things that have *shared distinctiveness* (that is, are infrequent). In this study, the members of the "minority group" (who were described only half as much as the "majority group") and the undesirable actions (which occurred only half as much as the desirable behaviors) were both distinctive aspects of this scenario. This shared distinctiveness resulted in their illusory correlation, a finding replicated in later studies (Mullen & Johnson, 1995).

Illusory Correlation

The belief that two variables are associated with one another when in fact there is little or no actual association.

CRITICAL *thinking*

Can you explain how the shared distinctiveness hypothesis might help in understanding why many non-Blacks overestimate the percentage of crime committed by African Americans relative to their own race?

FIGURE 4.2

Illusory Correlations and the Persistence of Stereotypes

In Hamilton and Gifford's (1976) study of illusory correlations, participants read sentences in which a person from Group A or Group B was associated with either a desirable or an undesirable behavior. As you can see in the actual correlation graph, both groups were described with the same proportion of desirable and undesirable behaviors, but only one-third of the provided information was about Group B members, making them the "minority group." The illusory correlation graph indicates that participants later overestimated the number of undesirable behaviors in the minority group (Group B), which suggests that people tend to perceive an illusory correlation between variables that stand out because they are unusual or deviant.

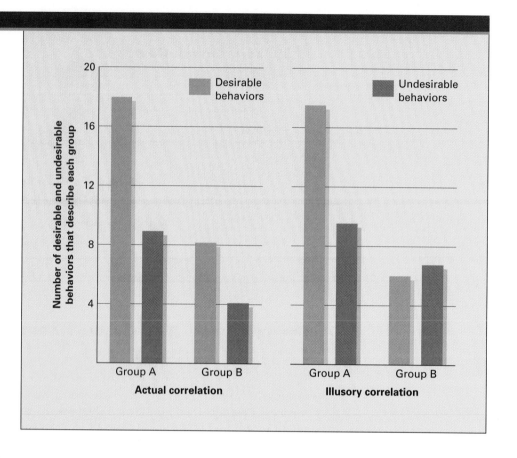

The research reviewed thus far suggests that selective attention to the infrequent behaviors of minority group members appears to set the stage for the illusory correlation effect. Yet, what would happen if people's attention was diverted while they were observing the minority group's actions? Would this minimize the tendency to perceive illusory correlations? Research by Steven Stroessner and his colleagues (1992) found that when people are in either a positive or a negative mood, they are less likely to perceive an illusory correlation between minority group members and infrequent (that is, negative) actions. Although there is still a great deal more to learn about the role that mood plays in illusory correlations, it is possible that emotional arousal interferes with the cognitive processing necessary to encode into memory this infrequent or distinctive information about the minority group. Without this encoding, the illusory correlation effect is diminished.

In both of the previously discussed studies, the participants had no preexisting attitudes or beliefs about the minority groups under scrutiny. However, as illustrated in our previous example of the person who had a negative stereotype about Jews, this is certainly not always the case in the real world. Further research indicates that people's preexisting attitudes and beliefs predispose them to perceive associations that are truly illusory (Berndsen et al., 1996). Once the stereotype is activated, the person engages in biased processing of social information by attending to information consistent with the stereotype and ignoring that which contradicts it (Greenberg & Pyszczynski, 1985). Through this process of selective attention to information consistent with the stereotype, the stereotype proves resistant to change (Dovidio et al., 1986). Thus, even if people are distracted due to their current mood, if they already have a negative stereotype about the minority group under scrutiny, what little they do attend to will likely be sufficient to reinforce their prior beliefs.

STEREOTYPICAL THINKING IS MORE CHARACTERISTIC OF THE POWERFUL

Studies by Susan Fiske and Eric Dépret indicate that the tendency to think in stereotypical terms is related to a person's level of social power (Fiske & Dépret, 1996; Fiske, 1993). For example, in a business firm, secretaries know more about their bosses' personal habits and preferences than vice versa. Why is this the case? It is so, Fiske and Dépret contend, because powerful individuals in a social group exercise a good deal of control over the less powerful members. Due to this control, it is in the powerless person's best interests to pay close attention to those who have power (Dépret & Fiske, 1993). What they pay particular attention to is information about the powerful person that is inconsistent with the stereotype of these individuals. This gives them knowledge about specific powerful persons they cannot receive through simple reliance on stereotypes. This knowledge is important, for it provides the powerless with some degree of power and control—power to better predict the powerful individuals' future actions, thus giving them a greater sense of control in their surroundings (Allen, 1996; Fiske & Dépret, 1996).

In contrast to the attentiveness of the powerless, research indicates that powerful people pay considerably less attention to those below them in the power hierarchy (Keltner & Robinson, 1997). When they do attend to those with little social power, the powerful are more likely to judge them based on social stereotypes. Fiske believes there are two primary reasons that people in power stereotype less powerful others. First, due to their high status position, more people are competing for their attention than is the case for the less powerful. Faced with time constraints brought on by these demands, the powerful are likely to rely on such cognitive shortcuts as stereotypes. A second reason they tend to ignore the individual qualities of the powerless is simply that there is less at stake—the powerless have relatively little impact on the lives of the powerful (Goodwin & Fiske, 1993).

The tendencies of those with social power to ignore the individual qualities of their subordinates does not mean that the powerful all engage in stereotypical thinking when judging those who fall below them in the status hierarchy. Research indicates that people, including the powerful, can be motivated to think of others in nonstereotypical ways by either appealing to their desire for accuracy (Neuberg, 1989), their concern for public accountability (Tetlock et al., 1989), their humanitarian or egalitarian values (Goodwin & Fiske, 1993), or their self-concepts as fair-minded and careful people (Fiske & Von Hendy, 1992). Again, these findings are consistent with the motivated-tactician model highlighted in this chapter: as flexible social thinkers, we change our cognitive strategies based on what is currently motivating us.

SECTION SUMMARY

The classification of people into groups based on their common attributes is known as *social categorization*. The socially shared beliefs concerning the personalities, abilities, and motives of people within social categories are known as *stereotypes*. Once social categorization occurs, stereotypes are most likely to be activated if the target person closely matches the prototype for that social category. A good deal of our knowledge about gender, for example, is based on stereotypes. Two functions of stereotyped thinking are that it is fast and efficient, but it also functions to inhibit thought, which, among other things, can lead to illusory correlations. The tendency to think in stereotypical terms is more characteristic of people who are in a position of social power.

MENTAL SHORTCUTS AND SIMULATIONS

As previously noted, when we adopt the strategy of a cognitive miser we are always on the lookout for timesaving mental shortcuts to help us make social judgments. Our social beliefs are also shaped by musing over imaginary scenarios. In this section, we will examine both *heuristics* and *mental simulations*.

HEURISTICS ARE TIMESAVING "RULES OF THUMB"

Heuristics

Timesaving mental shortcuts that reduce complex judgments to simple rules of thumb.

Amos Tversky and Daniel Kahneman (1974) called cognitive shortcuts **heuristics.** Heuristics require very little thought; people merely take the shortcut and make the judgment. One type of heuristic that we have already discussed is a *stereotype*. The advantage of stereotypes and all other mental shortcuts is that they allow us to make quick social judgments by ignoring a great deal of potentially relevant information in our environment. This advantage, however, is also a disadvantage, because these heuristics often result in biased and inaccurate information processing (Ajzen, 1996). Let's consider three commonly used mental shortcuts that social psychologists have identified and studied over the years.

THE REPRESENTATIVENESS HEURISTIC

Representativeness Heuristic

The tendency to judge the category membership of people based on how closely they match the "typical" or "average" member of that category.

During my first few years as an assistant professor, people often mistook me for a student when they encountered me on campus. Why was this the case? Well, to them I just didn't fit their image of what a university professor looked like. This judgment is an example of a cognitive shortcut often taken by people. The **representativeness heuristic** is the tendency to judge the category membership of people based on how closely they match the prototype of that category (Kahneman & Tversky, 1973). Because I looked younger than my age, and because I dressed casually and seldom wore suits or ties to work, people guessed I was a student.

The representativeness heuristic helps people to quickly decide in what categories to place others. In fact, it is essentially stereotyping operating in reverse. That is, when we stereotype someone, we first place them in a particular social category and then infer that they possess the personal attributes associated with people in that category. When we rely on the representativeness heuristic, we merely reverse this cognitive process: because a person possesses attributes we associate with a particular social category, we infer that they must be a member of that category.

The problem with this cognitive shortcut is that being a rapid method of identifying people, it doesn't take into account other important qualifying information. The most important information of this type relates to *base-rates*—the frequency with which some event or pattern occurs in the general population. The tendency to overlook base-rate information was demonstrated in a well-known study by Tversky and Kahneman (1973). Research participants were told that an imaginary person named Jack had been selected from a group of a hundred men. Some were told that thirty of the men were engineers (a base-rate for engineers of 30 percent), and others were told that seventy were engineers (a base-rate of 70 percent). Half the participants were given no other information, but the other half were given a description of Jack that either fit the common stereotype of engineers (for example, practical, likes to work with numbers) or did not. They were then asked to guess the probability that Jack was an engineer.

Results indicated that when participants received only information related to base-rates, they were more likely to guess that Jack was an engineer when the base-rate was 70 percent than when it was 30 percent. However, when they received information about Jack's personality and behavior, they tended to ignore the base-rate information and, instead, focus on whether Jack fit their image of an engineer. The tendency to ignore or underuse useful base-rate information and overuse personal descriptors of the individual being judged has been called the *base-rate fallacy*.

THE ANCHORING AND ADJUSTMENT HEURISTIC

Do you think the population of Cincinnati, Ohio, is more than 100,000? "Yes" is the correct answer. OK, now estimate Cincinnati's actual population, and then check on page 124 for the correct answer. If, instead of asking whether Cincinnati's population is *more than 100,000,* I had asked whether it is *less than 1,000,000,* your answer to the second question probably would have been higher. The reason this effect often happens is because quantitative judgments are often biased toward an initial anchor point—in our example, this was the 100,000 figure. Later when making our estimate, we use this anchor as our starting point and, thus, usually insufficiently adjust toward the correct answer. This mental bias is known as the **anchoring and adjustment heuristic.**

As demonstrated in a survey study by Scott Plous (1989), the anchoring and adjustment heuristic can affect our social judgments. Respondents were first asked whether they thought there was greater than a 1 percent chance of a nuclear war occurring soon. Other respondents were asked whether nuclear war had less than a 90 percent chance of occurring soon. All respondents were then asked to estimate the likelihood of such a war occurring soon. Those who "started" from the 1 percent anchor guessed at a 10 percent risk factor, while those who "started" from the 90 percent anchor estimated the risk of nuclear war to be 25 percent.

THE AVAILABILITY HEURISTIC

I have a friend who was planning to purchase a new car recently, and I asked her if she was considering a particular brand that had received excellent reliability ratings in *Consumer Reports'* annual review of new automobiles. Her reply was no, because she knew a few people who had that type of car and weren't satisfied with its reliability. In nixing this car from her list, my friend was basing her judgment on how easily she could recall those negative experiences of others. The **availability heuristic** is the tendency to judge the frequency or probability of an event in terms of how easy it is to think of examples of that event (Tversky & Kahneman, 1973). Thus, in judging the reliability of this car model, my friend quickly sampled the information accessible in her memory to see how many examples came to mind. If the information in memory had been reasonably representative of the actual reliability of these cars, relying on the availability heuristic would have resulted in an accurate assessment. Unfortunately, this was not the case here.

In the use of the availability heuristic, the most important factor for people is not the *content* of their memory recall but the *ease* with which this content comes to mind. For example, Norbert Schwarz and his colleagues (1991b) found that participants who were asked to recall twelve examples of their own assertive behaviors (a difficult cognitive task) subsequently rated themselves as less assertive than participants who were asked to recall only six examples (an easy cognitive task). Similar results were obtained for participants who were asked to recall examples of their unassertive behaviors (refer to figure 4.3). The implication here is that people pay attention to how easy or difficult it is for them to recall examples of a particular event or behavior in making attributions. They only rely on the content of their recall (for example, assertive behavior) if its implications are not called into question by the difficulty they experience in bringing the relevant material to mind. Thus, individuals would conclude that they must not be assertive if it is difficult to recall personal examples of assertive behavior in their past.

WHEN DO WE USE HEURISTICS?

With what frequency do we take mental shortcuts in making social judgments? Are we constantly cutting corners, or is it a rare occurrence? Common experience and social psychologists' best reasoned analysis suggest that people do not always rely on stereotypes and other heuristics. Often we systematically analyze a situation using a variety of information. Research has identified at least five conditions most likely to lead to the use of heuristics rather than more careful

---

Anchoring and Adjustment Heuristic

A tendency to be biased towards the starting value or anchor in making quantitative judgments.

Availability Heuristic

The tendency to judge the frequency or probability of an event in terms of how easy it is to think of examples of that event.

FIGURE 4.3

Ratings of Assertiveness Due to Ease of Recall

People judged themselves to be more or less assertive based on how many examples of assertive or unassertive behaviors they were asked to recall from their past. For example, when asked to recall six examples of assertive behavior, they subsequently rated themselves as more assertive than when asked to recall twelve examples. The same pattern of findings occurred for unassertive behavior. How do these findings support the existence of the availability heuristic?

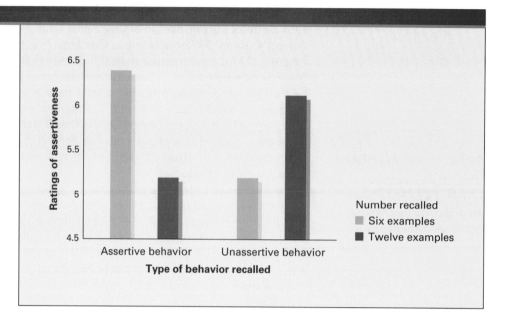

Cincinnati has a population of 364,000.

decision making (Macrae et al., 1993). The first condition in which these mental shortcuts will likely be used is when we simply don't have *time* to engage in systematic analysis. The second and third conditions are when we are *overloaded with information* so that it is impossible to process all that is meaningful and relevant, and/or when we consider the issues in question to be *not very important*. Finally, heuristics will often be relied on when we have *little other knowledge* or information to use in making a decision, or when something about the situation in question calls to mind a given heuristic, making it *cognitively available*. Thus, although basing decisions on heuristics may lead to errors and may be motivated by lazy thinking, relying on them can actually be adaptive under conditions where we don't have the luxury of systematically analyzing all our options (Johnston et al., 1997; Klein, 1996). For example, reacting quickly in an emergency based only on information that is most accessible from memory (the availability heuristic) may often be the difference between life and death. Thus, although heuristics can lead to sloppy decision making, their timesaving quality may sometimes be a lifesaver. It is this quality that makes heuristics such a valuable device in the motivated-tactician's cognitive "toolbox."

MENTALLY SIMULATING EVENTS CAN ALTER OUR SOCIAL THINKING

The previous section examined how the way that information is organized and retrieved from memory can shape social cognition. Yet, a number of researchers believe that memories of past events are less crucial to our social judgments than is our ability to imagine or *mentally simulate* these events (Kahneman & Tversky, 1982). Throughout our lives, we invent imaginary scenarios of past, future, and alternative social realities. To imagine an event, we must temporarily assume that it is true. This fact sometimes causes the line between real and imagined events to become blurred in memory. As a result, the more often we imagine a particular scenario, the more likely we are to believe that it is possible (Heath et al., 1991). For example, you may have never feared that your romantic partner might be unfaithful until your best friend's lover proves to be disloyal. Over the next few days, you may catch yourself imagining how you would react in a similar scenario.

Although your friend's betrayal does not involve you or your partner, simply imagining this event now leads you to be more likely than before to believe that your partner could be unfaithful.

MENTAL SIMULATIONS IN THE COURTROOM

Mental simulations play an important role in how jurors make decisions during courtroom trials. Beyond simply agreeing on the facts of the case, jurors must also agree on the *meaning* of those facts. Nancy Pennington and Reid Hastie (1992) believe that in attempting to impose this meaning on the presented evidence, individual jurors construct one or more plausible accounts or *stories* that explain the motives of the key players in the case. This *story model of juror decision making* hypothesizes that of the various stories jurors construct, the one that can organize the most evidence in the most cohesive fashion will be the one they use in rendering their final verdict. Research not only supports this hypothesis but also indicates that when evidence fits into a juror's cohesive story, that juror is more likely to consider it important, regardless of its actual strength or weakness (Pennington & Hastie, 1992). Based on this evidence, you might think that all attorneys would emphasize storytelling in presenting their cases to juries. To an extent, this is true—both sides in a trial have a story to tell. However, the *way* in which evidence is presented in a court case may either highlight the story or highlight the witnesses. In what is called the *story order,* attorneys present witnesses in the sequence corresponding to the story they want jurors to believe. In what is called the *witness order,* lawyers present witnesses in the sequence meant to have the greatest impact, even if this means that evidence is presented out of sequence to the story they want jurors to believe. For example, imagine that Spencer is charged with embezzling $25,000 from a bank where he was a cashier. The crime supposedly took place on September 18. A prosecuting attorney using a story order would present his witnesses in the following manner:

1. Spencer's girlfriend testifies that she threatened to leave him on September 15 because he never had any money to buy her "special" presents.
2. The bank janitor testifies that he saw a large sum of money in Spencer's gym bag at 3:00 p.m. on September 18.
3. The bank manager testifies that she noticed a $25,000 discrepancy in the bank books at 5:15 p.m. on September 18.
4. A local jeweler testifies that Spencer bought a $3,000 necklace from him at 6:30 p.m. on September 18, using cash in the transaction.

In contrast to this sequential presentation of the evidence, a prosecutor using a witness order might save his best witness, the bank janitor, for last, so that the trial ends with dramatic testimony. This sort of dramatic finish to a trial is the sort of presentation style commonly depicted in TV criminal law series (that's why they call them "dramas"). The question is, does one of these presentation styles lead to greater success than the other? Not surprisingly, Pennington and Hastie believe that the story order will be more convincing to a jury than the witness order.

To test this hypothesis, they asked mock jurors to listen to a simulated trial in which the defense attorney and the prosecuting attorney varied the *way* in which they presented their cases (Pennington & Hastie, 1988). In one condition the attorneys both used the story order, in another condition they both used the witness order, and in the two remaining conditions they used opposing presentation orders. Results indicated that presenting evidence in the sequence that events occurred in one's desired story was the best strategy, especially when the opposing attorney relied on witness impact rather than story order. As you can

TABLE 4.3

How Should Lawyers Present Their Evidence to the Jury?

Pennington and Hastie (1988) found that the best strategy for both prosecutors and defense attorneys was to present the evidence in the order that corresponds most closely to their desired story (story order), especially when the opposing attorney presented witnesses in the sequence meant to have the greatest impact (witness order).

Percentage of Jurors Voting to Convict Defendant

Prosecution Evidence	Defense Evidence	
	Story Order	Witness Order
Story order	59%	78%
Witness order	31%	63%

Source: Adapted from Pennington & Hastie, 1988.

Based on what you have learned about the presentation of evidence during a jury trial, how should attorneys present witnesses? In the sequence corresponding to the story they want jurors to believe (story order), or in the sequence meant to have the greatest impact (witness order)?

see in table 4.3, when the defense used the story order and the prosecutor used the witness order, the jurors voted to convict only 31 percent of the time. When the tables were reversed so that the prosecutor used the story order and the defense employed the witness order, jurors convicted 78 percent of the time. These findings suggest that although dramatic testimony plays well in front of juries on *Perry Mason* reruns, in real-life trials juries are more convinced by plausible stories.

THE HINDSIGHT BIAS

Another bias in social judgment is that, when recalling past events we tend to believe that we "knew all along" how things would turn out. After learning that your best friend's lover has been unfaithful, you might think, "I could see this coming for quite some time." Or after your favorite sports team narrowly

Hindsight Bias

The tendency, once an event has occurred, to overestimate our ability to have foreseen the outcome.

I just knew I should have picked door number two.

Let's Make a Deal TV-show contestant

defeats its archrival for the first time in years you exclaim, "All week long I could tell that my team would win!" In such instances, this after-the-fact over-estimation of our ability to have foreseen the outcome is known as the **hindsight bias** (Hawkins & Hastie, 1990). Why does it occur? Because in thinking about a past event, we tend to selectively recall information in constructing a plausible story that is consistent with the now-known outcome (Harvey & Martin, 1995). This "rewriting" of how events occurred allows us to insert the missing causal connections so that the story makes sense given the outcome. Although we actively rewrite these life stories, we generally are not aware that we are doing so (Wasserman et al., 1991).

If you were among a group of workers laid off at your place of employment, do you think you would be more or less likely to claim that "there were many warning signals" than if you were merely an unaffected observer of these layoffs? In one study that explored this question, people living near a factory were surveyed about their beliefs and opinions about recent factory layoffs (Mark & Mellor, 1991). Results indicated that townspeople who did not work at the factory and were not personally affected by the layoffs were most likely to claim that they knew the layoffs were coming (high hindsight bias). People who worked at the factory but kept their jobs were less likely to claim hindsight. Those who expressed the greatest surprise (no hindsight bias) were the workers who actually lost their jobs. What these results suggest is that, although we often engage in the hindsight bias when explaining past events, we are less likely to do so when those events affect us personally *and* are negative. One possible reason why we are less likely to claim hindsight for negative outcomes is that it allows us to avoid blaming ourselves: "If I couldn't foresee being laid off, I cannot be blamed for not working harder or changing jobs."

COUNTERFACTUAL THINKING

Besides our social judgments being shaped by simulating *actual* past events, they are also affected by the ease with which we can imagine *alternative* versions and outcomes of past events. Remember our chapter-opening imaginary scenario in which you learned about two people killed in a train crash, one a regular commuter and the other a first-time rider? Why did the first-time rider's death seem more tragic? Next, imagine the following day at the ski slopes:

> Hector loves to snow ski but is cautious and never goes down the expert slope. Yesterday, however, he tried it and broke his leg. Martina also loves to ski and frequently goes down the expert slope. Yesterday she broke her leg going down this slope.

Counterfactual Thinking

The tendency to evaluate events by imagining alternative versions or outcomes to what actually happened.

Research suggests that the vast majority of us believe that Hector will feel the greatest regret following his injury, and most of us will also express greater sympathy toward him than toward Martina, just as we will perceive the death of the first-time train rider as more tragic than that of the frequent rider (Roese & Olson, 1995a). The reason for these different judgments is that we engage in **counterfactual thinking,** which is the tendency to evaluate events by imagining alternative versions or outcomes (Kahneman, 1995). We are most likely to engage in counterfactual thinking following negative and unexpected events, and the thoughts that are generated usually deal with how the negative outcome might have been prevented (Mandel & Lehman, 1996; Sanna & Turley, 1996). Regarding Hector and Martina, it's easier for us to imagine that Hector would be uninjured if he had not deviated from his normal cautious skiing style than it is to imagine this altered outcome for Martina, given her tendency to take greater risks on the slopes. It's also easier to imagine that the first-time train rider would be alive if her regular form of transportation had been available than it is to imagine this altered outcome for the regular commuter. Because it is easier to "undo"

For Better or For Worse®   **by Lynn Johnston**

If we didn't have birthdays, you wouldn't be you.

If you'd never been born, well then what would you do?

If you'd never been born, well then what would you be?

You *might* be a fish! Or a toad in a tree!

Dr. Seuss, American children's author and cartoonist, 1904–1991

Hectors's broken leg and the first-time rider's death through counterfactual thinking ("If only they had stuck to their usual routines . . ."), we are more likely to feel sympathy for them. When our skiers engage in this same "What if . . .?" thinking, Hector will experience greater regret over his injury than Martina, for the same reasons as do we.

Why do we engage in counterfactual thinking? Neal Roese (1997) suggests two possible functions served by these "What if . . .?" thoughts. First, they may simply help us feel better following a negative outcome. That is, a negative event will be judged more favorably if we can imagine how things could have turned out even worse (Roese & Olson, 1997). Following a traffic accident in which your car is damaged, you may think, "At least I didn't get hurt." By imagining an even worse outcome, your accident seems less negative by contrast. Besides helping us emotionally cope in the present, a second function of counterfactual thoughts may be to better prepare us for the future. By considering alternatives to past actions, we can better understand our mistakes and thereby improve our chances for future success (Johnson & Sherman, 1990). For example, after doing poorly on an exam, you may mentally imagine alternative study strategies that you could have used, such as memorizing key terms or working through the study guide. If you implement these new strategies in preparing for your next exam, you may improve your grade. Summarizing these two functions, then, we can say that imagining alternative versions or outcomes to what actually happened may not only help us emotionally cope with negative events, but it may also help us to achieve success in the future.

Although there are benefits resulting from counterfactual thoughts, research indicates that excessive use of this type of thinking following traumatic life events can inhibit our ability to psychologically recover from the losses we incur. For instance, Christopher Davis and his coworkers (1995) interviewed people who had lost a spouse or a child in an accident. Results indicated that the more people imagined how the tragedy could have been averted by mentally undoing events preceding it, the more distress and guilt they felt. This tendency to engage in counterfactual thinking following traumatic life events also helps to explain why victims of crime often blame themselves for their victimization (C. Davis et al., 1996). That is, in attempting to understand how their plight could have been avoided, victims tend to focus on trivial aspects of their own behavior rather than on the causally more significant behavior of the perpetrator. If they can imagine some plausible way in which they *could* have prevented the crime, they may come to believe that they *should* have been able to prevent it. Although victims of crime who engage in such counterfactual thinking may not blame themselves for being the cause of their injuries, they may blame themselves for not avoiding the situation that was the cause (Miller & Turnbull, 1990).

SECTION SUMMARY

Although heuristics allow us to make quick judgments with minimal cognitive effort, they often result in biased and inaccurate information processing. The *representativeness heuristic* involves judging the category membership of people based on how closely they match the prototype for that category. Being biased toward the starting value or anchor in making quantitative judgments is known as the *anchoring and adjustment heuristic*. In the *availability heuristic*, we judge the probability of an event in terms of how easy it is to think of examples of it. We are most likely to use heuristics when we don't have time to engage in systematic analysis, when we have too much or too little information, when we consider the issue to be unimportant, or when something about the situation calls to mind a given heuristic, making it cognitively available. In shaping our social beliefs, memories of past events are less crucial than is our ability to mentally simulate being involved in these events. Once an event has occurred, overestimating our ability to have foreseen the outcome is known as the *hindsight bias*. Evaluating events by imagining alternative versions or outcomes is known as *counterfactual thinking*, and we may engage in this thinking to emotionally cope with negative events and to help achieve success in the future.

SOCIAL WORLD BELIEFS

Many of our social judgments are shaped by beliefs we hold about how the social world operates. In this section, we will examine our tendency to believe that others think and behave as we do (*false consensus*), our tendency to think and behave in ways that verify our beliefs (*confirmation bias* and *self-fulfilling prophecies*), our tendency to believe that the world is fair (*just-world belief*), and our tendency to stop trying after repeated failure (*learned helplessness*).

WE EXAGGERATE THE EXTENT TO WHICH OTHERS THINK AND ACT AS WE DO

If someone asked you to wear a sign around campus with a quirky message written on it like "Eat at Joe's," would you agree to do so? What percentage of your fellow students do you think would wear the sign? Although I don't know whether you would consent or refuse this hypothetical request, I am fairly confident that you think your peers would respond like yourself. My confidence is based on the fact that we tend to perceive our own behavior as fairly typical. In many instances, however, this perception is wrong. The tendency to believe that our own traits, actions, and choices are more common than they really are is known as the **false consensus effect** (Gross & Miller, 1997).

The first study to demonstrate the false consensus effect actually asked college students the question I asked you: Would you walk around campus for thirty minutes wearing a large sandwich board sign with the message, "Eat at Joe's" (Ross et al., 1977b)? Some students agreed and some refused. They were then asked to estimate the percentage of students who would make the same choice they made. Students who had agreed to wear the sign estimated that 62 percent of their peers would also agree, while those who had refused estimated that 67 percent of their peers would also refuse.

What explains the false consensus effect? One likely possibility is that false consensus is a product of the previously discussed availability heuristic. That is,

False Consensus Effect

The tendency to exaggerate how common one's own characteristics and opinions are in the general population.

A man never discloses his own character so clearly as when he describes another's.

Johann Richter, German author, 1763–1825

RITICAL *thinking*

Can you think of situations in your own life where the false consensus effect contributed to misunderstandings and conflicts between you and other people, such as your parents or your friends? How about instances in which it actually fostered smooth interactions?

Confirmation Bias

The tendency to seek information that supports our beliefs while ignoring disconfirming information.

When you look for the bad in mankind expecting to find it, you surely will.

Abraham Lincoln, sixteenth U.S. president, 1809–1865

the reason we often assume others share our characteristics and opinions may be because our own self-beliefs are easily recalled from memory. In a very real sense, then, our self-concept serves as the lens through which we view others (Alicke et al., 1996; Krueger & Clement, 1994). Consider again the characteristics you listed when describing yourself in chapter 2. It is likely that the attributes you listed as being important components of your own self-concept are ones that you are sensitive to in others as well (Dornbush et al., 1965). Returning to the "painter" analogy in chapter 2, if self-concept is the grand portrait we paint of ourselves, then the portraits we paint of others will often incorporate many of these same characteristic qualities. Just as painters have a distinct style that can be recognized from one painting to the next, so too do we all have distinctive styles of portraying ourselves and those around us. This tendency to "paint" another with the same characteristic qualities as we "paint" ourselves does not appear to be a deliberate or conscious process (Dunning & Hayes, 1996), but it is more likely to occur if we first actively imagine ourselves in the other person's shoes (M. Davis et al., 1996).

WE SEEK INFORMATION THAT SUPPORTS OUR BELIEFS

When you think you have a solution to a problem, you may fall victim to the **confirmation bias,** which is the tendency to seek only information that verifies your beliefs. Unfortunately, such selective attention inhibits problem solving when your solution is incorrect. In one confirmation-bias study, college students were given the three-number sequence, 2-4-6, and told to discover the rule used to generate it (Wason, 1960). Before announcing their beliefs about the rule (which is simply any three increasing numbers), students could make up their own number sequences, and the experimenter told them whether these sequences fit the rule. They were instructed to announce the rule only after receiving feedback from enough self-generated number sequences to feel certain that they knew the correct solution. True to the confirmation bias, 80 percent of the students convinced themselves of an incorrect rule. Typically, they would begin with a wrong hypothesis (for example, adding by twos) and then search only for confirming evidence (testing 8-10-12, 20-22-24, 19-21-23, etc.). Had they tried to disconfirm this hypothesis by testing other number sequences that simply increased in value (for example, 1-2-3 or 10-19-39), they would have realized their error. But their bias toward confirmation ruled out this important hypothesis-testing step.

How might this tendency to seek confirming information affect our social beliefs? In one experiment, Mark Snyder and William Swann (1978) asked research participants to find out whether the person they were about to interact with was an introvert, or an extravert, depending on the experimental condition. Consistent with the confirmation bias, the questions that participants asked their interaction partner were biased in the direction of the original question. For instance, if they had been asked to find out whether the person was an introvert, they asked questions such as, "What do you dislike about loud parties?" or "In what situations do you wish you could be more outgoing?" However, in the extravert condition, they asked questions such as, "How do you liven things up at a party?" or "What kind of situations help you to meet new people?" Because most people can recall both introverted and extraverted incidents from their past, the interaction partners' answers provided confirmatory evidence for either personality trait. Experiments like this indicate that one barrier to accurate social judgments can be our tendency to search for information that will confirm our beliefs more energetically than we pursue information that might refute them (Edwards & Smith, 1996). Such confirmation-seeking not only leads to mistakes about individuals, but also perpetuates incorrect stereotypes about social groups (Yzerbyt et al., 1996).

Although the confirmation bias is generally thought of as being caused by people taking cognitive shortcuts in problem solving (the cognitive miser perspective), another view is that in social interactions we may engage in the confirmation bias due to our desire to get along with others. Belgian social psychologists Jacques-Philippe Leyens and Benoit Dardenne argue that we sometimes adopt a confirmation-seeking strategy during getting-acquainted sessions in order to smooth the interaction and give others the impression that they are understood by us (Leyens, 1990; Leyens & Dardenne, 1994). For example, when a new acquaintance says that she prefers working alone and is shy, asking her *matching questions* (for example, "Do you prefer to spend your evenings reading a novel?") is more likely to result in a smooth and comfortable conversation than asking *nonmatching questions* (for example, "Do you like noisy and crowded parties?"). Research by Dardenne and Leyens (1995) indicates that such a matching strategy is more likely to be used by high self-monitoring individuals than those low in self-monitoring because high self-monitors know better what is appropriate to do with or say to others in specific social situations. What this suggests is that the interaction style adopted by socially skilled people is more likely to lead to a confirmation bias than the style adopted by those who are less socially skilled. The reason the socially skilled are more likely to use this flawed problem-solving strategy is not necessarily because they are lazy thinkers, but rather, because they desire to be liked by those they are getting to know. From this motivated-tactician perspective, instead of thinking of the confirmation bias as always being caused by flawed problem solving, we can also see it as sometimes being a by-product of exercising a social skill. As a motivated tactician, the socially skilled person sometimes adopts a flawed confirmation-seeking strategy because it helps them to better adjust to their immediate social surroundings: their desire to be liked supersedes their desire to be accurate.

Does this then mean that socially skilled people make more social judgment errors due to their interaction style? Not necessarily. According to Dardenne and Leyens, what social psychologists from the cognitive miser perspective identify as social judgment errors may often be very practical and useful cognitive strategies that not only lead to "good-enough" social judgments, but also promote liking for those who employ them because they make others feel socially at ease.

OUR EXPECTATIONS CAN BECOME SELF-FULFILLING PROPHECIES

The confirmation bias highlights how our *expectations* often become the blueprint in defining social reality. In 1948, sociologist Robert Merton introduced the concept of the **self-fulfilling prophecy** to describe a situation in which someone's expectations about a person or group actually lead to the fulfillment of those expectations. As Merton described it:

> The self-fulfilling prophecy is, in the beginning, a *false* definition of the situation evoking a new behavior which makes the originally false conception come *true*. The specious validity of the self-fulfilling prophecy perpetuates a reign of error. For the prophet will cite the actual course of events as proof that he was right from the very beginning. (Merton, 1948, p. 195)

More recent work indicates that the self-fulfilling prophecy involves a three-step process (refer to figure 4.4). First, the perceiver (the "prophet") forms an impression of the target person. Second, the perceiver acts toward the target person in a manner consistent with this first impression. In response, the target person's behavior changes to correspond to the perceiver's actions (Darley & Fazio, 1980; Snyder et al., 1977).

The most famous empirical demonstration of the self-fulfilling prophecy was a study conducted by Robert Rosenthal and Lenore Jacobson (1968) on teachers and students in a South San Francisco elementary school. In this study, the researchers first gave IQ tests to the children and then met with the teachers to share the results.

Self-Fulfilling Prophecy

The process by which someone's expectations about a person or group leads to the fulfillment of those expectations.

FIGURE 4.4

The Development of a Self-Fulfilling Prophecy

Self-fulfilling prophecies often develop as a three-step process. In step 1, the perceiver forms expectations about the target. In step 2, the perceiver behaves in a manner consistent with those expectations. In step 3, the target responds to the perceiver's actions in a manner that unwittingly confirms the perceiver's initial beliefs. The more interactions the target has with the perceiver, and the more this three-step process is repeated during those interactions, the more likely it is that the target will internalize the perceiver's expectations into his or her own self-concept. What personal qualities in a perceiver and in a target would make a self-fulfilling prophecy more or less likely?

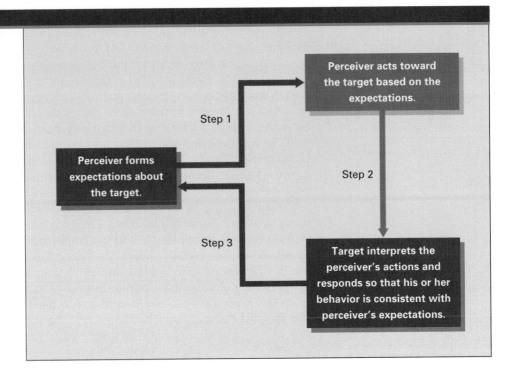

At these information sessions, the teachers were told that the tests identified certain students in their classroom as "potential bloomers" who should be expected to show substantial IQ gains during the remaining school year. In reality, this information was merely part of the experimental manipulation. The children identified as potential bloomers had been randomly selected by the researchers and did not differ from their classmates in any systematic way. Although the potential-blooming label was fabricated for these children (approximately 20 percent of the class), Rosenthal and Jacobson hypothesized that the teachers' subsequent expectations would be sufficient to enhance the academic performance of these students. Eight months later, when the students were again tested, this hypothesis was confirmed. Those children who had been identified as potential bloomers not only exhibited improved schoolwork, they also showed significantly higher gains on their IQ scores than those in the control group (see figure 4.5).

Follow-up studies indicated that students who are positively labeled in this manner tend to be treated differently by their teachers (Jussim, 1989; Meichenbaum et al., 1969). First, teachers tend to create a warmer *socioemotional climate* for these students than for those who are perceived less positively. Second, they provide these gifted students with more *feedback* on their academic performance than they do to their average students. Third, they *challenge* these positively labeled students with more difficult material than the rest of the class. Finally, they provide these students with a *greater opportunity to respond* to presented material in class. The result of this different form of treatment is that the positively labeled students are likely to assume either that the teacher especially likes them and has good judgment or that the teacher is a likable person. Whichever attribution is made, it's likely that the positively labeled students will work harder and begin thinking about themselves as high achievers. Through this behavioral and self-concept change, the prophecy is fulfilled.

Unfortunately, not all self-fulfilling prophecies are of the positive sort. Children who are negatively labeled as "troubled" or "disruptive" often are treated by teachers and fellow students in a way that reinforces the negative label so that it is more likely to be internalized. To better understand this sort of negative self-concept change, Monica Harris and her colleagues (1992) studied the impact of

FIGURE 4.5

Percentage of School Children Whose IQ Test Scores Improved Over the Course of the School Year Due to the Self-Fulfilling Prophecy

Those first- and second-grade students who were identified as "potential bloomers" showed a significant improvement in their IQ test scores during the course of the school year. In actuality, these students were randomly chosen for the "potential blooming" category—they did not differ from the other students in any way. Yet, their teachers' expectations that they were "gifted" resulted in those students being challenged more in class, which caused the bloomers to try harder and to learn more. The same social psychological mechanisms that result in beneficial self-fulfilling prophecies can also operate in reverse, causing normally capable children to believe that they are intellectually inferior to others. What types of schoolchildren do you think are most likely to be categorized in this negative manner?

Imaginations which people have of one another are the solid facts of society.

Charles Horton Cooley, American sociologist, 1864–1929

If three people say you are an ass, put on a bridle.

Spanish proverb

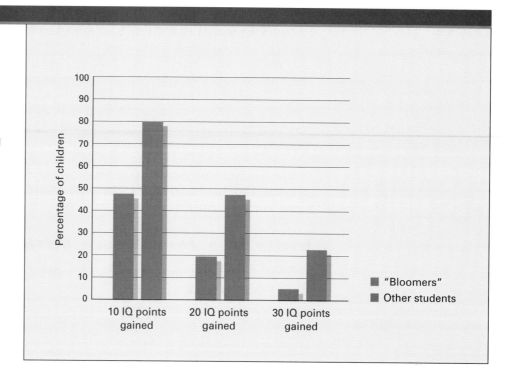

negative expectancies on children's social interactions. In their research, sixty-eight pairs of unacquainted boys in third through sixth grade played together on two different tasks. The researchers designated one of the boys in the pairing as the *perceiver* and the other boy the *target.* Half the target boys had been previously diagnosed as being hyperactive, and the rest of the participants—the remaining targets and all the perceivers—had no history of behavioral problems. Prior to playing together, perceivers in the *hyperactive expectancy condition* were told—independently of their partner's actual behavior—that their partner had a special problem and may give them a hard time: He disrupted class a lot, talked when he shouldn't, didn't sit in his chair, and often acted silly. In the *control condition,* the perceivers were not given this information.

One of the activities the two boys mutually engaged in was an unstructured, cooperative task in which they planned and built a design with plastic blocks; the other task was more structured and competitive—separately coloring a dinosaur as quickly as possible using the same set of crayons. The boys' behavior on both tasks was videotaped and later rated by judges on a number of dimensions, such as friendliness, giving commands, and offering plans or suggestions. The boys also reported their own feelings and reactions to the tasks.

Results indicated that the target boys whose partners had been led to believe that they had a behavioral problem (the *hyperactive expectancy condition*) enjoyed the tasks less, rated their own performances as poorer, and took less credit for success than the boys whose partners were in the *control condition.* Likewise, the boys who held the negative expectancies about their partners enjoyed the tasks less themselves, worked less hard on them, talked less, and liked their partners less and were less friendly to them than those perceivers who were not provided with negative expectancies. What these findings indicate is that when people have negative expectations about others, they are more likely to treat these individuals in a negative manner, which often results in the targets of such negative treatment reacting in kind, thus confirming the initial negative expectations. For half of the boys in this study, the negative expectations were groundless, but this did not alter the outcome of the interaction. Unfortunately, this form of self-fulfilling prophecy is all too common, and, over time it leads to negative self-beliefs and low self-esteem.

I'd like to have you think of instances in your own life where negative expectations of others may have created undesirable self-fulfilling prophecies. If you can identify someone whom you've viewed and treated in a negative fashion, try a little exercise to reverse this process. The next time you interact with them, put aside your negative expectations, and instead, treat them as if they were your best friend. Based on the research we have reviewed here, by redefining them in your own eyes, you may create a new definition of social reality in theirs as well. People you thought were unfriendly, and even hostile, may respond to your redefinition by acting warm and friendly. If successful in redefining this particular social reality, you will have fulfilled one of my own prophecies of readers of this text—namely, that those who learn about social psychological principles will use this knowledge to improve the quality of their social relationships. Does this sound like an expectation worth internalizing?

BELIEF IN A JUST WORLD BOTH COMFORTS US AND INFLUENCES HOW WE EXPLAIN OTHERS' MISFORTUNES

Just-World Belief

A belief system in which the world is perceived to be a fair and equitable place, with people getting what they deserve.

Do you believe the world is a "fair" place and that people get what they deserve in life? Before reading further, spend a few minutes answering the items in table 4.4. In many cultures throughout the world, people are taught from early childhood that the world naturally operates out of a sense of justice. Those who follow this **just-world belief** system, perceive the world as a fair and equitable place. In a just world, hard work and clean living will be rewarded, while laziness and sinful living will be punished. According to Melvin Lerner (1980), this naive belief system is simply a defensive reaction to the sometimes cruel twists of fate encountered in life, but it is comforting because most of us conceive ourselves to be good and decent people. By believing in a just world, we have the illusion that we have more control over our lives than we actually do.

Although an exaggerated sense of personal control could be dangerous if taken to extremes, in most instances, it is related to good psychological adjustment (Ormel & Schaufeli, 1991). This fact partly explains why people who believe in a just world tend to experience less depression and stress and greater life satisfaction than those who do not believe in a just world (Lipkus et al., 1996).

Another reason why the belief in a just world is related to psychosocial adjustment is due to its influence on the believers' approach to social relationships. Because they believe that good deeds will be rewarded and bad deeds will be punished, just-world believers are more likely than nonbelievers to develop an accommodating interpersonal style (Lipkus, 1991; Zuckerman & Gerbasi, 1977). Accommodation typically involves putting aside one's own immediate self-interests to satisfy other, long-term goals. When accommodation occurs in a social relationship, it is generally perceived by both the accommodator and the recipient as a positive deed that should be reciprocated. This greater willingness to accommodate may explain why just-world believers experience greater satisfaction in long-term romantic relationships than nonbelievers (Lipkus & Bissonnette, 1996). Simply put, their belief that relationship self-sacrifices will be rewarded motivates them to make concessions to their partners, which often are then reciprocated. It is this reciprocal accommodation that, over time, promotes romantic happiness.

Although just-world believers often psychologically benefit from their positive illusions about how the world operates, this social belief can lead to some unfortunate social judgments. One unfortunate consequence of believing in a just world is that we tend to make *defensive attributions* when explaining the plight of victims. In other words, we are prone to blame people for their misfortunes. Research demonstrates that this tendency to blame victims is strongest when we

TABLE 4.4

Do You Believe in a Just World?

Instructions

Read the statements below and decide which of these you tend to agree with and with which you disagree.

1. Good deeds often go unnoticed.
2. When parents punish their children it is almost always for good reason.
3. Many people suffer through absolutely no fault of their own.
4. By and large, people deserve what they get.
5. The political candidate who sticks up for his principles rarely gets elected.
6. Although evil men may hold political power for a while, in the general course of history good wins out.

Scoring

The more of the even numbered statements you agreed with and the more of the odd numbered statements you disagreed with, the stronger is your belief in a just world. How does the belief in a just world influence both psychosocial well-being and willingness to help victims of unfortunate circumstances?

Source: Items from the *Just World Scale*, Rubin and Peplau (1975).

feel personally threatened by an apparent injustice. Thus, accident victims are more likely to be blamed for their fate if they are similar to us on some relevant characteristic, or if their injuries are severe rather than mild (Burger, 1981). By disparaging the victim, we not only reassure ourselves that the world is just, but also that we aren't likely to fall victim to similar circumstances ("Because I'm really not like *them*"). In chapter 13, we will explore in more detail the link between just-world beliefs and helping.

REPEATED FAILURE OFTEN LEADS TO LEARNED HELPLESSNESS

You have seen how a belief in a just world fosters a sense of personal control that can promote psychological health. Yet, what happens when you repeatedly experience a lack of control in altering bad life circumstances? To help you envision this scenario, consider the present life of Desmond, a graduating college senior. During the past month, he was rejected from all twenty of the jobs for which he applied. With each rejection, Desmond felt his future slipping away. He now believes that he is not intellectually "fit" for any career success, and he envisions a life of endless failure and unhappiness. In such a state of mind, when Desmond is told about another job opportunity he thinks, "What's the use?"

When an unpleasant situation is perceived to be inescapable, humans and other animals develop the belief that they are helpless to alter their circumstances by means of any voluntary behaviors. Because of this *expectation* that one's behavior has no effect on outcome, the person or animal simply gives up trying to change the outcome. This psychological reaction, which is known as **learned help-lessness,** was first discovered in animal research. Martin Seligman and Steven Maier found that when dogs were unable to escape electrical shocks, they simply gave up trying, even when escape was later possible (Seligman & Maier, 1967). In human studies, those exposed to uncontrollable bad events at first feel angry and

Learned Helplessness

The passive resignation produced by repeated exposure to negative events that are perceived to be unavoidable.

anxious that their goals are being blocked. However, as the extent of uncontrollable events increases and they begin to feel helpless, the previous anger and anxiety is replaced with depression (Peterson et al., 1993). Learned helplessness explains why, for example, many unemployed workers eventually give up trying after repeatedly being passed over for new jobs. Unfortunately, by concluding that there is nothing they can do to change their current situation, these individuals often overlook real possibilities for change.

Not everyone who is placed in an uncontrollable situation experiences learned helplessness. According to Lyn Abramson and her colleagues (1978), people's *attributions* about what caused the initial lack of control will ultimately determine whether an uncontrollable event leads to learned helplessness and depression. If people believe that the cause of an uncontrollable event is *stable* (it will not change over time) and *global* (it extends across many events), they are more likely to expect future events to also be uncontrollable. When those future events arrive, these expectations cause them to act passively and helplessly. If people further believe that their lack of control is caused by *internal* factors, such as personal characteristics and behaviors, they are further likely to experience a loss of self-esteem. This stable, global, and internal attributional set describes how Desmond interpreted his job rejections. The Applications section at the end of this chapter examines an alternative attributional style that helps people weather these storms of failure.

MANY SEEMINGLY BIASED SOCIAL JUDGMENTS AND BELIEFS MAY ULTIMATELY BE BENEFICIAL

Based on what you have learned in both this chapter and chapter 3 about how we judge our social world, I trust that you now understand that social thinking involves many complex judgments that are fraught with potential errors and biases. Whether it is in first impressions, attributions, or beliefs about how our social world operates, there are many points in the social judgment process at which problems can arise. Because of these and other considerations, rational models are often inadequate in reliably describing the social judgmental process (Funder, 1987; Swann, 1984). Sometimes judgments have to be made very quickly and do not allow for careful observation and logical analysis. At other times, information in our social world is so unreliable, biased, and incomplete that a rational analysis is not possible. In such situations, heuristics and other mental shortcuts are typically relied on as a means to judge our world.

You may be wondering how we survive in a complex and ever changing world, given that we are so predisposed to make such a wide variety of errors. One thing to keep in mind is that our social world is much more flexible and dynamic than the static and artificial laboratory conditions that characterize social psychological research (Schliemann et al., 1997). In a laboratory study, once a research participant makes a judgmental error, it becomes a data point, frozen in time. But in the course of everyday life, people are constantly revising their social assessments due to feedback from the environment. As a result of this flexibility, many of the social judgment errors committed in the "real world" are corrected through normal interaction with others (Fiske & Haslam, 1996; Wegener & Petty, 1995b). For example, you may meet someone and, based on that limited encounter, form a certain impression. Another person, upon hearing of that impression, may provide new meaningful information that redefines your initial impression. This evolution of social reality is ongoing and can be extremely forgiving of individual judgmental errors, so that you can arrive at an "efficient definition" of others that can be used in the social world. Consistent with this view is a study by David Funder and C. Randall Colvin (1988) indicating that although we may have little success in judging the personality of strangers in a laboratory setting, we make relatively accurate judgments about the personalities of our own friends.

A second thing to keep in mind is how social cognitive theorists conceive of us as social thinkers. Whether we make careful and rational decisions or quick and sloppy ones is often determined by what motivates us in a given situation. The motivated-tactician model proposes that we are flexible social thinkers who choose among multiple cognitive strategies based on our current goals, motives, and needs. Central to the motivated-tactician model is the self. Unlike computers, we have an investment in our self-beliefs and our beliefs about others. This psychological fact makes motivational biases likely in social thinking. Through such biases we often can justify our self-concepts and our worldview, making it possible for us to more confidently engage in social interaction and meet daily challenges. Anthony Greenwald (1980), in an analysis of how the self figures into the social cognition equation, makes this very point. He argues that cognitive biases serve very useful and self-protective functions. Likening the self to a totalitarian government, Greenwald states that both are designed to manage (and distort) information so as to maintain a stable and efficiently functioning system. The distortion of reality is functional for both the self and the dictatorship. If this biasing did not occur, the system—either self or governmental—would likely collapse (see the Applications section that follows).

In the final analysis, our social judgments should not be expected to be any more accurate or efficient than our self judgments. Just as we have a need for consistency when assessing our own self-beliefs, we also express that need in our social judgments. When we are faced with contradictory information, our inclination is to distort or explain away the contradictions. As proposed by Greenwald (1980), these distortions may well have functional value, allowing us to maintain a set of beliefs and perceptions of the world that have proven useful and efficient in making everyday decisions. And just as there are individual differences in accuracy of self-assessments, there are variations in people's ability to judge their social surroundings.

SECTION SUMMARY

Our social judgments are shaped by how we think our social world operates. The belief that our own traits, actions, and choices are more common than they really are is known as the *false consensus effect.* One likely explanation for false consensus is that these self-beliefs are readily available in memory. When we think we have a solution to a problem, we may fall victim to the *confirmation bias,* in which we seek only information that verifies our beliefs. The confirmation bias can also lead to *self-fulfilling prophecies,* in which our expectations about a person or group actually lead to the fulfillment of those expectations. Those who believe in a *just world* believe that people get what they deserve in life. This self-protective way of thinking fosters less depression and stress and greater life satisfaction, but it also leads to greater victim blaming. Finally, when an unpleasant situation is perceived to be inescapable, we often develop *learned helplessness.* Because of this expectation that our behavior has no effect on outcome, we simply give up trying to change the outcome.

According to Lyn Abramson and her colleagues (1978), people differ in their attributional style, and these differences can affect how they respond to uncontrollable life events. As previously discussed, reactions to uncontrollable events are determined by three types of attributions: *internal versus external, stable versus unstable,* and *global versus specific* (that is, whether the event extends to many spheres of life or is confined to one sphere). Those who make *internal* attributions for uncontrollable events tend to experience more negative self-esteem. Individuals who make *stable* and *global* attributions for uncontrollable events are more likely to feel helpless in future events. When all three types of negative attributions are habitually used to explain stressful events in one's life, this attributional tendency is called the **pessimistic explanatory style,** and people who fit this pattern have been found to be at greater risk for depression (Nolen-Hoeksma et al., 1992; Sweeney et al., 1986). For them, an unfortunate event has an internal cause ("It's my fault"), a stable cause ("It will always be this way"), and a global cause ("It's this way in many different situations"). In contrast, when some-

Pessimistic Explanatory Style

A habitual tendency to attribute negative events to internal, stable, and global causes, and positive events to external, unstable, and specific causes.

thing positive happens to them, people with a pessimistic explanatory style tend to make external, unstable, and specific attributions.

An attributional style that contrasts sharply to the pessimistic style is the **optimistic explanatory style.** Optimists tend to explain negative events in terms of an external cause ("It's someone else's fault"), an unstable cause ("It won't happen again"), and a specific cause ("It's just in this one area"). On the other hand, when faced with positive events, optimists explain them by making internal, stable, and global attributions (Seligman, 1991). Do you think you tend to have an optimistic or a pessimistic explanatory style of explaining the causes of good and bad events? Spend a few minutes answering the questions in table 4.5.

Optimistic Explanatory Style

A habitual tendency to attribute negative events to external, unstable, and specific causes, and positive events to internal, stable, and global causes.

> The optimist sees the rose and not its thorns; the pessimist stares at the thorns, oblivious to the rose.
>
> *Kahlil Gibran, Lebanese poet, 1883–1931*

Christopher Peterson and Martin Seligman (1987) conducted a series of studies to better understand the relationship between explanatory style and illness. In one study,

What type of explanatory style does Earl likely possess?

TABLE 4.5

Do You Have a Pessimistic or an Optimistic Explanatory Style?

Directions

Imagine yourself in the two situations described below. Events often have many causes, but if these situations happened to you, what do you think would be the primary cause of each? Answer questions a–c about each situation by circling a number from 1 to 5 for each question.

Situation 1:

While eating at a restaurant, your dinner companion appears bored.

    a. Is this outcome caused by you or by the other person or the circumstances?

Completely caused by other people or circumstance	1	2	3	4	5	Completely caused by me

    b. Will this cause be present in the future?

Will never be present again	1	2	3	4	5	Will always be present

    c. Is this cause unique to this situation, or does it also affect other areas of your life?

Affects just this situation	1	2	3	4	5	Affects all situations in my life

Situation 2:

You receive an award for a university or community project.

    a. Is this outcome caused by you or by the other people or the circumstances?

Completely caused by other people or circumstances	1	2	3	4	5	Completely caused by me

    b. Will this cause be present in the future?

Will never be present again	1	2	3	4	5	Will always be present

    c. Is this cause unique to this situation, or does it also affect other areas of your life?

Affects just this situation	1	2	3	4	5	Affects all situations in my life

Scoring

For the negative outcome situation 1, high scores (4, 5) on questions a–c describe an internal, stable, and global attribution (pessimistic explanatory style). Low scores (1, 2) on these same questions describe an external, unstable, and specific attribution (optimistic explanatory style). For the positive outcome situation 2, high scores on questions a–c again describe an internal, stable, and global attribution, but now this indicates an optimistic explanatory style. Low scores indicate a pessimistic explanatory style.

they measured college students' attributional style and asked them to list all illnesses they had experienced during the previous month. They also completed this illness measure one year after the initial testing. Results indicated that even after controlling for the number of illnesses reported at the first session, students with an optimistic explanatory style reported fewer illnesses and fewer visits to a physician for diagnosis or treatment of an illness than did those with a pessimistic style.

In a second investigation, these same researchers used the responses that ninety-nine male college graduates gave in 1946 to an open-ended questionnaire about their wartime experiences to classify them in terms of their degree of pessimistic explanatory style (Peterson et al., 1988). Although style did not predict health in young adulthood—when nearly all the men were healthy—there was a link between explanatory style and illness by the age of 45, when health became more variable. After this age, the men who had a pessimistic explanatory style in their youth tended to have more health problems than those who had a more optimistic outlook.

Finally, Peterson and Seligman (1987) conducted an archival study on the deceased members of the Baseball Hall of Fame who played between 1900 and 1950. First, they searched the sports pages of old newspapers for the explanations these players gave of their successful and unsuccessful performances. Next, they had independent judges rate these quotes for internality, stability, and globality. Finally, they recorded the age at which each baseball player had died. Results indicated that players who made internal, stable, and global explanations for bad events died at a younger age, and those who explained positive events as being

 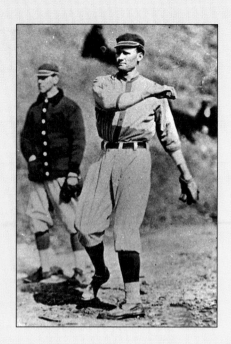

Peterson and Seligman (1987) found that Hall of Famer Zack Wheat (left) had a highly optimistic manner of explaining his baseball success (internal, stable, global). He stated "I'm a better hitter than I used to be because my strength has improved and my experience has improved." In contrast, Hall of Famer Walter Johnson (right) had a depressive style of explaining his failure late in his career (internal, stable, global). He stated, "I can't depend on myself to pitch well. I'm growing old. I have had my day." Based on their research on optimistic versus depressive attributional style, which player do you think died at the ripe old age of 83, and which died at the relatively young age of 59?

due to external, unstable, and specific factors died at a younger age. Overall, this study suggests that people with a pessimistic explanatory style live shorter lives than those with an optimistic style.

Although the findings from these studies are all impressive, they still do not answer the question of why explanatory style influences health. Peterson and Seligman offer several possibilities:

1. Optimists may have better immune systems than pessimists, making them less susceptible to diseases. This explanation is supported by at least one recent study that found that optimists have higher numbers of helper T cells that mediate immune reactions to infection (Segerstrom et al., 1998).

2. Pessimists may not be good problem solvers; they procrastinate in solving problems that eventually often become crises.

3. Pessimists may neglect their health and not obtain adequate sleep, nutrition, or exercise.

4. Pessimists may become passive when faced with disease. By not seeking medical attention or not following the prescribed medical treatment, their health deteriorates.

Regardless of the ultimate explanation for this relationship between explanatory style and health, what these findings suggest is that there is a propensity for certain individuals to be stress-prone (Räikkönen et al., 1999). A central feature in this susceptibility to stress is the *beliefs* that people develop about why both positive and negative events occur in their lives. In a very real sense, these findings point to the important role that people's *subjective interpretations* of events have on their health and behavior. Fortunately, people with a pessimistic explanatory style can be taught to change their self-attributions through cognitive therapy (Hollon et al., 1991). Typically, this therapy involves keeping a diary of daily successes and failures, and identifying how you contributed to your successes and how external factors caused your failures. Essentially, this therapy trains people to do what most of us do naturally, engage in the self-serving bias! The lesson to be learned here, regardless of your own explanatory style, is one of the basic truths of social psychology: your interpretation of events will profoundly influence your subsequent emotions and actions.

FEATURED STUDY
EXPLANATORY STYLE AND UNTIMELY DEATH

Peterson, C., Seligman, M. E P., Yurko, K. H., Martin, L. R., & Friedman, H. S. (1998). Catastrophizing and untimely death. *Psychological Science*, 9: 127–130.

People who provide internal, stable, and global explanations in response to bad events in their lives are said to have a *pessimistic explanatory style*. Although previous research has suggested that a pessimistic explanatory style is a risk factor for early death, these findings have been based on relatively small samples. This same research has raised the question of whether the link between explanatory style and health is the same or different for men versus women. The present study sought to provide a clearer picture of how explanatory style might influence mortality by analyzing the participants in the Terman Life-Cycle Study, an existing set of longitudinal data detailing the life experiences of more than 1,500 preadolescents from the 1920s to the present (Terman & Oden, 1947; Friedman et al., 1995).

METHOD

As formulated by the famed intelligence pioneer, Lewis Terman, the original objective of the Terman Life-Cycle Study was to examine the lives of California children who had been identified as above average in intelligence. Most of them were White and from middle-class families. Over the years, the data from this seventy-plus year longitudinal study has been used by numerous researchers—including the researchers in the current study—to investigate psychological phenomena far afield of intelligence. In 1936 and 1940, the Terman participants, who were then in their twenties, completed open-ended questionnaires about different life events. In the present study, bad life events for 1,182 participants were content-analyzed by eight judges for their causal explanation in terms of internality, stability, and globality. Death certificates for deceased participants were also obtained and coded for underlying cause of death. When death certificates were not available, cause of death was assigned based on information provided by relatives.

RESULTS AND DISCUSSION

When all three attributional dimensions of internality, stability, and globality were statistically analyzed to determine their association with the probability of early death, only globality was a significant predictor. In other words, when people habitually believed that a bad event in one specific life area would undermine everything else in their life, they were more likely to die at an early age. Men with this global explanatory style were at the highest risk for such death. Globality was also a significantly better predictor of deaths by accident or violence than deaths by cardiovascular disease or cancer. These findings persisted even when the mental health of the participants and their smoking habits were statistically controlled in the analyses.

The importance of the present findings are that they represent the first evidence from a large sample of initially healthy people that a dimension of pessimistic explanatory style, namely globality, is a risk factor for early death, especially among men. The fact that globality best predicted deaths by accident or violence suggests that expecting bad events to spread throughout one's life may lead to poor problem solving and risky decision making. That is, "being in the wrong place at the wrong time" may not simply be due to chance but may be partly a result of a pessimistic lifestyle. With men, this pessimism is more fatal than with women.

WEB SITES accessed through http://www.mhhe.com/franzoi2

Web sites for this chapter focus on social cognition topics, including judgment and decision making, social categorization, stereotyping, and counterfactual thinking.

Social Cognition Paper Archive and Information Center

This is a web page maintained at Purdue University which archives various abstracts of social cognition articles in such areas as judgment and decision making, social categorization, stereotyping, and person memory.

Counterfactual Research News

How might your life have unfolded differently? This is a web site which contains a bibliography of counterfactual publications, in press articles, and cartoons.

PART TWO

EVALUATING OUR SOCIAL WORLD

As a species, we not only have a desire to understand ourselves and others, but we also habitually evaluate our social world. Yet, how do we form our opinions? And how do we try to shape others' opinions?

Chapter 5 examines the nature of attitudes, including how they are formed and maintained. Does our behavior shape our attitudes, or do our attitudes shape our behavior? When do attitudes predict behavior? Is cognitive consistency an important aspect of attitude formation and change?

In chapter 6 we will analyze various theories on persuasion and attitude change. Specifically, how does the source of a persuasive message, its content, the manner of transmission, and the nature of the audience determine whether it will be effective? We will not only examine persuasion from the "outside" but also from the "inside," meaning we will explore the cognitive processes of the "persuadee."

Then, in chapter 7, we will tackle an issue that has quite possibly plagued humankind since the dawn of our species, namely prejudice and discrimination. How is stereotyping related to intergroup intolerance? What are the social causes of prejudice and discrimination? Are there ways to combat these negative intergroup evaluations and behavior?

CHAPTER 5

ATTITUDES

CHAPTER OUTLINE

ew issues today can arouse more passion among so many people than the issue of abortion. As the debate is currently framed, two basic human values are often at loggerheads—life versus liberty. Pro-life activists claim that the issue boils down to the right to life. On the other hand, pro-choice activists state that the real issue revolves around the woman's right to choose. Most Americans support a woman's right to have an abortion during the early stages of pregnancy, when the embryo is merely a tiny collection of cells with no discernible human features. Yet many of these same individuals express concerns about the more mature fetus, especially when it is capable of surviving outside the womb. Some people's attitudes, however, are not conflicted, and they feel so strongly that they publicly demonstrate their support for or against abortion rights. Two such individuals are Joan and Natasha, whom I interviewed as they stood outside a barricaded Milwaukee health clinic where abortions were performed.

Joan, a married woman in her midfifties, was active in the pro-life movement. Her reply to my question about why she held such strongly negative attitudes toward abortion was partly based on personal experience—she had an abortion forty years ago, when it was illegal:

> At the time I thought it was the right thing to do. Afterwards, I didn't think about it, I went on with my life. Much later I became a born-again Christian and began to rethink my action of forty years ago. Today, I believe I murdered my unborn child. Abortion is the killing of human life, done out of convenience. If I don't speak out against abortion now, young girls will also carry this burden the rest of their lives. I believe a woman has a choice before she gets pregnant, but not afterwards.

On the pro-choice side, Natasha, a single woman of 30, held a decidedly different attitude than Joan. Raised in Lebanon and Egypt during times of social conflict and war, she said these experiences shaped her current attitudes:

> Having lived throughout the world and experienced war, I see a woman's choice over her body as a much broader issue than women in Milwaukee getting into a clinic. I'm pro-life in the sense that I want to raise the quality of life of those who are born. I've had firsthand experience with others interfering with a woman's right to choose. When I lived in Egypt I was raped and became pregnant. Abortion is illegal in Egypt. I had an unsafe and illegal abortion, and I had it during the second trimester of pregnancy due to all the obstacles I faced. I just cannot believe that people would work so hard to take rights away from women.

Belief

An estimate of the probability that something is true.

Listening to both of these women articulate their abortion attitudes, I was struck by a number of similarities imbedded within their sharply contrasting perspectives. First, their attitudes were based on a number of **beliefs.** Second, these attitudes were associated with a good deal of emotion, or *affect*. Finally, their attitudes were based on their past behavior.

Strongly held attitudes can profoundly shape a person's actions and lifestyle choices. Are you the type of person who holds strong attitudes about many different things?

THE NATURE OF ATTITUDES

Over the years, social psychologists have attempted to explain how attitudes influence behavior. My goal in this chapter is to guide you through this "theoretical maze" so that you arrive at a greater appreciation of how people like Joan and Natasha—and you yourself—are shaped by these psychological factors. As Dorothy from *The Wizard of Oz* was instructed by the Good Witch Glinda prior to setting out in search of the mysterious and powerful wizard, "It's always best to start at the beginning." With this in mind, let's start with first defining the attitude concept itself.

ATTITUDES ARE POSITIVE OR NEGATIVE EVALUATIONS OF OBJECTS

One of the earliest uses of the term *attitude* came from the theater and dates back to the 1800s, where it described a physical posture or body position. An actor on stage would assume a certain body posture (for example, drooping shoulders and head), to signify the mental state of the character (dejection or sadness). Later this term was used to refer not to a body posture, but rather to a "posture of the mind." In 1935, in the *Handbook of Social Psychology*, Gordon Allport declared that attitude was social psychology's most indispensable concept:

> Without guiding attitudes the individual is confused and baffled. Some kind of preparation is essential before he can make a satisfactory observation, pass suitable judgment, or make any but the most primitive reflex type of response. Attitudes determine for each individual what he will see and hear, what he will think and what he will do. To borrow a phrase from William James, they "engender meaning upon the world"; they draw lines about and segregate an otherwise chaotic environment; they are our methods for finding our way about in an ambiguous universe. (Allport, 1935, p. 806)

Today, most social psychologists would still generally agree with this statement. The principal reason the attitude concept is so popular is that the aim of psychology

FIGURE 5.1

Three Different Types of Attitude Antecedents

Attitudes are believed to be formed through affective, behavioral, and cognitive processes. The assumption that attitudes are formed on the basis of affective or emotional experiences is reflected in classical conditioning principles and the mere exposure hypothesis. The idea that evaluations are based on behavioral responses is reflected in operant conditioning principles, self-perception theory, and the facial feedback hypothesis. Finally, the claim that attitudes derive from a process of cognitive learning can be seen in a host of theories, including the theory of planned behavior and cognitive dissonance theory.

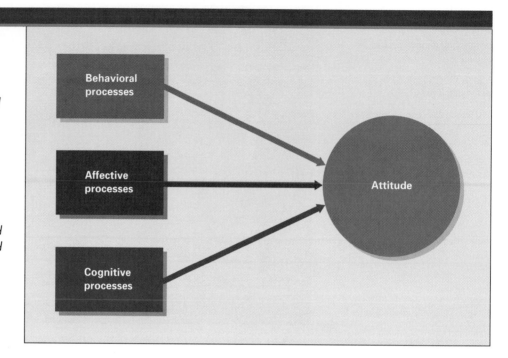

Attitude

A positive or negative evaluation of an object.

is to study behavior, and attitudes are supposed to influence behavior. To change an attitude is to often set in motion a modification of behavior. Any concept that is believed to have such power is bound to come under serious scrutiny by those who desire to unlock the mysteries of human functioning. Social psychologists are not alone in recognizing the importance of attitudes as a key to behavioral change. Most people believe that attitudes determine behavior, which explains why those who feel strongly about abortion, for example, voice their views in a public forum. They think that if they can influence people's attitudes, their behavior will follow.

Prior to the 1990s, attitudes were often defined in terms of three distinct components: beliefs, feelings, and behavioral intentions (Breckler, 1984). According to this multidimensional, or *tricomponent* view, attitudes are made up of our beliefs about an object, our feelings about the object, and our behavior toward the object. Although this definition is appealing because it so neatly carves up the attitude concept into three distinct categories, research indicates that not all three of these components need be in place for an attitude to exist (Eagly & Chaiken, 1993; Priester & Fleming, 1997). For example, you could develop a positive attitude toward a product you see on television without developing any beliefs about it or ever engaging in any behavior relevant to the product. As you will learn (see pp. 151–153), simply by repeatedly being exposed to the product, you can develop a positive attitude toward it.

Because the three aspects of the tricomponent definition are not always present in an attitude, many social psychologists have moved away from this elegant multidimensional view to an earlier, more basic unidimensional, or *single component*, definition in which *evaluation* is central. Here, **attitude** is simply defined as a positive or negative evaluation of an object (Schuman, 1995). "Objects" include people, things, events, and issues. When people use such words as *like, dislike, love, hate, good,* and *bad,* they are usually describing their attitudes. Social psychologists also use specialized terms to describe certain classes of attitudes. For example, an attitude toward the self is called *self-esteem* (chapter 2), negative attitudes toward groups are referred to as *prejudice* (chapter 7), and attitudes toward individuals are referred to as *interpersonal attraction* (chapter 10). The movement away from the tricomponent attitude definition does not mean that social psychologists no longer consider beliefs, feelings, and behavior important in explaining attitudes. Instead, as illustrated in figure 5.1, these three sources of evaluative judgment—beliefs, feelings, and past behavior—are thought of as determining attitudes singly or in combination.

PEOPLE DIFFER IN THEIR NEED TO EVALUATE

Social psychologists have long assumed that nearly all cognition and perception is evaluative, and that it is only rarely that we view people, things, or events without evaluating them in some way (Markus & Zajonc, 1985). Supporting this assumption is a wealth of empirical studies demonstrating that people not only appear to have little trouble reporting attitudes toward common objects, but they can also evaluate unfamiliar objects (see the *mere exposure effect*, pp. 151–153). Despite this research, W. Blair Jarvis and Richard Petty (1996) have recently offered evidence that just because people *can* evaluate with ease does not necessarily mean that they all *will* spontaneously and habitually evaluate. Their resulting *need to evaluate scale* (see table 5.1) measures individual differences in the tendency to engage in evaluation.

How do individuals with a high versus a low need to evaluate differ from one another? As would be expected, Jarvis and Petty found that people with a high need to evaluate are more likely to hold attitudes toward issues they have previously encountered and are more likely to describe daily events in evaluative terms than those with a low need to evaluate. Although research in this area is only just beginning, future studies are likely to explore how individual differences in the need to evaluate might affect how people respond to both positive and negative life events. For example, the impact that divorce or job loss might have on one's self-esteem or level of depression could be influenced by the degree to which one chronically evaluates these events. Insights into these possible relations await further research.

VALUES INDIRECTLY INFLUENCE BEHAVIOR THROUGH ATTITUDES

Values

Enduring beliefs about important life goals that transcend specific situations.

One psychological variable closely associated with attitudes is **values.** Although attitudes refer to evaluations of specific objects, values are enduring beliefs about important life goals that transcend specific situations (Rokeach, 1973). "Peace," "wisdom," "equality," and "happiness" are examples of values. Values constitute an important aspect of self-concept and serve as guiding principles for a person (Kristiansen & Hotte, 1996).

How are values specifically related to attitudes and behavior? Research by Pamela Homer and Lynn Kahle (1988) indicates that values indirectly influence behavior through their influence on attitudes. For example, suppose Mario values physical fitness. This means that maintaining his own fitness is an important life goal for him. Based on his valuing of fitness, Mario will probably have a positive attitude toward bicycling, an activity that promotes fitness. It is this positive attitude that should subsequently influence Mario's decision to exercise with a bike.

Although values can shape attitudes, this does not mean that values shape all attitudes. Your attitudes toward abortion are probably shaped by your values, but your preference for one brand of toothpaste over another is much less likely to be influenced by important life goals. Attitudes that are formed mainly through the influence of long-standing values internalized early in life are called *symbolic attitudes* (Sears & Funk, 1991). They are symbolic because the attitude object is perceived not merely as it is, but rather as a symbol of something else. This type of attitude is likely to be associated with social groups to which a person belongs, to involve a good deal of emotional intensity, and to be relatively unresponsive to rational arguments (Abelson, 1982). *Instrumental attitudes,* on the other hand, are those based on direct benefits and costs of the attitude object. This means that evaluations of the attitude object center solely on its utility for the person and not on its

TABLE 5.1

Measuring the Need to Evaluate

Instructions

The extent to which people chronically engage in evaluation is measured by items on the Need to Evaluate Scale (NES: Jarvis & Petty, 1996). To take the NES, read each item below and then indicate how well each statement describes you using the following scale:

1 = extremely uncharacteristic (very much unlike me)
2 = somewhat uncharacteristic (somewhat unlike me)
3 = uncertain
4 = somewhat characteristic (somewhat like me)
5 = extremely characteristic (very much like me)

_____ 1. I form opinions about everything.

_____ 2. I prefer to avoid taking extreme positions.*

_____ 3. It is very important to me to hold strong opinions.

_____ 4. I want to know exactly what is good and bad about everything.

_____ 5. I often prefer to remain neutral about complex issues.*

_____ 6. If something does not affect me, I do not usually determine if it is good or bad.*

_____ 7. I enjoy strongly liking and disliking new things.

_____ 8. There are many things for which I do not have a preference.*

_____ 9. It bothers me to remain neutral.

_____ 10. I like to have strong opinions even when I am not personally involved.

_____ 11. I have many more opinions than the average person.

_____ 12. I would rather have a strong opinion than no opinion at all.

_____ 13. I pay a lot of attention to whether things are good or bad.

_____ 14. I only form strong opinions when I have to.*

_____ 15. I like to decide that new things are really good or really bad.

_____ 16. I am pretty much indifferent to many important issues.*

Directions for Scoring

Several of the NTE items are reverse-scored; that is, for these items a lower rating actually indicates a higher level of evaluation need. Before summing the items, recode those with an asterisk ("*") so that 1 = 5, 2 = 4, 4 = 2, and 5 = 1. To calculate your need to evaluate score, add up your responses to the sixteen items.

When Jarvis and Petty developed the NTE in 1996, the mean score for college students was about 52. The higher your score is above this value, the greater is your motivation to evaluate objects and events. The lower your score is below this value, the less of this need to evaluate you probably possess.

Source: From Jarvis, W. B. G., & Petty, R. E. (1996). The need to evaluate. *Journal of Personality and Social Psychology, 70:* 172–194.

relation to long-standing values. The object is perceived as it is, rather than as a symbol. Your attitudes toward your favorite toothpaste are probably based on its utility—how well it brightens your teeth and prevents cavities. It is an "instrument" to meet those needs. Sometimes specific attitude objects are less easily identifiable as symbolic or instrumental. For example, voters may cast their ballots for candidates who will provide direct and immediate benefits to them in the form of tax

I happen to feel that the degree of a person's intelligence is directly reflected by the number of conflicting attitudes she can bring to bear on the same topic.

Lisa Alther, American novelist, 1976

CRITICAL *thinking*

Refer back to the "Values Hierarchy" questionnaire in chapter 1 (p. 18). This questionnaire provides you with information about whether individualist or collectivist values are more important to your self-concept. If individualist values are more central to how you view yourself, they will have greater influence in shaping your attitudes, and thus, your behavior. Which were more important for you? Can you identify ways in which these values have influenced your attitudes and behavior?

relief and governmental services (instrumentally based attitudes), whereas other people's electoral attitudes are based more on value considerations (symbolically based attitudes). A very different type of example would be consumers' decisions to buy or not buy fur coats based on their utility or comfort (instrumentally based attitudes) versus considerations of animal rights (symbolically based attitudes).

The importance that a person attaches to a particular value largely determines whether or not it will influence attitudes. For each individual, values are organized into a hierarchy from most important to least important to the self (Ball-Rokeach et al., 1984). Where a specific value falls in this hierarchy will often determine its influence on attitudes. Consider again the explanations the abortion activists gave about why they were either pro-choice or pro-life. To a considerable degree, these explanations hinged on where in their own values hierarchy the principles of "life," "liberty," and "quality of life" fell. When values of relatively equal importance (for example, life and liberty) conflict with one another on a particular issue, such as abortion, the person's subsequent attitudes tend to not only be complex but also ambivalent (Katz et al., 1986; Tetlock, 1989). A person who has complex and ambivalent attitudes toward abortion is unlikely to demonstrate outside a medical clinic—on either side of the issue.

> ### SECTION SUMMARY
>
> Attitudes are determined by a number of factors, including past behavior, emotions, and cognitions. People with a high *need to evaluate* are more likely to hold attitudes toward issues they have previously encountered and are more likely to describe daily events in evaluative terms. Although attitudes refer to evaluations of specific objects, *values* are enduring beliefs about important life goals that transcend specific situations. Values shape many, but not all, attitudes.

HOW ARE ATTITUDES FORMED AND MAINTAINED?

You might think that forming new attitudes is a fairly simple process. In some instances this is true. Yet remember that attitudes can develop from one's beliefs, one's feelings, and one's behavior, singly or in combination. Due to the various ways in which attitudes can be formed, social psychologists have generated or applied a number of theories to explain these various developmental processes. In this section of the chapter, we will first examine theories that explain fairly simple attitudes formed through *mere exposure* and *classical conditioning*. These largely feeling or *affect-based* explanations will then be followed by theories that involve more behavioral and/or cognitive sources (for example, *operant conditioning* and *self-perception theory*). We will also examine one perspective on attitude formation and change, the *functional approach*, that describes how the three sources of attitudes—feeling, thinking, and behavior—might differently come into play due to a person's current psychological needs.

MERE EXPOSURE CAN LEAD TO POSITIVE ATTITUDES

Larissa has developed a positive attitude toward an elderly man who lives in a nearby apartment. If you asked her why she likes this man, Larissa would be hard-pressed to give you a reason: she has never talked to the man and really knows

FIGURE 5.2

Frequency of Exposure and Liking

Research participants' attitudes toward Chinese-like characters became more positive as the frequency of their exposure to these stimuli increased. Can you think of how the mere exposure effect has influenced your own attitudes?

Source: Data from R. B. Zajonc, "Attitudinal Effects of Mere Exposure" in *Journal of Personality and Social Psychology Monograph Supplement, 9* (2, part 2):1–27, American Psychological Association, 1968.

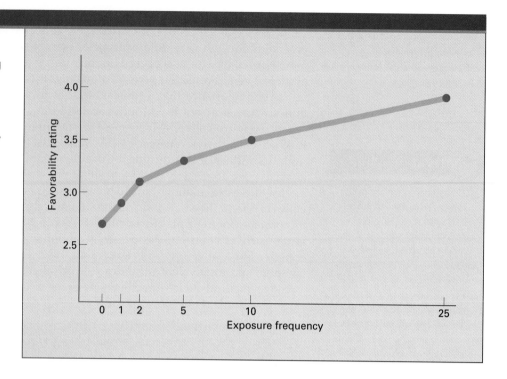

Mere Exposure Effect

The tendency to develop more positive feelings toward objects and individuals the more we are exposed to them.

nothing about him. The only way their lives intersect is that Larissa sees him every day on her way to and from work. With no actual contact, why did Larissa develop a liking for this man?

Larissa's positive attitude is best explained by a theory Robert Zajonc (pronounced like "science") first developed in 1968. Zajonc proposed that simply exposing people repeatedly to a particular object (such as an elderly man) will often lead them to develop a more positive attitude toward the object. This phenomenon, which he called the **mere exposure effect,** does not require any action toward the object, nor does it require the development of any beliefs about the object. Zajonc (1968) reported several experiments in which increased exposure resulted in greater liking for previously neutral objects. In one study in this series, college students were told that they were participating in an experiment to determine how people learn a foreign language. They were then shown ten Chinese-like characters for two seconds at a time, with instructions to pay close attention to them as they appeared on the screen. Two of the characters were presented only once, two others twice, two others five times, two others ten times, and a final two were presented twenty-five times. Besides these ten characters, Zajonc had two others that the participants did not see at all. Once the exposure trials were completed, participants were told that the characters were Chinese adjectives and they were now going to be asked to guess what the characters meant. The experimenter hastened to add that he realized that it would be virtually impossible for them to guess the exact adjective; therefore, he wanted them to merely indicate whether each character meant something good or bad in Chinese. Participants then rated the characters—including the two they had not seen—using a seven-point good-bad scale. The results, shown in figure 5.2, indicated that the more often a character was repeated, the more favorable participants estimated its meaning. Zajonc obtained similar findings by using nonsense syllables and facial photographs taken from a college yearbook. Although there are some limitations and qualifications to repeated exposure (which will be discussed in chapter 6), more than two hundred experiments have confirmed that the mere exposure effect can lead to greater liking (Bornstein, 1989).

One of the more interesting mere exposure studies was conducted by Theodore Mita and his coworkers (1977). They reasoned that people are more exposed to their mirrored facial images than they are to their true facial images, and thus, they should have more positive attitudes toward the former than the latter. To test this hypothesis, they photographed women students on campus and later showed each one her picture along with a mirror image print of it. When asked to indicate which of the two prints they "liked better," two-thirds of the women preferred the mirror print, while 61 percent of their close friends preferred the actual picture, a significant difference in preference. What is impressive about these findings is that the mirrored and true facial photographs were almost indistinguishable from one another, and no one suspected they were looking at altered images.

Overall, the significance of the mere exposure effect regarding our understanding of attitudes is that it illustrates how sometimes affect can become associated with an object independent of any knowledge about it. These feeling-based attitudes develop outside the realm of rational thoughts and represent a very basic and powerful form of evaluation. As a species, we seem to naturally develop a liking for those things that are repeatedly presented to us, be they a stranger in a nearby apartment or the very nose on our face. We simply like that which is familiar. Think about this effect the next time you gaze into a mirror. You're probably the only person who knows you well who prefers that image of your face.

ATTITUDES CAN FORM THROUGH CLASSICAL CONDITIONING

Now let's consider another life situation. Andrew and Coretta are two well-behaved and happy children who are members of a loving family. During the course of their young lives they have developed extremely negative attitudes toward various ethnic and racial groups. The curious thing about Andrew and Coretta's attitudes is that they are not based on any direct contact with anyone from these minority groups. What might have contributed to the development of these hostile attitudes? Partly, their hatred may have developed from listening to their parents and other adults continuously use negatively evaluated words such as *stupid, lazy, dishonest,* and *dirty* in referring to minority members. Through such **classical conditioning,** a previously neutral attitude object (the conditioned stimulus) can come to evoke an attitude response (the conditioned response) simply by being paired with some other object (the unconditioned stimulus) that naturally evokes the attitude response (the unconditioned response).

Arthur and Carolyn Staats were two of the first researchers to systematically test the classical conditioning of attitudes. In one study (Staats et al., 1962), they repeatedly presented participants with meaningful words (for example, *large*) paired with aversive unconditioned stimuli (shocks or loud noises). Later, the conditioned words were presented alone and the participants were asked to evaluate them on a seven-point unpleasant-pleasant scale. As they completed this task, the participants' physiological arousal was measured by monitoring their galvanic skin response. Consistent with the classical conditioning hypothesis, participants showed increased arousal in response to the presentation of the conditioned words, but little arousal in response to control words. Additionally, in comparison to a control group who had not undergone the experimental treatment, the participants also expressed more extreme negative attitudes toward the classically conditioned words.

If classical conditioning only resulted in people disliking certain words, this research would have limited importance. Yet the Staatses demonstrated that people could also be conditioned to develop negative attitudes toward specific social groups. In another experiment (Staats & Staats, 1958), they asked participants to remember words paired with various nationality names, such as "German–table," "French–with," "Dutch–gift," and "Swedish–failure." For one group of participants,

Classical Conditioning

Learning through association, when a neutral stimulus (conditioned stimulus) is paired with a stimulus (unconditioned stimulus) that naturally produces an emotional response.

FIGURE 5.3

Classical Conditioning of Attitudes to Nationality Names

Research by Staats and Staats (1958) demonstrated that classical conditioning could play a role in establishing some of the emotional components of attitudes and prejudice. Participants who heard favorable word pairings with "Dutch" and negative pairings with "Swedish" subsequently had more positive attitudes toward the Dutch and less positive attitudes toward the Swedes. Those individuals who had opposite word pairings later had more favorable attitudes toward the Swedes. Can you think of instances in your own life in which certain attitudes toward other social groups have been similarly classically conditioned?

Source: A. W. Staats and C. K. Staats, "Attitudes Established by Classical Conditioning" in *Journal of Abnormal and Social Psychology, 57:* 37–40, American Psychological Association, 1958.

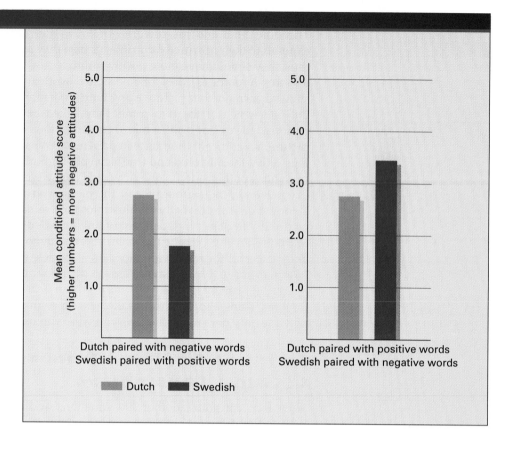

the target nationality "Dutch" was always followed by a word with a positive evaluative meaning, and the target nationality "Swedish" was always paired with negative words. This evaluative pairing was reversed for a second group of participants: "Dutch" was paired with negative words, and "Swedish" was followed by positive words. At the end of the experiment, each participant rated how they actually felt about the various nationality groups using a seven-point pleasant–unpleasant scale. As figure 5.3 shows, the group that heard favorable word pairings with "Dutch" and negative pairings with "Swedish" had more positive attitudes toward the Dutch and less positive attitudes toward the Swedes. These ratings were reversed for the group that had opposite word pairings. Although the attitude shifts were not extreme (participants didn't leave the lab hating one nationality and loving the other), the fact that this mild emotional stimuli produced significant attitude shifts caused attitude researchers to sit up and take notice. Classical conditioning could play a role in establishing some of the emotional components of attitudes and prejudice.

The Staats' research and other studies conditioned attitudes to familiar English words (Zanna et al., 1970). However, this effect is even stronger when the words are unfamiliar. John Cacioppo and his colleagues (1992) found stronger conditioning effects when electric shock was paired with unfamiliar nonsense words (for example, *tasmer*) as compared with meaningful words (for example, *finger*). This study suggests that classical conditioning is a more powerful determinant of attitude formation when people possess little knowledge about the attitude object.

Having reviewed research on the conditioning of attitudes, let's return to our children, Andrew and Coretta. How might they have acquired negative attitudes toward minority groups by simply hearing their parents use a number of negative adjectives (lazy, stupid, dangerous, greedy) in referring to these groups? As we have seen, the novel minority names (like Blacks or Jews) were initially neutral stimuli to the children, because they had not previously been associated with either positive or negative adjectives. However, once the negative adjectives were introduced, repeated pairings of the minority names with these negative adjectives caused Andrew and Coretta to acquire negative attitudes toward these people. They may never have met a Black or a Jew, but this attitude conditioning played a significant role in their aversion and hostility nonetheless.

REINFORCEMENT AND PUNISHMENT CAN SHAPE ATTITUDES

Operant Conditioning

A type of learning in which behavior is strengthened if followed by reinforcement and weakened if followed by punishment.

Because classical conditioning and mere exposure influence people's emotions, it appears to contribute most directly to shaping the *affective* component of attitudes. Yet one of the most powerful ways in which the *behavioral* component can shape attitudes is through **operant conditioning,** a form of learning extensively studied by such behavioral psychologists as Edward Thorndike (1911) and B. F. Skinner (1938). According to operant conditioning principles, when an action toward an object is rewarded or reinforced, the action will probably be repeated in the future. On the other hand, if behavior is not rewarded or is punished, similar future actions are less likely. Learning theorists who study attitudes contend that accompanying this increase or decrease of behavior will be an attitude consistent with the behavior. For example, if a child's parents and teachers praise her for doing well in math, she may redouble her efforts and develop a positive attitude toward mathematics in general. However, if the significant people in her life do not acknowledge these academic accomplishments, her interest in math may diminish and eventually extinguish. She probably will also develop a negative attitude toward the subject matter.

Although attitudes can develop by being directly rewarded and punished when interacting with the attitude object, they can also develop through the indirect means of *observational learning*. In such instances, attitudes are shaped by observing how other people are reinforced or punished when interacting with the attitude object (Rowe et al., 1996). Thus, for example, you might develop a dislike for rock climbing after watching a friend being injured while climbing. Although your friend's newly formed dislike for rock climbing is due to operant conditioning, your negative attitude is a result of observational learning.

SELF-PERCEPTION THEORY CONTENDS THAT BEHAVIOR CAUSES ATTITUDES

Self-Perception Theory

The theory that we often infer our internal states, such as our attitudes, by observing our behavior.

Self-knowledge is best learned, not by contemplation, but action.

Johann Wolfgang von Goethe, German author, 1749–1832

Our lives teach us who we are.

Salman Rushdie, Indian-born British author, 1990

Another theory that emphasizes how behavior shapes attitudes is Daryl Bem's **self-perception theory.** Influenced by Skinner's behaviorist perspective, Bem (1965, 1972) downplays the importance of introspection and self-awareness in the development of attitudes. Instead, he argues that we often do not know what our attitudes are and, instead, simply infer them from our behavior and the circumstances under which the behavior occurs. Bem's theory is a radical explanation of the attitude concept, because it contends that, instead of attitudes causing behavior, it is *behavior that causes attitudes*.

If this notion that we do not automatically understand our own internal states sounds strange to you, let me relate my own recent experience with self-perceptual processes. Last year, I was asked to teach a research methods course while the regular instructor was on leave, and I reluctantly agreed. Whenever my colleagues asked why I was teaching this course, I replied that my arm had been twisted. I taught the course, but I really did not develop a clear liking or disliking for it. Then today, while having lunch with my colleagues, we discussed how best to teach research methods. In the middle of this discussion, I realized that I was dominating the conversation. Why was I so enthusiastic about a course I had never placed high on my preferred teaching list? As I contemplated both my current behavior and my past actions in the course—involving numerous class projects—I literally thought, "Wow, maybe I do like teaching research methods!" According to self-perception theory, at that moment, I had formed an attitude by observing my behavior toward the attitude object.

FIGURE 5.4

Self-Perception of Environmental Attitudes

In a study of environmental attitudes, Chaiken and Baldwin (1981) found that when people were induced into reporting past personal behavior that was either proenvironment or antienvironment, they came to view themselves in ways consistent with this behavior, but only if their prior environmental attitudes were weak and vaguely defined. What limits does this suggest about the self-perception process in attitude formation?

Source: Data from S. Chaiken and M. W. Baldwin, "Affective-Cognitive Consistency and the Effect of Salient Behavioral Information on the Self-Perception of Attitudes" in *Journal of Personality and Social Psychology*, 41:1–12, American Psychological Association, 1981.

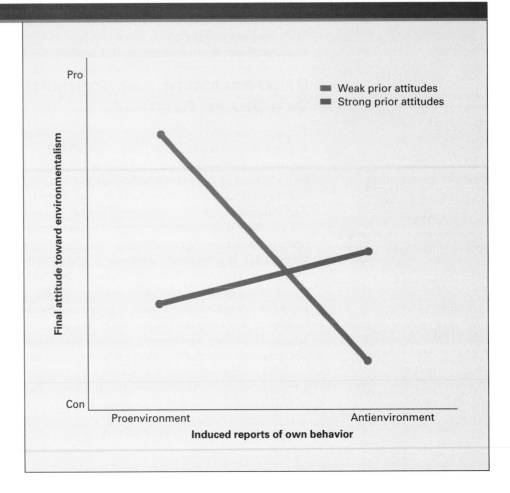

This process of inferring attitudes based on observing behavior should sound familiar, because it describes the attribution principles introduced in chapter 3. Self-perception theory contends that when we form attitudes, we function like an observer, watching our behavior and then attributing it to either an external (the situation) or internal (attitude) source. Comparable to the *discounting principle* in Kelley's covariation model of attribution (p. 96), Bem argued that we are more likely to make attitude inferences when our behavior is *freely chosen* rather than coerced. In my case, Bem would assert that the reason I didn't initially infer an attitude about teaching research methods was because I felt mildly coerced into teaching the course. I wasn't teaching research methods because I liked doing so (an internal attribution), but rather because I was yielding to someone's influence (an external attribution). At our luncheon discussion, however, no one was forcing me to talk about this course, and thus my enthusiasm could not be easily attributed to an external source.

Shelly Chaiken and Mark Baldwin (1981) conducted an interesting empirical demonstration of how the self-perception process influences attitudes. First, they separated participants into two groups: those who held strong, consistent, proenvironmental attitudes and those who had weak, inconsistent attitudes on this issue. They then induced participants to endorse either relatively proenvironment or relatively antienvironment behavioral statements on a questionnaire. They were able to secure the desired behavioral endorsements by inserting either the word *frequently* or *occasionally* into the questions. For example, participants who were asked "Do you occasionally carpool?" were more likely to answer "Yes" and perceive themselves as proenvironment. In contrast, those asked "Do you frequently carpool?" were more likely to answer "No" and feel somewhat antienvironment. Figure 5.4 shows that participants who were induced into reporting proenvironmental behaviors later

FIGURE 5.5

Ratings of Cartoon Funniness Due to Facial Feedback

Strack and his colleagues (1988) had participants rate cartoons on a scale from 0 to 9, where a higher value indicated greater funniness. Some participants read and rated the cartoons while holding a pen in their lips, others while holding a pen in their teeth, and others while holding it in their nondominant hand. Those who held a pen between their teeth expressed more positive attitudes toward the cartoon than those who held a pen between their lips. How do these findings support the facial feedback hypothesis?

Source: Data from F. Strack et al., "Inhibiting and Facilitating Conditions of Facial Expressions: A Non-Obtrusive Test of the Facial Feedback Hypothesis" in Journal of Personality and Social Psychology, 54:768–777, American Psychological Association, 1988.

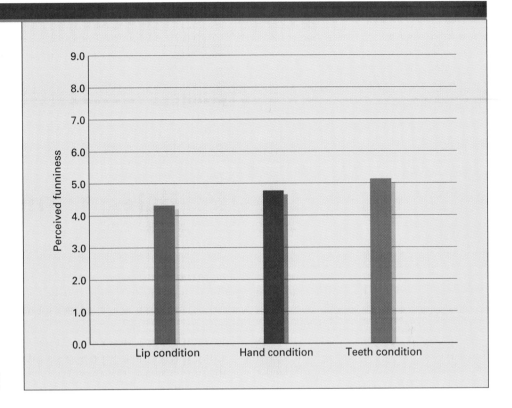

rated their attitude as more proenvironmental than those who were induced into reporting antienvironmental behaviors—but only if their initial environmental attitudes were weak and inconsistent. Among the participants whose prior attitudes were strong and consistently proenvironment, the manipulation of self-reported environmentalist behaviors had no significant impact on their attitudes.

Based on a number of such studies, it appears that Bem's self-perception theory provides an adequate explanation for how we can sometimes infer our attitudes from our behavior. People who have little prior experience with an attitude object, or whose attitudes are vaguely defined, tend to infer their attitudes by observing their behavior (Olson & Roese, 1995; Wilson & Hodges, 1992). However, when they possess well-defined attitudes on a particular topic, attending to their behavior is much less likely to influence any attitude change.

ATTITUDES ARE INFLUENCED BY CHANGES IN FACIAL EXPRESSION, HEAD MOVEMENT, AND BODY POSTURE

Related to self-perception theory is the view that people's emotions—and thus their attitudes—can be manipulated by changing their facial expressions, body posture, or other motor responses (Duclos et al., 1989). For example, in an innovative experiment, German psychologist Fritz Strack and his colleagues (1988) asked college students to hold a pen in their mouths while they were shown a series of amusing cartoons. Participants in the *lips condition* were instructed to hold the pen tightly with their lips, while those in the *teeth condition* were told to hold the pen with their front teeth (see photographs on p. 158). In a control condition, participants were told to hold the pen in their nondominant hand. After reading the cartoons, all students rated how funny they were using a ten-point scale. As you can see in figure 5.5, participants who held the pen between their teeth found the cartoons to be the most amusing, followed by those who held it in their hand.

The facial feedback hypothesis states that changes in facial expression can lead to corresponding changes in emotion. If this hypothesis is correct, what contrasting emotions might be elicited by holding a pen between one's teeth versus between one's lips?

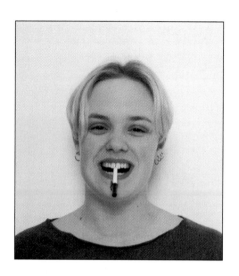 

Students who held the pen in their lips gave the cartoons the lowest ratings of amusement. Why do you think this was the case?

Based on your understanding of self-perception theory, you know that people will sometimes infer their attitudes based on their actions. You also can tell by looking at the photographs that holding a pen with the teeth causes a person to smile, while holding it with the lips prevents smiling. Could the participants have inferred their attitudes toward the cartoons based on their facial muscle movements? This is a possibility, referred to as the *facial feedback hypothesis,* and it would be consistent with self-perception theory. However, Robert Zajonc (1993) offers an alternative explanation, namely, the *vascular theory of emotion.* He contends that smiling causes facial muscles to increase the flow of air-cooled blood to the brain, which, in turn, produces a pleasant mood by lowering brain temperature. In contrast, frowning decreases blood flow, causing heightened brain temperature and an unpleasant mood. Supporting this hypothesis, Zajonc and his coworkers (1989) found that simply having people repeat a series of vowel sounds twenty times each was sufficient to change their forehead temperature and their mood: sounds such as *ah* and *e,* which caused the speakers to mimic smiling, decreased temperature and elevated mood, whereas the *u* and the Germanic *ü* sound, which mimic frowning, had the opposite effect. Regardless of whether these findings are due to increased blood flow to the brain, this study is important because it indicates that even when people are not aware they are wearing a particular expression, movement of facial muscles can alter their mood. In other words, self-perception processes may not be necessary for facial feedback to work.

Besides facial expressions, other expressive behaviors also appear to influence feelings. For instance, when people feel proud, they assume an erect, upright posture, whereas when dejected, their posture becomes slumped. Using this knowledge, Sabine Stepper and Strack (1993) manipulated people's body posture to determine what effect it would have on their feelings of pride following success on an achievement test. Posture was manipulated by having research participants take a test and then learn about their results while either sitting upright at a normal-height table or sitting slumped over at a short-legged table. Those who sat upright felt prouder after succeeding than those who were slumped over. Similarly, Gary Wells and Richard Petty (1980) asked students to "test the sound quality of headphones" by moving their heads either vertically up and down (nodding) or horizontally side to side (shaking) while listening to a taped editorial. Results indicated that the head nodders later expressed more positive attitudes toward the editorial than did the head shakers. Finally, John Cacioppo and his colleagues (Cacioppo et al., 1993; Priester et al., 1996) found that when research participants were presented with neutral or meaningless words and symbols while gently pressing their arms upward against a table (mimicking an inviting "approach" gesture), they expressed greater liking for the words and symbols than participants who gently pressed their arms downward on a table (mimicking a rejecting "avoidance" gesture).

Because participants in all these studies did not perceive a connection between their motor responses and their attitudes, this suggests that these findings cannot be explained by self-perception. Likewise, Zajonc's vascular theory cannot account for these findings. Instead, what may best explain these effects is classical conditioning (refer back to pp. 153–155), where an upright posture, head nodding, and "approach" arm movements have become associated with and facilitate the generation of favorable thoughts, while the reverse is true for a slumped posture, head shaking, and "avoidant" arm movements (Alluisi & Warm, 1990; Förster & Strack, 1996). Together, these studies suggest that performing actions associated with happiness cannot only cause you to feel happier, but it can also cause you to perceive other objects in your environment more favorably.

THE FUNCTIONAL APPROACH ASSERTS THAT ATTITUDES ARE FORMED TO SATISFY CURRENT NEEDS

All of the theories discussed thus far tend to emphasize one attitude component over others in explaining attitude formation. For example, the mere exposure effect and classical conditioning highlight the affective component, while operant conditioning and self-perception theory largely focus on the behavioral component. In an attempt to understand when one attitude component will exercise greater influence than others in shaping a particular attitude, a number of theorists have argued that the purpose or *function* of attitudes needs to be examined. The crux of their argument is that people hold attitudes that fit their current psychological needs, and when those needs change, so will their attitudes. From this perspective, people could have similar attitudes toward an object, but for different reasons. In this process of attitude development and change, the **functional approach** views the individual as an active participant, changing attitudes to satisfy current needs. For example, I might like to drink "Figzoi" soda because all my friends like it and I want to do things to win their approval (refer back to *instrumental attitudes*, p. 149). You, on the other hand, might like Figzoi because the company making it is environmentally conscious (a *symbolic attitude*). Our attitudes may be the same, but they are based on different psychological needs.

Now, imagine that the makers of Figzoi are bought out by an environmentally irresponsible corporation that invests their profits in strip mining and deforestation. Your attitude toward the soda is likely to change, because your support for the company's product is no longer in line with your desire to act in an environmentally responsible manner. I, on the other hand, am unlikely to change my attitude because it is based on a desire to gain acceptance and approval from my friends and not on a desire to act proenvironmentally. In the future, if my psychological needs change so that I no longer am so concerned about seeking others' approval, my attitudes toward Figzoi will more likely be based on the quality of the product itself, or perhaps, like you, on the way in which this product satisfies my socially conscious values. This belief that people are actively involved in developing and changing their own attitudes stands in sharp contrast to the previously discussed attitude theories, which view the person as rather passive in the attitude development process.

Early theorists, particularly Daniel Katz (1960) and M. Brewster Smith (Smith et al., 1956) proposed four psychological functions that attitudes may serve. These functions, listed in table 5.2, are closely associated with different theoretical perspectives in psychology and emphasize different components of attitudes.

Functional Approach

Attitude theories that emphasize that people develop and change their attitudes based on the degree to which they satisfy different psychological needs. To change an attitude, one must understand the underlying function that attitude serves.

TABLE 5.2

Psychological Functions of Attitudes

Type of Attitude	Function Served by Attitude	Psychological Perspective
Utilitarian	Helps the person to achieve rewards and gain approval from others	Behaviorist
Knowledge	Helps the person to structure the world so that it makes sense	Cognitive
Ego Defense	Helps the person protect himself or herself from acknowledging basic self-truths	Psychoanalytic
Value-Expression	Helps the person express important aspects of the self-concept	Humanistic

UTILITARIAN FUNCTION

Sometimes we develop certain attitudes toward objects because we associate them with either positive or negative outcomes. Consistent with the previously discussed operant conditioning principles of behavioral psychology, the *utilitarian* function (also referred to as the *adjustment* function or *instrumental* attitudes) presumes a basic need of self-interest—gaining rewards and avoiding punishments from the environment. Functional theorists contend that we develop positive attitudes toward those objects that are associated with rewards and develop negative attitudes toward those that are associated with punishment. Many children, for example, develop positive attitudes toward their parents because they have been rewarded by them much more than they have been punished. In contrast, these same children develop negative attitudes toward the neighborhood "bullies" because the reinforcement contingencies are reversed. In both instances, the attitudes that the children develop *function* to satisfy their utilitarian needs, by drawing them toward those individuals who have rewarded them in the past (their parents) and avoiding those (the bullies) who have punished them.

KNOWLEDGE FUNCTION

Besides the need to achieve rewards and avoid punishments, functional theorists further contend that people have a need to attain a meaningful, stable, and organized view of the world. Inspired by the insight of cognitive psychology, Katz (1960) stated that attitudes satisfy this *knowledge* function when they provide a "frame of reference" for organizing the world so that it makes sense. In this way, attitudes can serve the same function as the cognitive schemas described in chapter 2—by organizing information and providing stability to people's experience. How might the knowledge function influence actual attitudes? Let's consider college students' attitudes toward professors. You might hold positive attitudes toward certain professors because their courses helped you to make sense out of a particular topic of interest. On the other hand, certain professors' lectures or course organization may have left you confused, and therefore they did not satisfy your need for knowledge. You likely have less positive attitudes toward them.

Knowledge is happiness, because to have knowledge—broad, deep knowledge—is to know true ends from false, and lofty things from low.

Helen Keller, American author and humanitarian, 1880–1968

EGO-DEFENSIVE FUNCTION

Besides helping a person gain rewards and an organized view of the world, attitudes can also help a person cope with emotional conflicts and protect self-esteem. Consistent with the psychoanalytic principles of Freud, the *ego-defensive* function assumes that attitudes serve as defense mechanisms, shielding the self or ego from inner conflict and unpleasant truths (Kristiansen & Zanna, 1994). For example,

Justin may not be performing well on the job and may unjustly blame his problems on fellow coworkers or supervisors. The function of holding these negative attitudes toward others is that it allows Justin the opportunity to avoid acknowledging the real source of the problem—himself. An ego-defensive attitude, by its very nature, is not grounded in a realistic perception of the attitude object, yet the theory assumes that the person holding such an attitude is largely unaware of its ego-defensive function. Thus, when Justin expresses his negative attitudes toward others on the job, he is believed to be generally oblivious to the fact that he is distorting reality to protect his own self-esteem.

VALUE-EXPRESSIVE FUNCTION

Although ego-defensive attitudes prevent people from acknowledging unpleasant truths about themselves, other attitudes help them to give a positive expression to their central values and core aspects of their self-concept. For example, Joe may have a positive attitude toward his volunteer work in building low-cost housing because this activity allows him to express his sense of social responsibility, a value that is central to his self-concept. Expressing such important attitudes is inherently satisfying to Joe, reinforcing a sense of self-realization and self-expression. In assuming the human need for positive expression of core values, the *value-expressive* function (previously referred to as *symbolic attitudes*) emphasizes principles consistent with humanistic theories in psychology.

CONTEMPORARY CONCEPTIONS OF THE FUNCTIONAL APPROACH

The notion that people hold attitudes for different reasons has been an extremely important contribution to the discussion of attitudes. Unfortunately, the major stumbling block in the further development of this theory during the 1960s and 1970s was the failure of researchers to design measurement techniques to properly *assess* what functions particular attitudes serve for particular persons (Eagly & Chaiken, 1998). Fortunately, during the past twenty years, a number of researchers have devised a variety of measurement techniques that allow the assessment of underlying motives (Fazio, 1989; Murray et al., 1996). In one study, Gregory Herek (1987a) found that the attitudes of heterosexuals toward gay men and lesbians appeared to be primarily motivated by either utilitarian needs, ego-defensive needs, or value-expressive needs. For example, Jessie might have a negative attitude toward homosexual individuals because she once had an abrasive employer who was gay and a lesbian landlord who evicted her from her apartment. Jessie is hostile toward gay men and lesbians (a utilitarian function) because she generalizes her negative attitudes toward these people in her past to the entire gay and lesbian population. Another heterosexual, Gloria, might also have negative attitudes toward gay men and lesbians because her religion considers homosexuality to be immoral. The fact that she never had a bad experience with anyone who was gay or lesbian is irrelevant. Gloria's negative attitude satisfies her value-expressive function, allowing her to express an important value associated with a religious group with which she strongly identifies. Finally, Juan may be confused about his own sexual orientation, and as a result, he may develop a hostile stance to those who are openly expressing a lifestyle that he unconsciously desires. This negative attitude fulfills the ego-defensive function because it protects Juan from acknowledging a basic truth about an important self-aspect.

Herek's research highlights one of the most important contributions that the functional approach makes to the understanding of attitudes. Namely, it stresses that those interested in changing other people's attitudes must first determine what functions those attitudes serve for the targeted individuals (Herek & Capitanio, 1998). To increase the probability of successfully changing these people's attitudes so that they are more positive toward gay men and lesbians, different approaches would be needed. For Jessie, one would need to "recondition" her to the target group by perhaps having her experience positive social interactions with

Research by Prentice (1987)
indicates that we tend to perceive
our material possessions as
primarily satisfying either value-
expressive needs or utilitarian
needs. Which need do you think
these photographs most likely fulfill
for most people?

people who are gay. For Gloria, one might try to either change the attitude of her religious leaders toward homosexuality or attempt to detach her from this particular religious group and attach her to a new religion with more tolerant attitudes. For Juan, one would need to create an accepting environment for him to resolve the confusion surrounding his own sexual orientation. These attitude-change strategies will not guarantee success, but functional theorists contend that they would certainly improve the probability of success over the use of one single persuasion strategy on all three individuals.

In addition to investigating how attitude functions vary among people, modern functional researchers have also considered the possibility that different attitude objects may actually engage different functions for most people and, further, that people may differ in their inclination toward certain attitude functions. Regarding the first possibility, Deborah Prentice (1987) has found evidence that people tend to view their material possessions as primarily satisfying either value-expressive needs (for example, family heirlooms, diaries, old letters) or utilitarian needs (stereos, computers, televisions). This finding confirms an assumption that advertising agencies have operated on for many years: people purchase certain products to fulfill utilitarian needs and other products to satisfy value-expressive needs. Regarding the latter, Prentice also found that people who cherish value-expressive possessions over utilitarian possessions differ systematically in their attitudes and values from individuals who cherish most their utilitarian possessions. In one study, for example, people who were "value-expressive" possessors and people who were "utilitarian" possessors were presented with six different messages on current events (New Yorkers should be allowed to accept or reject the placement of a naval base on Staten Island), along with a proposed course of action and arguments supporting the action. Some participants received value-expressive arguments aimed at social ideals and symbolic values (that is, people should have a direct say in matters that affect their welfare); others received arguments that stressed the utilitarian benefits of the proposed course of action (that is, the plan would bring jobs to the New York area, which has an extremely high unemployment rate). Results indicated that those who were value-expressive possessors found the messages stressing symbolic values more appealing than the utilitarian messages. Research conducted by other investigators has yielded similar findings (Snyder & DeBono, 1989).

Overall, this research suggests that value-expressive and utilitarian orientations may represent general approaches people take toward organizing their life experiences. When you stop and think about this possibility, it does make sense. A person who highly cherishes possessions that are symbolic of the self (family heirlooms, souvenirs, diaries) should be drawn to life experiences that allow the positive expression of personal values. After all, personal values are also symbols of the self. On the other hand, people who are more "practical" in evaluating their possessions are likely to also carry this utilitarian orientation into other aspects of their lives, and their attitudes are likely to be influenced by similar considerations.

SECTION SUMMARY

Some attitudes are formed through simple emotional mechanisms. In the *mere exposure effect*, we develop more positive feelings toward objects the more frequently we are exposed to them. In *classical conditioning*, attitudes form when a previously neutral attitude object (the conditioned stimulus) comes to evoke an attitude response (the conditioned response) simply by being paired with some other object (the unconditioned stimulus) that naturally evokes the attitude response (the unconditioned response). One of the most powerful ways in which the behavioral component can shape attitudes is through *operant conditioning*, a form of learning extensively studied by behavioral psychologists. *Self-perception theory*, which could be described as having both a behavioral and cognitive orientation, contends that we infer our attitudes based on our behavior. Our emotions—and thus out attitudes—can also be manipulated by changing our facial expressions, body posture, or other motor responses. Finally, the *functional* approach asserts that we hold attitudes that fit our needs, and when those needs change, so will our attitudes. Early functional theorists proposed four psychological functions that attitudes may serve: utilitarian, knowledge, ego-defensive, and value-expressive.

WHEN DO ATTITUDES PREDICT BEHAVIOR?

One assumption underlying our discussion of attitudes has been that they do indeed influence behavior. To what extent is this true? How *strong* is the link between attitudes and behavior? During the 1970s, a "crisis of confidence" in the attitude concept developed because a number of studies had not found much of an association between attitudes and behavior (Wicker, 1969). Because attitudes failed to reliably predict behavior, many social scientists began to wonder whether attitudes still should be considered a central concept in social psychology (Abelson, 1972).

SEVERAL FACTORS DETERMINE THE ATTITUDE-BEHAVIOR RELATIONSHIP

The difficulty in predicting behavior from attitudes was first demonstrated in a classic study by sociologist Richard LaPiere in 1934. In the early 1930s, the majority of Americans held strongly negative attitudes toward Asians. Being aware of this racial prejudice, LaPiere, a white male, decided to use a three-month, cross-country automobile trip with a young Chinese couple to test how accurately attitudes

Without doubt, it is a delightful harmony when doing and saying go together.

Michel de Montaigne, French writer, 1533–1592

CRITICAL *thinking*

Before reading further, what are some possible confounding variables in the LaPiere study? That is, how might the "true" association between attitudes and behavior have been tainted by the way LaPiere conducted his study?

would predict behavior. His question: Would restaurant and hotel managers act on their negative attitudes toward Asians and refuse service to the Chinese couple?

Surprisingly, only one of the 66 hotels they stopped at turned them away, and none of the 184 restaurants refused them service. Later, LaPiere sent a letter to each establishment asking whether they would accept Chinese as guests. Of the 128 proprietors who replied, more than 90 percent said they would not serve Chinese. Why were the proprietors' attitudes toward Chinese so unreliable in predicting their actual behavior toward this particular Chinese couple? Forty years later, the questions raised by LaPiere's findings and those of other studies led to some fruitful research to determine the conditions under which attitudes might better predict behavior.

LEVEL OF ATTITUDE-BEHAVIOR SPECIFICITY

One problem in predicting behavior from attitudes has been the *level of specificity* at which attitudes and behavior are measured. Too often in the past, researchers have used very general measures of attitudes to predict a very specific form of behavior. This was one of the problems with the LaPiere study. The attitude questionnaire mailed to proprietors asked about Chinese guests in *general*, but their behavioral decision was based on a *specific* Chinese couple, who were well dressed, well spoken, and accompanied by a White person. More recent studies indicate that specific attitudes are much better predictors of behavior than more general attitudes (Newcomb et al., 1992; Weigel et al., 1974).

TIME FACTORS

Another variable that influences the success of attitudes in predicting behavior is *time*. The longer the time interval between measurements of attitude and behavior, the greater the probability that the person's attitude will change. As an example of how time influences attitudes, consider the electorate's opinions about political candidates. The accuracy of opinion polls (attitude and behavioral intention measures) one month before an election is lower than those taken one week before citizens cast their ballots (Fishbein & Coombs, 1974). Put simply, there is less time for attitudes to change during a week than during a month.

PRIVATE VERSUS PUBLIC SELF-AWARENESS

A third factor that influences the attitude-behavior association is *self-awareness*. As discussed in chapter 2 (pp. 44–45), people who are privately self-aware are more attentive to their personal standards of behavior, while those who are publicly self-aware are more attentive to public standards. In a two-stage experiment, William Froming and his colleagues (1982) demonstrated how attention to private versus public standards can either strengthen or undermine the association between attitudes and behavior. First, the researchers pretested college students regarding their attitudes toward physical punishment. Next, they selected students from this group who had negative attitudes toward punishment but who also believed that most people approved of such behavior. Thus, these students had a private attitude that differed from what they perceived to be the public standard. Weeks later, these same students participated in a study that required them to administer electric shocks to someone (in reality, a confederate) as part of a "learning" study. Because the students could control the intensity of the shocks, the dependent variable was the average shock intensity chosen (although no shocks were actually delivered). Some students administered shocks while facing a small mirror (*private self-awareness condition*), others did so while a small audience observed and evaluated them as "effective teachers" (*public self-awareness condition*), and still others delivered shocks with neither a mirror nor an audience present (*control condition*). As seen in figure 5.6, participants who were made privately self-aware by the presence of a small mirror behaved more in line with their previously expressed attitudes than did those in the control group. In contrast, those facing the audience behaved more in accordance with their perception of the public standard than did the controls. What

FIGURE 5.6

Attitude-Behavior Consistency Due to Type of Self-Awareness

In the Froming et al. (1982) study, the researchers selected students to be in an experiment in which their task was to deliver electric shocks to another person as part of a "learning" study. These students had previously expressed negative attitudes toward physical punishment, even though they believed that most others favored such punishment. Those who delivered the shocks while privately self-aware chose the lowest shock levels, whereas those who were publicly self-aware chose the highest shock levels. Based on these findings, which of the two types of self-awareness promotes attitude-behavior consistency?

Source: Data from W. J. Froming et al., "Public and Private Self-Awareness: When Personal Attitudes Conflict with Societal Expectations" in *Journal of Experimental Social Psychology*, 18:476–487, American Psychological Association, 1982.

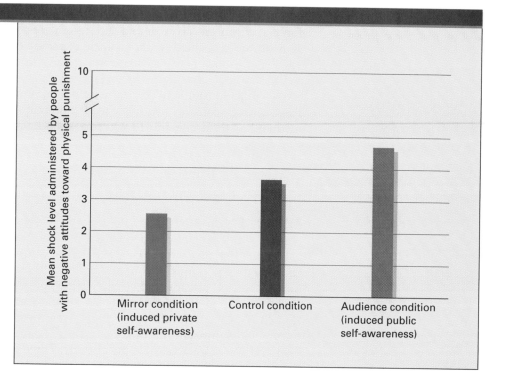

these and other studies suggest is that the *kind of self-awareness* people experience prior to engaging in an activity will significantly determine whether their behavior coincides with their privately held attitudes (Echabe & Garate, 1994).

ATTITUDE STRENGTH

Based on our previous discussion of abortion, it should come as no surprise to you that strongly held attitudes are the ones most influential in determining behavior and the ones most resistant to change (Judd & Brauer, 1995). But what makes an attitude "strong"? Research indicates that simply *acquiring more information* about an attitude object is often sufficient to strengthen people's attitudes (Chaiken et al., 1995; Wood et al., 1995). In one study, for instance, people were first questioned about their attitudes and knowledge about environmental issues, and later were asked to participate in pro-environmental activities (Kallgren & Wood, 1986). Those who knew a lot about environmental issues showed more consistency between their environmental attitudes and their behavior than those who were less informed. The fact that thinking more about something often results in greater attitude-behavior consistency is an important finding, and we will discuss it more extensively in chapter 6 when we examine the *elaboration likelihood model* of persuasion (p. 190).

Another source of attitude strength is the amount of *personal involvement* an individual has with the attitude object (Crano, 1995; Liberman & Chaiken, 1996). For example, in 1978, a ballot initiative in Michigan proposed raising the legal drinking age from 18 to 21. To study the effects that personal involvement would have on attitude strength, John Sivacek and William Crano (1982) contacted college students and asked them to volunteer to help campaign against the proposed law. Although almost all the students opposed the ballot initiative, only some of them (those younger than 20) had a personal stake in the outcome. As expected, the younger students were much more likely to agree to campaign against the law than those who would be unaffected by its passage. In other words, the attitudes of the more personally involved individuals were stronger predictors of behavior than the attitudes of the less involved.

If you want to know the taste of a pear, you must change the pear by eating it yourself. . . . All genuine knowledge originates in direct experience.

Mao Zedong, Chinese communist revolutionary, 1893–1976

Related to personal involvement is the fact that attitudes formed through *direct experience* are stronger and, as a result, are better predictors of later behavior than attitudes formed without such experience (Millar & Millar, 1996). One possible reason that direct experience leads to stronger attitudes is that such encounters are more likely to engage all three attitude components: affective, behavioral, and cognitive (Zanna & Rempel, 1988). Remember Joan and Natasha? Their strong abortion attitudes were not only based on their past behavior surrounding this issue, but also on corresponding beliefs and emotions.

This is certainly not meant to be an exhaustive list of the factors that contribute to attitude strength. The general point you should take from this discussion, however, is that the link between attitudes and behavior will be stronger when the attitude itself is strong.

ATTITUDE ACCESSIBILITY

One reason attitudes formed through direct experience have a powerful impact on behavior is that they tend to be highly *accessible;* that is, they are frequently thought about and come quickly to mind (Fazio, 1995; Smith et al., 1996). For example, during the 1984 presidential election campaign, Russell Fazio and Carol Williams (1986) measured the accessibility of people's attitudes toward then President Ronald Reagan. Attitude accessibility was measured by the *speed* with which respondents pressed buttons to answer Reagan questions: the quicker the response, the more accessible the attitude. Three months later, following the election, these people were recontacted and asked to reveal for whom they voted. Results indicated that those people with highly accessible attitudes toward Reagan showed a significantly stronger link between their attitudes and their voting behavior ($r = .89$) than those with low accessible attitudes ($r = .66$). This notion of attitude accessibility is similar to the concept of the *availability heuristic* discussed in chapter 4 (p. 123). Recall that the availability heuristic is the tendency to judge the frequency or probability of an event in terms of how easy it is to recall examples of the event. Similarly, the ease with which relevant attitudes come to mind will partly determine our perceptions of an attitude object. In both instances, the more readily information is activated in memory, the greater impact it will have on subsequent behavior (Wänke et al., 1996). According to Fazio, these more accessible attitudes can be spontaneously and automatically activated without our conscious awareness (Fazio, 1990). In other words, attitudes can guide our behavior without us necessarily being aware of their influence.

THE THEORY OF PLANNED BEHAVIOR ASSERTS THAT ATTITUDES INFLUENCE BEHAVIOR BY SHAPING INTENTIONS

Theory of Planned Behavior

The theory that people's conscious decisions to engage in specific actions are determined by their attitudes toward the behavior in question, the relevant subjective norms, and their perceived behavioral control.

During the 1970s, one product of the debate about whether attitudes determine behavior was the development of a new attitude theory by Martin Fishbein and Icek Ajzen (1975) called the *theory of reasoned action.* Later, Ajzen (1991) further developed this theory and renamed it the **theory of planned behavior.** By using the term *reasoned action* in the original theory and *planned behavior* in the updated version, Ajzen and Fishbein convey their belief that people rationally think about the consequences of their behavior prior to acting. In other words, behavior is *intended* to achieve certain outcomes, and cognition is the primary process of attitude development. By discovering the intentions of others in a particular situation, they argued that you could predict their behavior.

According to this perspective, the most immediate cause of behavior is not attitudes, but rather *behavioral intentions,* which are conscious decisions to carry out specific actions. Thus, the theory argues that attitudes influence behavior by their influence on intentions (Bagozzi et al., 1989). As you can see in figure 5.7, besides

FIGURE 5.7

Theory of Planned Behavior

The theory of planned behavior hypothesizes that the most immediate cause of behavior is not attitudes, but rather, behavioral intentions. According to this theory, what factors combine with attitudes to determine these intentions?

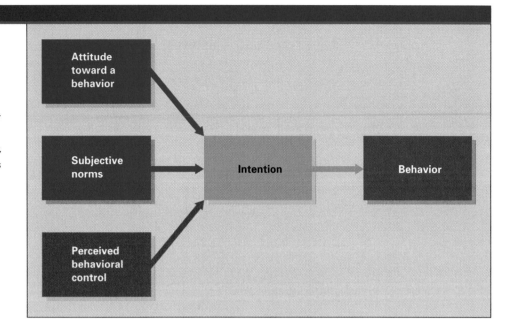

> The ancestor of every action is a thought.
>
> *Ralph Waldo Emerson, American philosopher/poet, 1803–1882*

a person's attitude toward the behavior, behavioral intention is also determined by *subjective norms* and *perceived behavioral control*.

DETERMINANTS OF ATTITUDES

As you might expect, Fishbein and Ajzen believe that an attitude toward performing a particular behavior is formed according to a fairly rational process and is the product of two factors: (1) one's beliefs about the consequences of performing the particular behavior, and (2) one's evaluation of those possible consequences. Returning to our previous discussion of abortion, Fishbein and Ajzen would argue that a woman's attitude toward being pregnant could be predicted by learning what she believes the consequences of having a child would be, and by discovering her evaluations of these beliefs. Table 5.3 outlines the consequences that a sample of childless married women believed would follow from having a baby in the next three years (Fishbein, 1980). Some of these women wanted to have a child during this time, while others had no intention of becoming pregnant anytime soon. In a questionnaire, both groups of women stated their beliefs about having a child and evaluated these beliefs using seven-point scales ranging from +3 (positive outcome or evaluation) to −3 (negative outcome or evaluation). As the table shows, more positive "Belief × Evaluation" products were associated with intentions to have children. That is, as Fishbein and Ajzen would predict, the women who intended to become pregnant believed that this event would have more positive consequences than women who had no intentions of becoming pregnant.

DETERMINANTS OF SUBJECTIVE NORMS

A *subjective* norm is a person's judgment about whether other people will approve of a particular behavior. Like attitudes, subjective norms are also a product of two factors: (1) the perceived expectations of significant others, and (2) one's motivation to conform to those expectations. Thus, a woman's subjective norm about having a child would be determined both by the beliefs that significant others have about her becoming pregnant (for example, "My husband wants to wait until we can afford our own house"; "My parents think a woman's first priority in marriage is to have children"), and her motivation to conform to their expectations (for example, "I want to please my husband"; "My parents' views are outdated").

TABLE 5.3

Attitudes of Women Intending and Not Intending to Have a Child Based on Their Mean Beliefs and Mean Evaluations

This table compares the attitude scores of women who intended and did not intend to have a child in the next three years. Their attitude scores are based on the product of their behavioral beliefs and evaluations of these beliefs, with higher (positive) values indicating more positive attitudes.

	Mean Belief × Evaluation Product	
	Intenders	Nonintenders
Having a child I could not afford	3.46	−2.57
Having a child while at a good age	7.13	2.95
Too much of an emotional strain	4.86	−0.97
A restriction on my freedom	0.22	−3.32
Stronger marriage	2.37	−3.62
Fulfillment of my family life	5.33	−1.41
An added responsibility	3.57	−4.14
Having less time for my own goals and plans	−0.56	−5.41

Source: Adapted from Fishbein, 1980.

How do attitudes and subjective norms influence behavioral intentions? When these two different factors are carefully measured, results have generally shown a high correspondence between intention and behavior (Sheppard et al., 1988). Research also indicates that, although behavioral intentions are generally more controlled by attitudes than by subjective norms, their individual contribution also depends on the particular attitude, setting, and population under study (Corby et al., 1996). For example, we have previously seen (p. 164) that situations which induce private self-awareness increase attitudes' influence on behavior, while situations which induce public self-awareness increase the influence of subjective norms. Further research indicates that the tendency for people to be more influenced by their attitudes or subjective norms is related to whether they have more of an individualist or collectivist orientation. The actions of individualists are more influenced by their attitudes, while collectivists' actions are more controlled by subjective norms (Trafimow & Finlay, 1996). Together, these studies demonstrate that even though attitudes and subjective norms determine behavioral intentions, their individual contributions to the intention equation can differ.

DETERMINANTS OF PERCEIVED CONTROL

In many instances, attitudes and subjective norms are adequate determinants of behavioral intention. Yet what about those cases in which people believe the behavior is difficult to control? Responding to this weakness in the original theory, Ajzen (1985, 1988) added the concept of *perceived behavioral control*, which is one's perception of how easy or difficult it is to perform the behavior. Ajzen argued that when people believe they have little control over performing a behavior because of a lack of ability or resources, then their behavioral intentions will be low regardless of their attitudes or subjective norms. For example, suppose that Lyle desires to quit his thirty-year smoking habit (positive attitude toward quitting smoking). In addition, he knows that his family and doctor approve of him quitting and he would like to please them (subjective norm). Over the course of time, however,

after realizing how ingrained this habit is in his everyday activities, Lyle may lose confidence in his ability to become a nonsmoker (low perceived behavioral control). Thus, despite the proper attitude and subjective norm, Lyle is likely to change his intention to quit smoking.

Another example of perceived control thwarting intention was demonstrated by my daughter Lillian when she was 3 years old. We'd been trying to get her to stop sucking her thumb and one day she said to me, "Dad, do you know . . . do you know . . . do you know why I don't like sucking my thumb anymore? Because . . . because . . . because I want to get big." I was pleased. It seemed our little talks were finally paying off: she understood and wanted to conform to our household's "no thumbsucking" norm. Later that night, however, I saw Lillian vigorously sucking her thumb. When I reminded her about her previous pronouncement, she first claimed that she wasn't sucking it, but merely giving it a "good cleaning." Then, in the exasperated anger typical of 3-year-olds, she blurted out, "But I *have* to suck my thumb!" Despite Lillian's attitude and subjective norm both pointing toward the termination of thumbsucking, at the end of a hard day's play she just didn't feel capable of keeping that thumb out of her mouth.

CRITICISMS OF THE THEORY OF PLANNED BEHAVIOR

Quite a few studies have tested the theory of planned behavior, and the general conclusion is that it does a good job of explaining behavior based on rational thinking and planning (Norman & Conner, et al., 1996 Reinecke et al., 1996). However, by placing intention after attitudes and before behavior, the theory ignores the possibility that attitudes sometimes result in spontaneous, *unintentional* behavior. For example, when I was 10 years old and at summer Bible camp, I developed a strong dislike for a tall, strong, and—as far as I was concerned— mean 11-year-old boy named Billy. One morning as he passed by me on the playgrounds, without provocation—and more important, without any deliberative thought—I pushed him. I distinctly remember this event because I was as surprised as anyone that I had instigated a physical confrontation with someone twice my size. Luckily, a camp counselor quickly intervened and prevented me from being rebaptized in the nearby lake at the hands of the irate "Pastor Billy." This example illustrates the fact that sometimes people act without thinking (refer back to *attitude accessibility*, p. 166). By confining their theory to volitional and deliberate actions, Fishbein and Ajzen would be hard-pressed to explain my behavior at camp. Nor could they explain how a person's hatred or love for another sometimes elicits sudden, spontaneous violence or affection.

Another class of behaviors that the planned behavior model cannot explain are well-established *habits* (Maddux & DuCharme, 1997). With habits, there is no assessment of attitudes and norms prior to behaving. There is no real planning or conscious intention. Instead, the behavior is performed in a relatively unthinking fashion, with little self-regulation (Langer, 1989). Research indicates that habits shape many different kinds of behavior, including using seat belts (Wittenbraker et al., 1983), donating blood (Bagozzi, 1981), attending college classes (Fredricks & Dossett, 1983), voting for a particular political party (Echabe et al., 1988), exercising (Bentler & Speckart, 1981), and choosing what mode of transportation to use while on vacation (Verplanken et al., 1998). At one time, all of these behaviors were exclusively under conscious, self-regulatory control. However, through repetition, they may have slipped into a rather "automatic" mode and thus are now less influenced by conscious intentions. Under these circumstances, this relatively *mindless behavior* limits the likelihood that we will act rationally. Ask anyone who has ever tried to break a bad habit, such as eating fatty foods or tailgating fellow motorists on the highway. They will attest to the power that habitual behavior can have in overriding rational action.

When one begins to live by habit and by quotation, one has begun to stop living.

James Baldwin, American expatriate civil rights author, 1924–1987

SECTION SUMMARY

Factors that increase the correspondence between attitudes and behavior include the level of attitude-behavior specificity, the time interval between the measurement of attitude and behavior, the type of self-awareness induced prior to behaving, and the strength and accessibility of the attitude itself. The *theory of planned behavior* contends that the most immediate cause of behavior is not your attitude, but rather your behavioral intention. Although this rational theory is not an adequate explanation for behavior that is spontaneous or habitual, it has been successful in finding a stronger correspondence between attitudes and deliberate behavior.

IS COGNITIVE CONSISTENCY AN IMPORTANT ASPECT OF ATTITUDES?

One of the most influential approaches in social psychology, especially in the study of attitudes, has been the notion that people are motivated to keep their own cognitions (beliefs, attitudes, self-perceptions) organized in a consistent and tension-free manner (refer to chapter 2, p. 58). This principle of **cognitive consistency** was first introduced by Fritz Heider (1946) and has its roots in the Gestalt belief that human beings not only expect and prefer their perceptions to be coherent and harmonious, but they are motivated to make them so (Koffka, 1935; Köhler, 1929). Consistency theories became popular in the late 1950s and shaped the study of attitudes for the following two decades. Even though this motivational approach toward understanding attitudes was eclipsed by the cognitive movement in the 1970s, it is still an influential perspective (Leippe & Eisenstadt, 1994).

Cognitive Consistency

The tendency to seek consistency in one's cognitions.

COGNITIVE DISSONANCE THEORY ASSERTS THAT RATIONALIZATION SHAPES ATTITUDES

The most influential of the consistency theories was developed in 1957 by Leon Festinger. Festinger's *cognitive dissonance theory* proposed that although we may generally appear logical in our thinking and behavior, we often engage in irrational and maladaptive behavior in order to maintain cognitive consistency. It also describes and predicts how we spend much of our time *rationalizing* our behavior rather than actually engaging in rational action. Let's examine in some detail this exceptionally prolific theory that has spawned so many experiments and countertheories over more than forty years.

FIGURE 5.8

Effects of Payment on Attitudes Toward a Dull Task

Festinger and Carlsmith (1959) predicted that participants who were given insufficient monetary justification for lying (the $1-liars) would experience greater cognitive dissonance and, thus, would express more liking for the dull task than those who received sufficient monetary justification (the $20-liars). Why would insufficient justification create greater dissonance?

Source: Data from L. Festinger and J. M. Carlsmith, "Cognitive Consequences of Forced Compliance" in *Journal of Abnormal and Social Psychology*, *47*: 382–389, American Psychological Association, 1959.

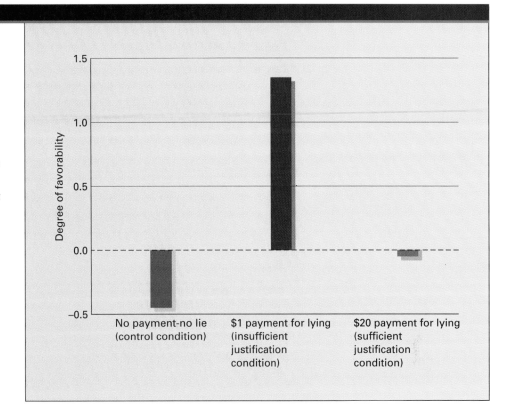

INSUFFICIENT JUSTIFICATION AND DISSONANCE

Imagine that you volunteer to participate in an experiment and, upon arriving at the lab, are asked to perform two 30-minute tasks. The first task consists of emptying and refilling a tray with spools, and the second consists of repeatedly turning forty-eight wooden pegs on a board. As you work on these tasks, you silently curse their monotony. Finally, when your hour of boredom ends, the experimenter tells you that the real purpose of the study is to determine if a person's performance is influenced by whether he's told beforehand that it will be "very enjoyable" and "fun," or, like yourself, is told nothing at all. Then he tells you that his assistant is not able to help him with the next participant who will be in the "favorable information condition." The experimenter then asks if you would tell the participant that you had just completed the task—a true statement—and that you found it to be extremely enjoyable—a lie. You agree to become the assistant and tell your lie to the waiting participant. When the participant completes the tasks and departs, the experimenter sends you to an office where an interviewer asks how fun and interesting you in fact found the tasks to be. Do you think your attitude toward these tasks would be influenced by whether the experimenter had promised you $1 versus $20 to tell your lie? If yes, which sum of money would lead to the greatest attitude shift?

This is the scenario of a classic cognitive dissonance experiment conducted by Festinger and J. Merrill Carlsmith (1959). As depicted in figure 5.8, participants who, for $1, told others (who were actually confederates) that the task was "very enjoyable" and "fun" came to believe that it was enjoyable to a far greater degree than those who said so for $20. These $1-liars also expressed greater enthusiasm for the task than a control group who were not asked to lie. Do these findings surprise you? They certainly surprised a lot of attitude researchers because it contradicted reward theories based on operant conditioning principles, which predicted that participants who were paid more to lie would exhibit greater attitude change than those who were paid less (see p. 155).

TABLE 5.4

Ways to Reduce Cognitive Dissonance

There are a number of ways to reduce dissonance. For example, consider people who have quit smoking cigarettes because of the health risks, but then, resume the habit. How might they reduce the dissonance aroused by the discrepancy between their attitude ("I don't like smoking") and their behavior ("I'm smoking again")?

Common Strategies	Examples
Changing attitudes: People can simply change their attitudes to make them consistent with discrepant attitudes or prior behaviors.	"I don't really need to quit. I like smoking."
Adding cognitions: If two discrepant thoughts cause dissonance, people can add more consonant thoughts.	"Smoking relaxes me and keeps my weight down, which benefits my health."
Altering the importance of the discrepancy: People can alter the importance of the consonant and discrepant thoughts.	"It's more important to stay relaxed and slim than to worry about maybe getting cancer thirty years from now."
Reducing perceived choice: People can convince themselves that they are not freely choosing to engage in the discrepant behavior.	"I have no choice but to smoke. I have so much stress in my life now that smoking is one of the only ways to calm my nerves."
Changing behavior: People can change their behavior so it no longer conflicts with their attitudes.	"I'm going to stop smoking again."

Cognitive Dissonance

A feeling of discomfort caused by performing an action that is inconsistent with one's attitudes.

Although these findings seemed surprising to many, they are consistent with cognitive dissonance theory. The theory states that if you simultaneously hold two cognitions that are inconsistent ("This was a boring task" and "I told someone it was very enjoyable"), this will thwart your desire for cognitive consistency. Recognizing that you have acted inconsistently, you will experience a feeling of discomfort known as **cognitive dissonance.** Festinger believed dissonance was analogous to hunger in its aversiveness; that is, people are naturally motivated to reduce or eliminate the dissonance. How is this cognitive dissonance eliminated or reduced? Table 5.4 lists some ways to reduce dissonance.

In the Festinger and Carlsmith study, only two dissonance-reducing outlets were available to the liars: (1) they could add a third cognition to make their attitude-behavior inconsistency less inconsistent, or (2) they could change their attitude about the task. The reason the "$1 participants" showed more attitude change toward the boring task than the "$20 participants" was that they experienced a greater *amount* of cognitive dissonance. Festinger and Carlsmith reasoned that the $20 participants would not need to change their attitudes because they could justify their actions and, thus, reduce dissonance by adding a third cognition that makes the original cognition less inconsistent: their high payment was *sufficient justification* for their counterattitudinal behavior. Thus, the $20 participants had a reasonable justification for lying. The same could not be said for the $1 participants. They were only given $1 for their lie. This amount of payment provided *insufficient justification* for their counterattitudinal behavior. According to Festinger, when people engage in a counterattitudinal behavior without receiving a large reward, they should experience cognitive dissonance. Faced with this dissonance, the $1 group strove to reduce the negative drive state. They couldn't deny that they lied, so instead they changed their attitude about the task: it wasn't so boring after all.

Just as the offer of a small reward is insufficient justification for engaging in counterattitudinal behavior, the threat of mild punishment is insufficient justification for *not* engaging in some desired action. In an experiment demonstrating this effect, 4-year-old children were prohibited by an adult from playing with a toy in a playroom (Aronson & Carlsmith, 1963). In one condition the prohibition was induced by a severe threat ("I don't want you to play with the toy on the table. If you play with it, I will be very angry. I will have to take all of my toys and go home!"). In another condition the threat was mild ("I don't want you to play with the toy on the table. If you play with it, I will be annoyed."). Even though all the children had previously stated that they liked this toy, all obeyed the adult's command.

Before reading further, based on your understanding of cognitive dissonance, how should these two groups of children have differed in their attitudes toward this toy after not playing with it? Remember, for both the mildly and severely threatened children, the attitude that "I like the toy on the table" was inconsistent with the realization that "I didn't play with the toy." Yet, for the children who received the severe threat, this was sufficient external justification for not engaging in the desired behavior, and therefore they shouldn't have experienced much dissonance. However, the mildly threatened children had insufficient justification for not playing with the desired toy, and therefore they should have experienced greater dissonance. The only way for them to reduce their dissonance was to devalue the forbidden toy. This is exactly what they did. No similar attitude change was found in the severely threatened group, or in a control group of children who received no threats. Forty-five days after the initial testing, the children who had been mildly threatened still had more negative attitudes toward this toy than did those who had been severely threatened. A replication of this study found that the tendency to shun the highly attractive toy persisted up to nine weeks after the presentation of the mild threat (Freedman, 1965).

This notion of insufficient justification is so important in understanding how cognitive dissonance operates that it bears reviewing. As Festinger stated, if the reasons for engaging in counterattitudinal behavior are strong (for example, "I was paid $20 to lie" or "I was severely threatened not to play with the toy"), little or no dissonance will be generated. But if these reasons are weak ("I was paid only $1 to lie" or "I was only mildly threatened"), then people are confronted with the dissonant-producing thought that they had no strong or clear basis for acting inconsistently with their attitudes. In other words, cognitive dissonance theory demonstrates that the *weaker* the reasons for acting inconsistently with one's attitudes, the *greater* the pressures to change the attitudes in question.

FREEDOM OF CHOICE AND DISSONANCE

Another factor that can lay the base for cognitive dissonance is freely choosing to engage in a counterattitudinal behavior. For example, let's suppose young Jack tells his grade-school friends that he hates girls, but later they see him sitting next to Betty Lou on the bus. If the bus driver forced Jack to sit next to Betty Lou, he can legitimately explain his close proximity to Betty Lou as being beyond his control. According to dissonance theory, due to Jack's lack of choice, it is unlikely that he will feel responsible for his actions, and therefore he will not experience much cognitive dissonance. However, if no one forced Jack to sit next to Betty Lou, then his behavior would likely be seen as freely chosen; therefore, he should experience discomfort due to his dissonant thoughts ("I hate girls, but I sat next to a girl").

Darwyn Linder and his colleagues (1967) conducted an experiment that demonstrated the role that choice plays in dissonance arousal. College students

FIGURE 5.9

Linder, Cooper, and Jones (1967) manipulated participants' freedom of choice and incentive. Consistent with cognitive dissonance theory, in the "free-choice" condition, low-incentive students expressed greater attitude change than high-incentive students. However, in the "no-choice" condition, reward or incentive effects occurred: low-incentive students showed less attitude change than high-incentive students. What do these results tell you about the role that perceived freedom of choice plays in attitude change?

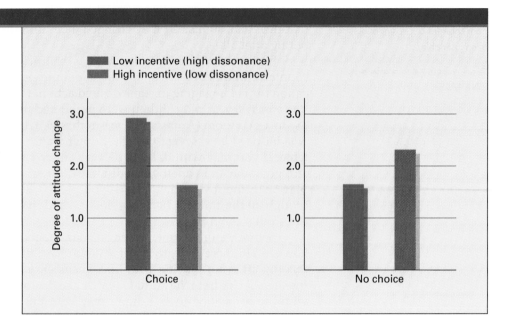

were asked to write essays in favor of a law barring controversial individuals from speaking on campus. This law, in fact, was actually being discussed in the state legislature, and almost all students opposed its passage. Students were offered either $.50 or $2.50 for their essays. In the "free-choice" condition, the experimenter stressed the students' freedom to refuse to write the essay, while in the "no-choice" condition, no mention was made about the students' right to refuse. Instead, the experimenter acted as if by volunteering to participate in the study, the students had committed themselves to its requirements.

As predicted by cognitive dissonance theory, when the students' free choice was stressed, the group that was paid $.50 changed their attitude toward the law so that it was more in line with the essay content, but the attitudes of the group paid $2.50 did not shift. In the "no-choice" condition, the exact opposite effects occurred: the larger amount of money produced greater attitude change (see figure 5.9). The attitude change in the "no-choice" condition does not conform to dissonance theory, but instead follows the principles of operant conditioning, in which external incentives shape attitudes. Thus, to experience cognitive dissonance, people must feel that they *freely chose* to behave in a counterattitudinal manner.

JUSTIFICATION OF EFFORT AND DISSONANCE

Although we have seen that the use of negative incentives—in the form of mild threats—can induce cognitive dissonance, which, in turn, results in less liking for the attitude object, negative incentives can also lead to *increased liking*. Recall the discussion in chapter 1 of my experiences with the Divine Light Mission. Here were people who had given up all their worldly possessions and had worked tirelessly for their 16-year-old Perfect Master, Guru Maharaj Ji. As the evidence mounted that their spiritual master was simply an overindulgent and spoiled teenager, many of these people surprisingly increased their psychological commitment to the Mission. Were they insane? Not according to cognitive dissonance theory. Dissonance theorists argue that when people have a bad experience with some group they have freely chosen to join, there is a natural tendency for them to try to transform the bad experience into a good one to reduce cognitive dissonance. In addition, the greater the sacrifice or hardship associated with the choice, the greater the level of dissonance people experience.

To better understand the actions of those who incur large costs in questionable ventures, let's look at an experiment carried out by Elliot Aronson and Judson Mills (1959) on the effects of the *severity of initiation* on liking for a group. Participants were college women who volunteered to take part in discussions of the psychology of sex. It was their false understanding that these discussions would be analyzed to better understand group dynamics. Prior to being admitted into the discussion group, each woman, except those in the control condition, was told that she would have to take an "Embarrassment Test" to assure the researchers that she could talk frankly and freely about this intimate topic. The real purpose of this test was to make the participants pay a different "price" to get into the group. Those women in the *severe initiation* condition were required to read aloud to the male experimenter a list of obscene words, as well as some extremely graphic sexual scenes from contemporary novels. (Keep in mind that this was the 1950s, when uttering obscene and sexually graphic words to a university psychologist would make most undergraduates extremely uncomfortable.) In the *mild initiation* condition, women were asked to read aloud such mildly sex-related words as *prostitute, virgin,* and *petting.* This group, then, paid a lower initiation "price" than the severe group. Regardless of how embarrassed the women were or how haltingly they read the words in either condition, all were told they had passed the test and could join the group. The women were then given earphones and instructed to listen in on the group they would soon be joining. What they heard was a discussion that Aronson and Mills described in the following manner:

> The participants spoke dryly and haltingly on secondary sex behavior in the lower animals, contradicted themselves and one another, mumbled several non sequiturs, started sentences that they never finished, hemmed, hawed, and in general conducted one of the most worthless and uninteresting discussions imaginable. (Aronson & Mills, 1959)

After listening to this discussion, the women were asked to rate both the discussion and the group members on such evaluative scales as "dull--interesting" and "intelligent–unintelligent." According to dissonance theory, the women in the severe initiation group should have experienced a pair of dissonant thoughts: "I willingly went through a very embarrassing initiation in order to join this sex discussion group"; "These group discussions are dull and worthless." To reduce the cognitive dissonance, these women had to alter one of these thoughts. Since they couldn't deny that they willingly paid a high price to join the group, the only thought they could reasonably alter was their group evaluation. In contrast to the severe initiation women, the women in the "mild" and "no initiation" groups had invested little, if anything, to join the group and, thus, should not have experienced much dissonance. Consistent with this reasoning, the severe initiation group gave significantly more positive evaluations of the discussion than those who were in either the mild initiation or the control groups (see figure 5.10).

Replications of this experiment have demonstrated that this effect is strong: the more you pay for something, the more you will come to like it (Axsom, 1989; Gerard & Mathewson, 1966). Is it any wonder that many of the devotees in the Divine Light Mission increased their allegiance to Guru Maharaj Ji when those outside the mission were calling him a fraud and a sham? To agree with this judgment would have called into question all that they had suffered for during the past few years. Faced with such a choice, there is some sense in

Those who have free seats at a play hiss first.

Chinese proverb

That which costs little is less valued.

Miguel de Cervantes, Spanish writer, 1547–1616

FIGURE 5.10

Cognitive Dissonance and the Effects of Initiations

Participants' attitudes toward the quality of the discussion in the Aronson and Mills (1959) experiment was significantly influenced by the "price" they had to pay to join the group. Based on cognitive dissonance theory, why did those women in the severe initiation condition express greater liking for the quality of the discussion?

Source: E. Aronson and J. Mills, "The Effect of Severity of Initiation on Liking for a Group" in *Journal of Abnormal and Social Psychology*, 59: 177–181, American Psychological Association, 1959.

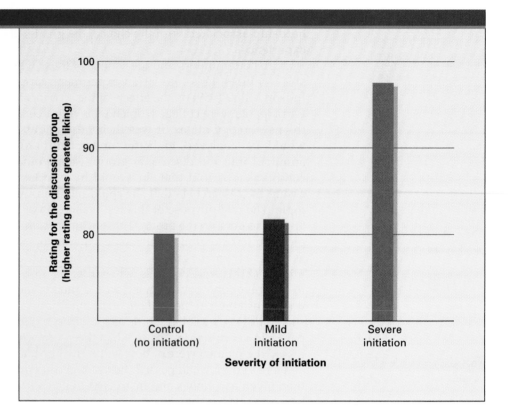

Imagine that you read a story in the newspaper about a woman who is the leader of a UFO cult.

She claims that beings from another planet have told her that the entire west coast of North and South America will be destroyed by a flood on a specific date. Based on this belief, many of her followers quit their jobs, sell their property, and leave their families. However, on the specified date, nothing happens. Based on cognitive dissonance theory, how do you think the leader of this cult and her followers will respond to this disconfirmation of their beliefs?

justifying to themselves not only the actions of their spiritual leader, but their own actions as well.

POSTDECISION DISSONANCE AND ALTERED PERCEPTIONS

A few years ago, a student in our department applied to several graduate programs in social psychology and was accepted into three of his top choices. Following a long process of weighing the strengths and weaknesses of each school, he made his choice. Shortly thereafter, I saw him on campus and asked if he had any regrets. "No, Dr. Franzoi," he said with genuine sincerity. "Since making my decision, I'm even more certain I made the right choice." Then, being the bright student that he was, he smiled and said, "Now I really understand the concept of postdecision dissonance."

What did this aspiring social psychologist mean by this last statement? He merely meant that he had firsthand experience with a phenomenon that Festinger first described in the 1950s. Festinger stated that making a decision often arouses dissonance. He explained that whenever we must decide between attractive alternatives, the final choice is to some extent inconsistent with some of our beliefs. That is, as soon as we *commit* ourselves to a particular course of action, the attractive aspects of the unchosen alternatives and the unattractive aspects of our choice are inconsistent with our decision. The more difficult or important the decision, the greater the amount of postdecision dissonance. Because of our tendency to react to decisions in this manner, we often try to reduce dissonance by *altering our perceptions* of the choices we had entertained prior to making our final choice. We do this by improving our evaluation of the chosen alternative and lowering our evaluations of the unchosen alternatives (Frenkl & Doob, 1976). Such after-the-fact, altered perceptions have been found in the behavior of consumers following product choices (Gilovich et al., 1995; Murphy & Miller, 1997), voters on election day (Regan & Kilduff, 1988), and even bettors at a racetrack (Knox & Inkster, 1968). Because votes, bets, and many product purchases cannot be changed once a decision has been made, people who commit themselves are motivated to reduce post-

decision dissonance. In these circumstances, the only way for people to reduce their dissonance is to convince themselves that they made the right choice.

COGNITIVE CONSISTENCY IS NOT A UNIVERSAL MOTIVE

In Festinger's initial formulation of his theory, he assumed that everyone has an equal desire to engage in cognitively consistent actions. However, Australian social psychologist Yoshihisa Kashima (1987) later suggested that this desire may be more descriptive of individualist cultures than those that have a collectivist orientation. He argued that this belief in the need for consistency is based on the premise that the person is an independent entity unaffected by the social context. In a series of survey studies of Australian (individualist) and Japanese (collectivist) college students, Kashima and his colleagues (1992) found support for this reasoning: the Australians held stronger beliefs about attitude-behavior consistency than did the Japanese. These results, and those of other studies (Heine & Lehman, 1997), suggest that people from collectivist cultures perceive behavior to be less consistent with attitudes, and thus, they may be less driven by the desire to maintain cognitive consistency.

An illustration of the weaker attitude-behavior consistency need can be seen in the Japanese notion of the self. In Japanese culture, there are two important aspects to the self: "omote" (front) is presented to the public as a socially acceptable aspect of the self, whereas "ura" (back) is that aspect of the self that is hidden from the public (Bachnik, 1992). The Japanese value both self-aspects and teach their young how to appropriately use them. Thus, when presenting omote, not acting according to one's true attitudes is perfectly acceptable and would not cause dissonance. For example, in one study, Japanese and American students read episodes in which hypothetical characters had to choose between honestly expressing their attitudes or not doing so to maintain social appropriateness (Iwao, 1989). As expected, American students were more likely to favor attitude-consistent choices than were their Japanese counterparts. For instance, in one hypothetical situation, a father privately disapproved of his daughter marrying someone of another race. Almost half of the American students (49 percent) stated that it would be wrong for the father to think to himself that he would never allow the marriage yet tell the couple that he favored it. On the contrary, less than 7 percent of the Japanese felt this sort of attitude-discrepant behavior was inappropriate. In summary, then, what many North Americans and other individualists consider to be discrepant and psychologically aversive—namely, believing one thing but saying something else—may not be as troubling to people from other cultures with a collectivist orientation.

If you are from an individualistic culture, you might be thinking, "I don't often get upset with acting differently from my attitudes. What gives?" My response would be that beyond cultural considerations, research also indicates that some people tolerate cognitive inconsistencies better than others. Spend a few minutes completing the *Preference for Consistency Scale* in table 5.5. Robert Cialdini and his colleagues (1995) have found that people who score high on this scale are highly motivated to keep their behavior consistent with their attitudes, as predicted by cognitive dissonance theory. In contrast, those who score low on this preference for consistency scale are much less bothered by inconsistent actions, and instead, appear open and oriented to flexibility in their behavior. Given these diverging motivational patterns, it isn't surprising that those with a high preference for consistency are more likely to experience cognitive dissonance than those with a low consistency preference.

In the final analysis, when we consider the universality of the cognitive consistency motive, it appears that at least two factors can derail expected cognitive dissonance effects when otherwise they should be aroused: a person's cultural upbringing may make attitude-discrepant behavior an appropriate and valued option, and a person's underlying psychological needs may reduce the aversiveness of attitude-discrepant acts.

SEVERAL THEORIES HAVE CHALLENGED COGNITIVE DISSONANCE THEORY

In addition to questioning the universality of the cognitive consistency motive, a number of other researchers have challenged different aspects of cognitive dissonance theory and have offered various alterations or outright replacements of the original model.

SELF-PERCEPTION EXPLANATIONS

The first and most serious challenge to cognitive dissonance theory came from Bem's self-perception theory. As you recall from our previous discussion, this theory claims that we infer our attitudes by observing our own behavior and the context in which it occurs, much as we do when perceiving other people's actions. According to Bem, when people behave inconsistently, they first seek explanations outside themselves for their behavior, and when they cannot find a probable *external* cause for their behavior, they assume that there must be an internal cause, namely an attitude. This search for a cause of behavior is not fueled by a need to reduce an unpleasant psychological state—as is assumed in cognitive dissonance theory—but rather, it is based on calm rationality.

To test his hypothesis, Bem (1967) had people simply read a description of the Festinger and Carlsmith (1959) study, in which a person performs a dull task and then is paid either $1 or $20 to tell someone else that it was fun and interesting. Based on their observation of this study's procedures, Bem had readers guess the person's attitude toward the task. Despite the fact that these people experienced no cognitive dissonance, the pattern of results duplicated that found in the original study. As the readers perceived the situation, the person who was paid $20 to say the task was interesting really was lying—he did it for the money. However, the person who was paid $1 must have been sincere, because the small amount of

TABLE 5.5

The Preference for Consistency Scale

Instructions

The extent to which people have a preference for consistency is measured by items on the Preference for Consistency Scale (PCS: Cialdini et al., 1995). To take the PCS, read each item below and then indicate how well each statement describes you using the following scale:

1 = Strongly disagree
2 = Disagree
3 = Somewhat disagree
4 = Slightly disagree
5 = Neither agree nor disagree
6 = Slightly agree
7 = Somewhat agree
8 = Agree
9 = Strongly agree

_____ 1. It is important to me that those who know me can predict what I will do.

_____ 2. I want to be described by others as a stable, predictable person.

_____ 3. The appearance of consistency is an important part of the image I present to the world.

_____ 4. An important requirement for any friend of mine is personal consistency.

_____ 5. I typically prefer to do things the same way.

_____ 6. I want my close friends to be predictable.

_____ 7. It is important to me that others view me as a stable person.

_____ 8. I make an effort to appear consistent to others.

_____ 9. It doesn't bother me much if my actions are inconsistent.

Directions for Scoring

The last PCS item (#9) is reverse-scored; that is, for this item a lower rating actually indicates a higher level of consistency preference. Before summing the items, recode item 9 so that 1 = 9, 2 = 8, 3 = 7, 4 = 6, 6 = 4, 7 = 3, 8 = 2, 9 = 1. To calculate your preference for consistency score, add up your responses to the 9 items.

When Cialdini and his colleagues developed the PCS in 1995, the mean score for college students was about 48. The higher your score is above this value, the greater is your preference for consistency. The lower your score is below this value, the less of this preference you probably possess.

Source: From Cialdini, R., Trost, M., & Newsom , J. (1995). Preference for consistency: The development of a valid measure and the discovery of surprising behavioral implications. *Journal of Personality and Social Psychology, 69:* 318–328.

money certainly wasn't enough to justify lying. What this study suggests is that cognitive dissonance may not be necessary in explaining how behavioral inconsistencies can cause attitude change. Table 5.6 compares the cognitive dissonance and self-perception theories.

Which of these two competing theories is correct? Based on a number of studies, it appears that *both* are correct, but in different situations. Fazio and his colleagues (1977) contend that people are most likely to experience dissonance, and respond in line with cognitive dissonance theory, when their behavior is sharply discrepant with their attitudes and there is no external justification for it. However, when the attitude-behavior inconsistency is only mild, these same

TABLE 5.6

Cognitive Dissonance and Self-Perception Theories Compared

Cognitive Dissonance Theory	Self-Perception Theory
Attitudes directly known	Attitudes inferred from behavior
Attitudes in "dissonance groups" are distortions	Attitudes in "dissonance groups" are rationally inferred
Unpleasant affect necessary for attitude formation	No unpleasant affect or negative drive state involved in attitude formation

When Is Dissonance or Self-Perception of Attitudes Most Likely?

Dissonance is most likely when the attitude in question is important to the self or the attitude-discrepancy is large	Self-perception of attitudes is most likely when the attitude-behavior discrepancy is small

people tend to behave in ways expected by self-perception theory. Put a slightly different way, Aronson (1969) suggests that what will determine which theory is the best explanation for attitude-behavior inconsistencies is whether the behavior in question is central to the self. According to Aronson, cognitive dissonance theory makes its strongest predictions when a person's freely chosen behavior is inconsistent with an important aspect of the self-concept. Thus, dissonance is likely if the attitude is important to the self or the discrepancy between attitude and behavior is substantial. When the issue is not important to the self or the attitude-behavior inconsistency is small, then self-perception processes are likely to operate.

SELF-AFFIRMATION EXPLANATIONS

Self-Affirmation Theory

A theory predicting that people will often cope with specific threats to the integrity of their self-concept by reminding themselves of other unrelated but cherished aspects of their self-concept.

Another interpretation of dissonance theory with a focus on the self is Claude Steele's **self-affirmation theory.** According to Steele (1988), when we act in a manner inconsistent with our sense of honesty or integrity, this causes a threat to our self-concept. We ask ourselves, "If I acted this way, am I really who I think I am?" Steele contends that when our self-concept is threatened in this manner, we often can reduce or entirely avoid the negative affect that Festinger called cognitive dissonance by affirming our integrity in some other unrelated area of our lives. This self-affirmation can be achieved in many ways and does not necessarily have to resolve the specific dilemma that threatened the self in the first place. Thus, according to self-affirmation theory, we can reduce dissonance without resolving the self-inconsistency that originally caused it.

In one study supporting the self-affirmation perspective (Steele & Liu, 1981), researchers induced participants to write an essay opposing state funding for handicapped services. Before writing this essay, some participants were told that they would later be asked to help a blind student, while others were not given this expectation. Results indicated that only those participants who were not given a chance to help the blind changed their attitudes to be more consistent with the essay. In other words, if people could reaffirm their sense of self-worth, they felt no need to resolve the specific inconsistency that initially threatened the self. This study and others suggest that inconsistency between our attitudes and our behavior may not be the motivating feature of cognitive dissonance (Aronson et al., 1995; Steele et al., 1993). Instead, *threats to the integrity of the self* may be the key motivator, and any response useful in restoring integrity reduces dissonance. Although research indicates that we often will self-affirm when our self-concepts are threatened, it is also true that *level of self-esteem* affects our ability to actually engage in self-affirmation. That is, because people with high self-esteem have more positive aspects of their self-concept to affirm than those low in self-esteem, they find self-affirmation easier to engage in than individuals with low self-esteem (Dodgson & Wood, 1998; Murray et al., 1998).

As you can see, cognitive dissonance theory is an excellent example of a "fertile" theory (see chapter 1) that continues to generate novel ways of understanding attitudes (Harmons-Jones et al., 1996; Shultz et al., 1999). What we now know is that cognitive dissonance does not always result when we act in a counterattitudinal manner. Whether dissonance is aroused depends not only on how central the need for cognitive consistency is in our thinking, but also on whether the attitude-behavior discrepancy is important to the self and is substantial. And even when the attitude-behavior discrepancy is important and substantial, dissonance might still be avoided if we can redirect self-awareness to some other valued self-aspects.

SECTION SUMMARY

An important motive in many people's attitudes and behavior is the need for *cognitive consistency. Cognitive dissonance theory* states that if people simultaneously hold two cognitions that are inconsistent, they will experience an unpleasant emotion known as cognitive dissonance, which they will attempt to reduce. Although cognitive dissonance theorists initially assumed that dissonance always results when one acts in a counterattitudinal manner, what we now know is that this is not the case. Dissonance is most likely to occur when the attitude in question is important to the self or the discrepancy between attitude and behavior is substantial.

A FINAL WORD ON THE ATTITUDE JOURNEY

My goal in this chapter was to guide you through the "theoretical attitude maze" so that you gained a greater understanding of how you and others evaluate your social world. Social psychologists' attempts to better understand the attitude concept has been a journey in which different theoretical perspectives have taken turns trying to make sense of the diverse empirical findings that had accumulated over the years (Eagly, 1992). In the 1960s, cognitive dissonance theory and other motivation-based theories held everyone's interest. In the 1970s and mid-1980s the cognitive approach was the perspective of choice among most attitude researchers. Now, as we begin the twenty-first century, besides the continued development of various cognitive theories, there has been a new wave of interest in the motivational point of view, as well as an attempt to integrate all the perspectives we have discussed into a unified analysis of attitude formation and change. Accompanying this increased theoretical sophistication and diversity is a renewed confidence that attitudes can substantially predict future behavior (Kraus, 1995). One of the most successful attempts at theoretical integration is the *elaboration likelihood model* of Richard Petty and John Cacioppo (1986), which we will closely examine in our chapter 6 analysis of persuasion.

APPLICATIONS

HOW DO REFERENCE GROUPS SHAPE YOUR SOCIAL AND POLITICAL ATTITUDES?

ave you ever observed pleasant dinner conversation change into bitter accusations and denunciations due to one person discovering that another held different attitudes about some political or social issue? Have you yourself been one of these dinner combatants?

Our values and many of our attitudes are often determined by the groups to which we seek membership or with which we identify. A **reference group** is a group to which people orient themselves, using its standards to judge themselves and the world. An important defining characteristic of a reference group is that people have an *emotional attachment* to it and refer to it for guidance, even if they are not actual members.[1] Reference groups can be large and inclusive, such as an entire nation or religion, but they can also be much smaller, such as one's family or friends.

Reference Group

A group to which people orient themselves, using its standards to judge themselves and the world.

One of the first and best studies investigating reference group influence on attitudes was the research of Theodore Newcomb in the 1930s documenting college students' shift from social and political conservatism when they entered college to liberalism when they graduated. Newcomb's research began in 1934 when he was hired as a young faculty member at the recently established Bennington College for women in Vermont. This new college was very exclusive, with almost all of the students coming from upper class, politically conservative New England families. In contrast, Newcomb and most of the other young faculty were very liberal in their social views. Thus, the first-year entering students were moving from one social context—a conservative family and social life— into a new context in which the authority figures and role models held exactly opposite social views.

Due to its small size (three hundred students and faculty) and its location in a relatively isolated

Political and social attitudes developed by many college students at Bennington College in the 1930s continued to influence their behavior throughout the rest of their lives.

area of rural Vermont, Bennington fostered a great deal of interaction between the faculty and the female student body. This unique convergence of circumstances prompted Newcomb to test a belief that he had about how a person's attitudes are influenced by changes in their reference groups. To accomplish this task, Newcomb (1943) tested the social and political attitudes of the arriving first-year students, and he remeasured their attitudes each year until they graduated. His findings indicated that with each passing semester, the students' social and political attitudes became increasingly liberal. As one student explained her shift in attitudes over the course of time, "I simply got filled with new ideas here, and the only possible formulation of all of them was to adopt a radical approach" (Newcomb, 1958, p. 273). Another stated, "I'm easily influenced by people whom I respect, and the people who rescued me when I was down and out, intellectually, gave me a radical intellectual approach" (Newcomb, 1958, p. 273).

Newcomb believed that this attitude change was due to the students' disengagement from their conservative hometown reference group and their integration into a new, more liberal reference group at Bennington. Yet, not all students experienced such a

---

[1]Because emotional attachment and not membership itself is the key factor in defining reference groups, they are broader in scope than ingroups, which are discussed in chapters 2, 7, and 9.

"radical" shift in their attitudes during their four years at Bennington. Indeed, some students maintained their conservative political perspective throughout their college years. How did these students differ from the rest of the Bennington population? Newcomb discovered that these students did not experience a shift in their reference groups. They spent their vacations with their parents and frequently traveled home on weekends, and therefore did not blend into the Bennington culture.

How might the Bennington study relate to your own college experience? During your time at college, have your social and political attitudes changed from what they were in high school? To what degree have these attitudes been shaped by your college experiences?

The importance of reference groups in maintaining attitudes even when the person is no longer immersed within the group itself was demonstrated by Newcomb in a twenty-five-year follow-up study of the women who attended Bennington College in the late 1930s (Newcomb et al., 1967). In the 1960s, these Bennington alumnae were in their 40s and 50s and were also in the top 1 percent of the population in socioeconomic status. Comparing them with non-Bennington-educated women of comparable wealth, age, religion, and geographic region, Newcomb found that the Bennington women's political attitudes and behavior were much more liberal. In addition, the Bennington women's selection of a spouse and friends was partly based on their liberal political preferences.

Other studies, testing different social groups, have replicated Newcomb's overall findings (Marwell et al., 1987; McAdam, 1989). Together, they illustrate the important role that reference groups play in shaping and maintaining social and political attitudes, as well as the role that these attitudes play in shaping the life course of those who hold them. To a substantial degree, when you select a college or a university to attend following high-school graduation, you may also be inadvertently choosing a new social and political perspective. Sometimes, these newly adopted political and social attitudes become the "little surprises" that young adults spring upon their parents around the dinner table during semester breaks and summer holidays. If you have had such conversations with your parents, or believe you will have some in the not-too-distant future, now you can also describe the social psychological dynamics of your political transformation as well. Pleasant dining!

FEATURED STUDY
THE PERSISTENCE OF POLITICAL ATTITUDES

Alwin, D. F., Cohen, R. L., & Newcomb, T. M. (1991). *Political attitudes over the life span: The Bennington women after fifty years.* Madison, WI: University of Wisconsin Press.

The first two studies of the women who attended Bennington College in the 1930s and 1940s are well-known contributions to the attitudes literature. During the 1980s, Newcomb and his coworkers again recontacted these former Bennington students, who were now in their 60s and 70s, to remeasure their political attitudes. In this third study, the researchers sought to more extensively analyze the patterns of stability and change in the women's attitudes in order to better understand the lifelong development of attitudes more generally.

METHOD

By the 1980s, of the 527 women who participated in the original studies, 77 had died and 51 could not be located or contacted. Ultimately, 335 agreed to complete a one-hour interview, as well as a self-report questionnaire. A major problem in attempting to measure social and political attitudes over a long time interval is in finding comparable attitude measures. That is, attitude measures

TABLE 5.7

Voting Preferences of Bennington Graduates in Presidential Elections

The liberal political attitudes that many Bennington students developed in the 1930s were maintained over the years and are reflected in their presidential preferences, where they consistently voted for the more liberal Democratic candidate in all elections studied. In contrast, women with similar educational background and age tended to prefer the more conservative Republican candidates. Where do you think your own university environment stacks up on the liberal-conservative dimension? Have your political attitudes shifted in the direction of this dominant campus view during your time in college?

Election Year	Conservative Candidate	Liberal Candidate
1952		
Bennington women	43%	57%
Comparable women	64%	36%
1960		
Bennington women	26%	74%
Comparable women	75%	25%
1968		
Bennington women	33%	67%
Comparable women	79%	19%
1976		
Bennington women	31%	69%
Comparable women	55%	45%
1984		
Bennington women	27%	72%
Comparable women	73%	26%

Source: Based on data from Alwin, Cohen, & Newcomb (1991) and the Institute for Social Research, *National Election Studies, 1952–1984.*

that were appropriate and valid in the 1930s may no longer be meaningful fifty years later because of drastic changes in social issues. Although the researchers were able to replicate some attitude measures exactly, others had to be created to equal the conceptual meaning of earlier measures. In crafting these new attitude measures, the researchers matched them to measures in an existing large national sample that was used as the comparison group in the study.

RESULTS AND DISCUSSION

The results supported Newcomb's initial hypothesis about the strength of reference groups. The women's liberal reference groups, forged during their college days a half century ago, still significantly influenced their lives. As you can see in table 5.7, when compared with other college-educated women in their same age group, the Bennington graduates consistently preferred the more liberal candidate in each presidential election from 1952 to 1984. They also expressed greater interest in following government affairs and political events. Despite the fact that college-educated women of the 1930s generation were much more likely than noncollege-educated women to align themselves with the more conservative Republican Party throughout their lives, this was not the case for the Bennington women. In fact, their social and political attitudes were even more intensely liberal than most women of their generation.

In summary, the present findings, combined with those from the previous two studies, highlight the important role that reference groups play in shaping life choices. Following their college days, the Bennington women to some extent selected social environments that were compatible with their own political orientations, which further strengthened those orientations and partially immunized them from alternative views. In this respect, the Bennington study nicely illustrates the role that attitudes play in regulating social relations.

 WEB SITES accessed through http://www.mhhe.com/franzoi2

Web sites for this chapter focus on attitude formation and change, including cognitive consistency theories and how consistency needs can be used to increase retail sales.

Theories of Cognitive Consistency

This web page analyzes cognitive consistency theories and explores the question of whether cognitive consistency needs can be used to increase retail sales.

Steve's Primer of Practical Persuasion and Influence

This web page discusses the elements of attitude theory, including vivid examples that demonstrate how attitudes function in daily living.

CHAPTER 6

PERSUASION

ormer dairy farmer Fred Tuttle is a man who can be easily under-estimated. At the age of 79, and with a worrisome health history of three heart attacks, cataracts, arthritis, diabetes, and prostate cancer, Tuttle is a most unlikely candidate for public office. Yet after playing the lead character in a low-budget movie about a retired farmer who runs for Congress, Fred decided to enter the 1998 Vermont Republican primary for the U.S. Senate. His opponent was Jack McMullen, an energetic 56-year-old millionaire who spent $475,000 on his bid for the nomination. Fred spent $200. McMullen has law and business degrees from Harvard. Fred was a tenth-grade dropout. McMullen crisscrossed the state pressing the flesh and putting out position papers on the issues. Fred basically sat on his porch, nursing his arthritic knee. In the movie, Fred's character wins the election by one vote, yet in real life, Fred beat McMullen, 24,561 votes to 19,962. Why was he able to persuade Vermont voters to elect him as the Republican Senate candidate?

As you can perhaps tell by the accompanying photo of Fred, one of his best assets as a persuader is his likability. His genuine grandpa cuddliness, combined with a winning smile, made Fred an extremely likable figure for many voters. Being a minor movie celebrity didn't hurt him, either. He also has in abundance something that McMullen has in very short supply: Vermont roots. While Fred was born in Vermont and can trace his state ancestry back to 1832, his opponent moved from Massachusetts just one year ago. In one of their debates, Fred humorously exposed McMullen's lack of knowledge about the state by asking him to pronounce the name of a fairly well-known Vermont town, Calais. When McMullen mispronounced it, Fred responded, "It may be cah-*lay* in France, but it is *cah*-las in Vermont." McMullen also mistakenly thought that cows, a Vermont fixture, had six teats instead of four. Following such gaffes, McMullen was perceived to be an outsider who thought his money could buy

Effective persuaders come in many forms. Just ask millionaire Jack McMullen who was overwhelmingly defeated by this man, Fred Tuttle, in the 1998 Vermont Republican primary for the U.S. Senate. Based on this photo, what quality of a good persuader does Tuttle appear to possess?

him the election. Fred's down-home quality made him an extremely likable candidate at the same time that McMullen's outsider status lowered his overall credibility.[1]

In this chapter, we are going to examine the psychological dynamics of **persuasion,** which is the process of consciously attempting to change attitudes through the transmission of some message. What I want you to understand from the outset is that it is not just the Fred Tuttles and the Jack McMullens of the world who try to change attitudes. We all engage in this universal avocation. If you doubt this assertion, read on and I will attempt to change your mind.

Persuasion

The process of consciously attempting to change attitudes through the transmission of some message.

THE EVOLUTION OF THEORY AND RESEARCH ON PERSUASION

There are many different ways to change attitudes. Yet before exploring these avenues, let us first examine how social psychologists' views of persuasion have changed over the years (Petty, 1997).

THE MESSAGE-LEARNING APPROACH IDENTIFIED WHAT STRENGTHENS AND WEAKENS A PERSUASIVE MESSAGE

One of the first and most influential research programs on attitude change was developed during and after World War II, under the direction of Carl Hovland at Yale University (McGuire, 1995). In this endeavor, Hovland collaborated with other prominent social psychologists such as Irving Janis, Harold Kelley, Herbert Kelman, and Muzafer Sherif (Hovland et al., 1949, 1953). Their *message-learning* approach to understanding persuasion, which was later elaborated and extended by William McGuire in the 1960s, employed basic principles of learning theory to explain the distinctions between effective and ineffective persuasive communications. As illustrated in figure 6.1, attitude change was assumed to follow a series of stages. First, we must pay *attention* to the message; second, we must *comprehend* the message; and third, we must *accept* the message. Each stage in this process is dependent on the preceding stage. Comprehension cannot occur, for example, if we do not pay attention to the message. Likewise, a message will not be accepted if it is not understood. However, if we do attend to and understand the message, acceptance will occur if the rewards or incentives for the new attitudinal position outweigh those associated with the old attitude.

To understand the process of attitude change, the Yale researchers conducted experiments that focused on four factors that influence persuasion: (1) *source variables,* (2) *message variables,* (3) *medium* or *channel variables,* and (4) *target variables.* They attempted to explain how a person or group (the source) communicates a message through some medium or channel to change the attitudes of some target person or group. Put simply, they studied *who* says *what* by *what means* and to *whom.*

THE COGNITIVE-RESPONSE APPROACH SEEKS TO IDENTIFY WHAT MAKES PEOPLE THINK ABOUT PERSUASIVE ARGUMENTS

The message-learning approach is generally credited with providing a good deal of insight into *when* and *how* persuasion occurs. In contrast, the more recent *cognitive-response* approach has been helpful in better understanding *why* people change

---

[1]Fred Tuttle later lost the Senate election to Democratic incumbent Patrick Leahy. His candidacy was seriously undercut by his family's concerns for his health ("I hope they have more sense than to vote for my husband," his wife declared) and his admission that Leahy not only knew how many teats there were on a cow, but that he had done a good job as senator and should be reelected!

FIGURE 6.1

The Message-Learning Approach to Understanding Persuasion

According to the message-learning approach to persuasion (Hovland et al., 1953), attitude change follows a series of stages: (1) attention to the message, (2) comprehension of the message, and (3) acceptance of the message.

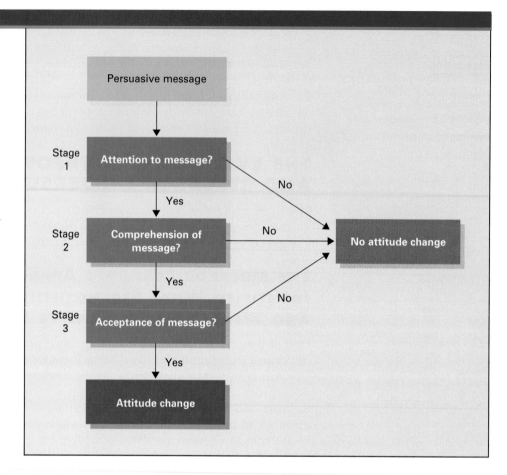

Elaboration Likelihood Model

A theory that there are two ways in which persuasive messages can cause attitude change, each differing in the amount of cognitive effort or elaboration they require.

Central Route to Persuasion

Persuasion that occurs when people think carefully about a communication and are influenced by the strength of its arguments.

Peripheral Route to Persuasion

Persuasion that occurs when people do not think carefully about a communication and instead are influenced by cues that are irrelevant to the content or quality of the communication.

their attitudes in response to persuasive messages (Chaiken, 1987; Petty & Cacioppo, 1986). Further, whereas the message-learning approach takes a relatively *passive* view of the recipient of persuasion, the cognitive-response approach conceives of people as being *active* participants in the persuasion process. That is, the thoughts that people generate in response to a message are believed to be the end result of information-processing activity (Chaiken & Trope, 1999). Social psychologists who adopt this perspective attempt to systematically analyze (1) what people attend to when they receive a persuasive communication, and (2) how their cognitive assessment of the appeal influences their current attitudes.

The most influential theory to develop out of the cognitive-response approach is Richard Petty and John Cacioppo's (1986) **elaboration likelihood model** (ELM), which assumes that people want to be correct in their attitudes. The term *elaboration likelihood* refers to the probability that the target of a persuasive message will elaborate (that is, carefully analyze and attempt to comprehend) the information contained in the message. According to the model, we tend to engage in either high or low elaboration when attending to and processing persuasive messages. When motivated and able to think carefully about the content of a message (high elaboration), we are influenced by the strength and quality of the arguments: Petty and Cacioppo say we have taken the **central route to persuasion.** However, when unable or unwilling to analyze message content, we take the **peripheral route to persuasion,** where we pay attention to cues that are irrelevant to the content or quality of the communication (low elaboration), such as the attractiveness of the communicator or the sheer amount of information presented. By attending to these peripheral cues, we can evaluate a message without engaging in any extensive thinking about the actual issues under consideration. This means that it isn't necessary for a person who takes the peripheral route to comprehend the content of a

FIGURE 6.2

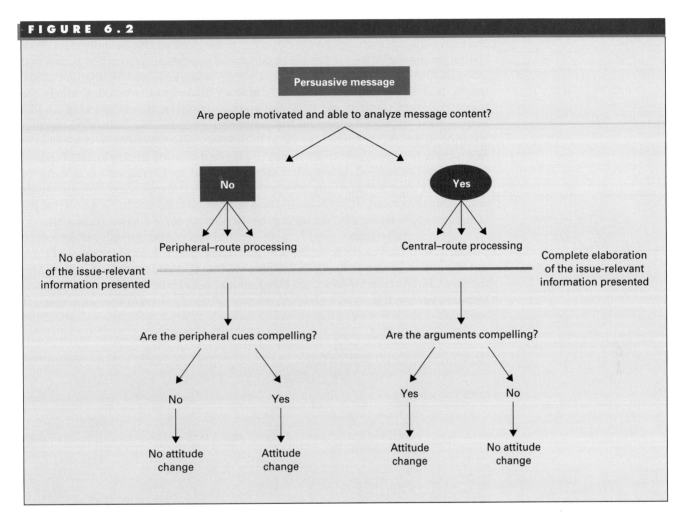

Persuasive message

Are people motivated and able to analyze message content?

No

Yes

Peripheral–route processing

Central–route processing

No elaboration of the issue-relevant information presented

Complete elaboration of the issue-relevant information presented

Are the peripheral cues compelling?

Are the arguments compelling?

No

Yes

Yes

No

No attitude change

Attitude change

Attitude change

No attitude change

Two Routes to Persuasion

The elaboration likelihood model describes how people evaluate persuasive messages based on their ability and motivation to analyze its contents. As the likelihood of thinking about the attitude object increases, the processes specified by the central route become more likely determinants of attitudes, and those specified by the peripheral route become less likely determinants. This process is reversed as the likelihood of thinking about the attitude object decreases. In central-route processing, message contents are carefully scrutinized before they are accepted. However, in peripheral-route processing, evaluation of the message is based on a more shallow analysis of incidental cues, such as the communicator's credibility, status, or likability. Of the two routes to persuasion, which do you think secures the most enduring attitude change?

Profound thoughts arise only in debate, with a possibility of counterargument, only when there is a possibility of expressing not only correct ideas, but also dubious ideas.

Andrei Sakharov, Russian scientist and social critic, 1921–1989

message: attitude change can occur without comprehension. This is one of the main differences between the cognitive-response approach and the message-learning approach.[2] Figure 6.2 depicts these two different persuasion routes.

Do these two different types of cognitive processes sound familiar? Think back to the chapter 4 discussion of social cognition. As flexible social thinkers, we sometimes carefully analyze all relevant factors and behave in a systematic and rational fashion, but at other times we try to save time by taking mental shortcuts. This "thoughtful" versus "lazy" way of thinking is essentially what comprises the two routes to persuasion.

[2]Although the elaboration likelihood model is the most influential of the cognitive-response theories, a related theory that also adds to our understanding of persuasion is the heuristic-systematic model developed by Shelly Chaiken (1980). Like the ELM, this model asserts that people either attempt to carefully and intentionally judge the truth of a persuasive message (systematic processing) or use simple decision rules, called heuristics, to spontaneously and automatically estimate the validity of a persuasive message (heuristic processing). Because these two theories are similar in many important ways, for simplicity's sake, I will use the ELM's terminology in describing the cognitive processing of persuasive messages.

According to the elaboration likelihood model and other cognitive-response theories, although attitude change can occur through either the thoughtful mode of central processing or the lazy mode of peripheral processing, research indicates that attitudes formed by means of the lazy route are weaker, less resistant to counterarguments, and less predictive of actual behavior than those formed through the thoughtful route (Petty et al., 1995). An analogy might be that if attitudes are like houses, then attitudes formed by the peripheral route are like houses made from straw or sticks. They require little effort to develop and are extremely vulnerable to destruction. In contrast, attitudes formed by the central route are like houses made of bricks. They take a good deal of effort to construct and are strong and durable. As we know from both childhood fairy tales and our own life experiences, well-built houses and highly elaborated attitudes are the best insurance against the huffing and puffing of someone with either a strong set of lungs or a strong set of counterarguments.

To more fully understand how thoughtful or lazy processing can influence people's perspectives on an issue, and how other psychological processes figure into the persuasion equation, let's examine the four related factors first explored by the Yale Communication Research Program and later elaborated by the cognitive-response perspective: *source variables, message variables, channel variables,* and *target variables.*

SECTION SUMMARY

The process of consciously attempting to change attitudes through the transmission of some message is known as *persuasion.* The *message-learning approach* is generally credited with providing a good deal of insight into *when* and *how* persuasion occurs, while the more recent *cognitive-response approach* has been helpful in better understanding *why* people change their attitudes in response to persuasive messages. Attitude researchers who adopt this cognitive perspective have attempted to systematically analyze what people attend to when they receive a persuasive communication, and how their cognitive assessment of the appeal influences their current attitudes. According to the *elaboration likelihood model,* people tend to engage in either high or low elaboration when attending to and processing persuasive messages. These two contrasting ways of thinking about a persuasive message are known respectively as the *central route* and the *peripheral route* to persuasion. Central-route processing involves a good deal of cognitive activity, whereas peripheral-route processing focuses on cues less central to the message content.

SOURCE VARIABLES: WHO IS COMMUNICATING?

One factor that is a peripheral cue to the actual content of the persuasive communication is the deliverer of the message. Research indicates that the *source* of a communication is important in determining whether the message will be effective in producing attitude change. This is especially true when the recipient lacks the motivation to process the message arguments carefully (Petty et al., 1981b). What is it that makes one source better at persuasion than another?

LOW CREDIBILITY IS A DISCOUNTING CUE

More than 2,300 years ago, the Greek philosopher Aristotle specified one of the critical elements in a communicator's ability to persuade:

We believe good men more fully and more readily than others; this is true generally whatever the question is, and absolutely true where exact certainty is impossible and opinions are divided . . . his character may almost be called the most effective means of persuasion he possesses. (Roberts, 1954, pp. 24–25)

Building on Aristotle's insights, contemporary researchers contend that those listening to the source of a persuasive message pay a good deal of attention to his or her *credibility* or believability (Cecil et al., 1996). The Yale group stated that credibility is mainly based on two factors: *expertise,* which is the amount of knowledge that a communicator is assumed to possess, and *trustworthiness,* which is the perceived intention of the communicator to deceive.

DISCOUNTING CUES

Not surprisingly, research has found that high-credibility sources are more effective in producing attitude change than are low-credibility sources, at least in the short run. A source's low credibility is a *discounting cue* that results in the audience rejecting the message. For example, in one study, Hovland and Walter Weiss (1951) asked American college students to read an article proposing that nuclear-powered submarines were both feasible and safe (at the time, no such submarines had yet been built). Some of those reading the article were told that the author was J. Robert Oppenheimer, the American physicist who supervised the construction of the atomic bomb. Others were told that the source was the Soviet newspaper *Pravda.* The researchers assumed that during the height of the Cold War, the average American would perceive Oppenheimer as a highly credible source and would consider *Pravda* a low-credibility source. True to expectations, readers who believed the article was written by the highly credible Oppenheimer were more persuaded by its message immediately after reading it than those who believed they were reading a Soviet article.

THE SLEEPER EFFECT

If this was all there was to learn about source credibility, we might conclude that persuasion seems pretty straightforward and uncomplicated. Yet four weeks after the initial reading of the submarine article, Hovland and Weiss again measured their participants' attitudes toward nuclear-powered submarines and found a surprise in the responses. As you can see in figure 6.3, the highly credible Oppenheimer had lost some of his persuasive power, whereas *Pravda* had actually gained in persuasiveness. Similar studies by Hovland and Weiss revealed the same delayed effects; highly credible sources are more persuasive immediately after the message presentation than less credible sources, but over time the credibility factor seems to weaken. The researchers called this enhanced, delayed effect that the low-credible source has on attitude change the **sleeper effect.**

What could explain the sleeper effect? Herbert Kelman and Hovland (1953) believed it occurs because people who receive a message from a low-credibility source eventually forget where they heard it and then are influenced by the message content alone. If true, this would also explain why the highly credible Oppenheimer lost some of his persuasive power over time—the credible source became disassociated from the message. To test this hypothesis, the researchers extended the Hovland and Weiss (1951) design by adding a condition in which participants were reminded of the source's identity before their attitudes were reassessed. If the sleeper effect occurred because people forgot that the persuasive message came from a low-credible source, then it could be eliminated by reestablishing this link. This is exactly what happened. Participants who were not reminded of the source showed the expected sleeper effect, but those who were reminded did not.

Sleeper Effect

The delayed effectiveness of a persuasive message from a noncredible source.

FIGURE 6.3

The Sleeper Effect

Immediately following the reception of a message, people are more likely to be persuaded by a highly credible source than one of low credibility. However, as Hovland and Weiss (1951) found, over time, the message becomes disassociated from its source, resulting in less agreement with the highly credible source and more agreement with the source having lower credibility. What is a possible explanation for this effect?

Source: Data from C. I. Hovland and W. Weiss, "The Influence of Source Credibility on Communication Effectiveness" in *Public Opinion Quarterly*, 15:635–650, University of Chicago Press, 1951.

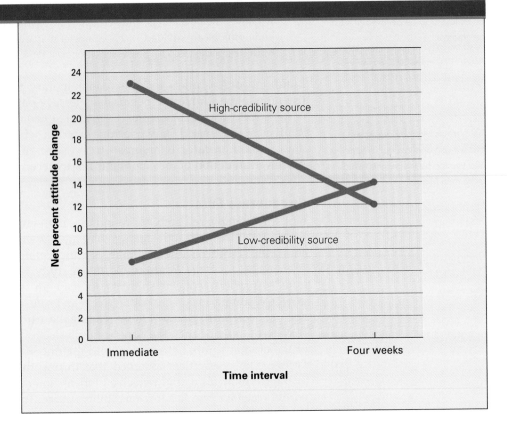

More recent studies on the sleeper effect (Gruder et al., 1978; Pratkanis et al., 1988) have found that it is most likely to occur when the following conditions have been met:

1. The message must be convincing enough by itself to lead to persuasion.
2. People are given information discounting the credibility of the source *following* the persuasive message, not before.
3. The impact of the discounting cue (the low-credibility information) decays in memory faster than the persuasive message.

If these conditions are met, although people who receive such persuasive messages are likely to initially dismiss them due to the noncredible source, over time they will be somewhat persuaded by the message content because they've forgotten where it originated.

ATTRACTIVENESS ENHANCES PERSUASIVENESS

During the 1920s, when feminists were demonstrating against women's inequality, Edward Bernays, the nephew of Sigmund Freud, was designing an ad campaign for the cigarette industry to persuade women to smoke cigarettes. He thought that cigarettes could serve as a "torch of freedom" symbol for women if he could somehow dramatically show attractive and "liberated" women using the product. Bernays arranged to have a group of attractive, "liberated," cigarette smoking women marching in the 1929 Easter Parade in midtown Manhattan (Greaves, 1996). Women throughout the country saw photographs of these women in their local newspapers and in national magazines, and many took up the "torch of freedom" habit. Advertisers also collected endorsements from female movie stars who extolled the virtues of various brands. The rest is history: the cigarette company's profits soared with this newfound, "liberated-female" market.

It is clear that an attractive communicator can be very persuasive (Stanton et al., 1996). But what exactly determines attractiveness? Research has demonstrated that a communicator's attractiveness can be based on a number of factors, including *physical appearance, likability,* and *similarity to the audience.*

PHYSICAL APPEARANCE

Several studies have found that physically attractive persons are more effective in changing others' attitudes than less attractive individuals (Dion & Stein, 1978; Shavitt et al., 1994). In one study by Shelly Chaiken (1979), university undergraduates attempted to persuade fellow students to sign a petition to get the university to stop serving meat during breakfast and lunch. Although less attractive persuaders were only able to secure signatures 32 percent of the time, the more attractive students convinced 41 percent of the students they approached to sign the petition. Other persuasion studies have found that good looks can sometimes even overcome a poor presentation style (Pallak, 1983).

LIKABILITY

As illustrated by Fred Tuttle's surprising primary victory, besides physical appearance, being likable can also increase attractiveness. Indeed, merely saying nice things to others is often enough to get them to like you and thereby increase your ability to persuade (Berscheid & Walster, 1978; Drachman et al., 1978). The power of being likable is not lost on those in the "image-making" business. Indeed, Roger Ailes, a well-known public relations adviser to both Presidents Reagan and Bush believes likability is a persuader's most important quality:

> If you could master one element of personal communication that is more powerful than anything we've discussed, it is the quality of being *likable.* I call it the magic bullet, because if your audience likes you, they'll forgive just about everything else you do wrong. If they don't like you, you can hit every rule right on target and it doesn't matter. (Ailes, 1988, p. 81)

SIMILARITY

With their preference for Vermont-born Fred Tuttle over newcomer Jack McMullen, Vermont voters demonstrated a third determinant of attractiveness: similarity. We tend to be attracted to those who are similar to us. As a general rule, this attraction also results in us being influenced by similar others (Budesheim et al., 1996). For example, Theodore Dembroski and his colleagues (1978) found that when African-American high-school students heard an appeal from a dentist to engage in proper dental care, the message was more persuasive when it came from a dentist who was also African American rather than White.

A communicator can be similar to her or his audience in a number of ways (McCroskey et al., 1975). One way is if the two share attitudes and values ("Does she think like me?" "Are his morals like mine?"). Another way is if they have similar backgrounds ("Is he of my race or from my hometown?"). A third way is in terms of appearance ("Does he look like me?"). Of the different ways in which people could be similar to one another, perceived similarity in attitudes and values appears to be the most important in enhancing persuasion (Simons et al., 1970). This is why politicians try to present themselves as having attitudes and values in step with the majority: they understand that perceived similarity will lead to increased liking and greater persuasive power.

CRITICAL *thinking*

Commercial advertisers are acutely aware of the similarity effect and tailor their ads to enhance liking for their products. For example, television commercials are constructed in ways that reinforce the image of gender most familiar to and comfortable for their target audience at a particular time of the day. Over the next few days, observe the content of TV commericals in the morning, evening, or during weekend sports shows. Are there differences in the way women and men are portrayed?

SECTION SUMMARY

When considering the source of a persuasive message, a number of factors influence persuasiveness. Highly *credible* sources are more likely to persuade, at least initially, than less credible ones. *Attractive* communicators are also more persuasive than those who are unattractive.

MESSAGE VARIABLES: WHAT IS THE CONTENT?

Another question the Yale researchers were interested in answering was, what makes a message persuasive in its own right, independent of the source? Over the years numerous studies have attempted to better understand the characteristics of a persuasive message, including such things as the effectiveness of using facts versus vivid images; fear and humor; the use of one-sided versus two-sided arguments; the order in which arguments are presented; and the number of times the message is repeated.

VIVIDNESS CAN MAKE SOLID EVIDENCE EVEN MORE PERSUASIVE, BUT SOMETIMES IT CAN UNDERMINE IT

In trying to enhance our persuasive arguments, we can cite facts and numerical data, or we can infuse our message with vivid and colorful stories that will attract and hold our audience's attention. Advertisers use both evidence-based appeals and vivid, graphic messages in trying to convince viewers to follow a certain course of action. For example, an evidence-based message attempting to reduce teenage drunk driving may state that *"Last year, 7,514 high-school students were killed in alcohol-related automobile accidents."* On the other hand, a vividness-based appeal (see photo at top of page 197) presents no data, but instead it may offer a jarring and disturbing image that makes the negative consequences of drunk driving immediate and memorable. Other advertisers may try to persuade by combining both types of appeals in a single message (see bottom photo on p. 197).

The research literature strongly supports the notion that evidence-based appeals are effective in enhancing persuasive messages. Yet while evidence enhances persuasion, not all evidence persuades. As we have already discussed, evidence is more immediately persuasive when attributed to a highly credible source rather than to one with low credibility (Reinard, 1988). Research also indicates that the persuasive power of evidence can be increased if it is combined with vivid imagery. For example, since 1978, utility companies have offered American consumers a free home audit to pinpoint how they can make their houses and apartments more energy-efficient. Despite the valuable information given to them in these audits, only 15 percent of those who requested such inspections actually followed the recommendations of the auditor. Why were people not persuaded to take action when presented with all this evidence? To answer this question, Marti Gonzales and her colleagues (1988) interviewed homeowners and discovered that most of them had a hard time believing that such things as a small crack under a few doors could appreciably decrease energy efficiency. Based on this information, the researchers trained a group of auditors to present their information in the following graphic and vivid terms:

> If you were to add up all the cracks around and under the doors of your home, you'd have the equivalent of a hole the size of a football in your living room wall.

Vivid, graphic messages of jarring and disturbing consequences can persuade without the use of empirical data.

Many advertisers combine a vivid image with statistics to increase the persuasive power of their advertisement.

Think for a moment about all the heat that would escape from a hole that size. That's precisely why I'm recommending that you install weatherstripping . . . And your attic totally lacks insulation. We call that a "naked attic." It's as if your home is facing winter not just without an overcoat, but without any clothing at all. (Gonzales et al., 1988, p. 1052)

Results indicated that auditors trained to use such vivid descriptions in presenting their evidence for greater energy efficiency dramatically increased their effectiveness in persuading consumers to have the recommended work done (61 percent compliance versus the previous 15 percent rate).

Although Gonzales's findings suggest that a vivid presentation can make solid evidence even more persuasive, further research indicates that under certain conditions, vividness can actually undermine the persuasiveness of a message. In one such study, Kurt Frey and Alice Eagly (1993) presented vivid or nonvivid persuasive messages to undergraduate volunteers about either airline terrorism or school privatization (see table 6.1). In one condition (*high attentional constraint*), students were instructed to pay close attention to this information, whereas in another condition (*low attentional constraint*), the information was presented as an incidental part of the laboratory situation with no instructions to pay attention to

TABLE 6.1

Vivid and Nonvivid Persuasive Messages

What constitutes a vivid versus a nonvivid persuasive message? Reprinted below are the vivid and nonvivid persuasive messages concerning airline terrorism that Frey and Eagly (1993) used in their study of how vividness can sometimes undermine persuasiveness. A similarly constructed persuasive message concerning school privatization was also used in this study. Attesting to the success of the vividness manipulation, research participants who heard the vivid versions rated them as bringing to mind more "concrete images and mental pictures" than those who listened to the nonvivid messages. However, the vivid and nonvivid versions were not rated as more or less interesting, understandable, professional, or intelligent from one another. Because of these findings, the researchers were confident that any differences in the persuasiveness of these two messages was due to differences in their vividness.

Airline Terrorism (Vivid Version)	Airline Terrorism (Nonvivid Version)
Terrorist threats and acts of violence against airlines are on the rise. The recent bombing of Pan Am Flight 103, in which 258 passengers were killed in a mid-air explosion over Lockerbie, Scotland, is an example of such ruthless terrorism. This cold-blooded killing of innocent people raises a vital question: Should airlines inform the public of terrorist threats they receive?	There has been an ever-growing increase in the number of terrorist threats and acts of violence against airlines. In recent years, a number of commercial flights have been targeted by such terrorism. The bombing of one flight resulted in the deaths of many of its passengers. The question that is being raised by many is whether or not airlines should inform the public of terrorist threats they receive.
There are a number of good reasons why airlines should not inform the public of terrorist threats. First, if airlines were to publicize every incoming threat, they would be doing exactly what terrorists want. These foaming martyrs would then increase the numbers of their threats. In fact, they would compete to see whose blood-chilling threats could make headlines in the *New York Times*.	There are a number of good reasons why airlines should not inform the public of terrorist threats. First, if airlines were to publicize every incoming threat, they would be doing exactly what terrorists want. Terrorists would then increase the number of their threats. In fact, they would compete with each other for news coverage.
Second, disclosure of threats to the public would encourage phony threats. Threats would be called in by just about anyone, from someone irate about having their patent leather luggage lost on a previous flight to someone trying to prevent a business rival from attending a power lunch on the West Coast.	Second, disclosure of threats to the public would encourage phony threats. Threats would be called in by just about anyone, from someone dissatisfied with the service they received on a previous flight to someone trying to interfere with another person's travel plans.
Third, announcing threats would disrupt airline operations. Imagine the confusion caused by hordes of shouting, terror-stricken people elbowing their way to the ticket counter to reschedule their flights every time a bomb threat was announced.	Third, announcing threats would disrupt airline operations. Imagine the confusion caused by hundreds of people trying to reschedule their flights every time a bomb threat was announced. The situation would be utterly chaotic.
Finally, most would-be flyers do not have the expertise to evaluate terrorist threats. Evaluating the danger of a threat would be like playing Russian roulette with a gun pointed at one's head.	Finally, most would-be flyers do not have the expertise to evaluate terrorist threats. If terrorist threats were publicized, ordinary travelers would be faced with decisions concerning the likelihood that a threat would be carried out and the danger involved if it were.
Countering terrorist threats will not be accomplished by warnings to the public. The real answer to airline terrorism lies in replacing yawning, zombie-like security guards with savvy, eagle-eyed experts. It also lies in replacing simplistic metal detectors that go "beep" with state-of-the-art scanners able to detect plastic explosives concealed, for example, in a pair of cowboy boots or a bottle of imported wine.	Countering terrorist threats will not be accomplished by warnings to the public. The real answer to airline terrorism lies in replacing bored security guards with better trained and more alert personnel. It also lies in replacing unsophisticated baggage inspection equipment with the modern technology that is necessary to detect even well-concealed plastic explosives.

Source: From K. P. Frey and A. H. Eagly. "Vividness Can Undermine the Persuasiveness of Messages" in *Journal of Personality and Social Psychology*, 65:32–44. Copyright © 1993 by the American Psychological Association. Reprinted by permission.

FIGURE 6.4

Mean Persuasion Due to Vividness and Attentional Constraint

Frey and Eagly (1993) presented vivid or nonvivid persuasive messages to people concerning either airline terrorism or school privatization. Some students closely focused their attention on this information (high attentional constraint), while for other students this information was merely an incidental part of the laboratory situation (low attentional constraint). Although vivid and nonvivid messages were equally persuasive under high constraint, nonvivid messages were more persuasive than the vivid ones under low constraint. In the figure, higher numbers indicate greater persuasion.

Source: Data from K. P. Frey and A. H. Eagly, "Vividness Can Undermine the Persuasiveness of Messages" in *Journal of Personality and Social Psychology*, 65:32–44, American Psychological Association, 1993.

There will be a giant sucking sound going south.

Ross Perot on American businesses moving plants to Mexico

You bought a front-row box seat and got a third-rate performance.

Ross Perot on tax dollars and educational achievement

There are two levers for moving man—interest and fear.

Napolean Bonaparte, French general and emperor, 1769–1821

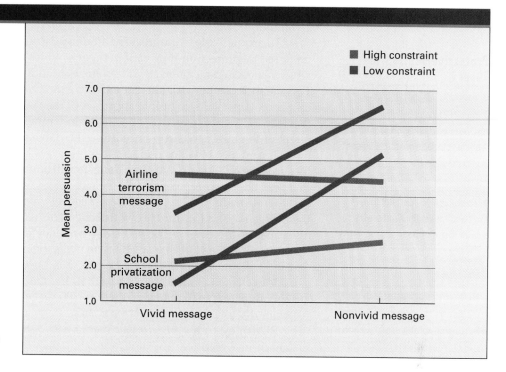

it. As you can see in figure 6.4, although vivid and nonvivid messages were equally persuasive when students were instructed to pay close attention to them, nonvivid messages were more persuasive than the vivid ones when incidentally presented.

What these results suggest is that vividness may undermine persuasiveness when vivid elements interfere with the full comprehension of the persuasive message. Such interference is most likely when people's attention has not been constrained. That is, when not admonished to "pay attention" to a message, vivid elements in the message itself may cause people's attention to wander off on tangents so they miss the essential meaning of the message. An example of vividness interfering with message comprehension was Ross Perot's speaking style during the 1992 and 1996 presidential campaigns. When I listened to him, I often missed the point of his argument because his colorful language and provocative metaphors distracted me.

FEAR APPEALS FACILITATE PERSUASION IF CERTAIN CONDITIONS ARE MET

Would-be persuaders, whether they are making evidence-based appeals or using more graphically oriented arguments, often try to evoke fear in order to persuade. An antismoking ad tells you how your nicotine habit will shorten life expectancy. An insurance agent conjures up the frightening image of your family being thrown out of their home if you don't purchase sufficient life-insurance coverage. A presidential candidate suggests that if his opponent is elected, the federal deficit will spiral out of control. There is no doubt that fear appeals are used quite frequently in persuasion. But do they work?

The early research on the use of fear in persuasion suggested that it might be counterproductive. For example, Irving Janis and Seymour Feshbach (1953) found that people who watched a graphic and frightening lecture on the dangers of poor oral hygiene were less likely to follow the lecture recommendations than were those who watched a less frightening lecture. Unfortunately, subsequent research generally was not able to replicate these findings and, instead, often found that

Protection-Motivation Theory

A theory proposing that fear induces both a self-protective response and an appraisal of whether the fear-arousing threat can be avoided.

People react to fear, not love—they don't teach that in Sunday school, but it's true.

Richard M. Nixon, U.S. president, 1913–1994

No passion so effectually robs the mind of all its powers of acting and reasoning as fear.

Edmund Burke, Irish philosopher, 1729–1797

greater aroused fear results in more—not less—effective persuasion (Janis, 1967; Leventhal, 1970).

To explain the contradictory findings, Ronald Rogers and his colleagues proposed a **protection-motivation theory,** which outlined the conditions under which fear would facilitate attitude change (Maddux & Rogers, 1983; Rogers, 1983). This theory hypothesizes that fear induces a motivation to protect the self, as well as influences a person's cognitive appraisal of the fear-arousing threat. Rogers argues that fear appeals can effectively persuade under the following four conditions: (1) the target of the message is convinced that the dangers mentioned are serious; (2) the target is convinced that the dangers are quite probable; (3) the target is convinced that the recommendations to avoid the dangers will be effective; and (4) the target believes that he or she can competently take the recommended action. Rogers believes that the first two elements in this persuasion process convince people that they should change their behavior, and the third and fourth elements reassure them that they are personally capable of changing the necessary behavior in order to avoid the danger. If a person's self-beliefs indicate an ability to make the necessary behavioral changes, the fear-inducing message will likely be effective. Does this notion of being personally capable of changing one's own behavior sound familiar? It should, because it bears a striking similarity to the concept of *perceived behavioral control* in the theory of planned behavior discussed in chapter 5 (see p. 168).

Returning to the previously mentioned dental hygiene study by Janis and Feshbach in which fear did not induce change, more recent studies suggest that this effect may have been due to the participants tuning the message out. That is, sometimes high fear appeal can cause so much anxiety that the audience is unable to process later information in the appeal about how to avoid the forthcoming danger. For example, Christopher Jepson and Chaiken (1990) measured participants' anxieties about cancer and then asked them to read and evaluate an article advocating regular checkups for cancer. Following this exercise, participants were asked to list all their thoughts about the article and as many of the arguments contained in the article. Those who were highly anxious about cancer listed fewer thoughts, remembered fewer arguments, and were ultimately less persuaded than those who were less anxious. This study, and others, suggest that if a fear-inducing message immobilizes its audience with anxiety, they may be unable to carefully process the message content concerning how to avoid the danger. Instead of promoting healthy change, the message may instead induce a feeling of helplessness. Although this is certainly an undesirable consequence of fear appeals, existing research indicates that if fear appeals are combined with information that one can do something about the danger, important behavioral changes can and do occur (Block & Keller, 1997; Mulilis & Duval, 1997).

HUMOR INCREASES ATTENTION TO A PERSUASIVE MESSAGE, BUT IT MAY INTERFERE WITH MESSAGE PROCESSING

Advertising executive David Martin, in his book *Romancing the Brand,* describes his favorite commercial (D. Martin, 1989). The commercial was designed to promote the use of an insecticide on one of farmers' most obscure crops: sunflowers. As the commercial begins, a tall, handsome, and healthy-looking man in a business suit begins talking to viewers. He is articulate and sincere. He is also a sunflower. His head is crowned with bright yellow sunflower petals.

Let's say I'm a sunflower and I was treated with Furadan insecticide.

Suddenly, an unkempt, sickly, short man wearing a wilted sunflower bonnet glumly stumbles into view. The tall, healthy sunflower glances at the intruder and continues:

Here's a sunflower that wasn't treated with Furadan. Just look what sunflower beetles and grasshoppers did to him. And those stem weevils got to him . . . well. . . .

The tall sunflower sighs and punches his sickly companion fondly on the shoulder.

If you were harvesting you'd run right over a little guy like that.

Upon receiving this mild playful punch, the sickly sunflower coughs, reaches desperately for some sort of support, and then falls to the ground with a loud thud. As the camera zooms in on the tall handsome sunflower, he shrugs knowingly, adjusts his tie, and says:

So take some advice from a sunflower who knows; use Furadan at planting. It's the best way I know to keep your heads up.

This humorous commercial was extremely popular with viewers, and this popularity translated into doubled sales for the insecticide. Advertising executives like Martin believe that humor can persuade consumers to buy their products, and that is why about 40 percent of all advertisements employ humor (Unger, 1996). Public relations consultants also believe that humor is an effective persuader, and they regularly recommend that their clients punch up their persuasive speeches with humorous anecdotes (Weinberger & Campbell, 1991). Are they correct in their beliefs?

One thing research clearly shows is that using humor in persuasive messages does increase people's *attention* to the message more than serious-sounding communication attempts (Duncan & Nelson, 1985). People are simply more likely to listen to someone who is trying to make them laugh, or at least smile, while trying to persuade them about a particular point of view. Persuaders who inject humor into their messages also tend to enhance their likability in the minds of the audience (Gruner, 1985). As we have already discussed, communicators can use this increased liking to persuade their audience to adopt their perspective on the issue under consideration, whether it is insecticide products or defense spending.

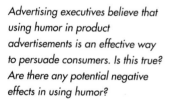

Advertising executives believe that using humor in product advertisements is an effective way to persuade consumers. Is this true? Are there any potential negative effects in using humor?

One of the problems with using humor, however, is that it may interfere with the listener's *comprehension* of the message, by directing attention away from the persuasive content (Cantor & Venus, 1983). That is, the jokes may be so funny that people only remember them and not the persuasive information. Thus, if a persuader merely wants to get people to notice the message, humor may be useful in this regard. However, as pointed out by the message-learning approach (refer back to figure 6.1), attending to the message is only the first step in persuasion. With no message comprehension (step 2), any attitude change is likely to be extremely vulnerable to a counterpersuasive attack (Haugtvedt & Petty, 1992).

Because enabling listeners to comprehend the message is important in securing durable attitude change, recent studies have more closely assessed the effects of humor on how people *process* persuasive messages. One such study, conducted by Steven Smith and his coworkers (1994) found that humor can either promote message processing or disrupt it. The key determining factor in whether processing or disruption occurs is the *relevance* of the humor to the evaluation of the message content. When humor is relevant to the content of the message, people appear to be more motivated to take a central route to persuasion and process the message arguments. However, when humor is irrelevant to the message content, people are likely to take a peripheral route and base their evaluation of the message merely on cues such as source credibility.

So what is the answer to the question of whether humor is helpful or hurtful to a persuasive message? Based on what we know so far, it seems to depend first on the *goal* of the persuasive message: humor will get you most people's attention, but it may interfere with them processing the important content of your persuasive message. However, it appears that you can circumvent this negative "humor effect" by employing humor that is *relevant* to your persuasive arguments. This relevant humor appears to motivate people to process the content of your message, which increases the likelihood that any ensuing attitude change will be less susceptible to decay.

Two-Sided Messages Can "Inoculate" Your Audience Against Opposing Views Better Than One-Sided Messages

Besides humor, another factor in determining whether a message will be persuasive has to do with whether you present a one-sided or a two-sided message. A *one-sided* message is one in which you try to convince others to adopt your perspective by presenting only your arguments. In contrast, a *two-sided* message involves you acknowledging the opposing arguments in your pitch and attempting to refute them.

Hovland and his colleagues (1949), in a study conducted during World War II, attempted to determine whether one-sided or two-sided messages were more effective audience persuaders. Working in the Army's Information and Education Division immediately after the surrender of Nazi Germany, their objective was to convince American soldiers that the war was far from over and that the armed conflict against Japan would last at least two more years. Some soldiers heard a one-sided message that did not bring up opposing viewpoints, and other soldiers heard a two-sided message that also mentioned and then refuted the opposing viewpoints. As illustrated in figure 6.5, the effectiveness of the appeal depended on who was listening. A one-sided appeal was most effective with those who already believed that the war would be long, while a two-sided appeal worked better with those who initially believed that the war would be over soon.

Later research found that two-sided messages tend to be more effective in persuading not only those who initially disagree, but also those people who are either well informed on the topic or are going to be exposed to opposing viewpoints in the future (Jones & Brehm, 1970; Lumsdaine & Janis, 1953). In such

FIGURE 6.5

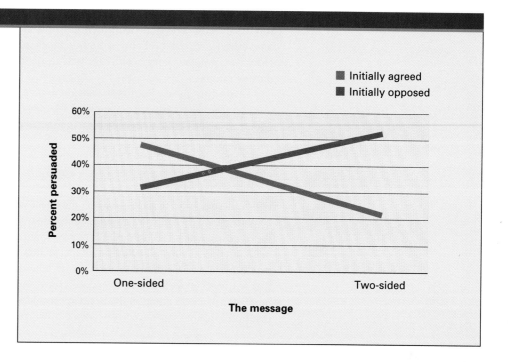

One-Sided Versus Two-Sided Appeals

Following Germany's defeat in World War II, American soldiers who initially agreed with a message that Japan was strong and that the war in the Pacific would last a long time were more persuaded by a one-sided appeal. In contrast, soldiers skeptical of this message were more persuaded by a two-sided appeal.

Source: Data from C. I. Hovland et al., *Experiments on Mass Communications,* Princeton University Press, 1949.

circumstances, mentioning the opposition's arguments may suggest that you are being an objective, fair-minded person, thereby increasing your trustworthiness and, thus, your effectiveness at persuasion.

Besides increasing communicator trustworthiness, there is another important factor operating in two-sided messages. For those who are soon going to hear the opposition state its case, raising and then refuting its arguments can *inoculate* these people against it, making it harder for them to be persuaded. This inoculation approach to persuasion was developed by William McGuire during the 1950s in partial response to Cold War fears about Americans' susceptibility to communist propaganda from the Soviet Union. McGuire reasoned that people become vulnerable to propaganda when they are raised in a society that overprotects them from hearing things that attack culturally shared beliefs. Using a biological analogy, he stated that people who are raised in such a "germ-free" environment would not have developed appropriate mechanisms to adequately defend themselves against attacking viruses (outside propaganda). However, just as administering a small dose of a dangerous virus will stimulate the body to develop defenses to fight off the disease, McGuire asserted that exposing people to a weakened dose of the attacking material would also stimulate the development of resistance-promoting counterarguments.

Research supports some of the basic elements of inoculation theory, and its principles have been effectively applied in many realms, including commercial advertising and political campaigning (McGuire & Papageorgis, 1961; Pfau & Burgoon, 1988). However, as the application of inoculation theory has spread, McGuire has had second thoughts about some of his basic theoretical assumptions. Two of his initial assumptions were that (1) outside beliefs were often dangerous and should be guarded against, and (2) the inoculation effect would only protect people from "dangerous" political perspectives, such as Soviet-style communism and other totalitarian belief systems; it could not be used to manipulate an audience. As you can see from the following commentary by McGuire, these early views are now recognized as being naive:

I must confess that I felt like Mr. Clean when I started this immunization work because while everybody else was studying how to manipulate people, I was studying how to keep them from being manipulated. But now I appreciate more that the person has to be open to outside influence: if one had to learn everything from one's own experience, one probably wouldn't survive. . . . Immunizing somebody against change isn't always very healthy for the reason that people do have to be open to outside influence.

I am also uneasy because subsequent developments in advertising show that our immunization research can be used for questionable purposes. I remember a call I got from an advertising agency bigwig just after this research was publicized. He said, "Very interesting, Professor. I was really delighted to read about it." Somewhat righteously I replied, "Very nice of you to say that, Mr. Bigwig, but I'm really on the other side. You're trying to persuade people, and I'm trying to make them more resistant." "Oh, don't underrate yourself, Professor," he said. "What you're doing will be very helpful to us in reducing the effectiveness of our competitors." And so it has turned out. Before our immunization research, advertisements always ignored the opposition as if it didn't exist. But now mentioning the other brands and deflating their claims is becoming almost standard in the advertising of many product classes. Our immunization research has brought home to the ad agencies that with audiences likely to be exposed to strong ads for competing brands, it is more efficacious to mention the opposition claims in advance, but in weakened form that builds up resistance to them. (Evans, 1980, pp. 179–180)

THE ORDER IN WHICH MESSAGES ARE PRESENTED CAN INFLUENCE THEIR PERSUASIVENESS

Is there any advantage in presenting your persuasive message before or after your rival's message when competing for the audience's favor? This is the dilemma often faced by prosecution and defense attorneys in a courtroom trial, as well as candidates in a political debate or sales representatives competing for a client's business. The dilemma boils down to whether the *primacy effect* is more important than the *recency effect* in persuasion. Recall from chapter 3 that if you believe that information presented first has more impact, you are stating a preference for the primacy effect. On the other hand, believing that later information has more influence is predicting a recency effect.

Research findings have been mixed in declaring either of these effects to be the most influential. The earliest persuasion studies found support for the primacy effect (Knower, 1936; Lund, 1925), while later studies sometimes yielded recency effects, sometimes primacy effects, sometimes both, and sometimes neither. One factor that appears to determine whether early or later information has more impact is *time*. For example, Norman Miller and Donald Campbell (1959) conducted a simulation jury study in which half the participants first read a summary of the plaintiff's case, then read a summary of the defendant's case, and finally made a decision on who to believe. The remaining participants in the study reversed this order of reading. The researchers also varied how much time elapsed between the two messages, as well as how much time separated the second message from the participants' decisions. When participants read the second message right after the first and then waited seven days before reporting their decision, the first message was more persuasive than the second: a primacy effect. In this condition, the seven-day waiting period caused both messages to decay equally in memory, leaving only the first-impressions effect intact. However, when participants read the second message one week after the first and then immediately made a decision, a recency effect occurred. In this condition, the second argument was more easily recalled from memory, and thus, its contents were more persuasive.

The findings of this study suggest that when two parties present their persuasive arguments back-to-back, and a good deal of time elapses between the presentations and the audience's decision, the first presenter will have an advantage due to the primacy effect. However, if the two parties are to make their presentations on different days or, even better, in different weeks, and if the audience is scheduled to make their decision immediately after hearing the last presentation, the smart persuader should try to go last and capitalize on the recency effect.

A second factor that appears to influence order effects is the *personal relevance* of the message to the audience. In one study, Curtis Haugtvedt and Daniel Wegener (1994) found that when the personal relevance of the two presented messages was high, the first message tended to be more persuasive (primacy effect). However, when the two persuasive messages were of low relevance, the second message had the edge (recency effect). As the researchers explain these findings, when the messages were of high personal relevance, the audience tended to think a lot about the first presented message (high elaboration), which made them more resistant to the second message. However, when the messages were not personally relevant to the audience, they didn't analyze them carefully (low elaboration) and, instead, were more persuaded by the last one they heard.

What this study suggests is that when you and your adversary on some issue are scheduled to present persuasive messages, it will be to your advantage to go first if the issue is something of importance to your audience. However, in those cases where your audience is not personally involved in the issue, go last, so that the last arguments this apathetic group hears is your own.

REPEATING A MESSAGE INCREASES ITS PERSUASIVE POWER

Have you ever wondered why advertisers keep repeating the same commercials on television? I was reminded of the answer to this question recently when I stumbled out of bed on a Saturday morning to find my two daughters already downstairs watching cartoons. Usually my wife and I limit their TV viewing, but this morning they literally caught us napping and had at least a sixty-minute dose of "Scoobie-Doo," "Land of the Lost," and numerous commercials. Apparently the Trix rabbit had figured prominently in commercial air time, for all my daughters wanted for breakfast was a bowl of Trix, "the fruity sweetened corn puff cereal with natural fruit flavors and eight essential vitamins and iron."

One reason television sponsors repeat their commercial messages is that repetition tends to increase liking for the product because of the *mere exposure effect* discussed in chapter 5. But despite the effectiveness that repetitive messages can have on liking and, thus, persuasion, there are limits to its power. Repeated exposure seems to increase liking for stimuli that are initially perceived as neutral or positive, but it has the opposite effect on stimuli that are initially perceived as negative (Cacioppo & Petty, 1989). This undoubtedly explains why I hate "Snuggles," the little animated, stuffed bear in the fabric softener commercials of the same name. I was irritated by its squeaky, giggly voice when the commercials first appeared in the early 1980s, and my negative attitude has increased through repeated exposures over the years.

Another limitation of the mere exposure effect is that even when it is effective, it increases liking only up to a point. After too much exposure, liking will level off and, in some instances, even decline, an effect advertisers call *wear-out* (Smith & Dorfman, 1975). Wear-out effects tend to occur with ads that attract a great deal of attention when they first appear, such as humorous ads. One technique that advertisers use to overcome wear-out effects is to engage in *repetition with variation* (Pratkanis & Aronson, 1992). In this technique, they present the same information repeatedly, but the format of the ad is varied. For example, during the course of an hour of television viewing, you might see as many as four Energizer battery commercials featuring the pink Energizer-operated toy bunny, but each time the pointy-eared toy is shown in a different humorous context. Research indicates that such variation in repetition does generally succeed in reducing wear-out effects, and it may accomplish this by causing viewers to further elaborate—and thereby strengthen—their attitudes toward the product (Haugtvedt et al., 1994; Schumann et al., 1990).

Repeated exposure to a product often leads to greater liking, except if one's initial reaction to the product is negative. Are there any products you dislike because the ads irritate you?

SECTION SUMMARY

Evidence-based appeals and those that use *vivid* images are both persuasive, but their individual power can increase if they are combined in one message. *Fear* can also persuade, yet it can also immobilize an audience with anxiety. However, if fear appeals are combined with information that one can do something to avoid the danger, important behavioral changes can occur. An opposite emotion to fear, namely *humor*, can also be used effectively in certain forms of persuasion, but it can also reduce the effectiveness of strong arguments by interfering with information processing. Besides facts, figures, and emotions, *two-sided messages* tend to be effective in persuading not only those who initially disagree but also those who are either well informed or are going to be exposed to opposing viewpoints in the future. Regarding *primacy* and *recency effects,* the question of whether one should present persuasive arguments before or after those of the opposition depends on when the audience is planning on making their decision. Finally, *message repetition* increases the persuasive power of the message due to the mere exposure effect.

CHANNEL VARIABLES: HOW IS THE MESSAGE TRANSMITTED?

Another important aspect of persuasion is the channel or medium of communication used to persuade an audience to adopt a particular attitude or course of action. In other words, how does the persuader deliver the message? Two aspects of the communication medium that have been investigated deal with the speed at which the message is delivered, and the style of speech that is used.

RAPID SPEECH CAN BENEFIT PERIPHERAL-ROUTE PERSUASION YET OFTEN HINDERS CENTRAL-ROUTE PROCESSING

Are fast-talking communicators any more successful at persuading an audience than those who speak more slowly? Research indicates that people who speak rapidly are generally more persuasive than those who speak more slowly because fast talkers convey the *impression* that they are more credible (Miller et al., 1976). Certain marketing studies also report this benefit of rapid speech—people seem to be more favorably disposed toward advertisements and the products advertised when the product spokesperson talks at a faster-than-normal rate of speech (LaBarbera & MacLachlan, 1979; Street & Brady, 1982). But is fast talking always beneficial to persuasion?

According to the elaboration likelihood model, fast talking will only be beneficial to the persuasive communicator when the audience's initial attitudinal position is *opposite* to that of the communicator. This hypothesis is derived from the belief that rapid speech makes it difficult for a listener to adequately process and critically analyze the content of the message. Because the audience's counterarguing is "short-circuited" by the sheer speed at which the opposing viewpoints are presented, audience members are more likely to be persuaded by the message than if they had more time to scrutinize it. Put another way, the difficulty in processing rapid speech prompts the audience to abandon the central route, and instead, they take the peripheral route to persuasion. In contrast to the hypothesized benefits of rapid speech when the audience opposes the communicator, the elaboration likelihood model further predicts that fast talking will hurt the persuasive power of the message when it is presented to an audience that favors the communicator's point of view. Why? Because the arguments are presented so quickly, the audience cannot adequately process them and incorporate them into their existing belief system to further bolster their current attitudes on the issue.

Steven Smith and David Shaffer (1991) found support for this explanation in a study in which college students listened to persuasive messages arguing for or against raising the legal drinking age to 20. A survey conducted prior to the study revealed that the overwhelming majority of undergraduates on campus opposed such a law. Students heard the persuasive arguments either at a slow, normal, or rapid rate of speech. Consistent with the elaboration likelihood hypothesis, when students listened to arguments counter to their perspective, rapid speech suppressed the tendency to rebut the counterattitudinal message, and hence, listeners were more susceptible to persuasion. However, when students listened to arguments consistent with their own attitudes toward the drinking-age law, rapid speech inhibited favorable elaboration of the proattitudinal message, thus undermining its persuasive impact. These findings suggest that rapid speech may either promote or inhibit persuasion through its impact on message elaboration.

POWERFUL SPEECH IS GENERALLY MORE PERSUASIVE THAN POWERLESS SPEECH

In addition to how fast a person talks, another speech-related factor influencing persuasion is the style in which a speech is delivered. For example, consider two people, Jessie and Tony, going to their boss to make persuasive arguments for a raise. First, let's see how Jessie states her case:

> "Uh . . . excuse me, sir? . . . Uh . . . could I have a minute of your time? . . . This may sound a little out of the ordinary, but, I've been with the company for one year now, you know, and . . . uhm, well, I was sort of wondering if we could talk about an increase in my salary? Uh . . . you know, since starting here, I've kind of been given a good deal of responsibilities that go beyond my job description, you know, and . . . uh . . . I've handled this additional work efficiently and professionally, you know, without complaining and without supervision, don't you think? I'm not an expert on how to run this company, you know, but I was wondering . . . uh . . . now that I have proven capable of handling this increased workload and responsibilities, you know, don't you think my salary should reflect this fact?"

CRITICAL *thinking*

When radio ads try to persuade you to buy tickets in state lotteries or to purchase their products in the hopes of later winning prizes, they are required by law to tell the listener the actual odds of winning. Have you noticed that when the spokespersons are trying to persuade you to spend your money they speak at a normal rate of speed, yet when they convey the odds of winning, their speech rate dramatically increases? Are they simply trying to save money by cutting down on the length of the commercial, or is there an equally important reason for this shift to fast-paced speech?

Now, let's see how Tony presents these same arguments to his boss:

> "Excuse me, sir? Could I have a minute of your time? I've been with the company for one year now, and I would like to talk to you about an increase in my salary. Since starting here I've been given a good deal of responsibilities that go well beyond my job description, and I've handled this additional work efficiently and professionally without complaining and without supervision. Now that I have proven capable of handling this increased work load and responsibilities, I would like to have my salary reflect this fact."

The factual content of both messages is the same, yet they differ markedly in how the content is presented. Sociolinguists would say that Jessie's presentation is an example of *powerless speech,* while Tony's embodies *powerful speech* (Newcombe & Arnkoff, 1979). Powerless speech includes the following language forms:

Hesitation Forms: "Uh" and "You know" indicate a lack of confidence or certainty.
Disclaimers: "This may sound out of the ordinary, but . . . " and "I'm not an expert, but . . ." ask the listener to be patient or refrain from criticism.
Qualifiers: "Sort of," "kind of," and "I guess" serve to tone down or blunt the force of an assertive statement.
Tag Questions: "I've handled this additional work efficiently and professionally, don't you think?" "That's the right thing to do, isn't it?" The added-on question turns an assertive statement into a plea for agreement.

Given the different delivery styles of Jessie and Tony, whom do you think is more likely to persuade their boss to give them the desired raise? Not surprisingly, research finds that when people use a powerful speaking style, they are generally judged much more competent and credible than when their style is powerless (Erickson et al., 1978; Newcombe & Arnkoff, 1979). This suggests that even when people have good and persuasive messages, they often fail to persuade if they weaken their message by the way they deliver it. Despite the fact that the use of powerful language forms adds an assertive "punch" to one's message, not everyone in society is taught to use this style of speech. Sociolinguist Robin Lakoff (1975) contends that because the status of women in society has been relatively powerless and marginal compared with men, they generally are not socialized nor expected to express themselves as assertively and forcefully as men. True to this gender expectation, in conversation, women are more likely than men to use qualifiers, ask tag questions, and use disclaimers (Crosby & Nyquist, 1977; Mulac & Lundell, 1986).

Although a powerful speaking style generally is more persuasive than a powerless one, under certain conditions, the sex of the communicator may reverse this effect. For example, Linda Carli (1990) found that when women tried to persuade men to change their attitudes, using powerless speech was more effective than employing a more assertive style. On the other hand, when trying to persuade other women, breaking with convention and adopting a more powerful speaking style was found to be more influential. The greater influence a powerless speaking style had on men occurred despite the fact that both male and female participants in this study believed that women who spoke tentatively were less competent and knowledgeable than women who spoke assertively! As you can see in table 6.2, men perceived the woman who talked tentatively to be more trustworthy and likable, while women judged her to be less likable and trustworthy.

This study clearly suggests that there is a double standard in speaking style for women and men. The use of tentative speech appears to enhance a woman's ability to persuade a man at the same time that it reduces her ability to persuade another woman. Why might these differences exist? One possibility is that because women typically have lower social status than men, they must first demonstrate in

TABLE 6.2

Gender Differences in Speech Style and Persuasiveness

Carli (1990) found that there appears to be a double standard in persuasive speaking style for women and men, with tentative speech enhancing a woman's ability to persuade a man at the same time that it reduces her persuasiveness with a woman. In the table, higher scores reflect greater trustworthiness and likableness, and greater agreement with the persuasive message. What might explain these differences?

Speaker	Sex of Listener					
	Agreement with Speaker		Speaker Trustworthiness		Speaker Likableness	
	Male	Female	Male	Female	Male	Female
Male						
Tentative language	4.13	4.07	6.73	6.73	5.93	6.53
Assertive language	3.80	5.20	6.80	7.00	6.40	6.93
Female						
Tentative language	5.00	3.13	8.40	5.47	8.00	5.80
Assertive language	2.93	5.93	6.33	7.27	6.53	7.73

Source: Data from L. L. Carli, "Gender, Language, and Influence" in *Journal of Personality and Social Psychology*, 59:941–951, American Psychological Association, 1990.

Public speaking is done in the public tongue, the national or tribal language; and the language of our tribe is the men's language. Of course women learn it. We're not dumb. If you can tell Margaret Thatcher from Ronald Reagan, or Indira Gandhi from General Somoza, by anything they say, tell me how. This is a man's world, so it talks a man's language.

Ursula LeGuin, U.S. author, 1983

conversations with them that they have no desire to compete for status—hence the use of powerless speech. When women conversationally acknowledge their lower status (for example, "I know I'm not an expert on this issue, but . . ." "Maybe we could . . ."), men may be more likely to consider their ideas and arguments (Meeker & Weitzel-O'Neill, 1977). Does this mean that women should adopt a powerless speaking style to improve their persuasive power with men? No. The use of such powerless language as a subtle persuasion technique will either compromise a woman's perceived competence or make it difficult for her to persuade an audience of both men and women. Instead, a follow-up study by Carli and her coworkers (1995) suggests that an alternative method for female persuaders to use with a male audience is to combine assertive language with a *social nonverbal style* that communicates friendliness and affiliation (relaxed forward-leaning, smiling face, moderate eye contact). In this study, men were more inclined to like and be persuaded by a competent woman when she was also sociable than when she was merely competent. For a male audience, then, a sociable nonverbal style appears to take the perception of threat out of a competent woman's self-presentation, making her an effective agent of persuasion.

SECTION SUMMARY

Research on the medium of communication indicates that *rapid speech* can either increase or decrease persuasibility, depending on the audience's initial position and the strength of the persuasive arguments being presented. *Speech style* also can boost or hinder the ability to change people's attitudes, with powerful speech increasing and powerless speech decreasing one's effectiveness in most instances.

AUDIENCE VARIABLES: TO WHOM IS THE MESSAGE DELIVERED?

Now that we have discussed the source, the message, and the channel of persuasion, let's analyze certain characteristics of the target of persuasion that can also influence how the message is received. Some of these characteristics have to do with the mood, involvement, personality, self-concept, and age of the target.

WHETHER GOOD MOODS HELP OR HINDER PERSUASION DEPENDS ON MESSAGE STRENGTH AND DEGREE OF MESSAGE ELABORATION

Early research on mood and persuasion indicated that people who are in a positive mood are more susceptible to persuasion than the average person. For example, Irving Janis and his colleagues (1965) had some people read persuasive messages while they ate a snack and drank soda, while others simply read the messages without the accompanying treats. Greater attitude change occurred among the "munchers" than among the "food-free" group. Similar effects were also found among people listening to pleasant music (Milliman, 1986).

Why do you think these effects might occur? Although some would contend that people in a good mood are easier to persuade than those in a bad mood simply because of classical conditioning principles (see chapter 5, pp. 153–155), the cognitive-response approach offers more complex explanations (Petty & Wegener, 1998). One of these explanations, the *feelings-as-information* view, argues that whereas negative moods signal to people that something is wrong in their environment and that some action is necessary, positive moods have the opposite effect: they signal that everything is fine and no effortful thought is necessary (Schwarz, 1990). As a result, people in a positive mood are more persuasible because they are less likely to engage in extensive processing of the presented arguments than those in a neutral or negative mood (Bohner et al., 1992). This does not mean, as classical conditional principles would suggest, that people in a bad mood are more likely to react negatively to any arguments presented. On the contrary, they are simply less likely than those in a positive mood to be influenced by poor arguments.

Although the feelings-as-information view contends that happy people tend to rely on peripheral-route processing, an alternative cognitive-response explanation, the *hedonic-contingency* view, asserts that this is not always the case (Wegener & Petty, 1994). According to this perspective, happy people will engage in cognitive tasks that allow them to remain happy and will avoid those tasks that lower their mood. Research investigating this possible effect indicates that a happy mood can indeed lead to *greater* message elaboration than a neutral or sad mood when the persuasive message is either uplifting or not mood threatening (Wegener et al., 1995). Thus, it appears that happy people do not always process information less than neutral or sad people.

Taken together, what these studies suggest is that although happy people are generally less likely to elaborate a persuasive message than neutral or sad persons, when the message does not threaten their good mood, happy listeners may carefully scrutinize it. Consider this the next time you are at a campaign rally about to listen to the candidate outline his or her stands on important political issues. The music preceding the speech, the euphoria permeating the assembled citizenry, and any free food and drink dispensed by campaign workers are all designed to put you in an upbeat, festive mood. Will your joy in the moment cause you to engage in a less critical analysis of just what the candidate is telling you? To a certain extent, it may depend on whether the message is consistent with your upbeat mood.

DEGREE OF MESSAGE ELABORATION IS SHAPED BOTH BY ISSUE AND IMPRESSION INVOLVEMENT

In some of the earliest work on how one's involvement in an issue can influence willingness to be persuaded, Muzafir Sherif and Hadley Cantril (1947) argued that attitudes that become closely associated with the self are highly resistant to change. Later studies by cognitively oriented researchers not only have supported this hypothesis, but also have identified at least two different types of involvement, each having a distinctly different effect on persuasion (Petty & Cacioppo, 1990; Zuwerink & Devine, 1996).

Issue involvement is a type of involvement in which the attitudinal issue under consideration has important consequences for the self. Involvement in an issue results in you being very attentive to the presented arguments and very active in critically analyzing their strengths and weaknesses (Petty & Cacioppo, 1979). A second type of involvement is *impression-relevant involvement* (also known as *response involvement*), in which the attitudinal issue does not have great personal relevance, but your attitudinal response will be scrutinized by others and receive either social approval or disapproval. In this form of involvement, you are more concerned about your self-presentation and the social acceptability of your attitudes than you are about the quality of the arguments surrounding the issue.

Michael Leippe and Roger Elkin (1987) conducted a study in which they sought to determine how these two different types of involvement might interact in a given situation. College students were first told that their university was seriously considering implementing comprehensive examinations. The researchers then manipulated issue involvement by either telling students that the policy, if adopted, would go into effect the following year and they would be participants in the process (*high issue involvement*), or that the policy would not be put into effect for some years (*low issue involvement*). Impression-relevant involvement was manipulated by telling some students they would discuss this issue with another student and a professor (*high impression-relevant involvement*), while others did not believe any public discussion would take place (*low impression-relevant involvement*). Which condition do you think yielded the most critical analysis? Actually, the only students who engaged in a critical analysis of the arguments were those who were both highly issue involved and weakly involved in terms of impression relevance. If students were strongly involved in terms of impression relevance, or weakly involved in terms of issue relevance, they largely ignored the strength of the arguments.

These findings suggest that if an issue has great personal relevance to an audience and they are not very concerned how others might judge their stance on the issue, they are likely to take a central route to persuasion. In such a scenario, the audience is most likely to be persuaded by strong, well-reasoned arguments. However, if issue relevance is low to an audience, or they are concerned how others might judge them, they are likely to take a peripheral route and be persuaded by a speaker who is popular and who can reassure them that this perspective is socially acceptable.

INDIVIDUAL DIFFERENCES AFFECT SUSCEPTIBILITY TO PERSUASION

Three individual difference variables that appear to make people more or less susceptible to persuasion are one's *need for cognition*, level of *self-monitoring*, and *age*.

NEED FOR COGNITION

Need for Cognition

An individual preference for and tendency to engage in effortful cognitive activities.

Involvement in an issue can be affected not only by the importance of the message to the self, but also by the tendency for people to desire cognitive challenges. The **need for cognition** is an individual preference for and tendency to engage in effortful cognitive activities. Cacioppo and Petty (1982) have designed a personality scale to measure

TABLE 6.3

Need for Cognition Scale: Sample Items

Directions

These are sample items taken from the Need for Cognition Sacle. If you agree with items 1, 3, 5, and 7 and disagree with items 2, 4, 6, and 8, you exhibit behaviors that are indicative of a person high in the need for cognition. If your responses to these items are exactly in the opposite direction, you may be low in the need for cognition. Based on your responses, which route to persuasion do you think you tend to take? [Items taken from Cacioppo & Petty, 1982]

1. I really enjoy a task that involves coming up with new solutions to problems.
2. Thinking is not my idea of fun.
3. The notion of thinking abstractly is appealing to me.
4. I like tasks that require little thought once I've learned them.
5. I usually end up deliberating about issues even when they do not affect me personally.
6. It's enough for me that something gets the job done; I don't care how or why it works.
7. I prefer my life to be filled with puzzles that I must solve.
8. I only think as hard as I have to.

Source: From J. T. Cacioppo and R. E. Petty, "The Need for Cognition" in *Journal of Personality and Social Psychology,* 42:116–131. Copyright © 1982 by the American Psychological Association. Reprinted by permission.

individual differences in this need for cognition. Table 6.3 lists some of the items from this scale. People who are high in the need for cognition (high NFC) like to work on difficult cognitive tasks, analyze situations, and make subtle cognitive distinctions (Petty & Jarvis, 1995). Research has shown that high-NFC persons tend to take the central route to persuasion. In contrast, individuals with a low need for cognition (low NFC) are more likely to take mental shortcuts and follow a peripheral route (Cacioppo et al., 1996; Priester & Petty, 1995). As a result, the attitudes of low NFCs are easier to change than those of high NFCs (Shestowsky et al., 1998).

How does need for cognition influence attention to political campaigns and stability of political attitudes? During the 1984 presidential and vice-presidential debates, voters high in the need for cognition were more likely to watch these events than were their low-NFC counterparts (Ahlering, 1987). Not only did they spend more time watching the debates, but the high-NFC voters also held more beliefs about the candidates than did those low in the need for cognition. The greater number of beliefs making up the overall attitudes held by the high-NFC voters toward the political candidates may well explain another finding that emerged from the 1984 election. Their attitudes toward the candidates eight weeks before the November election were significantly better predictors of their actual voting behavior than were the attitudes of the low NFCs (Cacioppo et al., 1986). This greater attitude-behavior persistence probably occurs because attitudes formed as a result of critically analyzing the relevant issues are more resistant to change than attitudes shaped by means of peripheral cues (Haugtvedt & Petty, 1992). In addition to the need for cognition, table 6.4 reviews some of the factors that influence central versus peripheral processing.

SELF-MONITORING

Another personality trait related to persuasion is *self-monitoring*. As discussed in chapters 3 and 4, people who are high in self-monitoring tend to use social cues to regulate their self-presentations, while low self-monitors are less concerned about

Man is but a reed, the weakest in nature, but he is a thinking reed.

Blaise Pascal, French scientist, 1625–1662

To most people nothing is more troublesome than the effort of thinking.

James Bryce, British statesman, 1838–1922

TABLE 6.4

Central Versus Peripheral Processing of Persuasive Messages

Route to Persuasion	Most Likely to Occur When	Effect on Attitudes?
Central Route		
The person carefully scrutinizes all the available information in the persuasion environment in an attempt to determine the merits of the presented arguments.	People find the message personally relevant and involving. People are high in need for cognition. People are in a neutral or mildly negative mood. The communicator speaks at a normal rate of speed.	Attitudes tend to be strong, resistant to counterarguments, and predictive of behavior.
Peripheral Route		
Instead of actively thinking about the attitude object, the person relies on incidental cues and simple rules of thumb, such as the attractiveness of the communicator or the length of the message.	People find the message to be irrelevant and noninvolving. People are low in need for cognition. People are in a positive mood. The communicator speaks rapidly.	Attitudes tend to be weak, susceptible to counterarguments, and not predictive of behavior.

the opinions of others and are more likely to behave according to their own personal preferences. Mark Snyder and Kenneth DeBono (1985) hypothesized that high and low self-monitors might differ in their susceptibility to two common persuasion techniques employed in advertising. One technique, the *soft sell*, emphasizes the visual image of the product or ad and is relatively unconcerned with the characteristics or ingredients of the product itself. The *hard sell*, on the other hand, is a technique that emphasizes the quality, value, and utility of the product and is less concerned with how the product is packaged. Snyder and DeBono believed that high self-monitors, who are sensitive to social cues indicating appropriate behavior in a particular setting, would be more persuaded by the soft-sell stress on images. On the other hand, they believed low self-monitors, who base their life choices more on their internal attitudes, would be more influenced by hard-sell ads that focus on information about the product. As predicted, results indicated that high self-monitors not only favored image-oriented ads and were more willing to buy products (coffee, cigarettes, and whiskey) using such an approach, but they also were willing to pay more money for such products. In contrast, low self-monitoring individuals were more influenced by information-oriented ads that stressed product quality and utility (refer to figure 6.6).

This is an interesting set of findings that has been supported in other studies as well (Celuch & Slama, 1995; Debono & Packer, 1991). It suggests that the image-conscious, high self-monitors will more likely be persuaded by the ad on the top of page 215 rather than the ad on the bottom. The reverse will be true for low self-monitoring persons. Yet, despite these differences in what persuasion techniques high and low self-monitors are likely to respond to, both are susceptible to persuasion. As the functional approach to attitudes suggested in chapter 5, if you want to

FIGURE 6.6

High and Low Self-Monitors' Susceptibility to Information-Oriented Versus Image-Oriented Ads

High and low self-monitors were asked how much they would pay for products presented in image-oriented or information-oriented ads. As predicted, high self-monitors were not only more willing than low self-monitors to purchase image-oriented products; they were willing to spend more money for such products. In contrast, low self-monitors were more influenced by the information-oriented ads that stressed product quality. Based on your knowledge of self-monitoring, how would you explain these findings?

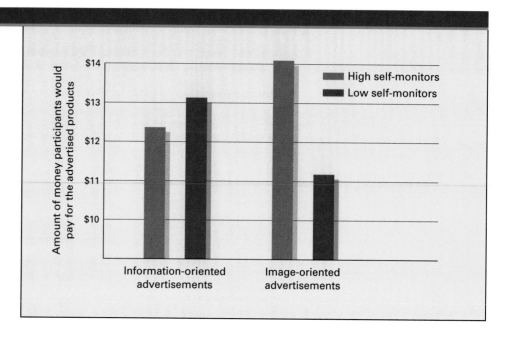

change someone's attitudes, you must first understand what the attitude does for the person—what *function* it serves.

AGE

I'm sure you've heard the old adage "You can't teach an old dog new tricks." In part, this saying reflects a common belief that while adolescents and young adults are highly susceptible to change, as people mature they become more fixed in their ways (Schuman & Scott, 1989). How true is this folk wisdom as it relates to persuasion?

According to the *impressionable years hypothesis,* it is during the formative years of adolescence and young adulthood that people are most impressionable and susceptible to persuasion (Dawson & Prewitt, 1969). This period of heightened susceptibility is thought to be caused by young people grappling for the first time with a wide range of social and political issues upon which they begin to formulate opinions. Once these basic social and political orientations are acquired, they remain largely unchanged throughout the remaining adult years. Jon Krosnick and Duane Alwin (1989) found support for this hypothesis when they analyzed survey data collected from twenty-five hundred Americans during national elections between 1956 and 1980. The attitudes of individual respondents toward several issues were measured at several points over a four-year period, and the results indicated that those 18 to 25 years old exhibited the most attitude change, followed by those 25 to 36 years old. No significant attitude change occurred among any of the older age groups (37 to 83 years old).

Although the impressionable years hypothesis seems a plausible explanation for this greater degree of attitude change among the young, a recent series of studies suggests that it provides an incomplete picture of attitude change over the life cycle. Penny Visser and Krosnick (1998) point out that previous investigations—including Krosnick and Alwin's own study—have mistakenly divided their samples into several discrete age groups and examined the average level of attitude change for each group. The problem with this technique of collapsing across a span of ages is that 65- to 80-year-olds often are grouped together. Because there are more 65-year-olds in the population than 80-year-olds, this grouping contains many more people at the younger end of the range than at the older end. Due to the relatively small number of truly old people in this "elderly" grouping, Visser and Krosnick suspected that averaging across these individuals masks changes that occur at the very end of the life cycle. To overcome this methodological problem, rather than arbitrarily breaking

Image-oriented ad.

Information-oriented ad.

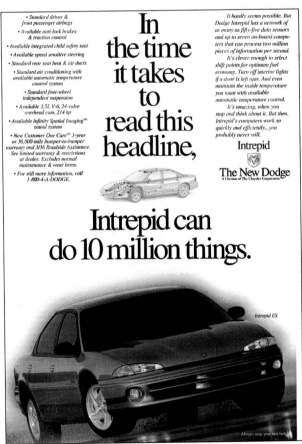

their samples into broad age subgroups, Visser and Krosnick used a more sophisticated statistical procedure (linear and nonlinear regression analysis) to allow them to use people's exact ages when assessing the relation between age and susceptibility to change. In six subsequent survey studies involving more than eighty-five hundred participants, Visser and Krosnick analyzed age differences in people's attitudes toward such social and political issues as crime, race relations, defense spending, and international affairs. Consistent with the impressionable years hypothesis, young adults' attitudes were more susceptible to change than middle-age adults' attitudes. However, counter to the impressionable years hypothesis, after about age 60, attitude change became increasingly common with increasing age.

What accounts for these results? As discussed earlier in the chapter (p. 192), strong attitudes are more resistant to change than weak attitudes. In chapter 5 you also learned that what makes an attitude strong is acquiring more relevant information about it and becoming more personally involved so that the attitude is more important to you (p. 165). Visser and Krosnick found that attitude importance and perceived knowledge about attitude issues rose in early adulthood, peaked at about age 50, and then began to fall after about age 65. Thus, resistance to attitude change may increase between early and middle adulthood because we attach more importance to our social and political attitudes and think more frequently about them. This same resistance appears to decline later in life because the importance of these attitudes and our knowledge about the relevant issues surrounding them also declines. Their *life-stages hypothesis* contends that the greater susceptibility to attitude change in young adulthood and old age is partly due to the many role transitions that often occur in these two age groups. As their social roles change, young and elderly adults' perceptions of their social and political worlds also change, thereby undermining the strength of their attitudes. In addition, for the elderly, a decline in cognitive skills may render them less able to actively resist persuasion through counterarguing. What these findings suggest is that we may need to revise our "old dog" folk saying. It isn't old dogs or young dogs who are most likely to resist learning new tricks. It's the middle-aged dogs who appear set in their ways.

CRITICAL *thinking*

If the life-stages hypothesis is correct that the attitudes of the young and the elderly are more susceptible to persuasion than the attitudes of middle-age adults, does this change any conclusions that we drew from the Bennington College study described in the Applications section of chapter 5?

SECTION SUMMARY

The audience is perhaps the most important factor in determining the outcome of a persuasive attempt. Audiences in a *positive mood* are generally more susceptible to persuasion than those in a neutral or somber mood. If an issue has a great deal of personal relevance to an audience (high *self-involvement*), they are likely to take a central route to persuasion and, thus, are most likely to be persuaded by strong, well-reasoned arguments. In contrast, people with a low *need for cognition* or those who are high *self-monitors* are more likely to be persuaded by peripheral cues. Researchers have also explored whether *age* affects susceptibility to persuasion. Although early results suggested that susceptibility to persuasion steadily decreased as people moved through adulthood, more recent studies suggest a life-stages explanation: middle-aged adults are most resistant to attitude change, while young adults and the elderly are more easily persuaded.

THE ROLE OF THE SELF IN PERSUASION

When discussing persuasion, it is technically incorrect to state that persuaders change people's minds. Persuaders can present their persuasive arguments, couch it in powerful language, and associate it with pleasing stimuli, but they cannot actually change people's attitudes. What successful persuaders do is create the

By persuading others, we convince ourselves.

Junius, eighteenth-century English political pundit

proper conditions under which individuals become *willing* to change their attitudes (Simons, 1971). This distinction may seem like hairsplitting, but it has raised important questions that have advanced our understanding of the persuasion process. At the heart of this discussion is the self.

SELF-GENERATED PERSUASION IS VERY EFFECTIVE

One of the first studies to explore the nature of self-generated persuasion was conducted by Kurt Lewin (1943, 1947) during World War II. The U.S. Department of Agriculture's Committee on Food Habits was attempting to increase the American public's consumption of meat products that, prior to the war, had generally been thrown away or used as pet food. These less desirable meats were kidneys, beef hearts, and intestines. The Agricultural Department asked Lewin to develop a way to persuade Americans that these undesirable foods were really not that bad. To accomplish this task, Lewin first enlisted a group of housewives as participants in the study and then divided them into two groups. The first group received a forty-five-minute lecture on the merits of intestinal meats. The speaker emphasized how eating these meats would provide more food for the troops overseas, which would greatly benefit the war effort. As recipes were distributed, the speaker described the many nutritional and economic advantages of intestinal meats and informed the women how she had successfully added them to her own family's diet.

In contrast to this first group, the second group of women received no lecture. Instead, after a brief introduction, the discussion leader asked the women, "Do you think that housewives like yourselves could be persuaded to participate in the intestinal meat program?" During the next forty-five minutes, the women brought up many of the same issues as in the lecture. The difference between the lecture and the discussion, however, was that the women in the discussion group were actively generating arguments for serving these relatively undesirable food products. What effect do you think this different information format had on their later culinary activities? While only 3 percent of the housewives in the lecture format group later served intestinal meats to their families, 32 percent of those who engaged in the self-persuasion discussion group served these food products.

As in most, if not all, of the persuasion techniques discussed thus far in the chapter, people who sell consumer products have learned how to employ the self-generated persuasion technique to boost sales. How might this work? Imagine that you are a door-to-door salesperson selling subscriptions to a local cable television network. Using the self-generated persuasion technique, you might knock on someone's door, introduce yourself and your product, and have the following conversation:

You: Mr. Pantouflard, I'd like you to take a moment and imagine how cable TV will provide *you* with broader entertainment value. For example, how do you think cable TV will save you money and make your life easier?

Mr. P.: Gee, let me think about that a bit. Hmm. Well, for one thing, if I had all those movies on HBO, I wouldn't have to waste time renting videos. I could just sit on my couch and tune in the flicks. That's appealing. Being a family man, I also wouldn't have to go to the movie theater and pay $30 for tickets and $20 for popcorn and refreshments. Heck, a night at the movies can cost more than an entire month's worth of cable TV and potato chips! Where do I sign up?!

Although this scene may be a bit exaggerated, it isn't too far off the mark from the actual technique employed by a group of door-to-door cable TV salespersons in Tempe, Arizona. These salespersons were part of a study conducted by Larry

Gregory and his colleagues (1982), in which some salespersons used the self-generated persuasion strategy, while others simply told customers about the advantages of having cable. The results indicated that although less than 20 percent of the customers subscribed when they passively received the information, almost 50 percent subscribed when they themselves were asked to imagine using the service.

Taken together, the studies first conducted by Lewin and those later carried out by others suggest that getting people to actively generate arguments in favor of a certain course of action makes it more likely that their attitudes will change in the direction of these self-generated arguments. Why are these self-generated arguments more persuasive? One fundamental reason is that manipulations that encourage self-persuasion serve to increase how deeply people delve into their attitude structures and, therefore, how many self-relevant connections they make. Another reason is that when someone is actively trying to persuade you by presenting a set of arguments, you may respond negatively to this perceived manipulation of your thoughts (Rhodewalt & Davison, 1983). However, when you are encouraged to generate your own arguments, there is a much greater likelihood that you will adopt these ideas because they have been conceived by a trustworthy and credible source—yourself. Astute persuaders, therefore, allow their audience's positive attitudes concerning their own ideas to move them toward adopting the persuaders' point of view.

EMPLOYING SUBTLE LABELS CAN NUDGE PEOPLE INTO ATTITUDE AND BEHAVIOR CHANGE

Another way in which the self can figure in persuasion is through the attribution process: an effective persuader may nudge people into a desired course of action by convincing them that they are the *sort of people* who engage in this type of activity. Daryl Bem's self-perception theory, discussed in chapter 5, is helpful in describing how this labeling process works. As you recall, Bem contends that people often come to know their own attitudes and dispositions by inferring them from observations of their past behavior. When others begin to attribute certain dispositional qualities to us, self-perception theory contends that we look to our behavior for confirmation of the validity of this labeling. For example, suppose a friend tells you that you are a very insightful and "deep" person. Even though you may never have thought of yourself in this way, you may now recall incidents from your past when you exhibited particular wisdom, understanding, or the ability to ask penetrating questions (for example, you were the first child in your neighborhood to wonder why Goofy, the Disney dog character, walked on his hind legs while Pluto, another Disney dog character, walked on all fours). This analysis of past behavior may lead you to conclude that your friend is correct—you are "deep."

Richard Miller and his coworkers (1975) conducted two interesting studies demonstrating the power of labels in changing an audience's behavior. Both studies took place in three fifth-grade classrooms in an inner-city Chicago public school. In the first study, the teachers in two of the three classrooms engaged in an eight-day ecology program, while the third classroom served as the control group. The teacher in the *attribution-persuasion* classroom first commended her students for being ecology minded and not throwing candy wrappers on the auditorium floor during that day's school assembly. She also told them that the janitor had said that their class was one of the cleanest in the building (this comment was a fabrication). During the week, whenever students picked up paper from the floor, the teacher would commend them for their ecology consciousness. During the middle of the school week, a large poster was pinned to the class bulletin board saying "We Are Anderson's Litter-Conscious Class." The next day, the principal visited their room, commented on how neat and orderly the students were, and then later sent a letter to the class stating:

> As I talked to your teacher, I could not help but notice how very clean and orderly your room appeared. A young lady near the teacher's desk was seen picking up around her desk. It is quite evident that each of you is very careful in your section.

On the eighth day, the janitor washed the classroom floor and left a note (actually written by the experimenters) telling the students it was easy to clean due to their neatness.

In the *information-persuasion* classroom, the students first went on a field trip during which their teacher talked about ecology and warned them of the dangers of littering and pollution. Following this lecture, the students pretended to be trash collectors and picked up litter as they came across it. During the week, the teacher talked about the importance of picking up litter and discussed with the students how they could improve their own classroom. She also told them that the school janitor had said he needed help from the students in keeping the floor clean, implying that such help would lead to adult approval. The next day the principal visited and commented about the need for tidy and neat classrooms, and later sent a letter stating:

> As I talked to your teacher, I could not help but notice that your room was in need of some cleaning. It is very important that we be neat and orderly in the upkeep of our school and classrooms. I hope each of you in your section will be very careful about litter.

The teacher also put up a large poster of a Peanuts character saying "Don't be a litterbug" with "Be neat" and "Don't litter" bordering it. Toward the end of the week, the teacher appointed several children to watch and see if people were neat outside the building as well as in the classroom. On the last day, a note was left on the board from the janitor (actually written by the experimenters) reminding the children to pick up papers off the floor.

Now in both classrooms, students learned that they should be ecology conscious and not litter. However, in the *attribution* classroom, students were repeatedly labeled as ecology minded, while no such labels were "pinned" on the *information* students. Figure 6.7 shows that students in the attribution classroom not only exhibited significantly greater nonlittering behavior two days after the eight-day treatment period, but their ecology mindedness was found to still be intact two weeks following the first posttest. Indeed, three months later the teacher of the attribution class reported that her students were still significantly neater than they had been prior to treatment.

Using a similar labeling procedure with second-graders in the same school, the researchers were also able to significantly increase students' performance in mathematics. These studies, along with others, indicate that when people (especially those whose opinions we respect) make dispositional attributions about our behavior, we often will accept the given label and act in accordance with it in the future (Jensen & Moore, 1977; Kraut, 1973). That is, when we incorporate the labels that others assign to us into our own self-concepts, we will likely also begin acting in ways consistent with the labels.

This self-attribution process, which we previously discussed in chapter 4 as the *self-fulfilling prophecy*, usually does not occur instantaneously. Returning to the ecology study, during the first two days of the treatment, many of the students in the attribution condition did not agree with the ecology label. When the teacher told them that they were not the type of children who would litter, the students disagreed and stated that they would and did indeed litter. However, after repeatedly being called ecology minded by others, and given some time to observe their own behavior, these children began to adopt the ecology label quite strongly. They had accepted the dispositional attribution of being ecology-conscious children.

FIGURE 6.7

Attribution Versus Information Persuasion as a Means for Modifying Behavior

Miller and his colleagues taught fifth-graders in two separate classrooms not to litter and to clean up after others. How were they taught? Students in the attribution classroom were repeatedly told they were neat and tidy people, while those in the persuasion classroom were told they should be neat and tidy. The students who were labeled as neat and tidy not only littered less two days after the eight-day treatment period, but their ecology-mindedness was still intact two weeks later.

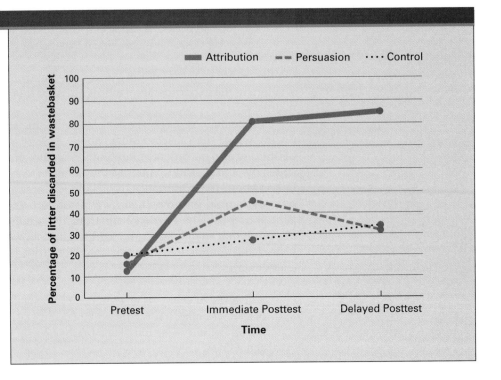

One of the advantages of using attributional statements in persuading people to change their attitudes and behavior is that in their guise as "truth statements," these labels may more easily slip past the defenses people ordinarily employ against more direct persuasive attempts. In other words, using attribution to persuade may be more successful because it is less easily recognized as persuasion, and thus, it is less likely to arouse resistance or counterarguing.

Having extolled the persuasive power of using labels to change people's attitudes and actions, it must be added that there are limits to this attributional power. Labels are often rejected. As you will recall from chapter 2, self-concept change generally occurs only on those self-aspects about which people hold uncertain beliefs (Swann & Ely, 1984). When people hold very definite beliefs about themselves, they are very likely to reject any labels that contradict those beliefs. Thus, persuading through labeling is generally only going to have a chance for success when the audience has vaguely formulated conceptions of their personal attributes in the area under scrutiny. The lesson to be learned here is that you can use labels to persuade if the focus of change is not some attitude or behavior strongly associated with a central aspect of a person's self-concept.

SECTION SUMMARY

Successful persuaders understand the role the self plays in the persuasion process. Getting people to actively generate arguments in favor of a certain course of action makes it more likely that they will persuade themselves. In addition, subtly labeling someone as being the type of person who would think or act in a certain way may be sufficient to persuade them to do so.

n the summer of 1957, advertising executive James Vicary claimed that he had induced customers at a New Jersey theater to dramatically increase their popcorn and coke purchases by secretly splicing the words *EAT POPCORN* and *DRINK COKE* into the Hollywood movie *Picnic* and flashing it before their eyes for a fraction of a second. These messages were *subliminal*, meaning that they were presented so fast or so faintly that they were just below the absolute threshold for conscious awareness. **Subliminal perception** is the processing of such information. Vicary's "study" created a sensation with the public, and, over the years, people commonly cite it when they either talk or write about the powerful influence that subliminal messages can have on thought and action (Key, 1989). What they don't realize is that James Vicary fabricated the entire study in an attempt to attract customers to his failing marketing business (Weir, 1984)!

Subliminal Perception

The processing of information that is just below the absolute threshold for conscious awareness.

A likely reason why Vicary's surprising claims were so uncritically accepted may be that they fit popular assumptions about the powers that new communication technologies can have over the attitudes and behavior of viewers (Wartella & Reeves, 1985). Indeed, almost 70 percent of people who have some knowledge of subliminal advertising believe that it can influence consumer buying habits (Zanot et al., 1983). Yet, is there any real scientific evidence that subliminal messages can influence attitudes or behavior?

Actually, there is a possibility that people can respond to stimuli without being aware that they are doing so. For example, in a series of studies, Robert Bornstein and his colleagues (1987) found evidence for a subliminal mere exposure effect. Participants who were repeatedly exposed to subliminal stimuli (abstract geometric figures or people's faces) later expressed greater liking for those stimuli. These findings, along with others (Krosnick et al., 1992), indicate that it is at least theoretically possible for a stimulus subliminally embedded in an advertisement to influence buyers' preferences. Yet before you demand that

laws be passed to restrict subliminal ads, let's examine some differences between the laboratory environment where these results were obtained and the real world where people would normally receive subliminal messages.

First, these effects were obtained in a carefully controlled lab study where participants paid a great deal of attention to the experimental stimuli. In watching the average media advertisement, people are much less attentive. Due to the viewer's wandering eye, it is doubtful that a subliminal stimulus embedded in an ad would be unconsciously processed. A second reason to doubt that these effects would occur outside the lab is that the duration of these subliminal effects may be very short, perhaps lasting only a few seconds. If the subliminal effects last only a short period of time, they are unlikely to influence product purchases. Consistent with this expectation, field studies of subliminal advertising in newspapers and on television have found no evidence that they have even a slight effect in persuading people to increase their product purchasing (DeFleur & Petranoff, 1959, 1992).

Despite the fact that research provides little evidence that subliminal messages can persuade people to change their attitudes or behavior, the marketplace is flooded with subliminal self-help audiotapes that claim amazing results. Is there any evidence that such claims are credible? Like the field studies of subliminal advertising, the results from a number of subliminal tape experiments suggest that whatever benefits people derive from such self-help products have little to do with the content of the subliminal messages themselves (Benoit & Thomas, 1992; Merikle & Skanes, 1992). Instead, people's expectations and their desire to reduce cognitive dissonance ("I invested a lot of time and money in this tape; it must be good!") appear to be the sole means of persuasion operating here. Thus, even though people can perceive stimuli just below their absolute threshold for conscious awareness, and although such subliminal exposure can sometimes briefly influence attitudinal preferences in laboratory settings, there is no evidence that subliminal messages have anything close to the persuasive power that some advertisers and merchandisers claim. When all is said and done, what very likely explains attitude and behavior change in those who use subliminal self-help products is good old-fashioned persuasion principles.

Despite the overwhelming weight of this scientific evidence, subliminal tapes will probably continue to do a fairly brisk business in the self-help marketplace. Fed by high expectations from the tapes' nonsubliminal persuasion tactics and sustained by the consumers' need to justify their purchases, product owners will convince themselves that their lives have been improved due to these subliminal messages. Armed with this firm, but false, belief in the tapes' subliminal powers, the proud owners of these products will become effective proselytizers to others who are unaware of the current scientific literature. Yet now that you know the scientific facts regarding subliminal perception, perhaps you can combine this with your newly learned knowledge of persuasion to dissuade others from wasting their money on such products.

> It is true that you may fool all the people some of the time; you can even fool some of the people all the time; but you can't fool all of the people all the time.
>
> *Abraham Lincoln, U.S. president, 1809–1865*

> You can fool all the people all the time if the advertising is right and the budget is big enough.
>
> *Joseph E. Levine, U.S. film producer, 1984*

Although subliminal self-help tapes do not improve memory or increase self-esteem, they continue to do a brisk business. Their staying power in the marketplace is probably due to two factors: (1) a misperception by the public that subliminal persuasion can influence this type of attitude and behavior change, and (2) self-persuasion of consumers who likely experience postdecision dissonance after purchasing such pricey products.

FEATURED STUDY
TESTING THE EFFECTIVENESS OF SUBLIMINAL SELF-HELP TAPES

Pratkanis, A. R., Eskenazi, J., & Greenwald, A. G. (1994). What you expect is what you believe (but not necessarily what you get): A test of the effectiveness of subliminal self-help audiotapes. *Basic and Applied Social Psychology, 15: 251–276.*

A likely mechanism underlying many consumers' beliefs in the usefulness of subliminal self-help audiotapes is the concept of an expectancy effect. In other words, people who buy these tapes convince themselves that their lives are better after using them. In the present study, the researchers evaluated the therapeutic claims made by marketers of such tapes and investigated the possibility that consumers' beliefs were based on an expectancy effect.

METHOD

Seventy-eight college students and community residents volunteered to participate in a study investigating the therapeutic value of subliminal tapes. Participants were pretested for their level of self-esteem and memory recall ability and then given a self-help audiotape containing various pieces of classical music. The tape manufacturers claimed that embedded within these tapes were subliminal messages designed either to increase self-esteem ("I have high self-worth and high self-esteem") or to increase memory ("My ability to remember and recall is increasing daily"). However, the researchers purposely mislabeled half of the tapes, leading participants who received them to believe they had a memory tape when they really had a self-esteem tape, or vice versa. The remaining participants received the rest of the tapes, with correct labels. Participants were randomly assigned to these experimental conditions. During the next five weeks, these volunteers listened daily to their respective tapes at home. After this exposure period, they were again given self-esteem and memory tests, and they were also asked whether they believed the tapes had been effective.

RESULTS AND DISCUSSION

Results indicated no self-esteem or memory increases: the subliminal tapes were utterly ineffective. These null findings, however, stood in sharp contrast to the participants' beliefs about the tapes. Those who thought they had received the self-esteem tape tended to believe their self-esteem had increased, and those who thought they had been given the memory tape were more likely to believe that their memory had improved. This was true even if they had received a mislabeled tape! According to the researchers, these findings indicate that users of self-help audiotapes expect self-improvement through their use, and actually convince themselves that the improvement has taken place, when, in fact, it has not.

 WEB SITES accessed through http://www.mhhe.com/franzoi2

Web sites for this chapter focus on persuasion, including an analysis of propaganda and recent research employing the elaboration likelihood model.

Propaganda Analysis Home Page

This web page contains an analysis of common propaganda techniques, historical examples, and a bibliography of relevant publications.

John Cacioppo's Home Page

John Cacioppo, co-creator of the elaboration likelihood model, has a home page where you can learn more about his recent research and ideas.

SMASH
GAY
RIGHTS
NOW
JEWISH MORA
COMMITTEE
SMILE
IF YOU HAVE
AIDS

CHAPTER 7

PREJUDICE AND DISCRIMINATION

CHAPTER OUTLINE

n October 12, 1998, Matthew Shepard died five days after slipping into a coma. The disease that caused his death cannot be found in any medical textbook, but it is a disease that permeates society. What caused his death was prejudice. Matthew was a freshman at the University of Wyoming in Laramie who was lured from a campus bar, pistol-whipped, burned, and tied to a split-rail fence like a scarecrow by two men who wanted to make an example out of him. His skull was so badly smashed that doctors could not perform surgery. What triggered such an intensely aggressive response in these men? One of the men told authorities he committed the crime because he thought Matthew was flirting with him in front of his friends. Compounding the grief and anger of Matthew's family and friends was the fact that his funeral was picketed by antigay protesters who carried signs such as "God Hates Fags" and "No Fags in Heaven." Despite the nationwide attention to Matthew's murder, in 1999 Wyoming lawmakers voted down for a fifth year legislation that would have increased the fine and prison terms for similar prejudice-based crimes.

Gay men are not the only targets of intolerance. The following incidents, all of which have occurred within the past five years, depict some of the awful manifestations of prejudice and discrimination:

> In Toronto, Ontario, a native Indian correctional officer was denied promotions, regularly called "Tomahawk," "Chief," and "Wagon Burner," and greeted with war whoops and dancing by his fellow officers.

> In Novato, California, a Chinese American man was repeatedly stabbed by an unemployed White man who told police he wanted to "kill me a Chinaman" because they "got all the good jobs."

> In Harlem, New York, a Jewish-owned store was picketed by Black residents following a dispute with a Black-owned business. Picketers frequently shouted anti-Semitic slurs, and one demonstrator fire-bombed the store, resulting in eight deaths.

> In Jasper, Texas, a Black man's body was literally torn to pieces after he was chained to a pickup truck by three White men and dragged along a winding rural road. One of the accused knew the victim since childhood.

Can you make sense of these people's behavior? Where do you stand in your own attitudes and actions toward members of other social groups? What about group-based antagonism at your own doorstep? College campuses are supposed to be bastions of tolerance, where people are accepted as individuals and judged on their intellectual merits. Has tolerance and acceptance been a hallmark of your college experience? Where have you noticed intergroup tension, and even hostility? Have you been the victim, and sometimes perhaps the perpetrator, of prejudice and discrimination? How do you understand these experiences?

The primary objective of this chapter is to analyze how we think, feel, and act in response to social group categories. These *category-based reactions of intolerance* encompass the concepts of *stereotyping* (first discussed in chapter 4), *prejudice*, and *discrimination*. Besides examining the social psychological dynamics of these three intertwined concepts and the various theories developed to explain them, we will also focus on three different forms of group intolerance: *racism*, which is intolerance based on skin color or ethnic heritage; *sexism*, which is intolerance based on

Twenty-one year-old Matthew Shepard, a student at the University of Wyoming, was murdered because he was a gay man. There are many "Matthews" on college campuses today. Their social "stigma" might be their sexual orientation, skin color, sex, religion, or some other characteristic that discredits them in others' eyes. To what degree is the prejudice and discrimination they elicit from others facilitated by cultural attitudes and beliefs?

sex; and *heterosexism,* which is intolerance based on sexual orientation. Our chapter inquiry will end with an exploration of ways that social scientists believe that prejudice and discrimination can be reduced.

PREJUDICE AND DISCRIMINATION DEFINED

We often use the terms *prejudice* and *discrimination* interchangeably, yet they are distinct concepts. Prejudice is a type of attitude; discrimination is a form of behavior.

PREJUDICE IS A NEGATIVE ATTITUDE AND DISCRIMINATION IS A NEGATIVE ACTION

Prejudice

A negative attitude directed toward people because they are members of a specific social group.

Prejudice is a negative attitude directed toward people because they are members of a specific social group. A person who is prejudiced toward some group tends to ignore the individual qualities of its members and prejudges them based on this negative evaluation.

Examination of the emotions underlying prejudicial attitudes suggests that they may lead to different behavioral consequences (Smith, 1993). Negative emotions such as anger and contempt often lead to movement *against* a social group, while emotions such as fear and disgust often lead to movement *away* from a negatively evaluated group. However, it must be kept in mind that prejudice does not actually involve behavior. Although it is an attitude of aversion, **discrimination** is a negative *action* toward members of a specific social group (see Brewer & Brown, 1998). This negative action could involve movement against a group—such as denying "them" good jobs and housing—but it could also involve movement away from the group—such as selling one's house when "they" move next door.

Discrimination

A negative action toward members of a specific social group.

Having stated that prejudicial attitudes often trigger discriminatory responses, I must hasten to remind you that behavior does not always follow attitude. For example, an Asian storeowner could be prejudiced against Blacks, but he may not overtly act on his negative attitudes because most of his customers are Black and he needs their business to survive financially. In this case, the subjective norm (see chapter 5, p. 167) dictates against the storeowner acting on his prejudice. It is also true that discrimination can occur without prejudice. For instance, sometimes people who are not prejudiced engage in *institutional discrimination* by carrying out the discriminatory guidelines of institutions. Even today in certain real-estate businesses, agents will show their African-American clients only houses located in Black or racially mixed neighborhoods. Many agents who have no personal animosity toward African Americans (and who may be Black themselves) carry out this institutional practice, known as *redlining*, merely because they are following the guidelines of their superiors, who believe that property values will be lowered by residential integration.

SECTION SUMMARY

While *prejudice* is a negative attitude directed toward people because they are members of a specific social group, *discrimination* is a negative action toward members of a specific group.

HOW IS STEREOTYPING RELATED TO PREJUDICE AND DISCRIMINATION?

A concept often associated with prejudice and discrimination is *stereotype*. As you may recall from our discussion in chapter 4, stereotypes are fixed ways of thinking about people that don't allow for individual variation. Although stereotypes can consist of positive traits (doctors, for example, are often thought of as intelligent, hard-working, caring, and wealthy), it is also true that people can and do associate extremely negative traits with other social groups (Krueger, 1996). These negative labels can form the basis for later prejudicial feelings and discriminatory actions (see Fiske, 1998). Therefore, even though stereotyping doesn't have to lead to prejudice and discrimination, it can provide the necessary foundation. Here's how the foundation can be set.

SOCIAL CATEGORIZATION CAN LEAD TO GROUP DISTORTIONS

Outgroup Homogeneity Effect

Perception of outgroup members as being more similar to one another than are members of one's ingroup.

How many times have you heard a woman say, "Well, you know men . . . They're all alike and they all want the same thing!" Likewise, how often have you heard men describing women in similar terms? This tendency to see members within a given outgroup as being more alike than members of one's ingroup is a consequence of social categorization. Research has shown that merely assigning people to different social groups can create this **outgroup homogeneity effect.** For example, Bernadette Park and Charles Judd found that on college campuses, sorority members, business majors, and engineering students all tend to perceive students in other campus social groups (those in other sororities or those with other majors) as more alike than those in their ingroup (Judd et al., 1991; Park & Rothbart, 1982).

What are some factors that influence our tendency to see outgroups as uniform? Research indicates that this *illusion* of outgroup homogeneity is more likely to occur among competing than noncompeting groups (Judd & Park, 1988). It is also more likely when there are relatively few members in the outgroup being judged (Mullen & Hu, 1989). Surprisingly, a person's familiarity or contact with the outgroup, such as the frequent and often intimate contact between men and women, does not appear to appreciably change this tendency to see them as more alike than different (Lorenzi-Cioldi, 1993; Park et al., 1992).

Although we tend to perceive outgroups as being fairly uniform, our view of ingroup members is generally that they are relatively *distinct* and *complex*. An example of this effect is the social perceptions of the young and old in our society. Young adults tend to perceive others of their age as having more complex personalities than the elderly, whereas older adults hold exactly opposite beliefs (Brewer

Test your knowledge of racial and ethnic group stereotypes by writing down what you think are some of the positive and negative characteristics typically associated with the following social groups in North American culture: Anglo-Whites, Asians, Blacks, Jews, and Latinos. Once you have listed characteristics for each group, compare them with the research findings summarized in Appendix A. Does your knowledge of group stereotypes tell us anything about your degree of prejudice toward these racial and ethnic groups?

& Lui, 1984; Linville, 1982). Interestingly, the outgroup homogeneity effect actually reverses and becomes an "ingroup homogeneity effect" when members of *small groups* or *minority groups* compare their own group with the majority outgroup on attributes *central* to their social identity (Castano & Yzerbyt, 1998; Simon, 1992b). In such instances, by emphasizing their similarities with fellow ingroup members, minority group members affirm their social identity.

One manifestation of the outgroup homogeneity effect is seen in our relative difficulty in correctly identifying people of other races. Perhaps you have had the embarrassing experience of confusing two people of another race, and having the misnamed person say to you, "We all look alike to you, don't we?" Numerous studies have found a weak to moderate tendency for people to more accurately recognize faces of members of their own race than those of another race (Anthony et al., 1992; Shapiro & Penrod, 1986). This *own-race bias* in facial recognition is not confined to one racial group, nor does it appear to be related to the perceiver's racial attitudes. Civil rights activists apparently can make this perceptual mistake as easily as members of the Ku Klux Klan (Platz & Hosch, 1988). Although racial attitudes seem to be unrelated to cross-race facial identification, *experience* may be an important factor. For example, June Chance (1985) found that White college students generally have difficulty recognizing individual Japanese faces. However, if these students are trained to notice differences in pairs of Japanese faces, their accuracy rate significantly increases. One implication of these findings is that people who live in more racially diverse settings may be less prone to see people of other races as "all looking alike."

FORMING STEREOTYPE SUBCATEGORIES FOSTERS THE RETENTION OF MORE GLOBAL STEREOTYPES

As observed earlier, many men and women often describe the other sex as fitting a particular stereotypical mold or as all having the same desires or characteristics. People expressing such views hold these stereotypical beliefs despite the fact that they probably have friends and lovers of the other sex whom they don't categorize in this manner. One question social psychologists have asked is why these nonstereotypical acquaintances don't serve as a catalyst to alter these people's stereotypes.

There is a tendency to perceive outgroup members as more similar to one another than members of one's own ingroup. This outgroup homogeneity effect can cause people to be more accurate in recognizing faces of members of their own race than those of other races. Have you had personal experience with this own-race bias in facial recognition?

One explanation for why stereotypes often survive such disconfirming evidence is that the global stereotype consists of a number of more limited, specific subtypes or *subcategories* (Hewstone et al., 1994). These subcategories give people who stereotype others a place to categorize those individuals of the stereotyped group whose personal characteristics don't correspond to those characteristics in the global stereotype (Lambert, 1995). For example, Kay Deaux and her colleagues (1985) found that American college students distinguish at least five different subcategories of women: housewives, career women, athletes, feminists, and sex objects. When a man with gender-stereotypical beliefs meets and learns to respect a woman who does not fit his gender stereotype, he may retain his prior gender beliefs by concluding that this particular woman is atypical of women in general. She is not "like the rest of them." Here, instead of revising his global stereotype of women, the man merely creates a new subcategory in which to place this particular woman, thus leaving his global gender stereotype essentially unchanged.

For some stereotypes that people hold about other groups, very little overlap exists between the global stereotypes and the specific subcategories within those groups. For example, many White Americans' global stereotype of African Americans tends to be primarily negative, while their stereotypes of African-American businesspersons or athletes are primarily positive (Devine & Baker, 1991). In categorizing African Americans who are either businesspersons or athletes, many White Americans are more likely to identify them with their occupational role (either businessperson or athlete) rather than with their race (Black). This is perhaps why professional athletes like Michael Jordan and Barry Sanders can be idolized by White fans who harbor negative racial stereotypes. For these fans, the Michael Jordans and the Barry Sanders of the world are not like most others of their race. Because these fans do not perceive them as representing the "average" African American, such athletes are unlikely to challenge the negative global stereotype these fans hold. Thus, even though subcategories often seem more positive than many global stereotypes, their very creation allows people who hold these stereotypes the opportunity to retain more rigid and unflattering views of the social group in question.

STIGMATIZED GROUPS RESPOND TO NEGATIVE STEREOTYPES WITH OPPOSITION AND ANXIETY

Stigma

An attribute that serves to discredit a person in the eyes of others.

A **stigma** is an attribute that serves to discredit a person or a social group in the eyes of others (Goffman, 1963). John Ogbu (1993) believes that some members of stigmatized ethnic groups respond to negative stereotypes and discrimination by developing an *oppositional* ethnic identity and cultural frame of reference that defensively opposes the rejecting dominant culture (see chapter 2 for a discussion of the *ethnic identity search* stage). This oppositional identity helps them cope with a hostile social environment by clearly defining their ingroup in contrasting ways with various outgroups. In this oppositional stance, people think, feel, and act the way they believe "authentic" members of their ingroup are supposed to act, and they judge other ingroup members by these same standards.

As a defensive strategy, oppositional identities can have both beneficial and hindering effects on oppressed groups (Crocker & Major, 1989). On the positive side, they function to psychologically insulate stigmatized people from some of the negative effects of social injustice, such as loss of self-esteem (Helms, 1990). On the negative side, however, immersion in an identity that defines itself in terms of opposition to the dominant outgroup will likely constrict one's personal identity. For example, according to this perspective, when an African-American's behavior or thinking falls within the forbidden White cultural frame of reference, she or he may be accused by other Blacks of "acting White" or being an "oreo" (being Black on the outside but White on the inside). These forbidden areas are those that have historically been reserved for White Americans, and where minorities have not been given an equal opportunity to excel. Academic tasks represent one of these cultural domains. For young African Americans who hold to an oppositional identity, committing themselves to academic excellence and learning to follow the academic standards of the school might be perceived as adopting a White American cultural frame of reference and forsaking their ethnic identity (Ford, 1996). Unfortunately, by rejecting certain activities perceived to be White, such as academic pursuits, many Blacks have hindered themselves from fully taking advantage of recent civil rights advances (Bankston & Caldas, 1997).

Although rejecting pursuits that are important to mainstream economic success is a problem in certain segments of American society, oppositional identities must be seen in a larger developmental context. As described in chapter 2, ethnic identity is conceived of as an ongoing developmental process, and this defensive oppositional identity is only one possible stage in the process. Many African Americans, for instance, do not identify at all with an oppositional identity, and others do so only marginally (Fordham, 1985). For them, pursuing academic excellence does not create psychological conflict with their Black social identity. Instead, it is consistent with a central feature of the civil rights movement of the 1960s, namely, social advancement through educational achievement.

In addition to the problem that oppositional identities pose to minority students' academic achievement, Claude Steele (1997) asserts that minority students enrolled in largely White schools and colleges carry the extra burden of "representing their race" in academic pursuits. By this, he means that these students are often one of only a few members of their race enrolled in a particular course, and their individual performance is often looked on by students not of their race as representing the typical student of that group. Accompanying this scrutiny is the added social stigma associated with the minority label, which often implies a suspicion of intellectual inferiority (Sigelman & Tuch, 1997).[1] Because these negative stereotypes are widely known throughout society, people who are their targets are susceptible to developing what Steele identifies as **stereotype threat**. Stereotype threat is a disturbing awareness among members of a negatively stereotyped group that anything one does, or anything about oneself that fits the stereotype, may confirm it as a self-characterization (Steele & Aronson, 1994).

Steele contends that faced with this sort of threatening scrutiny, and fearing that they may confirm others' negative perceptions of both themselves and their race, minority students often *disidentify* with achievement. That is, they change their self-concept so that academic achievement is no longer very important to their self-esteem. Adopting an oppositional identity that rejects academic pursuits as being "too White" further validates this disidentification process (Ford & Harris, 1992). As Steele describes the effects of disidentification on one particular student with whom he spoke:

> She may continue to feel pressure to stay in school—from her parents, even from the potential advantages of a college degree. But now she is psychologically insulated from her academic life, like a disinterested visitor. Cool, unperturbed. But, like a pain killing drug, disidentification undoes her future as it relieves her vulnerability. (Steele, 1992, p. 74)

Evidence for the stereotype threat effect among African-American college students comes from a series of experiments that Steele and Joshua Aronson (1995)

---

[1] Exceptions would be Asian students, who often are expected to perform better academically than others, including White students. Although this is a positive perception, it still burdens Asian students with the social pressure to positively represent their race in a way that White students rarely experience (Nakanishi & Nishida, 1995).

Stereotype Threat

A disturbing awareness among members of a negatively stereotyped group that anything one does, or anything about oneself that fits the stereotype, may confirm it as a self-characterization.

FIGURE 7.1

African-American Intellectual Test Performance and Stereotype Threat

Steele and Aronson (1995) administered a difficult English test to Black and White college students. When the test was described as a measure of intellectual ability (stereotype threat condition), Blacks performed worse than Whites. However, when it was not associated with ability (nonstereotype threat condition), no racial differences were found. How are these findings consistent with the stereotype threat hypothesis?

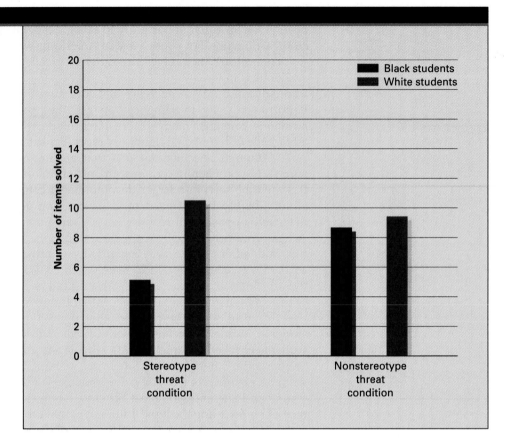

conducted. In one of these studies, Black and White student volunteers were given a difficult English test. In the *stereotype threat condition*, the test was described as a measure of intellectual ability, while in the *nonstereotype threat condition*, it was described as a laboratory problem-solving task that didn't measure intelligence. Because one of the more salient racial stereotypes is that Blacks are intellectually inferior to Whites, the researchers presumed that describing the test as an intellectual measure would make this negative stereotype relevant to the Black students' performance. In turn, researchers also expected this stereotype relevance to establish for these Black students a fear of confirming the stereotype ("If I do poorly, my performance will reflect badly on my race and on me"). Steele and Aronson hypothesized that the self-evaluation apprehension created by such thinking would interfere with the Black students' performance. In contrast, when the task was described as not measuring intelligence, researchers assumed that this would make the negative racial stereotype about ability *irrelevant* to the Black students' performance and, therefore, not arouse performance anxiety. As you can see in figure 7.1, consistent with the stereotype threat hypothesis, when the test was presented as a measure of ability, Blacks performed worse than Whites. However, when it was not associated with ability, no significant racial differences were found.

Further research indicates that the academic disidentification presumed to be caused by stereotype threat is much more common among African-American students than among White-American students (Osborne, 1995). For example, in one experiment with college students, Brenda Major and her coworkers (1998) manipulated success and failure feedback on a supposed test of intelligence. White students reacted with higher self-esteem after success than after failure, but Black students' self-esteem was unaffected. These findings are consistent with the hypothesis that Black students tend to disengage their self-esteem from academic performance. A second experiment in this series found

FIGURE 7.2

Stereotype Threat and Women's Math Performance

Spencer and his colleagues (1996) found that when a difficult math test was described as exhibiting gender differences (men outperforming women), women did indeed underperform. However, when the test was described as exhibiting no gender differences, women's underperformance disappeared. How do these results support the stereotype threat hypothesis?

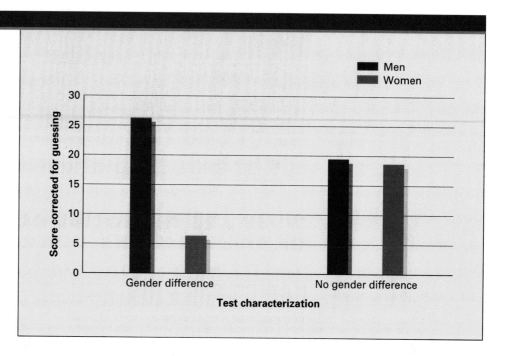

RITICAL *thinking*

Although stereotype threat is thought to be most noticeable and problematic among social groups that have been historically disadvantaged, it can also occur among members of privileged groups, such as White middle-class males. Can you think of a negative stereotype about White males that might cause them to experience stereotype threat in a particular area of pursuit, thereby motivating them to disidentify with this activity?

that, consistent with Steele's notion of stereotype threat, academic disidentification among African-American students is most likely to occur when negative racial stereotypes concerning Black intellectual inferiority are salient in an academic setting. Although such disidentification protects self-esteem and is a coping response to racial prejudice and discrimination, it also is one of the psychological factors that undermines African-American students' school achievement.

Academic disidentification not only occurs among African Americans, but also among American Indians, Hispanic Americans, lower-class Whites, and female students in male-dominated majors (Croizet & Claire, 1998). For example, Steven Spencer and his colleagues (1998) found that women performed as well as men on a difficult English test where they suffered no social stigma, but women underachieved relative to men on a comparably difficult math test where they are more vulnerable to suspicions of intellectual inferiority. In a follow-up to this study, the researchers gave male and female college students a difficult math test, but divided it into two halves and presented it as two distinct tests. Half of the students were told that the first test was one on which men outperformed women, and that the second test was one on which there were no gender differences. The other students were told the opposite—test 1 was described as exhibiting no gender differences, but men outperformed women on test 2. As you can see in figure 7.2, consistent with the stereotype threat hypothesis, when told that the test yielded gender differences, women greatly underperformed in relation to men. However, when the test was described as not exhibiting any gender differences, women's underperformance disappeared. This dramatic change occurred even though the two tests were the same! Similar to African-American students' disidentification process described earlier, women are most likely to disidentify with math and math-related careers when negative gender stereotypes are salient (cited in Steele, 1997).

Are all members of stigmatized groups equally likely to experience stereotype threat? No. A series of recent studies conducted by Elizabeth Pinel (1999) suggest that members of stigmatized groups are more likely to experience stereotype threat the more they have personally experienced discrimination.

WHAT ARE THE SOCIAL CAUSES OF PREJUDICE AND DISCRIMINATION?

In addition to the role that negative stereotypes play in both the causes and effects of prejudice and discrimination, powerful social variables also exert a significant influence in the creation of intergroup intolerance. In this section of the chapter we will examine some of these social causes.

PREJUDICE CAN DEVELOP AS A WAY TO JUSTIFY OPPRESSION

Social Dominance Theory

A theory contending that societal groups can be organized in a power hierarchy in which the dominant groups enjoy a disproportionate share of the society's assets and the subordinate groups receive most of its liabilities.

Power is a necessary condition for effective discrimination. In laboratory experiments, when groups are given different amounts of social power, members of high power groups discriminate more against outgroups than members of low power groups (Sachdev & Bourhis, 1987, 1991). **Social dominance theory** proposes that in all societies, groups can be organized in a hierarchy of power with at least one group being dominant over all others (Pratto, 1996; Sidanius, 1993). Dominant groups enjoy a lopsided share of the society's assets, such as wealth, prestige, education, and health. In contrast, subordinate groups receive most of the society's liabilities, such as poverty, social stigma, illiteracy, poor health, and high levels of criminal punishment. What history teaches us is that the negative stereotypes and prejudicial attitudes that dominant groups develop about those they oppress serve to justify their continued oppression (Sidanius et al., 1996).

The whites told only one side. Told it to please themselves. Told much that is not true. Only his own best deeds, only the worst deeds of the Indians, has the white man told.

Yellow Wolf of the Nez Perce Indians, 1940

Racism breeds racism in reverse.

Mary Brave Bird, Sioux (Lakota) Nation commentator, 1990

A good deal of the history of the United States rests on prejudice based on social dominance. Europeans who founded this country did not arrive on uninhabited shores in the "New World." These settlers used their superior weapons to dominate and conquer the indigenous people of North America. At the same time that Europeans were colonizing North America, they were also capturing and buying Africans and transporting them to the colonies as slaves. They justified the inhuman exploitation that took place by stigmatizing both Native Americans and Africans as inferior races who needed civilizing.

A number of experimental studies have demonstrated that developing prejudicial and dehumanizing attitudes toward the victims of one's own harmful actions is a common response (Glass, 1964). For example, Stephen Worchel and Virginia Mathie Andreoli (1978) found that when instructed to deliver electric shocks to a man when he responded incorrectly on a learning task, college students were more likely to dehumanize him than were students who were instructed to reward the man for correct answers. By dehumanizing and derogating their own victims, exploiters can not only avoid thinking of themselves as villains, but they can also justify further exploitation.

Old American textbooks illustrate the racist attitudes generated from such exploitation. For example, figure 7.3 is an excerpt from a popular high-school geography book published in 1880 devoted to the "Races of Man" around the

FIGURE 7.3

An Example of Racist Attitudes in an Old American Textbook

The characterization of the various races in Swinton's text conveys the ingroup biases of the author. In comparing our own beliefs against the beliefs of this author of the nineteenth century, before we smugly assume a superior attitude of intergroup tolerance, we must ask ourselves how our current attitudes and beliefs toward different social groups will be judged by future generations. What sort of overlooked ingroup prejudices and biases permeate the text you are reading at this very moment? As the author of this social psychology book, I am sure my ingroup biases have occasionally made their way into my writing. Later, when discussing ways to monitor stereotypical thinking, we will examine how becoming aware of our current prejudices can steer us toward nonprejudiced thinking.

Source: W. Swinton, *A Complete Course in Geography: Physical, Industrial, and Political.* New York: Ivison, Blakeman, Taylor, & Co., 1880.

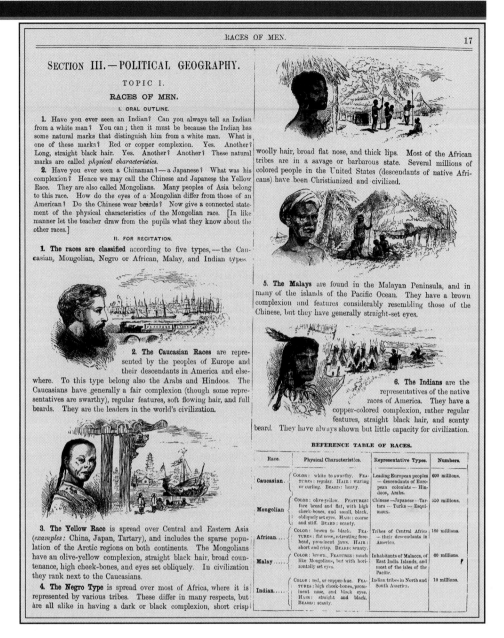

We first crush people to the earth, and then claim the right of trampling on them forever, because they are prostrate.

Lydia Maria Child, U.S. author and abolitionist, 1802–1880

globe. The five listed races are classified in a descending order of capacity for civilization—the *Caucasian* races, the *Yellow* race, the *Negro* type, the *Malays,* and the *Indians.* Can you guess the race of the author of this civilized hierarchy? Particularly interesting about this section is how the White-American author describes the two races that his social group had the most contact with, and with whom they had historically treated so harshly. African tribes are described as living in a "savage or barbarous state," while the descendants of native Africans had "been Christianized and civilized" by Whites. What about the representatives of the native races of America, whose land had been taken by the same European descendants as the author of the text? According to the author, American Indians "have always shown but little capacity for civilization" (Swinton, 1880, p. 17). In these characterizations, we see how an oppressor group justifies its exploitation of less powerful groups by denigrating them.

INTERGROUP COMPETITION CAN LEAD TO PREJUDICE

In 1996, "Beauty Island," a cosmetics store located in a predominantly Black Milwaukee neighborhood, was the target of boycotts, vandalism, and even attempted arson. The reason? Black community activists charged that the Korean-born owner's business was taking money out of the Black community. Amid a "BUY BLACK" message spray-painted on the side of the store and racial epithets hurled at the inhabitants, one protester stated, "This isn't just about Beauty Island, and it's not just about Milwaukee. It's about foreign merchants in the Black community." This example of racial prejudice and violence directed against a member of another social group can be at least partly explained by *intergroup competition*. That is, when two groups compete for a limited number of scarce resources such as jobs, housing, consumer sales, or even food, one group's success becomes the other's failure and creates a breeding ground for prejudice (Duckitt & Mphuthing, 1998; Quillian, 1995).

REALISTIC CONFLICT THEORY

Realistic Group Conflict Theory

The theory that intergroup conflict develops from competition for limited resources.

Examining the competitive roots for intergroup intolerance is exactly the perspective taken by **realistic group conflict theory** (Levine & Campbell, 1972). It argues that groups become prejudiced toward one another because they are in conflict over competition for scarce resources. The group conflict is considered "rational" or "realistic" because it is based on real competition. According to this theory, African-Americans' hostility toward Asian Americans will increase if they believe that Asian shopkeepers in their neighborhoods are taking business opportunities away from them. Similarly, White-Americans' prejudice toward African Americans will increase if Blacks are hired ahead of Whites due to affirmative-action programs.

Ethnocentrism

A pattern of increased hostility toward outgroups accompanied by increased loyalty to one's ingroup.

Realistic group conflict theory contends that when groups are in conflict, two important changes occur in each group. The first change involves increased hostility toward the opposing outgroup, and the second change involves an intensification of ingroup loyalty. This pattern of behavior is referred to as **ethnocentrism** (Sumner, 1906). To better understand how ethnocentrism can develop due to conflict, let's examine one of the first experimental studies involving this psychological phenomenon.

THE ROBBERS CAVE EXPERIMENT

What happens if you randomly place people into one of two groups and manipulate circumstances in a way that promotes intergroup competition? This was the central question surrounding a classic field experiment designed by Muzafer Sherif and his colleagues (Sherif et al., 1961; Sherif & Sherif, 1956). They conducted the study in the summer of 1961 at a densely forested and hilly 200-acre camp that the researchers had created at Robbers Cave State Park, which is 150 miles southeast of Oklahoma City. Participants were twenty White, middle-class, well-adjusted 11- and 12-year-old boys who had never met one another before. In advance, the researchers divided the boys into two groups, with one group leaving by bus for the camp a day before the other. Upon arrival, each group was assigned a separate cabin out of sight of the other, and thus, neither knew of the other's existence. The camp counselors were actually researchers who unobtrusively observed and recorded day-to-day camp events as the study progressed.

There were three phases to the study. The first phase was devoted to *creating ingroups*, the second was devoted to *instilling intergroup competition*, and the third phase involved *encouraging intergroup cooperation*. During the first week of ingroup creation, each group separately engaged in cooperative activities such as hiking, hunting for hidden treasures, making meals, and pitching tents. As the week progressed, each group developed its own leader and unique social identity. One group named itself the "Rattlers," established a tough-guy group norm, and spent a good deal of time cursing and swearing. The other group called itself the "Eagles," and they instituted a group norm forbidding profanity. As the first week drew to a close, each group became aware of the other's existence. How do you think they responded? By making clear and undeniable ingroup-outgroup statements: "*They* better not be in *our* swimming hole!" "*Those* guys are using *our* baseball diamond again!"

During the second phase of the study, Sherif tested his main hypothesis that intergroup competition would cause prejudice. To do this, he created a weeklong tournament between the two groups, consisting of ten athletic events such as baseball, football, and tug-of-war. The winner of each event received points, and at the end of the week the group with the most points received highly prized medals and impressive four-bladed pocket knives. True to Sherif's expectations, the intergroup conflict transformed these normal, well-adjusted boys into what a naive observer would have thought were "wicked, disturbed, and vicious" youngsters (Sherif, 1966, p. 58).

During this phase, the counselors heard a sharp increase in the number of unflattering names used to refer to outgroup members (for example, "pig" and "cheater"). The boys also rated their own group as being "brave," "tough," and "friendly," while those in the outgroup were "sneaky," "smart alecks," and "stinkers." This ingroup favoritism was also manifested in the boys' friendship preferences. Sherif, playing the role of camp handyman, asked the boys to tell him who their friends were at camp. The sharp division between the two groups was reflected in the fact that 93 percent of the friendship preferences were of the ingroup variety. If negative attitudes previously existed between ingroup members, they were now redirected against the outgroup. These findings indicate that one by-product of intergroup hostility is an increase in ingroup solidarity.

As the two groups competed in the various games, intergroup hostility quickly escalated from name-calling to acts of physical aggression. For example, at the end of the first tug-of-war contest, the losing Eagles demonstrated their outgroup attitudes by seizing and burning the Rattlers' group flag. Not to be outdone, the Rattlers raided the Eagles' cabin, overturning cots, ripping mosquito netting, and carrying off one of the Eagle's blue jeans as booty. The next day, armed with bats and sticks, the Eagles returned the favor. Then they retreated to their cabin and proceeded to stuff rocks in their socks, and waited for the next wave of Rattler reprisals.

Who ultimately won the valued prizes for which they were competing? The Eagles. Not surprisingly, the Rattlers thought they had been cheated. While the victors were taking a celebratory swim, the Rattlers stole their medals and knives. When the Eagles returned to find their prizes gone, the Rattlers admitted to the deed and told the incensed Eagles they could have them back . . . if they got down on their bellies and crawled for them! These are only a few of the incidents that occurred between the Eagles and the Rattlers. Intergroup hostility became so intense that members of the opposing groups held their noses whenever they passed by one another in camp.

This second phase of the study illustrates how easily hostility can develop between groups when they are brought into competition. The third phase of the experiment was designed to reverse the hostility, a task that proved to be much more difficult to accomplish. First, the researchers sought to determine whether simple noncompetitive contact between the groups would ease tensions. They tested this hypothesis during the first two days of phase three by bringing the groups together for some pleasant activity, such as a meal or a movie. The results were not encouraging. Both groups used each interaction as an opportunity to merely increase their mutual animosity for one another. During mealtimes, for example, food was more likely to be thrown at opposing group members than eaten.

This failure of simple contact to reduce hostility did not surprise Sherif and his colleagues. They hypothesized that to reduce intergroup conflict, they needed

Sherif and his colleagues (1961) created intergroup hostility between two groups of boys (the "Eagles" and the "Rattlers") at a summer camp by having them compete against one another. In the top photo shown here, the Eagles grab and burn the Rattlers' group flag after losing a tug-of-war contest. Later (bottom photo), the Rattlers hang from a pole an Eagle's pair of jeans upon which they have painted, "The Last of the Eagles." Can you recall incidents from your own life where competition with another group resulted in the development of prejudicial attitudes and discriminatory behavior?

Muzafer Sherif and Carolyn W. Sherif. Copyright 1948, 1956 by Harper & Brothers. Copyrights renewed 1976 by Muzafer Sherif. Reprinted by permission of Addison-Wesley Educational Publishers.

Superordinate Goal

A mutually shared goal that can be achieved only through intergroup cooperation.

to introduce what they called a **superordinate goal,** which is a mutually shared goal that can be achieved only through intergroup cooperation. To test this hypothesis, the researchers arranged for a series of problem situations to develop over the course of the next six days. Each problem was urgent and involved both groups. The first problem was the "failure" of the camp's water supply. The groups initially responded to this emergency by trying to solve it on their own, without the other group's assistance. However, after converging on the source of the water problem, the camp water tank's plugged faucet, they cooperated in fixing it. A few days later, the camp truck "broke down" while the two groups were on an overnight camping excursion, and all the boys had to work together to pull it up a steep hill. Following this incident of cooperation, name-calling and negative outgroup stereotypes declined. Sherif, still in his guise as the camp handyman, again asked the boys who their friends were. Now, outgroup friendships had grown from a measly 7 percent average at the end of phase one to a rather robust 30 percent average, a significant increase in outgroup liking. In keeping with this newfound outgroup appreciation, at their final campfire the two groups decided to put on a joint entertainment program, consisting of skits and songs. When departing from camp the following day, the two groups insisted on traveling home on the same bus. On the way home, the Rattlers used money they had won in their previous competitions with the Eagles to buy milk shakes for everyone.

Taken as a whole, the Robbers Cave experiment is an excellent example of how ethnocentrism can develop when two groups compete for scarce resources. It also demonstrates that having a superordinate goal can lead to peaceful coexistence between previously antagonistic groups. Although this study used children as participants, similar results have also been obtained with adult samples (Worchel et al., 1977). Together, they provide solid support for realistic group conflict theory.

A Desire to Enhance Social Identity Can Promote Prejudice

Realistic group conflict theory might leave you with the impression that competition is necessary for the development of a negative bias against outgroup members and a favorable bias toward one's ingroup. However, European social psychologist Henri Tajfel pointed out that competition is not necessary to create ethnocentrism. According to Tajfel, all that is necessary is to simply create two groups—the new members will take it from there.

Research on Minimal Groups

To support his claim that group membership is often sufficient to create ingroup favoritism, Tajfel and his colleagues created what they called *minimal groups,* which are groups selected from a larger collection of people using some trivial criterion such as eye color, a random number table, or the flip of a coin. The people comprising these newly created groups were strangers to one another and were never given the opportunity to get acquainted. In some studies, participants were individually taken into a room with the experimenter and asked how much money two other participants should be paid for a subsequent task. These two people were identified only by code numbers, indicating to the participant that one came from his or her own group and the other was a member of the other group. Although participants only knew the others' membership status, they proceeded to reward the ingroup person more than the outgroup person (Tajfel et al., 1971).

Research on minimal groups documents a general tendency for people to engage in what social psychologists have called **ingroup bias** in evaluating others. That is, if they observe two people performing the same task, one of whom is a member of their ingroup, their evaluations of the two people's performance will tend to be biased in favor of the ingroup member. This ingroup favoritism may manifest itself by people selectively remembering ingroup persons' good behavior and outgroup members' bad behavior, or by selectively forgetting or trivializing ingroup members' bad behavior and outgroup members' good behavior (Sherman et al., 1998). Such selective information processing results in an overestimation of ingroup performance relative to outgroup performance. Because of this ingroup biasing, ingroup members are consistently rewarded more than outgroup members. This ingroup favoritism in minimal groups has also been found in the assessment of people's personalities and in the recall of favorable and unfavorable behaviors, with ingroup members generally being given the benefit of the doubt over outgroup members (Otten et al., 1996).

Ingroup preference is so strong that simply using ingroup pronouns is often sufficient to arouse positive emotions, while using pronouns signifying outgroups can trigger negative emotions. Evidence for this effect comes from a series of studies conducted by Charles Perdue and his coworkers (1990), in which college students saw 108 seemingly randomly paired letter strings on a computer screen. Each pair of letter strings consisted of a nonsense syllable (*xeh, yof, laj*) presented with either an ingroup-designating pronoun (*we, us, ours*), an outgroup-designating pronoun (*they, them, theirs*), or, on the control trials, some other pronoun (*he, she, his,*

Ingroup Bias

The tendency to give more favorable evaluations and greater rewards to ingroup members than to outgroup members.

FIGURE 7.4

Us and Them: Ingroup Biasing

How pervasive is ingroup biasing? Perdue and colleagues (1990) found that nonsense words that had previously been paired with ingroup pronouns (e.g., us) were evaluated as more "pleasant" than nonsense words that had been paired with either outgroup pronouns (e.g., them) or control pronouns (e.g., hers). This study suggests that the ingroup-outgroup distinction has such emotional meaning to people that it can even shape their evaluation of unfamiliar words.

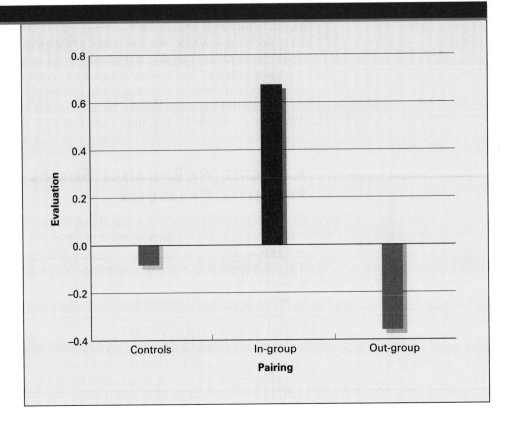

hers). Students were told to quickly decide which letter string in each pair was a real word (*we-xeh, they-yof*). Unbeknownst to the students, one nonsense syllable was consistently paired with ingroup pronouns and another with outgroup pronouns. After the trials, students were asked to rate each of the nonsense syllables in terms of its degree of pleasantness–unpleasantness. As you can see from figure 7.4, students evaluated the nonsense words that had previously been paired with the ingroup pronouns as more pleasant than those paired with either outgroup pronouns or with the control pronouns. These results suggest that merely associating a previously neutral stimulus to words that designate either ingroup or outgroup affiliations is sufficient to create biased emotional responses.

Research on minimal groups is important not only because it documents how ingroup biasing can be easily created but also because it specifically demonstrates how *social* and *cognitive* factors can work together in creating prejudicial evaluations. That is, people's identification with an ingroup (the social factor) causes them to selectively process information about ingroup and outgroup member performance (the cognitive factor) to reinforce their prevailing stereotypes and prejudices.

SOCIAL IDENTITY THEORY

Based on the minimal group studies, it is now known that ingroup biasing can occur without any apparent intergroup competition. One of the most popular explanations for *why* ingroup biasing occurs was offered by Tajfel and John Turner in their *social identity theory* (Tajfel & Turner, 1979; Turner, 1987). As you will recall from chapter 2, according to this theory, besides our personal identity, another important aspect of our self-concept is our social identity, which derives from the groups to which we belong. Our social identity establishes *what* and *where* we are in social terms. Because our social identity forms a central aspect of our own self-definition, our self-esteem is partly determined by the social esteem of our ingroups. When our ingroups succeed, or even when members of our ingroups achieve some level of personal success, we can bask in their reflected glory. Consistent with several self-

CRITICAL *thinking*

Based on the research you have just reviewed and the hypotheses derived from social identity theory, what is the relationship between "pride" and "prejudice"? How is this psychological process similar to the social reflection process (also known as "basking in reflected glory") observed in interpersonal relationships?

concept theories discussed in chapter 2, social identity theory asserts that people are motivated to achieve or maintain a high level of self-esteem. The theory predicts that when the social esteem of their ingroup is threatened, people will attempt to maintain a positive social identity by engaging in ingroup biasing.

Research generally supports social identity theory (Jackson et al., 1996; Weber, 1994). People who engage in ingroup biasing tend to experience an increase in self-esteem compared with those who are not given the opportunity to express this bias (Rubin & Hewstone, 1998). Also as expected, members of lower status groups—whose social esteem, by definition, is perpetually low—tend to engage in more ingroup biasing than members of higher status groups (Ellemers et al., 1997). Finally, people who exhibit great pride in their ingroups and believe these groups are a central component of their own self-concept are more likely to engage in ingroup biasing when placed in a minimal group situation than are those who don't identify so strongly with their ingroups (Crocker & Luhtanen, 1990).

AUTHORITARIANISM IS ASSOCIATED WITH HOSTILITY TOWARD OUTGROUPS

Although identification with a particular group can lead to ingroup biasing and prejudice, what about instances of horrific persecution and murder by one group against another? One of the most infamous examples of this form of intolerance was the mass genocide of millions of Jews and other "undesirables" during World War II by the Nazi regime in Germany. In response to this horrific manifestation of anti-Semitism, two social scientists who had fled Nazi Germany, Theodor Adorno and Else Frenkel-Brunswick, set out to discover how people with certain personality characteristics might be prone to such extreme intergroup hostility.

Along with their colleagues at the University of California at Berkeley, Adorno and Frenkel-Brunswick believed that the cause of extreme prejudice could be traced to personality conflicts developed during childhood (Adorno et al., 1950). Operating from a psychoanalytic perspective, and using survey, case study, and interview methods, they identified what they called the **authoritarian personality.** Based on their studies, the researchers concluded that authoritarians are submissive to authority figures and intolerant of those who are weak or different. They also conform rigidly to cultural values and believe that morality is a matter of clear right and wrong choices. The instrument developed to measure authoritarian tendencies was called the *F-scale* (short for *Fascism*). People who expressed strong agreement with items such as the ones that follow were classified as having an authoritarian personality:

> Obedience and respect for authority are the most important virtues children should learn.
> People can be divided into two distinct classes: the weak and the strong.
> Homosexuals are hardly better than criminals and ought to be severely punished.
> What this country needs most, more than laws and political programs, is a few courageous, tireless, devoted leaders in whom the people can put their faith.

Adorno and his colleagues believed that authoritarian personalities resulted from harsh childrearing practices that taught children to *repress* their hostility toward authority and, instead, to redirect or *displace* it onto less powerful targets who could not retaliate. Although this original theory is acknowledged as an important attempt to understand prejudice in terms of personality conflict and childrearing practices, questions about how people actually become authoritarians and criticisms of Adorno's research methods resulted in this approach losing credibility. Other research by Bob Altemeyer (1981, 1988) suggests that the origins of authoritarianism have less to do with personality conflicts from childhood and have more to do with learning a prejudicial style of thinking during adolescence.

Authoritarian Personality

A personality trait characterized by submissiveness to authority, rigid adherence to conventional values, and prejudice toward outgroups.

TABLE 7.1

Differences and Similarities in the Two Perspectives on Authoritarianism

The Original Psychoanalytic Perspective (Adorno et al., 1950)	The Revised Social Learning Perspective (Altemeyer, 1981, 1988)
Differences	
Origins	**Origins**
Personality conflicts with stern, harsh parents during early childhood	Social learning from parents and others, especially during adolescence
Superstitious mind-set	Lack of personal contact with unconventional people or minorities
Similar Effects	
Submission to established, legitimate authority figures	
Strong adherence to standard social conventions	
Hostility toward many outgroups different from one's own	

Operating from a social learning perspective, Altemeyer contends that people who are socialized by authoritarian and strict disciplinarians tend to develop similar tendencies because they model and reinforce this intolerant world-view. He further believes that most of this social learning occurs during adolescence, with the principal modelers being parents and peers. Isolated from personal contact with nonconventional people or minorities, adolescents in authoritarian environments learn that it is acceptable to express hostility against various outgroups. Table 7.1 outlines the similarities and differences between these two views of authoritarianism.

Regardless of whether researchers have taken a psychoanalytic or a social learning approach to this topic, studies have consistently found that authoritarians in many different societies not only express greater antipathy toward outgroups than the average person, but they are also more likely to act on their hostility (Duncan et al., 1997; Verkuyten & Hagendoorn, 1998). There also is a tendency for right-wing authoritarians to generalize their outgroup prejudices. For example, if they hate Blacks, they are also likely to express hostility toward Jews, feminists, gay men and lesbians, the homeless, and people with AIDS (McFarland et al., 1996; Peterson et al., 1993). Authoritarians' distaste for outgroups is also reflected in their greater support for their government's military actions against other countries during times of international tension. They not only support such actions, but they are also more likely to excuse atrocities committed by their own military forces during these interventions (Doty et al., 1997). On the homefront, persons high in authoritarianism have a general bias against defendants in criminal proceedings—a definite outgroup (Narby et al., 1993). They pay more attention to the prosecuting attorney's arguments against the defendant than to the arguments presented by the defense attorney, and they are more influenced by incriminating evidence than the average person (Garcia & Griffitt, 1978; Werner et al., 1982).

Besides identifying individual variations in authoritarianism, social scientists have also examined how it might vary on a societal level. One factor that has been found to be an important catalyst for the manifestation of societal authoritarianism is *perceived social threat* (Doty et al., 1991). That is, when societies undergo economic hardships and social upheaval, mildly authoritarian individuals may become motivated to adopt more dogmatic and rigid social attitudes that feed outgroup preju-

dices. This social threat hypothesis may well explain the resurgence in neo-Nazi popularity following the reunification of Germany in 1990. As reunification efforts led to high inflation and unemployment, Germany's large immigrant minority population became convenient scapegoats for people's frustration and anger.

THERE IS A POSITIVE CORRELATION BETWEEN RELIGIOUS BELIEFS AND PREJUDICE

Because religious teachings generally encourage love of one's neighbor, it seems reasonable to assume that people who belong to organized religions would be more tolerant of outgroups than those who have no religious affiliations. Despite the logic in such an assumption, this is not the case. Based on a review of thirty-eight studies conducted from 1940 to 1990, C. Daniel Batson and his colleagues (1993) found a positive relationship between amount of religious involvement and amount of prejudice. That is, belonging to an organized religion was associated with *increased*, not decreased, prejudice and bigotry. Similarly, in Israel, Joseph Schwarzwald and his colleagues (1992) found that in the army, soldiers who had previously attended religious schools expressed greater ethnic intolerance than those who had attended secular schools.

What may partly explain this positive association between religion and prejudice is that people belong to religious organizations for different reasons (Allport & Ross, 1967). Some people have a religious orientation that is primarily *extrinsic*, meaning that it is essentially a self-serving, instrumental way of gaining social rewards (for example, meeting people, making business contacts, pleasing parents). Others, in contrast, have an *intrinsic* religious orientation, in that their religion is a central part of their self-concept and its teachings provide them with guidance in living their lives. As Gordon Allport summarized these two religious orientations, "The extrinsically motivated person *uses* his religion, while the intrinsically motivated *lives* his religion" (Allport & Ross, 1967, p. 434).

Research seems to suggest that in some cases, intrinsically oriented persons express less prejudice than those who are extrinsically oriented, while in other cases, they express more prejudice. What may determine religious tolerance is which minority group is the target of attention. When studies have been conducted on racial tolerance, White intrinsics tend to express less prejudicial attitudes or behave in a less overtly discriminatory manner than White extrinsics (Batson et al.,

1986; Donahue, 1985). However, when the target group is lesbians and gay men, religious intrinsics who are members of conservative religions (for example, the Catholic or Baptist Churches) tend to be less tolerant (Herek, 1987c; McFarland, 1989). This might mean that when religious teachings encourage tolerance, as is often the case when race is an issue, intrinsic persons apparently attempt to live their religion by trying to be more accepting. However, when religious teachings do not encourage tolerance or encourage outright discrimination, as is the case with many contemporary religious views of homosexuality, intrinsics again live their religion and express hostility toward gay people. Thus, while some religious beliefs may reduce prejudice, other religious teachings fan the flames of intolerance and bigotry (Hunsberger, 1995).

SECTION SUMMARY

A number of crucial social variables can increase intergroup intolerance. *Social dominance theory* explains how dominant groups develop negative stereotypes and prejudicial attitudes toward those they oppress to justify their continued oppression. *Realistic group conflict theory* argues that groups become prejudiced toward one another because they are in conflict over competition for scarce resources. *Social identity theory* asserts that prejudice and discrimination can result from people trying to increase or maintain self-esteem. Extreme prejudice can also be traced to personality effects, in what came to be called *authoritarianism*. Finally, belonging to an organized religion is associated with increased prejudice.

HISTORICAL MANIFESTATIONS OF PREJUDICE AND DISCRIMINATION

Although an endless number of distinguishing qualities in the human population can trigger prejudice and discrimination, certain qualities have historically been associated with prejudice and discrimination and often sanctioned by societal institutions. A person's race, sex, and sexual orientation have been described as traditional master statuses in American society. A *status* is a socially defined position that a person occupies within society, whereas a **master status** is a status that is very important in shaping a person's self-concept and life choices (Becker, 1963). It generally overrides a person's other statuses and determines, more so than other statuses, how she or he will be treated. Put another way, once an individual is labeled as having a particular master status, perceptions of her or him are filtered through that status. Race, sex, and sexual orientation are *ascribed* master statuses in that in almost all instances, a person has no choice in assuming them. Exceptions would be (1) mixed-race individuals whose physical features are sufficiently ambiguous so that they can "pass" as members of more than one racial or ethnic group, (2) individuals who have had sex changes, or (3) lesbians and gay men who try to "pass" as heterosexuals to avoid the social stigma associated with homosexuality.

In theory, all members of a society can be categorized according to their race, sex, or sexual orientation. For certain groups, however, such categorization *stigmatizes* them in the larger society (Crocker et al., 1998). As defined earlier, a stigma is an attribute that serves to discredit a person or a group in the eyes of others. The stigmatizing attribute relegates the individual to an unequal status and puts her or him in opposition to the dominant group. For African Americans, Asian Americans, Hispanic Americans, and American Indians, the dominant group consists of White Americans. For women it is men, and for lesbians, gay men, and bisexuals the dominant group is made up of heterosexuals. In the following sections, we will

Master Status

A socially defined position occupied by a person in society that is very important in shaping his or her self-concept and life choices.

examine prejudice and discrimination caused by the stigmatization of race (*racism*), sex (*sexism*), and sexual orientation (*heterosexism*).

RACISM IS BASED ON OPEN HOSTILITY OR AVERSIVENESS

At the turn of the century, the famous African-American inventor Booker T. Washington encountered the White mayor of a small town he was passing through on his travels. Greeting Dr. Washington at the train station, the man said to him in a good-natured, backwoods fashion, "Y'u know, Booker, I been hear'n about you, and I been a-tellin' my friends about y'u. I been tellin' them you was one of the biggest men in this country today. Yes sir, one of the biggest men in the whole country." Being somewhat embarrassed by the enthusiasm of this man's greeting, Dr. Washington asked, "Well, what do you think about President Roosevelt?" With only a slight change in his voice, the mayor responded, "Oh! Hell, Roosevelt! Well, I used to be all for him until he let you eat dinner with him. That finished him as far as I'm concerned."[2]

OLD-FASHIONED RACISM

This White man's response to a Black man dining with the president was not uncommon during the first fifty years of the twentieth century. Historically, Blacks have been viewed by Whites as lazy and dependent slaves, carefree minstrels, and even potentially dangerous vagabonds (Jordan, 1968). American Indians have similarly been characterized by Whites as an uncivilized and lazy people who cannot take care of their own welfare (Trimble, 1988). These blatantly negative stereotypes based on beliefs in the racial superiority of one's own group (in this

Unfortunately, old-fashioned racism has been expressed throughout the history of the United States. Is this type of racism also found in other countries?

Old-Fashioned Racism

Blatantly negative stereotypes based on beliefs in the racial superiority of one's own group, coupled with open opposition to racial equality.

case, White people), coupled with open opposition to racial equality characterizes what is known as **old-fashioned racism** (McConahay, 1986). Old-fashioned racism tends to arouse emotions such as anger and contempt and often leads to movement *against* the despised group, including physical violence.

MODERN RACISM

Although old-fashioned racism typified the perspective of many White Americans toward other racial groups throughout most of the history of this country, the vast majority of Whites today cannot be classified in this simple and straightforward fashion (Cox et al., 1996). Instead, researchers such as Samuel Gaertner and John Dovidio (1986) and Irwin Katz and R. Glen Hass (1988) assert that the fundamental nature of White Americans' current attitudes toward many racial groups, but especially toward African Americans, is complex and conflicted. They contend that on the one hand, the majority of Whites hold to egalitarian values that stress equal treatment of all people and a sympathy for social groups who have been mistreated in the past. Therefore, they sympathize with the victims of racial prejudice and tend to support public policies that promote racial equality. On the other hand, because of exposure to unflattering stereotypes and media images depicting African Americans as lazy, unmotivated, and violent, and due to simple ingroup-outgroup biases, these researchers believe that many Whites come to possess negative feelings and beliefs about Blacks that directly contradict their egalitarian values. The American individualist value of the Protestant work ethic, which emphasizes self-reliance and individual initiative in pursuing life goals, reinforces these negative social perceptions about Blacks. Given their own relative lack of personal experience with the negative impact of racial prejudice, many Whites tend to believe that anyone who works hard has a good chance of succeeding in life. Therefore, many of them conclude that at least part of the source of continued racial inequality is what they perceive as a low level of motivation and effort on the part of Blacks and other disadvantaged groups, such as American Indians and Latinos (Biernat et al., 1996).

According to this perspective on modern racism, the negative feelings engendered by Whites' perceptions of these disadvantaged racial groups generally do not encompass anger or contempt, as in old-fashioned racism, but they do include such emotions as discomfort, uneasiness, and even fear. Due to the fact that an egalitarian value system plays an important role in their self-concepts, this perspective assumes that many White Americans typically are ashamed of these negative feelings and do not openly acknowledge them. Because interacting with members of these other racial groups tends to make Whites aware of their prejudicial attitudes, they avoid such interactions and, thus, avoid confronting their true feelings. This is why the combination of both positive and negative beliefs and feelings about a particular racial group is called **aversive racism.** Interracial encounters make salient the attitudinal conflict, and this awareness threatens one's self-concept as a fair-minded, yet discerning, person.

Aversive Racism

Attitudes toward members of a racial group that incorporate both egalitarian social values and negative emotions, causing one to avoid interaction with members of the group.

Now that this theoretical perspective has been described, what evidence is there to support it? One study, conducted by Katz and Hass (1988), suggests that White Americans may indeed have conflicting attitudes regarding African Americans. In this research, White college students first completed a questionnaire that either contained items measuring adherence to the individualist Protestant ethic of self-reliance, initiative, and hard work, or contained egalitarian and humanitarian items stressing equal treatment of all people and empathy for those who are less fortunate (see table 7.2). When participants completed the questionnaire, the researchers administered a second questionnaire that measured the participants' degree of racial prejudice toward Blacks. Because Katz and Hass believed that both sets of values were part of the participants' worldview, they predicted that their attitudes toward Blacks would be influenced by whichever of these two values were made salient. Consistent with their hypothesis, when Whites were first

TABLE 7.2

Racial Ambivalence and Conflicting American Values

People with a strong Protestant ethic would agree with the sample items from the first scale, while those with a strong humanitarianism-egalitarianism value orientation would agree with the sample items from the scale bearing its name. If a White American believes in both of these value orientations, according to Katz and Hass (1988), what sort of attitudinal conflict might this create in their overall perceptions of African Americans or American Indians?

The Protestant Ethic (Sample Items from Katz & Hass, 1988)	Humanitarianism-Egalitarianism (Sample Items from Katz & Hass, 1988)
1. Most people who don't succeed in life are just plain lazy.	1. One should find ways to help others less fortunate than oneself.
2. Anyone who is willing to work hard has a good chance of succeeding.	2. There should be equality for everyone—because we are all human beings.
3. If people work hard enough they are likely to make a good life for themselves.	3. Everyone should have an equal chance and an equal say in most things.
4. Most people spend too much time in unprofitable amusements.	4. Acting to protect the rights and interests of other members of the community is a major obligation for all persons.

Source: From I. Katz and R. G. Hass, "Racial Ambivalence and American Value Conflict: Correlation and Prime Studies of Dual Cognitive Structures" in *Journal of Personality and Social Psychology*, 55:893–905. Copyright 1988 by the American Psychological Association. Reprinted by permission.

primed by egalitarian statements, their subsequent prejudice scores went down. When they were primed by individualist work ethic statements, their prejudice scores went up. This is what one would expect if the participants held both value orientations. In any given situation, whichever one is made salient will exert the most influence over attitudes and behavior.

Katz and Hass believe that another consequence of having an ambivalent attitude toward a particular outgroup is that it can cause people to act in a more extreme manner toward outgroup members than they would to members of their own ingroup (Katz et al., 1986). This tendency for responses to become more extreme when one holds ambivalent attitudes is called *response amplification*, and it can occur in either a favorable or an unfavorable direction, depending on the social context (Hass et al., 1991). Thus, White individuals with ambivalent attitudes toward Blacks may act overfriendly and solicitous when being introduced to African Americans whom they perceive to be competent and ambitious. This is because such encounters discredit the negative components of their ambivalent attitudes. Likewise, they may react with great annoyance and anger when interacting with Blacks they judge to be incompetent and lazy, because the encounter discredits the positive component of their ambivalent attitudes. When either one of these components has been discredited in a given situation, the person's evaluative response is likely to be exaggerated in the opposing direction.

Taken as a whole, these research findings suggest that although many Whites have become more tolerant of Blacks during the past fifty years, racism still exists in this country. According to the aversive racism perspective, although the majority of Whites try to be open-minded and relaxed about racial issues, they still harbor prejudiced attitudes.

He flattered himself on being a man without any prejudices; and this pretension itself is a very great prejudice.

Anatole France, French novelist and poet, 1844–1924

You learn about equality in history and civics, but you find out life is not really like that.

Arthur Ashe, professional tennis player, 1943–1993

TABLE 7.3

A Stage Model of Racial Acceptance

Characteristics of Old-Fashioned Racism	Characteristics of Aversive Racism	Characteristics of Egalitarianism
Differences between ethnic groups are biological.	Differences between ethnic groups are learned.	Differences between ethnic groups are learned.
One's own ethnic group is superior.	There are no superior ethnic groups.	There are no superior ethnic groups.
Ethnic outgroups should not have equal rights.	Ethnic outgroups should have equal rights.	Ethnic outgroups should have equal rights.
There should only be minimal interracial contact.	Interracial contact is threatening.	There should be no separation between the races.
The ideal society would consist only of one's ingroup.	The ideal society would be where the ingroup's culture is dominant and accepted by the other ethnic groups.	The ideal society would be where the various cultures are accepted and respected by all members.

Source: Adapted from G. Kleinpenning and L. Hagendoorn, "Forms of Racism and the Cumulative Dimension of Ethnic Attitudes" in *Social Psychology Quarterly*, 56:21–36, American Sociological Association, 1993.

Is There a Progression of Racial Acceptance?

Some social scientists have argued that different forms of racism reflect different stages in the development of racial tolerance. Sociologist Herbert Blumer (1965), for one, proposed that ethnic minorities will first be accepted in the area of political rights (citizenship, the right to vote), then in the area of economic rights (equal employment opportunities), and finally in the area of private contacts (racially mixed neighborhoods, friendships and interracial marriages). Each stage in racial acceptance increases the minority group's access to the same opportunities and social networks of the dominant group.

In a similar vein, Dutch social psychologists Gerard Kleinpenning and Louk Hagendoorn (1993) contend that different forms of racism represent stages in the movement toward greater intergroup tolerance. I have outlined their stage model, with some adjustment, in table 7.3. The most basic form of racism involves a rejection of contact with racial groups, and a belief that one's own group is biologically superior. For a person with such beliefs, the ideal society would consist of only one's ingroup. This is *old-fashioned racism*. Later, as racial attitudes become more accepting, a new form of racism emerges, namely *aversive racism*. Here, there are no superior races, and any ethnic differences are believed to be learned, not innate. Although aversive racists believe that racial outgroups should have equal rights, interracial contact is threatening to them. For aversive racists, the ideal society would be one in which their ingroup's culture is either dominant or is accepted by the outgroups. Finally, in an *egalitarian* society, other racial groups would not be perceived as threatening but, rather, would be viewed as enriching the larger society. Here, there would be no cultural or physical separation between groups, and the ideal society would be one in which everyone accepts and respects ethnic differences.

If racial tolerance can be described in such a stage model, where are we in this progression? Kleinpenning and Hagendoorn offer a compelling answer. In the Netherlands, as well as in the United States, Germany, Canada, and other countries

Sexism

Any attitude, action, or institutional structure that subordinates a person because of her or his sex.

Ambivalent Sexism

Sexism directed against women based on both positive and negative attitudes (hostility and benevolence), rather than uniform dislike.

where various ethnic and racial groups reside, the dominant cultural norm often favors tolerance and opposes discrimination. Some people have internalized this norm, others comply with it but don't believe it, and others simply reject it. Based on our understanding of aversive racism, it is clear that even when people internalize this nondiscrimination norm, they do not always do it in a complete fashion (Monteith, 1996b). A person may have internalized the norm with respect to one domain of their worldview, such as civil rights, but not necessarily in another domain, such as interracial marriage. Kleinpenning and Hagendoorn believe this is where their own country and the United States are in terms of racial acceptance. The nondiscrimination norm is more internalized with respect to fundamental civil rights than with respect to private contacts. Unfortunately, in the private domain of our lives, many of us remain segregated and prejudiced (see the Featured Study at the end of the chapter).

SEXISM HAS BOTH A HOSTILE AND A BENEVOLENT COMPONENT

Sexism is any attitude, action, or institutional structure that subordinates a person because of her or his sex. Much as racism in Western societies is mostly discussed in terms of White hostility toward racial minority groups, sexism around the globe primarily focuses on the prejudice and discrimination that males direct at females. This is so because virtually all societies in the world are *patriarchal,* meaning that the social organization is such that males dominate females (Harris, 1991). Evolutionary theorists propose that the social dominance of men over women is probably due to the biology of human sexual reproduction, in which the competition between males for sexual access to females eventually resulted in men being more aggressive and having a stronger social dominance orientation than women. As outlined by social dominance theory (see p. 234), the patriarchal systems that resulted from males' greater dominance-seeking eventually led to the development of a sexist ideology to justify control over females (Sidanius et al., 1995). The basic storyline of this ideology is that women are inferior and irrational creatures who need to be controlled by men. This *hostile* component of sexism, which justifies continued oppression, has many psychological similarities to old-fashioned racism.

AMBIVALENT SEXISM

What distinguishes many expressions of sexism from virtually all types of racism is that sexism often has a *benevolent* side mirroring the hostile side. That is, unlike most dominant-subordinate relationships, in male-female relationships there is a great deal of intimacy: men are dependent on women as mothers, wives, and sexual/romantic partners. Historically, this intimacy has resulted in many sexist men idealizing women in traditional feminine roles: they cherish these women and want to protect them because these traditional relationships fulfill their dual desires for social dominance and intimacy. Peter Glick and Susan Fiske (1996, 1997) contend that this orientation toward women, which is based on both positive and negative attitudes (hostility and benevolence) rather than uniform dislike, constitutes **ambivalent sexism.** Recent studies indicate that the degree to which these views are held varies from culture to culture, as well as from individual to individual (see the Ambivalent Sexism Inventory in table 7.4). Although benevolent sexist beliefs lead people to express many positive attitudes about women, it shares common assumptions with hostile sexism; namely, that women belong in restricted domestic roles and are the "weaker" sex. Both beliefs serve to justify male social dominance.

Based on your understanding of cognitive dissonance theory (chapter 5, pp. 170–177), you might be wondering how ambivalent sexists avoid feeling conflicted about their positive and negative beliefs and attitudes toward women? Shouldn't people experience considerable dissonance if they simultaneously

TABLE 7.4

The Ambivalent Sexism Inventory

Instructions:

Below is a series of statements concerning men and women and their relationships in contemporary society. Please indicate the degree to which you agree or disagree with each statement using the following scale:

0 = Disagree strongly	3 = Agree slightly
1 = Disagree somewhat	4 = Agree somewhat
2 = Disagree slightly	5 = Agree strongly

_____ 1. No matter how accomplished he is, a man is not truly complete as a person unless he has the love of a woman.

_____ 2. Many women are actually seeking special favors, such as hiring policies that favor them over men, under the guise of asking for "equality."

_____ 3. In a disaster, women ought not necessarily be rescued before men.*

_____ 4. Most women interpret innocent remarks as being sexist.

_____ 5. Women are too easily offended.

_____ 6. People are often truly happy in life without being romantically involved with a member of the other sex.*

_____ 7. Feminists are not seeking for women to have more power than men.*

_____ 8. Many women have a quality of purity that few men possess.

_____ 9. Women should be cherished and protected by men.

_____ 10. Most women fail to appreciate fully all that men do for them.

_____ 11. Women seek to gain power by getting control over men.

_____ 12. Every man ought to have a woman whom he adores.

_____ 13. Men are complete without women.*

_____ 14. Women exaggerate problems they have at work.

_____ 15. Once a woman gets a man to commit to her, she usually tries to put him on a tight leash.

_____ 16. When women lose to men in a fair competition, they typically complain about being discriminated against.

_____ 17. A good woman should be set on a pedestal by her man.

_____ 18. There are actually very few women who get a kick out of teasing men by seeming sexually available and then refusing male advances.*

_____ 19. Women, compared with men, tend to have a superior moral sensibility.

_____ 20. Men should be willing to sacrifice their own well being in order to provide financially for the women in their lives.

_____ 21. Feminists are making entirely reasonable demands of men.*

_____ 22. Women, as compared with men, tend to have a more refined sense of culture and good taste.

Scoring Instructions

Before summing either scale, first reverse the scores for the "*" items:

$$0 = 5, 1 = 4, 2 = 3, 3 = 2, 4 = 1, 5 = 0.$$

Hostile Sexism Scale Score: Add items 2,4,5,7,10,11,14,15,16,18,21

The average score for men is about 29, while the average score for women is about 20. Higher scores indicate greater degrees of hostile sexism.

Benevolent Sexism Scale Score: Add items 1,3,6,8,9,12,13,17,19,20,22

The average score for men is about 28, while the average score for women is about 24. Higher scores indicate greater degrees of benevolent sexism.

Total Ambivalent Sexism Inventory Score: Sum the Hostile Sexism Scale score and the Benevolent Sexism Scale score.

The average score for men is about 57, while the average score for women is about 44. Higher scores indicate greater degrees of ambivalent sexism.

Source: Glick & Fiske, 1996.

But how can a man respect his wife
when he has a contemptible opinion
of her and her sex, when from his
own elevation he looks down on
them as void of understanding, full
of ignorance and passion, so that
folly and a woman are equivalent
terms with him?

*Mary Astell, English pamphleteer,
1666–1731*

I would just like to say that the first
time Adam had a chance he laid
the blame on woman.

*Lady Nancy Astor, first woman to sit in the
British House of Commons, 1879–1941*

The history of men's opposition to
women's emancipation is more
interesting perhaps than the story
of that emancipation itself.

*Virginia Woolf, U.S. novelist and critic,
1882–1941*

Sexual Harassment

*Unwelcome physical or verbal
sexual overtures that create an
intimidating, hostile, or offensive
social environment.*

believe that women are inferior, ungrateful, sexual teasers who are also refined, morally-superior goddesses? According to what we have already learned about the resiliency of negative stereotypes (refer back to p. 230), ambivalent sexists could avoid cognitive dissonance by splitting women into "good" and "bad" stereotype subcategories that embody the positive and negative aspects of sexist ambivalence. Having subcategorized women in this polarized manner, the ambivalent sexist could justify treating the "bad" women with hostility, while treating the "good" women with benevolence.

In two separate studies, Glick and his colleagues (1997) found support for this hypothesis. When asked to spontaneously list the different "types" they use to classify women, men who scored high and low on the Ambivalent Sexism Inventory (ASI) generated many of the same subcategories, but ambivalent sexists evaluated their traditional and nontraditional female subcategories in a more polarized fashion than did the nonsexists. Among ambivalent sexists, career women evoked negative feelings (fear, envy, competitiveness, intimidation), and these negative evaluations were significantly correlated with the Hostile Sexism Scale of the ASI (Mean $r = -.34$), but not with the ASI's Benevolent Sexism Scale (Mean $r = .12$). In contrast, homemakers elicited a variety of positive feelings (warmth, respect, trust, happiness), and these positive evaluations were significantly correlated with the Benevolent Sexism Scale (Mean $r = .21$), but not with the Hostile Sexism Scale (Mean $r = .02$). What these findings suggest is that, among ambivalent sexist men, specific female subcategories activate either hostility or benevolence, but not both. Apparently, reserving negative attitudes for nontraditional women and positive attitudes for those who are traditional allows sexist men to simultaneously hold contradictory views of women in general.

What about sexist women? Do they also evaluate traditional and nontraditional female subcategories in a polarized benevolent-hostile manner? When female participants completed this same task, although sexist—as compared with nonsexist—women also evaluated career women less favorably and reported more positive feelings for homemakers, the Benevolent Sexism Scale did not significantly correlate with evaluations of either subcategory. What these findings suggest is that the sexism of women against other women is not of the polarized variety seen in sexist men, but instead, simply constitutes an expression of hostility toward women who have not adopted traditional feminine roles. Thus, ambivalent sexism appears to exclusively be a male experience.

SEXUAL HARASSMENT

One manifestation of sexism is **sexual harassment,** which is unwelcome physical or verbal sexual overtures that create an intimidating, hostile, or offensive social environment. In the 1990s, sexual harassment charges against such high-profile public figures as President Clinton and Supreme Court Justice Clarence Thomas, along with numerous highly publicized cases within the armed services, served as a catalyst for national discussion of this form of sexism. Subsequent surveys of American and European working women estimated that 50 percent will experience harassment at some point in their careers, and the figure goes as high as 70 percent in Japan (Fitzgerald, 1993a). On college campuses, about 30 percent of undergraduate women experience sexual harassment by at least one of their male professors during the time they are pursuing their degree (Bogart et al., 1992). When the statistics include sexual harassment by fellow students, about half of all female college students report some experience with this type of sexism during their college years (McKinney & Maroules, 1991).

One problem in dealing with this issue is that sexual harassment is not an objective phenomenon: a behavior that is perceived as sexual harassment by one person may be casually shrugged off or viewed positively by others (Houston & Hwang, 1996). This problem in identifying an incident as harassment is more common among men then among women (Frazier et al., 1995), especially when the incident involves unwanted sexual attention (for example, persistent flirting) or gender-based insults (for example, "You and all other women are stupid"). However, when the behavior in question consists of sexual coercion (for example, "Have sex with me or lose your job"), men are as likely as women to label it as sexual harassment (Burgess & Borgida, 1997).

In most instances, sexual harassment involves the misuse of power. Although women can be sexual harassers and men can be victims, women are overwhelmingly underrepresented in careers with the organizational power that would allow them to coerce others for sexual favors (Charney & Russell, 1994). For this reason, sexual harassment is a social problem that women are much more likely to face than men. Although sexual harassment can occur in any work context, it is more common and is more likely to be overlooked when women are employed in traditionally all-male environments (Fitzgerald et al., 1997; Sheffey & Tindale, 1992). The typical harassment case involves a single woman under the age of 34 being the target of a male supervisor over the age of 35.

What type of man is most likely to engage in sexual harassment? Research indicates that men who associate sex with social dominance or power are most likely to sexually harass a coworker (Pryor et al., 1995). Although they engage in sexual harassment, these men generally don't perceive their actions as inappropriate or a misuse of power (Fitzgerald, 1993b). One reason for this lack of awareness is that, for these men, the connection between power and sex appears to be automatic and unconscious (Bargh et al., 1995). That is, the sexual harasser's tendency to automatically think in terms of sex in situations in which he has power, blinds him to the inappropriate nature of his behavior.

One way in which power and sex may become associated in the harasser's own thought processes is through the type of behaviors exhibited in dominant-subservient role relationships. That is, power holders are typically treated by subordinates in a friendly, appreciative, and sometimes even worshipful manner (Jones, 1964). Instead of attributing the cause for these behaviors to their more powerful social role, harassers interpret such actions by female subordinates as indicating sexual attraction (Fiske, 1993). This tendency, coupled with the fact that men generally tend to misperceive a woman's friendliness as indicating sexual interest (see chapter 11, p. 406), creates a work environment where harassers often respond with unwelcomed sexual overtures (Stockdale, 1993).

Another way in which this power-sex association may be formed is through real—not perceived—differences in the sexual interest shown by some women to men in power roles. As we will discuss more fully in chapter 10, a small minority of women are indeed attracted to men who have power, probably because women historically have only been able to secure economic resources through allying themselves with powerful men. Thus, men holding positions of power could form this power-sex association because of the way a few women react to their social role. Although powerful men may correctly interpret some women's friendly behavior as indicating sexual interest, other women's friendly behavior will carry no sexual implications. Yet because this power-sex association has been formed, sexual harassment becomes more likely.

Despite the negative impact sexual harassment has on their lives, most victims do not report these incidents (Paludi & Barickman, 1991). On college campuses, estimates are that only between 2 and 7 percent directly report confronting their harassers (Koss, 1990). Instead, students drop classes, discontinue research projects, and change their academic major and career aspirations (Glaser & Thorpe, 1986). In the workforce, only 40 percent tell the harasser to stop, and only 24 percent report the incident. A common reaction of victims is to experience guilt and self-blame, which is similar to the response that rape victims have (Dziech & Weiner, 1984). When victims do report harassment, all too often the charges are ignored or the offenders are given only token reprimands (Fitzgerald et al., 1995). In addition, one quarter of those who are harassed are either fired or forced to quit their jobs following the harassment (Sandroff, 1992). As one woman described her multiple experiences with sexual harassment on the job: "I lost or was forced out of my job each time, while my respective harassers are busily laying, tormenting, embarrassing, or firing people as we speak."

DETECTING SEXISM FROM UNEXPECTED SOURCES

Charges of sexism usually involve a man being accused of prejudice or discrimination against a woman. But what about women being biased against other women or men being biased against other men? In an exploration of sexist accusations, Robert Baron and his coworkers (1991) hypothesized that people are less likely to notice sexism when the protagonist and victim are of the same sex. The researchers based this prediction on their belief that people are aware of how ingroup biasing operates (refer back to pp. 239–241), and that they would more likely be attentive to discrimination against outgroup members (for example, men being biased against women, or women against men) than discrimination against ingroup members (for example, women being biased against other women).

In one study, male and female college students read a series of vignettes in which a protagonist derogated either women or men. Consistent with the ingroup/outgroup hypothesis, when the protagonist derogated women, 88 percent guessed that the person was a man. However, also as expected, when the protagonist derogated men, 93 percent believed the person was a woman. In a second study, college students read a new series of vignettes describing sexist actions against females by either a man or a woman. Again, consistent with the ingroup/outgroup hypothesis, both male and female respondents were eight times more likely to label the male protagonist as sexist than the female.

Taken together, what these and other studies (Inman & Baron, 1996) suggest is that prejudice and discrimination are less likely to be detected when they are initiated by an unexpected source rather than an expected source. One practical implication of these findings is that others are more likely to label the ambiguous remarks or actions about women that men make as being sexist. For example, a woman calling other women "girls" is less likely to raise eyebrows than if that term comes from the lips of a man.

HETEROSEXISM IS WOVEN INTO OUR CULTURAL FABRIC

Sarah, a 19-year-old student at Marquette University where I teach, is a lesbian. The most discouraging thing for her and other gay students on campus is that for the most part, people seldom talk about sexual orientation or acknowledge homosexuality. Lesbians and gay men are the "invisible people" on campus. When homosexuality does come up in conversation, it usually is through an offensive joke or remark concerning "faggots," "queers," or "dykes." Reflecting on these experiences, Sarah observed, "It's a very sensitive issue to me, and when people make jokes about it, it's kind of like, that's not funny, that's my life. I don't make jokes about their heterosexuality" (Mendenhall, 1993, p. 11).

ANTIGAY PREJUDICE AS A CULTURAL PHENOMENON

Sarah's experience of feeling like an invisible person reflects a common experience that lesbians and gay men have in living their lives in societies overwhelmingly dominated by heterosexuals who denigrate nonheterosexual lifestyles. For example, during the first seventy years of the twentieth century, the medical profession stigmatized lesbians and gay men as sexually deviant and mentally disturbed (Martin, 1993). When rigorous scientific studies found no evidence of an association between homosexuality and psychopathology, the American Psychiatric Association finally changed its opinion in the mid-1970s and removed homosexuality as a diagnostic category for mental illness (Bayer, 1987). Despite this

Though your tissues gel,
And you rot in hell,
Don't feel gloomy, friend—
It will never end.
Happy Death, Faggot Fool.

From "Death Threat Christmas Cards" sent to gay students by a hate group at the University of Chicago

clean bill of mental health from the scientific community, the Catholic Church has persisted in describing homosexual feelings as "ordered toward an intrinsic moral evil" and concludes that homosexuality "itself must be seen as an objective disorder" comparable to mental illness (Congregation for the Doctrine of the Faith, 1986, paragraph 3). Also, in the vast majority of states and municipalities, gay relationships have no legal status, and lesbians and gay men often lose the custody of their children when their homosexuality becomes known (Melton, 1989).

Social scientists observing the continued prejudice and discrimination directed at lesbians, gay men, and even bisexuals have increasingly explained it in terms of a particular cultural ideology. **Heterosexism** is a system of cultural beliefs, values, and customs that exalts heterosexuality and denies, denigrates, and stigmatizes any nonheterosexual form of behavior or identity (Herek et al., 1991). Heterosexism is a fairly new concept used to explain antigay prejudice. The more common term, *homophobia*, will not be used here for two reasons: (1) the term *phobia* implies that antigay prejudice is an irrational fear and a form of psychopathology, which, in fact, only explains a small percentage of cases, and (2) it focuses on the homophobe's own personal history rather than the larger cultural context in which antigay sentiments develop (Fernald, 1995).

How does heterosexism manifest itself? Overt and blatant expressions of antigay attitudes, such as someone calling another person a "faggot" or a "dyke," is certainly an example of heterosexism. However, heterosexism can also operate on a more subtle level (see figure 7.5). Like the fish that doesn't realize it's wet, heterosexuals are so used to defining heterosexual behaviors as normal and natural that they cease to think of them as being a manifestation of sexuality. For instance, heterosexuals who don't look twice at a man and woman holding hands, hugging, or even kissing in public, often react very differently if the couple is of the same sex. Gay couples expressing affection in public are typically criticized for flaunting their sexuality. As one heterosexual person expressed this sentiment, "Gay people have a right to live their own lives as long as they keep it to themselves and don't display the fact in public" (Herek, 1990, p. 320). Such condemnation of nonheterosexual behavior can make it dangerous for gay people to do anything in public that would define them by their master status, a fact that was highlighted by the murder of Matthew Shepard. This danger in identifying oneself as a lesbian or gay man not only restricts public self-presentations, it also renders gay people *invisible* as a group and denies them freedom to be seen as a whole person.

CHARACTERISTICS OF ANTIGAY INDIVIDUALS

Although many cultures encourage prejudicial attitudes and discriminatory behavior toward nonheterosexuals, heterosexuals differ in their level of antigay prejudice. Gregory Herek and other researchers have found that those who hold extremely negative attitudes toward gay men and lesbians differ in a number of ways from those with more accepting attitudes. In contrast to less-prejudiced individuals, heterosexuals who express antigay attitudes tend to

1. be male rather than female (Whitley & Kite, 1995).
2. hold traditional attitudes toward gender roles (Kite & Whitley, 1996).
3. be strongly religious and have membership in conservative religious organizations (Herek, 1984; VanderStoep & Green, 1988).
4. have friends who hold similarly negative attitudes (Herek, 1988).
5. be racially prejudiced and authoritarian (Haddock & Zanna, 1998).
6. have had less personal contact with gay men or lesbians (Herek & Capitanio, 1996).

These findings indicate that those who have the most negative attitudes toward lesbians and gay men are those who conform most to socially conservative—and even racist and sexist—value systems.

Heterosexism

A system of cultural beliefs, values, and customs that exalts heterosexuality and denies, denigrates, and stigmatizes any nonheterosexual form of behavior or identity.

❚ I just thought, "Oh God, What if they pick up that I'm gay?" It was that fear and shame. . . . I watched the whole Gay Pride march in Washington in 1993, and I wept when I saw that. I mean I cried so hard, thinking "I wish I could be there," because I never felt like I belonged anywhere.

Ellen DeGeneres, comedian and actor, 1996

CRITICAL *thinking*

Try the following exercise. Listen to some of your favorite songs with lyrics involving romance. Do you tend to automatically imagine the person singing the song is expressing his or her love for a person of the other sex? If you do, does this tell us anything about your level of heterosexism? Now, actively imagine that the song is about same-sex love. How do you react to these lyrics and any visual images that come to mind? On the other hand, if you regularly imagine that the lyrics of popular songs involve same-sex love, is this an automatic process or does it usually take more cognitive effort on your part? How does this exercise illustrate your own personal experience of heterosexism?

FIGURE 7.5

The pervasiveness of heterosexism in our society can be seen in the way the perceived superiority of heterosexuality over homosexuality is used to depict the concept of positive and negative charges in a high school physics textbook. "Attraction" is depicted as a man and a woman holding each other, while "repulsion" is depicted as two men or two women expressing disgust at the possibility of holding each other. Can you think of other ways in which homosexuality is depicted as being "repulsive" in everyday life?

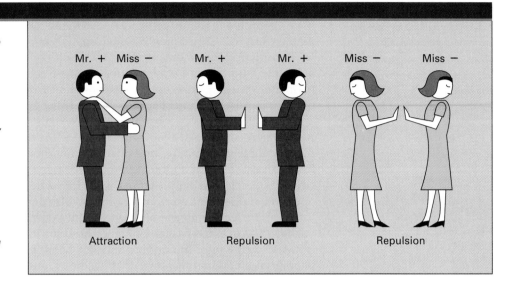

Mr. + Miss −   Mr. +   Mr. +   Miss −   Miss −

Attraction   Repulsion   Repulsion

Why do heterosexual men have more negative attitudes than heterosexual women? Herek believes that this gender difference exists because many cultures emphasize the importance of heterosexuality in the male gender role. A defining characteristic of this *heterosexual masculinity* is to reject men who violate the heterosexual norm, namely gay males. This is also why heterosexual males express more negative attitudes toward gay men than toward lesbians. They perceive a male transgression of the heterosexual norm to be a more serious violation than that of a female transgression. As we will discuss in chapter 11, concern for not straying from the narrowly defined boundaries of heterosexual masculinity is also believed to be the main reason heterosexual male same-sex friendships are often lacking in emotional tenderness (Rubin, 1985). This is especially true for males with strongly antigay attitudes (Devlin & Cowan, 1985).

The fact that people who hold strongly antigay attitudes also have friends who hold similar opinions is consistent with our previous discussion in chapter 5 (pp. 182–185) about the important role that reference groups play in the formation of attitudes. In the case of verbalizing antigay attitudes, Herek (1988) found that for men, but not for women, perceived social support in such attitude expression was significantly important. This gender difference suggests that expressing antigay attitudes helps some heterosexual males, especially those who are adolescents, to identify themselves as "real men" and be accepted into heterosexual friendship cliques.

HAVE ANTIGAY ATTITUDES AND BELIEFS CHANGED?

No other group of Americans is the object of such sustained, extreme, and intense distaste as gay men and lesbians. The only other social group that rivals gay people in being the target of hostility is illegal aliens (Sherrill, 1996). In a Gallup poll, for instance, only 6 percent of heterosexual Americans stated they felt "favorable and warm" toward gay people; 74 percent stated they felt "uncomfortable and don't care too much for" gay people (Yang, 1997). Similarly, a 1998 survey of potential U.S. jurors found that they were more than three times as likely to feel they could not be fair or impartial toward a gay or lesbian defendant than toward other minority group defendants (Associated Press, 1998). The astonishing fact about this data is that it represents a *decrease* in antigay attitudes from the 1970s and 1980s. These poll results indicate that, unlike racism and sexism, most prejudice based on sexual orientation is still of the "old-fashioned" hostile variety.

Interestingly, despite the persistence of strong antigay attitudes, 84 percent of Americans in 1996 stated that gay people should have equal rights in terms of job opportunities compared with 56 percent in 1977 (Saad, 1996). One reason

It wasn't easy telling my parents that I'm gay. I made my carefully worded announcement at Thanksgiving. I said, 'Mom, would you please pass the gravy to a homosexual.' Then my Aunt Lorraine piped in, 'Bob, you're gay. Are you seeing a psychiatrist?' I said, 'No, I'm seeing a lieutenant in the Navy.'

Comedian Bob Smith

heterosexuals have become more accepting of gay civil rights is that gay activists have attempted to identify their cause with the movements for racial equality and women's rights. Consequently, heterosexuals who consider egalitarianism to be an important component of their own self-concept may have adopted more accepting attitudes as a way of affirming their liberal social identities. This explanation for greater gay acceptance is consistent with the value-expressive function of attitudes discussed in chapter 5 (see p. 161).

Another catalyst for changing heterosexuals' attitudes and beliefs toward gay people has been the AIDS epidemic. Despite the heavy toll the disease has had in the gay male community, one positive consequence is that it has given many heterosexuals their first glimpse at nonstereotypical gay relationships. Numerous news articles, television programs, and Hollywood movies have documented the devotion and loving care that gay men with AIDS have received from their gay lovers and friends, often while being coldly rejected by their biological families. Such media coverage has not only increased the visibility of gay relationships, but it has also provided the opportunity for heterosexuals to feel empathy for gay people, an emotional response that has been found to improve attitudes toward stigmatized groups (Batson et al., 1997).

On the negative side, the AIDS crisis has also revealed the often deep-seated hostility that many heterosexuals still feel toward gay men (Crawford, 1996). For example, many antigay organizations used the specter of AIDS contamination to promote continued discrimination, and groups monitoring antigay violence reported an increase in physical assaults as public awareness about AIDS increased (Herek et al., 1997).

SECTION SUMMARY

Although *old-fashioned racism* has declined over the years in the United States, some social scientists contend that it has been replaced by a new form, *aversive racism*, which is a combination of both positive and negative beliefs and feelings about a racial group. The overt and blatant *sexism* of previous generations has also diminished during the past thirty years. However, although the benevolent sexist beliefs expressed in *ambivalent sexism* lead to more positive attitudes about women, it still serves to justify male social dominance. Finally, in contrast to existing social norms against open expression of racist or sexist sentiments, *heterosexism* permeates our culture to such a degree that most people are unaware of how it influences their own social perceptions. Given contemporary attitudes regarding homosexuality, heterosexuals still feel relatively free to socially reject gay men, lesbians, and bisexuals.

And if a house be divided against itself, that house cannot stand.

The New Testament, Mark, 3:24–25

Let's go hand in hand, not one before another.

William Shakespeare, English dramatist and poet, 1564–1616

COMBATING PREJUDICE

Having analyzed various forms of prejudice, and having examined the psychological and social mechanisms underlying intergroup intolerance, let us now explore the prospects for reducing prejudice. First, we will examine whether changing people's thinking can reduce prejudice (an *individual-based approach*), and then we will outline situational factors necessary to reduce intergroup intolerance (a *group-based approach*). Finally, we will end the chapter with a brief look at two social psychological attempts to remedy some of the negative consequences of prejudice and discrimination in our educational system.

Are stereotyping and prejudice inevitable? Some social scientists believe that because stereotyping is often an automatic process, prejudiced thinking cannot be changed. Others contend that prejudice can be reduced by monitoring stereotypical thinking.

SOCIAL SCIENTISTS DIFFER ON WHETHER STEREOTYPED THINKING CAN BE CHANGED

Because prejudice and discrimination are often based on stereotypical thinking, some experts have suggested that positive changes can occur if people make a conscious effort to think more rationally and deductively. Others argue that such efforts are futile. Let's briefly explore both viewpoints, beginning with the more pessimistic perspective that stereotyped thinking cannot be changed.

ONE VIEW: STEREOTYPING IS INEVITABLE

Anthropologist Robin Fox (1992) believes that stereotyped thinking is an adaptive mental strategy that has allowed us to survive as a species. Fox contends that due to our biological makeup, we are locked in stereotyped thinking and there is no magic key to help us escape this particular cognitive domain. According to Fox, sensitivity training, consciousness raising, and even taking a social psychology course will not remove stereotyping from our daily thought processes.

> The whole point of this argument has been to show that we have no choice but to think in stereotypes. That is what a lot of basic thinking is. What is more, we are "comfortable" with such stereotyping, and our better selves only deplore the fact when some particular stereotype lacks social approval or conflicts with our current moralistic stereotyping. As long as it does not, we are happy to sink into it. Thus, in certain circles, "All big corporations are polluters" would not be challenged, whereas "all gay men are untrustworthy" would evoke horror. In other circles, of course, this would be reversed . . . as long as perceivable differences exist, we can only hope constantly to revise our stereotypes in a more favorable direction, not try to outlaw what is evidently not a disease of the mind but part of its basic constitution. We have to come to terms with the idea that prejudice is not a form of thinking but that thinking is a form of prejudice. (Fox, 1992, pp. 149, 151)

Although thinking in terms of stereotypes may be an automatic and inevitable process (Macrae et al., 1994), and while it also is often socially beneficial, these advantages can, at times, be outweighed by the negative consequences of unmonitored stereotypical thinking. As we have already discussed, many stereotypes about various outgroups contain unflattering and demeaning characteristics. When they become activated, they can result in harmful biasing effects toward outgroup members who possess none of the objectionable qualities ascribed to their group. One of the disturbing possible implications of describing stereotyping as natural and inevitable is that it might appear to condone the prejudice and discrimination resulting from negative stereotypes. That is, some might conclude that we cannot—and we *should not*—do anything to change a type of thinking that helps us survive.

ANOTHER VIEW: STEREOTYPING CAN BE MONITORED

Not surprisingly, a number of social psychologists reject this conclusion. Michael Billig (1985), for example, argues that emphasizing categorization as the only useful and adaptive thought process in social cognition provides a one-sided account of human thinking. Although categorizing most certainly is useful, Billig contends that to *differentiate* between things within a given category is also useful. He asserts that it is too simplistic to think that it is always in a person's best interest to merely categorize.

Consistent with Billig's analysis, Patricia Devine (1989) believes that people can circumvent stereotypical thinking if they make a conscious effort to use more rational, inductive strategies. That is, even though individuals may have *knowledge* of a stereotype and may have relied on it in the past to make social judgments, their current *personal beliefs* may no longer be in agreement with the stereotype. Due to this change in circumstances, instead of making judgments based on the stereotype, they may now consciously decide to rely on their own personal beliefs (Devine & Monteith, 1999).

For example, imagine that Clayton has grown up being taught that women are intellectually inferior to men. However, during the course of his life, Clayton has been exposed to people who do not fit this gender stereotype. Because of these experiences, as well as his desire to perceive himself as nonsexist, Clayton may begin to adopt a more egalitarian view of women. Although Clayton no longer accepts this stereotype, he has not eliminated it from his memory. Quite the contrary. According to Devine, during his relearning process, this stereotype remains a well-organized, frequently activated cognitive structure, and it is more accessible than his newly adopted personal beliefs. In a very real sense, for a person like Clayton, censoring the negative stereotype and guarding against ingroup biasing takes conscious and deliberate attention—like trying to break a bad habit. As you may recall from chapter 5 (p. 169–170), because habits involve a good deal of automatic and unthinking responses, they are often difficult to break.

Figure 7.6 outlines how self-awareness and self-regulation (see chapter 2) may play a role in reducing prejudiced responses. Continuing with our example, whenever Clayton encounters a woman, the gender stereotype is involuntarily activated. If he does not consciously monitor his thoughts, he may automatically slip back into acting as though women were the intellectual inferiors of men (a *discrepant response*). Becoming aware of this discrepancy in his actions, Clayton will experience *discrepancy-associated consequences*. These include feelings of guilt and self-criticism that will in turn motivate him to heighten his self-awareness and search for situational cues that may have spontaneously triggered this prejudiced response (Zuwerink et al., 1996). Through such attentiveness to prejudice-triggering cues, Clayton will slowly build up self-regulatory mechanisms that should produce more controlled and careful responses on future occasions (Monteith, 1993; Monteith et al., 1998).

The importance of Devine's perspective for reducing prejudice and discrimination is that it doesn't assume that prejudice is an inevitable consequence of the natural process of social categorization. People can avoid prejudiced responding

FIGURE 7.6

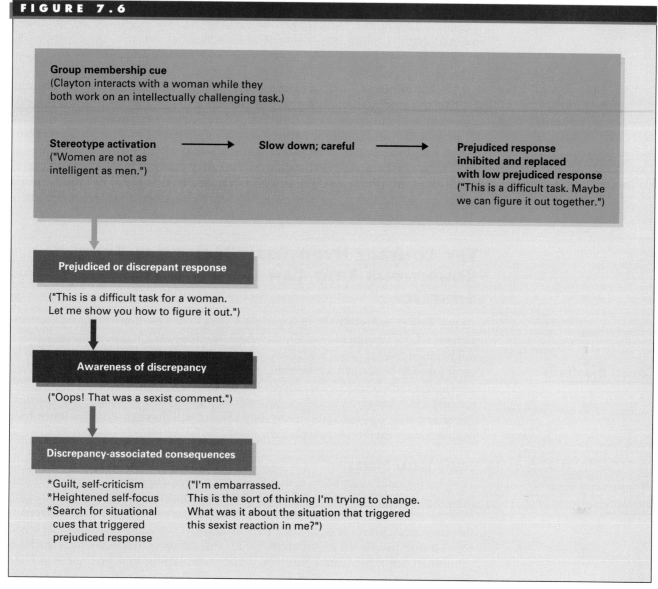

Reducing Prejudiced Responding Through Self-Regulation

According to Devine (1989) and Monteith (1993), when low prejudiced persons first begin to try to respond in a nonprejudiced manner toward previously denigrated outgroup members, stereotype activation often spontaneously triggers a discrepant (i.e., prejudiced) response, which subsequently triggers a series of discrepancy-associated consequences. This cognitive process is depicted by the arrows running vertically from top to bottom in the left side of the figure. Over time, through careful self-regulation of one's thoughts and attention to one's nonprejudiced standards, low prejudiced people break the "prejudice habit" and respond as depicted by the horizontal arrows at the top of the figure. If this model accurately describes how prejudiced behavior can be eliminated, what would be the first step you would need to take to reduce your own prejudiced responding?

Source: Adapted from M. J. Monteith, "Self-Regulation of Prejudiced Responses: Implications for Progress in Prejudice-Reduction Efforts" in *Journal of Personality and Social Psychology*, 65:469–485, American Psychological Association, 1993.

(that is, discrimination) if low-prejudiced standards are central to their self-concept *and* they bring these standards to mind before acting. Thus, although automatic stereotype activation makes nonprejudiced responding difficult, Devine's work indicates that people can inhibit such intolerance through conscious and deliberate self-regulation. However, the biggest stumbling block in unlearning prejudicial responding is that, as we discovered in chapter 2 (pp. 45–48), many people do not spontaneously engage in the self-awareness necessary to think about their own personal nonprejudiced standards (Monteith, 1996a): if they don't think about these standards, there will be no guilt and internal conflict when they respond in a prejudicial manner. Yet if people do engage in self-awareness, research indicates that they can avoid using stereotypes in their social judgments (Macrae et al., in press).

A further implication of Devine's perspective is that it does not assume, as does the theory of aversive racism (see pp. 246–247), that all White Americans are prejudiced toward minority group members. Instead of viewing Whites as people desperately trying to hide their racial prejudices from themselves and others, this perspective contends that many people, regardless of their race, sex, or sexual orientation, consciously attempt to develop nonprejudicial thinking (Plant & Devine, 1998). Viewed in this light, Devine is much more optimistic about the prospects of prejudice reduction than are the aversive racism theorists.

THE CONTACT HYPOTHESIS IDENTIFIES FOUR CONDITIONS THAT CAN REDUCE INTERGROUP CONFLICT

At the time of the original U.S. Supreme Court *Brown vs. Board of Education* decision on school desegregation, Gordon Allport (1954) outlined how desegregation might reduce racial prejudice. Later, other social psychologists also contributed to what came to be known as the **contact hypothesis** (Amir, 1969; Brewer & Miller, 1984). In certain respects, the contact hypothesis can be thought of as a guideline for reducing hostility between groups that have had a history of conflict. According to this perspective, intergroup contact will decrease hostility when four conditions are met (refer to table 7.5).

EQUAL SOCIAL STATUS

The first necessary condition is that the groups interacting must be roughly *equal in social status*. When this condition is not met and traditional status imbalances are maintained, long-standing stereotypes that are largely based on status discrepancies are generally not revised (Cohen, 1982). However, research indicates that when equal-status people from different racial and ethnic groups interact, such as soldiers in the U.S. Armed Services, racial stereotyping and prejudices decline (Pettigrew, 1969).

SUSTAINED CLOSE CONTACT

The second condition is that the two groups must have *sustained close contact*. Several public-housing studies conducted in the 1940s and 1950s demonstrated the importance of this condition in reducing prejudice. Reflecting upon these social experiments in racial integration, Stuart Cook stated:

> One of the clearest findings of studies on the relation between intergroup contact and attitude change is that, while individuals rather quickly come to accept and even approve of association with members of another social group in situations of the type where they have experienced such association, this approval is not likely to be generalized to other situations unless the individuals have quite close personal relationships with members of the other group. (Cook, 1964, pp. 41–42)

Similarly, survey studies in France, Great Britain, Germany, and the Netherlands confirm that intergroup friendships significantly reduce both subtle and blatant prejudice (Pettigrew, 1997). Experimental studies even suggest that the sustained close contact necessary to reduce prejudice does not have to be something that one directly experiences: simply knowing that some of your ingroup

Contact Hypothesis

The theory that under certain conditions, direct contact between antagonistic groups will reduce prejudice.

Only equals can be friends.

Ethiopian proverb

You cannot judge another person until you have walked a mile in his moccasins.

American Indian proverb

TABLE 7.5

Reducing Prejudice Through Social Contact

Now that you have learned how to develop an individual program to reduce your own prejudice (refer back to figure 7.6), let's now set to work on reducing prejudice on a group level. According to the contact hypothesis, intergroup prejudice can be reduced if the four conditions listed below are met. Think about intergroup hostilities on your own college campus or in your local community. Perhaps this conflict involves men and women, gays and heterosexuals, or people from different racial groups. How could you develop a "Tolerance Campaign" utilizing these four principal conditions?

Necessary Conditions

1. *Equal Social Status:* Members of groups in conflict should interact in settings where everyone has roughly equal status.

2. *Sustained Close Contact:* Interaction between members of different groups should be one-on-one and should be maintained over an extended period of time.

3. *Intergroup Cooperation:* Members of different groups should engage in joint activities to achieve superordinate goals.

4. *Social Norms Favoring Equality:* There must be a clear social perception, largely fostered by group authority figures, that prejudice and discrimination is not condoned.

members have outgroup friends is often sufficient to reduce prejudice toward that outgroup (Wright et al., 1997). Regarding school desegregation, one likely reason it has not produced significant reductions in racial prejudice is that students of different races generally avoid interacting with one another. That is, even though the school building is integrated, students segregate themselves on the bus and playground, and in the cafeteria and classroom. School officials often magnify the problem by separating students based on academic achievement, which results in advantaged White students and disadvantaged minority students having very little classroom contact (Epstein, 1985).

INTERGROUP COOPERATION

A third condition that can help reduce hostility is *intergroup cooperation.* As the Robbers Cave experiment demonstrated, animosity between the Rattlers and the Eagles subsided when they engaged in a joint activity to achieve mutually shared goals (*superordinate goals*). Similar results have been obtained in a variety of experimental and field settings, including school, work, and the armed forces (Desforges et al., 1997). One possible reason why cooperation reduces intergroup bias and hostility is that cooperating members of different social groups appear to cognitively *recategorize* one another into a new ingroup (Gaertner et al., 1996).

SOCIAL NORMS FAVORING EQUALITY

The final condition for successful conflict reduction is that there must be in place *social norms favoring equality* (Monteith et al., 1996). As demonstrated in chapter 5, social norms have a significant effect on determining people's behavioral intentions. Here is where authority figures and group leaders play a pivotal role. If they publicly state support for equality, others are likely to follow their lead. If they oppose intergroup contact, prejudice reduction is unlikely (Cook, 1984). This is one of the principal reasons why lesbians and gay men in the armed

Progress is a nice word, but change is its motivator. And change has its enemies.

Robert Kennedy, U.S. senator, 1925–1968

services continue to run the very real risk of physical and psychological abuse at the hands of fellow soldiers if their sexual orientation is revealed. Many of their superiors up the chain of command have consistently not favored acceptance or even tolerance for homosexual enlisted personnel (Herek et al., 1996). On the other hand, race, sex and even sexual orientation tensions have been successfully defused in many work environments when supervisors make it clear that prejudicial statements and discriminatory actions will not be tolerated.

BEYOND THE CONTACT HYPOTHESIS

One criticism of the contact hypothesis has been its overemphasis on changing the dominant group's prejudicial attitudes, while ignoring the attitudes of minority group members (Devine et al., 1995). Those who level this criticism suggest that to more effectively promote intergroup harmony, social scientists must also consider (1) the attitudes and beliefs of minority group members, and (2) the beliefs and anxieties of everyone involved in intergroup contact. For example, according to this perspective, during intergroup contact, minority group members may feel anxious because they fear being victimized and negatively evaluated (refer back to the *stereotype threat* discussion, p. 231), while dominant group members may be anxious from fear of saying or doing something that might be interpreted as a sign of prejudice (see the cartoon on this page). It is the combined effect of this **intergroup anxiety** that often creates difficulties in such social encounters, even in the absence of any real prejudicial attitudes (Stephan & Stephan, 1985, 1989a). When people experience this anxiety during intergroup exchanges, they often adopt a *protective self-presentation style*, in which they focus on trying not to make a bad impression, rather than trying to make a good one. Thus, they might talk less and generally act more cautiously than less anxious individuals. This strategy can backfire, however, because their outgroup partners may interpret their reticence as hostility. The good news is that if people place themselves in intergroup situations and have positive or even neutral contact with outgroup members, their intergroup anxiety will decrease (Britt et al., 1996; Stephan & Stephan, 1992).

In the final analysis, there is no single strategy to eliminate prejudice and discrimination from the vocabulary of intergroup relations. Because of the manner in which we as a species process information from our social world, and because of the importance we place on our group affiliations, we will always need to be attentive to the way we judge others. Although there is nothing inherently wrong with social stereotyping, it can easily diminish our ability to see the shared humanity in those who fall outside the favored category of "we."

Intergroup Anxiety

Anxiety due to anticipating negative consequences when interacting with an outgroup member.

If we accept and acquiesce in the face of discrimination, we accept the responsibility ourselves and allow those responsible to salve their conscience by believing that they have our acceptance and concurrence. . . . We should therefore, protest openly everything . . . that smacks of discrimination.

Mary McLeod Bethune, U.S. educator and civil rights activist, 1875–1955

SECTION SUMMARY

Although a difference of opinion exists among social scientists concerning the ability of people to stop stereotypical and prejudicial thinking, various techniques have been developed to reduce intergroup hostility, both on the individual and group level. One of the better-known strategies, the *contact hypothesis*, identifies four conditions that must be met before hostilities will decrease. These four conditions are: promote equal status interaction, encourage sustained close contact and intergroup cooperation, and put in place social norms favoring equality. More recently, researchers have also examined how the perceptions of minority group members and intergroup anxiety in general can hinder the development of greater understanding between various social groups.

APPLICATIONS

HOW CAN OUR SCHOOLS BOTH REDUCE INTERGROUP CONFLICT AND PROMOTE ACADEMIC ACHIEVEMENT?

 n 1971, Elliot Aronson was asked by the superintendent of the Austin, Texas, schools to devise a plan to reduce interracial tensions in the recently desegregated classrooms. After observing student interaction, Aronson realized that the social dynamics were strikingly similar to those described by Sherif in the Robbers Cave field experiment (refer back to pp. 236–239). Using that study as a guide, he and his colleagues developed a cooperative learning technique that came to be called the **jigsaw classroom** (Aronson et al., 1978b; Aronson & Thibodeau, 1992). The technique was so named because students had to cooperate in "piecing together" their daily lessons, much the way a jigsaw puzzle is assembled. Ten fifth-grade classrooms were introduced to this technique, and three additional classes served as control groups.

In the jigsaw classroom, students were placed in six-person, racially and academically mixed learning groups. The day's lesson was divided into six subtopics, and each student was responsible for learning one piece of this lesson and then teaching it to the other group members. With the lesson divided up in this manner, cooperation was essential for success. In contrast to traditional classroom learning, in which students compete against one another, the jigsaw classroom promoted superordinate goals. It also promoted racial harmony. Compared with students in the control classrooms in which traditional learning techniques were employed, students in the jigsaw groups showed a decrease in prejudice and an increase in liking for one another. Their liking for school also improved, as did their level of self-esteem. The cooperative learning also improved minority students' academic test scores, while White students' scores remained the same.

Since these studies were first conducted and reported meta-analysis of the results from similar cooperative classroom settings have found that the jigsaw method offers a promising way to improve race relations in desegregated schools by breaking down the "outgroup" barriers that drive a cognitive and emotional wedge between students (Miller & Davidson-Podgorny, 1987).

While the jigsaw classroom was specifically designed to reduce prejudice, a new—and still evolving—educational approach, known as *"wise"*

Jigsaw Classroom

A cooperative group-learning technique designed to reduce prejudice and raise self-esteem.

schooling, has been developed by Claude Steele to combat one of the effects of prejudice; namely, stereotype threat. Wise schooling combines the cooperative learning of the jigsaw classroom with attempts to defuse stereotype threat in academic settings. Instead of offering minority students stigmatizing remedial help, which often only reinforces doubts they may have about their academic ability, wise schooling invites minority students to participate in a racially integrated and intellectually challenging honors program. Working together, male and female students of different races and social class backgrounds receive the message that regardless of their current skill level, they are valued because of their academic potential. Results from such a program offered at the University of Michigan ("21st Century Program") are encouraging: both White and minority first-year students living together in a dormitory and participating in a wise schooling program achieved better academic scores than comparable students who were either involved in stigmatizing remedial education programs or not involved in cooperative learning programs (Steele, 1997). More importantly, this higher academic performance has persisted in subsequent years, and after four years, only one student has dropped out of school compared with a 25 percent drop-out rate for Black students in remedial education programs.

As these intervention programs demonstrate, there is room for guarded optimism about the outlook for not only reducing prejudice in our lives but also reducing some of its negative consequences (Prentice & Miller, 1999). Yes, it is true that we are far from being a nonprejudiced species. Our natural inclination to categorize people can indeed set the stage for prejudice. It is also true that competition, ingroup loyalties, and social ideologies can fan the flames of this tendency to see people as "them" rather than "us." However, as has been demonstrated throughout this text, our ability to reflect on our actions, our desire to act in ways consistent with our internalized personal beliefs, and our ability to reshape social reality means that prejudice can be reduced. If, as described in chapter 2, self-concept is truly a process of identification, what we need to do on an individual level is expand our ingroup identification to include humanity as a whole. In doing so, we will be able to see ourselves in those who were previously thought of as merely inferior "others." This is by no means an insignificant cognitive shift. For as you will discover in chapter 11, when we include others in our self-concept, our resources become theirs to share, and their successes and failures become our own. Therefore, the first step in achieving a community with a low level of prejudice is to monitor our own thinking and action. The second step is to work collectively to change the perceptions of others. The question to ask yourself is whether you are ready to take that first step.

FEATURED STUDY
STUDENT COOPERATION AND PREJUDICE REDUCTION

Van Oudenhoven, J. P., Groenewoud, J. T., & Hewstone, M. (1996). Cooperation, ethnic salience and generalization of interethnic attitudes. *European Journal of Social Psychology, 26,* 649–661.

Social identity theory asserts that social categorization often leads to a favoring of the ingroup and prejudice toward outgroups. This theory has led to two different strategies to improve intergroup relations. One strategy, called *personalization,* proposes that reducing the salience of social categories will shift people's attention to personal or individual information (Brewer & Miller, 1984). If the resulting interpersonal exchange is positive, which is likely in a cooperative setting, then intergroup relations should improve. In contrast, the other strategy, known as *generalization,* proposes that prejudice reduction will result from cooperation *only* when it is accompanied by actions that promote the generalization of the resulting positive attitudes toward specific individuals to the group from which the individuals come (Hewstone & Brown, 1986).

Which of these two strategies is most likely to reduce prejudice? With generalization, does it matter whether the *degree* of outgroup salience is medium or high? That is, should an outgroup member's social identity be made salient only after cooperation has begun to exert its positive influence on liking, or should the salience be established during initial introductions and be maintained until generalization of the positive attitudes toward the liked outgroup member is made to the outgroup as a whole?

In the present study, three hypotheses were tested:

1. Cooperation leading to success with a participating outgroup member will lead to more positive attitudes toward nonparticipating outgroup members in general.
2. Attitudes toward nonparticipating outgroup members will be more favorable if social categories are made salient than if the categories are kept nonsalient.
3. These attitudes will be most favorable if social categorization is not made salient until the second phase of the cooperation.

METHOD

Fifty-four unacquainted Dutch secondary school pupils (aged 14–16 years) participated in the study and were randomly assigned to one of three experimental conditions consisting of two Dutch students and a male Turkish confederate. Turks were chosen as the target outgroup because interethnic attitudes toward Turks in the Netherlands are rather negative. In the *High-High salience* condition, the confederate's ethnicity was made salient during both the introductory conversation and during the break between the two puzzle tasks. In the *Low-High salience* condition the confederate's ethnicity was only made salient during the break, while in the *Low-Low salience* condition his ethnicity was never made salient.

For two hours, each three-student group worked cooperatively together on two crossword puzzles. Similar to the jigsaw cooperative learning method, the conditions for cooperation were created by giving each student only a third of the information needed to solve the puzzles. Success was guaranteed by choosing a difficulty level in which all groups could nearly complete the puzzles. The success experience was further enhanced by the experimenter informing each group that they had worked faster and filled out more words than the average group.

Once the puzzles were completed, participants expressed their attitudes toward the Turkish and Dutch cooperation partner by completing a self-report questionnaire. Their attitudes toward Turks in general was obtained by next ushering them into another room and asking them to participate in "a different study" measuring the attitudes toward eleven different ethnic groups who lived in the Netherlands. After the main study was conducted, researchers also ran a second group of fifty-five students who only filled out the "Attitude Toward Turks in general" scale without any contact or cooperation.

RESULTS AND DISCUSSION

Consistent with hypothesis 1, students in the cooperative groups later expressed more positive attitudes toward Turkish outgroup members in general than students who had not experienced the contact or cooperation with the Turkish student. This finding that cooperation reduces prejudicial attitudes confirms one of the basic tenets of the contact hypothesis. In line with hypothesis 2, the most positive attitude toward Turks was obtained in the two conditions in which the cooperating Turk's ethnicity was made salient (*High-High salience* and *Low-High salience*). This finding suggests that ingroup members who have contact with likable outgroup members must, at some point, become aware of the outgroup members' social identity in order for their positive feelings to generalize to the outgroup. The fact that the *Low-Low salience* condition yielded little generalized attitude change suggests that the personalization strategy is not as effective as the generalization strategy in improving intergroup attitudes. Finally, according to hypothesis 3, attitudes should be most favorable if social categorization is not made salient until the second phase of cooperation. However, contrary to expectations, there were no differences between the *High-High salience* and *Low-High salience* conditions. The researchers suggest that a possible reason this expected effect was not found was because their research setting was not a threatening one, and thus, participants were unlikely to experience intergroup anxiety. Further research should explore whether the gradual introduction of outgroup categorization is more effective in generalizing positive attitudes under more threatening circumstances.

 WEB SITES accessed through http://www.mhhe.com/franzoi2

Web sites for this chapter focus on the nature of prejudice, including an analysis of ethnic stereotypes, sexual harassment, antigay prejudice, the history and psychology of hate crimes, and how to break prejudicial habits.

American Psychological Association

The American Psychological Association has web pages which explore a number of issues related to prejudice and discrimination. For example, one web page analyzes whether all of us have some degree of prejudice, as well as the possibility that we can break our prejudicial habits. Another web page explores the history of hate crimes, including its prevalence, perpetrators, and emotional effects.

Examining the Asian-Small Eye Syndrome

This web page analyzes stereotypes about Asians with humor and interesting personal and historical stories and illustrations.

American Association of University Women

This web site of the American Association of University Women has separate sites devoted to sexual harassment (Hostile Hallways: The AAUW Survey on Sexual Harassment in America's Schools) and gender discrimination in education ("Gender Gaps: Where Schools Still Fail Our Children").

Sexual Orientation: Science, Education, and Policy

This web site features the work of Dr. Gregory Herek, a noted authority on antigay prejudice, and his Northern California Community Research Group. A number of the studies conducted by Herek and this group are cited in the present chapter.

PART THREE

UNDERSTANDING OUR PLACE WITHIN THE GROUP

We, as individuals, are creatures of the group (Miller & Prentice, 1994). Or, as sociologist George Herbert Mead (1934) pointed out so many years ago, it is the internalization of the group into the mind of the individual that gives us selfhood. Group dynamics are just that—vibrant and ever changing.

Chapter 8 examines how social power is used to influence our thoughts and behavior. How do personal, social, and cultural factors impact conformity? What happens to nonconformists or those who hold minority opinions in groups? How can we get others to comply to our requests? And how susceptible are we to the destructive commands of authority figures?

Chapter 9 looks more closely at the psychology of the group. How do a collection of people become a group? How is the behavior of individual members shaped by the group? Do groups make more cautious or more risky decisions than individuals? How do leaders emerge in a group, and are there different types of leaders? Finally, what happens when group interests and individual interests conflict?

C H A P T E R   8

SOCIAL INFLUENCE

CHAPTER OUTLINE

"ONE MORNING"

ne morning a man awakens to find strings coming through his window attached to his hands and feet.

　　. . . I'm not a marionette, he says, his voice rising with the question, am I? Am I a marionette?

One of the strings loosens and jerks as he scratches his head.

　　. . . Hmmm, he says, I just wonder if I am a marionette?

And then all the strings pull and jerk and he is jumping out of bed.

Now that he's up he'll just go to the window and see who's doing tricks with him when he's half asleep . . .

He follows the strings up into the sky with his eyes and sees a giant hand sticking through a cloud, holding a crossbar to which the strings are attached . . .

Hmmm, he says, that's funny, I never saw that crossbar before . . . I guess I am a marionette . . .

This Russell Edson (1976) poem provides an apt description of the world of 30-year-old Truman Burbank in the 1998 movie *The Truman Show* starring Jim Carrey. Truman is a resident of the all-too-perfect small town of Seahaven, an island just off a Florida-like shore. What Truman does not know is that his entire life is being choreographed by an unseen hand. As the first person legally adopted by a corporation, his entire life is being chronicled on television and watched by billions of viewers around the world. Seahaven, in fact, is a TV studio enclosed within a huge dome, complete with its own artificial sun, moon, weather, and a distant horizon that is actually a painted wall. All the people in his life—parents, wife, friends, coworkers, even strangers on the street—are actors who have been hired to follow a set script revolving around the show's unwitting star, Truman. Every time he behaves in a way that does not conform to this prearranged script, some glitch pops up to steer him back to his normal routine.

Truman never ventures beyond the confines of this carefully controlled world because he has been psychologically conditioned not to do so. For example, as a youngster, his father "drowned" when he and Truman sailed too far out in the harbor, creating in the young boy an enduring phobia for the "ocean" surrounding Seahaven. In a more benign manner, he has been encouraged to internalize the message of his favorite television show, "Show Me the Way to Go Home," which trumpets the virtue and wisdom of remaining in your hometown.

Why does Truman not realize that his life is being manipulated and shaped on such a grand scale? As the godlike creator and director of this world explains while sitting in the show's control room located inside Seahaven's moon, "We accept the reality for which we are presented." As the movie progresses, however, Truman slowly begins to question his reality. Will this questioning reveal to him the truth about the social forces that shape his life? What will he do with this knowledge? Will he resign himself to his human marionette role, or will he strive to wrest the strings from the hidden hand? As you read this current chapter on social influence, I would like you to ask yourself the following question: To what degree are we all Truman Burbank?

In The Truman Show, Jim Carrey plays a character, Truman Burbank, who is unknowingly being followed on camera through every minute of his life in a made-for-TV community. In this ultimate social influence attempt, everyone Truman interacts with, from the news vendor on the street to his doting wife, are actors who follow a set script revolving around him. To what degree is your own life similar to the stage-managed life of Truman? Are you aware of the social forces that influence your everyday decisions and those with whom you interact?

DEFINITIONS OF SOCIAL INFLUENCE

As a way to begin answering this question, let's first define the chapter topic and related concepts.

SOCIAL INFLUENCE INVOLVES THE EXERCISE OF SOCIAL POWER

Social Influence

The exercise of social power by a person or group to change the attitudes or behavior of others in a particular direction.

Social Power

The force available to the influencer to motivate attitude or behavior change.

Social influence involves the exercise of social power by a person or group to change the attitudes or behavior of others in a particular direction. **Social power** refers to the force available to the influencer to motivate this change. This power can originate from having access to certain resources (for example, rewards, punishments, information) due to one's social position in society, or from being liked and admired by others (French & Raven, 1959; Tyler, 1997). In *The Truman Show,* the creator and director exercises an all-encompassing social power over Truman's life. Yet how far removed is this from the power that parents have over their children, or that societies' leaders exercise over their citizens? Is it merely a matter of degree how closely our lives parallel Truman's?

Consider for a moment one simple cultural ritual practiced throughout the world, namely, the singing of the national anthem. As sociologist Karen Cerulo (1989) points out, ruling bodies in a society use national anthems as a cultural tool to create bonds, retain loyalty, and reinforce goals among their citizens. Government leaders and their representatives diffuse these symbols throughout the culture by teaching the anthem and the pledge in schools, and using the anthem at all official occasions and ceremonies, including sporting events (Mead, 1980). During times of cultural strife, rituals become very important because member participation provides leaders some indication of their power base (Swidler, 1986).

Compliance

Publicly acting in accord with a direct request.

When you are asked to stand and sing the national anthem, this request illustrates one of the three main behavioral consequences of social influence; namely, compliance. **Compliance** is publicly acting in accord with a direct request. In compliance, people responding to a direct request may privately agree or disagree with the action they are engaging in, or they may have no opinion about their behavior. Complying with a request upon which you have no personal attitude is not uncommon. Do you really think about what passing the salt to a dinner companion implies about your relationship with this person or your own values? Probably not. You simply comply out of habit. Similarly, some people might stand and sing the *Star Spangled Banner* without considering the meaning of their actions.

To them, it is a ritual they habitually comply with before all sporting events, and they do so in a mindless fashion (Langer, 1989).

Have you ever granted a friend's request to copy your homework even though you believed it was the wrong thing to do? This *external compliance*—acting in accord with a direct request despite privately disagreeing with it—occurs because we are concerned how others might respond if we refuse them (Deutsch & Gerard, 1955). On the other hand, we often comply with a request because we have a personal allegiance to the values and principles associated with it. Such *internal compliance* (or *internalization*) involves both acting and believing in accord with a request (Kelman, 1958). When you agree to donate money to a social cause consistent with your own values, this is an instance of internal compliance. So is singing the national anthem to express your patriotism.

When we do not respond by complying with others' requests, they may up the ante by trying to secure a second behavioral consequence of social influence; namely, obedience. **Obedience** is the performance of an action in response to a direct order, usually from a person of high status or authority. Because most of us are taught from childhood to respect and obey authority figures (parents, teachers, police officers), obedience to those of higher status is common and is often taken to be a sign of maturity. What other factors shape your willingness to obey? We will explore this question later in the chapter.

The third main behavioral consequence of social influence focuses on **conformity,** which is a yielding to perceived group pressure by copying the behavior and beliefs of others. To what degree do you conform to others' social influence? Consider the clothing you wear, the food you eat, the music you prefer, the religion you practice, and so on. How are these areas of your life influenced by the social standards of your friends, family, and larger culture? What about when you actively defy a particular group's perceived influence? Are you then acting independently, or are you simply conforming to another group's standards? Sometimes it is difficult, if not impossible, to distinguish conformity from independence. Even though the former is a yielding to group standards and **independence** is not being subject to control by others, they often result in the same behavioral outcomes. We will discuss this issue and many others in more detail later in the chapter. In the meantime, has our discussion thus far caused you to see any similarities between your own life and the life of Truman Burbank?

Obedience

The performance of an action in response to a direct order.

Conformity

A yielding to perceived group pressure by copying the behavior and beliefs of others.

Independence

Not being subject to control by others.

SECTION SUMMARY

Social influence involves the exercise of social power by a person or group to change the attitudes or behavior of others in a particular direction. Conformity, compliance, and obedience represent the three main behavioral consequences of social influence. Each of these three often varies in the degree of social pressure preceding it. *Conformity* is a yielding to perceived group pressure, *compliance* is publicly acting in accord with a direct request, and *obedience* is the performance of an action in response to a direct order.

CLASSIC CONFORMITY RESEARCH

To better understand social influence, let's begin by analyzing three classic conformity studies conducted more than forty years ago: Muzafir Sherif's work on norm development, Solomon Asch's work on group pressure, and Stanley Schachter's work on how people react to nonconformists.

SHERIF'S NORM DEVELOPMENT RESEARCH ANALYZED CONFORMITY TO AN AMBIGUOUS REALITY

The first widely recognized conformity study was that of Turkish-born Muzafir Sherif, who in 1935 published his research on the development of social norms. Sherif's research was partly spurred by his disagreement with the prevailing individualist view of social psychology that a group was merely a collection of individuals and that no new group qualities arise when individuals form into a collective entity. Sherif countered that a group was more than the sum of its individuals' nongroup thinking. He set out to prove his point by demonstrating that when social norms develop in a group, it is a result of "a psychological atmosphere that is not inherent in its discrete parts" (Sherif, 1936, p. 15).

To document how group pressures influence the judgments of individuals in an ambiguous situation, Sherif enlisted college students into a visual perception experiment. Participants were individually placed in a small, totally darkened laboratory where, fifteen feet in front of them, a small dot of light appeared. They were told that after a short time the light would move, and their task would be to judge how far it moved. In all cases the light was left on for two seconds after the participants indicated the beginning of movement. Each participant made one hundred light movement judgments. Although they didn't realize it, the experimenter never actually moved the dot of light. What the participants perceived as light movement was really an optical illusion known as the autokinetic effect. The *autokinetic effect* refers to the fact that when someone stares at a stationary point of light in a darkened room where there is no frame of reference, it appears to move in various directions.

Each participant's first few guesses were generally quite different from one another. However, after a few more trials, they settled on a consistent range of light movement. Thus, even though this was an optical illusion, participants assigned some order to the visual chaos, zeroing in on a stable estimate as if they were actually mastering this perceptual task. Yet because the light movement was illusory, there wasn't much consistency between those making their isolated judgments. One person would settle on a stable range of about two inches, while another would make an estimate of six inches.

During the experiment's second phase, Sherif placed these same individuals together in groups of two and three and had them publicly announce their light movement estimates after each trial. What ensued was not a free-for-all bickering of light movement experts. Instead, all participants tended to gradually change their estimates to be more similar to the others. Moving from their individual standards, they converged on an expected standard established by the group, known as a **social norm** (figure 8.1).

This demonstration of the process by which social norms develop is also an illustration of the more general process of social influence (Cialdini & Trost, 1998). Participants were in a fluid and ambiguous situation, and they looked to the group to help them define reality. They all conformed to an emerging social norm that was different from their individually developed standards. Interestingly, even though the data clearly indicated such social influence occurred, most of Sherif's participants denied that the others had influenced their own judgments.

Sherif also found that the more uncertain participants were about the reality of the situation, the more they were influenced by others' opinions. For example, in a variation of the original experiment, Sherif had participants experience the autokinetic effect for the first time in a group setting rather than alone, and thus, they had not established their own individual norms. Under such circumstances, participants were even more influenced by others' view of reality, and convergence toward a common social norm occurred much faster than in the original group condition.

No written law has ever been more binding than unwritten custom supported by popular opinion.

Carrie Chapman Catt, U.S. women's suffrage and peace activist, 1859–1947

Social Norm

An expected standard of behavior and belief established and enforced by a group.

FIGURE 8.1

Norm Development

In Sherif's autokinetic experiments, when participants in three-person groups announced their individual judgments of light movement to one another, their initial divergent norms gradually converged over the course of the trials. In other words, in an ambiguous reality, the individuals established an expected standard (a social norm) of light movement. Can you think of instances in your own life where you and others established social norms to guide your own behavior and beliefs?

Source: Based from M. Sherif, "A Study of Some Social Factors in Perception" in *Archives of Psychology*, 2:187, 1935.

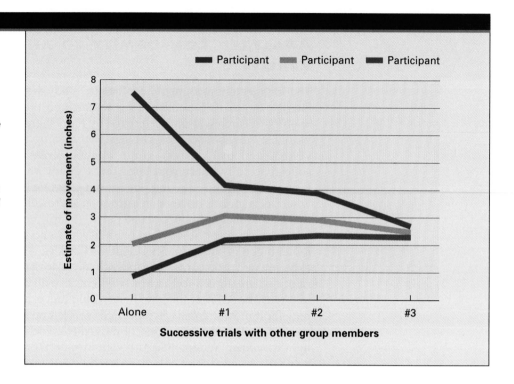

Never throw away hastily any old faith, tradition or convention . . . they are the result of the experience of many generations.

Sir Oliver Lodge, English physicist, 1851–1940

A stranger must conform to his host's customs.

Euripides, Greek dramatist, 5th century B.C.

To do exactly as your neighbors do is the only sensible rule.

Emily Post, U.S. hostess, 1873–1960

A third finding of Sherif's study was that when participants were uncertain about how to define reality, they were highly influenced by others who appeared confident. The basis for these findings came by placing a naive participant in the lab with a confederate who had been instructed to make all of his judgments within a predetermined range. As expected, the naive participants quickly adopted the confederate's range of judgments, and later used this social norm when placed in the autokinetic situation alone. In essence, faced with a confusing situation, people tended to conform to those who appeared confident in dealing with their surroundings, and they continued to be influenced by these opinions even in their absence.

The extent of the power that confident others can have over the less confident, and the durability of the social norms established in such a situation, was later explored by Robert Jacobs and Donald Campbell (1961). They exposed a single person to the autokinetic effect in the company of three confederates who made extreme judgments (light movement of sixteen inches). Even though these judgments were twelve inches larger than what people typically made, the participants strongly conformed, making judgments nearly as extreme as those of the confederates. Following the creation of the light movement norm in this "extreme" group, the researchers created successive generations of four-person groups to judge a series of thirty light movements, but in each generation they removed one of the extreme confederates and replaced him with a naive participant. By the fourth generation all confederates had been replaced, and the four-person group consisted of four actual participants. Although the extreme confederates were no longer in the group, their extreme group-derived norm continued to influence the judgment of successive generations of groups for quite some time. Jacobs and Campbell's study demonstrates experimentally a regularly occurring social phenomena—the views of past generations largely shape the thinking of current and future generations.

Taken together, these studies indicate that when faced with uncertainty about how to interpret or judge events in our lives, we are influenced by others, especially if they appear confident. Not only are we likely to conform to their view of reality, but we are likely to continue to use their perspective in rendering judgments even in their absence. This conformity forms the bedrock of the socialization process in all societies, and it goes a long way in explaining how a Truman Burbank character could be duped into accepting the artificial reality of Seahaven for thirty years.

ASCH'S LINE JUDGMENT RESEARCH ANALYZED CONFORMITY TO A UNANIMOUS MAJORITY

Although conformity due to uncertainty and the desire for accuracy may well be an understandable and even a sensible course of action in many situations, what about those situations in which we conform even though we do not agree with the group's judgment? What can explain our course of action?

In the spring of 1992, Los Angeles was rocked by its worst race riot in twenty-five years following a jury trial in which four White Los Angeles police officers were acquitted of using excessive force in the beating of Rodney King, a Black man.[1] The actual beating was captured on videotape, and most who viewed the tape believed that Mr. King was a victim of police brutality. One of the jurors, Virginia Loya, stated shortly after the trial that she initially favored a guilty verdict. Yet when the jury deliberated, the strength of her convictions waned as other jurors argued that King deserved the beating he received. In reflecting on her fellow jurors' thinking, Loya said, "The tape was the big evidence to me. They couldn't see. To me, they were people who were blind and couldn't get their glasses clean. If anything, I wish these people weren't so blind." Despite her belief that the other jurors were incorrectly assigning blame, Loya conformed to their judgment and changed her vote from guilty to not guilty on all counts but one. Why did she accept what she believed to be an incorrect judgment by the rest of the jurors? In attempting to understand her actions, we might be tempted to search for character flaws or an all-too-compliant personality structure. Yet in doing so, we would be

The beating of Rodney King by Los Angeles police officers was videotaped and shown to the jury at the officers' assault trial. Despite this graphic evidence, the first trial resulted in a "not guilty" verdict. Do you think you would have acted differently than Virginia Loya, a juror who changed her vote from guilty to not guilty due to social pressure from fellow jurors?

---

[1]The officers were later tried on charges that they violated Mr. King's civil rights. In this second trial, two of the officers were convicted and sentenced to prison.

In Asch's conformity experiments, individuals in seven-person groups publicly announced their judgments of which comparison line matched the standard line. Person 6, the only naive participant, appears perplexed and uneasy after the five people before him all chose the incorrect line. If you were in his place, would you have picked the correct line or conformed to the group's incorrect judgment?

overlooking the power of social influence and how group pressure can cause us to go against what our eyes tells about social reality.

This account of an important jury trial bears a striking resemblance to the experience of participants in a classic study of conformity conducted by Solomon Asch (1951, 1952, 1956) almost fifty years ago. In a series of experiments, college students volunteered for what was described as a visual perception experiment. Upon arriving at the lab, they discovered that six other students would also be participating in the study. In fact, all six were confederates who were given prior instructions by Asch to behave a certain way. After the assembled students were seated around a table, Asch placed a card on an easel and pointed to a vertical line on the card that he said was the standard line. On this same card were three more vertical lines labeled "a," "b," and "c" (see figure 8.2). Asch explained that the students' task was to call out the letter corresponding to the line that was the same length as the standard line. Participants made a total of eighteen different line judgments and were seated so that five of the six confederates stated their judgments before the actual participant gave an opinion.

Undoubtedly, all participants in this study must have initially thought that their task would be simple, for it was obvious that "c" was the correct answer. For the first two trials, confederates picked the correct line, but thereafter, on a prearranged basis, they unanimously chose a clearly incorrect line in twelve of the remaining sixteen problems. What would the second to last student—the only "real" participant—do when faced with this dilemma? Would he conform to the judgment of others, or would he stick with what his eyes told him?

Although participants did differ in their degree of conformity, overall they conformed by naming the same incorrect line as the confederates on over one-third (37 percent) of the critical trials. Further, a large majority (76 percent) conformed with the incorrect judgments on at least one of the critical trials (see figure 8.3). In contrast, when other participants in a control condition made their judgments privately, less than 1 percent made errors (Asch, 1951). Similar to juror Virginia Loya, Asch's research participants demonstrated that many people can be induced to forgo what their own eyes tell them and, instead, conform to the incorrect judgment of others. These findings are consistent with later research indicating that

FIGURE 8.2

Asch's Line Judgment Task

This is an example of the stimulus lines used in Asch's classic conformity experiments. Participants were asked to judge which of the three comparison lines were equal in length to the standard line.

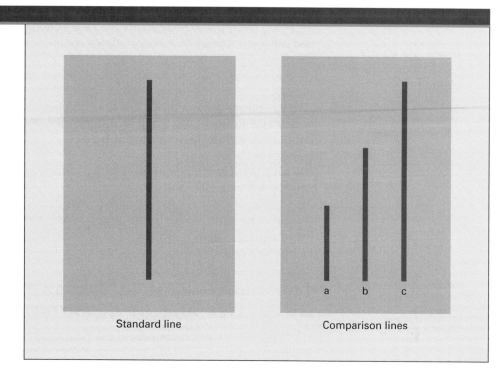

Standard line   Comparison lines

FIGURE 8.3

Degree of Conformity in Asch's Research

In judging line length, when faced with a group of people who picked incorrect lines, participants conformed to their false judgments on 33 percent of the trials. Although less than one-third conformed on more than half the judgmental trials, 76 percent conformed on at least one occasion. What type of social influence likely accounts for these effects?

Source: Data from S. E. Asch, 1956.

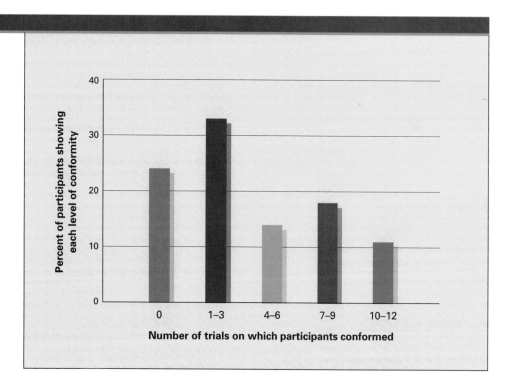

people often find it easier to conform rather than challenge the unanimous opinions of others (Tanford & Penrod, 1984).

As discussed in previous chapters, many people prefer their attitudes, beliefs, and actions to fit into a consistent pattern. If this is true, how do people typically react to the reality of their own conforming behavior, especially when it seems to run counter to their private views? Research suggests that when faced with the choice between admitting that one has arbitrarily conformed to a group standard and proving that agreement with that standard was forced by the facts, almost everyone attempts to reconstruct the facts (Buehler & Griffin, 1994). This sort of *postconformity change-of-meaning* allows conformers to justify their behavior and maintain cognitive consistency.

Although the Asch findings indicate the strength of social influence even when the group's judgment seems clearly misguided, they don't imply that we are merely slaves to others' judgments. As illustrated in figure 8.3, 24 percent of Asch's participants never followed the group on a single trial, and less than one-third conformed on more than half the trials. Likewise, in explaining why she dissented from the majority of the jurors on one count against one of the police officers after conforming to their not guilty judgment on all other counts, juror Loya stated, "They couldn't make me change my mind on guilty for [that officer]. I wasn't going to give in." As heartening as this act of independence may appear, the fact that people often are willing to go along with erroneous group judgments, or are willing to accept the judgments of others when they feel uncertain how to define their surrounding reality, suggests there are compelling social forces in need of further inquiry.

CONFORMITY CAN BE CAUSED BY BOTH NORMATIVE AND INFORMATIONAL INFLUENCE

Let's explore a bit further the differing dilemmas faced by the participants in the Sherif and Asch experiments. First, Sherif's participants found themselves in an ambiguous reality in which they undoubtedly felt less than confident about their own abilities to judge the movement of this fluctuating point of light. They could stumble along doing the best they could under the circumstances, or they could seek the guidance of others. In contrast, Asch's participants could clearly see which line was the correct match—there was no ambiguity. Yet for them, something strange was happening. Everyone else was picking the wrong line! Under such circumstances, they could either maintain their own judgment and thereby stick out like a sore thumb, or they could go along with the group and thus avoid the uncomfortable stares and raised eyebrows of others. In this latter case, by publicly adopting the opinions of others, participants demonstrated that "fitting in" was of greater concern to them than giving the correct answer. In the former case, however, adopting the opinions of others was the avenue participants followed in their search for the correct answer.

In trying to make sense of the different social pressures in these two studies, Morton Deutsch and Henry Gerard (1955) suggested that group pressure derives from two sources: normative and informational influence. **Normative influence** occurs when a person conforms, complies, or obeys to gain rewards or avoid punishments from another person or group. If Asch's participants changed their judgments because they were afraid others might laugh at them or evaluate them negatively, they were responding to normative pressure. However, if they modified their answers because they thought the unanimously responding confederates might have a more accurate view of the lines, then they were responding to informational pressure. **Informational influence** occurs when the individual conforms, complies, or obeys to gain accurate information. We often look to groups for information, especially if we doubt our own judgment (Campbell et al., 1986). Because it's unlikely that very many participants in the Asch studies actually believed that the group was correct in its line judgments, we're probably safe in concluding that their conformity was principally due to normative influence rather than informational influence. In the Sherif study, on the other hand, the conformity exhibited was more likely due to informational influence because light movement was extremely ambiguous.

These two different types of social influence reflect two different types of social dependence. Informational influence reflects a form of social dependence called *information dependence,* which is dependence upon others for information about the world that reduces uncertainty. Underlying normative influence is the

Normative Influence

Conformity, compliance, or obedience due to a desire to gain rewards or avoid punishments (outcome dependence).

Informational Influence

Conformity, compliance, or obedience due to a desire to gain information (information dependence).

Once conform, once do what other people do because they do it, and a lethargy steals over all the finer nerves and faculties of the soul. She becomes all outer show and inward emptiness; dull, callous, and indifferent.

Virginia Woolf, British novelist, 1882–1941

The fish dies because he opens his mouth.

Spanish proverb

Those who disobey authority figures run the very real risk of punishment and even expulsion from the group. For example, in 1989, after ruthlessly crushing the student pro-democracy protest in Tiananmen Square, the communist government in China arrested and imprisoned pro-democracy dissident Han Dongfang for 22 months. Eventually he was allowed to travel to the United States to seek treatment for tuberculosis. In 1993, when he tried to return to mainland China, the government refused him entry and threw him back over the border to Hong Kong. From there he continued his criticisms of the communists and attempted to organize unions back home. Now that Hong Kong has been taken over by the mainland, what do you think the government would like to do with Dongfang?

dependence upon others for positive outcomes or rewards, which is called *outcome dependence* (also known as *normative dependence*). Therefore, the need to reduce uncertainty in a given situation leads to information dependence, while the need to gain acceptance or approval results in outcome dependence. Although in some cases these two mechanisms of influence operate separately, in many others they function simultaneously (Insko et al., 1985). This is likely what occurred as Virginia Loya deliberated with her fellow jurors in the Rodney King case. Faced with fellow jurors who pressured her to accept defense claims that the videotape didn't tell the entire story (normative influence), the strength of her convictions weakened, and she may well have begun to more seriously consider their interpretation of events (informational influence).

SCHACHTER'S "JOHNNY ROCCO" STUDY INVESTIGATED THE REJECTION OF THE NONCONFORMIST

Thus far we've discussed the forces brought to bear on us so that we conform to the group's judgment. But what about those of us who do not knuckle under to this influence? How does a group typically respond to the nonconformist?

About the same time that Asch was conducting his group conformity research, Stanley Schachter (1951) provided an excellent experimental analysis of the consequences of not conforming to majority opinion. Schachter arranged for groups of eight to ten volunteers to form a "case study club" to discuss the case of a juvenile delinquent, Johnny Rocco, and then make a recommendation of what the authorities should do with Johnny. In making their recommendations, participants used a seven-point love-punishment rating scale ranging from a position 1 "loving" treatment of Johnny to a position 7 "punishment" treatment. Unknown to the naive participants, each group contained three confederates instructed to take a particular position in the discussion of Johnny. Expecting that the naive participants would select a position closer to the "loving" end of the scale, Schachter instructed his confederates to take differing positions. The "deviate" argued for position 7 throughout the discussion, acting unswayed by contrary opinions; the "slider" began at position 7, but "slid" toward the majority position of the group; the "mode" held the group's most agreed upon position throughout the discussion.

How do you think the naive participants reacted to these three different positions during discussion, and how do you think they dealt with the deviate at the end, when their best efforts at persuasion failed to secure conformity? At first, participants communicated a great deal with the deviate and slider in an attempt to convince them to change their minds about Johnny. During this same time period, very little attention was paid to the right-thinking mode. Once participants concluded that the deviate was not going to alter his judgment, and once the slider adopted the group's position, communication toward them dropped sharply. If you think of this communication as an indicator of social pressure, these findings suggest that those who hold minority opinions become the focus of influence attempts until they either conform or convince the group that such attempts are fruitless. This direct persuasive communication is a form of normative influence.

At the end of group discussion, Schachter informed everyone that the group was simply too large for their next discussion and that he wanted them to decide who to retain in the group. Participants' responses provided the answer to how groups respond to nonconformists—the deviate was excluded from future discussions. A more recent meta-analysis of twenty-three Schachter-like "deviant" studies found that rejection by the group is most likely when there are only one or two nonconformists rather than a more substantial number (Tata et al., 1996). Together, these and other studies provide compelling evidence that social rejection is the final, and perhaps most powerful, form of normative influence directed toward nonconformists (Williams, 1997). In adolescence, for example, to be popular with and accepted into a social clique, some teenagers conform to the group's standards of drinking beer and liquor, smoking cigarettes, and taking drugs. For other adolescents with different group standards, being accepted entails forgoing these forms of harmful indulgences. If the best group efforts at persuasion fail, the nonconformist is often branded a social pariah and is ostracized from future group activities (Zippelius, 1986). The bottom line is, if we are attracted to a group and if the group is an important part of our social identity, we will be greatly susceptible to its influence.

SECTION SUMMARY

Three classic sets of experiments illustrate how conformity has been studied and what factors contribute to this yielding to group pressure. Muzafir Sherif's research on social norm development demonstrated that when faced with uncertainty about how to interpret or judge events, pandemonium does not ensue. Instead, we look to others to determine how they are defining reality, and we are most likely to be influenced by others if they appear confident. This dependence upon others for accurate information is known as *informational influence.* On the other hand, Solomon Asch's experiments of visual perception demonstrated the strength of *normative influence,* even when the group's judgment was clearly incorrect. While the Sherif and Asch studies explored situational factors effecting conformity, Stanley Schachter investigated how a cohesive group reacts to a nonconformer. His findings indicate that the group first directs a great deal of persuasive communication toward the nonconformist, and then, if this proves unsuccessful, they cast the individual out of the group.

FACTORS THAT INFLUENCE CONFORMITY

Thus far, we have learned that people are likely to conform when they are uncertain about their own ability to make accurate judgments and others are confident, or when they are concerned about being negatively evaluated by others. What social and personal factors help create this uncertainty and concern?

SITUATIONAL FACTORS IMPACT CONFORMITY

In attempting to understand the conditions that facilitate conformity, social psychologists have paid particular attention to the social setting. The assumption is that these situational factors exert a social force on individuals that can cause uniform behavior.

FIGURE 8.4

Group Size and Conformity

In Asch's (1955) conformity research, when the number of unanimous confederates was varied from 1 to 15, conformity approached its maximum level when the number of confederates was between 3 and 4. Why do you think group size effects leveled off in this manner?

Source: Data from S. E. Asch, "Opinions and Social Pressure" in *Scientific American,* November 1955.

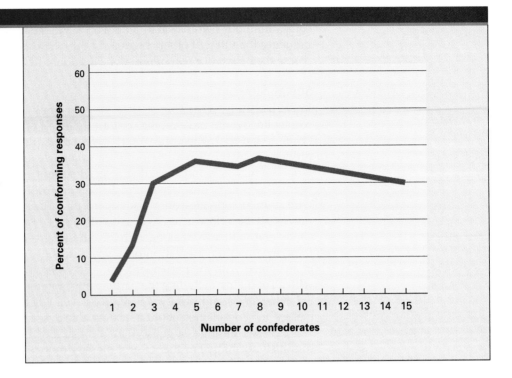

GROUP SIZE

One situational factor contributing to conformity is the size of the influencing group. When Asch (1955) varied the number of unanimous confederates from one to fifteen, he found that conformity increased as group size increased, but only up to a certain size (figure 8.4). Conformity was near its peak level when the number of confederates was between three and four, and then actually tapered off so that there was no greater conformity with a group of fifteen confederates than with a group of three.

Other research suggests that group size will only be a predictor of conformity levels in certain situations. Jennifer Campbell and Patricia Fairey (1989) found that group size is important when the social reality is clear (judgments are easy), but that the size of the group is relatively unimportant when the social reality is ambiguous (judgments are difficult). The explanation for this interaction effect has to do with what type of social influence is most potent in an ambiguous or clear reality. As previously discussed, when the reality is clear, whether you conform depends on the amount of normative influence the group can exert. Adding more people to the group (up to four or so) will increase normative influence, and thus, increase conformity. On the other hand, if the reality is ambiguous, informational influence is more of a factor than normative influence. In this state of information dependence, one or two people may influence you just as well as three, four, or twenty-four.

GROUP COHESIVENESS AND TOPIC RELEVANCE

A group is termed cohesive when its members are highly attracted to one another. In general, cohesive groups engender more conformity than noncohesive groups (Hogg, 1992). For example, in other conditions of Schachter's (1951) deviant study, he varied the cohesiveness of the group as well as the relevance of the contested discussion topic. When the group was highly cohesive and the topic was also highly relevant, the group exerted its greatest pressure on deviates and was most likely to reject nonconformists. These findings indicate that if groups with a strong sense of togetherness are discussing important topics, they will tend to be intolerant of those who hold differing opinions. The best examples of cohesive groups influencing members comes from our own friendship networks. We are much more likely to accept their influence than that of others because of our respect for their opinions, our desire to please them, and our fear of rejection (Crandall, 1988).

Social Support

In Asch's study, what sort of effect do you think a single confederate picking the correct line would have on the conformity levels of the participants? Actually, Asch (1956) found that when one of the confederates picked the correct line, conformity dropped dramatically, to one-fourth the original levels. Research by Vernon Allen and John Levine (1969) indicates that a social supporter reduces conformity by diminishing the group's normative influence. In one of their studies, participants worked with four confederates on a visual perception task. Three of the confederates had previously been instructed to consistently agree on incorrect judgments. The fourth confederate either went along with the others, agreed with the participant, or made a third, incorrect judgment. Conformity was not only reduced when the fourth confederate agreed with the participant, but also when this confederate merely disagreed with all opinions, including the participants' opinions. In a second experiment (Allen & Levine, 1971), conformity was reduced even when the social supporter wore thick glasses and complained about not being able to see the visual displays!

These findings suggest that almost any dissent from the majority can diminish normative influence and thereby reduce conformity. Although breaking social consensus appears to be the crucial factor here, receiving social support early is more effective than receiving such support after normative pressures have already built up (Morris et al., 1977). Unfortunately, if this support is later removed, normative influence again is exerted. In one of Asch's studies, when the confederate who had previously agreed with the participant switched and began to conform to the majority opinion, the participants' own level of conformity returned to near the levels observed in the original experiments (Asch, 1955). Thus, to promote nonconformity in others, one should voice dissent, and do so early and consistently. Remember this bit of advice, for it will be important when we later discuss how minorities can exert influence in not only resisting majority opinion, but actually changing it.

Personal Factors Influence Conformity

The general consensus is that situational forces are most important in determining whether we conform or not. Yet we are not machines who respond identically to these situational factors. Although specific personality traits related to conformity have been difficult to identify (McGuire, 1968), research does suggest that conforming to group pressure is related to our *values* and *self-concept*.

Self-Awareness

As noted in chapter 2, whether behavior is more influenced by personal or social standards is at least partially determined by what aspect of the self is salient (private or public). When people are privately self-aware, they tend to act in line with their own personal standards, but social standards are more influential when people are publicly self-aware (Carver, 1975; Froming et al., 1982). Thus, being privately self-aware reduces conformity, while being publicly self-aware increases conformity.

Self-Presentation

The irony of yielding to social influence out of concern for how others might evaluate you is that in many cultures it is not desirable to be recognized as a conformist. Robert Cialdini and his coworkers (1974), for example, found that American college students generally perceived people as more intelligent if they do not yield to social

Imagine that you are conducting an Asch-type conformity experiment, yet you also want to test whether you can increase nonconformity by inducing public self-presentation concerns in your participants. What variable could you add to the standard Asch research design to test this possibility? That is, how could you alter the standard procedure to induce public self-presentation concerns? Would public self-presentation concerns lead to greater nonconformity when the line judgments were clear and easy or ambiguous and difficult? How might public self-awareness effects contaminate the findings?

I'm not gonna change the way I look or the way I feel to conform to anything. I've always been a freak. So I've been a freak all my life and I have to live with that, you know. I'm one of those people.

John Lennon, English rock musician, 1940–1980

Theory of Psychological Reactance

The theory that people believe they possess specific behavioral freedoms, and that they will react against and resist attempts to limit this sense of freedom.

influence—unless, of course, they were the ones trying to get others to conform! Further research found that often underlying the conformity and independence responses of people are calculated assessments of the impressions they are making on those present (Collins & Brief, 1995; Santee & Maslach, 1982). Conformity is most likely to occur when self-presenters are alone with those trying to influence them and when the conformity will be viewed as indicating intelligence or open-mindedness. On the other hand, open defiance of influence attempts is most likely under two conditions (Baumeister, 1982): (1) when others not involved in the influence attempt are present, and (2) when the attitude of those exerting the influence makes any subsequent yielding seem like weak-kneed surrender rather than intelligent decision making. Under such conditions, it would be difficult to conform and still maintain a public image of independence and autonomy.

THE NEED FOR INDIVIDUATION

Besides desiring to retain a favorable self-presentation, another motive that influences conformity is the *need for individuation.* That is, sometimes people disagree with others to maintain a unique identity (Maslach et al., 1987). In one experiment, student volunteers were deceived into believing that their ten most important attitudes were either distinct from or nearly identical to the attitudes of ten thousand other students (Snyder & Fromkin, 1980). Later, when participating in a conformity experiment, those who had been informed that they were no different than most students were most likely to assert their individuality by not conforming to others' influence. Thus, although we often conform to avoid negative judgments, we sometimes do not conform simply to feel different from others.

THE DESIRE FOR PERSONAL CONTROL

Although the need for individuation may sometimes explain nonconformity, on other occasions we may resist social influence simply to feel that we personally control our own actions. Jack Brehm (Brehm, 1966; Brehm & Brehm, 1981) has proposed a **theory of psychological reactance,** which states that people believe they possess specific behavioral freedoms and that they will react against and resist attempts to limit this sense of freedom. For example, if parents demand that their daughter not date a certain boy, she might defy the parents as a way to restore a feeling of personal control over her own behavior. When reactance is aroused, the forbidden behavior (dating the disapproved boy) becomes more desirable. Similarly, if the daughter believes her parents are trying to coerce her into dating some other boy, reactance results in this boy becoming a much less desirable date than the forbidden male.

Is the son's behavior an example of independence or anticonformity? How could his mother manipulate him to do what she desires by arousing his need for individuation?

Reprinted with special permission of King Features Syndicate.

TABLE 8.1

Desire for Control and Conformity: Are Unfunny Cartoons Judged Funny Due to Others' Favorable Ratings?

When students rated the humor of previously identified "unfunny" cartoons, high and low desire for personal control (DPC) individuals didn't significantly differ when rating the cartoons alone (higher scores mean funnier ratings), but high DPCs were significantly less likely to agree with confederates' favorable ratings (the Group condition) than were low DPCs. Based on these findings, which of these two groups are better equipped to resist conformity?

		Mean Humor Scores	
		Desire for Personal Control	
		Low	**High**
	Alone	43.7	49.3
Condition			
	Group	73.2	62.1

Jerry Burger (1987) has found evidence indicating that individual differences in desire for personal control may partly explain susceptibility to social influence. In his study, he asked college students to rate the humor in a series of newspaper cartoons using a scale from 1 ("very unfunny") to 100 ("very funny"). In one condition, participants rated the cartoons alone, and in another condition, they rated them after hearing two other students' evaluations. These other students, being experimental confederates, had been instructed to rate the cartoons as being relatively funny (averaging 70 on the 100-point scale), even though Burger had specifically chosen cartoons that had previously been judged to be quite dull (average humor rating of only 25).

Prior to rating the cartoons, participants' desire for personal control (DPC) had been measured by a paper and pencil questionnaire. As you can see in table 8.1, although DPC did not predict how students rated the cartoons when they were alone (both groups rated them as not very funny), high DPC participants were less likely to agree with confederates' favorable ratings than were low DPCs. Although the high DPCs certainly were not immune to the confederates' influence, the results suggest that they appear to be better equipped to resist conformity than those who have a low desire for control.

Although individuals may not conform to social pressures due to their desire for personal control or individuation, this does not mean that they are necessarily acting independently. There are two different types of nonconformity responses. One is *independence*, which was previously defined as not being subject to others' control. The person who dates someone not because her parents approve or disapprove but because she genuinely likes her dating partner is demonstrating independence; psychological reactance does not play a factor in her behavioral choices. **Anticonformity,** on the other hand, is characterized by opposition to social influence on all occasions, and psychological reactance often explains these behavioral choices (Nail, 1986). The anticonformist would date people whom her parents disapproved and would not date those whom they approved. Thus, the actions of two people may be identical but may be motivated by very different desires. A person who has a strong desire for personal control could express this either through independence or anticonformity. The same is true for the desire for individuation. Some people "take the road less traveled" not because they disagree with the group's direction, but by disagreeing they can satisfy their need for uniqueness.

I wouldn't have turned out the way I was if I didn't have all those old-fashioned values to rebel against.

Madonna, American rock singer, 1990

The young always have the same problem—how to rebel and conform at the same time. They have now solved this by defying their parents and copying one another.

Quentin Crisp, British author, 1968

Anticonformity

Opposition to social influence on all occasions, often caused by psychological reactance.

GENDER AND CONFORMITY

Early social influence research found a slight tendency for women to conform more than men, but more recent studies find little, if any, gender differences (Eagly, 1987). Where small gender differences sometimes occur is in face-to-face encounters in which a person must openly disagree with others (Becker, 1986). Whatever small gender differences exist in susceptibility to influence appear to be due to the social roles that men and women have traditionally been socialized to assume in our culture, and to their concerns about self-presentation. That is, when people believe they are being observed, women tend to conform more and men tend to conform less than they do in more private settings (Eagly & Chravala, 1986). It's likely that in attempting to create a favorable impression when questions of conformity arise, people tend to fall back on well-learned patterns of behavior that are considered socially acceptable for their sex. If this analysis is correct, you would expect that as men and women adopt less traditional gender roles, such self-presentation concerns will cease to be important, and whatever conformity differences there are will disappear entirely.

INDIVIDUALISTS AND COLLECTIVISTS DIFFER IN THEIR CONFORMITY PATTERNS

Does knowing a person's cultural background give you any insight into how he or she might respond to social influence? A number of studies have investigated differences between individualist and collectivist cultures.

INDIVIDUALISM VERSUS COLLECTIVISM

The guiding principle of individualism is that individual interests are more important than those of the group. In decided contrast, collectivism asserts that group interests should guide the thinking and behavior of individual members (Ho & Chiu, 1994). According to Harry Triandis and his colleagues, people from collectivist cultures are more concerned than individualists with gaining the approval of their group and feel shameful if they fail to get it (Hui & Triandis, 1986; Triandis, 1989). A person from an individualist culture, on the other hand, has a higher need or preference for autonomy from the group and a desire to feel unique. As a result of these different orientations, people from collectivist cultures tend to be more conforming to their own group than individualists (Bond & Smith, 1996). This yielding to the group by collectivists is not considered to be a sign of weakness, as it is often perceived in our individualist culture, but rather it is believed to indicate self-control, flexibility, and maturity (White & LeVine, 1986).

Although these cultural differences suggest that conformity is generally more likely in a collectivist culture, this does not mean that collectivists submit to any and all group influence attempts. To better understand group influence in such a culture, we must be clear about just which groups are the focus of our attention. As described in chapter 2, an *ingroup* is a group to which a person belongs and which forms a part of his or her social identity. In understanding social influence, it is important to distinguish ingroups from *outgroups,* which are any groups to which a person does not belong. Research suggests that people from collectivist cultures perceive ingroup norms as universally valid and tend to automatically obey ingroup authorities (Shweder & LeVine, 1984). On the other hand, collectivists tend to distrust outgroup norms and, as a result, often are unwilling to yield to their influence (Triandis, 1972).

Most of the nonconformity that occurs in a collectivist culture is to the social norms of outgroups, not ingroups. This difference in the perceived validity of ingroup norms is one of the reasons that collectivist cultures tend to breed more conformity than individualist cultures. Therefore, a person from a collectivist culture such as traditional Greece might be very yielding to his family's and his

The man who never submitted to anything will soon submit to a burial mat.

Nigerian proverb

Cross-cultural research suggests that people from a collectivist culture, such as the Chinese pictured here, tend to be more influenced by ingroup norms than people from individualist cultures.

village's influence attempts (his ingroup), yet be staunchly defiant of any pressure exerted by the distant national authorities (a perceived outgroup). When we consider those who belong to an individualist culture, although they too tend to trust ingroup norms more than outgroup norms, they are more likely than collectivists to question ingroup norms as well, especially when they run counter to their self-interests or when adherence to these social norms makes them feel average or ordinary (that is, nonunique).

UNDER CERTAIN CONDITIONS, THE MINORITY CAN INFLUENCE THE MAJORITY

History is filled with stories of lone individuals or small, relatively powerless groups expressing unpopular views and enduring abuse from the majority until their views are eventually adopted. In commenting on what it takes to stand up to such social pressure, the nineteenth-century feminist Susan B. Anthony said, "Cautious, careful people always casting about to preserve their reputation and social standing, never can bring about a reform. Those who are really in earnest must be willing to be anything or nothing in the world's estimation." Social research bears out Ms. Anthony's pronouncement. People who dissent from the majority, although generally perceived as competent, often are heartily disliked (Bassili & Provencal, 1988).

How exactly does minority influence operate? Beginning in the late 1960s, the French social psychologist Serge Moscovici and other researchers conducted a series of experiments documenting the conditions under which minorities would be most likely to shift or *convert* majority beliefs. In articulating his *conversion theory* of minority influence, Moscovici (1980) first outlined how it differed from majority influence. As previously discussed, movement to the majority position is due to the common belief that there is truth in numbers (informational influence) and due to the concern for being accepted by those numbers (normative influence). Underlying this social influence is a generally positive judgment of and an attraction toward the majority by those being influenced (W. Wood et al., 1994, 1996). However, unlike the majority group, minority groups tend to be viewed negatively by others, and therefore, their viewpoints need greater time to register with group members (Mugny & Perez, 1991). Moscovici contended that the most important factor in determining the

Every society honors its live conformists and its dead troublemakers.

Mignon McLaughlin, U.S. author, 1963

FIGURE 8.5

Conformity to a Consistent and Inconsistent Minority

Moscovici, Lage, and Naffrechoux, (1969) found that the degree to which participants labeled a blue slide "green" was partly determined by whether they were tested alone (control condition), with a minority saying "green" inconsistently (inconsistent condition), or with a minority saying "green" consistently (consistent condition). Why is consistency so important for minority group influence?

Source: Data from S. Moscovici, E. Lage, and M. Naffrechoux, "Influences of a Consistent Minority on the Responses of a Majority in a Color Perception Task" in *Sociometry*, 32:365–380, 1969.

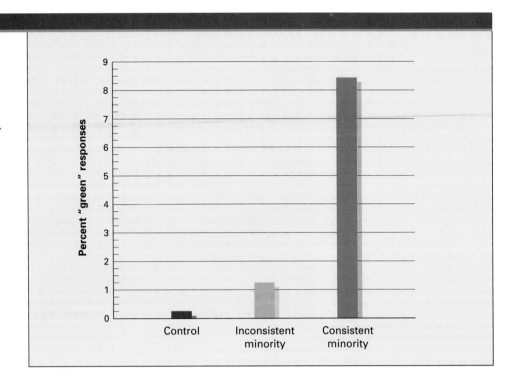

effectiveness of minority group influence is their *style of behavior* in presenting nonconforming views (Moscovici & Faucheux, 1972; Moscovici & Nemeth, 1974). For minorities to exert influence on majority members, they must consistently and confidently state their dissenting opinions (Moscovici & Mugny, 1983).

In a demonstration of the importance of consistency in minority group influence, Moscovici and his colleagues (1969) asked groups of individuals to judge whether the color of projected blue slides was blue or green. Each group consisted of four naive participants and two confederates. In the *inconsistent minority condition* the confederates randomly varied calling the blue slide green and blue, while in the *consistent minority condition* they always claimed that it was green. Figure 8.5 shows that when the confederates were inconsistent in labeling the blue slide green, their ability to influence the majority's opinion was negligible (1.25 percent). However, when the confederates were consistent, more than 8 percent of the time participants conformed to this minority point of view. In addition, after the color trials, those who were exposed to the consistent minority shifted the point on the blue-green color spectrum where they identified a color green instead of blue; now they called more stimuli "green" and fewer "blue." These findings not only suggest that a consistent minority can affect overt responses in the majority, but they also suggest that a unified minority can cause majority members to alter their private beliefs as well.

Although this research indicates that those sharing minority opinions must appear confident in consistently stating their views, other research indicates that minorities must walk a fine line in presenting their nonconforming opinions. They cannot appear dogmatic or rigid, for that will also reduce their influence (Nemeth et al., 1974). Therefore, for majority members to consider their perspective in the first place, the minority must come across as consistent and confident, but also flexible and open-minded. Nelson Mandela, a longtime opponent of the former apartheid government of South Africa, is perhaps the best recent example of a minority group leader (a minority in power but not in numbers) whose consistent, unwavering call for Black equality was combined with a nondogmatic approach to reform that won over many White South Africans. In 1994, he became the first president of a nonapartheid South Africa.

All men should have a drop of treason in their veins, if nations are not to go soft like so many sleepy pears.

Rebecca West, English novelist, 1892–1983

Nelson Mandela, longtime leader of the African National Congress, has been successful in changing the social and political landscape of South Africa despite his double minority status. One of his strengths was consistent and confident articulation of his ideas, coupled with a willingness to negotiate with white apartheid leaders.

CRITICAL *thinking*

Based on what you learned in chapter 6 about gender differences in the effects of powerful speech on the ability to persuade, what is an alternative—or additional— interpretation of the findings from the Maass et al. (1982) experiment?

The power of a movement lies in the fact that it can indeed change the habits of people. This change is not the result of force but of dedication, of moral persuasion.

Steve Biko, South African political leader, 1946–1977

One other factor that also affects the ability of the minority to influence the majority is the *degree of difference* between the minority and the majority. *Single minorities* are individuals who differ from the majority only in terms of their beliefs, while *double minorities* are those who differ from the majority in terms of both beliefs and group membership (Martin, 1988). An example of a single minority is a heterosexual arguing for equal rights for gay people to the heterosexual majority. A gay person advocating such rights is a double minority. Research indicates that single minorities are more likely to exert influence over the majority than are double minorities (Alvaro & Crano, 1997). For example, in one study (Maass et al., 1982), conservative male participants engaged in a discussion of abortion with either a single (male confederate) or double (female confederate) minority. In these discussions, the minority consistently defended a liberal position rather than the conservative viewpoint of the male participants. The results indicated that the male participants perceived the double minorities (the liberal females) as having a stronger self-interest in the discussion, and they were less influenced by them than they were by the single minorities (the liberal males). By perceiving self-interest in the position of a double minority, it appears that people can more easily discount their arguments. Nelson Mandela recognized this tendency to discount double minorities in the struggle to put Black South Africans on an equal footing with their White counterparts. Some of the most effective influencers of White public opinion were fellow Whites who expressed antiapartheid beliefs.

Finally, minorities have the strongest influence when they take positions in the same direction as evolving cultural norms, but they are relatively ineffective when they argue against these emerging norms (Kiesler & Pallack, 1975). For example, during the early stages of the civil rights movement in the United States, the Rev. Martin Luther King, Jr., and other civil rights activists espoused beliefs about equality and human justice that were in line with the emerging liberalism within the nation as a whole. Similarly, although Americans rejected the political views of Ronald Reagan and other conservative members of the Republican Party in the 1960s, they generally embraced them in the 1980s, when the prevailing norms shifted to a more conservative posture.

All these findings together indicate that minorities will be most successful in exerting influence on the majority when arguing for positions that are not too far from the prevailing majority position, and when they show a *consistent behavioral style* that the majority interprets as indicating *certainty* and *confidence*. On the other hand, minority influence will surely fail if the minority group *argues against evolving social norms* and exhibits a *rigid* style of negotiation with *inconsistently held beliefs.* In explaining why this is the case, Moscovici and Charlan Nemeth (1974) draw from the insights of Harold Kelley's attribution theory. As you remember from chapter 3, we tend to infer that the behavior of others is due to internal causes when (1) consensus is low (few others are behaving this way), (2) consistency is high (these people have behaved the same way over time), and (3) distinctiveness is low (they act this way in other situations). These conditions describe the behavior of strongly committed minorities. Not only are few others taking the belief position of the minority, but they consistently maintain this position over time and voice it in many varied situations. The logical conclusion that majority group members draw from all this information is that the voicing of such beliefs can only be due to deep and abiding personal convictions—convictions that perhaps should be seriously considered and scrutinized.

Even if minority groups follow a consistent avenue of persuasion, this does not mean that those holding majority beliefs will necessarily change. Remember, majority groups can impose sanctions and withdraw rewards from its members if they begin to espouse minority viewpoints, and this often is enough to maintain public compliance with majority opinions. Further, people's social identities generally consist of majority-held values and beliefs, and those aspects of the self-concept are resistant to change. However, although overt change toward minority positions may not readily take place, when majority members engage in critical analysis of these positions, it often stimulates *divergent thinking,* a cognitive process in which one considers a problem from varying perspectives (Legrenzi et al., 1991). What appears to initially motivate this enhanced scrutiny of the minority message is simply that it is different and unexpected (Baker & Petty, 1994). However, as we learned in chapter 6, increased analysis of a persuasive message places people on the *central route* to persuasion, in which argument strength is particularly important in securing attitude and behavior change. Therefore, one possible consequence of the increased scrutiny of minority points of view is that it can cause people to consider a wider variety of possible explanations or novel solutions to problems (Peterson & Nemeth, 1996). Often when majority opinions change due to the impact of the minority viewpoint, people are not aware that they were actually influenced by these previously divergent views (Personnaz, 1981), but change occurs nonetheless. (Refer to the *sleeper effect,* chapter 6, p. 193.)

SECTION SUMMARY

Situational forces that influence conformity are the *size* of the influencing group, its *cohesiveness,* and whether there is any *social support* for contrary positions. Regarding personal factors, those of us with a need for *individuation* or a desire for *personal control* are likely to be less conforming. Other factors related to conformity, but in less clear-cut ways, are *self-awareness* and *self-presentational* concerns. Although past research indicated that females are slightly more conforming than males, recent studies indicate that whatever small *gender* differences exist are likely due to the social roles that men and women have traditionally been socialized to assume. This cultural effect on conformity levels is not limited to gender. People from *collectivist* cultures are likely to be more conforming to their own ingroup than those from *individualist* cultures. Finally, *minority group influence* studies suggest that to persuade majority members to change their beliefs, the minority must consistently and confidently state their dissenting views and, at the same time, come across as flexible and open-minded. One positive consequence of the increased scrutiny given minority viewpoints is that majority members often entertain a wider variety of possible solutions to problems.

COMPLIANCE

In trying to "get our way" with others, sometimes we forget the most direct route—simply asking them to do what we desire. When we seek compliance to our requests, we use a variety of techniques. The sort of compliance strategy we employ often depends on to whom we are making the request, how well we know the person, our status in the relationship, our own personality, and the nature of the request (Buss et al., 1987).

THREE FACTORS THAT FOSTER COMPLIANCE ARE POSITIVE MOODS, RECIPROCITY, AND GIVING REASONS

When people are roughly equal in social status, establishing the correct atmosphere or mood is especially important to increase compliance. Three factors that help create the proper atmosphere are to make people feel good, to do something for them, and to give them reasons for compliance.

POSITIVE MOOD

In the course of making requests, people soon discover that others are more likely to comply when they are in a good mood, especially if the requests are prosocial, such as helping others (Forgas, 1998). One reason for this is that people who are in good moods are simply more likely to be active and, thus, are more likely to engage in a range of behaviors, including granting requests (Batson et al., 1979). A second reason is that pleasant moods activate pleasant thoughts and memories, which likely makes people feel more favorable toward those making requests (Carlson et al., 1988). A third reason is that people in a happy mood are often less likely to critically analyze events, including requests, and thus, are more likely to grant them (Bless et al., 1996).

Because of this general awareness that good moods help create compliance, we often try to "butter someone up" before making a request. As discussed in chapter 3, this self-presentation strategy of *ingratiation* is designed to get others to view us favorably (Liden & Mitchell, 1988). Although people may be suspicious of ingratiators' motives after receiving their requests, the preceding flattery is still often effective in securing compliance (Kacmar et al., 1992).

Don't open a shop unless you know how to smile.

Jewish proverb

RECIPROCITY

How often have strangers offered you small gifts, such as flowers, pencils, or flags, and then asked you to donate money to their organization? If so, they were hoping that the token would lower your resistance to their request. The hope rested on a powerful social norm that people in all cultures follow, namely the **reciprocity norm.** Although this unwritten social norm helps to maintain fairness in social relationships by prescribing that favors or good deeds should be reciprocated, it can also be used to increase compliance (Gouldner, 1960).

Laboratory research clearly demonstrates that giving someone a small gift or doing them a favor can easily lead to reciprocal compliance, especially if you seek compliance shortly after doing the good turn (Burger et al., 1997; Chartrand et al., 1999). For example, Dennis Regan (1971) had college students work on a task with another student (a confederate) who acted in either a friendly or unfriendly manner. During a break, the confederate left and returned a few minutes later either with a soft drink for the student participant or with nothing. Shortly afterward, the confederate asked the student to buy twenty-five-cent raffle tickets. Those who had been given the soft drink "gift" bought an average of two tickets, whereas those who had not been given a soft drink bought only one. The effect of reciprocity was so strong that the students returned the favor even when the

Reciprocity Norm

The expectation that one should return a favor or a good deed.

One does not give a gift without motive.

Mali proverb

A common technique to secure compliance from others is to first do them a favor or give them a gift. Due to the reciprocity norm, the recipients often then feel obligated to comply with a forthcoming request, such as a plea for monetary contributions.

confederate had previously acted in an unlikable manner. Because soft drinks only cost a dime in 1971, offering soft drinks increased raffle profits on average by 60 percent!

Given the power of the reciprocity norm, who is most likely to use it to secure compliance? Everyday experience tells us that reciprocity is commonly used as a strategy in making sales. On my birthday I receive almost as many cards from people who are trying to do business with me as I do from my friends and loved ones. Insurance agents give away free pens or calendars. Grocery stores provide free samples of their products. Car salespeople give potential customers new twenty-five-cent key rings—just right to hold the key to that new $25,000 automobile. All of these instances are examples of reciprocal compliance attempts (Howard, 1995).

But it is not just professional salespeople who employ such tactics. Those who habitually use reciprocity to secure compliance are called *creditors,* because they try to keep others in their debt so they can cash in when necessary. People who are creditors tend to agree with statements such as "If someone does me a favor, it's a good idea to repay that person with a greater favor." Creditors know the power of indebtedness, and they work hard to make sure they are on the influential side of the reciprocity equation (Eisenberger et al., 1987). And they know all too well the wisdom of the proverb, "Beware of strangers bearing gifts."

GIVING REASONS

In granting someone's request, we often require some reason for complying. For instance, if you are in line at a grocery store with a small number of food items, and someone with only one item asks to go ahead because his sick grandmother is waiting for her cold medicine, you are likely to grant the request. The explanation given for his request strikes a responsive chord within you—it is "reason-able." Ellen Langer and her colleagues (1978) found evidence for the power of reason giving in gaining compliance when they had confederates try to cut in line ahead of others at a photocopying machine. In one condition the confederates gave no reason, merely asking, "May I use the photocopying machine to make five copies?" Sixty percent of those waiting complied with this "no reason" request. In another condition, when the confederates gave an explanation for their request ("May I use the photocopying machine to make five copies because I'm in a hurry?"), compliance increased to 94 percent, a significant difference. What Langer was interested in determining at this point was whether the actual content of the reason was important or whether any reason at all would suffice. To test this, she had her confederates try a third version of the request, where the reason given for cutting in line was really no explanation at all; it was merely a restatement of their desire to make copies ("May I use the photocopying machine to make five copies because

I have to make copies?"). Surprisingly, this mere reiteration of a desire to make copies resulted in 94 percent compliance, identical to when an actual explanation was given ("I'm in a hurry").

Why does merely giving a reason—any reason—result in greater compliance? Giving reasons may be important because of our habitual desire to explain others' actions and our use of cognitive heuristics or "mental shortcuts" in arriving at these explanations (refer to chapter 4). We are especially likely to seek an explanation for behavior when it runs counter to the standard social norms (for example, cutting in front of someone in a line). We have also learned through experience that there are exceptions to these social norms, and when people ask to be granted an exception, it's expected that they will provide a reason why the exception should be granted. Because we believe that others are as concerned about acting appropriately as we are, we tend to assume that when someone gives us a reason for doing something, it must be worthy of an exception. As a result, we may often mindlessly grant a request accompanied by a reason because we assume the requester wouldn't ask if the request was illegitimate. When my daughter Lillian was 2 years old, she had already learned the importance of giving reasons when seeking compliance from her parents. In asking to go outside she would say, "Can I go outside and play? Because I have to go outside and play." Based on Langer's findings, when it comes to securing compliance, Lillian had already developed sufficient social skills to do quite nicely in the adult world.

A fair request should be followed by the deed in silence.

Dante Alighieri, Italian poet, 1265–1321

VARIOUS TWO-STEP COMPLIANCE STRATEGIES ARE EFFECTIVE FOR DIFFERENT REASONS

Earlier, we discussed how "creditors" secure compliance by keeping tabs on others' debts to them. Professional creditors, such as insurance agents, car dealers, or door-to-door salespersons rely on more than just indebtedness to secure compliance to their sales requests. In making sales, they realize that it often takes more than a single plea to win over a potential customer. Social psychologists have studied how multiple requests, employed in different ways, can result in some very effective compliance techniques.

He that does not ask will never get a bargain.

French proverb

FOOT-IN-THE-DOOR

In chapter 5, we saw that many people feel pressure to remain consistent in their beliefs. Salespersons, recognizing this need for consistency, often employ a two-step compliance strategy known as the **foot-in-the-door technique.** In this strategy, the person secures compliance with a small request and then follows it up later with a larger, less desirable request. For example, imagine that a young woman knocks on your door and tells you she is gathering signatures on a petition supporting environmental protection. Would you be willing to sign? This question represents the first small request. Being proenvironment, you readily agree. After signing, the woman says she is also seeking money for her organization to better fight for the environment, and would you be willing to make a contribution? This is the second, larger request. Chances are, if you signed the petition you will also contribute some money. Joseph Schwarzwald and his coworkers (1983) found that, using a very similar scenario, they were able to produce a 75 percent increase in donations over a comparison request strategy involving no prior petition signing.

Meta-analyses of studies using the foot-in-the-door technique indicate that it is fairly reliable in securing compliance (Beaman et al., 1983; Dillard, 1991). However, if people reject the small request, they are even less likely to comply with the larger request than those who were not approached with the small request (Snyder & Cunningham, 1975). Can you guess why? It appears that the foot-in-the-door effect causes a change in self-perception. In not granting the small first request, people may decide that they are not the type of person who grants those

Foot-in-the-Door Technique

A two-step compliance technique in which the influencer secures compliance to a small request, and then later follows this with a larger, less desirable request.

kinds of requests. Therefore, because of this new self-image, they are more likely to later reject the larger request. The same self-perception process operates for those who do grant the small request. They perceive themselves as cooperative, and therefore, later comply to the second, larger request in order to maintain their cooperative self-image. For this technique to work, the initial request must be large enough to cause people to think about the implications of their behavior, and they must believe they are freely complying (Dejong, 1979).

Although the foot-in-the-door technique is an effective form of strategic influence, there is an entire class of people who are not susceptible to its power. Can you identify these people? As a hint, note that in order for changes in self-perception to occur, people must have the cognitive ability to make inferences about their personality based on past behavior. Prior to the age of about 7, however, children do not have the necessary reasoning ability to make such self-attributions (Grusec & Redler, 1980). Because they lack basic reasoning skills, young children experience little internal pressure to be consistent, and thus, they are not susceptible to foot-in-the-door strategies (Eisenberg et al., 1987). Armed with this knowledge, the next time a solicitor comes to your door, if you want to hold on to your money, send the person who is watching "Sesame Street" on television to speak for the family. If you don't have a youngster available, then send someone who does not have a strong preference for consistency (refer to chapter 5, pp. 177–178): they are much less bothered by inconsistent actions, and thus, are less susceptible to the foot-in-the-door effect (Cialdini et al., 1995).

DOOR-IN-THE-FACE

A second compliance technique that also uses multiple requests is in some sense the reverse of the foot-in-the door strategy. In the **door-in-the-face technique,** the person seeking compliance starts by asking for a very large favor—one the recipient is almost certain to reject. When the rejection occurs, the request is changed to a much less costly request. Securing this second request was the objective of the influencer from the start. The first rejection is the door in the face, and it is presumed that the second request stands a better chance of being accepted if it's preceded by this rejection.

A study by Robert Cialdini and his colleagues (1975) illustrates the effectiveness of this compliance strategy. College students were approached by teams of confederates who asked them to volunteer to spend two hours a week over the next year as "big brothers" or "big sisters" to juveniles in need of older role models. Not surprisingly, no one agreed to this request, which is exactly what Cialdini expected. But the confederates then followed this rejection with a second request: Would the students be willing to spend two hours just once taking the same kids to the zoo? Fifty percent agreed to this request. In a control condition, when this smaller request had been presented without being preceded by the large request, less than 17 percent of the students agreed to comply.

For the door-in-the-face effect to occur, three conditions must be met. First, the initial request must be very large so that when people refuse they make no negative inferences about themselves (for example, "I'm not a very generous person"). Second, the interval between the first and second requests must be relatively short so that the feeling of obligation is still salient. In contrast, a longer interval (weeks or even months) between the two requests can still be effective for the foot-in-the-door technique. Finally, the third condition is that the subsequent smaller request must be made by the same person who made the first large request. People perceive this second request as a concession by the requester that the first request was too large. Once this perceived concession occurs, due to the reciprocity norm, people feel pressure to reciprocate with a concession of their own—agree to the second request. Of the two sequential compliance techniques discussed thus far, the "face" approach has been shown to be more effective than the "foot" technique (Harari et al., 1980).

CRITICAL *thinking*

How might the foot-in-the-door compliance strategy be combined with the effects of post-decision dissonance (see chapter 5, p. 176) to partly explain how some people initially become involved and then committed to religious or political cults?

Door-in-the-Face Technique

A two-step compliance technique in which, after having a large request refused, the influencer counteroffers with a much smaller request.

The door-in-the-face strategy is often used by both parties in negotiating contracts for such things as houses, cars, and salaries. Both parties begin with an economic position that is extremely favorable to themselves but very unfavorable to the other side. Following the initial proposal rejections, one or both of them might make concessions that are actually closer to what they really hope to obtain from the other. Often, those who make less reciprocal concessions and who are also less concerned with appearing unreasonable are the ones who secure the best deals (Pendleton & Batson, 1979).

THAT'S-NOT-ALL

That's-Not-All Strategy

A two-step compliance technique in which the influencer makes a large request, then immediately offers a discount or bonus before the initial request is refused.

Closely related to the door-in-the-face technique is the **that's-not-all strategy,** which involves the influencer making a large request, but then immediately offering a discount or bonus that makes the request more reasonable. Unlike the door-in-the-face technique, however, the person is not given the opportunity to reject the large request before it is reduced or "sweetened." Jerry Burger (1986) demonstrated the effectiveness of this tactic when he conducted a bake sale at Santa Clara University. On the table where the sale was taking place were a number of cupcakes with no indicated price. In one condition, when potential buyers asked how much one cupcake cost, they were given a high price. Then, before they could respond, they were also told that this price included a "bonus" bag of cookies. In a control condition, potential buyers were immediately shown the bag of cookies and told that they were included in the total price. Results indicated that 73 percent of those who experienced the *that's-not-all* tactic bought the sweets, versus only 40 percent of those who were offered everything up front.

In a second cupcake study, instead of the request being "sweetened" by a bonus, it was reduced in size. In the that's-not-all condition, people were told that the cupcakes cost $1.25 but that they would be sold to the buyer at $1.00, because the booth would be closing soon. In the control condition, people were merely told that the cupcakes cost $1.00. As shown in figure 8.6, the that's-not-all strategy was again more effective in selling cupcakes: 55 percent of those in this condition bought cupcakes, versus only 20 percent in the control condition.

Burger was also interested in determining whether the that's-not-all effect occurred only because the offered items were now a bargain, and so he created a third condition. In this *bargain* condition, the seller stated to the potential buyer that the cupcakes were now priced at $1.00, although formerly they were $1.25. The bargain condition only resulted in a 25 percent purchase rate (see figure 8.6). This finding suggests that the that's-not-all strategy is not just effective because it offers a bargain to the influence target, but there also appears to be a psychological potency created by the influencer personally sweetening the deal that lowers people's resistance to the request.

How exactly does the that's-not-all technique lower resistance? One possibility is that when the salesperson's request is reduced or sweetened, the customer may perceive this as a concession that the original request was unreasonable. Following the norm of reciprocity, the customer may now feel an increased obligation to reciprocate this act by agreeing to the better price (as in the door-in-the-face effect). Another possible way in which the that's-not-all technique may lower resistance is by altering the customer's "anchor point" against which the purchase decision is made (see chapter 4 discussion of the *anchoring and adjustment heuristic,* p. 123). That is, if customers are contemplating the purchase of a product for which they themselves don't have a fixed price in mind (such as cupcakes at a bake sale), the salesperson's costly first request sets the price standard, or anchor. When the second cheaper price immediately follows the costly price, it alters the anchor point and creates the impression that the product is a bargain.

Although the that's-not-all technique is effective, success appears to depend on targets responding rather mindlessly to the request (Pollock et al., 1998). For example, one recent study found that compliance occurs only when the initial

FIGURE 8.6

That's Not All!

The effectiveness of the "that's not all" compliance technique was demonstrated in a campus bake sale. By far, the highest percentage of potential customers purchased cupcakes when the deal was "sweetened" by first stating one price and then lowering it before the customer could respond. When customers were told that the price had already been lowered (bargain) or when they were merely given the low price right away (control), purchases were much less likely.

Source: Data from J. M. Burger, "Increasing Compliance by Improving the Deal: The That's-Not-All Technique" in *Journal of Personality and Social Psychology,* 52, 277–283, American Psychological Association, 1986.

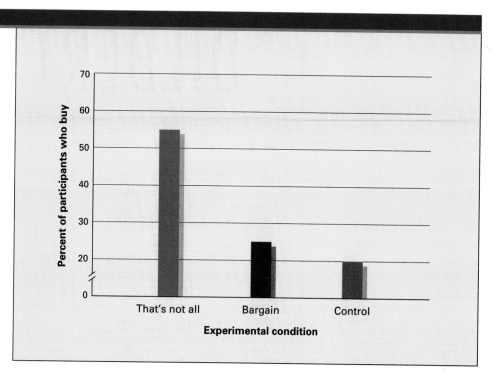

Low-Ball Technique

A two-step compliance strategy in which the influencer secures agreement with a request by understating its true cost.

request is within reason (Burger et al., in press). If you first ask people to buy cupcakes for the extremely high price of $3.00 apiece, lowering your price to $1.00 is unlikely to induce compliance because the initial request appears ridiculous, and it places potential customers on guard. Now, instead of engaging in the type of "lazy" thinking discussed in chapter 4 (*heuristics*) and chapter 6 (*peripheral route processing*), the target is motivated to more critically analyze the offer. Under this greater scrutiny, compliance decreases.

Low-Balling

A few years ago I went shopping for a new car to replace my badly rusted "old reliable." After test driving one car, I made an offer that included my car as a trade-in for $700. The salesperson said we had a deal; he just had to get the manager's OK. After ten minutes, however, the salesperson returned looking forlorn, saying the manager would only take my trade-in for $300. Then with a big smile he declared, "And that means you can have *your* new car for only $400 more!"

What happened here? In the vernacular of the car dealer, I had been "low-balled." The **low-ball technique** is a strategy in which an influencer secures agreement with a request by understating its true cost. When the size of the request is increased by revealing the hidden costs, even though most people are disappointed and even angry that the deal has been made less desirable, they often stick to their initial commitment and proceed with the new arrangement. Fortunately, I was aware of the research on low-balling and recognized the scam for what it was.

In one low-balling study, psychology students were phoned and asked to participate in an experiment (Cialdini et al., 1978). Some students were told before answering the request that the experiment would begin at the undesirable time of 7 A.M. Other students were first asked if they would agree to participate, and only after they had agreed were they told that the experiment began at such an early hour (the low ball). As testament to the power of low-balling, more than half of the students in the low-ball condition agreed to participate, while fewer than one-third of the control condition students did so. Furthermore, more than half of the low-balled students actually kept their 7 A.M. appointment, as opposed to less than one-quarter of the control condition students.

Low-balling taken to new heights.

DILBERT reprinted by permission of United Feature Syndicate, Inc.

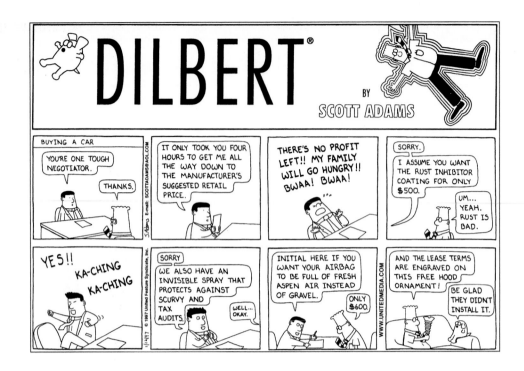

Why does the low-ball procedure work? One important factor is the psychology of commitment. Once people make a particular decision, they tend to justify it to themselves by thinking of its positive aspects. As they become increasingly committed to their course of action, they grow more resistant to changing their minds. This is why car dealers will let you, the prospective buyer, sit in the showroom for a while before telling you that they require more money. During that time, they are counting on you fantasizing so much about "your new car" that you will be willing to pay the extra money to drive it off the lot. Yet, if you spend that time reviewing what you've learned here, you stand a better chance of leaving the showroom with a deal to your liking. In this case, knowledge truly is power—social influence power.

SECTION SUMMARY

In seeking compliance from those who are roughly of our own social status, we employ a variety of tactics. First, we may attempt to create the proper "ambience" by fostering a *good mood* in the one we are attempting to influence. In addition, we may attempt to increase the likelihood that our request will be granted by first doing the other person some favor or good deed. Due to the *norm of reciprocity*, it is likely this person will then feel more obligated to grant the subsequent request. Those being influenced are also more likely to comply if a *reason* is given for why the request should be granted, even if the reason is only a reiteration of our desire to have the request granted. Finally, we may also employ some rather subtle, yet very effective, compliance techniques utilizing multiple requests. These include the *foot-in-the-door*, the *door-in-the-face*, the *that's not all*, and the *low-balling* strategies.

OBEDIENCE

As you can see from our overview of both conformity processes and compliance strategies, many social influence pressures are relatively hidden and subtly employed. In this respect, obedience differs from these other types of influence because it is overt and easily recognized as an exercise of power.

When people are ordered by an authority figure to engage in a particular behavior, you might expect that their need for personal control would result in a good deal of disobedience. If the order was to engage in behavior that appeared to pose serious health risks to others, you might predict that wide-scale disobedience would occur. Would it? What would you do under such circumstances? To answer this question, let's explore the most discussed social psychological study ever conducted (Miller et al., 1995).

MILGRAM'S RESEARCH SUGGESTS THAT OBEYING DESTRUCTIVE COMMANDS IS MORE THE RULE THAN THE EXCEPTION

Imagine that you have volunteered to participate in an experiment on learning. Upon arriving at the laboratory, you find that a 50-year-old man is also taking part in the study. The experimenter explains that the study will investigate the effects of punishment on the learning of word pairs. The punishment will be electrical shock. One of you will be the "teacher," and the other will be the "learner." A drawing of names determines that you will be the teacher. When the learner discovers that he will be receiving shocks, he tells the experimenter that he has a mild heart condition ("Nothing serious, but since electricity is being used I thought I should tell you"). The experimenter replies that while the shocks may be painful, they will not cause permanent tissue damage. The learner is then taken to an adjacent room where he is strapped into a chair and electrodes are attached to his arms. As this is being done, the experimenter explains that your task is to teach the learner a list of word pairs, to then test him on the list, and to administer punishment whenever he makes a mistake. In front of you is a shock generator, which has a row of thirty switches ranging from 15 to 450 volts. You are instructed to start at the lowest intensity level and to increase the shock by one switch (15 volts) for each subsequent learner error. To give you some idea of what the shock feels like, the experimenter gives you a 45-volt shock—and it hurts. You're a little nervous now, but you don't say anything.

Once the study begins, the learner makes many mistakes, and you respond by flipping the shock switches. Starting at 75 volts, you hear through the intercom system the learner grunting and moaning in pain whenever you deliver the shocks. At 150 volts he demands to be released, shouting, "Experimenter! That's all! Get me out of here. My heart's starting to bother me now. I refuse to go on!" Now your nervousness becomes nail-biting anxiety. At 180 volts he shouts that he can no longer stand the pain. At 300 volts he says that he absolutely refuses to provide any more answers. Responding to this attempt by the learner to halt the study, the experimenter instructs you to treat the absence of a response as equivalent to an error and to deliver the appropriate level of shock. Even though the learner no longer gives answers, he continues to scream in agony whenever your finger flips the shock generator switch. When you surpass the 330-volt switch, the learner not only does not give any answers, he falls silent, not to be heard from again. As you continue to increase the shock intensity, the labels under the switches now read, "Danger—Severe Shock" and you realize you are getting closer to the last switch, the 450-volt switch, which is simply labeled "XXX." You desperately want to stop, but when you hesitate, the experimenter first tells you, "Please continue," then "The experiment requires that you continue," then "It is absolutely essential that you go on," and finally, "You have no other choice, you must go on!"

(Top) Stanley Milgram and the "shock generator," which he used in his obedience experiments. (Bottom) In this replication of the obedience experiment, the teacher (participant) had to force the learner's (confederate's) hand onto a shock plate. Less than one-third obeyed the experimenter under these conditions.

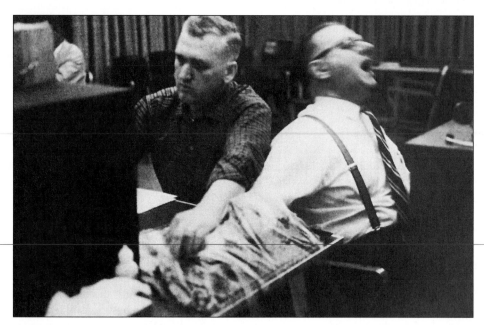

""Oh God, let's stop it."

A reluctant but obedient participant in the Milgram experiments, Milgram, 1963, p. 377

. . . **O**bedience, Bane of all genius, virtue, freedom, truth, makes slaves of men, and, of the human frame, a mechanized automaton.

Percy Bysshe Shelley, English poet, 1792–1822

What would you do? Would you disobey the experimenter's commands? When would you stop obeying? Is it possible that you would continue to deliver all the shocks, including the dangerous 450 volts, despite the learner's protests? How many of your friends do you think would obey the experimenter's orders if they were the teachers?

I'm guessing that your prediction is that you and your friends would disobey the experimenter's authority and refuse to continue the learning experiment well before the 450-volt limit. If this is your prediction, you are in good company, for widespread disobedience is exactly what was predicted by college students, middle-class adults, and psychiatrists who were presented with this hypothetical scenario (Milgram, 1963). People in all three groups guessed that they would disobey by about 135 volts, and none thought they would go beyond 300 volts. The psychiatrists, when asked about other people's level of obedience, predicted that

TABLE 8.2

Shock Levels at Which Milgram's Participants Disobeyed (n = 40) Compared to Predicted Disobedience by Psychiatrists

Voltage	Actual Number of Defectors	Percentage	Actual Cumulative % of Defectors	Predicted Cumulative % of Defectors
75	0	0.0	0.0	15
135	0	0.0	0.0	44
150	0	0.0	0.0	68
210	0	0.0	0.0	86
300	5	12.5	12.5	96
315	4	10.0	22.5	96
330	2	5.0	27.5	97
345	1	2.5	30.0	99
360–435	2	5.0	35.0	99
450[a]	0	0.0	35.0	99.9

[a]Although a team of psychiatrists predicted that only about one-tenth of 1 percent of the participants in the Milgram obedience research would fully obey the experimenter's commands and administer the highest shock level on the generator, in actuality, 65 percent of the participants fully obeyed the experimenter's commands. The first point at which participants began disobeying was when the learner refused or was unable to respond (the 300-volt level).

Source: Data from S. Milgram, *Obedience to Authority: An Experimental View*, Harper and Row, Publishers, Inc. 1974; and S. Milgram, *The Individual in a Social World: Essays and Experiments*, Addison-Wesley Publishing Company, 1992.

less than one-tenth of 1 percent of participants—one person out of one thousand—would obey the experimenter completely.

To determine the actual level of obedience, Milgram conducted this study at Yale University, using as his subjects forty adult males who ranged in age from 20 to 50 years and who came from all walks of life. There was a rigged drawing so that the naive participant always became the teacher. The learner was a confederate and received no actual shocks. Even his screams of protest and pain were prerecorded so that all participants heard exactly the same thing. To Milgram's astonishment, 65 percent of the participants (twenty-six out of forty) obeyed the experimenter completely, despite these convincing cries of agony from the learner. In fact, all participants who reached 450 volts obeyed the experimenter's command to continue with the procedure using the 450-volt switch until the experiment was halted a short time later. Table 8.2 provides a summary of when the disobedient participants refused to continue delivering shocks. As you can see, all obeyed up to 300 volts.

The simplest interpretation of these findings is that Milgram inadvertently recruited closet sadists who were more than willing to inflict pain on the hapless learner. However soothing this explanation would be to our collective psyches, it does not stand up to the available evidence (Darley, 1995). Milgram's participants were not suffering from any personality disorders that would cause them to enjoy their destructive obedience. In fact, their actions caused them a great deal of stress (Elms, 1995; Elms & Milgram, 1966). Participants were observed sweating, trembling, stuttering, biting their lips, and groaning as they struggled through the experimental procedure.

Some sense of their state of mind can be gleaned from remarks made by one of the fully obedient individuals who began the experiment calmly but became increasingly tense as the learner protested the shocks being delivered:

150 volts delivered: "You want me to keep going?"

165 volts delivered: "That guy is hollering in there. There's a lot of them here. He's liable to have heart condition. You want me to go?"

180 volts delivered: "He can't stand it! I'm not going to kill that man in there! You hear him hollering? He's hollering. He can't stand it. What if something happens to him? . . . I'm not going to get that man sick in there. He's hollering in there. You know what I mean? I mean I refuse to take the responsibility. He's getting hurt in there. He's in there hollering. Too many left here. Geez, if he gets them wrong. There's too many of them left. I mean who is going to take responsibility if anything happens to that gentleman?"

[The experimenter accepts responsibility]: "All right."

195 volts delivered: "You see he's hollering. Hear that. Gee, I don't know."

[The experimenter says, "The experimenter requires that you go on"]: "I know it does, sir, but I mean—hugh—he don't know what he's in for. He's up to 195 volts."

210 volts delivered.

225 volts delivered.

240 volts delivered: "Aw no. You mean I've got to keep going up with the scale? No sir. I'm not going to kill that man! I'm not going to give him 450 volts!"

[The experimenter says, "The experiment requires that you go on."]: "I know it does, but that man is hollering there, sir. . . ."

Because the findings were so unexpected, Milgram carried out a number of variations of his experiment to better understand the conditions under which obedience and disobedience would be most likely. When college students and women served as participants, the same level of destructive obedience was found (Milgram, 1974). Different researchers also obtained similar results in several other countries, suggesting that these high levels of obedience were not solely an American phenomenon. Australia had a 68 percent obedience level (Kilham & Mann, 1974), Jordan was at 63 percent (Shanab & Yahya, 1977), and Germany was the highest at 85 percent (Mantell, 1971).

Some critics initially suggested that the high obedience was due to the prestige of Yale University and the presumed belief by participants that no one at Yale would allow harm to come to anyone in the study (Baumrind, 1964; Orne, 1962). To test this possibility, Milgram (1965) moved the experimental site to a run-down office building in Bridgeport, Connecticut, with no noticeable affiliations with Yale. Although obedience decreased slightly, the difference was not significant—48 percent of the participants delivered the maximum shock level. Although switching locations from a prestigious to a nonprestigious institution did not have a significant effect on obedience, when the experimenter was replaced with an ordinary person (actually a confederate), obedience dropped to 20 percent. What these findings suggest is that the social role of "scientist" or "researcher" has sufficient prestige and authority to secure obedience, regardless of the social context (see Blass, 1996).

Although an authority figure is much more likely to be obeyed than a nonauthority, situational factors strengthen or weaken this influence. In a follow-up study, Milgram varied the proximity of the experimenter to the teacher. In one condition, the experimenter sat a few feet from the teacher as he delivered the electrical shocks to the learner. In a second condition, after giving initial instructions, the experimenter left the room and gave his orders by phone. In a third condition, the teacher received his instructions on a tape recorder and never actually met the experimenter. Findings from these three conditions indicated that obedience decreased as the distance to the experimenter increased. In fact, when the experimenter was absent, several participants administered shocks of a lower voltage than called for by the experimenter.

In another series of experiments, the proximity of the learner to the teacher was varied (Milgram, 1974). Under one condition, the learner and teacher were located in separate rooms without access to intercom systems, and thus, the teacher could not hear the learner's cries of protest and pain. The teacher's only knowledge of the victim's reaction was that he pounded on the adjoining wall at 300 volts and subsequently stopped responding to the word pairs. In another condition, the learner was seated in the same room only a few feet from the teacher. In a third condition, the learner sat right next to the teacher, resting his hand on a metal plate in order to receive the shock. At 350 volts, the learner refused to put his hand on the plate to receive the shock, and the experimenter then ordered the teacher to force the learner's hand onto the shock plate. In all of these studies, results indicated that the closer the teacher was to the learner, the lower the level of obedience.

In addition to testing for proximity and site effects, Milgram also investigated how group pressure might influence obedience. In one study, three teachers (two of them confederates) split up the duties previously assigned to one. The naive participant always was assigned the role of actually delivering the electrical shock, while the confederate-teachers read the word pairs and told the learner if his answers were correct. In one condition, the confederate-teachers simply followed the experimenter's commands and did not express any sympathy for the learner. In another condition, the confederates were openly rebellious—one refused to continue after 150 volts and the other quit at the 210-volt level. The first condition only slightly increased obedience (72 percent) above the original study's level, but the second condition resulted in complete obedience in only 10 percent of the participants.

The likely explanation for this sharp drop in obedience is that the open defiance of the confederates broke the social consensus of the situation and reduced the strength of the experimenter's social power. Did the participants in this study recognize the liberating effect that the rebellious confederate-teachers had on their own willingness to disobey the orders of the authority figure? No. Three-fourths of the participants who disobeyed believed that they would have stopped even without the other teachers' examples. Yet the previous studies strongly argue against this belief, suggesting that people seriously underestimate the impact that others have on their own behavior. Figure 8.7 summarizes the findings of some of these studies and identifies factors that foster and inhibit obedience.

ORDERS TO INFLICT PSYCHOLOGICAL HARM ON VICTIMS IS ALSO LIKELY TO BE OBEYED

Milgram's experiments demonstrated the frightening willingness of people to inflict physical pain upon innocent victims due to the commands of authority figures. Two Dutch social psychologists, Wim Meeus and Quinten Raaijmakers (1986), conducted a series of experiments to determine whether people would be equally willing to obey the commands of authority figures in inflicting psychological pain on others.

In one study, when participants arrived at the lab, they met a man who told them he was there to take a test as part of a job interview. The applicant further stated that obtaining the job depended on whether or not he passed the test. When the experimenter arrived, he took the participant aside and told him he was interested in people's ability to work under stress. To aid in this investigation, the participant was told to induce stress in the job applicant while he was taking the test. To induce

FIGURE 8.7

Some Factors That Influence Obedience and Disobedience to Authority

To determine what factors increase or decrease obedience beyond the baseline 65 percent level, Milgram varied the location of the experiment, the participant's proximity to the victim and the experimenter, and the presence of obedient or disobedient confederates. As you can see, all of these factors influenced obedience levels.

Source: Data from S. Milgram, *Obedience to Authority: An Experimental View*, Harper and Row, Publishers, Inc., 1974; and S. Milgram, *The Individual in a Social World: Essays and Experiments*, Addison-Wesley Publishing Company, 1992.

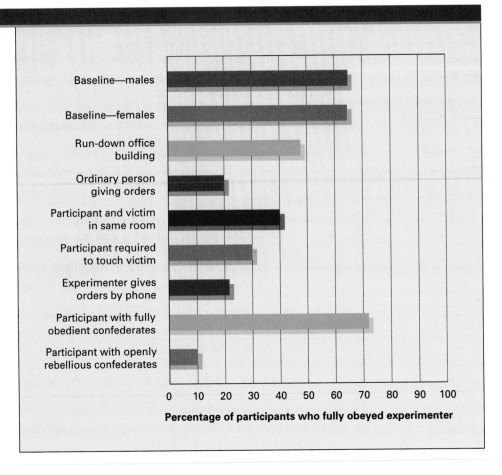

stress, the participant was instructed to make a series of fifteen increasingly negative remarks about the applicant's performance and abilities as he read him the test items. Examples of some of the "stress remarks" were, "If you continue like this, you will fail the test," and "This job is much too difficult for you. You are more suited for lower functions." In actuality, the applicant was a confederate who had been instructed to react to the stress remarks in a specified manner. First, he merely protested the distracting remarks. Next, he pleaded with the participant to stop making him nervous, and then he angrily refused to put up with such negative treatment. Finally, he fell into a state of despair. As the negative remarks escalated, the applicant's performance began to deteriorate and he eventually failed the test and lost the job. Whenever participants hesitated to deliver the next negative remark, the experimenter would order them to continue.

As in the Milgram studies, Meeus and Raaijmakers were interested in how many participants would follow the experimenter's orders through the entire set of stress remarks, despite the "fact" that their behavior was causing psychological harm to another (see Meeus & Raaijmakers, 1995). In a control condition in which the experimenter did not order hesitant participants to continue, everyone stopped before the fifteen stress remarks had been read. However, in the experimental condition in which orders were issued to reluctant participants, 92 percent of them—both males and females—obeyed fully.

In a follow-up to this study, Meeus and Raaijmakers (1987) attempted to determine whether obedience would be reduced if participants were forewarned about the nature of the task. With this in mind, they sent people a letter a day before they were to participate in the stress remark study and told them what they would be doing. This letter contained specific information that a job applicant might perform poorly on an exam due to their negative comments and thus lose a job he would normally obtain. Despite the opportunity to consider the implications of their actions away from the actual presence of the authority figure, the next day all participants fully obeyed the experimenters' commands.

In discussing the meaning of his obedience experiments, Milgram made the following remarks that would equally apply to Meeus and Raaijmakers's findings:

> The behavior revealed in the experiments reported here is normal human behavior but revealed under conditions that show with particular clarity the danger to human survival inherent in our make-up. And what is it we have seen? Not aggression, for there is no anger, vindictiveness, or hatred in those who shocked the victim. Men do become angry; they do act hatefully and explode in rage against others. But not here. Something far more dangerous is revealed: the capacity for man to abandon his humanity, indeed, the inevitability that he does so, as he merges his unique personality into larger institutional structures. This is a fatal flaw nature has designed into us, and which in the long run gives our species only a modest chance of survival. (1974, p. 188)

OBSERVING OTHERS DEFY AUTHORITY FIGURES SIGNIFICANTLY REDUCES OBEDIENCE

Milgram's commentary on his own obedience research paints a bleak picture of humankind's ability to resist destructive authoritarian pressure. Yet is the abandonment of our humanity as inevitable as Milgram suggests? Perhaps the depth of Milgram's pessimism is partly due to the special circumstances created in his research design. In most of the obedience studies discussed thus far, including Milgram's, a lone individual engages in destructive behavior after being placed in a situation in which he or she receives orders from an authority figure. What would happen if antisocial orders are delivered not to a lone individual but, rather, to an entire group of people? Would this collective be as malleable as the lone individual?

It was this question that William Gamson and his colleagues (1982) were interested in exploring when they recruited groups of people to participate in a purported discussion of community standards. Participants, scheduled in groups of nine, arrived at a local motel for the discussion and were greeted by the "coordinator." This coordinator told them that the proceedings would be videotaped for a large oil company that was being sued by a former manager of one of its local gas stations. This former employee had been fired after the company learned he was living with a woman to whom he was not married. The company justified its actions by stating that its representatives must be beyond moral reproach. Despite this explanation by the coordinator, participants soon learned some additional information that cast a different light on the firing—the manager was fired after appearing on local TV, where he spoke out against higher gas prices.

Shortly after discussion began about whether the manager's lifestyle was morally offensive to those in the community, the coordinator interrupted and told three group members to argue on camera as if they were offended by the manager's lifestyle. A short time later, he again interrupted and told three more members to also act offended. Soon the coordinator had instructed all members to act offended on camera concerning the manager's lifestyle and to state that they would not do business at his gas station. Then he told them there was an affidavit to be signed and notarized that gave the oil company the right to introduce the videotapes as evidence in court, editing them as they saw fit.

As originally designed, some discussion groups were to include a confederate member who would either take a more or less active role in mobilizing rebellion against the oil company's actions. However, as the malicious intent of the videotaped discussion began to dawn on the actual group participants, they

I hold it that a little rebellion now and then, is a good thing, and as necessary in the political world as storms in the physical. . . . It is a medicine for the sound health of government.

Thomas Jefferson, U.S. president, 1743–1826

Disobedience when it is not criminally but morally, religiously, or politically motivated is always a collective act and it is justified by the values of the collectivity and the mutual engagements of its members.

Social historian Michael Walzer, 1970

began to rebel on their own. One participant, when told to act offended before the videocamera, expressed his defiance by adopting a mocking, twangy accent and stating, "Next to ma waaf, ma car is my favritt thing, an ah ain't sending neither of 'em tuh that gas stoishen." Some groups became so outraged at the company's attempts to use them to discredit the former employee that they threatened to forcibly confiscate the videotapes and expose the company to the local news media. Confronted by one outraged group after another, the researchers were forced to terminate the experiment due to fears that it was causing too much stress on the participants.

Why did this experiment result in such open disobedience when Milgram's research produced such widespread obedience? In both studies there were agents of authority, the experimenter and the coordinator. In both studies the original intention of participants was to obey the instructions of these authorities. In both studies the authorities overstepped the proper moral boundaries and began to demand unjust actions by the participants. The basic difference between these studies is that Milgram's participants were alone, whereas Gamson's were in groups. Because eight or nine of Gamson's group members were naive participants, the possibility of collective action always existed. Milgram's design, on the other hand, has never been tried with more than one naive participant in the teacher role, and so the possibility of collective action here has never been studied.

Although the Milgram design never tested more than one participant at a time, in one of his experiments he did use two confederates who posed as coteachers along with the actual participant. As discussed previously (see p. 301), when the participant observed others openly defying the destructive commands of the authority figure, he became much more willing to disobey as well. In a very real psychological sense, the rebellious confederates served as models for the participant's own disobedience. Similar findings were also obtained in Asch's conformity studies: social support allowed others to more easily express their own opinions.

One who breaks an unjust law that conscience tells him is unjust, and who willingly accepts the penalty of imprisonment in order to arouse the consciousness of the community over its injustice, is in reality expressing the highest respect for the law.

Martin Luther King, Jr., U.S. civil rights leader, 1929–1968

SECTION SUMMARY

People's susceptibility to strong authority pressure was vividly and dramatically demonstrated by Stanley Milgram in his series of obedience experiments. Confronted with the demands of an authority figure to engage in destructive behavior toward an innocent victim, almost two-thirds obeyed. Further research suggests that one of the most important factors in determining whether one will obey or rebel against the destructive commands of an authority figure is the social support he or she may receive. As was found in the conformity research of Asch, obtaining social support for one's beliefs or behavioral inclinations allows people to more easily express themselves when confronted by social pressures from the majority or from those in power positions.

TOWARD A UNIFIED UNDERSTANDING OF SOCIAL INFLUENCE

Although different factors are involved in the various forms of social influence discussed in this chapter, the task of social scientists is to discover common principles operating in the exercise of social power. In this section, we will examine one theory that attempts to predict when influence attempts are most likely to succeed.

FIGURE 8.8

According to social impact theory, the impact of other people on the target person depends on (a) the number of people present (number of source circles), the strength or importance of these people (size of the source circles), and their immediacy to the target person (nearness of the source circles to the target). Social impact increases as source factors increase. In addition, the total impact of other people on target persons depends on (b) the number of target persons (number of target circles), the strength of these targets (size of target circles), and their immediacy (nearness to one another). Social impact decreases as target factors increase.

Social Impact Theory

The theory that the amount of social influence others have depends on their number, strength, and immediacy to those they are trying to influence.

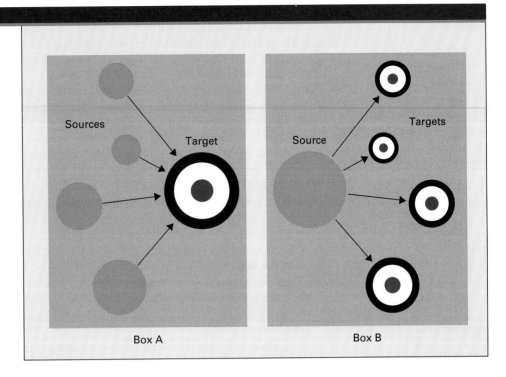

Box A

Box B

SOCIAL IMPACT THEORY STATES THAT INFLUENCE IS DETERMINED BY PEOPLE'S NUMBER, STRENGTH, AND IMMEDIACY

As developed by Bibb Latané (1981), **social impact theory** states that the amount of influence others have in a given situation (their social impact) is a function of three factors: their *number, strength,* and *immediacy.* This social impact operates like physical impact. For example, the amount of light falling on a surface depends not only on how many lights are turned on, but also on the strength or power of the bulbs and how close they are to the surface. Similarly, as illustrated in figure 8.8, Box A, a person will be more influenced by others when there are more of them, when they are stronger sources of influence, and when they are physically closer.

Although social impact theory predicts that people become more influential as their numbers increase, what about the "leveling off" effect found in the Asch (1956) conformity research? In that study, adding more confederates beyond three or four had little impact on conformity. Latané contends that this is due to another principle of social impact theory, which states that as the number of influencing persons increases, their individual impact decreases. Returning to the light bulb analogy, when you turn on a second light in a room that previously had only one bulb illuminating it, the increased impact the second light has on your sight is quite perceptible. Yet the impact of adding a fifteenth bulb to a room illuminated by fourteen lights is hardly seen at all. Latané claims that the same is true with individuals and their social impact on others: the second person has less impact than the first, and the nth person has less effect than the $(n-1)$th.

Regarding the strength of would-be influencers, Latané states that this depends on their status, expertise, and power. For example, in most circumstances, a police officer will have greater social impact than a mail carrier. Similarly, in the Milgram studies, the experimenter was more successful in securing obedience than an ordinary person. Finally, the immediacy of others is determined by their closeness to the individual in time or space. In other words, others will have greater social impact on you if they are actually present than if they are watching you on a monitor in another location or watching a videotape of your actions at a later date. In the obedience studies, people were more likely to obey the experimenter when he was physically present rather than when he gave orders over the phone.

Although social impact theory can explain the social influence exerted in the Asch and Milgram studies, how would it explain the *disobedience* in Gamson's oil company research? As you can see in figure 8.8, Box B, social impact theory also predicts that people are more likely to *resist* others' influence attempts when the social impact is dispersed among many strong and closely situated targets. In the oil company study, the social impact of the authority figure was divided among nine participants, not one, making disobedience easier. Similar disobedience occurred in the Milgram study when participants were in the presence of confederates who actively resisted the authority's orders. What these findings indicate is that when a group of individuals is confronted with the dictates of an immoral authority, there is always the possibility that the group will collectively redefine social reality and draw individual strength and conviction from the assembled others. With this group-originated conviction, they can more easily defy the social power of the authority. This same strength is simply not available to the lone individual, and therefore it is not surprising that obedience is more common here.

Having made the argument that groups can resist destructive obedience more effectively than the individual, I must also note that groups can often trigger destruction as well. You need only consider for a moment the death and suffering that has been caused by such group actions as lynchings, riots, and wars to recognize that groups are not a safeguard against destructive obedience. The power of groups can be used for either constructive or destructive purposes (see chapter 9). However, when prosocial values are made salient within a group setting, individual members can draw strength from those in their midst, enabling them to resist orders they consider immoral.

Social impact theory has been found to be useful in determining precisely *when* other people will exert influence over someone's actions (Latané & Nowak, in press). Although this theory has not gone unchallenged (Mullen, 1985), it does offer an avenue to better understand the social influence process, and it continues to generate new insights and alternative perspectives (Latané & L'Herrou, 1996; Sedikes & Jackson, 1990).

UNDERESTIMATING SITUATIONAL FACTORS MAKES YOU MORE SUSCEPTIBLE TO COERCIVE SOCIAL INFLUENCE

Earlier, when describing the situation confronting participants in Milgram's research, I asked whether you would have fully obeyed the commands of the experimenter. This is a question I have asked myself over the years. Most people emphatically believe that they would resist the destructive commands and openly rebel. They further believe that those who would obey fully must be more aggressive, cold, and unappealing than the average person (Miller et al., 1973). How do we reconcile these beliefs with the actual experimental findings?

To answer this question, let me return to information presented in chapter 3. There is a widely held assumption, more common in individualist cultures than in those that are collectivist, that people's actions are caused by internal dispositions rather than by external forces. This *fundamental attribution error* often results in a gross underestimation of the inherent power of the situation to shape behavior. The source for this belief in the power of the individual to act independent of situational forces resides in the desire of many people to believe that they have control over their own lives. This need to believe that the self is relatively uninfluenced by outside forces fosters a misrepresentation of how the social world actually operates.

Gunter Bierbrauer (1979) attempted to eliminate this misperception by having college students either observe a vivid reenactment of the Milgram experiment or play the role of obedient teachers themselves. Despite being exposed to the power that situational factors had in causing high levels of obedience, students still predicted that their friends would be only minimally obedient if they participated in Milgram's study. Despite being confronted by the social psychological facts, these students still essentially believed that only bad people do bad deeds, and good people only do good deeds. The danger in such a view of the social world is that it leaves us wide open to being manipulated by the very social forces we underestimate.

Previous chapters have documented how the self and self-beliefs shape our interpretation and response to our social surroundings. In the matter of social influence, it is our *misinterpretation* of how the social world is constituted that helps to explain how we are so often easily manipulated. If our own self-beliefs were not so firmly based on our power to remain uninfluenced by the wishes, desires, and dictates of others, we might be better able to recognize when we are in danger of falling prey to such social manipulation.

In closing this chapter on social influence, I'd like you to recall the main characters in both Russell Edson's poem, "One Morning," and in the film *The Truman Show,* for they represent two very different reactions to the knowledge of social influence. Upon discovering that he has strings tied to his hands and feet that are controlled from above by a giant hand, the unnamed character in the poem simply says, "Hmmm, that's funny, I never saw that crossbar before. . . . I guess I am a marionette." In contrast to this submission of will to the controlling hand from above, the Truman Burbank character fights to reassert control when he realizes how his life is being so thoroughly managed.

Based on your own newfound knowledge of the social influence process, you are undoubtedly more aware of the social strings to which you too are attached. The "anchor" for these social strings may well be based in an evolutionary past, predisposing you to be naturally receptive to others' influence. Keep in mind, however, that the difference between you and a marionette (and many other animal species) is that, like Truman Burbank, you can reflect on your own actions, and you can analyze the strings that bind you to your social world. Through such analysis, you can become less a puppet of other people's desires and more a coactor in a rich and interlocking web of social intercourse.

SECTION SUMMARY

In attempting to explain the common principles operating in social influence attempts, *social impact theory* has been successful in predicting when people will exert influence over others' actions. It contends that the amount of influence others have is a function of three factors: their number, their strength, and their immediacy. Beyond these factors, another reason we can sometimes be manipulated is simply because we underestimate the inherent power of the situation to shape our behavior.

COULD YOU BE PRESSURED TO FALSELY CONFESS TO A CRIME?

n 1986 following a brutal murder of a woman in Clearwater, Florida, police invited Thomas Sawyer, a neighbor of the victim, to assist them in the investigation. They first flattered Sawyer by asking him to provide his own theory on how the murder occurred, and then used leading questions to shape his responses so that it fit the actual crime. When he was first accused of committing the crime, Sawyer vehemently denied the charge. To support their claim, the police lied to Sawyer about having "a lot of evidence" that implicated him in the murder. After hours of this sort of interrogation, Sawyer began to doubt his innocence, saying, "I honestly believe that I didn't do it. . . . I don't remember doing it. . . . You almost got me convinced I did, but. . . ." Finally, after sixteen hours of interrogation, Sawyer confessed to a crime he did not commit, stating, "I guess all the evidence is in, I guess I must have done it."

Sawyer's nightmare is an excellent example of how unusual influence can sometimes cause *internal compliance* (see p. 272). Internal compliance occurs when police interrogators' influence techniques are so effective that innocent suspects not only confess, but actually come to believe that they are indeed guilty. The influence operating here, namely informational, was observed in Sherif's autokinetic studies on group norm formation described earlier in this chapter. In contrast, false confessions can also occur through *external compliance* (see p. 272), where innocent suspects admit to crimes they know they did not commit in order to avoid further aversive interrogation. This form of normative influence was illustrated in Asch's conformity studies. Do you think you could fall prey to either one of these influence processes if you were a suspect in a crime you didn't commit?

False confessions due to external compliance are generally made by suspects in exchange for penalty reductions (Bordens & Bassett, 1985). Here, their perceptions of the strength of the evidence against them—which police interrogators may highly exaggerate—significantly determines whether they will confess (Moston et al., 1992; Cassell & Hayman, 1996). Of course, many suspects will not falsely confess to a crime regardless of how strong the evidence appears. What distinguishes them from those who do? Not surprisingly,

"resisters" are less susceptible to normative influence in general than are "confessors" (Gudjonsson, 1991).

By far, the most psychologically interesting confession is the one in which innocent defendants—anxious, confused, and desperately trying to make sense out of their current situation—actually come to believe that they committed the crime. This internalization of guilt is closely related to the creation of false memories, a topic extensively studied in cognitive psychology (Read, 1996). For obvious ethical reasons, psychologists cannot attempt to implant false memories of murder or sexual assault in research participants. However, Elizabeth Loftus and

How do you think you would react to long hours of police interrogation, during which you were presented with damaging evidence linking you to a crime? Under such intense pressure from the authorities, are you certain that you would steadfastly maintain your innocence?

James Coan (1995) have successfully implanted less traumatic memories in five research participants ranging in age from 8 to 42. Following Loftus and Coan's instructions, trusted family members told these five individuals that, at age 5, they had been lost in a shopping mall for an extended time before being rescued by an elderly man. Following these suggestions, all participants became convinced that they indeed had been lost. These and other studies demonstrate that false memories can be implanted into the minds of both children and adults (Ceci & Bruck, 1993; Kassin, 1997). In fact, research indicates that simply repeating imaginary events to people causes them to become more confident that they actually experienced these events (Zaragoza & Mitchell, 1996). Once constructed, these false memories may feel as real as—or even more real than—genuine memories (Brainerd et al., 1995). Susceptibility to such false memory construction is especially likely when people have been deprived of sleep, which is often the state of mind of crime suspects who are interrogated late at night (Blagrove, 1996).

How often do false confessions lead to miscarriages of justice? Based on a review of more than four hundred cases in which innocent people were convicted of murder in the United States, Michael Radelet and his colleagues (1992) found that 14 percent (or fifty-six cases) were caused by false confessions. Although this figure is alarming, other research indicates that confessions in general are less important in securing a guilty verdict than is independent evidence. Few convictions are sustained on confession evidence alone, and it's estimated that a defendant's confession is pivotal in only 5 percent of cases (McConville, 1993).

Fortunately, few of you reading this text will ever be falsely accused of murder. However, all of you have been—and will continue to be—falsely accused of less serious transgressions. When facing your accusers, you will stand a better chance of successfully professing your innocence if you keep in mind the lessons of this chapter.

FEATURED STUDY
FALSELY ACCEPTING GUILT

Kassin, S. M., & Kiechel, K. L. (1996). The social psychology of false confessions: Compliance, internalization, and confabulation. *Psychological Science*, 7, 125–128.

Can people be induced to accept guilt for crimes they did not commit? In the present experiment, researchers tested the following two hypotheses: (1) The presentation of false evidence can lead people who are in a heightened state of uncertainty to confess to an act they did not commit, and (2) these "false confessors" will internalize the confession and create details in memory consistent with this new guilt.

METHOD

Seventy-nine college students (forty males and thirty-nine females) participated, for extra course credit, in what they thought was a reaction time experiment. Participants were randomly assigned to one of four experimental conditions involving either high or low vulnerability, and either the presence or absence of a false incriminating witness.

In each session, two people worked together on a computer "reaction" task. One of these people (a female confederate) read aloud a list of letters while the participant typed them on the computer keyboard. Before the session began, the participant was specifically warned not to press the "ALT" key because doing so would cause the program to crash and data to be lost. However, one minute after beginning work on the task, the computer ceased to function, and a highly agitated experimenter accused the participant of having pressed the forbidden key. In reality, the computer was rigged to stop functioning through no fault of the participant. When first accused, all participants denied responsibility for the computer damage. However, in the *false witness* condition, the confederate disputed the participant's denial, testifying that she saw the participant press the forbidden key. In the *no-witness* condition, the confederate did not challenge the participant's denial, but simply stated that she did not see the key pressed. The participant's vulnerability was manipulated by varying the pace of the task. In the *high vulnerability* condition the confederate—following the beat of a metronome—read the letters at a frenzied pace of sixty-seven letters per minute, while in the *low vulnerability* condition the pace was set at a leisurely forty-three letters per minute.

The dependent measures involved three forms of social influence. To measure *external compliance*, the experimenter asked participants to sign a handwritten confession stating that they had hit the ALT key and caused the program to crash. To assess *internal compliance*, participants' private descriptions of what happened—told to a second confederate waiting outside the lab— were recorded and later coded for whether they unambiguously internalized guilt for what happened. To measure the *creation of memories*, participants were also asked by the experimenter to "recall" specific details of how they caused the computer program to crash. At the end of the session, participants were fully and carefully debriefed.

RESULTS AND DISCUSSION

No gender differences were found on any of the dependent measures. Overall, 69 percent of the participants signed the confession, 28 percent exhibited internalization, and 9 percent created memories to support their false beliefs. As expected, participants in the high vulnerability condition were most susceptible to all three forms of social influence following the false accusation. In addition, regardless of the vulnerability condition, participants in the *false witness* conditions not only were more likely to sign a confession prepared by the experimenter, but they were also more likely to later admit their guilt to the second confederate. Finally, participants in the low vulnerability/no-witness condition were the least susceptible to these effects, while those in the high vulnerability/witness condition were the most susceptible. Although the false confessions coerced out of participants in this study are much less dramatic than many of the false confessions squeezed out of suspects in criminal cases, they do demonstrate that people can be induced to erroneously confess to crimes, and to believe in their own guilt, following the presentation of false evidence.

 WEB SITES accessed through http://www.mhhe.com/franzoi2

Web sites for this chapter focus on the psychological study of social influence, examining everyday and interpersonal influence, mindful versus mindless behavior, and the influence tactics used by cults.

Social Influence Web Site

This web site is devoted to the psychological study of social influence, examining everyday and interpersonal influence, mindful versus mindless behavior, and the influence tactics used by cults.

AFF Cult Group Information

This web site contains information about cults, mind control, and psychological manipulation. The recruitment and socialization practices of known cults are discussed, and former cult members tell their personal stories.

Social Psychology Network

Among other things, this large social psychology database offers links to other web sites dealing with social influence including those that discuss marketing and sales techniques, social influence counter-measures, and relevant research.

CHAPTER 9

GROUP BEHAVIOR

n 1978, boyhood friends Jerry Greenfield and Ben Cohen opened a small homemade food shop in a converted gas station in Burlington, Vermont, with the help of a $4,000 bank loan. Their business plan, if you could call it that, was to sell high-quality food in a "fun" way, while using part of their profits to improve the quality of life of the community. Greenfield was given the title of president because they had put Cohen's name first when naming the business. Having little cash to pay for the building's extensive renovations, the two young businessmen promised their building contractor "free food for life" and named him as the third member on their board of directors. Greenfield and Cohen also offered lifetime free food to friends who helped with the renovations. Once open, they even extended their free food offer to a customer who regularly played ragtime and boogie-woogie tunes on the foodshop's decrepit piano. Very quickly, this young business became a popular eating and entertainment spot, showing free summer movies on the outside wall of the store and having annual frog jumping, apple peeling, and stiltwalking contests. The unofficial motto of the business became, "If it's not fun, why do it?" Attracted by this philosophy and the commitment to social responsibility, employees worked long hours for little pay to make the business a success.

Although only a handful of people and two unconventional leaders made up this business group in 1978, twenty years later it employed more than seven hundred people, had 150 franchises, and sold shares of its company on the stock market. True to their commitment to give back to the community, 7.5 percent of annual profits are donated to employee-managed philanthropic causes in this country and abroad. Have you guessed yet what kind of food Cohen and Greenfield serve to their customers? Do their first names, Ben and Jerry, jog your memory? Yes, their product is ice cream. Today, "Ben & Jerry's Homemade" has annual sales over $170 million and is widely regarded as a model for other socially responsible businesses.

How does a collection of individuals like those that initially formed around Ben Cohen and Jerry Greenfield come to perceive themselves as a group? What effect does group membership have on their subsequent thinking and behavior? How does leadership style influence group performance? These are a few of the questions this chapter will address. But first, let's start with the most basic of questions: what is a group?

THE NATURE OF GROUPS

Group

Several interdependent people who have emotional ties and interact on a regular basis.

Although there is little agreement about how to precisely define a **group,** one common definition is that it consists of several interdependent people who have emotional ties, and who interact on a regular basis (Levine & Moreland, 1998; McGrath, 1984). By *interdependence,* I not only mean that members depend on one another to achieve group goals, but events that affect one member affect others as well. Therefore, members of Ben & Jerry's fledgling business not only relied on one another to create new marketing ideas and ice cream flavors, but they each were influenced by fellow members' personal joys and sorrows. Their lives were intertwined.

GROUPS DIFFER IN THEIR SOCIAL COHESIVENESS

Beyond this general definition, groups can be further distinguished by their *social cohesiveness,* or "groupiness." As social cohesion increases, people think, feel, and act more like group members and less like isolated individuals (Fine & Holyfield, 1996). Members of highly cohesive groups have a greater desire to retain their membership than do those in low cohesive groups, and this cohesiveness allows the group to exert more influence on its members, which often leads to greater productivity (Jehn & Shah, 1997; Langfred, 1998). Such cohesiveness epitomized the atmosphere of Ben & Jerry's during its formative years: employees felt like it was "their" company and that together they could make a difference in the world. Two factors that affect group cohesion are *group size* and *member similarity and diversity.*

GROUP SIZE

The size of a group typically changes over time, as witnessed by Ben & Jerry's growth spurt over the past twentysome years. Despite these size variations, the vast majority of groups contain less than four persons (Mullen & Copper, 1994). As a group grows, there's a tendency for member participation to decline, power to become concentrated in the hands of a few, conflicts to increase, and cooperation to decrease (Wagner, 1995; Widmeyer et al., 1995). One possible explanation for this negative relationship between group size and cohesiveness is that large groups simply make it harder for members to control what happens to them (Lawler, 1992). A related explanation is that, as group size increases, members become more selfish and less group-focused because they perceive the impact of their own behavior on group success or failure being weaker and less identifiable (see *social loafing,* pp. 324–326).

MEMBER SIMILARITY AND DIVERSITY

Within groups, members tend to be more similar than different (Jackson et al., 1991). One reason for this similarity characteristic is that membership in most groups involves the performance of specific activities (for example, members of an aerobics class all exercise), and thus, people are drawn toward a specific group because they mutually share an interest in that group's activities. Another reason for within-group similarity is socialization. That is, in the process of socializing new members, attempts are made to mold them to the group's way of thinking and acting (see "There Are Five Phases to Group Membership," pp. 317–319). As discussed in chapter 6 (p. 195), similarity is often the "glue" of affiliation and liking. Thus, it's no surprise that when group members are dissimilar rather than similar, conflict and turnover are more likely (Moreland et al., 1996).

Although member dissimilarity can be dangerous to groups, it can also provide benefits. As group tasks change and become more complex, and as the group's social environment changes, diversity among members gives the group more flexibility in adapting to these changes (Watson et al., 1993). For example, as North American culture has become more diverse and complex, many successful businesses have recognized the need to increase the diversity of their employees to better meet the needs of their customers. Research suggests that the negative effects of diversity can be minimized by educating members about their similarities and differences, encouraging tolerance, and improving social skills (Caudron, 1994). Recognizing that there are benefits to group diversity, homogeneous groups often try to *simulate diversity* by instructing some members to act as "devil's advocates" so that majority-held opinions will be challenged and critically analyzed (see *groupthink,* pp. 335–337). What these findings suggest is that, although similarity tends to promote group cohesion, diversity can promote flexibility in group functioning.

GROUP STRUCTURE DEVELOPS QUICKLY AND CHANGES SLOWLY

One characteristic upon which groups differ is *structure,* which are the regular, stable patterns of behavior between members (Wilke, 1996). These group behavior patterns generally develop quickly and change slowly. Consider, for example, the loose management structure at Ben & Jerry's compared with the high structure at most major corporations. Monthly board meetings were occasionally held in Ben's swimming pool and the lines of authority within the company were only vaguely defined. When the company needed to hire a new corporate executive officer in 1995, they held a national "Yo! I Want To Be CEO!" contest in which people were urged to send in 100-word applications.

In analyzing the structure of groups, social psychologists have identified a number of common elements. Three of the more important ones are social norms, social roles, and status systems.

SOCIAL NORMS

As defined in chapter 8, *social norms* are expected standards of behavior and belief established and enforced by a group. Some groups have norms for personal appearance (for example, shaved heads for Marine recruits), others have norms for opinions (for example, liberal views in environmental organizations), and most have norms for behavior (for example, profanity is forbidden in school classrooms). Sometimes, these norms are formally conveyed to group members in written guidelines, but most often, they are learned through everyday conversations or observing other members (Miller & Prentice, 1996). As demonstrated by Sherif's classic studies (see chapter 8), once norms are established, they tend to be stable over time, despite changes in group membership. Although social norms certainly increase conformity and reduce deviancy within groups, they also can enhance performance when structured in such a way as to reward effort, efficiency, and quality (Seashore, 1954).

SOCIAL ROLES

As defined in chapter 2, *social roles* are clusters of socially defined expectations that individuals in a given situation are expected to fulfill. In a group, roles often define the division of labor, and well-defined roles improve group dynamics and

Groups often differ in terms of the degree to which their norms, roles, and status systems are articulated. For example, monthly Ben & Jerry corporate board meetings occasionally took place in Ben's swimming pool. Can you imagine a similar group structure at IBM or the U.S. Supreme Court?

performance (Barley & Bechky, 1994). In some cases, social roles *evolve* during group interaction, while at other times, people *import* a role into their new group that they enjoyed playing in previous groups (Rose, 1994). For instance, if you were known as a "good listener" in your high school friendship groups, you may import this role into your college friendships. Likewise, others may try to shape their "comedian" friendship role into the "class clown" role at school.

STATUS SYSTEMS

The third aspect of group structure is its *status system,* which reflects the distribution of power among members (Robinson & Balkwell, 1995). Even in groups that don't have formal status systems, such as friendship cliques, members often differ in their prestige and authority. One way you can tell who has higher status in a group is by paying attention to verbal and nonverbal behavior: higher status members maintain greater eye contact, stand more erect, are more likely to criticize, command, or interrupt others, and not only speak more often, but they are also spoken to more often than those of lower status (Leffler, 1982). Although status can be *achieved* by helping a group reach its goals (Cohen & Zhou, 1991), it is often *ascribed* rather than earned: people are given higher status simply because of who or what they are (Ridgeway, 1991).

How exactly are these status differences created in the first place? According to Joseph Berger's **expectation states theory,** when group members first meet, they form expectations about each other's probable contributions to the achievement of group goals (Berger et al., 1985). These expectations are not only based on members' *task-relevant characteristics,* such as social skills and past experience, but also on *diffuse status characteristics,* such as race, sex, age, and wealth (Balkwell & Berger, 1996; Wittenbaum, 1998). Those members whose characteristics produce higher expectations in fellow members are assigned higher status in the group. Thus, for example, White, middle-aged, wealthy men might be perceived as better potential leaders by other group members than young, poor, Hispanic women. Although these initial status assignments can be later modified based on actual performance, members who are unfairly given an initially low status will have trouble proving their worth to the group (Ridgeway, 1982).

THERE ARE FIVE PHASES TO GROUP MEMBERSHIP

An important, and often overlooked, characteristic of group membership is that it is a *dynamic* process involving different *phases.* In an attempt to better understand this process, Richard Moreland and John Levine (1988) have examined not only how people are changed through their membership in a group, but also how the group is changed by members' ideas and actions. Three psychological processes that propel people into and out of groups are the *ongoing evaluations* the individual and the group make of one another, the *feelings of commitment* that follows these evaluations, and the *role transitions* that result from these changes in commitment (Moreland et al., 1993). The two faces of evaluation that occur during the course of group membership involve (1) the degree to which the individual meets the needs of the group, and (2) the degree to which the group meets the needs of the individual.

According to Moreland and Levine, the passage of the individual through the group generally occurs in an ordered set of five phases, with each phase associated with a different social role played by the individual. The movement from one membership phase to the next represents a role transition. In figure 9.1, the line of the bell-shaped curve represents the personal history of someone passing through all five phases of group membership. As people move up the line, their commitment to the group and the group's commitment to them strengthens. However, as they move down the line, this mutual commitment weakens.

In the *investigation phase,* the group seeks people who seem likely to be able to attain group goals, and prospective members look for groups that provide the

By whom?

U.S. critic Dorothy Parker, when told she was outspoken, 1893–1967

Expectation States Theory

A theory that states that the development of group status is based on members' expectations of others' probable contributions to the achievement of group goals. These expectations are shaped not only by members' task-relevant characteristics, but also by diffuse status characteristics, such as race, sex, age, and wealth.

CRITICAL *thinking*

In chapter 7 you learned how ingroup biases can lead to prejudice and discrimination. How might this knowledge help you better understand the process by which the *diffuse status characteristics* of group members significantly determines their power in the group?

FIGURE 9.1

A Temporal Model of Group Membership

Based on Moreland and Levine's (1982) model of the phases of group membership, in what phase is commitment the greatest?

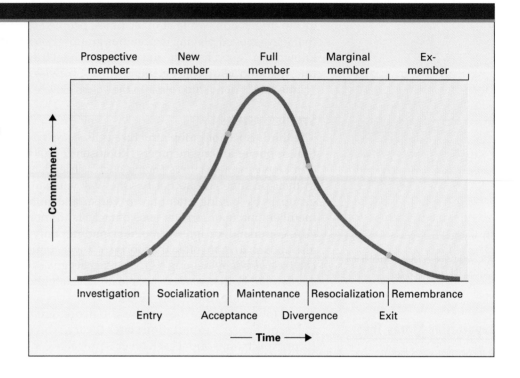

I don't care to belong to any club that will have me as a member.

Groucho Marx, U.S. comedian, 1875–1977

opportunity to satisfy personal needs. If both the individual's and the group's commitment levels are sufficiently strong, a prospective member enters the group. Although many groups have low entrance criteria and continually admit new members, other groups establish strict criteria and only periodically allow others to join. For these more formal groups, the entry of new members is almost always accompanied by some ceremony that acknowledges the newly established relationship between the group and the individual. Although many factors influence a group's tendency to be relatively open or closed to new members, groups that are unsuccessful or understaffed at key positions tend to be more accepting of new members than those that are successful or overstaffed (Cini et al., 1993).

In the *socialization phase*, the group tries to shape the new members' thinking and behavior so that they can and will make the maximum contribution to the group (Levine & Moreland, 1994). Groups accomplish this task through formal and informal indoctrination sessions and through "coaches" who model the appropriate thinking and behaviors (Shuval & Adler, 1980). While this socialization process is taking place the new members often try to change the group so that it will accommodate their needs. The socialization phase ends when the individual's and the group's commitment levels increase so that the individual becomes a full member of the group.

During the *maintenance phase,* the group attempts to define specialized roles for full members that maximizes their contributions to the group's goals. In contrast, the full members often try to define their roles in the group to maximize personal needs. If the social influence that both parties exert results in a mutually satisfying agreement on the full member's role, commitment is increased on both sides. However, if role negotiation fails, both the member and the group will regard the relationship as less rewarding, and commitment to one another will decrease. The individual will now be viewed as a marginal member.

When full group members are relabeled as marginal, they enter the *resocialization phase,* in which both parties once again try to persuade the other to meet their expectations. If the group or the individual succeeds in convincing the other to accept their role expectations, or if a mutually agreeable compromise can be

For many student groups on college campuses (for example, political and religious groups, service organizations), new members are continuously accepted with little fanfare and few entrance criteria. In more formal groups, such as fraternities and sororities, prospective members are often admitted only during designated times, and only after being closely scrutinized and voted in by full members. A formal induction ceremony usually ushers these new members into the group.

struck, the marginal member will once again be regarded as a full member. As figure 9.1 shows, this essentially means that the person moves backward on the curve toward a higher commitment level. If, however, no agreement can be reached, the individual's and the group's commitment levels will fall even further, prompting the individual to exit the group. In the resulting *remembrance phase*, the group develops a consensus concerning the ex-member's contributions to the group's goals, and similarly, the ex-member reminisces about the benefits and costs of being a member of the group.

How does this model fit your experiences with various groups in your own life? Undoubtedly, many of you are currently associated with various groups and are in different phases of membership with many of them. A number of the social psychological processes that unfold in the different phases of group membership, such as majority and minority influence, have been discussed in chapter 8. Perhaps some of you have also noticed that the dynamics of group membership bears a striking similarity to the dynamics of romantic relationships which we will discuss in chapter 11. The reason for this is simple: romantic relationships are often considered to be a type of group—the intimate dyad.

One last comment. Because American social psychologists developed this theory, its depiction of the phases of group membership has an individualist bent to it. That is, there is an assumption that members conceive of their own personal goals as often diverging from group goals. In a collectivist culture, phases of group membership would be less affected by individual-group tensions (Abrams et al., 1998; Markus & Kitayama, 1994).

GROUPS ACCOMPLISH INSTRUMENTAL TASKS AND SATISFY SOCIOEMOTIONAL NEEDS

Have you ever wondered why people join groups? Existing evidence suggests that they do so for several reasons, all of which can be traced to the accomplishment of *instrumental* tasks and the satisfaction of *socioemotional* or expressive needs (Schachter, 1959). Put simply, people often join groups because they desire to achieve certain task-oriented goals that they cannot attain alone. For example, you will have a much better chance of extinguishing the fire in a burning

The two principal functions of groups are to accomplish tasks and to deal with emotional and social relationships. Would you guess that this group has more of a task orientation or a socioemotional orientation?

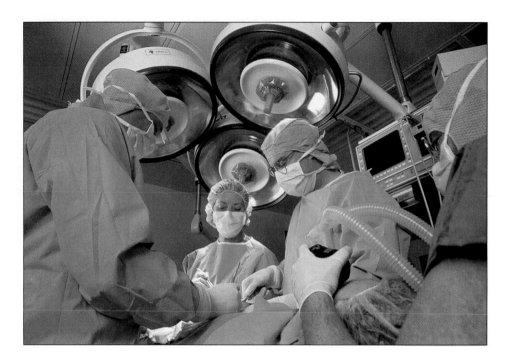

When spiders unite, they can tie down a lion.

Ethiopian proverb

building or of finding shelter for the homeless if you pursue these tasks within the supportive network of a group. In addition, becoming a group member provides people with the opportunity to satisfy such affiliative motives as the desire for approval, belonging, prestige, friendship, and even love. These mutual desires for task accomplishment and emotional fulfillment in a group setting are observed across many species and are an integral part of our evolutionary heritage.

The work of Robert Bales, which began in the late 1940s, suggests that *accomplishing tasks* and *dealing with emotional and social relationships* are indeed the two principal functions of groups (Bales, 1970; Bales & Slater, 1955). Some groups are primarily task-oriented, while others are principally constituted to foster social relationships. Examples of *task-oriented* groups are work groups, such as a surgical team operating on a patient or factory workers assembling automobiles. Examples of *socioemotional* groups are friendship and family groups nurturing and emotionally supporting fellow members or neighbors organizing a summer block party.

Although some groups can be identified as more oriented toward one function than the other, almost all groups engage in at least some degree of both task and socioemotional activity. Indeed, Bales contends that this continual oscillation between task and socioemotional activities is what characterizes group process. As a group engages in task-oriented activities, members' feelings tend to be neglected, and this inattention creates group tension in the socioemotional area. However, when the group attempts to reduce these socioemotional tensions by paying more attention to members' feelings, task goals become temporarily sidetracked and this, in turn, creates task tension. According to Bales, groups constantly strive to strike a proper balance between their attention to task and socioemotional concerns so that they can keep group tension to a minimum. For example, imagine that in the process of pushing to complete a group project in one of your classes, you rub some of your classmates the wrong way. To try to restore group cohesion, you might bring a bag of doughnuts to class or do something else that will salve emotional hurts.

Two heads are better than one.

North American folk saying

SECTION SUMMARY

A *group* consists of several interdependent people who have emotional ties, and who interact on a regular basis. Every group has a *structure*, consisting of social norms, social roles, and status systems. The passage of the individual through the group generally occurs in an ordered set of five phases, with each phase associated with a different social role played by the individual. The two main functions of groups are to accomplish instrumental tasks and satisfy socioemotional needs.

GROUP INFLUENCE ON INDIVIDUAL BEHAVIOR

If one of the main functions of groups is to perform tasks, what factors influence the ability of people to successfully engage in task activities? In this section, we will examine how the presence of others affects a person's work performance. The two types of situations to be investigated are: (1) an individual performing an activity in the presence of an audience (*social facilitation*), and (2) an individual performing an activity as part of a larger group of performers (*social loafing*). Finally, we will also examine how both being aroused and being hidden in the group can loosen one's behavioral inhibitions.

SOCIAL FACILITATION ENHANCES EASY TASKS AND INHIBITS DIFFICULT TASKS

As discussed in chapter 1, Norman Triplett (1897) conducted one of the first social psychological experiments to determine whether task performance was enhanced or inhibited by the presence of others. Subsequent experiments during the first quarter of the twentieth century found that the presence of others enhances the speed with which people perform relatively simple tasks but inhibits task efficiency in more complex activities (Allport, 1920; Travis, 1925). This *social facilitation* effect, as it came to be called, was also found in other animals, such as dogs, rats, birds, fish, and even ants and cockroaches (Chen, 1937; Gates & Allee, 1933). Although researchers extensively documented these divergent effects through the 1930s and 1940s, no one could explain *why* the presence of others would sometimes enhance and sometimes hinder individual performance. This explanatory conundrum ultimately led to a loss of interest in social facilitation as a research topic.

THE MERE-PRESENCE EXPLANATION

In the mid-1960s, Robert Zajonc (1965) renewed the field's interest in social facilitation by proposing a theory to reconcile the contradictory findings. His social facilitation theory involved three basic propositions or steps (see figure 9.2). First, he argued that all animals (including humans) are genetically predisposed to become physiologically aroused when around *conspecifics* (members of one's own species). This is so, he believed, because animals receive most of their rewards and punishments in life from conspecifics, and through the process of evolution have developed an innate arousal response due to their *mere presence*. Second, resurrecting an old behaviorist principle of learning (Hull, 1943), Zajonc stated that this physiological arousal enhances the performance of whatever response tendency is dominant (that is, well learned) in an animal. Third, and last, he contended that for well-learned tasks the correct responses are also the dominant responses, but for

FIGURE 9.2

Zajonc's Drive Theory of Social Facilitation

According to Zajonc (1965), the presence of other people increases arousal, which, in turn, enhances the performance of dominant responses. If the dominant responses are correct, performance will also be enhanced. However, if the dominant responses are incorrect, performance will be inhibited. Can you think of instances from your own life in which the presence of others had these two contrasting effects on your performance of different types of tasks?

Source: Adapted from R. B. Zajonc, "Social Facilitation" in *Science, 149*:269–274, American Association for the Advancement of Science, 1965.

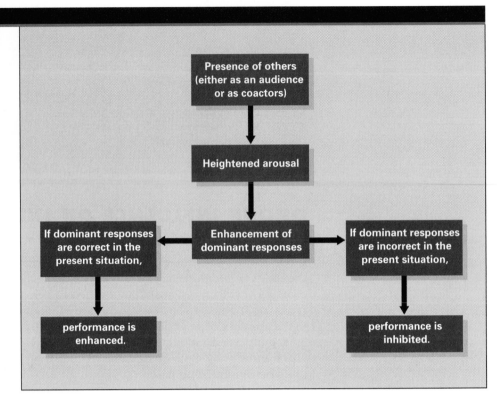

Social Facilitation

The enhancement of dominant responses due to the presence of others.

novel, unlearned tasks the dominant responses are the incorrect ones. What this means is that the presence of others will enhance correct execution of well-learned tasks, at the same time that it will interfere with or inhibit correct performance of novel, unlearned tasks.

Zajonc argued that when we perform a simple task like hand clapping, the mere presence of an audience increases our arousal, eliciting the dominant response, and we clap more vigorously than when we are alone and not aroused. Now, if instead, we calculated difficult math problems in front of others, our increased arousal would inhibit execution of this task because the correct answers are not dominant responses. They would only be dominant responses if we had them memorized. Taken together, these two different effects due to the presence of others—enhancement of correct performance on easy tasks and inhibition of correct performance on difficult tasks—are known as **social facilitation.** The reason the same term is used for both effects is that on both easy and difficult tasks, the performance of the dominant response is *facilitated* in others' presence. For easy tasks the correct response is dominant, and thus, the person's performance is enhanced. Yet for difficult tasks the correct response is not dominant, hence the decline in performance efficiency.

Numerous studies have been conducted to either specifically test Zajonc's theory or to more generally examine social facilitation. Two separate meta-analyses of more than three hundred experiments involving more than twenty-five thousand participants indicates that social facilitation does indeed exist (Bond & Titus, 1983; Guerin, 1986). For example, in one study of pool players in a college student union, researchers first unobtrusively identified those who were either above or below average in their ability to make shots (Michaels et al., 1982). After recording their shooting accuracy without an audience present, the researchers had four confederates walk up and closely watch these students play several more rounds. Results indicated that the good players' accuracy in making shots increased with an audience present (from 71 percent to 80 percent), while poor players' performances deteriorated (from 36 percent to 25 percent).

THE EVALUATION-APPREHENSION EXPLANATION

Although there is little dispute that the presence of others increases individual arousal, there is a good deal of debate concerning the nature of this arousal. Some have contended that rather than being due to the mere presence of others, arousal is a result of *evaluation apprehension*—concern over being judged by others (Aiello & Svec, 1993; Cottrell, 1972). In one study supporting this explanation, participants worked on a task either alone, in the presence of confederates who were also working on the task, or in the presence of blindfolded confederates who supposedly were preparing for a perception experiment (Cottrell et al., 1968). Results found that participants working on the task in the company of "seeing" confederates exhibited social facilitation effects when compared with those working alone. Both the evaluation-apprehension and the mere-presence explanations would predict this outcome. However, in the presence of blindfolded confederates, there was no evidence for social facilitation. Participants' dominant responses did not differ from those who were alone. Because the blindfolded confederates were physically present but could not evaluate the performance of participants, these findings support the evaluation-apprehension explanation at the same time they contradict the mere-presence explanation. Similar effects were found in other studies in which observers were present but not evaluating an individual's performance (Worringham & Messick, 1983). According to the evaluation-apprehension perspective, if people are present but not attending to another person's task performance, their presence is unlikely to produce social facilitation effects.

THE DISTRACTION-CONFLICT EXPLANATION

As appealing as the evaluation-apprehension explanation is, there seem to be social facilitation effects it cannot explain. Recall that social facilitation has been observed in such animals as ants and cockroaches. Does this mean that insects "worry" about other insects evaluating them? Because this possibility is unlikely, other social scientists have contended that heightened arousal is simply caused by a conflict between two tendencies (Baron, 1986). This *distraction-conflict theory* states that when an animal (human or other) is working on a task in the presence of other conspecifics, it experiences conflict regarding whether to attend to their companions or the task at hand. Distraction-conflict theorists contend that it is this conflict, and this conflict alone, that induces heightened arousal. Because conflict is a well-documented source of arousal, this perspective can explain both human and nonhuman social facilitation effects. In addition to social stimuli (that is, conspecifics) causing conflict, and thus arousal, the distraction-conflict theory hypothesizes that nonsocial objects that distract a performer can also induce conflict. True to this contention, loud noises and flashing lights have been found to produce the same enhancement/impairment effects produced by the presence of others (Pessin, 1933; Sanders & Baron, 1975). Therefore, the one advantage that the distraction-conflict theory has over the other two explanations is that it can explain task enhancement both in social and nonsocial settings (see figure 9.3).

Given the research discussed with the three theories of social facilitation, can we declare that one of them is clearly the best explanation of this phenomenon? Although the distraction-conflict theory can explain some instances of social facilitation that the other two theories cannot, no direct evidence indicates that conflict alone induces the heightened arousal we find in social situations. It is still possible, then, that conflict and evaluation apprehension just add to the arousal produced by mere presence. Currently, then, the most prudent conclusion to draw is that each theory adds to our understanding of social facilitation: others can affect our performance (1) by just being there, (2) as evaluators, and (3) by distracting us (Kent, 1996).

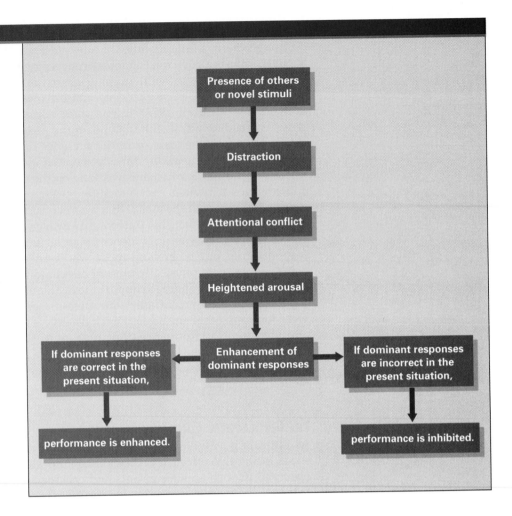

FIGURE 9.3

Distraction-Conflict Theory

According to the distraction-conflict theory, when one is working on a task, the presence of others or the presence of novel stimuli is distracting. This distraction produces a conflict between paying attention to the task and paying attention to these stimuli. This conflict causes arousal to increase, which leads to the social facilitation effects previously discussed.

Source: Adapted from R. S. Baron, "Distraction-Conflict Theory: Progress and Problems" in L. Berkowitz (Ed.), *Advances in Experimental Social Psychology*, 19:1–40, Academic Press, 1986.

Social Loafing

Group-induced reduction in individual output when performers' efforts are pooled and, thus, cannot be individually judged.

SOCIAL LOAFING OCCURS WHEN OUR INDIVIDUAL OUTPUT BECOMES "LOST IN THE CROWD"

Social facilitation research identifies the conditions under which the presence of others can motivate individuals to enhance their performance. Usually this enhancement occurs when a person's efforts can be individually evaluated. Yet, what if the performers' efforts are *pooled* so that individually judging them is difficult or even impossible? Do you know what often happens? If you guessed that individuals work less hard under these conditions than when performing alone, you are correct. This group-induced reduction in individual output is known as **social loafing** (Karau & Williams, 1995).

EARLY AND CONTEMPORARY RESEARCH

The first empirical study suggesting such an effect was conducted in the 1880s by French agricultural engineer Max Ringelman (1913). He found that people's efforts pulling on a rope or pushing a cart were less when they worked in a group than when they performed these tasks alone. More recently, social loafing has been documented in a host of behaviors. For example, Bibb Latané and his associates (1979) had six blindfolded college students sit in a semicircle and wear headphones that blasted sounds of people shouting into their ears. The students' task was to shout as loud as possible while listening to the headphone noise. On some trials, they believed that the five other students were also shouting, while on other trials they believed they were either shouting alone or with only one other person. In actuality, on all these trials only one student was performing. Consistent with what

Because of the diffusion of responsibility, people who perform a task as part of a group often exert themselves less than when they perform the task alone in front of others. How can the likelihood of social loafing be reduced?

you would expect due to social loafing, when students thought one other person was yelling, they shouted 82 percent as intensely as when alone, and when they believed everyone was yelling, they shouted 75 percent as intensely.

Social loafing is not restricted to simple motor tasks like rope pulling or cheering; it also takes place when people perform cognitive tasks (Weldon & Gargano, 1988). In addition, cross-cultural research (Gabrenya et al., 1985) indicates that social loafing occurs in both individualist and collectivist societies, although the effect is not as strong in the latter (Karau & Williams, 1993).

What might explain social loafing? A likely explanation is that when people work in a group, they realize that their individual output will be "lost in the crowd." As a result, they feel less personally responsible for the outcome, and their performance effort declines (Comer, 1995). The cognitive process that group performers go through in feeling less personally responsible for task outcomes is known as the **diffusion of responsibility,** and in chapter 13 (pp. 497–498) we will examine how it causes a variation of social loafing, namely, bystanders to an emergency failing to aid victims.

Diffusion of Responsibility

The belief that the presence of other people in a situation makes one less personally responsible for the events that occur in that situation.

REDUCING SOCIAL LOAFING

If social loafing is truly caused by a diffusion of responsibility, then it is also true that social loafing is not an inevitable consequence of people working together in groups. That is, if people's individual efforts can be judged while they work on a group task, they shouldn't lose personal responsibility for their actions, and there should be no social loafing. This is exactly what was found in a variation of the cheering study (Williams et al., 1981). Here, as before, participants shouted alone or in groups. In some conditions, shouters were led to believe that their individual performance was being monitored; in other conditions they believed their output was never identifiable. Results indicated that if participants believed their individual shouting was being monitored, no performance dropoff occurred in a group context. This study suggests that when group performers cannot conceal minimal effort from observers, social loafing is unlikely.

The fact that social loafing is greatly reduced when individual effort can be identified and evaluated suggests that evaluation apprehension can curtail minimal effort. But what if performers in a group are made aware of their own individual efforts or those of the group in comparison with a social standard without others being privy to this information? Would this private information still reduce social loafing on their part? Research indicates that it does (Harkins & Szymanski, 1989). What this finding suggests is that it isn't necessary to convince individuals that their efforts will be identified by others. Simply providing them with a standard to evaluate their own performance, or even that of the entire group, is often sufficient to prevent social loafing. Thus, providing the potential for *evaluation*—even if it is only self-evaluation—seems to be the key to reduce the loss of individual output on a group task.

Although informing group members of the potential for evaluation may generally reduce loafing, how should "known" social loafers be handled? Short of physically rejecting lazy workers from the group, one common technique to increase their output is to socially shun them until they conform to the group productivity norm. Yet is such *social ostracism* effective? In one recent experiment, Kipling Williams and Kristin Sommer (1997) found that the effectiveness of this technique was different for female and male loafers. The women loafers reacted to social ostracism by socially acknowledging their feelings of rejection and openly questioning their own attractiveness and abilities. When given a chance to get back into the good graces of the group, the women worked hard to do so. In contrast, the men appeared to cope with ostracism by redirecting their interests toward nontask objects in their surroundings. Also, their concern for impression management caused the men to hide their emotions and to reinterpret the situation: they tended to perceive their separation from the group as being due to their own personal choice rather than something imposed on them. By engaging in these face-saving coping strategies, the men now had a lower need to seek the group's approval, and hence, they were more likely to continue loafing. Williams and Sommer speculate that these gender differences are due to most societies socializing women to be emotionally expressive and men to be nonexpressive. That is, women's learned response of attending to and expressing their emotions enhances the effectiveness of social ostracism as a control technique. For men, however, their learned response of directing their attention away from their emotions to other environmental stimuli dilutes the effectiveness of ostracism. What these findings suggest is that, although social ostracism may be an effective control strategy for social loafing in people who regularly attend to and publicly express their emotions, it may be ineffective for those who are psychologically invested in controlling any such public displays.

CAN ANONYMITY SOMETIMES IMPROVE GROUP PERFORMANCE?

So far, all the group activities resulting in social loafing that we have examined involved simple tasks. But if evaluation apprehension—either of the "social" or "self" variety—is the key to social loafing, then would working together at a complex, poorly learned task lower evaluation apprehension and, therefore, lead to better individual performance? Researchers addressed this question in a study in which people worked on a complex computer maze alongside a coworker (Jackson & Williams, 1985). In one condition, participants were led to believe that their scores would be combined with their coworker's so that no single performance could be identified. In another condition, they were told their individual scores would be identifiable. Results indicated that participants performed better on this complex task when they believed their individual efforts would *not* be evaluated than when they thought they would be. These interesting findings suggest that under conditions that usually produce social loafing (when one's individual efforts seemingly cannot be identified and evaluated) performance can actually be enhanced. Again, as before, the key to understanding this effect is that group performance allows task outcome responsibility to be diffused among fellow coactors. On simple tasks this reduction in evaluation apprehension causes decreased output by individual actors. However, on poorly learned tasks the reduction in evaluation apprehension—and presumably arousal—allows more careful concentration on the task at hand.

CRITICAL *thinking*

Imagine that you have been hired to design a training course to teach company employees how to efficiently use a complex computer program. How can you use the findings of social loafing research to help you design a training course that not only facilitates quick learning, but also encourages high productivity following learning?

DEINDIVIDUATION INVOLVES THE LOSS OF INDIVIDUAL IDENTITY

One Halloween night a few years ago, I heard a noise outside my house. Looking out the window, I saw a group of teenagers in masks and costumes carrying pumpkins—my pumpkins. I quickly went to the front porch and noticed that my lamppost light had been shattered by one of the pumpkins being thrown against it. Although I was barefoot and dressed in pajamas, I gave chase after these "hooligans." As I sprinted toward them, they took off running. They ran faster than I sprinted and I abruptly gave up the chase. When I ended my pursuit they stopped, too, and turned back to check me out. Standing there in the cold and the dark, it suddenly dawned on me that I was their "old geezer"—the feeble, angry man who chases pranksters on Halloween night. At that moment, memories of my own youthful Halloween escapades came back to haunt me. Like me years ago, these "hooligans" were normally well-behaved adolescents who had been caught up in a one night antisocial neighborhood romp. What caused them (and me, at that age) to act this way? Have you ever been in a similar situation and later wondered why you behaved so contrary to acceptable standards?

GROUP-INDUCED LOWERING OF INHIBITIONS

Social facilitation research demonstrates that groups can arouse us. Social loafing studies indicate that groups can also diffuse responsibility and lower evaluation apprehension. What happens when groups diffuse responsibility and lower evaluation apprehension at the same time that they arouse us? In such circumstances, our normal inhibitions may diminish, and we may engage in behaviors we normally avoid. This state of mind has come to be called **deindividuation.**

Deindividuation

The loss of individual identity and a loosening of normal inhibitions against engaging in behavior that is inconsistent with internal standards.

Deindividuation not only helps to explain the vandalism of many Halloween pranksters, but it also provides insight into other forms of collective antisocial behavior. Philip Zimbardo (1969) outlined the antecedents and consequences of a deindividuated state, noting that important contributing factors are *arousal, anonymity,* and *diffused responsibility.* Zimbardo argued that when people become deindividuated—by a combination of these factors—their inhibitions will be lowered and they will be much more likely to impulsively engage in such antisocial behavior as vandalism, aggression, and rioting. Steven Prentice-Dunn and Ronald Rogers (1980) believe that *accountability cues,* such as anonymity, tell people how far they can go without being held responsible for their actions. These cues loosen restraints against deviant behavior by altering a person's *cost-reward calculations.* For example, during a riot, people often think they won't be caught and punished for engaging in illegal activities, and it is this reassessment of the costs and rewards that lowers their inhibitions. Although early investigators (Festinger et al., 1952) believed that deindividuation occurred only in groups, later research indicated that it could also be induced outside of a collective (Mullen, 1986).

One example of deindividuation causing antisocial consequences is when onlookers goad people who are threatening suicide. For example, while writing this chapter, I read a newspaper account of a distraught truck driver who committed suicide in his truck after passing motorists used citizens band radios to egg him on when they learned he was threatening to shoot himself. Similarly, in an analysis of newspaper accounts of people witnessing someone threatening suicide by jumping from a building or bridge, Leon Mann (1981) found that when a crowd of onlookers was large or "masked" by darkness (that is, deindividuated) they often jeered and encouraged the person to jump. Although large crowds and darkness facilitated the antisocial actions of onlookers during suicide attempts, when people were more easily identifiable—small crowds exposed by daylight—Mann found that they generally did not jeer the would-be jumper.

Because Halloween festivities tend to deindividuate celebrants, it's not surprising that researchers have used this annual event to investigate this process.

FIGURE 9.4

Effects of Deindividuation on Stealing Among Halloween Trick-or-Treaters

When trick-or-treating in a group or when anonymous, children were more likely to take extra Halloween candy. However, when both of these factors were present (group immersion and anonymity), candy stealing rose dramatically. What do these results tell us about the effects that deindividuation have on people's normal inhibitions?

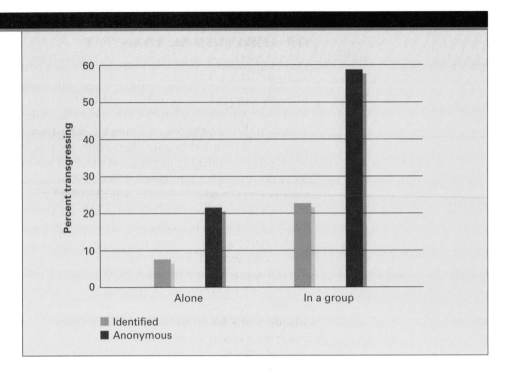

In one such study, Ed Diener and his colleagues (1976) set up testing sights in twenty-seven homes throughout Seattle and waited for young trick-or-treaters to come calling. Some children arrived alone, and others came in groups. On some trials, the experimenter asked the children their names and where they lived, and on other trials they remained anonymous. Then, the experimenter showed the children a bowl of candy and told them to "take *one* of the candies." They were then left alone with the candy bowl while hidden observers recorded how much candy the children actually took. The researchers discovered that children in a group were more than twice as likely to take extra candy than those who were alone. In addition, children who remained anonymous were also more than twice as likely to take more than one piece of candy than those who identified themselves. As you can see in figure 9.4, the greatest candy stealing occurred when children were in a group and remained anonymous.

CAN DEINDIVIDUATION UNLEASH POSITIVE BEHAVIOR?

If deindividuation causes us to act more impulsively, could it also unleash prosocial behavior that we might normally inhibit? In an investigation of this question, Kenneth Gergen and his coworkers (1973) individually ushered eight college students—four women and four men—into a totally darkened room, where they were to spend the next hour. None of these students knew one another and all were told, "There are no rules as to what you should do together. At the end you will be escorted alone from the room and there will be no opportunity to meet the other individuals." A control group spent a similar hour in a lighted room. If you were in the "dark room" group, how do you think you would respond? Remember, no one knows your name and no one can even see you.

In this deindividuated state, "dark room" participants' affiliation desires were unleashed. They talked less than the control group, but they rated their conversations as more important. Ninety percent purposefully touched others, 50 percent hugged, and some even kissed. No one in the control group engaged in any of these activities. Few of the "dark room" participants disliked their experience—in fact, most enjoyed it immensely, and many asked if they could participate again without pay! What this study and others indicate is that dein-

These trick-or-treaters may exhibit deindividuation: they may be more likely to "sneak" extra candy if their costumes or their group make them feel anonymous and less self-aware. What is a simple way to "individuate" them?

dividuation can encourage prosocial as well as antisocial behavior (Johnson & Downing, 1979; Spivey & Prentice-Dunn, 1990). Which type of behavior will occur depends on whether the situation encourages positive or negative actions.

DEINDIVIDUATION AND REDUCED SELF-AWARENESS

In explaining deindividuation, Diener (1980) argued that the crucial cognitive factor is a lack of self-awareness. Without such self-awareness, the deindividuated don't think of themselves as separate individuals and do not attend to their own inner values and behavioral standards (see chapter 2 for a discussion of self-awareness effects). To test this hypothesis, he and his coworkers conducted a second Halloween study in which, as before, experimenters waited for young trick-or-treaters to arrive to request candy (Beaman et al., 1979). After asking the children to give their names, they were told to take only one candy each and were then left alone by the candy bowl. On some trials, a mirror was placed behind the bowl so that when the children reached for the candy they saw their own image in the mirror. On other trials, no mirror was present. As you may recall from chapter 2, a mirror induces self-awareness, a psychological state in which one is aware of oneself as an object of attention and is also more attentive to behavioral standards. In such a state, one is not deindividuated. Not surprisingly, in the *mirror present* condition, only 12 percent of the children took extra candy, yet when the mirror was absent, candy stealing increased to 34 percent. These results, and those of other investigations, suggest that *reduced self-awareness* is a component of deindividuation (Diener & Wallbom, 1976; Prentice-Dunn & Rogers, 1982): the deindividuated lose their sense of personal identity in a group by not engaging in self-awareness. Here, as in other aspects of social behavior discussed throughout the text, people abdicate their personal standards of conduct and fall prey to the influence of the immediate situation when they fail to take themselves as objects of attention.

AN ALTERNATIVE EXPLANATION FOR DEINDIVIDUATION

Throughout the past fortysome years of deindividuation research, the prevailing view has been that it is an expression of antinormative and disinhibited behavior caused by a loss of personal identity. Recently, however, Dutch social psychologists

Tom Postmes and Russell Spears (1998) have proposed that what we call antinormative and disinhibited behavior in such situations may actually be a behavioral expression of *conformity* to group norms specific to the situation. They base their arguments on a meta-analysis of sixty studies in which deindividuation effects were found to be relatively small and most likely to occur in groups. Arguing from a social identity perspective (see chapter 2), Postmes and Spears assert that deindividuating settings do not lead to a loss of personal identity and an acting on impulse, but instead, they facilitate a transition from a personal to a more social identity. The so-called antinormative behavior is really an expression of whatever group norm is salient in the situation. Whether they are taking extra candy and stealing pumpkins as Halloween pranksters or touching and hugging strangers in a pitch-black room, the deindividuated are simply conforming to the prevailing group norm of the moment.

At present, Postmes and Spears's counterexplanation of deindividuation is best thought of as a "fly in the soup" of the prevailing view of this phenomenon. Future research will determine whether this particular fly is simply plucked out of the bowl or the soup is actually set aside in favor of an improved recipe. Such flies in the soup of scientific theory are what advance our knowledge.

SECTION SUMMARY

How does the presence of others affect individual behavior? In *social facilitation*, it enhances performance on easy tasks and inhibits performance on difficult tasks. It appears that others affect our performance by just being there, as evaluators, and by distracting us. In *social loafing*, the presence of coperformers reduces individual output. The key to understanding this effect is that group performance allows task outcome responsibility to be diffused among fellow coactors. Finally, in certain circumstances, people's normal inhibitions diminish due to a loss of individual identity, and they experience what has come to be called *deindividuation*. By inducing anonymity and reducing self-awareness, deindividuation can unleash both prosocial and antisocial tendencies.

DECISION MAKING IN GROUPS

The observation that groups sometimes influence people to behave in ways that are antisocial has been pointed to by some social scientists as evidence that people in groups think and behave more irrationally than they would alone. Although this belief in the inferiority of group thinking and action may be partly a function of the individualist bias of these scientists (Markus & Kitayama, 1994), it is also true that this view is not a new one in the social sciences, nor is it unique to North American scholars. As long ago as the late nineteenth century, French sociologists Gustave LeBon (1903) and Gabriel Tarde (1903) described people being magnetically drawn toward crowds, where they then develop a "collective mind." Although the research already discussed in this chapter indicates that people in groups can sometimes act in an inferior and impulsive manner (due to social loafing and deindividuation, respectively), you have learned in previous chapters that individuals acting alone can exhibit similar undesirable actions. Thus, group processes, like individual processes, are amply designed to foster both positive and negative outcomes (Kerr et al., 1996). In this chapter section, we will examine the decision-making process of groups and the conditions under which group decision making meets with success or failure.

FIGURE 9.5

The Stages of Group Decision Making

Group decision making typically moves through four distinct stages: orientation, discussion, decision, and implementation. In what two stages are members' social influence attempts—either normative or informational—most apparent?

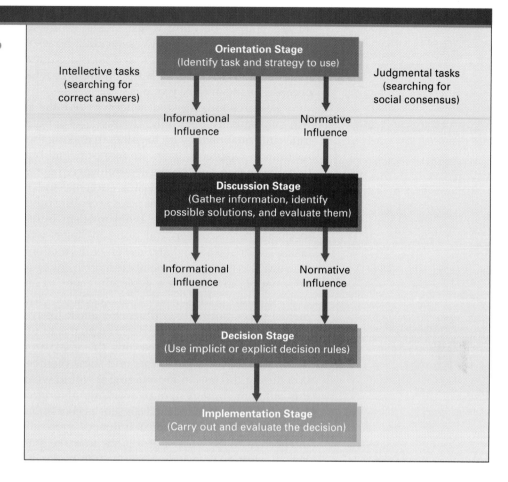

Group Decision Making Occurs in Stages and Involves Various Decision Rules

In making decisions, groups typically move through four distinct stages (Forsyth, 1990). As depicted in figure 9.5, the *orientation stage* involves the group identifying the task it is trying to accomplish and the strategy it will use to solve it. As you will shortly discover, the type of task presented to the group generally determines the strategy it chooses. In the *discussion stage,* the group gathers information, identifies possible solutions, and evaluates them. It is in this second stage and in the following *decision stage* that members' influence attempts—either normative or informational—are most apparent. In making decisions, the group relies on either implicit or explicit decision rules (see the section "Group Decision Rules"). Finally, in the *implementation stage,* the group first carries out the decision and then evaluates its effectiveness. Now that the stages have been outlined, let us examine the group dynamics in this process.

Two Types of Decision-Making Issues

To a good degree, *how* a group makes a decision depends on what *kind* of decision it is making. Many of the issues on which groups make decisions can be located on a continuum (Laughlin, 1996). At one end of the continuum are *intellective* issues for which there are demonstrably correct solutions. Here, the group's task is to discover the "true" or "correct" answer. Scientists searching for a cure for AIDS or campers trying to determine how to put together a tent are both examples of groups struggling with an intellective task. In contrast, at the other end of the continuum are *judgmental* issues involving behavioral, ethical, or aesthetic judgments for which there are no demonstrably correct answers. Examples of judgmental tasks are members of an arts council deciding which artists are most worthy of receiving monetary awards, or corporate executives deciding how to market their products. In these types of cases, although the groups' decisions often involve weighing facts, the ultimate decision is principally based on the appeal to social norms and the attainment of consensus within the group.

Research indicates that what type of issue a group believes it is working on will substantially determine the mode of influence members employ and how much information they try to gather in making their decision (Green, 1998). As you recall from chapter 8, there are two principal types of social influence: informational influence and normative influence. *Informational influence* occurs when a person accepts others' logical arguments and factual information in defining reality; *normative influence* involves accepting others' definition of reality based on the desire to win approval or avoid criticism. Informational influence is most likely to shape the discussion and decision stages when groups work on intellective tasks. The goal is to find and use any information that helps solve the problem. In reaching this goal, group members tend to engage in a thorough search for relevant information, and they are generally eager to share what they find with other members during the discussion stage. On the other hand, when working on judgmental tasks, normative influence is most likely to be used. Because there is no purely "correct" answer, the decision goal is to persuade other group members to accept your judgment. In reaching this goal, group members are less diligent in trying to uncover information, and some members may even withhold information during discussion if divulging it would weaken their arguments. Because of this different strategy, groups working on judgmental tasks tend to discuss only enough information to reach consensus (Wittenbaum & Stasser, 1996).

Although informational influence generally dictates decision making on intellective tasks, when a group has to make a quick decision, they often do not have the luxury of systematically searching for information during the discussion stage and instead must rely on more superficial or heuristic information processing (Karau & Kelly, 1992). In such instances, regardless of whether the task is judgmental or intellective, members tend to rely on normative influence in reaching a decision (Kelly et al., 1997).

MAJORITY INFLUENCE ON GROUP DECISIONS

Based on your previous reading of the social influence process in chapter 8, it should not be surprising that social psychologists have discovered that group decisions can be predicted with a good degree of accuracy from knowledge of members' initial preferences prior to a discussion of the issues (Davis, 1973). For example, interviews with members of 225 criminal juries found that, in 97 percent of the cases, the jury's final decision was the same as the one favored by a majority of the jurors on the initial vote (Kalven & Zeisel, 1966). Similar results have also been obtained in *mock* (simulated) jury trials (Tanford & Penrod, 1984). These findings suggest that if most of the group initially supports a particular position, discussion serves mainly to confirm or strengthen this popular view. Garold Stasser and his colleagues contend that the reason the initial majority opinion wins over the entire group is due to the greater informational influence and normative influence the majority members have at their disposal. That is, group discussion is more likely to focus on majority-held opinions rather than opinions shared by the minority, and those sharing the majority opinion exert greater pressure to conform than do those who hold minority positions (Stasser et al., 1989b).

GROUP DECISION RULES

Although group discussion can affect individual judgments due to informational and normative influence, it's also true that the rules governing those decisions affect group decisions. That is, because group decision making requires some level of agreement or consensus among members, groups develop rules that determine when a sufficient level of consensus has been reached. A *group decision rule* is simply the required number of group members that must agree with a position for the group as a whole to adopt it. Common decision rules include the following:

Unanimity rule: All group members must agree on the same position before a decision is finalized.

Majority-wins rule: A group opts for whatever position is held by more than 50 percent of its members.

Plurality-wins rule: When there is no clear majority, the group opts for the position that has the most support.

Decision rules may be explicit and formal, as is the case with the instructions given a jury to return a unanimous verdict, or they may be implicit and informal, such as a chairperson's intuitive assessment that the group sufficiently agrees on a previously disputed topic to consider it settled (Kaplan & Miller, 1983). Groups that use the unanimity rule are not only more thorough in discussing the issues than groups that employ the majority or plurality decision rules, but they also are more likely to use compromise in reaching a decision, which, not surprisingly, results in greater satisfaction with the final decision (Miller, 1989).

GROUP DISCUSSION ENHANCES THE INITIAL ATTITUDES OF PEOPLE WHO ALREADY AGREE

Imagine that you are on Ben & Jerry's board of directors and tomorrow will be voting on whether to buy brownies for your Chocolate Fudge Brownie Bar ice cream sandwich from supplier A, which is a traditional business, or get them for the same price from supplier B, which is employing the homeless and doing wonderful things in its community. At first, the choice seems like a no-brainer, because giving business to supplier B fulfills your company's goal of social responsibility. Upon closer inspection, however, you discover that the traditional supplier has years of experience producing both high volume and high quality brownies, but the nontraditional supplier has never attempted to produce brownies in such huge quantities. In choosing supplier B, you run the risk that your own product could be compromised if they cannot meet your high-volume, high-quality food requirements. In making a decision, what would be the *lowest* probabilities or odds of supplier B meeting your requirements you would consider acceptable? A five in ten chance? Seven in ten? Nine in ten? Would it surprise you to know that the level of risk you would settle on would likely be different if you made it on your own versus as part of the board?

ARE GROUP DECISIONS MORE OR LESS CAUTIOUS?

In the early 1960s, using hypothetical situations like the preceding one, James Stoner set out to test the commonly held belief that decision making by groups is more cautious than that made by individuals. To accomplish this task, Stoner (1961) asked management students to individually respond to twelve hypothetical dilemmas. When they completed these, he brought them together in groups with instructions to discuss each of the problems until they reached a unanimous decision as to what odds they would accept as a group. Unexpectedly, when Stoner compared the average odds of the groups with the average odds these people had endorsed as individuals, he found that the groups were actually *riskier* than the individuals on ten of the twelve items. During the next five years or so, subsequent research using similar hypothetical dilemmas found the same results across a wide variety of age and occupational groups and in dozens of different cultures—groups were riskier than individuals (Cartwright, 1971; Pruitt, 1971). This effect was initially known as the *risky shift.*

GROUP ENHANCEMENT OF INITIAL TENDENCIES

As researchers conducted more studies, they came to realize that not all decision dilemmas yielded a reliable risky shift. In fact, on some dilemmas, groups became reliably *more* cautious after discussion (Fraser et al., 1971; Knox & Safford, 1976). This was perplexing. How could group discussion produce both greater risk taking and greater conservativism? In time, researchers began to realize that what was occurring in these group discussions was not a consistent shift toward risk or caution but, rather, a tendency for discussion to *enhance* the initial attitudes of people who already agree (Moscovici & Zavalloni, 1969; Myers & Lamm, 1976). This group-produced enhancement or exaggeration of members' initial attitudes through discussion was called **group polarization.**

Group Polarization

Group-produced enhancement or exaggeration of members' initial attitudes through discussion.

Research indicates that group polarization is more likely to occur on important issues rather than trivial ones (Kerr, 1992). For example, based on high-school students' responses to a racial attitudes questionnaire, David Myers and George Bishop (1970) classified them as high, medium, and low on prejudice. Groups of like-minded students then met to discuss racial issues. The researchers found that students who were initially low in prejudice were even *less* so after the group discussion. On the other hand, those who were moderately or highly prejudiced became even *more* prejudiced. Similar strengthening of initial attitudes is also found in many other group settings. In juries, for instance, group discussion tends to lead individual members to more extreme opinions about a defendant's guilt or innocence than they initially held (Myers & Kaplan, 1976). Surprisingly, even terrorist groups' actions may be shaped by group polarization effects. An analysis of terrorist organizations around the world found that these groups typically become more extreme only gradually over time (McCauley & Segal, 1987). Being relatively isolated from those who hold more moderate views, terrorists become more extreme as they interact with one another. The result is increased violence, something the individual members may never have initially endorsed.

WHAT PRODUCES GROUP POLARIZATION?

Several different explanations have been offered for the group polarization effect, but the two receiving the most attention and support are the *social comparison* and *persuasive arguments* perspectives. The social comparison view stresses the role of normative influence in the polarization process, while the persuasive arguments view focuses more exclusively on informational influence.

As you may recall from chapter 2 (pp. 65–67), the social comparison perspective contends that we are motivated to self-evaluate, a process that we accomplish primarily by comparing ourselves with others (Festinger, 1954). Accordingly, during group discussion, members are concerned with how their positions on relevant issues compare with those of other group members (Goethals & Zanna, 1979). Most assume that they hold "better" views (more extreme in the valued direction) than others (Codol, 1975). However, through social comparison, individual members discover that they are not nearly as extreme in the socially valued direction as they initially thought. Because they want others to evaluate them positively (normative influence), discussants begin to shift toward even more extreme positions. Ultimately, this one-upmanship drives the group toward a decision that is either more conservative or more risky than individual members would otherwise have chosen (McGarty et al., 1992).

In contrast to this view, the persuasive arguments position states that group polarization involves *mutual persuasion*. According to this perspective, group discussion is not driven by the desire to be evaluated positively by oneself and others but by the desire to arrive at the correct or true solution. Here, the sheer strength of the arguments offered for certain decision choices is relevant (informational influence). Put simply, when people hear arguments from others, they learn new information. If even a slight majority of group members supports a particular position, most of the arguments presented will favor this view. Hearing more arguments in favor of their own position rather than against it, and hearing new supportive arguments that they had not initially considered, members gradually come to adopt even more extreme positions (Brauer et al., 1995).

Daniel Isenberg's (1986) meta-analysis of twenty-one different group polarization studies indicates that social comparison and persuasive argumentation often occur in combination to produce extreme group decisions. In an attempt to explain how these two forces could both produce group polarization, Martin Kaplan (1987) suggests that they may operate in different situations. That is, when the issue involves intellective tasks in which facts are weighed, group members will be primarily concerned with the information presented in people's arguments. In such a scenario, the persuasiveness of the arguments is what pushes their position toward extremity. However, when the issue involves judgmental tasks for which there are clearly no objectively right or wrong solutions, people are more likely to compare their views with those of others. Here, social comparison is more important in group polarization effects.

GROUPTHINK OCCURS WHEN CONSENSUS-SEEKING OVERRIDES CRITICAL ANALYSIS

On April 17, 1961, fourteen hundred American-armed Cuban exiles landed on the beaches of Cuba at the Bay of Pigs with the objective of overthrowing its communist government, led by Fidel Castro. The Central Intelligence Agency planned this counterrevolution, and President John Kennedy approved it after consulting with his advisers. Their belief was that the Cuban people would welcome the invading force and join them in overthrowing the communists. Nothing could have been further from the truth. Soon after landing on the beaches, loyal Castro forces captured the Cuban exiles. The Cuban citizenry rallied around their communist government, and the United States was humiliated on the world stage.

To say that the Kennedy administration had miscalculated Castro's internal support and had poorly planned the invasion would be a gross understatement. How could otherwise intelligent and competent people be party to such a monumentally terrible decision? In answering this question, Irving Janis (1982) contended that groups are sometimes susceptible to an extreme form of group polarization, which he called **groupthink.** This condition refers to a deterioration of mental efficiency, reality testing, and moral judgment in groups that have an excessive desire to reach consensus. According to Janis, groupthink emerges when maintaining a pleasant social atmosphere becomes more important than making the best decision.

Janis hypothesized that three major factors contribute to the development of groupthink. The first factor is *high group cohesiveness*. Although a high level of cohesiveness among group members would seem to be a very positive group characteristic, it also is associated with increased conformity. That is, when people are strongly attracted to a group and want badly to be accepted by it, they are more likely to allow group members to influence their thinking and actions (t'Hart et al., 1993). Janis believed that when high cohesiveness is combined with the other two factors, namely a *threatening situational context* and *structural and procedural faults*, groups become more susceptible to groupthink. Regarding the situational context, Janis contended that groups faced with a threatening or stressful situation may value speed of decision making over accuracy. In addition, as we will discuss in chapter 10 (pp. 358–361), during times of stress people become more dependent on the reassuring support of others, which should increase the group's influence on individual members. According to Janis, structural and procedural faults that contribute to groupthink are a lack of systematic procedures for making and reviewing decisions, the isolation of the group from others, and a strong, directive leader who lets other members know what his or her inclinations are regarding the group's final decision choice.

CRITICAL *thinking*

Based on the discussion of social influence processes in chapter 8, what type of individuals might be more susceptible to group polarization effects when working on judgmental tasks?

Groupthink

A deterioration of mental efficiency, reality testing, and moral judgment in a group that results from an excessive desire to reach consensus.

That is no use at all. What I want is men who will support me when I am in the wrong.

Lord Melbourne, British prime minister (1779–1848), reply to a politician's pledge: "I will support you as long as you are in the right."

When a group becomes more concerned with maintaining group consensus than in critically analyzing their proposed course of action, they often engage in the defective decision making known as groupthink. Such a situation characterized the group dynamics of President John F. Kennedy and his cabinet during their decision to invade Cuba in 1961. To best prevent groupthink, what stage in group decision making should be principally targeted?

SYMPTOMS OF GROUPTHINK

Janis believed there are three general ways (symptoms) to tell whether a group is suffering from groupthink. These are as follows:

1. *An overestimation of one's ingroup.* Members develop an illusion of invulnerability and an unquestioned belief in the ingroup's own morality. In the Bay of Pigs disaster, the Kennedy ingroup uncritically accepted the Central Intelligence Agency's hopelessly flawed plan (after all, we had the best intelligence agency in the world, didn't we?) and operated on the false assumption that they could keep their role in the invasion secret from the rest of the world.

2. *Close-mindedness.* Members rationalize the correctness of their decisions and develop a stereotyped view of their opponents. Prior to the invasion, Kennedy and his advisers spent far more time explaining and justifying their decisions than critically analyzing them. They convinced themselves that the Cuban military was so weak and Castro's support was so thin that a small invading force could easily overthrow the government.

3. *Increased conformity pressure.* Members reject those who raise doubts about the group's assumptions and decisions, and they censor their own misgivings. With all this conformity pressure, members develop an illusion that everyone is in agreement, which serves to confirm the group's ill-chosen decisions. During Cuban invasion discussions, Kennedy adviser Arthur Schlesinger, Jr., stated that there was "a curious atmosphere of assumed consensus." Schlesinger also noted that when he voiced objections, Attorney General Robert Kennedy took him aside and said, "You may be right or you may be wrong, but the President has made his mind up. Don't push it any further."

RESEARCH ON GROUPTHINK

One reason why Janis's formulation of groupthink is so appealing is that it seeks to understand how the high stakes and high-pressure decision making of powerful groups within society can sometimes go terribly wrong. Groupthink tendencies have been identified in such tragedies and political blunders as the decision to launch the space shuttle *Challenger* on its doomed mission in January of 1986 (Esser

& Lindoerfer, 1989; Moorhead et al., 1991) and the decisions made by President Nixon and his advisers following the Watergate burglary (McCauley, 1989). However, despite the appeal of Janis's model, surprisingly few studies have tested its viability (Herek et al., 1987; Moorhead & Montanari, 1986).

Perhaps the most comprehensive test of the Janis model was a study by Philip Tetlock and his colleagues (1992), in which they conducted a content analysis of the factual accounts of ten historic decisions that potentially involved groupthink. Consistent with Janis's model, results indicated that historic events involving disastrous decisions exhibited significantly more groupthink characteristics than those that led to successful decisions. Some of these groupthink characteristics were suspicion of outsiders, restriction of information exchange, and punishment of group dissenters. Also consistent with groupthink predictions, as groups became more concerned with maintaining group consensus, they began to exhibit more groupthink symptoms, which in turn resulted in more defective decision making. However, contrary to Janis's model, Tetlock and his colleagues did not find any evidence that group cohesiveness or situational threat were predictors of groupthink symptoms. In other words, highly cohesive groups and those under high stress were no more likely to fall prey to groupthink than those that were less cohesive or less stressed. What these and other findings suggest is that groupthink does exist, but it doesn't appear to function in the exact manner first proposed by Janis (Granström & Stiwne, 1998; Paulus, 1998).

Due to the potential harm generated by groupthink processes, what can groups do to prevent it? Based on the available evidence, the most important recommendation is to improve decision-making structures and procedures during the group's orientation stage (Schafer & Crichlow, 1996). Doing so will increase the likelihood that alternative perspectives will be fully weighed and considered during the discussion and decision stages. To facilitate this process, group leaders should encourage criticism and skepticism of all ideas, and once a decision has been reached, the group should return to the discussion stage so that members can express any lingering doubts. Approaching group decision making in this manner should facilitate the type of critical analysis that is the hallmark of success, both on the individual and the group levels (Michaelson et al., 1989).

SECTION SUMMARY

In reaching decisions, groups typically move through four distinct stages. How groups make decisions often depends on what kind of decisions they are making. Intellective decisions are generally reached through informational influence, while judgmental decisions typically rely on normative influence. Group decisions are also influenced by various formal and informal rules, as well as by members' initial positions prior to the deliberation process. When groups do meet to discuss an issue, the decision they ultimately reach is often more extreme than the initial positions of its members. This group-induced enhancement or exaggeration of individual opinion is called *group polarization*. An extreme form of group polarization, known as *groupthink*, refers to a deterioration of mental efficiency, reality testing, and moral judgment resulting from an excess desire to reach consensus.

LEADERSHIP

As previously mentioned, members of a group accept influence from others whom they believe to have greater ability (Foddy & Smithson, 1996). In this chapter section, we will examine these high status individuals and the nature of their relationship with those who have lower status.

A Leader Is an Influence Agent

Leader

The person who exerts the most influence and provides direction and energy to the group.

The person who exerts the most influence and provides direction and energy to the group is the **leader** (Jesuíno, 1996). This is the person who initiates action, gives orders, doles out rewards and punishments, settles disputes between fellow members, and pushes and pulls the group toward its goals. Many groups have only one leader; other groups have two or more individuals with equally high levels of influence. Generally, groups tend to have multiple leaders as their tasks become more diverse and complex.

In their position of social influence, leaders are called on to perform two basic types of activities. *Task leadership* consists of accomplishing the goals of the group, and *socioemotional leadership* involves an attention to the emotional and interpersonal aspects of group interaction (Bales, 1970; Hare & Kent, 1994). The necessary qualities for effective task leadership are efficiency, directiveness, and knowledge about the relevant group task. Task leaders tend to have a directive style, giving orders and being rather impersonal in their dealings with group members. In contrast, friendliness, empathy, and an ability to mediate conflicts are important qualities for effective socioemotional leadership. A socioemotional leader's style is more democratic, with greater emphasis on delegating authority and inviting input from others (Fiedler, 1987).

I am a leader by default, only because nature does not allow a vacuum.

Archbishop Desmond Tutu, Nobel Peace Prize winner and primate of the Anglican Church in South Africa, born 1931

In some groups, one person is the task leader and another person is the socioemotional leader (see the *contingency model*, pp. 339–341). At Ben & Jerry's, for example, Ben is more of a task leader than Jerry, who fits firmly in the mold of a socioemotional leader. Thus, early on they worked out an arrangement whereby affable Jerry did the hiring and, if things didn't work out, Ben did the firing. In other groups, one leader performs both functions. In such instances, the leader must know when to be the task master and when to be the supportive confidant—a difficult feat because the two leadership styles often conflict. Research indicates that individuals with a *flexible* leadership style know when to focus on task production and when to show concern for interpersonal relations. They also tend to receive the highest leadership ratings by other group members (Kirkpatrick & Locke, 1991).

Without a shepherd sheep are not a flock.

Russian proverb

One aspect of leadership that has not received adequate attention over the years is the role that *followers* play in legitimating the leader's influence. According to Edwin Hollander (1992), leaders and followers are involved in a *social exchange relationship*. The leader provides benefits to followers, such as direction, vision, and the opportunity to attain goals, and followers reciprocate by becoming more responsive to that leader's influence. Hollander (1961) describes this increased ability of the leader to influence group members as an accumulation of **idiosyncrasy credits.** These credits are earned over time by *competence* in helping the group achieve task goals and by *conformity* to group norms. Later on, these credits can be "cashed in" to prod group members into taking innovative actions that they would otherwise be reluctant to undertake. In a very real sense, early signs of competence and conformity by leaders earns the followers' confidence and trust, which later allows the leaders' nonconformity—that is, their innovation—to be tolerated by the group (Lombardo et al., 1988).

Idiosyncrasy Credits

Interpersonal influence that a group member (especially the leader) earns by helping the group achieve task goals and by conforming to group norms.

Transformational Leaders Take Heroic and Unconventional Actions

One of the earliest approaches to understanding leadership was to search for personality traits that caused some people and not others to become leaders. Unfortunately, few leader characteristics have been identified (Northouse, 1997). Leaders tend to be slightly more intelligent and taller than nonleaders, are more flexible and adaptable, and, not surprisingly, have a higher desire for power (Simonton, 1992, 1994). They also tend to be more charismatic, a quality that has

Transformational Leader

A leader who changes (transforms) the outlook and behavior of followers so that they move beyond their self-interests for the good of the group or society.

The charismatic leader gains and maintains authority solely by proving his strength in life.

Max Weber, German sociologist, 1864–1920

An army of sheep led by a lion would defeat an army of lions led by a sheep.

Arab proverb

The art of leadership . . . consists in consolidating the attention of the people against a single adversary and taking care that nothing will split up that attention. . . . The leader of genius must have the ability to make different opponents appear as if they belonged to one category.

Adolf Hitler, ruler of Nazi Germany, 1889–1945

Contingency Model of Leadership

The theory that leadership effectiveness depends both on whether leaders are task oriented or relationship oriented and on the degree to which they have situational control.

prompted a number of researchers to analyze the psychological dynamics of *charismatic* or **transformational leaders.**

A transformational leader is one who changes (transforms) the outlook and behavior of followers so that they move beyond their self-interests for the good of the group or society (Bass, 1997; House & Shamir, 1993). The great leaders of the twentieth century, such as Mahatma Ghandhi and Jawaharlal Nehru in India, Franklin Roosevelt and Martin Luther King, Jr., in the United States, Nelson Mandela in South Africa, and even Adolf Hitler in Germany, all inspired tremendous changes in their respective societies by making supporters believe that anything was possible if they collectively worked toward a common good (as defined by the leader). The general view of transformational leaders is that they are "natural born" influence agents who inspire high devotion, motivation, and productivity in group members (Lowe et al., 1996). Because transformational leaders often use unconventional strategies that put them at risk, it is not uncommon for them to face severe physical hardships—and even death—in moving the group to its goals.

Survey, interview, and experimental studies suggest there are at least three core components to transformational leadership (Bass & Avolio, 1993; Kirkpatrick & Locke, 1996):

1. *Ability to communicate a vision.* A vision, which is a future ideal state embodying shared group values, is the main technique that transformational leaders use to inspire followers. In communicating a vision, leaders convey the expectation of high performance among followers and a confidence that they have the ability to reach the vision.
2. *Ability to implement a vision.* Transformational leaders use a variety of techniques to implement a vision, such as clarifying how task goals are to be accomplished, serving as a role model, providing individualized support, and recognizing accomplishments.
3. *Demonstrating a charismatic communication style.* Transformational leaders have a captivating communication style, in which they make direct eye contact, exhibit animated facial expressions, and use powerful speech and nonverbal tactics (refer to chapter 6, pp. 207–209).

Although the concept of transformational leadership has stimulated renewed interest in the "trait" approach to understanding leader influence, it explains only a small number of leaders. Further, even theorists studying these charismatic types admit that they are most likely to emerge during times of change, growth, and crisis (Barbuto, 1997; Bass, 1985). What about times of relative stability, and what about the majority of leaders who do not have these special qualities?

THE CONTINGENCY MODEL HIGHLIGHTS PERSONAL AND SITUATIONAL FACTORS IN LEADER EFFECTIVENESS

Instead of simply attending to special personality characteristics, an alternative approach to understanding leadership—which draws inspiration from Kurt Lewin's notion of *interactionism* (see chapter 1, p. 9)—is to view it as a combination of personal and situational factors. Such an approach is offered by Fred Fiedler's (1967, 1993) **contingency model of leadership.** This contingency model contends that people do not become effective leaders because they possess a particular set of personality traits but, rather, because their particular personality matches the circumstances of a particular group. In other words, the traits that make a leader effective are *contingent* on the circumstances the leader encounters. Fiedler's model has four basic components, one dealing with leadership style and the other three encompassing the characteristics of the situation.

As this Far Side parody illustrates, transformational leaders often use simple emotional appeals when addressing followers. What current world leaders could be classified as "transformational".

THE FAR SIDE © 1985 FARWORKS, INC. Reprinted with permission. All rights reserved.

There is no such thing as a perfect leader either in the past or present, in China or elsewhere. If there is one, he is only pretending, like a pig inserting scallions into its nose in an effort to look like an elephant.

Liu Shao-ch'i, founding member of the Chinese Communist Party, 1898–1969

LEADERSHIP STYLE

Consistent with earlier research, Fiedler argued that there are two basic types of leaders. A *task-oriented leader* is one who gives highest priority to getting the work of the group accomplished and is much less concerned with the relations among group members. In contrast, *relationship-oriented leaders* assign highest priority to group relations, with task accomplishment being of secondary concern. Vince Lombardi, who coached the Green Bay Packers football team in the 1960s, was a task-oriented leader. In describing his focus of concern as a leader, he stated, "Winning isn't everything, it's the *only* thing." Although Lombardi's leadership style was instrumental in the Packers winning five championships in nine years, it is doubtful that his style would be effective with a children's team, where coaches must attend to players' feelings and relations. Instead, this situation requires a relationship-oriented leader, one who would describe his or her coaching philosophy as fostering positive social relationships first ("Having fun is more important than winning or losing"). Fiedler believed that these contrasting leadership styles were a product of enduring personality traits, and thus, would be difficult or impossible to change. To identify these two leadership styles, Fiedler developed the *Least Preferred Coworker Scale*, which asks leaders to evaluate the person in the group they like least. Fiedler found that leaders who evaluated their least preferred coworker (LPC) very negatively were primarily oriented to task success (task-oriented leaders), while those who evaluated their LPCs positively were more concerned with relationships among the group members (relationship-oriented leaders).

SITUATIONAL CONTROL

According to Fiedler, the favorability of the situation for task-oriented and relationship-oriented leaders will depend on the degree to which the situation allows them to exert influence over group members. This *situational control* depends on three factors:

1. *The leader's relations with the group.* The leader's personal relations with group members can range from very good to very poor and is similar to the previously discussed idiosyncrasy credits. Fiedler believes that leader/member relations is the single most important factor determining the leader's influence on followers (Fiedler, 1967).
2. *Task structure.* How clearly defined are the goals and the tasks of the group? The amount of structure can vary a great deal, from clear to unclear.
3. *The leader's position power.* The power and authority inherent in the leadership position. Does the organization back the leader? Does the leader have the power to reward and punish followers? The leader's position power can vary from strong to weak.

Taking these three situational factors into consideration, a leader has high situational control when the leader/member relations are good, there is clear task structure, and the leader has strong position power. In contrast, poor leader/member relations, an unstructured task, and weak position power indicate low situational control.

PREDICTING LEADER EFFECTIVENESS

How do leadership style and situational control interact to determine the effectiveness of a particular leader? As figure 9.6 shows, Fiedler hypothesizes that task-oriented (low-LPC) leaders are the most effective in situations in which they have either high or low situational control. In contrast, relationship-oriented (high-LPC) leaders should be associated with better group performance when they have only a moderate degree of control.

FIGURE 9.6

341

Predicting Group Effectiveness Based on Leadership Style and Situational Control

Based on your understanding of Fiedler's contingency theory of leadership and your reading of the figure, when are relationship-oriented leaders most effective in encouraging group productivity? How about task-oriented leaders?

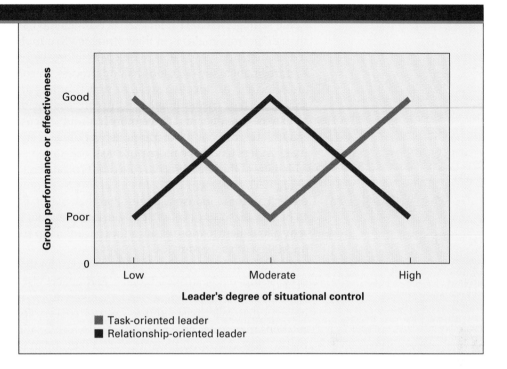

Why would this pattern of effectiveness be expected? Fiedler explains that under the difficult conditions of low situational control, a group needs guidance to be productive, which is exactly what a directive leader can best supply. In contrast, a relationship-oriented leader's more democratic style offers too little guidance in these low-control situations. When the situation in the group is very favorable, task-oriented leaders are again the most effective because their simple task-directed approach maximizes group productivity. On the other hand, the relationship-oriented leader's delight in delving into interpersonal matters can actually slow down the output of a smoothly functioning group. The relationship-oriented leader should be most effective when the situation is less favorable, such as when the task is unclear or the leader has little power. In such a moderate control situation, a considerate, open-minded management approach should be best at rallying group support and fostering creative solutions to problems.

The contingency model has been tested in many natural and laboratory settings, and results generally support the model as outlined by Fiedler (Peters et al., 1985; Schriesheim et al., 1994). What we can learn from this research is that there is no one style of leadership that is effective in all situations. Effective leadership requires a "good fit" between the leader's personal style and the demands of the situation. When the fit is not good, group productivity suffers (Ayman et al., 1995). And when a leader's style does not properly fit the situation, this mismatch also causes increased job stress and stress-related illnesses in the leader (Fiedler & Garcia, 1987). A bad situation for all concerned.

GENDER AND CULTURE CAN INFLUENCE LEADERSHIP STYLE

Many authors who have extensive experience in organizations and who write nontechnical books for management audiences and the general public argue that male leaders and female leaders substantially differ in their style or approach to leadership (Loden, 1985). Is this true? Although the answer is not an emphatic "no," research indicates that there are many more similarities than differences (Powell, 1990). In a meta-analysis of more than 150 studies of leadership in which men and women were compared, Alice Eagly and Blair Johnson (1990) found that in organizational settings, female leaders are as task oriented as their male counterparts. Where they differ from males is in their tendency to adopt a more democratic or participative leadership style. That is, women are more likely than men to invite subordinates to participate in the decision-making process. In contrast, male leaders tend to have an autocratic or directive style, in which orders are given rather than suggestions solicited. These leader differences are consistent with findings indicating that women tend to be friendlier and agree more in group discussions than men, and men tend to have higher rates of counterarguments (Johnson et al., 1996). Overall, it appears that male leaders tend to be more pure task-oriented types, while female leaders blend in a bit more of the interpersonal concerns typical of relationship-oriented leaders (Eagly et al., 1995; Helgesen, 1990). In explaining these small, yet significant, gender differences, Eagly and Johnson suggest that they may exist because women are more likely to be socialized to develop stronger interpersonal skills than men. This superiority may allow them to more easily adopt a leadership style employing considerable give-and-take with subordinates.

Moving from gender to cultural considerations, how might leadership style operate differently in individualist and collectivist societies? Harry Triandis (1993) hypothesizes that the "ideal" leader is likely to be different in these two cultures. He believes that collectivist cultures' greater concern for group needs and interpersonal relations may foster an environment in which relationship-oriented leaders are more highly desired by group members than they are in individualist cultures. Support for this belief comes from a handful of studies. In collectivist Iran, workers stated that "acting like a good boss" means being nurturant and supportive, "like a father" (Ayman & Chemers, 1983). In collectivist India, the leader who is most effective starts by being nurturant and *then* suggests to followers how the work is to be done (Sinha, 1986). In both countries, as well as in Japan and Hong Kong, nurturance appears to be a highly desired leadership quality (Smith et al., 1990). What about individualist cultures? Based on our previous discussion of the contingency model, we know that task-oriented leaders exhibit greater effectiveness in more varied situations than relationship-oriented leaders. Triandis suggests that this finding may be unique to individualist cultures. In individualist cultures, people are socialized to work alone, to concentrate on the task, and to emphasize achievement over socializing. This "training" may predispose individualists to be more responsive to task-oriented leaders.

SECTION SUMMARY

The decision making of groups is strongly shaped by the group's *leader*, who is the person who exerts the most influence and provides direction and energy to the group. Although the search for leader personality traits has been largely unfruitful, the analysis of *transformational leaders* is a notable exception. Transformational leaders are those who change the outlook and behavior of followers. Their attributes include the ability to communicate and implement a vision, and the ability to engage in charismatic communication. An alternative approach, the *contingency model*, emphasizes the interaction of personal and situational factors. The personal factor is *leadership style*, which involves two basic types: task-oriented and relationship-oriented leaders. The situational factors that provide the leader with *situational control* are (1) the leader's relations with the group, (2) the task structure, and (3) the leader's position power. It is the interaction of these three factors that determines the leader's effectiveness. Regarding cultural issues, although female leaders are as task oriented as male leaders, women tend to have a more democratic leadership style. Further, in collectivist cultures, relationship-oriented leaders may be more effective than they are in individualist cultures.

GROUP INTERESTS VERSUS INDIVIDUAL INTERESTS

The idea that followers' responsiveness to certain types of leaders may partly depend on whether they are individualists or collectivists has relevance to the final topic in this chapter: individual interests versus group interests. Whenever individuals are involved in group activities, the possibility always exists that they will be faced with a situation in which their own immediate interests diverge from those of the group. How individuals resolve this conflict has been the subject of a great deal of attention by social psychologists over the years.

SOCIAL DILEMMAS OCCUR WHEN SHORT-TERM AND LONG-TERM INTERESTS CONFLICT

Social Dilemma

Any situation in which the most rewarding short-term choice for an individual will ultimately cause negative consequences for the group as a whole.

A **social dilemma** is any situation in which the most rewarding short-term choice for an individual will ultimately cause negative consequences for the group as a whole (Pruitt, 1998). A classic example of a social dilemma is the "tragedy of the commons" described by ecologist Garret Hardin (1968). Imagine a small town with a communal piece of land—the commons—available to all the townspeople's cattle. For many years the commons has been able to grow enough grass to support fifty cattle, one for each farmer. Now suppose that one farmer selfishly adds another cow to the commons to increase his milk production. Other farmers, noticing this addition, also add more cattle. Soon the farmers reap the results of their selfishness and competitiveness—the commons dies and all the cattle perish. By pursuing short-term individual gains, the farmers orchestrated a collective disaster.

We read about numerous examples of real-life social dilemmas in the newspapers or confront them in our daily lives. The depletion of the South American rain forests brings timber companies short-term profits, but it poses a serious long-term threat to our environment. Even closer to home is the tendency for people to regularly use or benefit from certain public services, such as public radio or consumer groups, at the same time that they fail to contribute to their continued existence. If users don't contribute, the services will no longer be available. This willingness to use a public good, coupled with an unwillingness to contribute to it, has been called the *free-rider problem.*

Scientists believe that the short-term profits realized by companies overlogging the South American rain forests will ultimately lead to long-term negative environmental consequences for millions of people. This situation is an example of a social dilemma. What are some strategies to promote more cooperative behavior?

In all social dilemmas, people are in a situation of *mixed motives* in which it is to their advantage both to cooperate and to act selfishly. Their short-term interests will be advanced if they act selfishly, but their long-term interests and those of the group will be advanced if they cooperate. Although you might expect that people would cooperate when such cooperation will enhance their long-term interests, this is often not the case. For example, Julian Edney (1979) had college students play a game in which ten metal nuts were placed into a bowl. They were told that the goal of the game was for each student to gather as many nuts as possible. They were further told that they could remove as many nuts from the bowl as they wished, and every ten seconds the number of nuts remaining in the bowl would be doubled. Despite the fact that the most rational choice for individual players was to leave the nuts in the bowl for a period of time so that they would multiply in numbers, this was not the typical strategy gameplayers adopted. Instead, when the game started, most players simply grabbed as many nuts as they could snatch from the grasp of others. Sixty-five percent of Edney's groups didn't even make it past the first ten-second replacement period!

Have you noticed a psychological similarity between social dilemmas and the phenomenon of social loafing examined earlier? In social dilemmas, individuals deplete the group resource by taking from it more than their fair share, and in social loafing, individuals deplete group productivity (a group resource) by taking some of their own effort out of the collective effort. In both instances, being "lost in the crowd"—or deindividuated—allows members the protection necessary to behave selfishly (Williams et al., 1995). Although there are these similarities, research indicates that, unlike social loafing, fear and greed are two primary motives driving social dilemma decisions (Bruins et al., 1989). When people notice that others are taking a free ride or depleting collective resources, they abandon a socially responsible strategy and grab what they can (Kerr, 1983).

COOPERATION IS NECESSARY TO RESOLVE SOCIAL DILEMMAS

The basic problem in resolving a social dilemma is that it requires the cooperative efforts of many people. Yet all too often, people are unwilling to give up their short-term gain strategies until the social dilemma becomes quite serious (Yamagishi, 1988b). Although resolving social dilemmas is not easy under such conditions, research reveals several ways to promote cooperation (Messick & Liebrand, 1997).

SANCTIONING COOPERATIVE BEHAVIOR
Without a sanctioning system in place to regulate people's short-term interest strategies, cooperative group members are often taken advantage of by their more competitive neighbors (Yamagishi, 1988a). One way to increase the cooperation of selfish individuals is to *force* them to cooperate. Often this is accomplished by establishing an authority who will lead group members to set up guidelines of conduct that are consistent with the collective welfare of the group (Sato, 1987). Interestingly, people who tend to be less cooperative and less trusting of others' behavior are more willing to contribute money to establish an authority who will punish others for noncooperative behavior (Yamagishi, 1986).

EDUCATION
A second way to solve a social dilemma is to educate group members. For example, in one study using a laboratory simulation of a water shortage, participants were told that they could draw water from a hypothetical lake, which would then renew itself by a small amount, much as rain replenishes a real lake (Allison & Messick, 1985). Those who understood the consequences of their actions behaved in a more socially responsible manner. Similarly, in other studies in which participants were instructed about the negative consequences of selfish actions, there was a slight, but reliable, increase in cooperation (Rapoport, 1988a, 1988b).

GROUP IDENTIFICATION

Solutions to social dilemmas also may be achieved by encouraging the adoption of a meaningful group identity (Brewer, 1979; Kramer & Goldman, 1995). The reasoning here is that people are more likely to cooperate if they think of the other users of limited resources as being a part of their ingroup rather than as mere competitors. In support of this hypothesis, research has found that when the salience of people's group identity is manipulated, they are more likely to exercise personal restraint in their use of an endangered resource (Brewer & Kramer, 1986). These findings suggest that if groups can develop a "sense of community" in their members, they may be able to call on this group identification when it is crucial that individuals put collective needs ahead of immediate self-interest (Dawes et al., 1990).

PROMOTING A COOPERATIVE ORIENTATION

As we have already seen, not everyone automatically places cooperation ahead of competition when confronted with a social dilemma. This is so because people differ in their *social value orientation,* which is a person's rules specifying how outcomes or resources should be divided between oneself and others (Knight & Dubro, 1984; McClintock, 1978). Those with a *cooperative orientation* seek to maximize joint gains, those with an *individualistic orientation* try to maximize their own well-being regardless of what happens to others, and those with a *competitive orientation* strive to outdo others by as much as possible. It is far easier to solve a social dilemma when you are dealing with cooperators rather than individualists or competitors (De Dreu & McCusker, 1997). Recognizing this simple truth, and further realizing that a cooperative value system should be internalized early in life, educational programs have been established to teach children how to think and behave cooperatively rather than competitively in social interaction (Van Lange et al., 1997).

PROMOTING GROUP DISCUSSION

One final way to reduce the free-rider problem is simply to give people the opportunity to *discuss* the dilemma among themselves (Braver, 1995). Studies indicate that groups allowed to talk about the dilemma cooperate more than 95 percent of the time (van de Kragt et al., 1983, 1986). Why is discussion so effective? The most likely explanation appears to be that group discussion allows members to make explicit promises as to how they will behave, and these promises act as a binding social contract (Kiesler et al., 1996). If individual members hesitate to go along with this commitment to cooperate, group pressure is often sufficient to eventually secure compliance (Orbell et al., 1988).

Taking these strategies together, we can escape the destructive consequences of social dilemmas by (1) establishing guidelines and sanctions against self-serving behavior, (2) getting people to understand how their actions help or hurt everyone's long-term welfare, (3) encouraging people to develop a group identity, (4) fostering the internalization of social values that encourage cooperation rather than competition, and (5) promoting group discussion that leads to cooperation commitments.

SECTION SUMMARY

Whenever individuals become involved in group activities, there is always the possibility that they will be faced with a conflict between their short-term interests and the long-term interests of the group. Although these *social dilemmas* are difficult to resolve, various strategies have been found useful in encouraging people to cooperate rather than compete in such situations.

n the applications section of chapter 8, you learned how people can be coerced into confessing to a crime they didn't commit. In this section, let's examine how juries weigh the evidence presented by both prosecution and defense attorneys. What goes on behind those closed doors once the jury has gone into seclusion to deliberate? Unfortunately for those interested in better understanding the social psychological dynamics of this process, federal and virtually all state laws forbid eavesdropping on jury deliberations. Ironically, the catalyst for these laws was the public outrage that ensued when a judge in the 1950s allowed University of Chicago researchers to tape-record the deliberations of five juries (Ferguson, 1955).

Due to the inaccessibility of real juries, social scientists have resorted to alternative means of gaining insight into the inner workings of this group (Wrightsman et al., 1987). Some of these are: (1) interviewing jurors once a verdict has been reached, (2) analyzing court records, and (3) simulating the jury deliberation process by staging simulated trials using mock juries. What do these studies tell us about the jury as a decision-making group?

THE DELIBERATION PROCESS

As in most groups, juries move through distinct stages in making their decisions. During the orientation stage, jurors pick a foreperson, set an agenda, and begin to get to know one another. Next, in the discussion stage, they tackle the task of reviewing the evidence. This review process and the following decision stage can generate considerable tension because jurors often actively disagree with one another. As jurors move toward a decision in stage 3, the majority exerts pressure on dissenters to fall in line so that a unanimous verdict can be reached. Once consensus is within reach, the group tries to resolve the remaining differences and conflicts so that a verdict can be rendered. When no such consensus is reached, however, a jury does not have the option open to most other groups—rejecting nonconforming members. Instead, jurors who hold the majority opinion must continue to search for consensus with their minority counterparts. If after exhaustive and fruitless discussion, the jury proclaims itself "hung" and, if the judge agrees that further deliberation would be fruitless, a mistrial is declared.

Better understanding the group dynamics of juries is of central concern not only to social scientists but also to those who must try to persuade the group to believe their interpretation of the evidence presented to them, namely, prosecutors and defense attorneys.

As important as the deliberation process is to our legal system, in most cases the verdict is actually determined before the jurors even begin discussing the case (see p. 332). Although jurors holding minority viewpoints have little chance of dramatically shifting majority opinion, the research on minority influence described in chapter 8 suggests that jurors may be persuasive when their positions are not too far away from the prevailing majority position. Support for this hypothesis comes from a mock jury study that Nancy Pennington and Reid Hastie (1990) conducted, in which they found that a minority on a jury was often able to change the majority's minds on the *degree* of guilt of a defendant. What this suggests is that if ten out of twelve jurors believe a defendant is guilty of first-degree murder, though there is virtually no chance that the two dissenting jurors will be able to convince the majority that the defendant is innocent, they might be able to convince them to change their verdict to second-degree murder. Based on minority influence research, jurors holding minority positions would be most persuasive when they consistently and confidently state their dissenting views and, at the same time, come across as flexible and open-minded.

THE CONSEQUENCES OF SMALL JURIES AND NONUNANIMOUS VERDICTS

In the early 1970s, the U.S. Supreme Court ruled that in civil cases and state criminal cases not involving the death penalty, courts could use six-person juries instead of the traditional twelve. It also ruled that courts could accept verdicts based on less-than-unanimous majorities. In making their rulings, the Justices stated that there is no reason to believe that smaller juries, or those whose decisions are not unanimous, will arrive at different decisions than the traditional jury. Is this true?

Although research indicates that jury size does not appear to affect rates of convictions or acquittals, smaller juries do spend less time deliberating and recall less of the evidence (Saks, 1977). In addition, six-person juries are only half as likely to become hung than twelve-person juries (Kerr & MacCoun, 1985). Because trials resulting in hung juries often do so because of legitimate disagreements, it may be that smaller juries weaken a necessary safeguard in our legal system. One likely reason twelve-person juries are more likely to become deadlocked is that with more people in a group, there is a greater likelihood that more than one person will be dissenting from the majority. As Asch's (1956) conformity research suggests (see chapter 8, p. 282), when someone has a social supporter he or she is much more likely to resist majority pressure to conform.

Regarding less-than-unanimous verdicts, mock jury research indicates that majority-wins rule juries (two-thirds or five-sixths majority rule) are not only less likely to end up hung than unanimity-rule juries, but they are also likely to render harsher verdicts—and do so in a relatively short period of time using a bullying persuasive style rather than relying on carefully reasoned arguments (Hastie et al., 1983). Jurors who participate in these nonunanimous juries also emerge feeling less confident about their final decision (Nemeth, 1977). These findings suggest that allowing nonunanimous verdicts may decrease the robustness of the arguments heard in deliberation. This, in turn, may well hinder the minority's ability to persuade the majority.

Today, only two states permit nonunanimous verdicts in criminal trials, but thirty-three states permit such verdicts in civil cases. Most civil cases today also employ six-member juries. Based on the research conducted since the Supreme Court loosened the restraints on jury size and unanimity, it appears that these changes result in faster and harsher trials by encouraging closemindedness in jurors. The question we must ask ourselves is whether this is what we want to call "justice under the law."

FEATURED STUDY
FIRST-BALLOT JURY VOTES AND FINAL VERDICTS

Sandys, M., & Dillehay, R. C. (1995). First-ballot votes, predeliberation dispositions, and final verdicts in jury trials. *Law and Human Behavior, 19,* 175–195.

In their pioneering research on the role that first-ballot jury votes play in producing a final jury verdict, Kalven and Zeisel (1966) found that in 97 percent of the cases they reviewed, the jury's final decision was the same as the one favored by a majority of the jurors on the initial vote. Based on these findings, some social scientists have argued that the influence attempts that occur among jurors during deliberation have little impact on the initial majority opinion. Although this effect has also been found in mock juries, no study in almost thirty years has tried to replicate these results using samples of real juries. This was the primary objective of the present study.

A second purpose of the study was to determine whether final verdicts were influenced by *when* first-ballot votes were taken by the jury. This is known as the jury's deliberation style. In what is called *verdict-driven deliberations*, jury deliberation begins with first-ballot voting, and jurors cite evidence to support their individual verdict positions. In contrast, in *evidence-driven deliberations*, first-ballot voting occurs only late in deliberations, and thus, a good deal of evidence is reviewed without jurors announcing their positions. The question in the present study was whether final verdicts would be different based on which deliberation style was followed.

METHOD

Two hundred and thirteen adults who had served as jurors on fifty randomly selected felony cases in a Kentucky county were contacted by phone, and 142 of them (83 females, 59 males) agreed to participate in a thirty-minute interview regarding their jury experience. Consistent with the racial makeup of the county, the overwhelming majority of interviewees were White (94 percent). Their average age was 42 at the time of their jury duty.

RESULTS AND DISCUSSION

The present findings are remarkably similar to Kalven and Zeisel's (1966) results, in that a significant relationship was found between first-ballot votes and final verdicts. In fact, the final verdict was consistent with the initial majority in 93 percent of the trials. These results suggest that by the time the first vote is taken, the jury has generally already decided about the defendant's guilt. Regarding deliberation style and final verdicts, results indicate that first-ballot votes and final verdicts are significantly related for both verdict-driven and evidence-driven styles, as well as with mixed styles. These findings are consistent with the results from mock jury studies (Hastie et al., 1983).

Does this then mean that group discussion of the facts doesn't significantly influence individual juror opinions? The researchers don't think so, based largely on one particular set of analyses. Juror interviews revealed that even when first-ballot votes were taken before formal discussion of the evidence (verdict-driven juries), some informal discussion almost always took place among individual jurors. In such cases, it's possible that jurors were indeed influenced by the other jurors' opinions. In only 11 percent of the trials did the first ballot occur before any discussion or deliberation took place at all. These trials, then, represent individual juror first-ballot verdicts with the least amount of influence from other jurors. Did these individual first-ballot verdicts predict the jury's subsequent final verdicts? Interestingly, they did not. The researchers argue that these findings suggest that the deliberation process may play a more significant role in shaping the verdicts of juries than was previously thought to be the case.

 WEB SITES accessed through http://www.mhhe.com/franzoi2

Web sites for this chapter focus on why we form into groups, what needs and functions they serve, as well as the psychology of collective behavior and social institutions.

Why So Social an Animal?

This web site by Donelson Forsyth presents a thorough analysis of why we form into groups, what needs they satisfy, and what functions they perform.

Center for Leadership Studies

This web site for the Center for Leadership Studies contains the findings of recent studies on the social psychological dynamics of leaders as instruments of change within a group.

Self-Directed Work Teams

This web site analyzes self-directed work teams, discussing research on group work and how to improve teamwork.

PART FOUR

INTERACTING WITH OTHERS

In this final book section (Part Four), we will examine theory and research in the field of social psychology having to do with *how we interact with others*. Chapter 10 examines our desire to approach other individuals, to seek out their company. What are some basic reasons for seeking such affiliation? What characteristics of the situation and of others triggers our desire to affiliate? And what about those of us who have problems with social interaction?

Chapter 11 continues the analysis of social interaction by exploring how this interpersonal process can progress to friendship and romance. Do our early childhood experiences shape how we view intimacy? Do men and women differ in their friendship patterns? How can we understand the social psychology of love? What strengthens and weakens romantic relationships?

Chapter 12 explores the difficult issue of how social interaction can sometimes erupt into aggressive outbursts. To what degree are aggressive actions driven by our biology? What role do negative feelings play in the aggressive response? Should you act out your aggressive desires to "purge" yourself of their influence, or is this a strategy doomed to backfire on you? Is there a "culture of honor" in the southern states of this country that makes aggressive outbursts more likely than in the northern states? What influence does television and pornography have on your aggressive tendencies?

Finally, in Chapter 13 we will scrutinize the helping process by trying to answer five basic questions: Why do we help others? When do we help others? Who among us is most likely to help? Whom are we likely to help? And, are there hidden costs for receiving help?

CHAPTER 10

INTERPERSONAL ATTRACTION

Interpersonal Attraction

A person's desire to approach another individual.

here are many contradictory opinions on the nature of **interpersonal attraction,** which refers to a person's desire to approach another individual. For example, some people believe that "birds of a feather flock together," while others swear that "opposites attract." Where do you stand on some of these basic beliefs? Are longtime friends really as comfortable as old shoes, or does familiarity breed contempt?

As a way to help you ponder these questions, try the following exercise. Think about your best friend. How did you first meet? On paper, list up to ten reasons why you were initially attracted to this person. These reasons could be profound or mundane. Now think about a casual friend. In addition to listing factors that initially attracted you, also identify reasons why you think this relationship hasn't come close to achieving the level of "best friend." Finally, think about someone you dislike. List the factors that shaped the course of this bad relationship. Now compare the three lists. How are they different? How are they similar? Can you develop any hypotheses about the nature of interpersonal attraction based on any patterns you observe?

As we study the "chemistry" of interpersonal attraction in this chapter, keep these lists handy, for we will refer to them on more than one occasion. Following a discussion of two basic reasons why people affiliate, we will examine how personal characteristics of the individual, situational factors, and characteristics of others influence the attraction process. Then we will analyze how social interaction can be chronically problematic for some people, and end by discussing ways to improve the interpersonal skills of the socially anxious and lonely. Then, in chapter 11, we will investigate how this interpersonal process can progress—and sometimes deteriorate—in close friendships and other intimate relationships.

AFFILIATION NEEDS

Have you ever wondered why your need to be around other people often changes due to your daily experiences? Have you ever questioned why your overall need to socialize is different from the expressed need of some of your friends and acquaintances? I'm guessing that the answer to both of these questions is "yes." In this first section of chapter 10 you can explore how closely your personal musings on affiliation match the insights of social scientific theory and research.

TWO REASONS FOR AFFILIATION ARE COMPARISON AND EXCHANGE

Two factors that shape our affiliation desires involve the desire to gain knowledge about ourselves and the world through *social comparison,* and the desire to secure psychological and material rewards through *social exchange.* These two reasons for seeking out others relate to our dependence on others for information (information dependence) and our dependence on others for positive outcomes (outcome dependence) that we first discussed in chapter 8.

Social Comparison Theory

The theory that proposes that we evaluate our thoughts and actions by comparing them with those of others.

SOCIAL COMPARISON

According to Leon Festinger's (1954) **social comparison theory,** we human beings have a strong need to have accurate views, both about our social world and about ourselves. As you may recall from our discussion of the social comparison process in chapter 2, one way to know ourselves and better understand our place in the social environment is to compare ourselves with others. The information that such social comparison provides is used to evaluate the self. According to Festinger, social comparison is most likely when we are in a state of *uncertainty* concerning a relevant self-aspect. He further hypothesized that we generally prefer to compare ourselves with *similar* others. Why? Because the more similar people are to us, the more likely we will be able to use the information gained through social comparison in better understanding ourselves and our future plans of action.

To see how social comparison might be used, imagine trying to decide whether to take a particular course next semester. You know three people who were previously enrolled in the course: Juan, who is always the top student in every course; Vanessa, who usually receives similar grades as you; or Sarah, who is always on academic probation. Who would you seek out for information about the course? According to social comparison theory, you would go to Vanessa because of her academic similarity to you. Her opinions and observations, and her actual final grade, will be much more useful in predicting your own performance than information learned from Juan and Sarah.

A number of studies have confirmed this tendency to seek out similar others for comparison (Goethals, 1986; C. Miller, 1984). We use social comparison not only to judge—and improve—ourselves, but as you will see in later chapter sections, we also use it to provide information about our emotions and perhaps even to choose our friends (Helgeson & Mickelson, 1995; Wood, 1996). Today, our understanding of social comparison processes is more complex than originally formulated by Festinger, but it still conforms to the general principles outlined here.

SOCIAL EXCHANGE

Although the desire to evaluate ourselves through social comparison is one reason for affiliation, a second theory explaining affiliation focuses more closely on the *interactions* between people. According to **social exchange theory,** people seek out and maintain those relationships in which rewards exceed costs, and they avoid or terminate relationships when costs are greater than rewards (Berscheid & Lopes, 1997). The assumption underlying this perspective on affiliation is that people are basically *hedonists*—they seek to maximize pleasure and minimize pain, and to do so at minimum cost. Operating from this assumption, the theory also states that people will be attracted to those who are best able to reward them.

One of the earliest versions of social exchange theory was presented by sociologist George Homans (1958), who stated that all social relationships are like economic bargains in which each party has a value based on the goods they have to exchange. The "goods" exchanged could be either material (for example, money, flowers, food) or nonmaterial (for example, social influence, information, affection). For instance, teachers instruct students in various subjects (a nonmaterial good) in exchange for a certain amount of money from their school districts (a material good). Similarly, a husband may do the grocery shopping, daily food preparation, and weekly yard work, and in exchange, his wife may do the laundry, dinner cleanup, and weekly vacuuming and dusting. Social exchange theory assumes that people keep track of the goods they exchange, and on some level they know whether their rewards are exceeding their costs.

John Thibaut and Harold Kelley (1959) stated that, when people are deciding whether to remain in a certain relationship, they will not consider the rewards and costs in isolation. Instead, the level of costs and rewards accruing in the current

Social Exchange Theory

The theory that proposes that we seek out and maintain those relationships in which the rewards exceed the costs.

Almost all of our relationships begin and most of them continue as forms of mutual exploitation, a mental or physical barter, to be terminated when one or both parties run out of goods.

W. H. Auden, English poet, 1907–1973

Take out the three lists you created earlier for your best friend, casual friend, and disliked acquaintance. Examine your listed reasons for why each relationship developed in the way that it did. If you can, rank them in order of importance, with "1" being the "most important." Next, for each list, how many of your more important affiliation reasons (say, "1" through "5") can be identified as being primarily based on social comparison or social exchange needs? Finally, how are your three lists similar to or different from one another regarding social comparison and social exchange reasons?

relationship will be compared with the possible rewards and costs available in alternative relationships. If no alternative relationships are available, or none appear appreciably more rewarding than the current relationship, the person will make no changes. This is one reason why some people remain in dissatisfying or even harmful relationships—they would rather receive some rewards than run the risk of receiving none at all (Rusbult & Martz, 1995).

These two explanations for why we affiliate—the desire for social comparison and the desire for social exchange—do not exhaust the explanatory powers of current social psychological theories. Instead, they provide an anchoring point for the discussion that follows. With this in mind, let us now explore more specific aspects of interpersonal attraction.

MANY FACTORS INFLUENCE OUR AFFILIATION DESIRES

My father describes himself as a "real people person." He regularly organizes social activities, whether it's sporting events for neighborhood children or card clubs for fellow senior citizens. Are you like this, or do you instead prefer a more restricted range of social contact? Why do we differ in our general need for affiliation?

OUR EVOLUTIONARY HERITAGE

As a species, we are extremely social creatures. Indeed, our *need to belong* is a powerful, fundamental, and extremely pervasive motivation (Baumeister & Leary, 1995). For example, researchers have found that on average, adolescents spend about 75 percent of their waking time with other people (Larson et al., 1982). When with others, teenagers tend to be happier, more alert, and more excited than when they are alone. Social interaction, however, is not just important to this age group. In an analysis of institutionalized infant orphans, higher death rates were found among infants whose physical needs had been met but who received very little social interaction and nurturance from others (Spitz, 1945). Comparative studies of chimpanzees and monkeys suggest there is a biological basis for these affiliative needs (DeWaal, 1989). That is, our tendency to seek out others, to make friends, and to form enduring close relationships seems to be an inherited trait that has helped us to survive and reproduce.

PERSONALITY DIFFERENCES

Even though our attraction to others appears to be part of our genetic makeup, there is clear evidence, both anecdotal and scientific, that we differ in our motivation to seek social contact (Wong & Csikzsentmihalyi, 1991). People who have a high *need for affiliation* tend to be very active in pursuing social contacts and place a high premium on positive outcomes in such pursuits (Crouse & Mehrabian, 1977). In contrast, those with a low need for affiliation are less likely to respond negatively when their social interactions become less rewarding (Hill, 1991). High need for affiliation individuals are indeed "people persons"—they don't like being alone, and when interacting, they seek approval and avoid conflict (Stewart & Chester, 1982). Their desire for affiliation is also associated with being less competitive and less likely to talk negatively about others (McClelland et al., 1982).

Shawn O'Connor and Lorne Rosenblood's (1996) *social affiliation model* proposes that the process underlying everyday affiliation operates according to a homeostatic principle, meaning that we all seek to maintain an optimal range of social contact, but what is optimal differs for each of us. Compared with those who have a low need for affiliation, people with a high need simply have a higher optimal affiliation range. According to this model, when we deviate from our optimal affiliation range, we seek to reestablish it. Thus, excess contact causes us to seek solitude, while too much solitude causes us to pursue affiliation.

BIOLOGY AND AROUSABILITY

One possible biological cause of individual differences in the need for affiliation—that is also consistent with O'Connor and Rosenblood's social affiliation model—involves differences in *arousability*, which is the degree to which stimulation produces arousal of the central nervous system (Stelmack & Geen, 1992). Research inspired by Hans Eysenck's (1990) work on introversion and extroversion suggests that people who desire a great deal of social contact have a higher optimal arousal level for both social and nonsocial stimuli than those who desire less contact. In other words, it takes greater amounts of stimulation—either of the social or nonsocial variety—to arouse the central nervous system of people with a high need for affiliation (Depue et al., 1994). Their desire to reach this relatively high optimal level of arousal impels them to not only seek out others for social stimulation, but to also seek out other intense sources of excitement (Bullock & Gilliland, 1993). What this research suggests, then, is that each of us is born with a nervous system that causes us to have varying degrees of tolerance for the stimulation resulting from social interaction, and it is this biological difference that shapes our affiliation desires.

INDIVIDUALISM VERSUS COLLECTIVISM

Beyond biological causes, affiliation needs also appear to be shaped by cultural variables. Geert Hofstede's (1980) study of twenty-two countries found a positive relationship ($r = .46$) between a culture's degree of individualism and its citizens' affiliation needs: the more individualist cultures had higher needs for affiliation. In explaining this finding, Hofstede stated that in individualist cultures, people are generally expected to individually develop their own relationships and to do so in many varied social settings. Because they develop social ties with people in various social groups, their relationships may be numerous, but they are not particularly intimate.

This affiliative, yet nonintimate, approach to social relationships typifies our own culture. Individualist Americans have numerous relationships that are marked by friendliness and informality, but relatively few develop into deep and lasting friendships (Bellah et al., 1985; Stewart & Bennett, 1991). Whereas many Americans tend to restrict friendship to an area of common interest, collectivist Russians expect to form deep bonds with their friends and to have these intimate friendships extend over many years (Glenn, 1966). As Harry

Triandis observed in his analysis of these possible cross-cultural affiliation differences:

> People in individualist cultures often have greater skills in entering and leaving new social groups. They make "friends" easily, but by "friends" they mean nonintimate acquaintances. People in collectivist cultures have fewer skills in making new "friends" but "friend" in their case implies a life-long intimate relationship with many obligations. So the quality of the friendships is different. This difference in quality may complicate our understanding of the construct of collectivism, since people in individualistic cultures are likely to *appear* more sociable, while intimacy is not a readily observable attribute. (Triandis et al., 1988, p. 325)

Based on this brief overview of possible influences on affiliation needs, we can tentatively conclude that the desire for affiliation is an important defining characteristic of our species, yet individuals differ in the expression of this need. For some, our optimal affiliation range is fairly high, and we seek a great deal of social contact. For others, our affiliation range is relatively low, and we live our lives in a more socially introverted fashion. It appears that our biology—and perhaps even our culture—influence whether our optimal affiliation range is high or low.

SECTION SUMMARY

Two basic reasons for interpersonal attraction are *social comparison* and *social exchange*. According to social comparison theory, a good deal of our desire to be with others is due to our need to have an accurate self and worldview. We are more likely to gain such knowledge by comparing our reactions with those of others. In contrast, social exchange theory contends that we are attracted to others because of the social rewards that are exchanged in such interactions. These relationships are sought out and maintained if the rewards received in the interaction exceed the costs. Our tendency to be attracted toward others can also be understood by analyzing personal characteristics. Regarding social motives upon which people differ, those with a high *need for affiliation* tend to be very active in pursuing social contacts and emphasize positive outcomes in such pursuits. Whether our optimal affiliation range is high or low appears to be at least partly due to our biology and our cultural experiences.

CHARACTERISTICS OF THE SITUATION AND ATTRACTION

Individual differences can foster social contact or withdrawal, but a number of situational factors also can trigger affiliation needs and interpersonal attraction. In the following sections, we consider three of the more important situational factors: proximity, familiarity, and anxiety.

CLOSE PROXIMITY FOSTERS LIKING

One of the most powerful factors in determining whether you become friends with other people is their sheer *proximity* to you. Is this one of the reasons why you were initially attracted to your best friend? Chances are, most of your friends live in close proximity to you, or at least did so in the past.

Leon Festinger, Stanley Schachter, and Kurt Back (1950) conducted one of the earlier and better studies of how social relationships are influenced by proximity

FIGURE 10.1

Proximity and Friendship Development

This schematic diagram of an apartment building in the Festinger et al. (1950) study shows the two floors containing five apartments each, connected by two staircases. Within each floor, people were more likely to be nominated as close friends if they lived in the middle apartments on their floors (apartments 3 and 8) rather than in the end apartments. Further, those who lived in the first-floor apartments near the staircases (apartments 1 and 5) tended to be nominated more than those living farther away from the stairs. The reason for this effect was that the residents living near the staircase had less "functional distance" from others in the building; people were more likely to bump into them as they came and went during the day. If you live—or have lived in an apartment complex—does this pattern of results mirror your own friendship patterns?

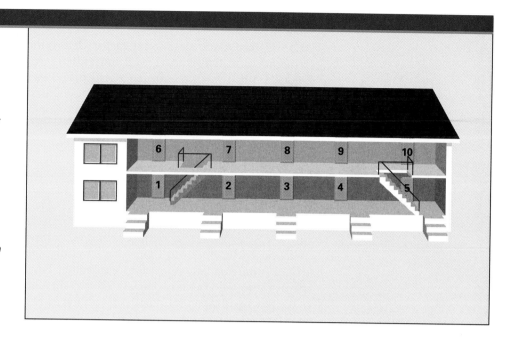

when they investigated the development of friendships in married graduate student housing at the Massachusetts Institute of Technology. Following World War II, the university had randomly assigned these student families to available apartments in seventeen different buildings; therefore, virtually none of the residents knew one another prior to moving in. When residents were asked to name their three closest friends in the housing units, physical proximity was the single most important determinant of friendship choices. Not only did about two-thirds of the listed friends reside in the same building as those who nominated them, but about two-thirds lived on the same floor (see figure 10.1). Similar proximity effects have been found in urban housing projects for the elderly (Nahemow & Lawton, 1975), in freshmen college dormitories (Priest & Sawyer, 1967), in office work environments (Conrath, 1973), and even in classroom settings (Segal, 1974). In the latter study, police academy trainees who were assigned classroom seats based on the alphabetical order of their last names made friends with those who sat adjacent to them.

Finally, for you romantics, there even is evidence that proximity can affect intimate relationships. In an early sociological study, James Bossard (1932) plotted the residences of each applicant on five thousand marriage licenses in Philadelphia and found a clear relation between proximity and love. Couples were more likely to get married the closer they lived to each other. This finding was replicated in later research as well (Ramsoy, 1966).

Based on the studies discussed in this section, you might think we have stumbled on a solution to the anger and violence in our world: Move enemies next door to one another and soon they will be friends! Before you act on this newfound belief, let's consider one last study. Ebbe Ebbesen and his colleagues (1976) found that residents in a California condominium complex not only established most of their friendships with people who lived in the same housing units, but they also developed most of their enemies close by as well. Was proximity one of the contributing factors in the development of your own "bad relationship" listed earlier? Ebbesen explains this effect by stating that those who live closer to you are better able than those living farther away to spoil your happiness and peace of mind by having loud parties late at night, throwing trash on your lawn, and just generally getting on your nerves. Thus, although proximity typically leads to liking, the lamb lying down next to the lion is not likely to develop anything that could be called a friendship.

FAMILIARITY BREEDS LIKING

Another important situational factor determining attraction is *familiarity*, the frequency of actual contact with individuals. As discussed in chapter 5, Robert Zajonc's (1968) *mere exposure hypothesis* proposes that repeated exposure to something or someone is sufficient, by itself, to increase attraction. This effect occurs in the absence of any information about the person or thing that is the object of attention, but it is strongest when somewhat positive feelings toward the person or thing already exist (Smith & Dorfman, 1975).

In one study examining mere exposure and liking for others, Susan Saegert and her colleagues (1973) asked undergraduate women to evaluate the taste of certain solutions, some that tasted good (various Kool-Aid flavors) and others that were rather unpleasant (vinegar, quinine, citric acid). The solutions were located in different rooms, which required participants to move from one tasting station to the next, sometimes being exposed to other tasters and other times tasting the solutions alone. The movement from room to room was carefully choreographed so that participants would be differentially exposed to one another. Finally, at the end of the testing, participants were asked to make one last set of evaluations—their degree of liking for each of the other participants. Consistent with the mere exposure effect, participants liked the people they had seen more often than those they had seen less frequently, regardless of the quality of the liquids they were tasting in the target person's presence.

The fact that familiarity leads to increased liking has not been lost on advertising executives, whose raison d'être is to get people to like whatever it is they are selling. Because we're discussing attraction to others, let's examine the electorate's exposure to political candidates during an election year. Joseph Grush and his colleagues (1978) analyzed the results from the 1972 congressional primaries and found that 83 percent of the primary winners could be predicted by the amount of media exposure they received! This candidate exposure effect has been replicated in numerous studies (Schaffner et al., 1981).

At present, it's not clear why familiarity leads to liking. One possibility is that it is part of our evolutionary heritage: we may have evolved to view unfamiliar objects or situations with caution, hesitation, and even fear (Bornstein, 1989). Such caution in the presence of the unfamiliar enhances our biological fitness because we are better prepared for danger. Only through repeated exposure to that which is unfamiliar does our caution and hesitation subside—the unfamiliar and potentially dangerous becomes familiar and safe, and thus, our positive feelings increase. Therefore, the mere exposure effect could have its roots in an evolutionarily adaptive tendency to be attracted toward those things that are familiar, because they are unlikely to pose a danger to our safety and health. According to this evolutionary perspective, then, familiarity doesn't breed contempt—it simply makes it more likely that we will breed!

OUR AFFILIATION DESIRES GENERALLY INCREASE WITH ANXIETY

Although individuals differ in their habitual desire for affiliation, external events can also motivate people to seek out others. Think about some event in your life that created a great deal of anxiety, such as the death or serious illness of a loved one, some local or international crisis, or even an important college exam. During such times of stress, we often seek out the company of others. Why is this the case? Does misery love company?

SCHACHTER'S ANXIETY RESEARCH
In the late 1950s, Stanley Schachter attempted to answer this question by bringing female college students into the laboratory and creating a stressful event. In his initial study, Schachter (1959) introduced himself to the women as "Dr. Gregor Zilstein" of the Neurology and Psychiatry Department. He told them that they would receive a

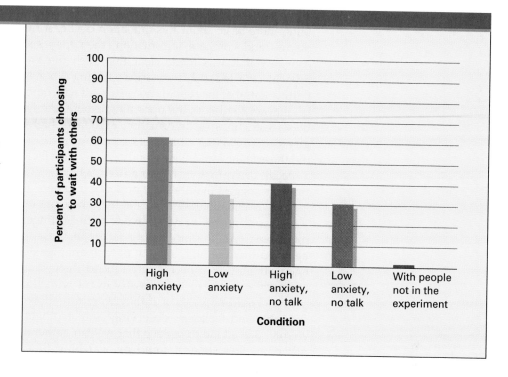

FIGURE 10.2

Desire to Affiliate Among High and Low Anxious Individuals

Schachter (1959) found that research participants' desire to be with others depended on their level of anxiety and the similarity of their potential "waiting mates." His findings indicated that when anxious or fearful, people desire to affiliate with others who are also experiencing similar feelings. Based on these findings, how would you amend the old folk saying "Misery loves company" to better reflect how we react to anxious situations?

Source: Data from S. Schachter, *The Psychology of Affiliation,* Stanford University Press, 1959.

series of electrical shocks as part of an experiment on their physiological effects. In the "high-anxiety" condition, participants were told that the shocks would be quite painful but would cause no permanent damage. In the "low-anxiety" condition, they were led to believe that the shocks were virtually painless, no worse than a little tickle. In actuality, no shocks were ever delivered—the intent was merely to cause participants to believe that they soon would be receiving these shocks.

After hearing this information, the women were told there would be a ten-minute delay while the equipment was set up. They could spend this time waiting either in a room alone or in a room with another participant in the study. Their stated preference was the dependent variable. As soon as participants stated their preference, they were told the true purpose of the study. As figure 10.2 shows, 63 percent of those in the high-anxiety condition chose to wait with others, while only 33 percent of the women in the low-anxiety condition did so. Thus, it appears that high anxiety caused people to seek out others. Misery does indeed appear to love company.

Yet why did they desire affiliation? Perhaps others serve as a *social distraction* to anxious individuals, temporarily taking their minds off their anxiety. If this is the case, then anyone would be an acceptable "waiting mate" for these anxious individuals. To test this hypothesis, Schachter (1959) conducted a follow-up study identical to the first experiment except for one important variation: some of the high-anxiety participants were told they could either wait alone or with other students who weren't in the experiment but were in the building to see their advisers. If anxious people merely want to be around others, regardless of who they are, then these nonanxious students would be acceptable "waiting mates."

Results did not support this reasoning: high-anxiety participants overwhelmingly wanted to wait with others undergoing the same stress, and they were not interested in waiting with students who were not in the experiment (see figure 10.2). Schachter somewhat facetiously asserted that these findings added a new wrinkle to the old "Misery loves company" proverb—misery appears to only love *miserable* company. Put another way, when anxious or fearful, people desire to affiliate with others who are also experiencing similar feelings. But why?

As you might have guessed, Schachter (1959) conducted a third experiment to determine whether anxious participants were motivated to seek out similarly anxious others to share their thoughts about the impending event, or whether there was something more basic about this affiliation desire. If they sought out others to verbally discuss and compare information, then they shouldn't bother seeking out this company if it was made clear that such information exchange wasn't allowed. Schachter created such a scenario by having "Dr. Zilstein" inform certain high-anxiety participants that they could choose to wait with other participants, but they would not be allowed to discuss the upcoming experiment while in their presence. Even with these restrictions on information exchange, high-anxiety participants exhibited a greater desire to wait with others experiencing the same anxiety-producing event than did those in the low-anxiety condition (again, refer to figure 10.2). Thus, in addition to a specific desire to discuss their anxiety with others who were similarly anxious, these findings suggest that the *mere* presence of others also motivates the affiliative need. Yet, of what possible benefit could their mere presence be to the anxious individuals?

Based on his previous work with Festinger, Schachter believed that *social comparison* was the motivating factor in these affiliation needs. Specifically, he believed that the high-anxiety participants wanted to wait with similarly threatened others not to necessarily talk to them, but rather, to compare the others' *emotional reactions* to the stressful event with their own. This social comparison process could occur even if they were not allowed to actually speak about their thoughts and feelings—observing similar others would suffice. As discussed in chapter 3, we tend to believe that we can gather a great deal of information about other people's state of mind by watching their nonverbal behavior. This was exactly what Schachter believed the anxious women in the "no-talking" condition were seeking when they chose to wait with other experimental participants. They could better evaluate their own emotional reactions to this experiment by comparing them with those of similarly distressed people.

Have you noticed that the information-seeking behavior exhibited by Schachter's research participants bears a striking similarity to those who participated in Sherif's autokinetic experiments, discussed in chapter 8? In Sherif's experiments, when faced with uncertainty about how to interpret events ("How far did the dot of light move?"), people became dependent on others for information. Likewise, in Schachter's research, when people faced an uncertain future ("How worried should I be about the impending painful electrical shocks?"), they too looked toward those who might help them evaluate their circumstances. Although Sherif's research demonstrated that *information dependence* makes us more susceptible to others' influence, Schachter's work indicates that it also causes us to be drawn toward others in the first place to gather the necessary information to make social judgments. In this regard, Schachter's anxiety research marked the first major extension of social comparison theory.

Common danger makes common friends.

Zora Neale Hurston, U.S. author, 1903–1960

LIMITATIONS AND WRINKLES IN THE ANXIETY-AFFILIATION EFFECT

Subsequent research has largely supported Schachter's general conclusion that stress increases the desire to affiliate (Rofé, 1984). However, one true limitation to this stress-induced affiliation response has to do with people who are faced with an upcoming embarrassing event. When college students were told that they would soon be expected to suck on large nipples and baby pacifiers in the presence of an experimenter, most preferred to wait alone for the commencement of this embarrassing event (Sarnoff & Zimbardo, 1961). Further, if they did choose to affiliate, they preferred to do so with people who were not going to be in the same embarrassing experiment (Firestone et al., 1973). Under these circumstances, the type of social dependence most likely influencing participants' behavior was not information dependence but *outcome dependence*. Participants avoided social contact because they did not want anyone to know that they were about to engage in a series of infantile acts. For these individuals, affiliation was expected to increase, not decrease, the negative impact of the stressful situation. They only chose to affiliate when others had no knowledge of their impending embarrassment.

When anxious or fearful, we often seek out others who are also experiencing similar feelings. What sort of social dependence is likely operating in these cases?

Besides this limitation to the anxiety-affiliation effect, there also is a "wrinkle" involved in this social comparison process. Although Schachter believed that anxious people affiliate with others who are similarly anxious in order to compare emotional states, this is not always so. Sometimes when anticipating a fearful event, people prefer not to be around those who are also fearful. Instead, they prefer someone who has already experienced the fearful event and who can tell them something about it. In such instances, people are seeking *cognitive clarity*—a desire to obtain information from others regarding the nature and dangerousness of the threat (Shaver & Klinnert, 1982). For example, a field study (Kulik & Mahler, 1989) found that the vast majority of hospital patients about to undergo coronary bypass surgery preferred to room with someone who had already undergone the procedure rather than with someone like them who had not yet had surgery (78 percent versus 22 percent). Subsequent research suggests that the cognitive clarity gained from having a postoperative heart patient as a roommate not only does the best job lowering anxiety, but it also results in faster recovery from surgery (Kulik et al., 1996). These findings and others like it suggest that our desire to affiliate when anxious is not only based on a need to compare our emotional state with others, but it is also fueled by our need to appraise the stressful situation itself—and such appraisal can provide us with both psychological and physical benefits (Kulik et al., 1994; Van der Zee et al., 1998).

SECTION SUMMARY

A number of situational factors determine why we choose certain individuals over others as social companions. One of the most powerful factors is *proximity*. Strangers become our friends and even our lovers partly due to their proximity to us. *Familiarity*, the frequency of actual contact with others, is a second important situational factor determining attraction. According to the mere exposure hypothesis, repeated exposure to someone or something is sufficient, by itself, to increase attraction. *Anxiety-inducing events* can also cause us to seek out the company of others (if they too are experiencing the anxiety-inducing event). Research suggests that the desire for social comparison motivates us to be attracted to similarly anxious others.

CHARACTERISTICS OF OTHERS AND ATTRACTION

In fourth grade, a number of us began to rate members of the other sex in terms of their interpersonal appeal. I don't recall how this "rating game" began, but I do distinctly recall Colleen McCash walking up to me one morning and telling me that she liked Walter first, Chuckie second, John third, and me fourth. Wow! I was number four on Colleen McCash's boyfriend chart! I immediately moved her up two notches on my own chart, from fourth to second, just behind Jane Hauserman. I didn't listen very attentively that morning as our teacher talked about the colonization of America or the rotation of the earth on its axis. No, as the Europeans sailed and as the world turned, I rearranged again and again my girlfriend chart and wondered what Colleen would do when I told her she was now "number two" with me.

Today, looking back on my first systematic attempt to evaluate why others appealed to me, I realize that a number of factors figured into my assessments. First there was the physical appearance of the girl—was she "cute?" Then, there was the matter of her personality—was she a "nice" person? Did we have similar interests? Finally, there was the consideration of her opinion of me—where did I fall on her "liking chart"? As you will see in the following sections, some of these qualities appear to be readily perceived and understood, while others are more subtle, requiring time by the perceiver to determine their presence or absence.

WE ARE DRAWN TOWARD THE PHYSICALLY ATTRACTIVE

As was mentioned in chapter 3, when we meet people, their physical appearance is generally the first thing we notice and remember (McArthur, 1982). What is the outcome of such attention to the physical self? Well, despite the frequently quoted folk-sayings that "beauty is only skin deep" and "you can't judge a book by its cover," we tend to pay little attention to whatever wisdom is contained within these phrases. Instead, research conducted over the past thirty-five years suggests that we operate according to Aristotle's two-thousand-year-old pronouncement that "personal beauty is a greater recommendation than any letter of introduction."

WHAT IS BEAUTIFUL IS GOOD

Physical Attractiveness Stereotype

The belief that physically attractive individuals possess socially desirable personality traits and lead happier lives than less attractive persons.

In one of the first studies of the **physical attractiveness stereotype,** Karen Dion, Ellen Berscheid, and Elaine [Walster] Hatfield (1972) asked college students to look at pictures of men and women who were either good-looking, average, or homely and to then evaluate their personalities. Results indicated that the students tended to assume that physically attractive persons possessed a host of socially desirable personality traits relative to those who were unattractive. This physical attractiveness effect has generally held up in subsequent research (Jackson et al., 1995), including a recent meta-analysis of thirty different stereotyping studies. Alan Feingold's (1992b) analysis revealed that physically attractive people are perceived to be more sociable, dominant, sexually warm, mentally healthy, intelligent, and socially skilled than those who are unattractive.

Although these findings are based solely on samples from individualist cultures, the physical attractiveness stereotype also occurs in collectivist cultures, but its content is a bit different (Chen et al., 1997b). For example, Ladd Wheeler and Youngmee Kim (1997) found that, as in individualist cultures, physically attractive Koreans are perceived to be more sexually warm, mentally healthy, intelligent, and socially skilled than unattractive Koreans. However, consistent with the greater emphasis on harmonious relationships in collectivist cultures, physically attractive Koreans are also assumed to have higher integrity and to be more concerned for others than those who are physically unattractive. What these findings suggest is that, although the physical attractiveness stereotype appears to be universal, its actual content is shaped by cultural values.

The positive glow generated by physical attractiveness is not reserved solely for adults. Attractive infants are perceived by adults as more likable, sociable, competent, and easy to care for than unattractive babies (Casey & Ritter, 1996; Karraker & Stern, 1990). In elementary school, cute children are more popular with their peers than unattractive children (Vaughn & Langlois, 1983), and there even is evidence that physical appearance may influence parents' and teachers' expectations (Martinek, 1981). For example, in one study by Dion (1972), female college students who were studying to become teachers read a negative evaluation of a child by her teacher after she had allegedly been caught throwing stones at a cat. Attached to each evaluation was a photo of either an attractive or unattractive child. When the child was attractive, the would-be teachers tended to excuse the negative behavior as being atypical, and they did not recommend punishment. However, the unattractive child was generally not given the benefit of the doubt—her negative behavior was more likely to be attributed to her personality. In a typical reaction to the attractive child's transgression, one of the college students remarked:

> She appears to be a perfectly charming little girl, well-mannered, basically unselfish. It seems that she can adapt well among children her age and make a good impression. . . . she plays well with everyone, but like anyone else, a bad day can occur. Her cruelty . . . need not be taken too seriously. (p. 211)

In contrast, the typical reaction to the unattractive child's negative behavior was captured in the following remark:

> . . . think the child would be quite bratty and would be a problem to teachers. . . . she would probably try to pick a fight with other children her own age. . . . she would be a brat at home. . . . all in all, she would be a real problem. . . . (p. 211)

Because people are favorably biased toward those who are good-looking, it should come as little surprise that physical appearance can have an impact on something that almost everyone cares about—their pocketbook (Collins & Ziebrowitz, 1995; Marlowe et al., 1996). For example, Irene Frieze and her coworkers (1991) obtained information on the career success of more than seven hundred former MBA graduates of the 1973 to 1982 classes at the University of Pittsburgh. They also judged former students' facial attractiveness based on photos taken during their final year in school. Results indicated that there was about a $2,200 difference between the starting salaries of good-looking men and those with below average faces. For women, facial attractiveness did not influence their starting salaries, but it did substantially impact their later salaries. Once hired, women who were above average in facial attractiveness typically earned $4,200 more per year than women who were below average in attractiveness. For attractive and unattractive men, this difference in earning power per year was $5,200. Further, although neither height nor weight affected a woman's starting salary, being 20 percent or more overweight reduced a man's starting salary by more than $2,000. These findings, supported by similar results in Canada (Roszell et al., 1990), indicate that physical appearance does indeed influence success on the job.

IS THE ATTRACTIVENESS STEREOTYPE ACCURATE?

Based on our analysis thus far, it is clear that we tend to give beautiful people high marks on many socially desirable personality traits and, as a result, give them high social exchange value. But do the beautiful really have more desirable personalities? Overall, the answer is clearly no. Feingold (1992b) also conducted a meta-analysis of more than ninety studies that investigated whether physically attractive and

Research indicates that physical attractiveness standards vary cross-culturally. Yet, despite this variability, evolutionary theorists believe there still may be evidence of some universal attractiveness standards. Can you guess what these standards might be?

C RITICAL *thinking*

Consider again the findings from the Snyder et al. (1977) experiment and the Anderson and Bem (1981) study. When people thought that the individuals they were interacting with were physically attractive, they acted more outgoing and sociable toward them, which, in turn, resulted in those individuals acting more warm, confident, animated, and attractive. How do these findings relate to one of the basic messages of social psychology? Further, how can you generalize these findings beyond physical attractiveness effects to create a more pleasant and rewarding social world for yourself?

physically unattractive people actually differed in their basic personality traits. His analysis indicated no significant relationships between physical attractiveness and such traits as intelligence, dominance, self-esteem, and mental health. Thus, even though we think good-looking people are more intelligent, dominant, happy, and mentally healthy than unattractive people, this is not really the case. Feingold did discover, however, that good-looking people do tend to be less socially anxious, more socially skilled, and less lonesome than those who are unattractive. One likely reason good-looking individuals are more at ease socially is that people generally seek out their company and respond favorably to them. As a result of this history of rewarding social encounters, the physically attractive have an increased sense of personal control when interacting with others (Diener et al., 1995).

Mark Snyder and his coworkers (1977) conducted an experimental demonstration of how such positive feedback can bolster social poise and confidence. They first gave college men information about a woman they soon would converse with on the telephone. Included in their information package was a photograph of the woman. Some of the men were given a photo of an attractive woman, while others saw an unattractive photo. Based on the research we have already discussed, Snyder and his colleagues assumed that the men would believe that the attractive woman would be more warm, likable, interesting, and outgoing than the unattractive woman. In reality, the women they talked to were not the women in either photo. As predicted, independent judges, who later listened to tape recordings of the phone conversations, rated the men who thought they were talking to an attractive woman as being more outgoing and sociable than those who believed they were conversing with an unattractive woman. Even more interesting was the response of the women on the other end of the line. Judges rated the women whose male partner thought they were attractive as being more warm, confident, animated, and attractive than the women whose partners thought they were unattractive. The same results were obtained in a related study when the roles were reversed and women were led to believe they were conversing with either an attractive or an unattractive man (Anderson & Bem, 1981). Together, these findings suggest that there is a *self-fulfilling prophecy* involved in the physical attractiveness stereotype. As discussed in chapter 4 (pp. 131–134), the self-fulfilling prophecy is the process by which someone's beliefs about another person can cause that person to behave in a manner that confirms those expectations. The apparent reason physically attractive people tend to be socially poised and confident is that those who interact with them convey the clear impression that they truly are very interesting and sociable individuals.

THERE ARE BOTH CROSS-CULTURAL DIFFERENCES AND SIMILARITIES IN ATTRACTIVENESS STANDARDS

Our examination of the research evidence thus far suggests that we are drawn to physically attractive people like bees to honey. Yet, what makes a person physically attractive? Is there a universal standard that can be identified and measured?

A landmark examination of 190 tribal societies by anthropologists Clelland Ford and Frank Beach (1951) did find that female physical attractiveness received more public attention and scrutiny than did male physical attractiveness, but did not find any universal standards of beauty (except if you consider cleanliness to be a beauty standard). Although Ford and Beach discovered no universal beauty standards, their finding that physical attractiveness—however defined—was more important for women than men bears comment, for it has been replicated in numerous studies of heterosexual attraction (Davis, 1990; Townsend & Wasserman, 1997). Curiously, however, this relation between the importance of physical attractiveness and gender is reversed for homosexual partners. Physical attractiveness is an important quality for gay men, yet it is a less important feature for lesbians (Harrison & Saeed, 1977). What this suggests is that men, regardless of their sexual orientation, place greater value on the physical appearance of a potential romantic partner than do either lesbians or heterosexual women.

In studying physical attractiveness standards, research indicates that within a particular culture and during a particular time period, people are generally in agreement about what defines physical attractiveness (Franzoi & Herzog, 1987). What is beautiful also often conforms to the current standards of the dominant social group. A good example of the influence that dominant group preferences often have on those of minority groups is the beauty standards of African Americans. Historically, fine facial features and light skin have been standards for physical attractiveness in North American culture, and African Americans mirrored these larger cultural preferences (Neal & Wilson, 1989). Light-skinned Blacks were not only more easily allowed into White society, they were also more likely to be accepted into the more affluent organized African-American social clubs. In fact, one common requirement for membership in these so-called blue vein societies was that one's skin tone had to be lighter than a paper bag or light enough to see the "blue" in one's veins (Okazawa-Rey et al., 1986). Although White-defined attractiveness preferences have been challenged by various Black activists over the years, lighter skin tones are still preferred by a majority of African-American college students today, especially males (Ross, 1997).

Searching through historical records for universal attractiveness standards also informs us that just as culture is not a static entity, neither is the concept of beauty. The Greeks revered the male body and, unlike our culture today, considered it more physically appealing than the female body (Fallon, 1990). During the Roman Empire, "thin was in," while being full-bodied was valued in the late Middle Ages (Garner et al., 1983). In the early to mid-nineteenth century, middle-class North American and European women strapped themselves into steel-framed corsets that, when tightened, would squeeze their waists to an eighteen-inch circumference to match the cultural ideal of the times—the delicate and frail Victorian woman. By the latter half of the century, the large influx of working-class immigrants to North America led to bustier, hippier, and heavy-legged women being the cultural ideal. This shift in attractiveness standards caused some young women to now worry about being too thin and frail. Acting on their concern, they ate more and often wore padding to make themselves look heavier. During the twentieth century, attractiveness standards for both women and men have continued to change, providing little evidence for a universal beauty standard, at least for body build. A recent cross-cultural study by Jeanine Cogan and her colleagues (1996), for example, found that in contrast to American college students, college students in the West African country of Ghana more often rated larger body sizes as ideal for women.

TABLE 10.1

Female Body Preferences Due to the Reliability of a Culture's Food Supply

Cross-cultural research indicates that heavy women are considered more attractive in societies with highly unreliable food supplies. Yet even in societies with very dependable food resources, female body "heftiness," though not as preferred, still is moderately popular. Evolutionary theorists believe this preference for heavy women over slender ones has an evolutionary basis and has fostered our species survival.

Standard of Beauty	Very Unreliable Food Supply n = 7	Moderately Unreliable Food Supply n = 6	Moderately Reliable Food Supply n = 36	Very Reliable Food Supply n = 5
Heavy Body	71%	50%	39%	40%
Moderate Body	29%	33%	39%	20%
Slender Body	0%	17%	22%	40%

Source: Data from Anderson et al., 1992.

No woman can be too slim . . .

Wallis Simpson, the Duchess of Windsor, 1896–1986

Besides being young, a desirable sex partner—especially a woman—should also be fat.

Observations of the seminomadic Siriono Indians of Bolivia, 1946

What might explain both these cross-cultural differences and intracultural changes in the *ideal* female body? Based on an analysis of female body size preferences in 54 different cultures, Judith Anderson and her colleagues (1992) found that female standards of beauty partly vary as a function of the reliability of the food supply. As you can see in table 10.1, although a reliable food supply did not necessarily encourage a slender beauty standard (40 percent preference), heavy women were strongly favored where the availability of food was highly unpredictable (71 percent preference). In addition, cross-culturally, heavy women were overwhelmingly preferred to slender women by a margin of two to one. The researchers believe that this preference for heavy women is evolutionarily adaptive because fat represents stored calories. Put simply, heavy women carry a built-in food supply that helps them to not only survive food shortages, but also be fertile and produce offspring. Thus, especially in cultures where the food supply is unreliable, their extra weight makes heavy women more desirable mates. However, as societies industrialize and food becomes more plentiful, fat becomes a less valued aspect of body attractiveness.

What these cross-cultural findings suggest is that earlier in human history, female body "heftiness" may have been a universal standard of beauty. If this indeed was the case, then traces of this universal standard can still be observed today in societies where food is not in abundant supply. In our own culture, however, this evolutionary-based beauty standard no longer has much influence, especially among White Americans (Cunningham et al., 1995).

Based on the research reviewed thus far, it would appear that despite the possible waning evolutionary influence on preferred female body size, physical attractiveness standards are strongly influenced by current cultural norms. Does this then mean that there are no universal standards of beauty? About the time that many social scientists were reaching this very conclusion (Hatfield & Sprecher, 1986), evidence began to accumulate indicating that there may be universal standards of *facial attractiveness*. For example, research suggests that we prefer faces in which the right and left sides are well matched, or *symmetrical* (Chen et al., 1997a; Mealey et al., 1999). Evolutionary psychologists contend that our preference for facial symmetry is due to the fact that symmetry generally indicates physical health and the lack of genetic defects, which are important attributes for a sexual partner to possess (Gangestad & Thornhill, 1998).

One possible universal standard of beauty in women is youthfulness, while physical maturity may be somewhat more appealing in men. How might you explain this gender difference from an evolutionary perspective? How about from a cultural perspective?

Besides symmetry influencing attractiveness, studies of people's perceptions of young men and women's individual faces and composite faces (computer-generated "averages" of all the individual faces), indicate that what people judge most attractive are faces that represent the "average" face in the population (Langlois et al, 1994). This tendency to define physical attractiveness according to the "average rule" has been found in many cultures around the world (Jones & Hill, 1993; Pollard, 1995). Why might we perceive average faces as more attractive than more unusual faces? Drawing upon the insights of the *mere exposure effect*, Carol Langlois and her colleagues (1994) maintain that average faces are more attractive because they are more prototypically facelike and, thus, seem more familiar to us.

Besides symmetry and normality, evolutionary psychologists further contend that youthfulness and maturity figure into facial attractiveness judgments. In American samples, for example, researchers found that possessing youthful or slightly *immature* facial features (large eyes, small nose, full lips, small chin, delicate jaw), enhanced female attractiveness, while *mature* facial characteristics related to social dominance (small eyes, broad forehead, thick eyebrows, thin lips, large jaw) increased the attractiveness of males (Cunningham, 1986; Keating, 1985). What caught the researchers' attention was that these preferences for mature facial features in males and slightly immature features in females suggested a dominant-submissive preference in heterosexual beauty standards. Although additional studies indicated that heterosexual women are also attracted to men with large eyes (an immature feature) and heterosexual men show a preference for women with high cheekbones (a mature feature), male preferences for youthfulness and female preferences for slightly more maturity appear to be the norm (Cunningham et al., 1990a).

What are the attributions people make of those with immature facial features? Based on their studies of infant faces, Leslie Zebrowitz (formerly McArthur) and her colleagues contend that immature features serve as cues to inform people that the observed individual is dependent and helpless—like an infant (Berry & McArthur, 1986; McArthur & Apatow, 1983/1984). Accompanying these perceptions are attributions that adults with immature features are weaker, less dominant, and less intelligent than the average adult. In the workplace, these attributions result in baby-faced applicants being recommended for lower-status jobs than applicants with mature-looking faces (Zebrowitz et al., 1991).

Taken as a whole, these findings point to a double bind that women face in their social lives. When they try to match physical attractiveness standards by using cosmetics to enlarge the appearance of their eyes and lips and make their eyebrows thin, others may perceive them as more beautiful, but also as more weak and helpless. Understanding the effects these facial qualities can have on other people's evaluations, career-oriented women may think twice about trying to match current cultural beauty standards. Conforming to such standards may place them at a competitive disadvantage with their male colleagues.

From what is currently known about physical attractiveness standards, four general conclusions present themselves. First, there is a great deal of cultural variability in what people find beautiful or handsome, yet within cultures, consensus typically reigns. Second, female physical attractiveness is given more attention and scrutiny than male physical attractiveness by heterosexual men and women, but the opposite appears to be true for gay men and lesbians. Another way to state this is that regardless of their sexual orientation, males value physical attractiveness in their partners more than females. Third, symmetrical and average faces tend to be judged more attractive than asymmetrical and unusual faces, perhaps because the former qualities are associated with greater health and genetic strength. Finally, mature facial features seem to enhance male attractiveness more than female attractiveness. Therefore, maturity in men and youthfulness in women may be universal beauty standards. In a later section (pp. 377–379), we will discuss the possible reasons for these gender differences. Before doing so, let's explore the effect that these differing attractiveness standards have on women's and men's body perceptions.

WOMEN'S BODIES AS OBJECTS OF BEAUTY

Our culture, like many around the world, places a premium on physically attractive women. Starting at a very young age, from the Barbie dolls and toy makeup cases girls are encouraged to play with, to the close attention given to clothing fashion and other bodily adornments, females are taught that their body as an *object* is a significant factor in how others will judge their overall value. The pervasiveness of this attention is seen in the message conveyed in television commercials and magazine advertisements, where difficult-to-attain standards of female beauty are established, especially relating to weight (Posavac & Posavac, 1998). One consequence of this greater attention to the female form is that women of all age groups are more aware of and influenced by attractiveness standards than are men, and this heightened focus has a lasting negative impact on their body attitudes, or **body esteem** (Rieves & Cash, 1996). Beginning in late childhood and early adolescence, girls not only experience more dissatisfaction with their bodies than do boys, but they also experience a steady increase in this dissatisfaction over time (Feingold & Mazzella, 1998). By adulthood, negative affect is a pervasive quality of female body esteem, and women are more likely to habitually experience what researchers identify as *social physique anxiety*—anxiety about others observing or evaluating their bodies (Fredrickson et al., 1998; Hart et al., 1989). The women most likely to be caught in this "beauty trap" are those with a traditional feminine gender role (Franzoi, 1995; Martz et al., 1995).

Although women generally express greater dissatisfaction toward their bodies than do men, there is evidence that Black women and lesbians feel less pressure to conform to the unrealistic standard of thinness in the larger culture than White heterosexual women (Hebl & Heatherton, 1998; Herzog et al., 1992). As a result, they are less concerned about dieting and weight loss (Gettelman & Thompson, 1993). This healthier perspective appears to be partly due to a greater valuing of large body sizes in the Black and lesbian culture, but it also may be a by-product of a more general tendency to reject White and heterosexual cultural standards, respectively (Kite & Deaux, 1987; Thompson et al., 1996). Yet, despite the fact that Black heterosexual women appear to have greater body satisfaction than White heterosexual women, this does not mean they are unconcerned about weight issues. In general, they are still more dissatisfied with their bodies—

Body Esteem

A person's attitudes toward his or her body.

particularly their weight—than are heterosexual Black men (Harris, 1995). Similar ambivalent feelings appear to describe lesbian body attitudes—interviews with young adult lesbians suggest they experience a conflict between mainstream and lesbian values about the importance of weight and overall physical appearance (Beren et al., 1997). What these findings suggest is that Black and lesbian cultural values are not enough to overcome the dominant White heterosexual cultural standard of female thinness.

MEN'S BODIES AS INSTRUMENTS OF ACTION

In contrast to the way that most females are socialized, males are taught to view their bodies not as static objects of aesthetic beauty but more as dynamic instruments used to accomplish tasks in the world. Boys are typically trained for a world of action, where the ability of the body to adeptly move through physical space is more important than how it looks as a stationary object (Langlois & Downs, 1980). Thus, similar to the manner in which a young boy views a battletank or a teenage mutant Ninja turtle, he is also taught that power and function are more important criteria than visual appearance for evaluating his physical self. As a result of the greater importance placed on the body as a functioning unit in the daily experiences of males, they are more likely than women to judge their bodies as a unified whole and less as a collection of parts (Fisher, 1964; Franzoi & Shields, 1984). Accompanying this more unified view of the body is a higher level of body esteem than typically found among women. One notable exception to this general finding is gay men. Like many heterosexual women, many gay men experience considerable pressure to conform to attractiveness standards that are difficult to attain (Silberstein et al., 1989). This heightened scrutiny of the body as a beauty object undoubtedly accounts for the lower levels of body esteem found in this population (Gettelman & Thompson, 1993). Before reading further, spend a few minutes completing and scoring the Body Esteem Scale in table 10.2.

OTHER PEOPLE'S PHYSICAL APPEARANCE INFLUENCES PERCEPTIONS OF OUR OWN ATTRACTIVENESS

Sometimes physical attractiveness judgments are influenced by factors other than one's actual appearance. In fact, sometimes it is the attractiveness of others that determines how we ourselves are judged. For example, people of average attractiveness tend to be judged more attractive when they are with a same-sex person who is very good-looking, but they are thought of as less attractive when with someone who is unattractive (Geiselman et al., 1984). This physical appearance *radiation effect* occurs when two people are observed simultaneously.

What happens when individuals are observed separately, one after the other? Interestingly, instead of sequential observations resulting in a radiation effect, they often lead to a *contrast effect*. People are generally judged more attractive after others have seen an unattractive same-sex person and less attractive when others have just seen someone who is very good-looking (Wedell et al., 1987). Consistent with earlier findings that men are more attentive to the physical attractiveness of potential and actual romantic partners, the contrast effect appears stronger in male than in female viewers (Kenrick et al., 1989).

Thus far we have only considered other people's judgments of our physical attractiveness. What about how we perceive our own physical appearance? In research conducted by Jonathan Brown and his colleagues (1992), female undergraduates evaluated their own physical attractiveness after being exposed to either an attractive or unattractive man or woman. Consistent with the contrast effect, participants' perceptions of their own beauty were greater after they were exposed to unattractive female targets than after they were exposed to attractive female

TABLE 10.2

What Are Your Attitudes Toward Your Body? The Body Esteem Scale

Instructions

Below are listed a number of body parts and functions. Please read each item and indicate how you feel about this part or function of your own body, using the following scale:

1 = Have strong negative feelings
2 = Have moderate negative feelings
3 = Have no feeling one way or the other
4 = Have moderate positive feelings
5 = Have strong positive feelings

_____ 1. body scent	_____ 13. chin	_____ 25. figure or physique
_____ 2. appetite	_____ 14. body build	_____ 26. sex drive
_____ 3. nose	_____ 15. physical coordination	_____ 27. feet
_____ 4. physical stamina	_____ 16. buttocks	_____ 28. sex organs
_____ 5. reflexes	_____ 17. agility	_____ 29. appearance of stomach
_____ 6. lips	_____ 18. width of shoulders	_____ 30. health
_____ 7. muscular strength	_____ 19. arms	_____ 31. sex activities
_____ 8. waist	_____ 20. chest or breasts	_____ 32. body hair
_____ 9. energy level	_____ 21. appearance of eyes	_____ 33. physical condition
_____ 10. thighs	_____ 22. cheeks/cheekbones	_____ 34. face
_____ 11. ears	_____ 23. hips	_____ 35. weight
_____ 12. biceps	_____ 24. legs	

Scoring Instructions and Standards

In 1984, Stephanie Shields and I developed the Body Esteem Scale (BES) which measures three different body esteem dimensions in men and women. For men, the dimensions are physical attractiveness, upper body strength, and physical condition, while for women they are sexual attractiveness, weight concern, and physical condition. To determine your score for each of the subscales for your sex, simply add up your responses for the items corresponding to each body esteem dimension. For example, for women, to determine self-judgments for the weight concern dimension of body esteem, add up the responses to the ten items comprising this subscale. For men, the items of "physical coordination" and "figure or physique" are on both the upper body strength and the physical condition dimensions. The subscale items—plus the means and standard deviations for 964 college men and women (Franzoi & Shields, 1984)—are listed below. How do you suppose your own body esteem has been influenced by your culture's physical attractiveness standards?

Women

Sexual attractiveness: *body scent, nose, lips, ears, chin, chest or breasts, appearance of eyes, cheeks/cheekbones, sex drive, sex organs, sex activities, body hair, face (Mean = 46.9, SD = 6.3)*

Weight concern: *appetite, waist, thighs, body build, buttocks, hips, legs, figure or physique, appearance of stomach, weight (Mean = 29.9, SD = 8.2)*

Physical condition: *physical stamina, reflexes, muscular strength, energy level, biceps, physical coordination, agility, health, physical condition (Mean = 33.3, SD = 5.7)*

Men

Physical attractiveness: *nose, lips, ears, chin, buttocks, appearance of eyes, cheeks/cheekbones, hips, feet, sex organs, face (Mean = 39.1, SD = 5.7)*

Upper body strength: *muscular strength, biceps, body build, physical coordination, width of shoulders, arms, chest or breasts, figure or physique, sex drive (Mean = 34.0, SD = 6.1)*

Physical condition: *appetite, physical stamina, reflexes, waist, energy level, thighs, physical coordination, agility, figure or physique, appearance of stomach, health, physical condition, weight (Mean = 50.2, SD = 7.7)*

FIGURE 10.3

Self-Ratings of Attractiveness Following Exposure to Attractive and Unattractive Same-Sex and Other-Sex Individuals

When women evaluated their own physical attractiveness after being exposed to either an attractive or unattractive man or woman, their perceptions of their own beauty were greater after they were exposed to unattractive female targets than after they were exposed to attractive female targets. Male targets' attractiveness did not influence the women's self-perceptions. What do these findings tell us about how social comparison influences self-perceptions of attractiveness?

Source: Data from J. D. Brown et al., "When Gulliver Travels: Social Context, Psychological Closeness, and Self-Appraisals" in *Journal of Personality and Social Psychology*, 62: 717–727, American Psychological Association, 1992.

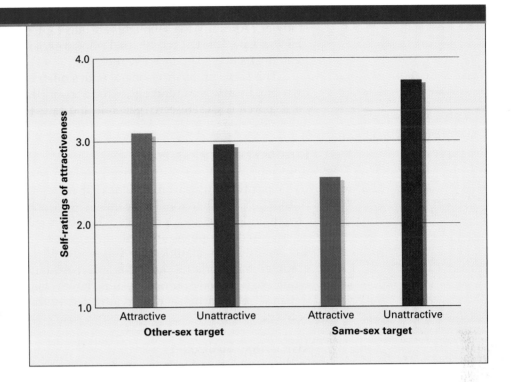

targets (refer to figure 10.3). Male targets did not influence the women's self-perceptions. These findings have been replicated in a number of studies and indicate that social comparison does indeed influence self-perceptions of attractiveness (Grogan et al., 1996; Thornton & Maurice, 1997). Put simply, we feel prettier or more handsome after seeing same-sex persons who fall well below conventional beauty standards.

Finally, I would like to mention social perceptions of "couple attractiveness." In heterosexual relationships, although people's overall impressions of a man appear to be influenced by his partner's physical attractiveness, the same effect does not hold for a woman (Sigall & Landy, 1973).[1] For example, in one study, participants were shown photos of supposedly married couples in which the wife and husband varied in physical attractiveness (Bar-Tal & Saxe, 1976). Results indicated that an unattractive man who had an attractive wife was judged to be the most intelligent and successful, and to have the highest income. In contrast, judgments of an unattractive woman were not influenced by her having an attractive husband. A likely explanation for this gender difference is that, as discussed previously, women have historically been viewed as aesthetic possessions of men. If people see a less-than-attractive man with a beautiful woman, they tend to infer that he was able to attract this woman to him—to *possess* her—because he has high social status. Such an inference is less likely to be made when an unattractive woman is seen with a handsome man because this pairing is not historically common.

BIRDS OF A FEATHER REALLY DO FLOCK TOGETHER

Imagine the following scene. It is the beginning of the fall semester in Ria's freshmen year, and she has just checked into her dormitory room and will soon meet her new roommate. As she unpacks, Ria wonders what her roommate will be like. What is her race and ethnic background? What sort of music does she like?

---

[1]Homosexual couples have not been studied in this area.

To like and dislike the same things, that is indeed true friendship.

Gaius Crispus, Roman historian & politician, 86–34 B.C.

Live with wolves, howl like a wolf.

Russian proverb

To what degree has the similarity effect influenced your own personal relationships? Consider once again your "best friend" and "casual friend" lists. With whom do you share more similarities? Do these similarities fall into a particular category, such as shared values versus shared preferences?

"I'm gonna like this new kid," thought General Manager Glenn Habner.

Similarity provides the basis for mutual attraction.

Reprinted with special permission of King Features Syndicate.

What are her politics? Does she like to party, or will she spend all her time studying? Abruptly, Ria's thoughts are interrupted by her new roommate entering. "Hi! I'm Kate," the tall, dark-haired woman exclaims as she smiles and extends her hand in greeting. "I guess we're roomies!"

This scene probably resonates with similar experiences you have had in your own life. In new surroundings, what sort of people do you typically seek out? Social psychological research generally indicates that we are attracted to those who are similar to us.

DEMOGRAPHIC SIMILARITY

Research on high school friendships found that students identified their best friends as those who were similar to them in sex, race, age, and year in school (Kandel, 1978). Theodore Newcomb (1961) further confirmed the magnetic-like power of similar demographics when he conducted a longitudinal study of friendship development in an all-male boardinghouse. The residents' liking for one another was significantly influenced by their sharing of similar demographic characteristics, and this effect extended beyond the initial getting-acquainted period. Similar results have also been obtained in studies of romantic relationships—we are attracted to those within our ingroups (Whitbeck & Hoyt, 1994).

ATTITUDINAL SIMILARITY

In Newcomb's boardinghouse study, similarity in age and family background not only influenced interpersonal attraction, but similarity in attitudes also provided mutual liking. Unlike physical and demographic characteristics, it generally takes time to learn another person's attitudes. In laboratory studies, Donn Byrne and his colleagues accelerated the getting-acquainted process by having participants complete attitude questionnaires and later "introducing" them to another person by having them read his or her responses to a similar questionnaire (Byrne & Nelson, 1965; Schoneman et al., 1977). As you might have already guessed, the researchers had actually filled out the questionnaire so that the answers were either similar or dissimilar to the participants' own attitudinal responses. As you can see from figure 10.4, participants expressed much stronger liking when they thought they shared a greater percentage of similar attitudes with the individual. This finding is important, for it suggests that the *proportion* of similar attitudes is more important than the actual *number* of similar attitudes. Thus, we should be more attracted to someone who agrees with us on four of six topics (66 percent similarity) than one with whom we share similar opinions on ten of twenty-five topics (40 percent similarity).

The attractive power of similar attitudes has not only been demonstrated in mixed and same-sex dyads, but also in various cultures throughout the world (Byrne et al., 1971). Indeed, as we learned in the "Johnny Rocco" study of chapter 8 (p. 279), our desire for attitudinal similarity is sufficiently strong that we will actively eject members from our groups if they refuse to share our attitudes on important issues. It isn't surprising then, that when trying to match people up into new friendship groups, we pay particular attention to their shared characteristics (Chapdelaine et al., 1994).

There is some evidence of a gender difference in what type of attitudinal similarity is most important in determining attraction. For example, in studies of college roommates, sharing common values was an important predictor of same-sex attraction among women, but shared activities (for example, music and sports preferences) were more important in determining men's same-sex preferences (Hays, 1985; Hill & Stull, 1981). This difference in what men and women attend to regarding attitudinal similarity in same-sex friendships will be discussed further in chapter 11.

FIGURE 10.4

Donn Byrne and his colleagues found that the greater the proportion of similar attitudes held by people, the greater their attraction to one another. Does this type of relationship between attitude similarity and attraction help explain why you are attracted to or repelled by certain people in your own life?

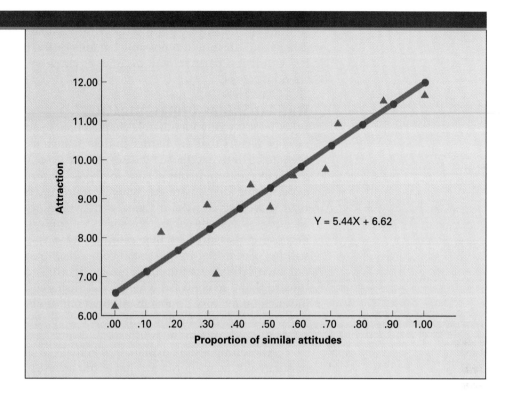

Matching Hypothesis

The proposition that people are attracted to others who are similar to them in particular characteristics.

SIMILARITY IN PHYSICAL ATTRACTIVENESS

Given that people generally favor the physically attractive, a visitor from outer space might guess that everyone on the planet would seek out the beautiful people and not be satisfied with anyone less than a perfect "10." Being earthlings with some degree of experience in these matters, we know this is not the case. In fact, researchers who have observed couples in public settings have found that they are remarkably well matched in physical attractiveness (Feingold, 1988). One possible reason *why* we are attracted to potential romantic partners who are similar to us in physical attractiveness is that we estimate they have about the same social exchange value as us. Therefore, we are less likely to be rejected. In other words, we learn not to reach too far beyond our own attractiveness value when seeking romance.

This tendency to be attracted to others who are similar to us in particular characteristics, such as physical attractiveness, is known as the **matching hypothesis,** and it appears to be a socially shared belief (Stiles et al., 1996). We expect that people who have similar levels of physical attractiveness will be more satisfied as couples than those who are physically mismatched (Garcia & Khersonsky, 1997). True to form, physically similar couples are more intimate (kissing, holding hands) in public settings and report greater love for one another than the mismatched (Murstein, 1972). And studies in North America, Europe, and Asia indicate that matched couples are more likely to get married and stay married than those who are physically mismatched (Peterson & Miller, 1980; White, 1980b).

The attraction of those with similar looks is not exclusive to romantic relationships but is also found in same-sex friendships (Cash & Derlega, 1978). For example, research by Linda Carli and her colleagues (1991) found that similarly attractive roommates were more satisfied, felt their roommates were more satisfied, and were more likely to want the same roommates the next year than those roommates who were physically mismatched. For friendships between people who differ in their physical attractiveness, these easily discernible differences may cause a strain in the relationship. On the one hand, the more attractive partner may view his or her less attractive friend as a social handicap in certain settings (for example, pairing up with possible dates in a singles bar). On the other hand, despite the possible benefits of the radiation effect (see p. 369), the less attractive partner may become envious of all the attention the attractive friend receives.

WHY ARE SIMILAR OTHERS ATTRACTIVE?

Whether it is easily identifiable characteristics such as physical attractiveness and race, or factors that are harder to detect, such as one's attitudes and values, we seem to be drawn to those who are similar to us. Why is this so?

One reason is our desire for social comparison. As Schachter's anxiety experiments demonstrated, when we are uncertain on how to define social reality, we are drawn to those with whom we can best compare ourselves. Meeting others who share our views on important issues makes us feel better because it reassures us that essential aspects of our self-concept have social validity. According to this social comparison perspective, when others validate our own self-beliefs through agreement, we should develop positive attitudes toward them. In contrast, when others disagree with us, this questioning of our judgment may raise doubts in our own minds about our self-concept and worldview. The negative feelings created by such nonagreement should cause us to avoid these people in the future.

A second possible explanation is that our affinity for similar others is part of our evolutionary heritage. That is, our ancestors may have used similarity cues (physical and attitudinal) to detect those who were genetically similar to themselves. John Rushton (1989), for example, has found that friends tend to be more similar to one another on certain genetically determined characteristics than one would expect by chance. It's possible that humans have unconsciously been attracted to similar others because they share many of the same genes. If we become friends with these people and provide them with help when they are in need, as friends often do, we are increasing the probability that genes like our own will find their way to succeeding generations. It is this biological predisposition that may cause us to respond positively to those who appear to have "a bit of us in them."

Another reason why we may be attracted to similar others is that we like that which is familiar. As we have already discussed (p. 358), it may have been evolutionarily adaptive to perceive unfamiliar others with caution and distrust because of the dangers inherent in dealing with the unfamiliar (Bornstein, 1989). Due to this biological predisposition, we may perceive similar others as attractive because they *mimic* familiarity. That is, their similarity to us makes them seemingly familiar creatures! Thus, similarity may lead to liking because the similar appear familiar.

Although these evolutionary-based explanations are intriguing and merit further scientific inquiry, an explanation that has received greater attention and interest by social psychologists over the years is Fritz Heider's (1946, 1958) **balance theory.** Heider proposed that people desire cognitive consistency or "balance" in their thoughts, feelings, and social relationships (refer to chapter 5, p. 170). Because of this desire for consistency, balanced relationships should be rewarding, while imbalanced relationships—those in which a person holds inconsistent or discrepant thoughts—should be unpleasant. Between two people, balance is created when both parties value the same things.

Consider again Ria and her new college roommate, Kate. As they get to know each other, imagine they discover that they both are feminists. According to balance theory, their mutual appreciation of the same social and political philosophy will facilitate the development of a mutual attraction toward one

Balance Theory

A theory that people desire cognitive consistency or balance in their thoughts, feelings, and social relationships.

Balanced relationships: "My enemy's enemy is my friend."

Nigerian proverb

The friends of our friends are our friends.

Congo proverb

another (see figure 10.5a). This is so, Heider contended, because people develop a liking relationship toward those things that are positively related to that which they value.

For the sake of further illustration of balance theory, let's now imagine that Ria detests feminist thinking. According to the theory, this attitude dissimilarity may well push the two women toward an antagonistic relationship because Ria doesn't value something that Kate does (figure 10.5b). Although they now dislike one another, this relationship is also balanced.

What would make this relationship imbalanced? Imagine that the two roommates strike up a friendship before they discuss politics. Then one day, Kate pulls out her copy of *Ms.* magazine, and Ria tells her how much she hates feminism. Now their relationship is imbalanced (figure 10.5c), because Ria's dislike of that which Kate values is inconsistent with Ria and Kate's mutual liking. Recall that imbalanced relationships are unpleasant. This unpleasantness, Heider states, will motivate people to restore balance by making relationship thoughts consistent. In this case, balance could be restored if the two women change their attitudes toward each other, or if one of them could change her attitude toward feminism. A simple way to determine whether a relationship is balanced or imbalanced is to multiply the affective signs on the three sides of the triangle. If the product is positive, the relationship is balanced:

a: $(+) \times (+) \times (+) = +$ and b: $(-) \times (+) \times (-) = +$

If it is negative, the relationship is imbalanced:

c: $(-) \times (+) \times (+) = -$

Don't try to make someone hate the person he loves, for he will go on loving, but he will hate you.

Senegalese proverb

Other ways in which the strain of imbalance can be reduced is if people reduce the *importance* of the topic about which they disagree, or reduce its *common relevance*. In the first instance, Kate and Ria could come to believe that differences in political philosophy are not as important as their friendship. In the second instance, both could conclude that the other's opinion on feminism is irrelevant.

FIGURE 10.5

Balanced and Imbalanced Relationships

According to Heider's balance theory, (a) two people who value the same thing (in this example, feminism) should develop a liking relationship with one another. However, (b) if one person values what the other detests, they should dislike one another. Both of these relationships are balanced because the people's feelings for one another are consistent with their attitudes toward the relevant topic (feminism). In addition, (c) if they mutually like one another but don't value the same thing, this should create a discomforting imbalance and a motivation to restore consistency and balance. How many different ways might Ria and Kate restore balance in their relationship?

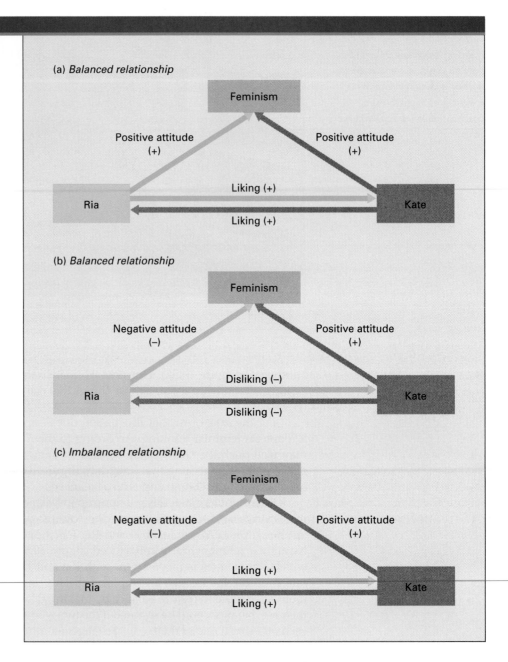

WE ARE ALSO ATTRACTED TO "COMPLEMENTARY" OTHERS

The tendency for similarity to lead to attraction is strong and pervasive. If you were asked to pick the most correct proverb describing the human condition, you would be well advised to choose "Birds of a feather flock together" over "Opposites attract." Having made this judgment, I must hasten to add that this does not mean that opposites cannot find affinity. According to the sociological theory of need *complementarity*, people choose relationships in which their basic needs can be mutually satisfied (Kerckhoff & Davis, 1962). Sometimes this results in people with complementary characteristics (some would call them opposite traits) being attracted to one another. For example, people who enjoy controlling social interactions (*dominants*) are more satisfied interacting with submissive people rather than dominant people (Dryer & Horowitz, 1997). Why? Because, in such situations, they are more likely to have their goal of control satisfied. The same is true of *submissives*. Their desire to have things decided for them is more likely to be satisfied when they interact with dominants, not submissives. This complementarity of personal traits is an example of a *compatible fit between differences*. Do you have any such complementary characteristics in your own best friendship?

MATE SELECTION BASED ON COMPLEMENTARY CHARACTERISTICS

Another example of complementary characteristics leading to attraction can be found in mate selection. As you learned earlier, in heterosexual relationships, men prefer a younger partner while women prefer older males. For example, David Buss (1989) found that in thirty-seven cultures around the world, men express a preference for women who are younger than themselves and women prefer men to be slightly older (except in Spain). This gender difference has recently been confirmed in both a large-scale national sample in the United States (Sprecher et al., 1994) and in a meta-analysis of forty different attractiveness studies including both North American and non–North American samples (Feingold, 1992a). In analyzing these findings (see figure 10.6), social scientists conclude that they reflect a *looks-for-status exchange* in mating relationships (Davis, 1990). Men are attracted to young women because female youth signifies beauty, and women are attracted to older men because male maturity signifies higher social status. Thus, even though similarity generally leads to attraction, sexual sparks often fly if someone possesses a characteristic that you value but do not possess yourself.

If the looks-for-status exchange exists in heterosexual relationships, then a man who is physically unattractive should still be able to attract beautiful women if he has high social status. Likewise, a woman who does not have high social status should still be able to attract high status men if she is physically attractive. One study confirming this particular type of complementarity in romantic relationships asked college students to evaluate, as potential marriage partners, strangers who varied in physical attractiveness and social status (Townsend & Levy, 1990). Results indicated that high status compensated for a lack of male attractiveness. High-status men who were only moderately attractive were as appealing to women as highly attractive but only moderately successful men. No such status trade-off occurred in men's ratings of women; they preferred highly attractive but lower-status women. In other words, men can trade status for looks and women can trade looks for status, but reversing the trade—a woman trading status for looks or a man trading looks for status—is not nearly so common.

Why do you think this looks-for-status complement exists worldwide? Do you think this effect is more influenced by biology or social conditions? The evolutionary perspective contends that what will be valued as desirable and attractive in men and women is that which increases their probability of producing offspring who will carry their genes to the next generation (Kenrick & Trost, 1989). Given the biological fact that women have a shorter time span to reproduce than do men, evolutionary psychologists assume that evolution predisposes men to perceive women who look *young* as being more desirable (that is, more physically attractive), because youth implies high reproductive potential (Alley & Cunningham, 1991). Using this same logic, evolutionary theorists also assume that women will instead favor male traits signifying an ability to provide and protect resources for them and their offspring. Thus, according to this perspective, instead of valuing youth in men, women should place more importance on status, ambition, and other signs of *social dominance*. As you might guess, the evolutionary perspective is not without its critics.

FIGURE 10.6

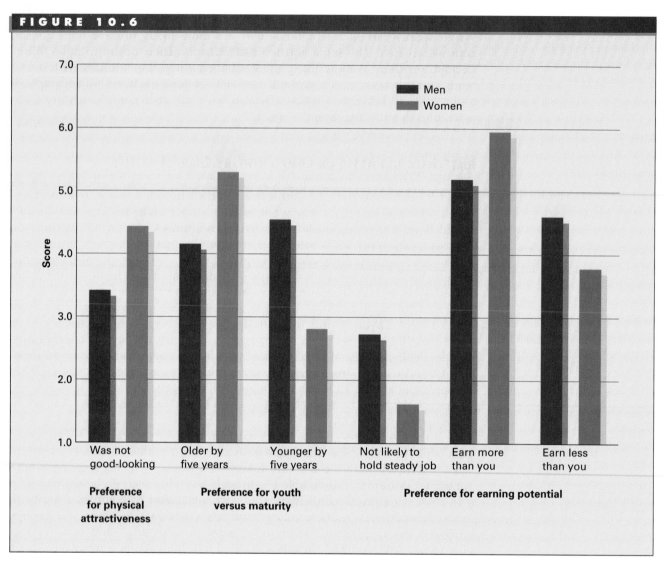

Gender Differences in Mate Selection Preferences

Sprecher, Sullivan, and Hatfield (1994) asked more than 1,300 English-speaking and Spanish-speaking Americans who were single and under the age of 35 to consider some possible assets and liabilities in a marriage partner and to indicate their willingness to marry someone possessing each of these characteristics. A score of "1" indicated "not at all," while a score of "7" indicated "very willing." All of the gender comparisons listed above are significant. What do these findings tell us about gender differences in heterosexual mate preferences?

Source: Data from S. Sprecher et al., "Mate Selection Preferences: Gender Differences Examined in a National Sample" in *Journal of Personality and Social Psychology*, 66: 1074–1080, American Psychological Association, 1994.

Some see it as a logical explanation for why physical attractiveness standards exist that locates the human species within a larger comparative analysis with other species. Others see it as a social scientific explanation that justifies the perpetuation of male dominance and female subservience based on "the natural order of things."

A second perspective that attempts to explain gender differences in mate selection, namely, the *sociocultural* viewpoint, maintains that men seek beauty in a woman and women seek power in a man because of the widely different social statuses they have historically held in society (Howard et al., 1987). This social-exchange explanation argues that women have historically been excluded from power and are viewed by men as objects of exchange in the social marketplace.

Men place a premium on the quality or the beauty of this exchange object, and that is why physical attractiveness is sought in a woman. Because of their historically low status and their restricted ability to socially advance based on their own individual skills, women have been forced to tie their social advancement with the status of their mate. Thus, women seek men who are socially dominant and can be "good providers" (Bernard, 1981).

Which of these perspectives provides the best explanation is currently a hotly debated topic. If the sociocultural perspective is correct, recent social advances made by many women in North American and European countries (higher pay and increased social status) may cause shifts in the attractiveness preferences of both women and men. Women may look for more "beauty" in men, and men may look for more "economic status" in women.

WE LIKE THOSE WHO LIKE US

So far, we have discussed how attraction can be based on a number of personal and situational factors. Yet, one very simple reason why people might make it on our "liking chart" is that we discover they like us. Research has shown that we like people who like us and say nice things about us (Wood & Kallgren, 1988). There is nothing surprising about reciprocal liking. Balance theory (Heider, 1958) asserts that we will develop a liking relationship toward anything that is positively related to something we value. Thus, if we learn that people like us, we should be more attracted to them because they value something we value—ourselves!

This notion that we are attracted to those who like us raises the possibility that it is our perceptions of their liking for us, and not necessarily their true attitudes, that matter. In an interesting study, Rebecca Curtis and Kim Miller (1986) examined how people's interaction style changes once they believe that another likes or dislikes them. Upon arriving at the lab, participants were paired up, asked to spend five minutes getting to know one another, and then were separated. One half of this interaction pair was assigned to the target group and told that their partners (the perceivers) either liked or disliked them based on false information provided by the experimenter. The experimenter stressed to the target person that she was interested in determining how the perceivers would act now that they had been given this false information about the targets. In actuality, the perceivers were never given any information at all. The experimenter's real goal was to manipulate the targets' perceptions, not the perceivers'. After this manipulation, the targets were asked to act as naturally as possible when they interacted again with the perceivers during a ten-minute discussion of current events.

Because this study is similar to the previously discussed phone experiments involving the physical attractiveness stereotype (Anderson & Bem, 1981; Snyder et al., 1977), it is not surprising that these false perceptions about the perceivers not only influenced the targets' behavior, they also influenced the perceivers' beliefs about their partner. Those targets who believed that the other person liked them disclosed more, had a more pleasant tone of voice and general attitude, and disagreed less with the perceiver than those who thought the perceiver disliked them. How did the perceivers evaluate their partners? They liked better those targets who had been led to believe that they were liked more than those who thought they were disliked. These findings suggest there is a *self-fulfilling prophecy* of liking, just as there is for the physical attractiveness stereotype. If we think others like us, we tend to act in ways that increase the likelihood that they will indeed like us. However, if we think they dislike us, our subsequent interaction style may fulfill the negative prophecy even if it is based on false information.

The only way to have a friend is to be one.

Ralph Waldo Emerson, U.S. poet, 1803–1882

SECTION SUMMARY

A third aspect of the social world that determines interpersonal attraction is the potential target of affiliation. Physically attractive people are perceived to possess more socially desirable personality characteristics and are thought to lead healthier, happier, and more fulfilling lives. This *physical attractiveness stereotype* generally gives "beautiful" people a decided edge in interpersonal exchanges, but these social perceptions are not grounded in reality. There is wide cultural variability in what people find beautiful or handsome, yet within cultures, consensus typically reigns. Regardless of sexual orientation, men place a higher value on a physically attractive partner than do women. Women are considered to be more attractive if they have immature and dependent-looking facial features, while men are considered more appealing with mature facial characteristics related to social dominance. The greater focus on the female body as an aesthetic object results in a decline in female *body esteem* starting in late childhood, especially among those with traditional feminine gender roles. Another factor influencing attraction is *similarity*. While there is ample evidence that "birds of a feather flock together," this does not mean that opposites cannot attract. Perhaps the best evidence for *complementary* characteristics leading to attraction is found in heterosexual mate selection, where men are attracted to female beauty and women are attracted to high male social status. The two most frequently mentioned explanations for this looks-for-status exchange are the *evolutionary* and the *sociocultural* perspectives. Finally, a simple reason why we may be attracted to some people over others is reciprocal liking.

WHEN SOCIAL INTERACTION BECOMES PROBLEMATIC

Throughout this chapter we have examined factors that prompt us to seek out others. However, whenever we approach others, we risk rejection. Even if others do accept our social overtures, there is the further possibility that we may commit a social blunder that will cause them to form a negative impression of us. How do we respond to these social "landmines"?

SOCIAL ANXIETY CAN KEEP US ISOLATED FROM OTHERS

Social Anxiety

The unpleasant emotion people experience due to their concern with interpersonal evaluation.

Social anxiety is the unpleasant emotion we experience due to our concern with interpersonal evaluation (Leary & Kowalski, 1995). This anxiety is what causes us to occasionally (or frequently) avoid social interaction. We can experience social anxiety even when alone: simply anticipating social interaction is often sufficient to arouse it. For example, do you remember how you have sometimes felt just before a "big date" or an important job interview? The social jitters you experience are due to you anticipating an interaction in which you have a vested interest.

When socially anxious, we are less likely to initiate interactions, and when in an interaction, we talk less, sometimes stammer and stutter when we do speak, disclose less about ourselves, and occasionally even withdraw from the anxiety-producing situation altogether (Daly et al., 1997; McCroskey, 1997). This tendency to socially withdraw is not an effect characteristic of anxiety per se. As you have already discovered (see pp. 358–361), when we are anxious due to nonsocial factors, we often affiliate more, not less (Schachter, 1959). Therefore, avoiding affiliation generally occurs only when the source of the anxiety involves other people, either real or imagined.

Although almost everyone occasionally experiences social anxiety, the unfortunate consequence of chronic social anxiety, or *social anxiousness*, is that it can trap a person into increasingly unpleasant social exchanges (DePaulo et al., 1990). Fearing negative reactions from others, individuals high in social anxiousness often act in ways—avoiding eye contact, appearing nervous and jittery—that fulfill the self-prophecy (Pozo et al., 1991).

To understand the nature of social anxiety, keep in mind something stated early in the text about the self: as self-reflective creatures, we actively construct our social reality. Schachter's anxiety-affiliation research indicated that in a given situation, when we are unsure about our own emotional reactions, we often compare them with the reactions of similar others. Schachter (1964) took this insight and expanded on it in his **two-factor theory of emotions.** He proposed that if people are emotionally aroused but are not sure what they are feeling, they will look for cues in their surroundings. If others are happy, they are likely to interpret their arousal as happiness. If others are anxious, they too are likely to feel anxious. Thus, according to Schachter, our emotions are based on two components: physiological arousal and cognitions about what that arousal means. Consistent with the two-factor theory of emotions, research has demonstrated that the attributions we make concerning our physiological responses to a particular stimulus will often, but not always, determine our emotional reactions (Reisenzein, 1983).

To illustrate how this self-attributional process might influence social anxiety, James Olson (1988) asked Canadian college students to read a speech while wearing headphones. Some participants believed that the noise they were hearing over the headphones contained a subliminal sound that would make them feel tense and anxious. A second group was told that this subliminal sound would make them feel pleasantly relaxed and calm, and the control group was told the noise would do nothing. Just before reading the speech, a video camera was pointed at them to further induce arousal. Results indicated that those who believed they would feel tense and anxious due to the subliminal sound gave smoother, more fluent speeches than either the participants who expected to feel calm or those who were given no expectations.

Are these results surprising to you? Why would those who thought the noise would make them feel tense and anxious behave so calmly when speaking? The reason for this effect is **misattribution of arousal,** in which the explanation of the physiological symptoms of arousal are switched from the real source to some external source. In Olson's experiment, the presence of what was thought to be arousing subliminal noise provided a convincing, neutral label for symptoms actually caused by the speech task. Believing their anxiety was due to an external source having no association with the upcoming speech, these participants were able to avoid the ever-increasing anxiety produced by fears of negative evaluation. Noticing their arousal, they told themselves: "This speech isn't making me anxious. My discomfort is caused by this noise." The other two groups could make no such attribution. Instead, after noticing their arousal, they were likely to think: "Gosh, I'm really anxious! I don't know if I can get through this speech!"

Although misattribution of arousal can reduce social anxiety and thereby increase social functioning, there are limits to its effectiveness. The crucial factor is that level of arousal must be relatively low so that its true cause is open to interpretation (Olson & Ross, 1988). When people are extremely aroused, they usually recognize its true source and, thus, are not likely to misattribute (Conger et al., 1976). Therefore, it is unlikely that prior to delivering a speech to a large audience, a person will incorrectly attribute her high anxiety to the distant sound of a droning lawnmower.

Two-Factor Theory of Emotions

A theory that emotional experience is based on two factors: physiological arousal and cognitive labeling of the cause of that arousal.

Misattribution of Arousal

A situation in which the explanation of the physiological symptoms of arousal is switched from the real source to another one.

Loneliness Is the Consequence of Social Isolation

Although the anticipation of evaluation can make us anxious, how do you think you would react to being cut off from meaningful interaction with others? Because of our need for others, the loss of meaningful social exchange would likely be quite detrimental.

Defining and Measuring Loneliness

Loneliness is defined as having a smaller or less satisfying network of social and intimate relationships than we desire (Marangoni & Ickes, 1989). In understanding loneliness, keep in mind that this is a subjective experience, reflecting what we feel and think about our interpersonal life, and, as such, is not the same thing as solitude or being alone. We can spend long periods of time alone without feeling lonely, and we can also feel terribly lonely in a crowd. In fact, research has shown that lonely and nonlonely people do not differ in the *quantity* of their social interaction, but rather in the *quality* of such exchanges. Lonely people spend more time with strangers and acquaintances and less time with friends and family than those who are not lonely (Jones et al., 1985).

Similar to social anxiety, we can experience loneliness as both a short-lived *state* and a chronic, long-term *trait*. For example, when you first arrived on campus in your freshman year, you may have experienced a temporary sense of loneliness until you became integrated into the college community. In contrast, some people suffer from chronic loneliness, regardless of the length of time they spend becoming acclimated to new social settings. Although loneliness is a subjective experience, social psychologists have developed objective measures to identify lonely people. One of the more commonly used measures is the UCLA Loneliness Scale (Russell et al., 1980), which asks people to indicate how often they experience such feelings. Spend a few minutes completing a variation of this scale in table 10.3, and then compare your score with the sample of other young adults.

Although almost everyone experiences loneliness, our recovery from it often depends on how we interpret and react to its perceived causes (Anderson et al., 1994). In an examination of the duration of loneliness experienced by first-year college students, Carolyn Cutrona (1982) found that it lasted longer among those who initially blamed themselves for their social isolation. That is, the chronically lonely made significantly more *internal, stable attributions* for their loneliness (for example, "I'm too shy" or "I don't know how to start a new relationship") than those who overcame their sense of isolation. Unfortunately, as can be seen in table 10.4, this sort of self-blaming can discourage people from seeking out others and can perpetuate their dissatisfaction with social relationships. On the other hand, Cutrona found that those who thought of loneliness as being caused by a combination of personal and external factors (for example, "I'm lonely because I don't know anyone here. Things will get better as I meet others") seemed to be more hopeful that they could make things change for the better. True to what would be expected from attribution theory (refer to chapter 3), these *external, unstable attributions* resulted in relatively short-lived loneliness for most of these students.

Age, Gender, and Loneliness

Who suffers the most from loneliness? Contrary to popular stereotypes, it is not the elderly. Numerous studies have identified the young—adolescents and young adults—as the loneliest age groups (Peplau et al., 1982). As people mature and move beyond the young adult years, their loneliness tends to decrease until relatively late in life, when factors such as poor health begin to restrict social activities (Schultz & Moore, 1984). One reason why adolescents and young adults may be more lonely than older individuals is that young people face many more social transitions, such as falling in and out of love for the first time, leaving family and

TABLE 10.3 **383**

Measuring Loneliness

Directions

Indicate how often each of the statements below is descriptive of you.

Circle one letter for each statement:

O indicates "I often feel this way"
S indicates "I sometimes feel this way"
R indicates "I rarely feel this way"
N indicates "I never feel this way"

1. How often do you feel unhappy doing so many things alone?	O	S	R	N
2. How often do you feel you have nobody to talk to?	O	S	R	N
3. How often do you feel you cannot tolerate being so alone?	O	S	R	N
4. How often do you feel as if nobody really understands you?	O	S	R	N
5. How often do you find yourself waiting for people to call or write?	O	S	R	N
6. How often do you feel completely alone?	O	S	R	N
7. How often do you feel you are unable to reach out and communicate with those around you?	O	S	R	N
8. How often do you feel starved for company?	O	S	R	N
9. How often do you feel it is difficult for you to make friends?	O	S	R	N
10. How often do you feel shut out and excluded by others?	O	S	R	N

Scoring

For each question, give yourself 1 point if you responded "never" (N), 2 points if you responded "rarely" (R), 3 points if you responded "sometimes" (S), and 4 points if you responded "often" (O). Your total loneliness score is computed by adding your score on each of the ten questions together.

Normative Data for This Loneliness Measure (Ten-Item Version)

Group	Average Score
College Students	20
Nurses	20
Public School Teachers	19
Elderly	16

Based on these normative data, a score above 30 in this version of the scale would indicate that the person is experiencing severe levels of loneliness.

Note: These are substitute items for the UCLA Loneliness Scale devised by Russell et al., 1980.
Source: From Russell, D., Peplau, L. A., & Ferguson, M. L. (1978). "Developing a Measure of Loneliness." *Journal of Personality Assessment*, 42:290–294. Copyright © Lawrence Erlbaum Associates. Reprinted by permission.

I see loneliness ooze damply from people's bodies, trail after them, trickling, widening, running deep, flowing on and on forever.

Kaneko Mitsuharu, 1977, Japanese poet

friends, and training and searching for a full-time job—all of which can cause loneliness. Another reason for this decrease in loneliness with age is that as we mature, we often settle into long-term romantic relationships and marriages, where the accompanying emotional bonds contribute to overall mental health (Russell, 1982).

There are clear age differences in loneliness, but gender differences are not as clear-cut. Some studies have found a slight tendency for women to report greater loneliness than men, yet other studies fail to find any differences at all (Archibald et al., 1995; Brage et al., 1993). Despite any firm evidence for gender differences in

TABLE 10.4

Causal Attributions for Loneliness

Stability	Locus of Causality	
	Internal	**External**
Stable	"I'm too shy." "I don't know how to start new relationships."	"Other people don't try to make friends."
Unstable	"I'm lonely because I haven't tried hard enough to meet others. I can change that by letting others know I'm fun to be around."	"I'm lonely because I don't know anyone here. Things will get better as I meet others."

Source: Based partly on Cutrona, 1982.

the *degree* of loneliness, there does appear to be evidence that males and females feel lonely for different *reasons*. Males tend to feel lonely when deprived of group interaction; females are more likely to feel lonely when they lack one-to-one emotional sharing (Stokes & Levin, 1986). This different pattern of loneliness reflects a difference in the friendship patterns of males and females that will be discussed in chapter 11.

SOCIAL SKILLS DEFICITS AND LONELINESS

Similar to the negative consequences of social anxiousness, chronically lonely people often think and behave in ways that reduce their likelihood of establishing new, rewarding relationships. Studies conducted with college students illustrate some of these self-defeating patterns of behavior. Typically, in these investigations, students who are strangers to one another are asked to briefly interact in either pairs or groups, after which they rate themselves and their partners on such interpersonal dimensions as friendliness, honesty, and openness. Compared with nonlonely individuals, lonely college students rate themselves negatively following such laboratory interactions. They perceive themselves as having been less friendly, less honest and open, and less warm (Christensen & Kashy, 1998; W. Jones et al., 1981, 1983). They also expect those who interact with them to perceive them in this negative manner. This expectation of failure in social interaction appears all the more hopeless to the chronically lonely because they believe that improving their social life is beyond their control (Duck et al., 1994).

If chronically lonely people were merely misperceiving their effect on others, you might expect that other people's positive feedback concerning their social competence would break down their misperceptions. The problem, however, is that the chronically lonely tend to lack social skills and, as a result, receive little positive reinforcement from others concerning their interaction style. Indeed, they are generally disliked or ignored by others, who see them as weak, unattractive, and insincere (Rotenberg et al., 1997).

What sort of social skills deficits do chronically lonely persons exhibit in their daily interactions? When conversing with another, the chronically lonely spend more time talking about themselves and take less interest in what their partner has to say than do nonlonely people (Jones et al., 1982). Consistent with the interaction style of those with low self-esteem, they also tend to perceive others in a negative light (Rotenberg & Kmill, 1992). When meeting such a person, new acquaintances often come away with negative impressions (Jones et al., 1983). Confronted with

. . . **S**itting down to one plate, that loneliest of all positions.

Caroline Gilman, U.S. author and educator, 1794–1888

the negative social judgments accompanying this sort of inept social style, lonely individuals often immerse themselves in their occupations, withdraw into wish-fulfilling fantasies, or engage in self-destructive activities such as alcohol and drug abuse. Not surprisingly, lonely people often use the television and radio as substitutes for interpersonal relationships. Unfortunately, the content of a good deal of mass media programming focuses on failed relationships and sadness, which actually can deepen one's sense of social isolation (Davis & Kraus, 1989).

SECTION SUMMARY

Many social psychological factors prompt us to seek out others, but *social anxiety* can cause us to avoid interaction. Although almost everyone occasionally experiences social anxiety, chronic social anxiety can trap a person into increasingly unpleasant social exchanges. When a person has a smaller or less satisfying network of social and intimate relationships than desired, he or she experiences *loneliness*. Adolescents and young adults are the loneliest age groups, but as people mature their loneliness tends to decrease until relatively late in life. People who are chronically lonely often lack social skills, which leads to many negative and rejecting social exchanges.

APPLICATIONS

HOW CAN SOCIAL SKILLS TRAINING IMPROVE YOUR LIFE?

ne of the most important obstacles that chronically lonely people must overcome is their lack of social skills (Solano & Koester, 1989). The same statement could also be made of those who experience high levels of social anxiousness, for they do not make good first impressions and often experience loneliness (Curran, 1977). This social deficiency is likely one of the more important causes of the low self-esteem of lonely and socially anxious individuals. It can also lead to a feeling of hopelessness and increased social withdrawal (Page, 1991). On the other hand, those who have well-developed social skills find it easy to talk to strangers, are perceived by others as friendly, are not easily angered, and possess high self-esteem (Reisman, 1984).

What makes a person socially skilled? One of the most important factors determining social skill is the *amount of personal attention given to one's partner* in interaction (Kupke et al., 1979). People who are judged

to be socially skilled direct more questions toward their conversational partners and make more positive personal statements about them. On the other hand, the unskilled are more self-focused and less responsive when conversing. Some social scientists suggest that this sort of "conversational narcissism," in which people habitually turn conversational topics to themselves without showing interest in their partners' topics, may be more prevalent in individualist cultures than in those with collectivist orientations (Vangelisti et al., 1990). These conversational narcissists have taken the individualist notion that personal needs are more important than group needs to the point where they ignore the interaction needs of others. The all-too-common price for such narcissism is social rejection.

A second factor related to social effectiveness is the *ability to recognize and conform to social norms.* People who have social skills problems often engage in situationally improper behavior. For example, they may make new acquaintances uncomfortable by disclosing very personal details about their lives. Although this sort of self-disclosure is important and valuable in intimate relationships, it is considered inappropriate when interacting with strangers and new acquaintances. Such norm violations generally discourage future encounters.

Given the fact that social skills promote greater relationship satisfaction, considerable research has been devoted to developing **social skills training** programs for both children and adults (Greca, 1993). These programs employ various learning techniques, including the observation and modeling of socially skilled trainers, role-playing various problematic social encounters, and observing one's own social interactions on videotape. The social skills taught in these training sessions cover such areas as initiating conversations, speaking fluently on the telephone, giving and receiving compliments, handling periods of silence, nonverbal methods of communication, and actively listening to what others have to say in conversation (Kelly, 1997).

Training is usually conducted in groups. In a typical session, the instructor might show a videotape of a model starting a conversation inappropriately or failing to respond to someone's compliment. The group might then discuss ways in which the model could have acted more appropriately. Following this discussion, another videotape might be shown in which the model performs more effectively. Each person in the training group might then role-play a conversation while others observe and then provide feedback. This role playing might even be videotaped so that group members can see exactly how they had interacted. The session might end with a homework assignment for group members to start a conversation with a stranger during the following week.

A growing body of research indicates that those who participate in such training exercises show improvements in their social skills and an increased level of social satisfaction (Erwin, 1994; Margalit, 1995). In one such intervention study, Warren Jones and his colleagues (1982) taught lonely college men to increase their personal attention shown to female strangers during a series of dyadic interactions. They were first given information on the importance of paying attention to others in conversation, and then they interacted individually with four women in successive five-minute, taped conversations. Following these four dyadic interactions, the lonely men were next instructed how to ask questions of their conversational partners, how to refer to their partners while talking to them, and how to discuss topics of interest with their partners. Training consisted of modeling, practice interaction, and feedback. Compared with two control groups of lonely men who did not receive instruction in personal attention, the trained students subsequently reported feeling less lonely, less self-conscious, and less shy.

The particular skills emphasized in many training programs appear best suited to facilitate the *initiation* of social relationships. Although this is a necessary starting point, it is also important for people to learn skills for "deepening" relationships and overcoming interpersonal conflict. One study that attempted to

Social Skills Training

A behavioral training program designed to improve interpersonal skills through observation, modeling, role-playing, and behavioral rehearsal.

Calvin and Hobbes   by Bill Watterson

YOU KNOW WHAT I LIKE TO DO WHEN SOMEONE'S TALKING TO ME? I STARE AT THE PERSON'S CHIN.

I'LL NOD AND RESPOND TO WHATEVER HE'S SAYING, BUT I KEEP LOOKING AT HIS CHIN AND CHANGING MY EXPRESSION.

I LOOK QUIZZICAL AT FIRST, THEN VAGUELY REPULSED, AND LATER, QUIETLY AMUSED. THEN I'LL SUDDENLY ARCH MY EYEBROWS AND BLINK A LOT, AND THEN I LOOK SKEPTICAL AND DISBELIEVING.

YOU GET BONUS POINTS EVERY TIME THE PERSON LOSES HIS TRAIN OF THOUGHT.

I'LL BET YOUR NATURAL CHARM HAS MADE YOU A GOOD SPRINTER.

© 1993 Watterson/Distributed by Universal Press Syndicate

People who possess the interpersonal skills necessary for daily living lead happier, more fulfilling lives than those who are lacking in these skills. Can you identify some of the more important factors determining social skills that Calvin has yet to master?

train such skills was conducted by Robin Cappe and Lynn Alden (1986). They recruited twenty-six men and twenty-six women who were at least moderately socially impaired and exposed them to different types of training programs. Some recruits were instructed on four human relations skills necessary in developing and strengthening friendships: *active listening, empathic responding, communicating respect,* and *self-disclosure.* The instructors discussed and modeled each skill. Participants then practiced their own problematic social situations and incorporated these new skills into each situation. In addition to learning these social skills, participants also learned how to relax when feeling anxious. A second group of recruits was not given any social skills training, but merely learned how to relax in anxiety-producing situations. Finally, a third group received no training at all. Results indicated that the shy, socially avoidant individuals who received a combination of social skills training and relaxation instruction reported significantly greater improve-

ments in their social functioning in the community than those who either received only relaxation training or no instruction at all. In addition, those who were given training in social skills were judged by independent observers to be more comfortable and skillful in social interactions than those in the other groups. A three-month follow-up assessment indicated that a greater proportion of those who had received the social skills training reported having made significant social changes in their lives. These events varied in social impact from minor ("I was able to join a club") to major ("I was able to date and am now engaged").

Taken together, what these studies indicate is that social skills training programs can, in a fairly short period of time, teach socially anxious and lonely people how to interact more effectively with others. The resulting interpersonal successes they experience can not only reduce their feeling of social isolation but can also boost their sense of social competence and their overall level of self-esteem.

FEATURED STUDY
MOOD REGULATION PRIOR TO SOCIAL INTERACTION

Erber, R., Wegner, D. M., & Therriault, N. (1996). On being cool and collected: Mood regulation in anticipation of social interaction. *Journal of Personality and Social Psychology, 70,* 757–766.

People who are socially skilled engage in many forms of mental control in preparing themselves for social interaction, with one of the primary forms being imposing constraints on their emotions. Such mood regulation is especially necessary when interacting with strangers, due to the importance of first impressions. In the present three-experiment investigation, the researchers hypothesized that when people anticipate interacting with a stranger, they would attempt to regulate their mood in the direction of *neutrality,* regardless of whether their current mood was positive or negative. This prediction of mood neutrality was made for at least two reasons. First, being perceived by new acquaintances as "cool" and "calm" is a socially desirable goal for most people, and a neutral mood is most consistent with attaining that goal. Second, during first encounters, arriving with a preexisting positive or negative mood might be interpreted by a new interaction partner as an attempt to impose one's own mood on her or him, which could lead to negative evaluations.

In Experiments 1 and 2, participants' moods were manipulated by the playing of either cheerful or sad music. The results indicated that, in preparing to interact with a stranger following these mood inductions, participants generally did indeed try to neutralize their moods: they chose to read happy newspaper articles when exposed to sad music and depressing stories when exposed to cheerful music. The only time neutralization did not occur was when (in Experiment 2) participants anticipated interacting with someone who already shared their mood and when happy participants were expecting to interact with a sad stranger.

The third experiment in this series, which is described next, did not manipulate participants' mood. Instead, it hypothesized that people who expected to interact with a stranger with an unknown mood would actively avoid exposing themselves to material that could change their mood in either a positive or negative direction.

METHOD

Participants were sixty undergraduate students (thirty-three female, twenty-seven male) who were told that they were taking part in an experiment to explore social interaction patterns and styles. Each participant was randomly assigned to watch either a happy or depressing video. The *happy video* contained a fifteen-minute clip of comedy routines by Robin Williams and Ellen DeGeneres, while the *depressing video* contained a fifteen-minute clip of a documentary on homelessness. Half of the participants watched the video with the expectation that they would subsequently meet another same-sex student and, after this interaction, give their opinion of it and the other person. The other half anticipated filling out questionnaires on their opinions about social interactions. In both conditions, the experimenter told participants to watch as much of the video as they wanted and to stop it when they had watched enough. Before leaving the room, the experimenter said she would return in ten minutes. The amount of time participants spent watching the video served as the dependent variable. When the experimenter returned, she fully debriefed the participants.

RESULTS AND DISCUSSION

Results indicated that participants spent less time watching the happy and depressing videos when they expected to interact with another person than when they expected to simply complete a social interaction questionnaire. This finding that participants reduced their exposure to potentially mood-altering information (the videos) when they expected to interact with another suggests that they may have tried to avoid attaining a mood that would be inappropriate for interacting with a stranger.

Overall, the findings from the three studies support the hypothesis that when people expect that they will soon be meeting someone they do not know, they consciously try to regulate their mood so that it is relatively neutral. The only times this does not appear to happen (Experiment 2) is when people know beforehand that the person they are about to meet shares their current mood, or when people are happy and they know that the person they are about to meet is depressed. In the latter instance, the researchers suggest that the failure to neutralize a happy mood might be a self-protective strategy employed by happy people. That is, they may not neutralize their positive emotions because they may believe that they will soon need their positive mood to buffer themselves against the contagious sadness of their interaction partner.

WEB SITES accessed through http://www.mhhe.com/franzoi2

Web sites for this chapter focus on research and theory on interpersonal relationships, as well as an analysis of shyness, social anxiety, and loneliness.

International Society for the Study of Personal Relationships

This web site for the International Society for the Study of Personal Relationships lists information about interpersonal relationship publications and conferences, as well as links to other relevant sites.

Shyness Institute

This web page is a gathering of network resources for people seeking information and services for shyness and social anxiety.

American Psychological Association

The American Psychological Association web site contains a web page which discusses research indicating that the internet increases social isolation among users.

C H A P T E R   1 1

INTIMATE RELATIONSHIPS

n Robert Munsch's (1986) children's book, *Love You Forever,* he tells a movingly offbeat story about a mother-son relationship. It begins with the mother holding her new baby and slowly rocking him back and forth while singing the following verse:

I'll love you forever,
I'll like you for always,
As long as I'm living
my baby you'll be.

As the child grows, he gets into all sorts of messes and squabbles and does a nice job aging the mother. Despite these hassles of childrearing, each night as he slept, the mother would look into his room, crawl across the floor, and look up over the side of the bed. If he was truly asleep, she carefully picked him up, slowly rocked him back and forth, and sang her song to him.

When he grew up and moved across town, sometimes the mother would strap a ladder to her car late at night, drive to her son's house, climb into his room and crawl to the foot of his bed. If he was truly asleep, she carefully picked up this full-grown man and slowly rocked him back and forth, singing her song as she gazed into his peaceful face.

Well, one day when the mother was old and feeble, she phoned her son and told him to come over quickly because she was very sick. When he arrived, the mother tried to sing her song but could not finish. Instead then, the grownup son carefully picked up his mother, held her in his arms, and began to slowly rock her back and forth. As he rocked her, he sang the following verse:

I'll love you forever,
I'll like you for always,
As long as I'm living
my Mommy you'll be.

Later, when he returned to his own home, he went to his newborn daughter's room where she peacefully slept. Reaching down, he gently picked her up in his arms, held her close, and slowly began to rock her back and forth. As he rocked her, he sang:

I'll love you forever,
I'll like you for always,
As long as I'm living
my baby you'll be.

The deeply tender and nurturing feelings expressed in Robert Munsch's story mirrors the story that psychologists tell about intimate relationships: children learn about intimacy and love during the first few years of life, and this forms the basis for how they will interact with others in later years.

In this chapter, we extend our discussion of interpersonal attraction by exploring the nature of close personal relationships. We examine the intimacy experienced in parent-child interactions, friendships, and romantic relationships,

Robert Munsch's book, Love You Forever, *is a funny but moving depiction of the positive emotional bonds that parents have with their children. What sort of attachment style (see pp. 396–399) do you think the son in this story developed?*

each of which offers its own unique contributions to our health and welfare (Davis et al., 1998). This is a journey we all have traveled before. Yet now, instead of trying to understand friendship and love simply by immersing ourselves in the experience, we survey the social psychological literature to better understand how scientists explain the communion of selves. Our social psychological journey begins with a discussion of what is encompassed in the term *intimacy.*

WHAT IS INTIMACY?

Imagine that you overhear another person make a disparaging remark about someone you love. How would you feel, and how might you respond? Now imagine that the one you care about has succeeded on an important task. Or done very poorly. How would this influence your mood? If you're like most people, you would *share* with that person the emotional highs and lows accompanying these events. **Intimacy** refers to sharing that which is inmost with others (McAdams, 1988, p. 18). The word itself is derived from the Latin *intimus,* which means "inner" or "inmost."

INTIMACY INVOLVES INCLUDING ANOTHER IN YOUR SELF-CONCEPT

As you recall from chapter 2, William James conceived of the "self as object" (or self-concept) as being a process of identification, expanding and contracting to include that which one values. Arthur Aron and Elaine Aron (1986, 1997) have adopted James's notion of *self-expansion* in their analysis of the experience of intimacy. They contend that in intimate relationships, people seek to psychologically expand themselves by acting as if some or all aspects of their partner are part of their own selves (Aron et al., 1992). Figure 11.1 provides a schematic illustration of different levels of intimacy through this self-expansion process.

This removal of psychological boundaries between people so that one experiences another as part of him- or herself is often identified as the most important distinguishing feature of intimacy (Harvey & Omarzu, 1997). Yet if intimacy is really an "inclusionary" experience, can researchers detect it by studying the structure and the process of the self? Let's examine various research areas where evidence for this inclusionary process has been found.

Intimacy

Sharing that which is inmost with others.

Each friend represents a world in us, a world possibly not born until they arrive, and it is only by this meeting that a new world is born.

Anaïs Nin, U.S. novelist, 1903–1977

A friend is, as it were, a second self.

Marcus Tullius Cicero, Roman statesman, 106–43 B.C.

FIGURE 11.1

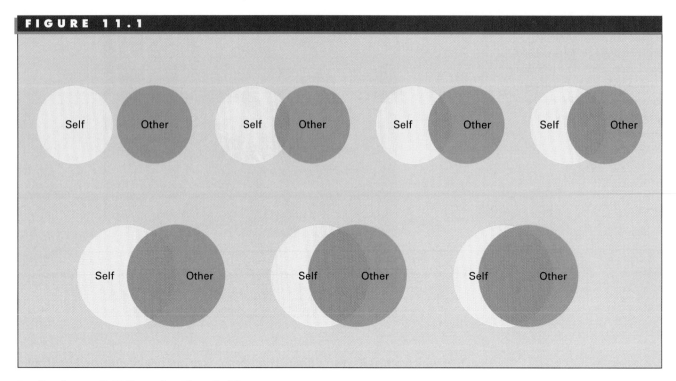

Inclusion of Other in the Self

This is a schematic illustration of seven different degrees of self-other relatedness, from no inclusion of the other in the self to an immersion of the other in one's self. Which of the pictures best describes different intimate relationships in your own life?

THE ATTRIBUTION PROCESS

One way intimacy manifests itself is in the attribution process. As discussed in chapter 3, when people make attributions about events, the perspective they have of their own versus others' behavior results in what is called the *actor-observer effect*—the tendency to attribute our own behavior to external causes but that of others to internal factors (Jones & Nisbett, 1971). This self-other discrepancy has been found to be significantly less pronounced when the "other" is more intimate with the self (Nisbett et al., 1973). In other words, when explaining the actions of someone for whom we care a great deal, the attributions we infer are more similar to those we would have for our own actions versus those of the average person on the street (Lavin, 1987).

RESOURCE ALLOCATION

Resource allocation is another way in which we include others within our self-concept. People in an intimate relationship make less of a distinction between self and other when allocating resources than do those who are less intimately acquainted (Aron et al., 1991). Why? Because if another is included in our self-concept, our resources are also the other's resources. Imagine two couples going out to dinner together, one pair deeply in love, the other pair on their first date. During the course of the meal, the two lovers eat from each other's plate, often reaching for morsels of food without asking permission. If, in a similar manner, one person from the nonintimate pair reached for the other's food, it would likely be interpreted as very bad manners. Regardless of who is paying for the meal, it would be an encroachment on the other's personal resources.

COMMUNAL VERSUS EXCHANGE RELATIONSHIPS

The different disbursement of resources to an intimate other naturally leads to another quality indicative of the "self-inclusion of other" perspective. In most of our everyday relationships, we operate on the principle of *exchange* by carefully

TABLE 11.1

Exchange Versus Communal Relationships

Exchange Relationships (Governed by concern for equity)	Communal Relationships (Governed by responsiveness to the other's needs)
1. Person motivated by a desire to have a "fair" relationship	1. Person motivated by a desire to please the other person
2. Person desires to be immediately repaid for favors	2. Person dislikes being immediately repaid for favors
3. Person feels exploited when favors are not returned	3. Person does not feel exploited when favors are not returned
4. Person keeps track of who is contributing what to the relationship	4. Person does not keep track of who is contributing what to the relationship
5. Helping one's partner doesn't elevate one's mood	5. Helping one's partner elevates one's mood

If I have no love, I am nothing. . . . Love is patient; love is kind and envies no one. Love is never boastful, nor conceited, nor rude; never selfish, not quick to take offence. Love keeps no score of wrongs; does not gloat over other men's sins, but delights in the truth. . . . Love will never come to an end.

I Corinthians 13

tallying our costs and balancing those against our rewards to determine whether we should maintain the relationship. However, Margaret Clark and Judson Mills have demonstrated that when we are involved in intimate relationships we often do not think about our rewards and costs as if we were balancing our bank accounts (Mills & Clark, 1994). Instead, these *communal relationships* are organized according to the principle that people are to be given what they need, with little concern for what we will receive in return (Clark et al., 1989). Thus, in intimate relationships, we treat our loved ones' needs as if they were our own. Because these intimate others are important elements in our own self-concept, our needs and their needs are intertwined and often indistinguishable. Table 11.1 summarizes the differences between these two different types of relationships.

SELF-SCHEMAS

A fourth way in which intimate relationships reflect the inclusion of the other in the self-concept is in what constitutes self-concept ingredients, or *self-schemas*. As discussed in chapter 2, traits that we identify as being important in our self-concepts are recognized as being self-descriptive more quickly than traits that are not relevant to our self-concepts (Markus, 1977). Research comparing the self-schemas of strangers, friends, and married couples has found that as the intimacy bond deepens between two people, they begin to incorporate some of the other's self-schemas into their own self-concepts. As a result of this cognitive blurring of the self-other distinction, people involved in intimate relationships need less time to recognize self-descriptive traits if the traits are also shared with their partner (Aron et al., 1991). For example, imagine that Ann and Stephanie are involved in an intimate relationship. Ann has self-schemas consisting of such traits as independent, tidy, and industrious. Stephanie sees herself as independent, industrious, and athletic. The speed at which they can individually process and recall self-descriptive traits will be faster for traits they share (independent, industrious) rather than those upon which they differ. Even though Ann has a self-schema for "tidy" and Stephanie has a self-schema for "athletic," because the intimate other does not share this trait it takes them longer to identify it as being self-descriptive.

We are molded and remolded by those who have loved us; and, though the love may pass, we are nevertheless their work, for good or ill.

Francois Mauriac, French novelist, 1885–1970

TRANSACTIVE MEMORY

Finally, a fifth way that the self-inclusion of the other is manifested is in the reliance on what has been called *transactive memory*. Daniel Wegner and his colleagues (1991) have found evidence that people in intimate relationships have a shared memory system for encoding, storing, and retrieving information that is greater than either of their individual memories. In this transactive memory, each partner enjoys the benefits of the pair's memory by taking responsibility for remembering just those items that fall clearly to her or him (Andersson & Rónnberg, 1997). For a romantic couple living together, this may involve one person assuming responsibility for remembering the proper place for all the workroom tools, while the other assumes responsibility for remembering where the special dinnerware and napkins are stored. If each person learns in a general way what the other knows in detail, the two can share the detailed memories enjoyed by both. Through updating one another on what is in each other's knowledge area, the partners further embellish their transactive memory (Engestrom et al., 1990).

In summary, these studies illustrate the utility of viewing close relationships as including the other in the self-concept. Partners who are high in intimacy are concerned about the other's welfare and happiness, often even more than their own. The rewards shared by intimates go far beyond "warm fuzzies." Numerous studies indicate that the quality of our personal relationships plays a vital role in our health and well-being (Lakey & Drew, 1997; Reis & Franks, 1994). Let us now examine the foundation for these intimacy beliefs.

SECTION SUMMARY

Intimacy is sharing that which is inmost with others, an inclusion of others in one's self-concept. Intimacy manifests itself in the attribution process, in resource allocation, in our self-schemas, and in the way in which we encode, store, and retrieve information from memory.

PARENT-CHILD ATTACHMENT AND LATER ADULT RELATIONSHIPS

The strong emotional bond that develops between infants and their caregivers is known as **attachment,** and it is considered to be the cornerstone for all other relationships in a child's life (Reis & Patrick, 1998). Based on his analysis of both orphaned children and other species, British psychiatrist John Bowlby (1969) proposed that attachment is part of many species' genetic heritage, and its evolutionary function is to keep immature animals close to their parents where they are better protected from predators. In other words, infants who cling to their parents stand a better chance of surviving to adulthood than those who wander away from their protective care.

CHILDREN DEVELOP DIFFERENT ATTACHMENT STYLES

Although our biological heritage may propel us toward our caregivers, the basic principles of reinforcement theory suggest that the caregiver's response will influence the strength of this desire to establish such proximity. Parent-child attachment research by Mary Ainsworth (1989) identified three types of relationships between infants and their mothers. Infants with a **secure attachment style** have caregivers who are sensitive and responsive to their signals of distress, happiness, and fatigue.

Knowledge is of two kinds. We know a subject ourselves or we know where we can find information about it.

Samuel Johnson, English author, 1709–1784

Attachment

The strong emotional bond an infant forms with its primary caregiver.

Secure Attachment Style

An expectation about social relationships characterized by trust, a lack of concern with being abandoned, and a feeling of being valued and well liked.

Avoidant Attachment Style

An expectation about social relationships characterized by a lack of trust and a suppression of attachment needs.

Anxious-Ambivalent Attachment Style

An expectation about social relationships characterized by a concern that others will not return affection.

This feeling of emotional security fosters a sense of trust in those close to them, a lack of concern with being abandoned, and a feeling that they are valued and well liked. Children with an **avoidant attachment style,** on the other hand, tend to have caregivers who behave aloof and distant, and they try to avoid their children's attempts to establish intimacy. As a result of this emotional distancing, the children develop a lack of trust in their social relationships and learn to suppress their attachment needs. Finally, children who form an **anxious-ambivalent attachment style** have caregivers who are inconsistent and overbearing in their affection, sometimes showering them with attention, while at other times expressing disinterest. Due to this inconsistent love, anxious-ambivalent children tend to be temperamental and anxious that others will not return their affection (Belsky & Cassidy, 1994).

Generally speaking, throughout childhood securely attached children exhibit greater social competence and higher levels of self-esteem and self-concept complexity than children in the two insecure groups (Schulman et al., 1994). Insecurely attached children often exhibit contradictory social behavior, sometimes initiating social contact, but then unexpectedly spurning others' social advances. This vacillating pattern of approach-avoidance invites social rejection from peers, which then serves to confirm the child's original sense of insecurity and distrust.

Although attachment appears to be a universal feature of human development, the nature of the attachment styles that children eventually develop also appears to be shaped by their culture (Harwood et al., 1995). For example, both U.S. and German children are far more likely than Japanese children to develop an avoidant attachment style (Cole, 1992). The reason for these cultural differences is probably due to different views on how to raise children. Parents in the United States and Germany try to foster independence at an earlier age, and thus, they discourage their children from staying near them and are more likely to give them toys or food when they cry rather than picking them up. In contrast, Japanese parents do not promote independence, and thus, they rarely leave their children alone and quickly pick them up when they cry.

CHILDHOOD ATTACHMENT STYLES INFLUENCE ADULT ROMANTIC RELATIONSHIPS

In an attempt to understand how these different attachment styles might affect adult intimate relationships, Cindy Hazan and Philip Shaver (1987) designed a "love quiz" and printed it in a local newspaper. Besides asking people questions about their current romantic relationships, they also asked respondents to choose one of the three descriptions shown in table 11.2 based on how they typically felt in these relationships. The results of this study and numerous others are consistent with attachment theory (Levy et al., 1998; Tidwell et al., 1998). Securely attached adults easily become close to others, expect intimate relationships to endure, perceive others as generally trustworthy, and handle relationship conflict constructively (Feeney & Kirkpatrick, 1996; Morrison et al., 1997). In contrast, avoidant adults are uncomfortable becoming intimate, find it hard to trust others, and often express hostility during relationship conflicts (Mikulincer, 1998). Because the avoidant style often prompts social rejection, it isn't surprising that avoidants report that they rarely find "true love." Similarly, anxious-ambivalent people also report having unsatisfactory intimate relationships, but, unlike the avoidants, they tend to be obsessed and preoccupied with their romantic partners, and they fear that their intense love will not be reciprocated (see p. 399).

Research that has examined the childhood experiences of adults who differ in attachment styles finds that the securely attached report positive family relationships when young, while the insecurely attached rate their childhood family environments

What is love? Ask him who lives, what is life. Ask him who adores, what is God . . . [Love] is that powerful attraction towards all that we conceive, or fear, or hope beyond ourselves, when we find within our own thoughts the chasm of an insufficient void, and seek to awaken in all things that are, a community with what we experience within ourselves.

Percy Bysshe Shelley, English poet, 1792–1824

TABLE 11.2

What Is Your Adult Attachment Style?

Hazan and Shaver (1987) placed a survey of attitudes toward love in a newspaper and invited readers to send in their responses. Included in this survey were these descriptions of different views of love, corresponding to different attachment styles. Interestingly, the percentages for the three groups is roughly equal to those obtained in studies of infant-parent attachment (Ainsworth et al., 1978; Campos et al., 1983). Which of these styles best describes your own experiences with love?

Secure Attachment Style (Frequency = 56%):

I find it relatively easy to get close to others and am comfortable depending on them and having them depend on me. I don't often worry about being abandoned or about someone getting too close to me.

Avoidant Attachment Style (Frequency = 25%):

I am somewhat uncomfortable being close to others; I find it difficult to trust them completely, difficult to allow myself to depend on them. I am nervous when anyone gets too close, and often, love partners want me to be more intimate than I feel comfortable being.

Anxious-Ambivalent Style (Frequency = 19%):

I find that others are reluctant to get as close as I would like. I often worry that my partner doesn't really love me or won't stay with me. I want to merge completely with another person, and this desire sometimes scares people away.

Source: Data from C. Hazan and Philip Shaver, "Romantic Love Conceputalized as an Attachment Process" in *Journal of Personality and Social Psychology*, 52:511–524, American Psychological Association, 1987.

Children who have sensitive and responsible parents develop a secure attachment style in which they feel valued, trust others, and can readily form intimate adult relationships. How do you think their adult romantic relationships are influenced by these childhood intimacy experiences?

as emotionally "cold" and openly conflicted (Klohnen & Bera, 1998). What these findings suggest is that securely attached people have learned how to foster intimacy, while both avoidant and anxious-ambivalent adults have learned how to destroy it. The avoidant lover tends to *starve* intimacy by being emotionally distant and aloof, and the anxious-ambivalent lover *smothers* intimacy by being overly possessive, jealous, and emotionally demanding. Given these different intimacy orientations, it isn't surprising

CRITICAL *thinking*

The self-sufficient cowboy who keeps to himself and doesn't engage in idle chitchat is one of the great icons of the American West. Hollywood actors John Wayne, Gary Cooper, and Clint Eastwood personified this extreme form of individualism in many of their film roles. Today, Hollywood uses this same rugged, individualist personality in creating the lead male role in action-adventure films (Bruce Willis, Sylvestor Stallone, John Travolta). What attachment style would you say these film characters most often represent? Is this an attachment style we should be placing in our male cultural role models?

that securely attached lovers are the most desired partners by the vast majority of adults, regardless of their own attachment style (Pietromonaco & Carnelly, 1994).

Not surprisingly, securely attached adults are attracted to one another and are the happiest couples (Senchak & Leonard, 1992). No such similarity effect is found for the two insecure attachment styles. In fact, these attachment pairings (*anxious-anxious* and *avoidant-avoidant*) are unlikely to progress beyond casual dating because partners with the same insecure attachment style violate each other's expectations of how an intimate partner should behave (Kirkpatrick & Davis, 1994). The anxious-ambivalent person expects partners to avoid intimacy and to be rejecting; the avoidant person expects partners to be clingy and dependent. Because of these patterns of expectations, anxious-ambivalent adults and those who are avoidant tend to be attracted to one another (Collins & Read, 1990). In heterosexual relationships, the most common anxious-avoidant pairing is an anxious-ambivalent woman and an avoidant man (Kirkpatrick & Davis, 1994; Simpson, 1990). In other words, women who fearfully expect that their love will not be reciprocated (*anxious-ambivalents*) tend to be attracted to men who will confirm this negative expectation (*avoidants*). Likewise, men who are concerned about too much intimacy and are uneasy about commitment (*avoidants*) tend to be attracted to women who thirst for such comfort (*anxious-ambivalents*).

Taken as a whole, the attachment research indicates that the seeking and avoiding of intimacy has its roots in childhood experience. These attachment experiences, in turn, shape individuals' self-concepts concerning their capacity and conscious desire for intimate social contact (Brennan & Shaver, 1995).

> ### SECTION SUMMARY
> Although intimacy needs likely have an evolutionary heritage, parent-child attachment patterns influence later childhood peer relations and intimate adult relationships. These parent-child attachment patterns appear to be partly shaped by culture, with the *avoidant attachment style* being more common in individualist than in collectivist societies. Children who have gained a sense of emotional security from their parents (*secure attachment style*) have more successful intimate relationships later in life than those who are emotionally insecure.

FRIENDSHIP

As children mature, they not only form emotional ties to family members, but they also form friendships with their peers. Although intimacy is expressed in both social arenas, friendship appears to have a very different function from that of family relationships (Elbedour et al., 1997). While relationships with relatives are based on nonvoluntary forces, relationships based on friendship are *voluntary* and *mutually satisfying.* The distinction between friends and family is summed up in the old saying, "you can pick your friends, but not your family."

SELF-DISCLOSURE SHAPES FRIENDSHIP DEVELOPMENT AND MAINTENANCE

Social scientists and the ordinary person generally make distinctions between two different levels of friendship (Blieszner & Adams, 1992). *Superficial friendships* are formed and maintained because they are rewarding, and are based on the principle of exchange. *Developed friendships,* in contrast, are based not only on rewards but also on friends' mutual concern for each other's welfare (Lydon et al., 1997). One of the

FIGURE 11.2

The Theory of Social Penetration

According to Altman and Taylor's (1973) theory of social penetration, the amount of information people disclose early in a relationship is rather narrow and shallow, yet as the relationship progresses, self-disclosure becomes broader (covering a wider range of topics) and deeper (revealing more personal information).

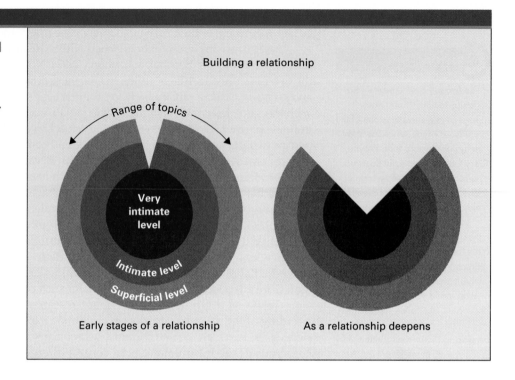

Building a relationship

Range of topics

Very intimate level

Intimate level

Superficial level

Early stages of a relationship

As a relationship deepens

Self-Disclosure

The revealing of personal information about oneself to other people.

Social penetration theory

A theory that describes the development of close relationships in terms of increasing self-disclosure.

prime avenues for creating developed friendships is through **self-disclosure,** which is the revealing of personal information about oneself to other people (Derlega et al., 1993). Individuals who do not avail themselves of this type of intimate communication tend to have dysfunctional relationships and experience greater loneliness than those who reveal their private self-aspects to friends and lovers (Stokes, 1987).

SOCIAL PENETRATION THEORY

Irving Altman and Dalmas Taylor (1973) sought to explain the self-disclosure process in their **social penetration theory.** According to Altman and Taylor, the development of a relationship is associated with communication moving gradually from a discussion of superficial topics to more intimate exchanges. When people first meet, they're likely to discuss such impersonal topics as the weather, sports events, or popular culture. If this superficial interaction is rewarding, they may broaden and deepen the social exchange by covering a wider range of topics and choosing to divulge more personal and sensitive information. As you can see in figure 11.2, when discussion topics move from the very narrow and shallow range to a broader and deeper scope, the intimacy level also increases (Laurenceau et al., 1998). In a very real sense, the process of relationship development involves the proper "pacing" of self-disclosure so that one avoids negative reactions if personal revelations are too large or too small.

During first meetings, new acquaintances usually follow the norm of *self-disclosure reciprocity*—they match each other's level of self-disclosure, revealing more when the other person does so, and decreasing personal revelations if the other person becomes reticent (Cunningham et al., 1986). In most first encounters, self-disclosure reciprocity is useful in building a mutually satisfying level of information exchange that benefits relationship development. However, if one person ignores this gradual self-disclosure process and instead reveals a great deal of personal information, there is a good chance the recipient will feel threatened with this premature rush to intimacy and will evaluate the discloser negatively (Kaplan et al., 1974). Once the relationship progresses beyond the superficial stage and intimacy barriers have been lowered, this tit-for-tat exchange of personal information is not as important and occurs much less frequently (Altman, 1973). In fact in an intimate relationship, instead of reciprocating with self-disclosure, a partner may simply offer support and understanding (Archer, 1979).

In addition to describing the process of social penetration, Altman and Taylor also discussed the dynamics of what they called *depenetration*, which is the disengagement from an intimate relationship. When intimate relationships are in trouble, some people emotionally withdraw by engaging in less breadth and depth in their personal revelations (Baxter, 1987). Other people reduce the number of topics they discuss, but increase the depth of their self-disclosure (Tolstedt & Stokes, 1984). The deeply personal feelings and beliefs that are disclosed are usually negative and are designed to accuse and hurt the other person. Thus, just as self-disclosure can build a relationship and provide it with a solid emotional foundation, it can also serve to weaken and tear it down.

Although social penetration theory's description of a gradual and orderly pattern of increasing self-disclosure fits most developing friendships and romantic relationships (Collins & Miller, 1994), not all intimate relationships progress in this fashion. In some, the type of intimate self-disclosure normally seen in long-term relationships develops almost immediately. For example, in studies of friends, roommates, and dating partners, John Berg found that some relationships just "click" right from the start rather than gradually becoming close over time (Berg, 1984; Berg & Clark, 1986). Berg explained that this early exchange of highly personal information occurs because the respective partners make quick judgments that the other person fits their prototype of the ideal friend or romantic partner. In situations in which people immediately become best friends or lovers, self-disclosure does not serve to deepen the relationship in the same way that it does in the more common and gradually developing relationships described by social penetration theory. Instead, when the partners recognize that this is an intimate relationship, the highly personal self-disclosure begins to flow.

CULTURAL DIFFERENCES IN SELF-DISCLOSURE

Research indicates that there are cultural differences in self-disclosure tendencies. North Americans tend to disclose more about themselves in a wider variety of social settings than people from collectivist cultures such as China, Japan, and the West African nation of Ghana (Sanders et al., 1991; Ting-Toomey, 1991). These differences in self-disclosure practices do not mean that Americans have more intimate relationships than people from China or Japan (refer to chapter 10, pp. 355–356), but they may be rooted in their respective individualist and collectivist orientations. For example, in chapter 2 (p. 55) and chapter 8 (p. 283), we discussed research indicating that many individualist Americans have a need to feel unique or distinct from others (Pratt, 1991; Triandis, 1989). Perhaps the willingness to reveal private self-aspects through self-disclosure provides individualists with the opportunity to identify and share their uniqueness.

These self-disclosure differences may also be partly due to preferred communication channels within the respective cultures. In Western cultures, social expressiveness tends to be a sign of social competence, yet in Eastern cultures such as Japan, China, and Korea, oral communication skills are not as highly valued. In fact, being socially *nonexpressive* is often interpreted as an indication of emotional strength and trustworthiness (Russell & Yik, 1996). Although great value is not placed on social expressiveness in these collectivist cultures, it is considered virtuous to be able to quickly and accurately interpret and respond to others' vaguely expressed feelings and desires before they have to be clearly articulated (Barnlund, 1989). In this kind of cultural context, self-disclosing one's desires or fears may be considered inappropriate, because others are expected to be able to "read" them through indirect means.

GENDER DIFFERENCES EXIST IN HETEROSEXUAL FRIENDSHIPS

Although both men and women value friendship throughout their lives, research suggests certain gender differences in heterosexual friendship patterns from childhood through adulthood (Winstead, 1986).

INTIMACY

One notable gender difference involves the level of emotional expressiveness within same-sex friendships. Put simply, women's friendships tend to be more intimate and involve more emotional sharing than men's friendships (Aukett et al., 1988; Veniegas & Peplau, 1997).

Initially, research conducted in the 1970s and 1980s suggested that in contrast to the friendships of women, men's friendships are more likely to revolve around shared activities (Sherrod, 1989). Paul Wright (1982) characterized this seemingly different orientation toward friendship as *face-to-face* versus *side-by-side:* women spend a good deal of time together talking about personal and intimate matters, and men spend the majority of their time together working or playing, with considerably less personal self-disclosure. Even though these contrasting descriptions of men's and women's friendships have an appealing simplicity, more recent studies suggest that they may be just that—too simplistic. Research by Steve Duck and Wright (1993) found that both women *and* men meet most often just to talk. They also discovered that although women are indeed more emotionally expressive than men in their friendships, they are just as likely as men to engage in shared activities. Therefore, it is misleading to describe men's friendships as being exclusively side-by-side encounters and women's friendships as being exclusively face-to-face interactions.

One important point to keep in mind is that even though women tend to have more intimate friendships than men, this does not mean that *all* men's friendships are less emotionally expressive than the average women's friendships. In all such comparisons, we are discussing *group averages.* The general consensus among social scientists is that these intimacy differences between men and women are not rooted in biology but, rather, are due to gender socialization. Indeed, Dorie Williams (1985) has found that both men and women who possess many feminine personality traits (see chapter 4, p. 116) report being more intimate in their same-sex friendships than men and women who exhibit

When same-sex friends get together, their main reason for doing so is to talk. The conversation of female friends, however, tends to be more intimate than that of male friends. What might explain these gender differences?

few feminine traits. Perhaps because women's same-sex friendships are generally more intimate, they also regard them more favorably than do men (Wright & Scanlon, 1991). This greater intimacy in female friendships is expressed in a number of ways.

SELF-DISCLOSURE

In a meta-analysis of 205 studies investigating gender differences in self-disclosure, Kathryn Dindia and Mike Allen (1992) found that women generally self-disclose more than men, especially in intimate relationships. Their analysis indicates that women self-disclose more than men to their same-sex friends and other-sex romantic partners, but men and women do not differ in their disclosure to male friends. They also found that these gender differences, although not as great as once thought, have shown no evidence of reduction during the past thirty years.

What is it about gender socialization that leads to less intimate self-disclosure among men? Research suggests that males in North American culture appear to be governed by a more rigid set of gender rules than females, especially regarding emotional expression (Timmers et al., 1998). As a result, a man is likely to have a harder time acting vulnerable and dependent. This restriction on male emotional expressiveness was demonstrated in a study in which male and female participants read a story about a man or a woman who appeared to be extremely upset while flying in a plane (Derlega & Chaikin, 1976). The reason this individual was so upset was that his or her mother had just suffered a nervous breakdown. Noticing this agitation, the person sitting next to the individual inquired as to whether he or she was anxious about flying. In one condition, participants read that the individual concealed the problem by replying, "Yes, I guess I am. I haven't flown that much before." In another condition, the character in the story revealed the actual problem. After reading the story, participants were asked to estimate the character's degree of psychological adjustment. Results indicated that if the character was depicted as a man, he was considered to be more unstable if he disclosed his mother's real problem than if he concealed it. For a female character, the results were exactly opposite: not disclosing was judged to be more indicative of maladjustment. It should also be noted that male and female participants did not differ in their assessments. Both men and women considered the emotionally expressive male and the inexpressive female to be maladjusted. These results, and similar findings from other studies, suggest that one important reason men disclose less than women is that for them to reveal tender and vulnerable feelings—to let down their emotional guard—is to run the risk of inviting negative evaluations from both men and women (Chelune, 1976).

Before reading further, take a few minutes and complete the self-disclosure questionnaire in table 11.3. If possible, ask some of your male and female friends to complete it as well, so that you can informally test for some of the gender differences we have discussed concerning friendship self-disclosure.

PHYSICAL TOUCHING

Beyond verbal communication, men and women also differ in the degree to which they engage in physical contact with a same-sex friend. In one study, Val Derlega and his colleagues (1989) asked friends and heterosexual dating partners to act out an imaginary scene where one person was greeting the other at the airport after returning from a trip. The greetings were photographed and later evaluated by judges for the intimacy of physical contact, ranging from no

TABLE 11.3

Do You Self-Disclose Differently to Your Male and Female Friends?

Instructions:

Think of a close male friend and a close female friend. Indicate for the topics listed below the degree to which you have disclosed to each person using the following scale:

Discussed not at all   0   1   2   3   4   Discussed fully and completely

Male Friend		Female Friend
_____	1. My personal habits.	_____
_____	2. Things I have done that I feel guilty about.	_____
_____	3. Things I wouldn't do in public.	_____
_____	4. My deepest feelings.	_____
_____	5. What I like and dislike about myself.	_____
_____	6. What is important to me in life.	_____
_____	7. What makes me the person I am.	_____
_____	8. My worst fears.	_____
_____	9. Things I have done that I am proud of.	_____
_____	10. My close relationships with other people.	_____
_____ Total score		Total score _____

You can determine your overall self-disclosure score for each of your friends by adding up the scores in the column. The higher the score, the greater the self-disclosure to the person. Is there an appreciable difference between these two scores? If there is a difference, does it correspond to what has been found in more systematic investigations of self-disclosure in intimate relationships?

Source: Adapted from L. C. Miller, J. H. Berg, and R. L. Archer, "Openers: Individuals Who Elicit Intimate Self-Disclosure" in *Journal of Personality and Social Psychology, 44*:1234–1244, American Psychological Association, 1983.

The locker room had become a kind of home to me. . . . I relax, my concerns lost among relationships that are warm and real, but never intimate, lost among the constants of an athlete's life. . . . We are at ease in the setting of satin uniforms and shower nozzles.

Bill Bradley, former professional basketball player and U.S. senator

touch at all to combinations of hugging and kissing. As figure 11.3 shows, dating partners exhibited the highest levels of physical intimacy: all of them engaged in a combination of hugging and kissing. When friendship touching was analyzed, male friends employed significantly less touching than did either female friends or mixed-sex friends. Further investigation of participants' perceptions of physical touch indicated that men were more likely than women to interpret touching as an indication of sexual desire.

The Avoidance of Intimacy in Male Friendships

Why are male friendships less intimate than female friendships, and why is there this social injunction against men being emotionally expressive? A number of social scientists contend that this avoidance of emotional expressiveness is due to males being socialized to conform to *heterosexual masculinity*, which entails valuing masculine traits related to power and control, while devaluing feminine traits related to the expression of tenderness and vulnerability (Herek, 1987b; Shields, 1987). This perspective on manhood especially denigrates male homosexuality, because it is perceived to be the antithesis of masculinity. For a man to express warmth, nurturance, or caring toward another man is often interpreted as an indication of homosexuality—which until recently was also considered to be a sign of psychological maladjustment (refer to chapter 7, p. 253). Thus, to be

FIGURE 11.3

*How do men and women differ
with respect to touching when
greeting a friend or dating
partner? In North American
cultures, physical intimacy is
highest among dating partners,
second highest among female
friends and mixed-sex friends, and
lowest among male friends. Have
you observed and/or experienced
such gender differences in your
own life?*

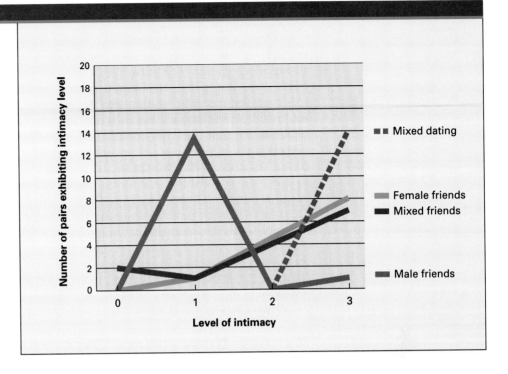

masculine requires men to avoid acting in ways that might indicate homosexuality, including expressing warmth, tenderness, and affection in friendships with other men (Rubin, 1985).

The contemporary conception of masculinity as not encompassing tenderness and affection in male friendships is a fairly recent historical development in Western culture, and one not shared by many non-Western societies (Williams, 1992). According to historians, until the late nineteenth century, a man could express tender affection for an intimate male friend without fearing the disapproval of others (Rotundo, 1989). This all changed around the 1880s, when *homosexuality* and *heterosexuality* came to be defined as clearly distinct and non-overlapping social roles. Masculinity was redefined to exclude "manly love" (Nardi, 1992a). As we enter the twenty-first century, the changes in gender roles may eventually lead men to feel less constrained in their expression of tenderness and affection toward other men. Until that time, however, male heterosexual friendships will generally lack the emotional intensity and gratification of the average female friendship.

CROSS-SEX HETEROSEXUAL FRIENDSHIPS GRAVITATE TO AN "INTIMACY MEAN"

From our review of past research, we can conclude that women's friendships are typically more intimate and openly expressive than those of men. Yet what happens when men and women are friends? Roughly 40 percent of young men and 30 percent of young women have one or more cross-sex friends. In these friendships, there appears to be a gravitation to the "intimacy mean." Men tend to be more emotionally open and self-disclosing than they are with their male friends, while women disclose less and are not as intimate as they are with their women friends (Block, 1980). Generally, heterosexual men believe their female friends provide more emotional support and security than their male friends, but not as much as women with whom they have romantic relationships (Wright, 1985). Women, on the other hand, do not perceive their cross-sex friendships as being that

Friendship is love without wings.

*George Gordon (Lord Byron), English
poet, 1788–1824*

intimate, and they are likely to turn to female friends for highly personalized interaction (Wright & Scanlon, 1991).

One impediment to cross-sex friendships—at least in North American culture—is that the language used to describe them is vague, confusing, and open to misinterpretation (O'Meara, 1994). For example, when describing a cross-sex friendship, people will often use the phrase "just a friend," which may imply that this is a failed romantic relationship. Accompanying the vague definition of cross-sex friendships is the fact that men not only tend to view sex as a primary means of achieving intimacy with women (Bell, 1981), but they also tend to misinterpret certain signs of affection (for example, physical touching) as indicating sexual desire. As a result, the issue of sexuality often has to be managed and negotiated in cross-sex friendships, and it can be an impediment to the development of platonic intimacy (Kaplan & Keys, 1997).

An important factor in fostering the development of cross-sex friendships is having a social environment that minimizes the relevance of the sexual dimension. Therefore, a man and a woman are more likely to develop a nonsexual friendship if they get to know one another at work or on the golf course rather than meeting at a "singles" bar. In the former instances, their shared roles as "coworkers" and "golfers" are likely to form the basis of their friendship, while in the latter case, their roles as "available romantic partners" will make the sexual dimension extremely salient.

GENDER DIFFERENCES DISAPPEAR IN SAME-SEX HOMOSEXUAL FRIENDSHIPS

There is reason to believe that *sexual orientation* influences the same-sex friendship patterns of men and women. One reason that a different friendship pattern is likely to be found is that heterosexual men appear to avoid intimacy in same-sex friendships out of fear of being labeled homosexual. Although many gay men are justifiably wary of expressing affection toward one another in clearly heterosexual surroundings because of fear of assault, no such anxiety should exist in the gay community. Another reason to expect greater intimacy among gay male friendships is that for both gay men and lesbians, gay friends are frequently viewed as family (Nardi, 1992c). This is so because their biological families often reject them or do not fully accept them as family members. Faced with these intimacy roadblocks, many gay people turn to friendships for their emotional well-being (Weston, 1991). As a gay man explained:

> Friends become part of my extended family. A lot of us are estranged from our families because we're gay and our parents don't understand or don't want to understand. . . . I can't talk to them about my relationships. I don't go to them; I've finally learned my lesson: family is out. Now I've got a close circle of friends that I can sit and talk to about anything, I learned to do without the family. (Kurdek & Schmitt, 1987, p. 65)

Because of the unusual importance of friendship in the gay population, Peter Nardi and Drury Sherrod (1994) hypothesized that same-sex friendships of gay men would be as intimate as those of lesbians. As you can see in table 11.4, their survey results support this hypothesis. Gay men and lesbians were equally open, disclosing, and satisfied with their casual, close, and best friendships.

Another possible difference in same-sex friendship patterns due to sexual orientation is that sexual intimacy should be more of an issue than in heterosexual same-sex friendships. In other words, just as sexual desires often become salient in heterosexual cross-sex friendships, they are likely to be a factor in homosexual same-sex friendships. In both cases, the sexual orientation of the two people could conceivably lead to sexual activity. Consistent with this possibility, Nardi and Sherrod (1994) found that about two-thirds of the gay men and about one-half of the lesbians reported having sex with their same-sex "close" or "best" friend. Another survey by Nardi (1992b) with only gay men as respondents similarly found that close friends

TABLE 11.4

Lack of Gender Differences in Gay and Lesbian Same-Sex Friendships

Nardi and Sherrod (1994) asked gay men and lesbians about their same-sex friendships in the gay community. Responses to the questions listed below range from 1 to 5, with higher scores indicating greater intimacy. None of these comparisons between men and women differs significantly. Thus, in contrast to the greater intimacy found in female heterosexual same-sex friendships when compared with male heterosexual same-sex friendships, gay men and lesbians appear to be equally intimate in their friendships.

		Means	
	Friendship Level	Men	Women
To what extent do you feel you are open, trusting, and "truly yourself" when with your friends?	Casual	3.05	2.76
	Close	4.12	4.25
	Best	4.57	4.68
	Friendship Level	Men	Women
How satisfied are you with the quality of your friendship?	Casual	3.35	3.36
	Close	3.69	3.90
	Best	4.16	4.37
	Friendship Level	Men	Women
How willing are you to self-disclose personal information in your friendship?	Casual	2.42	2.30
	Close	3.21	3.20
	Best	3.63	3.71

Source: Data from Nardi & Sherrod, 1994.

often had sex early in their relationship. Although generalizations from only two studies should be made with caution, these findings may indicate that sexual attraction plays an important role in homosexual same-sex friendships.

Does this mean that gay men and lesbians are having sex with most of their friends, or that friendship with a gay person will lead to sexual activity? The answer is no. Nardi's data indicates that most gay men and lesbians state they became friends *after* the sexual relationship ended. Thus, in contrast to heterosexual cross-sex friendships in which sex typically ends the friendship, for gay men and lesbians, sex often leads to friendship, which then marks the end of sexual activity between the now new friends. Perhaps the best way to understand the relationship between sex and gay friendships is to consider again the earlier description of gay friends being family. As Nardi (1992c) explains it, for most gay people, when sexual partners become friends, they become family members, and sex with family members is an incestuous taboo.

SECTION SUMMARY

One of the prime avenues for developing and maintaining friendship is *self-disclosure*. Social penetration theory describes the development of a relationship moving from superficial to more intimate levels of information exchange. There is evidence that people from individualist cultures may self-disclose more than those from collectivist societies, and that women self-disclose more than men. Although both men and women value friendship, female friendships tend to be more emotionally intimate. The exception is friendships of gay men, which are as intimate as those of lesbians.

ROMANTIC RELATIONSHIPS

About the time that my friends and I entered the fifth grade, we began to view girls as potential romantic partners. Being boys and having a history of doing things as a "pack," we often approached prepubescent romance as a group activity. Gathered in the basement of one of our houses, we would first discuss which girl in our class we would call on the phone, and then, which of us would be the group's offering to her. It was a simple game. Look up the phone number, make the call, ask the question, and then congratulate or tease the member of the group who had been either rejected or embraced (at this age, only in a social sense) by the girl on the other end of the line.

> "Hello, is this Marsha?"
> (Pause)
> "Never mind who this is. Listen, do you want to go with John Despins?"
> (Another pause, the length of which was positively correlated with impending rejection.)
> "What?! No?!!" (Then in a hurried attempt to save face for John, the caller turned the rejection on its head.) "Yeah, well he doesn't want to go with you either!"

To a certain degree, the collective esteem of the entire group rose slightly with each individual "phone embrace" and dipped a bit with each rejection. After all, it was an indication of our popularity as a group with the fifth-grade girls. If the girl said yes to our friend, perhaps one of her friends—maybe even the highly coveted Colleen McCash—would "go with" one of his lucky friends.

The psychological drama and tension generated in these early attempts at discovering where one stood in the minds of those who were confusingly and romantically coveted were played out in increasing degrees of sophistication in the coming years. Each time, psychological costs and rewards were riding on every attempt to secure the embrace of another. In the remaining sections of this chapter we turn our attention to the psychological nature of romantic love, and to the factors that foster and inhibit it.

MYTHS EXIST ABOUT THE NATURE OF ROMANTIC LOVE

Prior to delving into the psychological aspects of romantic relationships, it might prove beneficial to dispel three common misconceptions; namely, that (1) love can only be experienced in a heterosexual relationship, (2) romantic beliefs are similar in all historical periods, and (3) all cultures view love in the same way.

MYTH #1: TRUE ROMANTIC LOVE IS EXCLUSIVELY HETEROSEXUAL

Until fairly recently, virtually all research on romantic relationships focused on heterosexual dating and marriage. However, it has been variously estimated that between 2 percent and 10 percent of the world's adult population is primarily or exclusively attracted to their own sex (Gonsiorek & Weinrich, 1991). The lack of research on homosexual romantic relationships has allowed cultural stereotypes to shape social perceptions by creating myths about the gay lifestyle (Herek, 1991).

One of the main myths is that people who are gay drift from one sexual liaison to another and are unsuccessful in developing enduring, committed romantic relationships (De Cecco, 1988). Yet, actual surveys indicate that between 40 and 60 percent of gay men and between 45 and 80 percent of lesbians are currently in a steady relationship (Peplau et al., 1997). It is true that gay and lesbian couples break up more frequently than married couples, but this is also true of heterosexual couples who also don't have the formal institution of marriage to stabilize their relationships (Adams & Jones, 1997; Kurdek, 1998).

FIGURE 11.4

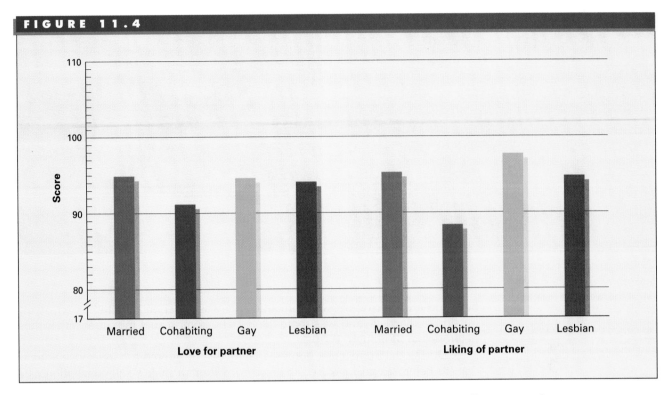

Expressed Love and Liking in Homosexual and Heterosexual Romantic Relationships

In a study of married, heterosexual cohabiting, gay, and lesbian monogamous couples, Kurdek and Schmitt (1986) obtained a liking and a loving score from each partner, which could range from a low of 17 to a high of 117. Higher scores indicated greater liking/loving. Results indicated that there were no differences in expressed love for one's partner between any of the different types of romantic relationships. In addition, the married, gay, and lesbian relationships expressed equally high amounts of liking of their partners. In contrast, heterosexual cohabiting couples had lower liking scores than the other couples. This study and others of its kind have dispelled the myth that gay couples are less capable of developing satisfying romantic relationships than are heterosexual couples.

Source: Data from L. A. Kurdek and J. P. Schmitt, "Relationship Quality of Partners in Heterosexual Married, Heterosexual Cohabiting, and Gay and Lesbian Relationships" in *Journal of Personality and Social Psychology,* 51:711–720, American Psychological Association, 1986.

As you can see in figure 11.4, lesbians, gay men, and heterosexuals involved in monogamous romantic relationships all tend to score high on scales that evaluate liking and love for one's partner, and all tend to be equally well adjusted and satisfied (Eldridge & Gilbert, 1990; Kurdek & Schmitt, 1986). In fact, based on our previous discussion of heterosexual males being less emotionally expressive, it isn't surprising to find that homosexual romantic love—especially lesbian love—tends to be *more* emotionally intimate than heterosexual love (Schreurs & Buunk, 1994). What these findings indicate is that, counter to cultural stereotypes, many lesbians and gay men establish lifelong partnerships, and the psychological dynamics in these relationships are more similar to than different from married heterosexual partnerships (Kurdek, 1997; McWhirter & Mattison, 1984). Regardless of whether we are heterosexual or homosexual, our romantic relationships follow a similar psychological course and are influenced by many of the same personal, situational, and cultural factors.

Myth #2: Historical Beliefs About Romance Are Unchanging

A second common misconception of love is that it has had an unchanging nature from one historical epoch to another. In Western culture, for example, it is true that romantic love can be found in all recorded time periods, but it is also true that it has undergone numerous social transformations (Beall & Sternberg, 1995; Gergen & Gergen, 1995). The ancient Greeks considered romantic love to be a form of madness that would "wound" you, and thus, the Greek god of love (Eros) was armed with a

Contrary to popular beliefs in the heterosexual world, gay couples are as capable of forming long-lasting, happy, romantic relationships as heterosexual couples.

Love is a kind of warfare.

Ovid, Ars Amatoria, II, Roman poet, 43 B.C.–A.D. 17

Whoever indulges in love without sense or moderation recklessly endangers his life; such is the nature of love that no one involved with it can keep his head.

Marie de France, French/English noble, 1160–1215

Marriage is a noose.

Miguel de Cervantes Saavedra, Spanish novelist, 1547–1616

bow and a quiver of arrows. Romantic love was experienced almost exclusively outside of marriage and was more likely to be homosexual in nature rather than heterosexual (Bullough, 1976).

During the Roman era, homosexual love—considered a "Greek vice"—gave way to heterosexual love. Yet, the free-born Roman male's self-conception as a world conqueror led him to view romantic love as a game played outside of marriage. Keeping with this view of love as a game, the Romans were one of the first Western societies to institutionalize divorce (Gathorne-Hardy, 1981). Later, as Christianity became more entrenched as an institution within Roman society, sex came to be viewed as a corrupting influence, tolerated only in marriage. Romantic love was not highly valued.

During the Middle Ages (1000–1300 A.D.), a new conception of love took hold among European aristocrats—the practice of courtly love. Romance was no longer a game, even though it still occurred outside of marriage. Courtly love was considered majestic and spiritual, and in theory, was never to be consummated (Murstein, 1974). In the twelfth century, Countess Marie de France codified an elaborate etiquette to guide the behavior of lovers (de Rougemont, 1940). According to the countess, courtly love struck at first sight, conquered all, accepted no substitutes, and was a consuming passion of both agony and ecstasy.

Cross-cultural research indicates that associating romantic love with marriage typically occurs when people are free to choose their own partners (Rosenblatt & Cozby, 1972), although for centuries before and after courtly love, marriage was arranged by parents and based almost exclusively on political and property considerations. Beginning in the seventeenth and eighteenth centuries, as these more traditional considerations declined in importance, romantic love began to make some limited headway into marital arrangements (Stone, 1977). This new association of love and marriage first appeared in England but spread faster in the New World of North America, where social class considerations were not so rigidly defined.

Although love was now considered possible—and perhaps even desirable—within marriage, early-twentieth-century marriage educators in America still counseled against basing marital choice on this "romantic impulse" (Burgess, 1926). The irrational nature of romantic love was believed to dangerously undermine what should be a very serious, prudent, and rational decision. However, as marriages became more egalitarian and more focused on mutual satisfaction, romance became even more attractive. With this increased desire for romance within marriage came a greater willingness to end marriages that had lost their romantic spark (Scanzoni, 1979).

Today, our Western conception of romantic love is an amalgam of past formulations. It is generally not considered to be a form of madness, but it is something many of us believe we "fall into" and cannot control. Love leads to happiness, but we can also be hurt in love. Love is possible both within and outside of marriage, and it can be either heterosexual or homosexual in nature.

MYTH #3: CULTURAL VIEWS OF ROMANCE ARE UNCHANGING

In general, people from Western cultures view love as a positive experience. However, in a cross-cultural study of love, Philip Shaver and his coworkers (1991) found that not all contemporary cultures share this perspective. In fact, inhabitants of the country with the world's largest population, namely, China, have a more pessimistic outlook on romantic love than most Western cultures (Rothbaum & Tsang, 1998). Consistent with ancient Chinese traditions, where love is equated with sadness, most contemporary Chinese associate romance with sorrow, pain, and unfulfilled affection. What do they think of the Western view of love? They regard it as unrealistically optimistic. In a very real sense, how we experience love speaks volumes about who we are as individuals and what we are as a culture (Dion & Dion, 1991).

A recent study by Robert Levine and his colleagues (1995) examined the importance of love as a basis for marriage in both individualist and collectivist cultures. Results indicated that there are cross-cultural differences in the perceived importance of romantic love. Individualist countries such as the United States, England, and Australia placed great importance on love in marriage, while collectivist countries such as India, Pakistan, Thailand, and the Philippines rated it as much less important. These beliefs appear to have behavioral consequences as well. Those countries placing great importance on love had higher marriage rates, lower fertility rates, and higher divorce rates. Other studies indicate that collectivists tend to select mates who will best "fit in" to the extended family; individualists are more likely to select a mate who is physically attractive or has an "exciting" personality. This does not mean, however, that love is not a part of a collectivist marriage. Instead, it means that, compared with individualist cultures, in collectivist cultures it is more common for people to get married, and then to fall in love.

One question raised by these studies is whether there isn't an inherent conflict between individualist values and the interdependence necessary to maintain romantic love (Agnew & Le, 1997). That is, if you were raised to be autonomous and independent, wouldn't you tend to have difficulty maintaining an intimate relationship that is defined by partners depending on each other? The curious irony is that although individualists are more likely to marry due to romantic love, the way they've been socialized may make it less likely that their marriages will survive and their love will be nurtured.

INITIAL ROMANTIC ENCOUNTERS ARE OFTEN AMBIGUOUS

Although cultural differences exist concerning the nature of romantic love, one quality of romance is universal: when two people who are potential romantic partners meet for the first time, their social reality is often ambiguous. One of them might develop an interest in the other without knowing whether it will be reciprocated.

READING SIGNALS OF ATTRACTION

Faced with this uncertainty, people tend to exchange information (Sprecher & Duck, 1994). Yet, due to the high risk of rejection in such encounters, the information exchanged tends to be subtle and discreet. By using nonverbal behavior and "verbal indirectness," the other's level of interest can be gauged while exposing oneself to the minimal self-esteem threat (Symonds, 1972). For example, imagine two strangers, Joyce and Louis, who catch each other's attention. At this moment, either could take the direct approach and walk up to the other and express their romantic desires. Instead, they will likely avert their gaze when making initial eye contact. If interested, one or both of them may then slowly position themselves for an introduction.

In such introductions, opening lines are important in creating a favorable first impression (Kleinke et al., 1986). The safest and most effective opening lines tend to be fairly innocuous and nonthreatening ("Could you tell me what time it is?" "Do you come here often?") because they do not offend, and they also protect the user against rejection. Opening remarks that are direct but inoffensive may also be effective ice breakers ("I don't have anybody to introduce me, but I'd really like to get to know you"), but there is more inherent risk of rejection as well. Finally, using crude and flippant remarks is the surest route to social rejection, especially if a man directs them toward a woman ("Hey gorgeous, if I say I love your body, would you hold it against me?").

Returning to our example, if Joyce is interested in Louis, she may frequently look down during their conversation and position her body so that Louis sees it in profile. If Louis finds Joyce appealing, he may look directly at her while thrusting his head slightly forward and opening up his body posture (Grammer, 1990). It is through such indirect and subtle means that strangers judge the romantic interest of others.

THE DISTRESS OF UNREQUITED LOVE

Research and personal experience indicates that loving someone who doesn't love you or being loved but not returning the love occurs much more frequently than reciprocated love (Baumeister & Wotman, 1992). Not surprisingly, people with an anxious-ambivalent attachment style are most likely to be the victims of unrequited love (Aron et al., 1998). Based on an analysis of self-reports from would-be lovers and rejectors, Roy Baumeister and his coworkers (1993) discovered that rejected love is a negative experience for both parties. Although self-esteem might be slightly bolstered by the adoration, guilt about hurting the other person is the most common emotion. This guilt is accompanied by an uncertainty about how to deliver the bad news, and by annoyance when the would-be lover does not accept no for an answer. Baumeister contends that the uncertainty about how to reject love occurs because there are so few competent cultural role models to show how to effectively spurn unwanted romantic overtures. Indeed, when popular culture does focus on the rejector's viewpoint—as in the movie *Fatal Attraction*—it tends to dwell on the futility and danger inherent in rejecting others' romantic desires.

In contrast to the rejector's lack of cultural role models, the would-be lover can draw upon literally thousands of different "scripts" for how to play his or her role. If you doubt this assertion, turn on the radio and listen to love songs. Most of them describe someone's experiences either in pursuing love or having love rejected. A familiar theme in these songs calls for the brokenhearted to grieve, assign blame, accept the failure, and get on with their lives. However, other cultural scripts call for the would-be lover to show persistence to the point of stalking, as is illustrated in such movies as *Addicted To Love* and *There's Something About Mary*. Baumeister found that would-be lovers tend to look back on their experience with both positive and negative emotions. The rejection was a blow to their self-esteem, but they recalled events in such a way as to recover a certain degree of self-worth and to also retain a degree of affection for the person who rejected them.

Based on these findings, it seems that being at either end of unrequited love is a distressing experience. Both parties become victims, with the rejector experiencing guilt and the rejected losing self-esteem. As we will see in the following sections, it is not the giving or the receiving of love alone that provides satisfaction and fulfillment in romantic relationships; rather, it is the

I know I am but summer to your heart,
And not the full four seasons of the year.

Edna St. Vincent Millay, U.S. poet, 1892–1950

To love someone who doesn't love you is like shaking a tree to make the dewdrops fall.

Congo proverb

Where love is not, there can be no pleasures.

Russian proverb

FIGURE 11.5

Sternberg (1988) conceives of different kinds of love being a combination of the three basic components of intimacy, passion, and commitment.

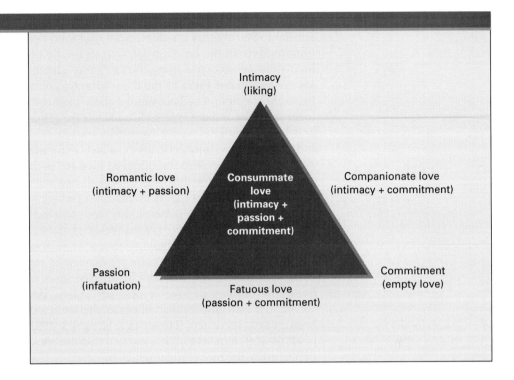

mutual giving and receiving—the inclusion of the other in one's self-concept—that provides happiness.

SOCIAL SCIENTISTS IDENTIFY DIFFERENT TYPES OF ROMANTIC LOVE

What does love feel like? How do we experience it? When people in one study were asked to list different types of love, they produced 205 distinct attributes (Fehr & Russell, 1991)! Acknowledging that there is more than one way to experience love, social scientists have developed multidimensional theories that identify various forms or styles of love (Harter et al., 1997; Meyers & Berscheid, 1997).

A TRIANGULAR THEORY OF LOVE

Robert Sternberg (1986) has proposed that love can be thought of as a triangle, with its three corners consisting of the three components of passion, intimacy, and commitment (figure 11.5). According to Sternberg, there are seven distinct kinds of love made up of different combinations and proportions of these components:

Liking: the experience of intimacy without passion and commitment (for example, friendship)

Infatuated love: the experience of passion without intimacy and commitment (for example, "puppy love")

Empty love: the experience of commitment without passion and intimacy (for example, stagnant marriages)

Romantic love: the experience of passion and intimacy without commitment (for example, extramarital affairs)

Companionate love: the experience of intimacy and commitment without passion (for example, many long-term, happy marriages)

Fatuous love: the experience of passion plus commitment without intimacy (for example, love at first sight)

Consummate love: the experience of intimacy, passion, and commitment (good luck!)

Love Styles

Similar to Sternberg, Canadian sociologist John Lee (1977) contends there is no one type of love. In his typology of love styles, he identifies three primary styles of love—*eros* (passionate love), *ludus* (game-playing love), and *storge* (friendship love)—and likens them to the three primary colors of red, yellow, and blue. Like these three colors, Lee believes the three primary love styles can be combined to form three secondary love styles: *pragma* (pragmatic love), which contains storge and ludus elements; *mania* (possessive love), which is a compound of eros and ludus; and *agape* (altruistic love), which combines elements of eros and storge. According to Lee, all of the different love styles are equally valid ways of loving, and it is the relationship that is styled, not the lover. Thus, one could have a romantic relationship that is intense and passionate (eros), and then develop one that starts as a friendship and slowly leads to a lasting commitment (storge). Clyde and Susan Hendrick (1986) have developed questionnaires to assess Lee's different love styles. Table 11.5 lists sample items for each style.

As you can see from this brief overview of multidimensional theories of love, social scientists believe that people can experience many different kinds during their lives. The number of love "types" or "styles" depends on what theory is being considered, and empirical attempts to pin down a specific set of categories have not been entirely successful (Hendrick & Hendrick, 1992; Levy & Davis, 1988). However, of all the different love styles, the two that are consistently found in all studies and appear to be the most fundamental are *passionate love* and *companionate love.*

Passionate Love Is Most Intense Early in a Romantic Relationship

When love is not madness, it is not love.

Spanish proverb

Joyce and Louis have been dating for three weeks now and are passionately in love. The last thing Joyce thinks about before falling asleep and the first thing she thinks about upon awakening is her Louis. Across town, Louis is trying to stay awake while he feigns interest in his coworker's latest design project. The previous night, he tossed and turned for hours in bed, being both exhilarated by his love for Joyce and riddled with anxiety that she might not feel the same toward him. Now, in less than five hours, twenty-six minutes, and thirty-two seconds he will see her again.

Does this sound familiar? Do Louis and Joyce's feelings bring a pleasant, perhaps even pained, smile of recognition to your face? If so, you are a member of that not-so-elite group who since time immemorial have experienced something deliciously joyful and painful: passionate love. According to Elaine Hatfield (1988), **passionate love** is "a state of intense longing for union with another" (p. 193). It is a type of love that we feel with our bodies—a warm-tingling, body rush, stomach-in-a-knot kind of love. Indeed, some physiologists

Passionate Love

A state of intense longing for union with another.

What type of romantic love is being experienced here? Based on research, and perhaps your own personal experiences, are these specific love symptoms likely to be long-lasting or relatively short-lived? How might an evolutionary theorist explain the duration of this particular love effect?

© Lynn Johnston Productions Inc./Dist. by United Feature Syndicate, Inc.

TABLE 11.5

Measuring Six Basic Styles of Love

Listed below are sample items from Hendrick and Hendrick's love scale, which was designed to measure the six styles of love identified by Lee (1977). Read through the various items and think about your current or past relationships. Which style or styles characterize each of these relationships? According to Lee, people could experience many different styles of love during their lives.

Eros

1. My lover and I were attracted to each other immediately after we first met.
2. Our lovemaking is very intense and satisfying.
3. My lover fits my ideal standards of physical beauty/handsomeness.

Ludus

1. I try to keep my lover a little uncertain about my commitment to him/her.
2. I have sometimes had to keep two of my lovers from finding out about each other.
3. I enjoy playing the "game of love" with a number of different partners.

Storge

1. It is hard to say exactly when my lover and I fell in love. (Our friendship merged gradually into love over time.)
2. Love is really a deep friendship, not a mysterious, mystical emotion.
3. My most satisfying love relationships have developed from good friendships.

Pragma

1. I consider what a person is going to become in life before I commit myself to him/her.
2. I try to plan my life carefully before choosing a lover.
3. A main consideration in choosing a lover is how he/she reflects on my family.

Mania

1. Sometimes I get so excited about being in love that I can't sleep.
2. When I am in love, I have trouble concentrating on anything else.
3. If my lover ignores me for a while, I sometimes do stupid things to get his/her attention back.

Agape

1. I would rather suffer myself than let my lover suffer.
2. I cannot be happy unless I place my lover's happiness before my own.
3. I would endure all things for the sake of my lover.

Source: Adapted from C. Hendrick and S. Hendrick, 1986.

When you are beside me my heart sings; a branch it is, dancing, dancing before the Wind Spirit in the moon of strawberries. When you frown upon me, beloved, my heart grows dark. . . . the shadows of clouds darken, then with your smile comes the sun.

Anonymous Ojibway poem

argue that passionate love produces changes in brain chemistry, which brings on a sense of giddiness in the "love-struck" comparable to an amphetamine high (Liebowitz, 1983). Passionate love is experienced most intensely during the early stages of a romantic relationship. According to Ellen Berscheid and Hatfield (1974), passionate love is produced, or at least enhanced, during these first romantic encounters due to a rather interesting transference of arousal from one stimulus to another. As a way to introduce you to this phenomenon, let me tell you how I met my wife.

PASSIONATE LOVE CAN BE TRIGGERED BY EXCITATION TRANSFER

In the winter of 1982 I had recently arrived in Bloomington, Indiana, to begin a three-year postdoctoral fellowship at Indiana University. One evening I attended a modern dance concert. When I purchased my ticket, the ticketer ripped it in two and gave me half, instructing me to remember the number on my ticket stub because it would later be used as part of the performance. Indeed. The dance company's performance pieces were extremely avant-garde, and just before beginning the last one, they brought a hat on stage filled with all the ticket stubs. If your ticket stub number was called, you were supposed to walk on stage and become part of the performance.

Upon hearing this, I instinctively sunk lower in my seat. Ever since my sister had tried to teach me to dance the "twist" and the "pony" in the early 1960s—while laughing uncontrollably—I have always felt self-conscious on the dance floor (an excellent example of classical conditioning). As luck would have it, my number was called by one of the performers, a tall attractive woman, with long blonde hair. Maybe this wouldn't be so bad after all, I thought as I walked on stage. But what did she want me to do? You guessed it, learn a complicated dance step in front of the entire audience. My heart began to beat rapidly and my face became flushed, but I concentrated as best I could as she led me through the steps. Halfway through the routine, in the middle of a big leg swing, my brand new reversible belt buckle popped completely off my belt and shot across the dance floor! The dancer laughed, the audience roared. I was mortified. Somehow I finished the dance routine and sat down. Later, whenever I would see this dancer around town, my heart would race and my face would become flushed as I relived "the incident." She never took notice of me during these near encounters, but now I certainly had her number. What were my feelings toward her? Attraction coupled with anxiety. Eight months later, I finally introduced myself when our paths crossed again, and we began dating. A year and a half later we were married.

In explaining the initial encounter with my future wife, social psychological research suggests that my acute embarrassment may have actually sparked a romantic attraction toward her. Drawing on Schachter's (1964) two-factor theory of emotion described in chapter 10 (p. 381), Berscheid and Hatfield (1974) contend that passionate love is likely to occur when three conditions are met. The first condition is that you must learn what love is and come to expect that you will eventually fall in love. Second, you must meet someone who fits your preconceived beliefs of an appropriate lover. And third, while in this person's presence, you must experience a state of physiological arousal. How does this arousal become passionate love? Recall that Schachter's theory of emotion asserts that people use external cues to label their arousal states. When arousal occurs in the presence of an appropriate love object, you may well interpret this arousal as romantic and sexual attraction. If the true source of arousal is something other than the attractive person, passionate love is simply a *misattribution*. What if you are sexually attracted to the other person *and* you are also aroused by some other source (as was the case when I first met my wife)? Dolf Zillman (1984) has called this psychological process—in which arousal caused by one stimulus is transferred and *added* to arousal elicited by a second stimulus—**excitation transfer.** In such instances, our increased romantic interest can be traced to the transfer of arousal from one source to the object of our newfound affections.

Excitation Transfer

A psychological process in which arousal caused by one stimulus is transferred and added to arousal elicited by a second stimulus.

Capilano Canyon Suspension Bridge, Vancouver, British Columbia.

We don't believe in rheumatism and true love until after the first attack.

Marie von Ebner-Eschenbach

Donald Dutton and Arthur Aron (1974) conducted the first test of this romantic attribution of arousal hypothesis on two bridges at a popular tourist site in North Vancouver, British Columbia. One of the bridges, the Capilano Canyon Suspension Bridge, is 5 feet wide, 450 feet long, and constructed of wooden boards attached to wire cables that span the Capilano River at a height of 230 feet. This bridge is not for those with a fear of heights—it wobbles as you walk on it and sways in the wind. Nearby, there is another bridge that does not set your heart aflutter. It is solidly built out of heavy wood and stands only ten feet above a small, peaceful stream.

In their experiment, whenever an unaccompanied male began to walk across either bridge, he was approached by a male or female research assistant and asked to write an imaginative story in response to a picture while standing on the bridge. The assistant also told the man that if he wanted to receive information about the study's results he could give her (or him) a phone call. Dutton and Aron found that the men who were approached by a woman on the suspension bridge told stories with the highest sexual imagery of all the experimental groups. As you can see in figure 11.6, these men were also more likely than any of the other groups to call the assistant. Apparently, they had attributed their arousal, which was undoubtedly principally caused by the swaying bridge, to the female assistant.

Although this is one interpretation of the results, can you think of another possibility? Perhaps the men who chose to walk across the dangerous-looking suspension bridge were generally more adventurous, both sexually and physically, than the men who chose the safer bridge. If this were the case, then it was their more adventurous personalities that caused both the bridge choice and the phoning of the female assistant. Dutton and Aron ruled out this possibility by repeating the experiment, but this time using only the suspension bridge. Half of the men were asked to write their stories as they stood on the bridge, while the others were approached after they had completed their walk and had calmed down. As expected, increased sexual imagery and phone calls were only associated with the condition in which men were approached as they

FIGURE 11.6

Sexual Attraction Under Conditions of High Anxiety

A male or female research assistant asked men to write an imaginative story in response to a picture while either standing on a solid 10-foot-high bridge or a wobbly 230-foot-high bridge. Men who were approached by the female assistant on the wobbly bridge were much more likely to later call her, supposedly to learn more about the study's findings. These men's imaginative stories also contained the highest sexual imagery of all the groups. How do these findings support the misattribution of arousal hypothesis?

Source: Data from D. G. Dutton and A. P. Aron, "Some Evidence for Heightened Sexual Attraction under Conditions of High Anxiety" in *Journal of Personality and Social Psychology,* 30:510–517, American Psychological Association, 1974.

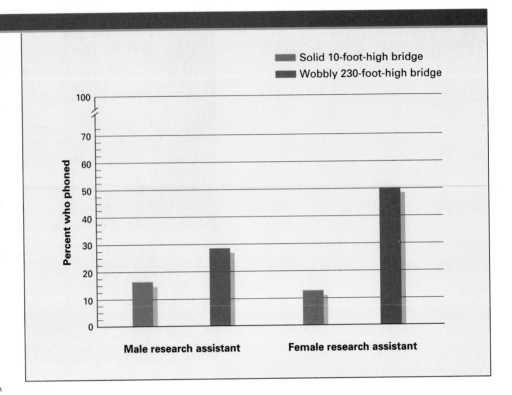

Will he always love me?
I cannot read his heart.
This morning my thoughts
Are as disordered
As my black hair.

Harikawa, Japanese poet, 1135–1165

crossed the bridge. Misattribution, not adventurous personalities, explained the men's actions.

The two-factor theory of emotion emphasizes the role our thoughts and beliefs play in accounting for our states of arousal. Yet other social psychologists have suggested that a different mechanism may explain why fear and anxiety intensifies romantic feelings (Kenrick & Cialdini, 1977; Riordan & Tedeschi, 1983). Referring to the anxiety-affiliation studies discussed in chapter 10, Douglas Kenrick and Robert Cialdini (1977) proposed that in some circumstances the presence of others tends to calm anxious people. They argued that the reason the men on the suspension bridge were attracted to the female assistant was not because they mistakenly thought she aroused them, but because she in fact calmed them down. The men associated her with a reduction of anxiety, and that led to greater liking for her. Therefore, it is not misidentified or transferred arousal that increases romantic feelings, but it is the emotional "comfort" people provide that increases their attractiveness.

This explanation of romantic attraction, although providing an alternative interpretation of the Dutton and Aron findings, soon ran into trouble based on the findings of another series of arousal studies. In one experiment, male participants' arousal was manipulated by having them run in place for either two minutes or fifteen seconds (White et al., 1981). As soon as the men completed this exercise, they watched a videotape of a woman they expected to meet sometime later. In one condition, the woman was made to look and sound attractive, while in another condition she appeared unattractive. After watching the videotape, the men rated the woman's attractiveness.

One thing to keep in mind about this experiment is that the men who participated did not experience any anxiety or fear, and thus Kenrick and Cialdini's arousal reduction explanation would predict no differences due to this exercise-induced arousal. Yet, this arousal did indeed heighten the men's emotional responses toward the target woman. Men who had exercised for two minutes evaluated the physically attractive woman as more attractive and the physically unattractive woman as less attractive than those who had exercised for only fifteen seconds. Later studies indicated that misattribution was most likely to occur when the actual source of the arousal (exercise, for example) was less salient than the target person (White & Kight, 1984). Together these studies suggest that arousal from a nonsexual stimulus can intensify a person's initial emotional reaction to a potential romantic partner, be it either positive or negative.

The basic premise underlying the misattribution of arousal effect is that people are fooled into believing their arousal is caused by something other than the actual source. Misattribution shouldn't occur if you actually know the true source of the arousal (see chapter 10, p. 381). Yet, a subsequent study by Kenrick and his colleagues indicates that heightened emotional responses toward someone can sometimes occur even when we are made aware that something other than that person is causing our arousal (Allen et al., 1989). In such circumstances, no misattribution occurs. What then explains the heightened emotions? Kenrick believes that the *social facilitation* effect discussed in chapter 9 may provide the answer. That is, physiological arousal simply enhances any response we are currently having toward the object of our attention. This facilitation effect does not involve any cognitive attributions on our part; it's merely a physiological reaction. Perhaps this noncognitive activity partly explains passionate love.

So where are we in our understanding of the arousal of passion? Under certain circumstances we can be fooled into attributing our arousal to an incorrect source and, therefore, experience heightened feelings of passion. At other times, we may be aware that some other source is causing our arousal, but we are enjoying the increased passionate feelings too much to care. On a date, the physiological arousal generated by seeing a thrilling adventure movie or riding on a roller coaster at an amusement park, for example, may be transferred to our feelings for the person we are with. Perhaps the lesson here is that when our ticket is pulled out of the hat of romance, we may not care whether our romantic feelings are triggered by a reflex action, a misattribution of arousal, or "the real thing," but we'd better hope that our potential romantic partner's initial reaction toward us is one of attraction rather than repulsion, for excitation transfer may heighten either to equal degrees.

COMPANIONATE LOVE IS MORE STABLE AND ENDURING THAN PASSIONATE LOVE

Let's consider again the romantic relationship of Joyce and Louis. Yes, they did become more certain about each other's love. Yet as time has passed, the hot flames of passion have cooled to warm embers. Having grown up watching movie stars convulse with passion whenever they embrace on the silver screen, Joyce and Louis are disillusioned to discover that the intensity of their feelings no longer matches Hollywood's depiction of love. They feel very close, like best buddies, but the passion ebbs and flows. They wonder to themselves, "Is this what love becomes?" Social psychologists investigating the course of romantic relationships might reply, "Yes, in most cases, this is what becomes of romantic love . . . if you're lucky." Why is this the case?

One reason the emotional roller-coaster ride of early love slows over time to a more smooth and steady experience is the fact that passion generally burns itself out. Passionate love is considered to be a relatively short-lived type of love, more typical of the early stages of a romantic relationship when one's partner's love is less certain (Brehm, 1988). Indeed, passionate love thrives on the thrill and uncertainty of winning over another's affections. As we settle into a romantic relationship, the

I am your clay.
You are my clay.
In life we share a single quilt.
In death we will share our coffin.

Kuan Tao-sheng, Chinese poet and painter, 1262–1319

As a romantic relationship grows, the emotional highs and lows of passionate love subside. What then predicts relationship satisfaction and longevity is the couple's degree of companionate love.

emotional freshness and uncertainty of passionate love is replaced by a more certain and dependable type of love—if love survives at all.

Some social scientists explain this diminution of passion as being genetically predetermined. Passion is adaptive early in a relationship because it frequently results in children, yet once born, the infants' survival is aided by the parents becoming less obsessed with one another (Kenrick & Trost, 1987). In defining this less impassioned, more enduring **companionate love,** Hatfield (1988) states that it is "the affection we feel for those with whom our lives are deeply entwined" (p. 205). Companionate love exists between close friends as well as between lovers. It develops out of a sense of certainty in one another's love and respect, and a feeling of genuine mutual understanding (Hecht et al., 1994).

Another difference between passionate love and companionate love is the beliefs that one has about one's partner. In the early stages of romantic relationships, when passions run high, lovers tend to see their partners through rose-colored glasses (Brehm, 1988). Their partners are "perfect," the "ideal man or woman," their "dream come true." As passion fades and couples develop companionate love based on mutual understanding, this idealization of one's beloved often gives way to a more realistic view. Yet, as we will discuss more fully later in the chapter (p. 422), although companionate love is a more reality-based love, successful and happy romantic partners are those who tend to see each others' imperfections in the best possible light.

WOMEN AND MEN MAY DIFFER IN THEIR EXPERIENCE OF LOVE

Thus far we have discussed how love is influenced by cultural and historical factors, situational influences, and even the passage of time in the relationship itself. Another important factor in how love is approached and experienced is gender. For example, studies conducted with American college students found that heterosexual men have a more romantic view of love than heterosexual women (Hobart, 1958; Spaulding, 1970). That is, men are more likely to believe in love at first sight, in love as the basis for marriage and for overcoming obstacles, and to believe that their romantic partners and their relationships will be perfect (Hendrick et al., 1984). True to these beliefs, other studies indicate that men tend to fall in love faster and fall out of love more slowly than women (Dion & Dion, 1985). They also are less likely than women to break up a premarital romance (Hill et al., 1979).

The fact that men seem to enter heterosexual romantic relationships with higher expectations and a greater willingness to let their emotions guide their behavior does not mean that women are unromantic. Women are typically as emotionally involved as their partners once they fall in love. In fact, they are more likely than men to report feeling intense romantic sensations such as euphoria and giddiness for their partner, and to have more vivid memories of past romantic relationships (Dion & Dion, 1973; Harvey et al., 1986). In assessing these findings as a whole, one possible interpretation is that men appear more eager to fall in love than women, but once a man and woman take the plunge they seem to both be very emotionally involved in the ensuing romantic intimacy. If this indeed is the way men and women typically approach romance, the next question comes begging. Why is it that men appear very willing to fall in love, while women initially take a more cautious approach?

One possible answer centers on the different social statuses that men and women traditionally enjoy in most cultures (Howard et al., 1987). Typically, young men have greater expectations about their social and economic security than young women. Men may therefore feel they can afford to let their emotions rule their mate selection: their status will be determined by them alone, and not their partner's status. On the other hand, being aware of the sexual inequality in their

Companionate Love

The affection we feel for those with whom our lives are deeply entwined.

To be in love is merely to be in a state of perpetual anesthesia—to mistake an ordinary young woman for a goddess.

H. L. Mencken, U.S. social critic, 1880–1956

Rank creates its rules: A woman is asked about her husband, a man is asked about his rank.

From the Palace of Nefertari, 1554–1070 B.C.

Might the different lengths of men's and women's reproductive cycles cause different mating strategies?

From *i need help* by Vic Lee, Andrews and McMeel, 1996. Reprinted with special permission of King Features Syndicate.

Marriage, to women as to men, must be a luxury, not a necessity; an incident of life, not all of it. And the only possible way to accomplish this great change is to accord to women equal power in the making, shaping and controlling of the circumstances of life.

Susan B. Anthony, U.S. women's rights pioneer, 1820–1906

culture, women might be more likely to believe that their future status will be determined more by their mates' status than their own. Women may therefore believe they cannot afford the luxury of only following their emotions and may adopt a more pragmatic approach to love. This sociocultural explanation is consistent with the data presented in chapter 10 indicating that men place more importance on physical attractiveness in choosing a partner, while women emphasize social status.

An alternative perspective is to look at our biology rather than our culture (Wilson, 1978). Evolutionary theorists contend that the different approaches to love that men and women exhibit are principally due to the different investment the two sexes have in the results of sexual bonding, namely, the children that are born. To maximize the probability that his genes will live on in future generations, it is to a man's advantage to establish sexual intimacy as quickly as possible in a relationship and to have frequent sexual encounters with many different women. If a man can establish sexual intimacy early in a relationship, he could theoretically court one woman after another and therefore be a big winner in reproductive fitness. For a woman, a more discriminating approach is needed in choosing a mate because she has a limited number of eggs that can be fertilized during her time of reproduction. This biological limitation means the best strategy for women is to carefully judge their potential partners' strengths and weaknesses so they can identify men with the best genes. Thus, according to evolutionary theorists, it is adaptive for men to fall in love quickly, while the female evolutionary injunction is to move slowly in matters of love.

Although the evolutionary approach provides a plausible explanation for why men fall in love quickly while women are more cautious, how might it explain the fact that men are more reluctant than women to end a romantic relationship? From an evolutionary perspective, it might seem to make more sense for men to fall in and out of love quickly, because such a strategy of numerous, short romantic relationships will maximize their chances of passing their genes on to future generations. One possible explanation offered by evolutionary theorists about why men fall out of love more slowly than women is that they have less to lose in a romantic relationship. Because they don't have to worry about a ticking biological clock and the risks of pregnancy, they can waste more time than women in a relationship that is going nowhere.

In contrast to the evolutionary perspective's explanation of this gender difference, the sociocultural perspective suggests that heterosexual men may fall in love quickly and out of love slowly because they are starved for intimacy due to their inability to express love and tenderness to their male friends. As discussed earlier, because males are socialized to value heterosexual masculinity, their same-sex friendships tend to lack intimacy. Therefore, often the only outlet they have to express warmth, tenderness, and deep affection is in a romantic relationship with a woman. This greater dependency on romantic relationships for emotional support is true for both married and unmarried heterosexual men (Tschann, 1988). Thus, it may be that heterosexual men tend to fall in love more quickly and be less willing to end a romantic relationship because they place all their emotional "eggs" in this romantic basket. In contrast, women are more likely to spread their emotional eggs around, placing a number of them in their same-sex friendships.

SECTION SUMMARY

The experience of romantic love and the beliefs surrounding it are shaped by both cultural and historical forces. However, counter to cultural stereotypes, the psychological dynamics in homosexual and heterosexual romantic relationships are more similar to than different from one another. Current theories have identified various forms of romantic love, with the two most common being *passionate love* and *companionate love*. Passionate love is a relatively short-lived type of love, more typical of the early stages of romance, when one's partner's love is less certain. Companionate love, on the other hand, develops more slowly and is more enduring. It develops out of a sense of certainty in each other's love and respect, and a feeling of genuine mutual understanding.

WILL LOVE ENDURE?

More than one million divorces occur each year in the United States, and more than half of all marriages end in divorce (U.S. Bureau of the Census, 1998). Outside of marriage, the mortality rate of romantic relationships is even higher. Although the odds that love will endure are not good, we all know people who have built loving and satisfying relationships lasting many years. In this section we examine some of the most common factors that contribute to satisfaction and conflict in romance.

PERCEIVING PARTNERS IN THE BEST POSSIBLE LIGHT LEADS TO SATISFYING RELATIONSHIPS

My parents have been married for more than fifty years. For me, they epitomize the happily married couple, and I use their photo on p. 419 to illustrate companionate love. Over the years, one thing that I have noticed about my parents' love is how it seems to be partly based on *positive illusions*. Example. Although I believe my mother is a truly wonderful person, the way my father describes her would lead you to conclude that she is simultaneously being considered for both sainthood and "Ms. Universe." With apologies to my mother, the questions this example begs are the following: Are my father's embellishments of my mother's virtues a healthy ingredient in their relationship? Does it promote a happier marriage?

For many years, most psychologists asserted that lasting satisfaction in romantic relationships depends on people understanding their partners' real strengths and weaknesses (Brickman, 1987; Swann et al., 1994). Although it is hard to argue against the benefits of an occasional good dose of reality, a number of studies suggest that we have a need to perceive our romantic relationships as being better than others' (Buunk & van der Eijnden, 1997; Van Lange & Rusbult, 1995). Yet how can we satisfy this need if we insist on scrutinizing our partners' flaws? The answer to this question is that, if we want to be happy in love, we should allow our desire to feel good about our romantic relationships to dominate our desire to critically analyze relationship imperfections (Bradbury & Fincham, 1990; Sedikides et al., 1998). Just as there is a *self-serving bias* that leads people with high self-esteem to see themselves in the best possible light (see chapter 3, p. 103), people in happy romantic relationships tend to attribute their partners' positive behaviors to dispositional causes ("their wonderful personality") and their negative behaviors to situational factors ("a bad day"). This *partner-enhancing bias* not only makes lovers feel better, but recent research suggests that it can also create a self-fulfilling prophecy.

In a series of studies, Sandra Murray and her colleagues discovered that an important component of a satisfying, stable romantic relationship is the ability to mix positive illusion with sober reality when perceiving one's partner. That is, those who can see virtues in their partners that their partners cannot even see in themselves tend to be happier with the relationship than those who perhaps have a more realistic view (Murray et al., 1996a). For instance, in one longitudinal study, dating couples who idealized one another more during the initial stages of their romance reported greater increases in satisfaction and decreases in conflicts and doubts over the course of a year than couples who saw each other in a more realistic light (Murray et al., 1996b). In addition, during the year, the targets of these positive illusions actually incorporated these idealized images into their own self-concepts. Similar findings were also obtained with married couples (Murray & Holmes, 1997). What these studies suggest is that couples who idealize one another often create a self-fulfilling prophecy. By taking a "leap of faith" and seeing imperfect relationships in somewhat idealized ways, people not only satisfy their need to feel that their relationships are better than most other relationships, but they create the conditions necessary for their positive illusions to become realized.

PARTNERS ARE SATISFIED WHEN THE RATIO BETWEEN THEIR REWARDS AND COSTS ARE SIMILAR

As stated in chapter 10, social exchange theory is based on the assumption that all relationships are like economic bargains in which each party tries to maximize their rewards while minimizing their costs. Although intimate relationships tend to be based on attention to other people's needs rather than one's own, it would be naive to believe that once people fall in love they cease to consider their relationship rewards and costs. Indeed, one important factor determining whether a romantic relationship will endure is the perception the partners have about what they give to and receive from one another. How are these rewards and costs tabulated?

One theory that provides a sensible explanation for how rewards and costs are analyzed in an intimate relationship is a special type of exchange model known as **equity theory** (Adams, 1965). This theory contends that people in a romantic relationship don't try to maximize their rewards and minimize their costs but, instead are most satisfied when the *ratio* between the rewards and costs is similar for both partners. If one partner receives more rewards from the relationship but also makes greater contributions to it, the relationship is still equitable.

For the sake of illustration, consider again our imaginary couple, Joyce and Louis, who are now married and have a young baby. Joyce has put her career on hold to stay home, and despite the drudgery of household duties, she derives great pleasure in witnessing her child's development. Regarding Louis's perceptions, his career is advancing nicely, but it keeps him from his family for extended periods.

C RITICAL *thinking*

Earlier in the chapter you learned that passionate love is associated with perceiving one's partner through rose-colored glasses. This idealization, however, often gives way to a more realistic view with the development of companionate love. Yet, if companionate love is more enduring than passionate love, how can the present findings—that perceiving one's partner in somewhat ideal terms leads to greater romantic happiness than perceiving her/him realistically—be explained?

Equity Theory

The theory that people are most satisfied in a relationship when the ratio between rewards and costs is similar for both partners.

Yet overall, he too is still pleased with their marriage. Employing some arbitrary numbers to describe these costs and rewards, let's say that Joyce's rewards equal 40, and Louis's benefits amount to 25. Even though Joyce receives more relationship rewards than Louis, the relationship is equitable because her costs are higher: 32 to Louis's 20. As you can see, the basic equation suggests a balanced or equitable relationship:

$$\frac{40}{32} \quad = \quad \frac{25}{20} \quad = \quad \frac{5}{4}$$

Joyce's ratio   Louis's ratio   Relationship ratio

If these two ratios were not equal, equity theory would predict that both partners would become distressed and would try to restore balance. How would this distress be manifested? The partner who is *overbenefited* should feel guilty about the inequity, while the one who is *underbenefited* should experience anger and depression. Research indicates that inequity does indeed produce these negative emotions in both dating and married couples (Hatfield et al., 1982; Schafer & Keith, 1980). However, although people who are overbenefited tend to feel guilty, they generally are very satisfied and contented with the relationship. This is not the case for the underbenefited. Their anger and depression cause a great deal of dissatisfaction with the relationship (Sprecher, 1992). Given the stress that this inequity produces, it is not surprising that inequitable relationships are less likely to endure (Walster et al., 1978).

SOCIAL SUPPORT PREDICTS RELATIONSHIP SATISFACTION

In the majority of Western cultures, most people involved in long-term romantic relationships consider their partners to be their best friends and the persons they would most likely turn to for support in times of need (Pasch et al., 1997). Receiving such support has three important benefits: the *stress* of the partner in need decreases while her or his *satisfaction* and *commitment* to the relationship increases (Sprecher et al., 1995). Of course, when couples are angry with one another, they are less likely to seek or provide support, and this nonsupport can be very damaging to the relationship (Abbey et al., 1985).

In heterosexual romance, men rely more on their partners for social support than do women, who tend to also depend on a variety of sources, including friends, relatives, and neighbors (Cutrona, 1996). Despite this wider variety of support outside the romantic relationship, a woman's psychological well-being is still closely linked to the support she receives from her romantic partner. For example, a longitudinal study of married couples found that lower levels of depression were associated with both women and men receiving a good deal of *emotional support* (tenderness and understanding) and *information support* (advice and guidance) from their partners during the previous six months (Cutrona & Suhr, 1994).

Unfortunately for women involved in heterosexual romantic relationships, their skill in providing social support appears to be greater than that of their male partners (Vinokur & Vinokur-Kaplan, 1990; Wheeler et al., 1983). The most common explanation for this gender difference is the greater childhood training girls receive in the caretaking role and in emotional attentiveness. Whereas female socialization fosters the development of these *relationship-enhancing* behaviors, male socialization is more likely to promote the development of *individual-enhancing* behaviors, such as independence and control. This gender difference may explain why marriage is more beneficial to men than to women: men marry people who, on average, have a good deal of training and experience in providing care and nurturance to others, while women marry people who, on average, have spent a lot of time learning how to be independent of others!

How does this gender socialization difference influence social support among lesbian and gay couples? A five-year longitudinal study by Lawrence Kurdek (1998) suggests that although the "double dose" of relationship-enhancing skills that lesbians bring to romantic relationships results in somewhat higher levels of intimacy than that found among heterosexual couples, it doesn't lead to higher levels of relationship satisfaction. For gay couples, while their "double dose" of individual-enhancing skills may explain why they tend to have a higher need for autonomy than heterosexual couples, it doesn't lead to lower levels of relationship satisfaction.

Taken as a whole, this discussion of gender differences in social support may remind you of our previous discussion of how the socialization practice of raising people to be autonomous and independent in individualist cultures may be less conducive to maintaining intimate relationships than collectivist social-ization practices (p. 411). Because males are the dominant sex in virtually all soci-eties, their gender socialization more closely mirrors the dominant values of the culture than does female socialization. As our society becomes more egalitarian on gender issues, it's possible that these gender differences may diminish as we socialize boys and girls in more similar ways. The question is, in which direction will the shift take place? Will it move toward more relationship-enhancing behaviors or toward more individual-enhancing behaviors? The answer to this question will be partly determined by the values you bring to future romantic relationships, and the extent to which you shape the gender and relationship beliefs of coming generations.

WE ARE MEANER TO THOSE WE LOVE THAN WE ARE TO STRANGERS

Despite the many emotional joys we derive from long-term intimate relation-ships, this closeness can also be the source of frequent frustrations and annoy-ances. A common reaction to these "aggravations of the heart" is to emotionally lash out at those we profess to love (Miller, 1997). For example, studies of married people interacting with either their spouses or strangers during casual conversa-tion and while working on a problem-solving task found that they were much more polite, agreeable, and attentive to the strangers than to their spouses (Birchler et al., 1975). They not only interrupted their spouses, but they also often openly criticized and belittled them. The communication problems that result from this social insensitivity can gradually weaken lovers' emotional bonds (Kurdek, 1991, 1994).

A number of studies indicate that couples headed for a breakup tend to be unable or unwilling to terminate the expression of negative emotions (Halford et al., 1990). For example, in a four-year longitudinal study of married couples, John Gottman and Robert Levenson (1992) discovered that those relationships that end in divorce tend to involve people who nag and whine a great deal and don't listen very well to their partner's concerns. When troubled couples interact, they often fall into what Gottman (1979) calls a *negative reciprocity cycle,* where positive behaviors tend to be ignored and negative behaviors are reciprocated. Although troubled couples may realize the damage they are inflicting on their relationship with each glare, harsh word, and slammed door, they nevertheless persist in these destructive actions. Happy couples, on the other hand, argue in a more constructive fashion (Blais et al., 1990). When they complain to each other, they also recognize the validity of the other person's feelings and viewpoint (Koren et al., 1980). This tendency to take their partner's point of view when arguing (a psychological state known as *perspective-taking*) is important in maintaining relationship health (Arriaga & Rusbult, 1998).

You are inventing all sorts of feelings for me such as I have never really had at all, and then getting cross with me for having them. That is not a very amiable proceeding, is it?

Murasaki Shikaba, Japanese poet, 974-1031

FIGURE 11.7

In dealing with relationship conflict people employ different strategies, which differ in terms of the dimensions of active-passive and constructive-destructive. In dealing with dissatisfactions in romantic relationships in your own life, which of these four basic strategies have you used?

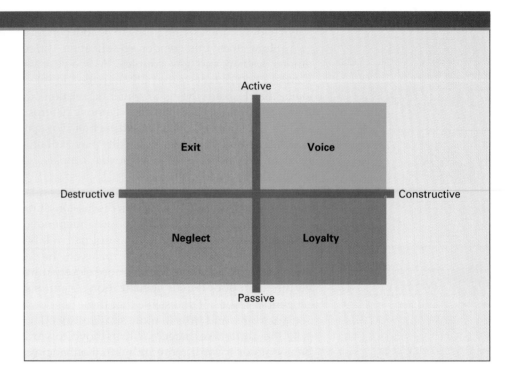

Love doesn't just sit there, like a stone, it has to be made, like bread; re-made all the time, made new.

Ursula K. LeGuin, U.S. science fiction writer, b. 1929

PEOPLE USE DIFFERENT STRATEGIES TO COPE WITH A TROUBLED RELATIONSHIP

How do people typically react when a romantic relationship becomes dissatisfying? Caryl Rusbult and her coworkers have identified four strategies people use in coping with a troubled relationship (Rusbult et al., 1986a, 1987). Their level of commitment to the relationship influences the strategies they choose, or find themselves using. The more satisfied and the more invested partners are, the more committed they will be to work on solutions to maintain and improve the relationship (Bui et al., 1996). Figure 11.7 illustrates the primary qualities of these four strategies.

In dealing with conflict, Rusbult contends that some people may take a passively constructive approach by exhibiting *loyalty*. They simply wait, hoping that things will improve on their own. Individuals who adopt this strategy are often afraid to "rock the boat," so they say nothing, and pray that their loyalty will keep the relationship afloat. Others, especially men, adopt the passively destructive strategy of *neglect*. They "clam up" and ignore their partners, or spend less time with them. When together, neglectful persons often treat their partners poorly by constantly criticizing them for things unrelated to the real problem. Those who don't know how to deal with their negative emotions, or aren't motivated to improve the relationship but also aren't ready to end it, tend to employ this strategy. When people do conclude that the relationship is not worth saving, they *exit*, which is an active, yet destructive, strategy. A much more constructive and active strategy used to deal with conflict in a relationship is *voice*. People discuss their problems, seek compromises, consult therapists, and attempt to salvage a relationship they still highly value.

Rusbult and her colleagues (1986b) have found that one determinant of the strategies that people choose to employ in dealing with their dissatisfaction is their level of psychological masculinity and femininity (see chapter 4, p. 117). In survey studies involving lesbian, gay male, and heterosexual women and men, individuals with many feminine personality traits were much more likely to react constructively to relationship problems. They either actively searched for an

CRITICAL *thinking*

acceptable resolution, or, if a solution did not seem possible, they remained quietly loyal to the relationship. In contrast, those who had many masculine traits and few feminine traits tended to respond destructively when trouble developed in their relationships. They either passively neglected the problems and allowed things to deteriorate further, or they actively threatened to exit. These patterns were true for both men and women, regardless of sexual orientation. More generally, other studies indicate that high levels of femininity in one or both partners are associated with higher levels of relationship satisfaction and commitment (Lamke et al., 1994; Stets & Burke, 1996). In addition, longitudinal studies of married couples indicate that masculinity's negative impact on relationship satisfaction is due to the influence of the undesirable masculine personality traits in men (but not in women) related to arrogance and aggressiveness, and not due to the more desirable masculine traits related to independence and assertiveness (Bradbury et al., 1995).

Overall, these findings suggest that through the acquisition of feminine personality traits, people learn to react to relationship problems in a constructive manner (Ickes, 1985). On the other hand, acquiring undesirable masculine traits is downright destructive to relationship survival. Why might this be the case? As already mentioned, feminine traits are characterized by a communal orientation of warmth, intimacy, and a concern with interpersonal relations. On the other hand, masculine traits are characterized by a more individualistic orientation of power, dominance, and a concern with achieving instrumental (that is, work) goals. People with many feminine personality characteristics appear to be more interested in resolving conflict through emotional sharing and compromise, whereas those with mostly masculine characteristics, especially those that are undesirable, prefer reaching decisions on their own and imposing their will on others. When described in this manner, it isn't surprising that these two gender orientations often achieve different results when conflicts arise in romance.

ROMANTIC BREAKUPS OFTEN CAUSE EMOTIONAL DISTRESS

When romantic relationships fail, it is relatively rare that the breakup is mutually desired. In both heterosexual dating relationships and marriages, women tend to initiate the breakup (Hagestad & Smyer, 1982; Rubin et al., 1981). One possible reason for this gender difference is that women appear to be more attentive to and sensitive about relationship problems (Ptacek & Dodge, 1995).

In both heterosexual and homosexual relationships, the partner who initiates the breakup tends to suffer less distress, but this effect is much more apparent for men than women in heterosexual romance (Frazier & Cook, 1993; Helgeson, 1994). Men also tend to suffer more than women when they are romantically rejected. A possible explanation for this effect involves the traditional gender roles taught to men and women. First, because power and control are central aspects of the traditional male gender role (Garfinkel, 1985), men may experience greater self-esteem threat and emotional distress when their partner takes relationship control away from them by ending the romance. Second, because heterosexual men tend to place all their emotional eggs in their romantic baskets, they may suffer more emotional pain when the bottom falls out of the relationship and those eggs are smashed (Barbee et al., 1990).

A similar effect is found regarding the ideologies of individualism and collectivism. In a study of romantic breakups in both the United States and Puerto Rico, Harry Triandis and his colleagues (1988) found that people with a more individualist orientation were the loneliest following a breakup. Individualists, Triandis explained, tend to have a less extensive social support network than collectivists, and thus, they have little to rely on when their romantic relationships fall apart.

In coping with the loss of love, men and women are equally likely to spend considerable time talking to themselves about the relationship ("I'm lucky to have dumped that jerk!" "I've learned a valuable lesson"), distracting themselves by engaging in physical activities or doing things to improve their looks and sex appeal. However, women are more likely than men to cry, talk things over with their friends, read self-help books, and consult a therapist to better understand their feelings (Orimoto et al., 1993). These results suggest that women, more than men, tend to spend time following a breakup attending to their emotional needs in ways that may promote increased understanding so future relationships can be more satisfying.

People who deal best with the loss of romantic love are those who have a supportive social network; that is, friends and family from whom they can receive emotional sustenance and encouragement (Holahan et al., 1997; Milardo & Allan, 1997). In such times of stress, this support network provides the recent victims of love with a "buffer" from the full force of their loss (Thoits, 1982). The support that a social network offers could be either emotional or financial assistance, and its purpose is to help people overcome their loss and reestablish a sense of normalcy in their daily activities.

Despite the turmoil that love often brings to our lives, most of us yearn for romance even after experiencing romantic failure. Some call this persistence a form of addiction, but others describe the desire for romantic intimacy as an expression of one of the most basic human needs, the desire to share and immerse oneself as completely as possible in the life and love of another who has become an integral part of one's self-concept.

When a romantic relationship ends, social support received from friends and family can help people cope with their emotional pain.

SECTION SUMMARY

Several factors determine whether love will endure or fade. First, couples who idealize one another tend to have happier relationships than those who have more realistic views. Second, romantic relationships are happiest when the ratio between the rewards and costs is similar for both partners. Third, receiving social support from one's partner increases satisfaction and commitment to the relationship. When arguments do lead to serious trouble, it is often because couples are unable or unwilling to terminate the expression of negative emotions toward one another, and because each person views the other as being motivated by selfish concerns and negative intentions. In dealing with relationship dissatisfaction, we typically employ four distinct strategies: *loyalty, neglect, voice,* or *exit.* When romance does end, those who cope best tend to be the ones with a supportive social network that can partially buffer them from the full force of the loss.

esides the many other problems that can besiege an intimate relationship, jealousy can also contribute to relationship failure. **Jealousy** is the negative emotional reaction experienced when a relationship that is important to a person's self-concept is threatened by a real or imagined rival (Parrott & Smith, 1993). In most cases, the threat is another person, but people can also feel jealous about their partner's time involvement with work, hobbies, and family obligations (Buunk & Bringle, 1987). Some people mistakenly believe that jealousy indicates the depths of a partner's love, and thus, is a healthy sign in romantic relationships. In actuality, research demonstrates that it indicates the degree of a lover's dependence and, thus, is a sign of relationship insecurity (Salovey & Rodin, 1991). It also triggers a host of negative feelings and behaviors and tends to lower self-esteem (Mathes et al., 1985). Not surprisingly, people with chronically low self-esteem are more susceptible to jealousy than those with high self-esteem (Nadler & Dotan, 1992).

Jealousy

The negative emotional reaction experienced when a relationship that is important to a person's self-concept is threatened by a real or imagined rival.

O! Beware my lord, of jealousy; It is the green-eyed monster which doth mock.

William Shakespeare, English dramatist, 1564–1616, from Othello

Despite the negative and unpleasant effects brought on by jealousy, some people consciously try to manipulate situations to make their partners jealous. For example, a survey of college students found that one-third of young women and one-fifth of young men flirt with others or talk about former lovers in an attempt to gain their current lover's attention and to strengthen the relationship (White, 1980a). Those who tried to induce jealousy stated they were more involved in the relationship than were their partners. In most cases, however, the actual consequences of these tactics were that they hurt, not helped, the relationship.

What types of coping strategies, both of the constructive and destructive variety, could you employ in contending with your own jealousy? Jeff Bryson (1977) suggests that all jealousy-coping strategies boil down to two major goal-oriented behaviors:

1. Attempts to maintain the relationship
2. Attempts to maintain one's own self-esteem

As can be seen in table 11.6, if jealous individuals desire to maintain both the relationship and their self-esteem, they will try to negotiate a mutually satisfying solution with their partners. This constructive and active strategy corresponds to Rusbult's notion of relationship *voice*. However, if jealous individuals desire to maintain their romantic relationships regardless of the loss of self-esteem, they may swallow their pride and put up with the jealousy-inducing behavior. This passive approach corresponds to Rusbult's notion of relationship *loyalty*. In contrast to these relationship-maintaining strategies, those who are more concerned with self-esteem maintenance often use verbal and physical attacks against their partner or rival. Likewise,

TABLE 11.6

Different Ways of Coping with Jealousy

		Relationship Maintaining Behaviors	
		Yes	**No**
Self-Esteem Maintaining Behaviors	**Yes**	Negotiating a mutually acceptable solution	Verbal/physical attacks against the partner or rival
	No	Clinging to the relationship	Self-destructive behaviors

Source: Adapted from J. B. Bryson, "Situational Determinants of the Expression of Jealousy" in H. Sigall (chair), Sexual Jealousy, symposium presented at the annual meeting of the American Psychological Association, San Francisco, 1977.

jealous people who are not principally attempting to either maintain the relationship or bolster their self-esteem often employ self-destructive behavior.

In commenting on these different coping strategies, Sharon Brehm (1992) brings up a good point: The jealous should think about both the short-term and long-term consequences of their coping responses *before* acting. For example, verbally or physically attacking partners may temporarily intimidate them into staying in the relationship while it also shores up your own sagging self-esteem, but in the long run, it will push partners away and lower your self-worth. Similarly, begging and pleading with your partner to end another romance may succeed in the short run, but it will threaten your self-esteem as it reduces your partner's attraction to you.

A survey of young adults conducted by Peter Salovey and Judith Rodin (1988) found that the strategy of *self-reliance* was the most effective in reducing jealousy. This strategy involved jealous individuals *containing emotional outbursts, maintaining daily routines*, and *reevaluating the importance of the relationship*. Another strategy that reduced depression and anger among the jealous was *self-bolstering*, which involved thinking positively about oneself and doing nice things for oneself. Similarly, Elaine Hatfield and Richard Rapson (1993) found that encouraging people to make new friends, or to get a job, or to go back to school helped them to think better of themselves, which in turn reduced their jealousy.

The general recommendations coming from all this jealousy work is that the best antidotes to the "green-eyed monster" are to (1) avoid emotional outbursts that are destructive to you and others, and (2) develop a feeling of self-confidence about your ability to act and survive independent of the relationship. In the final analysis, even though intimacy involves an inclusion of the other in our self-concepts, our own health and the health of the relationship depends on our ability to develop a sense of self independent of our partners.

FEATURED STUDY

GENDER DIFFERENCES IN JEALOUS RESPONDING

Nadler, A., & Dotan, I. (1992). Commitment and rival attractiveness: Their effects on male and female reactions to jealousy arousing situations. *Sex Roles, 26,* 293–310.

Romantic jealousy is associated with two kinds of threats: (1) a threat to the present relationship, and (2) a threat to the jealous person's self-esteem. Due to the different ways in which women and men are socialized, researchers hypothesized that women would expect jealous women to be more concerned with the ending of a romantic relationship, while men would expect jealous men to be more concerned with self-esteem loss.

METHOD

Participants were seventy-six women and seventy-five men (age range 27–45) from various adult education courses in Tel Aviv, Israel. All volunteers were from the middle and upper socioeconomic classes and had been married between five and twenty years. Each participant read four story vignettes describing jealousy-provoking situations. For female participants, the vignettes involved a wife discovering that her spouse was romantically involved in an extramarital affair, while for male participants the roles were reversed. The rivals' attractiveness and the degree of perceived commitment of the spouses to the rival relationships were varied between the stories. Following each story, participants filled out a questionnaire in which they rated how the betrayed spouse would react.

RESULTS AND DISCUSSION

As predicted, results indicated that male and female participants expected the betrayed spouse to feel and behave differently. Although both female and male participants expected their same-sex protagonists to generally respond more intensely to an attractive rival than to an unattractive rival, *when* they expected them to respond most intensely differed.

Female participants expected the spouse (a woman) to feel the worst, and experience the most negative arousal, when the rival was attractive and the rival relationship was of long duration (high commitment). They attributed significantly lower negative feelings and negative arousal to the wife when the rival was attractive but the relationship was of low commitment (a brief affair). The researchers interpret these results as supporting their hypothesis that jealous women are more concerned with salvaging a valued, yet troubled, romantic relationship than with trying to recover lost self-esteem: when their romantic relationships are most seriously threatened, women's negative emotional arousal is at its peak.

In contrast to these findings, male participants expected the spouse (a man) to feel the worst when his wife had a brief affair (low commitment) with an attractive rival. When the unfaithful spouse was described as having an affair of long duration (high commitment) with an attractive rival, male participants expected the betrayed spouse to be relatively unattracted to his wife. The researchers interpret these findings as supporting their hypothesis that jealous men are more concerned with the loss of self-esteem than with trying to salvage a troubled romantic relationship: when their romantic relationships are most seriously threatened, men seem to emotionally disassociate themselves from their partners.

Together, these findings suggest that both women and men seem sensitive to the threat to romantic relationships, but they tend to cope differently with this threat. When threatened, jealous women tend to emotionally focus on their relationship, which may help to salvage it; jealous men tend to emotionally distance themselves from their relationship, which may serve to protect their self-esteem.

 WEB SITES accessed through http://www.mhhe.com/franzoi2

Web sites for this chapter focus on research and theory on adult attachment dynamics and the psychology of personal relationships.

Adult Attachment Lab

This web page for the Adult Attachment Lab, which is directed by Dr. Phillip Shaver at the University of California at Davis, advances understanding of adult attachment dynamics. Here you will find an overview of self-report measures of adult attachment security, as well as recent studies conducted from the lab.

International Society for the Study of Personal Relationships

The International Society for the Study of Personal Relationships has a web site which endeavors to stimulate and support scholarship and research on personal relationships.

Social Cognition and Personal Relationships

At this web site you can learn about the formation, evolution, maintenance, and dissolution of intimate relationships.

C H A P T E R   1 2

AGGRESSION

itchell Johnson, age 13, was angry after being "dumped" by his girlfriend. He was mad at everybody, and he told some of his classmates at Westside Middle School in Jonesboro, Arkansas that he was going to shoot all the girls who had ever broken up with him. "Tomorrow you all find out if you live or die," he bragged. Eleven-year-old Andrew Golden, also of Jonesboro, was already known in his neighborhood as a bully who regularly threatened other children. He also was well tutored by his father, an official of a local gun club, in shooting rifles, shotguns, and pistols. On the afternoon of March 24, 1998, these two boys executed a plan that relied on Andrew's deadly expertise to fulfill Mitchell's promise of revenge. Shortly after lunch, dressed in camouflage clothing and armed with their families' handguns and semiautomatic rifles, Mitchell and Andrew lured the student body of the middle school onto the playground with a false fire alarm and then opened fire from a nearby woods. Their weapons were aimed at girls, the target of Mitchell's anger. Within fifteen seconds, four students and one teacher had been fatally shot, and eleven others had been wounded, including Mitchell's former girlfriend. All the victims were female.

Following the Westside Middle School shootings, and the even more deadly April 1999 shooting spree at a Colorado high school that left 15 dead and 28 wounded, people have understandably tried to make sense of such aggression. What could cause people, much less children, to behave so violently? Biology? Family environment? Culture? These are some of the questions we address in this chapter. Hopefully, by its end, we will have a better understanding of the social psychology of aggression.

WHAT IS AGGRESSION?

Before we try to understand aggression similar to the Westside Middle School shootings, we first need to define the concept. What is aggression, and how can we distinguish between different types? Also, what is the nature of gender and self-esteem differences in aggressive responding?

On the afternoon of March 24, 1998, Mitchell Johnson and Andrew Golden shot and killed four students and one teacher, and wounded ten others at the Westside Middle School in Jonesboro, Arkansas. The motive for the shooting was revenge for Mitchell being "dumped" by his girlfriend, a classmate at the school. Can social psychological research and theory make sense out of this seemingly senseless act of violence?

Social Psychologists Define Aggression as "Intentional Harm"

Aggression

Any form of behavior that is intended to harm or injure some person, oneself, or an object.

Although there is no universally agreed upon definition of **aggression**, one of the more common ones used by social psychologists is that it is any form of behavior that is intended to harm or injure some person, oneself, or an object (Björkqvist & Niemelä, 1992). Using this definition, we can clearly conclude that Mitchell Johnson and Andrew Golden committed an aggressive act against students and teachers at the middle school. In firing their weapons, they *intended* to harm the people on the playground.

To test whether you can identify other aggressive actions based on this definition, read the following vignette and try to identify five acts of aggression.

> A thief fires a gun at a man he is trying to rob, but the bullet misses the mark and the man is uninjured. Panicked, the man accidentally knocks down a young girl as he flees the scene, and she badly cuts her knee on the pavement. Later, the girl screams in pain as a doctor puts five stitches in her knee to stop the bleeding. Upon finishing, the doctor asks the girl how badly it hurts. Still crying and now very angry, she grabs his moustache and yanks with all her might and snears, "That's how much it hurts!" The next day, the thief is arrested and his cellmate verbally berates him for being such an inept burglar. Depressed and angry, the thief smashes his fist into the concrete cell wall, fracturing three fingers. While in the infirmary being treated for his injury the thief angrily destroys a medicine cabinet.

Can you correctly identify the five aggressive acts in this injury-filled story? What about the thief shooting but missing his intended victim? No harm, no aggression? Even though the bullet missed its mark, this is still an aggressive action because it was the *intention* of the thief to harm the man. In the second action, although the robbery victim's behavior caused injury to the girl, this is not an example of aggression because the man had no intention of hurting the child or anyone else. Neither is the behavior of the doctor treating the girl's wound an aggressive action. Although his actions caused pain and he performed those actions intentionally, the goal was to help the girl recover from her previous injury. Although the man and the doctor did not perform any aggressive actions, the little girl did. In pulling the doctor's moustache, she intentionally tried to seek retribution for the hurt she believed he caused. What about the thief's cellmate? The psychological harm intended in such verbal abuse qualifies this as an aggressive action. The fourth instance of aggression involved the prisoner's self-inflicted injury: intentional actions that cause harm to oneself are considered aggressive, even if they are impulsive. Finally, aggression can be directed against inanimate objects, as was the case when the thief destroyed the medicine cabinet.

The wish to hurt, the momentary intoxication with pain, is the loophole through which the pervert climbs into the minds of ordinary men.

Jacob Bronowski, British biologist

You cannot shake hands with a clenched fist.

Indira Gandhi, India's first woman prime minister, 1917–1984

Social Psychologists Make a Distinction Between "Instrumental" and "Hostile" Aggression

Instrumental Aggression

The intentional use of harmful behavior so that one can achieve some other goal.

Traditionally, social psychologists have distinguished between two "types" of aggression, namely, *instrumental* and *hostile* (Geen, 1990). The aggression the thief used in his robbery attempt is an example of instrumental aggression. **Instrumental aggression** is the intentional use of harmful behavior so that one can achieve some other goal. In the robbery attempt, the thief used aggression as an *instrument* to achieve his real goal, which was obtaining the victim's money. The aggression that occurs in a military context is also often instrumental in nature. Here, the principal goal may be either to defend one's own territory or to confiscate the enemy's land. As a general rule, aggressive acts carried out with the objective of gaining material, psychological, or social benefits all fit our instrumental definition.

In contrast to this type of aggression, the Westside Middle School shootings and most of the other aggressive instances in the imaginary vignette were examples of hostile aggression. **Hostile aggression** is triggered by anger, and the goal of the intentionally harmful behavior is simply to cause injury or death to the victim. Mitchell Johnson's goal was to kill those who had angered him. Similarly, the girl attacking the doctor, the thief smashing his hand against the wall, and the thief then destroying a medicine cabinet were all instances in which the aggressor's principal goal was to cause injury to another person or thing.

In thinking about instrumental and hostile aggression, it is important to keep in mind how they differ. Instrumental aggression is motivated by the anticipation of rewards or the avoidance of punishment. In that sense, it can be thought of as being relatively deliberate and rational. On the other hand, hostile aggression is not really motivated by the anticipation of rewards or the avoidance of punishments, even though these may indeed be ultimate consequences of the aggressive act. Instead, this type of aggression is often impulsive and irrational. There is a goal, but it is simply the desire to cause harm to the victim.

Research suggests that highly aggressive individuals can be distinguished by the degree to which they engage in instrumental and hostile aggression (Berkowitz, 1994b). *Instrumental aggressors* tend to use "proactive" force in a cool and collected manner to attain their objectives. Many robbers and school-yard bullies fall into this category. In contrast, *hostile aggressors* tend to use "reactive" force in a highly emotional and impulsive manner. Their crimes often entail excessive use of violence due to their tempers getting out of hand. Hostile aggressors are especially likely to perceive danger in their world and to respond to ambiguous stimuli with aggression (Bushman, 1996).

Although the distinction between instrumental and hostile aggression is often useful, many aggressive actions cannot be neatly placed into only one of the categories. For example, a child may angrily hit another child who has taken her

Hostile Aggression

The intentional use of harmful behavior, triggered by anger, in which the goal is simply to cause injury or death to the victim.

Anger is a short madness.

Quinus Horatius Flaccus, Roman poet, 65–8 B.C.

Is this primarily an example of instrumental or hostile aggression?

Reprinted with special permission of King Features Syndicate, Inc.

Carl's wife offers him proof that, yes, she was planning to serve "that stupid stringy Italian stuff" again.

favorite toy, and then she may retrieve the toy while the victim cries. The motives underlying this aggression are both the infliction of pain (hostile aggression) *and* the recovery of the favored toy (instrumental aggression). In such instances, no clear distinctions can be made between hostile and instrumental aggression. In other instances, aggression might start out instrumentally, yet then turn hostile. For example, a soldier's "cool" and methodical firing of a weapon at a hidden enemy may turn into impulsive rage when one of his comrades is killed.

GENDER AND PERSONALITY MODERATE THE EXPRESSION OF AGGRESSION

Research has found considerable evidence that individual differences in aggression are relatively stable, meaning that some people tend to be more prone to aggressive outbursts than others (Farrington, 1994). Attempts to better understand these individual differences have resulted in studies examining gender and personality as variables likely to *moderate* the expression of aggression.

GENDER

A widespread belief in our culture is that men are more aggressive than women. Does social psychological research support this cultural belief? The answer is yes and no. Meta-analytic studies indicate that males and females do differ in one important kind of aggression: *physical aggression.* That is, males are more likely than females to engage in aggression that produces pain or physical injury (Eagly & Steffen, 1986a). This gender difference in willingness to cause physical injury is more pronounced (1) among children than adults (Hyde, 1984), and (2) for unprovoked aggression than for provoked aggression (Bettencourt & Miller, 1996). In contrast, men and women are very similar to one another in their *verbal* aggression and in expressing feelings of anger (Tavris, 1989).

Although gender differences are considerably smaller than what gender stereotypes suggest, women and men do appear to have different *social representations* of their physical aggression. In a series of studies, British social psychologist Anne Campbell and her colleagues found that women tend to view their aggression as being stress-induced and precipitated by a loss of self-control that erupts into an antisocial act (Campbell et al., 1996, 1997b). Their expressions of aggression were uniformly seen as a negative experience. Men, in contrast, perceived their aggression as a means of exerting control over others and reclaiming power and self-esteem. Unlike women, men often believed that resorting to physical violence was a positive experience. The researchers contend that these gender differences in the experience of physical aggression may mean that the more spontaneous and unplanned behaviors typical of *hostile aggression* are more descriptive of the antisocial actions of women, while the more planned and calculated actions of *instrumental aggression* are more descriptive of male aggression.

One form of aggression that researchers have largely ignored until recently is *indirect aggression,* a form of social manipulation in which the aggressor attempts to harm another person without a face-to-face encounter. Gossiping, spreading bad or false stories about someone, telling others not to associate with a person, and revealing someone's secrets are all examples of indirect aggression. Field studies by Kaj Björkqvist and Kirsti Lagerspetz (see figure 12.1) suggest that among adolescents in Finland, girls are more likely than boys to use indirect aggression (Björkqvist et al., 1992; Lagerspetz et al., 1988). Their research further indicates that while male physical aggression decreases significantly during adolescence, teenage Finnish girls continue to exhibit higher levels of indirect aggression at all age levels. Anthropologist Douglas Fry (1992) has found similar preferences for indirect aggression among peasant women in the Mexican state of Oaxaca. Although more studies need to be conducted on

FIGURE 12.1

Gender Comparisons in Aggressive Strategies

In a study of the aggressive styles used by adolescents in Finland, Björkqvist and his colleagues (1992) found that verbal aggression (for example, yelling, insulting, name-calling) is the most used by both boys and girls. Boys display more physical aggression (hitting, kicking, shoving), whereas girls utilize more indirect forms of aggression (gossiping, writing nasty notes about another, telling bad or false stories).

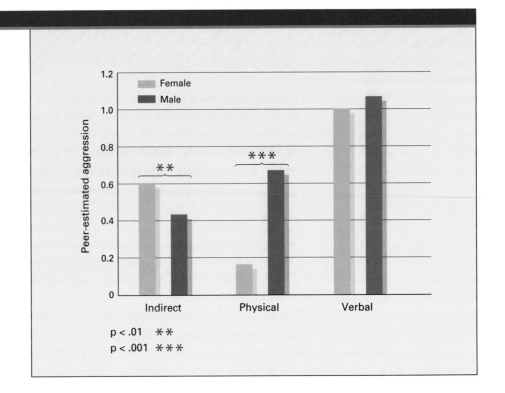

indirect aggression, these findings are important because they suggest we need to reexamine the "peaceful female" stereotype.

One important question emerging from these studies is: Why might females be more likely to choose indirect rather than direct aggressive means? Björkqvist and Lagerspetz suggest four possible reasons. One explanation is that girls tend to be discouraged more than boys from engaging in direct acts of aggression. Because of this different gender socialization pattern, females may use more indirect aggression simply because it is more socially acceptable. Another possibility involves the *social structure* of same-sex peer groups during childhood and adolescence. Girls typically form small, intimate play groups, while boys' groups tend to be bigger and less defined (Maccoby, 1990). Björkqvist and Lagerspetz suggest that indirect aggression may be more effective in the intimate social settings usually inhabited by girls because such surroundings create greater opportunities to discover and pass on personal information about others. A third possibility has to do with the *relative physical strengths* of the two sexes. Women, typically being smaller than men, may have learned that indirect forms of aggression are more effective and less costly than direct personal attack. Finally, because research indicates that indirect retaliation to aggression is more common in older than in younger children, Lagerspetz and Björkqvist (1994) suggest that the greater use of indirect means by females during adolescence may reflect their earlier social maturation.

In our examination of gender differences in aggression, we must also consider the impact that *culture* has on females' willingness to act in an aggressive manner. Although a good deal of cross-cultural research indicates that women are less physically aggressive than men and less likely to commit homicide (Daly & Wilson, 1988), a number of societies encourage and teach women to be physically aggressive. For example, in her study of aggression among the islanders of Margarita, Venezuela, anthropologist H. B. Kimberley Cook (1992) discovered that aggression was an integral aspect of being a woman in Margarita. As one elderly woman told her:

Although males appear to be more physically aggressive than females, research suggests that females may engage in more indirect aggression, such as spreading bad or false stories about others, or revealing someone's secrets. Why might these gender differences exist?

Women in Margarita are *"guapa"* (physically strong). When we fight, we punch and tear each other's hair. A long time ago, I had a fight with a woman. I chased her all around the ranchería. When I caught her, I grabbed her by the hair and pushed her face into the mud. She was screaming, but I wouldn't let go. I was stronger and I laughed. She didn't talk to me for years afterwards, but later we became friends again. (Cook, 1992, p. 156)

Unlike many women in North America, Margariteño women do not relate their aggression to a loss of self-control. Instead, their antisocial actions are an *exercise of control,* usually employed against other women in disputes over authority or jealousy concerning a man. When combined with the findings from other cross-cultural aggression studies (Burbank, 1987), Cook's observations illustrate that although women are less *lethal* and generally less physically aggressive than men, they are by no means the "gentle sex." As a species, we all share the capacity to cause harm to one another.

PERSONALITY

A major program of research conducted by Italian social psychologist Gian Vittorio Caprara and his associates (1994, 1996) indicates that three personality traits most consistently related to aggression are *irritability* (the tendency to explode at the slightest provocation), *rumination* (the tendency to retain feelings of anger following provocation), and *emotional susceptibility* (the tendency to experience feelings of discomfort and inadequacy). These findings clearly suggest that highly aggressive people have a hard time controlling their emotions: they not only have quick tempers, but they also "stew in their own angry juices" following a confrontation.

The fact that aggressive-prone individuals tend to experience feelings of inadequacy is relevant to research discussed in chapter 2 (p. 62) suggesting that aggression is one means by which some people seek to maintain or restore their *self-esteem.* For many years, it was thought that only low self-esteem individuals were susceptible to these types of aggressive outbursts. However, it now appears that aggression is more commonly a result of threats to highly favorable views of the self and is most likely to occur when a person's high self-esteem is fragile and unstable (Baumeister et al., 1996). Apparently, in these instances, aggression is a defensive reaction to avoid having to make any downward revision of self-esteem (Tangney et al., 1992).

> ## SECTION SUMMARY
>
> *Aggression* is any form of behavior that is intended to harm or injure some person, oneself, or an object. Social psychologists have investigated two basic types of aggression: *instrumental aggression* is the use of harmful behavior to achieve some other goal, whereas *hostile aggression* is where harming another is the goal of the attack. Regarding gender differences, men are more physically aggressive, but women engage in more indirect aggression. Both sexes appear to express equal levels of verbal aggression. Three personality traits found in aggressive-prone persons are irritability, rumination, and emotional susceptibility.

THE BIOLOGY OF AGGRESSION

It has been estimated that more than 17 million people have died in wars fought since World War II. In the United States, approximately twenty-three thousand deaths per year are due to violent assaults, the prime targets being minority groups, men, and the young (Rosenberg & Mercy, 1991). Even when people do not directly participate in aggressive acts themselves, many enjoy watching others do so in action adventure films or sporting events (Mustonen, 1997). Aggression even manifests itself in the play guns and toy soldiers we produce and purchase for our children's enjoyment. And judging from their faces as they play with these toys, enjoyment is what it often brings them. Based on these observations, is it reasonable to conclude that the human race has an inborn tendency for aggression?

EVOLUTION MAY HAVE SHAPED OUR AGGRESSIVE BEHAVIOR PATTERNS

A number of social scientists concur with the judgment that we are an innately aggressive species. In fact, for more than one hundred years, many biologically oriented scientists have argued that aggression in humans—as well as aggression in other species—can be understood as an adaptive response to the environment. Evolutionary psychologists and sociobiologists believe that males of many species, including our own, are more aggressive and have a stronger social dominance orientation than females (see chapter 7) because aggression and dominance-seeking have been the primary ways males have gained sexual access to females (Pratto et al., 1993). That is, by physically intimidating—and sometimes even killing—less aggressive males, the more aggressive males became socially dominant, and thus, were more likely to sexually reproduce. Unlike males, females' reproductive success did not depend on their level of aggression. Over many generations, this difference in the importance of aggression and dominance-seeking in male and female reproductive success led to genetically based differences in male and female aggression.

One important point to keep in mind about evolutionary theory is that it assumes that aggression increases the likelihood that an individual will survive and successfully reproduce. However, unlike earlier *instinct theories* that emphasized individual survival (Lorenz, 1966), modern evolutionary theories stress *genetic* survival (Buss & Shackelford, 1997). From this perspective, genetic survival

FIGURE 12.2

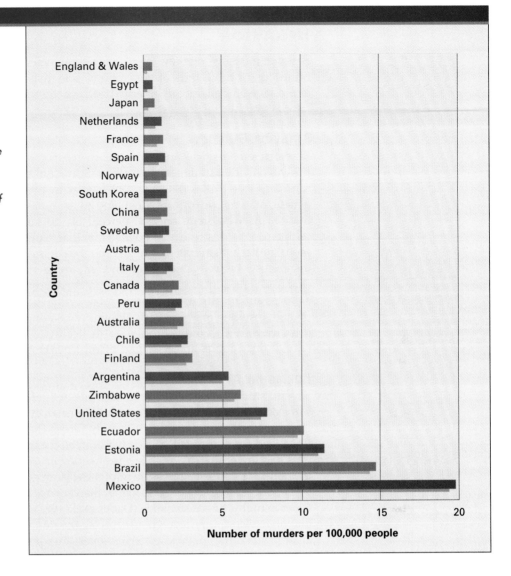

Murder Rates Around the Globe

A United Nations study reported that not only does the murder rate vary widely from country to country, but also that the murder rates within many countries change substantially from year to year. Do these data suggest that evolutionary-based explanations of aggression are false? How might you explain the data by considering both evolutionary and cultural factors in your analysis?

Source: Data from United Nations, 1991.

necessitates that aggression should be selective because relatives share many more of the same genes than strangers. In other words, relatives should not be attacked, for this reduces the likelihood that one's gene pool will be passed on to future generations. In general, research supports this hypothesis: aggression is much more likely to be directed against nonrelatives, and when relatives are attacked, they tend to be "relatives by marriage." For example, stepchildren, who by definition do not have genetic ties to one of their parents, are much more likely to be abused and killed than are other children (Daly & Wilson, 1991). A similar pattern is found in other animal species (Lore & Schultz, 1993).

One problem with solely relying on an evolutionary-based explanation for aggression in humans is that—as figure 12.2 illustrates—levels of aggression vary so widely across cultures. A related problem is that wide differences in aggression occur *within* cultures *over time*. For example, three hundred years ago, Sweden had one of the highest documented rates of interpersonal violence in the Western world, and today it has one of the lowest (Lagerspetz, 1985). Genetic changes in human groups over such a short (in terms of evolution) time period are simply not possible. Instead, social and cultural factors are the more likely causes. Of course, this does not mean that evolutionary factors do not influence human aggression. It simply means that evolutionary forces, by themselves, cannot adequately explain human aggression.

War nourishes war.

Johann Schiller, German writer & philosopher, 1759–1805

BIOLOGICAL FACTORS INFLUENCE AGGRESSIVE BEHAVIOR

Beyond focusing on how aggressive tendencies may have been shaped over hundreds of thousands of generations, scientists also study whether individual aggressive tendencies are inherited and whether hormonal fluctuations influence later aggressive responses.

BEHAVIOR GENETICS

Research on identical and fraternal twins in the field of behavior genetics has provided evidence suggesting that our individual aggressiveness may be partly due to inheritance (Miles & Carey, 1997). That is, twins who share exactly the same genetic material (identical twins) tend to have more similar aggressive tendencies than twins who share only 50 percent of the same genes (fraternal twins). The problem with this research, however, is that parents tend to treat identical twins more similarly than fraternal twins, and thus, it is difficult for twin studies to clearly distinguish between biological and environmental determinants of aggression (McCord, 1994). In addition, animal studies suggest that environmental factors, such as stress and nutrition, can actually cause certain genes to become activated or deactivated, resulting in even identical twins not having the same *active* genetic makeup (McClearn, 1993). For the time being, then, although heritability undoubtedly influences human aggression, its degree of influence is still unknown (Plomin et al., 1990).

HORMONAL ACTIVITY

Several studies suggest that chemical messengers in the bloodstream, known as *hormones,* influence human aggression (Berman et al., 1993; Campbell at al., 1997a; Loosen, 1994). For example, one study found that people who had been institutionalized for attempted suicide (self-directed aggression) or extreme aggressiveness had lower than average levels of *serotonin,* a hormone that is associated with the ability to control aggressive impulses (Marazzitti et al., 1993).

Other studies have found higher than normal levels of the male hormone *testosterone* in highly aggressive men (Dabbs et al., 1987). Although these findings suggest that high testosterone levels may cause aggression, there is also evidence suggesting an opposite causal path: testosterone levels are sometimes affected by the *outcome* of competition. For example, in one study of male tennis players, winners' testosterone levels increased after the match while losers' hormonal levels decreased (Mazur & Lamb, 1980). Similar hormonal changes occur among nonhuman primates following competition in which they either gain or lose status in their social groups. Among humans, the positive and negative emotions accompanying success and failure appear to be what cause the changes in testosterone level (McCaul et al., 1992).

What these studies suggest is that there is no simple causal relationship between hormone levels and aggression in humans or other animals. Heightened testosterone levels may make aggression more likely, but aggression—or even nonaggressive competition—may cause changes in testosterone levels. The message that can be taken from this research and the other studies reviewed in this section is that biological variables—evolutionary history, genetic inheritance, and level of hormone activity—contribute to the general "aggressiveness" of the person (Geen, 1998). Unlike early instinct theories, contemporary biologists and evolutionary theorists do not argue that aggressive behavior is determined by some inborn fixed tendency. Instead, they propose that these biological "background" variables influence how we respond to situational provocations. Although a growing number of social psychologists are acknowledging the impact that biological factors can have on our *capacity* for aggression, the vast majority still believe that the *form* that the aggression takes, as well as its *intensity,* is influenced most by the many psychological, social, and cultural forces that we will discuss in the remaining chapter sections (Hinde, 1990; Robarchek, 1989).

SECTION SUMMARY

Although scientists once believed that human beings possessed an innate aggressive instinct, this perspective has been modified by evolutionary theorists, who contend that aggressive tendencies are selective and based on the principle of genetic survival. Biological research further suggests that individual differences in aggressiveness may be partly due to inheritance and hormonal changes.

AGGRESSION AS A REACTION TO NEGATIVE AFFECT

Japanese are world-famous for their politeness. One notable exception to this courteous behavior is a two-hundred-year-old event that takes place just before midnight on New Year's Eve in Ashikaga, a city fifty miles north of Tokyo. In what outsiders might consider to be a very strange festival, people walk in a procession up a dark mountain road to the Saishoji Temple, screaming curses at those who have frustrated them during the previous twelve months. *"You idiot!" "Give me a raise!" "My teacher is stupid!"* Although these words of blame, hostility, and anger would almost never be directed at the real sources of the Japanese's frustration, participants believe the screaming is beneficial. Is such behavior really beneficial to people? Does it reduce aggressive tendencies?

THE FRUSTRATION-AGGRESSION HYPOTHESIS ASSERTS THAT AGGRESSION IS ALWAYS THE PRODUCT OF FRUSTRATION

Frustration-Aggression Hypothesis

The theory that frustration causes aggression.

Catharsis

The reduction in the aggressive drive following an aggressive act.

If you had asked a group of social psychologists these questions in 1939, they most likely would have replied that releasing pent-up frustrations in this manner was a very good idea. At that time, John Dollard, Neal Miller, Leonard Doob, O. H. Mowrer, and Robert Sears had just published their now classic monograph, *Frustration and Aggression,* which outlined what came to be the most popular theory of aggression in the social sciences, namely the **frustration-aggression hypothesis.** They defined *frustration* as any external condition that prevents you from obtaining the pleasures you had expected to enjoy. In other words, if you are prevented from doing something that you want to do, you become frustrated. The original theory had three main propositions. The first proposition was that frustration will *always* elicit the drive to attack others. The second proposition was that *every* act of aggression could be traced to some previous frustration (this essentially meant that all aggression is of the "hostile" variety). The third proposition was that engaging in aggression causes **catharsis,** which is the reduction in the aggressive drive following an aggressive act.

A number of studies have supported the general proposition that frustration can cause aggression. For example, in an archival analysis of the relationship between cotton prices and the lynching of African Americans in the South during the late 1800s and early 1900s, Hovland and Sears (1940) found that lower cotton prices were significantly correlated with more lynchings. A drop in the price of cotton indicated regional economic depression, producing frustration among White southerners, which in turn heightened their aggressive behavior. African Americans were the scapegoats of this White displaced aggression (see also Hepworth & West, 1988). Other studies have found a correlation between the loss of jobs in communities and an increase in child abuse and other violent behavior (Catalano et al., 1993; Steinberg et al., 1981).

Although these studies indicate that a link exists between frustration and aggression, shortly after the theory was first proposed, Neal Miller (1941) conceded that frustration does not always produce an aggressive drive. Later research found that frustration is most likely to produce an inclination to aggress when the person believes the hindrance was unfair and deliberate (Averill, 1983). Thus, if someone catches your heel and sends you tumbling to the ground, you are less likely to hold it against him if you believe it was an accident rather than deliberate.

Another basis for criticizing the theory was its contention that frustration was the root cause of *all* aggression. Subsequent research has clearly shown that frustration is simply one cause among many causes of aggression.

Finally, the claim that aggressive tendencies are reduced following the expression of aggression has been subjected to a great deal of scientific scrutiny. Although this notion of catharsis reflects a common belief that people can purge themselves of powerful emotions by "letting off steam" or "getting it off their chests," little empirical evidence supports this proposition. For example, in one representative study, Shahbaz Mallick and Boyd McCandless (1966) had third-grade girls and boys work on a block-construction task in pairs. What the young participants didn't realize, however, was that the child working with them was a confederate who had been instructed to either allow participants to complete the block-construction task or to act very clumsy and impede completion. Immediately following this frustrating or nonfrustrating experience, participants performed an intervening activity for about eight minutes. This activity either involved shooting a toy gun at a target or talking with the experimenter. Half of the children who talked with the experimenter were told during the course of the conversation that their partner had been tired and upset, while the rest merely engaged in neutral talk with the experimenter. At the end of this intervening activity, the young confederate was brought into another room, supposedly to work on another block-construction task. Each of the naive participants then was given an opportunity to hinder the confederate's progress by pushing a "hurt" button that would disrupt the confederate's work. Aggression was measured by the number of times the child pushed the button.

As figure 12.3 shows, frustration generally increased aggression, except when participants were told that fatigue and emotional strain caused the confederate's clumsiness. This finding suggests that when someone frustrates us, we are much more likely to respond aggressively if we believe the person frustrated us *intentionally* rather than unintentionally. More important for our discussion of catharsis, however, is the fact that children's aggressive play did not result in any reduction in the number of attacks on the frustrator. Put simply, there is no evidence in these findings for catharsis. Engaging in make-believe violence does not purge aggressive drives.

Direct acts of aggression also do not cause catharsis. In fact, a number of experiments indicate that people who are given the opportunity to aggress directly against someone who has frustrated them often become *more* aggressive, not less so (Buss, 1966; Geen, 1968). Sociologist Murray Straus (1974) observed that this sort of escalation of aggression is a common pattern found in domestic violence. His research indicates that family conflicts often begin with verbal quarreling, which then escalates to screaming and yelling, and finally to physical aggression (Straus et al., 1980). In contrast, households that engage in little or no verbal aggression rarely ever experience physical violence (less than half of 1 percent). These findings not only run directly counter to the catharsis hypothesis, but they also directly contradict a number of aggression- and conflict-reducing strategies often recommended by mental health professionals. For example, a common belief among many marriage counselors is that "couples who fight [verbally] together, stay together"— as long as they don't engage in vindictive verbal attacks. As Straus points out, however, the research literature indicates that once verbal aggression begins, it's

I have enjoyed all the pleasures that revenge can give.

Marie Madeleine de La Fayette, French countess and novelist, 1634–1692

No more tears now. I will think about revenge.

Mary, Queen of Scots, 1542–1587

FIGURE 12.3

Does Children's Aggressive Play Have a Cathartic Effect?

In contradiction to the catharsis hypothesis, Mallick and McCandless (1966) found that children who had been frustrated by a "clumsy" child confederate showed no reduction in their aggressive responses after engaging in imaginary aggression. What did reduce aggression in the frustrated children was being told that the confederate's clumsiness had been caused by fatigue and strain (talking and explaining condition). What do these findings suggest about recommendations that aggression can be decreased by having people engage in make-believe violence?

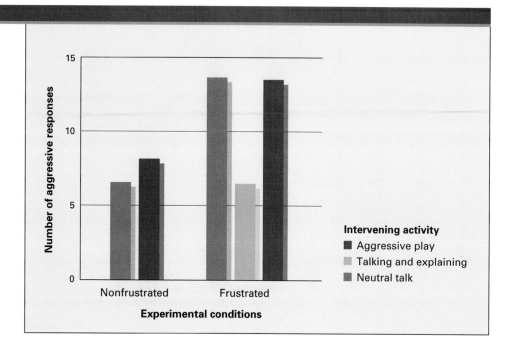

difficult to keep it within manageable bounds. This doesn't mean we should keep our frustrations and anger bottled up inside ourselves. Rather, Straus believes we should try to convey these feelings calmly and clearly, without being hurtful.

THE COGNITIVE-NEOASSOCIATIONIST MODEL EXPLAINS OUR INITIAL REACTION TO PROVOCATION

Realizing that the frustration-aggression hypothesis overstated the association between frustration and aggression, Leonard Berkowitz (1969, 1989) developed a new theory to explain how *hostile aggression* is often triggered by circumstances that arouse negative feelings. He asserted that frustration is just one of many factors that can stimulate negative affect. Besides frustration, other aversive factors such as pain, extreme temperatures, and encountering disliked people can also cause negative affect. It is this negative affect, and not frustration itself, that stimulates the inclination to aggress. The stronger the negative affect, whether it's caused by frustration or by some other aversive experience, the greater the aggressive inclination.

COGNITIVE-ASSOCIATIVE NETWORKS

Cognitive-Neoassociationist Model

A theory of impulsive aggression that aversive events produce negative affect, which stimulates the inclination to aggress.

Berkowitz named his theory the **cognitive-neoassociationist model** because he believes that when we experience negative affect due to some unpleasant condition, this affect is encoded into memory and becomes *cognitively associated* with specific types of negative thoughts, emotions, and reflexive behaviors. Although these cognitive-associative networks are initially weak, the more they are activated, the stronger they become (Ratcliff & McKoon, 1994). When these associations are sufficiently strong, activating any one of them will likely activate the others, a process known as *cognitive priming.* Thus, when we recall a past occasion in which we were extremely angry, this memory may prime hostile thoughts, angry feelings, and even anger/aggression-related reflexive actions, such as clenched fists and gritted teeth. One important implication of this theory is that even when our surroundings don't elicit negative affect, simply thinking about aggression can set us on the path to its activation.

FIGURE 12.4

Cognitive-Neoassociationist Model of Hostile Aggression

Leonard Berkowitz's theory of impulsive aggression states that aversive events produce negative affect. This negative affect, in turn, stimulates the inclination to aggress. How can this aggressive inclination be "short-circuited"?

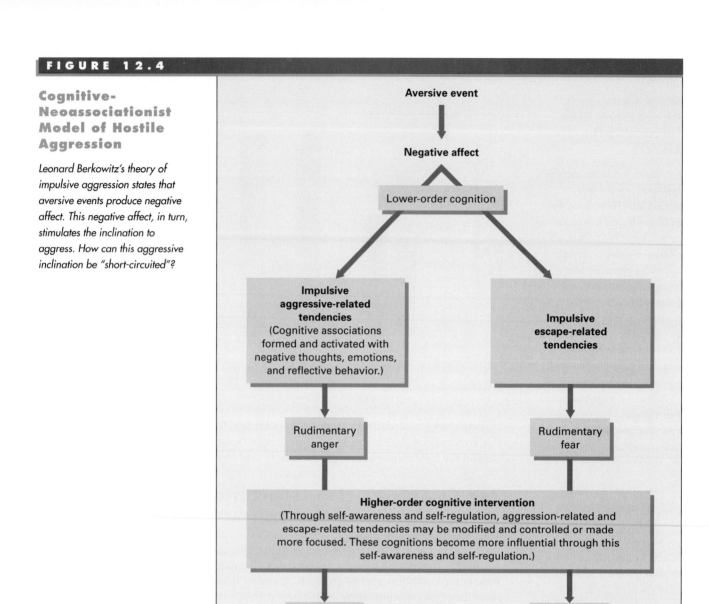

INITIAL "FIGHT" OR "FLIGHT" TENDENCIES

In addition to describing how cognitive-associative networks are formed, the cognitive associationist model (figure 12.4) further proposes that an aversive event initially activates, not one, but two different networks at the same time. One network is related to the impulsive aggression-related tendencies already described (the *fight response*); the other is related to impulsive escape-related tendencies (the *flight response*). Whether we react to negative affect with "fight" or "flight" depends on (1) our biological "background" variables, (2) our prior conditioning and learning, and (3) our attention to aspects of the situation that facilitate or inhibit aggression (Berkowitz, 1993). Because our present objective is to understand how aversive events often lead to aggression, we will concentrate on the fight-response side of this model (the left side of figure 12.4).

"UNTHINKING" AGGRESSIVE RESPONSES

One thing to keep in mind is that the cognitive processes discussed thus far are simply impulsive reactions to negative affect, and thus, they represent only the potential first stage in aggression. The negative thoughts, emotions, and reflexive actions evoked in the cognitive-associative networks at this stage are primitive, or *rudimentary*, and have yet to be shaped and developed by higher-order cognitive processes. If this more-sophisticated thinking does not come into play, we may simply lash out with anger or aggression. According to Berkowitz (1994a), this type of "unthinking" or impulsive aggression is most likely to occur when we are engaged in highly routine activities and thus are not consciously monitoring our thoughts, feelings, or actions.

HIGHER-ORDER COGNITIVE INTERVENTION

Although aggression is likely if we reflexively respond to negative affect, a very different outcome often occurs if higher-order cognitive processes are activated. This represents stage two in the aggressive response. The cognitive-neoassociationist model contends that if these aggression-related tendencies are subjected to higher-level thinking, they are often modified and controlled. What causes the aggression-related tendencies in stage one to come under the control of the more complex cognitive processes of stage two? Research suggests that these cognitive control mechanisms are activated when we become self-aware and attend to what we are thinking, feeling, and doing (Mischel et al., 1996). Thus, when frustrated, we may try to make sense of our negative feelings before acting. If we conclude that no one is to blame for the aversive event, our anger will likely subside. Similarly, we may assign blame to a particular person but still conclude that retaliation is an inappropriate response. Because of these cognitive control mechanisms in higher-order thinking, negative affect does not always lead to aggression. Of course, after thinking things over we may still strike out at those we blame. Higher-order thinking doesn't guarantee a nonaggressive response, but it does make it more likely.

THE "HEAT HYPOTHESIS"

Beyond providing a better explanation for the association between frustration and aggression, the primary importance of the cognitive-neoassociationist model is in its explanation of our *impulsive* and *affect-driven* reactions to aggression. One very common unpleasant situation that has often been associated with such aggressive responses is hot weather. Consistent with the cognitive-neoassociationist model, laboratory experiments have demonstrated that hot temperatures increase hostile thoughts and feelings (Anderson et al., 1995). Also consistent with the model is the finding of an *upward spiral effect*, in which the extreme discomfort caused by high temperatures is related to increased levels of aggression (Cohn & Rotton, 1997). For example, archival studies suggest that the urban riots that erupted in many American cities in the 1960s were most likely to occur on exceptionally hot days and then to diminish in intensity as the weather cooled (Carlsmith & Anderson, 1979). This effect also occurs for such aggressive behaviors as murder, assault, rape, and spousal abuse (Anderson & Anderson, 1984, 1996). The positive relationship between hot weather and hot tempers is even found in sporting events: as temperatures climb during the hot summer months, major league baseball pitchers become more aggressive, hitting more batters at the plate (Reifman et al., 1991).

The fact that hot temperatures appear to increase impulsive, hostile aggression has some interesting practical implications. First, it suggests that the frequency of hostile outbursts could be reduced in temperature-controlled environments. For example, using air conditioning in prisons might reduce the problems of inmate violence. Similar reductions of hostile aggression might also be achieved by controlling the temperatures in schools and work environments. Of course, air conditioning will not create harmony in these settings, but it may make it easier for people to curb their impulse to lash out when annoyed or provoked.

TABLE 12.1

Facts Concerning Firearm Violence in the U.S.: Aggression-Eliciting Cues?

1. Over 35 percent of U.S. households contain at least one firearm, and in half of those housholds the guns are loaded and ready to fire.

2. Guns kept in the home for self-protection are 43 times more likely to kill someone you know than to kill in self-defense.

3. By the teen years, most homicides and suicides occur with firearms.

4. The risk of homicide in the home is three times greater and the risk of suicide in the home is five times greater for those households with guns.

5. Almost half of all deaths among African-American male teenagers involve firearms.

6. Handguns are increasingly being marketed as tools of self-defense for women. However, crime statistics indicate that for every one instance that a woman uses a handgun to kill a stranger in self-defense, 239 women are murdered with handguns. Often, the handguns used in these murders came from the woman's own household.

Source: Diaz (1999), O'Donnell (1995), Vassar & Kizer (1996).

Second, the heat hypothesis has obvious implications for global warming. By the middle of the twenty-first century, we can expect global temperatures to increase by two to eight degrees, which means there will be many more hot days in the summer months (U.S. House of Representatives, 1994). Craig Anderson and his colleagues (1997) estimate that such temperature increases could increase annual serious and deadly assaults by almost forty-three incidents per one hundred thousand people. Unless we discover some way to "air condition" the planet, future generations may become all too familiar with the negative effects of the heat hypothesis.

AGGRESSIVE CUES AS "TRIGGERS" OF AGGRESSION

Man only becomes dangerous when he is equipped with weapons.

Sir Edmund Leach, British social anthropologist, b. 1910

One question many people were asking following the Westside Middle School shootings was whether the presence of guns in the two boys' homes actually "triggered" their aggression. Leonard Berkowitz would certainly consider this a distinct possibility. In addition to anger eliciting aggression, Berkowitz believes that the presence of aggression-associated cues in the environment can act as triggers for hostile outbursts. An aggression-associated cue is anything that is associated with either violence or unpleasantness. The most obvious aggressive cues are weapons, such as guns, knives, and clubs (Anderson et al., 1998). Less obvious aggressive cues are negative attitudes and unpleasant physical characteristics.

Aggression-associated cues can not only trigger aggression but also heighten it. In a meta-analysis of twenty-three studies, Michael Carlson and his coworkers (1990) found strong support for the hypothesis that aggression-associated cues enhance aggressiveness among people who are already angry. This finding may go a long way in explaining the fact that a handgun kept in the home for self-protection is forty-three times more likely to kill a friend or family member than to be used in killing intruders (refer to table 12.1). When domestic disputes erupt, the presence of firearms may enhance the aggressiveness of the angry parties, resulting in tragic consequences. As Berkowitz explains this effect, "Guns not only permit violence, they can stimulate it as well. The finger pulls the trigger, but the trigger may also be pulling the finger" (Berkowitz, 1968, p. 22).

What are some ways researchers believe alcohol increases aggressive outbursts?

ALCOHOL CONSUMPTION INCREASES THE LIKELIHOOD OF AGGRESSION

...  thou invisible spirit wine,
if thou hast no name to be known by,
let us call thee devil! ...
O God, that men should put an enemy
in their mouths to steal away their brains!
That we should, with joy, pleasure, revel
and applause, transform into beasts!

William Shakespeare, Othello (II, iii)

Although weapons may trigger aggressive outbursts in those who are already angry, it has long been assumed that the consumption of alcohol causes people to become more easily angered and hostile. Correlational research provides support for this assumption. Numerous studies conducted in various countries around the world have found a strong correlation between alcohol intoxication and a host of different types of aggression, including domestic abuse, assault, rape, and homicide (Leonard & Quigley, 1999; Zhang et al., 1997). Experimental studies have also found that when people drink beverages containing enough alcohol to make them legally intoxicated, they tend to behave more aggressively or respond more strongly to provocation than do persons who consume nonalcoholic drinks (Giancola & Zeichner, 1997).

Why does the consumption of alcohol increase aggression? Few researchers contend that alcohol provides a *direct* biochemical stimulus to aggression. Instead, the general view is that alcohol weakens people's restraints against aggression (Ito et al., 1996). Some researchers believe that this weakening of restraints, or *disinhibition*, is caused by an interruption of one's ability to process and respond to the meaning of complex and subtle situational cues (Hull & Bond, 1986; Steele & Josephs, 1988). In other words, when provoked, people who are drunk are much less attentive than those who are sober to such inhibiting cues as the provocateur's intent and the possible negative consequences of violence. For example, in a shock-competition experiment, Kenneth Leonard (1989) found that alcohol did not influence participants' reactions to their competitors' *explicit* aggressive or nonaggressive signals, but it did interfere with their understanding of *subtle* aggressive signals. That is, following an aggressive exchange, intoxicated participants were more likely than those who were sober to misinterpret their competitors' subtly announced intentions of nonaggression as being aggression-as-usual.

Disinhibition can also be caused by inattention to personal and social standards of nonviolence. As discussed in chapter 2 (pp. 44–45), we are more attentive to personal and social standards of behavior when self-aware. However, alcohol consumption reduces self-awareness (Hull, 1981; Hull et al., 1986), and this can lead to impulsive, nonnormative actions, such as aggression. Thus, intoxicated people not only have problems attending to external cues that might defuse their inclinations to aggress, but they also have problems attending to internalized behavioral standards that might also inhibit aggression.

A third way in which this disinhibition effect may sometimes occur is through people's *expectations* of how behavior will be affected by alcohol. Perhaps you have heard people excuse a drunken individual's verbal aggression by saying,

CRITICAL *thinking*

The proportion of men who have been physically violent toward their wives is at least four times higher among married men in treatment for alcoholism than among demographically similar nonalcoholic men (O'Farrell & Murphy, 1995). How might alcohol impair judgment and, thus, lead to such aggressive outbursts?

"It's the liquor talking." Such statements imply that it isn't the drunken person misbehaving, but rather, it is the alcohol that is to blame. If people learn that normally inappropriate behaviors may be excusable when performed under the influence of alcohol, they may engage in those behaviors when drinking (Gelles, 1993). From this perspective, alcohol's effect on aggression is due to a *learned disinhibition*. In support of this viewpoint, research indicates that people sometimes become more aggressive not just when they have consumed alcohol, but also when they *think* they have consumed it (Lang et al., 1975). There is also evidence that some men who ordinarily disapprove of hitting a woman believe that being in an intoxicated state gives them a socially acceptable excuse to abuse their spouses (Straus & Gelles, 1990).

Undoubtedly, both the chemically induced disinhibiting effects of alcohol and its learned disinhibiting effects offer us possible explanations of why alcohol consumption causes aggression. Alcohol not only reduces self-awareness and disrupts our ability to adequately process situational cues that would normally inhibit our aggressive behavior, but it also provides us with a ready excuse for responding in such an antisocial manner.

EXCITATION TRANSFER CAN INTENSIFY HOSTILITY-BASED AGGRESSION

You may recall that in chapter 11 (pp. 416–419) we discussed how passionate love can sometimes be kindled by transferring emotional arousal from one source to the love object. Dolph Zillmann (1994) called this psychological process—in which arousal caused by one stimulus is transferred and added to arousal elicited by a second stimulus—*excitation transfer.* According to Zillmann, excitation transfer isn't restricted to romantic attraction; it can also explain aggressive outbursts.

For example, in one study, male participants were either provoked or treated in a neutral manner by an experimental confederate (Zillmann et al., 1972). Then, half of them engaged in strenuous physical exercise while the rest did not. Following a brief delay, participants were then given the opportunity to shock the confederate they had interacted with earlier (of course, no actual shocks were actually delivered). As expected, angered men who had exercised chose stronger shock levels than did those who had not been angered or who had not exercised. In other words, the elevation of excitation due to physical exertion "energized" aggression only in those who had been angered. No longer thinking about the arousing effects of the exercise, it was fairly easy for these previously angered men to transfer this arousal to the now-salient disliked confederate. In the unangered men, however, the increased excitation had no consequence because they had not experienced any feelings, either positive or negative, toward the confederate.

Besides physical exercise, increased aggression through excitation transfer can also occur due to such arousing stimuli as loud noise, vigorous music, violent movies, and even sexual scenes (Anderson, 1997; Zillmann, 1983). Thus, no matter what produces heightened excitation, the arousal can energize whatever aggressive urges we may be having at the moment. Excitation transfer may partly explain why violence sometimes erupts among sports fans of rival teams during games. Aroused by the excitement of the contest, ordinarily civilized fans may become violent when angered by an incident on or off the field of play. Excitation transfer is an even more likely explanation for why warriors throughout the ages have engaged in such energizing practices as dancing, chanting, and drum beating before going into battle. Undoubtedly, they discovered that such activities intensified their anger and aggressive inclinations.

SECTION SUMMARY

One of the best-known theories to explain hostile aggression is the *frustration-aggression hypothesis*, which states that blocking a person's goal-directed behavior produces frustration which, in turn, increases the aggressive drive. A more recent revision of this theory, the *cognitive-neoassociationist model*, asserts that frustration is just one of many factors that can stimulate negative affect, and it is this negative affect that stimulates the inclination to aggress. These aggressive tendencies are often modified by higher-level thinking. Consistent with this model, research demonstrates that hot temperatures increase hostile thoughts, feelings, and actions. Other ways in which hostile aggression can be sparked and enhanced are through alcohol intoxication and excitation transfer.

LEARNING AGGRESSIVE BEHAVIOR

Now that we have examined how negative affect can sometimes trigger aggressive outbursts, let us now explore how our social environment can shape aggressive behavior. The facts are that in families where adults use violence, children grow up being much more likely to use it themselves (Patterson et al., 1989). In communities where aggression is considered to be a sign of manhood, aggressive behaviors are eagerly and consciously transmitted from generation to generation, especially among males (Rosenberg & Mercy, 1991). Yet how does this learning take place?

SOCIAL LEARNING THEORY EMPHASIZES THE ACQUISITION AND MAINTENANCE OF AGGRESSIVE BEHAVIOR

Social Learning Theory

A theory that proposes that social behavior is primarily learned by observing and imitating the actions of others, and secondarily by being directly rewarded and punished for our own actions.

Albert Bandura, one of the leading proponents of **social learning theory,** contends that people learn *when* to aggress, *how* to aggress, and against *whom* to aggress (Bandura, 1979; Bandura & Walters, 1963). This social learning of appropriate behavior, shaped by operant conditioning principles (see chapter 5, p. 155), occurs through both direct and indirect means.

THE REWARDS OF AGGRESSION

Any behavior that is rewarded, or reinforced, is more likely to occur in the future. Therefore, if people act aggressively and receive rewards, they are more likely to act aggressively at some later date. The rewards could be material, such as candy or money, or they could be social, such as praise or increased status and self-esteem (Branscombe & Wann, 1994). When behavior, like aggression, is repeatedly not rewarded, or is even punished, this will generally lead to a reduction in the frequency of the behavior. Psychologists call this weakening and eventual termination of the tendency to engage in a behavior *extinction*. Extinction of aggressive actions is exactly what parents are aiming at when they give children "time-outs" following harmful outbursts.

Although withdrawing rewards can lead to the extinction of aggressive behavior, an inconsistent pattern of reward withdrawal can do more harm than good. This is because like any behavior that people learn and utilize, aggression does not have to be rewarded each time it occurs. In fact, an important principle of learning is that both people and other animals show greater resistance to the extinction of a behavior when it has been rewarded only intermittently rather than continuously. In one study demonstrating this principle, young children were rewarded for hitting a doll (Cowan & Walters, 1963). Half were rewarded every time they acted aggressively, but the others were rewarded only periodically. In both instances, the rewards increased the children's aggressive behavior. However, when the experimenters stopped the rewards, the children who had been only periodically reinforced continued to hit the doll longer than those whose aggressiveness had been continuously reinforced. Because in real life people are not always reinforced for their aggressive activities, this study suggests that such periodic reinforcement is ideally suited to the *prevention* of extinction, not the weakening of aggressive behavior.

OBSERVATIONAL LEARNING

Although learning does occur through direct reinforcement, we most often learn by watching and imitating others without being directly rewarded for doing so. This *observational learning* is also known as social *modeling,* because the learner imitates the model. Children are most likely to pay attention to and model the behavior of those with whom they have a nurturing relationship and who also have social control over them (Bandura & Huston, 1961). Parents are prime candidates as role models, but behavior can also be observed and modeled from television, books, and other mass media sources (Basow, 1986).

In perhaps the most well-known series of observational learning experiments, Bandura and his colleagues (1961) set out to determine whether children would imitate the behavior of an aggressive adult model. In these studies, a child was first brought into a room to work on an art project. In another part of the room, an adult was playing quietly with Tinker Toys. Near these toys was a mallet and a Bobo doll, which is a big, inflatable clownlike toy that is weighted at the bottom so that when it is pushed or punched down it will quickly bounce back to an upright position. In the experimental condition, after playing with the Tinker Toys for a minute, the adult stood up, walked over to the Bobo doll, and began to attack it. She punched the doll, kicked it, hit it with the mallet, and even sat on it. As she pummeled the clown doll, she yelled out, "Sock him in the nose! . . . Kick him! . . . Knock him down!" In the control condition, the adult simply played quietly and nonaggressively with her toys for ten minutes. After witnessing either the aggressive or nonaggressive adult model, the child was led into another room filled with many wonderful toys. However, before the child could play with these treasures, the experimenter aroused frustration by saying that these were her best toys and she must "save them for the other children." The child was then led to a third room, containing both aggressive and nonaggressive toys, including a Bobo doll.

What did children typically do in this third room? If they had witnessed the nonaggressive adult model, they played calmly. However, if they had been exposed to the aggressive adult, they were likely to beat up the Bobo doll, often shouting the same things at the clown during their attack as the previous adult model. Similar results were obtained when the child had no direct exposure to the adult but merely saw a film of the adult attacking the doll. Other experimental variations demonstrated that children were more likely to imitate same-sex models (boys imitating men and girls imitating women) than those of the other sex. Taken as a whole, these studies indicate that observing adult aggression can not only lower children's aggressive inhibitions; it can also teach them how to aggress.

As with direct aggression, the observational learning experiments demonstrated that children are much more likely to imitate others' aggressive acts if social models are rewarded for their behavior. For example, Mary Rosekrans and Willard Hartup (1967) had preschool children watch an adult model aggress against a Bobo doll. These aggressive actions were either praised by another adult ("Good for you! I guess you really fixed him that time") or scolded ("Now look what you've done, you've ruined it"). After watching this interaction, the children were allowed to play with the same toys. Another group of children who had not been exposed to

Bandura's Bobo doll studies clearly indicate that children can learn aggressive behavior through modeling the aggressive actions of an adult.

the aggressive model also played with the toys. Results indicated that the children who had watched the aggressive model being rewarded were significantly more aggressive in their play behavior than the children in the other two groups (refer to figure 12.5). This study and others reveal that children do not unthinkingly imitate a model's actions. Rather, they copy the actions of others who have been rewarded, not punished.

Although these findings might leave you with the impression that aggressive models who are punished have little negative impact on children's later behavior, this is not necessarily the case. The research demonstrates that children are less likely to *imitate* the actions of punished aggressors. Does this mean these children fail to learn the aggressive behavior, or does it mean they simply *inhibit* the expression of these behaviors? In a study similar to Rosekrans and Hartup's experiment, Bandura (1965) offered all the children in the study a reward if they could imitate the aggressive behavior of the model that they had previously observed. Every single one of the participants could mimic the model's aggressive actions, even those who had seen the punished model. Thus, observing someone being punished for aggression doesn't prevent the *learning* of aggression—it simply inhibits its *expression* in certain circumstances. When children believe aggressive expression will lead to rewards, their inhibitions generally evaporate.

THE FORMATION OF AGGRESSIVE SCRIPTS

Borrowing a concept from cognitive psychology, Rowell Huesmann (1986b, 1988) has proposed that aggressive behavior, like other social behavior, is controlled by *cognitive scripts*. A script is a preconception about how a series of events is likely to occur, which is developed and stored in memory and used as a guide for behavior and problem solving. Based on many social learning experiments (for example, Bandura's Bobo doll studies), Huesmann contends that children's **aggressive scripts** are often derived by observing the aggressive actions of others. For instance, if children learn from their parents or friends that the proper way to respond to insults or other social slights is to physically or verbally assault their protagonists, when they are later actually insulted by someone, an aggressive

Aggressive Script

A guide for behavior and problem solving that is developed and stored in memory and is characterized by aggression.

FIGURE 12.5

Children were much more likely to imitate the aggressive behavior of an adult model if the adult had been rewarded rather than punished. Can you imagine how these social learning principles might exert their influence among children playing on a grade-school playground?

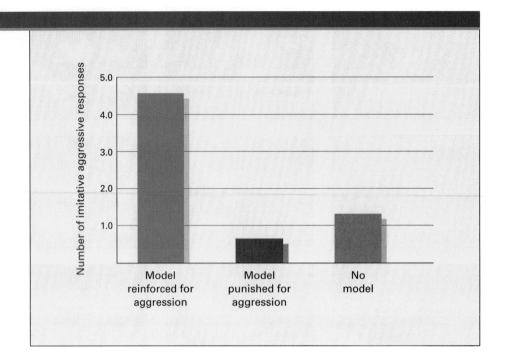

script may be recalled from memory. This script not only provides the child with a prediction about what is likely to happen in this situation, but it also prescribes the proper way to act. Huesmann believes that the more exposure children have to aggressive role models, the greater the number of detailed aggressive scripts they will encode into memory. Those with strongly developed aggressive scripts are likely to choose an aggressive solution to social conflict because it will seem to them to be the "best" and most "natural" way to respond to such circumstances.

OBSERVING MEDIA VIOLENCE MAY FOSTER AGGRESSIVE BEHAVIOR

Facts: Prime-time TV averages five violent acts per hour, while Saturday-morning children's shows transmit an astounding twenty-five acts of aggression per hour (Gerbner & Signorielli, 1990). With children in developed countries watching an average of around thirty hours of TV per week, this means that they observe more than ten thousand violent acts every year through this medium (Tangney & Feshbach, 1988).

Although aggressive scripts are most commonly formed by observing people with whom we regularly interact, Huesmann believes they also can develop by viewing violence on television and in the movies. Evidence supporting this claim comes from experiments indicating that immediately after watching violent shows on television, children tend to act more aggressively in their play behavior and are more likely to choose aggressive solutions to social problems than are children not exposed to TV violence (Leifer & Roberts, 1972; Liebert & Sprafkin, 1988). Further, a meta-analysis of twenty-eight laboratory and field experiments found that exposure to media violence significantly enhanced children's and adolescents' aggression in interactions with strangers, classmates, and friends (Wood et al., 1991).

Longitudinal studies have also found a link between TV violence and aggression. In perhaps the best of these studies—previously discussed in chapter 1—Leonard Eron and Huesmann collected data on people when they were about 8 years old, then again when they were 19, and finally when they were about 30 years of age (Eron & Huesmann, 1984; Huesmann, 1986a). Their results: Early exposure to TV violence was related to later aggression, but only among the males. Boys who

FIGURE 12.6

Boys who show a high preference for violent television shows at age 8 have been found to exhibit greater aggressive behavior later in life, as indicated by the number of criminal convictions by age 30. Does this mean that TV violence caused their later aggression?

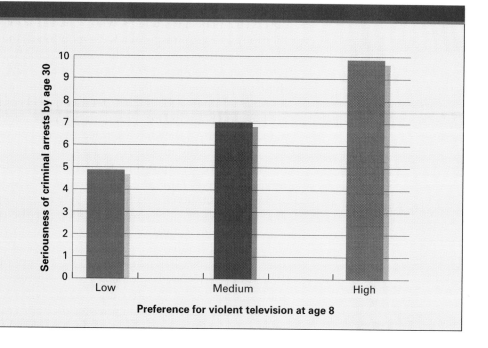

preferred to watch violent television shows when they were 8 years of age were significantly more aggressive ten years later, even after controlling for their initial level of aggressiveness. In addition, as figure 12.6 illustrates, the 8-year-old boys who had the strongest preference for violent shows were much more likely to have been convicted of a serious crime by the time they reached the age of 30. These findings suggest that the frequent viewing of televised violence does seem to contribute to later aggressive behavior beyond what you would expect due to stable aggressive traits.

Because most of the media violence studies have been conducted in the United States and Canada, Huesmann and Eron (1986) sought to determine whether these results would also be found in other countries. With the cooperation of psychologists in Australia, Finland, Israel, and Poland, they repeatedly interviewed and tested children and their parents in these countries, as well as children living in the Chicago area, over a three-year period. Results partially replicated their earlier research. In all the countries except Australia, the early TV habits of children significantly predicted their later aggressive behavior, even after statistically controlling for their initial aggressiveness. What appeared to influence children's later aggressiveness was their *identification* with aggressive TV characters. That is, those children who watched a lot of TV violence when they were young *and* identified with aggressive TV characters were most likely to become highly aggressive later in life. One finding that was not replicated was the gender difference in media effects initially found in the United States. In other words, no evidence indicated that TV violence had a greater impact on boys than on girls. Due to these contradictory findings, currently there is no consensus concerning the role that gender plays in exposure to TV violence.

Based on these lab, field, and longitudinal studies, the least that can be concluded is that repeated exposure to violence on television does not have any known social benefits. A more bold, but still relatively safe, conclusion is that such exposure may well encourage children to develop aggressive scripts that make later antisocial conduct more likely (Huesmann & Miller, 1994).

Beyond the learning of aggressive scripts, another possible effect of watching a great deal of media violence is emotional blunting or *desensitization*, which means simply becoming indifferent to aggressive outbursts. For example, in a series of experiments conducted by Ronald Drabman and Margaret Thomas, children who had just watched a violent movie were less concerned when they later observed other youngsters fighting and were slower to stop the fight than a control group of children who had not seen the movie. This desensitization to violence was also observed in college students who watched a lot of violent TV programs. When their physiological responses were monitored, the heavy consumers exhibited the weakest levels of arousal as they observed both fictional and realistic aggression (Drabman & Thomas, 1975; Thomas et al., 1977). Thomas and Drabman believe these findings indicate that people who watch a lot of media-generated violence become habituated to violence in other aspects of their lives. Because they are less anxious and bothered by aggressive behavior, they may be more inclined to use the aggressive scripts they have learned as a means to solve social confrontations.

Another way in which media violence may increase aggression is through cognitive priming. According to Berkowitz (1984), the aggression-associated cues in television programs and films can cognitively prime a host of aggressive ideas and violent emotions, which in turn may trigger aggressive actions. Brad Bushman and Russell Geen (1990) found support for the cognitive priming hypothesis in experiments investigating the effects that media violence have on viewers' thoughts and emotional responses. In these studies, college students wrote down the thoughts they had while watching excerpts from such violent movies as *48 Hours* and *The French Connection*. A control group watched a nonviolent scene from the TV series *Dallas*. Results indicated that viewers who watched the most aggressive episodes had the most aggressive thoughts, experienced the strongest increase in anger-related feelings, and had the greatest physiological arousal.

Of course, this does not mean that all or even most children who view violent TV programs will begin terrorizing their schools and neighborhoods. It also does not mean that TV violence is a *primary* cause of aggression in children. However, when violence is regularly depicted and glamorized on television, should we really be surprised that impressionable minds are influenced by what they see?

The "Culture of Honor" Encourages Male Violence

Cross-cultural research suggests that societies in which the economy is based on the herding of animals have more male violence than farming societies. For example, among the Native American cultures of North America, the herding Navajos were famous for their warring tendencies, while the farming Zunis tended to be nonviolent (Farb, 1978). Within given societies, researchers have also observed this contrast in aggression. In East African cultures, for instance, herders are easily provoked to violence, while farmers go out of their way to get along with their neighbors (Edgerton, 1971). Social psychologists Richard Nisbett and Dov Cohen (1996) believe that the greater violence exhibited by herding people is due to their **culture of honor,** which is a belief system that prepares men to protect their reputation by resorting to violence. In cultures that place a high value on honor, males learn from childhood that it is important to project a willingness to fight to the death against insults and to vigorously protect their property—specifically, their animals—from theft. Nisbett and Cohen hypothesize that this culture of honor is more necessary in herding than in farming societies because herders' assets (animals) are more vulnerable to theft—and thus, more in need of aggressive protection—than are the assets of farmers (land).

How does this culture of honor theory relate to contemporary violence in the United States? First, in an archival analysis of crime statistics in this country, Nisbett and Cohen found that the southern and western states, which were settled by people whose economy was originally based on herding, have higher levels of current violence related to honor than the northern states, which were originally settled by farmers (Cohen, 1996; Cohen & Nisbett, 1994). Honor-related violence involves arguments, brawls, and lovers' triangles where a person's public prestige and honor have been challenged. Second, the cultures of the South and West are also more likely to approve of violence as indicated by viewership of violent TV

Culture of Honor

A belief system in which males are socialized to protect their reputation by resorting to violence.

programs, subscriptions to violent magazines, hunting license applications, and national guard enrollments (Baron & Straus, 1989; Lee, 1995b). Third, in a series of experimental studies, Cohen and Nisbett also found that, when insulted, young White men from the South not only became more stressed and angry than young White men from the North, but they also were more prepared to respond to insults with aggression (Cohen et al., 1996).

What these multimethod studies suggest is that southern and western White men tend to be more physically aggressive than northern White men in certain situations because they have been socialized to live by a code of honor that calls for quick and violent responses to threats to their property or personal integrity. Although the vast majority of these men no longer depend on herding for their livelihood, they still live by the culture of honor of their ancestors, and this code of conduct continues to be legitimated by cultural institutions (Cohen, 1998; Cohen & Vandello, 1998).

As you recall from the chapter-opening vignette, 13-year-old Mitchell Johnson vowed to kill the girls who spurned his affections. The subsequent murders he and Andrew Golden committed outside the Arkansas middle school are an example of honor-related violence. Is the fact that this incident occurred in a southern state simply a coincidence? Following the shootings, there was a great deal of media discussion concerning the degree to which "Southern male culture" contributed to these murders. This discussion was fueled by similar school shootings committed by white teenaged boys in Mississippi and Kentucky. In all these cases, revenge was the apparent motive and murder the chosen solution. Further, all three of these southern states allow children of all ages to use rifles. Were these boys taught an "honor code" that made their violence more likely? Although one must be extremely cautious in drawing conclusions about individuals—much less an entire region of the country—based on a few violent incidents, Cohen and Nisbett's analysis of many violent incidents does suggest that honor-related violence may be more likely among southern White males than among their northern counterparts.

Interestingly, a similar regional difference in violence is not found among young African-American males: Black southern men are not more violent than Black northern men. Thus, this hypothesized culture of honor in the south is unique to White males. Having stated this, however, both psychologists and sociologists note that the higher incidence of violence among inner-city African-American males than among African-American males in rural or suburban areas may be partly related to a similar honor code (Anderson, 1994; Cohen et al., 1998). Thus, just as a culture of honor may exist among southern White men, in the inner-city "street" culture there may also be a culture of honor that makes violent outbursts more likely. That is, in the inner city, where it is extremely difficult to pull oneself out of poverty by legal means, and where police provide little protection from crime and physical attack, young Black males may strive to gain and maintain respect by responding violently to any perceived insults.

SECTION SUMMARY

Social learning theory proposes that aggression occurs because it has been either rewarded in the past or the aggressor has observed someone else being rewarded for an aggressive act and is now imitating these actions. Observational learning also fosters the development of *aggressive scripts*. Both correlational and experimental research indicate that exposure to television and other media violence does teach and encourage children and adults to engage in antisocial modes of conduct. Aggression is also learned and encouraged in a *culture of honor*, which is a belief system that prepares men to protect their reputation by resorting to violence.

SEXUAL AGGRESSION

Would it surprise you to know that since 1977 forcible rape has increased by 21 percent, making it the largest increase among all major crimes (Von et al., 1991)? Or what about the fact that more than a hundred thousand women in this country report being raped each year—about one every six minutes (Federal Bureau of Investigation, 1998)? Does this fact surprise you? These statistics are grim reminders concerning the dangers women face in our society. Yet rape is certainly not confined to our borders. It is a worldwide phenomenon, most common in societies characterized by male violence and a social ideology of male dominance (Deming & Eppy, 1981; Sanday, 1981). In this section we analyze three possible determinants of sexual aggression, namely *pornography*, *sexual scripts*, and *jealousy*.

PORNOGRAPHY PROMOTES A BELIEF IN THE "RAPE MYTH" AND MAY INCREASE MALE VIOLENCE AGAINST WOMEN

Pornography

The combination of sexual material with abuse or degradation in a manner that appears to endorse, condone, or encourage such behavior.

According to Diana Russell (1993), while *erotica* is sexually suggestive or arousing material that is nonviolent and respectful of all persons portrayed, **pornography** is the combination of sexual material with abuse or degradation in a manner that appears to endorse, condone, or encourage such behavior. Pornography is objectionable not for its sexual content, but rather, its abusive and degrading portrayal of another person, usually a female. Experimental studies demonstrate that exposure to erotic material generally elicits a pleasant emotional response and increased sexual arousal in both men and women, which usually results in them being less aggressive (Davis & Bauserman, 1993; Donnerstein et al., 1987). A different pattern appears to hold for people's response to pornography, as you will soon discover.

THE RAPE MYTH

In a content analysis of 428 pornographic paperback books, sociologist Donald Smith (1976) found that physical abuse was a common theme in sexual encounters between men and women. Twenty percent of all sex episodes depicted in these books involved rape. The storyline focused on the victim's initial fear and terror at being attacked, followed by an awakening of her sexual desire as it proceeded. In more than 97 percent of these rape depictions, the victims experienced an orgasm during the sexual assault. Similar story themes are found in sexually oriented home videos (Cowan & Campbell, 1994).

Rape Myth

The false belief that deep down, women enjoy forcible sex and find it sexually exciting.

This false belief that deep down, women enjoy forcible sex and find it sexually exciting, is known as the **rape myth** (Lonsway & Fitzgerald, 1994). Not surprisingly, convicted rapists tend to believe in this myth (Scully, 1985), but more disturbingly, there is evidence that exposure to pornography also increases ordinary men's rape myth beliefs. In one such study, Neil Malamuth and James Check (1981) arranged for Canadian college students to attend commercial movies at campus theaters. Half of the students saw two nonviolent romantic movies, *A Man and a Woman* and *Hooper*. The other students saw two sexually aggressive films, *Swept Away* and *The Getaway*, in which women characters in both films become sexually aroused by a sexual assault and romantically attracted to their assailant. Several days later, these same students were asked to complete a class questionnaire about their attitudes toward rape and other forms of aggression against women (refer to table 12.2 and table 12.3). None of the students realized that the questionnaire and the movies were connected in any way.

Results indicated that exposure to the two films portraying sexual aggression increased male viewers' acceptance of interpersonal aggression against women

Everyone knows that murder is wrong, but a strange myth has grown up, and been seized on by filmmakers, that rape is really not so bad, that it may even be a form of liberation for the victim, who may be acting out what she secretly desires—and perhaps needs—with no harm done.

Lord Harlech, British Film Board

TABLE 12.2

Rape Myth Acceptance Scale

Directions

There are nineteen items on this scale. For items 1 to 11, use the following seven-point scale to indicate your degree of agreement or disagreement:

Strongly disagree   1   2   3   4   5   6   7   Strongly agree

_____ 1. A woman who goes to the home or apartment of a man on their first date implies that she is willing to have sex.

_____ 2. Any female can get raped.

_____ 3. One reason that women falsely report a rape is that they frequently have a need to call attention to themselves.

_____ 4. Any healthy woman can successfully resist a rapist if she really wants to.

_____ 5. When women go around braless or wearing short skirts and tight tops, they are just asking for trouble.

_____ 6. In the majority of rapes, the victim is promiscuous or has a bad reputation.

_____ 7. If a girl engages in necking or petting and she lets things get out of hand, it is her own fault if her partner forces sex on her.

_____ 8. Women who get raped while hitchhiking get what they deserve.

_____ 9. A woman who is stuck-up and thinks she is too good to talk to guys on the street deserves to be taught a lesson.

_____ 10. Many women have an unconscious wish to be raped, and may then unconsciously set up a situation in which they are likely to be attacked.

_____ 11. If a woman gets drunk at a party and has intercourse with a man she's just met there, she should be considered "fair game" to other males at the party who want to have sex with her too, whether she wants to or not.

Note: For items 12 and 13, use the following scale to answer the questions:

1 = About 0%   2 = About 25%   3 = About 50%   4 = About 75%   5 = About 100%

_____ 12. What percentage of women who report a rape would you say are lying because they are angry and want to get back at the man they accuse?

_____ 13. What percentage of reported rapes would you guess were merely invented by women who discovered they were pregnant and wanted to protect their own reputation?

Note: For items 14 to 19, read the statement below and use the following scale to indicate your response:

1 = Always   2 = Frequently   3 = Sometimes   4 = Rarely   5 = Never

A person comes to you and claims s/he was raped. How likely would you be to believe their statement if the person were

_____ 14. your best friend?

_____ 15. an Indian woman?

_____ 16. a neighborhood woman?

_____ 17. a young boy?

_____ 18. a Black woman?

_____ 19. a White woman?

Note: Once you have indicated your response to each item, reverse the scoring for item 2 (1 = 7, 2 = 6, 3 = 5, 5 = 3, 6 = 2, 7 = 1). Then add up your total score. The higher your total score, the greater your belief in the rape myth. The mean total score in Burt's (1980) original sample of 598 American adults (average age of 42 years) was 86.6, with a standard deviation of 11.9. How does your total score compare with Burt's original sample? Are you more or less likely to believe in the rape myth than these American adults? Have your friends complete this scale as well. How do your beliefs about the rape myth compare with their beliefs?

Total score: _____

Source: Adapted from Martha Burt, "Cultural Myths and Supports for Rape" in Journal of Personality and Social Psychology, 38:217–230. Copyright 1980 by the American Psychological Association. Reprinted by permission.

TABLE 12.3

Acceptance of Interpersonal Violence Scale

Directions

Use the following seven-point scale to indicate your degree of agreement or disagreement to the six items on this scale:

Strongly disagree   1   2   3   4   5   6   7   Strongly agree

_____ 1. People today should not use "an eye for an eye and a tooth for a tooth" as a rule for living.

_____ 2. Being roughed up is sexually stimulating to many women.

_____ 3. Many times a woman will pretend she doesn't want to have intercourse because she doesn't want to seem loose, but she's really hoping the man will force her.

_____ 4. A man is never justified in hitting his wife.

_____ 5. Sometimes the only way a man can get a cold woman turned on is to use force.

_____ 6. A wife should move out of the house if her husband hits her.

Note: *Once you have indicated your response to each item, reverse the scoring for items 1, 4, and 6 (1 = 7, 2 = 6, 3 = 5, 5 = 3, 6 = 2, 7 = 1). Then add up your total score. The higher your total score, the greater your acceptance of interpersonal violence. The mean total score for Burt's (1980) sample of 598 American adults was 29.8 and a standard deviation of 5.9. How does your score compare to this sample? What about your friends? How do your beliefs about interpersonal violence compare with theirs?*

Total score: _____

Source: Adapted from Martha Burt, "Cultural Myths and Supports for Rape" in *Journal of Personality and Social Psychology, 38*:217–230. Copyright 1980 by the American Psychological Association. Reprinted by permission.

and tended to increase their acceptance of rape myths (see figure 12.7). In contrast, females' acceptance of interpersonal aggression against women and of rape myths decreased after watching these sexually aggressive films. These data indicate that exposure to films that seem to condone sexual violence against women can cause men to become more accepting of such violence. Another disturbing fact about these findings is that they were not obtained by exposing men to pornographic material typically found in adult X-rated movies, but rather were obtained from exposure to commercially successful R-rated films that contained pornographic elements in their story lines.

DOES PORNOGRAPHY PROVOKE MALE AGGRESSION AGAINST WOMEN?

Thus far, we have learned that exposure to sexually violent films can cause men to become more accepting of false beliefs about rape and to have greater tolerance for violence against women. However, does this translate into men actually becoming more aggressive toward women? In an attempt to answer this question, social psychologists have conducted two separate lines of research: (1) lab experiments in which exposure to violent pornography is manipulated to see how it affects laboratory aggression, and (2) survey research on whether the prevalence of pornography in a particular geographic region is related to sexual assault.

Regarding lab experiments, a series of studies conducted by Edward Donnerstein suggests that although male-to-male aggression is no greater after exposure to violent pornography, male-to-female aggression is significantly increased (Donnerstein, 1983b). In one representative study, Donnerstein and Leonard Berkowitz (1981) demonstrated that *how* rape is depicted in films is crucial in determining male viewers' later aggression. First, male participants were either angered or not by either a male or a female confederate and then were shown either a neutral, erotic, or one of two violent pornographic films. In both the sexually violent films, a woman was raped by two men, but each film had a different

FIGURE 12.7

The Effects of Mass Media Exposure on Acceptance of Violence Against Women

Malamuth and Check (1981) found that men who had watched sexually violent commercial films were more accepting of interpersonal violence against women and were more accepting of the rape myth than men who were not exposed to such violent entertainment. What effect did such exposure have on women viewers?

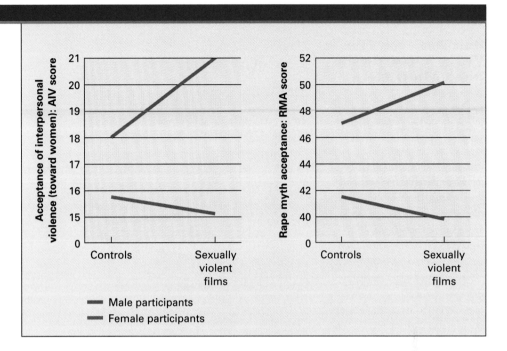

— Male participants
— Female participants

ending. In one ending shown to some participants, the victim is smiling and not resisting as she experiences sexual gratification at being raped (*rape myth ending*). In the other ending, the victim is in obvious pain and emotional turmoil, and conveys disgust and humiliation at being raped (*realistic negative ending*).

As can be seen in figure 12.8, males who had been angered by the female confederate and who had watched a sexually violent film administered more intense shocks to the female confederate, regardless of the film victim's own emotional reaction to being raped. However, when they were not angry, males who had been exposed to the rape film delivered intense shocks to the female confederate only when the film depicted the woman as enjoying the experience. These results are consistent with other investigations of aggression of a nonsexual nature, in which for nonangered individuals, victim pain cues tend to *reduce* aggression by inducing empathy. However, for highly angered individuals, a victim's pain can actually *provoke increased* aggression (Geen, 1978). Why this is the case is a matter of speculation. One possible explanation is that anger raises the threshold for empathy toward the victim's plight (Hartmann, 1969). Another explanation is Berkowitz's notion of aggression-associated cues (p. 448). For males who have been angered, watching a woman become the victim of sexual aggression may not only cause arousal, but it may also associate women with aggression. Later, in a situation in which aggression is a behavioral option, the presence of a woman might be a sufficient aggression-eliciting cue for the already aroused male.

Although Donnerstein's overall findings and those of other experiments (Hui, 1986) suggest that men who watch violent pornography are more likely to engage in aggressive behaviors toward women, survey studies of actual sex crimes do not generally support this conclusion. For example, Danish social psychologist Berl Kutchinsky (1971, 1985) reasoned that if pornography increases male sexual aggression against women, then sexual crimes should rise when pornography laws are relaxed. In an early test of this hypothesis, he gathered crime statistics for the time periods prior to and following the legalization of hard-core pornography in Denmark in the late-1960s. What he found was exactly opposite of what would be expected based on the experimental literature: the increased availability of pornography coincided with a *decrease* in sex

FIGURE 12.8

How Does the Film Victim's Reaction to Rape Affect Male Viewers' Subsequent Level of Aggression Toward Women?

Men who had been angered by a female confederate and who had then watched a sexually violent film administered more intense shocks to the female confederate, regardless of the film victim's own emotional reaction to being raped. How were these men's reactions different from males who were not angered by the female confederate, but who also were exposed to one of the two rape films?

Source: Data from E. Donnerstein and L. Berkowitz, "Victim Reactions in Aggressive Erotic Films As a Factor in Violence Against Women" in *Journal of Personality and Social Psychology,* 41:710–724, American Psychological Association, 1981.

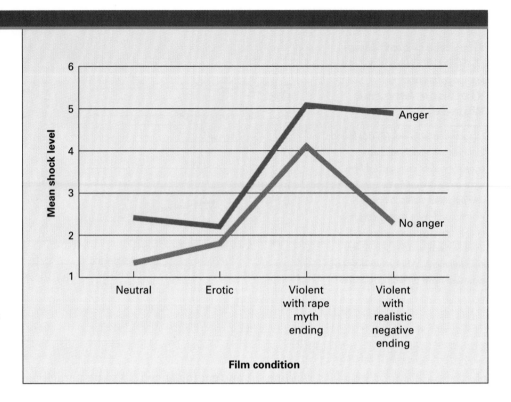

offenses against children, while the number of reported rapes remained unchanged. Kutchinsky (1991) later extended his research by looking at rates of rape and nonsexual assault from 1964 to 1984 in Denmark, Sweden, Germany, and the United States. In all four countries, new laws made pornography much more available during the late 1960s and early 1970s. Did this increased availability of pornography coincide with an increase in sexual assault? Crime statistics indicate that rape rates only increased in the United States, but this change coincided with a similar increase in nonsexual violent crimes. Kutchinsky argued that this simultaneous increase in rapes and assaults is consistent with the belief that rape is primarily an act of violence rather than of sexual arousal. What these results seem to suggest is that the increased availability of pornography does not seem to directly contribute to increased sexual offenses (Bauserman, 1996).

So where are we in our understanding of the effects of pornography on men's sexual beliefs and aggressive actions toward women? There appears to be generally good support for the hypothesis that exposure to violent pornography increases men's acceptance of the rape myth. However, the contradictory findings in the experimental and survey literature regarding a possible pornography-aggression link suggest that additional research is necessary before we can reach any firm conclusions. In the meantime, research by Murray Straus and his colleagues has led them to suggest that rape rates are shaped by two sets of social forces (Baron & Straus, 1987, 1989). The first is *social disorganization,* which is brought about as a society experiences increases in poverty, urbanization, and divorce—the very social ills that the United States has increasingly experienced since the 1960s. The second is *hypermasculinity,* which is the desire to exercise power and dominance over women. The rape myth is a product of this hypermasculinity. The role that hypermasculinity plays in acquaintance rape is one of the primary topics of the next chapter section.

CULTURE-BASED SEXUAL SCRIPTS MAKE ACQUAINTANCE RAPE MORE LIKELY

Acquaintance Rape

Forced sexual intercourse that occurs either on a date or between people who are acquainted or romantically involved. Also known as date rape.

Forced sexual intercourse that occurs either on a date or between people who are acquainted or romantically involved is known as **acquaintance rape** (or *date rape*). On American college campuses, acquaintance rapes account for 84 percent of all rapes or attempted rapes (Koss et al., 1987). In a 1992 survey of more than two thousand of the brightest high-school juniors and seniors in the country, 31 percent said they knew someone who had been the victim of acquaintance rape. Although 95 percent of the males and 97 percent of the females agreed that sexual advances should stop when a woman says no, nearly half stated that they believed that when a woman says no she doesn't always mean it (Cox News Service, November 18, 1992).

One explanation for this belief that no doesn't always mean no comes from the sexual scripts that adolescents learn as they mature. As discussed earlier in the chapter, scripts provide guidance for people in their social behavior, enabling them to anticipate the goals, behaviors, and outcomes likely to occur in a particular setting. Much like the way children can learn aggressive scripts by watching violent television programs, adolescents and adults can also learn societal *sexual scripts* that make sexual aggression more likely in a dating relationship.

THE RESISTANT FEMALE ROLE

The common belief that no doesn't always mean no is based on the traditional sexual script in which the woman's role is to act resistant to sex and the man's role is to persist in his sexual advances despite the woman's protests (Alksnis et al., 1996). Research by Charlene Muehlenhard and Lisa Hollabaugh (1988) found that some women do indeed appear to sometimes go along with this traditional sexual script in their relationships with men. In a questionnaire administered to more than six hundred undergraduate women, the researchers asked them to recall whether they had ever been in the following situation with a man:

> You were with a guy who wanted to engage in sexual intercourse and you wanted to also, but for some reason you indicated that you didn't want to, although *you had every intention to and were willing to engage in sexual intercourse.* In other words, you indicated "no" and you meant "yes."

Thirty-nine percent of the respondents reported that they had indeed been in such a situation at least once with a man—saying no to sexual intercourse when they really meant yes. More recent studies suggest that the true instances of token resistance to sex by women are closer to 10 percent rather than the 39 percent figure reported by Muehlenhard and Hollabaugh, and they are most likely to occur in later-stage dating relationships (Shotland & Hunter, 1995).

Even if this lower estimate is accurate, why might one in ten women put up this sort of token resistance to sex? One possible explanation has to do with our culture's double standard for sexual activity between men and women. Put simply, frequent sexual activity outside of marriage has always been more socially acceptable for men than for women. Although it is socially acceptable for women to appear "sexy," they run the risk of being negatively labeled "promiscuous" or "loose" if they appear to be too sexually eager. Faced with this double standard, some women may see engaging in token resistance as a rational behavior to deflect this sort of negative social attribution.

The danger in employing this sexual script, however, is that it not only discourages honest communication between men and women, but it also perpetuates restrictive gender roles and encourages men to ignore women's refusals.

Having encountered a woman who employed token resistance to sex might reinforce a man's belief in the rape myth—that is, he may believe that all a woman needs is a little encouragement or even force to overcome her inhibitions. This belief, in turn, may precipitate later acquaintance rapes. Thus, the small minority of women who use token resistance not only put themselves in danger, but they also endanger the majority of women who mean no when they say no.

THE PREDATOR MALE ROLE

Even though evidence shows that some women send mixed signals regarding their own sexual desires, this in no way justifies forced sex. It cannot be stressed enough that acquaintance rape occurs when a man refuses to stop his sexual aggression. Surveys on college campuses indicate that roughly 12 to 15 percent of male respondents admit having used force or violence to try to obtain sex against another's will (Sigelman et al., 1984). In an even more alarming series of survey findings, when asked to rate their likelihood of raping a woman if they could be absolutely assured that they would not be arrested or punished, between 35 and 51 percent of college male respondents state that there is at least "some possibility" of them doing so (Malamuth, 1981).

Although sexual gratification is clearly a motive in rape, studies of convicted rapists have found that they view rape as an aggressive conquest that validates their sense of hypermasculinity (Groth, 1979). Based on this work, social scientists have identified the desire to exercise power and dominance over women as key factors in sexual aggression (Malamuth & Thornhill, 1994). Similarly, in studies using college samples, men who either had a history of sexual aggression or were more accepting of violence against and dominance over women were also more likely to be sexually aroused by depictions of rape and to be insensitive to others' feelings (Dean & Malamuth, 1997; Porter & Critelli, 1994).

In an analysis of acquaintance rape, Julie Allison and Lawrence Wrightsman (1993) identify characteristics of both the victimizer and the victim that closely correspond to the sexual scripts already discussed. A victim often does not clearly communicate the limits of acceptable behavior to someone who persists after initial sexual advances have been discouraged. Instead of employing the highly effective tactic of declaring to her attacker, "This is rape and I'm calling the cops," a victim of acquaintance rape tends to be nonassertive or in the habit of giving mixed messages. The victim of acquaintance rape often has problems with forcefully conveying a clear message of no, and the victimizer often misperceives the actions of the victim, interpreting passivity as permission. He tends to be more sexually active than other men and treats women as if they were his property. An acquaintance rapist also generally has a history of antisocial behavior and displays a lot of anger toward women. Because he believes that women often need a little force to enjoy sex, the victimizer does not believe that acquaintance rape is rape, even after he has committed this crime.

SEXUAL JEALOUSY OFTEN LEADS TO INTIMATE VIOLENCE

Sexual aggression does not entail only sexual assault and rape. As discussed in chapter 11, jealousy between lovers or former lovers can often lead to aggression. More American and Canadian women are injured by men with whom they have a romantic relationship than are injured in automobile accidents, armed robberies, and stranger rape combined (Grandin & Lupri, 1997; Zlotnick et al., 1998). The prime reason given for such aggression by the victims and the victimizers is sexual jealousy (Daly & Wilson, 1996). In Canada, 39 percent of all women murdered in 1990 were killed by a current or former male lover (Toronto Globe & Mail, Jan. 18, 1993). In the United States, more than half of all women murdered are the victims

Brute force, the law of violence, rules to a great extent in the poor man's domicile; and woman is little more than his drudge.

Sarah Moore Grimké, U.S. abolitionist and feminist, 1792–1873

Learning and practicing sexual scripts in which men act as "predators" and women play the "resistant" role promotes sexual aggression and acquaintance rape. Couples who are sexually attracted to one another should put aside these traditional, limiting gender roles and engage in open, honest communication. In such exchanges, a refusal of sexual intimacy should be accepted as such.

of partner homicide (Browne & Williams, 1989). Similarly, a woman who kills her male lover generally does so to protect herself from his jealousy-induced physical assaults (see table 12.4).

The fact that heterosexual men have a greater tendency to respond violently when they discover or suspect their romantic partner of infidelity may be because society has historically sanctioned this sort of response in males but not in females. Indeed, wife beating occurs in more societies around the globe than any other type of family violence (Levinson, 1989).

Although virtually all research investigating jealousy and violence has focused on heterosexual relationships, recent studies have also documented the occurrence of violence in relationships of gay men and lesbians (Levy & Lobel, 1991; Waterman et al., 1989). Like their heterosexual counterparts, gay men and lesbians who batter seek to achieve, maintain, and demonstrate power over their partners to meet their own needs and desires. Surprisingly, however, lesbians appear to be at least as likely as gay men to victimize their partners (Waldner-Haugrud et al., 1997). Given the previously reported findings that women tend to be less physically aggressive than men (p. 437), why would lesbian relationships not have lower abuse levels? Several researchers suggest that it might be due to the tendency for lesbian couples to socially isolate themselves more from society than gay couples (Lockhart et al., 1994; Renzetti, 1993). This kind of isolation tends to lead to an overdependency on one's partner and, borrowing from research on heterosexual couples, increases the likelihood of relationship violence (Pagelow, 1984). What these findings suggest is that, regardless of sexual orientation, when couples become overly dependent on one another, jealousy-based abuse becomes more likely.

In a study of relationship violence among college students, James Makepeace (1989) found evidence to suggest two distinct types of courtship violence, one more

TABLE 12.4

Domestic Abuse Among Couples in the United States and Canada

Some Facts

Women are the victims of abuse eleven times more often than men.

One out of ten men carries out at least one violent act toward his wife or live-in girlfriend each year.

Two million women are beaten every year, one every sixteen seconds.

Approximately fourteen hundred women are killed by their husbands each year.

The U.S. Surgeon General has ranked abuse by husbands and partners as the leading cause of injuries to women aged 15 to 44.

Statistically, one woman in four will be physically assaulted by a partner or ex-partner during her lifetime.

Risk Factors*

Previous domestic abuse is the highest risk factor for future violence. Couples with any two of the factors listed below are twice as likely to experience violence as those with none. For those with seven or more of these factors, the abuse rate is 40 times higher.

- Male unemployed
- Male uses illegal drugs at least once each year
- Partners have different religious backgrounds
- Male saw father hit mother
- Couple isolates themselves within the relationship
- Male has blue-collar occupation, if employed
- Male did not graduate from high school
- Male is between 18 and 30 years of age
- Male or female uses severe violence toward children in home
- Total family income is below the poverty line

Getting Help

The national information and referral centers listed below handle domestic-violence calls from male and female victims as well as abusers, whether gay or straight.

In the United States:

National Domestic Violence Hotline, Phone #: 1-800-799-SAFE
National Center for Victims of Crime, Phone #: 1-800-FYI-CALL

In Canada:

CAVEAT (Canadians Against Violence Everywhere Advocating for its Termination), Phone #: 1-800-622-8328
Or contact local mental health organizations.

Source: *Partly based on R. J. Gelles et al., "Riskmarkers of Men Who Batter: A 1994 Analysis" in *Newsweek*, July 4, 1994.

typical of early-stage relationships and the other more characteristic of later stages. In early-stage romantic relationships, especially first dates, *predatory* violence appears to be most common. The primary motivation of the aggressor is to sexually exploit his partner. Physical aggression is used to gain sex, and thus, this violence describes the previously discussed acquaintance rape. These relationships usually break up. Those romantic relationships that advance to the more intimate stages of steady dating, and later, engagement and living together, increasingly focus the couple's attention on how to socialize as a couple and how to define the status of the relationship itself. Here, the violence that occurs tends to be *relational;* that is, primarily motivated by jealousy and rejection. What is disturbing about relational violence is that the victims often fail to leave their relationships, and they tend not to notify authorities or seek professional help.

A likely reason why the victims of relational violence fail to terminate these destructive relationships has to do with their heavy psychological and emotional involvement with their partners. Evidence for this explanation comes from Makepeace's finding that the victims of relational violence who were engaged or living with their victimizer were much less likely to end the relationship than those who were only steadily dating. Makepeace believes that in the advanced stages of courtship, the costs of walking away from a relationship, however abusive, are substantially higher compared with earlier stages. Victimizers, realizing that their abused partners are now less likely to leave, become less restrained in acting on their aggressive tendencies. Unfortunately, an escalation of physical and psychological abuse often results.

SECTION SUMMARY

Sexual aggression has increased in frequency in our society. Experimental studies suggest that exposure to violent *pornography* increases men's acceptance of rape myths. Although experimental studies also suggest that violent pornography may increase men's aggressive tendencies toward women, survey research does not generally support this conclusion. Sexual aggression may also be fostered, especially in acquaintance rapes, through the learning of cultural sexual scripts in which women are expected to act resistant to sex and the man's role is to persist in his sexual advances despite the woman's protests. Sexual jealousy also accounts for a high number of instances of sexual aggression. Relational aggression caused by sexual jealousy is more likely to occur in the more advanced stages of romantic relationships.

REDUCING AGGRESSION

As you see from our review, many different causes underlie human aggression. The resulting psychological and physical injury has naturally led social psychologists to try to determine how aggressive responses can be minimized. In this final section, we examine some strategies that have been found to be relatively effective.

PUNISHMENT CAN BOTH DECREASE AND INCREASE AGGRESSION

Punishment is the most common treatment societies have employed to control aggression. Following such timeworn prescriptions as "an eye for an eye and a tooth for a tooth," legal systems throughout the world often use aggression to punish violent criminals, sometimes resorting to the ultimate punishment—death. Exercising this extreme form of punishment will certainly "relieve" convicted criminals of their aggressive tendencies, but short of killing aggressors, is punishment a truly effective technique?

Three conditions appear to be necessary for punishment to have a chance of being effective (Bower & Hilgard, 1981). First, the punishment must be *prompt,* administered quickly after the aggressive action. Second, it must be *relatively* strong so that its aversive qualities are duly noted by the aggressor. And third, it must be *consistently applied* so that the aggressor knows that punishment will likely follow future aggressive actions. But even if these conditions are met, reduced aggression is not guaranteed. If potential aggressors are extremely angry, threats of punishment *preceding* an attack are unlikely to inhibit aggression (Baron, 1973). Here, the strength of the anger supersedes any concerns about the negative consequences of aggression. Likewise, the cognitive-neoassociationist model would suggest that punishment *following* aggression may actually provoke counteraggression in the aggressor-turned-victim, because such punishment might provoke even more intense anger.

In further considering the effectiveness of using punishment to reduce aggression, one should be even more wary of using aggression in doling out punishment. Based on the research inspired by social learning theory, it is entirely possible that employing violent punishment as a treatment for aggression may simply teach and encourage observers to copy these violent actions. That is, the aggressive punisher may serve as an aggressive model. This is exactly the process underlying the continuing cycle of family violence—observing adult aggression appears to encourage rather than discourage aggression in children (Hanson et al., 1997).

Taking these factors into account, even though punishment may reduce aggressive behavior under certain circumstances, it does not teach the aggressor new prosocial forms of behavior. The aggressive behaviors are not being replaced by more productive kinds of actions, but are most likely only being temporarily suppressed. For this reason, punishment by itself is unlikely to result in long-term changes in behavior.

INDUCING INCOMPATIBLE RESPONSES CAN INHIBIT AGGRESSION

Have you ever been in a situation in which you were about to hit or verbally lash out at someone, when suddenly someone breaks the tension and dissipates your anger by making you laugh? As a youngster, my father often used this strategy whenever I became angry with all the "injustices" that he and my mother imposed upon me. As I stood there red-faced and fuming, he might make a funny gesture or suggest that my face looked as though it was about to explode like a firecracker. Suddenly my anger was transformed into giggles, and my parents were no longer the enemy who needed to be vanquished.

Using a well-established principle in psychology that states that all organisms are incapable of engaging in two incompatible responses, or of experiencing two incompatible emotions at the same time, Robert Baron (1983) has argued that inducing responses or emotions incompatible with anger or overt aggression may effectively deter such actions. In one field experiment that encapsulates the basic findings of many other studies investigating this *incompatible response strategy*, Baron (1976) instructed a research confederate driving a car near campus to frustrate other male motorists. The confederate accomplished this task by stopping at a traffic light and then hesitating for fifteen seconds before driving on when the light turned from red to green. Because motorists honk their horns frequently to express irritation (Turner et al., 1975), two observers sitting in a nearby parked car recorded whether the frustrated drivers honked their horns. This was the dependent measure of aggression.

Three different stimuli were introduced when the light was still red in order to determine whether incompatible responses would reduce the motorists' tendencies to aggress (honk). In one experimental condition, the induced incompatible response was *empathy*—a female confederate wearing a bandage on her leg hobbled across the street on crutches. In the second condition, *humor* was induced by having this same confederate cross the street wearing an outlandish clown mask. Finally, in the third experimental condition,

TABLE 12.5

Aggression-Inhibiting Influence of Incompatible Responses

Inducing empathy, humor, and mild sexual arousal in frustrated drivers resulted in less horn honking and a greater delay in horn honking than in the control and distraction conditions. How do these findings support the incompatible response hypothesis?

Dependent Measure	Experimental Conditions				
	Control	Distraction	Empathy	Humor	Mild Sexual Arousal
Percentage of drivers honking	90	89	57	50	47
Latency of honking (seconds)	7.19	7.99	10.73	11.94	12.16

Source: Data from C. W. Turner, J. F. Layton, and L. S. Simons, "Naturalistic Studies of Aggressive Behavior: Aggressive Stimuli, Victim Visibility, and Horn Honking" in *Journal of Personality and Social Psychology*, 31:1098–1107, American Psychological Association, 1975.

CRITICAL *thinking*

"Road rage" has unfortunately become an all-too-familiar term we read and hear about to describe violent outbursts by people driving cars. If you were the mayor of a large city and wanted to try to reduce the likelihood of such aggressive outbursts on your streets and highways, how could you use social psychological knowledge to help meet this goal?

mild sexual arousal was induced—the female confederate wore a very brief and revealing outfit while crossing the street. In addition to these experimental conditions, Baron also included two control conditions. In one (*distraction*), the confederate crossed the street dressed in conservative clothing, while in the other (*control*), she was absent entirely from the scene. As you can see in table 12.5, consistent with the incompatible response hypothesis, inducing empathy, humor, and mild sexual arousal resulted in less horn honking and a greater delay in horn honking than in either of the control conditions. These findings suggest that inducing incompatible responses in potential aggressors can inhibit overt aggressive behavior.

TEACHING NONAGGRESSIVE RESPONSES TO PROVOCATION CAN EFFECTIVELY CONTROL AGGRESSION

Beyond the rather simple strategies of punishment and induction of incompatible emotions, social psychologists have also relied on the considerable cognitive abilities of human beings in constructing more elaborate techniques for controlling aggression.

SOCIAL MODELING: TEACHING BY EXAMPLE

Just as destructive models can teach people how to act aggressively, social learning theorists contend that nonaggressive models can urge observers to exercise restraint in the face of provocation. In an experiment supporting this claim, research participants who watched a nonaggressive model exhibit restraint in administering shocks to a "victim" in a learning experiment were subsequently less aggressive than those who observed an aggressive model (Baron & Kepner, 1970).

Besides reducing aggression by modeling nonaggressive behavior, aggression can also be controlled by having an authority figure condemn the behavior of aggressive individuals. For example, research demonstrates that if a child watches violence on television in the presence of an adult who condemns the violence, the child is less likely to later imitate this aggression (Hicks, 1968; Horton & Santogrossi, 1978). This bit of knowledge has not been lost on my wife and me in raising our own children. On more than one occasion while watching television with our daughters, the screen has suddenly erupted with violent images so quickly that we don't have time to change the channel. Each time this has happened we condemned the violence. These efforts do have an impact. When Lillian was 4 years old, we were watching a Looney Toons cartoon and Elmer Fudd suddenly pulled out a shotgun and blew the head off of Daffy Duck. Without missing a beat Lillian turned to us and said, "Boy, that wasn't very nice was it? People shouldn't be so mean."

Internalizing Antiaggression Beliefs

As we have discussed throughout the text, when people internalize certain beliefs and attitudes into their self-concept, they are more likely to act in ways consistent with those beliefs and attitudes. Recognizing the important role that the self plays in behavior change, social scientists have devised a cognitive strategy to facilitate the internalization of antiviolent beliefs by simply having people think of reasons why aggression is a bad idea. For example, in one study, when children were prompted to generate reasons why it was bad to imitate TV violence, this intervention was effective in later reducing the impact that TV violence had on their attitudes and behavior regarding aggression (Huesmann et al., 1983). Generating these antiviolent beliefs apparently caused the children to incorporate them into their self-concepts and overall worldview. The subsequent reduction in aggression through this "belief ownership" was still measurable two years after the initial intervention.

Apologies as Aggression Controllers

The fact that people can reason and develop explanations for their actions and those of others also explains why apologies can effectively reduce anger and aggression. An experiment by Ken-ichi Ohbuchi and his coworkers (1989) demonstrated this aggression-reducing effect of apologies. In the experiment, Japanese college students were embarrassed by their poor performance while working on a complex experimental task. The reason they did so poorly was that the experimenter's assistant committed a series of errors in presenting the experimental materials to them. When the experimenter learned of each participant's poor performance, he roundly criticized the assistant, who then either apologized for causing the participants to fail, or said nothing. After this, participants were asked to rate the assistant on several dimensions and were told that these ratings would be used as a basis for the assistant's grade. A public apology in the experimenter's presence significantly reduced the participants' hostility in these ratings. This study is important because it suggests that merely offering an apology can defuse another's hostile aggression.

Social Skills Training

The art of apologizing is just one skill in a larger repertoire of interpersonal skills learned through the process of socialization. As children mature, their impulsive aggressive reactions to anger and conflict are often replaced by more socially acceptable responses, such as negotiation, compromise, and cooperative problem solving. However, children with low intelligence are less likely to learn these prosocial skills and, therefore, are more likely to retain a combative interpersonal style that invites aggression and further interferes with their intellectual development (Huesmann et al., 1987). For these antisocial children, and for adults who have trouble managing their own aggression, deliberately and consciously teaching them alternative nonaggressive strategies can be extremely beneficial.

Social skills training can take many forms, including the role-playing of nonaggressive behaviors, modeling the prosocial actions of others, or generating nonaggressive alternative solutions to conflict. In one twelve-session intervention program employing some of these cognitive strategies, Nancy Guerra and Ronald Slaby (1990) found that male and female juvenile delinquents not only showed increased skills in solving social problems, but they also exhibited a significant decrease in their aggressive beliefs and actions. This study, and others like it (Feldman et al., 1983), indicate that aggressive behavior can be changed by teaching people to replace maladaptive thoughts and behaviors with ones that foster social harmony and conflict resolution.

ONE FINAL WORD ON CONTROLLING AGGRESSION

> Nonviolence is the answer to the crucial political and moral questions of our time; the need for man to overcome oppression and violence without resorting to oppression and violence. Man must evolve for all human conflict a method which rejects revenge, aggression and retaliation. The foundation of such a method is love.
> (Rev. Martin Luther King, Jr., 1964)

If we could point to one single strategy to effectively control aggression in a wide range of settings, it would simply be the adoption of the nonviolent philosophy practiced by civil rights leader Martin Luther King. Unfortunately, because it is highly unlikely that this philosophical transformation will take place anytime soon, we are left with a number of imperfect intervention strategies, each of which has a reasonable chance of reducing aggression when certain conditions are met.

Although our present ability to control aggression may seem meager at best, keep in mind that our analysis of aggression in this chapter reveals that this is a highly complex phenomenon. It not only springs from several psychological sources (for example, anger, fear of punishment, desire for rewards), but it also appears to be shaped by a variety of environmental factors. For me, in some respects, the various forms of aggression in society today seem like a modern-day Hydra. In Greek mythology, the Hydra was a terribly dangerous nine-headed serpent that was exceedingly difficult to kill. Whenever one head was chopped off, two grew back. Fortunately for the ancient Greeks, the Hydra was finally destroyed by their superhero, Hercules. There are no superheroes in contemporary social psychology, nor in the larger society. Yet if we ever hope to slay our Hydra, it will entail a Herculean task by all elements of society.

SECTION SUMMARY

Social psychologists have attempted to determine how aggressive responses can be minimized. Various techniques appear to have some success under certain conditions, including punishment, inducing incompatible responses, and teaching people nonaggressive responses to provocation.

he most common stereotype of a rapist is a sociopathic man hiding behind the bushes, waiting to attack an unsuspecting woman. Operating from this stereotype, many rape prevention programs have stressed the installation of outdoor lights and alarm systems, the trimming of bushes, and the teaching of self-defense to women (Warshaw, 1988). Yet as previously noted (p. 463), the vast majority of women who are raped know their attacker. Given that sexual assault is all too commonly found within dating relationships, an increasing number of rape prevention programs are being developed to not only train women how to protect themselves, but also change the attitudes, beliefs, and behaviors of potential rapists, namely, ordinary men. Listed here are some of the common elements in these acquaintance rape prevention programs (Abbey et al., 1996; Lonsway, 1996).

Targeting the rape myth: Targeting the misinformation of rape mythology is one of the most widely used—and effective—techniques in rape education programs (Fonow et al., 1992). Generally, participants first read or view fictional depictions of women becoming sexually aroused while being raped, followed by the presentation of the scientific and medical facts of rape trauma.

Sexual communication training: As previously discussed, men are more likely than women to misinterpret friendliness from an other-sex person as sexual interest. Educating people about how such sexual misunderstandings come about has been shown to have a positive influence on beliefs and attitudes about rape and violence (Dallager & Rosen, 1993).

Discussing negative sexual scripts: Many programs accompany sexual communication training with discussions of the contrasting sexual scripts learned by most women and men that contribute to acquaintance rape.

Inducing empathy: *Empathy* is a feeling of compassion and tenderness for people who experience pain, loss, or other unfortunate circumstances in their lives. Because people who

Effective acquaintance rape prevention programs are designed to accomplish numerous goals, including debunking the rape myth, increasing sexual communication, learning about negative sexual scripts, and inducing empathy for sexual assault victims. When presenting these programs to mixed-sex groups, should trainers use confrontational tactics with male participants?

experience empathy are less likely to believe that victims caused their own plight, it's reasonable to hypothesize that inducing empathy will make participants in rape prevention programs more sympathetic to victims of sexual assault. Unfortunately, empirical research more clearly supports this hypothesis for women than for men (Ellis et al., 1992; Gilbert at al., 1991). One possible explanation for this gender difference is that women tend to spontaneously empathize with victims more than men, and thus, they may simply be better able to "feel others' pain." A second related explanation is that women may find it easier to emotionally identify with rape victims because almost all imagined scenarios of rape in these training programs use a female victim.

Nonconfrontational approaches: When discussing rape myths, male misperceptions, and male "predators," trainers must be careful not to cast male participants into the "enemy" camp. Inducing defensiveness and alienation in male participants is one of the surest ways to guarantee that desirable changes will not take place (Dallager & Rosen, 1993). Instead, effective trainers adopt a nonconfrontational approach.

When discussing cultural ideologies that promote rape, they emphasize the point that men are also victims of these ideologies because they are taught to behave according to a very restrictive hypermasculine role.

These are some of the basic elements in many acquaintance rape prevention programs. Yet, an effective program has more than just these elements—*time duration* of the training is also important. Rape education researchers contend that training programs that meet only once or twice are vastly insufficient for the task of challenging rape-supportive ideology (Schaeffer & Nelson, 1993). Instead, they strongly recommend that these programs consist of classes that meet weekly over several months. Such a format is ideally suited for a college course. Kimberly Lonsway and her colleagues (1998) recently evaluated one such semester-long college program (*Campus Acquaintance Rape Education,* or *CARE*) that incorporates the course elements just listed. Their findings—which are described in the Featured Study section—indicate that it is effective in changing beliefs and behaviors regarding sexual communication and sexual assault.

FEATURED STUDY
OUTCOMES OF A RAPE PREVENTION EDUCATION PROGRAM

Lonsway, K. A., Klaw, E. L., Berg, D. R., Waldo, C. R., Kothari, C., Mazurek, C. J., & Hegeman, K. E. (1998). Beyond "no means no": Outcomes of an intensive program to train peer facilitators for campus acquaintance rape education. *Journal of Interpersonal Violence, 13,* 73–92.

The purpose of the present study was to conduct an evaluation of the Campus Acquaintance Rape Education (CARE) program, which is a semester-long university course that trains undergraduates to facilitate peer rape education workshops. The researchers investigated the short-term and long-term effects that this college course had on students' attitudes and behavioral intentions regarding rape.

METHOD

A semester-long human sexuality course served as the comparison group in this program evaluation study. Participants in the CARE course consisted of seventy-four undergraduates (fifty-three women and twenty-one men), while participants in the human sexuality course consisted of ninety-six students (fifty-eight women and thirty-eight men). Pre- and posttest data on rape-supportive attitudes and beliefs were collected at the beginning and end of the semester in each class. In addition, CARE students responded to videotaped sexual conflict scenarios both at the beginning and end of the semester. These scenarios portrayed a heterosexual couple involved in conflict with varying levels of sexual coercion by the male. At various points, the tape was stopped, and viewers were asked to write down what they would say or do if they were the person of their sex involved in this conflict.

Two years after taking their respective courses, students were mailed a questionnaire in which they were asked to participate in a survey conducted by the university administration to assess current and former students' attitudes toward controversial social issues. Items measuring rape-supportive attitudes and beliefs were embedded among items measuring race relations and sexual orientation. Later phone interviews with several participants suggested that none guessed that this follow-up survey was related to their previous research participation.

RESULTS AND DISCUSSION

Results indicated that although students in the CARE and human sexuality courses did not significantly differ in their rape-supportive attitudes and beliefs at the beginning of the semester, they did so at the end of the semester. On all measures, the CARE students reported less acceptance of cultural rape myths and less endorsement of adversarial sexual beliefs (predator male and resistant female roles). Analysis of CARE students' responses to the sexual conflict videos further suggested that both women and men became more willing and able to directly express themselves and assert their needs in ways that facilitated increased sexual communication in a dating relationship. Finally, the follow-up survey two years later revealed that CARE participants remained less accepting of cultural rape myths than students who were enrolled in the human sexuality course, but there were no group differences in endorsement of adversarial sexual beliefs. Although more research is needed in how to best design and implement rape prevention training programs, the present study suggests that the changes that take place in such venues can have a lasting, positive impact.

WEB SITES accessed through http://www.mhhe.com/franzoi2

Web sites for this chapter focus on research and theory on family violence, acquaintance rape, violence on television, and recommendations on how to control anger before it leads to aggression.

Minnesota Center Against Violence and Abuse

This is the web site for the Minnesota Center Against Violence and Abuse listing links to education and training resources, papers and reports on aggression, and resource materials for teaching about family violence.

American Psychological Association

The American Psychological Association web site has a number of relevant web pages, including one that examines research on the psychological effects of television violence and another on how to control anger before it leads to aggression.

"Friends" Raping Friends: Could It Happen to You?

This is a web site devoted to the facts about acquaintance rape, including its causes and consequences, and how to avoid situations that might lead to acquaintance rape.

Center for the Study and Prevention of Violence

This is the web site for the Center for the Study and Prevention of Violence which has fact sheets on violence, research summaries, and a list of papers you can request.

National Consortium on Violence Research

This is the web site for the National Consortium on Violence Research which is a research and training center specializing in violence research. The mission of the consortium is to advance basic scientific knowledge about the causes or factors contributing to interpersonal violence.

Contemporary Conflicts

This web site provides information and news updates on armed international and civil conflicts in Europe, Africa, Asia, and South America.

CHAPTER 13

PROSOCIAL BEHAVIOR: HELPING OTHERS

t was midafternoon and the 12-year-old boy, clad only in pajamas, clung to the sloping roof of the ramshackle house, watching the horrifying scene below. There were soldiers everywhere rounding up the boy's neighbors. He witnessed a child being repeatedly stabbed with a bayonet, and another thrown from a second-story window. The boy had been on the roof since dawn, awakened from a deep sleep by his parents, who told him to run for his life just before they were taken by the soldiers.

The inhabitants of this village were the "undesirables" of the country, and the soldiers' actions were meant to cleanse the country of this human blight. Many undesirables were killed in their homes, but most were herded into trucks and taken to a nearby forest, where they were thrown into huge pits and machine-gunned. Near nightfall, the soldiers left, and it was only then that the boy climbed down from his hiding place and began searching the empty houses for warmer clothes and temporary shelter. That night he slept in a small closet.

The following morning the boy awoke early and walked to a nearby village where his father's friend, Balwina Piecuch, lived. Although the boy did not know this woman well, he went to her because she was not an "undesirable." She was his only hope. He also knew that this woman could get a reward for turning him in to the authorities. When he knocked on her door and identified himself, she said, "For heaven's sake, what are you doing here? It's very dangerous. Hurry, come on in." Balwina Piecuch and her family kept the boy hidden in their attic for several days, feeding him, listening to his tragic story, and drying his tears. During that time, if the soldiers had discovered that an undesirable was being sheltered by this household, the Piecuch family would have perished along with the boy. To reduce this possibility, the family taught the boy how to pass as a "desirable" and helped him secure a job on a nearby farm. In helping the boy survive, Balwina Piecuch and her family had nothing tangible to gain and every-thing to lose. Yet they helped. Why?

Today, sixty years later, the boy of this story, now known by the name Samuel Oliner, is a professor of sociology at Humboldt State University in California. The origin of his undesirability was the fact that he was a Jew in Nazi-occupied Poland. With a few detail changes, this story could also be about a child in any corner of the globe and at any given time period. In chapters 7 and 12 we explored many of the factors that cause the Samuel Oliners of this world to become victims of perse-cution and violence. This chapter is only incidentally about the victims of such antisocial behavior. In the following pages, the principal analysis will focus on the many different Balwina Piecuchs of the world who provide aid and comfort to those in need. We will address and try to answer five basic questions concerning prosocial behavior. First, why do we help? Second, when do we help? Third, who is most likely to help? Fourth, whom do we help? And fifth, are there hidden costs for those who receive help?

WHAT IS PROSOCIAL BEHAVIOR?

Before tackling these five helping questions, let's begin by defining our topic and briefly discussing the notion that there may be two basic forms of helpful actions.

PROSOCIAL ACTION IS VOLUNTARY AND BENEFITS OTHERS

Prosocial Behavior

Voluntary behavior that is carried out to benefit another person.

Prosocial behavior is voluntary behavior that is carried out to benefit another person (Batson, 1998). This definition excludes beneficial actions that are not performed voluntarily or are not performed with the intention of helping another. Thus, if the young boy in our story had come to Balwina's house and forced her at gunpoint to help him, her actions would not be considered prosocial because she really would have had no *choice* in rendering assistance. Likewise, if a soldier had tossed a half-eaten sandwich along the roadside and the passing boy retrieved it for his evening meal, the soldier's actions also would not be prosocial because his *intention* in throwing the food away was not to benefit another. On the other hand, Balwina's actions and those of her family—freely providing shelter, safety, food, and emotional comfort—perfectly fit our definition because they were freely chosen and the intention was to benefit another.

All of us have had personal experiences of helping and being helped by others. Sometimes our prosocial actions involve little cost, while at other times our helping can entail considerable time, money, and even personal danger. Have you ever wondered how your own degree of helpfulness compares with that of others' prosocial tendencies? If you have, spend a few minutes responding to the Helping-Orientation Questionnaire items (Romer et al., 1986) in table 13.1.

Beyond the basic definition, philosophers and a number of social scientists have traditionally described two forms of helpful behavior that are based on very different motives. For example, nineteenth-century philosopher Auguste Comte (1875) contended that **egoistic helping**—in which the person wants something in return—is based on *egoism*, because the ultimate goal of the helper is to increase his or her own welfare. In contrast, Comte stated that **altruistic helping,** in which the person expects nothing in return, is based on *altruism*, because the ultimate goal is to increase another's welfare.

Egoistic Helping

A form of helping in which the ultimate goal of the helper is to increase his or her own welfare.

Altruistic Helping

A form of helping in which the ultimate goal of the helper is to increase another's welfare without expecting anything in return.

As we discuss later in the chapter, social scientists disagree on whether any useful distinctions can be made between egoistic and altruistic helping, and some argue that all helping is ultimately egoistic in nature. Based on your responses to the questionnaire, what best describes your reactions to others in need of help? Are you generally helpful? If you are, do you think any of your helpfulness could be described as ultimately motivated by altruism rather than mere egoism?

GENDER INFLUENCES HELPING

Beyond egoism and altruism, do you think your willingness to help is influenced by whether you are a woman or a man? Alice Eagly and Maureen Crowley's (1986) meta-analytic review of 172 helping behavior studies indicates that men and women differ in their willingness to engage in certain prosocial actions: men generally help more than women, and they are more likely than women to help strangers. These gender differences are greatest when there is an audience, when there is potential danger involved in helping, and when the person in need is female. Although these differences appear real, they apply most to nonroutine prosocial acts such as offering help to strangers in distress. When other forms of prosocial behavior—such as helping a friend or caring for children—are studied, women generally prove to be more helpful than men. For example, women are more likely than men to provide social and emotional support to others (Shumaker & Hill, 1991), and they also are more willing to serve as caretakers for children and the elderly (Trudeau & Devlin, 1996). In addition, among children, there are few gender differences in helping, and the few differences that have been found indicate that girls tend to be a bit more helpful than boys (Eisenberg et al., 1996).

TABLE 13.1

Helping-Orientation Questionnaire

Directions

While reading these descriptions of hypothetical situations, imagine yourself in each of them and pick the action that best describes what you would do:

1. You have come across a lost wallet with a large sum of money in it, as well as identification of the owner. You
   A. return the wallet without letting the owner know who you are.
   B. return the wallet in hopes of receiving a reward.
   C. keep the wallet and the money.
   D. leave the wallet where you found it.
2. A person in one of your classes is having trouble at home and with schoolwork. You
   A. help the person as much as you can.
   B. tell the person not to bother you.
   C. leave the person alone to work out his or her own problems.
   D. agree to tutor the person for a reasonable fee.
3. When it comes to cooperation when you would rather not, you usually
   A. cooperate if it is helpful to others.
   B. cooperate if it is helpful to yourself.
   C. refuse to get involved.
   D. avoid situations where you might be asked to cooperate.
4. A neighbor calls you and asks for a ride to a store that is six blocks away. You
   A. refuse, thinking you will never need a favor from him (or her).
   B. explain that you are too busy at the moment.
   C. immediately give the ride and wait while the neighbor shops.
   D. consent if the neighbor is a good friend.
5. You are approached by someone asking for a contribution to a well-known charity. You
   A. give if there is something received in return.
   B. refuse to contribute.
   C. give whatever amount you can.
   D. pretend you are in a hurry.
6. You are in a waiting room with another person. If you heard a scream in the adjoining room and the other person failed to respond, you would
   A. help the screaming person whether the other person helps or not.
   B. help the screaming person only if the other person does too.
   C. wait to see if the screaming continues.
   D. leave the room.
7. When asked to volunteer for a task in which you will receive no pay, you
   A. avoid or put off answering.
   B. explain that you don't agree with the objectives to be accomplished and therefore couldn't volunteer.
   C. compromise and help if you will receive some recognition.
   D. volunteer without question.

Scoring

The information below shows which answers on the Helping-Orientation Questionnaire indicate altruistic helping, egoistic helping, and unhelpful behavior. It also shows the percentage of people who gave each answer in a recent survey. Do your responses indicate that your helping orientation is predominantly altruistic, egoistic, or unhelpful?

Item	Altruistic Helping	Egoistic Helping	Unhelpful Behavior
1.	A (38%)	B (47%)	C,D (15%)
2.	A (86%)	D (4%)	B,C (10%)
3.	A (61%)	B (20%)	C,D (19%)
4.	C (33%)	D (56%)	A,B (11%)
5.	C (70%)	A (4%)	B,D (26%)
6.	A (50%)	B (10%)	C,D (40%)
7.	D (35%)	C (27%)	A,B (39%)

Men are more likely to help when assistance involves an element of danger. Does this mean men are generally more helpful, or that they are generally more willing to take risks?

RITICAL *thinking*

What sort of cultural role models might influence the "helping habits" of boys and girls? Can you identify any of these role models depicted in the news or in Hollywood movies? If gender roles continue to become more flexible, how might this influence male and female helping tendencies?

Based on these findings, we can make two tentative conclusions. First, women and men appear to be helpful in different ways. Second, these differences become stronger from childhood to adulthood and are most apparent when gender roles are salient. Consistent with the culturally valued male role of heroic rescuer, men are more likely than women to place themselves in danger when rendering assistance. In contrast, women are more likely than men to provide longer-term help involving empathy and caretaking, qualities consistent with the feminine gender role.

SECTION SUMMARY

Prosocial behavior is voluntary behavior that is carried out to benefit another person. When we engage in *egoistic helping* our ultimate goal is to increase our own welfare, while in *altruistic helping* we expect nothing in return and our ultimate goal is simply to increase another's welfare. Social scientists disagree on whether any useful distinctions can be made between these two forms of helping. Regarding gender differences, women and men appear to be helpful in different ways.

WHY DO WE HELP?

As already noted, some social scientists believe that people sometimes help solely to benefit another, while at other times they help in order to achieve some personal gain. In addition, it has also been suggested that because of inborn characteristics, people may be *predisposed* to prosocial behavior.

HELPING IS CONSISTENT WITH EVOLUTIONARY THEORY

As discussed in previous chapters, one principle of evolutionary theory is that any social behaviors that enhance reproductive success (the conception, birth, and survival of offspring) will continue to be passed on from one generation to the next. However, in order to reproduce, an animal must first survive. Often, an animal's survival depends on how well it can compete with other members of its own species for limited resources. This evolutionary fact would seem to dictate that animals should be selfish, looking out first and foremost for themselves. Yet what of the seemingly selfless act of helping?

Ethologists and evolutionary psychologists have documented countless instances in which animals have put their own lives at risk to protect other members of their own species from danger (Fouts, 1997; Wilson, 1996). For example, a chimpanzee foraging for food with its troop will often emit a warning call to alert the others about a nearby predator. By calling out, this chimp is the one most likely to be caught by the predator. As this example illustrates, helping others can be downright deadly. When you're dead, your reproductive days are over. Thus, from an evolutionary perspective, how could helping be advantageous to reproduction?

KIN SELECTION

As previously outlined in the chapter 12 discussion of aggression, evolutionary theorists contend that it is not individual survival that is important, but rather, it is *gene* survival that promotes reproductive fitness (Archer, 1991). Because your blood relatives share many of your same genes, by promoting their survival you can also preserve your genes even if you don't survive the helpful act. This principle of **kin selection** states that you will exhibit preferences for helping blood relatives because this will increase the odds that your genes will be transmitted to subsequent generations (Burnstein et al., 1994).

Although the principle of kin selection explains why we are more likely to help those who are related to us by blood, it doesn't explain the countless incidents of people helping total strangers. Stranger helping is also found in other animals as well. Ethologist Jane Goodall (1986) describes observing one such incident involving Washoe, an adult female chimp at a fenced-in chimpanzee colony:

> Washoe spent some time at Norman, Oklahoma, on an island ringed with an electric fence. One day a three-year-old female, Cindy, somehow jumped this fence. She fell into the moat, splashed wildly, and sank. As she reappeared, Washoe leaped over the fence, landed on the narrow strip of ground at the water's edge, and, clinging tightly to a clump of grass, stepped into the water and managed to seize one of Cindy's arms as the infant surfaced again. [Yet] Washoe was not related to Cindy and had not known her for very long. At Lion Country Safaris in Florida a number of [similar] rescues or attempted rescues have been observed. p. 378

Stranger helping is found not only among primates but among other species as well. For example, female lions, dolphins, and bluebirds have been observed taking care of nonrelated newborns deserted by their mothers (Conner & Norriss,

Kin Selection

A theory that people will exhibit preferences for helping blood relatives because this will increase the odds that their genes will be transmitted to subsequent generations.

1982). Given this fact, how can evolutionary theorists explain prosocial behavior that extends beyond one's family?

RECIPROCAL HELPING

Robert Trivers (1971) has described a way in which helping strangers could have arisen through natural selection. This principle, which he called *reciprocal altruism*, involves mutual helping, usually separated in time. However, because "altruism" refers to motives and Trivers was merely referring to behavior, we will use the more accurate term **reciprocal helping** when referring to this mutual helping.

According to this principle, people are likely to help strangers if it is understood that the recipient is expected to return the favor at some time in the future. In such a world of reciprocal helping, the "cost" of aiding another is more than offset by the later returned help (Vos & Zeggelink, 1997). Trivers contended that for reciprocal helping to evolve, the benefit to the recipient must be high and the cost to the helper must be relatively low. In addition, the likelihood of their positions being reversed in the future must also be high, and there must be a way to identify "cheaters"—those who do not reciprocate help.

A good example of reciprocal helping is *social grooming*. In many species, one individual cleans the other's fur or feathers, and later, the "groomee" returns the favor (DeNault & MacFarlane, 1995). Grooming is a low-cost activity (only time lost) that returns high benefits to the recipient (removing disease-carrying parasites). Trivers (1983) believes that reciprocal helping is most likely to evolve in a species when certain conditions exist. Three of these conditions are (1) *social group living,* so that individuals have ample opportunity to give and receive help, (2) *mutual dependence,* in which species survival depends on cooperation, and (3) the *lack of rigid dominance hierarchies,* so that reciprocal helping will enhance each animal's power.

Considerable research supports both kin selection and reciprocal helping among humans and other animals. For example, when threatened by predators, squirrels are much more likely to warn genetically related squirrels and squirrels with whom they live than unrelated squirrels or those from other areas (Sherman, 1985). Similarly, across a wide variety of human cultures, relatives receive more help than nonrelatives, especially if the help involves considerable costs, such as being a kidney donor (Borgida et al., 1992). Reciprocal helping is also common in humans, and, consistent with evolutionary-based mechanisms to prevent cheating, when people are unable to reciprocate, they tend to experience guilt and shame (Wonderly, 1996).

Taken together, this research suggests that there may be mechanisms for the genetic transmission of helpful inclinations from generation to generation. Yet unlike many species where altruistic behavior is closely tied to genetic heritage, human genes influence behavior in a more indirect manner. As I have stated throughout this text, although ancient evolutionary forces may have left us with *capacities* (such as the capacity to behave altruistically), current social and environmental forces encourage or discourage the actual development and use of those capacities.

SOCIAL NORMS DEFINE THE "RULES" OF HELPING OTHERS

Although prosocial behavior may well have a genetic basis, it makes sense that social mechanisms would develop to help enforce these evolutionarily adaptive helping strategies (Simon, 1990). Chapter 8 discussed how general rules of conduct, known as *social norms*, prescribe how people should generally behave. These shared expectations are backed up by the proverbial carrot and stick: the threat of group punishment if the norms are not obeyed and the promise of rewards if one conforms. Prosocial norms are expectations to behave selflessly in bestowing benefits on others. Three social norms that serve as guidelines for prosocial behavior deal with *reciprocity, responsibility,* and *justice.*

RECIPROCITY

The first of these prosocial norms, the *norm of reciprocity,* is based on maintaining fairness in social relationships. As discussed in chapters 8 and 11, this norm prescribes that people should be paid back for whatever they give us. Regarding prosocial behavior, this means helping those who help us (Gouldner, 1960; Wilke & Lanzetta, 1982). As mentioned in the previous section, this norm also explains the discomfort that people typically experience when they receive help but cannot give something back in return (Nadler et al., 1985).

SOCIAL RESPONSIBILITY

In comparison to the reciprocity norm, the other two prosocial norms dictate that people should help due to a greater awareness of what is right. For instance, the **norm of social responsibility** states that we should help when others are in need and dependent on us (Schwartz, 1975). Acting on this norm, adults feel responsible for the health and safety of children, teachers have a sense of duty and obligation to their students, and soldiers believe they must help one another even at the risk of their own lives. This social responsibility norm requires help-givers to render assistance regardless of the recipient's worthiness and without an expectation of being rewarded (Nunner-Winkler, 1984). Unfortunately for the needy of the world, even though most people endorse the social responsibility norm, they often do not act in accordance with it.

SOCIAL JUSTICE

One reason people often do not adhere to the social responsibility norm is that they believe in social justice. In contrast to the dependent-driven social responsibility norm, the **norm of social justice** stipulates that people should help only when they believe that others *deserve* assistance (Lerner & Meindl, 1981). How does one become a "deserving" person? Melvin Lerner (1980) contends that at least in North American society, people become entitled to the deserving label by either possessing socially desirable personality characteristics or by engaging in socially desirable behaviors. Thus, according to the social justice norm, if "good" people encounter unfortunate circumstances, they deserve our help and we have a duty to render assistance.

CULTURAL DIFFERENCES

Research conducted in both individualist and collectivist cultures indicate that the norm of reciprocity may be universal (Gergen et al., 1975). Regarding the norm of social responsibility, a number of cross-cultural studies have found that adult members of collectivist cultures are not only more likely to help others of their ingroup than are members of individualist cultures, but they also express greater enjoyment in meeting these social obligations than do individualists (Bontempo et al., 1990). Similar cross-cultural differences have also been obtained when studying children's prosocial actions. For example, children from the collectivist cultures of Kenya, Mexico, and the Philippines were found to be much more helpful than children from the United States (Whiting & Edwards, 1988). A likely reason for this difference is that collectivists are much more likely than individualists to stress ingroup cooperation and individual sacrifice. In such a context, people may feel greater moral obligation to help than if they grew up in a less group-oriented environment.

Joan Miller and her colleagues (1990) found support for this perspective in a study of the moral reasoning of Hindus in India and of Americans. Participants read a series of hypothetical situations in which the main character in the story failed to help someone experiencing either a life-threatening, a moderately serious, or a minor need. The needy person was either the main character's child, best friend, or

If you don't look out for others, who will look out for you?

Whoopi Goldberg, comedian, actress and social activist for the homeless, b. 1949

Norm of Social Responsibility

A social norm stating that we should help when others are in need and dependent on us.

Help the weak ones that cry for help, help the prosecuted and the victim . . . they are the comrades that fight and fall.

Nicola Sacco, Italian-born anarchist, 1891–1927

If a free society cannot help the many who are poor, it cannot save the few who are rich.

John F. Kennedy, 35th U.S. President, 1917–1963

Norm of Social Justice

A social norm stating that we should help only when we believe that others deserve our assistance.

TABLE 13.2

Percentage of Hindus and Americans Saying People Have an Obligation to Help Others

When asked to state their opinion on people's social responsibility to help, collectivist Hindus believed that helping was one's responsibility as a parent, friend, and stranger, even when the need was minor. In contrast, Americans believed the social responsibility norm only extended to life-threatening situations or when parents had children with moderately serious needs.

	Hindus			Americans		
	Parent	**Friend**	**Stranger**	**Parent**	**Friend**	**Stranger**
Extreme need	99	99	100	100	98	96
Moderate need	98	100	99	95	78	55
Minor need	96	97	88	61	59	41

Source: Data from J. G. Miller, D. M. Bersoff, & R. L. Harwood, "Perceptions of Social Responsibilities in India and in the United States: Moral Imperatives or Personal Decisions?" in *Journal of Personality and Social Psychology*, 58:33–47, American Psychological Association, 1990.

Does research suggest that people from a collectivist culture like India are more or less likely to give assistance to a stranger than people from the individualist-oriented United States? Does the severity of the need appear to matter in willingness to help in these two cultures?

a stranger. As table 13.2 shows, Hindu respondents tended to perceive helping as the main character's social responsibility in all conditions, even when the need was minor. This means they believed that in all situations, giving help should be dictated by social norms and not by the personal norms of the potential helper. In comparison, American respondents believed that the norm of social responsibility should only be dictated in life-threatening cases or when parents were faced with moderately serious needs of their children. In all other instances, Americans believed that the main character's decision to help should be based on his or her own personal norms of help giving and should not be subject to social regulation.

These findings suggest that collectivist Indian culture holds to a broader and more stringent view of social responsibility than does the individualist American culture (Miller, 1994). For life-threatening needs of both strangers and loved ones and for moderately serious needs of one's family members, both Indians and Americans are likely to subscribe to the social responsibility norm. However, for nonthreatening needs, Americans are less influenced by social norms and, instead, are more affected by personal norms. It should be noted, however, that these cultural differences appear to apply only to ingroup helping. When those needing help are clearly members of an outgroup, research suggests that collectivists may actually be less helpful than individualists (L'Armand & Pepitone, 1975; Moghaddam et al., 1993).

CENTRAL PERSONAL HELPING NORMS ARE MORE LIKELY TO BE FOLLOWED

Miller's research points out one of the limitations of looking to social norms for explanations of prosocial action, especially in individualist cultures. Although social norms may be useful predictors of helping in life-threatening situations, they appear to be less effective in explaining people's actions in less serious circumstances. In addition to this problem, anyone who has read or heard news accounts of unhelpful bystanders in emergencies realizes that even in life-threatening situations, social norms do not always explain the behavior of people. The simple fact is that even though most people subscribe to many of the same social norms, they differ in their tendencies to act consistently with these norms.

Israeli social scientist Shalom Schwartz (1977) suggests that one way researchers can better predict how norms influence helping is by shifting attention from general norms of conduct to more specific personal norms. *Personal norms* are an individual's feelings of moral obligation to provide help to specific others in specific situations (Schwartz & Howard, 1982). According to Schwartz, personal norms are based on personally held *values.* As discussed in chapter 5, each person has a unique organized structure of values that vary in their importance to the self-concept. In addition, some values are particularly relevant to moral choices and helping (for example, compassion, a world of peace), while others are not (for example, industriousness, knowledge). Schwartz contends that values central to the self-concept will arouse stronger emotions when they become salient in a given situation than less central values. When central values are salient, we will feel self-satisfied if we intend to act consistent with these values, but we will experience shame and a loss of self-esteem if we intend to behave inconsistently. In essence, Schwartz's self-based model specifies how a motivation to help—in the form of a specific personal norm—is activated in a situation, and how this activation leads to behavior that is either consistent or inconsistent with a more general norm of social responsibility.

As an example of how personal norms might influence helping, consider Jesus' parable of the Good Samaritan. In this story, as the Samaritan is walking from Jerusalem to Jericho, he comes across a badly beaten man who has been robbed and stripped of his clothing and left for dead. Two other men, a priest and a Levite, have already passed by without providing aid. In contrast, the Samaritan is moved with pity and bandages the man's wounds, then takes him to an inn and cares for him. The next day, before continuing his journey, the Samaritan gives the innkeeper money and says, "Take care of him; and whatever you spend, I will repay you when I come back" (Luke 10:30–35). Analyzing this parable from the perspective of personal norms, the Good Samaritan's value of compassion—a central aspect of his self-concept—became salient when he encountered the beaten man. This value was consistent with the social responsibility norm, and thus, helping filled him with self-satisfaction. Not helping, on the other hand, was inconsistent with this core value and would have caused him great shame. Here, then,

An individual has not started living until he can rise above the narrow confines of his individualistic concerns to the broader concerns of all humanity.

Martin Luther King, Jr., African-American civil rights leader, 1929–1968

his personal norm was to help this man. The priest and the Levite, in contrast, responded differently because compassion was not a central value to either of them. Thus, even though the social responsibility norm may have been salient to them, they did not act consistent with this general social norm.

Individuals whose central values are irrelevant to moral choices (the priest and the Levite) are less likely to act consistently with prosocial norms when someone needs their help than are those whose central values are relevant to moral choices (the Samaritan). Schwartz has found that in such situations, nonhelpful people often reduce their own feelings of moral obligation with various psychological defenses, such as denial of responsibility (Schwartz & Howard, 1980).

The development of values relevant to moral choices begins in the preschool years (Eisenberg & Mussen, 1989). These prosocial values play a significant role in shaping children's personal norms. A good example of how prosocial values and personal norms influence decisions to help was provided by my daughter Amelia when she was 7 years old. In response to my question about why she helped other children when they needed assistance, Amelia said, "Because I want to be a good person on the inside and the outside, too."

One can see the operation of this internal motivation to help in the small minority of our population who regularly donate blood. Research suggests that over time, these persistent donors come to view giving blood as an affirmation of an important aspect of their self-concepts (Piliavin & Callero, 1991). On self-report questionnaires, these repeat donors are more likely than others to agree that "blood donation is an important part of who I am" and that "for me, being a blood donor means more than just donating blood." For them, acting in this prosocial manner is their way of being a good person on the inside and the outside, too.

If I can stop one Heart from breaking
I shall not live in vain
If I can ease one Life the Aching
Or cool one Pain
Or help one fainting Robin
Unto his Nest again
I shall not live in Vain.

Emily Dickinson, American poet, 1830–1886

LEARNING TO BE A HELPER INVOLVES BOTH OBSERVATION AND DIRECT REINFORCEMENT

The internalization of values consistent with prosocial norms does not occur in a social vacuum. In various ways, parents, teachers, and peers can be extremely influential, making it more or less likely that children will construct prosocial personal norms in needy situations. Just as chapter 12 outlined how aggression can be learned through modeling and direct reinforcement, we now examine how prosocial behavior is similarly learned.

OBSERVATIONAL LEARNING IN CHILDREN

According to social learning theorists, such as Albert Bandura (1986) and J. Philippe Rushton (1980), observational learning or modeling can influence the development of helping in at least two ways. First, it can initially teach children how to engage in helpful actions. Second, it can show children what is likely to happen when they actually engage in helpful (or selfish) behavior. In this learning process, what models *say* and what they *do* both shape the observers' prosocial behaviors.

For example, in one study, sixth-grade girls played a game to win chips that could be traded for candy and toys (Midlarsky et al., 1973). Prior to actually playing, each of the girls watched a woman play the game. In the *charitable* condition, the adult put some of the chips she won into a jar labeled "money for poor children" and then urged the girl to think about the poor children who would "love to receive the prizes these chips can buy." In the *selfish* condition, the adult model also urged the child to donate chips to the poor children, but she did so after putting all her chips into a jar labeled "my money." Results indicated a clear effect of prosocial modeling. Girls who had observed the charitable model donated more chips to the poor than those who had seen the selfish model.

Although this study demonstrates that what one does has more effect on children than what one says, subsequent studies have shown that *preaching* can

FIGURE 13.1

Immediate and Long-Term Effects of Modeling and Preaching on Children's Generosity

Children observed an adult model acting either generously or selfishly and also listened to them preach either generosity or selfishness. How did the model's behavior and preaching influence the children's immediate willingness to donate tokens? What about their willingness to donate two months later?

Source: Data from J. P. Rushton, "Generosity in Children: Immediate and Long-Term Effects of Modeling, Preaching, and Moral Judgment" in *Journal of Personality and Social Psychology*, 31:459–466, American Psychological Association, 1975.

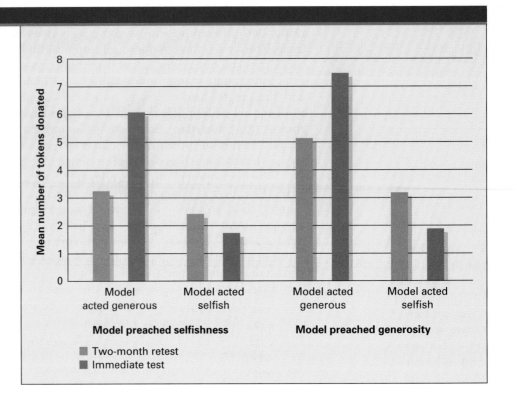

have a delayed effect in influencing prosocial behavior. In one of these studies, Rushton (1975) had children observe a same-sex adult model being either generous or selfish with her or his winning tokens from a game. Regardless of their actual behavior, some of the models told the watching child that one should be generous ("We should share our tokens . . ."), while others preached that one should be selfish ("We should not share our tokens . . ."). As in the previous study, the models' behavior had clear effects on the children's immediate helping, but what the models said had little immediate impact (see figure 13.1). However, two months later, in a retest of their willingness to help, something interesting happened. Although the children who had observed the charitable models were still more helpful than those who had watched the selfish models, children exposed to the models who preached generosity now donated more of their winnings to charity than those children who heard models preach selfishness. By far the most generous were those children previously exposed to models who had acted consistently with their prosocial preachings. In addition, the models preaching generosity but behaving selfishly produced the most giving in the selfish model condition.

This study, along with others (Moore & Eisenberg, 1984), suggests that although children are more likely to be influenced by adults' deeds rather than their words, over the course of time, preaching generosity can have some positive effect on children's prosocial tendencies, even if it comes from people who don't practice what they preach. The finding that selfish people can, over time, promote prosocial behavior by preaching generosity is interesting, but why might this be the case? Wouldn't a hypocrite's words simply be discounted by listeners?

The answer to this question is that in the short run, a hypocrite's preachings do appear to be discounted. However, in chapter 6 we learned that although people with low credibility (like a hypocrite) are not very persuasive immediately after they present their message, over time listeners forget where they heard it and then are influenced by the message content alone. This delayed effectiveness of a persuasive message from a noncredible source is known as the *sleeper effect* (see p. 193). In Rushton's study, although the children initially seemed to dismiss the selfish models' preachings of generosity, over time they were somewhat persuaded by the message content because they forgot where it originated.

PROSOCIAL MODELING IN ADULTS

Modeling prosocial behavior is not confined to children. In one study conducted in a natural setting, motorists who simply saw someone helping a woman change a flat tire were more likely to later stop and assist a second woman who was in a similar predicament (Bryan & Test, 1967). In another experiment (Rushton & Campbell, 1977), female college students interacted with a friendly woman as part of a "study" on social interaction (this was not the true purpose, and the woman was a confederate of the researchers). When the fabricated study was completed, the two women left the lab together and passed a table staffed by people asking for blood donations. When participants were asked first, only 25 percent agreed, and none actually followed through on their pledge six weeks later. However, when the confederate was asked first and signed up to donate blood, 67 percent of the participants also agreed to give blood, and 33 percent actually fulfilled their commitment.

THE LASTING CONSEQUENCES OF MODELING

At the beginning of this chapter, you read about the boyhood experience of Samuel Oliner and how he was protected from the Nazis by his father's friend, Balwina Piecuch. Later in life, Oliner and his wife, Pearl Oliner, conducted an extensive international study of more than four hundred rescuers of Jews during World War II and a matched sample of nonrescuers (Oliner & Oliner, 1988). In-depth interviews revealed the critical importance that prosocial parental modeling played in the lives of the rescuers. In contrast to the nonrescuers, the rescuers were more likely to say that they learned generosity and caring from their parents:

> It begins in close family relationships in which parents model caring behavior and communicate caring values. . . . They implicitly or explicitly communicate the obligation to help others in a spirit of generosity, without concern for external rewards or reciprocity. Parents themselves model such behaviors, not only in relation to their children but also toward other family members and neighbors. (Oliner & Oliner, 1988, pp. 249–250)

In a similar study of civil rights activists in the late 1950s and 1960s, researchers found that previous parental modeling of prosocial behavior distinguished those who made many personal sacrifices from those who participated in only one or two freedom rides or marches. The fully committed activists had parents who had been excellent prosocial models when the activists were children, whereas the parents of the partially committed tended to be inconsistent models, often preaching prosocial action but not actually practicing it (Rosenhan, 1970). These findings mesh nicely with the previously discussed experiment by Rushton (1975). Combined with other studies, they indicate that adults' modeling of altruism can have a powerful effect on the altruistic tendencies of children that can last well into adulthood (Fogelman, 1996).

Based on this knowledge, social scientists believe they can make a clear recommendation to parents on how to raise children who will help those in need. Put simply, parents who try to instill prosocial values only by preaching and not by modeling altruism will likely raise children who are only weakly altruistic. Parents who not only preach altruism, but also let their prosocial actions serve as guidelines for their children's behavior, are much more likely to foster altruism in the next generation. In a very real sense, to be effective altruistic teachers, one must not only "talk the talk," but also "walk the walk."

FIGURE 13.2

The Effects of Positive Reinforcement and Punishment on Model-Induced Generosity in Children

Do rewards and punishment affect children's willingness to help others? Rushton and Teachman (1978) either praised, criticized, or said nothing to children who donated tokens to an orphan named Bobby. How did these different consequences influence the children's subsequent willingness to donate tokens?

Source: Data from J. P. Rushton and G. Teachman, "The Effects of Positive Reinforcement, Attributions, and Punishment on Model-Induced Altruism in Children" in *Journal of Personality and Social Psychology*, 4:322–325, American Psychological Association, 1978.

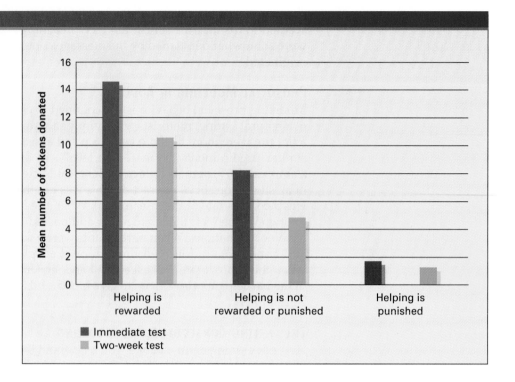

REWARDING PROSOCIAL BEHAVIOR

Although observing the prosocial actions of others can shape children's and adults' own helping, the *consequences* of their actions will often determine whether they continue to engage in prosocial behavior. Social rewards, such as praise, are generally more effective reinforcers than material rewards, such as money (Grusec, 1991). In one such "praise" experiment conducted by Rushton and Goody Teachman (1978), children were first induced to behave generously by having generosity modeled to them as in the previously described game-token studies. When the children donated some of their winnings to an orphan named Bobby, the model either praised the child for his or her imitative generosity (*reward condition*) by saying "Good for you, that's really nice of you," or scolded the child (*punishment condition*) by saying "That's kind of silly for you to give to Bobby. Now you will have fewer tokens for yourself." There was also a no-reinforcement condition in which the adult said nothing. As you can see in figure 13.2, children who were praised gave more to Bobby on later trials than did children who were scolded. The effects of being either rewarded or punished for prosocial behavior were so strong that they still influenced how much the children gave to Bobby two weeks later. This study demonstrates that verbal praise or scolding by an adult model can either strengthen or weaken children's level of generosity.

Reinforcement also influences adult helping. For example, imagine yourself walking along the main street in your hometown and being approached by a woman who asks how to get to a local department store. After giving her directions you continue along your way. Shortly, you pass by another woman who accidentally drops a small bag and continues walking, unaware that she has lost this possession. Would you return the bag to her? Do you think your decision to help the second woman would be influenced by how the first woman responded to your attempt to help her?

This was the question researchers asked in a naturalistic study conducted on the streets of Dayton, Ohio, using just this scenario (Moss & Page, 1972). In the *reward* condition, the woman asking for directions rewarded her helper by saying,

"Thank you very much, I really appreciate this." In contrast, in the *punishment* condition the woman responded to help by saying, "I can't understand what you're saying, never mind, I'll ask someone else." Researchers found that when people were rewarded by the first woman, 90 percent of them helped the second woman. However, when they were punished by the first woman, only 40 percent helped in the later situation. As in the study with children, this adult study suggests that people's future decisions to help are often influenced by the degree to which current helpful efforts are met by praise or rebuke.

SECTION SUMMARY

According to the evolutionary principle of *kin selection*, we exhibit preferences for helping blood relatives because this increases the odds that our genes will be transmitted to subsequent generations. Evolutionary theorists further explain that helping strangers can also be adaptive because any helpful act or favor is expected to be returned (*reciprocal helping*). Regarding cultural factors, social scientists point to relevant social norms, such as *reciprocity, social responsibility,* and *social justice,* as serving as guidelines for prosocial action. Although the reciprocity norm may be universal, collectivist societies may hold to a broader and more stringent view of social responsibility than individualist societies. People in individualist cultures appear to be less influenced by social norms, and more affected by *personal norms.* Finally, another reason people engage in prosocial behavior is that they have either observed others helping or they have been previously reinforced for helping. Children who become altruistic adults tend to have parents who model prosocial behavior for them.

While her neighbors listened to her cries for help, Kitty Genovese was repeatedly stabbed outside of her apartment building on the night of March 31, 1964. Despite this obvious emergency, no one came to her aid and no one even called the police until she had already died from her wounds. This incident prompted social psychologists John Darley and Bibb Latané to study the conditions that inhibit bystanders from helping in emergencies.

WHEN DO WE HELP?

In chapter 1, you learned how social psychological research is sometimes motivated by the researcher's desire to explain some real-life incident that has received wide news coverage. One of the most memorable examples of a real-life event spurring social psychological research was the Kitty Genovese case, which occurred on March 13, 1964, in the New York City borough of Queens. At 3:20 a.m. Kitty Genovese was returning home from her job as a bar manager when a man attacked her with a knife near her apartment building. She screamed, "Oh, my God! He stabbed me. Please help me!" As her cry rang out in the night, at least thirty-eight of her neighbors went to their windows to see what was going on. Within moments, Kitty Genovese's assailant stabbed her again, and then got into his car and drove away.

Despite the fact that Ms. Genovese was on the ground and in obvious need of help, not one of her neighbors came to her aid. No one called the police or an ambulance, but one couple did pull up chairs to their window and turn out the lights to see better. Fifteen minutes passed. As Ms. Genovese was crawling toward the back of her apartment building in search of safety, the assailant returned again. Now a watching neighbor reached for the phone to call police, but his wife told him, "Don't; thirty people have probably called by now." Yet no one had alerted the police. Within seconds, the killer, finding Ms. Genovese slumped against the stairs, struck again, this time stabbing her eight times and sexually assaulting her. Twenty minutes after she died, someone finally phoned the police, who arrived on the scene within two minutes.

Bystander Intervention Involves a Series of Decisions

The apathy of Kitty Genovese's neighbors was the topic of news stories, commentaries, religious sermons, and dinner conversation for some time. The question everyone was asking was "Why were these bystanders so callous to her suffering?" Two people who discussed the murder at length were social psychologists John Darley and Bibb Latané. Years later, Darley recalled the content of their discussion:

> Latané and I, shocked as anybody else, met over dinner a few days after this terrible incident had occurred and began to analyze this process in social psychological terms. . . . First, social psychologists ask not how are people different or why are the people who failed to respond monsters, but how are all people the same and how might anybody in that situation be influenced not to respond. Second, we asked: What influences reach the person from the group? We argued for a several-step model in which a person first had to define the situation. Emergencies don't come wearing signs saying "I am an emergency." In defining an event as an emergency, one looks at other people to see their reactions to the situation and interpret the meaning that lies behind their actions. Third, when multiple people are present, the responsibility to intervene does not focus clearly on any one person. . . . You feel a diffusion of responsibility in that situation and you're less likely to take responsibility. We argued that these two processes, definition and diffusion, working together, might well account for a good deal of what happened. (Evans, 1980, pp. 216–217)

Bystander Intervention Model

A theory that whether bystanders intervene in an emergency is a function of a five-step decision-making process.

According to the **bystander intervention model,** which eventually emerged as a result of this dinner discussion, being helpful during an emergency involves not just one decision, but a series of five decisions. As you can see from figure 13.3, at each point in this 5-step process, one decision results in no help being given, while the other decision takes the bystander one step closer to intervention.

The first thing that you, as a potential helper, must do is *notice that something unusual is happening.* Unfortunately, in many social settings, we are inundated by countless sights and sounds. Because it is impossible to attend to all this stimuli, and because we may be preoccupied with something else, a cry for help could conceivably go completely unnoticed. This *stimulus overload effect* is more likely to occur in densely populated urban environments than in rural settings (Milgram, 1970). Indeed, it is one of the likely reasons why there is a negative correlation between population density and helping (Levine et al., 1994; Yousif & Korte, 1995). That is, throughout the world, people who live in more crowded cities are less likely to help strangers in need of assistance than those who live in less densely populated urban centers. Another reason it is sometimes difficult to notice things out of the ordinary is that what is unusual in one setting may be a normal occurrence in another. For example, in some neighborhoods, a person lying unconscious on the sidewalk may be extremely unusual and cause passersby to take notice. Yet, in other neighborhoods, this same person may be one of many streetpeople who live and sleep outdoors much of the year—an all too common sight that passersby generally would take little, if any, notice of.

As a bystander to an emergency, if you do indeed notice that something unusual is happening, you move to the second step in the decision-making process: *deciding whether something is wrong and help is needed.* Returning to the previous example, if you pass by an unconscious man on the sidewalk you may ask yourself, "Did he suffer a heart attack or is he merely sleeping?" This is an extremely important decision, because if you decide he is merely sleeping you will continue on your way. But what if you are mistaken? One evening a few years ago, students in a fraternity house at the University of Wisconsin saw a man and a woman having sex near their residence. They quickly realized this was highly unusual behavior (the first decision step), but they did not define the situation as

FIGURE 13.3

The Model of Bystander Intervention: A Five-Step Decision Process

As outlined by Latané and Darley (1970), the decision to help someone involves a five-step process. At any step, a bystander's decision could lead to either further analysis of the situation or to nonintervention.

Source: Data from B. Latané and J. M. Darley, *The Unresponsive Bystander: Why Doesn't He Help?* Prentice-Hall, Inc., 1970.

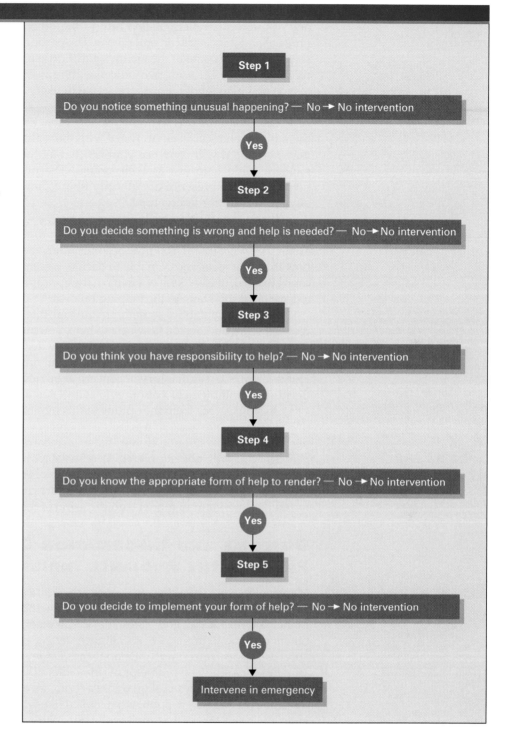

Step 1

Do you notice something unusual happening? — No → No intervention

Yes

Step 2

Do you decide something is wrong and help is needed? — No → No intervention

Yes

Step 3

Do you think you have responsibility to help? — No → No intervention

Yes

Step 4

Do you know the appropriate form of help to render? — No → No intervention

Yes

Step 5

Do you decide to implement your form of help? — No → No intervention

Yes

Intervene in emergency

an emergency (the second decision step). Instead of intervening in what they perceived to be consensual sex, the onlookers yelled encouragement to the couple below. Only later did they learn that they were actually watching a rape. Incorrectly defining the situation led to their nonintervention.

When you define the situation as an emergency, the bystander intervention model states that the third decision you must make is *determining the extent to which you have responsibility to help.* According to Latané and Darley, one factor that may play a role in your decision to help or not is whether an appropriate authority figure is nearby. For instance, imagine sitting in your car at a busy intersection and noticing that in the car ahead of you, two people are arguing heatedly. Suddenly, one of these quarrellers begins hitting the other with a club. This is definitely unusual and it is clearly an emergency. The pertinent question now is, do you have responsibility to come to the victim's aid? Further, imagine that to your immediate right is a police car with two officers sitting inside. If you decide that it is their responsibility to render assistance, you will likely assume the role of an unresponsive bystander.

Let's continue this hypothetical emergency situation, but now imagine that there is no police car in sight. Faced with the reality of a clear emergency, you still may not help if you convince yourself that all the other motorists watching this incident could help just as well as you. The presence of these other potential helpers, like the presence of authority figures, may cause you to feel less personally responsible for intervening.

If you assume responsibility for helping, a fourth decision you must make is *the appropriate form of assistance to render.* But in the heat of the moment, what if you aren't sure what to do? You may become paralyzed with uncertainty about exactly how to render assistance. Unable to decide, you may not offer any help at all. Children are particularly likely not to have the appropriate skills or confidence to make a decision at this stage in the helping process.

Finally, if you notice something unusual, interpret it as an emergency, assume responsibility, and decide how best to help, you must still decide whether to *implement your course of prosocial action.* If you have decided to run to the car where the person is being beaten and intervene, you must now act on this intention. However, due to fear of injury or concern about testifying at a future trial, you may decide not to implement your previous decision and remain a passive bystander.

As you can see from the outline of this model, Latané and Darley believe that the decision to intervene in a possible emergency involves a rather complex set of decisions. As a bystander, if you make an incorrect decision at any point in this process, you will not intervene. Two social psychological processes that often operate in emergency situations are the *audience inhibition effect* and the *diffusion of responsibility.* The inhibition effect can short-circuit helping at step 2 in the bystander intervention model, and diffusion of responsibility occurs in step 3.

OUTCOME AND INFORMATION DEPENDENCE PRODUCE THE AUDIENCE INHIBITION EFFECT

Many emergency situations are not clearly defined as such, but rather, have some degree of ambiguity. You may realize that something unusual is happening (step 1 in the model), but you aren't sure that it's an emergency (step 2). How do you and others respond to this sort of social uncertainty? In one study designed to investigate bystander uncertainty, Latané and Darley (1968) recruited male college students for a study on problems of urban life. When a research participant arrived at the laboratory, he was ushered into a room, given a questionnaire, and then was left alone to complete it. Soon, what looked like white smoke (but wasn't) began to enter the room through a small wall vent. Within six minutes, the smoke was so thick it was difficult to see. The dependent variable was whether or not the participant would leave the room to report the problem before the six minutes had elapsed. What do you think happened?

When working alone, most participants usually hesitated a moment upon first seeing the smoke, but then walked over to the vent to investigate. In 75 percent of the trials, the participant finally left the room to report the emergency. In a second experimental condition, groups of three naive participants were seated in the room when smoke began to pour from the vent. In all trials, participants looked to one another to help them decide if there was an emergency, but in only 38 percent of these three-person groups did even a single person report the incident

FIGURE 13.4

The Audience Inhibition Effect

When a room began filling with white smoke, people were much less likely to report the incident—and did so more slowly—when they were with others rather than alone. What two types of social dependence are interacting here to create the audience inhibition effect?

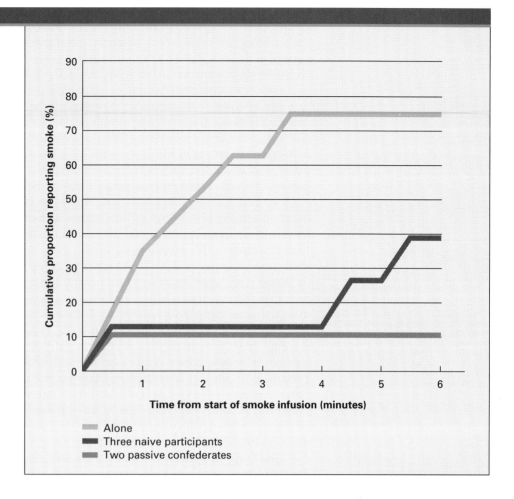

- Alone
- Three naive participants
- Two passive confederates

Audience Inhibition Effect

People are inhibited from helping for fear that other bystanders will evaluate them negatively if they intervene and the situation is not an emergency.

before the six-minute mark. Although 55 percent of the participants in the *alone* condition reported the smoke within the first two minutes, only 12 percent of the three-person groups did so. Finally, in a third condition, two confederates, acting like research participants, joined the one real participant in the room. As it began to fill with smoke, the confederates acted unconcerned. If the real participant asked them any questions, they replied "I dunno" and continued working on the questionnaire. In the presence of these unconcerned confederates, only 10 percent of the participants reported the smoke. The other 90 percent coughed, rubbed their eyes, and opened the window, but they did not leave the room. These findings, summarized in figure 13.4, indicate that when others are present, people not only are less likely to define a potentially dangerous situation as an emergency, but they also respond more slowly to the possible emergency. This **audience inhibition effect** is particularly likely when other people are acting calmly.

In another investigation of the inhibition effect, Latané and Judith Rodin (1969) set up a situation in which some other person, besides the research participant, was in possible danger. First, a female researcher set participants to work on a questionnaire and then left through a collapsible curtained doorway to work in an adjoining office. From their room, participants could hear her shuffling papers and opening and closing drawers. After four minutes, the researcher turned on a tape recorder that broadcast the sound of her climbing on a chair to reach a stack of papers on a bookcase. Participants then heard the researcher's scream, quickly followed by a loud crash. "Oh, my God, my foot. . . . I . . . I . . . can't move . . . it," she moaned. "Oh . . . my ankle. . . . I . . . can't get this . . . thing . . . off me." After about two minutes of moaning, the woman could be heard dragging herself out of her office.

Seventy percent of the participants who were in the room alone tried to help by pulling open the curtain or running out the other door to find help. Consistent with the audience inhibition effect, when two strangers were sitting in the room, only 40 percent of the time did either of them help. When the two people sitting in the room were friends, at least one of them helped in 70 percent of the trials. Even though this is the same percentage of helping as in the *alone* condition, it still indicates an inhibition effect because two people were present. If these two friends didn't inhibit each other's response, then helping should have occurred in 91 percent of the trials ($70\%_{friend\,1}$ + (70% × remaining $30\%_{friend\,2}$) = 91%).[1] Finally, in the last condition, a naive participant sat in the room with a confederate who acted unconcerned and nonchalant about the ruckus behind the curtain. Again, consistent with the inhibition effect, in this setting the participant tried to help only 7 percent of the time.

To better understand why the inhibition effect occurs, let's return to two concepts previously discussed in chapter 8, namely *information dependence* and *outcome dependence*. As discussed in that chapter, when we are not clear about how to define a particular situation, we are likely to become dependent on others for a definition of social reality. Thus, when a group of people witnesses a possible emergency, each person bases his or her interpretation of the event partly or exclusively on the reaction of others (information dependence). The problem with this information seeking in an emergency is that in our culture we have learned that it is not socially acceptable to "lose your cool." If we become agitated and excitable during a crisis, we run the risk of being negatively evaluated by others. Due to this concern with how others might evaluate us (outcome dependence), we will often pretend to be calm while witnessing an emergency. Acting cool and calm, they then observe others' behavior as a clue as how to define what they all are witnessing. However, because everyone else is also assuming this calm exterior, what we observe is a group of calm bystanders who, by their nonplussed demeanor, are defining the situation as a nonemergency.

In ambiguous emergency situations, then, the fear of being negatively evaluated (outcome dependence), combined with the tendency to look to others for further information (information dependence), results in the audience inhibition effect. In both the "smoke" study and the "woman in distress" study, the presence of others and their behavior significantly inhibited helping. Postexperimental debriefings indicated that some of those who did not intervene claimed they were either unsure of what had occurred or didn't think the situation was very serious.

Russell Clark and Larry Word (1972), in a replication of the Latané and Rodin study, made the situation even less ambiguous by allowing participants in the adjoining room to not only hear the crash of the person (this time a man) falling and his subsequent moaning, but now they could also feel the floor shake with the force of the crash. With this reduction in ambiguity, every single participant helped, regardless of the number of bystanders. However, when the situation was made more ambiguous (the victim did not cry out in pain), helping occurred only 30 percent of the time. In addition, as with the previous studies, participants in groups were less likely to help than those who were alone. This study clearly indicates that the audience inhibition effect is driven by our fear of being negatively evaluated. Indeed, those of us who are especially sensitive to embarrassment are the most likely to experience inhibition in emergencies (Tice & Baumeister, 1985). Thus, in an ambiguous emergency situation, we seem to be saying to ourselves, "What if I cause a big fuss by intervening and there is no emergency? I'll look like a fool and be mortified." However, if that fear of committing a social faux pas is

---

[1] Why would less inhibition occur in a friend's presence than in a stranger's presence? Shortly, I will discuss the likely reason for the inhibition effect. For now, suffice it to say that as opposed to being with strangers, with friends we are generally less likely to be concerned about embarrassing ourselves by overreacting to a situation.

reduced due to clear "emergency" signals, our inhibitions are greatly reduced and we are more likely to help.

DIFFUSION OF RESPONSIBILITY INCREASES WITH THE NUMBER OF BYSTANDERS

Fear of embarrassment is one reason we don't intervene in some emergencies, but what about those situations in which someone clearly needs help but no one raises a finger to come to the victim's aid? Surely some other social psychological factor is operating. For example, the neighbors of Kitty Genovese, sitting in their own separate apartments, heard her cries for help and correctly understood what was happening. However, they knew—or assumed—that others were also watching this drama unfold below them. Darley and Latané believed that this realization that others could also help diffused the neighbors' own feelings of individual responsibility (step 3 in the model). They called this response to others' presence the *diffusion of responsibility*—the belief that the presence of other people in a situation makes one less personally responsible for events that occur in that situation (see chapter 9, p. 325).

In an attempt to simulate the social psychological factors present in the Genovese case, Darley and Latané (1968) designed an experiment in which they placed people in separate areas from which they then heard a "victim" cry for help. In this study, New York University students thought they were participating in a discussion about the kinds of personal problems undergraduates typically face in a large urban environment. They were also told that to avoid embarrassment, they each would be placed in separate booths and would talk to one another using an intercom system. To further ensure they wouldn't be inhibited, the experimenter said he would not eavesdrop on their conversation. The way the intercom system worked was that only one person could speak at a time, and the others had to merely listen.

The study included three different conditions. Some participants were told the discussion would be with just one other student, while others were told they were either part of a three-person or a six-person group. In reality, all the other discussion participants were merely tape recordings. Discussion began with the first speaker stating that he was an epileptic who was prone to seizures when studying hard or when taking exams. When everyone else had spoken, the first speaker began to talk again, but now he was speaking in a loud and increasingly incoherent voice:

> I-er-um-I think I-I need-er-if-if could-er-er-somebody er-er-er-er-er-er-er give me a little-er-give me a little help here because-er-I-er-I'm-er-er-h-h-having a-a-a real problem-er-right now and I-er-if somebody could help me out it would-it would-er-er s-s-sure be-sure be good . . . because-er-there-er-er-a cause I-er-I-uh-I've got a-a one of the-er-sei——-er-er-things coming on and-and-and I could really-er-use some help so if somebody would-er-give me a little h-help-uh-er-er-er-er-er c-could somebody-er-er-help-er-uh-uh-uh (choking sounds). . . . I'm gonna die-er-er-I'm . . . gonna die-er-help-er-er-seizure-er-[chokes, then quiet]. (Darley & Latané, 1968, p. 379)

How did participants respond to this concocted, yet convincing, emergency? It depended on the number of bystanders they thought were also aware of the epileptic's seizure. When participants thought they were the only ones listening to the emergency unfold, 85 percent of them left their booths to help before the victim's pleas for help were choked off. When they thought they were one of five bystanders, only 31 percent reacted in a similar prosocial manner. When participants thought there was one other bystander aware of the emergency, helping was intermediate, with 62 percent helping. Not only was helping less likely as the number of bystanders increased, but the *speed* of rendering assistance was significantly slower as well. As you can see from figure 13.5, when participants thought

Where are they who claim kindred with the unfortunate?

Caroline Lamb, English novelist, 1785–1828

FIGURE 13.5

The Diffusion of Responsibility Effect

When participants heard over an intercom system someone having a seizure, how did the number of perceived bystanders influence their speed and willingness to help the victim?

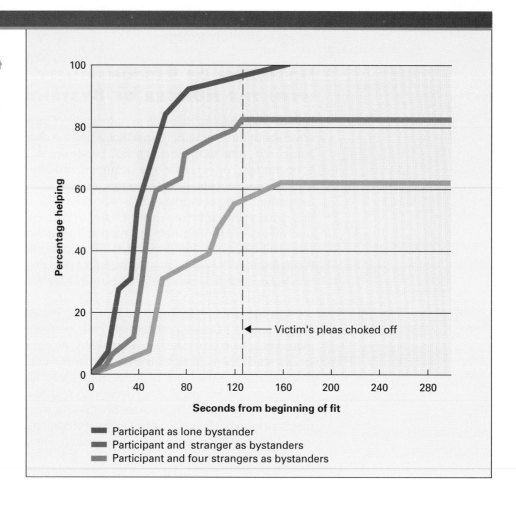

Participant as lone bystander
Participant and stranger as bystanders
Participant and four strangers as bystanders

 RITICAL *thinking*

To what degree do you think you would find these same bystander effects among people whose jobs regularly deal with helping others, such as nurses, doctors, and police officers? Would they be less likely to define an emergency as a nonemergency, or to diffuse responsibility? Do you think their tendency to diffuse responsibility would be influenced by whether their "helping" social role was currently salient or not salient to them? Would the type of help needed in the situation influence whether or not they actually helped? How might you test these hypotheses in an actual experiment?

there were four other bystanders, it took them three times longer to take any action (if they helped at all) than it did in the alone condition.

More than fifty subsequent laboratory and naturalistic studies have confirmed this diffusion of responsibility effect (Latané & Nida, 1981). On average, when participants believed they were the only bystander to an emergency, 75 percent of them helped, compared with only 53 percent who were in the presence of others. Despite the clear evidence that the presence of others influences people's decision to help, in postexperimental interviews the participants in all of Latané and Darley's experiments tended to deny that others' assumed presence had any effect on their actions (or inactions). As discussed in chapter 8, underestimating the effect that others have on your behavior makes it more likely that you will fall prey to their influence. After all, how can you guard against not falling into the nonhelpful mode when you don't recognize how the simple presence of others can change your feelings of personal responsibility?

BYSTANDER INTERVENTION IS ALSO SHAPED BY EMOTIONAL AROUSAL AND COST-REWARD ASSESSMENTS

Latané and Darley's bystander intervention model is best at explaining why people in a group of bystanders often don't interpret an event as an emergency, as well as why they often don't help even when it's clearly defined. Although this model provides a number of important pieces to the bystander puzzle, its focus is on the social problem of *nonintervention*. Yet why *do* we often decide to actually intervene in an emergency?

How might information dependence and outcome dependence inhibit bystanders from defining a situation as an emergency? If they do define the situation as an emergency, how might the presence of others inhibit intervention?

Arousal: Cost-Reward Model

A theory that helping or not helping is a function of emotional arousal and analysis of the costs and rewards of helping.

Jane Piliavin and her colleagues (1981) attempted to answer this question by developing a theory of bystander intervention that extends and complements Latané and Darley's model. These researchers added to the decision-making equation a consideration of bystanders' emotional arousal during an emergency and their assessment of the costs of helping and not helping. Essentially, their work focuses on the second half of Latané and Darley's model, namely, deciding on personal responsibility (step 3), deciding what to do (step 4), and implementing action (step 5).

According to their **arousal: cost-reward model** of helping, witnessing an emergency is emotionally arousing and is generally experienced as an uncomfortable tension that we, as bystanders, seek to decrease (Gaertner & Dovidio, 1977). This tension can be reduced in several different ways. We could intervene and thereby decrease our arousal, but we could also reduce arousal by either ignoring danger signs or benignly interpreting them as nothing to worry about. In addition to these avenues of action, we could reduce arousal by simply fleeing the scene. Which behavior we choose will be a function of our analysis of the costs and rewards for helping and for not helping.

What are the costs to the bystander for helping? This could involve a host of expenditures, including loss of time, energy, resources, health (even life), as well as the risk of social disapproval and embarrassment if the help is not needed or is ineffective. Counterbalancing the costs of helping are the costs of not helping. These might include serious harm to the ignored victim and subsequent public scorn of the nonhelpful bystander. Realizing that one didn't render assistance could also lead bystanders to engage in self-blame and experience loss of self-esteem.

According to Piliavin and her colleagues (refer to figure 13.6), if the costs of helping are low and the costs of not helping are high, bystanders will likely intervene. In contrast, if these costs are reversed (high helping costs and low not-helping costs), bystanders are unlikely to render assistance. If both types of costs are low, intervention will depend on the perceived social norms in the situation. The most difficult situation for bystanders is one in which the costs for helping and for not helping are both high. Here, the arousal:cost-reward model suggests two possible courses of action. One is for the bystanders to intervene indirectly by calling the police, an ambulance, or some other professional helping source. Another course of action is for bystanders to redefine the situation in a way that

FIGURE 13.6

The Influence of Costs and Rewards on Direct Helping

According to Piliavin and Piliavin (1972), the type of response a moderately aroused observer will have to someone's need for help will be influenced by his or her assessment of the combination of personal costs for direct help and costs for no help to the victim. According to this model, when are bystanders most and least likely to help?

Source: Adapted from J. A. Piliavin and I. M. Piliavin, "The Effect of Blood on Reactions to a Victim" in *Journal of Personality and Social Psychology*, 23:253–261, American Psychological Association, 1972.

		Costs for direct help		
		Low	High	
Costs for no help to victim	High	Direct intervention	Indirect intervention or →	Redefinition of the situation, disparagement of victim, etc., which lowers costs for no help, allowing
	Low	Variable: will be largely a function of perceived norms in situation		Leaving the scene, ignoring, denial

results in them not helping. Here, they could decide there really is no emergency after all, or that someone else will help, or that the victim deserves to suffer.

To help you better understand how consideration of these two cost factors might influence your own decision to intervene in an emergency, imagine that you are walking down the street when you hear a child screaming in pain. Directing your gaze toward the screams, you see a lone young girl who has slammed a car door on one of her hands. In this situation, you will likely directly intervene because: (1) the costs of not helping are high—the girl may seriously injure her hand if it is not removed from the door's grip soon, and you will experience terrible guilt if you don't help; and (2) the costs of helping are low—opening the car door will require little effort or loss of time, and helping will not put you in any danger.

Now, imagine that the child is not screaming in pain because her hand is caught in a door, but rather because an adult is beating her with a stick. Now, what will you do? Here, both the costs of not helping and helping are high—the girl may be seriously hurt and you will experience guilt if you don't stop the beating, but the adult could seriously injure you if you intervene. Faced with these high costs, you may help indirectly by calling the police or by yelling from a safe distance for the adult to stop. Sadly, you might also convince yourself that the child must deserve the beating she is getting and continue on your way.

Now, imagine that the child is screaming in pain because an adult is spanking her bottom with moderate force. In this situation, both the costs of not helping and helping are probably low. Not intervening will probably not cause serious physical injury to the child, and intervening may only result in the adult telling you to mind your own business. If your perception of cultural norms is that spanking children is an unacceptable response to misbehavior, you may try to stop the punishment. Otherwise, you are unlikely to intervene.

Finally, imagine the same scene as in the previous paragraph, but now let's add that you are rushing to an important job interview. If you try to stop the spanking you run the very real risk of arriving late. Here, your costs for helping are high and the costs for not helping are low. Weighing these factors, you are likely to continue on your way, perhaps muttering about the misguided actions of the adult but justifying your nonintervention to yourself ("If I didn't have this appointment, I'd give that adult a piece of my mind!").

A number of studies support the arousal:cost-reward model's hypothesis that people often weigh the costs of helping and not helping prior to rendering assistance (see Dovidio et al., 1991). For example, Lance Shotland and Margaret Straw (1976) staged a realistic fight between a man and a woman on an elevator. In one condition, 65 percent of the time bystanders intervened when the woman shouted, "Get away from me! I don't know you!" However, in another condition bystanders helped only 19 percent of the time when the woman shouted, "Get away from me! I don't know why I ever married you!" These differences in helping were apparently due to perceived costs. People who watched videotapes of the fights perceived the woman as being in greater danger when with the "stranger" than when with the "husband." They also believed that the combatants would be more likely to turn on them if they tried to intervene in the domestic fight rather than the "stranger" fight. Thus, the "stranger" condition was perceived to involve higher costs for not helping and lower costs for helping than the "husband" condition.

Another study investigating the costs for helping and the costs for not helping was conducted on the Philadelphia subway system when a male confederate carrying a cane collapsed (Piliavin & Piliavin, 1972). In one condition, the "victim" had a thin trickle of fake blood slip from his mouth as he fell, while in a second condition he did not. The researchers assumed that the presence of blood would increase the costs of intervening, because contact with blood for most people is repulsive. It was further assumed that bystanders would interpret the presence of blood to mean that the victim was in more danger than if no blood was visible. Thus, the "blood" condition was hypothesized to cause conflicting thoughts that would impede intervention ("The man needs help, but yikes! Look at that blood!"). True to these predictions, the unbloodied victim was directly helped more often (95 percent of the time) and more quickly than the bloody victim (helped 65 percent of the time). In one trial of the study, two teenagers witnessed the man collapse and rose to help but then saw the blood. "Oh, he's bleeding!" gasped one of them. Both promptly sat down.

Positive and Negative Moods Can Either Increase or Decrease Helping

Beyond the influence that fellow bystanders and perceived costs can have on prosocial behavior, research also demonstrates that people's willingness to help is affected by the mood they happen to be in when assistance is needed.

Good Moods and Generosity

Imagine this scene. Ralph bounds out of his psychology class feeling on top of the world because he has achieved one of the highest scores on his midterm exam. As he happily walks back to his apartment, he notices a woman carrying a tall stack of papers. Suddenly, the stack slips from her grasp and begins flying in all directions across campus. Without hesitation, Ralph springs into action and helps retrieve the errant papers.

Would Ralph have been so willing to help if he was in a less positive mood? Perhaps not. Research consistently indicates that good moods lead to more prosocial behavior. For example, in one study, Alice Isen (1970) administered a series of tests to college students and teachers, later telling them they had either performed very well or very poorly. Still others were told nothing at all about their performance. In addition to these three experimental conditions, a control group was not administered any tests at all. The participants who had "succeeded" at the tests were later more likely to help a woman struggling with an armful of books than any of the other participants. Further research indicates that people are more likely to help others on sunny days than on cloudy ones (Cunningham, 1979), after finding money or being offered a tasty treat (Isen & Levin, 1972), and even after listening to a comedian deliver a funny routine (Wilson, 1981).

What accounts for this *good mood effect?* Several possibilities have been offered. One is that when we are in a positive mood, we are more likely to perceive other people as "nice," "honest," and "decent," and thus deserving of our help (Isen, 1987). Another possibility is that we help others to enhance or prolong our good mood (Wegener & Petty, 1994). A third reason might be that, when happy, we are less likely to be absorbed in our own thoughts ("stewing in our own juices"), and thus, we are more attentive to others' needs (McMillen et al., 1977). A fourth possibility is that good moods increase the likelihood that we think about the rewarding nature of social activities in general. With the rewarding properties of helping being salient, our helping becomes more likely (Cunningham et al., 1990b). This enhanced attentiveness to the rewarding properties of helping may explain why good moods increase helpfulness only when the helpful task is expected to be pleasant. If helping is expected to entail unpleasant and aversive experiences, happy people are no more helpful than others (Isen & Simmonds, 1978; Rosenhan et al., 1981).

BAD MOODS AND SEEKING RELIEF

What about negative moods and helping? Rewind your thoughts to Ralph and his psychology midterm. As the "string-puller" of all fictional characters in this text, I will now change Ralph's exam grade from "A" to "F." Now, instead of bounding out of class, he trudges. Given his present somber mood, will he still dart around campus retrieving wayward sheets of paper? Surprisingly, he might. Isen and her coworkers (1973) found that people who believed they had failed at an experimental task were more likely to help another person than those who did not experience failure. Although this response certainly seems to contradict the good mood effect just described, one possible link between the two is the rewarding properties of helping. Because helping others often makes us feel good about ourselves, when feeling bad we may help as a way of *escaping* our mood—just as we help when we are in a good mood to maintain that mood.

Feeling guilty can also increase helping. Michael Cunningham and his colleagues (1980) conducted a field study in which people were individually approached on the street by a young man who asked them to use his camera to take his picture for a class project. The problem for the would-be helpers was that the camera had been rigged to malfunction. When the helpers realized the camera wasn't working, the young man examined it closely and asked the helpers if they touched any of the dials. He then informed them that it would have to be repaired. The researchers assumed that such an encounter would induce a certain degree of guilt in these individuals. As they continued on their way, these now guilty people passed a young woman who suddenly dropped a file folder containing some papers. How do you think they responded to this needy situation? Eighty percent of those who were led to believe that they had broken the young man's camera helped the female stranger pick up her papers. Only 40 percent of the passersby who had no broken-camera experience paused to help. Another field study found that Roman Catholics were more likely to donate money to a charity just prior to making their confession of sins to a priest—when their guilt level should have been high—rather than immediately after being absolved of those sins (Harris et al., 1975).

Although these studies demonstrate that negative moods can lead to prosocial behavior, other studies suggest that when we experience extremely negative moods, such as grief or depression, we may be so focused on our own emotional state that we simply don't notice others' needs and concerns (Carlson & Miller, 1987). Still other studies suggest that even when experiencing less severe negative moods, we are less likely to help than those who are in good moods (Isen, 1984). Robert Cialdini and Douglas Kenrick (1976) attempted to explain why this is the case by proposing that when we are in a bad mood, our decision to help is often based on a simple self-serving question: Will helping make us feel better? This **negative state relief model** asserts that when we are in a bad mood, if the perceived benefits for helping are high and the costs are low, the expected *reward value* for helping will be high, and thus, we will likely help to lift our own spirits. However, if the perceived benefits and costs are reversed so that the reward value is low, we are unlikely to help. Essentially, this model predicts that bad moods are more likely to lead to helping than neutral moods when helping is easy and highly rewarding.

Negative State Relief Model

A theory suggesting that for those in a bad mood, helping others may be a way to lift their own spirits if the perceived benefits for helping are high and the costs are low.

How might inducing guilt prompt people to help others? What might be the motivation of the helper in such a situation?

Although the negative state relief model has generated considerable scientific debate over whether it accurately depicts foul mood effects, even its proponents have pointed out the limits of its application (Cialdini & Fultz, 1990). First, research indicates that increased helping due to bad moods is much more common among adults than children (Kenrick et al., 1979). One probable explanation for this age difference is that children are less likely to have learned the self-rewarding properties of helping—that it can pull one out of a bad mood. A second limitation is that the model specifies that only mildly negative feelings such as sadness, guilt, and temporary depression will increase helping. More intense negative emotions, such as hostile anger and resentment, result in decreased helping. Finally, because the helping exhibited by adults in a bad mood is of a self-serving nature, if sad or guilty people get their spirits raised from some other source (such as being complimented or hearing a funny joke), they will no longer have a need to help others (Cunningham et al., 1980). Figure 13.7 summarizes the effects that both bad moods and good moods have on helping.

> ## SECTION SUMMARY
> Various theories have been proposed to predict the conditions under which we are likely to help. The *model of bystander intervention* and the *arousal:cost-reward model* focus attention, respectively, on the influence that fellow bystanders and perceived costs can have on prosocial behavior. Both models describe the cognitive steps we go through in deciding whether help is needed and whether we have responsibility to act. Two important social psychological processes that often negatively influence helping in such situations are the *audience inhibition effect* and the *diffusion of responsibility.* Beyond the influence of these factors, research also demonstrates that the mood we happen to be in during times of need will also affect our willingness to help. Sometimes, greater helping follows good moods, while, in other instances, we seemingly try to eliminate our negative moods by engaging in prosocial actions.

FIGURE 13.7

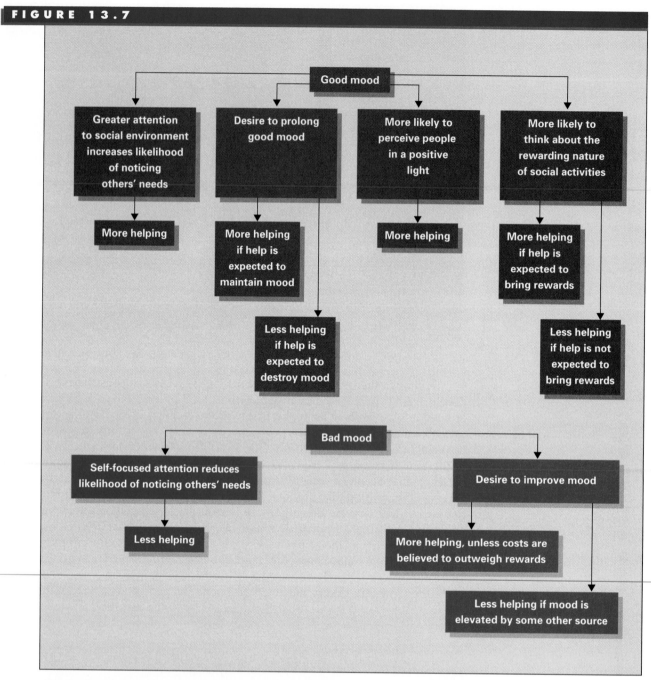

The Varied Effects of Mood on Helping

Depending on the circumstances, positive and negative moods can either increase or decrease helping.

DOES TRUE ALTRUISM REALLY EXIST?

The three previously discussed explanations of the conditions under which people are most likely to help others (arousal:cost-reward model, good mood effect, and negative state relief model), all assume there is an *egoistic* motive underlying prosocial behavior. All three explanations contend that helpful bystanders are ultimately trying to improve their own well-being by helping. Even Schwartz's value-driven notion of *personal norms,* discussed earlier in the chapter, could ultimately be fed by one's egoistic desire to avoid shame and enhance self-esteem through helping. Is egoism all there is underlying prosocial action?

Empathy-Altruism Hypothesis

A theory proposing that experiencing empathy for someone in need produces an altruistic motive for helping.

Personal Distress

An unpleasant state of arousal in which people are preoccupied with their own emotions of anxiety, fear, or helplessness upon viewing a victim's plight.

Empathy

A feeling of compassion and tenderness upon viewing a victim's plight.

Although not denying that helping is often motivated by a desire to fulfill egoistic needs, Daniel Batson (1991) and others (Hoffman, 1981; Krebs, 1975) have argued that sometimes our prosocial actions are truly *altruistic* (motivated solely by the desire to increase the welfare of another). In Batson's **empathy-altruism hypothesis,** he proposes that we typically experience two kinds of emotional reactions upon witnessing someone else suffer. One reaction, **personal distress,** is an unpleasant state of arousal in which we become preoccupied with our own anxiety upon viewing the victim's plight. Another reaction, **empathy,** is a feeling of compassion and tenderness for the victim. Batson contends that these two contrasting emotional reactions to a victim's plight—one focused on our own well-being (personal distress) and the other focused on the victim's (empathy), result in very different motivations.

Regarding the negative arousal state of personal distress, the greater our personal distress as a bystander, the more we will be motivated to have it reduced. Batson believes that Piliavin's arousal:cost-reward model does a good job of explaining how we respond to personal distress. Because reduction of this unpleasant arousal state is the primary motivation underlying personal distress, we will likely flee the stress-producing situation if at all possible. However, if we cannot easily escape, we will likely lend assistance in order to reduce our own unpleasant arousal. Described in this manner, one can clearly see that helping caused by personal distress is egoistic in nature.

Like personal distress, empathy for someone who is suffering will likely be an unpleasant emotion. However, unlike personal distress, empathy will not be satisfied by flight. Instead, Batson's empathy-altruism hypothesis contends that when we experience empathy, the stronger the feelings of compassion for the victim, the greater our motivation to help. Thus, when we feel great empathy, we are motivated more by our desire to improve the victim's welfare than attend to our own.

Support for the empathy-altruism hypothesis has been found in a number of studies in which bystanders' empathy or personal distress have been manipulated. In one of these studies, Batson and his coworkers (1981) had pairs of female college students participate in a task seemingly investigating how people work under aversive conditions. One participant was the "worker" and received electric shocks at random intervals during two trial periods; the other student observed the worker on a closed-circuit television as she performed the task. In actuality, the worker was a confederate. When the first aversive work trial began, the worker's facial expressions and body movements indicated that she found the shocks to be extremely uncomfortable. At the end of this trial, the worker explained that as a child she had been traumatized by electric shocks in an accident and, now, even mild shocks were often very painful. Responding to this "dilemma," the researcher asked the observer—who was naturally disturbed by this story—whether she would be willing to help the woman by trading places with her on the last trial. Batson and his colleagues predicted two factors would determine how participants responded to this dilemma: (1) whether or not they felt personal distress or empathy, and (2) whether or not they could flee this aversive situation.

Regarding the first factor, the experimenters assumed that everyone would experience arousal when witnessing the victim's plight, and that they would naturally attribute this arousal both to sympathy for the victim (empathy), and to personal discomfort (personal distress). To more clearly direct participants' interpretation of their arousal, the experimenters gave them a fictional drug, "Millentana" (a cornstarch placebo), as part of another study just prior to observing their partner being shocked. All participants were told that Millentana had a side effect. In the *empathy* condition, Batson and his coworkers wanted the participants to misattribute any feelings of personal distress to the drug and not to the victim's plight. To achieve this result, they said that the drug "produces a clear feeling of

TABLE 13.3

Percentage of Participants Willing to Help Due to Their Emotional Response to the Victim and Their Ability to Escape

Participants who experienced empathy when observing the victim's suffering were more likely to help regardless of whether it was easy or difficult to escape the situation. In contrast, those who experienced personal distress generally helped only when escape was difficult. How do these findings support the empathy-altruism hypothesis?

Escape Condition	Predominant Emotional Response	
	Personal Distress	Empathy
Easy	33	83
Difficult	75	58

Source: Data from C. D. Batson et al., "Is Empathic Emotion a Source of Altruistic Motivation?" in *Journal of Personality and Social Psychology*, 40, 290–302, American Psychological Association, 1981.

uneasiness and discomfort, a feeling similar to that you might experience while reading a particularly distressing novel." Due to this misattribution of personal distress to Millentana, the researchers assumed that participants in the empathy condition would perceive their emotional response to the victim to be primarily empathy. In contrast, those in the *personal distress condition* were told that the drug "produces a clear feeling of warmth and sensitivity, a feeling similar to that you might experience while reading a particularly touching novel." Following a similar logic, the experimenters assumed that these people would misattribute feelings of empathy to Millentana and perceive their emotional response to the victim to be primarily personal distress. Participants' subsequent self-reports indicated that the experimenters were successful in manipulating the women's emotional responses in the desired directions.

Regarding the second factor, ease of escape was manipulated by the instructions participants had previously received concerning their role as observer. In the *easy-escape* condition, they were told they would observe only the first trial, while in the *difficult-escape* condition, participants were told they would observe both trials.

How do you think these different emotional reactions affected willingness to help the victim? As can be seen in table 13.3, regardless of whether escape was difficult or easy, empathic observers tended to help by deciding to trade places with the confederate. On the other hand, the personally distressed observers chose to flee when fleeing was easy; they helped only if that was the only way to relieve their own discomfort. These findings are perfectly consistent with the empathy-altruism hypothesis.

In a replication of this experiment, instead of manipulating empathy and personal-distress arousal by giving people a placebo drug, Batson and his coworkers (1983) asked participants to describe their emotions after watching the confederate suffer. Based on these responses, participants were categorized as being either personally distressed or empathic. As in the previous experiment, the empathic observers chose to help regardless of how easy or difficult it was to escape. Likewise, those who experienced personal distress tended to flee if they could, and only helped if fleeing was not an option. Overall, the pattern that emerged in five separate studies is that, regardless of ease or difficulty of escape, empathic individuals provided help about 75 percent of the time. Likewise, those who experienced personal distress and could not escape easily tended to help at approximately the same level, about 79 percent. In contrast, when escape was easy for the personally distressed, their level of helping dropped dramatically, to only about 30 percent.

CRITICAL *thinking*

Imagine that you have been given the assignment to gather donations at a local community center to help starving people in a foreign country. As you prepare your donation pitch, you realize that when you talk to your audience and show them images of starving children and adults, some will react with empathy, while others will react with personal distress. Given these circumstance, what could you do to maximize the likelihood that your audience will donate money?

Based on these and other findings that are consistent with the empathy-altruism hypothesis (Batson et al., 1997; Sibicky et al., 1995), can we conclude that people who help due to empathy are motivated by true altruism? Certainly, Batson and many other social scientists think there is compelling evidence for this view (see Davis, 1996, for a review). Although some researchers still contend that the case for genuine altruism is still to be proven (Cialdini et al., 1997), the general consensus is that this sort of selfless helping does exist and is a part of human nature.

THERE ARE INDIVIDUAL DIFFERENCES IN EMPATHIC RESPONDING

In addition to exploring the role that *situational* empathy and personal distress play in prosocial behavior, researchers have also examined whether we differ in our habitual tendencies to experience these contrasting emotions. In other words, can these different emotional experiences be thought of as personality *traits?* Mark Davis (1980) has developed a personality measure that assesses individual differences in empathy (what he calls *empathic concern*) and personal distress. People who score high on empathic concern are those who habitually feel warmth and compassion for unfortunate others, while those who score high on personal distress tend to become anxious and uneasy when seeing others in need of help.

Studies of fraternal and identical twins indicate that individual differences in empathy and personal distress may be partly due to genetic factors (Davis et al., 1994; Zahn-Wexler et al., 1992). That is, high empathy and high personal distress people appear to have an inherited sensitivity to emotional experiences that causes them to react more strongly to the observed experiences of others. Before reading further, spend a few minutes answering the items in table 13.4. Based on your responses, are you high or low on empathic concern and personal distress?

Research indicates that individuals high in empathic concern not only are more willing to put themselves in situations in which the experience of sympathy for another is likely, but they also are generally more willing to help people in trouble than are those low in empathic concern (Unger & Thumuluri, 1997). For example, in an analysis of people's responses to the annual Jerry Lewis muscular dystrophy telethon, Davis (1983) found that people with high empathic concern were more likely to watch the telethon and to contribute their time, effort, and money as a result. In contrast, people high in personal distress showed no such tendency. What we can conclude from this research is that people who typically feel compassion for unfortunate others tend to be drawn toward situations in which their feelings of sympathy will be aroused. When exposed to others' misfortunes, they don't remain passive bystanders, but rather, they tend to take action to try to relieve the suffering. In this regard, the experience of caring for others represents a central self-concept value for those high in empathic concern (Emmons & Diener, 1986).

Because the experience of empathy seems to motivate us to help, isn't it possible that at times, we might be wary of feeling empathy out of concern for the costs of helping? This *empathy-avoidance hypothesis* assumes that we have an implicit knowledge of the empathy-helping relationship, and it is this knowledge that sometimes causes us to actively avoid feeling empathy when we believe the cost of helping will be high. Research indicates that empathy avoidance may well explain some instances of nonintervention. For example, in a series of experiments, when people believed that helping a homeless man would entail considerable time and effort, they actively avoided situations in which their empathy for this man would be aroused (Shaw et al., 1994). What these findings suggest is that even normally soft-hearted people can steel themselves to the suffering of others if they avoid an empathic connection. Consider this the next time you pass a homeless person on the street. Are you actively avoiding an empathic response because the perceived costs of helping are too great?

TABLE 13.4

Measuring Empathic Concern and Personal Distress

Instructions

To discover your level of empathic concern and personal distress, read each item below and then, using the following response scale, indicate how well each statement describes you.

0 = Extremely uncharacteristic (not at all like me)
1 = Uncharacteristic (somewhat unlike me)
2 = Neither characteristic nor uncharacteristic
3 = Characteristic (somewhat like me)
4 = Extremely characteristic (very much like me)

Empathic Concern Scale

_____ 1. When I see someone being taken advantage of, I feel kind of protective toward them.

_____ 2. When I see someone being treated unfairly, I sometimes don't feel very much pity for them.*

_____ 3. I often have tender, concerned feelings for people less fortunate than me.

_____ 4. I would describe myself as a pretty soft-hearted person.

_____ 5. Sometimes I don't feel very sorry for other people when they are having problems.*

_____ 6. Other people's misfortunes do not usually disturb me a great deal.*

_____ 7. I am often quite touched by things that I see happen.

Personal Distress Scale

_____ 1. When I see someone who badly needs help in an emergency, I go to pieces.

_____ 2. I sometimes feel helpless when I am in the middle of a very emotional situation.

_____ 3. In emergency situations, I feel apprehensive and ill-at-ease.

_____ 4. I am usually pretty effective in dealing with emergencies.*

_____ 5. Being in a tense emotional situation scares me.

_____ 6. When I see someone hurt, I tend to remain calm.*

_____ 7. I tend to lose control during emergencies.

Scoring Your Responses

Several of the items on these two scales are reverse-scored; that is, for these items a lower rating actually indicates a higher level of empathic concern or personal distress. Before summing the items, recode those with an asterisk (*) so that 0 = 4, 1 = 3, 3 = 1, 4 = 0.

Gender Differences in Empathic Concern and Personal Distress

Davis (1980) has found the following gender differences in levels of empathic concern and personal distress.

Empathic concern	Personal distress
Male mean = 19.04	Male mean = 9.46
Female mean = 21.67	Female mean = 12.28

Are your scores above or below the mean for your sex?

Source: From Mark H. Davis, "Interpersonal Reactivity Index" in Empathy: A Social Psychological Approach. Copyright ©1996. Boulder, CO: Westview Press.

The fact that we sometimes help to raise our bad moods or maintain our good moods has raised the question whether all helping is motivated by *egoistic* rather than *altruistic* concerns. The *empathy-altruism hypothesis* contends that bystanders who experience *empathy* due to another's plight are likely to help to provide comfort for the victim. In contrast, those who experience *personal distress* will not be motivated by altruistic concerns but, rather, by an egoistic desire to reduce their own negative arousal state. Because empathy motivates us to help, we may sometimes actively avoid experiencing it when the cost of helping is high.

WHOM DO WE HELP?

Thus far we have examined the *why, when,* and *who* of helping. Now it is time to ask the question, *whom* do we help? Are some people more likely to receive help than others?

WE TEND TO HELP SIMILAR OTHERS

Perceiving a needy person as similar to us tends to increase our willingness to lend assistance (Taormina & Messick, 1983). What kind of similarity is important? One salient characteristic is the clothes a needy person wears. For example, in one study conducted on college campuses in the early 1970s, researchers had confederates ask fellow students for a dime to make a phone call. The confederates asked for this help when either dressed conservatively or in a countercultural ("hippie") fashion. Fewer than half the students gave the dime to those dressed differently from themselves. Two-thirds did so for those dressed similarly (Emswiller et al., 1971). It's likely that the would-be helpers made assumptions about the social and political beliefs of the person-in-need based on what they wore. Clothing was a "symbol" for these hidden qualities.

Similarity of beliefs does indeed influence help giving. During the 1972 presidential campaign, Stuart Karabenick and his colleagues (1973) convinced Nixon and McGovern workers to "accidentally" drop campaign leaflets as people walked by on their way to vote. If passersby supported the candidate of the needy campaign worker, they were much more likely to help pick up the spilled leaflets than if they supported the other candidate.

One characteristic that exhibits an inconsistent, yet intriguing, pattern of similarity bias is *race.* In a review of helping studies investigating race as a predictor of aid giving, Faye Crosby and her colleagues (1980) found a same-race helping bias in less than half the studies. The remaining studies either showed no discrimination or a different-race helping bias. Does this inconsistent and even contradictory pattern of findings mean that no relation exists for race? Not necessarily. The studies that found greater different-race helping than same-race helping generally involved face-to-face interactions. As discussed in chapter 7, in most social quarters it's no longer acceptable to publicly engage in racial discrimination. It's possible that people today are generally biased toward their own race but hide this bias to avoid social disapproval. In fact, at times, they may even bend over backward to prove that they are not prejudiced. If this explanation is true, then people should be less likely to help someone from another race if they can attribute their unhelpful response to factors other than race.

This is exactly what has been found in a number of studies. For example, Samuel Gaertner and John Dovidio (1977) found that White female college students were less likely to help a needy Black woman than a needy White woman if they could diffuse responsibility among other bystanders. When they were the only bystander to the female victim's plight, and thus unable to diffuse responsibility, there was no difference in their help giving. Studies like this one, then, suggest that race similarity does increase helping. Or, looking at this similarity effect as a *dissimilarity* effect, when people are provided with an excuse not to help, racial discrimination in helping is more likely.

Although similarity may generally lead to greater helping, even a casual observer of the cultural scene can tell you that this is not the case when we consider whom male helpers prefer to assist. In a review of twenty-five studies that compared help received by male and female victims, Alice Eagly and Maureen Crowley (1986) found there was an overall tendency for men to provide more frequent help to women, not men. Women helpers, in contrast, did not show any gender bias. Although male helpers are acting out of line with the similarity effect, they are behaving perfectly in accord with the male gender role, which nurtures helping that is heroic and chivalrous—and is generally directed toward the benefit of female victims. In many cases, the help that men offer to women is clearly egoistic in nature; they more frequently help attractive than unattractive women (West & Brown, 1975).

WE HELP "DESERVING" OTHERS, BUT WE ALSO BLAME VICTIMS

Whether people receive help in times of need will partly depend on others' inferences about the causes of their troubles. Following the principles of attribution theory discussed in chapter 3, we are more likely to help someone if we attribute the cause of their problems to external or uncontrollable factors rather than internal ones. For example, college students state that they would be more willing to lend an acquaintance money or give them their lecture notes if the need arose due to an uncontrollable cause, such as illness, rather than an internal, controllable cause, such as laziness (Weiner, 1980). Put simply, if we believe the person could not have prevented the predicament, we are more likely to help.

The reason we are more likely to help "deserving" others is due to the *norm of social justice* discussed earlier in the chapter. However, the problem in making inferences about the cause of a victim's troubles, and thereby deciding if she or he deserves our help, is that most of us believe in a just world. As discussed in chapter 4, (p. 134) the *just-world belief* is a belief that the world is a fair and equitable place, with people getting what they deserve (Lerner, 1980). One unfortunate consequence of this belief is that we tend to make defensive attributions when explaining the plight of victims. That is, we blame people for their misfortunes, and by doing so, we reassure ourselves that the world is just and that we aren't likely to fall victim to similar circumstances.

Although many people believe in a just world, individual differences exist in the extent to which this belief is held (refer back to table 4.4, p. 135). Because those with a strong just-world belief are more likely to be unsympathetic to victims, it's not surprising to find that they generally are also less likely to help those in need. Does this mean that people who are strong believers in a just world are always unhelpful bystanders? No. When a victim's suffering can be easily and promptly corrected, strong believers in a just world are much more likely to help than when the problems are of a widespread and enduring nature (Bierhoff et al., 1991). The likely reason for this effect is that helping someone who needs just a little bit of assistance to get back on track confirms the just-world believer's perception that the truly deserving will not be unfairly punished. Thus, firm believers in a just world are much more likely to be onetime contributors to little Billy's heart operation fund than they are to be continuing contributors to a fund in search of a cure for AIDS or a program to promote affordable housing for the poor.

SECTION SUMMARY

Research indicates that we are most likely to help similar others. One exception to this similarity effect is that men tend to provide more frequent help to women, not other men. We also are most likely to help those we believe are deserving. However, one unfortunate consequence of believing in a just world is that we tend to blame people for their misfortunes.

ARE THERE HIDDEN COSTS FOR HELP RECIPIENTS?

Throughout the chapter we have examined some of the factors that inhibit bystanders to provide assistance to others, but, what if help is given? How do recipients typically respond? And what might prevent a person in need from asking for help?

BEING UNABLE TO RECIPROCATE HELP CAN CREATE STRESS

. . . It is natural to avoid those to whom we have been too much obliged.

Héloise, French abbess, 1098–1164

Throughout the world, people recognize that receiving help is a mixed blessing. Those who receive help often respond with feelings of relief and gratitude, but they also often feel embarrassed, indebted, and even inferior (Nadler, 1991). The contradictory feelings that often flow from prosocial actions help to explain why victims are sometimes less than gracious recipients of a helping hand. The potential that help giving has for producing resentment and hostility is aptly recognized in an Indian proverb that states, "Why do you hate me? I never even helped you" (Nadler & Fisher, 1986, p. 82).

In attempting to explain why receiving help may at times evoke unpleasant emotions, social psychologists have turned their attention to the fact that in exchange relationships (refer to chapter 11, p. 000), people are especially attentive to *reciprocity*—a mutual exchange of resources. *Equity theory* (chapter 11, p. 423) contends that people seek to maintain equity in their social relationships by keeping the exchange ratio of resources balanced, and they feel distressed when inequity exists (Hatfield et al., 1978). When people receive help, they commonly experience a feeling of inequity, because by definition, they realize they have a more favorable ratio of rewards to contributions than does the helper. Under such circumstances, recipients of help are motivated to restore actual equity by trying to return the favor (Greenberg & Frisch, 1972). But what happens if they cannot reciprocate?

Research indicates that recipients not only find nonreciprocal helping distressful, but they also are less likely to ask for assistance in the first place if they don't think they can repay the person in some way (Riley & Eckenrode, 1986). If they aren't in a position to refuse the help, they also might sometimes deal with their inability to restore equity by resenting the helper (Gross & Latané, 1974). In essence, help-givers may be resented if they don't allow recipients to restore equity in some way and thereby allow those who have been helped to live up to the reciprocity norm.

RECEIVING HELP CAN ALSO THREATEN SELF-ESTEEM

The notion that receiving help may produce inequity and feelings of distress in a relationship suggests that it may also pose a threat to the recipient's self-esteem. For instance, in our individualistic culture we place a high premium on self-reliance, and this value often is a key defining feature of our self-concept.

Threat-to-Self-Esteem Model

A theory stating that if receiving help contains negative self-messages, recipients are likely to feel threatened and respond negatively.

A charitable deed must be done as a duty which man owes to man, so that it conveys no idea of the superiority of the giver or the inferiority of the receiver.

The Koran 2:262, Sacred Scripture of Islam

Receiving help from someone puts us into a dependent role that is contrary to this individualistic value. According to Jeffrey Fisher and Arie Nadler's **threat-to-self-esteem model,** if receiving help contains such negative self-messages, we are likely to feel threatened and respond negatively (Nadler & Fisher, 1986). More specifically, this model states that when receiving help, we can perceive it as either *self-supporting* or *self-threatening.* Aid will be supportive to the extent that it (1) conveys caring for the recipient, and (2) provides real benefits (Dakof & Taylor, 1990). It will be threatening to the extent that it (1) implies an inferiority-superiority relationship between recipient and helper and (2) conflicts with important cultural values of self-reliance and independence (Dunkel-Schetter et al., 1992).

Beyond the qualities of the help itself, qualities of the helper and the recipient's own level of self-esteem will also determine whether aid is seen as supportive or threatening. Being helped by a friend, sibling, or a *similar* person is more likely to prompt social comparison, which in turn may call into question the recipient's level of competence (Searcy & Eisenberg, 1992). This is especially true when the helpful task involves something important to the recipient's self-concept. For example, if you are an aspiring psychologist who doesn't understand the subtleties of a particularly complex theory, asking a fellow student probably would be more threatening to your self-esteem than to ask your psychology professor. Why? The threat-to-self-esteem model would hypothesize that asking a fellow student for help would be more likely to reflect negatively on your own level of competence in this area than seeking help from the professor, a person who is clearly dissimilar to you in psychological training and knowledge (Nadler et al., 1983).

In one experiment testing this hypothesis, Nadler (1987) asked Israeli high school students to solve a series of anagrams when working alongside a same-sex partner. While describing the anagrams task the researchers told half of the students that their performance would provide accurate information on their intelligence and creativity. The rest were told that the task had no association with any important intellectual qualities. All the students were also told that during the task, they could ask their partner for help if they wished. Just before they began the anagrams, they were shown an attitude questionnaire their

When we need help on a task, we prefer that it comes from someone similar to us, such as a friend. The dilemma we sometimes face, however, is that if this task requires skills important to our self-esteem, we may feel threatened and, as a result, come to resent the help and the helper. Whom do you think is most likely to react in this manner, those high in self-esteem or those low in self-esteem?

partner had supposedly completed a few minutes earlier. Half of these questionnaires were constructed to be similar to the participants' own attitude questionnaire responses, while the others were dissimilar in content. The question of interest was under what conditions the students would be most likely to avoid help seeking.

Consistent with the threat-to-self-esteem model, students were less likely to seek help from their partners when they believed they were similar to them, especially when the task was defined as requiring skills important to self-esteem, namely, intelligence and creativity. This reluctance to ask for help from similar others was greatest among adolescents high in self-esteem, who supposedly had the most self-regard to lose on these important personal qualities. One positive consequence of this self-esteem threat is that people who feel threatened in this manner become motivated to develop the necessary skills so that in the future, they will not have to seek help.

Given our previous discussion of gender differences in providing aid (with men tending to assume the role of the chivalrous helper of women), it isn't surprising to find that men are more reluctant than women to ask for help (Barbee et al., 1993; Corney, 1990). After all, how often do you see Bruce Willis or Sylvestor Stallone–type characters asking for help in the movies? Such help seeking is more frowned upon for men than women and therefore poses a more serious threat to their self-esteem (Smith & DeWine, 1991). Evidence also shows that when heterosexual individuals seek help from someone of the other sex, men are more likely to prefer that it come from an unattractive woman, and women are more likely to prefer help from an attractive man (Nadler et al., 1982). This different pattern of help seeking can be explained as a function of traditional gender roles and self-esteem threat. For a traditional (masculine) heterosexual man, acting dependent toward an attractive woman would be perceived as imperiling his "macho" image in her eyes, but for a traditional (feminine) heterosexual woman, acting dependent toward an attractive man would be thought of as increasing, not decreasing, her appeal. In summary, then, our assessments of what effect such help seeking will have on our self-esteem will largely determine whether and from whom we will seek help.

SECTION SUMMARY

Although people generally appreciate others' help, they also often experience negative emotions due to this assistance. People may resent help-givers if they don't allow recipients to return the favor in some way. The *threat-to-self-esteem model* hypothesizes that if receiving help poses a threat to a person's self-esteem, he or she may respond negatively, disparaging the help and the helper.

*A*s you have already discovered in reading this chapter, many factors influence prosocial action. In this final section, I would like to revisit two areas of inquiry, namely, *observational learning* and *bystander intervention* research, in order to explore how helping behavior might be increased in two different age groups: children and adults.

TELEVISION FOSTERING PROSOCIAL BEHAVIOR IN CHILDREN

Earlier in the chapter, you read that observational learning or modeling can have a powerful effect on children's prosocial behavior. In chapter 12, you also learned that television violence can promote aggressive behavior in children. Because of these two sets of findings, it's only natural to wonder whether prosocial content on television can promote helpful behavior.

Over the years, a consistently excellent example of a program that attempts to enhance young children's prosocial development is public television's *Mister Rogers' Neighborhood*. In a series of studies, Lynette Friedrich and Aletha Stein (1973, 1975) found that preschool children who watched *Mister Rogers'* episodes not only remembered its prosocial content, but their later behavior was also more cooperative and helpful than that of children who watched shows with either aggressive or neutral content. The researchers further discovered that the socially desirable effects of such television exposure could be further enhanced if children later enacted (*role-played*) events and dialogue depicted on the show.

Studies of older children have also found similar results. For example, in one study, a group of first-graders saw an episode of *Lassie* in which a boy risked his life to save a puppy from a mine shaft. In contrast, children in two control groups saw either another *Lassie* episode with no altruism, or an episode of the situation comedy *The Brady Bunch*. Later, each child had the opportunity to help some distressed puppies. The catch was that to help the puppies the child had to stop playing a game in which the winner received a valuable prize. As you can see in figure 13.8, children who had watched the altruistic *Lassie* episode spent more time helping the puppies than did the other children (Sprafkin et al., 1975).

What these and other studies indicate is that viewing prosocial television programs can facilitate the acquisition or enhancement of prosocial behavior

---

FIGURE 13.8

The Effect of Prosocial Television on Children's Altruism

Children who watched an episode of Lassie *in which a child saves a puppy were more likely to later spend a greater amount of time helping real puppies than children who watched programs without any "helping themes." Are these prosocial effects of television viewing at least as powerful as the antisocial effects of TV violence?*

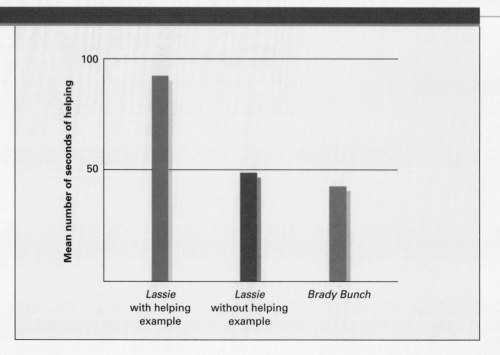

(Forge & Phemister, 1987). Indeed, in an analysis of more that a hundred studies investigating the effects of prosocial programs on children's behavior, Susan Hearold (1986) found that the effect that prosocial TV had on prosocial behavior was almost double the effect of TV violence on aggressive behavior. Based on these findings, Hearold recommends that groups and organizations currently working to pressure the television industry to remove violence from their shows due to its detrimental effects should apply an equal amount of effort to persuade industry executives to create more shows with prosocial themes.

LEARNING ABOUT THE BARRIERS TO HELPING

Regarding adults, perhaps the most disturbing set of findings discussed thus far is the tendency of bystanders to fail to act when someone is in need of help. Because emergencies are often not clearly defined as such, and because of the potential for embarrassment if one intervenes and there is no actual emergency, the presence of others inhibits prosocial responding. In light of this finding, what social changes might increase the tendency of bystanders to respond in a prosocial way when someone needs their help?

Bibb Latané, codeveloper of the bystander intervention model, believes the simplest and most direct change is to do what you have done in reading this chapter, namely, become aware of the inhibiting effects of other bystanders:

> To the extent that people become aware of the fact that the presence of others may inhibit their acting as they would want to act, they will better see the situation as it is and act the way they would like to. What can make them aware? Books. Articles. TV documentaries. Education in general. (Hunt, 1990, p. 207)

In an empirical demonstration of the empowering effects of knowledge, Arthur Beaman and his coworkers (1978) randomly assigned students to listen to either a lecture on Latané and Darley's bystander intervention research or to a topic irrelevant to helping. Two weeks later, while participating in a seemingly unrelated study, these same students walked past a person lying on the ground. A confederate who accompanied the student acted uncon-

cerned at this possible emergency. How did the students react? Only 25 percent of those not previously exposed to the bystander intervention lecture stopped to offer assistance. This low prosocial response rate is consistent with Latané and Darley's own findings. Undoubtedly, these students took their cue from their unconcerned companion and defined the situation as a nonemergency. In contrast, students who had previously learned about the paralyzing effects of fellow bystanders on the intervention process acted very differently. Forty-three percent stopped to help the person. These findings suggest that simply knowing about the social barriers to helping can free one from their antisocial effects.

Jane Piliavin, codeveloper of the arousal: cost-reward model, believes that in addition to this knowledge-created awareness of the social dynamics of emergency situations, we must also understand that in our individualistic society we have been socialized to leave people alone and to mind our own business. Such training can effectively inhibit intervention:

> In our society, we are trained from an early age to see the problems of other people as "none of our business," to close our feelings off from others' experiences. We have only recently "discovered" child abuse, spouse abuse, incest, and other family "traditions" because of the sanctity of the home and respect for others' privacy. This tendency saves all of us a great deal of emotional distress, but it contributes to the bureaucratization of helping in our society and, we believe, to the increasing alienation and self-absorption of which we all are currently being accused. We may need more training as busybodies; respect for privacy prevents empathic arousal, and directs one's attention to the costs of intervention, specifically the cost of being thought "intrusive." (Piliavin et al., 1981, p. 254)

Piliavin and her colleagues state that in classes in which they have discussed the social psychological research and theories of helping, students repeatedly report an increased attentiveness and responsiveness to emergencies. In a very real and important sense, then, making people aware of the social dynamics of emergencies and the inhibiting effects of socialization may be an important key to unlocking people's prosocial tendencies.

FEATURED STUDY

PRIOR EXPERIENCE WITH A NEED AND EMPATHY

Batson, C. D., Sympson, S. C., Hindman, J. L., Decruz, P., Todd, R. M., Weeks, J. L., Jennings, G., & Burris, C. T. (1996). "I've been there, too": Effect on empathy of prior experience with a need. *Personality and Social Psychology Bulletin, 22,* 474–482.

In attempting to better understand how willingness to help those in need can be increased, researchers have increasingly studied situations that evoke empathic responding. Within popular culture, there is a commonly expressed belief that a past experience with a need facilitates, or even creates, empathy for other people experiencing that need. To what degree is this true? The purpose of the present investigation was to provide evidence concerning the effect of prior experience on empathy. In two separate studies, researchers tested the hypothesis that prior experience with a given need will lead to increased feelings of empathy when witnessing another person experiencing that need. Study 2 is described in the following sections.

METHOD

Volunteers were eighty-eight introductory psychology students (forty-eight women, forty men) who earned partial course credit for their participation. The researchers told participants they wanted them to help select materials for use in a study of esteem-threatening life events during adolescence. This cover story allowed researchers to ask participants to read and react to transcripts of a same-sex adolescent's description of a stressful life event. Half the participants read about an adolescent's experience with severe acne, while the other half read about an adolescent's experience being rejected by a long-term dating partner. These two esteem-threatening events were chosen because it was anticipated that a substantial percentage of the participants would have had similar prior life experiences. None of the participants indicated any suspicion about the cover story.

After reading the transcript, participants indicated on a questionnaire the degree to which they were experiencing various empathic emotions (for example, *softheartedness, tenderness, compassion*) as a result of what they read. These ratings of emotions were used as the dependent measure of experienced empathy. A background questionnaire also assessed whether participants had had a similar experience to the one they had read about, and if so, how stressful had it been. After completing the questionnaires, participants were debriefed. Some of the debriefings were lengthy because participants wanted to talk about their own prior stressful experiences. No participants appeared upset with these recollections.

RESULTS AND DISCUSSION

The results of Study 2 were very similar to those of Study 1. Among women, reported similarity of prior experience was highly correlated with reported empathy ($r = .53$). However, no such significant correlation was found for men ($r = .06$). In other words, these findings provide support for the hypothesis that prior experience with a need increases empathy for another experiencing that need, but only among women.

What might explain these gender differences in empathic responding? The researchers suggest that it might reflect a difference in how males and females have been socialized to respond to esteem-threatening experiences. That is, girls in North American culture are socialized to value *emotional relatedness* to others, causing them to deal with suffering by moving toward others and seeking social support. In contrast, boys are socialized to devalue emotional expression, and instead, value *independence* and *self-defense.* This causes them to deal with suffering by pulling away from others. The researchers recommend further studies to more fully test this gender socialization explanation.

 WEB SITES accessed through http://www.mhhe.com/franzoi2

Web sites for this chapter focus on research and theory on helping, including how to raise children to be more altruistic and personal lifestories of people who help others.

American Psychological Association

The American Psychological Association has a web page which offers suggestions on how to raise children to be more altruistic, and supports the suggestion with relevant theories.

Giraffe Project Heroes Program

This web site highlights the personal life stories of people who stick their necks out for the common good.

CHAPTER 14

THE PERSONAL RELEVANCE OF SOCIAL PSYCHOLOGY

CHAPTER OUTLINE

hortly after 6 p.m. on September 5, 1993, a nude man was seen running through Cornell University's campus. Suddenly, he stopped at the College Avenue Bridge and began climbing over the railing so that he could jump into the deep gorge below. Yet before he could commit suicide, some students grabbed and held him to the ground until police arrived. Although hundreds of people saw him run past and head toward the bridge, only a handful chose to intervene. These Good Samaritans later admitted that they might not have helped if not for the quick thinking of Gretchen Goldfarb. "Something just clicked," Goldfarb said, in explaining how she realized that this was an emergency and not simply a prank. What was it that "clicked" in her mind? Social psychological knowledge. A few days earlier, she had learned in her psychology class about Darley and Latané's bystander intervention research (see chapter 13, pp. 492–498), which demonstrated that people will often not help in emergencies unless someone first takes action. Armed with this knowledge, she admonished fellow bystanders to grab the man. In that moment, her application of social psychological knowledge played a pivotal role in saving a life.[1]

Social psychology is a scientific discipline that studies how we, as individuals, are influenced by other people. Wherever and whenever we associate with others, or even think about interacting, social psychological processes come into play. Because of the fact that the *social* is such a crucial dimension of our existence, social psychology holds out the promise that it can answer some fundamental questions concerning what it means to be a person in a particular situation. The possibility that a social psychology course can reveal insights into our everyday lives is undoubtedly one of its primary attractions on college campuses. The application of these insights may seldom have as dramatic effects as Gretchen Goldfarb experienced, but it can enhance the quality of your life. Throughout this book, I have sprinkled questionnaires for you to answer and score in the hopes that this exercise would help you to not only better understand the nature of social behavior, but also yourself as a social creature. Now that you have reviewed the discipline as a whole, how will you use this knowledge in your everyday living?

PERCEIVING PEOPLE AND EVENTS

One of the great gifts you have as a member of the human species is that you can psychologically step outside yourself and contemplate what and who you are. Think about this a minute. Because of your ability to engage in self-awareness, you can reflect on your actions, contemplate possible future realities, and change your behavior to bring you closer to a reality you desire. As a self-reflective creature, you have the ability to actively create and re-create yourself and your social world. Of course, this construction is not undertaken by you alone. It is a *social construction* in the truest sense. Look again at your responses to the Twenty Statements Test that opened chapter 2. These are the things with which you emotionally identify. By examining them you will better understand what constitutes the important elements of your self-concept. How far away are these elements from your ideal self?

[1]Thank you to Professor Ken Savitsky at Williams College for relating this story to me.

Research suggests that there are two basic self-motives, namely, the desire to enhance self-esteem and the desire to verify self-concept. When given praise that contradicts your self-concept, how do you typically resolve the conflict? Are you receptive to revising your self-beliefs upward (*self-enhancement*), or do you feel more comfortable rejecting the praise (*self-verification*)? Similarly, are you willing to put your self-esteem on the line to achieve success in some area of your life, or do you tend to treat your self-esteem as an endangered resource that you must protect at all costs? These are important questions, for they will shape your life decisions. If you consistently shy away from risks that hold the possibility of enticing rewards, in the short run you may guard against self-esteem threats due to failure. However, over time, you will lose opportunities to experience self-enhancing grand success. In contrast, every time you take risks and succeed, you reduce your self-discrepancies and move closer to realizing your ideal self.

Your self-esteem can also be reinforced by associating yourself with others' successes. In a psychological sense, those others with whom you strongly identify are part of your self-concept. When you judge their actions, you tend to ascribe their positive behaviors to internal factors and their negative behaviors to external factors. In so doing, you can "bask in the reflected glory" of their accomplishments and experience some self-esteem benefits. Which route to self-esteem enhancement do you typically take? Do you prefer being the active risk-taker or do you prefer hooking your self-esteem to someone else's success? Although you can certainly take both routes, your self-esteem is most likely to benefit from your own accomplishments.

SELF-PRESENTATION AND SOCIAL PERCEPTION

You are probably familiar with William Shakespeare's line, "All the world's a stage, and all the men and women merely players." Regardless of how devoted you are to wearing the "masks" of social interaction, while on stage you undoubtedly endeavor to maintain competent and appropriate self-presentations. What strategic self-presentations are you most comfortable employing in your everyday interactions? Self-promotion? Modesty? Ingratiation? Are these the same self-presentations you prefer others to employ? Remember, there is nothing necessarily unsavory about strategic self-presentations—we all use them, especially when interacting with strangers or casual acquaintances. How do you think your own upbringing—perhaps your parents' influence and your gender learning—shaped your preferences for certain self-presentation strategies?

Although we all play roles on the social stage, some of us live according to this metaphor with greater "due diligence" than others. Return now to the *Self-Monitoring* items listed on p. 81. Does your behavioral style run more toward the low or high end of this trait? Have you ever thought that your level of self-monitoring might make you better suited for certain types of careers over others? Actually, it appears that those high in self-monitoring prefer jobs with clearly defined occupational roles, while low self-monitors prefer occupational roles coinciding with their own attitudes and beliefs so they can "be themselves" on the job (Snyder & Gangestad, 1982). This finding suggests that high self-monitors may be more willing to mold and shape themselves "to fit" their chosen occupational roles than low self-monitors. Careers in law, politics, public relations, and the theater—where social chameleon abilities are often necessary—may be particularly attractive to them. Another type of job that is uniquely suited to the skills of the high self-monitor are the so-called boundary spanning jobs in which individuals must interact and communicate effectively with two or more parties who, because of their conflicting interests, often cannot deal directly with one another (Caldwell & O'Reilly, 1982). In such work settings, high self-monitors are less likely than low self-monitors to allow their personal feelings to affect their social interactions. Examples of boundary spanning jobs would be the mediator in a dispute between management and labor, a real estate agent who negotiates the transfer of property from seller to buyer, or a university administrator who deals with students, faculty, and alumni.

As an actor on the social stage, you are also assessing your fellow actors while simultaneously trying to make sense of the play. In forming personality impressions,

You are both an actor and the audience on the social interaction stage. To what degree are you going to use the knowledge you have learned from the discipline of social psychology to help create the social reality you desire?

you learned in chapter 3 that there appears to be operating a principle of *evaluative consistency*—a tendency to view others in a way that is internally consistent. As a result, you may often assume that all good traits occur together in persons and that all bad traits do so as well, with little overlap between the two. This tendency to organize your understanding of others' personalities around this consistency principle often leads to faulty impressions.

You also learned how we explain the unfolding of behavior and events in our world. This tendency to emphasize internal causes over external causes when explaining others' actions is more common among those of us with an individualist rather than a collectivist orientation. Which orientation dominates your view of social life? For most of us, individualism significantly shapes our thinking due to our cultural upbringing, but review again your responses to the "Values Hierarchy Exercise" on p. 18. Members of individualist cultures not only give people too much credit for good things that happen to them, but also too much blame for the bad things that come their way. Put simply, they seek too many answers in people's personalities. This *fundamental attribution error* generally does not extend to explaining one's own actions. Instead, individualists tend to blame their setbacks and failures on external causes, while taking credit for positive behaviors and events. Although these *self-serving biases* provide us with a less-than-accurate view of ourselves, they do help us maintain high self-esteem so that we remain optimistic about the possibility of future success. Thus, positive self-illusions can be beneficial.

SOCIAL COGNITION

As a social thinker, you and those with whom you interact are remarkably flexible, choosing among multiple strategies based on your current goals, motives, and needs. For instance, if your primary goal in a given situation is to make accurate social judgments, you will probably carefully assess information. However, if you need to make a quick decision, if you are overloaded with information or have little information at all, or if the issue in question is not that important to you, you will probably take cognitive shortcuts. One of the best-known shortcuts is *stereotyping*. Although stereotyping is often beneficial because it is fast and allows you to redirect your energies to other tasks, the cost is that you may often make faulty judgments about whomever you stereotype. Because of this increased potential for error, should you avoid these mental shortcuts when judging events? Often, that's simply not a viable option. Sometimes you have to make snap judgments and cannot engage in logical analysis. At other times, the available information is so unreliable, biased, and incomplete that a rational analysis is not possible. In such situations, economical thinking may save the day.

In the final analysis, your social judgments should not be expected to be any more accurate or efficient than your self-judgments. Just as you probably have a need for consistency when assessing your own self-beliefs, you also express that need in your social judgments. When faced with contradictory information, your inclination is to distort or explain away the contradictions. Further, your expectations about how the world operates and who you and others are as individuals often become the blueprint in defining social reality. Among these expectations is a tendency to believe that others think and behave as you do (*false consensus*), a tendency to think and behave in ways that verify your beliefs (*confirmation bias* and *self-fulfilling prophecies*), and a tendency to believe that the world is fair (*just-world belief*). These distortions may well have functional value, allowing you to maintain a sense of optimism about your social performance, the competency of your fellow actors, and the worthiness of the play itself.

EVALUATING YOUR SOCIAL WORLD

Based on your responses to the *Need to Evaluate Scale* (p. 150), are you the type of person who forms opinions about everything, or are there many things for which you do not have a preference? On what basis do you form your attitudes?

ATTITUDES

Like everyone else, you develop positive attitudes toward those things that are rewarding and negative attitudes toward those things that are punishing. Yet prior to reading this book, were you aware that simply being repeatedly exposed to something can lead you to like it more? This *mere exposure effect* does not require any action on your part, nor does it require the development of any beliefs about the object. What about the value-expressive nature of your attitudes? Do you cherish certain possessions because they reflect something about who you are as a person? Or are you more practical, basing most of your attitudes on the usefulness of objects? Pay attention to the product advertisements you see on television or read in magazines: they are often tailored to appeal to either your value-expressive or utilitarian desires. In addition, they all are repeatedly thrust into your awareness to cash in on the mere exposure effect.

Just as you tend to seek consistency when forming impressions of people's personalities, you also may seek consistency between your thoughts and behavior. This need for consistency sometimes leads you to develop attitudes that appear— to an outside observer—to be based on irrational thinking. *Cognitive dissonance theory* asserts that when you have a bad experience with some "thing" you have freely chosen, you may try to convince yourself that the bad experience was really good in order to reduce your distress. Thus, you convince yourself that you really do like the "thing" that any rational person should dislike. The greater the investment, the greater your need to rationalize your situation. The bad investment could be an oppressive job that you've worked hard to attain, a new car plagued with problems, or an emotionally abusive romantic relationship. Do you know people who stay in unhealthy relationships because they cannot admit to themselves that they made a mistake? You will be faced with bad investments a number of times in your own life. Knowing the psychological dynamics underlying such situations may not ease your pain, but it can help you to make wiser choices.

PERSUASION

Although attitude research suggests that you may sometimes deceive yourself when evaluating personally important things in your life, in general, you want to be correct in your attitudes. What this means is that you can be persuaded to change your attitudes, and you can persuade others to do the same. In this persuasion process, you sometimes carefully analyze information and behave in a systematic and rational fashion; at other times, you try to save time by taking mental shortcuts. This "thoughtful" versus "lazy" way of thinking is what comprises two very different routes to persuasion. When motivated and able to think carefully about the content of a message (high elaboration), you are likely to be influenced by the strength and quality of the arguments; that is, you take the *central route to persuasion.* However, when unable or unwilling to analyze message content, you probably take the *peripheral route to persuasion,* where you pay attention to cues that are irrelevant to the content or quality of the communication (low elaboration), such as the attractiveness of the communicator or the sheer amount of information presented. By attending to these peripheral cues, you can evaluate a message without engaging in any extensive thinking.

Although evaluating things without thinking about them is definitely a quality we all possess, it isn't one that too many of us brag about. As stated in chapter 6, if attitudes are like houses, then attitudes formed by the peripheral route are like houses made from straw or sticks. They require little effort to develop and are extremely vulnerable to destruction. In contrast, attitudes formed by the central route are like houses made of bricks. They take a good deal of effort to construct and are strong and durable.

While it is true that, on any given topic, you might take the central or peripheral route to persuasion, another nugget of knowledge mined through social psychological research is that people vary in their *need for cognition.* What did your own responses to the Need for Cognition Scale (p. 212) suggest about your desire for critical thinking? Is it high or low on your personal priority list? There is nothing necessarily wrong with what we call "lazy" thinking. The ability to make quick decisions without carefully analyzing all the facts is critical to our survival. Similarly, being able to take mental shortcuts, to rely on hunches, and to even act on beliefs derived from group stereotypes can be useful at times. Yet, effortful, careful thinking is also an essential human feature, and it is especially important when the personal stakes are high and you have enough time to analyze the information before you. If you tend to be a less effortful thinker, this does not mean that you cannot engage in critical thinking, but rather, that you simply do not do it as often as many other people.

PREJUDICE AND DISCRIMINATION

Perhaps the most sinister type of attitudes are those based on *prejudice,* not simply because they involve a negative evaluation of an entire group of people, but because they also often lead to *discrimination.* Did you recall any expressions of prejudice on your own part while reading chapter 7? If so, were you able to identify the social and psychological factors that shaped your prejudice? If you have been the target of intolerance, how have you responded? Anger and opposition? Anxiety and insecurity?

If you have been the target of biased evaluations due to prejudice, it is important to understand the negative impact this can have on your life choices. As an example of subtle bias, consider gender studies that find that a woman's success on a masculine task tends to be attributed not to her ability, but to the ease of the task or to her extreme effort (Swim et al., 1989; Swim & Sanna, 1996). The more masculine the task, the more likely it is that a woman's performance will be devalued (Eagly et al., 1992; Foschi, 1996). Thus, if a female computer programmer can identify and neutralize a computer virus as quickly as her male coworkers, it generally will take longer for her skills to be recognized relative to her male peers. No similar bias is found for men's successes on feminine tasks. Despite the fact that these gender-based evaluation biases are relatively small, Janet Swim and Lawrence Sanna (1996) contend that these small effects could accumulate over time, and that the lifetime effect may significantly influence women's life choices. Support for this possibility comes from self-attribution studies indicating that although boys and men explain their own successful performances relatively more in terms of ability, girls and women tend to explain their successes more in terms of luck (Burgner & Hewstone, 1993; Wang & Creedon, 1989). Further research indicates that these gender differences in performance self-attributions are limited only to masculine tasks and do not occur for feminine and neutral tasks (Beyer & Bowden, 1997). Together, what these studies suggest is that even subtle manifestations of prejudicial bias can discourage otherwise talented people from following up their successes with even greater challenges.

UNDERSTANDING YOUR PLACE WITHIN THE GROUP

You are a unique individual in your own right, but you are most certainly a creature of the group. In a psychological sense, you are not fully mature until you have internalized the group into your everyday thinking. An important aspect of group living is the process of *social influence*. When faced with uncertainty about how to accurately interpret or judge events in your life, you are particularly susceptible to others' influence, especially if they appear confident. Likewise, the need to belong is a powerful, fundamental, and extremely pervasive motivation "pulling" you into others' orbits of influence. There is nothing inherently wrong with such influence—in fact, it is the social "stitching" that organizes the fabric of everyday life. Yet, in our individualist culture, the group has often been viewed with distrust and even condescension. It is true that you can sometimes act in an inferior and impulsive manner when in a group (due to *social loafing* and *deindividuation*, respectively), but you can also exhibit similar undesirable actions when acting alone. Thus, group processes, like individual processes, are amply designed to foster both positive and negative outcomes.

SOCIAL INFLUENCE

Whatever your attitudes toward "groupy" things, there is no denying the fact that within the not-too-distant-future you will hopefully be joining a very important new group—the company or organization that will employ you in your new career. Keep in mind that this new group membership will be a dynamic process involving different phases. Can you identify the social roles that you have previously played in groups? Perhaps you were the good listener, the clown, the carefree spirit, the idea person, or the wallflower. Were these roles associated with high or low status? Are they worth trying to "import" into your future career or do you want to distance yourself from them? It is usually during the early phases of group membership (*investigation* and *socialization*) that you are in the best position to create the social roles you desire. What self-presentation and social influence strategies might help you to create these new roles? The better you understand the conditions under which you and others are more or less susceptible to social influence, the better equipped you will be to actively shape your new surroundings to your liking.

As discussed in chapter 8, most people believe that it is inconceivable that they would ever knowingly hurt another person simply because someone in authority gives an order. Was this your own conclusion after reading the Milgram studies? In pondering this question, keep in mind this relevant social psychological fact: situational pressures can simultaneously be both powerful and subtle. For example, do you recall the *foot-in-the-door* compliance technique in which the influencer secures compliance to a small request, and then later follows this with a larger, less desirable request? Besides explaining certain types of everyday compliance, the foot-in-the-door effect might help you to better understand how you might, over time and by small steps, become an instrument of destructive obedience. John Darley (1995) points out that many people who participate in horrendous acts of organized torture and murder do so after complying to small-scale aggressive requests or orders from authority figures (Darley, 1995). Once complying to these less violent requests (for example, "Deliver 15 volts of shock" or "Tie the prisoners up"), they are far more likely to agree to more demanding requests at a later time ("Deliver 350 volts!" "Hit them until they talk!"). As this "ratcheting-up" of destructive requests/orders continues, the implications of engaging in such immoral behavior is often not fully realized until it is too late.

It's quite likely that you will never be ordered to inflict physical harm on another person. Yet you will certainly be faced with decisions on whether to follow the orders, requests, or expectations of people whose intentions are less than benign. Now that you know how the social influence process operates, you are in a much better position to free yourself from its destructive elements—that is, if you take the time to critically analyze the social psychological dynamics of the situation.

Our general desire to be liked and accepted by others and our general desire to have an accurate view of things significantly shape our self-concepts, our social judgments and evaluations, our susceptibility to social influence, and our desire for affiliation. There are no "islands" where others do not affect our thoughts, feelings, and actions. In living your life, because you have no choice but to play the "social creature" game, doesn't it make sense to understand as best you can its rules and strategies?

GROUP BEHAVIOR

Beyond simply deciding whether to follow the directions of authorities or group majorities, you also have the option of trying to persuade them to change their course so that it is more in line with your own. Although you risk rejection if you defy their desires, you will be more likely to actually convert them to your way of thinking under certain conditions. These conditions are (1) when your position is not too far from their own, and (2) when you display a consistent behavioral style that is interpreted as indicating certainty and confidence. Yet, what if your own position is considerably different from the majority or those in power? Does this mean you cannot steer them toward what you believe is best for the group? Although your prospects are substantially diminished under these circumstances, you still might be able to persuade them if you try to do so in small increments over time. . . that is, if you can first plant your psychological foot firmly in their minds' door.

Finally, whenever you become involved in a group, the possibility always exists that your own personal, self-focused interests will diverge from those of the collective. In such *social dilemmas,* your short-term interests will be advanced if you act selfishly, but your long-term interests and those of the group will be advanced if you cooperate. Resolving social dilemmas—and maintaining group membership itself—may be harder for individualists than collectivists. Again, based on your responses to the "Values Hierarchy Exercise" on p. 18, do you think it would be difficult or easy for you to work to resolve social dilemmas when they arise in your own groups? If you are trying to get other group members to act more cooperatively, what actions might you take to increase your likelihood of success? As discussed on pages 343–345, social dilemmas can be resolved by (1) establishing guidelines and sanctions against self-serving behavior, (2) by getting people to understand how their actions help or hurt everyone's long-term welfare, (3) by encouraging people to develop a group identity, (4) by fostering the internalization of social values that encourage cooperation rather than competition, and (5) by promoting group discussion that leads to cooperation commitments.

INTERACTING WITH OTHERS

As you have studied social psychology, have you become aware of a recurring set of psychological principles that appear to shape people's thoughts and actions? These two psychological cousins are the general desire to be liked and accepted by others and the general desire to have an accurate view of things. They correspond to the "hot" and "cold" perspectives on the nature of human behavior first mentioned in chapter 1. You can see these two principles operating in your self-enhancement and self-verification motives, in your social judgments, and in your ability to exert and to be susceptible to social influence. These principles also shape your attraction to others. According to *social exchange theory*, you seek out and maintain those relationships that make you feel good about yourself and bring you more rewards than costs. According to *social comparison theory*, you seek out similar others for accurate comparison so that you can judge and improve yourself.

INTERPERSONAL ATTRACTION

What you have learned about the psychology of relationships should prove useful in the coming years. As you seek the company of others, remember that there is a self-fulfilling prophecy associated with the "desire to be liked" principle: if you approach new social settings thinking that others will like you, you will probably act in ways that increase the likelihood that they will indeed like you. However, if you think they will dislike you, your subsequent interaction style may fulfill the negative prophecy, even if it is based on false information.

Also keep in mind that although almost everyone experiences loneliness, your recovery often depends on how you interpret and react to its perceived causes. People who make *internal, stable attributions* for their loneliness ("I just don't know how to make new friends") tend to be chronically lonely, while those who make *external, unstable attributions* ("I'm lonely because I don't know anyone here") are generally only temporarily lonely. Of the two social realities that you could create for yourself, which one of them do you think is related to mental health? The words of advice to be gleaned from this research is that you should be careful *what* you think you are, for you will likely behave consistent with those self-beliefs.

INTIMATE RELATIONSHIPS

Regarding intimacy, some people believe that this is an area that is fruitless to scientifically study because romantic love just "happens" and cannot be rationally understood, much less consciously worked on and improved. Others worry that if you examine love too closely; you risk destroying its essential mystery and excitement. An alternative view—and one that permeates social psychology—is that love and romance are too important not to study. Through studying the patterns and dynamics of intimate relationships, you will better understand the "hows" and "whys" of human communion so that the very real pain and misery brought on by failed relationships can, in some cases, be avoided or reduced.

So what have you learned about love? In contrast to the common Hollywood depiction of passion being the cornerstone of romantic love, research clearly indicates that companionship is what best supports an enduring romantic relationship. Of course, passion is important, but its primary function is not to sustain your romantic relationship as much as it is to spark the initial attraction toward your partner. As the relationship progresses and is sustained by your mutual companionship, passion will diminish, but it will probably also sporadically reignite, reminding each of you about your sensual chemistry. Hopefully, this knowledge will inoculate you against habitually entering and leaving relationships in search of the fantasy lover whose passion never fades.

Although "true love" usually does not match the idealized Hollywood version, an important component of a satisfying, stable romantic relationship is the ability to mix positive illusion with sober reality when perceiving your partner. As with your own self-perceptions, overlooking faults and exaggerating virtues in your partner will not only satisfy the need to feel that your relationship is better than most others, but it can actually create the conditions necessary for your positive illusions to become realized. Here again is an example of how you can shape your social reality.

Although you have the power to substantially shape the course of your intimate relationships, you can run into problems if you believe that your relationships are invulnerable to outside influences (Berscheid, 1998). For example, despite the folk-saying that "no third party can break up a happy relationship," research suggests that friends' and family members' approval or disapproval of your romantic relationships will significantly determine whether they survive or fail (Sprecher & Felmlee, 1992). In addition, although you might believe that "love conquers all," numerous studies indicate that outside influences such as money problems and job stress not only promote hostility in romantic relationships, but they also make partners less emotionally supportive of one another, all of which contribute to breakups (Lynch et al., 1997).

Given the potential negative impact of certain outside influences, have you considered how you plan to balance the demands of love and family responsibilities with those of work? The amount of attention you have devoted to this question might be related to your gender socialization (Yoder & Schleicher, 1996). Young women tend to learn that their plans for work and family will be interdependent, with a great deal of trade-off occurring in how best to balance both roles. Young men, on the other hand, generally learn to view work and family decisions as independent issues (Spade & Reese, 1991; Stevens et al., 1992). How do these findings fit your own circumstances?

Interestingly, this anticipation of conflict between occupational and family goals appears to be less of an issue among Black than White college women (Bridges & Etaugh, 1994; Granrose & Cunningham, 1988). Why might this be the case? One possibility is that out of economic necessity, Black female college students are more likely to have mothers who worked outside the home. As a result, juggling these two roles seems more natural and less stressful for young African-American women than it currently does for young White American women. In the coming years, regardless of your sex or race, the way you handle work and family demands will influence the quality of your life and largely determine how the next generation views these issues.

AGGRESSION

Turning from liking and loving to hurting and helping, you have learned that prosocial and antisocial behaviors can become conditioned responses if they are repeatedly reinforced by the social environment. Although learning does occur through direct reinforcement, most learning occurs by watching and imitating others. To what degree have you observed helpful versus harmful models within your own family or among your friends? Were you aware before reading this book that observing someone being punished for aggression doesn't prevent the *learning* of aggression—it simply inhibits its *expression* in certain circumstances? What implications might this finding have for allowing children to watch violent TV shows and movies?

The more exposure people have to aggressive role models, the greater the number of detailed aggressive scripts they will encode into memory. Those with strongly developed aggressive scripts are likely to choose an aggressive solution to social conflict because it will seem to them to be the "best" and most "natural" way to respond to such circumstances. Fortunately, the same is true for helpful role models. If you desire to promote prosocial behavior in others—especially in children—you can do so by (1) becoming a prosocial model yourself and (2) monitoring their exposure to aggressive models.

Regarding monitoring your own aggression, research suggests that *hostile aggression* is often triggered by circumstances that arouse negative feelings. The stronger your negative affect, the greater your aggressive inclination. Further, even when your surroundings don't elicit negative affect, simply thinking about aggression can set you on the path to its activation. According to the *cognitive-neoassociationist model*, this type of impulsive aggression is most likely to occur when you are engaged in highly routine activities and, thus, are not consciously monitoring your thoughts, feelings, or actions. However, if these aggression-related tendencies are subjected to higher-level thinking, you can often modify and control them. What causes these aggression-related tendencies to come under the control of more complex cognitive processes? Self-awareness, one of your great human gifts. Use this gift to control your aggression. When you become angry, try to make sense of your negative feelings before reacting. Analyze the implications of your actions and consider alternative nonaggressive responses. By bringing into play these cognitive control mechanisms, the link between negative affect and aggression can be short-circuited.

PROSOCIAL BEHAVIOR

Finally, in discussing ways to increase helpful responding during emergencies, let's turn the tables a bit: what if *you* are the one who needs help? How can you use your knowledge of the *bystander intervention model* to increase the likelihood that others will assist you? Remember, deciding to intervene in a possible emergency involves a rather complex set of decisions. If bystanders make an incorrect decision at any point in this process, they will not intervene. Faced with these facts, as the victim, you must attack and neutralize the psychological factors that cause nonintervention. The first psychological hurdle is the *audience inhibition effect,* in which the fear of being negatively evaluated, combined with the tendency to look to others for further information, leads bystanders to identify emergencies as nonemergencies. As the victim, you can eliminate this inhibition by clearly letting everyone know that this is an emergency and you need help. Yet even after clearing this hurdle, you must next attack the *diffusion of responsibility,* which is bystanders' tendency to believe they are less personally responsible for helping when others are present. Here, you should implore specific people to help you, because it's hard to deny assistance when singled out of the crowd. Finally, because some people may want to help but are unsure what to do, you can overcome this last hurdle by specifically giving them instructions ("You! Call an ambulance!" You! Gather my belongings and bring them to me!"). Using your most authoritative voice will further increase obedience. And obedience is exactly what you are seeking here. In all likelihood, you probably won't need to direct everyone who is assisting you. Once you get the ball rolling, others are likely to spring into action on their own. However, the more quickly you consciously transform the social dynamics to facilitate helping, the better off you will be. Gretchen Goldfarb can attest to this social fact.

A FINAL WORD ON BEING A PERSON IN A WORLD OF GROUPS

What I hope you understand by this time is that you are a creature of your social surroundings (Miller & Prentice, 1994). Contemporary social science confirms that the group fabric of human nature is strong. Yet, within the fabric of the group, you will find the creative weaving of the many interconnected selves. This unique blending of the self with others makes up the content of social psychology. When you respond to others, you are actively creating and re-creating your social reality—yet you are often unaware of the situational forces that help shape this reality. Despite the fact that you may think of yourself as being a relatively autonomous creature, your current understanding of the social process should tell you that much of this self-perceived independence is illusory. The simple fact is that regardless of your culture of origin, you are influenced by others, both singly and collectively. One of the most important goals of social psychology as a discipline is to increase knowledge of how the person—as a self—helps to weave the fabric of group life and how the paths of these individual life threads are influenced by one another. The better you understand the complex nature and influence of the group fabric, the better you will be able to weave your own unique, yet group-influenced, patterns.

I want, by understanding myself, to understand others. I want to be all that I am capable of becoming. . . . This all sounds very strenuous and serious. But now that I have wrestled with it, it's no longer so. I feel happy—deep down. All is well.

English writer Katherine Mansfield's last journal entry, 1888–1923

THE PROFESSION OF SOCIAL PSYCHOLOGY

At this point, some of you might be wondering how people become social psychologists and where they typically find employment today. Actually, there is no simple answer to either question, but let's briefly explore the typical path to a career in social psychology.

BECOMING A SOCIAL PSYCHOLOGIST

The vast majority of today's social psychologists majored in psychology as undergraduates. In their senior year many of them then applied to graduate programs in social psychology or social/personality psychology (sometimes these two areas of study are merged). Although master's degree programs do exist, almost all psychologists who identify themselves as social psychologists have a Ph.D. Earning a doctorate in social psychology generally takes at least four years of graduate training and entails extensive coursework in theory, statistics, and research methodology.

In graduate school, budding social psychologists often begin specializing in a particular area of the discipline, such as attitude change, social influence, or self-esteem. They then create a *research program* in which hypotheses are systematically tested and theories developed or extended. The graduate student's dissertation generally represents the clearest articulation of this research program. Often the dissertation builds on the research program of the more experienced social psychologists who trained the graduate student. Once social psychologists earn a Ph.D., they either seek employment in their profession or go on for further training. This *postdoctoral training,* if pursued, is often made possible by government-sponsored research grants offered at various universities. In these postdoctoral programs, social psychologists continue to develop their research programs and gain greater expertise in their field of specialization.

WHO EMPLOYS THE SOCIAL PSYCHOLOGIST?

Although becoming an expert in one's chosen field has its own intrinsic rewards, most people would lose sight of these inner perks if there was no accompanying job. Let's spend some time on the all-important second question of employment possibilities for the social psychologist. The answer to this question depends, to a great extent, on whether the work of the social psychologist is mainly geared toward theory testing and knowledge advancement or whether it entails mostly applying such knowledge to real-life situations. As can be seen in figure 14.1, most of the social psychologists with Ph.D.s—roughly 75 percent—are employed by colleges or universities (APA Education Directorate, 1995; Stapp & Fulcher, 1981). There, social psychologists spend the majority of their time conducting basic research, teaching undergraduates about their discipline's insights, and training future social psychologists in their graduate programs. It is in these academic pursuits that the knowledge base of the field is principally developed.

Once enough has been learned about a specific topic that is relevant to current problems in society, academic social psychologists may attempt to apply this knowledge to promote human welfare. This wedding of basic and applied scientific interests and activities was first championed by Kurt Lewin in the 1940s (see chapter 1, p. 9). What he called *action research* combines basic theoretical research and social action in a coordinated program. Although in recent years academic social psychologists have shown an increased interest in such action research, in general, it does not dominate the daily schedule of the average academician.

Those social psychologists who devote most of their energies to applying their knowledge of social behavior to real-life situations are much more likely to be

FIGURE 14.1

Where Do Social Psychologists Work?

Approximately 75 percent of social psychologists with Ph.D.'s work at colleges or universities, where their duties include teaching courses in psychology and conducting basic research. Most of the remaining social psychologists are employed in business and government jobs, where their work often involves using the findings from basic research to solve real-world problems.

Source: Data from J. Stapp and R. Fulcher, "The Employment of APA Members" in *American Psychologist, 36*: 1263–1314, 1981.

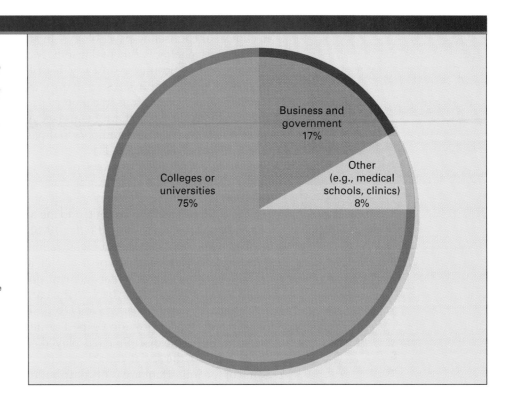

employed outside academic settings. Instead of trying to primarily develop theories of social behavior as academic social psychologists often do, nonacademic applied social psychologists typically utilize already formulated theories to effect changes in the social world (Posavec, 1992). Listed below are brief descriptions of seven of the more prominent applied areas where academic action researchers and nonacademic applied social psychologists are working and having an impact.

Crime and the legal system: Up until twenty-five years ago, the only psychologists regularly consulted by the courts were clinical psychologists (Kagehiro & Laufer, 1992). However, since the mid-1970s, an increasing number of social psychologists have studied and applied their knowledge to many different aspects of the legal system (Ellsworth & Mauro, 1998). Some of their primary areas of contribution have been in better understanding police interrogation, jury selection and decision making, eyewitness testimony, legal bargaining and negotiation, and the fairness of bail-setting and sentencing procedures (see Applications, chapters 8 and 9).

Health and health care: Most of the diseases that lead to deaths in our society are largely caused by human behaviors. As the discipline that analyzes the dynamic interplay between the person and the situation, social psychology is uniquely qualified to assist people in changing their unhealthy lifestyles (Salovey et al., 1998). Currently, social psychological work on health behavior emphasizes three different approaches: (1) applying existing theories to health problems (for example, the *theory of planned behavior,* see pp. 166–170), (2) developing new theories specifically to solve health problems (for example, *protection-motivation theory,* see p. 200) and (3) identifying specific social and personality factors that affect health (for example, *optimistic and pessimistic explanatory style,* see pp. 138–141).

Counseling and mental health: Social psychology shares a great deal of common ground with both counseling and clinical psychology. In recent years, a growing number of social psychologists have begun working with both clinical and counseling psychologists—or have actually received training in clinical or counseling psychology—in an attempt to better understand the social psychology of mental health (Moore et al., 1997; Snyder, 1997). As with general health care already described, social psychological work on mental health emphasizes applying existing theories to health problems (see Applications in chapter 2), developing new theories specifically to solve health problems (see Applications in chapter 10), and identifying specific social and personality factors that affect mental health (see Applications in chapter 11).

Organizational behavior: More than 90 percent of the people living in the United States will work for an organization during their lifetime. From personnel selection and training to leadership and labor-management relations, social psychology has greatly contributed to the understanding and improvement of organizational functioning (Pfeffer, 1998). Some of the topics studied by applied social psychologists in organizational settings involve group structure and leadership (see pp.338–342), the phases of membership (see pp. 317–319), participative management, and job satisfaction.

Education and learning: Dating back to the famous 1954 Supreme Court school desegregation case, *Brown v. Board of Education,* in which many eminent social psychologists provided expert testimony (Clark & Clark, 1947; Stephan, 1980), the discipline has played an important role in understanding the social variables that can facilitate and impede learning. Some of the important areas of contribution have been in understanding classroom self-fulfilling prophecies (see pp. 131–134), the benefits of cooperative learning (see pp. 263–266), and how to educate students with differing abilities.

Environmental effects: Largely an offshoot of social psychology, *environmental psychology* studies the interactions and relations between people and their environments (McAndrew, 1993). Traditionally, most of the work in this area has emphasized how the physical environment influences people's thoughts, feelings, and behavior (see *temperature and aggression,* pp. 447–448). However, more recent work has examined how human actions can affect the environment (refer to *social dilemmas,* pp. 343–345).

Politics and Public Policy: Social psychologists have worked to gain insight into the political process by studying such topics as political reference groups (see Applications, chapter 5), negative campaigning (see p. 90), and international negotiating. In relation to directly influencing public policy, some social psychologists adopt an *advocacy role*—speaking and working for particular social reforms—by using their expertise to mobilize legislators, courts, or disadvantaged groups to enact social changes (Lee et al., 1994). Some areas where social psychologists have attempted—with varying degrees of success—to influence public policy has been in pornography (see pp. 458–462), gun control (see p. 448), school desegregation (see pp. 260–262), and hate-crime legislation.

POSSIBLE FUTURE CONNECTIONS

Regardless of whether social psychologists work in an applied setting or a university environment, their ultimate goal is to use the scientific discipline's body of knowledge to improve the quality of people's lives. What future connections might both basic and applied social psychologists make with other disciplines, both within and outside the social and behavioral sciences? Part of Steven Breckler's job as the Social Psychology Program Director at the National Science Foundation is to try to answer this very question. Recently, he offered his observations (personal communication, October 9, 1998) concerning two very interesting new connections that are likely to develop as we enter the twenty-first century:

Social neuroscience: Social psychology is poised for increasing integrative efforts with biology. Already, evolutionary theory has made its mark on the discipline in attempting to explain various social phenomena, such as physical attractiveness standards (chapter 10, pp. 366–368), aggression (chapter 12, pp. 440–441), and helping behavior (chapter 14, pp. 482–483). Now, a handful of attitude researchers are beginning to explore how electrical activity in the brain is associated with attitude formation and change (Crites et al., 1995). Similarly, recent studies are also revealing insights into the psychobiology underlying the influences of positive affect on motivated cognition (Ashby et al., in press). This increased collaboration between social psychology and neuroscience is largely due to the development of more accurate measures of physiological changes. Although the numbers of social psychologists who pursue such research will probably be few over the next decade, the knowledge they acquire concerning the biology of social behavior will undoubtedly play a role in reshaping existing theories.

Computer science: The Internet and other electronic communication media are altering the way we interact and influence one another. Social psychological theory and research in such areas as group dynamics and interpersonal attraction will provide much needed insights into knowledge networking in the computer sciences. For example, how might access to the Internet both promote and reduce feelings of loneliness? Similarly, how can video-conferencing be made more effective? What social formats are good for such meetings? To what degree will these "virtual groups" operate according to the same social psychological principles as normal groups? Social psychologists are in a unique position to explore these questions.

As you can see, social psychology continues to expand its areas of inquiry, developing more sophisticated methods and theories that hopefully will provide greater insights into the social process. For those of you who might be interested in obtaining more information about graduate programs and career opportunities in social psychology, contact the Society for Personality and Social Psychology (SPSP) and the American Psychological Association (APA) through their web sites.

 WEB SITES accessed through http://www.mhhe.com/franzoi2

Web sites for this chapter offer information about graduate programs and career opportunities in social psychology, including typical salaries and future employment opportunities.

Society for Personality and Social Psychology (SPSP)

The Society for Personality and Social Psychology (SPSP) offers a web site for those who might be interested in obtaining more information about graduate programs and career opportunities in social psychology. Membership in SPSP is open to students as well as professionals—anyone interested in social psychology and personality is welcome to join.

American Psychological Association (APA)

The American Psychological Association offers a web page containing suggestions on career planning in psychology, including what are the typical salaries in psychology and what nonacademic careers are available to people.

A P P E N D I X   A
POSSIBLE ANSWERS FOR THE CRITICAL THINKING EXERCISES

A NOTE FROM THE AUTHOR

Appendix A contains possible answers to the critical thinking sidebars in chapters 1 to 13. In reading and comparing them with your own responses, analyze each answer's strengths and weaknesses. If you would like to help me improve my responses for the next edition, please drop me a line with your suggestions (or questions) using my e-mail address (franzois@vms.csd.mu.edu). For those critical thinking sidebar questions that asked you to provide personal recollections from your own experiences, I have understandably not provided a possible answer.

CHAPTER 1: SOCIAL PSYCHOLOGY AS A DISCIPLINE

Why do you think that some social psychologists have named Adolf Hitler as the one person who had the greatest impact on the development of social psychology?

Possible Answer: Adolf Hitler had a profound, albeit indirect, impact on the development of social psychology. As the leader of Nazi Germany during World War II, his persecution of Jews and intellectuals resulted in the mass exodus of many of Europe's leading scholars from Germany and other Nazi-occupied countries to the United States. Upon arriving in this country, these scholars exerted an immediate and lasting influence on their respective fields of study, including social psychology, which was still in its infancy as a science. Yet these refugees from Hitler's persecution not only shaped the direction and content of theory and research in social psychology. They also became mentors for many of the young American social psychologists who were able to attend college and graduate school under the G.I. Bill after serving as soldiers overseas fighting Hitler's armies. In addition, because of World War II, social psychology in the United States was able to demonstrate to the government that its theories and findings could be put to practical use in solving problems that aided the war effort against Hitler's Germany (and Japan). These wartime successes led to increased government funding of social psychological research when the war was over, which proved vital to the field's development. For these reasons, Hitler can be given indirect credit for shaping the field of social psychology.

Prior to conducting research, what precautions do you think social psychologists should take to ensure that the people who participate in their research will not be harmed? Should they be allowed to study people without their consent?

Possible Answer: Just as you can never guarantee that someone won't be hurt taking a walk around the block, you cannot guarantee that participants in a social scientific study will never be harmed. However, what you can do is examine all aspects of your study so that all reasonable precautions are taken to minimize participant risk. Whenever the choice is between securing the welfare of the study or the welfare of the participant, you must always place the participant's welfare first. This means that some studies will simply not be conducted.

In most cases, social scientists should only study people with their "informed consent," meaning that they are provided with enough information about the research to be able to make a conscious choice to participate or not. In some cases, however, it may be necessary to study people without their informed consent. For instance, when researchers study helping behavior, they may stage a fake emergency in a public setting—for example, a person collapsing on the street—and then observe the responses of bystanders. In such a natural setting, you cannot ask people for permission to include them in the study beforehand.

If you were a member of your college's institutional review board and a research proposal similar to the Milgram obedience study was submitted for approval, what questions would you ask to determine its risk/benefit ratio? Based on your assessment, would you approve the study?

Possible Answer: Using the risk/benefit ratio, you would weigh the potential risks to the participants against the study's potential benefits to society, with greater weight given to the participants' welfare. While assessing a Milgram-type study proposal, you might ask whether there was any other way the researchers could conduct the study to minimize participant stress. In essence, because of the deception being used, full informed consent could not be obtained. As such, you might ask the researchers whether they were going to let the participants know up front that they could not reveal all the details of the purpose and procedures to be used in the study. You might also ask the researchers how they would respond to a participant who asked them to stop the study. Would they stop the study after the first request? Because of the deception and the destructive obedience that is being studied, you would probably also ask the researchers to specifically detail their debriefing procedures, because these would need to be as sensitive and detailed as possible. You might also require follow-up interviews with participants to determine whether there were any delayed stress responses and further require that free counseling opportunities with a mental health professional be made available to participants if they wanted to discuss their research experience.

Would you approve a Milgram-type study? You might decide to do so only if it was seeking to shed light on an aspect of obedience that had not already been investigated. Given the fact that there already have been a number of Milgram obedience replications, you might find it difficult to justify approving another replication of the original study given the possible harm to participants. However, in considering your own answer to this question, keep in mind the following thought: the decision not to grant a request to conduct research on a particular topic also has ethical implications. If you do not allow certain research to be conducted because the behavior in question is socially undesirable or destructive when it naturally occurs in the "real world," the social sciences are likely to have crucial gaps in their knowledge base, and these gaps may prevent scientists from developing useful intervention strategies to lessen people's future suffering. What will be potentially lost by not allowing this study to go forward? These are just a few of the tough questions that you would grapple with as a member of an Institutional Review Board.

Chapter 2: The Self

According to the strength model of self-regulation, when would a parent or a spouse be most likely to engage in domestic violence due to losing control of their emotions?

Possible Answer: According to this theory, each act of self-regulation depletes the limited energy available for this purpose. Thus, immediately after exercising self-regulation in one activity, people will find it harder to regulate their behavior in an unrelated activity. From this perspective, domestic violence is most likely to occur when self-regulatory resources have been recently depleted. Thus, when abusers have just finished controlling or regulating their behavior—for example, working hard to prepare a meal when they would rather be relaxing, or holding their temper in check when talking to their employer on the phone—they are more susceptible to not being able to control their aggressive tendencies toward family members.

How would you design a study, using Markus's "me"/"not me" response format, to document the disappearance of a specific self-schema—say "sexiness"—from people's self-concept along the lines of James's notion of emotional identification? Would this be a longitudinal study or would you instead test people of different age groups?

Possible Answer: You could first identify young adult participants who were either schematic or aschematic for this particular self-attribute and then periodically test their response latencies for sexiness-related words that were embedded within a long list of nonrelated words. You might also test their recall of past incidents in which they acted in a sexy manner. Of course, this memory probing would also have to be embedded within many other memory probes in order not to raise participants' suspicions about all these "sexiness" questions. This retesting could be done over the course of many years, and you might hypothesize that the latencies would become longer and the recall of incidents more infrequent as they age. Given the amount of time, money, and energy necessary to conduct such a longitudinal study, you might decide to go forward with this project only if it was part of a much larger study of these individuals involving other research hypotheses so that you would get more of a "return" on your research investment.

A far simpler study could be conducted using what is called a cross-sectional design, in which you simultaneously test participants from different age groups. You might simply hypothesize that young adult participants would be more self-schematic for "sexiness" than older adults. The problem with this cross-sectional design is that you probably would have a harder time interpreting your results compared with the previously described longitudinal format. For instance, if you did find evidence to support your hypothesis, it might be difficult to determine whether this effect was due to age differences or generational differences. Is it that people's emotional identification with "sexiness" lessens with age, or is it perhaps that the elderly grew up in a time where "sexiness" was associated with sinfulness, and thus, they were much less likely to emotionally identify with it than young adults today? Teasing apart these two possibilities is much harder in a cross-sectional study.

Ask your grandparents (or others in this age group) to complete the TST and then code their responses. If "social self" descriptions dominate their responses, is this consistent with the "historical effects" hypothesis? How might their age—that is, their current point in the life cycle—account more for their responses than *when* they were born?

Possible Answer: Louis Zurcher hypothesized that a shift in young adults' self-concepts from the social self to the attributive self occurred in the United States due to widespread cultural changes and upheavals beginning in the mid-1960s. For most of you, your grandparents were young adults before the 1960s. If Zurcher's historical effects hypothesis is true, and your grandparents were less affected by these historical forces, then "social self" descriptions may still dominate their TST responses.

However, you could also argue that there will be an age effect working here as well. That is, as people become elderly, a number of their social roles "die" or become "inactive" (for example, employee, boss, son/daughter), which may result in "social self" descriptions actually declining on the elderly's TSTs. Because I don't think anyone has conducted a study to explore this particular issue, we're only dealing with educated guesses here.

If your ethnic heritage is relevant to who you think you are, what stage are you at in Phinney's model? Is this model an accurate portrayal of your own ethnic identity development?

This answer will be unique to your personal experiences.

CHAPTER 3: SELF-PRESENTATION AND SOCIAL PERCEPTION

Of the different self-presentation strategies that you employed today, under what circumstances and with whom were they used? Which ones achieved the desired effect? Was there one strategy that you frequently employed? If you didn't use any, why was this the case?

This answer will be unique to your personal experiences.

How might an evolutionary theorist explain the gender differences in decoding nonverbal communication? That is, from an evolutionary perspective, why would it be more beneficial for females than males to have good nonverbal skills?

Possible Answer: *According to the evolutionary perspective, human beings, along with all other species on the planet, have evolved in ways that maximize the chances of their genes being passed on to their offspring so that these gene traits survive from generation to generation. Because only women could bear and breast-feed infants, evolutionary theorists contend that they evolved to take on the more nurturing and empathic role of domestic caretaker. To be a good nurturer of infants who cannot yet convey their desires through spoken language, being very attentive to nonverbal signals of sickness or distress would be very beneficial. Thus, women who were nonverbally skilled would be most likely to have offspring who survived through this vulnerable age period. Over thousands of generations, a sex difference may have emerged based on this natural selection pressure on women.*

Why might someone argue that correspondent inference theory would not have been developed in a collectivist culture? Put another way, what individualist assumption is at the core of this theory?

Possible Answer: *A correspondent inference is an inference that the action of an actor corresponds to, or is indicative of, a stable personal characteristic. In developing correspondent inference theory, Jones and Davis assumed that people have a preference for explaining people's behavior in terms of their personalities, and that external attributions are merely default options, made only when internal causes cannot be found. This assumption makes perfect sense in an individualist culture, in which people are socialized to think of themselves and others as personally controlling their own actions, and that their rights and desires are at least as important as those of the group. Yet in a collectivist culture, where people are socialized to think first about the rights and desires of the group, it's likely that much greater attention would be paid to external causes of behavior than in an individualist culture. Because of these differences in cultural orientation, it's likely that correspondent inference theory would not have been developed in a collectivist culture.*

CHAPTER 4: SOCIAL COGNITION

What could you actively do to prevent other-sex individuals from negatively stereotyping you, knowing in advance of interacting with them that they are members of a group widely known to hold negative stereotypes toward your sex?

Possible Answer: *In a situation where your sex is in the numerical minority, you will not only receive a lot of attention, but you also are more likely to be evaluated in a gender-stereotypical fashion. In this particular situation, the people you will meet already are known to gender stereotype, so you will be fighting an uphill battle to defuse negative stereotypes. What you do know is that individuals whose physical and/or behavioral characteristics do not closely match their culture's prototype for their sex are less likely to be gender stereotyped. So you might wear clothes inconsistent with gender stereotypes: this will be easier to do for women than men, because there are a greater array of traditional and nontraditional clothes available to women. You might also let those in attendance know ahead of time, perhaps by some strategic self-disclosures, that your interests and hobbies are inconsistent with gender stereotypes (for example, football and fishing for women, cooking and modern dance for men). When you arrive at the gathering, you might also bring with you members of your own sex who also do not fit cultural gender stereotypes to further dampen stereotype activation.*

Can you explain how the shared distinctiveness hypothesis might help in understanding why many non-Blacks overestimate the percentage of crime committed by African Americans relative to their own race?

Possible Answer: *In real life, negative events such as crime occur less frequently than positive or neutral events, and thus, they are high in distinctiveness. In addition, African Americans are a minority group, and as such, they too are highly distinct relative to White Americans. When news reports describe African Americans being arrested for crimes, these two bits of information command greater attention and may be remembered more clearly due to their shared distinctiveness. It is the greater ease in recalling such negative incidents involving African Americans that may lead to the overestimation of crime in the Black community.*

Can you think of personal life situations in which the false consensus effect contributed to either misunderstandings and conflicts between you and other people or smoother interactions?

Possible Answer: *The tendency to believe that your own traits, actions, and choices are more common than they really are is known as the false consensus effect. Some possible social misunderstandings due to the false consensus effect might involve angry responses from others due to you acting on your assumptions that most people you meet share your political or social attitudes and beliefs. However, it is also possible that, due to your false consensus assumptions, you act more warm and personable toward others, which results in them responding in kind. If the truth about the false consensus is not discovered, your false assumptions would promote smooth interactions.*

CHAPTER 5: ATTITUDES

Which values on the Values Hierarchy questionnaire were more important for you? Can you identify ways in which these values have influenced your attitudes and behavior?

This answer will be unique to your personal experiences.

Is there any wisdom in parents admonishing their children to straighten their posture and to avoid slouching? How might the manner in which parents try to correct slouching destroy these possible benefits?

Possible Answer: *Yes there is, because studies suggest that upright postures cannot only cause you to feel happier, but they can also cause you to have a more favorable attitude toward things in general. Yet these are subtle effects and could be easily destroyed by parents forcing their children to engage in this behavior. In such instances, the feeling of children that their parents are trying to control their behavior may well be sufficient to create the exact opposite mood! Thus, to capitalize on these positive posture effects, parents should steer clear of orders and threats.*

What are some possible confounding variables in the LaPiere study?

Possible Answer: *One problem with the LaPiere study was that the behavioral measures of actually serving the Chinese couple when they showed up at managers' doorsteps created a conflict between the managers' positive attitudes toward making money versus their negative attitudes toward serving Chinese. In contrast, the previously obtained self-report measures concerning whether the managers would serve Chinese presented no such conflict for them because it was simply a hypothetical situation. Another possible problem was that LaPiere did not know whether the person who responded to the mailed questionnaire was the same person who decided whether to serve LaPiere's Chinese companions when they arrived at the manager's place of business.*

CHAPTER 6: PERSUASION

Advertisers design their ads to capitalize on the similarity effect. Did you observe differences in the way women and men are portrayed in TV ads that correspond to this effect?

Possible Answer: *Even with the more balanced portrayal of the two sexes in TV commercials today, they are still constructed in ways that reinforce the image of gender most familiar to and comfortable for their target audience at a particular time of the day. For example, R. Stephen Craig (1992) found that daytime ads, which are typically aimed at the female homemaker, focus on images of the traditional American household, with the wife taking care of the domestic family needs and the husband holding a position of authority at home and at the office. In contrast, weekend commercials targeted at the male sports viewer frequently exclude women and children altogether. These ads— dominated by alcohol and automotive products—stress traditional stereotypes of masculinity, such as the importance of being strong, daring, rugged, independent, and competitive. When women do appear in weekend commercials, they are generally portrayed in either subservient roles to men (for example, secretary or flight attendant) or as sexual objects. The traditional gender stereotyping in daytime and weekend commercials stands in sharp contrast to those shown during the evening and geared toward dual-career couples and single working women. Here, women are more likely to be portrayed in positions of authority and in settings away from home than they are in daytime ads. Men, in contrast, are more likely to be portrayed as a parent or spouse, and more in settings at home than they are on weekend TV. Thus, Craig's analysis suggests that how men and women are portrayed in North American TV ads today depends on who is watching. Evening commercials represent a more sophisticated and balanced portrayal of gender roles, but daytime and weekend ads reflect more traditional orientations.*

Why is it that when radio lottery advertisers are trying to persuade you to spend your money they speak at a normal rate of speed, yet when they convey the odds of winning their speech rate dramatically increases? Are they simply trying to save money by cutting down on the length of the commercial, or is there an equally important reason for this shift to fast-paced speech?

Possible Answer: *Although research indicates that fast talkers are generally more persuasive than slow talkers due to listeners' impressions that they are more credible, this is not why fast talking is used when announcing the odds of winning. Instead, a message that is presented very quickly is difficult to process and critically analyze, and this is exactly what the advertisers are counting on. They don't want listeners to elaborate on the message that their chances of winning the lottery are about equal to the likelihood that they will be struck by lightning while sitting in their living rooms!*

If the hypothesis is correct that the greater attitude change among the young isn't due to an age difference in openness to change, but rather is due to young adults encountering more negative experiences than their elders, does this change any conclusions that we drew from the Bennington College study?

Possible Answer: *The Bennington College study demonstrated the important role that reference groups can play in attitude formation and attitude endurance. Although Duane Alwin and his colleagues (1991) asserted that their Bennington College findings were consistent with the "impressionable years" hypothesis, these findings are also consistent with the more recent "negative experiences" hypothesis. Whether inducements to change attitudes are from greater impressionability among young adults or from greater negative experiences they encounter does not change the basic conclusions regarding the importance of reference groups in attitude formation and endurance.*

CHAPTER 7: PREJUDICE AND DISCRIMINATION

What do you think are the stereotypes associated with Anglo-Whites, Asians, Blacks, Jews, and Latinos in North American culture? Does your knowledge of these stereotypes tell us anything about your degree of prejudice toward these racial and ethnic groups?

Racial and Ethnic Stereotypes

Anglo-Whites	Asians	Blacks	Jews	Latinos
ambitious	hardworking	lazy	ambitious	lazy
intelligent	intelligent	ignorant	intelligent	ignorant
conceited	quiet	loud	pushy	loud
prejudiced	law-abiding	athletic	dishonest	proud
selfish		stupid	greedy	emotional
cruel		rhythmic	clannish	rude
industrious		funny		aggressive
nervous		criminal		inefficient
sly		hostile		unreliable
corrupt		corrupt		family-oriented
rich		poor		poor
greedy		friendly		messy

Sources: Allen, 1996; Fiske, 1998; Krueger, 1996; Mackie et al., 1996; Wuthrow, 1982.

Possible Answer: *Sometimes, people will deny knowledge of negative stereotypes of other groups out of fear that admitting to such knowledge is a sign of their own personal prejudice toward these groups. However, by itself, knowledge of these stereotypes tells us nothing about a person's degree of prejudice toward these racial and ethnic groups. Indeed, due to its personal relevance, you may have more extensive knowledge about the negative stereotypes associated with your own group than any other groups.*

Can you think of a negative stereotype about White males that might cause them to experience stereotype threat in a particular area of pursuit, thereby motivating them to disidentify with this activity?

Possible Answer: *A common negative stereotype about White males is that they do not have the physical skills to compete against Black males in certain sports, such as basketball. This was the primary theme in the movie White Men Can't Jump. When competing against Black basketball players, White players may become aware of this negative stereotype, experience stereotype threat, and underperform. One consequence of regularly experiencing this particular stereotype threat is that an increasing number of White males appear to have disidentified with basketball and chosen to identify with and participate in other sports, such as soccer. In other words, they changed their self-concept so that achievement in basketball was no longer very important to their self-esteem. Of course, this disidentification process does not have the negative impact on White males' future career prospects as does many Black males' disidentification with academic achievement. Why? Because basketball performance, unlike academic performance, is seldom associated with career success in adulthood.*

How would social identity theory explain the relationship between "pride" and "prejudice"?

Possible Answer: *There is a positive correlation between pride and prejudice. To indirectly increase or protect our own self-esteem, we try to bask in the reflected glory of our own group's esteem. To increase this group esteem, we may disparage and discriminate against other groups whose successes might reflect negatively on our own group's accomplishments. This intergroup process is psychologically identical to what we do in our interpersonal relationships when our friends are competing against other people for material and social rewards. In judging the competition, we tend to highlight our friends'* good points and their competitors' bad points, while downplaying or forgetting our friends' bad points and their competitors' good points. In both cases, the result is that we actively construct a negative bias against other groups and individuals whose successes might indirectly threaten our own self-esteem.*

Do you automatically imagine that popular songs are about other-sex love? If you do, does this tell us anything about your level of heterosexism? How do you react to these lyrics when you imagine that they are about same-sex love? If you regularly imagine that popular songs involve same-sex love, does this usually take more cognitive effort on your part?

Possible Answer: *Whether or not you automatically imagine the lyrics of romantic songs are about heterosexual love tells us little, if anything, about your level of heterosexism. Instead, regardless of your sexual orientation, such imagining simply illustrates how our culture is dominated by heterosexual assumptions about romantic relationships. Yet, it's likely that how you react to imagining homosexual romance in these same lyrics does provide some indication of your level of heterosexism. Given the fact that heterosexual romantic love is our cultural norm, if you regularly imagine that popular songs involve same-sex love, this probably takes more cognitive effort, or at least it may have in the past.*

CHAPTER 8: SOCIAL INFLUENCE

What variable could you introduce to the standard Asch research design to test the possibility that inducing public self-presentation concerns in your participants would increase nonconformity?

Possible Answer: *Because nonconformity may increase when others not involved in the influence attempt are present, you could have an experimental condition in which nonparticipants observe the line judgment tasks. If public self-presentation concerns significantly influence conformity, then this condition should result in greater nonconformity than in the standard Asch condition. This effect should occur when the line judgments are clear and easy, but probably won't occur when judgments are ambiguous and difficult. Instead, because the presence of an audience also induces public self-awareness—which leads to greater conformity to social standards—it's possible that ambiguous and difficult judgmental tasks will lead to greater conformity than in the standard Asch condition.*

What is an alternative—or additional—interpretation of the findings from the Maass et al. (1982) experiment that relate to the chapter 6 discussion of gender differences in the effects of powerful speech on persuasion?

Possible Answer: Linda Carli's (1990) research found that women who use a powerful speaking style when trying to persuade men to change their attitudes may be less successful than male persuaders due to the male audience being "put off" by the assertive female persuader. It's possible that the "double minority" results in the Maass et al. experiment are partly due to this gender bias effect. That is, the conservative male participants in this experiment are the sort of men who would most likely be defensive when listening to an assertive woman's persuasive message.

How might the foot-in-the-door compliance strategy be combined with the effects of postdecision dissonance to partly explain how some people initially become involved and then committed to religious or political cults?

Possible Answer: In the foot-in-the-door strategy, a person who complies with a small request is more likely to later comply to a larger, less desirable request from the same person. Converts to cults are initially drawn to them by agreeing to read the cult's literature or agreeing to attend one meeting. The compliance with these small requests are used by cult members to secure even greater degrees of compliance later on. Of course, cult members also tend to act very warm and accepting toward possible recruits, thus making it more likely that they will want to seek greater ties to this group.

When the recruits do commit themselves to the cult, postdecision dissonance may exert its influence. Now, the attractive aspects of not joining and the unattractive aspects of joining are inconsistent with the decision to join the cult. Because this is viewed by new recruits as an important life decision, they will likely experience quite a bit of postdecision dissonance. According to cognitive dissonance theory, the new members will try to reduce the dissonance by only focusing on the positive aspects of the cult, while simultaneously focusing on only the negative aspects of their previous life. Other cult members, both new and old, will eagerly reinforce this sort of thinking—often because they too need to justify their own decision to join—and the new members' allegiance to the cult is immensely strengthened.

CHAPTER 9: GROUP BEHAVIOR

In chapter 7 you learned how ingroup biases can lead to prejudice and discrimination. How might the knowledge of how ingroup biases can lead to prejudice and discrimination help you better understand the process by which the *diffuse status characteristics* of group members significantly determines their power in the group?

Possible Answer: When observing an ingroup member and an outgroup member performing the same task, performance evaluations will tend to be biased in favor of the ingroup member. This ingroup bias may manifest itself by people selectively remembering ingroup members' good behavior and outgroup members' bad behavior, or by selectively forgetting or trivializing ingroup members' bad behavior and outgroup members' good behavior. In a group, the ingroup biasing that will usually have the biggest consequences for how much power and status members individually attain is the biasing exhibited by those members who hold "gatekeeping" roles. Gatekeepers are usually high-status members who give other members access to similar high-status positions. Gatekeepers will tend to single out those members in the group whom they perceive to be "one of them." Often this means they will prefer members who are similar to them on such diffuse status characteristics as race, sex, age, and wealth.

How can you use the findings of social loafing research to design a computer training course that not only facilitates quick learning, but also encourages high productivity following learning?

Possible Answer: Research indicates that people can learn complex tasks more quickly when they believe their individual efforts are not being evaluated, such as when they are performing as part of a larger group. This is the type of situation that also often leads to social loafing on well-learned tasks. In both situations, group performance allows task outcome responsibility to be diffused among fellow coperformers. To facilitate employees learning a complex computer program, you could design the training so that their individual efforts are not evaluated. This could be accomplished by training employees in a group setting. Group coperformance should reduce their evaluation apprehension—and presumably their arousal—and allow them to more carefully concentrate on the task at hand.

Once the employees have mastered the computer program, you could then either monitor their individual performance to reduce social loafing, or—if you didn't want to be so Orwellian—you could simply allow them to monitor their own performance by providing them with individual performance feedback. Both strategies have been found to be effective in reducing social loafing.

Based on social influence research, what type of individuals might be more susceptible to group polarization effects when working on judgmental tasks?

Possible Answer: When the task is judgmental, people who are more concerned with how others will evaluate them will be more influenced by others' opinions. If they sense that the "socially acceptable" judgment is in a particular direction, they are likely to leapfrog over others to arrive at the most group-praiseworthy position. It's also possible that people with a high need for individuation—a desire to feel unique—may try to grab the most extreme position in the socially acceptable direction to "stand on top of the crowd."

CHAPTER 10: INTERPERSONAL ATTRACTION

How many of your more important affiliation reasons for your lists can be identified as being primarily based on social comparison or social exchange needs? How are your three lists similar to or different from one another regarding social comparison and social exchange reasons?

This answer will be unique to your personal experiences.

How do the findings from the Snyder et al. (1977) experiment and the Anderson and Bem (1981) study relate to one of the basic messages of social psychology? Further, how can you generalize these findings beyond physical attractiveness effects to create a more pleasant and rewarding social world for yourself?

Possible Answer: *One of the basic messages of social psychology is that we actively create and re-create our social reality. The better you understand the psychological dynamics of this social constructive process, the better equipped you will be to shape your reality in the manner you desire. In a larger sense, the findings from these two studies point out that if you treat other people as if they are attractive and a joy to be around, they not only will appreciate and seek out your company, but—if they weren't before—they are now more likely to become people who really are attractive and a joy to be around! This topic also relates to the "We like those who like us" discussion later in the chapter (p. 379).*

How has the similarity effect influenced your own personal relationships?

This answer will be unique to your personal experiences.

CHAPTER 11: INTIMATE RELATIONSHIPS

What attachment style would you say the self-sufficient cowboy/action film characters most often represent? Is this an attachment style we should be placing in our male cultural role models?

Possible Answer: *Securely attached adults easily become close to others, expect intimate relationships to endure, perceive others as generally trustworthy, and handle relationship conflict constructively. This type of an adult would*

be a very positive role model as a Hollywood movie figure. Unfortunately, this is definitely not how male cowboy/action film characters are typically portrayed. Thus, you already know that these characters are not the best role models for children and adults regarding intimate relationships. Yet it gets even worse. These male film characters represent the absolute worst attachment style for intimacy, namely, an avoidant one. Avoidant adults are uncomfortable with intimacy, have a hard time trusting others, and often express hostility during relationship conflicts. I guess that last difficulty would explain all the dead bodies that they leave in their wake. These cowboy/action characters sometimes tug at the audience's heartstrings by disclosing that "true love" is very hard to find and hold onto. Usually, there is a woman in their past who emotionally scarred them by either dying or rejecting them. Adults who watch these movies with children would be well advised to point out to the children afterward why Mr. Cowboy/Action Figure has such a hard time finding true love, and why imitation is not recommended.*

If companionate love is more enduring than passionate love, how can you explain the findings that perceiving one's partner in somewhat ideal terms leads to greater romantic happiness than perceiving her/him realistically?

Possible Answer: *The giddy, roller-coaster emotional ride associated with passionate love doesn't usually endure in a romantic relationship, but, rather, gives way to a more emotionally balanced form of romantic love, namely, companionate love. Passionate love can still exert its influence, but companionate love is the most influential. Yet, even with these romantic facts generally recognized, one manifestation of the importance of passion in an intimate relationship is revealed in the findings we are presently discussing. Put simply, those romantic relationships that have this "partner idealization" tendency appear to be the extra special romantic relationships, the ones that are perhaps closest to the enduring and happy relationships depicted in Hollywood movies (not necessarily including all the heavy breathing). They also would fall into the category that Sternberg (p. 413) calls "consummate love" and that Lee (p. 414) calls "agape" (altruistic love).*

In heterosexual relationships, the most common anxious-avoidant pairing is for anxious-ambivalent women to be attracted to avoidant men. Although these "oil and water" relationships are generally unsatisfying, why do they tend to be surprisingly stable? In contrast, why are relationships involving anxious-ambivalent men and avoidant women extremely unstable?

Possible Answer: *Kirkpatrick and Davis (1994) believe that these gender-influenced stability differences occur in* anxious-avoidant relationships because women are typically the maintainers and the breakers of relationships. Because an anxious woman's central concern is fear of abandonment, she would be accommodating and active in trying to maintain an unsatisfying romantic relationship, and she is unlikely to exit. In contrast, because an avoidant woman's central concern is a partner wanting too much intimacy, she is unlikely to possess, or even desire to use, relationship-enhancing skills. Instead of exercising voice, an avoidant is more likely to engage in either of the destructive strategies of neglect or exit.

CHAPTER 12: AGGRESSION

How might alcohol impair judgment and, thus, lead to the aggressive outbursts found in domestic violence cases?

Possible Answer: When people are intoxicated with alcohol, they are less likely to engage in self-awareness. Because self-awareness is necessary for self-regulation, and because self-regulation is part of the higher-level thinking necessary to control aggressive impulses, intoxication will make aggressive outbursts more likely.

In addition to excitation transfer, how else might violence erupt among rival sports fans?

Possible Answer: One obvious factor is the negative affect sports fans experience following a bad turn of events for their team or an outright defeat. The aggressive tendencies sparked by this negative affect are less likely to be modified by higher-level thinking due to the fans' high arousal level. In addition, sporting events often take place outdoors in hot weather or indoors in hot, cramped facilities. Both arenas could heighten aggression due to the heat effect. Finally, avid sports fans strongly identify with their teams, and this social identity can lead to strong prejudices against the fans of rival teams, which can erupt into discriminatory violence.

How could you use social psychological knowledge to reduce the likelihood of "road rage" on city streets and highways?

Possible Answer: You could employ Robert Baron's incompatible response strategy, in which you induce some emotional response in drivers that is likely to be incompatible with anger-induced aggression. Brooklyn, New York, has recently employed this strategy by posting signs along the highway containing "knock-knock" jokes. You could also encourage radio stations with "happy" programming formats to advertise their dial numbers on billboards that drivers could see. Another way to use billboards would be to use the insights of social learning theory: remind adults that they are role models for children and how they behave while

driving will be observed and learned by younger passengers and drivers. This strategy might engage higher-order cognitive processes in angry drivers—as proposed by Berkowitz's cognitive-neoassociationist model—so that their anger doesn't precipitate aggression.

CHAPTER 13: PROSOCIAL BEHAVIOR: HELPING OTHERS

What sort of cultural role models might influence the "helping habits" of boys and girls? How might greater gender role flexibility influence male and female helping tendencies?

Possible Answer: Social modeling studies suggest that children are most likely to imitate the behavior of people with whom they strongly identify, and for most children, this means same-sex adults. Thus, to foster good helping habits in children, existing cultural role models for boys and girls could be enlisted to convey this message to children in public service announcements.

In Hollywood movies, most leading-male actors play the traditional masculine role of helping people in dangerous situations, while being rather unwilling or ineffective in providing more mundane, long-term help, such as caring for children and the elderly. The underlying message in many of these movies is that this kind of assistance is unmanly and less important. Yet, in everyday living, this form of help is needed far more frequently than dangerous helping.

In contrast, most leading-female actors play characters with less gender stereotyped roles. As such, they are often depicted as being willing to intervene in both dangerous situations and in those requiring nurturance and long-term care to needy others. This greater flexibility in helping responses reflects the greater gender flexibility available to women in contemporary culture. For instance, girls are generally allowed to engage in more nontraditional gender behavior than boys. As a result, you might expect that girls will learn to help in a wider variety of situations than boys.

Do you think you would find these same bystander effects among people whose jobs regularly deal with helping others? How might you test whether the situational context or the salience of their "helping" social roles would influence their tendency to intervene?

Possible Answer: You probably would not find the same degree of bystander effects among nurses, doctors, and police officers because their experience and skill at handling emergencies would make it less likely that they would (1) worry about overreacting in possible emergency situations and (2) assume that other bystanders have as much *responsibility to help as them. It's likely that their tendency to diffuse responsibility would be further reduced if their "helping" social roles were currently salient to them, because they would be even more aware of the social norms regarding helping for their occupations. It's also likely that doctors' and nurses' willingness to help will be greater in those situations in which their occupations best prepare them, namely, emergencies involving medical attention. However, because police officers are trained to intervene in both physically dangerous and medical emergencies, it's likely that there would be few differences in their willingness to respond. You might test these hypotheses in an experiment by having doctors, nurses, and police officers participate in a typical bystander intervention study, but (1) vary the degree to which their occupations are socially salient, and (2) vary the type of emergency (medical or physical endangerment) that they witness.*

How could you design a donation pitch to members of a local community center to help starving people in a foreign country, knowing that some message receivers will react with empathy, while others will react with personal distress?

Possible Answer: *First, you want to convey an emotionally arousing message concerning how desperately these people need the audience's help. For those individuals who experience empathy, you can simply ask for their donations. However, for those who experience personal distress, you have to deal with the fact that they will try to escape the situation to reduce their distress. Thus, you need to make it difficult for them to escape the distress without donating money. You might set up your talk so that it precedes a dinner or event that everyone in attendance generally enjoys. Then, inform the audience that the enjoyable event will commence as soon as the donations reach a specified amount. This scenario is admittedly heavy-handed, but it should induce those who are experiencing personal distress to help in order to facilitate their own escape from this unpleasantly arousing situation.*

GLOSSARY

A

Acquaintance Rape
Forced sexual intercourse that occurs either on a date or between people who are acquainted or romantically involved. Also known as date rape.

Actor-Observer Effect
The tendency for people to attribute their own behavior to external causes but that of others to internal factors.

Aggression
Any form of behavior that is intended to harm or injure some person, oneself, or an object.

Aggressive Script
A guide for behavior and problem solving that is developed and stored in memory and is characterized by aggression.

Altruistic Helping
A form of helping in which the ultimate goal of the helper is to increase another's welfare without expecting anything in return.

Ambivalent Sexism
Sexism directed against women based on both positive and negative attitudes (*hostility* and *benevolence*), rather than uniform dislike.

Anchoring and Adjustment Heuristic
A tendency to be biased toward the starting value or anchor in making quantitative judgments.

Anticonformity
Opposition to social influence on all occasions, often caused by psychological reactance.

Anxious/Ambivalent Attachment Style
An expectation about social relationships characterized by a concern that others will not return affection.

Applied Research
Research designed to increase the understanding of and solutions to real-world problems by using current social psychological knowledge.

Arousal: Cost-Reward Model
A theory that helping or not helping is a function of emotional arousal and analysis of the costs and rewards of helping.

Attachment
The strong emotional bond between an infant and a caregiver.

Attitude
A positive or negative evaluation of an object.

Attribution
The process by which people use information to make inferences about the causes of behavior or events.

Audience Inhibition Effect
People are inhibited from helping for fear that other bystanders will evaluate them negatively if they intervene and the situation is not an emergency.

Authoritarian Personality
A personality trait characterized by submissiveness to authority, rigid adherence to conventional values, and prejudice toward outgroups.

Availability Heuristic
The tendency to judge the frequency or probability of an event in terms of how easy it is to think of examples of that event.

Aversive Racism
Attitudes toward members of a racial group that incorporate both egalitarian social values and negative emotions, causing one to avoid interaction with members of the group.

Avoidant Attachment Style
An expectation about social relationships characterized by a lack of trust and a suppression of attachment needs.

B

Balance Theory
A theory that people desire cognitive consistency or balance in their thoughts, feelings, and social relationships.

Basic Research
Research designed to increase knowledge about social behavior.

Belief
An estimate of the probability that something is true.

Body Esteem
A person's attitudes toward his or her body.

Bystander Intervention Model
A theory that whether bystanders intervene in an emergency is a function of a 5-step decision-making process.

C

Catharsis
The reduction in the aggressive drive following an aggressive act.

Central Route to Persuasion
Persuasion that occurs when people think carefully about a communication and are influenced by the strength of its arguments.

Central Traits
Traits that exert a disproportionate influence on people's overall impressions, causing them to assume the presence of other traits.

Classical Conditioning
Learning through association, when a neutral stimulus (conditioned stimulus) is paired with a stimulus (unconditioned stimulus) that naturally produces an emotional response.

Cognitive Consistency
The tendency to seek consistency in one's cognitions.

Cognitive Dissonance
A feeling of discomfort caused by performing an action that is inconsistent with one's attitudes.

Cognitive-Neoassociationist Model
A theory of impulsive aggression that aversive events produce negative affect, which stimulates the inclination to aggress.

Collectivism
A philosophy of life stressing the priority of group needs over individual needs, a preference for tightly knit social relationships, and a willingness to submit to the influence of one's group.

Companionate Love
The affection we feel for those with whom our lives are deeply entwined.

Compliance
Publicly acting in accord with a direct request.

Confederate
An accomplice of an experimenter whom research participants assume is a fellow participant or bystander.

Confirmation Bias
The tendency to seek information that supports our beliefs while ignoring disconfirming information.

Conformity
A yielding to perceived group pressure.

Contact Hypothesis
The theory that under certain conditions, direct contact between antagonistic groups will reduce prejudice.

Contingency Model of Leadership
The theory that leadership effectiveness depends both on whether leaders are task oriented or relationship oriented, and on the degree to which they have situational control.

Control Theory of Self-Regulation
A theory contending that, through self-awareness, people compare their behavior to a standard, and if there is a discrepancy, they work to reduce it.

Correlation Coefficient
A statistical measure of the direction and strength of the linear relationship between two variables, which can range from -1.00 to $+1.00$.

Correlational Studies
Research designed to examine the nature of the relationship between two or more naturally occurring variables.

Correspondent Inference
An inference that the action of an actor corresponds to, or is indicative of, a stable personal characteristic.

Counterfactual Thinking
The tendency to evaluate events by imagining alternative versions or outcomes to what actually happened.

Covariation Principle
A principle of attribution theory stating that for something to be the cause of a particular behavior, it must be present when the behavior occurs and absent when it does not occur.

Culture
The total lifestyle of a people from a particular social grouping, including all the ideas, symbols, preferences, and material objects that they share.

D

Debriefing
A procedure at the conclusion of a research session in which participants are given full information about the nature and hypotheses of the study.

Deception
A research technique that provides false information to persons participating in a study.

Deindividuation
The loss of a sense of individual identity and a loosening of normal inhibitions against engaging in behavior that is inconsistent with internal standards.

Dependent Variable
The experimental variable that is measured because it is believed to depend on the manipulated changes in the independent variable.

Diffusion of Responsibility
The belief that the presence of other people in a situation makes one less personally responsible for the events that occur in that situation.

Discounting Principle
A principle of attribution theory stating that whenever there are several possible causal explanations for a particular event, people tend to be much less likely to attribute the effect to any particular cause.

Discrimination
A negative action toward members of a specific social group.

Door-in-the-Face Technique
A two-step compliance technique in which, after having a large request refused, the influencer counteroffers with a much smaller request.

E

Egoistic Helping
A form of helping in which the ultimate goal of the helper is to increase his or her own welfare.

Elaboration Likelihood Model
A theory that there are two ways in which persuasive messages can cause attitude change, each differing in the amount of cognitive effort or elaboration they require.

Embarrassment
An unpleasant emotion experienced when we believe that we cannot perform coherently in a social situation.

Empathy
A feeling of compassion and tenderness upon viewing a victim's plight.

Empathy-Altruism Hypothesis
A theory proposing that experiencing empathy for someone in need produces an altruistic motive for helping.

Equity Theory
The theory that people are most satisfied in a relationship when the ratio between rewards and costs is similar for both partners.

Ethnic Identity
An individual's sense of personal identification with a particular ethnic group.

Ethnocentrism
A pattern of increased hostility toward outgroups accompanied by increased loyalty to one's ingroup.

Excitation Transfer
A psychological process in which arousal caused by one stimulus is transferred and added to arousal elicited by a second stimulus.

Expectation States Theory
A theory that states that the development of group status is based on members' expectations of others' probable contributions to the achievement of group goals. These expectations are shaped not only by members' *task-relevant characteristics* but also by *diffuse-state characteristics,* such as race, sex, age, and wealth.

Experimental Methods
Research designed to test cause-effect relationships between variables.

External Attribution
An attribution that locates the cause of an event to factors external to the person, such as luck, or other people, or the situation.

External Validity
The extent to which a study's findings can be generalized to people beyond those in the study itself.

F

False Consensus Effect
The tendency to exaggerate how common one's own characteristics and opinions are in the general population.

Foot-in-the-Door Technique
A two-step compliance technique in which the influencer secures compliance to a small request, and then later follows this with a larger, less desirable request.

Frustration-Aggression Hypothesis
The theory that frustration causes aggression.

Functional Approach
Attitude theories that emphasize that people develop and change their attitudes based on the degree to which they satisfy different psychological needs. To change an attitude, one must understand the underlying function that attitude serves.

Fundamental Attribution Error
The tendency to make internal attributions over external attributions in explaining the behavior of others.

G

Gender Identity
The knowledge that one is a male or a female and the internalization of this fact into one's self-concept.

Gender Schema
A mental framework for processing information based on its perceived male or female qualities.

Group
Two or more people who interact with and influence one another over a period of time, and who depend on one another and share common goals and a collective identity.

Group Polarization
Group-produced enhancement or exaggeration of members' initial attitudes through discussion.

Groupthink
A deterioration of mental efficiency, reality testing, and moral judgment in a group that results from an excessive desire to reach consensus.

H

Heterosexism
A system of cultural beliefs, values, and customs that exalts heterosexuality and denies, denigrates, and stigmatizes any nonheterosexual form of behavior or identity.

Heuristics
Timesaving mental shortcuts that reduce complex judgments to simple rules of thumb.

Hindsight Bias
The tendency, once an event has occurred, to overestimate our ability to have foreseen the outcome.

Hostile Aggression
The intentional use of harmful behavior in which the goal is simply to cause injury or death to the victim.

Hypotheses
Specific propositions or expectations about the nature of things derived from a theory.

I

Ideology
A set of beliefs and values held by the members of a social group, which explains its culture both to itself and to other groups.

Idiosyncrasy Credits
Interpersonal influence that a leader earns by helping the group achieve task goals and by conforming to group norms.

Illusory Correlation
The belief that two variables are associated with one another when in fact there is little or no actual association.

Implicit Personality Theory
Assumptions or naive belief systems people make about which personality traits go together.

Impression Formation
The process by which one integrates various sources of information about another into an overall judgment.

Independence
Not being subject to control by others.

Independent Variable
The experimental variable that the researcher manipulates.

Individualism
A philosophy of life stressing the priority of individual needs over group needs, a preference for loosely knit social relationships, and a desire to be relatively autonomous of others' influence.

Informational Influence
Conformity, compliance, or obedience due to a desire to gain information (information dependence).

Informed Consent
A procedure by which people freely choose to participate in a study only after they are told about the activities they will perform.

Ingroup
A group to which a person belongs and that forms a part of his or her social identity.

Ingroup Bias
The tendency to give more favorable evaluations and greater rewards to ingroup members than to outgroup members.

Instrumental Aggression
The intentional use of harmful behavior so that one can achieve some other goal.

Interactionism
An important perspective in social psychology that emphasizes the combined effects of both the person and the situation on human behavior.

Intergroup Anxiety
Anxiety due to anticipating negative consequences when interacting with an outgroup member.

Internal Attribution
An attribution that locates the cause of an event to factors internal to the person, such as personality traits, moods, attitudes, abilities, or effort.

Internal Validity
The extent to which cause-and-effect conclusions can validly be made in a study.

Interpersonal Attraction
A person's desire to approach another individual.

Intimacy
Sharing that which is inmost with others.

J

Jealousy
The negative emotional reaction experienced when a relationship that is important to a person's self-concept is threatened by a real or imagined rival.

Jigsaw Classroom
A cooperative group-learning technique designed to reduce prejudice and raise self-esteem.

Just-World Belief
A belief that the world is a fair and equitable place, with people getting what they deserve in life.

K

Kin Selection
A theory that people will exhibit preferences for helping blood relatives because this will increase the odds that their genes will be transmitted to subsequent generations.

L

Leader
The person who exerts the most influence on group behavior and beliefs.

Learned Helplessness
The passive resignation produced by repeated exposure to negative events that are perceived to be unavoidable.

Loneliness
Having a smaller or less satisfactory network of social and intimate relationships than one desires.

Low-Ball Technique
A two-step compliance strategy in which the influencer secures agreement with a request by understanding its true cost.

M

Master Status
A socially defined position occupied by a person in society that is very important in shaping his or her self-concept and life choices.

Matching Hypothesis
The proposition that people are attracted to others who are similar to them in particular characteristics, such as attitudes and physical attractiveness.

Mere Exposure Effect
The tendency to develop more positive feelings toward objects and individuals the more we are exposed to them.

Meta-Analysis
A statistical technique for combining information from many empirical studies on a topic to objectively estimate the reliability and overall size of the effect.

Misattribution of Arousal
A situation in which the explanation of the physiological symptoms of arousal is switched from the real source to another one.

Motivated-Tactician Model
An approach to social cognition that conceives of people as being flexible social thinkers who choose among multiple cognitive strategies based on their current goals, motives, and needs.

N

Need for Cognition
An individual preference for and tendency to engage in effortful cognitive activities.

Negative State Relief Model
A theory suggesting that for those in a bad mood, helping others may be a way to lift their own spirits if the perceived benefits for helping are high and the costs are low.

Negativity Effect
The tendency for negative traits to be weighted more heavily than positive traits in impression formation.

Nonverbal Behavior
Communicating feelings and intentions without words.

Norm of Social Justice
A social norm stating that we should help only when we believe that others deserve our assistance.

Norm of Social Responsibility
A social norm stating that we should help when others are in need and dependent on us.

Normative Influence
Conformity, compliance, or obedience due to a desire to gain rewards or avoid punishments (outcome dependence).

O

Obedience
The performance of an action in response to a direct order.

Old-Fashioned Racism
Blatantly negative stereotypes based on White racial superiority, coupled with open opposition to racial equality.

Operant Conditioning
A type of learning in which behavior is strengthened if followed by reinforcement and weakened if followed by punishment.

Optimistic Explanatory Style
A habitual tendency to attribute negative events to external, unstable, and specific causes, and positive events to internal, stable, and global causes.

Outgroup
Any group with which a person does not share membership.

Outgroup Homogeneity Effect
Perception of outgroup members as being more similar to one another than are members of one's ingroup.

P

Passionate Love
A state of intense longing for union with another.

Peripheral Route to Persuasion
Persuasion that occurs when people do not think carefully about a communication and instead are influenced by cues that are irrelevant to the content or quality of the communication.

Personal Distress
An unpleasant state of arousal in which people are preoccupied with their own emotions of anxiety, fear, or helplessness upon viewing a victim's plight.

Persuasion
The process of consciously attempting to change attitudes through the transmission of some message.

Pessimistic Explanatory Style
A habitual tendency to attribute negative events to internal, stable, and global causes, and positive events to external, unstable, and specific causes.

Physical Attractiveness Stereotype
The belief that physically attractive individuals possess socially desirable personality traits and lead happier lives than less attractive persons.

Pornography
The combination of sexual material with abuse or degradation in a manner that appears to endorse, condone, or encourage such behavior.

Positivity Bias
The tendency for people to evaluate individual human beings more positively than groups or impersonal objects.

Prejudice
A negative attitude directed toward people simply because they are members of a specific social group.

Primacy Effect
The tendency for the first information received to carry more weight than later information on one's overall impression.

Prosocial Behavior
Voluntary behavior that is carried out to benefit another person.

Protection-Motivation Theory
A theory proposing that fear induces both a self-protective response and an appraisal of whether the fear-arousing threat can be avoided.

Prototype
The most representative member of a category.

Psychological Femininity
Possession of expressive personality traits.

Psychological Masculinity
Possession of instrumental personality traits.

R

Random Assignment
Placement of research participants into experimental conditions in a manner that guarantees that all have an equal chance of being exposed to each level of the independent variable.

Rape Myth
The false belief that deep down, women enjoy forcible sex and find it sexually exciting.

Realistic Group Conflict Theory
The theory that intergroup conflict develops from competition for limited resources.

Recency Effect
The tendency for the last information received to carry greater weight than earlier information.

Reciprocal Helping
(Also known as reciprocal altruism.) A sociobiological principle stating that people expect that anyone helping another will have that favor returned at some future time.

Reciprocity norm
The expectation that one should return a favor or a good deed.

Reference Group
A group to which people orient themselves, using its standards to judge themselves and the world.

Representativeness Heuristic
The tendency to judge the category membership of people based on how closely they match the "typical" or "average" member of that category.

S

Schemas
Organized systems of beliefs about some stimulus object, which are built up from experience and which selectively guide the processing of new information.

Secure Attachment Style
An expectation about social relationships characterized by trust, a lack of concern with being abandoned, and a feeling of being valued and well liked.

Self
A symbol-using individual who can reflect on his/her own behavior.

Self-Affirmation Theory
A theory predicting that people will often cope with specific threats to their self-esteem by reminding themselves of other unrelated but cherished aspects of their self-concept.

Self-Awareness
A psychological state in which one takes oneself as an object of attention.

Self-Concept
The sum total of a person's thoughts and feelings that defines the self as an object.

Self-Consciousness
The habitual tendency to engage in self-awareness.

Self-Disclosure
The revealing of personal information about oneself to other people.

Self-Discrepancies
Discrepancies between our self-concept and how we would ideally like to be (*ideal self*) or believe others think we should be (*ought self*).

Self-Enhancement
The process of seeking out and interpreting situations so as to attain a positive view of oneself.

Self-Esteem
A person's evaluation of his or her self-concept.

Self-Evaluation Maintenance Model
A theory predicting under what conditions people are likely to react to the success of others with either pride or jealousy.

Self-Fulfilling Prophecy
The process by which someone's expectations about a person or group leads to the fulfillment of those expectations.

Self-Handicapping
Actions that people take to sabotage their performance and enhance their opportunity to excuse anticipated failure.

Self-Monitoring
The tendency to use cues from other people's self-presentations in controlling one's own self-presentations.

Self-Perception Theory
The theory that we often infer our internal states, such as our attitudes, by observing our behavior.

Self-Regulation
The ways in which people control and direct their own actions.

Self-Schemas
The many beliefs people have about themselves that constitute the "ingredients" of the self-concept.

Self-Serving Bias
The tendency to assign an internal locus of causality for our positive outcomes and an external locus for our negative outcomes.

Self-Verification
The process of seeking out and interpreting situations so as to confirm one's self-concept.

Sexism
Any attitude, action, or institutional structure that subordinates a person because of her or his sex.

Sexual Harassment
Unwelcome physical or verbal sexual overtures that create an intimidating, hostile, or offensive social environment.

Sleeper Effect
The delayed effectiveness of a persuasive message from a noncredible source.

Social Anxiety
The unpleasant emotion people experience due to their concern with interpersonal evaluation.

Social Categorization
The classification of people into groups based on their common attributes.

Social Cognition
The way in which we interpret, analyze, remember, and use information about the social world.

Social Comparison Theory
The theory that proposes that we evaluate our thoughts and actions by comparing them to those of others.

Social Dilemma
Any situation in which the most rewarding short-term choice for an individual will ultimately cause negative consequences for the group as a whole.

Social Dominance Theory
A theory contending that societal groups can be organized in a power hierarchy in which the dominant groups enjoy a disproportionate share of the society's assets and the subordinate groups receive most of its liabilities.

Social Exchange Theory
The theory that proposes that we seek out and maintain those relationships in which the rewards exceed the costs.

Social Facilitation
The enhancement of dominant responses due to the presence of others.

Social Identities
Aspects of a person's self-concept based on his or her group memberships.

Social Impact Theory
The theory that the amount of social influence others have depends on their number, strength, and immediacy to those they are trying to influence.

Social Influence
The exercise of social power by a person or group to change the attitudes or behavior of others in a particular direction.

Social Learning Theory
A theory that proposes that social behavior is primarily learned by observing and imitating the actions of others, and secondarily by being directly rewarded and punished for our own actions.

Social Loafing
Group-induced reduction in individual output when performers' efforts are pooled, and thus, cannot be individually judged.

Social Norm
An expected standard of behavior and belief established and enforced by a group.

Social Penetration Theory
A theory that describes the development of close relationships in terms of increasing self-disclosure.

Social Perception
The way we seek to know and understand other persons and events.

Social Power
The force available to the influencer to motivate attitude or behavior change.

Social Psychology
The scientific discipline that attempts to understand and explain how the thought, feeling, and behavior of individuals are influenced by the actual, imagined, or implied presence of others.

Social Role
A cluster of socially defined expectations that individuals in a given situation are expected to fulfill.

Social Role Theory
The theory that virtually all of the documented behavioral differences between males and females can be accounted for in terms of cultural stereotypes about gender and the resulting social roles that are taught to the young.

Social Skills Training
A behavioral training program designed to improve interpersonal skills through observation, modeling, role playing, and behavioral rehearsal.

Stereotype
A fixed way of thinking about people that put them into categories and don't allow for individual variation.

Stereotype Threat
A disturbing awareness among members of a negatively stereotyped group that anything one does, or anything about oneself that fits the stereotype, may confirm it as a self-characterization.

Stigma
An attribute that serves to discredit a person in the eyes of others.

Strategic Self-Presentation
Conscious and deliberate efforts to shape other people's impressions in order to gain power, influence, sympathy, or approval.

Subliminal Perception
The processing of information which is below one's threshold of conscious awareness.

Superordinate Goal
A mutually shared goal that can be achieved only through intergroup cooperation.

Symbolic Interaction Theory
A contemporary sociological theory, inspired by Mead's insights and based on the premise that the self and social reality emerge due to the meaningful communication among people.

T

That's-Not-All Strategy
A two-step compliance technique in which the influencer makes a large request, then immediately offers a discount or bonus before the initial request is refused.

Theory
An organized system of ideas that seeks to explain why two or more events are related.

Theory of Planned Behavior
The theory that people's conscious decisions to engage in specific actions are determined by their attitudes toward the behavior in question, the relevant subjective norms, and their perceived behavioral control.

Theory of Psychological Reactance
The theory that people believe they possess specific behavioral freedoms, and that they will react against and resist attempts to limit this sense of freedom.

Threat-to-Self-Esteem Model
A theory stating that if receiving help contains negative self-messages, recipients are likely to feel threatened and respond negatively.

Transformational Leader
A leader who changes (transforms) the outlook and behavior of followers (also referred to as a charismatic leader).

Two-Factor Theory of Emotions
A theory that emotional experience is based on two factors: physiological arousal and cognitive labeling of the cause of that arousal.

V

Values
Enduring beliefs about important life goals that transcend specific situations.

REFERENCES

Abbey, A. (1987). Perceptions of personal avoidability versus responsibility: How do they differ? *Basic and Applied Social Psychology, 8,* 3–19.

Abbey, A., Abramis, D. J., & Caplan, R. D. (1985). Effects of different sources of social support and social conflict on emotional well-being. *Basic and Applied Social Psychology, 6,* 111–129.

Abbey, A., Ross, L. T., McDuffie, D., & McAuslan, P. (1996). Alcohol and dating risk factors for sexual assault among college women. *Psychology of Women Quarterly, 20,* 147–169.

Abelson, R. P. (1972). Are attitudes necessary? In B. T. King & E. McGinnies (Eds.), *Attitudes, conflicts, and social change.* New York: Academic Press.

Abelson, R. P. (1982). Three modes of attitude-behavior consistency. In M. P. Zanna, E. T. Higgins, & C. P. Herman (Eds.), *Consistency in social behavior: The Ontario symposium* (Vol. 2, pp. 131–147). Hillsdale, NJ: Erlbaum.

Abrams, D., Ando, K., & Hinkle, S. (1998). Psychological attachment to the group: Cross-cultural differences in organizational identification and subjective norms as predictors of workers' turnover intentions. *Personality and Social Psychology Bulletin, 24,* 1027–1039.

Abramson, L. Y., Seligman, M. E. P., & Teasdale, J. (1978). Learned helplessness in humans: Critique and reformulation. *Journal of Abnormal Psychology, 87,* 358–372.

Adams, J. M., & Jones, W. H. (1997). The conceptualization of marital commitment: An integrative analysis. *Journal of Personality and Social Psychology, 73,* 1177–1196.

Adams, J. S. (1965). Inequity in social exchange. In L. Berkowitz (Ed.), *Advances in experimental social psychology* (Vol. 2, pp. 267–299). New York: Academic Press.

Adorno, T. W., Frenkel-Brunswik, E., Levinson, D., & Sanford, R. (1950). *The authoritarian personality.* New York: Harper.

Agnew, C. R., & Le, B. (1997). *Individualism in romantic relationships: Associations with commitment, satisfaction, and self-other inclusion.* Paper presented at the annual meeting of the American Psychological Society, Washington, DC.

Ahlering, R. F. (1987). Need for cognition, attitudes, and the 1984 presidential election. *Journal of Research in Personality, 21,* 100–102.

Aiello, J. R., & Svec, C. M. (1993). Computer monitoring of work performance: Extending the social facilitation framework to electronic presence. *Journal of Applied Social Psychology, 23,* 537–548.

Ailes, R. (1988). *You are the message.* New York: Doubleday.

Ainsworth, M. D. S. (1989). Attachments beyond infancy. *American Psychologist, 44,* 709–716.

Ajzen, I. (1985). From intentions to actions: A theory of planned behavior. In J. Kuhl & J. Beckmann (Eds.), *Action control: From cognition to behavior* (pp. 11–39). New York: Springer-Verlag.

Ajzen, I. (1988). *Attitudes, personality, and behavior.* Chicago: Dorsey.

Ajzen, I. (1991). The theory of planned behavior. *Organizational Behavior and Human Decision Processes, 50,* 179–204.

Ajzen, I. (1996). The social psychology of decision making. In E. T. Higgins & R. M. Sorrentino (Eds.), *Handbook of motivation and cognition: Foundations of social behavior* (Vol. 2, pp. 297–325). New York: Guilford.

Ajzen, I., & Holmes, W. H. (1976). Uniqueness of behavioral effects in causal attribution. *Journal of Personality, 44,* 98–108.

Alicke, M. D., LoSchiavo, F. M., Zerbst, J., & Zhang, S. (1997). The person who outperforms me is a genius: Maintaining perceived competence in upward social comparison. *Journal of Personality and Social Psychology, 73,* 781–789.

Alicke, M. D., Yurak, T. J., & Vredenburg, D. S. (1996). Using personal attitudes to judge others: The roles of outcomes and consensus. *Journal of Research in Personality, 30,* 103–119.

Alksnis, C., Desmarais, S., & Wood, E. (1996). Gender differences in scripts for types of dates. *Sex Roles, 34,* 321–336.

Allen, B. P. (1996). African Americans' and European Americans' mutual attributions: Adjective generation technique (AGT) stereotyping. *Journal of Applied Social Psychology, 26,* 884–912.

Allen, J. B., Kenrick, D. T., Linder, D. E., & McCall, M. A. (1989). Arousal and attraction: A response facilitation alternative to misattribution and negative reinforcement models. *Journal of Personality and Social Psychology, 57,* 261–270.

Allen, V. L., & Levine, J. M. (1969). Consensus and conformity. *Journal of Experimental Social Psychology, 5,* 389–399.

Allen, V. L., & Levine, J. M. (1971). Social support and conformity: The role of independent assessment of reality. *Journal of Experimental Social Psychology, 7,* 48–58.

Alley, T. R., & Cunningham, M. R. (1991). Averaged faces are attractive, but very attractive faces are not average. *Psychological Science, 2,* 123–125.

Allison, J. A., & Wrightsman, L. S. (1993). *Rape: The misunderstood crime.* Newbury Park: Sage.

Allison, S. T., & Messick, D. M. (1985). Effects of experience on performance in a replenishable resource trap. *Journal of Personality and Social Psychology, 49,* 943–948.

Allport, F. H. (1920). The influence of the group upon association and thought. *Journal of Experimental Psychology, 3,* 159–182.

Allport, F. H. (1924). *Social psychology.* Boston: Houghton Mifflin.

Allport, G. W. (1935). Attitudes. In C. Murchison (Ed.), *The handbook of social psychology* (pp. 798–844). Worcester, MA: Clark University Press.

Allport, G. W. (1985). The historical background of social psychology. In G. Lindzey & E. Aronson (Eds.), *Handbook of social psychology* (Vol. I, 3rd ed., pp. 1–46). New York: Random House.

Allport, G. W., & Ross, J. M. (1967). Personal religious orientation and prejudice. *Journal of Personality and Social Psychology, 5,* 432–443.

Alluisi, E. A., & Warm, J. S. (1990). Things that go together: A review of stimulus-response compatibility and related effects. In R. W. Proctor & T. G. Reeve (Eds.), *Stimulus-response compatibility: An integrated perspective* (pp. 3–30). Amsterdam: North Holland.

Altemeyer, B. (1981). *Right-wing authoritarianism.* Winnipeg: University of Manitoba Press.

Altemeyer, B. (1988). *Enemies of freedom: Understanding right-wing authoritarianism.* San Francisco: Jossey-Bass.

Altman, I. (1973). Reciprocity of interpersonal exchange. *Journal of Theory of Social Behavior, 3,* 249–261.

Altman, I., & Taylor, D. A. (1973). *Social penetration theory: The development of interpersonal relationships.* New York: Holt, Rinehart, & Winston.

Alvaro, E. M., & Crano, W. D. (1997). Indirect minority influence: Evidence for leniency in source evaluation and counterargumentation. *Journal of Personality and Social Psychology, 72,* 949–964.

Alwin, D. F., Cohen, R. L., & Newcomb, T. M. (1991). *Political attitudes over the life span: The Bennington women after fifty years.* Madison: University of Wisconsin Press.

American Psychological Association. (1982). *Ethical principles in the conduct of research with human participants.* Washington, DC: Author.

Amir, Y. (1969). Contact hypothesis in ethnic relations. *Psychological Bulletin, 71,* 319–342.

Amsterdam, B. (1972). Mirror self-image reactions before age two. *Developmental Psychobiology, 5,* 297–305.

Anderson, C. A. (1997). Effects of violent movies and trait hostility on hostile feelings and aggressive thoughts. *Aggressive Behavior, 23,* 161–178.

Anderson, C. A., & Anderson, D. C. (1984). Ambient temperature and violent crime: Tests of the linear and curvilinear hypotheses. *Journal of Personality and Social Psychology, 46,* 91–97.

Anderson, C. A., & Anderson, K. B. (1996). Violent crime rate studies in philosophical context: A destructive testing approach to heat and Southern culture of violence effects. *Journal of Personality and Social Psychology, 70,* 740–756.

Anderson, C. A., & Bushman, B. J. (1997). External validity of "trivial" experiments: The case of laboratory aggression. *Review of General Psychology, 1,* 19–41.

Anderson, C. A., Benjamin, A. J., & Bartholow, B. D. (1998). Does the gun pull the trigger? Automatic priming effects of weapon pictures and weapon names. *Psychological Science, 9,* 308–314.

Anderson, C. A., Bushman, B. J., & Groom, R. W. (1997). Hot years and serious and deadly assault: Empirical tests of the heat hypothesis. *Journal of Personality and Social Psychology, 73,* 1213–1223.

Anderson, C. A., Deuser, W. E., & DeNeve, K. M. (1995). Hot temperatures, hostile affect, hostile cognition, and arousal: Tests of a general model of affective aggression. *Personality and Social Psychology Bulletin, 21,* 434–448.

Anderson, C. A., Miller, R. S., Riger, A. L., Dill, J. C., & Sedikides, C. (1994). Behavioral and characterological attributional styles as predictors of depression and loneliness: Review, refinement, and test. *Journal of Personality and Social Psychology, 66,* 549–558.

Anderson, E. (1994). The code of the streets. *Atlantic Monthly, 5,* 81–94.

Anderson, J. L., Crawford, C. B., Nadeau, J., & Lindberg, T. (1992). Was the Duchess of Windsor right? A cross-cultural review of the socioecology of ideals of female body shape. *Ethology and Sociobiology, 13,* 197–227.

Anderson, J. R. (1993). To see ourselves as others see us: A response to Mitchell. *New Ideas in Psychology, 11,* 339–346.

Anderson, N. H. (1965). Averaging vs. adding as a stimulus-combination rule in impression formation. *Journal of Experimental Psychology, 70,* 394–400.

Anderson, N. H. (1968). A simple model for information integration. In R. B. Abelson, E. Aronson, W. J. McGuire, T. M. Newcomb, M. J. Rosenberg, & P. H. Tannenbaum (Eds.), *Theories of cognitive consistency: A sourcebook* (pp. 731–743). Chicago: Rand McNally.

Anderson, N. H. (1981). *Foundations of information integration theory.* New York: Academic Press.

Anderson, S. M., & Bem, S. L. (1981). Sex typing and androgyny in dyadic interaction: Individual differences in responsiveness to physical attractiveness. *Journal of Personality and Social Psychology, 41,* 74–86.

Andersson, J., & Rònnberg, J. (1997). Cued memory collaboration: Effects of friendship and type of retrieval cue. *European Journal of Cognitive Psychology, 9,* 273–287.

Andrews, J. D. W. (1989). Psychotherapy of depression: A self-confirmatory model. *Psychological Review, 96,* 576–607.

Ansolabehere, S., & Iyengar, S. (1995). *Going negative: How attack ads shrink and polarize the electorate.* New York: The Free Press.

Anthony, T., Cooper, C., & Mullen, B. (1992). Cross-racial facial identification: A social cognitive integration. *Personality and Social Psychology Bulletin, 18,* 296–301.

APA Education Directorate. (1995). *Five years of growth and change (1990–1995): Advancing the science and practice of psychology for benefit of the public through educational institutions and programs.* Washington, DC: American Psychological Association.

Archer, J. (1991). Human sociobiology: Basic concepts and limitations. *Journal of Social Issues, 47,* 11–26.

Archer, R. L. (1979). Role of personality and the social situation. In G. J. Chelune (Ed.), *Self-disclosure* (pp. 28–58). San Francisco: Jossey-Bass.

Archibald, F. S., Bartholomew, K., & Marx, R. (1995). Loneliness in early adolescence: A test of the cognitive discrepancy model of loneliness. *Personality and Social Psychology Bulletin, 21,* 296–301.

Arkin, R., & Duval, S. (1975). Focus of attention and causal attributions of actors and observers. *Journal of Experimental Social Psychology, 11,* 427–438.

Aron, A., & Aron, E. N. (1986). *Love as the expansion of self: Understanding attraction and satisfaction.* New York: Hemisphere.

Aron, A., & Aron, E. N. (1997). Self-expansion motivation and including other in the self. In S. Duck (Ed.), *Handbook of personal relationships: Theory, research and interventions* (2nd ed., pp. 251–270). Chichester, England: Wiley.

Aron, A., Aron, E. N., & Allen, J. (1998). Motivations for unreciprocated love. *Personality and Social Psychology Bulletin, 24,* 787–796.

Aron, A., Aron, E. N., & Smollan, D. (1992). Inclusion of other in the self scale and the structure of interpersonal closeness. *Journal of Personality and Social Psychology, 63,* 596–612.

Aron, A., Aron, E. N., Tudor, M., & Nelson, G. (1991). Close relationships as including other in the self. *Journal of Personality and Social Psychology, 60,* 241–253.

Aronoff, J., Woike, B. A., & Hyman, L. M. (1992). Which are the stimuli in facial displays of anger and happiness? Configurational bases of emotion recognition. *Journal of Personality and Social Psychology, 62,* 1050–1066.

Aronson, E. (1969). The theory of cognitive dissonance: A current perspective. In L. Berkowitz (Ed.), *Advances in experimental social psychology* (Vol. 4, pp. 1–34). New York: Academic Press.

Aronson, E., & Carlsmith, J. M. (1963). Effect of the severity of threat on the devaluation of a forbidden behavior. *Journal of Abnormal and Social Psychology, 66,* 584–588.

Aronson, E., & Mills, J. (1959). The effect of severity of initiation on liking for a group. *Journal of Abnormal and Social Psychology, 59,* 177–181.

Aronson, E., & Thibodeau, R. (1992). The jigsaw classroom: A cooperative strategy for reducing prejudice. In J. Lynch, C. Modgil, & S. Modgil (Eds.), *Cultural diversity in the schools.* London: Falmer Press.

Aronson, E., Stephan, C., Sikes, J., Blaney, N., & Snapp, M. (1978b). *The jigsaw classroom.* Beverly Hills, CA: Sage.

Aronson, J., Blanton, H., & Cooper, J. (1995). From dissonance to disidentification: Selectivity in the self-affirmation process. *Journal of Personality and Social Psychology, 68,* 986–996.

Arriaga, X. B., & Rusbult, C. E. (1998). Standing in my partner's shoes: Partner perspective taking and reactions to accommodative dilemmas. *Personality and Social Psychology Bulletin, 24,* 927–948.

Asch, S. E. (1946). Forming impressions of personality. *Journal of Abnormal and Social Psychology, 41,* 258–290.

Asch, S. E. (1951). Effects of group pressure upon the modification and distortion of judgments. In H. Guetzkow (Ed.), *Groups, leadership, and men.* Pittsburgh, PA: Carnegie Press.

Asch, S. E. (1952). *Social psychology.* New York: Prentice-Hall.

Asch, S. E. (1955, November). Opinions and social pressure. *Scientific American,* 31–35.

Asch, S. E. (1956). Studies of independence and conformity: A minority of one against a unanimous majority. *Psychological Monographs, 70,* (Whole No. 416).

Ash, M. G. (1992). Cultural contexts and scientific change in psychology: Kurt Lewin in Iowa. *American Psychologist, 47,* 198–207.

Ashby, F. G., Isen, A. M., & Turken, A. U. (in press). A neuropsychological theory of positive affect and its influence on cognition. *Psychological Review.*

Ashmore, R. D., & Jussim, L. (1997). Introduction: Toward a second century of the scientific analysis of self and identity. In R. Ashmore & L. Jussim (Eds.), *Self and identity: Fundamental issues* (pp. 1–19). New York: Oxford University Press.

Ashton, M. C., & Esses, V. M. (1999). Stereotype accuracy: Estimating the academic performance of ethnic groups. *Personality and Social Psychology Bulletin, 25,* 225–236.

Aukett, R., Ritchie, J., & Mill, K. (1988). Gender differences in friendship patterns. *Sex Roles, 19,* 57–66.

Averill, J. R. (1983). Studies on anger and aggression: Implications for theories of emotion. *American Psychologist, 38,* 1145–1160.

Axsom, D. (1989). Cognitive dissonance and behavior change in psychotherapy. *Journal of Experimental Social Psychology, 21,* 149–160.

Axtell, R. E. (1991). *Gestures: The do's and taboos of body language around the world.* New York: John Wiley.

Ayman, R., & Chemers, M. M. (1983). The relationship of supervisory behavior ratings to work group effectiveness and subordinate satisfaction among Iranian managers. *Journal of Applied Psychology, 68,* 338–341.

Ayman, R., Chemers, M. M., & Fiedler, F. (1995). The contingency model of leadership effectiveness: Its level of analysis. Special Issue: Leadership: The multiple-level approaches (Part I). *Leadership Quarterly, 6,* 147–167.

Bachnik, J. M. (1992). The two "faces" of self and society in Japan. *Ethos, 20,* 3–32.

Backman, C. W. (1983). Toward an interdisciplinary social psychology. In L. Berkowitz (Ed.), *Advances in experimental social psychology* (Vol. 14, pp. 219–261). New York: Academic Press.

Bagozzi, R. P. (1981). Attitudes, intentions, and behavior: A test of some key hypotheses. *Journal of Personality and Social Psychology, 41,* 607–627.

Baker, S. M., & Petty, R. E. (1994). Majority and minority influence: Source-position imbalance as a determinant of message scrutiny. *Journal of Personality and Social Psychology, 67,* 5–19.

Bales, R. F. (1970). *Personality and interpersonal behavior.* Fort Worth, TX: Holt, Rinehart & Winston.

Bales, R. F., & Slater, P. E. (1955). Role differentiation. In T. Parsons & R. F. Bales (Eds.), *Family, socialization, and interaction processes* (pp. 259–306). Glencoe, IL: Free Press.

Balkwell, J. W., & Berger, J. (1996). Gender, status, and behavior in task situations. *Social Psychology Quarterly, 59,* 273–283.

Ball-Rokeach, S. J., Rokeach, M., & Grube, J. W. (1984). *The great American values test: Influencing behavior and belief through television.* New York: The Free Press.

Bandura, A. (1965). Influences of models' reinforcement contingencies on the acquisition of initiative responses. *Journal of Personality and Social Psychology, 1,* 589–593.

Bandura, A. (1979). The social learning perspective: Mechanism of aggression. In H. Toch (Ed.), *Psychology of crime and criminal justice.* New York: Holt, Rinehart & Winston.

Bandura, A. (1986). *Social foundations of thought and action: A social cognitive theory.* Englewood Cliffs, NJ: Prentice-Hall.

Bandura, A., & Huston, A. C. (1961). Identification as a process of incidental learning. *Journal of Abnormal and Social Psychology, 63,* 575–582.

Bandura, A., Ross, D., & Ross, S. A. (1961). Transmission of aggression through imitation of aggressive models. *Journal of Abnormal and Social Psychology, 63,* 575–582.

Bandura, A., & Walters, R. H. (1963). *Social learning and personality development.* New York: Holt, Rinehart, & Winston.

Bankston, C. L. III, & Caldas, S. J. (1997). The American school dilemma: Race and scholastic performance. *The Sociological Quarterly, 38,* 423–429.

Barbee, A. P., Cunningham, M. R., Winstead, B. A., Derlega, V. J., Gulley, M. R., Yankeelov, P. A., & Druen, P. B. (1993). Effects of gender role expectations on the social support process. *Journal of Social Issues, 49,* 175–190.

Barbee, A. P., Gulley, M. R., & Cunningham, M. R. (1990). Support seeking in personal relationships. *Journal of Social and Personal Relationships, 7,* 531–540.

Barbuto, J. E., Jr. (1997). Taking the charisma out of transformational leadership. *Journal of Social Behavior and Personality, 12,* 689–697.

Bargh, J. A., & Raymond, P., Pryor, J. B., & Strack, F. (1995). Attractiveness of the underling: An automatic power-sex association and its consequences for sexual harassment and aggression. *Journal of Personality and Social Psychology, 68,* 768–781.

Barley, S. R., & Bechky, B. A. (1994). In the backrooms of science: The work of technicians in science labs. *Work and Occupations, 21,* 85–126.

Barnlund, D. C. (1989). *Communicative styles of Japanese and Americans.* Belmont, CA: Wadsworth.

Baron, L., & Straus, M. A. (1987). Four theories of rape: A macrosociological analysis. *Social Problems, 34,* 467–489.

Baron, L., & Straus, M. A. (1989). *Four theories of rape in American society: A state-level analysis.* New Haven, CT: Yale University Press.

Baron, R. A. (1973). Threatened retaliation from the victim as an inhibitor of physical aggression. *Journal of Research in Personality, 7,* 103–115.

Baron, R. A. (1976). The reduction of human aggression: A field study of the influence of incompatible reactions. *Journal of Applied Social Psychology, 6,* 260–274.

Baron, R. A. (1983). The control of human aggression: A strategy based on incompatible responses. In R. G. Geen & E. I. Donnerstein (Eds.), *Aggression: Theoretical and empirical reviews* (Vol. 2, pp. 173–190). New York: Academic Press.

Baron, R. A. (1986). Self-presentation in job interviews: When there can be "too much of a good thing." *Journal of Applied Social Psychology, 16,* 16–28.

Baron, R. A., & Kepner, C. R. (1970). Model's behavior and attraction toward the model as determinants of adult aggressive behavior. *Journal of Personality and Social Psychology, 14,* 335–344.

Baron, R. S. (1986). Distraction-conflict theory: Progress and problems. In L. Berkowitz (Ed.), *Advances in experimental social psychology* (Vol. 19, pp.1–40). New York: Academic Press.

Baron, R. S., Burgess, M. L., & Kao, C. F. (1991). Detecting and labeling prejudice: Do female perpetrators go undetected? *Personality and Social Psychology Bulletin, 17,* 115–123.

Barsalou, L. W. (1991). Deriving categories to achieve goals. In Posner, M. I. (Ed.), *The psychology of learning and motivation* (Vol. 27, pp. 1–64). New York: Academic Press.

Bar-Tal, D., & Saxe, L. (1976). Perceptions of similarly and dissimilarly attractive couples and individuals. *Journal of Personality and Social Psychology, 33,* 772–781.

Basow, S. A. (1986). *Gender stereotypes: Traditions and alternatives* (2nd ed.). Monterey, CA: Brooks/Cole.

Bass, B. M. (1985). *Leadership and performance beyond expectations.* New York: Free Press.

Bass, B. M. (1997). Does the transactional/transformational leadership paradigm transcend organizational and national boundaries? *American Psychologist, 52,* 130–139.

Bass, B. M., & Avolio, B. J. (1993). Transformational leadership: A response to critiques. In M. M. Chemers & R. Ayman (Eds.), *Leadership theory and research: Perspectives and directions* (pp. 49–80). San Diego, CA: Academic Press.

Bassili, J. N., & Provencal, A. (1988). Perceiving minorities: A factor-analytic approach. *Personality and Social Psychology Bulletin, 14,* 5–15.

Batson, C. D. (1991). *The altruism question: Toward a social psychological answer.* Hillsdale, NJ: Lawrence Erlbaum.

Batson, C. D. (1998). Prosocial behavior and altruism. In D. T. Gilbert, S. T. Fiske, & G. Lindzey (Eds.), *The handbook of social psychology* (4th ed., pp. 282–316). New York: McGraw-Hill.

Batson, C. D., Coke, J. S., Chard, F., Smith, D., & Taliaferro, A. (1979). Generality of the ``glow of goodwill'': Effects of mood on helping and information acquisition. *Social Psychology Quarterly, 42,* 176–179.

Batson, C. D., Duncan, B. D., Ackerman, P., Buckley, T., & Birch, K. (1981). Is empathic emotion a source of altruistic motivation? *Journal of Personality and Social Psychology, 40,* 290–302.

Batson, C. D., Flink, C. H., Schoenrade, P. A., Fultz, J., & Pych, V. (1986). Religious orientation and overt versus covert racial prejudice. *Journal of Personality and Social Psychology, 50,* 175–181.

Batson, C. D., O'Quinn, K., Fultz, J., Vanderplas, N., & Isen, A. M. (1983). Influence of self-reported distress and empathy on egoistic versus altruistic motivation to help. *Journal of Personality and Social Psychology, 45,* 706–718.

Batson, C. D., Polycarpou, M. P., Harmon-Jones, E., Imhoff, H. J., Mitchener, E. C., Bednar, L. L., Klein, T. R., & Highberger, L. (1997). *Journal of Personality and Social Psychology, 72,* 105–118.

Batson, C. D., Sager, K., Garst, E., Kang, M., Rubchinsky, K., & Dawson, K. (1997). Is empathy-induced helping due to self-other merging? *Journal of Personality and Social Psychology, 73,* 495–509.

Batson, C. D., Schoenrade, P., & Ventis, W. L. (1993). *Religion and the individual: A social psychological perspective.* New York: Oxford University Press.

Batson, C. D., Sympson, S. C., Hindman, J. L., Decruz, P., Todd, R. M., Weeks, J. L., Jennings, G., & Burris, C. T. (1996). "I've been there, too": Effect on empathy of prior experience with a need. *Personality and Social Psychology Bulletin, 22,* 474–482.

Baumeister, R. F. (1982). A self-presentational view of social phenomena. *Psychological Bulletin, 91,* 3–26.

Baumeister, R. F. (1991). *Escaping the self: Alcoholism, spirituality, masochism, and other flights from the burden of selfhood.* New York: Basic Books.

Baumeister, R. F. (1993). Understanding the inner nature of low self-esteem: Uncertain, fragile, protective, and conflicted. In R. F. Baumeister (Ed.), *Self-esteem: The puzzle of low self-regard* (pp. 201–218). New York: Plenum Press.

Baumeister, R. F. (1998). The self. In D. T. Gilbert, S. T. Fiske, & G. Lindzey (Eds.), *The handbook of social psychology* (4th ed., Vol. 1, pp. 680–740). New York: McGraw-Hill.

Baumeister, R. F., & Heatherton, T. F. (1996). Self-regulation failure: An overview. *Psychological Inquiry, 7,* 1–15.

Baumeister, R. F., & Ilko, S. A. (1995). Shallow gratitude: Public and private acknowledgment of external help in accounts of success. *Basic and Applied Social Psychology, 16,* 191–209.

Baumeister, R. F., & Jones, E. E. (1978). When self-presentation is constrained by the target's knowledge: Consistency and compensation. *Journal of Personality and Social Psychology, 36,* 608–618.

Baumeister, R. F., & Leary, M. R. (1995). The need to belong: Desire for interpersonal attachments as a fundamental human motivation. *Psychological Bulletin, 117,* 497–529.

Baumeister, R. F., & Scher, S. J. (1988). Self-defeating behavior patterns among normal individuals: Review and analysis of common self-destructive tendencies. *Psychological Bulletin, 104,* 3–22.

Baumeister, R. F., & Wotman, S. R. (1992). *Breaking hearts: The two sides of unrequited love.* New York: Guilford Press.

Baumeister, R. F., Bratslavsky, Muraven, M., & Tice, D. M. (1998). Ego depletion: Is the active self a limited resource? *Journal of Personality and Social Psychology, 74,* 1252–1265.

Baumeister, R. F., Heatherton, T. F., & Tice, D. M. (1993). When ego threats lead to self-regulation failure: Negative consequences of high self-esteem. *Journal of Personality and Social Psychology, 64,* 141–156.

Baumeister, R. F., Hutton, D. G., & Tice, D. M. (1989). Cognitive processes during deliberate self-presentation: How self-presenters alter and misinterpret the behavior of their interaction partners. *Journal of Experimental Social Psychology, 25,* 59–78.

Baumeister, R. F., Smart, L., & Boden, J. M. (1996). Relation of threatened egotism to violence and aggression: The dark side of high self-esteem. *Psychological Review, 103,* 5–33.

Baumeister, R. F., Tice, D. M., & Hutton, D. G. (1989). Self-presentational motivations and personality differences in self-esteem. *Journal of Personality, 57,* 547–579.

Baumrind, D. (1964). Some thoughts on ethics of research: After reading Milgram's "Behavioral Study of Obedience." *American Psychologist, 19,* 421–423.

Bauserman, R. (1996). Sexual aggression and pornography: A review of correlational research. *Basic and Applied Social Psychology, 18,* 405–427.

Baxter, L. A. (1987). Self-disclosure and relationship disengagement. In V. Derlega & J. H. Berg (Eds.), *Self-disclosure: Theory, research, and therapy* (pp. 155–174). New York: Plenum.

Bayer, R. (1987). *Homosexuality and American psychiatry: The politics of diagnosis* (2nd ed.). Princeton, NJ: Princeton University Press.

Beall, A. E., & Sternberg, R. J. (1995). The social construction of love. *Journal of Social and Personal Relationships, 12,* 417–438.

Beaman, A. L., Barnes, P. J., Klentz, B., & McQuirk, B. (1978). Increasing helping rates through information dissemination: Teaching pays. *Personality and Social Psychology Bulletin, 9,* 181–196.

Beaman, A. L., Cole, M., Preston, M., Klentz, B., & Steblay, N. M. (1983). Fifteen years of the foot-in-the-door research: A meta-analysis. *Personality and Social Psychology Bulletin, 9,* 181–186.

Beaman, A. L., Klentz, B., Diener, E., & Svanum, S. (1979). Self-awareness and transgression in children: Two field studies. *Journal of Personality and Social Psychology, 37,* 1835–1846.

Becker, B. J. (1986). Influence again: Another look at studies of gender differences in social influence. In J. S. Hyde & M. C. Linn (Eds.), *The psychology of gender: Advances through meta-analysis.* Baltimore: Johns Hopkins University Press.

Becker, H. S. (1963). *Outsiders: Studies in the sociology of deviance.* New York: Free Press.

Bednar, R., Wells, G., & Peterson, S. (1989). *Self-esteem: Paradoxes and innovations in clinical theory and practice.* Washington, DC: American Psychological Association.

Bell, K. L., & DePaulo, B. M. (1996). Liking and lying. *Basic and Applied Social Psychology, 18,* 243–266.

Bell, R. (1981). *Worlds of friendship.* Beverly Hills, CA: Sage.

Bellah, R., Madsen, R., Sullivan, W., Swindler, A., & Tipton, S. (1985). *Habits of the heart: Individualism and commitment in American life.* Berkeley, CA: University of California Press.

Belsky, J., & Cassidy, J. (1994). Attachment: Theory and evidence. In M. Rutter & D. Hay (Eds.), *Development through life: A handbook for clinicians* (pp. 373–402). Oxford, England: Blackwell.

Bem, D. (1972). Self-perception theory. In L. Berkowitz (Ed.), *Advances in experimental social psychology* (Vol. 6). New York: Academic Press.

Bem, D. J. (1965). An experimental analysis of self-persuasion. *Journal of Experimental Social Psychology, 1,* 199–218.

Bem, D. J. (1967). Self-perception: An alternative interpretation of cognitive dissonance phenomena. *Psychological Review, 74,* 183–200.

Bem, S. L. (1981). Gender schema theory: A cognitive account of sex typing. *Psychological Review, 88,* 354–364.

Bem, S. L. (1985). Androgyny and gender schema theory: A conceptual and empirical integration. In T. B. Snodegegger (Ed.), *Nebraska symposium on motivation: Psychology and gender* (pp. 179–226). Lincoln: University of Nebraska Press.

Benoit, S. C., & Thomas, R. L. (1992). The influence of expectancy in subliminal perception experiments. *Journal of General Psychology, 119,* 335–341.

Bentler, P. M., & Speckart, G. (1981). Attitudes "cause" behaviors: A structural equation analysis. *Journal of Personality and Social Psychology, 40,* 226–238.

Beren, S. E., Hayden, H. A., Wilfley, D. E., & Striegel-Moore, R. H. (1997). Body dissatisfaction among lesbian college students. *Psychology of Women Quarterly, 21,* 431–445.

Berg, J. H. (1984). The development of friendships between roommates. *Journal of Personality and Social Psychology, 46,* 346–356.

Berg, J. H., & Clark, M. S. (1986). Differences in social exchange between intimate and other relationships: Gradually evolving or quickly apparent? In V. J. Derlega & B. A. Winstead (Eds.), *Friendship and social interaction* (pp. 101–128). New York: Springer-Verlag.

Berger, J., Wagner, D. G., & Zelditch, M. (1985). Expectation states theory: Review and assessment. In J. Berger & M. Zelditch (Eds.), *Status, rewards, and influence* (pp. 1–72). San Francisco: Jossey-Bass.

Berglas, S., & Jones, E. E. (1978). Drug choice as a self-handicapping strategy in response to noncontingent success. *Journal of Personality and Social Psychology, 36,* 405–417.

Berkowitz, L. (1968, September). Impulse, aggression and the gun. *Psychology Today,* pp. 18–22.

Berkowitz, L. (1969). The frustration-aggression hypothesis revisited. In L. Berkowitz (Ed.), *Roots of aggression* (pp. 1–28). New York: Atherton.

Berkowitz, L. (1984). Some effects of thoughts on anti- and prosocial influences of media events: A cognitive-neoassociation analysis. *Psychological Bulletin, 95,* 410–427.

Berkowitz, L. (1989). Frustration-aggression hypothesis: Examination and reformulation. *Psychological Bulletin, 106,* 59–73.

Berkowitz, L. (1993). *Aggression: Its causes, consequences, and control.* New York: McGraw-Hill.

Berkowitz, L. (1994a). Is something missing? Some observations prompted by the cognitive-neoassociationist view of anger and emotional aggression. In L. R. Huesmann (Ed.), *Aggressive behavior: Current perspectives* (pp. 35–57). New York: Plenum.

Berkowitz, L. (1994b). On the escalation of aggression. In M. Potegal & J. F. Knutson (Eds.), *The dynamics of aggression: Biological and social processes in dyads and groups* (pp. 33–41). Hillsdale, NJ: Erlbaum.

Berkowitz, L., & Devine, P. G. (1995). Has social psychology always been cognitive? What is "cognitive" anyhow? *Personality and Social Psychology Bulletin, 21,* 696–703.

Bernard, J. (1981). The good-provider role: Its rise and fall. *American Psychologist, 36,* 1–12.

Berndsen, M., Spears, R., & Van Der Pligt, J. (1996). Illusory correlation and attitude-based vested interest. *European Journal of Social Psychology, 26,* 247–264.

Bernstein, W. M., Stephan, W. G., & Davis, M. H. (1979). Explaining attributions for achievement: A path analytic approach. *Journal of Personality and Social Psychology, 37,* 1810–1821.

Berscheid, E. (1998). The greening of relationship science. Distinguished Scientific Contribution Award Address at the American Psychological Association Convention, San Francisco.

Berscheid, E., & Hatfield (Walster), E. (1974). A little bit about love. In T. Huston (Ed.), *Foundations of interpersonal attraction* (pp. 355–381). New York: Academic Press.

Berscheid, E., & Hatfield, E. (1969). *Interpersonal attraction.* Reading, MA: Addison-Wesley.

Berscheid, E., & Lopes, J. (1997). A temporal model of relationship satisfaction and stability. In R. J. Sternberg & M. Hojjat (Eds.), *Satisfaction in close relationships* (pp. 129–159). New York: Guilford Press.

Berscheid, E., & Walster [Hatfield], E. (1978). *Interpersonal attraction* (2nd ed.). New York: McGraw.

Bettencourt, B. A., & Miller, N. (1996). Gender differences in aggression as a function of provocation: A meta-analysis. *Psychological Bulletin, 119,* 422–447.

Beyer, S., & Bowden, E. M. (1997). Gender differences in self-perceptions: Convergent evidence from three measures of accuracy and bias. *Personality and Social Psychology Bulletin, 23,* 157–172.

Bhargava, R. (1992). *Individualism in social science: Forms and limits of a methodology.* Oxford: Clarendon Press.

Bierbauer, G. (1979). Why did he do it? Attribution of obedience and the phenomenon of dispositional bias. *European Journal of Social Psychology, 9,* 67–84.

Bierhoff, H. W., Klein, R., & Kramp, P. (1991). Evidence for the altruistic personality from data on accident research. *Journal of Personality, 59,* 263–280.

Biernat, M., Vescio, T. K., & Theno, S. A. (1996). Violating American values: A "value congruence" approach to understanding outgroup attitudes. *Journal of Experimental Social Psychology, 32,* 387–410.

Billig, M. (1985). Prejudice, categorization and particularization: From a perceptual to a rhetorical approach. *European Journal of Social Psychology, 15,* 79–104.

Björkqvist, K., & Niemelä, P. (1992). New trends in the study of female aggression. In K. Björkqvist & P. Niemelä (Eds.), *Of mice and women: Aspects of female aggression* (pp. 3–16). San Diego, CA: Harcourt Brace Jovanovich.

Björkqvist, K., Lagerspetz, K. M. J., & Kaukiainen, A. (1992). Do girls manipulate and boys fight? Developmental trends regarding direct and indirect aggression. *Aggressive Behavior, 18.*

Blagrove, M. (1996). Effects of length of sleep deprivation on interrogative suggestibility. *Journal of Experimental Psychology: Applied, 2,* 48–59.

Blaine, B., & Crocker, J. (1993). Self-esteem and self-serving biases in reactions to positive and negative events: An integrative review. In R. Baumeister (Ed.), *Self-esteem: The puzzle of low self-regard* (pp. 55–85). New York: Plenum.

Blais, M. R., Sabourin, S., Boucher, C., & Vallerand, R. J. (1990). Toward a motivational model of couple happiness. *Journal of Personality and Social Psychology, 59,* 1021–1031.

Blake, R. R., & Mouton, J. S. (1979). Intergroup problem solving in organization: From theory to practice. In W. G. Austin & S. Worchel (Eds.), *The social psychology of intergroup relations* (pp. 19–32). Monterey, CA: Brooks/Cole.

Blass, T. (1984). Social psychology and personality: Toward a convergence. *Journal of Personality and Social Psychology, 47,* 1013–1027.

Blass, T. (1996). Attribution of responsibility and trust in the Milgram obedience experiment. *Journal of Applied Social Psychology, 26,* 1529–1535.

Bless, H., Clore, G. L., Schwarz, N., Golisano, V., Rabe, C., and Wölk, M. (1996). Mood and the use of scripts: Does a happy mood really lead to mindlessness? *Journal of Personality and Social Psychology, 71,* 665–679.

Blier, M. J., & Blier-Wilson, L. A. (1989). Gender differences in self-rated emotional expressiveness. *Sex Roles, 21,* 287–295.

Blieszner, R., & Adams, R. G. (1992). *Adult friendship.* Newbury Park, NJ: Sage.

Block, J. D. (1980). *Friendship: How to give it, how to get it.* New York: Macmillan.

Block, L. G., & Keller, P. A. (1997). Effects of self-efficacy and vividness on the persuasiveness of health communication. *Journal of Consumer Psychology, 6,* 31–54.

Blumer, H. (1965). The future of the color line. In J. C. McKinney & E. T. Thompson (Eds.), *The south in continuity and change.* Durham, NC: Seeman.

Bobo, L. (1988). Group conflict, prejudice, and the paradox of contemporary racial attitudes. In P. A. Katz & D. A. Taylor (Eds.), *Eliminating racism: Profiles in controversy* (pp. 85–114). New York: Plenum Press.

Bodenhausen, G. V. (1988). Stereotypic biases in social decision making: Testing process models of stereotype use. *Journal of Personality and Social Psychology, 55,* 726–737.

Bogart, K., Simmons, S., & Stein, N. (1992). Breaking the silence: Sexual and gender-based harassment in elementary, secondary, and postsecondary education. In S. S. Klein (Ed.), *Sex equity and sexuality in education* (pp. 191–221). Albany, NY: State University of New York Press.

Bohner, G., Crow, K., Erb, H., & Schwarz, N. (1992). Affect and persuasion: Mood effects on the processing of message content and context cues and on subsequent behaviour. *European Journal of Social Psychology, 22,* 511–530.

Bond, C. F., Jr., & Titus, L. J. (1983). Social facilitation: A meta-analysis of 241 studies. *Psychological Bulletin, 94,* 265–292.

Bond, R., & Smith, P. B. (1996). Culture and conformity: A meta-analysis of studies using Asch's (1952b, 1956) line judgment task. *Psychological Bulletin, 119,* 111–137.

Bontempo, R., Lobel, S., & Triandis, H. (1990). Compliance and value internalization in Brazil and the U.S. *Journal of Cross-Cultural Psychology, 21,* 201–213.

Bordens, K. S., & Bassett, J. (1985). The plea bargaining process from the defendant's perspective: A field experiment. *Basic and Applied Social Psychology, 6,* 93–110.

Borgida, E., Conner, C., & Manteufel, L. (1992). Understanding living kidney donation: A behavioral decision-making perspective. In S. Spacapan & S. Oskamp (Eds.), *Helping and being helped* (pp. 183–212). Newbury Park, CA: Sage.

Bornstein, R. F. (1989). Exposure and affect: Overview and meta-analysis of research, 1968–1987. *Psychological Bulletin, 106,* 265–289.

Bornstein, R. F., Leone, D. R., & Galley, D. J. (1987). The generalizability of subliminal mere exposure effects: Influence of stimuli perceived without awareness on social behavior. *Journal of Personality and Social Psychology, 53,* 1070–1079.

Bossard, J. (1932). Residential propinquity as a factor in marriage selection. *American Journal of Sociology, 38,* 219–224.

Bower, G. H., & Hilgard, E. R. (1981). *Theories of learning* (5th ed.). Englewood Cliffs, NJ: Prentice Hall.

Bowlby, J. (1969). *Attachment and loss.* Vol. I. *Attachment.* New York: Wiley.

Bradbury, T. N., & Fincham, F. D. (1990). Attributions in marriage: Review and critique. *Psychological Bulletin, 107,* 3–33.

Bradbury, T. N., Campbell, S. M., & Fincham, F. D. (1995). Longitudinal and behavioral analysis of masculinity and femininity in marriage. *Journal of Personality and Social Psychology, 68,* 328–341.

Brage, D., Meredith, W., & Woodward, J. (1993). Correlates of loneliness among midwestern adolescents. *Adolescence, 28,* 685–693.

Brainerd, C. J., Reyna, V. F., & Brandse, E. (1995). Are children's false memories more persistent than their true memories? *Psychological Science, 6,* 359–364.

Brauer, M., Judd, C. M., & Gliner, M. D. (1995). The effects of repeated expressions on attitude polarization during group discussions. *Journal of Personality and Social Psychology, 68,* 1014–1029.

Braver, S. L. (1995). Social contracts and the provision of public goods. In D. A. Schroeder (Ed.), *Social dilemmas: Perspectives on individuals and groups* (pp. 69–86). Westport, CN: Praeger.

Breckler, S. J. (1984). Empirical validation of affect, behavior, and cognition as distinct components of attitude. *Journal of Personality and Social Psychology, 52,* 384–389.

Brehm, S. S. (1988). Passionate love. In R. J. Sternberg & M. L. Barnes (Eds.), *The psychology of love* (pp. 232–263). New Haven, CT: Yale University Press.

Brehm, S. S. (1992). *Intimate relationships.* New York: McGraw-Hill.

Brehm, S. S., & Brehm, J. W. (1981). *Psychological reactance: A theory of freedom and control.* New York: Academic Press.

Brennan, K. A., & Shaver, P. R. (1995). Dimensions of adult attachment, affect regulation, and romantic relationship functioning. *Personality and Social Psychology Bulletin, 21,* 267–283.

Brewer, M. B. (1979). Ingroup bias in the minimal intergroup situation: A cognitive-motivational analysis. *Psychological Bulletin, 86,* 307–324.

Brewer, M. B., & Brown, R. J. (1998). Intergroup relations. In D. T. Gilbert, S. T. Fiske, & G. Lindzey (Eds.), *The handbook of social psychology* (4th ed.). New York: McGraw-Hill.

Brewer, M. B., & Kramer, R. K. (1986). Choice behavior in social dilemmas: Effects of social identity, group size, and decision framing. *Journal of Personality and Social Psychology, 50,* 543–549.

Brewer, M. B., & Lui, L. (1984). Categorization of the elderly by the elderly: Effects of perceiver's category membership. *Personality and Social Psychology Bulletin, 10,* 585–595.

Brewer, M. B., & Miller, N. (1984). Beyond the contact hypothesis: Theoretical perspectives on desegregation. In N. Miller & M. B. Brewer (Eds.), *Groups in contact: The psychology of desegregation* (pp. 281–302). New York: Academic Press.

Brickman, P. (1987). *Commitment, conflict, and caring.* Englewood Cliffs, NJ: Prentice-Hall.

Bridges, J. S., & Etaugh, C. (1994). Black and White college women's perceptions of early maternal employment. *Psychology of Women Quarterly, 18,* 427–431.

Briggs, S. R., & Cheek, J. M. (1988). On the nature of self-monitoring: Problems with assessment, problems with validity. *Journal of Personality and Social Psychology, 54,* 663–678.

Britt, T. W., Boniecki, K. A., Vescio, T. K., Biernat, M., & Brown, L. M. (1996). Intergroup anxiety: A person × situation approach. *Personality and Social Psychology Bulletin, 22,* 1177–1188.

Brockner, J. (1979). Self-esteem, self-consciousness, and task performance: Replications, extensions, and possible explanations. *Journal of Personality and Social Psychology, 37,* 447–461.

Brody, L. R. (1993). On understanding gender differences in the expression of emotion: Gender roles, socialization and language. In S. Ablom, D. Brown, E. Khantzian, & J. Mack (Eds.), *Human feelings: Exploration in affect development and meaning.* New York: Analytic Press.

Brody, L. R., & Hall, J. A. (1993). Gender and emotion. In M. Lewis & J. M. Haviland (Eds.), *Handbook of emotions* (pp. 447–460). New York: Guilford.

Brookins, C. C., Anyabwile, T. M., & Nacoste, R. (1996). Exploring the links between racial identity attitudes and psychological feelings of closeness in African-American college students. *Journal of Applied Social Psychology, 26,* 243–264.

Broverman, I. K., Vogel, S. R., Broverman, D. M., Clarkson, F. E., & Rosenkrantz, P. S. (1972). Sex role stereotypes: A current appraisal. *Journal of Social Issues, 28,* 59–79.

Brown, J. D. (1993). Motivational conflict and the self: The double-bind of low self-esteem. In R. F. Baumeister (Ed.), *Self-esteem: The puzzle of low self-regard* (pp. 117–130). New York: Plenum Press.

Brown, J. D., & Rogers, R. J. (1991). Self-serving attributions: The role of physiological arousal. *Personality and Social Psychology Bulletin, 17,* 501–506.

Brown, J. D., Novick, N. J., Lord, K. A., & Richards, J. M. (1992). When Gulliver travels: Social context, psychological closeness, and self-appraisals. *Journal of Personality and Social Psychology, 62,* 717–727.

Browne, A., & Williams, K. R. (1989). Exploring the effect of resource availability and the likelihood of female-perpetrated homicides. *Law and Society Review, 23,* 75–94.

Bruins, J. J., Liebrand, W. P., & Wilke, H. A. (1989). About the saliency of fear and greed in social dilemmas. *European Journal of Social Psychology, 19,* 155–162.

Bruner, J. S., Goodnow, J. J., & Austin, G. A. (1956). *A study of thinking.* New York: Wiley.

Bryan, J. H., & Test, N. A. (1967). Models and helping: Naturalistic studies in aiding behavior. *Journal of Personality and Social Psychology, 6,* 400–407.

Bryson, J. B. (1977). Situational determinants of the expression of jealousy. In H. Sigall (Chair), *Sexual jealousy.* Symposium presented at the Annual Meeting of the American Psychological Association, San Francisco.

Buck, R. (1977). Nonverbal communication of affect in preschool children: Relationships with personality and skin conductance.

Journal of Personality and Social Psychology, 35, 225–236.

Buck, R. (1984). *The communication of emotion.* New York: Guilford Press.

Budesheim, T. L., Houston, D. A., & DePaola, S. J. (1996). Persuasiveness of in-group and out-group political messages: The case of negative political campaigning. *Journal of Personality and Social Psychology, 70,* 523–534.

Buehler, R., & Griffin, D. (1994). Change-of-meaning effects in conformity and dissent: Observing construal processes over time. *Journal of Personality and Social Psychology, 67,* 984–996.

Bui, K.-V. T., Peplau, L. A., & Hill, C. T. (1996). Testing the Rusbult model of relationship commitment and stability in a 15-year study of heterosexual couples. *Personality and Social Psychology Bulletin, 22,* 1244–1257.

Bullock, W. A., & Gilliland, K. (1993). Eysenck's arousal theory of introversion-extroversion: A converging measures investigation. *Journal of Personality and Social Psychology, 64,* 113–123.

Bullough, V. L. (1976). *Sexual variance in society and history.* Chicago: University of Chicago Press.

Burbank, V. K. (1987). Female aggression in cross-cultural perspective. *Behavior Science Research, 21,* 70–100.

Burger, J. M. (1981). Motivational biases in the attribution of responsibility for an accident: A meta-analysis of the defensive-attribution hypothesis. *Psychological Bulletin, 90,* 496–512.

Burger, J. M. (1986). Increasing compliance by improving the deal: The that's-not-all technique. *Journal of Personality and Social Psychology, 51,* 277–283.

Burger, J. M. (1987). Desire for control and conformity to a perceived norm. *Journal of Personality and Social Psychology, 53,* 355–360.

Burger, J. M., Horita, M., Kinoshita, L., Roberts, K., & Vera, C. (1997). Effects of time on the norm of reciprocity. *Basic and Applied Social Psychology, 19,* 91–100.

Burger, J. M., Reed, M., DeCesare, K., Rauner, S., & Rozolis, J. (in press). The effects of initial request size on compliance: More about the that's-not-all technique. *Basic and Applied Social Psychology.*

Burgess, D., & Borgida, E. (1997). Sexual harassment: An experimental test of sex-role spillover theory. *Personality and Social Psychology Bulletin, 23,* 63–75.

Burgess, E. W. (1926). The romantic impulse and family disorganization. *Survey, 57,* 290–294.

Burgner, D., & Hewstone, M. (1993). Young children's causal attributions for success and failure: 'Self-enhancing' boys and 'self-derogating' girls. *British Journal of Developmental Psychology, 11,* 125–129.

Burnstein, E., Crandall, C., & Kitayama, S. (1994). Some neo-Darwinian decision rules for altruism: Weighing cues for inclusive fitness as a function of the biological importance of the decision. *Journal of Personality and Social Psychology, 67,* 773–789.

Burt, M. (1980). Cultural myths and supports for rape. *Journal of Personality and Social Psychology, 38,* 217–230.

Bushman, B. J. (1996). Individual differences in the extent and development of aggressive cognitive-associative networks. *Personality and Social Psychology Bulletin, 22,* 811–819.

Bushman, B. J., & Baumeister, R. F. (1998). Threatened egotism: Narcissism, self-esteem, and direct and displaced aggression: Does self-love or self-hate lead to violence? *Journal of Personality and Social Psychology, 75,* 219–229.

Bushman, B. J., & Geen, R. G. (1990). Role of cognitive-emotional mediators and individual differences in the effects of media violence on aggression. *Journal of Personality and Social Psychology, 58,* 156–163.

Buss, A. H. (1966). Instrumentality of aggression, feedback, and frustration as determinants of physical aggression. *Journal of Personality and Social Psychology, 3,* 153–162.

Buss, A. H. (1980). *Self-consciousness and social anxiety.* San Francisco: W. H. Freeman.

Buss, D. M. (1989). Sex differences in human mate preferences: Evolutionary hypotheses tested in 37 cultures. *Behavioral and Brain Sciences, 12,* 1–49.

Buss, D. M., & Shackelford, T. K. (1997). Human aggression in evolutionary psychological perspective. *Clinical Psychology Review, 17,* 605–619.

Buss, D. M., Gomes, M., Higgins, D. S., & Lauterbach, K. (1987). Tactics of manipulation. *Journal of Personality and Social Psychology, 52,* 1219–1229.

Buunk, B., & Bringle, R. G. (1987). Jealousy in love relationships. In D. Perlman & S. Duck (Eds.). *Intimate relationships: Development, dynamics, and deterioration* (pp. 123–147). Newbury Park, CA: Sage.

Buunk, B. P., & van der Eijnden, R. J. J. M. (1997). Perceived prevalence, perceived superiority, and relationship satisfaction: Most relationships are good, but ours is the best. *Personality and Social Psychology Bulletin, 23,* 219–228.

Byrne, D. (1971). *The attraction paradigm.* New York: Academic Press.

Byrne, D., & Nelson, D. (1965). Attraction as a linear function of proportion of positive reinforcements. *Journal of Personality and Social Psychology, 1,* 659–663.

Byrne, D., Gouaux, C., Griffitt, W., Lamberth, J., Murakawa, N., Prasad, M. B., & Ramirez, M., III. (1971). The ubiquitous relationship: Attitude similarity and attraction. A cross-cultural study. *Human Relations, 24,* 201–207.

Byrne, D., Rasche, L., & Kelley, K. (1974). When "I like you" indicates disagreement. *Journal of Research in Personality, 8,* 207–217.

Cacioppo, J. T., & Petty, R. E. (1982). The need for cognition. *Journal of Personality and Social Psychology, 42,* 116–131.

Cacioppo, J. T., & Petty, R. E. (1989). Effects of message repetition on argument processing, recall, and persuasion. *Basic and Applied Social Psychology, 10,* 3–12.

Cacioppo, J. T., Marshall-Goodell, B. S., Tassinary, L. G., & Petty, R. E. (1992). Rudimentary determinants of attitudes: Classical conditioning is more effective when prior knowledge about the attitude stimulus is low than high. *Journal of Experimental Social Psychology, 28,* 207–233.

Cacioppo, J. T., Petty, R. E., Feinstein, J. A., & Jarvis, W. B. G. (1996). Dispositional differences in cognitive motivation: The life and times of individuals varying in need for cognition. *Psychological Bulletin, 119,* 197–253.

Cacioppo, J. T., Petty, R. E., Kao, C. F., & Rodriguez, R. (1986). Central and peripheral routes to persuasion: An individual differences perspective. *Journal of Personality and Social Psychology, 51,* 1032–1043.

Cacioppo, J. T., Priester, J. R., & Berntson, G. G. (1993). Rudimentary determinants of attitudes II: Arm flexion and extension have differential effects on attitudes. *Journal of Personality and Social Psychology, 65,* 5–17.

Caldwell, D. F., & O'Reilly, C. A., III. (1982). Boundary spanning and individual performance: The impact of self-monitoring. *Journal of Applied Psychology, 67,* 124–127.

Campbell, A., Muncer, S., & Odber, J. (1997a). Aggression and testosterone: Testing a bio-social model. *Aggressive Behavior, 23,* 229–238.

Campbell, A., Muncer, S., Guy, A., & Banim, M. (1996). Social representations of aggression: Crossing the sex barrier. *European Journal of Social Psychology, 26,* 135–147.

Campbell, A., Sapochnik, M., & Muncer, S. (1997b). Sex differences in aggression: Does social representation mediate form of aggression? *British Journal of Social Psychology, 36,* 161–171.

Campbell, J. D., & Fairey, P. J. (1989). Informational and normative routes to conformity: The effect of faction size as a function of norm extremity and attention to the stimulus. *Journal of Personality and Social Psychology, 57,* 457–468.

Campbell, J. D., Chew, B., & Scratchley, L. S. (1991). Cognitive and emotional reactions to daily events: The effects of self-esteem and self-complexity. *Journal of Personality, 59,* 473–505.

Campbell, J. D., Tesser, A., & Fairey, P. J. (1986). Conformity and attention to the stimulus: Some temporal and contextual dynamics. *Journal of Personality and Social Psychology, 51,* 315–324.

Cantor, J. R., & Venus, P. (1983). The effect of humor on recall of a radio advertisement. *Journal of Broadcasting, 24*, 13–22.

Caplan, N., & Nelson, S. D. (1973). On being useful: The nature and consequences of psychological research on social problems. *American Psychologist, 28*, 199–211.

Cappe, R. F., & Alden, L. E. (1986). A comparison of treatment strategies for clients functionally impaired by extreme shyness and social avoidance. *Journal of Consulting and Clinical Psychology, 54*, 796–801.

Caprara, G. V., Barbaranelli, C., & Zimbardo, P. G. (1996). Understanding the complexity of human aggression: Affective, cognitive, and social dimensions of individual differences in propensity toward aggression. *European Journal of Personality, 10*, 133–155.

Caprara, G. V., Perugini, M., & Barbaranelli, C. (1994). Studies of individual differences in aggression. In M. Potegal & J. F. Knutson (Eds.), *The dynamics of aggression: Biological and social processes in dyads and groups* (pp. 123–153). Hillsdale, NJ: Erlbaum.

Carli, L. L. (1990). Gender, language, and influence. *Journal of Personality and Social Psychology, 59*, 941–951.

Carli, L. L., Ganley, R., & Pierce-Otay, A. (1991). Similarity and satisfaction in roommate relationships. *Personality and Social Psychology Bulletin, 17*, 419–426.

Carli, L. L., LaFleur, S. J., & Loeber, C. C. (1995). Nonverbal behavior, gender, and influence. *Journal of Personality and Social Psychology, 68*, 1030–1041.

Carlsmith, J. M., & Anderson, C. A. (1979). Ambient temperature and the occurrence of collective violence: A new analysis. *Journal of Personality and Social Psychology, 37*, 337–344.

Carlson, M., & Miller, N. (1987). Explanation of the relation between negative mood and helping. *Psychological Bulletin, 102*, 91–108.

Carlson, M., Charlin, V., & Miller, N. (1988). Positive mood and helping behavior: A test of six hypotheses. *Journal of Personality and Social Psychology, 55*, 211–299.

Carlson, M., Marcus-Newhall, A., & Miller, N. (1990). The effects of situational aggressive cues: A quantitative review. *Journal of Personality and Social Psychology, 58*, 622–633.

Cartwright, D. (1971). Risk taking by individuals and groups: An assessment of research employing choice dilemmas. *Journal of Personality and Social Psychology, 20*, 245–261.

Carver, C. S., & Scheier, M. F. (1981a). *Attention and self-regulation: A control-theory approach to human behavior.* New York: Springer-Verlag.

Carver, C. S., & Scheier, M. F. (1990b). Origins and functions of positive and negative affect: A control-process view. *Psychological Review, 97*, 19–35.

Casey, R. J., & Ritter, J. M. (1996). How infant appearance informs: Child care providers' responses to babies varying in appearance of age and attractiveness. *Journal of Applied Developmental Psychology, 17*, 495–518.

Cash, T. F., & Derlega, V. J. (1978). The matching hypothesis: Physical attractiveness among same-sexed friends. *Personality and Social Psychology Bulletin, 4*, 240–243.

Cassell, P. G., & Hayman, B. S. (1996). Police interrogation in the 1990s: An empirical study of the effects of *Miranda. UCLA Law Review, 43*, 839–931.

Castano, E., & Yzerbyt, V. Y. (1998). The highs and lows of group homogeneity. *Behavioural Processes, 42*, 219–238.

Catalano, R., Dooley, D., Novaco, R. W., Wilson, G., & Hough, R. (1993). Using ECA survey data to examine the effect of job layoffs on violent behavior. *Hospital and Community Psychiatry, 44*, 874–879.

Caudron, S. (1994). Diversity ignites effective work teams. *Personnel Journal, 73*, 54–63.

Caughey, J. L. (1984). *Imaginary social worlds: A cultural approach.* Lincoln: University of Nebraska Press.

Ceci, S. J., & Bruck, M. (1993). Suggestibility of the child witness: A historical review and synthesis. *Psychological Bulletin, 113*, 403–439.

Cecil, H., Evans, R. I., & Stanley, M. A. (1996). Perceived believability among adolescents of health warning labels on cigarette packs. *Journal of Applied Social Psychology, 26*, 502–519.

Celuch, K., & Slama, M. (1995). "Getting along" and "getting ahead" as motives for self-presentation: Their impact on advertising effectiveness. *Journal of Applied Social Psychology, 25*, 1700–1713.

Cerulo, K. A. (1989). Sociopolitical control and the structure of national symbols: An empirical analysis of national anthems. *Social Forces, 68*, 76–99.

Chaiken, S. (1979). Communicator physical attractiveness and persuasion. *Journal of Personality and Social Psychology, 37*, 1387–1397.

Chaiken, S. (1987). The heuristic model of persuasion. In M. P. Zanna, J. M. Olson, & C. P. Herman (Eds.), *Social influence: The Ontario symposium* (Vol. 5, pp. 3–39). Hillsdale, NJ: Erlbaum.

Chaiken, S., & Baldwin, M. W. (1981). Affective-cognitive consistency and the effect of salient behavioral information on the self-perception of attitudes. *Journal of Personality and Social Psychology, 41*, 1–12.

Chaiken, S., & Trope, Y. (1999). (Eds.). *Dual-process theories in social psychology.* New York: Guilford.

Chaiken, S., Pomerantz, E. M., & Giner-Sorolla, R. (1995). Structural consistency and attitude strength. In R. E. Petty & J. A. Krosnick (Eds.), *Attitude strength: Antecedents and consequences* (pp. 387–412). Mahwah, NJ: Erlbaum.

Chance, J. E. (1985). Faces, folklore, and research hypotheses. Presidential address to the Midwestern Psychological Association convention.

Charney, D., & Russell, R. (1994). An overview of sexual harassment. *American Journal of Psychiatry, 151*, 10–17.

Chartrand, T., Pinckert, S., & Burger, J. M. (1999). When manipulation backfires: The effects of time delay and requester on the foot-in-the-door technique. *Journal of Applied Social Psychology 29*, 211–221.

Chelune, G. J. (1976). Reactions to male and female disclosure at two levels. *Journal of Personality and Social Psychology, 34*, 1000–1003.

Chen, A. C., German, C., & Zaidel, D. W. (1997a). Brain asymmetry and facial attractiveness: Facial beauty is not simply in the eye of the beholder. *Neuropsychologia, 35*, 471–476.

Chen, H., Yates, B. T., & McGinnies, E. (1988). Effects of involvement on observers' estimates of consensus, distinctiveness, and consistency. *Personality and Social Psychology Bulletin, 14*, 468–478.

Chen, N. Y., Shaffer, D. R., & Wu, C. (1997b). On physical attractiveness stereotyping in Taiwan: A revised sociocultural perspective. *Journal of Social Psychology, 137*, 117–124.

Chen, S., Shecter, D., & Chaiken, S. (1996). Getting at the truth or getting along: Accuracy-versus impression-motivated heuristic and systematic processing. *Journal of Personality and Social Psychology, 71*, 262–275.

Chen, S. C. (1937). Social modification of the activity of ants in nest-building. *Physiological Zoology, 10*, 420–436.

Chiu, C., Hong, Y., & Dweck, C. S. (1997). Lay dispositionism and implicit theories of personality. *Journal of Personality and Social Psychology, 73*, 19–30.

Christensen, L. (1988). Deception in psychological research: When is its use justified? *Personality and Social Psychology Bulletin, 14*, 664–675.

Christensen, P. N., & Kashy, D. A. (1998). Perceptions of and by lonely people in initial social interaction. *Personality and Social Psychology Bulletin, 24*, 322–329.

Cialdini, R., Trost, M., & Newsom, J. (1995). Preference for consistency: The development of a valid measure and the discovery of surprising behavioral implications. *Journal of Personality and Social Psychology, 69*, 318–328.

Cialdini, R. B., & Fultz, J. (1990). Interpreting the negative mood-helping literature via "mega" analysis: A contrary view. *Psychological Bulletin, 107*, 210–214.

Cialdini, R. B., & Kenrick, D. T. (1976). Altruism as hedonism: A social development perspective on the relationship of negative mood state and helping. *Journal of Personality and Social Psychology, 34,* 907–914.

Cialdini, R. B., & Trost, M. R., (1998). Social influence: Social norms, conformity, and compliance. In D. T. Gilbert, S. T. Fiske, & G. Lindzey (Eds.), pp. 151–192. *The handbook of social psychology* (4th ed.). New York: McGraw-Hill.

Cialdini, R. B., Borden, R. J., Thorne, A., Walker, M. R., Freeman, S., & Sloan, L. R. (1976). Basking in reflected glory: Three (football) field studies. *Journal of Personality and Social Psychology, 34,* 366–375.

Cialdini, R. B., Braver, S. L., & Lewis, S. K. (1974). Attributional bias and the easily persuaded other. *Journal of Personality and Social Psychology, 30,* 631–637.

Cialdini, R. B., Brown, S. L., Lewis, B. P., Luce, C., & Neuberg, S. L. (1997). Reinterpreting the empathy-altruism relationship: When one into one equals oneness. *Journal of Personality and Social Psychology, 67,* 481–494.

Cialdini, R. B., Cacioppo, J. T., Bassett, R., & Miller, J. A. (1978). Low-ball procedure for producing compliance: Commitment then cost. *Journal of Personality and Social Psychology, 36,* 463–476.

Cialdini, R. B., Vincent, J. E., Lewis, S. K., Catalan, J., Wheeler, D., & Darby, B. L. (1975). Reciprocal concessions procedure for inducing compliance: The door-in-the-face technique. *Journal of Personality and Social Psychology, 31,* 206–215.

Cini, M. A., Moreland, R. L., & Levine, J. M. (1993). Group staffing levels and responses to prospective and new group members. *Journal of Personality and Social Psychology, 65,* 723–734.

Clark, K. B., & Clark, M. (1947). Racial identification and preferences in Negro children. In T. M. Newcomb & T. L. Hartley (Eds.), *Readings in social psychology* (pp. 167–178). New York: Holt.

Clark, K. B., & Clark, M. P. (1939). The development of self and the emergence of racial identifications in Nego preschool chidlren. *Journal of Social Psychology, 10,* 591–599.

Clark, M. S., Mills, J., & Corcoran, D. M. (1989). Keeping track of needs and inputs of friends and strangers. *Personality and Social Psychology Bulletin, 15,* 533–542.

Clark, R. D., III, & Word, L. E. (1972). Why don't bystanders help? Because of ambiguity? *Journal of Personality and Social Psychology, 24,* 392–400.

Coats, E. J., & Feldman, R. S. (1996). Gender differences in nonverbal correlates of social status. *Personality and Social Psychology Bulletin, 22,* 1014–1022.

Codol, J. P. (1975). On the so-called "superior conformity of the self" behavior: Twenty experimental investigations. *European Journal of Social Psychology, 5,* 457–501.

Cogan, J. C., Bhalla, S. K., Sefa-Dedeh, A., & Rothblum, E. D. (1996). A comparison study of United States and African students on perceptions of obesity and thinness. *Journal of Cross-Cultural Psychology, 27,* 98–113.

Cohen, A. T., & Zhou, X. (1991). Status processes in enduring work groups. *American Sociological Review, 56,* 179–188.

Cohen, D. (1996). Law, social policy, and violence: The impact of regional cultures. *Journal of Personality and Social Psychology, 70,* 961–978.

Cohen, D. (1998). Culture, social organization, and patterns of violence. *Journal of Personality and Social Psychology, 75,* 408–419.

Cohen, D., & Nisbett, R. E. (1994). Self-protection and the culture of honor: Explaining southern violence. *Personality and Social Psychology Bulletin, 20,* 551–567.

Cohen, D., & Vandello, J. A. (1998). Meanings of violence. *Journal of Legal Studies, 27,* 501–518.

Cohen, D., Nisbett, R. E., Bowdle, B., & Schwarz, N. (1996). Insult, aggression, and the southern culture of honor: An "experimental ethnography." *Journal of Personality and Social Psychology, 70,* 945–960.

Cohen, D., Vandello, J. A., & Rantilla, A. K. (1998). The sacred and the social: Cultures of honor and violence. In P. Gilbert & B. Andrews (Eds.), *Shame: Interpersonal behavior, psychpathology, and culture* (pp. 261–282). Oxford: Oxford University Press.

Cohen, E. G. (1982). Expectation states and interracial interaction in school settings. *Annual Review of Sociology, 8,* 209–235.

Cohn, E. G., & Rotton, J. (1997). Assault as a function of time and temperature: A moderator-variable time-series analysis. *Journal of Personality and Social Psychology, 72,* 1322–1334.

Coker, D. R. (1984). The relationships among gender concepts and cognitive maturity. *Sex Roles, 10,* 19–31.

Cole, M. (1992). Culture in development. In M. H. Bornstein & M. E. Lamb (Eds.), *Developmental psychology: An advanced textbook* (3rd ed.). Hillsdale, NJ: Erlbaum.

Collins, B. E., & Brief, D. E. (1995). Using person-perception vignette methodologies to uncover the symbolic meanings of teacher behaviors in the Milgram paradigm. *Journal of Social Issues, 51,* 89–106.

Collins, M. A., & Ziebrowitz, L. A. (1995). The contributions of appearance to occupational outcomes in civilian and military settings. *Journal of Applied Social Psychology, 25,* 129–163.

Collins, N. L., & Miller, L. C. (1994). Self-disclosure and liking: A meta-analytic review. *Psychological Bulletin, 116,* 457–475.

Collins, N. L., & Read, S. J. (1990). Adult attachment, working models, and relationship quality in dating couples. *Journal of Personality and Social Psychology, 58,* 644–663.

Collins, R. L. (1996). For better or worse: The impact of upward social comparison on self-evaluations. *Psychological Bulletin, 119,* 51–69.

Colombo, J. (1995). Cost, utility, and judgments of institutional review boards. *Psychological Science, 6,* 318–319.

Comer, D. R. (1995). A model of social loafing in real work groups. *Human Relations, 48,* 647–667.

Comte, I. A. (1875). *Systems of positive polity* (Vol. 1). London: Longmans, Green. (First published 1851.)

Conger, J. D., Conger, A. J., & Brehm, S. S. (1976). Fear level as a moderator of false feedback effects in snake phobics. *Journal of Consulting and Clinical Psychology, 44,* 135–141.

Congregation for the Doctrine of the Faith. (1986). *Letter to the bishops of the Catholic church on the pastoral care of homosexual persons.* Vatican City: Author.

Conner, R. C., & Norriss, K. S. (1982). Are dolphins reciprocal altruists? *American Naturalist, 119,* 358–374.

Conrath, D. W. (1973). Communication patterns, organizational structure, and man: Some relationships. *Human Factors, 15,* 459–470.

Cook, H. B. K. (1992). Matrilocality and female aggression in Margariteño society. In K. Björkqvist & P. Niemelä (Eds.), *Of mice and women: Aspects of female aggression* (pp. 149–162). San Diego, CA: Harcourt Brace Jovanovich.

Cook, S. W. (1964). Desegregation: A psychological analysis. In W. W. Charters, Jr., & N. L. Gage (Eds.), *Readings in the social psychology of education.* Boston: Allyn & Bacon.

Cook, S. W. (1984). Cooperative interaction in multiethnic contexts. In N. Miller & M. Brewer (Eds.), *Groups in contact: The psychology of desegregation.* New York: Academic Press.

Cook, T. D., & Shadish, W. R. (1994). Social experiments: Some developments over the past fifteen years. *Annual Review of Psychology, 45,* 545–580.

Cooley, C. H. (1902). *Human nature and the social order.* New York: Scribner's Press.

Corby, N. H., Jamner, M. S., & Wolitski, R. J. (1996). Using the theory of planned behavior to predict intention to use condoms among male and female injecting drug users. *Journal of Applied Social Psychology, 26,* 52–75.

Corney, R. (1990). Sex differences in general practice attendance and help seeking for minor illness. *Journal of Psychosomatic Research, 34,* 525–534.

Cottrell, N. B. (1972). Social facilitation. In C. G. McClintock (Ed.), *Experimental social psychology* (pp. 185–236). New York: Holt.

Cottrell, N. B., Wack, D. L., Sekerak, G. J., & Rittle, R. H. (1968). Social facilitation of dominant responses by the presence of an audience and the mere presence of others. *Journal of Personality and Social Psychology, 9*, 245–250.

Cowan, G., & Campbell, R. R. (1994). Racism and sexism in interracial pornography: A content analysis. *Psychology of Women Quarterly, 18*, 323–338.

Cowan, P. A., & Walters, R. H. (1963). Studies of reinforcement of aggression: I. Effects of scheduling. *Child Development, 34*, 543–551.

Cox, C. L., Smith, S. L., & Insko, C. A. (1996). Categorical race versus individuating belief as determinants of discrimination: A study of Southern adolescents in 1966, 1979, and 1993. *Journal of Experimental Social Psychology, 32*, 39–70.

Craig, R. S. (1992). The effect of television day part on gender portrayals in television commercials: A content analysis. *Sex Roles, 26*, 197–211.

Crandall, C. S. (1988). Social contagion of binge eating. *Journal of Personality and Social Psychology, 55*, 588–598.

Crano, W. D. (1995). Attitude strength and vested interest. In R. E. Petty & J. A. Krosnick (Eds.), *Attitude strength: Antecedents and consequences* (pp. 131–157). Mahwah, NJ: Erlbaum.

Crary, W. G. (1966). Reactions to incongruent self-experiences. *Journal of Consulting Psychology, 30*, 246–252.

Crawford, A. M. (1996). Stigma associated with AIDS: A meta-analysis. *Journal of Applied Social Psychology, 26*, 398–416.

Crick, N. R., Casas, J. F., & Mosher, M. (1997). Relational and overt aggression in preschool. *Developmental Psychology, 33*, 579–588.

Crites, S. L., Cacioppo, J. T., Gardner, W. L., & Berntson, G. G. (1995). Bioelectrical echoes from evaluative categorization: II. A late positive brain potential that varies as a function of attitude registration rather than attitude report. *Journal of Personality and Social Psychology, 68*, 997–1013.

Crocker, J., & Luhtanen, R. (1990). Collective self-esteem and ingroup bias. *Journal of Personality and Social Psychology, 58*, 60–67.

Crocker, J., & Major, B. (1989). Social stigma and self-esteem: The self-protective properties of stigma. *Psychological Review, 96*, 608–630.

Crocker, J., Luhtanen, R., Blaine, B., & Broadnax, S. (1994). Collective self-esteem and psychological well-being among White, Black, and Asian college students. *Personality and Social Psychology Bulletin, 20*, 503–513.

Crocker, J., Major, B., & Steele, C. (1998). Social stigma. In D. T. Gilbert, S. T. Fiske, & G. Lindzey (Eds.), *The handbook of social psychology* (4th ed.). New York: McGraw-Hill.

Croizet, J-C., & Claire, T. (1998). Extending the concept of stereotype threat to social class: The intellectual underperformance of students from low socioeconomic backgrounds. *Personality and Social Psychology Bulletin, 24*, 588–594.

Crosby, F., & Nyquist, L. (1977). The female register: An empirical study of Lakoff's hypothesis. *Language in Society, 6*, 313–322.

Crosby, F., Bromley, S., & Saxe, L. (1980). Recent unobtrusive studies of black and white discrimination and prejudice: A literature review. *Psychological Bulletin, 87*, 546–563.

Cross, S. E., & Madson, L. (1997). Models of the self: Self-construals and gender. *Psychological Bulletin, 122*, 5–37.

Crouse, B. B., & Mehrabian, A. (1977). Affiliation of opposite-sexed strangers. *Journal of Research in Personality, 11*, 38–47.

Cunningham, J. D., Strassberg, D. S., & Haan, B. (1986). Effects of intimacy and sex-role congruency on self-disclosure. *Journal of Social and Clinical Psychology, 4*, 393–401.

Cunningham, M. R. (1979). Weather, mood, and helping behavior: Quasi-experiments with the sunshine samaritan. *Journal of Personality and Social Psychology, 37*, 1947–1956.

Cunningham, M. R. (1986). Measuring the physical in physical attractiveness: Quasi-experiments on the sociobiology of female facial beauty. *Journal of Personality and Social Psychology, 50*, 925–935.

Cunningham, M. R., Barbee, A. P., & Pike, C. L. (1990a). What do women want: Facialmetric assessment of multiple motives in the perception of male physical attractiveness. *Journal of Personality and Social Psychology, 59*, 61–72.

Cunningham, M. R., Roberts, A. R., Barbee, A. P., Druen, P. B., & Wu, C.-H. (1995). "Their ideas of beauty are, on the whole, the same as ours": Consistency and variability in the cross-cultural perception of female physical attractiveness. *Journal of Personality and Social Psychology, 68*, 261–279.

Cunningham, M. R., Shaffer, D. R., Barbee, A. P., Wolff, P. L., & Kelley, D. J. (1990b). Separate processes in the relation of elation and depression to helping: Social versus personal concerns. *Journal of Experimental Social Psychology, 26*, 13–33.

Cunningham, M. R., Steinberg, J., & Grev, R. (1980). Wanting to and having to help: Separate motivation for positive mood and guilt-induced helping. *Journal of Personality and Social Psychology, 38*, 181–192.

Curran, J. P. (1977). Skills training as an approach to the treatment of heterosexual-social anxiety: A review. *Psychological Bulletin, 84*, 140–157.

Curtis, R. C., & Miller, K. (1986). Believing another likes or dislikes you: Behaviors making the beliefs come true. *Journal of Personality and Social Psychology, 51*, 284–290.

Cutrona, C. (1982). Transition to college: Loneliness and the process of social adjustment. In L. A. Peplau & D. Perlman (Eds.), *Loneliness: A sourcebook of current theory, research and therapy* (pp. 291–309). New York: John Wiley.

Cutrona, C. E. (1996). *Social support in couples.* Thousand Oaks, CA: Sage.

Cutrona, C. E., & Suhr, J. A. (1994). Social support communication in the context of marriage: An analysis of couples' supportive interactions. In B. B. Burleson, T. L. Albrecht, & I. G. Sarason (Eds.), *Communication of social support: Messages, relationships, and community* (pp. 113–135). Thousand Oaks, CA: Sage.

Dabbs, J. M., Frady, R. F., Carr, T. S., & Besch, N. F. (1987). Saliva testosterone and criminal violence in young adult prison inmates. *Psychosomatic Medicine, 49*, 174–182.

Dakof, G. A., & Taylor, S. E. (1990). Victims' perceptions of social support: What is helpful from whom? *Journal of Personality and Social Psychology, 58*, 80–89.

Dallager, C., & Rosen, L. A. (1993). Effects of a human sexuality course on attitudes toward rape and violence. *Journal of Sex Education & Therapy, 19*, 193–199.

Daly, J. A., Caughlin, J. P., & Stafford, L. (1997). Correlates and consequences of social-communicative anxiety. In J. A. Daly, J. C. McCroskey, J. Ayres, T. Hopf, & D. M. Ayres (Eds.), *Avoiding communication: Shyness, reticence, and communication apprehension* (2nd ed., pp. 21–71). Creskill, NJ: Hampton Press.

Daly, M., & Wilson, M. (1988). *Homicide.* New York: Aldine De Gruyer.

Daly, M., & Wilson, M. (1991). A reply to Gelles: Stepchildren are disproportionately abused, and diverse forms of violence can share causal factors. *Human Nature, 2*, 419–426.

Daly, M., & Wilson, M. I. (1996). Violence against stepchildren. *Current Directions in Psychological Science, 5*, 77–81.

Dana, E. R., Lalwani, N., & Duval, S. (1997). Objective self-awareness and focus of attention following awareness of self-standard discrepancies: Changing self or changing standards of correctness. *Journal of Social and Clinical Psychology, 16*, 359–380.

Dardenne, B., & Leyens, J.-P. (1995). Confirmation bias as a social skill. *Personality and Social Psychology Bulletin, 21*, 1229–1239.

Darley, J. M. (1995). Constructive and destructive obedience: A taxonomy of principal-agent relationships. *Journal of Social Issues, 51*, 125–154.

Darley, J. M., & Fazio, R. (1980). Expectancy confirmation processes arising in the social interaction sequence. *American Psychologist, 35*, 867–881.

Darley, J. M., & Latané, B. (1968). Bystander intervention in emergencies: Diffusion of responsibility. *Journal of Personality and Social Psychology, 8*, 377–383.

Darwin, C. (1872). *Expression of emotion in man and animals.* London: Murray.

Davies, M. F. (1994). Private self-consciousness and the perceived accuracy of true and false personality feedback. *Personality and Individual Differences, 17,* 697–701.

Davis, C. G., Lehman, D. R., Silver, R. C., Wortman, C. B., & Ellard, J. H. (1996). Self-blame following a traumatic life event: The role of perceived avoidability. *Personality and Social Psychology Bulletin, 22,* 557–567.

Davis, C. G., Lehman, D. R., Wortman, C. B., Silver, R. C., & Thompson, S. C. (1995). The undoing of traumatic life events. *Personality and Social Psychology Bulletin, 21,* 109–124.

Davis, C. M., & Bauserman, R. (1993). Exposure to sexually explicit materials: An attitude change perspective. In J. Bancroft (Ed.), *Annual Review of Sex Research* (Vol. 4, pp. 121–209). Mt. Vernon, IA: Society for the Scientific Study of Sex.

Davis, J. H. (1973). Group decision and social interaction: A theory of social decision schemes. *Psychological Review, 80,* 97–125.

Davis, M. H. (1980). A multidimensional approach to individual differences in empathy. *Psychological Documents, 10,* 85.

Davis, M. H. (1983). Empathic concern and the muscular dystrophy telethon: Empathy as a multidimensional construct. *Personality and Social Psychology Bulletin, 9,* 223–229.

Davis, M. H. (1996). *Empathy: A social psychological approach.* Boulder, CO: Westview Press.

Davis, M. H., & Franzoi, S. L. (1986). Adolescent loneliness, self-disclosure, and private self-consciousness: A longitudinal investigation. *Journal of Personality and Social Psychology, 51,* 595–608.

Davis, M. H., & Franzoi, S. L. (1991). Stability and change in adolescent self-consciousness and empathy. *Journal of Research in Personality, 25,* 70–87.

Davis, M. H., & Kraus, L. A. (1989). Social contact, loneliness, and mass media use: A test of two hypotheses. *Journal of Applied Social Psychology, 19,* 1100–1124.

Davis, M. H., Conklin, L., Smith, A., & Luce, C. (1996). Effect of perspective taking on the cognitive representation of persons: A merging of self and other. *Journal of Personality and Social Psychology, 70,* 713–726.

Davis, M. H., Luce, C., & Kraus, S. J. (1994). The heritability of characteristics associated with dispositional empathy. *Journal of Personality, 62,* 369–391.

Davis, M. H., Morris, M. M., & Kraus, L. A. (1998). Relationship-specific and global perceptions of social support: Associations with well-being and attachment. *Journal of Personality and Social Psychology, 74,* 468–481.

Davis, S. (1990). Men as success objects and women as sex objects: A study of personal advertisements. *Sex Roles, 23,* 43–50.

Davis, T. L. (1995). Gender differences in masking negative emotions: Ability or motivation? *Developmental Psychology, 31,* 660–667.

Dawes, R., van de Kragt, A. J. C., & Orbell, J. M. (1990). Cooperation for the benefit of us—not me, or my conscience. In J. J. Mansbridge (Ed.), *Beyond self-interest* (pp. 97–110). Chicago: University of Chicago Press.

Dawson, R. E., & Prewitt, K. (1969). *Political socialization.* Boston: Little, Brown and Company.

De Cecco, J. P. (1988). *Gay relationships.* Binghampton, NY: Haworth.

De Dreu, C. K. W., & McCusker, C. (1997). Loss frames and cooperation in two-person social dilemmas: A transformational analysis. *Journal of Personality and Social Psychology, 72,* 1093–1106.

de Rougemont, D. (1940). *Love in the Western world.* New York: Harcourt.

Dean, K. E., & Malamuth, N. M. (1997). Characteristics of men who aggress sexually and of men who imagine aggressing: Risk and moderating variables. *Journal of Personality and Social Psychology, 72,* 449–455.

Deaux, K. (1985). Sex and gender. In M. R. Rosenzweig & L. W. Porter (Eds.), *Annual review of psychology* (Vol. 36). Palo Alto, CA: Annual Reviews, Inc.

Deaux, K. (1996). Social identification. In E. T. Higgins & A. W. Kruglanski (Eds.), *Social psychology: Handbook of basic principles* (pp. 777–798). New York: Guilford Press.

Deaux, K., & Kite, M. (1993). Gender stereotypes. In F. L. Denmark & M. A. Paludi (Eds.), *Psychology of women: A handbook of issues and theories* (pp. 107–139). Westport, CT: Greenwood Press.

Deaux, K., & Major, B. (1987). Putting gender into context: An interactive model of gender-related behavior. *Psychological Review, 94,* 369–389.

Deaux, K., Reid, A., Mizrahi, K., & Ethier, K. A. (1995). Parameters of social identity. *Journal of Personality and Social Psychology, 68,* 280–291.

Deaux, K., Winton, W., Crowley, M., & Lewis, L. L. (1985). Levels of categorization and content of gender stereotypes. *Social Cognition, 3,* 145–167.

Debono, K., & Packer, M. (1991). The effects of advertising appeal on perceptions of product quality. *Personality and Social Psychology Bulletin, 17,* 194–200.

DeFleur, M. L., & Petranoff, R. M. (1959). A televised test of subliminal persuasion. *Public Opinion Quarterly, 23,* 168–180.

Dejong, W. (1979). An examination of self-perception mediation of the foot-in-the-door effect. *Journal of Personality and Social Psychology, 37,* 2221–2239.

Delgado-Gaitan, C. (1994). Socializing young children in Mexican-American families: An intergenerational perspective. In P. M. Greenfield & R. R. Cocking (Eds.), *Cross-cultural roots of minority child development* (pp. 55–86). Hillsdale, NJ: Erlbaum.

Dembroski, T. M., Lasater, T. M., & Ramirez, A. (1978). Communicator similarity, fear arousing communications, and compliance with health care recommendations. *Journal of Applied Social Psychology, 8,* 254–269.

Deming, M. B., & Eppy, A. (1981). The sociology of rape. *Sociology and Social Research, 65,* 357–380.

DeNault, L. K., & McFarlane, D. A. (1995). Reciprocal altruism between male vampire bats, Descodus yrotundus. *Animal Behaviour, 49,* 855–856.

DePaulo, B. M. (1992). Nonverbal behavior and self-presentation. *Psychological Bulletin, 111,* 230–243.

DePaulo, B. M., & Pfeifer, R. L. (1986). On-the-job experience and skill at detecting deception. *Journal of Applied Social Psychology, 16,* 249–267.

DePaulo, B. M., Charlton, K., Cooper, H. M., Lindsay, J. J., & Muhlenbruck, L. (1997). The accuracy-confidence correlation in the detection of deception. *Personality and Social Psychology Review, 1,* 346–357.

DePaulo, B. M., Epstein, J. A., & LeMay, C. S. (1990). Responses of the socially anxious to the prospect of interpersonal evaluation. *Journal of Personality, 58,* 623–640.

DePaulo, B. M., Kashy, D. A., Kirkendol, S. E., Wyer, M. M., & Epstein, J. A. (1996). Lying in everyday life. *Journal of Personality and Social Psychology, 70,* 979–995.

Dépret, E. F., & Fiske, S. T. (1993). Social cognition and power: Some cognitive consequences of social structure as a source of control deprivation. In G. Weary, F. Gleicher, & K. Marsh (Eds.), *Control motivation and social cognition* (pp. 176–202). New York: Springer-Verlag.

Depue, R. A., Luciana, M., Arbisi, P., Collins, P., & Leon, A. (1994). Dopamine and the structure of personality: Relation to agonist-induced dopamine activity to positive emotionality. *Journal of Personality and Social Psychology, 67,* 485–498.

Derlega, V., & Chaikin, A. L. (1976). Norms affecting self-disclosure in men and women. *Journal of Consulting and Clinical Psychology, 44,* 376–380.

Derlega, V. J., Lewis, R. J., Harrison, S., Winstead, B. A., & Costanza, R. (1989). Gender differences in the initiation and attribution of tactile intimacy. *Journal of Nonverbal Behavior, 13,* 83–96.

Derlega, V. J., Metts, S., Petronio, S., & Margulis, S. T. (1993). *Self-disclosure.* Newbury Park, NJ: Sage.

Dervin, B. (1981). Mass communicating: Changing conceptions of the audience. In R. E. Rice & W. J. Paisley (Eds.), *Public communication campaigns* (pp. 71–87). Beverly Hills, CA: Sage.

Desforges, D. M., Lord, C. G., Pugh, M. A., Sia, T. L., Scarberry, N. C., & Ratcliff, C. D. (1997). Role of group representativeness in the generalization part of the contact hypothesis. *Journal of Applied Social Psychology, 19,* 183–204.

Deutsch, M., & Gerard, H. B. (1955). A study of normative and informational social influence upon individual judgment. *Journal of Abnormal and Social Psychology, 51,* 629–636.

Devine, P. G. (1989). Stereotypes and prejudice: Their automatic and controlled components. *Journal of Personality and Social Psychology, 56,* 5–18.

Devine, P. G., & Baker, S. M. (1991). Measurement of racial stereotype subtyping. *Personality and Social Psychology Bulletin, 17,* 44–50.

Devine, P. G., & Monteith, M. J. (in press). Automaticity and control in stereotyping. In S. Chaiken & Y. Trope (Eds.), *Dual process theories in social psychology.* New York: Guilford.

Devine, P. G., Evett, S. R., & Vasquez-Suson, K. A. (1995). Exploring the interpersonal dynamics of intergroup contact. In R. Sorrentino & E. T. Higgins (Eds.), *Handbook of motivation and cognition: The interpersonal context* (Vol. 3). New York: Guilford.

Devlin, P. K., & Cowan, G. A. (1985). Homophobia, perceived fathering, and male intimate relationships. *Journal of Personality Assessment, 49,* 467–473.

DeVos, G. (1985). Dimensions of the self in Japanese culture. In A. Marsella, G. DeVos, & F. L. K. Hsu (Eds.), *Culture and self* (pp. 149–184). London: Tavistock.

DeWaal, F. (1989). *Peacemaking among primates.* Cambridge, MA: Harvard University Press.

Diaz, T. (1999). *Making a killing: The business of guns in America.* Free Press.

Diener, E. (1980). Deindividuation: The absence of self-awareness and self-regulation in group members. In P. B. Paulus (Ed.), *Psychology of group influence* (pp. 209–242). Hillsdale, NJ: Lawrence Erlbaum.

Diener, E., & Wallbom, M. (1976). Effects of self-awareness on antinormative behavior. *Journal of Research in Personality, 10,* 107–111.

Diener, E., Fraser, S. C., Beaman, A. L., & Kelem, R. T. (1976). Effects of deindividuation variables on stealing among Halloween trick-or-treaters. *Journal of Personality and Social Psychology, 33,* 178–183.

Diener, E., Wolsie, B., & Fujita, F. (1995). Physical attractiveness and subjective well-being. *Journal of Personality and Social Psychology, 69,* 120–129.

Dijker, A. J., & Koomen, W. (1996). Stereotyping and attitudinal effects under time pressure. *European Journal of Social Psychology, 26,* 61–74.

Dijksterhuis, A., & Knippenberg, A. V. (1996). The knife that cuts both ways: Facilitated and inhibited access to traits as a result of stereotype activation. *Journal of Experimental Social Psychology, 32,* 271–288.

Dillard, J. P. (1991). The current status of research on sequential-request compliance

techniques. *Personality and Social Psychology Bulletin, 17,* 283–288.

Dindia, K., & Allen, M. (1992). Sex differences in self-disclosure: A meta-analysis. *Psychological Bulletin, 112,* 106–124.

Dion, K. K. (1972). Physical attractiveness and evaluations of children's transgressions. *Journal of Personality and Social Psychology, 24,* 285–290.

Dion, K. K., & Dion, K. L. (1985). Personality, gender, and the phenomenology of romantic love. In P. R. Shaver (Ed.), *Self, situations and behavior: Review of personality and social psychology* (Vol. 6, pp. 209–239). Beverly Hills, CA: Sage.

Dion, K. K., & Dion, K. L. (1991). Psychological individualism and romantic love. *Journal of Social Behavior and Personality, 6,* 17–33.

Dion, K. K., & Stein, S. (1978). Physical attractiveness and interpersonal influence. *Journal of Experimental Social Psychology, 14,* 97–109.

Dion, K. K., Berscheid, E., & [Walster] Hatfield, E. (1972). What is beautiful is good. *Journal of Personality and Social Psychology, 24,* 285–290.

Dion, K. L., & Dion, K. K. (1973). Correlates of romantic love. *Journal of Consulting and Clinical Psychology, 41,* 51–56.

Dodgson, P. G., & Wood, J. V. (1998). Self-esteem and the cognitive accessibility of strengths and weaknesses after failure. *Journal of Personality and Social Psychology, 75,* 178–197.

Dollard, J., Doob, L. W., Miller, N. E., Mowrer, O. H., & Sears, R. R. (1939). *Frustration and aggression.* New Haven, CT: Yale University Press.

Donahue, M. J. (1985). Intrinsic and extrinsic religiousness: Review and meta-analysis. *Journal of Personality and Social Psychology, 48,* 400–419.

Donnerstein, E. (1983b). Erotica and human aggression. In R. Geen & E. Donnerstein (Eds.), *Aggression: Theoretical and empirical reviews* (pp. 127–154). New York: Academic Press.

Donnerstein, E., & Berkowitz, L. (1981). Victim reactions in aggressive erotic films as a factor in violence against women. *Journal of Personality and Social Psychology, 41,* 710–724.

Donnerstein, E., Linz, D., & Penrod, S. (1987). *The question of pornography.* New York: Free Press.

Dornbush, S. M., Hastorf, A. H., Richardson, S. A., Muzzy, R. E., & Vreeland, R. S. (1965). The perceiver and the perceived: Their relative influence on the categories of interpersonal cognition. *Journal of Personality and Social Psychology, 1,* 434–440.

Doty, R. M., Peterson, B. E., & Winter, D. G. (1991). Threat and authoritarianism in the United States, 1978–1987. *Journal of Personality and Social Psychology, 61,* 629–640.

Doty, R. M., Winter, D. G., Peterson, B. E., & Kemmelmeier, M. (1997). Authoritarianism and American students' attitudes about the

Gulf War, 1990–1996. *Personality and Social Psychology Bulletin, 23,* 1133–1143.

Dovidio, J. F., Evans, N., & Tyler, R. B. (1986). Racial stereotypes: The contents of their cognitive representations. *Journal of Experimental Social Psychology, 22,* 22–37.

Dovidio, J. F., Piliavin, J. A., & Clark, R. D., III (1991). The arousal:cost reward model and the process of intervention: A review of the evidence. In M. S. Clark (Ed.), *Review of personality and social psychology: Vol. 12. Prosocial behavior* (pp. 86–118).

Drabman, R. S., & Thomas, M. H. (1975). Does TV violence breed indifference? *Journal of Communications, 25*(4), 86–89.

Drachman, D., DeCarufel, A., & Insko, C. A. (1978). The extra credit effect in interpersonal attraction. *Journal of Experimental Social Psychology, 14,* 458–467.

Dryer, D. C., & Horowitz, L. M. (1997). When do opposites attract? Interpersonal complementarity versus similarity. *Journal of Personality and Social Psychology, 72,* 592–603.

Duck, S., & Wright, P. H. (1993). Reexamining gender differences in same-gender friendships: A close look at two kinds of data. *Sex Roles, 28,* 709–727.

Duck, S., Pond, K., & Leatham, G. (1994). Loneliness and the evaluation of relational events. *Journal of Social and Personal Relationships, 11,* 253–276.

Duckitt, J., & Mphuthing, T. (1998). Group identification and intergroup attitudes: A longitudinal analysis in South Africa. *Journal of Personality and Social Psychology, 74,* 80–85.

Duclos, S. E., Laird, J. D., Schneider, E., Sexter, M., Stern, L., & Van Lighten, O. (1989). Emotion-specific effects of facial expressions and postures on emotional experience. *Journal of Personality and Social Psychology, 57,* 100–108.

Dunbar, R. I. M. (1993). Coevolution of neocortical size, group size and language in humans. *Behavioral and Brain Sciences, 16,* 681–735.

Duncan, C. P., & Nelson, J. E. (1985). Effects of humor in a radio advertising experiment. *Journal of Advertising, 14,* 33–40.

Duncan, L. E., Peterson, B. E., & Winter, D. G. (1997). Authoritarianism and gender roles: Toward a psychological analysis of hegemonic relationships. *Personality and Social Psychology Bulletin, 23,* 41–49.

Dunkel-Schetter, C., Blasband, D. E., Feinstein, L. G., & Herbert, T. B. (1992). Elements of supportive interactions: When are attempts to help effective? In S. Spacapan & S. Oskamp (Eds.), *Helping and being helped: Naturalistic studies* (pp. 83–114). Newbury Park, CA: Sage.

Dunning, D., & Hayes, A. F. (1996). Evidence for egocentric comparison in social judgment. *Journal of Personality and Social Psychology, 71,* 213–229.

Dunning, D., Leuenberger, A., & Sherman, D. A. (1995). A new look at motivated inference: Are self-serving theories of success a product of motivational forces? *Journal of Personality and Social Psychology, 69*, 58–68.

Dutton, D. G., & Aron, A. P. (1974). Some evidence for heightened sexual attraction under conditions of high anxiety. *Journal of Personality and Social Psychology, 30*, 510–517.

Duval, S., & Wicklund, R. A. (1972). *A theory of objective self-awareness.* New York: Academic Press.

Dziech, B. W., & Weiner, L. (1984). *The lecherous professor: Sexual harassment on campus.* Boston, MA: Beacon Press.

Eagly, A. H. (1987). *Sex differences in social behavior: A social-role interpretation.* Hillsdale, NJ: Erlbaum.

Eagly, A. H. (1992). Uneven progress: Social psychology and the study of attitudes. *Journal of Personality and Social Psychology, 63*, 693–710.

Eagly, A. H. (1996). Differences between women and men: Their magnitude, practical importance, and political meaning. *American Psychologist, 50*, 158–159.

Eagly, A. H., & Chaiken, S. (1993). *The psychology of attitudes.* Fort Worth, TX: Harcourt Brace Jovanovich.

Eagly, A. H., & Chaiken, S. (1998). Attitude structure and function. In D. Gilbert, S. Fiske, & G. Lindzey (Eds.), *The handbook of social psychology* (4th ed.). New York: McGraw-Hill.

Eagly, A. H., & Chravala, C. (1986). Sex differences in conformity: Status and gender-role interpretations. *Psychology of Women Quarterly, 10*, 203–220.

Eagly, A. H., & Crowley, M. (1986). Gender and helping behavior: A meta-analytic review of the social psychological literature. *Psychological Bulletin, 100*, 283–308.

Eagly, A. H., & Johnson, B. T. (1990). Gender and leadership style: A meta-analysis. *Psychological Bulletin, 108*, 233–256.

Eagly, A. H., & Kite, M. E. (1987). Are stereotypes of nationalities applied to both women and men? *Journal of Personality and Social Psychology, 53*, 457–462.

Eagly, A. H., & Steffen, V. J. (1986a). Gender and aggressive behavior: A meta-analytic review of the social psychological literature. *Psychological Bulletin, 100*, 309–330.

Eagly, A. H., Karau, S. J., & Makhijani, M. G. (1995). Gender and the effectiveness of leaders: A meta-analysis. *Psychological Bulletin, 117*, 125–145.

Eagly, A. H., Makhijani, M. G., & Konsky, B. G. (1992). Gender and the evaluation of leaders: A meta-analysis. *Psychological Bulletin, 111*, 3–22.

Ebbesen, E. B., Kjos, G. L., & Konecni, V. J. (1976). Spatial ecology: Its effects on the choice of friends and enemies. *Journal of Experimental Social Psychology, 12*, 505–518.

Echabe, A. E. & Garate, J. F. V. (1994). Private self-consciousness as moderator of the importance of attitude and subjective norm: The prediction of voting. *European Journal of Social Psychology, 24*, 285–293.

Echabe, A. E., Rovira, D. P., & Garate, J. F. V. (1988). Testing Ajzen and Fishbein's attitudes model: The prediction of voting. *European Journal of Social Psychology, 18*, 181–189.

Edgerton, R. (1971). *The individual in cultural adaptation.* Berkeley: University of California Press.

Edney, J. J. (1979). The nuts game: A concise commons dilemma analog. *Environmental Psychology and Nonverbal Behavior, 3*, 252–254.

Edson, R. (1976). *The intuitive journey and other works.* New York: Harper & Row.

Edwards, K., & Smith, E. E. (1996). A disconfirmation bias in the evaluation of arguments. *Journal of Personality and Social Psychology, 71*, 5–24.

Eisenberg, N., & Mussen, P. H. (1989). *The roots of prosocial behavior in children.* Cambridge, England: Cambridge University Press.

Eisenberg, N., Martin, C. L., Fabes, R. A. (1996). Gender development and gender effects. In D. C. Berliner & R. C. Calfee (Eds.), *Handbook of educational psychology* (pp. 358–396). New York: Prentice-Hall.

Eisenberger, R., Cotterell, N., & Marvel, J. (1987). Reciprocation ideology. *Journal of Personality and Social Psychology, 53*, 743–750.

Ekman, P. (1994). Strong evidence for universals in facial expressions: A reply to Russell's mistaken critique. *Psychological Bulletin, 115*, 268–287.

Ekman, P., & Friesen, W. V. (1974). Detecting deception from the body or face. *Journal of Personality and Social Psychology, 29*, 288–298.

Ekman, P., & O'Sullivan, M. (1991). Who can catch a liar? *American Psychologist, 46*, 913–920.

Ekman, P., Friesen, W. V., & O'Sullivan, M. (1988). Smiles when lying. *Journal of Personality and Social Psychology, 54*, 414–420.

Ekman, P., Friesen, W. V., O'Sullivan, M., Chan, A., Diacoyanni-Tarlatzis, I., Heider, K., Krause, R., LeCompte, W. A., Pitcairn, T., Ricci-Bitti, P. E., Scherer, K., Tomita, M., & Tzavaras, A. (1987). Universals and cultural differences in the judgments of facial expressions of emotion. *Journal of Personality and Social Psychology, 53*, 712–717.

Elbedour, S., Shulman, S., & Kedem, P. (1997). Adolescent intimacy: A cross-cultural study. *Journal of Cross-Cultural Psychology, 28*, 5–22.

Eldridge, N. S., & Gilbert, L. A. (1990). Correlates of relationship satisfaction in lesbian couples. *Psychology of Women Quarterly, 14*, 43–62.

Ellemers, N., Rijswijk, W. V., Roefs, M., & Simons, C. (1997). Bias in intergroup perceptions: Balancing group identity with social reality. *Personality and Social Psychology Bulletin, 23*, 186–198.

Ellis, A. L., O'Sullivan, C. S., & Sowards, B. A. (1992). The impact of contemplated exposure to a survivor of rape on attitudes toward rape. *Journal of Applied Social Psychology, 22*, 889–895.

Ellsworth, P. C., & Mauro, R. (1998). Psychology and law. In D. T. Gilbert, S. T. Fiske, & G. Lindzey (Eds.), *The handbook of social psychology* (4th ed., Vol. 2, pp. 684–732). New York: McGraw-Hill.

Elms, A. C. (1975). The crisis of confidence in social psychology. *American Psychologist, 30*, 967–976.

Elms, A. C. (1994). Keeping deception honest: Justifying conditions for social scientific research strategems. In E. Erwin, S. Gendin, & L. Kleiman (Eds.), *Ethical issues in scientific research: An anthology* (pp. 121–140). New York: Garland.

Elms, A. C. (1995). Obedience in retrospect. *Journal of Social Issues, 51*, 21–31.

Elms, A. C., & Milgram, S. (1966). Personality characteristics associated with obedience and defiance toward authoritative command. *Journal of Experimental Research in Personality, 1*, 282–289.

Emmons, R. A., & Diener, E. (1986). A goal-affect analysis of everyday situational choices. *Journal of Research in Personality, 20*, 309–326.

Emswiller, T., Deaux, K., & Willits, J. E. (1971). Similarity, sex, and requests for small favors. *Journal of Applied Social Psychology, 1*, 284–291.

Engel, J. W. (1988). Work values of American and Japanese men. *Journal of Social Behavior and Personality, 3*, 191–200.

Engestrom, Y., Brown, K., Engestrom, R., & Koistinen, K. (1990). Organizational forgetting: An activity-theoretical perspective. In D. Middleton & D. Edwards (Eds.), *Collective remembering* (pp. 137–168). Newbury Park, CA: Sage.

Epley, N., & Huff, C. (1998). Suspicion, affective response, and educational benefit as a result of deception in psychology research. *Personality and Social Psychology Bulletin, 24*, 759–768.

Epstein, J. L. (1985). After the bus arrives: Resegregation in desegregation schools. *Journal of Social Issues, 41*, 23–43.

Epstein, S. (1973). The self-concept revisited, or a theory of a theory. *American Psychologist, 28*, 404–416.

Epstein, S., & Morling, B. (1995). Is the self motivated to do more than enhance and verify itself? In M. H. Kernis (Ed.), *Efficacy, agency, and self-esteem* (pp. 9–30). New York: Plenum Press.

Erber, R., Wegner, D. M., & Therriault, N. (1996). On being cool and collected: Mood regulation in anticipation of social interaction. *Journal of Personality and Social Psychology, 70*, 757–766.

Erickson, B., Lind, E. A., Johnson, B. C., & O'Barr, W. M. (1978). Speech style and impression formation in a court setting: The effects of "powerful" and "powerless" speech. *Journal of Experimental Social Psychology, 14*, 266–279.

Eron, L. D. (1963). Relationship of TV viewing habits and aggressive behavior in children. *Journal of Abnormal and Social Psychology, 67*, 193–196.

Eron, L. D., & Huesmann, L. R. (1984). The control of aggressive behavior by changes in attitudes, values, and the conditions of learning. In R. J. Blanchard & D. C. Blanchard (Eds.), *Advances in the study of aggression* (Vol. 1, pp. 139–171). New York: Academic Press.

Eron, L. D., Huesmann, L. R., Lefkowitz, M. M., & Walder, L. O. (1972). Does television violence cause aggression? *American Psychologist, 27*, 253–263.

Erwin, P. G. (1994). Effectiveness of social skills training with children: A meta-analytic study. *Counseling Psychology Quarterly, 7*, 305–310.

Esser, J. K., & Lindoerfer, J. S. (1989). Groupthink and the space shuttle Challenger accident: Toward a quantitative case analysis. *Journal of Behavioral Decision Making, 2*, 167–177.

Evans, R. I. (1980). *The making of social psychology: Discussions with creative contributors.* New York: Gardner Press.

Exline, J. J., & Lobel, M. (1997). Views of the self and affiliation choices: A social comparison perspective. *Basic and Applied Social Psychology, 19*, 243–259.

Eysenck, H. J. (1990). Biological dimensions of personality. In L. A. Pervin (Ed.), *Handbook of personality theory and research* (pp. 244–276). New York: Guilford Press.

Fagot, B. I. (1985). Changes in thinking about early sex role development. *Developmental Review, 5*, 83–98.

Fallon, A. (1990). Culture in the mirror: Sociocultural determinants of body image. In T. F. Cash & T. Pruzinsky (Eds.), *Body images: Development, deviance, and change* (pp. 80–109). New York: Guilford.

Farb, P. (1978). *Man's rise to civilization: The cultural ascent of the Indians of North America.* New York: Penguin.

Farr, R. M. (1996). *The roots of modern social psychology.* Cambridge, MA: Blackwell.

Farrington, D. P. (1994). Childhood, adolescent, and adult features of violent males. In L. R. Huesmann (Ed.), *Aggressive behavior: Current perspectives* (pp. 215–240). New York: Plenum.

Fazio, R. H. (1989). On the power and functionality of attitudes: The role of attitude accessibility. In A. R. Pratkanis, S. J. Breckler, & A. G. Greenwald (Eds.), *Attitude structure and function* (pp. 153–179). Hillsdale, NJ: Erlbaum.

Fazio, R. H. (1990). Multiple processes by which attitudes guide behavior: The MODE model as an integrative framework. In M. P. Zanna (Ed.), *Advances in experimental social psychology* (Vol. 23, pp. 75–109). New York: Academic Press.

Fazio, R. H. (1995). Attitudes as object-evaluation associations: Determinants, consequences, and correlates of attitude accessibility. In R. E. Petty & J. A. Krosnick (Eds.), *Attitude strength: Antecedents and consequences* (pp. 247–282). Mahwah, NJ: Erlbaum.

Fazio, R. H., & Williams, C. J. (1986). Attitude accessibility as a moderator of the attitude-perception and attitude-behavior relations. *Journal of Personality and Social Psychology, 51*, 505–514.

Fazio, R. H., Zanna, M. P., & Cooper, J. (1977). Dissonance and self-perception: An integrative view of each theory's proper domain of application. *Journal of Experimental Social Psychology, 13*, 464–479.

Feeney, B. C., & Kirkpatrick, L. A. (1996). Effects of adult attachment and presence of romantic partners on physiological responses to stress. *Journal of Personality and Social Psychology, 70*, 255–270.

Fehr, B., & Russell, J. A. (1991). The concept of love viewed from a prototype perspective. *Journal of Personality and Social Psychology, 60*, 425–438.

Fein, S., & Spencer, S. J. (1997). Prejudice as self-image maintenance: Affirming the self through negative evaluations of others. *Journal of Personality and Social Psychology, 73*, 31–44.

Feingold, A. (1988). Matching for attractiveness in romantic partners and same-sex friends: A meta-analysis and theoretical critique. *Psychological Bulletin, 104*, 226–235.

Feingold, A. (1992a). Gender differences in mate selection preferences: A test of the parental investment model. *Psychological Bulletin, 112*, 125–139.

Feingold, A. (1992b). Good-looking people are not what we think. *Psychological Bulletin, 111*, 304–341.

Feingold, A., & Mazzella, R. (1998). Gender differences in body image are increasing. *Psychological Science, 9*, 190–195.

Feldman, R. A., Caplinger, T. E., & Wodarski, J. S. (1983). *The St. Louis conundrum: The effective treatment of antisocial youths.* Englewood Cliffs, NJ: Prentice-Hall.

Felson, R. B. (1989). Parents and the reflected appraisal process: A longitudinal analysis. *Journal of Personality and Social Psychology, 57*, 965–971.

Fenigstein, A., & Vanable, P. A. (1992). Paranoia and self-consciousness. *Journal of Personality and Social Psychology, 62*, 129–138.

Fenigstein, A., Scheier, M. F., & Buss, A. H. (1975). Public and private self-consciousness: Assessment and theory. *Journal of Consulting and Clinical Psychology, 43*, 522–527.

Ferguson, G. (1955). Legal research on trial. *Judicature, 39*, 78–82.

Fernald, J. L. (1995). Interpersonal heterosexism. In B. Lott, & D. Maluso (Eds.), *The social psychology of interpersonal discrimination* (pp. 80–117). New York: Guilford Press.

Festinger, L. (1954). A theory of social comparison processes. *Human Relations, 7*, 117–140.

Festinger, L. (1957). *A theory of cognitive dissonance.* Stanford, CA: Stanford University Press.

Festinger, L., & Carlsmith, J. M. (1959). Cognitive consequences of forced compliance. *Journal of Abnormal and Social Psychology, 47*, 382–389.

Festinger, L., Pepitone, A., & Newcomb, T. (1952). Some consequences of deindividuation in a group. *Journal of Abnormal and Social Psychology, 47*, 382–389.

Festinger, L., Schachter, S., & Back, K. (1950). *Social pressures in informal groups: A study of a housing community.* New York: Harper.

Fiedler, F. E. (1967). *A theory of leadership effectiveness.* New York: McGraw-Hill.

Fiedler, F. E. (1987, September). When to lead, when to stand back. *Psychology Today*, pp. 26–27.

Fiedler, F. E. (1993). The leadership situation and the black box in contingency theories. In M. M. Chemers & R. Ayman (Eds.), *Leadership theory and research: Perspectives and directions* (pp. 1–28). San Diego, CA: Academic Press.

Fiedler, F. E., & Garcia, J. E. (1987). *New approaches to effective leadership.* New York: Wiley.

Fine, G. A., & Holyfield, L. (1996). Secrecy, trust, and dangerous leisure: Generating group cohesion in voluntary organizations. *Social Psychology Quarterly, 59*, 22–38.

Firestone, I. J., Kaplan, K. J., & Russell, J. C. (1973). Anxiety, fear, and affiliation with similar state versus dissimilar state others: Misery sometimes loves miserable company. *Journal of Personality and Social Psychology, 26*, 409–414.

Fishbein, M. (1980). A theory of reasoned action: Some applications and implications. In H. E. Howe, Jr. & M. M. Page (Eds.), *Nebraska symposium on motivation, 1979,* (Vol. 27, pp. 65–116). Lincoln: University of Nebraska Press.

Fishbein, M., & Ajzen, I. (1975). *Beliefs, attitude, intention, and behavior: An introduction to theory and research.* Reading, MA: Addison-Wesley.

Fishbein, M., & Coombs, F. S. (1974). Basis for decision: An attitudinal analysis of voting behavior. *Journal of Applied Social Psychology, 4*, 95–124.

Fisher, S. (1964). Sex differences in body perception. *Psychological Monographs, 78*, 1–22.

Fiske, A. P., & Haslam, N. (1996). Social cognition is thinking about relationships. *Current Directions in Psychological Science, 5*, 143–148.

Fiske, S. T. (1993). Controlling other people: The impact of power on stereotyping. *American Psychologist, 48,* 621–628.

Fiske, S. T. (1998). Stereotyping, prejudice, and discrimination. In D. T. Gilbert, S. T. Fiske, & G. Lindzey (Eds.), *The handbook of social psychology* (4th ed.). New York: McGraw-Hill.

Fiske, S. T., & Cox, M. G. (1979). Person concepts: The effect of target familiarity and descriptive purpose on the process of describing others. *Journal of Personality, 47,* 136–161.

Fiske, S. T., & Dépret, E. (1996). Control, interdependence and power: Understanding social cognition in its social context. In W. Stroebe & M. Hewstone (Eds.), *European review of social psychology* (Vol. 7, pp. 31–61). New York: Wiley.

Fiske, S. T., & Neuberg, S. L. (1990). A continuum model of impression formation, from category-based to individuating processes: Influence of information and motivation on attention and interpretation. In M. P. Zanna (Ed.), *Advances in experimental social psychology* (Vol. 23). New York: Academic Press.

Fiske, S. T., & Taylor, S. E. (1991). *Social cognition.* New York: McGraw-Hill.

Fiske, S. T., & Von Hendy, H. M. (1992). Personality feedback and situational norms can control stereotyping processes. *Journal of Personality and Social Psychology, 62,* 577–596.

Fitzgerald, L. F. (1993a). Sexual harassment: Violence against women in the workplace. *American Psychologist, 48,* 1070–1076.

Fitzgerald, L. F. (1993b, February). *The last open secret: The sexual harassment of women in the workplace and academia.* Edited transcript of a Science and Public Policy Seminar presented by the Federation of Behavioral, Psychological, and Cognitive Sciences, Washington, DC.

Fitzgerald, L. F., Drasgow, F., Hulin, C. L., Gelfand, M. J., & Magley, V. J. (1997). Antecedents and consequences of sexual harassment in organizations: A test of an integrated model. *Journal of Applied Psychology, 82,* 578–589.

Fitzgerald, L. F., Swan, S., & Fischer, K. (1995). Why didn't she just report him? The psychological and legal implications of women's responses to sexual harassment. *Journal of Social Issues, 51,* 117–138.

Foddy, M., & Smithson, M. (1996). Relative ability, paths of relevance, and influence in task-oriented groups. *Social Psychology Quarterly, 59,* 140–153.

Fogelman, E. (1996). Victims, perpetrators, bystanders, and rescuers in the face of genocide and its aftermath. In C. B. Strozier & M. Flynn (Eds.), *Genocide, war, and human survival* (pp. 87–97). Lanham, MD: Rowman & Littlefield.

Fonow, M. M., Richardson, L., & Wemmerus, V. A. (1992). Feminist rape education: Does it work? *Gender & Society, 6,* 108–121.

Ford, C. S., & Beach, F. A. (1951). *Patterns of sexual behavior.* New York: Harper & Row.

Ford, D. Y. (1996). *Reversing underachievement among gifted Black students: Promising practices and programs.* New York: Teachers College Press.

Ford, D. Y., & Harris, J. J., III. (1992). The American achievement ideology and achievement differentials among preadolescent gifted and nongifted African-American males and females. *Journal of Negro Education, 61*(1), 45–64.

Fordham, S. (1985). *Black student school success as related to fictive kinship: Final report.* The National Institute of Education, Washington, D.C.

Forgas, J. P. (1998). Asking nicely? the effects of mood on responding to more or less polite requests. *Personality and Social Psychology Bulletin, 24,* 173–185.

Forge, K. L., & Phemister, S. (1987). The effect of prosocial cartoons on preschool children. *Child Development Journal, 17,* 83–88.

Förster, J., & Strack, F. (1996). Influence of overt head movements on memory for valenced words: A case of conceptual-motor compatibility. *Journal of Personality and Social Psychology, 71,* 421–430.

Forsyth, D. R. (1990). *Group dynamics* (2nd ed.). Pacific Grove, CA: Brooks/Cole.

Foschi, M. (1996). Double standards in the evaluation of men and women. *Social Psychology Quarterly, 59,* 237–254.

Fouts, R. (1997). *Next of kin: What chimpanzees have taught me about who we are.* New York: William Morrow.

Fox, D. R. (1985). Psychology, ideology, utopia, and the commons. *American Psychologist, 40,* 48–58.

Fox, R. (1992). Prejudice and the unfinished mind: A new look at an old failing. *Psychological Inquiry, 3,* 137–152.

Frank, M. G., & Gilovich, T. (1989). Effect of memory perspective on retrospective causal attributions. *Journal of Personality and Social Psychology, 57,* 399–403.

Franzoi, S. L. (1995). The body-as-object versus the body-as-process: Gender differences and gender considerations. *Sex Roles, 33,* 417–437.

Franzoi, S. L., & Herzog, M. E. (1987). Judging physical attractiveness: What body aspects do we use? *Personality and Social Psychology Bulletin, 13,* 19–33.

Franzoi, S. L., & Shields, S. A. (1984). The body esteem scale: Multidimensional structure and sex differences in a college population. *Journal of Personality Assessment, 48,* 173–178.

Fraser, C., Gouge, C., & Billig, M. (1971). Risky shifts, cautious shifts, and group polarization. *European Journal of Social Psychology, 1,* 7–30.

Frazier, P. A., & Cook, S. W. (1993). Correlates of distress following heterosexual relationship dissolution. *Journal of Social and Personal Relationships, 10,* 55–67.

Frazier, P. A., Cochran, C. C., & Olson, A. M. (1995). Social science research on lay definitions of sexual harassment. *Journal of Social Issues, 51,* 21–37.

Fredricks, A. J., & Dossett, D. L. (1983). Attitude-behavior relations: A comparison of the Fishbein-Ajzen and the Bentler-Speckart models. *Journal of Personality and Social Psychology, 45,* 501–512.

Fredrickson, B. L., Roberts, T., Noll, S. M., Quinn, D. M., & Twenge, J. M. (1998). That swimsuit becomes you: Sex differences in self-objectification, restrained eating, and math performance. *Journal of Personality and Social Psychology, 75,* 269–284.

Freedman, J. L. (1965). Long-term behavioral effects of cognitive dissonance. *Journal of Experimental Social Psychology, 1,* 145–155.

Freedman, J. L. (1984). Effect of television violence on aggressiveness. *Psychological Bulletin, 96,* 227–246.

French, J. R. P., & Raven, B. H. (1959). The bases of social power. In D. Cartwright (Ed.), *Studies in social power.* Ann Arbor: University of Michigan Press.

Frenkl, O. J., & Doob, A. N. (1976). Post-decision dissonance at the polling booth. *Canadian Journal of Behavioral Science, 8,* 347–350.

Freud, S. (1920). *A general introduction to psychoanalysis.* London: Bonji & Liveright.

Frey, K. P., & Eagly, A. H. (1993). Vividness can undermine the persuasiveness of messages. *Journal of Personality and Social Psychology, 65,* 32–44.

Friedman, H. S., & Miller-Herringer, T. (1991). Nonverbal display of emotion in public and private: Self-monitoring, personality, and expressive cues. *Journal of Personality and Social Psychology, 61,* 766–775.

Friedman, H. S., Tucker, J. S., Schwartz, J. E., Tomlinson-Keasy, C., Martin, L. R., Wingard, D. L., & Criqui, M. H. (1995). Psychosocial and behavioral predictors of longevity: The aging and death of the "Termites." *American Psychologist, 50,* 69–78.

Friedrich, L. K., & Stein, A. H. (1973). Aggressive and prosocial television programs and the natural behavior of preschool children. *Monographs of the Society for Research in Child Development, 38* (4, Serial No. 151), 1–64.

Friedrich, L. K., & Stein, A. H. (1975). Prosocial television and young children: The effects of verbal labeling and role playing on learning and behavior. *Child Development, 46,* 27–38.

Frieze, I. H., Olson, J. E., & Russell, J. (1991). Attractiveness and income for men and women in management. *Journal of Applied Social Psychology, 21,* 1039–1057.

Froming, W. J., Corley, E. B., & Rinker, L. (1990). The influence of public self-consciousness and the audience's characteristics on withdrawal from embarrassing situations. *Journal of Personality, 58,* 603–622.

Froming, W. J., Nasby, W., & McManus, J. (1998). Prosocial self-schemas, self-awareness, and children's prosocial behavior. *Journal of Personality and Social Psychology, 75,* 766–777.

Froming, W. J., Walker, G. R., & Lopyan, K. J. (1982). Public and private self-awareness: When personal attitudes conflict with societal expectations. *Journal of Experimental Social Psychology, 18,* 476–487.

Fry, D. P. (1992). Female aggression among the Zapotec of Oaxaca, Mexico. In K. Björkqvist & P. Niemelä (Eds.), *Of mice and women: Aspects of female aggression* (pp. 187–199). San Diego, CA: Harcourt Brace Jovanovich.

Funder, D. C. (1987). Errors and mistakes: Evaluating the accuracy of social judgment. *Psychological Bulletin, 101,* 75–90.

Funder, D. C., & Colvin, C. R. (1988). Friends and strangers: Acquaintanceship, agreement, and the accuracy of personality judgment. *Journal of Personality and Social Psychology, 55,* 149–158.

Gabrenya, W. K., Jr., Wang, Y. E., & Latané, B. (1985). Social loafing on an optimizing task: Cross-cultural differences among Chinese and Americans. *Journal of Cross-Cultural Psychology, 16,* 223–242.

Gaertner, S. L., & Dovidio, J. F. (1977). The subtlety of white racism, arousal, and helping behavior. *Journal of Personality and Social Psychology, 35,* 691–707.

Gaertner, S. L., & Dovidio, J. F. (1986). The aversive form of racism. In J. F. Dovidio & S. L. Gaertner (Eds.), *Prejudice, discrimination, and racism: Theory and research* (pp. 61–89). Orlando, FL: Academic Press.

Gaertner, S. L., Rust, M. C., Dovidio, J. F., Bachman, B. A., & Anastasio, P. A. (1996). The contact hypothesis: The role of a common ingroup identity on reducing intergroup bias among majority and minority group members. In J. L. Nye & A. M. Brower (Eds.), *What's social about social cognition? Research on socially shared cognition in small groups* (pp. 230–260). Thousand Oaks, CA: Sage.

Gaines, S. O., Jr. (1995). Relationships between members of cultural minorities. In J. T. Wood & S. Duck (Eds.), *Understudied relationships: Off the beaten track* (pp. 51–88). Thousand Oaks, CA: Sage.

Gallup, G. G., Jr. (1977). Self-recognition in primates: A comparative approach to the bidirectional properties of consciousness. *American Psychologist, 32,* 329–338.

Gallup, G. G., Jr., & Povinelli, D. J. (1993). Mirror, mirror on the wall, which is the most heuristic theory of them all? A response to Mitchell. *New Ideas in Psychology, 11,* 327–335.

Gamson, W. A., Fireman, B., & Rytina, S. (1982). *Encounters with unjust authority.* Homewood, IL: Dorsey Press.

Gangestad, S. W., & Thornhill, R. (1998). Human sexual selection and developmental stability. In J. A. Simpson & D. T. Kenrick

(Eds.), *Evolutionary social psychology.* Mahwah, NJ: Erlbaum.

Gannon, L., Luchetta, T., Rhodes, K., Pardie, L., & Segrist, D. (1992). Sex bias in psychological research: Progress or complacency? *American Psychologist, 47,* 389–396.

Garcia, L. T., & Griffitt, W. (1978). Evaluation and recall of evidence: Authoritarianism and the Patty Hearst case. *Journal of Research in Personality, 12,* 57–67.

Garcia, S. D., & Khersonsky, D. (1997). "They are a lovely couple": Further examination of perceptions of couple attractiveness. *Journal of Social Behavior and Personality, 12,* 367–380.

Garfinkel, P. (1985). *In a man's world.* New York: New American Library.

Garner, D. M., Garfinkel, P. E., & Olmsted, M. P. (1983). An overview of sociocultural factors in the development of anorexia nervosa. In P. L. Darby, P. E. Garfinkel, D. M. Garner, & D. V. Coscina (Eds.), *Anorexia nervosa: Recent developments in research.* New York: Alan R. Liss.

Gates, M. F., & Allee, W. C. (1933). Conditioned behavior of isolated and grouped cockroaches on a simple maze. *Journal of Comparative Psychology, 15,* 331–358.

Gathorne-Hardy, J. (1981). *Marriage, love, sex and divorce.* New York: Summit Books.

Gecas, V., & Burke, P. J. (1995). Self and identity. In K. S. Cook, G. A. Fine, & J. S. House (Eds.). (1995). *Sociological perspectives on social psychology* (pp. 41–67). Boston: Allyn & Bacon.

Geen, R. G. (1968). Effects of frustration, attack, and prior training on aggressiveness upon aggressive behavior. *Journal of Personality and Social Psychology, 9,* 316–321.

Geen, R. G. (1978). Some effects of observing violence upon the behavior of the observer. In B. Maher (Ed.), *Progress in experimental personality research* (Vol. 8). New York: Academic Press.

Geen, R. G. (1990). *Human aggression.* Stony Stratford: Open University Press.

Geen, R. G. (1998). Aggression and antisocial behavior. In D. T. Gilbert, S. T. Fiske, & G. Lindzey (Eds.), *The handbook of social psychology* (4th ed.). New York: McGraw-Hill.

Geen, R. G., & O'Neal, E. C. (1969). Activation of cue-elicited aggression by general arousal. *Journal of Personality and Social Psychology, 11,* 289–292.

Geiselman, R. E., Haight, N. A., & Kimata, L. G. (1984). Context effects in the perceived physical attractiveness of faces. *Journal of Experimental Social Psychology, 20,* 409–424.

Gelles, R. J. (1993). Alcohol and other drugs are associated with violence: They are not its cause. In R. J. Gelles & D. R. Loseke (Eds.), *Current controversies on family violence* (pp. 182–196). Newbury Park, CA: Sage.

Gelles, R. J., Lackner, R., & Wolfner, G. D. (1994). Men who batter: The risk markers. *Violence Update, 4,* pp. 1ff.

Gerard, H. B., & Mathewson, G. C. (1966). The effects of severity of initiation on liking for a group: A replication. *Journal of Experimental Social Psychology, 2,* 278–287.

Gerbner, G., & Signorielli, N. (1990). Violence profile 1967 through 1988–89: Enduring patterns. Unpublished manuscript, Annenberg School of Communications, University of Pennsylvania.

Gergen, K. J., Ellsworth, P., Maslach, C., & Seipel, M. (1975). Obligation, donor resources, and reactions to aid in 3 cultures. *Journal of Personality and Social Psychology, 43,* 462–474.

Gergen, K. J., Gergen, M. M., & Barton, W. H. (1973). Deviance in the dark. *Psychology Today, 7,* 129–130.

Gergen, K. J., Gulerce, A., Lock, A., & Misra, G. (1996). Psychological science in cultural context. *American Psychologist, 51,* 496–503.

Gergen, M. M., & Gergen, K. J. (1995). What is this thing called love? Emotional scenarios in historical perspective. *Journal of Narrative and Life History, 5,* 221–237.

Gettleman, T. E., & Thompson, J. K. (1993). Actual differences and stereotypical perceptions in body image and eating disturbance: A comparison of male and female heterosexual and homosexual samples. *Sex Roles, 29,* 545–562.

Giancola, P. R., & Zeichner, A. (1997). The biphasic effects of alcohol on human physical aggression. *Journal of Abnormal Psychology, 106,* 598–607.

Gibbons, F. X., & McCoy, S. B. (1991). Self-esteem, similarity, and reactions to active versus passive downward comparison. *Journal of Personality and Social Psychology, 60,* 414–424.

Gibbons, F. X., Benhow, C. P., & Gerrard, M. (1994). From top dog to bottom half: Social comparison strategies in response to poor performance. *Journal of Personality and Social Psychology, 67,* 638–652.

Gibbons, F. X., Carver, C. S., Scheier, M. F., & Hormuth, S. E. (1979). Self-focused attention and the placebo effect: Fooling some of the people some of the time. *Journal of Experimental Social Psychology, 15,* 263–274.

Giddens, A. (1981). *Profiles and critiques of social theory.* London: MacMillan.

Gilbert, B. J., Heesacker, M., & Gannon, L. J. (1991). Changing the sexual aggression-supportive attitudes of men: A psychoeducational intervention. *Journal of Counseling Psychology, 38,* 197–203.

Gilbert, D. T., & Hixon, J. G. (1991). The trouble of thinking: Activation and application of stereotypic beliefs. *Journal of Personality and Social Psychology, 60,* 509–517.

Gilovich, T., Medvec, V. H., & Chen, S. (1995). Commission, omission, and dissonance reduction: Coping with regret in the

"Monty Hall" problem. *Personality and Social Psychology Bulletin, 21*, 182–190.

Glaser, R. D., & Thorpe, J. S. (1986). Unethical intimacy: A survey of sexual contact and advances between psychology educators and female graduate students. *American Psychologist, 40*, 43–51.

Glass, D. C. (1964). Changes in liking as a means of reducing cognitive discrepancies between self-esteem and aggression. *Journal of Personality, 32*, 531–549.

Glenn, E. S. (1966). *Mind, culture and politics.* Cited in Stewart, E. C., & Bennett, M. J. (1991). *American cultural patterns: A cross-cultural perspective* (p. 102). Yarmouth, ME: Intercultural Press.

Glick, P., & Fiske, S. T. (1996). The ambivalent sexism inventory: Differentiating hostile and benevolent sexism. *Journal of Personality and Social Psychology, 70*, 491–512.

Glick, P., & Fiske, S. T. (1997). Hostile and benevolent sexism: Measuring ambivalent sexist attitudes toward women. *Psychology of Women Quarterly, 21*, 119–135.

Glick, P., Diebold, J., Bailey-Werner, B., & Zhu, L. (1997). The two faces of Adam: Ambivalent sexism and polarized attitudes toward women. *Personality and Social Psychology Bulletin, 23*, 1323–1334.

Glick, P., Zion, C., & Nelson, C. (1988). What mediates sex discrimination in hiring decisions? *Journal of Personality and Social Psychology, 55*, 178–186.

Godfrey, D. K., Jones, E. E., & Lord, C. G. (1986). Self-promotion is not ingratiating. *Journal of Personality and Social Psychology, 50*, 106–115.

Goethals, G. R. (1986). Social comparison theory: Psychology from the lost and found. *Personality and Social Psychology Bulletin, 12*, 261–278.

Goethals, G. R., & Zanna, M. P. (1979). The role of social comparison in choice shifts. *Journal of Personality and Social Psychology, 37*, 1469–1476.

Goffman, E. (1959). *The presentation of self in everyday life.* Garden City, NY: Doubleday.

Goffman, E. (1963). *Stigma: Notes on the management of spoiled identity.* Englewood Cliffs, NJ: Prentice-Hall.

Gonsiorek, J. C., & Weinrich, J. D. (1991). The definition and scope of sexual orientation. In J. C. Gonsiorek & J. D. Weinrich (Eds.), *Homosexuality: Research implications for public policy* (pp. 1–12). Newbury Park, CA: Sage.

Gonzales, M. H., Aronson, E., & Costanzo, M. (1988). Increasing the effectiveness of energy auditors: A field experiment. *Journal of Applied Social Psychology, 18*, 1049–1066.

Goodall, J. (1986). *The chimpanzees of Gombe.* Cambridge, MA: Harvard University Press.

Goodwin, S. A., & Fiske, S. T. (1993). *Impression formation in asymmetrical power relationships: Does power corrupt absolutely?* Unpublished

manuscript, University of Massachusetts at Amherst.

Gordon, R. A. (1996). Impact of ingratiation on judgments and evaluations: A meta-analytic investigation. *Journal of Personality and Social Psychology, 71*, 54–70.

Göregenli, M. (1997). Individualist-collectivist tendencies in a Turkish sample. *Journal of Cross-Cultural Psychology, 28*, 787–794.

Gottman, J. M. (1979). *Marital interaction.* New York: Academic Press.

Gottman, J. M., & Levenson, R. W. (1992). Marital processes predictive of later dissolution: Behavior, physiology, and health. *Journal of Personality and Social Psychology, 63*, 221–233.

Gouldner, A. W. (1960). The norm of reciprocity: A preliminary statement. *American Sociological Review, 25*, 161–178.

Graham, S. R. (1992). What does a man want? *American Psychologist, 47*, 837–841.

Grammer, K. (1990). Strangers meet: Laughter and nonverbal signs of interest in opposite-sex encounters. *Journal of Nonverbal Behavior, 14*, 209–236.

Grandin, E., & Lupri, E. (1997). Intimate violence in Canada and the United States: A cross-national comparison. *Journal of Family Violence, 12*, 417–443.

Granrose, C. S., & Cunningham, E. A. (1988). Postpartum work intentions among Black and White college women. *Career Development Quarterly, 37*, 49–64.

Granström, K., & Stiwne, D. (1998). A bipolar model of groupthink: An expansion of Janis's concept. *Small Group Research, 29*, 32–56.

Greaves, L. (1996). *Smoke screen: Women's smoking and social control.* Halifax, Canada: Fernwood Publishing.

Greca, A. M. la. (1993). Social skills training with children: Where do we go from here? *Journal of Clinical Child Psychology, 22*, 288–298.

Green, C. W. (1998). Normative influence on the acceptance of information technology: Measurement and effects. *Small Group Research, 29*, 85–123.

Green, L. W., & McAlister, A. (1984). Macro-intervention to support health behavior: Some theoretical perspectives and practical reflections. *Health Education Quarterly, 11*, 323–339.

Greenberg, J., & Pyszczynski, T. (1985). The effect of an overheard slur on evaluations of the target: How to spread a social disease. *Journal of Experimental Social Psychology, 21*, 61–72.

Greenberg, M. S., & Frisch, D. M. (1972). Effects of intentionality on willingness to reciprocate a favor. *Journal of Experimental Social Psychology, 8*, 99–111.

Greenfield, P. M. (1994). Independence and interdependence as developmental scripts: Implications for theory, research, and

practice. In P. M. Greenfield & R. R. Cocking (Eds.), *Cross-cultural roots of minority child development* (pp. 1–37). Hillsdale, NJ: Erlbaum.

Greenwald, A. G. (1980). The totalitarian ego: Fabrication and revision of personal history. *American Psychologist, 35*, 603–618.

Greenwald, A. G., & Pratkanis, A. R. (1984). The self. In R. S. Weyer & T. K. Srull (Eds.), *The handbook of social cognition* (Vol. 3). Hillsdale, NJ: Erlbaum.

Greenwald, A. G., McGhee, D. E., & Schwartz, J. L. K. (1998). Measuring individual differences in implicit cognition: The implicit association test. *Journal of Personality and Social Psychology, 74*, 1464–1480.

Gregory, W. L., Cialdini, R. B., & Carpenter, K. M. (1982). Self-relevant scenarios as mediators of likelihood estimates and compliance: Does imagining make it so? *Journal of Personality and Social Psychology, 43*, 89–99.

Grogan, S., Williams, Z., & Conner, M. (1996). The effects of viewing same-gender photographic models on body esteem. *Psychology of Women Quarterly, 20*, 569–575.

Gross, A. E., & Latané, J. G. (1974). Receiving help, reciprocation, and interpersonal attraction. *Journal of Applied Social Psychology, 4*, 210–223.

Gross, S. R., & Miller, N. (1997). The "golden section" and bias in perceptions of social consensus. *Personality and Social Psychology Review, 1*, 241–271.

Groth, A. N. (1979). *Men who rape: The psychology of the offender.* New York: Plenum.

Gruder, C. L., Cook, T. D., Hennigan, K. M., Flay, B. R., Alessis, C., & Halamaj, J. (1978). Empirical tests of the absolute sleeper effect predicted from the discounting cue hypothesis. *Journal of Personality and Social Psychology, 36*, 1061–1074.

Gruner, C. R. (1985). Advice to the beginning speaker on using humor: What the research tells us. *Communication Education, 34*, 142–147.

Grusec, J. E. (1991). The socialization of empathy. In M. S. Clark (Ed.), *Review of personality and social psychology: Vol. Prosocial behavior* (pp. 9–33). Newbury Park, CA: Sage.

Grusec, J. E., & Redler, E. (1980). Attribution, reinforcement, and altruism: A developmental analysis. *Developmental Psychology, 16*, 525–534.

Grusec, J. E., Saas-Kortsaak, P., & Simutis, Z. M. (1978b). The role of example and moral exhortation in the training of altruism. *Child Development, 49*, 920–923.

Grush, J. E., McKeough, K. L., & Ahlering, R. F. (1978). Extrapolating laboratory exposure to actual political elections. *Journal of Personality and Social Psychology, 36*, 257–270.

Gudjonsson, G. H. (1991). Suggestibility and compliance among alleged false confessors and resisters in criminal trials. *Medicine, Science, and the Law, 31*, 147–151.

Guerin, B. (1986). Mere presence effects in humans: A review. *Journal of Personality and Social Psychology, 22,* 38–77.

Guerra, N. G., & Slaby, R. G. (1990). Cognitive mediators of aggression in adolescent offenders: 2. Intervention. *Developmental Psychology, 26,* 269–277.

Haddock, G., & Zanna, M. P. (1998). Authoritarianism, values, and the favorability and structure of antigay attitudes. In G. M. Herek (Ed.), *Stigma and sexual orientation: Understanding prejudice against lesbians, gay men, and bisexuals. Psychological perspectives on lesbian and gay issues* (Vol. 4, pp. 82–107). Thousand Oaks, CA: Sage.

Hagestad, G. O., & Smyer, M. A. (1982). Dissolving long-term relationships: Patterns of divorcing in middle age. In S. Duck (Ed.), *Personal relationships, 4: Dissolving relationships* (pp. 155–188). New York: Academic Press.

Halford, W. K., Hahlweg, K., & Dunne, M. (1990). The cross-cultural consistency of marital communication associated with marital distress. *Journal of Marriage and the Family, 52,* 487–500.

Hall, J. A. (1978). Gender effects in decoding nonverbal cues. *Psychological Bulletin, 85,* 845–875.

Hall, J. A. (1984). *Nonverbal sex differences: Communication accuracy and expressive style.* Baltimore: Johns Hopkins University Press.

Hamilton, D. L., & Gifford, R. K. (1976). Illusory correlation in interpersonal judgments. *Journal of Experimental Social Psychology, 12,* 392–407.

Hamilton, D. L., & Sherman, S. J. (1996). Perceiving persons and groups. *Psychological Review, 103,* 336–355.

Hampson, S. E. (1988). The dynamics of categorization and impression formation. In T. K. Srull & R. S. Wyer, Jr., (Eds.), *Advances in social cognition, Vol. 1: A dual process model of impression formation* (pp. 77–82). Hillsdale, NJ: Lawrence Erlbaum.

Hansen, C. H., & Hansen, R. D. (1988). Finding the face in the crowd: An anger superiority effect. *Journal of Personality and Social Psychology, 54,* 917–924.

Hanson, R. K., Cadsky, O., Harris, A., & Lalonde, C. (1997). Correlates of battering among 997 men: Family, history, adjustment, and attitudinal differences. *Violence and Victims, 12,* 191–208.

Harari, H., Mohr, D., & Hosey, K. (1980). Faculty helpfulness to students: A comparison of compliance techniques. *Personality and Social Psychology Bulletin, 6,* 373–377.

Hardin, G. (1968). The tragedy of the commons. *Science, 162,* 1243–1248.

Hare, A. P., & Kent, M. V. (1994). Leadership. In A. P. Hare, H. H. Blumberg, M F. Davies, & M. V. Kent (Eds.), *Small group research: A handbook* (pp. 155–166). Norwood, NJ: Ablex.

Harkins, S., & Szymanski, K. (1989). Social loafing and group evaluation. *Journal of Personality and Social Psychology, 56,* 934–941.

Harmons-Jones, E., Brehm, J. W., Greenberg, J., Simon, L., & Nelson, D. E. (1996). Evidence that the production of aversive consequences is not necessary to create cognitive dissonance. *Journal of Personality and Social Psychology, 70,* 5–16.

Harré, R. (1984). *Personal being: A theory for individual psychology.* Cambridge, MA: Harvard University Press.

Harrigan, J. A. (1985). Self touching as an indicator of underlying affect and language processing. *Social Science and Medicine, 20,* 1161–1168.

Harrigan, J. A., Lucic, K. S., Kay, D., McLaney, A., & Rosenthal, R. (1991). Effect of expresser role and type of self-touching on observers' perceptions. *Journal of Applied Social Psychology, 21,* 585–609.

Harris, M. (1991). *Cultural anthropology* (3rd ed.). New York: HarperCollins.

Harris, M. B., Benson, S. M., & Hall, C. L. (1975). The effects of confession on altruism. *Journal of Social Psychology, 96,* 187–192.

Harris, M. J., Milich, R., Corbitt, E. M., Hoover, D. W., & Brady, M. (1992). Self-fulfilling effects of stigmatizing information on children's social interactions. *Journal of Personality and Social Psychology, 63,* 41–50.

Harris, S. M. (1995). Family, self, and sociocultural contributions to body-image attitudes of African-American women. *Psychology of Women Quarterly, 19,* 129–145.

Harrison, A., & Saeed, L. (1977). Let's make a deal: An analysis of revelations and stipulations in lonely hearts advertisements. *Journal of Personality and Social Psychology, 35,* 257–264.

Hart, E. A., Leary, M. R., & Rejeski, W. J. (1989). The measurement of social physique anxiety. *Journal of Sport and Exercise Psychology, 11,* 94–104.

Harter, S., Waters, P. L., Pettitt, L. M., Whitesell, N., Kofkin, J., & Jordan, J. (1997). Autonomy and connectedness as dimensions of relationship styles in men and women. *Journal of Social and Personal Relationships, 14,* 147–164.

Hartley, W. S. (1970). *Manual for the twenty statements problem.* Kansas City, MO: Department of Research, Greater Kansas City Mental Health Foundation.

Hartmann, D. P. (1969). Influence of symbolically modeled instrumental aggression and pain cues on aggressive behavior. *Journal of Personality and Social Psychology, 11,* 280–288.

Harvey, J. H., & Martin, R. (1995). Celebrating the story in social perception, communication, and behavior. In R. S. Wyer & T. K. Srull (Eds.), *Knowledge and memory: Advances in social cognition* (Vol. 8). Hillsdale, NJ: Erlbaum.

Harvey, J. H., & Omarzu, J. (1997). Minding the close relationship. *Personality and Social Psychology Review, 1,* 224–240.

Harvey, J. H., Flanary, R., & Morgan, M. (1986). Vivid memories of vivid loves gone by. *Journal of Social and Personal Relationships, 3,* 359–373.

Harvey, O. J., Hunt, D. E., & Schroder, H. M. (1961). *Conceptual systems and personality organization.* New York: Wiley.

Harwood, R. L., Miller, J. G., & Irizarry, N. L. (1995). *Culture and attachment: Perceptions of the child in context.* New York: Guilford Press.

Hass, R. G., Katz, I., Rizzo, N., Bailey, J., & Eisenstadt, D. (1991). Cross-racial appraisal as related to attitude ambivalence and cognitive complexity. *Personality and Social Psychology Bulletin, 17,* 83–92.

Hastie, R., Penrod, S., & Pennington, N. (1983). *Inside the jury.* Cambridge, MA: Harvard University Press.

Hastorf, A., & Cantril, H. (1954). They saw a game: A case study. *Journal of Abnormal and Social Psychology, 49,* 129–134.

Hatfield, E. (1988). Passionate and companionate love. In R. J. Sternberg & M. L. Barnes (Eds.), *The psychology of love* (pp. 191–217). New Haven, CT: Yale University Press.

Hatfield, E., Aronson, E., Abrahams, D., & Rottman, L. (1966). The importance of physical attractiveness in dating behavior. *Journal of Personality and Social Psychology, 4,* 508–516.

Hatfield, E., Greenberger, E., Traupmann, J., & Lambert, P. (1982). Equity and sexual satisfaction in recently married couples. *Journal of Sex Research, 18,* 18–32.

Hatfield, E., & Rapson, R. L. (1993). *Love, sex, and intimacy: Their psychology, biology, and history.* New York: HarperCollins.

Hatfield, E., Walster, G. W., & Piliavin, J. (1978). Equity theory and helping relationships. In L. Wispé (Ed.), *Altruism, sympathy and helping* (pp. 115–139). New York: Academic Press.

Hatfield, S., & Sprecher, S. (1986). *Mirror, mirror: The importance of looks in everyday life.* Albany, NY: State University of New York.

Hau, K. T., & Salili, F. (1991). Structure and semantic differential placement of specific causes: Academic causal attributions by Chinese students in Hong Kong. *International Journal of Psychology, 26,* 175–193.

Haugtvedt, C. P., & Petty, R. E. (1992). Personality and persuasion: Need for cognition moderates the persistence and resistance of attitude changes. *Journal of Personality and Social Psychology, 63,* 308–319.

Haugtvedt, C. P., & Wegener, D. T. (1994). Message order effects in persuasion: An attitude strength perspective. *Journal of Consumer Research, 21,* 205–218.

Haugtvedt, C. P., Schumann, D. W., Schneier, W. L., & Warren, W. L. (1994). Advertising repetition and variation strategies: Implications for understanding attitude strength. *Journal of Consumer Research, 21,* 176–189.

Hawkins, S. A., & Hastie, R. (1990). Hindsight: Biased judgments of past events after the outcomes are known. *Psychological Bulletin, 107,* 311–327.

Hays, R. B. (1985). A longitudinal study of friendship development. *Journal of Personality and Social Psychology, 48,* 909–924.

Hazan, C., & Shaver, P. (1987). Romantic love conceptualized as an attachment process. *Journal of Personality and Social Psychology, 52,* 511–524.

Hearold, S. (1986). A synthesis of 1043 effects of television on social behavior. In G. Comstock (Ed.), *Public communication and behavior* (Vol. 1). Orlando, FL: Academic Press.

Heath, L., Acklin, M., & Wiley, K. (1991). Cognitive heuristics and AIDS risk assessment among physicians. *Journal of Applied Social Psychology, 21,* 1859–1867.

Heatherton, T. F., & Baumeister, R. F. (1991). Binge eating as escape from self-awareness. *Psychological Bulletin, 110,* 86–108.

Hebl, M. R., & Heatherton, T. F. (1998). The stigma of obesity in women: The difference is black and white. *Personality and Social Psychology Bulletin, 24,* 417–426.

Hecht, M. L., Marston, P. J., & Larkey, L. K. (1994). Love ways and relationship quality in heterosexual relationships. *Journal of Social and Personal Relationships, 11,* 25–43.

Heider, F. (1946). Attitudes and cognitive organization. *Journal of Psychology, 21,* 107–112.

Heider, F. (1958). *The psychology of interpersonal relations.* New York: Wiley.

Heine, S. J., & Lehman, D. R. (1997). Culture, dissonance, and self-affirmation. *Personality and Social Psychology Bulletin, 23,* 389–400.

Helgesen, S. (1990). *The female advantage: Women's ways of leadership.* New York: Doubleday.

Helgeson, V. S. (1994). Long-distance romantic relationships: Sex differences in adjustment and breakup. *Personality and Social Psychology Bulletin, 20,* 254–265.

Helgeson, V. S., & Mickelson, K. D. (1995). Motives for social comparison. *Personality and Social Psychology Bulletin, 21,* 1200–1209.

Helms, J. E. (1990). *Black and white racial identity: Theory, research, and practice.* New York: Greenwood Press.

Hendrick, C., & Hendrick, S. (1986). A theory and method of love. *Journal of Personality and Social Psychology, 50,* 392–402.

Hendrick, C., Hendrick, S., Foote, F. H., & Slapion-Foote, M. J. (1984). Do men and women love differently? *Journal of Social and Personal Relationships, 1,* 177–195.

Hendrick, S. S., & Hendrick, C. (1992). *Romantic love.* Newbury Park, CA: Sage.

Hepworth, J. T., & West, S. G. (1988). Lynchings and the economy: A time-series reanalysis of Hovland and Sears (1940). *Journal of Personality and Social Psychology, 55,* 239–247.

Herek, G. M. (1984). Beyond "homophobia": A social psychological perspective on attitudes toward lesbians and gay men. *Journal of Homosexuality, 10,* 1–21.

Herek, G. M. (1987a). Can functions be measured? A new perspective on the functional approach to attitudes. *Social Psychology Quarterly, 50,* 285–303.

Herek, G. M. (1987b). On heterosexual masculinity: Some psychical consequences of the social construction of gender and sexuality. In M. Kimmel (Ed.), *Changing men: New directions in research on men and masculinity* (pp. 68–82). Newbury Park, CA: Sage.

Herek, G. M. (1987c). Religious orientation and prejudice: A comparison of racial and sexual attitudes. *Personality and Social Psychology Bulletin, 13,* 34–44.

Herek, G. M. (1988). Heterosexuals' attitudes toward lesbians and gay men: Correlates and gender differences. *Journal of Sex Research, 25,* 451–477.

Herek, G. M. (1990). The context of anti-gay violence: Notes on cultural and psychological heterosexism. *Journal of Interpersonal Violence, 5,* 316–333.

Herek, G. M. (1991). Myths about sexual orientation: A lawyer's guide to social science research. *Law and Sexuality: A Review of Lesbian and Gay Legal Issues, 1,* 133–172.

Herek, G. M., & Capitanio, J. P. (1996). "Some of my best friends": Intergroup contact, concealable stigma, and heterosexuals attitudes toward gay men and lesbians. *Personality and Social Psychology Bulletin, 22,* 412–424.

Herek, G. M., & Capitanio, J. P. (1998). Symbolic prejudice or fear of infection? A functional analysis of AIDS-related stigma among heterosexual adults. *Basic and Applied Social Psychology, 20,* 230–241.

Herek, G. M., Gillis, J. R., Cogan, J. G., & Glunt, E. K. (1997). Hate crime victimization among lesbian, gay, and bisexual adults: Prevalence, psychological correlates, and methodological issues. *Journal of Interpersonal Violence, 12,* 195–215.

Herek, G. M., Janis, I. L., & Huth, P. (1987). Decision making during international crises: Is quality of process related to outcome? *Journal of Conflict Resolution, 31,* 203–226.

Herek, G. M., Jobe, J. B., & Carney, R. (1996). *Out in force: Sexual orientation and the military.* Chicago: University of Chicago Press.

Herek, G. M., Kimmel, D. C., Amaro, H., & Melton, G. B. (1991). Avoiding heterosexist bias in psychological research. *American Psychologist, 46,* 957–963.

Hermans, H. J. M., Kempen, H. J. G., & Van Loon, R. J. P. (1992). The dialogical self: Beyond individualism and rationalism. *American Psychologist, 47,* 23–33.

Herzog, D. B., Newman, K. L., Yeh, C. J., & Warshaw, M. (1992). Body image satisfaction in homosexual and heterosexual women. *International Journal of Eating Disorders, 11,* 391–396.

Hewstone, M. (1988). Causal attribution: From cognitive processes to collective beliefs. *The Psychologist, 8,* 323–327.

Hewstone, M., & Brown, R. J. (1986). Contact is not enough: An intergroup perspective on the 'contact hypothesis'. In M. Hewstone, & R. Brown (Eds.), *Contact and conflict in intergroup encounters* (pp. 1–44). Oxford: Basil Blackwell.

Hewstone, M., Macrae, C. N., Griffiths, R., Milne, A. B., & Brown, R. (1994). Cognitive models of stereotype change: Measurement, development, and consequences of subtyping. *Journal of Experimental Social Psychology, 30,* 505–526.

Hicks, D. (1968). Short- and long-term retention of affectively-varied modeled behavior. *Psychonomic Science, 11,* 369–370.

Higbee, K. L., Millard, R. J., & Folkman, J. R. (1982). Social psychology research during the 1970s: Predominance of experimentation and college students. *Personality and Social Psychology Bulletin, 8,* 180–183.

Higgins, E. T. (1987). Self-discrepancy: A theory relating self and affect. *Psychological Review, 94,* 319–340.

Higgins, E. T. (1996). The "self digest": Self-knowledge serving self-regulatory functions. *Journal of Personality and Social Psychology, 71,* 1062–1083.

Higgins, E. T., Bond, R. N., Klein, R., & Strauman, T. (1986). Self-discrepancies and emotional vulnerability: How magnitude, accessibility, and type of discrepancy influence affect. *Journal of Personality and Social Psychology, 51,* 5–15.

Higgins, E. T., Roney, C. J. R., Crowe, E., & Hymes, C. (1994). Ideal versus ought predilections for approach and avoidance: Distinct self-regulatory systems. *Journal of Personality and Social Psychology, 66,* 276–286.

Higgins, R. L., & Harris, R. N. (1988). Strategic "alcohol" use: Drinking to self-handicap. *Journal of Social and Clinical Psychology, 6,* 191–202.

Hill, C. A. (1991). Seeking emotional support: The influence of affiliative need and partner warmth. *Journal of Personality and Social Psychology, 60,* 112–121.

Hill, C. T., & Stull, D. E. (1981). Sex differences in effects of social and value similarity in same-sex friendship. *Journal of Personality and Social Psychology, 41,* 488–502.

Hill, C. T., Rubin, Z., & Peplau, L. A. (1979). Breakups before marriage: The end of 103 affairs. In G. Levinger & O. C. Moles (Eds.),

Divorce and separation (pp. 64–82). New York: Basic Books.

Hilton, J. L., & Hippel, W. V. (1996). Stereotypes. *Annual Review of Psychology, 47,* 237–271.

Hinde, R. A. (1990). The interdependence of the behavioural sciences. *Philosophical Transactions of the Royal Society of London, B 329,* 217–227.

Hirt, E. R., Deppe, R. K., & Gordon, L. J. (1991). Self-reported versus behavioral self-handicapping: Empirical evidence for a theoretical distinction. *Journal of Personality and Social Psychology, 61,* 981–991.

Hirt, E. R., Zillmann, D., Erickson, G. A., & Kennedy, C. (1992). Costs and benefits of allegiance: Changes in fans' self-ascribed competencies after team victory versus defeat. *Journal of Personality and Social Psychology, 63,* 724–738.

Ho, D. Y.-F., & Chiu, C.-Y. (1994). Component ideas of individualism, collectivism, and social organization: An application in the study of Chinese culture. In U. Kim, H. C. Triandis, C. Kâğitçibaşi, S. C. Choi, & G. Yoon (Eds.), *Individualism and collectivism: Theory, method, and applications* (pp. 137–156). Thousand Oaks, CA: Sage.

Hobart, C. W. (1958). The incidence of romanticism during courtship. *Social Forces, 36,* 364–367.

Hoffman, L. E. (1992). American psychologists and wartime research on Germany, 1941–1945. *American Psychologist, 47,* 264–273.

Hoffman, M. L. (1981). Is altruism part of human nature? *Journal of Personality and Social Psychology, 40,* 121–137.

Hogg, M. A. (1992). *The social psychology of group cohesiveness: From attraction to social identity.* London: Harvester-Wheatsheaf.

Hogg, M. A., & Abrams, D. (1988). *Social identifications: A social psychology of intergroup relations and group processes.* London: Routledge.

Holahan, C. J., Moos, R. H., & Bonn, L. (1997). Social support, coping, and psychological adjustment: A resource model. In G. R. Pierce, B. Lakey, I. G. Sarason, & B. R. Sarason (Eds.), *Sourcebook of social support and personality,* (pp. 169–186). New York: Plenum Press.

Hollander, E. P. (1961). Some effects of perceived status on responses to innovative behavior. *Journal of Abnormal and Social Psychology, 63,* 247–250.

Hollander, E. P. (1992). The essential interdependence of leadership and followership. *Current Directions in Psychological Science, 1,* 71–75.

Hollon, S. D., Shelton, R. C., & Loosen, P. T. (1991). Cognitive therapy and pharmacotherapy for depression. *Journal of Consulting and Clinical Psychology, 58,* 88–99.

Homans, G. C. (1958). Social behavior as exchange. *American Journal of Sociology, 63,* 597–606.

Homer, P. M., & Kahle, L. R. (1988). A structural equation test of the value-attitude-behavior hierarchy. *Journal of Personality and Social Psychology, 54,* 638–646.

Horton, R. W., & Santogrossi, D. A. (1978). The effect of adult commentary on reducing the influence of televised violence. *Personality and Social Psychology Bulletin, 4,* 337–340.

House, R. J., & Shamir, B. (1993). Toward the integration of transformational, charismatic, and visionary theories. In M. M. Chemers & R. Ayman (Eds.), *Leadership theory and research: Perspectives and directions* (pp. 81–107). San Diego, CA: Academic Press.

Houston, S., & Hwang, N. (1996). Correlates of the objective and subjective experiences of sexual harassment in high school. *Sex Roles, 34,* 189–204.

Hovland, C. I., & Sears, R. R. (1940). Minor studies in aggression: VI. Correlation of lynchings with economic indices. *Journal of Personality, 9,* 301–310.

Hovland, C. I., & Weiss, W. (1951). The influence of source credibility on communication effectiveness. *Public Opinion Quarterly, 15,* 635–650.

Hovland, C. I., Janis, I. L., & Kelley, H. H. (1953). *Communication and persuasion.* New Haven, CT: Yale University Press.

Hovland, C. I., Lumsdaine, A. A., & Sheffield, F. D. (1949). *Experiments on mass communication.* Princeton, NJ: Princeton University Press.

Howard, D. J. (1995). "Chaining" the use of influence strategies for producing compliance behavior. *Journal of Social Behavior and Personality, 10,* 169–185.

Howard, J. A., Blumstein, P., & Schwartz, P. (1987). Social evolutionary theories? Some observations on preferences in human mate selection. *Journal of Personality and Social Psychology, 53,* 194–200.

Huesmann, L. R. (1986a). The effects of film and television violence among children. In S. J. Katz & P. Vesin (Eds.), *Children and the media* (pp. 101–128). Paris: Centre International de l'Enfance.

Huesmann, L. R. (1986b). Psychological processes promoting the relation between exposure to media violence and aggressive behavior by the viewer. *Journal of Social Issues, 42,* 125–140.

Huesmann, L. R. (1988). An information processing model for the development of aggression. *Aggressive Behavior, 14,* 125–139.

Huesmann, L. R., & Eron, L. D. (Eds.). (1986). *Television and the aggressive child: A cross-national comparison.* Hillsdale, NJ: Erlbaum.

Huesmann, L. R., & Miller, L. S. (1994). Long-term effects of repeated exposure to media violence in childhood. In L. R. Huesmann (Ed.), *Aggressive behavior: Current perspectives* (pp. 153–186). New York: Plenum.

Huesmann, L. R., Eron, L. D., & Yarmel, P. W. (1987). Intellectual functioning and aggression. *Journal of Personality and Social Psychology, 52,* 232–240.

Huesmann, L. R., Eron, L. D., Klein, R., Brice, P., & Fischer, P. (1983). Mitigating the imitation of aggressive behaviors by changing children's attitudes about media violence. *Journal of Personality and Social Psychology, 44,* 899–910. Conceptual model. *Psychological Bulletin, 107,* 156–176.

Hui, C. H. (1986). Fifteen years of pornography research: Does exposure to pornography have any effects? *Bulletin of the Hong Kong Psychological Society, 14,* 41–62.

Hui, C. H., & Triandis, H. C. (1986). Individualism-collectivism, a study of cross-cultural researchers. *Journal of Cross-Cultural Psychology, 17,* 225–248.

Hull, C. L. (1943). *Principles of behavior: An introduction to behavior theory.* New York: Appleton-Century-Crofts.

Hull, J. G. (1981). A self-awareness model of the causes and effects of alcohol consumption. *Journal of Abnormal Psychology, 90,* 586–600.

Hull, J. G., & Bond, C. F., Jr. (1986). Social and behavioral consequences of alcohol consumption and expectancy: A meta-analysis. *Psychological Bulletin, 99,* 347–360.

Hull, J. G., Reilly, N. P., & Ennis, L. C. (1990). Self-consciousness, role discrepancy, and depressive affect. In R. Schwarzer & R. Wicklund (Eds.), *Anxiety and self-focused attention* (pp. 27–40). London: Harwood Academic Publishers.

Hull, J. G., & Young, R. D. (1983). Self-consciousness, self-esteem, and success-failure as determinants of alcohol consumption in male social drinkers. *Journal of Personality and Social Psychology, 44,* 1097–1109.

Hull, J. G., Young, R. D., & Jouriles, E. (1986). Applications of the self-awareness model of alcohol consumption: Predicting patterns of use and abuse. *Journal of Personality and Social Psychology, 51,* 790–796.

Hunsberger, B. (1995). Religion and prejudice: The role of religious fundamentalism, quest, and right-wing authoritarianism. *Journal of Social Issues, 51,* 113–129.

Hunt, M. (1990). *The compassionate beast: What science is discovering about the humane side of humankind.* New York: William Morrow.

Hutnik, N. (1991). *Ethnic minority identity: A social psychological perspective.* New York: Oxford University Press.

Hyde, J. S. (1984). How large are gender differences in aggression? A developmental meta-analysis. *Developmental Psychology, 20,* 722–736.

Ickes, W. (1985). Sex-role influences in dyadic interaction: A theoretical model. In C. Mayo & N. Henley (Eds.), *Compatible and incompatible relationships* (pp. 187–208). New York: Springer-Verlag.

Ingram, R. E. (1990). Self-focused attention in clinical disorders: Reviews and a conceptual model. *Psychological Bulletin, 107,* 156–176.

Inman, M. L., & Baron, R. S. (1996). Influence of prototypes on perceptions of prejudice. *Journal of Personality and Social Psychology, 70,* 727–739.

Inman, M. L., Reichl, A. J., & Baron, R. S. (1993). Do we tell less than we know or hear less than we are told? Exploring the teller-listener extremity effect. *Journal of Experimental Social Psychology, 29,* 528–550.

Insko, C. A., Smith, R. H., Alicke, M. D., Wade, J., & Taylor, S. (1985). Conformity and group size: The concern with being right and the concern with being liked. *Personality and Social Psychology Bulletin, 11,* 41–50.

Intons-Peterson, M. J. (1988). *Children's concepts of gender.* Norwood, NJ: Ablex.

Ip, G. W. M., & Bond, M. H. (1995). Culture, values, and the spontaneous self-concept. *Asian Journal of Psychology, 1,* 29–35.

Isen, A. M. (1970). Success, failure, attention, and reactions to others: The warm glow of success. *Journal of Personality and Social Psychology, 15,* 294–301.

Isen, A. M. (1984). Toward understanding the role of affect in cognition. In S. R. Wyer & T. K. Srull (Eds.), *Handbook of social cognition* (Vol. 3, pp. 179–236). New York: Academic Press.

Isen, A. M. (1987). Positive affect, cognitive processes, and social behavior. In L. Berkowitz (Ed.), *Advances in experimental social psychology* (Vol. 20, pp. 203–253). New York: Academic Press.

Isen, A. M., & Levin, P. A. (1972). Effect of feeling good on helping: Cookies and kindness. *Journal of Personality and Social Psychology, 21,* 384–388.

Isen, A. M., & Simmonds, S. F. (1978). The effect of feeling good on a helping task that is incompatible with good mood. *Social Psychology Quarterly, 41,* 346–349.

Isen, A. M., Horn, N., & Rosenhan, D. L. (1973). Effects of success and failure on children's generosity. *Journal of Personality and Social Psychology, 27,* 239–247.

Isenberg, D. (1986). Group polarization: A critical review and meta-analysis. *Journal of Personality and Social Psychology, 50,* 1141–1151.

Ishii-Kuntz, M. (1989). Collectivism or individualism? Changing patterns of Japanese attitudes. *Social Science Review, 73,* 174–179.

Ito, T. A., Miller, N., & Pollock, V. E. (1996). Alcohol and aggression: A meta-analysis on the moderating effects of inhibitory cues, triggering effects, and self-focused attention. *Psychological Bulletin, 120,* 60–82.

Iwao, S. (1989). Social psychology's models of social behavior: Is it not time for West to meet East? Unpublished manuscript. Keio University, Institute for Communications Research, Tokyo, Japan.

Izard, C. E. (1994). Innate and universal facial expressions: Evidence from developmental and cross-cultural research. *Psychological Bulletin, 115,* 288–299.

Jackson, J., & Williams, K. D. (1985). Social loafing on difficult tasks: Working collectively can improve performance. *Journal of Personality and Social Psychology, 49,* 937–942.

Jackson, L. A., Hunter, J. E., & Hodge, C. N. (1995). Physical attractiveness and intellectual competence: A meta-analytic review. *Social Psychology Quarterly, 58,* 108–122.

Jackson, L. A., Sullivan, L. A., Harnish, R., & Hodge, C. N. (1996). Achieving positive social identity: Social mobility, social creativity, and permeability of group boundaries. *Journal of Personality and Social Psychology, 70,* 241–254.

Jackson, S. E., Brett, J. F., Sessa, V. I., Cooper, D. M., Julin, J. A., & Peyronnin, K. (1991). Some differences make a difference: Individual dissimilarity and group heterogeneity as correlates of recruitment, promotions, and turnover. *Journal of Applied Psychology, 76,* 675–689.

Jacobs, R. C., & Campbell, D. T. (1961). The perpetuation of an arbitrary tradition through several generations of a laboratory microculture. *Journal of Abnormal and Social Psychology, 62,* 649–658.

Jamieson, D. W., Lydon, J. E., & Zanna, M. P. (1987). Attitude and activity preference similarity: Differential bases of interpersonal attraction for low and high self-monitors. *Journal of Personality and Social Psychology, 53,* 1052–1060.

Janis, I. L. (1967). Effects of fear arousal on attitude change: Recent developments in theory and experimental research. In L. Berkowitz (Ed.), *Advances in experimental social psychology* (Vol. 3, pp. 166–224). New York: Academic Press.

Janis, I. L. (1982). *Groupthink* (2nd ed.). Boston: Houghton Mifflin.

Janis, I. L., & Feshbach, S. (1953). Effects of fear-arousing communications. *Journal of Abnormal and Social Psychology, 48,* 78–92.

Janis, I. L., Kaye, D., & Kirschner, P. (1965). Facilitating effects of "eating while reading" on responsiveness to persuasive communications. *Journal of Personality and Social Psychology, 1,* 17–27.

Janoff-Bulman, R., & Lang-Gunn, L. (1988). Coping with disease, crime, and accidents: The role of self-blame attributions. In L. Y. Abramson (Ed.), *Social cognition and clinical psychology: A synthesis* (pp. 116–147). New York: Guilford.

Jarvis, W. B. G., & Petty, R. E. (1996). The need to evaluate. *Journal of Personality and Social Psychology, 70,* 172–194.

Jehn, K. A., & Shah, P. P. (1997). Interpersonal relationships and task performance: An examination of mediating processes in friendship and acquaintance groups. *Journal of Personality and Social Psychology, 72,* 775–790.

Jenson, R. E., & Moore, S. G. (1977). The effect of attribute statements on cooperativeness and competitiveness in school-age boys. *Child Development, 48,* 305–307.

Jepson, C., & Chaiken, S. (1990). Chronic issue-specific fear inhibits systematic processing of persuasive communications. *Journal of Social Behavior and Personality, 5,* 61–84.

Jesuíno, J. C. (1996). Leadership: Micro-macro links. In E. Witte & J. Davis (Eds.), *Understanding group behavior: (Vol. 2): Small group processes and interpersonal relations* (pp. 93–125). Hillsdale, NJ: Erlbaum.

Joe, J. R. (1994). Revaluing Native-American concepts of development and education. In P. M. Greenfield & R. R. Cocking (Eds.), *Cross-cultural roots of minority child development* (pp. 107–113). Hillsdale, NJ: Erlbaum.

John, O. P., Cheek, J. M., & Klohnen, E. C. (1996). On the nature of self-monitoring: Construct explication with Q-sort ratings. *Journal of Personality and Social Psychology, 71,* 763–776.

Johnson, C., Clay-Warner, J., & Funk, S. J. (1996). Effects of authority structures and gender on interaction in same-sex task groups. *Social Psychology Quarterly, 59,* 221–236.

Johnson, M. K., & Sherman, S. J. (1990). Constructing and reconstructing the past and the future in the present. In E. T. Higgins & R. M. Sorrentino (Eds.), *Handbook of motivation and cognition: Foundations of social behavior* (Vol. 2, pp. 482–526). New York: Guilford Press.

Johnson, R. D., & Downing, R. L. (1979). Deindividuation and valence of cues: Effects of prosocial and antisocial behavior. *Journal of Personality and Social Psychology, 37,* 1532–1538.

Johnston, J. H., Driskell, J. E., & Salas, E. (1997). Vigilant and hypervigilant decision making. *Journal of Applied Psychology, 82,* 614–622.

Jones, D., & Hill, K. (1993). Criteria of facial attractiveness in five populations. *Human Nature, 4,* 271–296.

Jones, E. E. (1964). *Ingratiation.* New York: Appleton-Century-Crofts.

Jones, E. E. (1990). *Interpersonal perception.* New York: W.H. Freeman.

Jones, E. E. (1998). Major developments in five decades of social psychology. In D. T. Gilbert, S. T. Fiske, & G. Lindzey (Eds.), *The handbook of social psychology* (4th ed., Vol. 1, pp. 3–57). New York: McGraw-Hill.

Jones, E. E., & Davis, K. E. (1965). A theory of correspondent inferences: From acts to dispositions. In L. Berkowitz (Ed.), *Advances in experimental social psychology* (Vol. 2, pp. 219–266). New York: Academic Press.

Jones, E. E., & Harris, V. A. (1967). The attribution of attitudes. *Journal of Experimental Social Psychology, 3*, 1–24.

Jones, E. E., & Nisbett, R. E. (1971). *The actor and the observer: Divergent perceptions of the cases of behavior.* Morristown, NJ: General Learning Press.

Jones, E. E., & Nisbett, R. E. (1972). The actor and the observer: Divergent perceptions of the causes of behavior. In E. E. Jones, D. E. Kanouse, H. H. Kelley, R. E. Nisbett, S. Valins, & B. Weiner (Eds.), *Attribution: Perceiving the causes of behavior* (pp. 79–94). Morristown, NJ: General Learning Press.

Jones, E. E., & Pittman, T. S. (1982). Toward a general theory of strategic self-presentation. In J. Suls (Ed.), *Psychological perspectives on the self.* Hillsdale, NJ: Erlbaum.

Jones, E. E., & Wortman, C. (1973). *Ingratiation: An attributional approach.* Morristown, NJ: General Learning Press.

Jones, E. E., Davis, K. E., & Gergen, K. J. (1961). Role playing variations and their informational value for person perception. *Journal of Abnormal and Social Psychology, 63*, 302–310.

Jones, E. E., Rock, L., Shaver, K. G., Goethals, G. R., & Ward, L. M. (1968). Pattern of performance and ability attribution: An unexpected primacy effect. *Journal of Personality and Social Psychology, 10*, 317–340.

Jones, R. A., & Brehm, J. W. (1970). Persuasiveness of one- and two-sided communications as a function of awareness: There are two sides. *Journal of Experimental Social Psychology, 6*, 47–56.

Jones, S. C. (1973). Self and interpersonal evaluations: Esteem theories versus consistency theories. *Psychological Bulletin, 79*, 185–199.

Jones, W. H., Carpenter, B. N., & Quintana, D. (1985). Personality and interpersonal predictors of loneliness in two cultures. *Journal of Personality and Social Psychology, 48*, 1503–1511.

Jones, W. H., Hobbs, S. A., & Hockenbury, D. (1982). Loneliness and social skills deficits. *Journal of Personality and Social Psychology, 42*, 682–689.

Jones, W. H., Sansone, C., & Helm, B. (1983). Loneliness and interpersonal judgments. *Personality and Social Psychology Bulletin, 9*, 437–441.

Jordan, W. D. (1968). *White over Black: American attitudes toward the Negro, 1550–1812.* Chapel Hill: University of North Carolina Press.

Josephs, R. A., Larrick, R. P., Steele, C. M., & Nisbett, R. E. (1992). Protecting the self from the negative consequences of risky decisions. *Journal of Personality and Social Psychology, 62*, 26–37.

Judd, C. M., & Park, B. (1988). Out-group homogeneity: Judgments of variability at the individual and group levels. *Journal of Personality and Social Psychology, 54*, 778–788.

Judd, C. M., Ryan, C. S., & Park, B. (1991). Accuracy in the judgment of in-group and out-group variability. *Journal of Personality and Social Psychology, 61*, 366–379.

Judd, M., & Brauer, M. (1995). Repetition and evaluative extremity. In R. E. Petty & J. A. Krosnick (Eds.), *Attitude strength: Antecedents and consequences* (pp. 43–71). Mahwah, NJ: Erlbaum.

Jussim, L. (1989). Teacher expectations: Self-fulfilling prophecies, perpetual biases, and accuracy. *Journal of Personality and Social Psychology, 57*, 469–480.

Jussim, L., Yen, H., & Aiello, J. R. (1995). Self-consistency, self-enhancement, and accuracy in reactions to feedback. *Journal of Experimental Social Psychology, 31*, 322–356.

Kacmar, K. M., Delery, J. E., & Ferris, G. R. (1992). Differential effectiveness of applicant impression management tactics on employment interview decisions. *Journal of Applied Social Psychology, 22*, 1250–1272.

Kagehiro, D. K., & Laufer, W. S. (Eds.). (1992). *Handbook of psychology and the law.* New York: Springer-Verlag.

Kahneman, D. (1995). Varieties of counterfactual thinking. In N. J. Roese & J. M. Olson (Eds.), *What might have been: The social psychology of counterfactual thinking* (pp. 375–396). Hillsdale, NJ: Erlbaum.

Kahneman, D., & Tversky, A. (1973). On the psychology of prediction. *Psychological Review, 80*, 237–251.

Kahneman, D., & Tversky, A. (1982). The simulation heuristic. In D. Kahneman, P. Slovic, & A. Tversky (Eds.), *Judgment under uncertainty: Heuristics and biases.* New York: Cambridge University Press.

Kallgren, C. A., & Wood, W. (1986). Access to attitude-relevant information in memory as a determinant of attitude-behavior consistency. *Journal of Experimental Social Psychology, 22*, 328–338.

Kalven, H., Jr., & Zeisel, H. (1966). *The American Jury.* Boston: Little, Brown.

Kanazawa, S. (1992). Outcome or expectancy? Antecedent of spontaneous causal attribution. *Personality and Social Psychology Bulletin, 18*, 659–668.

Kandel, D. B. (1978). Similarity in real-life adolescent friendship pairs. *Journal of Personality and Social Psychology, 36*, 306–312.

Kaplan, D. L., & Keys, C. B. (1997). Sex and relationship variables as predictors of sexual attraction in cross-sex platonic friendships among young heterosexual adults. *Journal of Social and Personal Relationships, 14*, 191–206.

Kaplan, K. J., Firestone, I. J., Degnore, R., & Morre, M. (1974). Gradients of attraction as a function of disclosure probe intimacy and setting formality: On distinguishing attitude oscillation from attitude change— Study one. *Journal of Personality and Social Psychology, 30*, 638–646.

Kaplan, M. F. (1987). The influencing process in group decision making. In C. Hendrick (Ed.), *Review of personality and social psychology: Group processes* (Vol. 8, pp. 189–212). Beverly Hills, CA: Sage.

Kaplan, M. F., & Miller, C. E. (1983). Group discussion and judgment. In P. B. Paulus (Ed.), *Basic group processes* (pp. 65–94). New York: Springer-Verlag.

Karabenick, S. A., Lerner, R. M., & Beecher, M. D. (1973). Relation of political affiliation to helping behavior on election day, November 7, 1972. *Journal of Social Psychology, 91*, 223–227.

Karasawa, K. (1995). An attributional analysis of reactions to negative emotions. *Personality and Social Psychology Bulletin, 21*, 456–467.

Karau, S. J., & Kelly, J. R. (1992). The effects of time scarcity and time abundance on group performance quality and interaction process. *Journal of Experimental Social Psychology, 28*, 542–571.

Karau, S. J., & Williams, K. D. (1993). Social loafing: A meta-analytic review and theoretical integration. *Journal of Personality and Social Psychology, 65*, 681–706.

Karau, S. J., & Williams, K. D. (1995). Social loafing, research findings, implications, and future directions. *Current Directions in Psychological Science, 4*, 134–140.

Karlins, M., Coffman, T., & Walters, G. (1969). On the fading of social stereotypes: Studies in three generations of college students. *Journal of Personality and Social Psychology, 13*, 1–16.

Karraker, K. H., & Stern, M. (1990). Infant physical attractiveness and facial expression: Effects on adult perceptions. *Basic and Applied Social Psychology, 11*, 371–385.

Kashima, Y. (1987). Conceptions of person: Implications in individualism/collectivism research. In C. Kâğitçibaşi (Ed.), *Growth and progress in cross-cultural psychology* (pp. 104–112). Lisse, The Netherlands: Swets & Zeitlinger.

Kashima, Y., & Kerekes, A. R. Z. (1994). A distributed memory model of averaging phenomena in person impression formation. *Journal of Experimental Social Psychology, 30*, 407–455.

Kashima, Y., & Triandis, H. C. (1986). The self-serving bias in attributions as a coping strategy: A cross-cultural study. *Journal of Cross-Cultural Psychology, 17*, 83–97.

Kashima, Y., Siegel, M., Tanaka, K., & Kashima, E. S. (1992). Do people believe behaviours are consistent with attitudes? Towards a cultural psychology of attribution processes. *British Journal of Social Psychology, 31*, 111–124.

Kashima, Y., Yamaguchi, S., Kim, U., Choi, S-C., Gelfand, M. J., & Yuki, M. (1995). Culture, gender, and self: A perspective from individualism-collectivism research. *Journal of Personality and Social Psychology, 69,* 925–937.

Kashy, D. A., & DePaulo, B. M. (1996). Who lies? *Journal of Personality and Social Psychology, 70,* 1037–1051.

Kassin, S. M. (1997). The psychology of confession evidence. *American Psychologist, 52,* 221–233.

Kassin, S. M., & Kiechel, K. L. (1996). The social psychology of false confessions: Compliance, internalization, and confabulation. *Psychological Science, 7,* 125–128.

Katz, D. (1960). The functional approach to the study of attitudes. *Public Opinion Quarterly, 24,* 163–204.

Katz, I., & Hass, R. G. (1988). Racial ambivalence and American value conflict: Correlational and prime studies of dual cognitive structures. *Journal of Personality and Social Psychology, 55,* 893–905.

Katz, I., Wackenhut, J., & Hass, R. G. (1986). Racial ambivalence, value duality, and behavior. In J. F. Dovidio & S. L. Gaertner (Eds.), *Prejudice, discrimination, and racism* (pp. 35–60). New York: Academic Press.

Katz, P. (1986). Gender identity: Development and consequences. In R. Ashmore & F. Del Boca (Eds.), *The social psychology of female-male relations* (pp. 21–67). Orlando, FL: Academic Press.

Keating, C. F. (1985). Gender and the physiognomy of dominance and attractiveness. *Social Psychology Quarterly, 48,* 61–70.

Keating, C. F., Mazur, A., Segall, M. H., Cysneiros, P. G., DiVale, W. T., Kilbride, J. E., Komin, S., Leahy, P., Thurman, B., & Wirsing, R. (1981). Culture and the perception of social dominance from facial expression. *Journal of Personality and Social Psychology, 40,* 601–614.

Kelley, H. H. (1950). The warm-cold variable in first impressions of persons. *Journal of Personality, 18,* 431–439.

Kelley, H. H. (1967). Attribution theory in social psychology. In D. L. Vine (Ed.), *Nebraska symposium on motivation.* Lincoln: University of Nebraska Press.

Kelley, H. H. (1972). Causal schemata and the attribution process. In E. Jones, D. Kanouse, H. Kelley, R. Nisbett, S. Valms, & B. Weiner (Eds.), *Attribution: Perceiving the causes of behavior.* Morristown, NJ: General Learning Press.

Kelly, J. R., Jackson, J. W., & Hutson-Comeaux, S. L. (1997). The effects of time pressure and task differences on influence modes and accuracy in decision-making groups. *Personality and Social Psychology, 23,* 10–22.

Kelly, K. M., & Jones, W. H. (1997). Assessment of dispositional embarrassability. *Anxiety, Stress, and Coping, 10,* 307–333.

Kelly, L. (1997). Skills training as a treatment for communication problems. In J. A. Daly,

J. C. McCroskey, J. Ayres, T. Hopf, & D. M. Ayres (Eds.), *Avoiding communication: Shyness, reticence, and communication apprehension* (2nd ed., pp. 331–365). Creskill, NJ: Hampton Press.

Kelman, H. C. (1958). Compliance, identification and internalization: Three processes of attitude change. *Journal of Conflict Resolution, 2,* 51–60.

Kelman, H. C. (1998). The place of ethnic identity in the development of personal identity: A challenge for the Jewish family. *Studies in Contemporary Jewry: An Annual.* (pp. 3–26). New York: Oxford University Press.

Kelman, H. C., & Hovland, C. I. (1953). "Reinstatement" of the communicator in delayed measurement of opinion change. *Journal of Abnormal and Social Psychology, 48,* 327–335.

Keltner, D., & Buswell, B. N. (1997). Embarrassment: Its distinct form and appeasement functions. *Psychological Bulletin, 122,* 250–270.

Keltner, D., & Robinson, R. J. (1997). Defending the status quo: Power and bias in social conflict. *Personality and Social Psychology Bulletin, 23,* 1066–1077.

Keltner, D., Young, R. C., & Buswell, B. N. (1997). Appeasement in human emotion, social practice, and personality. *Aggressive Behavior, 23,* 359–374.

Kenrick, D. T., & Cialdini, R. B. (1977). Romantic attraction: Misattribution versus reinforcement explanations. *Journal of Personality and Social Psychology, 35,* 381–391.

Kenrick, D. T., & Trost, M. R. (1987). A biosocial theory of heterosexual relationships. In K. Kelly (Ed.), *Females, males, and sexuality.* Albany: State University of New York Press.

Kenrick, D. T., Baumann, D. J., & Cialdini, R. B. (1979). A step in the socialization of altruism as hedonism: Effects of negative mood on children's generosity under public and private conditions. *Journal of Personality and Social Psychology, 37,* 747–755.

Kenrick, D. T., Gutierres, S. E., & Goldberg, L. L. (1989). Influence of popular erotica on judgments of strangers and mates. *Journal of Experimental Social Psychology, 25,* 159–167.

Kent, M. V. (1996). Presence of others. In A. P. Hare, H. H. Blumberg, M. F. Davies, & M. V. Kent (Eds.), *Small groups: An introduction* (pp. 41–57). Westport, CN: Praeger.

Kerckhoff, A. C., & Davis, K. E. (1962). Value consensus and need complementarity in mate selection. *American Sociological Review, 27,* 295–303.

Kernis, M. H., & Waschull, S. B. (1995). The interactive roles of stability and level of self-esteem: Research and theory. In M. P. Zanna (Ed.), *Advances in experimental social psychology* (Vol. 27, pp. 93–141). San Diego: Academic Press.

Kernis, M. H., Cornell, D. P., Sun, C. R., Berry, A. J., & Harlow, T. (1993). There's more to

self-esteem than whether it is high or low: The importance of stability of self-esteem. *Journal of Personality and Social Psychology, 65,* 1190–1204.

Kerr, N. L. (1983). Motivation losses in small groups: A social dilemma. *Journal of Personality and Social Psychology, 45,* 819–828.

Kerr, N. L. (1992). Issue importance and group decision making. In S. Worchel, W. Wood, & J. A. Simpson (Eds.), *Group process and productivity* (pp. 68–88). Newbury Park, CA: Sage.

Kerr, N. L., & MacCoun, R. J. (1985). The effects of jury size and polling method on the process and product of jury deliberation. *Journal of Personality and Social Psychology, 48,* 349–363.

Kerr, N. L., MacCoun, R. J., & Kramer, G. P. (1996). "When are N heads better (or worse) than one?": Biased judgment in individuals versus groups. In E. Witte & J. Davis (Eds.), *Understanding group behavior: (Vol. 1): Small group processes and interpersonal relations* (pp. 105–136). Hillsdale, NJ: Erlbaum.

Key, W. B. (1989). *The age of manipulation.* New York: Holt.

Kiesler, C. A., & Pallak, M. S. (1975). Minority influence: The effect of majority reactionaries and defectors, and minority and majority compromisers, upon majority opinion and attraction. *European Journal of Social Psychology, 5,* 237–256.

Kiesler, S., Sproull, L., & Waters, K. (1996). A prisoner's dilemma experiment on cooperation with people and human-like computers. *Journal of Personality and Social Psychology, 70,* 47–65.

Kilham, W., & Mann, L. (1974). Level of destructive obedience as a function of transmitter and executant roles in the Milgram obedience paradigm. *Journal of Personality and Social Psychology, 29,* 696–702.

Kim, U. (1994). Individualism and collectivism: Conceptual clarification and elaboration. In U. Kim, H. C. Triandis, C. Kâğitçibaşi, S. Choi, & G. Yoon (Eds.), *Individualism and collectivism: Theory, method, and applications* (pp. 19–40). Thousand Oaks, CA: Sage.

Kim, U., & Choi, S.-H. (1994). Individualism, collectivism, and child development: A Korean perspective. In P. M. Greenfield & R. R. Cocking (Eds.), *Cross-cultural roots of minority child development* (pp. 227–257). Hillsdale, NJ: Erlbaum.

Kimble, D. L., Covell, N. H., Weiss, L. H., Newton, K. J., & Fisher, J. D. (1992). College students use implicit personality theory instead of safer sex. *Journal of Applied Social Psychology, 22,* 921–933.

Kimble, G. A. (1989). Psychology from the standpoint of a generalist. *American Psychologist, 44,* 491–499.

Kinder, D. R. (1998). Attitude and action in the realm of politics. In D. T. Gilbert, S. T. Fiske, & G. Lindzey (Eds.), *The handbook of social psychology* (4th ed., Vol. 2, pp. 778–867). New York: McGraw-Hill.

Kirkpatrick, L. A., & Davis, K. E. (1994). Attachment style, gender, and relationship stability: A longitudinal analysis. *Journal of Personality and Social Psychology, 66*, 502–512.

Kirkpatrick, S. A., & Locke, E. A. (1991). Leadership: Do traits matter? *Academy of Management Executives, 5(2)*, 48–60.

Kirkpatrick, S. A., & Locke, E. A. (1996). Direct and indirect effects of three core charismatic leadership components on performance and attitudes. *Journal of Applied Psychology, 81*, 36–51.

Kite, M. E., & Deaux, K. (1987). Gender belief systems: Homosexuality and the implicit inversion theory. *Psychology of Women Quarterly, 11*, 83–96.

Kite, M. E., & Whitley, B. E., Jr., (1996). Sex differences in attitudes toward homosexual persons, behaviors, and civil rights: A meta-analysis. *Personality and Social Psychology Bulletin, 22*, 336–353.

Klein, G. (1996). The effect of acute stressors on decision making. In J. Driskell & E. Salas (Eds.), *Stress and human performance* (pp. 49–88). Mahwah, NJ: Erlbaum.

Kleinke, C. L., Meeker, F. B., & Staneski, R. A. (1986). Preference for opening lines: Comparing ratings by men and women. *Sex Roles, 15*, 585–600.

Kleinpenning, G., & Hagendoorn, L. (1993). Forms of racism and the cumulative dimension of ethnic attitudes. *Social Psychology Quarterly, 56*, 21–36.

Klohnen, E. C., & Bera, S. (1998). Behavioral and experiential patterns of avoidantly and securely attached women across adulthood: A 31-year longitudinal perspective. *Journal of Personality and Social Psychology, 74*, 211–223.

Knapp, M. L., Stafford, L., & Daly, J. A. (1986). Regrettable messages: Things people wish they hadn't said. *Journal of Communication, 36*, 40–58.

Knee, C. R., & Zuckerman, M. (1996). Causality orientations and the disappearance of the self-serving bias. *Journal of Research in Personality, 30*, 76–87.

Knight, G. P., & Dubro, A. F. (1984). Cooperative, competitive, and individualistic social values: An individualized regression and clustering approach. *Journal of Personality and Social Psychology, 46*, 98–105.

Knower, F. H. (1936). Experimental studies of changes in attitudes: I. A study of the effect of oral argument on changes of attitude. *Journal of Social Psychology, 6*, 315–347.

Knox, R. E., & Inkster, J. A. (1968). Postdecision dissonance at post-time. *Journal of Personality and Social Psychology, 8*, 319–323.

Knox, R. E., & Safford, R. K. (1976). Group caution at the race track. *Journal of Experimental Social Psychology, 12*, 317–324.

Koch, S. (1981). Psychology and its human clientele: Beneficiaries or victims? In R. A. Kasschau & F. S. Kessel (Eds.), *Psychology and society: In search of symbiosis* (pp. 24–47). New York: Holt, Rinehart & Winston.

Koestner, R., Bernieri, F., & Zuckerman, M. (1992). Self-regulation and consistency between attitudes, traits, and behaviors. *Personality and Social Psychology Bulletin, 18*, 52–59.

Koffka, K. (1935). *Principles of gestalt psychology.* London: Routledge & Kegan Paul.

Köhler, W. (1929). *Gestalt psychology.* New York: Liveright.

Komatsu, L. K. (1992). Recent reviews of conceptual structure. *Psychological Bulletin, 112*, 500–526.

Koren, P., Carlton, K., & Shaw, D. (1980). Marital conflict: Relations among behaviors, outcomes, and distress. *Journal of Consulting and Clinical Psychology, 48*, 460–468.

Koss, M. P. (1990). Changed lives: The psychological impact of sexual harassment. In M. A. Paludi (Ed.), *Ivory power: Sexual harassment on campus* (pp. 73–92). Albany, NY: State University of New York Press.

Koss, M. P., Gidycz, C. A., & Wisniewski, N. (1987). The scope of rape: Incidence and prevalence of sexual aggression and victimization in a national sample of higher education students. *Journal of Consulting and Clinical Psychology, 55*, 162–170.

Kramer, R. M., & Goldman, L. (1995). Helping the group or helping yourself? Social motives and group identity in resource dilemmas. In D. A. Schroeder (Ed.), *Social dilemmas: Perspectives on individuals and groups* (pp. 49–67). Westport, CN: Praeger.

Kraus, S. J. (1995). Attitudes and the prediction of behavior: A meta-analysis of the empirical literature. *Personality and Social Psychology Bulletin, 21*, 58–75.

Kraut, R. E. (1973). Effects of social labeling on giving to charity. *Journal of Experimental Social Psychology, 9*, 551–562.

Krebs, D. L. (1975). Empathy and altruism. *Journal of Personality and Social Psychology, 32*, 1134–1146.

Kristiansen, C. M., & Hotte, A. M. (1996). Morality and the self: Implications for the when and how of value-attitude behavior relations. In C. Seligman, J. Olson, & M. P. Zanna (Eds.), *The psychology of values: The Ontario symposium* (Vol. 8). Mahwah, NJ: Erlbaum.

Kristiansen, C. M., & Zanna, M. P. (1994). The rhetorical use of values to justify social and intergroup attitudes. *Journal of Social Issues, 50*, 47–65.

Krosnick, J. A., & Alwin, D. F. (1989). Aging and susceptibility to attitude change. *Journal of Personality and Social Psychology, 59*, 1140–1152.

Krosnick, J. A., Betz, A. L., Jussim, L. J., & Lynn, A. R. (1992). Subliminal conditioning of

attitudes. *Personality and Social Psychology Bulletin, 18*, 152–162.

Krueger, J. (1996). Personal beliefs and cultural stereotypes about racial characteristics. *Journal of Personality and Social Psychology, 71*, 536–548.

Krueger, J. (1998). Enhancement bias in descriptions of self and others. *Personality and Social Psychology Bulletin, 24*, 505–516.

Krueger, J., & Clement, R. W. (1994). The truly false consensus effect: An ineradicable and egocentric bias in social perception. *Journal of Personality and Social Psychology, 67*, 596–610.

Krueger, J., Ham, J. J., & Linford, K. M. (1996). Perceptions of behavioral consistency: Are people aware of the actor-observer effect? *Psychological Science, 7*, 259–264.

Kruglanski, A. W. (1996). Motivated social cognition: Principles of the interface. In E. T. Higgins & A. W. Kruglanski (Eds.), *Social psychology: Handbook of basic principles* (pp. 493–520). New York: Guilford Press.

Kruglanski, A. W., & Freund, T. (1983). The freezing and unfreezing of lay inferences: Effects on impressional primacy, ethnic stereotyping, and numerical anchoring. *Journal of Experimental Social Psychology, 19*, 448–468.

Krull, D. S., & Dill, J. C. (1996). On thinking first and responding fast: Flexibility in social inference processes. *Personality and Social Psychology Bulletin, 22*, 949–959.

Kuhn, M. H., & McPartland, T. S. (1954). An empirical investigation of self-attitudes. *American Sociological Review, 19*, 68–76.

Kuhn, T. (1977). *The essential tension.* Chicago: University of Chicago Press.

Kulik, J. A., & Gump, B. B. (1997). Affective reactions to social comparison: The effects of relative performance and related attributes information about another person. *Personality and Social Psychology Bulletin, 23*, 452–468.

Kulik, J. A., & Mahler, H. I. M. (1989). Stress and affiliation in a hospital setting: Preoperative roommate preferences. *Personality and Social Psychology Bulletin, 15*, 183–193.

Kulik, J. A., Mahler, H. I. M., & Earnest, A. (1994). Social comparison and affiliation under threat: Going beyond the affiliate-choice paradigm. *Journal of Personality and Social Psychology, 66*, 301–309.

Kulik, J. A., Mahler, H. I. M., & Moore, P. J. (1996). Social comparison and affiliation under threat: Effects on recovery from major surgery. *Journal of Personality and Social Psychology, 71*, 967–979.

Kupke, T., Hobbs, S. A., & Cheney, T. H. (1979). Selection of heterosocial skills: I. Criterion-related validity. *Behavior Therapy, 10*, 327–335.

Kurdek, L. A. (1991). The dissolution of gay and lesbian couples. *Journal of Social and Personal Relationships, 8*, 265–278.

Kurdek, L. A. (1994). Areas of conflict for gay, lesbian, and heterosexual couples: What couples argue about influences relationship satisfaction. *Journal of Marriage and the Family, 56,* 923–934.

Kurdek, L. A. (1997). Adjustment to relationship dissolution in gay, lesbian, and heterosexual partners. *Personal Relationships, 4,* 145–161.

Kurdek, L. A. (1998). Relationship outcomes and their predictors: Longitudinal evidence from heterosexual married, gay cohabiting, and lesbian cohabiting couples. *Journal of Marriage and the Family, 60,* pp. 553–568.

Kurdek, L. A., & Schmitt, J. P. (1986). Relationship quality of partners in heterosexual married, heterosexual cohabiting, and gay and lesbian relationships. *Journal of Personality and Social Psychology, 51,* 711–720.

Kurdek, L. A., & Schmitt, J. P. (1987). Perceived emotional support from families and friends in members of homosexual, married, and heterosexual cohabiting couples. *Journal of Homosexuality, 14(3/4),* 57–68.

Kutchinsky, B. (1971). Towards an explanation of the decrease in registered sex crimes in Copenhagen. *Technical report of the commission on obscenity and pornography* (Vol. 7, pp. 263–310). Washington, DC: U.S. Government Printing Office.

Kutchinsky, B. (1985). Pornography and its effects in Denmark and the United States: A rejoinder and beyond. *Comparative Social Research, 8,* 301–330.

Kutchinsky, B. (1991). Pornography and rape: Theory and practice? *International Journal of Law and Psychiatry, 14,* 47–64.

Kutner, N. G., & Levinson, R. M. (1978). The toy salesperson: A voice for change in sex-role stereotypes? *Sex Roles, 4,* 1–8

LaBarbera, P., & MacLachlan, J. (1979). Time compressed speech in radio advertising. *Journal of Marketing, 43,* 30–36.

Labov, W. (1973). The boundaries of words and their meanings. In C. J. N. Bailey & R. W. Shiny (Eds.), *New ways of analyzing variation in English (Vol. 1).* Washington, DC: Georgetown University Press.

Lagerspetz, K. (1985). Are wars caused by aggression? In F. L. Denmark (Ed.), *Social/ecological psychology and the psychology of women.* New York: Elsevier (North-Holland).

Lagerspetz, K. M. J., Björkqvist, K. (1994). Indirect aggression in boys and girls. In L. R. Huesmann (Ed.), *Aggressive behavior: Current perspectives* (pp. 131–150). New York: Plenum.

Lagerspetz, K. M. J., Björkqvist, K., & Peltonen, T. (1988). Is indirect aggression typical of females? Gender differences in aggressiveness in 11- to 12-year-old children. *Aggressive Behavior, 14,* 403–414.

Lakey, B., & Drew, J. B. (1997). A social-cognitive perspective on social support. In G. R. Pierce, B. Lakey, I. G. Sarason, & B. R. Sarason (Eds.), *Sourcebook of social support and personality* (pp. 107–140). New York: Plenum Press.

Lakoff, R. T. (1975). *Language and woman's place.* New York: Harper & Row.

Lambert, A. J. (1995). Stereotypes and social judgment: The consequences of group variability. *Journal of Personality and Social Psychology, 68,* 388–403.

Lamke, L. K., Sollie, D. L., Durbin, R. G., & Fitzpatrick, J. A. (1994). Masculinity, femininity and relationship satisfaction: The mediating role of interpersonal competence. *Journal of Social and Personal Relationships, 11,* 535–554.

Lang, A. R., Goeckner, D. J., Adesso, V. J., & Marlatt, G. A. (1975). Effects of alcohol on aggression in male social drinkers. *Journal of Abnormal Psychology, 84,* 508–518.

Langer, E. J. (1989). Minding matters: The consequences of mindlessness-mindfulness. In L. Berkowitz (Ed.), *Advances in experimental social psychology* (Vol. 22, 137–173). San Diego: Academic Press.

Langfred, C. W. (1998). Is group cohesiveness a double-edged sword? An investigation of the effects of cohesiveness on performance. *Small Group Research, 29,* 124–143.

Langlois, J. H., Roggman, L. A., & Musselman, L. (1994). What is average and what is not average about attractive faces? *Psychological Science, 5,* 214–220.

Langolis, J. H., & Downs, A. C. (1980). Mothers, fathers, and peers as socialization agents of sex-typed behaviors in young children. *Child Development, 51,* 1237–1247.

Lanzetta, J. T., & Orr, S. P. (1986). Excitatory strength of expressive faces: Effects of happy and fear expressions and context on the extinction of a conditioned fear response. *Journal of Personality and Social Psychology, 50,* 190–194.

LaPiere, R. T. (1934). Attitudes vs. actions. *Social Forces, 13,* 230–237.

L'Armand, K., & Pepitone, A. (1975). Helping to reward another person: A cross-cultural analysis. *Journal of Personality and Social Psychology, 31,* 189–198.

Larson, R., Csikszentmihalyi, M., & Graef, R. (1982). Time alone in daily experience: Loneliness or renewal? In L. A. Peplau & D. Perlman (Eds.), *Loneliness: A sourcebook of current theory, research and therapy* (pp. 40–53). New York: Wiley-Interscience.

Latané, B. (1981). The psychology of social impact. *American Psychologist, 36,* 343–356.

Latané, B., & Darley, J. M. (1968). Group inhibition of bystander intervention in emergencies. *Journal of Personality and Social Psychology, 10,* 215–221.

Latané, B., & Darley, J. M. (1970). *The unresponsive bystander: Why doesn't he help?* Englewood Cliffs, NJ: Prentice-Hall.

Latané, B., & L'Herrou, T. (1996). Spatial clustering in the conformity game: Dynamic social impact in electronic groups. *Journal of Personality and Social Psychology, 70,* 1218–1230.

Latané, B., & Nida, S. (1981). Ten years of research on group size and helping. *Psychological Bulletin, 89,* 308–324.

Latané, B., & Nowak, A. (in press). Self-organizing social systems: Necessary and sufficient conditions for the emergence of consolidation and clustering. In G. Barnett & F. Boster (Eds.), *Progress in communication science: Persuasion.* Norwood, NJ: Ablex.

Latané, B., & Rodin, J. (1969). A lady in distress: Inhibiting effects of friends and strangers on bystander intervention. *Journal of Experimental Social Psychology, 5,* 189–202.

Latané, B., Williams, K., & Harkins, S. (1979). Many hands make light the work: The causes and consequences of social loafing. *Journal of Personality and Social Psychology, 37,* 822–832.

Laughlin, P. R. (1996). Group decision making and collective induction. In E. Witte & J. Davis (Eds.), *Understanding group behavior: (Vol. 1): Small group processes and interpersonal relations* (pp. 61–80). Hillsdale, NJ: Erlbaum.

Laurenceau, J. P., Barrett, L. F., & Pietromonaco, P. R. (1998). Intimacy as an interpersonal process: The importance of self-disclosure, partner disclosure, and perceived partner responsiveness in interpersonal exchanges. *Journal of Personality and Social Psychology, 74,* 1238–1251.

Lavin, T. J. (1987). Divergence and convergence in the causal attributions of married couples. *Journal of Marriage and the Family, 49,* 71–80.

Lawler, E. J. (1992). Affective attachments to nested groups: A choice-process theory. *American Sociological Review, 57,* 327–339.

Lazarus, R. S. (1984). On the primacy of cognition. *American Psychologist, 39,* 124–129.

Leary, M. R. (1996). *Self-presentation: Impression management and interpersonal behavior.* Boulder, CO: Westview Press.

Leary, M. R., & Kowalski, R. M. (1995). *Social anxiety.* New York: Guilford Press.

Leary, M. R., Nezlek, J. B., Downs, D., Radford-Davenport, J., Martin, J., & McMullen, A. (1994). Self-presentation in everyday interactions: Effects of target familiarity and gender composition. *Journal of Personality and Social Psychology, 67,* 664–673.

LeBon, G. (1903). *Psychologie des foules [The psychology of the crowd].* Paris: Alcan.

Lee, F., Hallahan, M., & Herzog, T. (1996). Explaining real-life events: How culture and domain shape attributions. *Personality and Social Psychology Bulletin, 22,* 732–741.

Lee, J. A. (1977). A typology of styles of loving. *Personality and Social Psychology Bulletin, 3,* 173–182.

Lee, J. A., DeLeon, P. H., Wedding, D., & Nordal, K. (1994). Psychologists' role in influencing Congress: The process and the players. *Professional Psychology—Research & Practice, 25,* 9–15.

Lee, R. S. (1995). Regional subcultures as revealed by magazine circulation patterns. *Cross-Cultural Research, 29,* 91–120.

Lee, Y.-T., Jussim, L. J., & McCauley, C. R. (Eds.), (1995). *Stereotype accuracy: Toward appreciating group differences.* Washington, DC: American Psychological Association.

Leffler, A., Gillespie, D. L., & Conaty, J. C. (1982). The effects of status differentiation on nonverbal behavior. *Social Psychology Quarterly, 45,* 153–161.

Legrenzi, P., Butera, F., Mugny, G., & Perez, J. (1991). Majority and minority influence in inductive reasoning: A preliminary study. *European Journal of Social Psychology, 21,* 359–363.

Leifer, A. D., & Roberts, D. F. (1972). Childrens' response to television violence. In J. P. Murray, E. A. Rubinstein, & G. A. Comstock (Eds.), *Television and social behavior (Vol. 2): Television and social learning.* Washington, DC: U.S. Government Printing Office.

Leippe, M. R., & Eisenstadt, D. (1994). The generalization of dissonance reduction: Decreasing prejudice through induced compliance. *Journal of Personality and Social Psychology, 67,* 395–413.

Leippe, M. R., & Elkin, R. A. (1987). When motives clash: Issue involvement and response involvement as determinants of persuasion. *Journal of Personality and Social Psychology, 52,* 269–278.

Leonard, K. (1989). The impact of explicit aggressive and implicit nonaggressive cues on aggression in intoxicated and sober males. *Personality and Social Psychology Bulletin, 15,* 390–400.

Leonard, K. E., & Quigley, B. M. (1999). Drinking and marital aggression in newlyweds: An event-based analysis of drinking and the occurrence of husband marital aggression. *Journal of Studies on Alcohol, 60.*

Lerner, M. J. (1980). *The belief in a just world: A fundamental delusion.* New York: Plenum.

Lerner, M. J., & Meindl, J. R. (1981). Justice and altruism. In J. P. Rushton & R. M. Sorrentino (Eds.), *Altruism and helping behavior: Social, personality, and developmental perspectives* (pp. 213–232). Hillsdale, NJ: Lawrence Erlbaum.

Leventhal, H. (1970). Findings and theory in the study of fear communications. In L. Berkowitz (Ed.), *Advances in experimental social psychology* (Vol. 5, pp. 119–186). New York: Academic Press.

Levine, J. M., & Moreland, R. L. (1994). Group socialization: Theory and research. In W.

Stroebe & M. Hewstone (Eds.), *The European review of social psychology* (Vol. 5, pp. 305–336). Chichester, England: John Wiley.

Levine, J. M., & Moreland, R. L. (1998). Small groups. In D. Gilbert, S. T. Fiske, & G. Lindzey (Eds.), *Handbook of social psychology* (4th ed.). New York: McGraw-Hill.

Levine, R., Sata, S., Hashimoto, T., & Verma, J. (1995). Love and marriage in eleven cultures. *Journal of Cross-Cultural Psychology, 26,* 554–571.

Levine, R. A., & Campbell, D. T. (1972). *Ethnocentrism.* New York: Wiley.

Levine, R. V., Martinez, T. S., Brase, G., & Sorenson, K. (1994). Helping in 36 U.S. cities. *Journal of Personality and Social Psychology, 67,* 69–82.

Levinson, D. (1989). *Family violence in cross-cultural perspective* (Vol. 1). Newbury Park: Sage.

Levy, B., & Lobel, K. (1991). Lesbian teens in abusive relationships. In B. Levy (Ed.), *Dating violence: Young women in danger* (pp. 203–208). Seattle, WA: Seal Press.

Levy, K. N., Blatt, S. J., & Shaver, P. R. (1998). Attachment styles and parental representations. *Journal of Personality and Social Psychology, 74,* 407–419.

Levy, M. B., & Davis, K. E. (1988). Love styles and attachment styles compared: Their relation to each other and to various relationship characteristics. *Journal of Social and Personal Relationships, 5,* 429–471.

Lewin, K. (1943). Forces behind food habits and methods of change. *Bulletin of the National Research Council, 8,* 35–65.

Lewin, K. (1947). Group decision and social change. In T. M. Newcomb & E. L. Hartley (Eds.), *Readings in social psychology* (pp. 330–344). New York: Holt.

Lewin, K. (1951). Problems of research in social psychology. In D. Cartwright (Ed.), *Field theory in social science* (pp. 155–169). New York: Harper & Row.

Lewis, M., & Brooks, J. (1978). Self-knowledge in emotional development. In M. Lewis & L. Rosenblum (Eds.), *The development of affect* (pp. 205–226). New York: Plenum.

Lewis, M., & Weinraub, M. (1979). Origins of early sex-role development. *Sex Roles, 5,* 135–153.

Leyens, J.-P. (1990). Intuitive personality testing: A social approach. In J. Extra, A. van Knippenberg, J. van der Pligt, & M. Poppe (Eds.), *Fundamentele sociale psychologie* [Basic social psychology] (Vol. 4, pp. 3–20). Tilburg, The Netherlands: Tilburg University Press.

Leyens, J.-P. (Ed.). (1991). Prolegomena for the concept of implicit theories of personality. *European Bulletin of Cognitive Psychology, 11,* 131–136.

Leyens, J.-P., & Dardenne, B. (1994). La perception et connaissance d'autrui [People perception]. In M. Richelle, J. Requin, & M. Robert (Eds.), *Traité de psychologie*

expérimentale [Handbook of experimental psychology] (Vol. 2, pp. 81–132). Paris: Presses Universitaires de France.

Leyens, J.-P., Camino, L., Parke, R. D., & Berkowitz, L. (1975). Effects of movie violence on aggression in a field setting as a function of group dynamics and cohesiveness. *Journal of Personality and Social Psychology, 32,* 346–360.

Liberman, A., & Chaiken, S. (1996). The direct effect of personal relevance on attitudes. *Personality and Social Psychology Bulletin, 22,* 269–279.

Liden, R. C., & Mitchell, T. R. (1988). Ingratiatory behaviors in organizational settings. *Academy of Management Review, 13,* 572–587.

Liebert, R. M., & Sprafkin, J. (1988). *The early window* (3rd ed.). New York: Pergamon Press.

Liebowitz, M. R. (1983). *The chemistry of love.* Boston: Little, Brown.

Linder, D. E., Cooper, J., & Jones, E. E. (1967). Decision freedom as a determinant of the role of incentive magnitude in attitude change. *Journal of Personality and Social Psychology, 6,* 245–254.

Linville, P. W. (1982). The complexity-extremity effect and age-based stereotyping. *Journal of Personality and Social Psychology, 42,* 193–211.

Lipkus, I. M. (1991). The construction and preliminary validation of a Global Belief in a Just World Scale and the exploratory analysis of the Multidimensional Belief in a Just World Scale. *Personality and Individual Differences, 12,* 1171–1178.

Lipkus, I. M., & Bissonnette, V. L. (1996). Relationships among belief in a just world, willingness to accommodate, and marital well-being. *Personality and Social Psychology Bulletin, 22,* 1043–1056.

Lipkus, I. M., Dalbert, C., & Siegler, I. C. (1996). The importance of distinguishing the belief in a just world for self versus for others: Implications for psychological well-being. *Personality and Social Psychology Bulletin, 22,* 666–677.

Lockhart, L. L., White, B. A., Causby, V., & Isaac, A. (1994). Letting out the secret: Violence in lesbian relationships. *Journal of Interpersonal Violence, 9,* 469–492.

Locksley, A., Borgida, E., Brekke, N., & Hepburn, C. (1980). Sex stereotypes and social judgment. *Journal of Personality and Social Psychology, 39,* 821–831.

Loden, M. (1985). *Feminine leadership or how to succeed in business without being one of the boys.* New York: Times Books.

Loftus, E. F., & Coan, D. (1995). The construction of childhood memories. In D. Peters (Ed.), *The child witness in context: Cognitive, social and legal perspectives.* New York: Kluwer.

Lombardo, M. M., Ruderman, M. N., & McCauley, C. D. (1988). Explanations of success and derailment in upper-level management positions. *Journal of Business and Psychology, 2,* 199–216.

Lonsway, K. A. (1996). Preventing acquaintance rape through education. *Psychology of Women Quarterly, 20,* 229–265.

Lonsway, K. A., & Fitzgerald, L. F. (1994). Rape myths: In review. *Psychology of Women Quarterly, 18,* 133–164.

Lonsway, K. A., Klaw, E. L., Berg, D. R., Waldo, C. R., Kothari, C., Mazurek, C. J., & Hegeman, K. E. (1998). Beyond "no means no": Outcomes of an intensive program to train peer facilitators for campus acquaintance rape education. *Journal of Interpersonal Violence, 13,* 73–92.

Loosen, P. T. (1994). Effects on behavior of modulation of gonadal function in men with gonadotropin-releasing hormone antagonists. *American Journal of Psychiatry, 151,* 271–273.

Lord, C. G., & Saenz, D. S. (1985). Memory deficits and memory surfeits: Differential cognitive consequences of tokenism for tokens and observers. *Journal of Personality and Social Psychology, 49,* 918–926.

Lord, C. G., Desforges, D. M., Ramsey, S. L., Trezza, G. R., & Lepper, M. R. (1991). Typicality effects in attitude-behavior consistency: Effects of category discrimination and category knowledge. *Journal of Experimental Social Psychology, 27,* 550–575.

Lore, R., & Schultz, L. A. (1993). Control of human aggression: A comparative perspective. *American Psychologist, 48,* 16–25.

Lorenz, K. (1966). *On aggression.* New York: Harcourt, Brace & World.

Lorenzi-Cioldi, F. (1993). They all look alike, but so do we . . . sometimes: Perceptions of in-group and out-group homogeneity as a function of sex and context. *British Journal of Social Psychology, 32,* 111–124.

Lottes, I. L., & Kuriloff, P. J. (1994). The impact of college experience on political and social attitudes. *Sex Roles, 31,* 31–54.

Lowe, K. B., Kroeck, K. G., & Sivasubramaniam, N. (1996). Effectiveness correlates of transformational and transactional leadership: A meta-analytic review. *Leadership Quarterly, 7,* 385–391.

Lumsdaine, A., & Janis, I. (1953). Resistance to counterpropaganda produced by a one-sided versus a two-sided propaganda presentation. *Public Opinion Quarterly, 17,* 311–318.

Lund, F. H. (1925). The psychology of belief: IV. The law of primacy in persuasion. *Journal of Abnormal and Social Psychology, 20,* 183–191.

Lydon, J. E., Jamieson, D. W., & Holmes, J. G. (1997). The meaning of social interactions in the transition from acquaintanceship to friendship. *Journal of Personality and Social Psychology, 73,* 536–548.

Lynch, J. W., Kaplan, G. A., & Shema, S. J. (1997). Cumulative impact of sustained economic hardship on physical, cognitive, psychological, and social functioning. *New England Journal of Medicine, 337,* 1889–1895.

Ma, V., & Schoeneman, T. J. (1997). Individualism versus collectivism: A comparison of Kenyan and American self-concepts. *Basic and Applied Social Psychology, 19,* 261–273.

Maadux, J. E., & Rogers, R. W. (1983). Protection motivation and self-efficacy: A revised theory of fear appeals and attitude change. *Journal of Experimental Social Psychology, 19,* 469–479.

Maass, A., Clark, R. D., III, & Haberkorn, G. (1982). The effects of differential ascribed category membership and norms on minority influence. *European Journal of Social Psychology, 12,* 89–104.

Maccoby, E. E. (1990). Gender and relationships: A developmental account. *American Psychologist, 45,* 513–520.

Mackie, D. M., Hamilton, D. L., Susskind, J., & Rosselli, F. (1996). Social psychological foundations of stereotype formation. In C. N. Macrae, C. Stangor, & M. Hewstone (Eds.). *Stereotypes and stereotyping* (pp. 41–78). New York: Guilford.

Macrae, C. N., Bodenhausen, G. V., & Milne, A. B. (in press). Saying no to unwanted thoughts: Self-focus and the regulation of mental life. *Journal of Personality and Social Psychology.*

Macrae, C. N., Bodenhausen, G. V., Milne, A. B., & Jetten, J. (1994a). Out of mind but back in sight: Stereotypes on the rebound. *Journal of Personality and Social Psychology, 67,* 808–817.

Macrae, C. N., Hewstone, M., & Griffiths, R. J. (1993). Processing load and memory for stereotype-based information. *European Journal of Social Psychology, 23,* 77–87.

Macrae, C. N., Milne, A. B., & Bodenhausen, G. V. (1994b). Stereotypes as energy-saving devices: A peek inside the cognitive toolbox. *Journal of Personality and Social Psychology, 66,* 37–47.

Maddux, J. E., & DuCharme, K. A. (1997). Behavioral intentions in theories of health behavior. In D. S. Gochman (Ed.), *Handbook of health behavior research I: Personal and social determinants* (pp. 133–151). New York: Plenum.

Major, B., Spencer, S., Schmader, T., Wolfe, C., & Crocker, J. (1998). Coping with negative stereotypes about intellectual performance: The role of psychological disengagement. *Personality and Social Psychology Bulletin, 24,* 34–50.

Makepeace, J. (1989). Dating, living together, and courtship violence. In M. A. Pirog-Good & J. E. Stets (Eds.), *Violence in dating relationships: Emerging social issues.* (pp. 94–107). New York: Praeger.

Malamuth, N. M. (1981). Rape fantasies as a function of exposure to violent sexual stimuli. *Archives of Sexual Behavior, 10,* 33–47.

Malamuth, N. M., & Check, J. V. P. (1981). The effects of mass media exposure on acceptance of violence against women: A field experiment. *Journal of Research in Personality, 15,* 436–446.

Malamuth, N. M., & Thornhill, N. W. (1994). Hostile masculinity, sexual aggression, and gender-based domineeringness in conversations. *Aggressive Behavior, 20,* 185–193.

Mallick, S. K., & McCandless, B. R. (1966). A study of catharsis of aggression. *Journal of Personality and Social Psychology, 4,* 591–596.

Mandel, D. R., & Lehman, D. R. (1996). Counterfactual thinking and ascriptions of cause and preventability. *Journal of Personality and Social Psychology, 71,* 450–463.

Mann, L. (1981). The baiting crowd in episodes of threatened suicide. *Journal of Personality and Social Psychology, 41,* 703–709.

Mantell, D. M. (1971). The potential for violence in Germany. *Journal of Social Issues, 27,* 101–112.

Marangoni, C., & Ickes, W. (1989). Loneliness: A theoretical review with implications for measurement. *Journal of Social and Personal Relationships, 6,* 93–128.

Marazziti, D., Rotondo, A., Presta, S., Pancioloi-Guadagnucci, M. L., Palego, L., & Conti, L. (1993). Role of serotonin in human aggressive behavior. *Aggressive Behavior, 19,* 347–353.

Marcus, D. K., Wilson, J. R., & Miller, R. S. (1996). Are perceptions of emotion in the eye of the beholder? A social relations analysis of judgments of embarrassment. *Personality and Social Psychology Bulletin, 22,* 1220–1228.

Margalit, M. (1995). Effects of social skills training for students with an intellectual disability. *International Journal of Disability, Development and Education, 42,* 75–85.

Mark, M. M., & Mellor, S. (1991). Effect of self-relevance of an event on hindsight bias: The foreseeability of a layoff. *Journal of Applied Psychology, 76,* 569–577.

Markus, H. (1977). Self-schemata and processing information about the self. *Journal of Personality and Social Psychology, 35,* 63–78.

Markus, H., & Zajonc, R. B. (1985). The cognitive perspective in social psychology. In G. Lindzey & E. Aronson (Eds.), *Handbook of social psychology* (Vol. 1, pp. 137–230). Hillsdale, NJ: Erlbaum.

Markus, H., Smith, J., & Moreland, R. L. (1985). Role of the self-concept in the perception of others. *Journal of Personality and Social Psychology, 49,* 1494–1512.

Markus, H. R., & Kitayama, S. (1991). Culture and the self: Implications for cognition, emotion, and motivation. *Psychological Review, 98,* 224–253.

Markus, H. R., & Kitayama, S. (1994). A collective fear of the collective: Implications for selves and theories of selves. *Personality and Social Psychology Bulletin, 20,* 568–579.

Markus, H. R., Kitayama, S., & Heiman, R. J. (1996). Culture and "basic" psychological principles. In E. T. Higgins & A. W. Kruglanski (Eds.), *Social psychology: Handbook of basic principles* (pp. 857–913). New York: Guilford Press.

Marlowe, C. M., Schneider, S. L., & Nelson, C. E. (1996). Gender and attractiveness biases in hiring decisions: Are more experienced managers less biased? *Journal of Applied Psychology, 81*, 11–21.

Marrow, A. J. (1969). *The practical theorist: The life and work of Kurt Lewin.* New York: Basic Books.

Martin, D. N. (1989). *Romancing the brand: The power of advertising and how to use it.* New York: American Management Association.

Martin, K. A. (1993). Gender and sexuality: Medical opinion on homosexuality, 1900–1950. *Gender and Society, 7*, 246–260.

Martin, R. (1988). Ingroup and outgroup minorities: Differential impact upon public and private responses. *European Journal of Social Psychology, 18*, 39–52.

Martinek, T. J. (1981). Physical attractiveness: Effects on teacher expectations and dyadic interactions in elementary school children. *Journal of Sport Psychology, 3*, 196–205.

Martz, D. M., Handley, K. B., & Eisler, R. M. (1995). The relationship between feminine gender role stress, body image, and eating disorders. *Psychology of Women Quarterly, 19*, 493–508.

Marwell, G., Aiken, M. T., & Demerath, N. J., III. (1987). The persistence of political attitudes among 1960s civil rights activists. *Public Opinion Quarterly, 51*, 383–399.

Maslach, C., Santee, R. T., & Wade, C. (1987). Individuation, gender role, and dissent: Personality mediators of situational forces. *Journal of Personality and Social Psychology, 53*, 1088–1093.

Maslow, A. H. (1970). *Motivation and personality.* New York: Harper & Row.

Mathes, E. W., Adams, H. E., & Davies, R. M. (1985). Jealousy: Loss of relationship rewards, loss of self-esteem, depression, anxiety, and anger. *Journal of Personality and Social Psychology, 48*, 1552–1561.

Matlin, M., & Stang, D. (1978). *The pollyanna principle: Selectivity in language, memory, and thought.* Cambridge, MA: Schenkman.

Matsumoto, D. (1992). American-Japanese cultural differences in the recognition of universal facial expressions. *Journal of Cross-Cultural Psychology, 23*, 72–84.

Mazur, A., & Lamb, T. A. (1980). Testosterone, status, and mood in human males. *Hormones and Behavior, 14*, 236–246.

McAdam, G. (1989). The biographical consequences of activism. *American Sociological Review, 54*, 744–760.

McAdams, D. P. (1988). Personal needs and personal relationships. In S. Duck (Ed.), *Handbook of personal relationships: Theory, research, and interventions* (pp. 7–22). New York: Wiley.

McAndrew, F. T. (1993). *Environmental psychology.* Pacific Grove, CA: Brooks/Cole.

McArthur (Zebrowitz), L. Z. (1982). Judging a book by its cover: A cognitive analysis of the relationship between physical appearance and stereotyping. In A. H. Hastorf & A. M. Isen (Eds.), *Cognitive social psychology* (pp. 149–211). New York: Elsevier/North Holland.

McArthur (Zebrowitz), L. Z., & Apatow, K. (1983/1984). Impressions of baby-faced adults. *Social Cognition, 2*, 315–342.

McCaul, K. D., Gladue, B. A., & Joppa, M. (1992). Winning, losing, mood, and testosterone. *Hormones and Behavior, 26*, 486–504.

McCauley, C. (1989). The nature of social influence in groupthink: Compliance and internalization. *Journal of Personality and Social Psychology, 57*, 250–260.

McCauley, C. R., & Segal, M. E. (1987). Social psychology of terrorist groups. In C. Hendrick (Ed.), *Group processes and intergroup relations: Review of personality and social psychology* (Vol. 9, pp. 231–256). Newbury Park, CA: Sage.

McClearn, G. E. (1993). Behavioral genetics: The last century and the next. In R. Plomin & G. E. McClearn (Eds.), *Nature, nurture, and psychology.* Washington, DC: American Psychological Association.

McClelland, D. C., Constantian, C., Pilon, D., & Stone, C. (1982). Effects of child-rearing practices on adult maturity. In D. C. McClelland (Ed.), *The development of social maturity.* New York: Irvington.

McClintock, C. G. (1978). Social values: Their definition, measurement, and development. *Journal of Research Development in Education, 12*, 121–137.

McConahay, J. B. (1986). Modern racism, ambivalence, and the modern racism scale. In S. L. Gaertner & J. Dovidio (Eds.), *Prejudice, discrimination, and racism: Theory and research.* New York: Academic Press.

McConville, M. (1993). *Corroboration and confession: The impact of a ride requiring that no conviction can be sustained on the basis of confession evidence alone.* London: HMSO. (Royal Commission on Criminal Justice Research Study No. 13).

McCord, J. (1994). Aggression in two generations. In L. R. Huesmann (Ed.), *Aggressive behavior: Current perspectives* (pp. 241–251). New York: Plenum.

McCroskey, J. C. (1997). Willingness to communicate, communication apprehension, and self-perceived communication competence: Conceptualizations and perspectives. In J. A. Daly, J. C. McCroskey, J. Ayres, T. Hopf, & D. M. Ayres (Eds.), *Avoiding communication: Shyness, reticence, and communication apprehension* (2nd ed., pp. 75–108). Creskill, NJ: Hampton Press.

McCroskey, J. C., Richmond, V. P., & Daly, J. A. (1975). The development of a measure of perceived homophily in interpersonal communication. *Human Communication Research, 1*, 325–332.

McDougall, W. (1908). *An introduction to social psychology.* London: Methuen.

McFarland, S. G. (1989). Religious orientation and the targets of discrimination. *Journal for the Scientific Study of Religion, 28*, 324–336.

McFarland, S. G., Ageyev, V. S., & Djintcharadze, N. (1996). Russian authoritarianism two years after communism. *Personality and Social Psychology Bulletin, 22*, 210–217.

McGarty, C., & Haslam, S. A. (1997). Introduction and a short history of social psychology. In C. McGarty & S. A. Haslam (Eds.), *The message of social psychology: Perspectives on mind in society* (pp. 1–19). Cambridge, MA: Blackwell.

McGarty, C., Turner, J. C., Hogg, M. A., David, B., & Wetherell, M. S. (1992). Group polarization as conformity to the prototypical group member. *British Journal of Social Psychology, 31*, 1–19.

McGrath, J. E. (1984). *Groups: Interaction and performance.* Englewood Cliffs, NJ: Prentice-Hall.

McGuire, W. J. (1964). Inducing resistance to persuasion. In L. Berkowitz (Ed.), *Advances in experimental social psychology* (Vol. 1). New York: Academic Press.

McGuire, W. J. (1968). Personality and susceptibility to social influence. In E. F. Borgatta & W. W. Lambert (Eds.), *Handbook of personality theory and research.* Chicago: Rand McNally.

McGuire, W. J. (1995). The communication and attitude change program at Yale in the 1950s. In E. E. Dennis & Wartella (Eds.), *American communication research: The remembered history.* Hillsdale, NJ: Erlbaum.

McGuire, W. J., & Papageorgis, D. (1961). The relative efficacy of various types of prior belief-defense in producing immunity against persuasion. *Journal of Abnormal and Social Psychology, 62*, 327–337.

McGuire, W. J., McGuire, C. V., Child, P., & Fujioka, T. (1978). Salience of ethnicity in the spontaneous self-concept as a function of one's ethnic distinctiveness in the social environment. *Journal of Personality and Social Psychology, 36*, 511–520.

McKelvie, S. J. (1993). Stereotyping in perception of attractiveness, age, and gender in schematic faces. *Social Behavior and Personality, 21*, 121–128.

McKinney, K., & Maroules, N. (1991). Sexual harassment. In E. Grauerholz & M. A. Koralewski (Eds.), *Sexual coercion* (pp. 29–44). Lexington, MA: Lexington Books.

McMillen, D. L., Sander, D. V., & Solomon, G. S. (1977). Self-esteem, attentiveness, and helping behavior. *Personality and Social Psychology Bulletin, 3*, 257–261.

McMullin, E. (1983). Values in science. In P. D. Asquith & T. Nickles (Eds.), *Proceedings of* the 1982 Philosophy of Science Association (Vol. 2, pp. 3–23). East Lansing, MI: Philosophy of Science Association.

McWhirter, D. P., & Mattison, A. M. (1984). *The male couple: How relationships develop.* Englewood Cliffs, NJ: Prentice-Hall.

Mead, G. H. (1934). *Mind, self, and society.* Chicago: University of Chicago Press.

Mead, R. (1980). The national anthem. In S. Sadie (Ed.), *Groves dictionary of music and musicians.* New York: Macmillan, 46–75.

Mealey, L., Bridgstock, R., & Townsend, G. C. (1999). Symmetry and perceived facial attractiveness: A monozygotic co-twin comparison. *Journal of Personality and Social Psychology, 76,* 151–158.

Meeker, B. F., & Weitzel-O'Neill, P. A. (1977). Sex roles and interpersonal behavior in task-oriented groups. *American Sociological Review, 42,* 91–105.

Meeus, W. H. J., & Raaijmakers, Q. A. W. (1986). Administrative obedience: Carrying out orders to use psychological administrative violence. *European Journal of Social Psychology, 16,* 311–324.

Meeus, W. H. J., & Raaijmakers, Q. A. W. (1987). Administrative obedience as a social phenomenon. In W. Doise & S. Moscovici (Eds.), *Current issues in European social psychology, Vol. 2* (pp. 183–230). Cambridge, England: Cambridge University Press.

Meeus, W. H. J., & Raaijmakers, Q. A. W. (1995). Obedience in modern society: The Utrecht studies. *Journal of Social Issues, 51,* 155–175.

Mehlman, R. C., & Snyder, C. R. (1985). Excuse theory: A test of the self-protective role of attributions. *Journal of Personality and Social Psychology, 49,* 994–1001.

Mehrabian, A. (1972). *Nonverbal communication.* Chicago: Aldine-Atherton.

Meichenbaum, D. H., Bowers, K. S., & Ross, R. R. (1969). A behavioral analysis of teacher expectancy effects. *Journal of Personality and Social Psychology, 13,* 306–316.

Melton, G. B. (1989). Public and private prejudice: Psychology and law on gay rights. *American Psychologist, 44,* 384–399.

Mendenhall, M. (1993, April). Lesbian student faces Marquette's homophobia. *Harbinger: The alternative voice for the Marquette community,* p. 11.

Merikle, P. M., & Skanes, H. E. (1992). Subliminal self-help audiotapes: A search for placebo effects. *Journal of Applied Psychology, 77,* 772–776.

Merton, R. (1948). The self-fulfilling prophecy. *Antioch Review, 8,* 193–210.

Messick, D. M., & Liebrand, W. B. G. (1997). Levels of analysis and the explanation of the costs and benefits of cooperation. *Personality and Social Psychology Review, 1,* 129–139.

Meyer, J. P., & Koebl, S. L. M. (1982). Dimensionality of students' causal attributions for test performance. *Personality and Social Psychology Bulletin, 8,* 31–36.

Meyers, S. A., & Berscheid, E. (1997). The language of love: The difference a preposition makes. *Personality and Social Psychology Bulletin, 23,* 347–362.

Michaels, J. W., Blommel, J. M., Brocato, R. M., Linkous, R. A., & Rowe, J. S. (1982). Social facilitation and inhibition in a natural setting. *Replications in Social Psychology, 2,* 21–24.

Michaelson, L. K., Watson, W. E., & Black, R. H. (1989). A realistic test of individual versus group consensus decision making. *Journal of Applied Psychology, 74,* 834–839.

Midlarsky, E., Bryan, J. H., & Brickman, P. (1973). Aversive approval: Interactive effects of modeling and reinforcement on altruistic behavior. *Child Development, 44,* 321–328.

Mikulincer, M. (1998). Adult attachment style and individual differences in functional versus dysfunctional experiences of anger. *Journal of Personality and Social Psychology, 74,* 513–524.

Milardo, R. M., & Allan, G., (1997). Social networks and marital relationships. In S. Duck (Ed.). *Handbook of personal relationships: Theory, research and interventions* (2nd ed., pp. 506–522). Chichester, England: John Wiley & Sons.

Miles, D. R., & Carey, G. (1997). Genetic and environmental architecture of human aggression. *Journal of Personality and Social Psychology, 72,* 207–217.

Milgram, S. (1963). Behavioral study of obedience. *Journal of Abnormal and Social Psychology, 67,* 371–378.

Milgram, S. (1965). Some conditions of obedience and disobedience to authority. *Human Relations, 18,* 57–76.

Milgram, S. (1970). The experience of living in cities. *Science, 167,* 1461–1468.

Milgram, S. (1974). *Obedience to authority: An experimental view.* New York: Harper & Row.

Milgram, S. (1992). *The individual in a social world: Essays and experiments.* Reading, MA: Addison-Wesley.

Millar, M. G., & Millar, K. U. (1996). The effects of direct and indirect experience on affective and cognitive responses and the attitude-behavior relation. *Journal of Experimental Social Psychology, 32,* 561–579.

Miller, A. G., Collins, B. E., & Brief, D. E. (1995). Perspectives on obedience to authority: The legacy of the Milgram experiments. *Journal of Social Issues, 51,* 1–19.

Miller, A. G., Gillen, B., Schenker, C., & Radlove, S. (1973). Perception of obedience to authority. *Proceedings of the 81st Annual Convention of the American Psychological Association, 8,* 127–128.

Miller, C. E. (1989). The social psychological effects of group decision rules. In P. B. Paulus (Ed.), *Psychology of group influence* (2nd ed., pp. 327–355). Hillsdale, NJ: Erlbaum.

Miller, C. T. (1984). Self-schemas, gender, and social comparison: A clarification of the related attributes hypothesis. *Journal of Personality and Social Psychology, 46,* 1222–1229.

Miller, C. T., & Felicio, D. M. (1990). Person-positivity bias: Are individuals liked better than groups? *Journal of Experimental Social Psychology, 26,* 408–420.

Miller, D. T., & Prentice, D. A. (1994). The self and the collective. *Personality and Social Psychology Bulletin, 20,* 451–453.

Miller, D. T., & Prentice, D. A. (1996). The construction of norms and standards. In E. T. Higgins & A. W. Kruglanski (Eds.), *Social psychology: Handbook of basic principles* (pp. 799–829). New York: Guilford Press.

Miller, D. T., & Turnbull, W. (1990). The counterfactual fallacy: Confusing what might have been with what ought to have been. *Social Justice Research, 4,* 1–19.

Miller, H. G., Turner, C. F., & Moses, L. E. (Eds.). (1990a). *AIDS: The second decade.* Washington, DC: National Academy.

Miller, J. G. (1984). Culture and the development of everyday social explanation. *Journal of Personality and Social Psychology, 46,* 961–978.

Miller, J. G. (1988). Bridging the content-structure dichotomy: Culture and the self. In M. H. Bond (Ed.), *The cross-cultural challenge to social psychology* (pp. 266–281). Beverly Hills, CA: Sage.

Miller, J. G. (1994). Cultural diversity in the morality of caring: Individually oriented versus duty-based interpersonal moral codes. *Cross-Cultural Research, 28,* 3–39.

Miller, J. G., Bersoff, D. M., & Harwood, R. L. (1990). Perceptions of social responsibilities in India and in the United States: Moral imperatives or personal decisions? *Journal of Personality and Social Psychology, 58,* 33–47.

Miller, L. C., Berg, J. H., & Archer, R. L. (1983). Openers: Individuals who elicit intimate self-disclosure. *Journal of Personality and Social Psychology, 44,* 1234–1244.

Miller, L. C., Cooke, L. L., Tsang, J., & Morgan, F. (1992). Should I brag? Nature and impact of positive and boastful disclosures for women and men. *Human Communication Research, 18,* 364–399.

Miller, M. L., & Thayer, J. F. (1989). On the existence of discrete classes in personality: Is self-monitoring the current joint to carve? *Journal of Personality and Social Psychology, 57,* 143–155.

Miller, N., & Campbell, D. T. (1959). Recency and primacy in persuasion as a function of the timing of speeches and measurements. *Journal of Abnormal and Social Psychology, 59,* 1–9.

Miller, N., & Davidson-Podgorney, G. (1987). Theoretical models of intergroup relations and the use of cooperative teams as an intervention for desegregated settings. In C.

Hendrick (Ed.), *Group Processes and Intergroup Relations: Review of Personality and Social Psychology* (Vol. 9, pp. 41–67). Beverly Hills, CA: Sage.

Miller, N., Maruyama, G., Beaber, R. J., & Valone, K. (1976). Speed of speech and persuasion. *Journal of Personality and Social Psychology, 34,* 615–624.

Miller, N. E. (1941). The frustration-aggression hypothesis. *Psychological Review, 48,* 337–342.

Miller, R. S. (1995). Embarrassment and social behavior. In J. P. Tangney & K. W. Fischer (Eds.), *Self-conscious emotions: The psychology of shame, guilt, embarrassment, and pride* (pp. 322–339). New York: Guilford Press.

Miller, R. S. (1997). We always hurt the ones we love: Aversive interactions in close relationships. In R. M. Kowalski (Ed.), *Aversive interpersonal behaviors* (pp. 11–29). New York: Plenum Press.

Miller, R. S., & Schlenker, B. R. (1985). Egotism in group members: Public and private attributions of responsibility for group performance. *Social Psychology Quarterly, 48,* 85–89.

Miller, S. A. (1995). Parents' attributions for their children's behavior. *Child Development, 66,* 1557–1584.

Milliman, R. E. (1986). The influence of background music on the behavior of restaurant patrons. *Journal of Consumer Research, 13,* 286–289.

Mills, J., & Clark, M. S. (1994). Communal and exchange relationships: Controversies and research. In R. Erber & R. Gilmour (Eds.), *Theoretical frameworks for personal relationships* (pp. 29–42). Hillsdale, NJ: Erlbaum.

Mischel, W. (1996). From good intentions to willpower. In P. Gollwitzer & J. Bargh (Eds.), *The psychology of action* (pp. 197–218). New York: Guilford Press.

Mischel, W., Cantor, N., & Feldman, S. (1996). Principles of self-regulation: The nature of willpower and self-control. In E. T. Higgins & A. W. Kruglanski (Eds.), *Social psychology: Handbook of basic principles* (pp. 329–360). New York: Guilford Press.

Mita, T. H., Dermer, M., & Knight, J. (1977). Reversed facial images and the mere-exposure hypothesis. *Journal of Personality and Social Psychology, 35,* 597–601.

Moghaddam, F. M., Taylor, D., & Wright, S. C. (1993). *Social psychology in cross-cultural perspective.* New York: W. H. Freeman.

Monahan, B. (1983). *A dictionary of Russian gesture.* Ann Arbor, MI: Hermitage.

Money, J., & Ehrhardt, A. A. (1972). *Man and woman, boy and girl.* Baltimore: Johns Hopkins University Press.

Monteith, M. J. (1993). Self-regulation of prejudiced responses: Implications for progress in prejudice-reduction efforts. *Journal of Personality and Social Psychology, 65,* 469–485.

Monteith, M. J. (1996a). Affective reactions to prejudice-related discrepant responses: The impact of standard salience. *Personality and Social Psychology Bulletin, 22,* 48–59.

Monteith, M. J. (1996b). Contemporary forms of prejudice-related conflict: In search of a nutshell. *Personality and Social Psychology Bulletin, 22,* 461–473.

Monteith, M. J., Deneen, N. E., & Tooman, G. D. (1996). The effect of social norm activation on the expression of opinions concerning gay men and blacks. *Basic and Applied Social Psychology, 18,* 267–288.

Monteith, M. J., Sherman, J. W., & Devine, P. G. (1998). Suppression as a stereotype control strategy. *Personality and Social Psychology Review, 2,* 63–82.

Montepare, J. M., & Zebrowitz-McArthur, L. (1988). Impressions of people created by age-related qualities of their gaits. *Journal of Personality and Social Psychology, 55,* 547–556.

Moore, B. S., & Eisenberg, N. (1984). The development of altruism. *Annals of Child Development, 1,* 107–174.

Moore, M. A., Britt, T. W., & Leary, M. R. (1997). Integrating social and counseling psychological perspectives on the self. *The Counseling Psychologist, 25,* 220–239.

Moore, T. E. (1992). Subliminal perception: Facts and fallacies. *Skeptical Inquirer, 16,* 273–281.

Moorhead, G., & Montanari, J. R. (1986). An empirical investigation of the groupthink phenomenon. *Human Relations, 39,* 399–410.

Moorhead, G., Ference, R., & Neck, C. P. (1991). Group decision fiascoes continue: Space shuttle Challenger and a revised groupthink framework. *Human Relations, 44,* 539–550.

Moreland, R. L., & Levine, J. M. (1982). Socialization in small groups: Temporal changes in individual group relations. In L. Berkowitz (Ed.), *Advances in experimental social psychology* (Vol. 15). New York: Academic Press.

Moreland, R. L., & Levine, J. M. (1988). Group dynamics over time: Development and socialization in small groups. In J. E. McGrath (Ed.), *The social psychology of time* (pp. 151–181). Newbury Park, CA: Sage.

Moreland, R. L., Levine, J. M., & Cini, M. (1993). Group socialization: The role of commitment. In M. A. Hogg & D. Abrams (Eds.), *Group motivation: Social psychological perspectives* (pp. 105–129). New York: Harvester Wheatsheaf.

Moreland, R. L., Levine, J. M., & Wingert, M. L. (1996). Creating the ideal group: Composition effects at work. In E. Witte & J. Davis (Eds.), *Understanding group behavior: (Vol. 2): Small group processes and interpersonal relations* (pp. 11–35). Hillsdale, NJ: Erlbaum.

Morf, C. C., & Rhodewalt, R. (1993). Narcissism and self-evaluation maintenance: Explorations in object relations. *Personality and Social Psychology Bulletin, 19,* 668–676.

Morling, B., & Epstein, S. (1997). Compromises produced by the dialectic between self-verification and self-enhancement. *Journal of Personality and Social Psychology, 73,* 1268–1283.

Morris, M. W., & Larrick, R. P. (1995). When one cause casts doubt on another: A normative analysis of discounting in causal attribution. *Psychological Review, 102,* 331–355.

Morris, M. W., & Peng, K. (1994). Culture and cause: American and Chinese attributions for social and physical events. *Journal of Personality and Social Psychology 67,* 949–971.

Morris, W. N., Miller, R. S., & Spangenberg, S. (1977). The effects of dissenter position and task difficulty on conformity and response to conflict. *Journal of Personality, 45,* 251–266.

Morrison, T., Conaway, W. A., & Borden, G. A. (1994). *Kiss, bow, or shake hands: How to do business in sixty countries.* Holbrook, MA: Adams Media Corporation.

Morrison, T. L., Urquiza, A. J., & Goodlin-Jones, B. L. (1997). Attachment, perceptions of interaction, and relationship adjustment. *Journal of Social and Personal Relationships, 14,* 627–642.

Moscovici, S. (1980). Toward a theory of conversion behavior. In L. Berkowitz (Ed.), *Advances in experimental social psychology* (Vol. 13, pp. 2209–2239). New York: Academic Press.

Moscovici, S. (1989). Preconditions for explanation in social psychology. *European Journal of Social Psychology, 19,* 407–430.

Moscovici, S., & Faucheux, C. (1972). Social influence, conformity bias and the study of active minorities. In L. Berkowitz (Ed.), *Advances in experimental social psychology* (Vol. 6, pp. 149–202). New York: Academic Press.

Moscovici, S., & Mugny, G. (1983). Minority influence. In P. B. Paulus (Ed.), *Basic group processes* (pp. 41–64). New York: Springer-Verlag.

Moscovici, S., & Nemeth, C. (1974). Social influence II: Minority influence. In C. Nemeth (Ed.), *Social psychology: Classic and contemporary integrations* (pp. 217–249). Chicago: Rand McNally.

Moscovici, S., & Zavalloni, M. (1969). The group as a polarizer of attitudes. *Journal of Personality and Social Psychology, 12,* 125–135.

Moscovici, S., Lage, E., & Naffrechoux, M. (1969). Influences of a consistent minority on the responses of a majority in a color perception task. *Sociometry, 32,* 365–380.

Moss, M. K., & Page, R. A. (1972). Reinforcement and helping behavior. *Journal of Applied Social Psychology, 2,* 360–371.

Moston, S., Stephenson, G. M., & Williamson, T. M. (1992). The effects of case characteristics on suspect behavior during police questioning. *British Journal of Criminology, 1,* 23–40.

Muehlenhard, C. L., & Hollabaugh, L. C. (1988). Do women sometimes say no when they mean yes? The prevalence and correlates of women's token resistance to sex. *Journal of Personality and Social Psychology, 54,* 872–879.

Mugny, G., & Perez, J. A. (1991). *The social psychology of minority influence.* Cambridge, England: Cambridge University Press.

Mulac, A., & Lundell, T. L. (1986). Linguistic contributors to the gender-linked language effect. *Journal of Language and Social Psychology, 5,* 81–101.

Mulilis, J-P., & Duval, T. S. (1997). The PrE model of coping and tornado preparedness: Moderating effects of responsibility. *Journal of Applied Social Psychology, 27,* 1750–1766.

Mullen, B. (1985). Strength and immediacy of sources: A meta-analytic evaluation of the forgotten elements of social impact theory. *Journal of Personality and Social Psychology, 48,* 1458–1466.

Mullen, B. (1986). Atrocity as a function of lynch mob composition: A self-attention perspective. *Personality and Social Psychology Bulletin, 12,* 187–197.

Mullen, B., & Copper, C. (1994). The relation between group cohesiveness and performance: An integration. *Psychological Bulletin, 115,* 210–227.

Mullen, B., & Hu, L. (1989). Perceptions of ingroup and outgroup variability: A meta-analytic integration. *Basic and Applied Social Psychology, 10,* 233–252.

Mullen, B., & Johnson, C. (1995). Cognitive representation in ethnophaulisms and illusory correlation in stereotyping. *Personality and Social Psychology Bulletin, 21,* 420–433.

Mullen, B., & Riordan, C. A. (1988). Self-serving attributions for performance in naturalistic settings: A meta-analytic review. *Journal of Applied Social Psychology, 18,* 3–22.

Mullen, B., & Suls, J. (1982). Know thyself: Stressful life changes and the ameliorative effect of private self-consciousness. *Journal of Experimental Social Psychology, 18,* 43–55.

Munsch, R. (1986). *Love you forever.* Ontario, Canada: Firefly Books, Limited.

Muraven, M., Tice, D. M., & Baumeister, R. F. (1998). Self-control as limited resource: Regulatory depletion patterns. *Journal of Personality and Social Psychology, 74,* 774–789.

Murphy, P. L., & Miller, C. T. (1997). Postdecisional dissonance and the commodified self-concept: A cross-cultural examination. *Personality and Social Psychology Bulletin, 23,* 50–62.

Murray, S. L., & Holmes, J. G. (1997). A leap of faith? Positive illusions in romantic relationships. *Personality and Social Psychology Bulletin, 23,* 586–604.

Murray, S. L., Haddock, G., & Zanna, M. P. (1996). On creating value-expressive attitudes: An experimental approach. In C. Seligman, J. Olson, & M. P. Zanna (Eds.), *The psychology of values: The Ontario symposium* (Vol. 8, pp. 107–133). Mahwah, NJ: Erlbaum.

Murray, S. L., Holmes, J. G., & Griffin, D. W. (1996a). The self-fulfilling nature of positive illusions in romantic relationships: Love is not blind, but prescient. *Journal of Personality and Social Psychology, 71,* 1155–1180.

Murray, S. L., Holmes, J. G., & Griffin, D. W. (1996b). The benefits of positive illusions: Idealization and the construction of satisfaction in close relationships. *Journal of Personality and Social Psychology, 70,* 79–98.

Murray, S. L., Holmes, J. G., MacDonald, G., & Ellsworth, P. C. (1998). Through the looking glass darkly? When self-doubts turn into relationship insecurities. *Journal of Personality and Social Psychology, 75,* 1459–1480.

Murstein, B. I. (1972). Physical attractiveness and marital choice. *Journal of Personality and Social Psychology, 22,* 8–12.

Murstein, B. I. (1974). *Love, sex, and marriage through the ages.* New York: Springer.

Mustonen, A. (1997). Nature of screen violence and its relation to program popularity. *Aggressive Behavior, 23,* 281–292.

Myers, D. G., & Bishop, G. D. (1970). Discussion effects on racial attitudes. *Science, 169,* 778–789.

Myers, D. G., & Kaplan, G. D. (1976). Group-induced polarization in simulated juries. *Personality and Social Psychology Bulletin, 2,* 63–66.

Myers, D. G., & Lamm, H. (1976). The group polarization phenomenon. *Psychological Bulletin, 83,* 602–627.

Nadler, A. (1987). Determinants of help seeking behaviour: The effects of helper's similarity, task centrality and recipient's self-esteem. *European Journal of Social Psychology, 17,* 57–67.

Nadler, A. (1991). Help-seeking behavior: Psychological costs and instrumental benefits. In M. S. Clark (Ed.), *Prosocial behavior: Review of personality and social psychology* (Vol. 12, pp. 290–311). Newbury Park, CA: Sage.

Nadler, A., & Dotan, I. (1992). Commitment and rival attractiveness: Their effects on male and female reactions to jealousy arousing situations. *Sex Roles, 26,* 293–310.

Nadler, A., & Fisher, J. D. (1986). The role of threat to self-esteem and perceived control in recipient reactions to help: Theory development and empirical validation. In L. Berkowitz (Ed.), *Advances in experimental social psychology* (Vol. 19, pp. 81–122). New York: Academic Press.

Nadler, A., Fisher, J. D., & Ben-Itzhak, S. (1983). With a little help from my friend: Effects of single or multiple act aid as a function of donor and task characteristics. *Journal of Personality and Social Psychology, 44,* 310–321.

Nadler, A., Mayseless, O., Peri, N., & Chemerinski, A. (1985). Effects of opportunity to reciprocate and self-esteem on help-seeking behavior. *Journal of Personality, 53,* 23–35.

Nadler, A., Shapiro, R., & Ben-Ttzhak, S. (1982). Good looks may help: Effects of helper's physical attractiveness and sex of helper on males' and females' help-seeking behavior. *Journal of Personality and Social Psychology, 42,* 90–99.

Nahemow, L., & Lawton, M. P. (1975). Similarity and propinquity in friendship formation. *Journal of Personality and Social Psychology, 32,* 205–213.

Nail, P. R. (1986). Toward an integration of some models and theories of social response. *Psychological Bulletin, 100,* 190–206.

Nakanishi, D.-T., & Nishida, T. Y. (Eds.). (1995). *The Asian American educational experience.* New York: Routledge.

Narby, D. J., Cutler, B. L., & Moran, G. (1993). A meta-analysis of the association between authoritarianism and jurors' perceptions of defendant culpability. *Journal of Applied Psychology, 78,* 34–42.

Nardi, P. M. (1992a). Seamless souls: An introduction to men's friendships. In P. M. Nardi (Ed.), *Men's friendships* (pp. 1–14). Newbury Park, CA: Sage.

Nardi, P. M. (1992b). Sex, friendship, and gender roles among gay men. In P. M. Nardi (Ed.), *Men's friendships* (pp. 173–185). Newbury Park, CA: Sage.

Nardi, P. M. (1992c). That's what friends are for: Friends as family in the gay and lesbian community. In K. Plummer (Ed.), *Modern homosexualities* (pp. 108–120). New York: Routledge.

Nardi, P. M., & Sherrod, D. (1994). Friendship in the lives of gay men and lesbians. *Journal of Social and Personal Relationships, 11,* 185–199.

Neal, A. M., & Wilson, M. L. (1989). The role of skin color and features in the Black community: Implications for Black women and therapy. *Clinical Psychology Review, 9,* 323–333.

Nelson, T. E., Acker, M., & Manis, M. (1996). Irrepressible stereotypes. *Journal of Experimental Social Psychology, 32,* 13–28.

Nemeth, C. (1977). Interactions between jurors as a function of majority vs. unanimity decision rules. *Journal of Applied Social Psychology, 7,* 38–56.

Nemeth, C. J. (1992). Minority dissent as a stimulant to group performance. In S. Worchel, W. Wood, & J. A. Simpson (Eds.), *Group processes and productivity.* Newbury Park, CA: Sage.

Nemeth, C. J., Swedlund, M., & Kanki, B. (1974). Patterning of the minority's responses and their influence on the majority. *European Journal of Social Psychology, 4,* 53–64.

Neuberg, S. L. (1989). The goal of forming accurate impressions during social interactions: Attenuating the impact of negative expectancies. *Journal of Personality and Social Psychology, 56,* 374–386.

Newcomb, M. D., Rabow, J., & Hernandez, A. C. R. (1992). A cross-national study of nuclear attitudes, normative support, and activist behavior: Addictive and interactive effects. *Journal of Applied Social Psychology, 22,* 780–800.

Newcomb, T. M. (1943). *Personality and social change: Attitude formation in a student community.* New York: Dryden.

Newcomb, T. M. (1951). Social psychological theory: Integrating individual and social approaches. In J. Rohrer & M. Sherif (Eds.), *Social psychology at the crossroads.* New York: Harper.

Newcomb, T. M. (1958). Attitude development as a function of reference groups. In E. E. Maccoby, T. M. Newcomb, & E. L. Hartley (Eds.), *Readings in social psychology* (3rd ed., pp. 265–275). New York: Holt, Rinehart & Winston.

Newcomb, T. M. (1961). *The acquaintance process.* New York: Holt, Rinehart & Winston.

Newcomb, T. M., Koenig, K. E., Flacks, R., & Warwick, D. P. (1967). *Persistence and change: Bennington College and its students after twenty-five years.* New York: Wiley.

Newcombe, N., & Arnkoff, D. B. (1979). Effect of speech style and sex of speaker on person perception. *Journal of Personality and Social Psychology, 37,* 1293–1303.

Nisbett, R. E. (1990). Evolutionary psychology, biology, and cultural evolution. *Motivation and Emotion, 14,* 255–264.

Nisbett, R. E., & Cohen, D. (1996). *Culture of honor: The psychology of violence in the south.* Boulder, CO: Westview Press.

Nisbett, R. E., Caputo, C., Legant, P., & Marecek, J. (1973). Behavior as seen by the actor and as seen by the observer. *Journal of Personality and Social Psychology, 27,* 154–164.

Nix, G., Watson, C., Pyszcznski, T., & Greenberg, J. (1995). Reducing depressive affect through external focus of attention. *Journal of Social and Clinical Psychology, 14,* 36–52.

Nolen-Hoeksma, S., Girgus, J. S., & Seligman, M. E. P. (1992). Predictors and consequences of childhood depressive symptoms: Five year longitudinal study. *Journal of Abnormal Psychology, 101,* 405–422.

Norman, P., & Conner, M. (1996). Predicting health-check attendance among prior attenders and nonattenders: The role of prior behavior in the theory of planned behavior. *Journal of Applied Social Psychology, 26,* 1010–1026.

Northouse, P. G. (1997). *Leadership: Theory and practice.* Thousand Oaks, CA: Sage.

Nunner-Winkler, G. (1984). Two moralities? A critical discussion of an ethic of care and responsibility versus an ethic of rights and justice. In W. M. Kurtines & J. L. Gewiirtz (Eds.), *Morality, moral behavior and moral development* (pp. 348–361). New York: Wiley.

O'Connor, S. C., & Rosenblood, L. K. (1996). Affiliation motivation in everyday experience: A theoretical comparison. *Journal of Personality and Social Psychology, 70,* 513–522.

O'Donnell, C. R. (1995). Firearm deaths among children and youth. *American Psychologist, 50,* 771–776.

O'Farrell, T., & Murphy, C. M. (1995). Marital violence before and after alcoholism treatment. *Journal of Consulting and Clinical Psychology 63,* 256–262.

Ogbu, J. U. (1993). Differences in cultural frame of reference. *International Journal of Behavioral Development, 16,* 483–506.

Ohbuchi, K., Kamdea, M., & Agarie, N. (1989). Apology as aggression control: Its role in mediating appraisal of and response to harm. *Journal of Personality and Social Psychology, 56,* 219–227.

Okazawa-Rey, M., Robinson, T., & Ward, J. V. (1986). Black women and the politics of skin color and hair. *Women's Studies Quarterly, 14,* 13–14.

Oliner, S. P., & Oliner, P. M. (1988). *The altruistic personality: Rescuers of Jews in Nazi Europe.* London: Free Press.

Olson, J. M. (1988). Misattribution, preparatory information, and speech anxiety. *Journal of Personality and Social Psychology, 54,* 758–767.

Olson, J. M., & Roese, N. J. (1995). The perceived funniness of humorous stimuli. *Personality and Social Psychology Bulletin, 21,* 908–913.

Olson, J. M., & Ross, M. (1988). False feedback about placebo effectiveness: Consequences for the misattribution of speech anxiety. *Journal of Experimental Social Psychology, 24,* 275–291.

O'Meara, D. J. (1994). Cross-sex friendship and the communication challenge: Uncharted terrain for exploration. *Personal Relationship Issues, 2,* 4–7.

Orbell, J. M., van de Kragt, A. J. C., & Dawes, R. M. (1988). Explaining discussion-induced cooperation. *Journal of Personality and Social Psychology, 54,* 811–819.

Orimoto, L., Hatfield, E., Yamakawa, R., & Denney, C. (1993). Gender differences in emotional reactions and coping strategies following a break-up. Reported in E. Hatfield & R. Rapson (1996), *Love, sex, and intimacy: Their psychology, biology, and history* (p. 231). Neeham Heights, MA: Allyn & Bacon.

Ormel, J., & Schaufeli, W. B. (1991). Stability and change in psychological distress and their relationship with self-esteem and locus of control: A dynamic equilibrium model. *Journal of Personality and Social Psychology, 60,* 288–299.

Orne, M. T. (1962). On the social psychology of the psychological experiment: With particular reference to demand characteristics and their implications. *American Psychologist, 17,* 776–783.

Ortmann, A., & Hertwig, R. (1997). Is deception acceptable? *American Psychologist, 52,* 746–747.

Osborne, J. W. (1995). Academics, self-esteem, and race: A look at the underlying assumptions of the disidentification hypothesis. *Personality and Social Psychology Bulletin, 21,* 449–455.

Otten, S., Mummendey, A., & Blanz, M. (1996). Intergroup discrimination in positive and negative outcome allocations: Impact of stimulus valence, relative group status, and relative group size. *Personality and Social Psychology Bulletin, 22,* 568–581.

Oyserman, D. (1993). The lens of personhood: Viewing the self and others in a multicultural society. *Journal of Personality and Social Psychology, 65,* 993–1009.

Oyserman, D., & Packer, M. J. (1996). Social cognition and self-concept: A socially contextualized model of identity. In J. L. Nye & A. M. Brower (Eds.), *What's social about social cognition: Research on socially shared cognition in small groups* (pp. 175–201). Thousand Oaks, CA: Sage.

Oyserman, D., Sakamoto, I., & Lauffer, A. (1998). Cultural accommodation: Hybridity and the framing of social obligation. *Journal of Personality and Social Psychology, 74,* 1606–1618.

Page, R. M. (1991). Loneliness as a risk factor in adolescent hopelessness. *Journal of Research in Personality, 25,* 189–195.

Pagelow, M. (1984). *Family violence.* New York: Praeger.

Pallak, S. R. (1983). Salience of a communicator's physical attractiveness and persuasion: A heuristic versus systematic processing interpretation. *Social Cognition, 2,* 158–170.

Paludi, M., & Barickman, R. B. (1991). *Academic and workplace sexual harassment.* Albany, NY: State University of New York Press.

Park, B., & Rothbart, M. (1982). Perception of out-group homogeneity and levels of social categorization: Memory for the subordinate attributes of ingroup and outgroup members. *Journal of Personality and Social Psychology, 42,* 1051–1068.

Parrott, W. G., & Smith, R. H. (1993). Distinguishing the experiences of envy and jealousy. *Journal of Personality and Social Psychology, 64,* 906–920.

Pasch, L. A., Bradbury, T. N., & Sullivan, K. T. (1997). Social support in marriage: An analysis of intraindividual and interpersonal components. In G. R. Pierce,

B. Lakey, I. G. Sarason, & B. R. Sarason (Eds.), *Sourcebook of social support and personality* (pp. 229–256). New York: Plenum Press.

Patterson, G. R., DeBaryshe, B. D., & Ramsey, E. (1989). A developmental perspective on antisocial behavior. *American Psychologist, 44,* 329–335.

Paulhus, D. L., & Levitt, K. (1987). Desirable responding triggered by affect: Automatic egotism? *Journal of Personality and Social Psychology, 52,* 245–259.

Paulhus, D. L., & Martin, C. L. (1988). Functional flexibility: A new conception of interpersonal flexibility. *Journal of Personality and Social Psychology, 55,* 88–101.

Paulus, P. B. (1998). Developing consensus about groupthink after all these years. *Organizational Behavior and Human Decision Processes, 73,* 1–13.

Pelham, B. W., & Wachsmuth, J. O. (1995). The waxing and waning of the social self: Assimilation and contrast in social comparison. *Journal of Personality and Social Psychology, 69,* 825–838.

Pendleton, M. G., & Batson, C. D. (1979). Self-presentation and the door-in-the-face technique for inducing compliance. *Personality and Social Psychology Bulletin, 5,* 77–81.

Pendry, L. F., & Macrae, C. N. (1994). Stereotypes and mental life: The case of the motivation but thwarted tactician. *Journal of Experimental Social Psychology, 30,* 303–325.

Pennington, N., & Hastie, R. (1988). Explanation-based decision making: Effects of memory structure on judgment. *Journal of Experimental Psychology: Learning, Memory, and Cognition, 14,* 521–533.

Pennington, N., & Hastie, R. (1990). Practical implications of psychological research on juror and jury decision making. *Personality and Social Psychology Bulletin, 16,* 90–105.

Pennington, N., & Hastie, R. (1992). Explaining the evidence: Tests of the story model for juror decision making. *Journal of Personality and Social Psychology, 62,* 189–206.

Peplau, L. A., Bikson, T. K., Rook, K. S., & Goodchilds, J. D. (1982). Being old and living alone. In L. A. Peplau & D. Perlman (Eds.), *Loneliness: A sourcebook of current theory, research and therapy* (pp. 327–347). New York: John Wiley.

Peplau, L. A., Cochran, S. D., & Mays, V. M. (1997). A national survey of the intimate relationships of African American lesbians and gay men: A look at commitment, satisfaction, sexual behavior and HIV disease. In B. Greene & G. Herek (Eds.), *Psychological perspectives on lesbian and gay issues: Ethnic and cultural diversity among lesbians and gay men.* Newbury Park: Sage.

Perdue, C. W., Dovidio, J. F., Gurtman, M. B., & Tyler, R. B. (1990). Us and them: Social categorization and the process of

intergroup bias. *Journal of Personality and Social Psychology, 59,* 475–486.

Personnaz, B. (1981). Study in social influence using the spectrometer method: Dynamics of the phenomena of conversion and covertness in perceptual responses. *European Journal of Social Psychology, 11,* 431–438.

Pessin, J. (1933). The comparative effects of social and mechanical stimulation on memorizing. *American Journal of Psychology, 45,* 263–270.

Peters, L. H., Hartke, D. D., & Pohlmann, J. T. (1985). Fiedler's contingency theory of leadership: An application of the meta-analytic procedures of Schmidt and Hunter. *Psychological Bulletin, 97,* 274–285.

Peterson, B. E., Doty, R. M., & Winter, D. G. (1993). Authoritarianism and attitudes toward contemporary social issues. *Personality and Social Psychology Bulletin, 19,* 174–184.

Peterson, C., & Seligman, M. E. P. (1987). Explanatory style and illness. *Journal of Personality, 55,* 237–265.

Peterson, C., Maier, S. F., & Seligman, M. E. P. (1993). *Learned helplessness: A theory for the age of personal control.* New York: Oxford University Press.

Peterson, C., Seligman, M. E. P., & Vaillant, G. E. (1988). Pessimistic explanatory style is a risk factor for physical illness: A thirty-five-year longitudinal study. *Journal of Personality and Social Psychology, 55,* 23–27.

Peterson, C., Seligman, M. E. P., Yurko, K. H., Martin, L. R., & Friedman, H. S. (1998). Catastrophizing and untimely death. *Psychological Science, 9,* 127–130.

Peterson, J. L., & Miller, C. (1980). Physical attractiveness and marriage adjustment in older American couples. *Journal of Psychology, 105,* 247–252.

Peterson, R. S., & Nemeth, C. J. (1996). Focus versus flexibility: Majority and minority influence can both improve performance. *Personality and Social Psychology Bulletin, 22,* 14–23.

Pettigrew, T. F. (1969). Racially separate or together? *Journal of Social Issues, 25,* 43–69.

Pettigrew, T. F. (1997). Generalized intergroup contact effects on prejudice. *Personality and Social Psychology Bulletin, 23,* 173–185.

Petty, R. E. (1997). The evolution of theory and research in social psychology: From single to multiple effect and process models of persuasion. In C. McGarty & S. A. Haslam (Eds.), *The message of social psychology: Perspectives on mind in society* (pp. 268–290). Oxford, England: Blackwell.

Petty, R. E., & Cacioppo, J. T. (1979). Issue involvement can increase or decrease persuasion by enhancing message-relevant cognitive responses. *Journal of Personality and Social Psychology, 37,* 1915–1926.

Petty, R. E., & Cacioppo, J. T. (1986). *Communication and persuasion: Central and peripheral routes to attitude change.* New York: Springer-Verlag.

Petty, R. E., & Cacioppo, J. T. (1990). Involvement and persuasion: Tradition versus integration. *Psychological Bulletin, 107,* 367–374.

Petty, R. E., & Jarvis, W. B. G. (1995). Individual differences in the motivation to think and evaluate: Implications for surveys. In S. Sudman & N. Schwarz (Eds.), *Methods for determining cognitive processes in answering questions.* San Francisco: Jossey-Bass.

Petty, R. E., & Wegener, D. T. (1998). Attitude change: Multiple roles for persuasion variables. In D. Gilbert, S. Fiske, & G. Lindzey (Eds.), *The handbook of social psychology* (4th ed., pp. 323–390). New York: McGraw-Hill.

Petty, R. E., Haugtvedt, C. P., & Smith, S. M. (1995). Elaboration as a determinant of attitude strength: Creating attitudes that are persistent, resistant, and predictive of behavior. In R. E. Petty & J. A. Krosnick (Eds.), *Attitude strength: Antecedents and consequences.* Hillsdale, NJ: Erlbaum.

Petty, R. E., Ostrom, T. M., & Brock, T. C. (1981b). Historical foundations of the cognitive response approach to attitudes and persuasion. In R. E. Petty, T. M. Ostrom, & T. C. Brock (Eds.), *Cognitive responses in persuasion* (pp. 5–29). Hillsdale, NJ: Lawrence Erlbaum.

Pfau, M., & Burgoon, M. (1988). Inoculation in political campaign communication. *Human Communication Research, 15,* 91–111.

Pfeffer, J. (1998). Understanding organizations: Concepts and controversies. In D. T. Gilbert, S. T. Fiske, & G. Lindzey (Eds.), *The handbook of social psychology* (4th ed., Vol. 2, pp. 733–777). New York: McGraw-Hill.

Phinney, J. (1993). A three-stage model of ethnic identity development. In M. Bernal & G. Knight (Eds.), *Ethnic identity: Formation and transmission among Hispanics and other minorities* (pp. 61–79). Albany, NY: State University of New York Press.

Phinney, J., & Kohatsu, E. (1997). Ethnic and racial identity and mental health. In J. Schulenberg, J. Maggs, & K. Hurrelmann (Eds.), *Health risks and developmental transitions during adolescence,* pp. 420–443. New York: Cambridge University Press.

Phinney, J., Cantu, C. L., & Kurtz, D. A. (1997). Ethnic and American identity and self-esteem. *Journal of Youth and Adolescence, 26,* 165–185.

Phinney, J. S. (1989). Stages of ethnic identity in minority group adolescents. *Journal of Early Adolescence, 9,* 34–49.

Phinney, J. S. (1991). Ethnic identity and self-esteem: A review and integration. *Hispanic Journal of Behavioral Sciences, 13,* 193–208.

Pietromonaco, P. R., & Carnelley, K. B. (1994). Gender and working models of attachment: Consequences for perception of self and romantic relationships. *Personal Relationships, 1,* 3–26.

Piliavin, J. A., & Callero, P. L. (1991). *Giving blood: The development of an altruistic identity.* Baltimore, MD: Johns Hopkins University Press.

Piliavin, J. A., & Piliavin, I. M. (1972). The effect of blood on reactions to a victim. *Journal of Personality and Social Psychology, 23,* 253–261.

Piliavin, J. A., Dovidio, J. F., Gaertner, S. L., & Clark, R. D., III. (1981). *Emergency intervention.* New York: Academic Press.

Pinel, E. C. (1999). Stigma consciousness: The psychological legacy of social stereotypes. *Journal of Personality and Social Psychology, 76,* 114–128.

Pion, G. M., Mednick, M. T., Astin, H. S., Hall, C. C. I., Kenkel, M. B., Keita, G. P., Kohut, J. L., & Kelleher, J. C. (1996). The shifting gender composition of psychology: Trends and implications for the discipline. *American Psychologist, 51,* 509–528.

Plant, E. A., & Devine, P. G. (1998). Internal and external motivation to respond without prejudice. *Journal of Personality and Social Psychology, 75,* 811–832.

Platz, S. J., & Hosch, H. M. (1988). Cross-racial/ethnic eyewitness identification: A field study. *Journal of Applied Social Psychology, 18,* 972–984.

Pleban, R., & Tesser, A. (1981). The effects of relevance and quality of another's performance on interpersonal closeness. *Social Psychology Quarterly, 44,* 278–285.

Plomin, R., Nitz, K., & Rowe, D. C. (1990). Behavior genetics and aggressive behavior in childhood. In M. Lewis & S. Miller (Eds.), *Handbook of developmental psychopathology* (pp. 119–133). New York: Plenum.

Plous, S. (1989). Thinking the unthinkable: The effects of anchoring on likelihood estimates of nuclear war. *Journal of Applied Social Psychology, 19,* 67–91.

Pollard, J. S. (1995). Attractiveness of composite faces: A comparative study. *International Journal of Comparative Psychology, 8*(2), 77–83.

Pollock, C. L., Smith, S. D., Knowles, E. S., & Bruce, H. J. (1998). Mindfulness limits compliance with the That's-not-all technique. *Personality and Social Psychology, 24,* 1153–1157.

Porter, J. F., & Critelli, J. W. (1994). Self-talk and sexual arousal in sexual aggression. *Journal of Social and Clinical Psychology, 13,* 223–239.

Porter, S., & Yuille, J. C. (1996). The language of deceit: An investigation of the verbal clues to deception in the interrogation context. *Law and Human Behavior, 20,* 443–458.

Posavac, H. D., & Posavac, S. S. (1998). Exposure to media images of female attractiveness and concern with body weight among young women. *Sex Roles, 38,* 187–201.

Posavec, E. J. (1992). Communicating applied social psychology to users: A challenge and an art. In F. B. Bryant, J. Edwards, R. S. Tinsdale, E. J. Posavec, L. Heath, E. Henderson, & Y. Suarez-Balcazar (Eds.), *Methodological issues in applied social psychology* (pp. 269–294). New York: Plenum.

Postmes, T., & Spears, R. (1998). Deindividuation and antinormative behavior: A meta-analysis. *Psychological Bulletin, 123,* 238–259.

Powell, G. N. (1990). One more time: Do female and male managers differ? *Academy of Management Executive, 4,* 68–75.

Powers, T. A., & Zuroff, D. C. (1988). Interpersonal consequences of overt self-criticism: Comparison with neutral and self-enhancing presentations of self. *Journal of Personality and Social Psychology, 54,* 1054–1062.

Powlishta, K. K. (1995). Intergroup processes in childhood: Social categorization and sex role development. *Developmental Psychology, 31,* 781–788.

Pozo, C., Carver, C. S., Wellens, A. R., & Scheier, M. F. (1991). Social anxiety and social perception: Construing others' reactions to the self. *Personality and Social Psychology Bulletin, 17,* 355–362.

Pratkanis, A. R., & Aronson, E. (1992). *Age of propaganda: The everyday use and abuse of persuasion.* New York: W.H. Freeman.

Pratkanis, A. R., Eskenazi, J., & Greenwald, A. G. (1994). What you expect is what you believe (But not necessarily what you get): A test of the effectiveness of subliminal self-help audiotapes. *Basic and Applied Social Psychology, 15,* 251–276.

Pratkanis, A. R., Greenwald, A. G., Leippe, M. R., & Baumgardner, M. H. (1988). In search of reliable persuasion effects: III. The sleeper effect is dead. Long live the sleeper effect. *Journal of Personality and Social Psychology, 54,* 203–218.

Pratt, D. D. (1991). Conceptions of self within China and the United States: Contrasting foundations for adult education. *International Journal of Intercultural Relations, 15,* 285–310.

Pratto, F. (1996). Sexual politics: The gender gap in the bedroom, the cupboard, and the cabinet. In D. Buss & N. Malamuth (Eds.), *Sex, power, and conflict: Evolutionary and feminist perspectives* (pp. 179–230). New York: Oxford University Press.

Pratto, F., & John, O. P. (1991). Automatic vigilance: The attention-grabbing power of negative social information. *Journal of Personality and Social Psychology, 61,* 380–391.

Pratto, F., Sidanius, J., & Stallworth, L. M. (1993). Sexual selection and the sexual and ethnic basis of social hierarchy. In L. Ellis (Ed.). *Social stratification and socioeconomic inequality: Vol. 1: A Comparative biosocial analysis.* (pp. 111–137). Westport, CT: Praeger.

Prentice, D. A. (1987). Psychological correspondence of possessions, attitudes, and values. *Journal of Personality and Social Psychology, 53,* 993–1003.

Prentice, D. A., & Miller, D. T. (1999). (Eds.). *Cultural divides: Understanding and overcoming group conflict.* New York: Russell Sage Foundation.

Prentice-Dunn, S., & Rogers, R. W. (1980). Effects of deindividuating situational cues and aggressive models on subjective deindividuation and aggression. *Journal of Personality and Social Psychology, 39,* 104–113.

Prentice-Dunn, S., & Rogers, R. W. (1982). Effects of public and private self-awareness on deindividuation and aggression. *Journal of Personality and Social Psychology, 43,* 503–513.

Priest, R. F., & Sawyer, J. (1967). Proximity and peership: Bases of balance in interpersonal attraction. *American Journal of Sociology, 72,* 633–649.

Priester, J. R., & Fleming, M. A. (1997). Artifact or meaningful theoretical constructs? Examining evidence for nonbelief- and belief-based attitude change processes. *Journal of Consumer Psychology, 6,* 67–76.

Priester, J. R., & Petty, R. E. (1995). Source attributions and persuasion: Perceived honesty as a determinant of message scrutiny. *Personality and Social Psychology Bulletin, 21,* 637–654.

Priester, J. R., Cacioppo, J. T., & Petty, R. E. (1996). The influence of motor processes on attitudes toward novel versus familiar semantic stimuli. *Personality and Social Psychology Bulletin, 22,* 442–447.

Pruitt, D. G. (1971). Choice shifts in group discussion: An introductory review. *Journal of Personality and Social Psychology, 20,* 339–360.

Pruitt, D. G. (1998). Social conflict. In D. Gilbert, S. T. Fiske, & G. Lindzey (Eds.), *Handbook of social psychology* (4th ed.). New York: McGraw-Hill.

Pryor, J. B., Giedd, J. L., & Williams, K. B. (1995). A social and psychological model for predicting sexual harassment. *Journal of Social Issues, 51,* 69–84.

Ptacek, J. T., & Dodge, K. L. (1995). Coping strategies and relationship satisfaction in couples. *Personality and Social Psychology Bulletin, 21,* 76–84.

Pye, L. W. (1996). The state and the individual: An overview interpretation. In B. Hook (Ed.), *The individual and the state in China* (pp. 16–42). Oxford: Clarendon Press.

Pyszczynski, T., & Greenberg, J. (1992). *Hanging on and letting go: Understanding the onset, maintenance, and remission of depression.* New York: Springer-Verlag.

Quillian, L. (1995). Prejudice as a response to perceived group threat: Population composition and anti-immigrant and racial prejudice in Europe. *American Sociological Review, 60,* 586–611.

Räikkönen, K., Matthews, K. A., Flory, J. D., Owens, J. F., & Gump, B. B. (1999). Effects of optimism, pessimism, and trait anxiety on ambulatory blood pressure and mood during everyday life. *Journal of Personality and Social Psychology, 76,* 104–113.

Radelet, M. L., Bedau, H. A., & Putnam, C. E. (1992). *In spite of innocence: Erroneous convictions in capital cases.* Boston: Northeastern University Press.

Ramsoy, N. R. (1966). Assortive mating and the structure of cities. *American Journal of Sociology, 31,* 773–786.

Rapoport, A. (1988a). Experiments with N-person social traps: I. Prisoner's dilemma, weak prisoner's dilemma, volunteer's dilemma, and largest number. *Journal of Conflict Resolution, 32,* 457–472.

Rapoport, A. (1988b). Experiments with N-person social traps: II. Tragedy of the commons. *Journal of Conflict Resolution, 32,* 473–488.

Ratcliff, R., & McKoon, G. (1994). Retrieving information from memory: Spreading-activation theories versus compound-cue theories. *Psychological Review, 101,* 177–184.

Read, J. D. (1996). From a passing thought to a false memory in 2 minutes: Confusing real and illusory events. *Psychonomic Science and Review, 3,* 105–111.

Regan, D. T. (1971). Effects of a favor and liking on compliance. *Journal of Experimental Social Psychology, 7,* 627–639.

Regan, D. T., & Kilduff, M. (1988). Optimism about elections: Dissonance reduction at the ballot box. *Political Psychology, 9,* 101–107.

Reifman, A. S., Larrick, R. P., & Fein, S. (1991). Temper and temperature on the diamond: The heat-aggression relationship in major league baseball. *Journal of Personality and Social Psychology, 17,* 580–585.

Reinard, J. C. (1988). The empirical study of the persuasive effects of evidence: The status after fifty years of research. *Human Communications Research, 15,* 3–59.

Reinecke, J., Schmidt, P., & Ajzen, I. (1996). Application of the theory of planned behavior to adolescents' condom use: A panel study. *Journal of Applied Social Psychology, 26,* 749–772.

Reis, H. T., & Franks, P. (1994). The role of intimacy and social support in health outcomes: Two processes or one? *Personal Relationships, 1,* 185–197.

Reis, H. T., & Patrick, B. C. (1998). Attachment and intimacy: Component processes. In E. T. Higgins & A. Kruglanski (Eds.), *Social psychology: Handbook of basic principles* (pp. 523–563). New York: Guilford.

Reisenzein, R. (1983). The Schachter theory of emotion: Two decades later. *Psychological Bulletin, 94,* 239–264.

Reisman, J. M. (1984). Friendliness and its correlates. *Journal of Social and Clinical Psychology, 2,* 143–155.

Renzetti, C. (1993). Violence in lesbian relationships. In M. Hensen & M. Hareway (Eds.), *Battering and family therapy: A feminist perspective* (pp. 188–199). Newbury Park, CA: Sage.

Reynolds, D. L., Chambers, L. W., & Devilliaer, M. (1992). Measuring alcohol abuse in the community: Consumption, binge drinking, and alcohol-related consequences ("alcoholism"). *Canadian Journal of Public Health, 83,* 441–447.

Rhodewalt, F., & Davison, J., Jr. (1983). Reactance and the coronary-prone behavior pattern: The role of self-attribution in response to reduced behavioral freedom. *Journal of Personality and Social Psychology, 44,* 220–228.

Ridgeway, C. L. (1982). Status in groups: The importance of motivation. *American Sociological Review, 47,* 76–88.

Ridgeway, C. L. (1991). The social construction of status value: Gender and other nominal characteristics. *Social Forces, 70,* 367–386.

Rieves, L., & Cash, T. F. (1996). Social developmental factors and women's body-image attitudes. *Journal of Social Behavior and Personality, 11,* 63–78.

Riley, D., & Eckenrode, J. (1986). Social ties: Subgroup differences in costs and benefits. *Journal of Personality and Social Psychology, 51,* 770–778.

Ringelmann, M. (1913). Research on animate sources of power: The work of man. *Annales de l'Institut National Agronomique, 2e serietome XII,* 1–40.

Riordan, C. A., & Tedeschi, J. T. (1983). Attraction in aversive environments: Some evidence for classical conditioning and negative reinforcement. *Journal of Personality and Social Psychology, 44,* 683–692.

Robarchek, C. (1989). Primitive warfare and the ratomorphic image of mankind. *American Anthropologist, 91,* 903–920.

Roberts, B. W., & Helson, R. (1997). Changes in culture, changes in personality: the influence of individualism in a longitudinal study of women. *Journal of Personality and Social Psychology, 72,* 641–651.

Roberts, R. E., Phinney, J. S., Masse, L., Chen, Y. R., Roberts, C., & Romero, A. (in press). The structure of ethnic identity in young adolescents from diverse ethnocultural groups. *Journal of Early Adolescence.*

Roberts, W. R. (1954). *Aristotle.* New York: Modern Library.

Robins, R. W., Gosling, S. D., & Craik, K. H. (1999). An empirical analysis of trends in psychology. *American Psychologist, 54.*

Robins, R. W., Spranca, M. D., & Mendelsohn, G. A. (1996). The actor-observer effect revisited: Effects of individual differences and repeated social interactions on actor and observer attributions. *Journal of Personality and Social Psychology, 71,* 375–389.

Robinson, D. T., & Balkwell, J. W. (1995). Density, transitivity, and diffuse status in task-oriented groups. *Social Psychology Quarterly, 58,* 241–254.

Roese, N. J. (1997). Counterfactual thinking. *Psychological Bulletin, 121,* 133–148.

Roese, N. J., & Olson, J. M. (1995a). Counterfactual thinking: A critical overview. In N. J. Roese & J. M. Olson (Eds.), *What might have been: The social psychology of counterfactual thinking* (pp. 1–55). Hillsdale, NJ: Erlbaum.

Roese, N. J., & Olson, J. M. (1997). Counterfactual thinking: The intersection of affect and function. In M. P. Zanna (Ed.), *Advances in experimental social psychology* (Vol. 29, pp. 1–59). New York: Academic Press.

Rofé, Y. (1984). Stress and illness: A utility theory. *Psychological Review, 91,* 235–250.

Rogers, C. R. (1947). Some observations on the organization of personality. *American Psychologist, 2,* 358–368.

Rogers, R. W. (1983). Cognitive and psychological processes in fear appeals and attitude change: A revised theory of protection motivation. In J. Cacioppo & R. Petty (Eds.), *Social psychophysiology: A sourcebook* (pp. 153–176). New York: Guilford.

Rokeach, M. (1973). *The nature of human values.* New York: Free Press.

Romer, D., Gruder, C. L., & Lizzadro, T. (1986). A person-situation approach to altruistic behavior. *Journal of Personality and Social Psychology, 51,* 1001–1012.

Rosch, E. H. (1978). Principles of categorization. In E. Rosch & B. L. Lloyd (Eds.), *Cognition and categorization.* Hillsdale, NJ: Erlbaum.

Rose, J. (1994). Communication challenges and role functions of performing groups. *Small Group Research, 25,* 411–432.

Rosekrans, M., & Hartup, W. (1967). Imitative influences of consistent and inconsistent response consequences to a model on aggressive behavior in children. *Journal of Personality and Social Psychology, 7,* 429–434.

Rosenberg, M. (1979). *Conceiving the self.* New York: Basic Books.

Rosenberg, M. L., & Mercy, J. A. (1991). Assaultive violence. In M. L. Rosenberg & M. A. Fenley (Eds.), *Violence in America: A public health approach* (pp. 14–50). New York: Oxford University Press.

Rosenblatt, P. C., & Cozby, P. C. (1972). Courtship patterns associated with freedom of choice of spouse. *Journal of Marriage and the Family, 34,* 689–695.

Rosenhan, D. L. (1970). The natural socialization of altruistic autonomy. In J. Macaulay & L. Berkowitz (Eds.), *Altruism and helping behavior.* New York: Academic Press.

Rosenhan, D. L., Salovey, P., & Hargis, K. (1981). The joys of helping: Focus of attention mediates the impact of positive affect on altruism. *Journal of Personality and Social Psychology, 40,* 899–905.

Rosenthal, R. (1974). On the social psychology of the self-fulfilling prophecy: Further evidence for Pygmalion effects and their mediating mechanisms. *MSS Modular Publications*, New York, Module 53, 1–28.

Rosenthal, R. (1984). *Meta-analytic procedures for social research*. Beverly Hills, CA: Sage.

Rosenthal, R. (1991). Teacher expectancy effects: A brief update 25 years after the Pygmalion experiment. *Journal of Research in Education, 1*, 3–12.

Rosenthal, R., & Jacobson, L. (1968). *Pygmalion in the classroom: Teacher expectation and pupils' intellectual development*. New York: Holt.

Ross, E. A. (1908). *Social psychology: An outline and sourcebook*. New York: Macmillan.

Ross, L. (1977). The intuitive psychologist and his shortcomings: Distortions in the attribution process. In L. Berkowitz (Ed.), *Advances in experimental social psychology* (Vol. 10, pp. 174–221). New York: Academic Press.

Ross, L., Amabile, T. M., & Steinmetz, J. L. (1977a). Social roles, social control, and biases in social perception processes. *Journal of Personality and Social Psychology, 35*, 485–494.

Ross, L., Greene, D., & House, P. (1977b). The "false consensus effect": An egocentric bias in social perception and attribution processes. *Journal of Experimental Social Psychology, 13*, 279–301.

Ross, L. E. (1997). Mate selection preferences among African-American college students. *Journal of Black Studies, 27*, 554–569.

Roszell, P., Kennedy, D., & Grabb, E. (1990). Physical attractiveness and income attainment among Canadians. *Journal of Psychology, 123*, 547–559.

Rotenberg, K. J., & Kmill, J. (1992). Perception of lonely and non-lonely persons as a function of individual differences in loneliness. *Journal of Social and Personal Relationships, 9*, 325–330.

Rotenberg, K. J., Bartley, J. L., & Toivonen, D. M. (1997). Children's stigmatization of chronic loneliness in peers. *Journal of Social Behavior and Personality, 12*, 577–584.

Rothbaum, F., & Tsang, B. Y-P. (1998). Lovesongs in the United States and China: On the nature of romantic love. *Journal of Cross-Cultural Psychology, 29*, 306–319.

Rotundo, A. (1989). Romantic friendships: Male intimacy and middle-class youth in the northern United States, 1800–1900. *Journal of Social History, 23*, 1–25.

Rowatt, W. C., Cunningham, M. R., & Druen, P. B. (1998). Deception to get a date. *Personality and Social Psychology Bulletin, 24*, 1228–1242.

Rowe, D. C., Chassin, L., Presson, C., & Sherman, S. J. (1996). Parental smoking and the "epidemic" spread of cigarette smoking. *Journal of Applied Social Psychology, 26*, 437–454.

Rubin, L. (1985). *Just friends: The role of friendship in our lives*. New York: Harper & Row.

Rubin, M., & Hewstone, M. (1998). Social identity theory's self-esteem hypothesis: A review and some suggestions for clarification. *Personality and Social Psychology Review, 2*, 40–62.

Rubin, Z., & Peplau, L. A. (1975). Who believes in a just world? *Journal of Social Issues, 31*, 65–89.

Rubin, Z., Peplau, L. A., & Hill, C. T. (1981). Loving and leaving: Sex differences in romantic attachments. *Sex Roles, 7*, 821–835.

Ruble, T. L. (1983). Sex stereotypes: Issues of change in the 1970s. *Sex Roles, 9*, 397–402.

Rusbult, C. E., & Martz, J. M. (1995). Remaining in an abusive relationship: An investment model analysis of nonvoluntary dependence. *Personality and Social Psychology Bulletin, 21*, 558–571.

Rusbult, C. E., Johnson, D. J., & Morrow, G. D. (1986a). Impact of couple patterns of problem solving on distress and nondistress in dating relationships. *Journal of Personality and Social Psychology, 50*, 744–753.

Rusbult, C. E., Morrow, G. D., & Johnson, D. J. (1987). Self-esteem and problem-solving behaviour in close relationships. *British Journal of Social Psychology, 26*, 293–303.

Rusbult, C. E., Zembrodt, I., & Iwaniszek, J. (1986b). The impact of gender and sex-role orientation on responses to dissatisfaction in close relationships. *Sex Roles, 15*, 1–20.

Rushton, J. P. (1975). Generosity in children: Immediate and long term effects of modeling, preaching, and moral judgment. *Journal of Personality and Social Psychology, 31*, 459–466.

Rushton, J. P. (1980). *Altruism, socialization, and society*. Englewood Cliffs, NJ: Prentice-Hall.

Rushton, J. P. (1989). Genetic similarity in male friendships. *Ethology and Sociobiology, 10*, 361–373.

Rushton, J. P., & Campbell, A. C. (1977). Modeling, vicarious reinforcement and extraversion on blood donating in adults: Immediate and long term effects. *European Journal of Social Psychology, 7*, 297–306.

Rushton, J. P., & Teachman, G. (1978). The effects of positive reinforcement, attributions, and punishment on model-induced altruism in children. *Personality and Social Psychology Bulletin, 4*, 322–325.

Russell, D. (1982). Types of loneliness. In L. A. Peplau & D. Perlman (Eds.), *Loneliness: A sourcebook of current theory, research and therapy* (pp. 81–104). New York: John Wiley.

Russell, D., Peplau, L. A., & Cutrona, C. E. (1980). The revised UCLA Loneliness Scale: Concurrent and discriminant validity evidence. *Journal of Personality and Social Psychology, 39*, 472–480.

Russell, D. E. H. (1993). *Making violence sexy: Feminist views on pornography*. New York: Teachers College Press.

Russell, J. A., & Yik, S. M. (1996). Emotion among the Chinese. In M. H. Bond (Ed.), *The handbook of Chinese psychology*. Hong Kong, China: Oxford University Press.

Russo, V. (1987). *The celluloid closet: Homosexuality in the movies* (2nd ed.). New York: Harper & Row.

Ryckman, R. M., Robbins, M. A., Thornton, B., Kaczor, L. M., Gayton, S. L., & Anderson, C. V. (1991). Public self-consciousness and physique stereotyping. *Personality and Social Psychology Bulletin, 17*, 400–405.

Saad, L. (1996, December). Americans growing more tolerant of gays: But still resist official sanctioning in the law. *The Gallup Poll Monthly*, pp. 12–14.

Sachdev, I., & Bourhis, R. Y. (1987). Status differentials and intergroup behaviour. *European Journal of Social Psychology, 17*, 277–293.

Sachdev, I., & Bourhis, R. Y. (1991). Power and status differentials in minority and majority group relations. *European Journal of Social Psychology, 21*, 1–24.

Saegert, S. C., Swapp, W., & Zajonc, R. B. (1973). Exposure, context, and interpersonal attraction. *Journal of Personality and Social Psychology, 25*, 234–242.

Saks, M. (1977). *Jury verdicts*. Lexington, MA: Lexington Books.

Salovey, P., & Rodin, J. (1988). Coping with envy and jealousy. *Journal of Social and Clinical Psychology, 7*, 15–33.

Salovey, P., & Rodin, J. (1991). Provoking jealousy and envy: Domain relevance and self-esteem threat. *Journal of Social and Clinical Psychology, 10*, 395–413.

Salovey, P., Rothman, A. J., & Rodin, J. (1998). Health behavior. In D. T. Gilbert, S. T. Fiske, & G. Lindzey (Eds.), *The handbook of social psychology* (4th ed., Vol. 2, pp. 633–683). New York: McGraw-Hill.

Sampson, E. E. (1988). The debate on individualism: Indigenous psychologies of the individual and their role in personal and societal functioning. *American Psychologist, 43*, 15–22.

Sanday, P. (1981). The socio-cultural context of rape: A cross-cultural study. *Journal of Social Issues, 37*, 5–27.

Sanders Thompson, V. L. (1991). Perceptions of race and race relations which affect African-American identification. *Journal of Applied Social Psychology, 21*, 1502–1516.

Sanders, G. S., & Baron, R. S. (1975). The motivating effects of distraction on task performance. *Journal of Personality and Social Psychology, 32*, 956–963.

Sanders, J. A., Wiseman, R. L., & Matz, S. I. (1991). Uncertainty reduction in acquaintance relationships in Ghana and the United States. In S. Ting-Toomey & F. Korsenny (Eds.), *Cross-cultural interpersonal communication* (pp. 79–98). Newbury Park, CA: Sage.

Sandroff, R. (1992, June). Sexual harassment: The inside story. *Working Woman*, pp. 47–51.

Sandys, M., & Dillehay, R. C. (1995). First-ballot votes, predeliberation dispositions, and final verdicts in jury trials. *Law and Human Behavior, 19*, 175–195.

Sanna, L. J., & Mark, M. M. (1995). Self-handicapping, expected evaluation, and performance: Accentuating the positive and attenuating the negative. *Organizational Behavior and Human Decision Processes, 64*, 84–102.

Sanna, L. J., & Pusecker, P. A. (1994). Self-efficacy, valence of self-evaluation, and performance. *Personality and Social Psychology Bulletin, 20*, 82–92.

Sanna, L. J., & Turley, K. J. (1996). Antecedents to spontaneous counterfactual thinking: Effects of expectancy violation and outcome valence. *Personality and Social Psychology Bulletin, 22*, 906–919.

Santee, R. T., & Maslach, C. (1982). To agree or not to agree: Personal dissent amid social pressure to conform. *Journal of Personality and Social Psychology, 42*, 690–700.

Sarnoff, I., & Zimbardo, P. G. (1961). Anxiety, fear, and social affiliation. *Journal of Abnormal and Social Psychology, 62*, 356–363.

Sato, K. (1987). Distribution of the cost of maintaining common resources. *Journal of Experimental Social Psychology, 23*, 19–31.

Savin, H. B. (1973). Professors and psychological researchers: Conflicting values in conflicting roles. *Cognition, 2*, 147–149.

Scanzoni, J. (1979). Social exchange and behavioral interdependence. In R. L. Burgess & T. L. Huston (Eds.), *Social exchange in developing relationships*. New York: Academic Press.

Schachter, S. (1951). Deviation, rejection and communication. *Journal of Abnormal and Social Psychology, 46*, 190–207.

Schachter, S. (1959). *The psychology of affiliation.* Stanford, CA: Stanford University Press.

Schachter, S. (1964). The interaction of cognitive and physiological determinants of emotional state. In L. Berkowitz (Ed.), *Advances in experimental social psychology* (Vol. 1, pp. 49–80). New York: Academic Press.

Schaeffer, A. M., & Nelson, E. S. (1993). Rape-supportive attitudes: Effects of on-campus residence and education. *Journal of College Student Development, 34*, 175–179.

Schafer, M., & Crichlow, S. (1996). Antecedents of groupthink: A quantitative study. *Journal of Conflict Resolution, 40*, 415–435.

Schafer, R. B., & Keith, P. M. (1980). Equity and depression among married couples. *Social Psychology Quarterly, 43*, 430–435.

Schaffner, P. E., Wandersman, A., & Stang, D. (1981). Candidate name exposure and voting: Two field studies. *Basic and Applied Social Psychology, 2*, 195–203.

Schaufeli, W. B. (1988). Perceiving the causes of unemployment: An evaluation of the causal dimensions scale in a real-life situation. *Journal of Personality and Social Psychology, 54*, 347–356.

Scheier, M. F. (1980). Effects of public and private self-consciousness on the public expression of personal beliefs. *Journal of Personality and Social Psychology, 39*, 514–521.

Scheier, M. F., & Carver, C. S. (1977). Self-focused attention and the experience of emotion: Attraction, repulsion, elation, and depression. *Journal of Personality and Social Psychology, 35*, 625–636.

Scheier, M. F., & Carver, C. S. (1980). Private and public self-attention, resistance to change, and dissonance reduction. *Journal of Personality and Social Psychology, 39*, 390–405.

Scheier, M. F., & Carver, C. S. (1983). Two sides of the self: One for you and one for me. In J. Suls & A. G. Greenwald (Eds.), *Psychological perspectives on the self* (Vol. 2). Hillsdale, NJ: Lawrence Erlbaum.

Schlenker, B. R. (1980). *Impression management: The self-concept, social identity, and interpersonal relations.* Monterey, CA: Brooks/Cole.

Schlenker, B. R., & Leary, M. R. (1982). Audiences' reactions to self-enhancing, self-denigrating, and accurate self-presentations. *Journal of Experimental Social Psychology, 18*, 89–104.

Schliemann, A. D., Carraher, D. W., & Ceci, S. . (1997). Everyday cognition. In J. W. Berry, P. R. Dasen, & T. S. Saraswathi (Eds.), *Handbook of cross-cultural psychology, Vol. 2: Basic processes and human development* (pp. 177–216). Boston: Allyn & Bacon.

Schmidt, F. L. (1992). What do data really mean? Research findings, meta-analysis, and cumulative knowledge in psychology. *American Psychologist, 47*, 1173–1181.

Schmidt, G., & Weiner, B. (1988). An attributional-affect-action theory of behavior: Replications of judgments of helping. *Personality and Social Psychology Bulletin, 14*, 610–621.

Schneller, R. (1992). Many gestures, many meanings: Nonverbal diversity in Israel. In F. Poyatos (Ed.), *Advances in nonverbal communication: Sociocultural, clinical, esthetic and literary perspectives* (pp. 213–233). Philadelphia: John Benjamins.

Schoneman, P. H., Byrne, D., & Bell, P. A. (1977). Statistical aspects of a model for interpersonal attraction. *Bulletin of the Psychonomic Society, 9*, 243–246.

Schreurs, K. M. G., & Buunk, B. P. (1994). Intimacy, autonomy, and relationship satisfaction in Dutch lesbian couples and heterosexual couples. *Journal of Psychology and Human Sexuality, 7*(4), 41–57.

Schriesheim, C. A., Tepper, B. J., & Tetrault, L. A. (1994). Least preferred coworker score, situational control, and leadership effectiveness: A meta-analysis of contingency model performance predictions. *Journal of Applied Psychology, 79*, 561–573.

Schulman, S., Elicker, J., & Sroufe, A. (1994). Stages of friendship growth in preadolescents as related to attachment history. *Journal of Social and Personal Relationships, 11*, 341–361.

Schultz, N. R., & Moore, D. (1984). Loneliness: Correlates, attributions, and coping among older adults. *Personality and Social Psychology Bulletin, 10*, 67–77.

Schultz, T. R., Léveillé, E., & Lepper, M. R. (1999). Free choice and cognitive dissonance revisited: Choosing "lesser evils" versus "greater goods." *Personality and Social Psychology Bulletin, 25*, 40–48.

Schuman, H. (1995). Attitudes, beliefs, and behavior. In K. S. Cook, G. A. Fine, & J. S. House (Eds.), *Sociological perspectives on social psychology* (pp. 68–89). Boston: Allyn & Bacon.

Schuman, H., & Scott, J. (1989). Generations and collective memories. *American Sociological Review, 54*, 359–381.

Schumann, D. W., Petty, R. E., & Clemons, D. S. (1990). Predicting the effectiveness of different strategies of advertising variation: A test of the repetition-variation hypotheses. *Journal of Consumer Research, 17*, 192–202.

Schuster, B., Forsterling, F., & Weiner, B. (1989). Perceiving the causes of success and failure: A cross-cultural examination of attributional concepts. *Journal of Cross-Cultural Psychology, 20*, 191–213.

Schwartz, S. H. (1975). The justice of need and the activation of humanitarian norms. *Journal of Social Issues, 31*, 111–136.

Schwartz, S. H. (1977). Normative influences on altruism. In L. Berkowitz (Ed.), *Advances in experimental social psychology* (Vol. 10, pp. 221–279). New York: Academic Press.

Schwartz, S. H., & Howard, J. A. (1980). Explanations of the moderating effect of responsibility denial on the personal-norm behavior relationship. *Social Psychology Quarterly, 43*, 441–446.

Schwartz, S. H., & Howard, J. A. (1982). Helping and cooperation: A self-based motivational model. In V. J. Derlega & J. Grzelak (Eds.), *Cooperation and helping behavior: Theories and research* (pp. 327–353). New York: Academic Press.

Schwarz, N. (1990). Feelings as information: Informational and motivational functions of affective states. In E. T. Higgins & R. M. Sorrentino (Eds.), *Handbook of motivation and cognition: Foundations of social behavior* (Vol. 2, pp. 527–561). New York: Guilford.

Schwarz, N., Bless, H., Strack, F., Klumpp, G., Rittenauer-Schatka, & Simons, A. (1991b). Ease of retrieval as information: Another look at the availability heuristic. *Journal of Personality and Social Psychology, 61,* 195–202.

Schwarzwald, J., Amir, Y., & Crain, R. L. (1992). Long-term effects of school desegregation experiences on interpersonal relations in the Israeli defense forces. *Personality and Social Psychology Bulletin, 18,* 357–368.

Schwarzwald, J., Bizman, A., & Raz, M. (1983). The foot-in-the-door paradigm: Effects of second request size on donation probability and donor generosity. *Personality and Social Psychology Bulletin, 9,* 443–450.

Scully, D. (1985). *The role of violent pornography in justifying rape.* Paper prepared for the Attorney General's Commission on Pornography Hearings, Houston, TX.

Searcy, E., & Eisenberg, N. (1992). Defensiveness in response to aid from a sibling. *Journal of Personality and Social Psychology, 62,* 422–433.

Sears, D. O. (1983). The person-positivity bias. *Journal of Personality and Social Psychology, 44,* 233–250.

Sears, D. O., & Funk, C. L. (1991). The role of self-interest in social and political attitudes. In M. Zanna (Ed.), *Advances in experimental social psychology* (pp. 2–91). San Diego: Academic Press.

Seashore, S. E. (1954). *Group cohesiveness in the industrial work group.* Ann Arbor, MI: Institute for Social Research.

Sedikedes, C., & Skowronski, J. J. (1997). The symbolic self in evolutionary context. *Personality and Social Psychology Review, 1,* 80–102.

Sedikides, C. (1993). Assessment, enhancement, and verification determinants of the self-evaluation process. *Journal of Personality and Social Psychology, 65,* 317–338.

Sedikides, C., & Strube, M. J. (1997). Self-evaluation: To thine own self be good, to thine own self be sure, to thine own self be true, and to thine own self be better. In M. P. Zanna (Ed.), *Advances in experimental social psychology* (Vol. 29, pp. 209–269). San Diego: Academic Press.

Sedikides, C., Campbell, W. K., Reeder, G. D., & Elliot, A. J. (1998). The self-serving bias in relational context. *Journal of Personality and Social Psychology, 74,* 378–386.

Sedikes, C., & Jackson, J. M. (1990). Social impact theory: A field test of source strength, source immediacy and number of targets. *Basic and Applied Social Psychology, 11,* 273–281.

Seeman, M. (1997). The elusive situation in social psychology. *Social Psychology Quarterly, 60,* 4–13.

Segal, M. W. (1974). Alphabet and attraction: An unobtrusive measure of the effect of propinquity in a field setting. *Journal of Personality and Social Psychology, 30,* 654–657.

Segerstrom, S. C., Taylor, S. E., Kemeny, M. E., & Fahey, J. L. (1998). Optimism is associated with mood, coping, and immune change in response to stress. *Journal of Personality and Social Psychology, 74,* 1646–1655.

Seligman, M. E. P. (1991). *Learned optimism.* New York: Alfred A. Knopf.

Seligman, M. E. P., & Maier, S. F. (1967). Failure to escape traumatic shock. *Journal of Experimental Psychology, 74,* 1–9.

Senchak, M., & Leonard, K. E. (1992). Attachment styles and marital adjustment among newlywed couples. *Journal of Social and Personal Relationships, 9,* 51–64.

Setterlund, M. B., & Niedenthal, P. M. (1993). "Who am I? Why am I here?": Self-esteem, self-clarity, and prototype matching. *Journal of Personality and Social Psychology, 65,* 769–780.

Shanab, M. E., & Yahya, K. A. (1977). A behavioral study of obedience in children. *Journal of Personality and Social Psychology, 35,* 530–536.

Shapiro, P. N., & Penrod, S. (1986). Meta-analysis of facial identification studies. *Psychological Bulletin, 100,* 139–156.

Shaver, P., & Klinnert, M. (1982). Schachter's theories of affiliation and emotion: Implications of developmental research. In L. Wheeler (Ed.), *Review of personality and social psychology* (Vol. 3). Beverly Hills, CA: Sage.

Shaver, P. R., Wu, S., & Schwartz, J. C. (1991). Cross-cultural similarities and differences in emotion and its representation: A prototype approach. In M. S. Clark (Ed.), *Review of personality and social psychology* (Vol. 13, pp. 175–212). Beverly Hills, CA: Sage.

Shavitt, S., Swan, S., Lowery, T. M., & Wänke, M. (1994). The interaction of endorser attractiveness and involvement in persuasion depends on the goal that guides message processing. *Journal of Consumer Psychology, 3,* 137–162.

Shaw, L. L., Batson, C. D., & Todd, R. M. (1994). Empathy avoidance: Forestalling feeling for another in order to escape the motivational consequences. *Journal of Personality and Social Psychology, 67,* 879–887.

Sheffey, S., & Tindale, R. S. (1992). Perceptions of sexual harassment in the workplace. *Journal of Applied Social Psychology, 22,* 1502–1520.

Sheppard, B. H., Hartwick, J., & Warshaw, P. R. (1988). The theory of reasoned action: A meta-analysis of past research with recommendations for modifications and future research. *Journal of Consumer Research, 18,* 321–334.

Sherif, M. (1935). A study of some social factors in perception. *Archives of Psychology, 27* (187), 1–60.

Sherif, M. (1936). *The psychology of social norms.* New York: Harper.

Sherif, M. (1966). *In common predicament: Social psychology of intergroup conflict and cooperation.* Boston: Houghton Mifflin.

Sherif, M., & Cantril, H. (1947). *The psychology of ego-involvements: Social attitudes and identifications.* New York: Wiley.

Sherif, M., & Sherif, C. W. (1956). *An outline of social psychology.* New York: Harper & Brothers.

Sherif, M., Harvey, O. J., White, B. J., Hood, W. R., & Sherif, C. (1961). *Intergroup conflict and cooperation: The Robbers' Cave experiment.* Norman, OK: Oklahoma Book Exchange.

Sherman, J. W., & Klein, S. B. (1994). Development and representation of personality impressions. *Journal of Personality and Social Psychology, 67,* 972–983.

Sherman, J. W., Klein, S. B., Laskey, A., & Wyer, N. A. (1998). Intergroup bias in group judgment processes: The role of behavioral memories. *Journal of Experimental Social Psychology, 34,* 51–65.

Sherman, P. W. (1985). Alarm calls of Belding's ground squirrels to aerial predators: Nepotism or self-preservation? *Behavioral Ecology and Sociobiology, 17,* 313–323.

Sherrill, K. (1996). The political power of lesbians, gays, and bisexuals. *PS: Political Science and Politics, 24,* 469–471.

Sherrod, D. (1989). The influence of gender on same-sex friendships. In C. Hendrick (Ed.), *Review of personality and social psychology: Vol. 10. Close relationships* (pp. 164–186). Newbury Park, CA: Sage.

Shestowsky, D., Wegener, D. T., & Fabrigar, L. R. (1998). Need for cognition and interpersonal influence: Individual differences in impact on dyadic decisions. *Journal of Personality and Social Psychology, 74,* 1317–1328.

Shields, S. A. (1987). Women, men, and the dilemma of emotion. In P. R. Shaver & C. Hendrick (Eds.), *Sex and gender* (Review of Personality and Social Psychology, Vol. 7, pp. 229–250). Beverly Hills, CA: Sage.

Shoda, Y., Mischel, W., & Peake, P. K. (1990). Predicting adolescent cognitive and self-regulatory competencies from preschool delay of gratification: Identifying diagnostic conditions. *Developmental Psychology, 26,* 978–986.

Shotland, R. L., & Hunter, B. A. (1995). Women's "token resistant" and compliant sexual behaviors are related to uncertain sexual intentions and rape. *Personality and Social Psychology Bulletin, 21,* 226–236.

Shotland, R. L., & Straw, M. K. (1976). Bystander response to an assault: When a man attacks a woman. *Journal of Personality and Social Psychology, 34,* 990–999.

Shrauger, J. S. (1975). Responses to evaluation as a function of initial self-perceptions. *Psychological Bulletin, 82,* 581–596.

Shumaker, S. A., & Hill, D. R. (1991). Gender differences in social support and physical health. *Health Psychology, 10,* 102–111.

Shuval, J. T., & Adler, I. (1980). The role of models in professional socialization. *Social Science & Medicine, 14,* 5–14.

Shweder, R. A., & LeVine, R. A. (Eds.). (1984). *Culture theory: Essays on mind, self, and emotion.* New York: Cambridge.

Sibicky, M. E., Schroeder, D. A., & Dovidio, J. F. (1995). Empathy and helping: Considering the consequences of intervention. *Basic and Applied Social Psychology, 16,* 435–453.

Sidanius, J. (1993). The psychology of group conflict and the dynamics of oppression: A social dominance perspective. In S. Iyengar & W. J. McGuire (Eds.), *Explorations in political psychology* (pp. 183–219). Durham, NC: Duke University Press.

Sidanius, J., Pratto, F., & Bobo, L. (1996). Racism, conservatism, affirmative action, and intellectual sophistication: A matter of principled conservatism or group dominance? *Journal of Personality and Social Psychology, 70,* 476–490.

Sidanius, J., Pratto, F., & Brief, D. (1995). Group dominance and the political psychology of gender: A cross-cultural comparison. *Political Psychology, 16,* 381–396.

Sigall, H., & Landy, D. (1973). Radiating beauty: The effects of having a physically attractive partner on person perception. *Journal of Personality and Social Psychology, 28,* 218–224.

Sigelman, C. K., Berry, C. J., & Wiles, K. A. (1984). Violence in college students' dating relationships. *Journal of Applied Social Psychology, 5,* 530–548.

Sigelman, L., & Tuch, S. A. (1997). Metastereotypes: Blacks' perceptions of Whites' stereotypes of Blacks. *Public Opinion Quarterly, 61,* 87–101.

Silberstein, L. R., Mishkind, M. E., Striegel-Moore, R. H., Timko, C., & Rodin, J. (1989). Men and their bodies: A comparison of homosexual and heterosexual men. *Psychosomatic Medicine, 51,* 337–346.

Simon, B. (1992b). Intragroup differentiation in terms of ingroup and outgroup attributes. *European Journal of Social Psychology, 22,* 407–413.

Simon, H. (1990). A mechanism for social selection and successful altruism. *Science, 250,* 1665–1668.

Simons, H. W. (1971). Persuasion and attitude change. In L. L. Barker & R. J. Kibler (Eds.), *Speech communication behavior: Perspectives and principles* (pp. 227–248). Englewood Cliffs, NJ: Prentice-Hall.

Simons, H. W., Berkowitz, N. N., & Moyer, R. J. (1970). Similarity, credibility, and attitude change: A review and a theory. *Psychological Bulletin, 73,* 1–16.

Simonton, D. K. (1985). Intelligence and personal influence in groups: Four nonlinear models. *Psychological Review, 92,* 532–547.

Simonton, D. K. (1994). *Greatness: Who makes history and why?* New York: Guilford Press.

Simonton, D. K. (1998). Historiometric methods in social psychology. *European Review of Social Psychology, 9,* 267–293.

Simpson, J. A. (1990). Influence of attachment styles on romantic relationships. *Journal of Personality and Social Psychology, 59,* 971–980.

Singelis, T. M., Triandis, H. C., Bhawuk, D. S., & Gelfand, M. (1995). Horizontal and vertical dimensions of individualism and collectivism: A theoretical and measurement refinement. *Cross-Cultural Research, 29,* 240–275.

Sinha, D., & Tripathi, R. C. (1994). Individualism in a collectivist culture: A case of coexistence of opposites. In U. Kim, H. C. Trandis, Ç. Kâğitçibaşi, S. Choi, & G. Yoon (Eds.), *Individualism and collectivism: Theory, method, and applications* (pp. 123–136). Thousand Oaks, CA: Sage.

Sinha, J. B. P. (1986, July). Concepts and controversies in Indian organizational psychology. Invited Address, International Congress of Applied Psychology, Jerusalem.

Sivacek, J., & Crano, W. D. (1982). Vested interest as a moderator of attitude-behavior consistency. *Journal of Personality and Social Psychology, 43,* 210–221.

Skinner, B. F. (1938). *The behavior of organisms.* New York: Appleton-Century-Crofts.

Smith, A., & Berard, S. P. (1982). Why are human subjects less concerned about ethically problematic research than human subjects committees? *Journal of Applied Social Psychology, 12,* 209–221.

Smith, D. (1976, August). *Sexual aggression in American pornography: The stereotype of rape.* Paper presented at the American Sociological Association meetings, New York City.

Smith, E. R. (1993). Social identity and social emotions: Toward new conceptualizations of prejudice. In D. Mackie & D. Hamilton (Eds.), *Affect, cognition, and stereotyping,* (pp. 297–315). San Diego: Academic Press.

Smith, E. R., & Henry, S. (1996). An ingroup becomes part of the self: Response time evidence. *Personality and Social Psychology Bulletin, 22,* 635–642.

Smith, E. R., Fazio, R. H., & Cejka, M. A. (1996). Accessible attitudes influence categorization of multiply categorizable objects. *Journal of Personality and Social Psychology, 71,* 888–898.

Smith, G. F., & Dorfman, D. D. (1975). The effect of stimulus uncertainty on the relationship between frequency of exposure and liking. *Journal of Personality and Social Psychology, 31,* 150–155.

Smith, G. L., & DeWine, S. (1991). Perceptions of subordinates and requests for support: Are males and females perceived differently when seeking help? *Organizational Studies, 16,* 408–427.

Smith, G. T., Hohlstein, L. A., & Atlas, J. G. (1989, August). *Race differences in eating disordered behavior and eating-related experiences.* Paper presented at the 97th Annual Convention of the American Psychological Association, New Orleans, LA.

Smith, M. B., Bruner, J. S., & White, R. W. (1956). *Opinions and personality.* New York: Wiley.

Smith, P. B., Peterson, M. F., Bond, M., & Misumi, J. (1990). Leadership style and leader behaviour in individualistic and collectivist cultures. In S. Iwawaki, Y. Kashima, & K. Leung (Eds.), *Innovations in cross-cultural psychology* (pp. 76–85). Amsterdam: Swets & Zeitlinger.

Smith, S. M., Haugtvedt, C. P., & Petty, R. E. (1994). Humor can either enhance or disrupt message processing: The moderating role of humor relevance. Unpublished manuscript.

Smith, S. M., Shaffer, D. R. (1991). Celerity and cajolery: Rapid speech may promote or inhibit persuasion through its impact on message elaboration. *Personality and Social Psychology Bulletin, 17,* 663–669.

Smith, S. S., & Richardson, D. (1983). Amelioration of deception and harm in psychological research: The important role of debriefing. *Journal of Personality and Social Psychology, 44,* 1075–1082.

Snodgrass, J. G., & Thompson, R. L. (1997). *The self across psychology: Self-recognition, self-awareness, and the self-concept.* New York: New York Academy of Sciences.

Snodgrass, S. E. (1992). Further effects of role versus gender on interpersonal sensitivity. *Journal of Personality and Social Psychology, 62,* 154–158.

Snyder, C. R. (1997). "I've led three lives," but is there a life for the interface? *The Counseling Psychologist, 25,* 256–265.

Snyder, C. R., & Fromkin, H. L. (1980). *Uniqueness: The pursuit of difference.* New York: Plenum.

Snyder, M. (1974). The self-monitoring of expressive behavior. *Journal of Personality and Social Psychology, 30,* 526–537.

Snyder, M. (1979). Self-monitoring processes. In L. Berkowitz (Ed.), *Advances in experimental social psychology* (Vol.12, pp. 86–131). New York: Academic Press.

Snyder, M. (1987). *Public appearances/private realities: The psychology of self-monitoring.* New York: Freeman.

Snyder, M., & Cunningham, M. R. (1975). To comply or not to comply: Testing the self-perception explanation of the foot-in-the-door phenomenon. *Journal of Personality and Social Psychology, 31,* 64–67.

Snyder, M., & DeBono, K. G. (1985). Appeals to image and claims about quality: Understanding the psychology of advertising. *Journal of Personality and Social Psychology, 49,* 586–597.

Snyder, M., & DeBono, K. G. (1989). Understanding the functions of attitudes:

Lessons for personality and social behavior. In A. R. Pratkanis, S. J. Breckler, & A. G. Greenwald (Eds.), *Attitude structure and function* (pp. 339–359). Hillsdale, NJ: Lawrence Erlbaum.

Snyder, M., & Gangestad, S. (1982). Choosing social situations: Two investigations of self-monitoring processes. *Journal of Personality and Social Psychology, 43,* 123–135.

Snyder, M., & Simpson, J. A. (1984). Self-monitoring and dating relationships. *Journal of Personality and Social Psychology, 47,* 1281–1291.

Snyder, M., & Swann, W. B. (1978). Hypothesis-testing processes in social interaction. *Journal of Personality and Social Psychology, 36,* 1202–1212.

Snyder, M., Tanke, E. D., & Berscheid, E. (1977). Social perception and interpersonal behavior: On the self-fulfilling nature of social stereotypes. *Journal of Personality and Social Psychology, 35,* 656–666.

Solano, C. H., & Koester, N. H. (1989). Loneliness and communication problems: Subjective anxiety or objective skills? *Personality and Social Psychology Bulletin, 15,* 126–133.

Spade, J. Z., & Reese, C. A. (1991). We've come a long way, maybe: College students' plans for work and family. *Sex Roles, 24,* 309–321.

Spaulding, C. (1970). The romantic love complex in American culture. *Sociology and Social Research, 55,* 82–100.

Spencer, S. J., Fein, S., Wolfe, C. T., Fong, C., & Dunn, M. A. (1998). Automatic activation of stereotypes: The role of self-image threat. *Personality and Social Psychology Bulletin, 24,* 1139–1152.

Spencer, S. J., Steele, C. M., & Quinn, D. M. (1998). Under suspicion of inability: Stereotype threat and women's math performance. Manuscript submitted for publication.

Spitz, R. A. (1945). Hospitalism: An inquiry into the genesis of psychiatric conditions in early childhood. In A. Freud (Ed.), *The psychoanalytic study of the child* (Vol. 1, pp. 53–74). New York: International Universities Press.

Spivey, C. B., & Prentice-Dunn, S. (1990). Assessing the directionality of deindividuated behavior: Effects of deindividuation, modeling, and private self-consciousness on aggressive and prosocial responses. *Basic and Applied Social Psychology, 11,* 387–403.

Sprafkin, J. N., Liebert, R. M., & Poulos, R. W. (1975). Effects of a prosocial televised example on children's helping. *Journal of Experimental Child Psychology, 20,* 119–126.

Sprecher, S. (1992). How men and women expect to feel and behave in response to inequity in close relationships. *Social Psychology Quarterly, 55,* 57–69.

Sprecher, S., & Duck, S. (1994). Sweet talk: The importance of perceived communication for romantic and friendship attraction experienced during a get-acquainted date. *Personal and Social Psychology Bulletin, 20,* 391–400.

Sprecher, S., & Felmlee, D. (1992). The influence of parents and friends on the quality and stability of romantic relationships: A three wave longitudinal investigation. *Journal of Marriage and the Family, 54,* 888–900.

Sprecher, S., Metts, S., Burleson, B., Hatfield, E., & Thompson, A. (1995). Domains of expressive interaction in intimate relationships: Associations with satisfaction and commitment. *Family Relations, 44,* 1–8.

Sprecher, S., Sullivan, Q., & Hatfield, E. (1994). Mate selection preferences: Gender differences examined in a national sample. *Journal of Personality and Social Psychology, 66,* 1074–1080.

Staats, A. W., & Staats, C. K. (1958). Attitudes established by classical conditioning. *Journal of Abnormal and Social Psychology, 57,* 37–40.

Staats, A. W., Staats, C. K., & Crawford, H. L. (1962). First-order conditioning of meaning and the parallel conditioning of a GSR. *Journal of General Psychology, 67,* 159–167.

Stagner, R. (1986). Reminiscences about the founding of SPSSI. *Journal of Social Issues, 42,* 35–42.

Stangor, C., Lynch, L., Duan, C., & Glass, B. (1992). Categorization of individuals on the basis of multiple social features. *Journal of Personality and Social Psychology, 62,* 207–218.

Stanton, W. R., Currie, G. D., Oei, T. P. S., & Silva, P. A. (1996). A developmental approach to influences on adolescents' smoking and quitting. *Journal of Applied and Developmental Psychology, 17,* 307–319.

Stapp, J., & Fulcher, R. (1981). The employment of APA members. *American Psychologist, 36,* 1263–1314.

Stasser, G., Taylor, L. A., & Hanna, C. (1989b). Information sampling in structured and unstructured discussions of three- and six-person groups. *Journal of Personality and Social Psychology, 57,* 67–78.

Steele, C. M. (1988). The psychology of self-affirmation: Sustaining the integrity of the self. In L. Berkowitz (Ed.), *Advances in experimental social psychology* (Vol. 21, pp. 261–302). New York: Academic Press.

Steele, C. M. (1992). Race and the schooling of Black Americans. *The Atlantic Monthly,* April, 68–78.

Steele, C. M. (1997). A threat in the air: How stereotypes shape intellectual identity and performance. *American Psychologist, 52,* 613–629.

Steele, C. M., & Aronson, J. (1994). Stereotype vulnerability and intellectual performance. Paper presented at the Western Psychological Association meeting, Hawaii, April 29.

Steele, C. M., & Aronson, J. (1995). Contending with stereotypes: African-American Intellectual test performance and stereotype vulnerability. Submitted for publication.

Steele, C. M., & Josephs, R. A. (1988). Drinking your troubles away. I: The psychology of drunken excess. *Journal of Personality and Social Psychology, 48,* 18–34.

Steele, C. M., & Josephs, R. A. (1990). Alcohol myopia: Its prized and dangerous effects. *American Psychologist, 45,* 921–933.

Steele, C. M., & Liu, T. J. (1981). Making the dissonant act unreflective of self: Dissonance avoidance and the expectancy of a value-affirming response. *Personality and Social Psychology Bulletin, 7,* 393–397.

Steele, C. M., Spencer, S. J., & Lynch, M. (1993). Self-image resilience and dissonance: The role of affirmational resources. *Journal of Personality and Social Psychology, 64,* 885–896.

Steinberg, L. D., Catalano, R., & Dooley, D. (1981). Economic antecedents of child abuse and neglect. *Child Development, 52,* 975–985.

Stelmack, R. M., & Geen, R. G. (1992). The psychophysiology of extraversion. In A. Gale & M. W. Eysenck (Eds.), *Handbook of individual differences: Biological perspectives* (pp. 227–254). New York: Wiley.

Stephan, C. W., & Stephan, W. G. (1992). Reducing intercultural anxiety through intercultural contact. *International Journal of Intercultural Relations, 16,* 89–106.

Stephan, W. G. (1980). A brief historical overview of school desegregation. In W. G. Stephan & J. R. Feagin (Eds.), *School desegregation: Past, present, and future* (pp. 3–24). New York: Plenum.

Stephan, W. G., & Stephan, C. W. (1985). Intergroup anxiety. *Journal of Social Issues, 41,* 157–175.

Stephan, W. G., & Stephan, C. W. (1989a). Antecedents of intergroup anxiety in Oriental-Americana and Hispanics. *International Journal of Intercultural Communication, 13,* 203–219.

Stepper, S., & Strack, F. (1993). Proprioceptive determinants of emotional and nonemotional feelings. *Journal of Personality and Social Psychology, 64,* 211–220.

Sternberg, R. J. (1986). A triangular theory of love. *Psychological Review, 93,* 119–135.

Sternberg, R. J. (1988). Triangulating love. In R. J. Sternberg & M. L. Barnes (Eds.), *The psychology of love* (pp. 119–138). New Haven, CT: Yale University Press.

Stets, J. E., & Burke, P. J. (1996). Gender, control, and interaction. *Social Psychology Quarterly, 59,* 193–220.

Stevens, C. J., Puchtell, L. A., Ryu, S., & Mortimer, J. T. (1992). Adolescent work and boys' and girls' orientations to the future. *Sociological Quarterly, 33,* 153–169.

Stevens, C. K., & Kristof, A. L. (1995). Making the right impression: A field study of applicant impression management during job interviews. *Journal of Applied Psychology, 80,* 587–606.

Stewart, A. J., & Chester, N. L. (1982). Sex differences in human social motives: Achievement, affiliation and power. In A. J. Stewart (Ed.), *Motivation and society.* San Francisco: Jossey-Bass.

Stewart, E. C., & Bennett, M. J. (1991). *American cultural patterns: A cross-cultural perspective.* Yarmouth, ME: Intercultural Press.

Stiff, J. B., Miller, G. R., Sleight, C., Mongeau, P. L., Garlick, R., & Rogon, R. (1989). Explanations for visual cue primacy in judgments of honesty and deceit. *Journal of Personality and Social Psychology, 56,* 555–564.

Stiles, W. B., Walz, N. C., Schroeder, M. A. B., Williams, L. L., & Ickes, W. (1996). Attractiveness and disclosure in initial encounters of mixed-sex diads. *Journal of Social and Personal Relationships, 13,* 303–312.

Stockdale, M. S. (1993). The role of sexual misperceptions of women's friendliness in an emerging theory of sexual harassment. *Journal of Vocational Behavior, 42,* 84–101.

Stokes, J. P. (1987). The relation of loneliness and self-disclosure. In V. J. Derlega & J. H. Berg (Eds.), *Self-disclosure: Theory, research, and therapy* (pp. 175–202). New York: Plenum.

Stokes, J., & Levin, I. (1986). Gender differences in predicting loneliness from social network characteristics. *Journal of Personality and Social Psychology, 51,* 1069–1074.

Stone, J., Wiegand, A. W., Cooper, J., & Aronson, E. (1997). When exemplification fails: Hypocrisy and the motive for self-integrity. *Journal of Personality and Social Psychology, 72,* 54–65.

Stone, L. (1977). *The family, sex and marriage in England: 1500–1800.* New York: Harper & Row.

Stoner, J. A. F. (1961). *A comparison of individual and group decisions involving risk.* Unpublished master's thesis, M. I. T., Cambridge, MA.

Storms, M. D. (1973). Videotape and the attribution process: Reversing actors' and observers' points of view. *Journal of Personality and Social Psychology, 27,* 165–175.

Strack, F., Martin, L. L., & Stepper, S. (1988). Inhibiting and facilitating conditions of facial expressions: A nonobtrusive test of the facial feedback hypothesis. *Journal of Personality and Social Psychology, 54,* 768–777.

Straus, M. A. (1974). Leveling, civility, and violence in the family. *Journal of Marriage and the Family, 36,* 12–29.

Straus, M. A., & Gelles, R. J. (1990). *Physical violence in American families: Risk factors and adaptations to violence in 8,145 families.* New Brunswick, NJ: Transaction.

Straus, M. A., Gelles, R. J., & Steinmetz, S. K. (1980). *Behind closed doors: Violence in the American family.* Garden City, NY: Doubleday/Anchor.

Street, R. L., Jr., & Brady, R. M. (1982). Speech rate acceptance ranges as a function of evaluative domain, listener speech rate, and communication context. *Communication Monographs, 49,* 290–308.

Striegel-Moore, R. H., Silberstein, L. R., & Rodin, J. (1993). The social self in bulimia nervosa: Public self-consciousness, social anxiety, and perceived fraudulence. *Journal of Abnormal Psychology, 102,* 297–303.

Stroessner, S. J., Hamilton, D. L., & Mackie, D. M. (1992). Affect and stereotyping: The effect of induced mood on distinctiveness-based illusory correlations. *Journal of Personality and Social Psychology, 62,* 564–576.

Stryker, S. (1989). The two social psychologies. *Social Forces, 68,* 45–54.

Stryker, S. (1997). "In the beginning there is society": Lessons from a sociological social psychology. In C. McGarty & S. A. Haslam (Eds.), *The message of social psychology: Perspectives on mind in society* (pp. 315–327). Cambridge, MA: Blackwell.

Suls, J., & Fletcher, B. (1985). Self-attention, life stress, and illness: A prospective study. *Psychosomatic Medicine, 47,* 469–481.

Sumner, W. (1906). *Folkways.* New York: Ginn.

Swann, W. B., De La Ronde, C., & Hixon, J. G. (1994). Authenticity and positive strivings in marriage and courtship. *Journal of Personality and Social Psychology, 66,* 857–869.

Swann, W. B., Jr. (1984). Quest for accuracy in person perception: A matter of pragmatics. *Psychological Review, 91,* 457–477.

Swann, W. B., Jr. (1990). To be adored or to be known? The interplay of self-enhancement and self-verification. In E. T. Higgins & R. M. Sorrentino (Eds.), *Handbook of motivation and cognition: Foundations of social behavior* (Vol. 2, pp. 408–448). New York: Guilford Press.

Swann, W. B., Jr. (1997). The trouble with change: Self-verification and allegiance to the self. *Psychological Science, 8,* 177–183.

Swann, W. B., Jr., & Ely, R. J. (1984). A battle of wills: Self-verification versus behavioral confirmation. *Journal of Personality and Social Psychology, 46,* 1287–1302.

Swann, W. B., Jr., Griffin, J. J., Predmore, S., & Gaines, B. (1987). The cognitive-affective crossfire: When self-consistency confronts self-enhancement. *Journal of Personality and Social Psychology, 52,* 881–889.

Sweeney, P. D., Anderson, K., & Bailey, S. (1986). Attributional style in depression: A meta-analytic review. *Journal of Personality and Social Psychology, 50,* 974–991.

Swidler, A. (1986). Culture in action: Symbols and strategies. *American Sociological Review, 51,* 273–286.

Swim, J., Borgida, E., Maruyama, G., & Myers, D. G. (1989). Joan McKay vs. John McKay: Do gender stereotypes bias evaluations? *Psychological Bulletin, 105,* 409–429.

Swim, J. K., & Sanna, L. J. (1996). He's skilled, she's lucky: A meta-analysis of observers' attributions for women's and men's successes and failures. *Personality and Social Psychology Bulletin, 22,* 507–519.

Swinton, W. (1880). *A complete course in geography: Physical, industrial, and political.* New York: Ivison, Blakeman, Taylor, & Co.

Symonds, C. (1972). A vocabulary of sexual enticement and proposition. *The Journal of Sex Research, 8,* 136–139.

't Hart, P., Rosenthal, U., & Kouzmin, A. (1993). Crisis decision making: The centralization thesis revisited. *Administration & Society, 25,* 12–45.

Tajfel, H., & Turner, J. (1979). An integrative theory of intergroup conflict. In W. G. Austin & S. Worchel (Eds.), *The social psychology of intergroup relations.* Monterey, CA: Brooks/Cole.

Tajfel, H., Billig, M. G., Bundy, R. P., & Flament, C. (1971). Social categorization and intergroup behavior. *European Journal of Social Psychology, 1,* 149–178.

Tanford, S., & Penrod, S. (1984). Social influence model: A formal integration of research on majority and minority influence. *Psychological Bulletin, 95,* 189–225.

Tangney, J. P., & Feshbach, S. (1988). Children's television viewing frequency: Individual differences and demographic correlates. *Personality and Social Psychology Bulletin, 14,* 145–158.

Tangney, J. P., Wagner, P., Fletcher, C., & Gramzow, R. (1992). Shamed into anger? The relation of shame and guilt to anger and self-reported aggression. *Journal of Personality and Social Psychology, 62,* 669–675.

Taormina, R. J., & Messick, D. M. (1983). Deservingness for foreign aid: Effects of need, similarity, and estimated effectiveness. *Journal of Applied Social Psychology, 13,* 371–391.

Tarde, G. (1903). *The laws of imitation.* (Elsie Clews Parson, Trans.). New York: Henry Holt. (Original work published in 1890).

Tata, J., Anthony, T., Lin, H., Newman, B., Tang, S., Millson, M., & Sivakumar, K. (1996). Proportionate group size and rejection of the deviate: A meta-analytic integration. *Journal of Social Behavior and Personality, 11,* 739–752.

Tavris, C. (1989). *Anger: The misunderstood emotion.* New York: Touchstone Books.

Taylor, J., & Riess, M. (1989). "Self-serving" attributions to valenced causal factors: A field experiment. *Personality and Social Psychology Bulletin, 15,* 337–348.

Taylor, S. E. (1998). The social being in social psychology. In D. T. Gilbert, S. T. Fiske, & G. Lindzey (Eds.), *The handbook of social psychology* (4th ed., pp. 58–95). New York: McGraw-Hill.

Taylor, S. E., & Brown, J. D. (1999). Illusion and well-being: A social psychological perspective on mental health. *Psychological Bulletin, 103,* 193–210.

Taylor, S. E., & Fiske, S. T. (1975). Point of view and perceptions of causality. *Journal of Personality and Social Psychology, 32,* 439–445.

Terman, L. M., & Oden, M. H. (1947). *Genetic studies of genius: IV. The gifted child grows up: Twenty-five years follow-up of a superior group.* Stanford, CA: Stanford University Press.

Tesser, A. (1988). Toward a self-evaluation maintenance model of social behavior. In L. Berkowitz (Ed.), *Advances in experimental social psychology* (Vol. 21, pp. 181–227). New York: Academic Press.

Tesser, A., & Campbell, J. (1982). Self-evaluation maintenance and the perception of friends and strangers. *Journal of Personality and Social Psychology, 50,* 261–279.

Tetlock, P. E. (1989). Structure and function in political belief systems. In A. R. Pratkanis, S. J. Breckler, & A. G. Greenwald (Eds.), *Attitude structure and function* (pp. 129–151). Hillsdale, NJ: Lawrence Erlbaum.

Tetlock, P. E., & Kim, J. I. (1987). Accountability and judgment processes in a personality prediction task. *Journal of Personality and Social Psychology, 52,* 700–709.

Tetlock, P. E., Peterson, R. S., McGuire, C., Chang, S., & Feld, P. (1992). Assessing political group dynamics: A test of the groupthink model. *Journal of Personality and Social Psychology, 63,* 403–425.

Tetlock, P. E., Skitka, L., & Boettger, R. (1989). Social and cognitive strategies for coping with accountability: Conformity, complexity, and bolstering. *Journal of Personality and Social Psychology, 57,* 632–640.

Tharp, R. G. (1994). Intergroup differences among Native Americans in socialization and child cognition: An ethnogenetic analysis. In P. M. Greenfield & R. R. Cocking (Eds.), *Cross-cultural roots of minority child development* (pp. 87–105). Hillsdale, NJ: Erlbaum.

Thibaut, J. W., & Kelley, H. H. (1959). *The social psychology of groups.* New York: Wiley.

Thoits, P. A. (1982). Conceptual, methodological, and theoretical problems in studying social support as a buffer against life stress. *Journal of Health and Social Behavior, 23,* 145–159.

Thomas, M. H., Horton, R. W., Lippincott, E. C., & Drabman, R. S. (1977). Desensitization to portrayals of real-life aggression as a function of exposure to television violence. *Journal of Personality and Social Psychology, 35,* 450–458.

Thompson, S. H., Sargent, R. G., & Kemper, K. A. (1996). Black and White adolescent males' perceptions of ideal body size. *Sex Roles, 34,* 391–406.

Thorndike, E. L. (1911). *Animal intelligence: Experimental studies.* New York: Macmillan.

Thornton, B., & Maurice, J. (1997). Physique contrast effect: Adverse impact of idealized body images for women. *Sex Roles, 37,* 433–439.

Tice, D. M. (1991). Esteem protection or enhancement? Self-handicapping motives and attributions differ by trait self-esteem. *Journal of Personality and Social Psychology, 60,* 711–725.

Tice, D. M. (1993). The social motivations of people with low self-esteem. In R. F. Baumeister (Ed.), *Self-esteem: The puzzle of low self-regard* (pp. 37–53). New York: Plenum Press.

Tice, D. M., & Baumeister, R. F. (1985). Masculinity inhibits helping in emergencies: Personality does predict the bystander effect. *Journal of Personality and Social Psychology, 49,* 420–428.

Tice, D. M., Butler, J. L., Muraven, M. B., & Stillwell, A. M. (1995). When modesty prevails: Differential favorability of self-presentation to friends and strangers. *Journal of Personality and Social Psychology.*

Tidwell, M.-C. O., Reis, H. T., & Shaver, P. R. (1998). Attachment, attractiveness, and social interaction: A diary study. *Journal of Personality and Social Psychology, 75.*

Timmers, M., Fischer, A. H., & Manstead, A. S. R. (1998). Gender differences in motives for regulating emotions. *Personality and Social Psychology Bulletin, 24,* 974–985.

Ting-Toomey, S. (1991). Intimacy expressions in three cultures: France, Japan, and the United States. *International Journal of Intercultural Relations, 15,* 29–46.

Tolstedt, B. E., & Stokes, J. P. (1984). Self-disclosure, intimacy, and the depenetration process. *Journal of Personality and Social Psychology, 46,* 84–90.

Tower, R. K., Kelly, C., & Richards, A. (1997). Individualism, collectivism and reward allocation: A cross-cultural study in Russia and Britain. *British Journal of Social Psychology, 36,* 331–345.

Townsend, J. M., & Levy, G. D. (1990). Effects of potential partners' physical attractiveness and socioeconomic status on sexuality and partner selection. *Archives of Sexual Behavior, 19,* 149–164.

Townsend, J. M., & Wasserman, T. (1997). The perception of sexual attractiveness: Sex differences in variability. *Archives of Sexual Behavior, 26,* 243–268.

Trafimow, D., & Finlay, K. A. (1996). The importance of subjective norms for a minority of people: Between-subjects and within-subjects analyses. *Personality and Social Psychology Bulletin, 22,* 820–828.

Travis, L. E. (1925). The effect of a small audience upon eye-hand coordination. *Journal of Abnormal and Social Psychology, 20,* 142–146.

Triandis, H. C. (1972). *The analysis of subjective culture.* New York: Wiley.

Triandis, H. C. (1989). The self and social behavior in differing cultural contexts. *Psychological Review, 96,* 506–520.

Triandis, H. C. (1993). The contingency model in cross-cultural perspective. In M. M. Chemers & R. Ayman (Eds.), *Leadership theory and research: Perspectives and directions* (pp. 167–188). San Diego, CA: Academic Press.

Triandis, H. C., Botempo, R., Villareal, M. J., Asai, M., & Lucca, N. (1988). Individualism and collectivism: Cross-cultural perspectives on self-ingroup relationships. *Journal of Personality and Social Psychology, 54,* 323–338.

Triplett, N. (1897). The dynamogenic factors in pacemaking and competition. *American Journal of Psychology, 9,* 507–533.

Trivers, R. L. (1971). The evolution of reciprocal altruism. *Quarterly Review of Biology, 46,* 35–57.

Trivers, R. L. (1983). The evolution of cooperation. In D. L. Bridgeman (Ed.), *The nature of prosocial development.* New York: Academic Press.

Trudeau, K. J., & Devlin, S. (1996). College students and community service: Who, with whom, and why? *Journal of Applied Social Psychology, 26,* 1867–1888.

Tschann, J. M. (1988). Self-disclosure in adult friendship: Gender and marital status differences. *Journal of Social and Personal Relationships, 5,* 65–81.

Turner, C. W., Layton, J. F., & Simons, L. S. (1975). Naturalistic studies of aggressive behavior: Aggressive stimuli, victim visibility, and horn honking. *Journal of Personality and Social Psychology, 31,* 1098–1107.

Turner, J. C. (1985). Social categorization and the self-concept: A social cognitive thory of group behavior. In E. J. Lawler (Ed.), *Advances in group processes* (Vol. 2, pp. 77–122). Greenwich, CT: JAI Press.

Turner, J. C. (1987). *Rediscovering the social group: A self-categorization theory.* Oxford, England: Basil Blackwell.

Tversky, A., & Kahneman, D. (1973). Availability: A heuristic for judging frequency and probability. *Cognitive Psychology, 5,* 207–232.

Tversky, A., & Kahneman, D. (1974). Judgment under uncertainty: Heuristics and biases. *Science, 185,* 1124–1131.

Tyler, T. R. (1997). The psychology of legitimacy: A relational perspective on voluntary deference to authorities. *Personality and Social Psychology Review, 1,* 323–345.

Tyler, T. R., & Schuller, R. A. (1991). Aging and attitude change. *Journal of Personality and Social Psychology, 61,* 689–697.

U.S. Bureau of the Census. (1998). *Statistical abstract of the United States (118th ed.)*. Washington, DC: U.S. Government Printing Office.

U.S. House of Representatives. (1994). *Climate change action plan and assessment: Hearing before the Committee on Science, Space, and Technology, 103rd Congress, First Session* (Publication No. 79–623). Washington, DC: U.S. Government Printing Office.

Unger, L. S. (1996). The potential for using humor in global advertising. *Humor: International Journal of Humor Research, 9*, 143–168.

Unger, L. S., & Thumuluri, L. K. (1997). Trait empathy and continuous helping: The case of voluntarism. *Journal of Social Behavior and Personality, 12*, 785–800.

United Nations. (1991). Special topic: International migration studies. In *United Nations demographic year book*. New York: Author.

Vala, J., Lima, M. L., & Caetano, A. (1996). Mapping European social psychology: Co-word analysis of the communications at the 10th general meeting of the EAESP. *European Journal of Social Psychology, 26*, 845–850.

van de Kragt, A. J. C., Dawes, R. M., Orbell, J. M., Braver, S. R., & Wilson, L. A. (1986). Doing well and doing good as ways of resolving social dilemmas. In H. A. M. Wilke, D. M. Messick, & C. G. Rutte (Eds.), *Experimental social dilemmas* (pp. 177–204). Frankfurt: Verlag Peter Lang.

van de Kragt, A. J. C., Orbell, J. M., & Dawes, R. M. (1983). The minimal contributing set as a solution to public goods problems. *American Political Science Review, 77*, 112–122.

Van der Zee, K., Oldersma, F., Buunk, B. P., & Bos, D. (1998). Social comparison preferences among cancer patients as related to neuroticism and social comparison orientation. *Journal of Personality and Social Psychology, 75*, 801–810.

Van Lange, P. A. M., & Rusbult, C. E. (1995). My relationship is better than—and not as bad as—yours is: The perception of superiority in close relationships. *Personality and Social Psychology Bulletin, 21*, 32–44.

Van Lange, P. A. M., Otten, W., De Bruin, E. M. N., & Joireman, J. A. (1997). Development of prosocial, individualistic, and competitive orientations: Theory and preliminary evidence. *Journal of Personality and Social Psychology, 73*, 733–746.

Van Oudenhoven, J. P., Groenewoud, J. T., & Hewstone, M. (1996). Cooperation, ethnic salience and generalization of interethnic attitudes. *European Journal of Social Psychology, 26*, 649–661.

Vandereycken, W. (1994). Emergence of bulimia nervosa as a separate diagnostic entity: Review of the literature from 1960 to 1979. *International Journal of Eating Disorders, 16*, 105–116.

VanderStoep, S., & Green, C. (1988). Religiosity and homonegativism: A path analytic study. *Basic and Applied Social Psychology, 9*, 135–147.

Vangelisti, A. L., Knapp, M. L., & Daly, J. A. (1990). Conversational narcissism. *Communication Monographs, 57*, 251–274.

Vassar, M. J., & Kizer, K. W. (1996). Hospitalizations for firearm-related injuries: A population-based study of 9,562 patients. *Journal of the American Medical Association, 275*, 1734–1739.

Vaughn, B. E., & Langlois, J. H. (1983). Physical attractiveness as a correlate of peer status and social competence in preschool children. *Developmental Psychology, 19*, 561–567.

Veniegas, R. C., & Peplau, L. A. (1997). Power and the quality of same-sex friendships. *Psychology of Women Quarterly, 21*, 279–297.

Verkuyten, M., & Hagendoorn, L. (1998). Prejudice and self-categorization: The variable role of authoritarianism and in-group stereotypes. *Personality and Social Psychology Bulletin, 24*, 99–110.

Verplanken, B., Aarts, H., & Knippenberg, A. V., Moonen, A. (1998). Habit versus planned behaviour: A field experiment. *British Journal of Social Psychology, 37*, 111–128.

Vinokur, A. D., & Vinokur-Kaplan, D. (1990). In sickness and in health: Patterns of social support and undermining in older married couples. *Journal of Aging and Health, 2*, 215–241.

Visser, P. S., & Krosnick, J. A. (1998). The development of attitude strength over the life cycle: Surge and decline. *Journal of Personality and Social Psychology, 75*, 1389–1410.

Von, J. M., Kilpatrick, D. G., Burgess, A. W., & Hartman, C. R. (1991). Rape and sexual assault. In M. L. Rosenberg & M. A. Fenley (Eds.), *Violence in America: A public health approach* (pp. 95–122). New York: Oxford University Press.

Vonk, R. (1993). The negativity effect in trait ratings and in open-ended descriptions of persons. *Personality and Social Psychology Bulletin, 19*, 269–278.

Vonk, R., & Kippenberg, A. van (1995). Processing attitude statements from ingroup and outgroup members: Effects of within-group and within-person inconsistencies on reading times. *Journal of Personality and Social Psychology, 68*, 215–227.

Vos, H., & Zeggelink, E. (1997). Reciprocal altruism in human social evolution: The viability of reciprocal altruism with a preference for "old-helping-partners." *Evolution and Human Behavior, 18*, 261–278.

Wagner, J. A. (1995). Studies of individualism-collectivism: Effects on cooperation in groups. *Academy of Management Review, 38*, 152–172.

Walkner-Haugrud, L. K., Gratch, L. V., & Magruder, B. (1997). Victimization and perpetration rates of violence in gay and lesbian relationships: Gender issues explored. *Violence and Victims, 12*, 173–184.

Walster [Hatfield], E., Walster, G. W., & Traupmann, J. (1978). Equity and premarital sex. *Journal of Personality, 36*, 82–92.

Wang, T. H., & Creedon, C. F. (1989). Sex role orientations, attributions for achievement, and personal goals of Chinese youth. *Sex Roles, 20*, 473–486.

Wänke, M., Bless, H., & Biller, B. (1996). Subjective experience versus content of information in the construction of attitude judgments. *Personality and Social Psychology Bulletin, 22*, 1105–1113.

Warshaw, R. (1988). *I never called it rape: The "Ms." report on recognizing, fighting, and surviving date and acquaintance rape*. New York: Harper & Row.

Wartella, E., & Reeves, B. (1985). Historical trends in research on children and the media: 1900–1960. *Journal of Communication, 35*, 118–133.

Wason, P. C. (1960). On the failure to eliminate hypotheses in a conceptual task. *Quarterly Journal of Experimental Psychology, 12*, 129–140.

Wasserman, D., Lempert, R. O., & Hastie, R. (1991). Hindsight and causality. *Personality and Social Psychology Bulletin, 17*, 30–35.

Waterman, C. K., Dawson, L. J., & Bologna, M. J. (1989). Sexual coercion in gay male and lesbian relationships: Predictors and implications for support services. *Journal of Sex Research, 26*, 118–124.

Watkins, M. (1986). *Invisible guests: The development of imaginal dialogues*. Hillsdale, NJ: Erlbaum.

Watson, W. E., Kumar, K., & Michaelsen, L. K. (1993). Cultural diversity's impact on interaction process and performance: Comparing homogeneous and diverse task groups. *Academy of Management Journal, 36*, 590–602.

Weber, J. G. (1994). The nature of ethnocentric attribution bias: Ingroup protection or enhancement? *Journal of Experimental Social Psychology, 30*, 482–504.

Wedell, D. H., Parducci, A., & Geiselman, R. E. (1987). A formal analysis of ratings of physical attractiveness: Successive contrast and simultaneous association. *Journal of Experimental Social Psychology, 23*, 230–249.

Wegener, D. T., & Petty, R. E. (1994). Mood management across affective states: The hedonic contingency hypothesis. *Journal of Personality and Social Psychology, 66*, 1034–1048.

Wegener, D. T., & Petty, R. E. (1995a). Effects of mood on persuasion processes: Enhancing, reducing, and biasing scrutiny of attitude-relevant information. In L. L. Martin & A. Tesser (Eds.), *Striving and feeling: Interactions between goals and affect*. Hillsdale, NJ: Erlbaum.

Wegener, D. T., Petty, R. E., & Smith, S. M. (1995). Positive mood can increase or decrease message scrutiny: The hedonic contingency view of mood and message processing. *Journal of Personality and Social Psychology, 69*, 5–15.

Wegner, D. M. (1994). Ironic processes of mental control. *Psychological Review, 101*, 34–52.

Wegner, D. M., Erber, R., & Raymond, P. (1991). Transactive memory in close relationships. *Journal of Personality and Social Psychology, 61*, 923–929.

Weinberger, M. G., & Campbell, L. (1991). The use and impact of humor in radio advertising. *Journal of Advertising Research, 30*, 44–52.

Weiner, B. (1980). A cognitive (attribution)-emotion-action model of motivated behavior: An analysis of judgments of help-giving. *Journal of Personality and Social Psychology, 39*, 186–200.

Weiner, B. (1982). The emotional consequences of causal attributions. In M. S. Clark & S. T. Fiske (Eds.), *Affect and cognition: The 17th annual Carnegie symposium on cognition* (pp. 185–210). Hillsdale, NJ: Lawrence Erlbaum.

Weiner, B. (1986). *An attribution theory of motivation and emotion.* New York: Springer-Verlag.

Weiner, B., Amirkhan, J., Folkes, V. S., & Verette, J. A. (1987). An attributional analysis of excuse-giving: Studies of a naive theory of emotion. *Journal of Personality and Social Psychology, 52*, 316–324.

Weiner, B., Frieze, I., Kukla, A., Reed, L., Rest, S., & Rosenbaum, R. M. (1972). Perceiving the causes of success and failure. In E. E. Jones, D. E. Kanouse, H. H. Kelley, R. E. Nisbett, S. Valins, & B. Weiner (Eds.), *Attribution: Perceiving the causes of behavior* (pp. 95–120). Morristown, NJ: General Learning Press.

Weir, W. (1984, October 15). Another look at subliminal "facts." *Advertising Age*, p. 46.

Weldon, E., & Gargano, G. M. (1988). Cognitive loading: The effects of accountability and shared responsibility on cognitive effort. *Personality and Social Psychology Bulletin, 14*, 159–171.

Wells, G. L., & Petty, R. E. (1980). The effects of overt head movements on persuasion: Compatibility and incompatibility of responses. *Basic and Applied Social Psychology, 1*, 219–230.

Werner, C. M., Kagehiro, D. K., & Strube, M. J. (1982). Conviction proneness and the authoritarian juror: Inability to disregard information or attitudinal bias? *Journal of Applied Psychology, 67*, 629–636.

West, S. G., & Brown, T. J. (1975). Physical attractiveness, the severity of the emergency and helping: A field experiment and interpersonal simulation. *Journal of Experimental Social Psychology, 11*, 531–538.

Weston, K. (1991). *Families we choose: Gays, lesbians, and kinship.* New York: Columbia University Press.

Wheeler, L., & Kim, Y. (1997). What is beautiful is culturally good: The physical attractiveness stereotype has different content in collectivist cultures. *Personality and Social Psychology Bulletin, 23*, 795–800.

Wheeler, L., Reis, H., & Nezlek, J. (1983). Loneliness, social interaction, and sex roles. *Journal of Personality and Social Psychology, 45*, 943–953.

Whitbeck, L. B., & Hoyt, D. R. (1994). Social prestige and assortive mating: A comparison of students from 1956 and 1988. *Journal of Social and Personal Relationships, 11*, 137–145.

White, G. L. (1980a). Inducing jealousy: A power perspective. *Personality and Social Psychology Bulletin, 6*, 222–227.

White, G. L. (1980b). Physical attractiveness and courtship progress. *Journal of Personality and Social Psychology, 39*, 660–668.

White, G. L., & Kight, T. D. (1984). Misattribution of arousal and attraction: Effects of salience of explanation of arousal. *Journal of Experimental Social Psychology, 20*, 55–64.

White, G. L., Fishbein, S., & Rutstein, J. (1981). Passionate love: The misattribution of arousal. *Journal of Personality and Social Psychology, 41*, 56–62.

White, M., & LeVine, R. A. (1986). What is an *Ii ko* (good child)? In H. Stevenson, H. Azuma, & K. Hakuta (Eds.), *Child development and education in Japan* (pp. 55–62). New York: Freeman.

Whiting, B. B., & Edwards, C. P. (1988). *Children of different worlds: The foundation of social behavior.* Cambridge, MA: Harvard University Press.

Whitley, B. E., & Kite, M. E. (1995). Sex differences in attitudes toward homosexuality: A comment on Oliver and Hyde (1993). *Psychological Bulletin, 117*, 146–154.

Wicker, A. W. (1969). Attitude versus actions: The relationship of verbal and overt behavioral responses to attitude objects. *Journal of Social Issues, 25*(4), 41–78.

Widmeyer, W. N., Brawley, L. R., & Carron, A. V. (1995). The effects of group size in sport. *Journal of Sport and Exercise Psychology, 12*, 177–190.

Widom, C. S. (1989). Does violence beget violence? A critical examination of the literature. *Psychological Bulletin, 106*, 3–28.

Wilke, H., & Lanzetta, J. T. (1982). The obligation to help: The effects of amount of prior help on subsequent helping behavior. *Journal of Experimental Social Psychology, 6*, 483–493.

Wilke, H. A. M. (1996). Status congruence in small groups. In E. Witte & J. Davis (Eds.), *Understanding group behavior: (Vol. 2): Small group processes and interpersonal relations* (pp. 67–91). Hillsdale, NJ: Erlbaum.

Williams, D. G. (1985). Gender, masculinity-femininity, and emotional intimacy in same-sex friendship. *Sex Roles, 12*, 587–600.

Williams, J. E., & Best, D. L. (1982). *Measuring sex stereotypes: A thirty nation study.* Beverly Hills, CA: Sage.

Williams, K. D. (1997). Social ostracism. In R. M. Kowalski (Ed.), *Aversive interpersonal behaviors* (pp. 133–170). New York: Plenum.

Williams, K. D., & Sommer, K. L. (1997). Social ostracism by coworkers: Does rejection lead to loafing or compensation? *Personality and Social Psychology Bulletin, 23*, 693–706.

Williams, K. D., Harkins, S., & Latané, B. (1981). Identifiability as a deterrent to social loafing: Two cheering experiments. *Journal of Personality and Social Psychology, 40*, 303–311.

Williams, K. D., Jackson, J. M., & Karau, S. J. (1995). Collective hedonism: A social loafing analysis of social dilemmas. In D. A. Schroeder (Ed.), *Social dilemmas: Perspectives on individuals and groups* (pp. 116–141). Westport, CT: Praeger.

Williams, W. L. (1992). The relationship between male-male friendship and male-female marriage. In P. M. Nardi (Ed.), *Men's friendships* (pp. 186–200). Newbury Park, CA: Sage.

Wilson, D. W. (1981). Is helping a laughing matter? *Psychology, 18*, 6–9.

Wilson, E. O. (1978). *On human nature.* Cambridge, MA: Harvard University Press.

Wilson, E. O. (1996). *In search of nature.* Washington, DC: Island Press.

Wilson, M. I., & Daly, M. (1996). Male sexual proprietariness and violence against wives. *Current Directions in Psychological Science, 5*, 2–7.

Wilson, T. D., & Hodges, S. D. (1992). Attitudes as temporary constructions. In L. L. Martin & A. Tesser (Eds.), *The construction of social judgments.* Hillsdale, NJ: Erlbaum.

Windschitl, P. D., & Wells, G. L. (1997). Behavioral consensus information affects people's inferences about population traits. *Personality and Social Psychology Bulletin, 23*, 148–156.

Winstead, B. A. (1986). Sex differences in same-sex friendships. In V. J. Derlega & B. A. Winstead (Eds.), *Friendship and social interaction* (pp. 81–100). New York: Springer-Verlag.

Wittenbaum, G. M. (1998). Information sampling in decision-making groups: The impact of members' task-relevant status. *Small Group Research, 29*, 57–84.

Wittenbaum, G. M., & Stasser, G. (1996). Management of information in small groups. In J. L. Nye & A. M. Brower (Eds.), *What's social about social cognition? Research on socially shared cognition in small groups* (pp. 3–28). Thousand Oaks, CA: Sage.

Wittenbraker, J., Gibbs, B. L., & Kahle, L. R. (1983). Seat belt attitudes, habits, and behaviors: An adaptive amendment to the Fishbein model. *Journal of Applied Social Psychology, 13*, 406–421.

Wonderly, D. M. (1996). *The selfish gene pool: An evolutionarily stable system.* Lanham, MD: University Press of America.

Wong, M. M., & Csikszentmihalyi, M. (1991). Loneliness, social interaction, and sex roles. *Journal of Personality and Social Psychology, 60,* 154–164.

Wood, J. V. (1996). What is social comparison and how should we study it? *Personality and Social Psychology Bulletin, 22,* 520–537.

Wood, J. V., Giordano-Beech, M., Taylor, K. L., Michela, J. L., & Gaus, V. (1994). Strategies of social comparison among people with low self-esteem: Self protection and self-enhancement. *Journal of Personality of Social Psychology, 67,* 713–731.

Wood, W., & Kallgren, C. A. (1988). Communicator attributes and persuasion: Recipients' access to attitude-relevant information in memory. *Personality and Social Psychology Bulletin, 14,* 172–182.

Wood, W., Lundgren, S., Ouellette, J. A., Busceme, S., & Blackstone, T. (1994). Minority influence: A meta-analytic review of social influence processes. *Psychological Bulletin, 115,* 323–345.

Wood, W., Pool, G. J., Leck, K., & Purvis, D. (1996). Self-definition, defensive processing, and influence: The normative impact of majority and minority groups. *Journal of Personality and Social Psychology, 71,* 1181–1193.

Wood, W., Wong, F. Y., & Chachere, J. G. (1991). Effects of media violence on viewers' aggression in unconstrained social interaction. *Psychological Bulletin, 109,* 371–383.

Wood, W. L., Rhodes, N., & Biek, M. (1995). Working knowledge and attitude strength: An information-processing analysis. In R. E. Petty & J. A. Krosnick (Eds.), *Attitude strength: Antecedents and consequences* (pp. 283–313). Mahwah, NJ: Erlbaum.

Worchel, S. (1994). You can go home again: Returning group research to the group contest with an eye on developmental issues. *Small Group Research, 25,* 205–223.

Worchel, S., & Andreoli, V. M. (1978). Facilitation of social interaction through deindividuation of the target. *Journal of Personality and Social Psychology, 36,* 549–556.

Worchel, S., Andreoli, V. A., & Folger, R. (1977). Intergroup cooperation and intergroup attraction: The effect of previous intersection and outcome combined effort. *Journal of Experimental Social Psychology, 13,* 131–140.

Worchel, S., Coutant-Sassic, D., & Grossman, M. (1992). A developmental approach to group dynamics: A model and illustrative research. In S. Worchel, W. Wood, & J. A. Simpson (Eds.), *Group process and productivity* (pp. 181–202). Newbury Park, CA: Sage.

Worchel, S., Grossman, M., & Coutant, D. (1994). Minority influence in the group context: How group factors affect when the minority will be influential. In S. Moscovici, A. Mucchi-Faina, & A. Maass (Eds.), *Minority influence* (pp. 97–114). Chicago: Nelson-Hall.

Worringham, C. F., & Messick, D. M. (1983). Social facilitation of running: An unobtrusive study. *Journal of Social Psychology, 121,* 23–29.

Wosinska, W., Dabul, A. J., Whetstone-Dion, R., & Cialdini, R. B. (1996). Self-presentational responses to success in the organization: The costs and benefits of modesty. *Basic and Applied Social Psychology, 18,* 229–242.

Wright, E. F., Lüüs, C. A. E., & Christie, S. D. (1990). Does group discussion facilitate the use of consensus information in making causal attributions? *Journal of Personality and Social Psychology, 59,* 261–269.

Wright, P. H. (1982). Men's friendships, women's friendships and the alleged inferiority of the latter. *Sex Roles, 8,* 1–20.

Wright, P. H. (1985). The acquaintance description form. In S. Duck & D. Perlman (Eds.), *Understanding personal relationships: An interdisciplinary approach.* London: Sage.

Wright, P. H., & Scanlon, M. B. (1991). Gender role orientations and friendship: Some attenuation, but gender differences abound. *Sex Roles, 24,* 551–566.

Wright, S. C., Aron, A., McLaughlin-Volpe, T., & Ropp, S. A. (1997). The extended contact effect: Knowledge of cross-group friendships and prejudice. *Journal of Personality and Social Psychology, 73,* 73–90.

Wrightsman, L. S., Kassin, S. M., & Willis, C. S. (1987). *In the jury box: Controversies in the courtroom.* Thousand Oaks, CA: Sage.

Wuthrow, R. (1982). Anti-Semitism and stereotyping. In A. G. Miller (Ed.), *In the eye of the beholder: Contemporary issues in stereotyping* (pp. 137–187). New York: Praeger.

Wyer, R. S., Jr. (1988). Social memory and social judgment. In P. R. Solomon, G. R. Goethals, C. M. Kelley, & B. R. Stephens (Eds.), *Perspectives on memory research.* New York: Springer-Verlag.

Yamagishi, T. (1986). The provision of a sanctioning system as a public good. *Journal of Personality and Social Psychology, 51,* 110–116.

Yamagishi, T. (1988a). The provision of a sanctioning system in the United States and Japan. *Social Psychology Quarterly, 51,* 265–271.

Yamagishi, T. (1988b). Seriousness of social dilemmas and the provision of a sanctioning system. *Social Psychology Quarterly, 51,* 32–42.

Yang, A. S. (1997). The polls-trends: Attitudes toward homosexuality. *Public Opinion Quarterly, 61,* 477–507.

Yoder, J. D., & Schleicher, T. L. (1996). Undergraduates regard deviation from occupational gender stereotypes as costly for women. *Sex Roles, 34,* 171–188.

Yoshitake, K. (1990). The effects of group consensus formation patterns and public self-consciousness in group members' judgments. *The Japanese Journal of Experimental Social Psychology, 29* (3), 71–77.

Yousif, Y., & Korte, C. (1995). Urbanization, culture, and helpfulness: Cross-cultural studies in England and the Sudan. *Journal of Cross-Cultural Psychology, 26,* 474–489.

Yzerbyt, V. Y., Rocher, S., & Schadron, G. (1996). Stereotypes as explanations: A subjective essentialistic view of group perception. In R. Spears, P. J. Oakes, N. Ellemers, & S. A. Haslam (Eds.), *The social psychology of stereotyping and group life.* Cambridge: Blackwell.

Zahn-Wexler, C., Robinson, J., & Emde, R. N. (1992). The development of empathy in twins. *Developmental Psychology, 28,* 1038–1047.

Zajonc, R. B. (1965). Social facilitation. *Science, 149,* 269–274.

Zajonc, R. B. (1968). Attitudinal effects of mere exposure. *Journal of Personality and Social Psychology Monograph Supplement, 9*(2, Part 2), 1–27.

Zajonc, R. B. (1984). On the primacy of affect. *American Psychologist, 39,* 117–123.

Zajonc, R. B. (1993). Brain temperature and subjective emotional experience. In M. Lewis & J. M. Haviland (Eds.), *Handbook of emotions* (pp. 209–220). New York: Guilford.

Zajonc, R. B., Murphy, S. T., & Inglehart, M. (1989). Feeling and facial efference: Implications of the vascular theory of emotion. *Psychological Review, 96,* 395–416.

Zanna, M. P., Kiesler, C. A., & Pilkonis, P. A. (1970). Positive and negative attitudinal affect established by classical conditioning. *Journal of Personality and Social Psychology, 14,* 321–328.

Zanot, E. J., Pincus, J. D., & Lamp, E. J. (1983). Public perceptions of subliminal advertising. *Journal of Advertising, 12,* 37–45.

Zaragoza, M. S., & Mitchell, K. J. (1996). Repeated exposure to suggestion and the creation of false memories. *Psychological Science, 7,* 294–300.

Zebrowitz, L. A., & Montepare, J. M. (1992). Impressions of babyfaced individuals across the life span. *Developmental Psychology, 28,* 1143–1152.

Zebrowitz, L. A., Tenenbaum, D. R., & Goldstein, L. H. (1991). The impact of job applicants' facial maturity, sex, and academic achievement on hiring recommendations. *Journal of Applied Social Psychology, 21,* 525–548.

Zebrowitz, L. A., Voinescu, L., & Collins, M. A. (1996). "Wide-eyed" and "crooked-faced":

Determinants of perceived and real honesty across the life span. *Personality and Social Psychology Bulletin, 22,* 1258–1269.

Zhang, L., Wieczorek, W. F., & Welte, J. W. (1997). The nexus between alcohol and violent crime. *Alcoholism, Clinical and Experimental Research, 21,* 1264–1271.

Zhongyang, J. K. Y. (Ed.). (1984). *Song Qingling lun shaonian ertong jiaouya (Song Qingling's essays on education for youth and children).* Beijing: Jiaoyu chubanshe.

Zillman, D. (1984). *Connections between sex and aggression.* Hillsdale, NJ: Lawrence Erlbaum.

Zillman, D. (1994). Cognition-excitation interdependencies in the escalation of anger and angry aggression. In M. Potegal & J. F. Knutson (Eds.), *The dynamics of aggression: Biological and social processes in dyads and groups* (pp. 45–71). Hillsdale, NJ: Lawrence Erlbaum.

Zillmann, D. (1983). Arousal and aggression. In R. G. Geen & E. I. Donnerstein (Eds.), *Aggression: Theoretical and empirical reviews: Vol. 1. Theoretical and methodological issues* (pp. 75–101). New York: Academic Press.

Zillmann, D., Katcher, A. H., & Milavsky, B. (1972). Excitation transfer from physical exercise to subsequent aggressive behavior. *Journal of Experimental Social Psychology, 8,* 247–259.

Zimbardo, P. (1969). The human choice: Individuation, reason, and order versus deindividuation, impulse, and chaos. In W. J. Arnold & D. Levine (Eds.), *Nebraska Symposium on Motivation, Vol. 17.* Lincoln, NE: University of Nebraska Press.

Zimbardo, P. G. [Producer]. (1972). *The Stanford prison experiment.* [Slide/tape presentation].

Zippelius, R. (1986). Exclusion and shunning as legal and social sanctions. *Ethology and Sociobiology, 7,* 159–166.

Zlotnick, C., Kohn, R., Peterson, J., & Pearlstein, T. (1998). Partner physical victimization in a national sample of American families: Relationship to psychological functioning, psychosocial factors, and gender. *Journal of Interpersonal Violence, 13,* 156–166.

Zuckerman, M., & Gerbasi, K. C. (1977). Belief in a just world and trust. *Journal of Research in Personality, 11,* 306–317.

Zuckerman, M., DePaulo, B. M., & Rosenthal, R. (1981). Verbal and nonverbal communication of deception. In L. Berkowitz (Ed.), *Advances in experimental social psychology, 9,* 292–296.

Zurcher, L. A. (1977). *The mutable self.* Beverly Hills, CA: Sage.

Zuwerink, J. R., & Devine, P. G. (1996). Attitude importance and resistance to persuasion: It's not just the thought that counts. *Journal of Personality and Social Psychology, 70,* 931–944.

Zuwerink, J. R., Devine, P. G., Monteith, M. J., & Cook, D. A. (1996). Prejudice toward Blacks: With and without compunction? *Basic and Applied Social Psychology, 18,* 131–150.

CREDITS

CHAPTER 1

Table 1.4: D. Chan, K.-S. (1994). COLINDEX: A refinement of three collectivism measures. In Kim, H.C., Triandis, H.C., Kagitcibasi, C., Choi, S.-C., Yoon, G. *Individualism and Collectivism: Theory, Method, and Applications,* pp. 200–210. Selection "Public Announcement" from *Obedience to Authority* by Stanley Milgram. Copyright © 1974 by Stanley Milgram. Reprinted by permission of HarperCollins Publishers, Inc.

CHAPTER 2

Figure 2.1: Source: Data from Calbris, 1990; Monahan, 1983; and Schneller, 1992.
Table 2.2: From M. Rosenberg, *Conceiving the Self.* Copyright © 1979 Basic Books, New York, NY. Reprinted by permission.
Table 2.3: From M. Rosenberg, *Conceiving the Self.* Copyright © 1979 Basic Books, New York, NY. Reprinted by permission.
Table 2.4: From A. Fenigstein, M.F. Scheier, and A.H. Buss, "Public and Private Self-Consciousness: Assessment and Theory" in *Journal of Consulting and Clinical Psychology, 43:* 522–527. Copyright © 1975 by The American Psychological Association. Reprinted by permission.
Figure 2.3: From H. Markus, "Self-Schemata and Processing Information About the Self" in *Journal of Personality and Social Psychology, 35:* 63–78, 1977. Copyright © 1977 by the American Psychological Association. Reprinted by permission.
Table 2.5: "I wish you from your early age . . ." from Zhongyang, J.K.Y. (Ed.). (1984). *Song Qingling lun shaonian ertong jiaouyu* (Song Qingling's essays on education for youth and children.) Beijing: Jiaoyu chubanshe.
Figure 2.4: From H.R. Markus and S. Kitayama, "Culture and the Self: Implications for Cognition, Emotion, and Motivation" in *Psychological Review, 98:*224–253, 1991. Copyright © 1991 by the American Psychological Association. Reprinted by permission.
Figure 2.6: Source: Data from R.A. Josephs et al., "Protecting the Self from the Negative Consequences of Risky Decisions" in *Journal of Personality and Social Psychology, 62:*26–37, 1992.
Table 2.6: Source: Based on Phinney, 1989.
Poem from "Chinatown Talking Story" by Kitty Tsui in *Making Waves: An Anthology of Writings By and About Asian American Women,* ed. Asian Women United of California, Boston: Beacon Press, 1989, p. 135.

CHAPTER 3

Table 3.2: From K.M. Kelly & W.H. Jones, "Assessment of Dispositional Embarrassability," *Anxiety, Stress, and Coping, 10:* 307–333. Reprinted by permission of Gordon and Breach Publishers.
Table 3.3: From P. Ekman, et al., "Universals and Cultural Differences in the Judgments of Facial Expressions of Emotion" in *Journal of Personality and Social Psychology,* 53:712–717, 1987. Copyright © 1987 by the American Psychological Association. Reprinted by permission.
Figure 3.3: From L. Ross, T.M. Amabile, and J.L. Steinmetz, "Social Roles, Social Control, and Biases in Social Perception Processes" in *Journal of Personality and Social Psychology* 35:485–494, 1977. Copyright © 1977 by the American Psychological Association. Reprinted by permission.
Figure 3.5: From J.G. Miller, "Culture and the Development of Everyday Social Explanation" in *Journal of Personality and Social Psychology,* 46:961–978, 1984. Copyright © 1984 by the American Psychological Association. Reprinted by permission.
Figure 3.6: From M.D. Storms, "Videotape and the Attribution Process: Reversing Actors' and Observers' Points of View" in *Journal of Personality and Social Psychology,* 27:165–175, 1973. Copyright © 1973 by the American Psychological Association. Reprinted by permission.

CHAPTER 4

Table 4.1: Source: Data from J. E. Williams and D. L. Best, *Measuring Sex Stereotypes: A Thirty Nation Study,* Sage Publications, Inc., 1982.
Figure 4.1: From A.H. Eagley and M.E. Kite, "Are Stereotypes of Nationalities Applied to Both Women and Men?" in *Journal of Personality and Social Psychology,* 5e:457–462, 1987. Copyright © 1987 by the American Psychological Association. Reprinted by permission.
Figure 4.2: D.L. Hamilton and R.K. Gifford, "Illusory Correlation in Interpersonal Judgments" in *Journal of Experimental Social Psychology,* 12:392–407, 1976.
Figure 4.3: From N. Schwarz, H. Bless, F. Strack, G. Klumpp, Rittenauer-Schatka, and A. Simon, "Ease of Retrieval as Information: Another Look at the Availability Heuristic" in *Journal of Personality and Social Psychology,* 61:195–202, 1991. Copyright © 1991 by the American Psychological Association. Reprinted by permission.
Table 4.3: Source: Data from N. Pennington and R. Hastie, "Explanation-Based Decision Making: Effects of Memory Structure on Judgment" in *Journal of Experimental Psychology: Learning, Memory, and Cognition,* 14:521–533, American Psychological Association, 1988.
Figure 4.5: From *Pygmalion in the Classroom: Teacher Expectation and Pupils' Intellectual Development* by Robert Rosenthal and Lenore Jacobson, copyright © 1968 by Holt, Rinehart and Winston, Inc., reproduced by permission of the publisher.
Table 4.4: From Z. Rubin and L. A. Peplau, Just World Scale, "Who Believes In a Just World?" in *Journal of Social Issues,* 31:65–89, 1975. Reprinted by permission of Blackwell Publishers and the author.

CHAPTER 5

Table 5.1: From W.B.G. Jarvis & R.E. Petty in "The need to evaluate" in *Journal of Personality and Social Psychology, 70,* 172–194, 199, 1996. Copyright © 1996 by the American Psychological Association. Reprinted by permission.

Figure 5.2: Source: Data from R.B. Zajonc, "Attitudinal Effects of Mere Exposure" in *Journal of Personality and Social Psychology Monograph Supplement, 9*(2, part 2): 1–27, American Psychological Association, 1968.

Figure 5.3: Source: Data from A. W. Staats and C.K. Staats, "Attitudes Established by Classical Conditioning" in *Journal of Abnormal and Social Psychology, 57*:37–40, American Psychological Association, 1958.

Figure 5.4: Source: Data from S. Chaiken and M.W. Baldwin, "Affective-Cognitive Consistency and the Effect of Salient Behavioral Information on the Self-Perception of Attitudes" in *Journal of Personality and Social Psychology, 41*:1–12, American Psychological Association, 1981.

Figure 5.5: Source: Data from F. Strack, et al., "Inhibiting and Facilitating Conditions of Facial Expressions: A Non-Obtrusive Test of the Facial Feedback Hypothesis" in *Journal of Personality and Social Psychology, 54*:768–777, American Psychological Association, 1988.

Figure 5.6: Source: Data from W.J. Froming et al., "Public and Private Self-Awareness: When Personal Attitudes Conflict with Societal Expectations" in *Journal of Experimental Social Psychology, 18*:476–487, American Psychological Association, 1982.

Table 5.3: Source: Data from M. Fishbein, "A Theory of Reasoned Action: Some Applications and Implications" in Howe and Page (eds.), Nebraska Symposium on Motivation, 1979, Vol. 27:65–116, University of Nebraska Press, 1980.

Figure 5.8: Source: Data from L. Festinger and J. M. Carlsmith, "Cognitive Consequences of Forced Compliance" in *Journal of Abnormal and Social Psychology, 47*:382–389, American Psychological Association, 1959.

Figure 5.9: From D.E. Linder, J. Cooper, and E.E. Jones, "Decision Freedom As a Determinant of the Role of Incentive Magnitude in Attitude Change" in *Journal of Personality and Social Psychology, 6*:245–254, 1967. Copyright © 1967 by the American Psychological Association. Reprinted by permission.

Figure 5.10: Source: Data from E. Aronson and J. Mills, "The Effect of Severity of Initiation on Liking for a Group" in *Journal of Abnormal and Social Psychology, 59*:177–181, American Psychological Association, 1959.

Table 5.5: From R. Cialdini, M. Trost, & J. Newsom in "Preference for consistency: The development of a valid measure and the discovery of surprising behavioral implications" in *Journal of Personality and Social Psychology, 69*:318–328, 1995. Copyright © 1995 by the American Psychological Association. Reprinted by permission.

Table 5.7: Source: Data from D. F. Alwin, L.C. Cohen, and T. M. Newcomb, *Political Attitudes Over the Life Span: The Bennington Women After Fifty Years,* University of Wisconsin Press, 1991; and the Institute for Social Research, National Election Studies, 1952–1984.

CHAPTER 6

Figure 6.3: Source: Data from C. I. Hovland and W. Weiss, "The Influence of Source Credibility on Communication Effectiveness" in *Public Opinion Quarterly, 15*:635–650, University of Chicago Press, 1951.

Table 6.1: From K.P. Frey and A.H. Eagly, "Vividness Can Undermine the Persuasiveness of Messages" in *Journal of Personality and Social Psychology, 65*:32–44, 1993. Copyright © 1993 by the American Psychological Association. Reprinted by permission.

Figure 6.4: Source: Data from K. P. Frey and A. H. Eagly, "Vividness Can Undermine the Persuasiveness of Messages" in *Journal of Personality and Social Psychology, 65*:32–44, American Psychological Association, 1993.

Excerpt: Copyright FMC Corporation. Reprinted by permission.

Figure 6.5 Source: Data from C. I. Hovland et al., Experiments on Mass Communication, Princeton University Press, 1949.

Excerpt: From R.I. Evans, *The Making of Social Psychology: Discussions with Creative Contributors.* Copyright © 1980 Gardner Press, Lake Worth, FL. Reprinted by permission.

Table 6.2: Source: Data from L.L. Carli, "Gender, Language, and Influence" in *Journal of Personality and Social Psychology, 59*:941–951, American Psychological Association, 1990.

Table 6.3: From J.T. Cacioppo and R.E. Petty, "The Need for Cognition" in *Journal of Personality and Social Psychology, 42*:116–131, 1982. Copyright © 1982 by the American Psychological Association. Reprinted by permission.

Figure 6.6: From M. Snyder and K.G. DeBono, "Appeals to Image and Claims About Quality: Understanding the Psychology of Advertising" in *Journal of Personality and Social Psychology, 49*:586–597, 1985. Copyright © 1985 by the American Psychological Association. Reprinted by permission.

Figure 6.7: From R.L. Miller, P. Brickman, and D. Bolen, "Attribution versus Persuasion as a Means for Modifying Behavior" in *Journal of Personality and Social Psychology, 31*:430–441, 1975. Copyright © 1975 by the American Psychological Association. Reprinted by permission.

CHAPTER 7

Figure 7.1: Source: Data from C. M. Steele and J. Aronson, "Contending with Stereotypes: African-American Intellectual Test Performance and Stereotype Vulnerability," 1994.

Figure 7.2: Source: Data from S. J. Spencer and C. M. Steele, "Under Suspicion of Inability: Stereotype Vulnerability and Women's Math Performance," 1994.

Figure 7.3: Source: W. Swinton, *A Complete Course in Geography: Physical, Industrial, and Political.* New York: Ivison, Blakeman, Taylor, & Co., 1880.

Figure 7.4: From C.W. Perdue, J.F. Dovidio, M.B. Gurtman, and R.B. Taylor, "Us and Them: Social Categorization and the Process of Intergroup Bias" in *Journal of Personality and Social Psychology, 59*:475–486, 1990. Copyright © 1990 by the American Psychological Association. Reprinted by permission.

Table 7.2: From I. Katz and R.G. Hass, "Racial Ambivalence and American Value Conflict: Correlation and Prime Studies of Dual Cognitive Structures" in *Journal of Personality and Social Psychology, 55*:893–905, 1988. Copyright © 1988 by the American Psychological Association. Reprinted by permission.

Table 7.3: Source: Adapted from G. Kleinpenning and L. Hagendoorn, "Forms of Racism and the Cumulative Dimension of Ethnic Attitudes" in *Social Psychology Quarterly, 56*:21–36, American Sociological Association, 1993.

Table 7.4: From Peter Glick and Susan T. Fiske, "The Ambivalent Sexism Inventory: Differentiating Hostile and Benevolovent Sexism" in *Journal of Personality and Social Psychology, 70*:491–512, 1996. Copyright © 1996 by the American Psychological Association. Reprinted by permission.

Figure 7.6: Source: Adapted from M. J. Monteith, "Self-Regulation of Prejudiced Responses: Implications for Progress in Prejudiced-Reduction Efforts" in *Journal of*

Personality and Social Psychology, 65:469–485, American Psychological Association, 1993.
Poem: From *The Intuitive Journey and Other Works* by Russell Edson. Copyright © 1976 by Russell Edson. Reprinted by permission of Georges Borchardt, Inc. for the author.

CHAPTER 8

Figure 8.1: Source: Data from M. Sherif, "A Study of Some Social Factors in Perception" in *Archives of Psychology*, 2:187, 1935.
Figure 8.3: Source: Data from S.E. Asch, 1957.
Figure 8.4: Source: Data from S.E. Asch, "Opinions and Social Pressure" in *Scientific American*, 31–35, November 1955.
Table 8.1: Source: Data from Jerry Burger, 1987.
Figure 8.5: Source: Data from S. Moscovici, E. Lage, and M. Naffrechoux, "Influences of a Consistent Minority on the Responses of a Majority in a Color Perception Task" in *Sociometry*, 32:365–380, 1969.
Figure 8.6: Source: Data from J.M. Burger, "Increasing Compliance by Improving the Deal: The That's-Not-All Technique" in *Journal of Personality and Social Psychology*, 51:277–283, American Psychological Association, 1986.
Table 8.2: Source: Data from S. Milgram, *Obedience to Authority: An Experimental View*, Harper and Row Publishers, 1974; and S. Milgram, *The Individual in a Social World: Essays and Experiments*, Addison-Wesley Publishing Company, 1992.
Excerpt: Experiment excerpt from *Obedience to Authority* by Stanley Milgram. Copyright © 1974 by Stanley Milgram. Reprinted by permission of HarperCollins Publishers, Inc.
Figure 8.7: Source: Data from S. Milgram, *Obedience to Authority: An Experimental View*, Harper and Row Publishers, Inc., 1974; and S. Milgram, *The Individual in a Social World: Essays and Experiments*, Addison-Wesley Publishing Company, 1992.

CHAPTER 9

Figure 9.1: From R.L. Moreland and J.M. Levine, "Socialization in Small Groups: Temporal Changes in Individual Group Relations," *Advances in Experimental Social Psychology*, Volume 15, p. 153, edited by L. Berkowitz, © Academic Press,1982. Reprinted by permission of Academic Press and the author.
Figure 9.2: Source: Adapted from R.B. Zajonc, "Social Facilitation," in *Science*, 149:269–274, American Association for the Advancement of Science, 1965.
Figure 9.3: Source: Adapted from R.S. Baron, "Distraction-Conflict Theory: Progress and Problems" in L. Berkowitz (ed.), *Advances in Experimental Social Psychology*, 19:1–40, Academic Press, 1986.
Figure 9.4: From E. Diener, S.C. Fraser, A.L. Beaman, and R.T. Kelem, "Effects of Deindividuation Variables on Stealing Among Halloween Trick-or-Treaters" in *Journal of Personality and Social Psychology*, 33:178–183, 1976. Copyright © 1976 by the American Psychological Association. Reprinted by permission.

CHAPTER 10

Figure 10.1: Reprinted from *Social Pressures In Informal Groups* by Leon Festinger, Stanley Schachter and Kurt Back with the permission of the publishers, Stanford University Press. Copyright © 1950 by Leon Festinger, Stanley Schachter and Kurt Back.
Figure 10.2: Source: Data from S. Schachter, *The Psychology of Affiliation*, Stanford University Press, 1959.
Table 10.1: Source: Data from Anderson et al., 1992.
Figure 10.3: Source: Data from J.D. Brown et al., "When Gulliver Travels: Social Context, Psychological Closeness, and Self-Appraisals" in *Journal of Personality and Social Psychology*, 62:717–727, American Psychological Association, 1992.
Figure 10.4: From D. Byrne and D. Nelson, "Attraction As a Linear Function of Proportion of Positive Reinforcements" in *Journal of Personality and Social Psychology, 1*:659–663, 1965. Copyright © 1965 by the American Psychological Association. Reprinted by permission.
Figure 10.6: Source: Data from S. Sprecher et al., "Mate Selection Preferences: Gender Differences Examined In a National Sample" in *Journal of Personality and Social Psychology*, 66:1074–1080, American Psychological Association, 1994.
Table 10.3: From D. Russell, L.A. Peplau, and M.L. Ferguson, "Developing a Measure of Loneliness" in *Journal of Personality Assessment*, 42:290–294, 1978. Reprinted by permission of Lawrence Erlbaum Associates, Inc.
Excerpt: Excerpt from *Love You Forever* by Robert Munsch, 1990. Copyright © Bob Munsch Enterprises Ltd. Reprinted by permission.

CHAPTER 11

Figure 11.1: From A. Aron, E.N. Aron, and D. Smollan, "Inclusion of Other In the Self Scale and the Structure of Interpersonal Closeness" in *Journal of Personality and Social Psychology*, 63:597, 1992. Copyright © 1992 by the American Psychological Association. Reprinted by permission.
Table 11.2: Source: Data from C. Hazan and Philip Shaver, "Romantic Love Conceptualized as an Attachment Process" in *Journal of Personality and Social Psychology*, 52:511–524, American Psychological Association, 1987.
Figure 11.2: From I. Altman and D.A. Taylor, *Social Penetration Theory: The Development of Interpersonal Relationships*. Reprinted by permission of Dr. Irwin Altman.
Table 11.3: Source: Adapted from L.C. Miller, J.H. Berg, and R.L. Archer, "Openers: Individuals Who Elicit Intimate Self-Disclosure" in *Journal of Personality and Social Psychology*, 44:1234–1244, American Psychological Association, 1983.
Figure 11.3: From V. Derlaga, R.J. Lewis, S. Harrison, B.A. Winstead, and R. Costanza, "Gender Differences in the Initiation and Attribution of Tactile Intimacy" in *Journal of Nonverbal Behavior*, 13:83–96, 1989. Reprinted by permission of Plenum Publishing Corporation.
Table 11.4: Source: Data from Nardi and Sherrod, 1994.
Figure 11.4: Source: Data from L.A. Kurdek and J.P. Schmitt, "Relationship Quality of Partners in Heterosexual Married, Heterosexual Cohabiting, and Gay and Lesbian Relationships" in *Journal of Personality and Social Psychology*, 51:711–720, American Psychological Association, 1986.
Figure 11.5: From R.J. Sternberg, "Triangulating Love" in R.J. Sternberg and M.L. Barnes (eds.), *The Psychology of Love*, 1988. Reprinted by permision of Yale University Press.
Table 11.5: Source: Adapted from C. Hendrick and S. Hendrick, 1986.
Figure 11.6: Source: Data from D.G. Dutton and A.P. Aron, "Some Evidence for Heightened Sexual Attraction Under

Conditions of High Anxiety" in *Journal of Personality and Social Psychology,* 30:510–517, American Psychological Association, 1974.

Figure 11.7: Source: C.E. Rusbult, "The Constructive/Destructive and Active/Passive Dimensions of Exit, Voice, Loyalty, and Neglect," paper presented at Society of Southeastern Social Psychologists meeting, Atlanta, GA.

Table 11.6: Source: Adapted from J.B. Bryson, "Situational Determinants of the Expression of Jealousy" in H. Sigall (chair), Sexual Jealousy, symposium presented at the annual meeting of the American Psychological Association, San Francisco, 1977.

CHAPTER 12

Figure 12.1: From K. Bjorkqvist, K. Osterman, and A. Kaukiainen, "The Development of Direct and Indirect Aggressive Strategies in Males and Females" in *Of Mice and Women: Aspects of Female Aggression* edited by K. Bjorkqvist and P. Niemele. Copyright © Academic Press, 1992. Reprinted by permission of Academic Press and the author.

Figure 12.2: Source: Data from United Nations, 1991.

Figure 12.3: From S.K. Mallick and B.R. McCandless, "A Study of Catharsis of Aggression" in *Journal of Personality and Social Psychology,* 4:591–596, 1966. Copyright © 1966 by the American Psychological Association. Reprinted by permission.

Table 12.1: Sources: *Kids Killing Kids,* Arnold Shapiro Productions, Inc., 1994; *The Milwaukee Journal,* July 19, 1994; and Jones, 1994.

Figure 12.5: From M. Rosekrans and W. Hartup, "Imitative Influences of Consistent and Inconsistent Response Sequences to a Model on Aggressive Behavior in Children" in *Journal of Personality and Social Psychology,* 7:429–434, 1967. Copyright © 1967 by the American Psychological Association. Reprinted by permission.

Figure 12.6: Based on Figure 3 from L.R. Huesmann, "Psychological Processes Promoting the Relation Between Exposure to Media Violence and Aggressive Behavior by the Viewer" in *Journal of Social Issues,* 42:125–140, 1986. Reprinted by permission of Blackwell Publishers and L. Rowell Huesmann.

Table 12.2: From Martha Burt, "Cultural Myths and Supports for Rape" in *Journal of Personality and Social Psychology,* 38:217–230, 1980. Copyright © 1980 by the American Psychological Association. Reprinted by permission.

Table 12.3: From Martha Burt, "Cultural Myths and Supports for Rape" in *Journal of Personality and Social Psychology,* 38:217–230, 1980. Copyright © 1980 by the American Psychological Association. Reprinted by permission.

Figure 12.7: From N.M. Malamuth and J.V.P. Check, "The Effects of Mass Media Exposure on Acceptance of Violence Against Women: A Field Experiment" in *Journal of Research in Personality,* 15:436–446. Copyright © Academic Press, 1981.

Figure 12.8: Source: Data from E. Donnerstein and L. Berkowitz, "Victim Reactions in Aggressive Erotic Films As a Factor in Violence Against Women" in *Journal of Personality and Social Psychology,* 41:710–724, American Psychological Association, 1981.

Table 12.4: Table "Ten Risk Factors" adapted from R.J. Gelles et al., "Riskmarkers of Men Who Batter: A 1994 Analysis" from *Newsweek,* July 4, 1994. Copyright © 1994 Newsweek Inc. All rights reserved. Reprinted by permission.

Table 12.4b: "Getting Help" adapted from R.J. Gelles et al., "Riskmarkers of Men Who Batter: A 1994 Analysis" from *Newsweek,* July 4, 1994. Copyright © 1994 Newsweek Inc. All rights reserved. Reprinted by permission.

Table 12.5: Source: Data from C.W. Turner, J.F. Layton, and L.S. Simons, "Naturalistic Studies of Aggressive Behavior: Aggressive Stimuli, Victim Visibility, and Horn Honking," in *Journal of Personality and Social Psychology,* 31:1098–1107, American Psychological Association, 1975.

CHAPTER 13

Table 13.1: From D. Romer, C.L. Gruder, and T. Lizzadro, "A Person-Situation Approach to Altruistic Behavior" in *Journal of Personality and Social Psychology,* 51:1001–1012, 1986. Copyright © 1986 by the American Psychological Association. Reprinted by permission.

Table 13.2: Source: Data from J.G. Miller, D.M. Bersoff, and R.L. Harwood, "Perceptions of Social Responsibilities in India and in the United States: Moral Imperatives or Personal Decisions?" in *Journal of Personality and Social Psychology,* 58:33–47, American Psychological Association, 1990.

Figure 13.1: Source: Data from J.P. Rushton, "Generosity in Children: Immediate and Long-Term Effects of Modeling, Preaching, and Moral Judgment" in *Journal of Personality and Social Psychology,* 31:459–466, American Psychological Association, 1975.

Figure 13.2: Source: Data from J.P. Rushton and G. Teachman, "The Effects of Positive Reinforcement, Attributions, and Punishment on Model-Induced Altruism in Children" in *Journal of Personality and Social Psychology,* 4:322–325, American Psychological Association, 1978.

Figure 13.3: Source: Data from B. Latane and J.M. Darley, *The Unresponsive Bystander: Why Doesn't He Help?,* Prentice-Hall, Inc., 1970.

Figure 13.4: From B. Latane and J.M. Darley, "Group Inhibition of Bystander Intervention in Emergencies" in *Journal of Personality and Social Psychology,* 10:218, figure 1, 1968. Copyright © 1968 by the American Psychological Association. Reprinted by permission.

Figure 13.5: From B. Latane and J.M. Darley, "Group Inhibition of Bystander Intervention in Emergencies" in *Journal of Personality and Social Psychology,* 10:218, figure 1, 1968. Copyright © 1968 by the American Psychological Association. Reprinted by permission.

Figure 13.6: Source: Adapted from J.A. Piliavin and I.M. Piliavin, "The Effect of Blood on Reactions to a Victim" in *Journal of Personality and Social Psychology,* 23:253–261, American Psychological Association, 1972.

Table 13.3: Source: Data from C.D. Batson et al., "Is Empathic Emotion a Source of Altruistic Motivation?" in *Journal of Personality and Social Psychology,* 55:52–77, American Psychological Association, 1981.

CHAPTER 14

Figure 14.1: Source: Data from J. Stapp and R. Fulcher, "The Employment of APA Members" in *American Psychologist,* 36:1263–1314, 1981.

PHOTO CREDITS

CHAPTER 1

p. 1 © Bob Thomas/Tony Stone Images, **p. 5** Corbis-Bettmann, **p. 7** © Disney Enterprises, Inc., **p. 8** Archives of the History of American Psychology, University of Iowa Libraries Record, **p. 9** AP/Wide World Photos, Inc., **p. 15** © Dr. John Drew/Image Artist, **p. 19** © Shooting Star, **p. 30** From OBEDIENCE TO AUTHORITY AN EXPERIMENTAL VIEW; Stanley Milgram; Harper & Row Publishers; Copyright 1974. Reprinted by permission of HarperCollins Publishers, Inc., **p. 30** (both) Copyright 1965 by Stanley Milgram from the film OBEDIENCE distributed by Penn State Media Sales, **p. 32** Courtesy of Dalmas Taylor

CHAPTER 2

p. 36 © Don Klumpp/The Image Bank, **p. 32** University of Chicago Library, Special Collection, **p. 40** Archives of the History of American Psychology Photographic

CHAPTER 3

p. 72 © AFP/Corbis Media, **p. 75**, AP/Wide World Photos

CHAPTER 4

p. 110 © Joe Traver/Liaison International, **p. 114**, © Tom McCarthy/Unicorn Stock Photos, **p. 126** © David Young-Wolff/Tony Stone Images, **p. 140** (both) National Baseball Library and Archive, Cooperstown, NY

CHAPTER 5

p. 144 © Bob Daemmrich/Stock, Boston/PNI, **p. 147** © Robert Ginn/Unicorn Stock Photos, **p. 162** © David Young-Wolff/PhotoEdit, **p. 169** © Josh Pulman/Tony Stone Images, **p. 182** Courtesy of Bennington College

CHAPTER 6

p. 186 © Jacques M. Chenet/Corbis Media, **p. 188** AP/Wide World Photos, **p. 197** (both) The Advertising Council, **p. 201** Courtesy FMC Corporation, **p. 215** Permission of Ebel USA, Inc./Photo by Firooz Zahedi/Don Henley's Fees donated to charity, The Walden Woods Project/Isis Fund, **p. 215** Courtesy of the Chrysler Corporation, **p. 222** © Deborah Davis/PhotoEdit

CHAPTER 7

p. 224 © Owen Franken/Stock, Boston, **p. 227** AP/Wide World Photos, **p. 238** (both) AN OUTLINE OF SOCIAL PSYCHOLOGY, REVISED EDITION by MUZAFER SHERIF and CAROLYN W. SHERIF. Copyrights renewed 1976 by Muzafer Sherif. Reprinted by permission of HarperCollins Publishers, Inc., **p. 243** © Joel Dexter/Unicorn Stock Photos, **p. 245** Corbis-Bettmann, **p. 257** Digital Stock CD

CHAPTER 8

p. 268 © Bob Daemmrich/Stock, Boston, **p. 271** © Shooting Star, **p. 275** Sygma, **p. 276**, William Vandivert, **p. 279**

Courtesy Asian-American Free Labor Institute, **p. 286** © 1989 Thaine Manske/The Stock Market, **p. 288** A Corbis-Bettmann, **p. 291** Liaison International, **p. 298** (top) Courtesy Alexandra Milgram, **p. 298** (bottom) Copyright 1965 by Stanley Milgram from the film OBEDIENCE distributed by Penn State Media Sales

CHAPTER 9

p. 312 © Ron Sherman/Tony Stone Images, **p. 316** © Ben & Jerry's Homemade Holdings, Inc. Used with permission of Ben & Jerry's Homemade Holdings, Inc., 1999, **p. 319** © Jay Foreman/Unicorn Stock Photos, **p. 320** Uniphoto, **p. 325** Uniphoto, **p. 336** Corbis-Bettmann, **p. 343** © Yann Arthus-Bertrand/Corbis Media, **p. 346** © Alan Klehr/Tony Stone Images

CHAPTER 10

p. 350 © Stewart Cohen/Tony Stone Images, **p. 355** © Lindsay Hebberd/Corbis Media, **p. 361** © Piero Pompani/Gamma Liaison, **p. 364** (all) Corel CD, **p. 367** (left) © Bill Losh/FPG International, **p. 367** (right) © Antony Nagelmann/FPG International, **p. 375** © Tom McCarty/Unicorn Stock Photos

CHAPTER 11

p. 390 © Stewart Cohen/Tony Stone Images, **p. 393** Courtesy of Sheila McGraw/Firefly Books LTD and Robert Munsch, **p. 398** © Aneal Vohra/Unicorn Stock Photos, **p. 402** © Stephanie Maze/Corbis Media, **p. 410** (left) Photri, Inc., **p. 410** (right) © Jean Higgins/Unicorn Stock Photos, **p. 417** © Thomas Kitchin, **p. 428** © Philip Gould/Corbis Media

CHAPTER 12

p. 432 12 © Curt Hodges/Jonesboro Sun/Sygma, **p. 434** © David Stout/Sygma, **p. 439** © Michelle Bridwell/PhotoEdit, **p. 449** © Bob Daemmrich/Stock, Boston, **p. 453** Courtesy of Albert Bandura, **p. 465** Uniphoto

CHAPTER 13

p. 476 © Noel Quidu/Gamma Liaison, **p. 481** © Frank Fournier/Contact Press Images/PNI, **p. 485** Corbis-Bettmann, **p. 491** AP/Wide World Photos, Inc., **p. 499** © Robert Brenner/PhotoEdit, **p. 503** © Aneal Vohra/Unicorn Stock Photos, **p. 512** © Richard Lindsey/Unicorn Stock Photos

CHAPTER 14

p. 518 © Mitchell Funk/The Image Bank, Chicago, **p. 522** © Daniel Bosler/Tony Stone Images, **p. 526** © R. Ian Lloyd/Corbis Media
Any photos not listed within the credits section have been supplied by the author.

N A M E   I N D E X

Miller, L. C., 76, 77, 401
Miller, L. S., 455
Miller, M. L., 82
Miller, N., 129, 204, 207, 260, 263, 265, 437, 502
Miller, N. E., 444
Miller, R. L., 218
Miller, R. S., 77, 78, 104, 425
Miller-Herringer, T., 85
Milliman, R. E., 210
Mills, J., 17, 395
Mischel, W., 41, 48, 447
Mita, T. H., 153
Mitchell, K. J., 308
Mitchell, T. R., 290
Moghaddam, F. M., 486
Money, J., 53
Montanari, J. J., 337
Monteith, M. J., 249, 258, 260, 261
Montepare, J. M., 84, 106
Moore, B. S., 488
Moore, D., 382
Moore, M. A., 532
Moore, S. G., 219
Moorhead, G., 337
Moreland, R. L., 50, 314, 315, 317, 318
Morf, C. C., 66
Morling, B., 60
Morris, M. W., 96, 100
Morris, W. N., 282
Morrison, T. L., 397
Moscovici, S., 6, 286, 287, 289, 334
Moss, M. K., 490
Moston, S., 308
Mphuthing, T., 236
Muehlenhard, C. L., 463
Mugny, G., 286, 287
Mulac, A., 208
Mullen, B., 46, 104, 119, 228, 306, 315, 327
Munsch, R., 392
Muraven, M., 49, 71
Murphy, P. L., 176
Murray, S. L., 161, 181, 423
Murstein, B. I., 373, 410
Mussen, P. H., 487
Mustonen, A., 440
Myers, D. G., 334

Norman, P., 169
Norriss, K. S., 482–483
Northouse, P. G., 338
Nowak, A., 306
Nunner-Winkler, G., 484
Nyquist, L., 208

O

O'Connor, S. C., 354
Oden, M. H., 141
Ohbuchi, K., 470
Okazawa-Rey, M., 365
Oliner, S. P., 489
Olson, J. M., 103, 127, 128, 157, 381
Omarzu, J., 393
O'Meara, D. J., 406
Orbell, J. M., 345
O'Reilly, C. A., III, 521
Orimonto, L., 428
Ormel, J., 134
Orne, M. T., 300
Orr, S. P., 84
Ortmann, A., 31
Osborne, J. W., 232
O'Sullivan, M., 106, 107, 409
Otten, S., 239
Oyserman, D., 41, 56, 57

P

Paalhus, D. L., 42
Packer, M. J., 41, 213
Page, R. A., 490
Page, R. M., 385
Pagelow, M., 465
Pallak, M. S., 288
Pallak, S. R., 195
Papageorgis, D., 203
Park, B., 87, 228
Parrott, W. G., 429
Pasch, L. A., 424
Patrick, B. C., 396
Patterson, G. R., 451
Pauldi, M., 252
Paulhus, D. L., 59
Paulus, P. B., 337
Pelham, B. W., 66
Pendleton, M. G., 294
Pendry, L. F., 116
Peng, K., 100
Pennington, N., 125, 346
Penrod, S., 229, 277, 332
Pepitone, A., 486
Peplau, L. A., 382, 402, 408
Perdue, C. W., 239
Perez, J. A., 286
Personnaz, B., 289
Pessin, J., 323
Peters, L. H., 341
Peterson, B. E., 136, 242
Peterson, C., 138, 139, 141
Peterson, J. L., 373
Peterson, R. S., 289
Petranoff, R. M., 221
Pettigrew, T. F., 260
Petty, R. E., 136, 149, 158, 189, 190, 192, 202, 205, 210, 211, 212, 289, 501
Pfau, M., 203
Pfeffer, J., 532
Pfeifer, R. L., 107
Phemister, S., 515
Phinney, J. S., 63, 64
Pietromonaco, P. R., 399

Piliavin, I. M., 501
Piliavin, J. A., 487, 499, 501, 515
Pinel, E. C., 233
Pion, G. M., 11
Plant, E. A., 260
Platz, S. J., 229
Pleban, R., 67
Plomin, R., 442
Plous, S., 123
Pollard, J. S., 367
Pollock, C. L., 294
Porter, J. F., 464
Porter, S., 107
Posavac, H. D., 368
Posavec, E. J., 531
Postmes, T., 330
Povinelli, D. J., 44
Powell, G. N., 341
Powers, T. A., 77
Powlishta, K. K., 56
Pozo, C., 381
Pratkanis, A. R., 50, 194, 205
Pratt, D. D., 56, 401
Pratto, F., 90, 234, 440
Prentice, D. A., 15, 162, 264, 267, 316, 529
Prentice-Dunn, S., 327, 329
Prewitt, K., 214
Priest, R. F., 357
Priester, J. R., 148, 158, 212
Provencal, A., 286
Pruitt, D. G., 343
Pryor, J. B., 252
Ptacek, J. T., 427
Pye, L. W., 56
Pyszczynski, T., 68, 120

Q

Quigley, B. M., 449
Quillian, L., 236

R

Raaijmakers, Q. A. W., 302
Radelet, M. L., 308
Räikkönen, K., 140
Ramsoy, N. R., 357
Rapoport, A., 344
Rapson, R. L., 430
Ratcliff, R., 445
Raven, B. H., 271
Read, J. D., 308
Read, S. J., 399
Redler, E., 293
Reese, C. A., 528
Reeves, B., 221
Regan, D. T., 176, 290
Reifman, A. S., 447
Reinard, J. C., 196
Reinecke, J., 169
Reis, H. T., 396
Reisenzein, R., 381
Reisman, J. M., 385
Rempel, J. K., 166
Renzetti, C., 465
Reynolds, D. L., 68
Rhodewalt, F., 218
Rhodewalt, R., 66
Richardson, D., 32
Ridgeway, C. L., 317
Riess, M., 104
Rieves, L., 368
Riley, D., 511
Ringelmann, M., 324

Riordan, C. A., 104, 418
Ritter, J. M., 363
Robarchek, C., 442
Roberts, B. W., 54
Roberts, D. F., 454
Roberts, R. E., 64
Roberts, W. R., 193
Robins, R. W., 18, 103
Robinson, D. T., 317
Robinson, R. J., 121
Rodin, J., 429, 430, 495
Roese, N. J., 127, 128, 157
Rofé, Y., 360
Rogers, C. R., 45
Rogers, R. J., 104
Rogers, R. W., 200, 327, 329
Rokeach, M., 149
Romer, D., 479
Rónnberg, J., 396
Rosch, E. H., 113
Rose, J., 317
Rosekrans, M., 452
Rosen, L. A., 472
Rosenberg, M. L., 440, 451
Rosenblatt, P. C., 410
Rosenblood, L. K., 354
Rosenhan, D. L., 489, 502
Rosenthal, R., 14, 131
Ross, J. M., 243
Ross, L., 98, 129
Ross, L. E., 365
Ross, M., 103, 381
Roszell, P., 363
Rotenberg, K. J., 384
Rothbaum, F., 411
Rotton, J., 447
Rotundo, A., 405
Rowatt, W. C., 81
Rowe, D. C., 155
Rubin, L., 255, 405
Rubin, M., 241
Rubin, Z., 427
Ruble, T. L., 116
Rusbult, C. E., 354, 423, 425, 426
Rushton, J. P., 374, 487, 488, 489, 490
Russell, D., 382, 383
Russell, D. E. H., 458
Russell, J. A., 401, 413
Russell, R., 252
Ryckman, R. M., 48

Waterman, C. K., 465
Watkins, M., 6
Watson, W. E., 315
Weber, J. G., 241
Wedell, D. H., 369
Weeks, J. L., 516
Wegener, D. T., 136, 205, 210, 501
Wegner, D. M., 69, 387, 396
Weigel, R. H., 164
Weinberger, M. G., 201
Weiner, B., 78, 93–94
Weiner, L., 252
Weir, W., 221
Weiss, W., 193
Weitzel-O'Neill, P. A., 209
Weldon, E., 325
Wells, G. L., 97, 158
Werner, C. M., 242
West, S. G., 443, 510
Weston, K., 406
Wheeler, L., 362, 424
Whitbeck, L. B., 372
White, G. L., 373, 418, 419, 429
White, M., 285
Whiting, B. B., 484

Whitley, B. E., 254
Whitley, B. E., Jr., 254
Wicker, A. W., 163
Wicklund, R. A., 45
Widmeyer, W. N., 315
Widom, C. S., 25
Wilke, H. A. M., 316, 484
Williams, C. J., 166
Williams, D. G., 402
Williams, J. E., 116
Williams, K. D., 280, 324, 325, 326, 344
Williams, K. R., 465
Williams, W. L., 405
Wilson, D. W., 501
Wilson, E. O., 421, 482
Wilson, M., 438, 441
Wilson, M. I., 464
Wilson, M. L., 365
Wilson, T. D., 157
Windschild, P. D., 97
Winstead, B. A., 402
Wittenbaum, G. M., 317, 332
Wittenbraker, J., 170
Wonderly, D. M., 483
Wong, M. M., 354

Wood, J. V., 181, 286, 353
Wood, W. L., 61, 165, 286, 379, 454
Worchel, S., 234, 239
Word, L. E., 496
Worringham, C. F., 323
Wortman, C., 77
Wosinska, W., 77
Wotman, S. R., 412
Wright, E. F., 97
Wright, P. H., 402, 403, 405, 406
Wright, S. C., 261
Wrightsman, L. S., 346, 464
Wyer, R. S., Jr., 114

Y

Yahya, K. A., 300
Yamagishi, T., 344
Yang, A. S., 255
Yik, S. M., 401
Yoder, J. D., 528
Yoshitake, K., 46
Yousif, Y., 492
Yuille, J. C., 107
Yurko, K. H., 141
Yzerbyt, V. Y., 130, 229

Z

Zahn-Wexler, C., 507
Zajonc, R. B., 17, 149, 152, 158, 321, 358
Zanna, M. P., 154, 160, 166, 254, 334
Zanot, E. J., 221
Zaragoza, M. S., 308
Zavalloni, M., 334
Zebrowitz, L. A., 106, 367
Zebrowitz-McArthur, L., 84
Zeggelink, E., 483
Zeichner, A., 449
Zeisel, H., 332, 347, 348
Zhang, L., 449
Zhou, X., 317
Ziebrowitz, L. A., 363
Zillmann, D., 416, 450
Zimbardo, P. G., 30, 327, 360
Zippelius, R., 280
Zlotnick, C., 464
Zuckerman, M., 103, 107, 134
Zurcher, L. A., 54
Zuroff, D. C., 77
Zuwerink, J. R., 211, 258

SUBJECT INDEX

A

Accountability cues, 327
Achieved ethnic identity, 64
Achieved status, 317
Acquaintance rape
  prevention of, 472
  sexual scripts and, 463–464
Action research, 530
Actor-observer effect
  attributions and, 101–103
  intimacy and, 394
Actual self, ideal self contrasted
    with, 48–49
Additive model of trait influence on
    impression formation,
    87–88
Adjustment function of attitudes, 160
Affiliation need, anxiety and,
    358–361
Affiliation needs, 352–356
  factors influencing, 354–356
  social comparison and, 352, 353
  social exchange and, 352,
    353–354
African Americans. See Prejudice
    and discrimination; Race;
    Racism
Agape, 414
Age. See also Children
  loneliness related to, 382–383
  persuasion and, 214, 216
Aggression, 433–474, 528–529
  alcohol consumption and,
    449–450
  biology of, 440–443
  cognitive-neoassociationist
    model of, 445–448
  definition of, 435
  excitation transfer and, 450
  frustration-aggression
    hypothesis of, 443–445
  gender differences in, 437–439
  high self-esteem and, 62
  instrumental versus hostile,
    435–437
  as intentional harm, 435
  male, "culture of honor" and,
    456–457
  observational learning and,
    454–456
  personality and, 439–440
  reducing, 467–473
  rewards of, 451–452
  sexual. See Rape; Sexual
    aggression
  social learning theory of, 451–454
Aggressive scripts, 453–454
Alcohol consumption, aggression
    and, 449–450
Altruism. See also Prosocial behavior
  reciprocal, 483
Altruistic helping, 479
Altruistic love, 414

Ambivalent sexism, 249–251
Anchoring and adjustment
    heuristic, 123
Anonymity, group performance
    and, 326
Anticonformity, 285
Anxiety
  affiliation need and, 358–361
  intergroup, 262
  social, isolation due to, 380–381
  social physique, 368
Anxious-ambivalent attachment
    style, 397
Apologies, as aggression
    controllers, 470
Applied research, 19
Appraisal, reflected, 40
Archival information for research, 22
Arousability, affiliation need and, 355
Arousal: cost-reward model of
    helping, 498–501
Arousal, misattribution. See
    Misattribution arousal
Ascribed status, 317
Asian Americans. See Prejudice and
    discrimination; Race;
    Racism
Attachment. See Parent-child
    attachment
Attitude(s), 145–185, 523
  accessibility of, 166
  behavior as cause of, 155
  beliefs and, 146
  changing. See Persuasion
  cognitive consistency and,
    170–181
  cognitive dissonance theory and.
    See Cognitive dissonance
  definition of, 147–149
  determinants of, 167
  enhancement by group
    decisions, 333–335
  toward groups. See
    Heterosexism; Prejudice
    and discrimination;
    Racism; Sexism
  toward individuals. See
    Interpersonal attraction
  instrumental, 149–151, 160
  need to evaluate and, 149
  political, 183–185
  prediction of behavior from,
    163–170
  reference groups and, 182–183
  research on, 183–185
  toward self. See Self-esteem
  similarity of, interpersonal
    attraction and, 372
  strength of, 165–166
  symbolic, 149, 161
  tricomponent view of, 148
  values related to, 149–151
Attitude formation
  functional approach to, 159–163

mere exposure effect and,
    151–153
  nonverbal behavior and, 157–159
  self-perception theory of,
    155–157
  through classical conditioning,
    153–155
  through operant conditioning, 155
Attraction. See Interpersonal
    attraction; Physical
    appearance
Attributions, 92–104, 527
  actor-observer effect and,
    101–103
  correspondent inference and,
    94–96
  covariation principle and, 96–98
  defensive, of victims' plight,
    134–135
  definition of, 92
  fundamental attribution error
    and, 98–101
  intimacy and, 394
  locus of causality and, 92–94
  self-serving bias and, 103–104
Audience, persuasion and. See
    Persuasion
Audience inhibition effect,
    494–497, 529
Authoritarian personality, 10
  definition of, 241
  hostility toward outgroups and,
    241–243
Autokinetic effect, 273
Availability heuristic, 123
Averaging model of trait influence
    on impression formation,
    87–88
Aversive racism, 246, 248
Avoidant attachment style, 397

B

Balance theory, 374–375
Base-rate fallacy, 122
Basic research, 19
Basking in reflected glory
    (BIRGing), 65
Beauty, physical attractiveness
    stereotype and, 362–364
Behavior. See also specific behaviors
  as cause of attitudes, 155
  planned, theory of, 166–170
  prediction by attitudes, 163–170
  unintentional, 169
Behavioral factors, activating
    stereotypes, 115
Behavioral intentions, 166–167
Behavioral self-handicapping, 80
Behavior genetics, aggression
    and, 442
Beliefs, 146
  antiaggression, internalizing, 470
  in just world, 134–135, 510

religious, prejudice correlated
    with, 243–244
Biases
  in attribution, 98–105, 306–307, 522
  beneficial aspects of, 136–137
  hindsight, 126–127
  ingroup, 104, 239–240
  own-race, 229
  partner-enhancing, endurance of
    romantic relationships
    and, 423
  personality judgments and, 89–91
  self-serving, 522
    endurance of romantic
    relationships and, 423
Biculturalism, self-concept related to,
    56–57
Binge behavior, 68–69
Bisexuals. See Heterosexism;
    Homosexuality
Blacks. See Prejudice and
    discrimination; Race;
    Racism
Body esteem, 368
Body movements, impression
    formation and, 84
Body posture, attitude formation
    and, 158–159
Bystander intervention model,
    491–501, 529
  audience inhibition effect and,
    494–497
  diffusion of responsibility and,
    497–498
  emotional arousal and cost-
    reward assessments and,
    498–501

C

Careers in social psychology,
    530–533
Categorization, social, 113–114
  stereotyping and, 114–116
Catharsis, 443–445
Causality, locus of, attributions and,
    92–94
Cause-effect relationships, 26–29
Central route to persuasion, 190,
    191–192, 207, 289
Central traits, impression formation
    and, 88–89
Charismatic leaders, 338–339
Children
  attachment of. See Parent-child
    attachment
  fostering prosocial behavior in,
    514–515
  observational learning of
    prosocial behavior in,
    487–491
Choice
  correspondent inference and,
    94–95

authoritarian, 10
judgments of, biased thinking as
basis of, 89–91
Personality theory, implicit, 89–90
Personality traits, impression
formation and, 87–89
Personalization as prejudice
reduction approach,
265–266
Personal relevance, persuasion
and, 205
Person attribution, 92–94
Persuasion, 187–223, 523–524
attractiveness of communicator
and, 194–195
central route to, 190, 191–192,
207, 289
cognitive-response approach to,
189–192
credibility of communicator and,
192–194
definition of, 189
fear appeals for, 199–200
group polarization due to,
334–335
humor for, 200–202
individual differences in
susceptibility to,
211–216
involvement of audience and,
211
labels for, 218–220
message-learning approach
to, 189
mood of audience and, 210
order of message presentation
for, 204–205
peripheral route to, 190–192,
206–207
powerful speech for, 207–209
repetition of messages for, 205
research on, 222–223
self-generated, 217–218
subliminal messages for, 221–223
two-sided messages for, 202–204
vividness of message and,
196–199
Pessimistic explanatory style,
138–140
Physical aggression. *See also*
Aggression
gender differences in, 437
Physical appearance, 362–371
cross-cultural differences and
similarities in
attractiveness standards
and, 365–369
persuasion and, 195
physical attractiveness
stereotype and, 362–364
of self, attractiveness of others
and, 369, 371
similarity of, interpersonal
attraction and, 373–374
Physical attractiveness stereotype,
362–364
Physical features, social
categorization based
on, 114
Physical touching, gender
differences in, 403–404
Planned behavior, theory of, 166–170
Political attitudes, research on,
183–185

Pornography, 458–462
definition of, 458
promotion of male aggression
against women by,
460–462
rape myth and, 458–460
Positivity bias in personality
judgments, 90
Postdoctoral training for social
psychologists, 530
Power
social. *See* Social power
of speech, persuasion and,
207–209
Pragma (pragmatic love), 414
Prejudice and discrimination,
225–266, 524. *See also*
Heterosexism; Racism;
Sexism
authoritarianism as basis for,
241–243
combating, 256–266
definition of, 227
differentiation between, 227–228
enhancement of social identity as
basis for, 239–241
history of, 244–256
intergroup competition leading
to, 236–239
as justification for oppression,
234–235
religious beliefs correlated with,
243–244
research on, 264–266
stereotyping related to, 228–234
Primary effect
in personality judgments, 90–91
persuasion and, 204–205
Private self-awareness, 44–45
attitudes as predictors of behavior
and, 164–165
Private self-consciousness, 46
Prosocial behavior, 477–517, 529
barriers to, 515
bystander intervention. *See*
Bystander intervention
model
costs to recipients of, 511–513
definition of, 479
empathy-altruism hypothesis of,
505–507
enhancing, 514–515
evolutionary perspective on,
482–483
gender differences in, 479, 481
individual differences in, 507
learning of, 487–491
moods and, 501–503
recipients of, 509–513
research on, 516–517
rewarding, 490–491
social norms and, 483–487
Protection-motivation theory, 200
Prototypes, social categorization
and, 114
Proximity, interpersonal attraction
and, 356–357
Psychological distancing, 65
Psychological femininity, 116–117
Psychological masculinity, 116–117
Psychological reactance, theory of,
283
Psychological social psychology, 7
Public self-awareness, 44–45

attitudes as predictors of
behavior and, 164–165
Public self-consciousness, 46–48
Punishment
attitude formation through, 155
increases and decreases in
aggression related to,
467–468

R

Race
helping behavior and, 509–510
own-race bias and, 229
Racism, 245–249. *See also* Prejudice
and discrimination
aversive, 246, 248
modern, 246–247
old-fashioned, 245–246, 248
progression of racial acceptance
and, 248–249
Radiation effect, physical appearance
and, 369
Random assignment, 28
Rape
acquaintance, 463–464, 472
pornography and, 460–462
prevention of, 472–473
rape myth and, 458–460
sexual scripts and, 463–464
Rape myth, 458–460
Rationalization, cognitive dissonance
theory and. *See* Cognitive
dissonance
Realistic group conflict theory,
236–239
Reasoned action, theory of, 166
Recency effect
in personality judgments, 90–91
persuasion and, 204–205
Reciprocal helping, 483
Reciprocity
helping behavior and, 511
interpersonal attraction and, 379
negative, romantic relationships
and, 425
of self-disclosure, 400–401
Reciprocity norm, 484
compliance and, 290–291
Redlining, 228
Reference groups, 182–183
Reflected appraisal, 40
Reinforcement, attitude formation
through, 155
Relationship-oriented leaders, 340
Relevance, personal, persuasion
and, 205
Religious beliefs, prejudice
correlated with, 243–244
Remembrance phase of group
membership, 318–319
Repetition, persuasion and, 205
Representativeness heuristic, 122
Research, 19–29
action, 530
on anxiety and affiliation need,
358–361
applied, 19
on attitudes, 183–185
basic, 19
on compliance, 308–310
correlational, 22, 23–26
ethics in, 29–33
experimental, 21–22, 26–29

on explanatory style, 141
in graduate programs, 530
on group decision making by
juries, 347–348
on groupthink, 336–337
on intergroup competition,
236–239
on interpersonal attraction,
387–388
on jealousy, 430–431
on lying, 107–108
meta-analysis in, 29
on obedience, 297–303
on persuasion, 222–223
on political attitudes, 183–185
on prejudice and discrimination,
264–266
on prosocial behavior, 516–517
on rape prevention, 473
on self-regulation, 70–71
on social identity and prejudice,
239–240
on social influence, 309–310
on social loafing, 324–325
steps in, 20–23
Resocialization phase of group
membership, 318–319
Resource allocation, intimacy
and, 394
Response amplification, 247
Response involvement, persuasion
and, 211
Responsibility, diffusion of, 325,
497–498, 529
Reverse-causality problem, 24–25
Rewards
of aggression, 451–452
for prosocial behavior, 490–491,
498–501
Risk, self-concept and willingness to
take, 60–62
Risky shift, 333
Robbers Cave experiment, 236–239
Roles, social, 87
Romantic love, 413
Romantic relationships, 408–428
childhood attachment style
effects on, 397–399
companionate love and, 419–420
distress caused by breakup of,
427–428
endurance of, 422–428
gender differences in experience
of love and, 420–422
myths about, 408–411
passionate love and, 414–419
reading signs of attraction and,
411–412
troubled, strategies for coping
with, 426–427
types of love and, 413–414
unrequited love and, 412–413

S

Schemas, 50–54
definition of, 50
gender schemas, 53–54
in personality judgments, 91
self-schemas, 51–52, 395
Schools, reduction of intergroup
conflict in, 263–265
Scripts, aggressive, 453–454
Secure attachment style, 396–397

Self, 37–71, 521
  attitude toward. *See* Self-esteem
  as both target of attention and
      active agent, 43–50
  contemporary theories of,
      39–42
  definition of, 38
  development of, 39–40
  escaping from, 68–69
  ideal *versus* actual, 48–49
  as knowledge structure, 50–58
  nature of, 38–43
  as process of identification, 40–41
  role in persuasion, 216–220
  as social being, 38, 63–67
  social environment and, 14
Self-affirmation theory, 180–181
Self-awareness, 38–39, 44–45
  actor-observer effect and, 102
  attitudes as predictors of
      behavior and, 164–165
  conformity and, 282
  definition of, 44
  effects of, 44–45
  reduced, deindividuation
      and, 329
Self-concept, 14
  cultural influences on, 54–57
  definition of, 41–42
  gender schemas and, 53–54
  including another in, 393–396
  self-schemas as ingredients of,
      51–52
Self-consciousness, 45–48
  definition of, 45
  effects of, 46–48
Self-consistency, 58–60
Self-disclosure, 399–401
  cultural differences in, 401
  gender differences in, 403
  reciprocity of, 400–401
Self-discrepancies, 48–49
Self-enhancement, 58–60
Self-esteem
  aggression and, 439–440
  definition of, 42
  high, aggression related to, 62
  maintenance through social
      reflection and social
      comparison, 65–67
  receiving help and, 511–513
  threats to, stereotyping and, 115
  willingness to take risks and,
      60–62
Self-evaluation maintenance model,
      65–66
Self-fulfilling prophecy, 131–134
  endurance of romantic
      relationships and, 423
  of liking, 379
  persuasion and, 219–220
  in physical attractiveness
      stereotype, 364
Self-handicapping as self-
      presentation strategy,
      80–81
Self-monitoring, 81–82
  persuasion and, 212–214
Self-perception, cognitive dissonance
      and, 178–180
Self-perception theory of attitude
      formation, 155–157
Self-presentation(s), 74–82, 521. *See
      also* Social perception

conformity and, 282–283
failed, embarrassment and
      excuse making following,
      77–81
  self-monitoring and, 81–82
  strategic, 76–77
Self-promotion as self-presentation
      strategy, 76
Self-regulation, 48–50
  definition of, 48
  research on, 70–71
Self-reporting handicapping, 80
Self-reports for research, 22
Self-schemas, 51–52
  intimacy and, 395
Self-serving bias, 103–104, 522
  endurance of romantic
      relationships and, 423
Self-verification, 58–60
Serotonin, aggression and, 442
Sexism, 249–253. *See also* Prejudice
      and discrimination
  ambivalent, 249–251
  definition of, 249
  sexual harassment and, 251–253
  from unexpected sources, 253
Sexual aggression, 458–467. *See also*
      Rape
  intimate violence and, 464–467
  pornography and, 458–462
Sexual harassment, 251–253
Sexual orientation. *See* Heterosexism;
      Homosexuality
Sexual scripts, acquaintance rape
      and, 463–464
Shared distinctiveness, illusory
      correlation and, 119–120
Similarity
  helping behavior and, 509–510
  interpersonal attraction and,
      371–375
  persuasion and, 195
Situational control, leadership
      and, 340
Situational factors
  activating stereotypes, 115
  conformity and, 280–282
  underestimation of,
      susceptibility to coercive
      social influence and,
      306–307
Situation attribution, 92–94
Sleeper effect, 193–194
Social affiliation model, 354
Social anxiety, isolation due to,
      380–381
Social behavior, culture and, 14–17
Social categorization, 113–114
  stereotyping and, 114–116
Social cognition, 111–142, 522–523
  alteration by mental simulations,
      124–128
  categorization and, 113–116
  definition of, 112
  explanation of negative effects
      and, 138–141
  heuristics and, 122–124
  stereotyping and, 116–121
  world beliefs and. *See* World
      beliefs
Social cohesiveness of groups, 315
Social comparison, 65–67
  affiliation needs and, 352, 353
  group polarization due to, 334

perceptions of own physical
      appearance and, 369, 371
Social construction(s), 520
Social constructionist perspective, 41
Social desirability of behavior,
      correspondent inference
      and, 94
Social dilemmas, 343–345, 526
Social disorganization, rape and, 462
Social dominance theory, 234–235
Social environment, self and, 14
Social exchange relationships, 338
Social exchange theory, 352, 353–354
Social facilitation, 321–323
  triggering of passionate love
      by excitation transfer
      and, 419
Social grooming, 483
Social identities, 63–65
  enhancement of, prejudice
      promoted by, 239–241
  ethnic, 63–64
  of groups, to solve social
      dilemmas, 345
  ingroup and outgroup and,
      64–65
  research on, using minimal
      groups, 239–240
Social identity theory, 240–241
Social impact theory, 305–306
Social influence, 269–310, 525
  compliance and. *See* Compliance
  conformity and. *See* Conformity
  definitions of, 271–272
  false confessions and, 308–310
  informational, 278, 279
  line judgment research on,
      275–278
  of majority on group
      decisions, 332
  normative, 278–279
  norm development research on,
      273–275
  obedience and. *See* Obedience
  research on, 272–280, 309–310
  social impact theory of, 305–306
  social power and, 271–272
  underestimation of situational
      factors and, 306–307
Social isolation, 380–385
  loneliness due to, 382–385
  social anxiety as cause of,
      380–381
Socialization phase of group
      membership, 318
Social justice, norm of, 484
Social learning theory, 451–454
  prosocial behavior and, 487–491
  reducing aggression and,
      469–470
Social loafing, 324–326
Social norms
  conformity and, 273–275
  definition of, 273
  favoring equality, 261–262
  in groups, 316
  helping behavior and, 483–487
  of reciprocity, 290–291
Social penetration theory, 400–401
Social perception, 521–522. *See also*
      Self-presentation(s)
Social physique anxiety, 368
Social power
  definition of, 271

social influence and, 271–272
  stereotyping and, 121
Social psychology
  careers in, 530–533
  definition of, 6
  history of, 7–11
  psychological and sociological, 7
  as value-free science, 32–33
Social reflection, 65–67
Social responsibility, norm of, 484
Social roles, 87
  in groups, 316–317
Social role theory, 87
Social skills deficits, loneliness
      related to, 384–385
Social skills training
  to improve interpersonal
      relationships, 385–387
  to reduce aggression, 470–471
Social status, 244
  contact hypothesis and, 260
  gender differences in love
      experience and, 420–421
  in groups, 317
  master, 244
Social support
  conformity and, 282
  endurance of romantic
      relationships and,
      424–425
Social threat, perceived,
      authoritarianism
      associated with, 242–243
Social value orientations, 345
Sociocultural perspective
  on gender differences in love
      experience, 422
  on interpersonal attraction,
      378–379
Socioemotional groups, 319–320
Socioemotional leadership, 338
Sociological social psychology, 7
Soft sell, 213
Source, persuasive. *See* Persuasion
Specificity, attitudes as predictors of
      behavior and, 164
Speech
  power of, persuasion and,
      207–209
  rate of, persuasion and, 206–207
Statistical significance, 22
Statistics, 22
Status. *See* Social status
Stereotypes, 114–116, 522
  factors activating, 115
  functions of, 115–116
  gender, 116–117
  illusory correlations as basis of,
      119–120
  outgroup homogeneity effect
      and, 228–229
  physical attractiveness, 362–364
  as probability judgments, 115
  reducing stereotyping and,
      257–260
  social power and, 121
  stigmatized groups' responses
      and, 230–233
  subcategories and globalization
      of, 229–230
Stereotype threat, 231–233
Stigma, 244
  definition of, 230
  response to, 230–233